PAROLE FEMINE

Words and Lives of the Woman's
Literary Club of Baltimore

nomination; and Mrs. McGaw was also unanimously elected, - and her acceptance was received.

The President spoke of the December Salon on the last day of year 1907; and also of the New Year's celebration on January 7th, 1908. For the latter she said the President pro tempore would of course call a meeting of the Board to arrange its details. = The meeting adjourned (or proposition had been made to have a reception on December 31st, 1907, in honor of our Honorary members, but other things - after this meeting - interfering, it was given up, by general agreement, - in favor of the usual monthly Salon.) (Written during a domestic crisis - falling ceilings - and physical disablement, when I was afraid it would never be written at all, L.C.)

Board of Management Meeting.
November 26th, 1907.

(Mrs. William Paret, First Vice President pro tempore at Annapolis this meeting, - will of onwards.)

The Board of Management of the Woman's Literary Club of Baltimore met on Tuesday, November 26th, 1907, in the library of the Academy of Sciences Building. The President pro tempore presented, from the Corresponding Secretary, the resignation of membership by Mrs. W. S. Belding. She wrote that she was going abroad on account of the state of her husband's health; and felt obliged to resign, for the present year, at any rate, with the hope of probably returning at a future time. The acting President proposed that a note be sent to Mrs. Belding expressing our regret for her leaving us, and for its cause, but also our hope for her return among us again. The proposal received the consent of the members present.

A note from our President, Mrs. Worthall was received, with regard to the presentation of the name

At the end of the Board of Managers Meeting Minutes for November 18, 1907, the Woman's Literary Club of Baltimore's longtime Recording Secretary, Lydia Crane, explains how domestic disturbances intruded upon her duties to the Club. Woman's Literary Club of Baltimore collection, Maryland Historical Society.

PAROLE FEMINE

Words and Lives of the Woman's Literary Club of Baltimore

Jean Lee Cole, Lead Editor

Research and Editorial Team

Loyola University Maryland

Stephen Cole Barrett

Tara Brooky

Mary Cronin

Francesca D'Aloia

Matthew Dabrowski

Nicole Day

Marina Fazio

Jonathan Flink

Hunter Flynn

Jill Fury

Alessia Hughes

Megan Hultberg

Sydney Johnson

Katie Kazmierski

Kate Kutch

Clara Love

Monica Malouf

Katherine Marrinan

Claire McElduff

Ju'waun Morgan

Natalie Muñoz

Miranda Nolan

Madeline Pikus

Cynthia Requardt

Ellen Roussel

Alyssa Schilke

Katie Shiber

For all the women who have been lost to history

First Edition

Paperback ISBN: 978-1-62720-252-7

Design by Molly Werts

Published by Apprentice House

Apprentice
House Press
Loyola University Maryland

Apprentice House
Loyola University Maryland
4501 N. Charles Street
Baltimore, MD 21210
410.617.5265 • 410.617.2198 (fax)
www.ApprenticeHouse.com
info@ApprenticeHouse.com

Contents

Dedication

The bird gives its songs to the day,
  The blossom its bloom to the sky,
The fountain out-tosses its spray
  As a call to the cloud that goes by.
The star on its glimmering path
  Pays toll to the sovereign night
Of the uttermost good that it hath,
  In a tribute of tremulous light.

What though the bird's carol be faint.
  The blossom be naught but a weed,
And the garb of the fountain be quaint,
  And the heavens too distant to heed?
What though the wan gleam of the star
  Be lost in the fulness of day?
Evermore to the power afar
  Each offers the thing that it may.

So I, like the star and the fount.
  The reiterant bird and the flower,
Telling o'er the inadequate count
  Of the fruits of my harvesting hour,
Fain to glean what I may from its store
  Before the brief reaping-time ends,
With a sigh that the gift be no more,
  Lay my sheaf at the feet of my friends.

—Grace Denio Litchfield

Acknowledgments

This project began nearly ten years ago when I stumbled across the Woman's Literary Club of Baltimore papers at the Maryland Historical Society. Since then, this project has been enabled, shaped, pushed forward, and lifted up by many hands.

Courtney Cousins, Loyola Class of 2014, was the first student to work on this project and the first person to dig into the WLCB collection at the Maryland Historical Society. Her passion for the collection and especially, the WLCB minutes, drove me to engage more deeply and more fully with the Club and its activities. Courtney, you provided the spark that launched the entire endeavor.

The Center for Humanities and especially, the ongoing support of Mark Osteen, kept the flame alive with periodic and absolutely necessary funding that stoked the furnace of student research, course development, and the creation of the project website and this anthology.

The Maryland Historical Society—especially, David Armenti, Director of Education, and Special Collections staff—welcomed Loyola student researchers with open arms, provided invaluable training and assistance to fledgling researchers, and provided opportunities to share our work through MDHS publications, events, and the museum shop. The summer 2017 researchers would specifically like to thank Scott "The Sticker Guy" Rubin for *all the stickers*.

The Loyola-Notre Dame Library has provided a home for the WLCB project website and helped to turn it into a navigable, content-rich resource that I hope will give many more students and researchers access to the activities, thoughts, writings, and lives of this fascinating group of women. Thanks especially to Matt Treskon, Technology Librarian; Clara Love, Technology Resources Assistant (and member of the research team); Sarah Espinosa, Cataloging and Metadata Librarian; Zachary Gahs-Bucchieri, Interlibrary Loan Assistant; Katie O'Neill, Associate Director; and Barbara Preece for committing support for this project and cheerfully providing ongoing assistance as the website has grown and evolved.

I would also like to thank several individuals who have become involved with the project over the past few years. In April 2018, Jon Kusckar and Emily Levenson (and their children Caroline & Ellen) graciously gave us a tour of their home, which happened to be the former home of WLCB member Christine Ladd Franklin, giving us a chance to walk the paths the women took within their domestic spaces. More recently, Eric Pope, great-grandson of first Club president Francese Litchfield Turnbull and great-great-nephew of Turnbull's sister, honorary member Grace Denio Litchfield, shared family papers and photographs of Turnbull, Litchfield, and Turnbull's daughter Grace Hill Turnbull, seeding future research on these three women. Participants at the Bmore Historic Unconference held every September at Baltimore's Museum of Industry have offered insights, resources, and general enthusiasm about the Club and Loyola students' engagement with local Baltimore history, and members of the Society for the Study of American Women Writers have done likewise at conferences and online.

Finally, the project would not be anywhere close to its current state without the on-going, diligent efforts of Cynthia Requardt, who researched Club member biographies, provided insight into nineteenth- and early-twentieth century Baltimore society, and transcribed hundreds (perhaps thousands) of pages of documents. Thank you, Cynthia!

Jean Lee Cole
Lead Editor

Women of the Woman's Literary Club of Baltimore. Left to right, top to bottom:
WLCB co-founder Hester Crawford Dorsey, Christine Ladd-Franklin, Lizette
Woodworth Reese, Alice M. Lord, Louise Malloy, Annie Leakin Sioussat

Introduction

I'm nobody! Who are you?
Are you nobody, too?
Then there's a pair of us—don't tell!
They'd banish us, you know!
—Emily Dickinson[1]

In early 1890, two Baltimore women hatched a plan. Hester Crawford Dorsey had made a splash that winter writing pert commentaries on gender roles and expectations under the name "Selene," for the *Baltimore American* newspaper. Louisa Courtauld Osburne Haughton, a teacher and neighbor, also had literary aspirations. Both were educated, nearing thirty years of age, and unmarried. Both also had the advantages of wealth and heritage. Dorsey was descended from a colonial-era Eastern Shore family that traced its roots to the Darcys of England, while Haughton's English roots were more recent; she had been born in England and was brought to Baltimore as a child by her father, a shipping clerk attracted to the bustling mid-Atlantic port city. While both women, given their economic status and gender ideology of the time, presumably sought to establish themselves as society wives, in the winter of 1889-1890 they wrote to friends and acquaintances—all women—enlisting their support for their idea: a society, made up solely of women, that would "further greater intellectual development of the women of Baltimore and to promote social relations among those of similar tastes." Nearly forty women attended the Club's first meeting, held on March 19, 1890, at the recently established Goucher College for Women.[2]

All of those who attended that first meeting were already published authors. Mary Spear Tiernan published her novel *Homoselle* with the venerable Boston firm Ticknor and Company in 1881 and had published other novels as well as short fiction in highly respected monthly magazines including *Harper's, Scribner's,* and the *Century.* Louise Clarkson had published nearly a dozen books of illustrated poetry.

Elizabeth Turner Graham was an officer in the General Federation of Women's Clubs and founder of Maryland's oldest women's club, the Lend-a-Hand Club, in nearby Mount Washington, and wrote poetry, which she also illustrated. A number of the women, including Marguerite Easter, Alice Sauerwein Lord, and Lydia Crane, had published fugitive verse in local and regional publications, including the *Sun* and the *American*. Other early members included Lizette Woodworth Reese, who became Maryland's poet laureate in 1931; Christine Ladd-Franklin, the first woman to complete the requirements for a PhD at Johns Hopkins; May Garrettson Evans, the first woman reporter at the *Baltimore Sun*; and Henrietta Szold, a Jewish American teacher and translator who would eventually establish the Zionist women's organization, Haddassah.

They decided at the outset that "those only should belong who had sufficient interest in literature to have devoted some time and thought to original work for either newspapers and magazines or of a more lasting nature."[3] After debating several possibilities for names, which included "The Writer's Club," "The Literary League," "Contemporary Women," "The Nineteenth Century," and "The Sphynx," they eventually settled upon the "Woman's Literary Club of Baltimore"—though they would continue to deliberate about whether to be a "Women's" literary club or a "Woman's" one.[4] They chose their club color: violet. And they adopted a motto, *Parole Femine*, the second half of the Maryland state motto "Fatti maschii, parole femine" ("Manly deeds, womanly words"), aligning themselves with women, writers, and proud Marylanders.[5]

Club history and structure

The WLCB sprung forth from America's women's club movement, which flourished in late nineteenth-century America. Historian Anne Ruggles Gere estimates that some two million women across the country and from a wide range of religious, social, and ethnic-racial groups were involved in some aspect of the movement over the course of its history.[6] A number of literary societies founded throughout the country during this time provided women a chance to read and discuss literature in a supportive setting. These clubs originated to fill a void left by the limited educational opportunities for girls. The members of the WLCB didn't just read and study literature, however. They also wrote their own "womanly words," and sought to shepherd them into print. The group that founded the Baltimore club provided mutual support for one another, not just in their study of literature but to support each other's efforts in pursuing literary careers.

After that initial March 1890 meeting, the WLCB would continue meeting for the next five decades, almost without interruption. The Club met weekly on Tuesday afternoons between October and May, leaving the summer months free for members to escape the city heat in travel or stays at summer homes. They remained a fairly small group, capping their membership at one hundred, and while doing so allowed them enough funding (in the form of membership dues) for their activities, it did not support the purchase and maintenance of a building, as was common for many women's clubs at the time. Instead, the group affiliated with the Maryland Academy of Sciences in 1891 as associate members and were allowed to establish their meeting room in the Academy's building. The Academy moved several times in the Club's early years, but when they finally moved to 105 West Franklin Street, the former mansion of Maryland governor Thomas Swann, the Club was provided with a comfortable meeting space until 1921, when they began meeting in a room at the Arundell Club at 1000 N. Charles Street.

The heart of the Woman's Literary Club of Baltimore was its committees, where the members tested their literary works to be presented at the weekly meetings. Each member was required to belong to at least one committee and to present—when called upon—at least one "paper" or "article" per year. Committee chairs selected the topics of each meeting and organized the discussions, debates and critical analysis of members' work. The committee setting was where the members presented their work and received, as one member put it, "a baptism of friendly criticism."[7] In committee sessions some members shared poems, short stories, book chapters, translations, or an act from a play. Others wrote papers on artistic movements, music and musicians, or historical events. After thorough vetting by the committee, papers deemed ready for wider hearing were selected by the committee chair and presented at a weekly meeting of the Club.

The committees shifted from season to season, but there were usually around ten of them; their plans of work varied from year to year depending on the chair. The committees that presented programs to the Club most often were those dealing with literature: Fiction, Modern Poetry, Drama, Essays, Current Criticism and Translation. Three long-standing committees were Art, Music, and Education. American history was of great interest to the members, supporting committees in Colonial and Revolutionary History, Letters and Autographs, and "Unfamiliar Records." The Club sustained a Committee on Current Events for many years, but the Club generally refrained from discussing volatile political topics. Archaeology, the specialty of longtime Club president Letitia Yonge Wrenshall, was a longstanding committee.

At each session, the Club's president would call the meeting to order, the secretary would read the minutes of the previous meeting, and then the program organized by the committee of the week would commence. Articles of the program usually took the form of Club members reading aloud fiction, poetry, or an essay that fell under the committee's jurisdiction. These works were written either by prominent authors of the day or by Club members themselves. Some women read their own work; some chose to have another member read it for them. Articles sometimes took other forms—they could consist of the sharing of a photograph or piece of art, a letter from an important figure, or a musical performance. In addition to these weekly meetings, the Club also hosted monthly Salons, social gatherings with musical programs and refreshments to which the exclusive Club's members were allowed to bring guests.

To provide inspiration for members, the Club maintained a library of books written by themselves as well as their fellow Maryland authors. The library was established sometime before 1892, and quickly became a valued extension of the Club. It functioned, in many ways, as a repository of female intellect and symbol of female creativity and imagination, what Virginia Woolf would characterize nearly four decades later as "a room of one's own." By May 1893, the Club library had amassed two hundred volumes, which Club librarian, Virginia Woodward Cloud, excitedly reported at the Club's 25th Salon on May 20, 1893, when she read the entire list of volumes that had been acquired and expressed sincere "gratitude to our members, and to our other friends" who had donated books. Meeting after meeting, news of their swelling library thrilled members of the Club, and like everything the Club undertook, it was taken very seriously. Their library demonstrated a sense of pride and ownership in an age where even wealthy women did not have much they could really, truly call their own.[8]

During much of its history, the Club organized lavish Twelfth Night celebrations in January, which commemorated the Epiphany in music, literary recitations, and a huge cake, reminiscent of today's Mardi Gras King Cake. The *Sun* described one of these cakes as having baked into it "Twelfth Night symbols, eagerly looked for by the younger guests to indicate their fortunes, the ring, the piece of money, bean, thimble and pen."[9] A characteristic feature of several of the Twelfth Night celebrations in the early 1900s was the presentation of a "stuffed peacock in a nest of Christmas greens,"[10] which appeared to serve as a sort of mascot for the Club. On All Souls' Day, November 2, Club members also decorated the graves of authors and artists buried in Maryland. Among those honored were Edgar Allan Poe, Junius Brutus Booth, John Pendleton Kennedy, Sidney Lanier, Richard Malcolm Johnston, William H. Rinehart, and founding Club member Mary Spear Tiernan.[11] In 1907, members of the WLCB organized the Edgar Allan Poe Memorial Association in advance of the centennial of his birth in 1909.

The Woman's Literary Club of Baltimore completed its final season in May 1941. Louisa Haughton, one of the originators of the Club, served as President during the Club's final two seasons, and had served as Vice President during many of the years when she wasn't president. Haughton clearly played an important role in the Club's stability and unswerving purpose. Unfortunately, little is known about her tenure as president, or about the Club's decision to dissolve, as the records of the Club housed at the Maryland Historical Society end with the 1920 season. Nevertheless, notices of meetings and events published in the Baltimore *Sun* indicate that the Club stayed true to its mission of supporting women writers and their literary pursuits throughout its existence. The Club's final meeting celebrated National Poetry Week with a contest for the best poem written by a Club member.

By all measures, the Club succeeded in producing published authors. Of the three hundred or so active members that have been documented, over fifty were published authors, with over a thousand discrete publications to their names—not counting the news assignments and regular columns produced by journalists in the group, which would certainly push the total number of publications into the thousands. Their meeting programs (which were printed weekly, in Club violet and always featuring the Club crest) showcased members' original literature and essays side by side with the likes of the Elizabeth Barrett and Robert Browning, William Shakespeare, and their favorite Southern poet, Sidney Lanier, next to whom one Club president is buried. They wrote novels and short stories across a range of genres, including not just what literary historian Nina Baym described as "woman's fiction," but also historical fiction set in in US and around the world, female *bildungsromans,* social reform novels, mysteries, and memoir; formal and free verse in lyric, dramatic, narrative, and comic modes; translations of works written by French, Italian, German, Russian, and Jewish authors, and dramatic works ranging from topical one-acts to dramatic monologues to full-length musical comedies. Following the conventions of the time, they also published works that we might not consider "literary" today: philosophical treatises, history, musical and dramatic criticism, and biography, among others. We have attempted to include in this anthology at least one example from each member whose works were pub-

lished between 1890-1920—corresponding to the years for which we have Club records—across the wide range of forms and genres they represent.[12]

The Aperio Project: Recovering Words, Lives, History

The history we have just outlined has been buried under decades of forgetting. This forgetting has been aided and abetted by both the continuing dominance of male-centered historiography and the female Club members' internalization of patriarchy. Periodic Club profiles appeared in the *Baltimore Sun* on important anniversaries and other Club milestones, most of them authored by member Emily Emerson Lantz, a longtime reporter for the newspaper. Otherwise, the WLCB's activities and accomplishments were documented only in brief notes appearing on the *Sun*'s social pages. No mention of the Club exists in histories of Maryland or Baltimore. Even literary histories such as Frank Shivers's *Maryland Wits and Baltimore Bards* mention it only in passing.[13]

Even though the Club stands as a clear and noteworthy example of women's leadership and intellect, women's accomplishments have not been recognized as a through-line for *human* history; the dominant narratives, by and large and to the present day, have told the story of nation-states, the actions of political and religious leaders, and the conflicts between them. The figures involved in these narratives—queens excluded, perhaps—have been men. Yet the history of women is crucial to understanding human history;

women, after all, have always made up at least half of the human population.

The notion that women's history has been lost—that it went unrecorded, that women left no traces of their activities, their art, their thought—has been painstakingly dismantled by feminist historians who have gleaned historical information from clothing and home furnishings, located diaries, journals, artworks, and unpublished manuscripts in archives and attics, and read between the lines of historical accounts passed down by male historians to trace the women moving the levers of state behind the scenes (or sometimes, in plain sight). And as historian Bonnie G. Smith reminds us, "thousands of histories of women" had already been written before 1950.[14] The documents preserved from the WLCB, held at the Maryland Historical Society in Baltimore, are a rich example of this extant history. The Club carefully—and copiously—took down its history, in the form of detailed meeting minutes, membership lists and dues records, printed programs, and privately published Club documents, including its constitution, guest invitations, ballot sheets, and a Club manual. Altogether, the WLCB collection at the Maryland Historical Society comprises some 3,000 pages of minutes stretching from the Club's foundation in 1890 through 1920, programs from each of the over 1,000 meetings held between 1890 and 1914, copies of the Club's constitution, member log books, and two large scrapbooks containing newspaper clippings about the Club and other news relating to women.

Gere writes that "such records show clubwomen making their own history and defining their own cultural identity." At the same time, they insisted that this history be presented "on their own terms."[15] As a result, they were highly protective of their documents—and their meetings—carefully controlling who had access and how documents would be used. Gere notes that record books from women's clubs across the country and throughout the nineteenth century "contain frequent references to clubwomen insisting that their deliberations remain beyond the gaze of nonmembers";[16] the WLCB was no exception, including a clause in their constitution stating that "no report of the meetings be given to the press without the approval of an officer" of the Club.[17] While it may seem presumptuous to us now to assume that the media would be interested in the goings-on of a group of women discussing literature, the fact that they expressed serious concerns about how their statements, actions, or motives might be misrepresented shows that the very occasion of women gathering together to discuss intellectual matters might be seen as newsworthy or controversial.

The WLCB documents at the Maryland Historical Society were first noticed by Cynthia Requardt, a young historian who had been hired in the mid-1970s by the University of Minnesota to locate archival collections relating to women. This collection, she wrote, like others she documented in the Maryland Historical Society holdings, showed "women who accepted the restrictions of a 'woman's sphere.'" While such collections might be unappealing to researchers in the present day seeking examples of female rebellion and precursors to the feminist movement, she maintained, "A study of women's past is not complete if historians concentrate solely on feminists who rebelled against these restrictions. Equally revealing is the way the majority of women accepted and coped with the restrictions placed on their lives."[18] Nevertheless, after publishing her report, the collection languished, unprocessed and unexplored, until 2010, when Jean Lee Cole, an American literature professor at Loyola University in Baltimore, stumbled upon it while looking for local literary societies. One of Cole's students, Courtney Cousins, Class of 2012, volunteered to do research in the collection as part of a class assignment, and convinced Cole of the significance of the material for future research. With the invaluable assistance of Loyola's Center for the Humanities Aperio Series in Humane Texts program and a Center for Humanities grant to fund the project, Cole undertook, with the help of dozens of students from Loyola as well as seniors attending Friends School just north of the university, what has become a two-year-long sequence of activities that have included summer research internships, two undergraduate seminar courses on textual recovery and editing, and an independent study in digital humanities to develop online research materials for the project. In a supremely fitting example of "closing the loop," Cynthia Requardt happened to run across a blog post about the project in fall 2017. Requardt had retired from a long career as a manuscripts librarian at the Maryland Historical Society and at Johns Hopkins University, and now had the time to sign on as a volunteer researcher. In that role, she has transcribed records, compiled biographical profiles of Club members, and provided ongoing assistance throughout the project.

During the initial research phase (Summer 2017-Spring 2018), team members transcribed documents from the Maryland Historical Society collection. All of the programs and nearly all of the meeting minutes were transcribed. Membership book data was deciphered and entered onto a spreadsheet to determine who belonged to the Club and when; we mapped Club members' addresses to confirm that the geographical center of the Club began Baltimore's Mount Vernon and Bolton Hill neighborhoods, and gradually shifted and extended to the northwest as upper-middle-class whites gradually migrated away from the city center. Five Summer 2017 research interns worked with Cole to decide how to present this information online, and one of these interns, Clara Love, learned about website development, metadata, and database construction, and worked with Cole during the fall and winter of 2017-2018 to create the online Woman's Literary Club of Baltimore archive, hosted by the Loyola Notre Dame Library. (After she graduated, Love was hired on by the Library and has continued to refine and expand the archive.)

During the initial phases of the project, we were constantly struck by how much Baltimore had changed in the intervening hundred years. References to streets and buildings that no longer existed; writers who are no longer favored; contemporary political figures and members of the Baltimore social scene—all of these made Baltimore seem like a foreign country. We were also struck by the fact that our research failed to provide basic information about who the Club members were. One of the first things one learns in a foreign language is how to tell someone your name, but these records failed to reveal even that. Although only women belonged to the Club, and even though the Club minutes and records were considered private documents, nearly all Club members were referred to by their husband's names. Unmarried members were simply referred to by "Miss," omitting their first names and making them virtually impossible to locate in historical records such as the census and contemporary newspapers. Because most Club members did not undertake paid employment, they were not included in city directories (the pre-telephone version of the phone book). We found a number of members' first names on a signed pledge that happened to be included in the middle of an otherwise empty membership roll book; we also found first names occasionally included in Club minutes, newspaper articles, obituaries (most frequently of their husbands, fathers, or other male relatives), census records, headstones on findagrave.com. We even took a field trip to Green Mount cemetery in Baltimore to find actual headstones; this is how we discovered Alice Emma Sauerwein Lord (Mrs. Charles W. Lord in Club documents)—as well as the fact that she was Charles W. Lord's *second* wife. If we had known, conceptually, that

women's history and women's stories had been effaced from the historical record, this absence became viscerally felt on an almost daily basis.

One of the most tantalizingly obscure figures we encountered was Lydia Crane, who served as the Recording Secretary of the Club from 1892 until 1913. The Recording Secretary was responsible for taking the minutes of each meeting, and while the minutes had to be approved by the Club members before being accepted into the record, she obviously wielded great power in representing the Club by being the person to describe the Club's activities, deciding how much detail to include, and what to omit. Every single person who has worked on this project has gotten to know Lydia's unique voice—articulate and always very proper, while also conveying a warm affection for her fellow Club members—with which she recorded the Club minutes. Full of detail and incorporating anecdotes and notes of her own, Lydia's voice lends color and character to the highly organized and rigidly procedural Club meetings. Taken together, Lydia's minutes take up over a thousand pages of the extant minutes; these minutes also document more than a decade of her life during which she devoted herself to recording the proceedings of the Club. Crane's style and tone set the precedent for all of the Recording Secretaries who followed her. When she gave up her post in 1913 due to failing eyesight, she was made Honorary Recording Secretary by acclamation, a position she held until her death in 1916. Ironically, she never published anything of her own aside from a few "fugitive verses" in local publications—none of which we have been able to locate. Even her tombstone in Green Mount Cemetery is illegible due to erosion. The only piece of writing we have recovered is a biographical sketch of her sister, novelist Anne Moncure Crane Seemuller, which Crane presented at an 1895 meeting and then meticulously copied into the minutes. Yet as her personhood has been erased from even the stone memorials of history, her voice dominates our understanding of the Club. Women like Lydia exemplify the goal of the Aperio project.

Yet Lydia Crane's sense of propriety was also responsible for some of our difficulties in understanding the Club's history. Most obvious was her reluctance, if not outright refusal, to use the given names of married members of the Club. We were both shocked and elated, when we discovered that Mrs. Fabian Franklin, a founding member who was a vocal and regular contributor to meetings during the Club's first decade, was also known as Christine Ladd-Franklin, the first woman to complete PhD requirements in mathematics at Johns Hopkins and a respected scholar in the disciplines of mathematics and psychology. Several other members were better known in public under their given names but appear in Club documents only as the "missus" of their husbands.

Crane also sought to smooth over differences and minimize conflict, and frequently omitted points of view or perspectives with which she disagreed. For example, while we now know that a number of the Club's members (including Christine Ladd-Franklin, for example) supported suffrage, the very idea of the women's vote was hardly ever mentioned. This was true even in the winter months of 1906, when the National American Women's Suffrage Association, headlined by Susan B. Anthony, held its national convention just blocks away from the Club's meeting rooms. The convention was almost certainly attended by Club members, but it is not even mentioned in the minutes.

Crane was especially circumspect when relating disagreements among Club members. One of the most contentious moments in the Club history erupted in 1893, when a group led by First Vice-President Elizabeth T. King sought to revise the Club Constitution so that it would permit the inclusion of non-literary subjects and activities, and to expand the membership to those who did not seek to publish their writings. After all, the Club constitution had indicated that meetings would engage in "discussion of the questions of the day—literary, artistic, social and political"; why not invite those actively involved in social and political pursuits to participate in those discussions? Over the course of several months, the question was studied, debated and voted upon. While Crane's minutes dutifully record the submissions of reports from "Majority" and "Minority" factions, votes taken, and statements made by individual members, the actual points of disagreement are described in such vague terms that it is difficult to tell why they are even disagreeing. It takes reading very carefully between the lines to understand that King's group, while representing the majority of the Club, was undermined by the more conservatively-minded minority through manipulations of parliamentary procedure. In the end, it was the minority faction, implicitly supported by Crane, who ended up carrying the day. This faction sought no change to the constitution and no change was made.

In the ensuing weeks, over a dozen members resigned from the Club, including King as well as others who are recorded as supporting expansion of the Club. These members ended up forming the core of a new club, the Arundell Club, and it is actually in their own history that the clearest representation of the schism can be found: "Philanthropy . . . was not smiled upon [by the WLCB] and there were suggestions detrimental to the feelings of some of us that history was not literature, whilst sociology naturally was anathema."[19] The Arundell Club, responding directly to this stance, offered its three hundred members public meetings, sectional study groups, committees for public work, field days, social entertainments and musicales. Gere writes that the desire to maintain amity at almost any cost was common to women's clubs throughout this period; "expressions of dissent and difficulty between members appear to have been deliberately downplayed." Rather than detail personal animosity and conflict, Gere argues, club women used the minutes to show how women were able "to transcend conflicts and reinforce commonalities so that they could stay emotionally connected to one another despite differences in ideas and beliefs."[20]

Despite Lydia Crane's limitations as a reliable Club historian, one thing rapidly became clear: the WLCB was not, as we had originally suspected, an organization simply interested in "self-culture." One of the first and most important things we noticed when transcribing was how frequently women presented their own original writing to the Club. These women were not passive observers of culture but were actively producing their own art and analysis.

We soon realized further that Club members were not just sharing this work with one another, they also published it—and not just locally, but with some of the most respected presses and magazines in the US. As we learned the Club members' names, interests, and histories, we noticed that published volumes were donated to the Club library. Reviews, short fiction, or poetry appearing in magazines were frequently mentioned during Club announcements. A work presented on one occasion would be mentioned months or sometimes years later as having appeared in print. This understanding led to a commitment to recovering as many of their publications as possible. Each student in the Spring 2018 class was assigned between two and four authors to research in library catalogues and databases and in online archive sites. We found that these women produced far more in print than we expected. Some of these women had practically countless publications, like Louise Malloy, who wrote daily jokes for a newspaper under the name Josh Wink; or Grace Denio Litchfield, whose poems were widely reprinted in newspapers across the country.

Our next step was to actually track down either physical or digital copies of these works. These were collected into the Virtual Library in the online WLCB archive, which we initially conceived of as replicating the Club library, which had been lost. But once we realized we would not be able to include more than a fraction of the Club's published output in an anthology, the Virtual Library became the means by which access could be provided to as many of their publications as possible. The Virtual Library is continuing to be updated as new works—and authors—are discovered. Collecting all of their works in one place also made it possible for the class to read and comment on the works together. For it remained important for us to publish a print anthology of their works. Club members expressed a desire to publish a volume of Club writings or a magazine from the first years of the WLCB's existence, but for whatever reason, none was ever produced. *Parole Femine* is the long-awaited fulfillment of that desire.

The Spring 2018 class spent a significant portion of the semester reading through the "slush pile" of publications we had recovered, recommending some for review by the entire class, and evaluating each other's selections. Having noticed a uniformity of worldview in the Club minutes, we were surprised to find that their published writings reflected a much wider range of attitudes toward gender roles—and pretty much everything else. While some defended the domestic values of True Womanhood, others espoused the social, economic, and intellectual freedom represented by the figure of the New Woman, who lived alone or with other women, sought an education and a career, and asserted an independent identity as a voting citizen. We decided to select works that demonstrated that range of views. We also decided to restrict the historical scope of the anthology to members belonging to the Club between the years 1890-1920; despite the sheer quantity of the archival materials held at the Maryland Historical Society, records dating after about 1915 are incomplete, and are essentially non-existent after 1920. In order to be able to contextualize the selected works within the history of the Club itself, we needed to restrict ourselves to this time period. Within this scope, however, *Parole Femine* represents Club members' diverse fields of interest and expertise. We selected at least one work from each writer, and we took into account whether a work had been read or discussed in a meeting, and what its critical or outside reception had been.

What we had more difficulty knowing what to do with was our dawning realization that many Club members, including those in high leadership positions, espoused views aligned with Lost Cause ideology: views that the Civil War, fought more than two decades before but with long lasting effects, had destroyed "the Southern way of life"; that slavery had been a benevolent institution, bringing benighted Africans and their descendants to Christian salvation and providing means for these helpless people to be provided for by caring, altruistic whites; that the Anglo-Saxon "race" was destined to reign over all others, due to their inherent superiority. The Club did not admit black members, and more than a few Club members were members of another organization that emerged at the same time, the Daughters of the Confederacy. Club programs included stories and poems featuring exaggerated dialects for non-white characters (at least one of these was likely read or performed in blackface), travel pieces treating the voyeuristic observation of native peoples as entertainment, articles celebrating the virtues and indomitability of the Aryan race, and anthropological pieces critiquing African-American or Native cultures through a white supremacist lens. A noticeable portion of their published works fell neatly in line with Lost Cause ideology, depicting grateful former slaves who remained on the "old plantation" with "missus" or "massa" because life elsewhere could be no better, and refined Southern families' lives destroyed through the rapaciousness of crass Northerners. It was difficult to reconcile these beliefs with these women we had come to know and to whom we had dedicated so much time and energy. At the same time, some of these members also supported philanthropic efforts to support the formerly enslaved, and others may even have supported racial equality—a daring view for a white person to hold in Maryland during the years when Jim Crow segregation became entrenched.

How could we create an anthology that acknowledged all of these contradictions, all this baggage? In the end, we decided that although certainly not every Club member held these views, it would be impossible and irresponsible to present our research about this Club without talking about this side of its legacy. Goodness knows, practically every Southern family had an enslaved person in their family tree and, to paraphrase literary historian Tony Horwitz, at least one Confederate in every attic. One cannot depict Southern culture of the time without encountering the anxious hegemony of white supremacy. At the same time, we emphasize that this anthology presents an incomplete cross-section of women's lives in Baltimore during this time. At the same time that the WLCB was forming, a formidable group of black women, including Anna Church Terrell, Anna Julia Cooper, Frances Ellen Watkins Harper, and Pauline Hopkins were organizing and publishing in nearby Washington, DC and Philadelphia. In Baltimore, Augusta Chissell formed the Colored Women's Suffrage Club in 1915, and wrote for the Baltimore *Afro-American*. None of these women would have been admitted to a WLCB meeting or Salon, and their names do not appear in the minutes. It is perhaps poetic justice that these African American women are now better-known than their white sisters.

The project's goal at its beginning was to recover the lost literary lives of Baltimore women, to recover their stories and voices from the dustbin of history. And we have done that. We do not shy away from including those works that made the women's racism apparent; to ignore those works in favor of a more palatable anthology would have been irresponsible. Instead, we used the headnote introducing each author to discuss her work, explain how it represents its contemporary moment, and how it is likely to be viewed today. It is important not to sanitize these women's legacy, because for so many of them, it is a legacy of Confederate sympathy, of romanticization of the old South, and of racism. Including and discussing these works lets us give an accurate picture of what the social views of educated middle- and upper-middle-class Baltimore women were really like at this time, and can even give us some historical context for our present-day discussions about Confederate monuments, many of which were built in Baltimore during the era when the WLCB was most visible on the public stage, and other lingering wounds from a national cataclysm that still has not been completely resolved.

In short, we have attempted to bring these women's voices into the light, even if they weren't saying what we had hoped or expected.

Travelers, Crusaders, Singers, Chroniclers, Elegists

When deciding how to structure the content within the anthology, the Spring 2018 class debated whether to authors in alphabetical order, chronological order by birthdate or publication date, or by genre. We wondered if we should simply select a single representative work from each member or try to fit as much as we possibly could into the book. In the end, we decided to present a capacious volume organized by theme and grouping the authors loosely within each category by date of first publication. These themes reflect the writerly personas projected by Club authors—those whose attention remained focused on local concerns; those who wrote about their travels around the world, whether literal or imaginative; social crusaders and critics; singers in the lyric poetry tradition; observers of natural phenomena and human behavior; chroniclers of the domestic arena and phases of women's lives ranging from girlhood through courtship, marriage, motherhood, and widowhood; and finally, those who paid tribute to fellow artists in the form of elegy and ode. Each section has its own introduction, and each author included also has her own headnote, written by the student who worked to recover her works and biography. We believe that this organization best conveys both the individual personalities and careers of the authors of the Woman's Literary Club of Baltimore, and a sense of the Club as a whole: a Club that worked collectively, as a Club and through its different committees, to realize a vision of female intellect and female participation in American print culture.

Parole Femine: Words and Lives of the Woman's Literary Club of Baltimore is the culmination of years of thinking, researching, and editing, and it is the work of many, many hands. As we complete the editorial work on this project, however, we are consistently reminded that this edition, and its companion online archive, constitutes a beginning rather than an end. Many new directions for further research and editorial work have been opened up by this project. Most obviously, a second volume with works from 1920-1941 is called for, and Professor Cole is already at work gathering publications from this period as well as what remains of the Club records, which are scattered in the papers of individual members, left in traces in newspaper accounts of meetings, and possibly, remembered by living descendants of Club members.

This project has also revealed the existence of several writers whose work calls for closer scrutiny and deeper exploration. To name just a few examples: Emily Emerson Lantz's profiles of Baltimore streets and neighborhoods are full of human and architectural detail and provide present-day readers and historians a vivid alternative perspective on a period of Baltimore history that has been dominated by figures such as H. L. Mencken. Louise Malloy has been recognized as a journalistic trailblazer but also wrote several plays, at least one of which was staged on Broadway, that show a sharp ear for witty dialogue and a strong sense of history. Grace Denio Litchfield was prolific and widely read alongside poets like Sarah Teasdale and Edna St. Vincent Millay, poets who were dismissed as hopelessly "middlebrow" by the academic establishment of the mid-twentieth century but are now receiving renewed attention by feminist literary scholars. Katharine Pearson Woods stood alongside fellow Christian Socialist Edward Bellamy during his lifetime but, like him, fell by the literary wayside when socialism in all of its forms became suspect during and after World War II. We hope that this anthology introduces scholars to the works of all of these writers and spurs them to bring them back into the classroom, scholarship, and American literary history.

Editorial note

Texts included in *Parole Femine* have been minimally edited, although those originally appearing in newspapers have been edited to conform to the *Chicago Manual of Style*, 17th Edition. Street names are capitalized, and military ranks and titles are spelled out. British spellings have been changed to conform to American usage, and obvious errors in spelling and punctuation have been silently corrected. The serial or Oxford comma is used throughout. Contemporary spellings of words such as "to-day" and "some one" have been retained as they appear in the copy-text.

Readers are encouraged to consult the digitized images of the original texts collected in the Virtual Library section of the Woman's Literary Club of Baltimore online archive, http://loyolanotredamelib.org/Aperio/WLCB/.

Local Favorites

Many of the women of the Woman's Literary Club of Baltimore weaved a strong sense of place into their writing. Those we have gathered here—poets, historians, journalists, and short story writers—all felt especially strong connections to the city of Baltimore. As a collective, the club took pride in the literary and historical legacy of their city.

One of the most obvious ways they showed their local pride was their obsession with the poetry of Edgar Allan Poe. Although not a native of Baltimore himself, Poe's family had strong ties to the city. At a time when Poe's work was frequently maligned, the women of the club did what they could to recognize his connection with Baltimore—going so far as to erect a literal monument to him.

Their relationship with Sidney Lanier, another poet who relocated to Baltimore, was hardly different. Lanier's wife, Mary Day Lanier, was an honorary member of the club. Their first president, Francese Litchfield Turnbull, and her husband Lawrence, were among the poet's closest associates in the city and were even buried alongside him.

In one of their most cherished traditions, the Club decorated the graves of "authors and artists of Maryland" every November. Poe and Lanier were among those whose graves they decorated annually—as was the grave of Club member Mary Spear Tiernan. But the club was not only concerned with literary figures who called Baltimore their home. They frequently recounted with humor the story of the novelist Henry James's brief visit to the city. James wrote of walking up North Charles Street and being distinctly unimpressed by the area—as though he had seen all Baltimore had to offer. They loved to recall Francis Scott Key's composition of the "Star-Spangled Banner" while he floated on Baltimore waters, or the Marquis de Lafayette's special fondness for the hospitality of Baltimore women.

All of this left an indelible impact on their writing. Jane Zacharias's short novel *The Newsboys' Christmas Party* is rife with imagery of Mount Vernon in snowfall. Then among Baltimore's most fashionable neighborhoods, the area's wealth contrasts with the poverty of the newspaper boys. In this story, Zacharias points to the uneven distribution of wealth in the city, and implicitly encourages her readers to do something about it.

Lucy Meacham Thruston was concerned less with Baltimore in particular and more with the region as a whole. Her volume of poetry, *Songs of the Chesapeake*, depicts the state's wetlands in verse. She didn't only write poetry, however; she also wrote novels, including a lengthy novelization of the life of Margaret Brent—among the most celebrated female figures in colonial Maryland. She shared this interest in Brent with fellow club member Elizabeth Lester Mullin, whose short story, "Mistress Brent's Bluff," provides a briefer glimpse into the life and character of this historically significant Marylander.

Then there were those who preferred to stick to the realm of nonfiction. Emily Lantz, longtime contributor to the *Baltimore Sun*, boasted an encyclopedic knowledge of the history of the city and the surrounding area. In addition to her extensive work in genealogy, Lantz documented the growth of Baltimore's suburbs, and uncovered the histories of the city's most famous thoroughfares. Annie Leakin Sioussat's text *Old Baltimore*, excerpted in this volume, is a comprehensive history of the city from its earliest settlement.

The Woman's Literary Club of Baltimore celebrated the culture of the city they inhabited. And through their writings, they also shaped it—crystallizing Baltimore's literary and historical legacy for posterity.

Jane Zacharias (1843-1906)

Jane Zacharias, born in Frederick, Maryland, was fondly known as "Miss Jane" or "Janie" by the newsboys who came to know her. Remaining unmarried her entire life, she was known for her artistic ability, musical talents, and philanthropic pursuits. Zacharias organized musicals and played the organ in several area churches. She was also one of several members of the Woman's Literary Club of Baltimore who also belonged to the Baltimore Folk-Lore Society.[1]

Zacharias's only known published literary work was *The Newsboys' Christmas Par-* *ty*. Zacharias volunteered for local organizations that established the Newsboys' Association and the Newsboys' Reading Rooms, and also established an annual Christmas dinner for the local newspaper boys in Baltimore, as she depicts in this semi-autobiographical account. According to the *Baltimore Sun*, the newsboys considered her "something good and wonderful, yet human enough to understand their trials and joys"; one of them commented, "She was the whole show."[2]
—J. Morgan and J. L. Cole

"HURR'LD, SUN, EN' ERMERRIEKIN!"

"Hurr'ld, Sun, en' Ermmerriekin!" Special Collections and University Archives, University of Maryland Libraries.

The Newsboys' Christmas Party (1899)

To
My little friends
The newsboys and bootblacks of Baltimore
on each returning Christmas Eve
makes "Merrie Christmas"
all the year 'round
for "Miss Janey"

Chapter I

It was early in the morning just three weeks before Christmas.

All through the night the snow had been falling, for the streets were seamed deep with ruts from the early milk-wagons and the pavements were white, inches deep, with an unbroken crust. Certainly Jack Frost had been busy long before the dawn: the window panes were full of pictures framed in bands of white fur, the sills were covered high to keep out the cold, and the little children still were fast asleep.

Fast asleep, in bare rooms on narrow streets, where broken windows were pasted with paper or stuffed with old clothes; fast asleep, in beautiful homes around Mt. Vernon Place,[3] and along the pretty streets were—asleep, behind dainty lace curtains, and so the little ones could not know of the finer lace work wrought outside. Good old Jack knew how and when to weave and had slipped out of sight with all his tools.

But Nota had wakened very early and was standing at her window looking out upon the dancing snow. Before her rose the roofs piled high with eider-down, all the chimney-pots covered up in soft white hoods. They looked like little people peeping from under blankets and brought to mind two little girls she once had known who popped up in bed suddenly one Christmas Eve long ago, listening while they looked towards the fireplace where the stockings were hanging. It seemed to her she still could hear them exclaim mysteriously: "What's that!" and, bobbing down as suddenly, clutch at each other's little gowns, ever so glad, but pretending to be afraid. It started her to thinking of Christmas time and little children.

When her glance wandered to the pavement below her, she saw that a single track had made on the opposite side—the track of short steps but big shoes—and while she was wondering who the early bird might be she heard a high voice calling through the wintry air: "Hurr'ld, Sun, en' Ermerriekin!"[4] She threw open the window and hardly had

time to look out when a little newsboy, in very big clothes, answered the sound of the rising window by an upward look, calling out again: "Hurr'ld, Sun, en' Ermerriekin!" Under one arm he carried a bundle of papers, while the other had partly disappeared in the depths of a pocket in his big jacket. Tossed on the back of his head was a slouch hat framing tangled dark hair blowing about with the wind; an old calico shirt was opened wide at his throat, the buttonless lap gaping over his thin white breast.

Nota quickly waved her hand to him and started to go down stairs as the boy came across the street, his big shoes, with the tongues hanging out, flapping after him over the snow.

Now, when the little fellow had looked back at the lady standing at the window, he said to himself, "My! But folks who live in big houses must be happy!"

When Nota had felt the cold air as she looked across the street at Pilkey in his shabby clothes so loose and thin, she felt great pity and expected to see a sad little face as she hurried down to meet him.

But when they met as she opened the hall door they just changed places: the boy's face was so bright and eager it gave her a surprise; while he, on his part, fell to wondering why she should look "sorry like," as he said to the newsboys when he was telling them about it in the afternoon:

"No, 'twas n't 'er black dress," he explained, "but sumpin' made 'er look so; ennyhow 'n she ast me 'f I'd enny breakfus 'n I showed 'er the raw turnip I was finishin' up and said 'yes'm, you may n't b'lieve me, but she set to cry'n'—'Front street theater,[5] las' act?'—well I reckon not; them was reel tears, fell clean down 'er face—'Cawphy'? you bet, an' roll all smokin' hot, an' then—but I ain't goin' to tell the res', cos' it's a secret an' I promused 'er. But," he continued, "she bought six Suns en' Ermerriekins—an' 't wasn't no murder er sooaside in either on 'em," he exclaimed triumphantly. "Mebbe you think Crismus ain't cumin'," he added, with a mysterious air as he gathered up his papers and started off for the afternoon sale.

When the hall door had closed on Pilkey in the morning, Nota went back to her chamber and sat for a long time before the open fire, with her head leaning on her hand, thinking. Suddenly she left her chair and began preparations for going out. "Let me see," she began, as she sat upon a low cushion to draw on her rubbers, "let me see; Mr. Lartell is the very one; he knows all about the business part of the city—and then, he has such a big heart," she added, drawing a fur cloak around her. After this she took up an umbrella in a snug silk case and a pretty little muff, but she laid her muff down, asking herself: "do I need this?" "No"—she thought gravely—"and yet I have it": just then she seemed to have seen Pilkey right before her in his thin clothes. She looked very hard at the muff and said half aloud: "If one muff costs thirty dollars—what about one thin old jacket—?" She did not finish what she started to say, but hurried out and was soon moving briskly along the snowy pavement.

Mr. Lartell's house was only a few blocks away, and on reaching it Nota told the servant to say that she wished to see him for a few minutes; "alone," she added, stepping into the library, a pleasant room looking out upon a grove of pine trees covered with snow.

"Good morning, Miss Nota," said Mr. Lartell, entering and holding both hands toward her in welcome.

"I know you will pardon the early hour," she rejoined placing her hands in those of her father's friend, "I feared missing you, and there is something special in this call."

"What can I do for you?" he asked cordially.

"More than anyone else just at this moment," she exclaimed, looking up into his kind face; then sitting near him, they spent ten or fifteen minutes talking in low voices.

"You are quite right about it," she said rising to go, "some one connected with the newspapers is the best source for information in this matter and I will see about it at once; you know we cannot lose a day."

"No, for it is only three weeks off, is it not?" he inquired in a lower tone.

"Sh!" retorted Nota, putting her fingers to her lips.

"I had forgotten, but trust me," Charles Lartell continued, "I shall keep your secret."

Nota laughingly lifted her finger again and started homeward as fast as the snow would permit.

"How delightful is this air on my face!" she thought, gliding over the slippery pavement. A voice at her side seemed to say:

"Yes, on the face when wrapped in furs, but how would it feel through a thin old jacket?"

A shiver crept over her as she thought of that, even on entering her own warm, bright home, where she lost but a few moments before sitting at her writing-table and addressing this note:

"My Dear Mr. Hendon:

One year ago among the evergreen garlands in the church, you asked me to call upon you if you could serve me in any way, especially at the Christmas–Tide.

I need very much to have your advice in a little matter that may become a big one before we are through with it; and as it concerns Christmas, which is so near at hand, as soon as you can spare an hour from that busy office of yours, will you call to see me? –and I can then explain fully what I can now only hint to you.

And believe me sincerely yours,

Nota Shelburne."

Then calling the maid and telling her to see that it was mailed immediately, she sat by the window and looked out.

The snow was still falling and had turned the tree before her into a mass of white blossoms. They hung on every twig just as in May-time, while in and out among the boughs a snow-bird swept his wings or stopped to listen, as though he could hear the snow falling as it touched the branches on its way to the street. Her face wore a glad look and she was busy thinking. She must have been planning something, for between smiles she would say:

"Yes, that will do, I am sure"; or, "plain pure candies may be much less by the quan-

tity"; "oranges are high and scarce just now, but we'll see Darby & Co.[6] about that"; and many little sentences scattered all about that no one else could possibly understand.

The morning soon passed and early in the afternoon of the same day a card was handed Nota:

Mr. William Hendon,
Of *The American*

She hastened down to meet him and as she extended her hand told him how pleased she felt as his prompt response to her note.

"It reached me only an hour ago," he responded, "and I felt so interested I came at once. What is it that you will let me do for you?" he asked, his fine dark eyes looking as eager as her own.

"O Mr. Hendon," She replied earnestly, "it is something I have set my heart on doing without knowing just how to begin—"

"And you would like to have me show you," he rejoined; "do you think I can?"

"I feel sure that you can," she said confidently: "You must know all about newsboys, don't you?"

"Newsboys!" he exclaimed, "it is a pretty difficult matter to know one newsboy well, though I see many every day. But what is it you would know about them?"

"Why, this," said Nota, speaking in a low tone; "has there ever been anything done for them at Christmas here in Baltimore?"

"No," he replied, "all that has been given them, that I have heard of, has been an occasional Thanksgiving Dinner."

"Then you are sure nothing has been thought of for Christmas?"

"Absolutely sure," he repeated; "it is so

Why They Beg on the Streets for a "Starter." Special Collections and University Archives, University of Maryland Libraries.

near the season that the press would know something of it."

"Well, then," she continued, "this is what I wish to see done them—" and the words came fast as he listened, attentive, following what she said with comments on its possibilities.

"But how do you expect to accomplish it in so short a time?" he asked; "there are fully three hundred newsboys and but three weeks for everything."

"I do not know *how* I shall do it," she retorted with a firm smile, "but I intend to—someway."

"Bravo!" cried William Hendon, and extending his hand he said gravely: "I will stand by you through all of it—when shall we begin?"

"When can we, how soon?" she asked eagerly.

He answered slowly: "At half past two

tomorrow afternoon, if you will meet me at Sutro's music store on Baltimore Street,[7] and from there we will go to find the newsboys—I will tell you all about it later," he continued, and in answer to her questioning glance he said: "We will first partly tell the boys our plans, and then the papers, and the papers will tell the people."

"And the people?—" she asked with a puzzled air.

"Will send in the money through the papers!—Oh! I am sure of it," he added hopefully, "but if they should fail, you may count on me for the hall."

Nota fairly clapped her hands, she was so pleased.

"Well, then, on me for —— and all its belongings," she said in laughing under-tones.

"And on me for teaching how to *sing* the carols," she retorted, suddenly going to the piano and beginning to sing from "Good King Wenceslaus":

"'Bring me flesh and bring me wine,
Bring me pine-logs hither;
Thou and I will see him dine
When we bear them thither.'
Page and monarch, forth they went,
Forth they went together;
Through the rude wind's wild lament
And the bitter weather."

After William Hendon had gone, Nota sat a long time before the open fire, now and then turning her head towards the window near her. In the bright coals and beyond the window she saw something that was not there and in the midst of it all, Pilkey, warm and happy.

Chapter II

Down near the corner of South and German Streets,[8] there was once an old court. Into it looked back windows from deserted warehouses, printing shops and saloons. Many of the broken windows were stuffed with rags and papers, but that day the snow had beautified everything it could rest upon, excepting the pavement of the court whose cobblestones were nearly covered with mud and slush. It was the day on which Nota had promised to meet Mr. Hendon, and just as "Big Sam," the clock on the City Hall, struck three, they entered the court together.

This was the rendezvous for the newsboys of South Baltimore, and the hour for gathering to the afternoon papers.

But not a boy was in sight.

"Where are they?" asked Nota.

"Wait a minute," Mr. Hendon explained, "you will see them; you can't tell where they come from—the little moles—" he added laughing. He had hardly spoken when they heard a quick, low whistle—presently out from a doorway that had once been painted blue a newsboy sprang, both feet squared together, over the three flagstone steps. He was followed by a second who jumped over the bent back of the first in a game of leap-frog. Tumbling over each other, one after another tilted into the court, and snowballs were seen flying at all points of the compass. "Boys," cried Mr. Hendon, at the top of his voice: "A lady is here!"

"Wot!" responded the latest comer, "Where?"

"Behind that wall, take care!" He exclaimed as another ball flew through the air.

"Where's a leddy?" cried out a boot-black, who with his box and strap, strung over his shoulder, had come in from the street side.

It flew like prairie-fire that a lady was in the court, and out of windows, door-ways and basement, one after another appeared. In a few moments fully a hundred boys were around William Hendon, who said to them: "Boys, a lady really is here. There is something she intends to do that you will like; but she will also need your help—will you behave like gentlemen while she is here?"

"Yes, sir, yes, sir!" rang through the air with tossing of caps, clog-dancing and a rush towards Mr. Hendon.

"No, boys, not until you show respect shall you see the lady or hear anything more of what we have come to tell you."

"Where's yer manners?" cried out Dick, a leader among the "boots"; "Where's yer manners? Git back! Git *back*, I say," creating a stir, as he pushed to the right and left of the mob of boys, while Mr. Hendon stepped up to where Nota was standing, looking on the rough little crowd, and led her out among them, when Pilkey made a circle in the melted snow underfoot, pre-scribing a line of distance from her.

"Now, boys," asked Mr. Hendon, "how far off is Christmas?"

"Crismus!"

"Hear that, *Crismus*!" accenting with a ball aimed at the opposite corner of the court.

"Crismus ain't three weeks," said Pilkey, slyly glancing at Nota.

One thing she learned then and there; that there was no enthusiasm about Christmas in that little crowd; it meant for them no especial joy: only a few more pennies here or there in the holiday number of papers.

"Well, people are happy at Christmas, are they not?" continued Mr. Hendon.

"Sum is," answered Dick, "them what's got hollidays and sleds."

At this Nota exclaimed: "Why, you are merry as Christmas yourselves to-day," smiling on the groups about her, while she scanned the eager faces, until her glace rested on Pilkey, ready to exchange with a knowing look.

The boys drew nearer curiously. She began to talk to them as though she had always known them; and with that keen and fair insight she learned afterwards to recognize in them, they established an un-derstanding free from words, and entered into a compact to practice the carols, and indeed were ready to promise anything when she asked them to meet her at Raine's Hall on Postoffice Avenue,[9] the next Sun-day afternoon, when they were to be told more about the plans for Christmas.

From this point Mr. Hendon went with Nota in the street cars out to Fre-mont Street, where the newsboys of West Baltimore collected together to get the af-ternoon papers. Only two boys were vis-ible as they approached, but in the same way as in the court there was a sudden ap-pearance of two and three at a time from near corners and alleys, soon increasing to a crowd, as it passed, on seeing elec-tric lines, that "some one" wanted to see them. They had gathered in front of a high brick wall that shut from view gar-dens and grounds belonging to a private house, and in an angle protected from the street, Nota stood, looking on while Mr. Hendon explained that "something" they should know about later was to happen at Christmas, and if they wished hear more about it they should meet the rest of the boys the next Sunday at Raine's Hall.[10]

Just then the wagon bringing the papers arrived, and the little street merchants with an eye to trade, left him standing alone, while they swarmed around the wagon bargaining for papers and running off to get the first chances at a sale for them on the cars and streets; but not before they understood where and when to meet again. The two friends of the boys again took a car for the shot-tower on Fayette Street,[11] the gathering place for the newsboys of East Baltimore. Here they were surprised at finding that the news had reached the place before they did, and a large crowd, many of whom were bootblacks, were waiting for them.

It had been decided the bootblacks were to "belong" as well as newsboys, Pilkey having explained: "fer it's all one trade ennyhow, Miss Nota, fer from a-sellin' papers they gener'ly goes to shinin'."

Nota asked: "And how long do they keep to selling papers?"

Mr. Hendon heard her, and replied: "Until they are about fourteen"; he seemed always to know about their ways as well as how to make friends of them.

The shot-tower looked tall and dark that afternoon, as it always does excepting when the sun shoots a long gilt arrow over the rising streets of East Baltimore at sunset.

All around it were machine-shops and crossing railroad lines; the boys liked that and anything besides—that looked like

bustle. It seemed as though the little fellows had always been in the busy lines of life, and were happiest, they said, "where lots is goin' on." The same divided attention between business, fun, and curious interest, marked the throng around the tower, and Nota with Mr. Hendon stayed until the wagons with the papers broke up the noisy groups and scattered the boys rapidly, here and there running away with bundles of papers under their arms.

The next day this is what appeared in the morning papers:

FOR THE NEWSBOYS.

"A small number of ladies and gentlemen interested in the newsboys and the bootblacks of Baltimore, have begun preparations for their entertainment on Christmas Eve, and to carry out their plans several hundred dollars will be required. The whole matter will be given to the public in detail later. Meanwhile any contributions of money, promised donations of candies, fruit, etc., will be received at the offices of *The American*, *Sun* and *Herald*, and be placed in the hands of the committee having the arrangements in charge. It is hoped that the public will respond heartily to this appeal and make these industrious little fellows as happy at Christmas as any tenderly cared-for child in the town."

Chapter III

On Sunday afternoon, two days later, several ladies were seen rapidly making their way towards Raine's Hall. When two or three blocks away they heard an unusual sound, a din softened by distance; "What can that be?" they questioned of each other.

"It sounds like an army of locusts or katydids," Nota remarked to her friend Julia Annalea, who had entered with enthusiasm on the undertaking for Christmas and with Nota was on her way to meet the boys for the first rehearsal of the carols. Julia exclaimed: "Can it be a fire?"

"I am afraid it is nothing more nor less than a demonstration from our saucy crowd," Nota said hurriedly, as they drew near the source of the sounds. There could be no doubt—it did come from Raine's Hall, but what could it be?

As they entered they saw William Hendon at the opposite end of the hall, his arms raised frantically above his head and judging from the movements of his lips he was speaking. Nota told him afterwards she could not at the moment imagine why he was trying to get his coat off though she knew warm work was going on.

Three hundred newsboys and bootblacks were in the hall and joining with one consent in a "Louisiana Tiger,"[12] the crescendo and diminuendo regulated by a leader known among the "boots" as "Cherry-ripe." The young mob was moving up and down the hall like swarming bees; fairly in for fun, they were forming in line in and out of the rows of benches and chairs, now using the latter as muskets in a drill, now breaking ranks and falling in heaps on the slippery floor, which was regularly used for dancing and had been waxed to a fine point.

Nearly all of the three hundred cop-ies of carols that had been printed for rehearsing were lying about, twisted into cigarettes, muddy with the imprint of shoes or pasted against the window panes, while the organ which had been sent with the compliments of Messrs. Sutro & Co., had been attacked and the whole top lifted off.

It was certainly discouraging. The ladies had evidently reckoned without their host. Both had known from experience the boys of mission schools, and had a general theory that street boys at least could be classified as to management.

They learned a lesson that afternoon and the newsboys taught it to them.

Mr. Hendon's first comment was: "We will have to learn a new way from the boys themselves, I suppose," as he sank exhausted into a chair, declaring it was the hardest day's work of his life. It was spoken in a whisper, all shade of a voice being lost through the continual effort to be heard during the last half-hour.

Suddenly in the midst of the din Nota thought of the organ and seating herself at it, she began to play in a spirited way the prettiest of the carols. The boys were taken by surprise. Arrested by the music they stood about in groups, looking at her, listening to the catching melody and gradually subsiding into order.

As the music ceased, without the boys having a moment for a chance at uprising, Mr. Hendon said kindly: "Boys, we won't scold for your being so noisy, so rude above all to the ladies, nor do we intend all through the whole thing to call in any policeman to keep you in order, but if you do not show by your conduct that you meant what you said when you promised to behave like gentlemen before the ladies there will be nothing more said about Christmas." A sudden silence fell over the room. Unknown to themselves they recognized the appeal to their chivalry and self-respect and there was a desperate effort to keep up the spell his words had thrown over them. The beginning of a promise for order would have been fulfilled, had not the "boots brigade" at that moment given a sly signal that drew nearly every boy in the hall to the long row of windows facing the street and with a cry of "Fire!" hats were thrown from the windows, followed down the stairs by every pair of legs that belonged to the owners until, the pavement reached, they fell over each other in a medley of claims for ownership. What rival claims there were for the dirty little slouches with the jagged brims! The typical newsboy hat! Upstairs, pell-mell into the hall the merry crowd scampered, noisier than ever, more than ever bent on having their fun out.

In the midst of it all, Nota began to sing, softly at first, walking down the aisle, looking the boys in the face with a smile as they made way for her; and these were the words she sang:

"There's a wonderful tree
The happy children rejoice to see,
Spreading its branches from year to year,
It comes from the forest to flourish here;
O this wonderful tree, with its
    branches wide,
Is always blooming at Christ-
    mas-tide!"[13]

There was not a boy in the hall who failed to listen and grow quiet as she passed up another aisle and down again, singing. In silence they gradually took seats and then still singing, without a pause, she sat as the organ and played an accompaniment to the song. When sure of her audience she told them they were to learn that carol, and the other carols as well, and the way to sing them beautifully—and without a second's loss she had them repeating the words after her.

They got to work in earnest, for after all they are an industrious little lot and work appeals to them. Patiently they went through the carol, catching the melody in a short time. They were repaid by Julia telling them after this, about the festival which she said was coming off on Christmas Eve; that they were to give the music themselves; that there would be a tree all their own, no other boys to take any part; it was to be just their own Christmas Party, and to learn more about it they must come to the next rehearsal. As the hall emptied of its cheery crowd Julia said: "No wonder they are hard to handle, they are their own masters so soon in life, and trying to be heard above the din of the streets doubtless makes noise their natural expression."

"True," Mr. Hendon rejoined, "besides of course they are real boys and in love with mischief, though to have fun they are dependent on what they can make for themselves."

"After all," Nota continued, "was it not downright lovely the way they simmered down under the carol?"

"Yes, it was," he returned, "and music is our dependence for order in the future; they'll come out all right," he added, "though we cannot at all tell what they will do on Christmas Eve when once started," and laughingly continued: "they'll make it merry for us, I fear." The next day the papers all came out with accounts of the meeting with the boys, reading like this:

"About three hundred newsboys and bootblacks met on Sunday afternoon at Raine's Hall to practice carols for the festival on Christmas Eve. The boys are wild with enthusiasm over the idea of their '*own* Christmas Party,' and of doing the entertaining on the occasion instead of being entertained; and so the 'carols' constitute the central figure of the whole affair. The results can be best imagined— but the occupants of the neighborhood were safely out of the way until Monday.

"It is the idea of the ladies who have the arrangements in hand, to draw the boys by the rehearsing of carols, and influence them to come each time by the anticipation of what each meeting will reveal, and so by degrees learn to know something of their ways and what may please and hold them—as it is hoped that the coming festival will be only the beginning of contact with the life of this little community of our streets and resolve into something permanent—" and this was followed with a list of contributions received on Saturday.

And here is what the *American* said about rehearsing the carols: "It is rather a difficult feat to sing well when you are flattened up against a side wall, all the wind knocked out of you by a dozen boys behind; but they managed to do it and didn't seem to mind. In front were a lot of little tackers not much higher that a duck. They sing in the chorus. There was one larger boy for whom the tune was too much. He couldn't keep it, but when they came to 'Carol, Brothers,'[14] he

was all right. Now, if the whole three hundred start off straight on the word 'Carol,' it's dollars to nickels they all get to the last word on time. But if the bootblacks start on 'Carol,' and the middle lot of newsboys on 'Brothers,' and the front seat of kids not certain where to start, it's dollars to coppers they don't know when they'll get there or how; for there's a little wrinkle in the tune at the end of the second line that breaks the boys up, but they get over it successfully and come in on the homestretch all together:

'Carol, Brothers, carol, for Christmas come again.'"

Chapter IV

On an afternoon several days after this, a party of ladies met in one of the prettiest drawing-rooms in Baltimore—at the house of Mrs. Annalea, who was well known for her unselfish life among those in need and her constant words and acts of kindness; so that the best thing about her beautiful home was her sweet self, making it always a pleasure to be with her. The most delicate flowers were clustered on mantels and tables, dainty glass baskets on little mirrors reflecting the maidenhair fern that was growing in them, while here and there a slender vase held long spikes of rare orchids that had been brought from her country home about six miles from town. Through the influence of her daughter Julia, Mrs. Annalea had consented to become treasurer for the festival fund, and her name brought in contributions rapidly. She had called a meeting of the few interested actively in the matter, and when she entered to greet them her fine face lighted up with pleasure as she announced the notes she had received from different parts of Baltimore wishing all success to the undertaking and enclosing sums of money to be used for the festival, with "Christmas greeting to the ladies" in charge of arrangements. Mr. Hendon had advised that the whole enterprise should continue in the ladies' hands as they had started it and seemed to have most influence with the boys. Mrs. Annalea offered her house for all meetings of the committee, for making ornaments for the tree and anything that it was possible to do there.

The next evening the work was begun. What a Christmas look the room wore when the ladies were at work using up the pretty materials! Colored card-board and fancy scrap pictures were lying on the tables; bright-colored tarlatans and ribbons were tossed among silver and gold papers, and in the midst of the variegated confusion one of the ladies had planted a Santa Claus holding a tiny Christmas tree.

Every one turned child that night and told Christmas legends while the scissors moved among the gauzes and fancy papers, transforming them into a variety of shapes; while at another table others were working with an alphabet of cardboard, making letters of many colors and frosting a number of stars that looked like snow with moon light on it.

It was like having Christmas before it came, for after all the real joy at Christmas-tide lies in giving it to others.

After this there was something of fresh interest daily. Gifts for the festival were arriving; the postman would leave every morning a bundle of notes addressed to "Mrs. Annalea, Treasurer of Newsboys' Christmas Fund." The boys were meeting twice a week to rehearse the carols and building air-castles about Christmas Eve, while the ladies visited the markets to see what was the best they could do about the tree and evergreens.

The public gave liberally for the short time they were made aware; for the generous charity spirit of Baltimore is taxed to its utmost at Christmas, and many had already decided to what cause their contributions should be given.

Then the boys were holding enthusiastic meetings along the curbstones to speculate on the outcome of "The Christmas Party," and vote upon the best "solo" voices with very forcible opinions on the subject.

One day this reached a heated point in the argument. "You call Chippie a bass, do you?" Said Dick, very red in the face. "Mebbe he is, an' mebbe he's th' bes' *bass*, but when I say Rob's th' boss voice o' th' gang, I'm talkin' about a *tener*!"

"I don't keer if he's a *fifteen-er*," came hot and fast from the first, "he ain't nowheres aside o' Chippie. Now there's a voice fer yer; y' kin hear him clean above th' whole gang, an' th' orgin an' ladies."

The rehearsals were hard work. Keeping quiet for an hour was harder than "hustling" all day with papers, and when to this was added the enterprise of turning a tune it became a question of downright labor.

But for all that the boys came regularly and the ladies began to know them better, and got to be closer friends with them, besides making it more possible to have some order, at least, on the evening of the Party.

Chapter V

Finally the day of the festival was at hand. The night before a small number of ladies

were met at Raine's Hall by as many gentlemen to decorate it with evergreens, working
hard to make it look "Christmasie" for their
little friends, who someway were gradually
growing to think more about the event itself
than simply what they were to get.

On the morning of the day, the same
party met at the hall to complete the
preparations for the evening, and were in
the midst of their work, bundles and boxes
arriving every few minutes, when three or
four of their little friends tumbled in the
doorway, following close upon men bringing boxes of oranges from Darby & Co.

Now, the ladies had tried their best to
keep the boys away until evening, so that
the whole effect should be a surprise; but
this was a "committee" appointed from their
own ranks to watch for an opportunity of
getting information and report it to a crowd
waiting in the court. Regular reporters they
were, getting in skillfully at the wrong moment and finding out all they were after in a
shorter time than it takes to tell.

THE UMPIRE.

The Umpire. Special Collections and University Archives, University of Maryland
Libraries.

But the ladies had begun by this time to understand too, so the door was locked on them and the small committee held prisoners. They were quite merry over this, walking about the room, making free comments and a full inspection, at the same time offering their services in the distribution of the contents of the various boxes and passing judgment on the quality whenever it struck their fancy.

One of them, holding his palms over a great bag of roasted peanuts, declared: "You can't trust these 'ere Light Street houses;[15] ten to one these ain't fresh," adding with a quizzical look, "I can't really tell 'till I taste 'em." Meanwhile under the tree, which as yet was untrimmed and had just been fastened securely to the stage, stood a second member of the committee, not over seven years old, hands in pockets, turning an apple face up towards the branches, red hair, freckles, saucy nose and keen, blue eyes, all called upon in a comical, critical survey. Nota was standing near and said:

"Well, my little man, are you really coming tonight?"

"Dunno," he replied with an indifferent air, his gaze roaming over the tree; "Wot cher goin' to hev?"

"I am sure you wouldn't be rude for the world," Nota responded, looking down into the mischievous, up-turned face, "why do you ask?"

The little fellow met the gaze undaunted and answered:

"'Cos I jus' thought ef it's to be *turkeys*, I'm in fer—" and lifting above his head two wide apart, chubby fingers, intimated how many he could manage, while a great open smile of fun brought forgiveness in its wake.

"No, there will be no supper to-night," Nota explained: "this is our first festival you know, and there was not time enough to have all we would like for you—but besides what *would* we do with all of you around tables?" she asked laughing, "it would be like three hundred tenpins all in a minute!"

"But never mind," she continued, as a look of disappointment showed itself in the boy's eyes, "we have a Christmas every year and this is only the first one."

"That's all right," he exclaimed in a manly way, "I guess I'll cum's evenin'."

Julia turned to him just then and said quietly: "This time we want you to learn what Christmas means and I am sure you will all be happy to-night even without the turkeys."

The only response to this word of comfort came from eyes devoutly raised to the ceiling, while their corners were being drawn down by the brown fingers, the dimpled corners of his mouth at the same moment curving downward in a mischievous protest. It was "Little-Liberty-Alley," whose real name was John Thomas, the youngest, most popular and sauciest boy in the trade.

Julia knew that he meant no rudeness; he was always brimming with fun and was a leader among the boys who had all helped to spoil him. He lived in the streets and a year before, when only six years old, had created a corner in *Heralds* twice in one week, but he was always ready to divide a turnover-pie or his last cigarette with any one who chanced to be near him. How the boys loved the generous comrade who at one moment had daubed the nearest nose with a paste-brush, and in the next offered to share with the victim his penny lunch to the last bit! Nota and he became fast friends after that first Christmas Eve together, and for many years he came to the festivals and was an active member of "The Newsboys' Club and Reading Rooms" that grew out of the newsboys' first Christmas festival.

All morning the boys worked with hearty good will, carrying packages from one end of the room to the other, clearing the floors of loose evergreen branches and making themselves useful in many ways. "What kin I do fer yer, to-night?" asked Rob, the "Tenor," as the morning wore on, bunching some spruce and handing it to Julia. "Be good!" said Nota promptly.

This was too much for Harry, a little cripple who, nevertheless, was moving rapidly about with the help of a short cane, his bent back and head often lost sight of in the heaps of evergreens that were strewn about the floor. He looked up with bright dark eyes lighting a delicate face, old with suffering but running over with fun, as he retorted in a flash: "Look 'ere, now, Miss Nota, ef *you're* goin' to talk about Heav'n, *I'm* goin' home!"

"Oh!" said Nota quickly, "that reminds me of something—what do you think Heaven is like?"

"I dun—no," was the slow reply.

"But suppose you try to think—I'll think too—."

After a puzzled silence in the group one of the boys suddenly cried out: "I bet it's like a pile o' white clouds wif' angels on top an' the devil underneath."

"But we don't want to think about what is beneath, do we?" asked Julia; "let us choose the angels, because you know Christmas Eve is the angels' time."

"So it is," Harry responded, "but-don't-le's-talk-about-it-now."

Julia agreed, but added: "Some time we will, shall we not?" smiling on the bent little figure that partly raised itself with the retort: "O, yaas," in a drawling way—adding briskly, "but le's keep it fer Sundays."

At this moment "Slouchy," the most ragged member of the party, cried out: "Oh! 'scuse me, ladies—really I mus' ast ye' to 'scuse me," as he clapped his hands on either side of his trousers and diving into the fathomless pocket of a newsboy's outfit, stuck five fingers through a rent in the end of an out-turned pocket: "'scuse me, but I mus' go home right now," continuing an apparent search for a lost article among the shreds of his clothes.

"What is it?" inquired on of the ladies, "have you lost your earnings?"

"No, not at all, but I fine' that," running his fingers through his hair, plunging his hands down into his untied shoes, going through a vigorous pantomime of searching—"I fine' I've lef' me pocket-book at home on the *pianner*."

The ladies joined heartily in the laugh that went around the room, one of them suggesting that he bring his piano to the festival.

Twelve o'clock came and the little prisoners were released. As they left the hall they promised faithfully not to tell the other boys what they had seen of the preparations—"anyway," Harry said demurely, "they're all gone now,"—and to come in the evening with clean faces, brushed hair and a "shine" on their shoes.

They were thought wholly out of the

way when Harry came back, limping on his stick, and standing in the doorway, said with a perfectly grave face, that he had been "'pointed to thank the ladies for a very pleasint mornin' quite onexpected."

Chapter VI

It was nearly six o'clock on Christmas Eve.

The street lamps were all lighted; the shop windows held myriads of twinkling lights; flambeaux were blazing and smoking in the gay garlanded markets and even the pea-nut-stand had its torch and bunch of green. The sky rejoiced in a goodly company of stars that watched over the city full of Christmas Light, and lifted out of darkness even the dim aisles of Greenmount,[16] where here and there bits of spruce had fallen along the ave-nues, from laden hands on their way to ivied mounds, where now a cross or anchor of im-mortelles stood out from the darkness and hinted of remembrance and a better Hope.

Through the streets of the town the crowds were hurrying, most of them turn-ing towards home with eager steps while many were joining the throng moving to-wards Lexington Market, where the carni-val centers and grows and lengthens from early evening to midnight. Here and there uptown a partly raised drapery at brilliant windows revealed pictures and doorways of beautiful rooms, framed in sprigs of holly and airy tendrils of ground-ivy. Now and then in darkened streets a narrow door opened and closed as a working man passed within, carrying a small basket packed high with homely food, relieved on top by a few bananas or apples, or perhaps a pint of cranberries and a tiny bunch of half-green celery. Along many pavements of the down-town streets, slim cedar trees were planted near the edge, and stood blooming with the shining fruits and gay flowers that wake up every Christmas-tide from a year's long sleep. Saloon and shop and stall rejoice in festoonings of evergreen as graceful as any on the illuminated business-houses.

Before the churches, wagons full of palms and lilies, garlands and wreaths, were unloading their bright burden, the opening and closing doors giving happy glimpses of busy hands adding here and there a finish-ing touch to altar and chancel, while the choir at its final rehearsal joined the organ in a *Jubilate* through the nave and arches.

Everywhere it was Christmas Eve. Where life was busiest and din was loudest, in among the passing throng were seen and heard the newsboys, hustling to get off the evening pa-pers and turning in squads towards Postoffice Avenue where Raine's Hall stood out a blaze of light amid the closed warehouses and dark thoroughfares around it.

Many had arrived at the hall long be-fore six o'clock, the hour for beginning "The Party," and had time to warm up be-fore the arrival of the late comers. Most of the latter had put a financial valuation upon an hour spent in waiting for the doors to open and decided it too heavy a cost for even a front seat. But Pilkey was not among these. Stiff yet in the legs from a long wait in the cold, jammed against the closed door from four o'clock, he was now triumphantly seated on the first bench, nearest the stage.

Down the hall they all were looking with expectant faces.

Presently there was a sound of scraping

feet and eager voices; Chippie was entering, leading in about twenty bootblacks.

"It's warm and jolly!" he called to those back of him, his following the lines of the gaily wreathed room.

"Beats th' gang for shinin'!" exclaimed Dick, settling his box and brushes under a seat in a row filled with bootblacks.

The scene filled them with surprise and delight; jostling each other like the merry crowds in the streets, they were finally seated and eagerly taking in all the novel charm of their own Christmas Party.

"Hello, Pilkey! *you're* stuck," cried out Slouchy from the lower end of the Hall. "No, I ain't," Pilkey called out, "I'll hustle afterwards"—finding under the seat, a place for his unsold papers, out of sight and free from further comment.

"Las' edishon!" shouted the latest arrival, with one paper under his arm and scrambling for a top seat. Soon the boys came in crowds and the room was rapidly filled. Mr. Hendon led the ladies up the middle aisle amidst tremendous cheer.

The hall was fairly quivering in the light from chandeliers and many side-lights, every jet glittering among the evergreens. Garlands of trailing pine were swung from the central chandelier and caught up, along the side walls with bunches of spruce full of spicy odors. Over the tall windows were boughs of laurel and holly with clusters of red berries standing out of the dark green, and all of it bending and bowing as in the forest when the wind has swept by. On the walls were letters of red-card board bordered with ivy and the boys were spelling out the texts for themselves: "Christ is Born," "The Star of Bethlehem," "Infant of Days," "The Shepherds Heard the Angels sing," "Glory to God in the Highest," and many others, while on the wall facing the boys were the words: "Holy Child Jesus." These were in very large letters of evergreen bordered with holly-berries.

The tree stood in the middle of the stage and was decorated with many shining strands thrown from bough to bough over the ornaments the ladies had made.

Fairies in spangled white dresses were swinging among the branches and every twig bent under the weight of gilded nuts and silver stars; the faces of cherubs were peeping out here there between their wings, and in the center of the tree a large star was suspended over many tiny banners of white silk, that were hung by slender gilt chains, each having a text painted in gold letters. Some of them were: "The Babe of Bethlehem," "Emanuel," "Peace on Earth," "The Prince of Peace," "Ancient of Days," "Good-will to Men," and many other inscriptions. These had been made by a very young man, a bookkeeper belonging to a large business-house near the hall. He had asked the ladies to allow him to contribute them to the festival, saying as he had not money to give he would like to give his work. He always worked at his books after business hours, so that by the time he had taken dinner it was after nine o'clock before he could work on the banners. But for all that—the ladies found out—he sat up often until midnight to have them finished in time for Christmas Eve. For they were delicately painted and very beautiful—just as perfect and beautiful as though they were going to a little Prince; and indeed they were to do honor to the Birth Day of the Prince of the House of David.[17]

Every one was sorry the tree could not be lighted with candles, but this could not be done for fear of fire. But it had been placed under a graceful chandelier with many prisms and when these were swaying and catching the light all around, it was almost as pretty as candles—though there is really nothing for a Christmas tree like candles.

Between the tree and the chandelier were the words: "Merrie Christmas," in red letters bordered with gold color and swung on wires. At the side of the stage the organ was placed nearly covered with boughs of the dogwood tree, full of red berries, and slim stems of "The Burning Bush"[18] gleaming from under cedar branches. Tables covered in white, bordered with myrtle, held the gifts, hundreds of packages wrapped with bright colors, and a perfect rainbow of candy-bags heaped on bunches of laurel. So everything was in readiness for the

"THE CHRISTMAS TREE IS AN EVERGREEN, IT BLOOMS WHERE FROST AND SNOW ARE SEEN."

"The Christmas Tree Is an Evergreen, It Blooms Where Frost and Snow Are Seen"
Special Collections and University Archives, University of Maryland Libraries.

little guest from the streets. Looking about them, the boys were too busy for mischief, and so all was quiet when Mr. Hendon stood before them saying:

"Before we begin our program you must be told that a prize will be given to the boy who shall behave the best this evening—but it will be hard to decide among so many who will doubtless deserve it, so we—"

"Let Liberty-Alley have it," cried out one of the boys.

Mr. Hendon, taken by surprise, answered quickly: "Not unless he is the best boy of the evening"; fully aware of the reputation of their favorite comrade.

"Ef he's good, we'll all be," shouted another from the end of the hall.

At this moment the little fellow himself came slowly walking up an aisle towards the stage, keeping his eyes fixed on the floor and finally sitting demurely on the bench immediately in front of Mr. Hendon; there, still without looking up, he leaned over until his elbows rested on his knees, and, holding his face between the palms of his hands intimated without so much as a side glance, that he had taken his position for the evening.

Good order seemed really assured. The ladies grouped themselves about the organ and began to sing beautifully the opening carol; "Carol, Brothers, Carol"—the boys rising and joining in with all their might when they came to their favorite verse:

"At the merry table
Think of those who've none:
The orphan and the widow,
Hungry and alone—
Bountiful your offerings,

To the altar bring,
Let the poor and needy
Christmas carols sing."

nearly lifting the roof at the chorus: "Carol, Brothers, car*roll.*"

The next line in the chorus ran this way: "And pray a gladsome Christmas"—but with all the rehearsing it came out "handsome Christmas," each time; the boys liked it better that way and when it came out just then there could be no lack of understanding clearly that they meant it to be "han'some," and "han'some" it was.

Next came the part of the evening Mr. Hendon most feared—the saying of The Lord's Prayer. But every one had a surprise in that. Nota moved forward to the front bench and knelt with the boys. When she saw them all so quiet, the lines of little heads dropping over folded hands red with the cold of the long day; the tired legs all bended at the ragged knees; the long rows of wet, worn shoes of all sizes facing her—all trying so hard to be good—something dim fell between her gaze and them, swaying the garlands in a misty light, until she had to close her eyes tight and keep them so, even after the reached the scattered, shy, "Amen."

There was the sound of many shuffling feet as they rose with considerable energy and joined with pent-up enthusiasm in singing:

"I know where the green leaves grow,
When the fields without are bare,
Where a sweet perfume of the woodland's bloom
Is afloat on the wintry air."

After this there was a short address: a happy little speech about Christmas, when

Mr. Hendon told them briefly about the surprise the shepherds had so many hundred years ago; when they saw the Great Light all around them and heard the kind Angel tell them not to be afraid but to listen to the Good News and Song from the sky.

"Now, boys," he continued, "you all know how it is about *news*, for you are spreading it all the time yourselves; but would it be of any use for you to sell the papers if people should not read them?"

"No Sir," responded rather a small voice near Mr. Hendon; but it was heard too far: *"No, Sir!"* "NO, SIR!" was heard successively through all parts of the hall, until it grew into a full chorus of uproarious assent.

When silence was regained he continued, telling them that if the shepherds had not listened to The Angel and then gone to tell it in Bethlehem we might never have heard the first Christmas Carol:

"Glory to God in the highest;
On earth peace, good-will to men;"[19]

—that the shepherds were messengers as well as The Angel, and that newsboys are messengers too; and so when they left the festival, they should carry the news with them and help to spread the best news that ever came to earth.

Then they were told all about the Holy Child and His gentle Mother; and the wonderful kings that came from a far country with gifts and how the Mother showed them The Baby in His straw cradle; gradually giving them all of the story of the first Christmas Eve.

The boys liked it immensely and wanted to applaud all through, but they had been asked to wait until the "speech" was over; and someway at the end of it they forgot about applauding and sat still with bright eyes looking earnestly at Mr. Hendon.

There was a busy rattling of papers as the boys took up the programmes again and with drawn-up faces eagerly scanned the lines for the words of the next carol. Hard spelling was going on among the little ones, who for the most part could only join in the choruses. They were none the less intent, however, for they were not to be outdone by the equally concentrated effort among the bootblacks, who were old enough to read straight on, and time enough to spare for looking from the corners of mischievous eyes at the small partners in trade looking so wise and learned behind programmes upside down, but for all that held conspicuously high, shutting out the little faces all puckered in the effort to get "the words."

This carol was: *The Christmas Tree.*[20]

It must have been heard blocks away, for they fairly swung themselves about when they came to the chorus:

"O this wonderful tree,
With its branches wide,
Is always blooming at Christmas-tide."

But the boys liked: "Is always a'blooming at Christmas-tide," and the ladies let them have it so. "Always" was repeated often in the music, and this was the chance for the five-year old "pardners," who made their knowledge tell at that point.

Among the guest was a gentleman who had been asked to talk a little to the boys about their business; he was getting on finely when he chanced to say:

"Ah! I see a little fellow back there who

knows what I mean—" Before he could finish the sentence every boy in the room but Liberty-Alley turned his head towards the point indicated and gradually rising from their seats cried out: "Where!" "Le's see him;" "Wait till we catch him outside,"—full of suppressed fun and ready for another demonstration.

"It won't do to ask questions, I see," the speaker continued when quiet was restored, "so I'll keep to the text," he added, laughing; but before he had spoken twenty words he started them again:

"I know you are not all newsboys—the ladies tell me many of you are bootblacks.

Now a bootblack—" he began—

"Have a shine, Sir?" echoed and re-echoed through the hall, one of the number swaggering up the aisle with his strap and box: "Have a shine, Sir?" he said, with a low bow.

"Not now, thank you—at another time I'll accept your offer, but now I must finish what I want to say, as something is coming you are all waiting for."

This proved another torpedo; the whole room rose on tiptoe while a threatening sound from shifting chairs and debating voices started the ladies into an impromptu beginning of the next carol, and the eager little crowd were

"THEY SAT STILL WITH BRIGHT EYES LOOKING EARNESTLY AT MR. HENDON."

They sat still with bright eyes looking earnestly at Mr. Hendon. Special Collections and University Archives, University of Maryland Libraries.

soon at work on their programmes again, this time singing, "Wonderful Night."

> "Wonderful night!
> Let me as long as life lingers
> Chant with the cherubim singers,
> 'Glory to God in the Height!'
> Wonderful night!"[21]

While they were absorbed in this, the gay parcels under the tree were being placed on trays to be given to the boys in their seats; for as the evening wore on it was found that nothing could be attempted that would cause moving about, as this was sure to result in confusion beyond control.

With most of them there would be nothing to make Christmas but what they brought from the festival, and the ladies wanted to have it all come with a Christmas touch into the poor homes, and run over to the next day; so everything was in shape to carry away when they should leave the hall.

But the vision of Julia and Nota among the presents was too much for the waiting audience; too eager for longer waiting, the carol was hardly ended before they rose in a mass and surged towards the stage, an uncontrollable little mob once more. No voice could be heard above the repeated: "Oh! Gi' me mine;" "they ain't 'nuff to go 'round;" "*Please* gi' me one;" "It's my turn, 'deed i'tis." It was not fun this time—no mischievous device to keep things going their own way; unmindful of all else, each one fought for his own chances; and there was danger through it all; more for the little ones being crushed in the upheaval that now was reaching from the end of the hall to the stage, sweeping over the backs of benches and chairs, climbing with extend-

ed arms over those ahead—the goal of all, the stage with its tree and gifts.

It was only by quickly gathering these and carrying them out of sight back of the stage and tree that there was any check to the wild confusion, and, with great effort order finally restored. "Hark! Hark, the sweet chiming of Merry Christmas Bells,"[22] one of the ladies began to sing in a low voice—the boys heard it as she sang on and work on the programs began again while Julia and Mr. Hendon stepped into a side room to consult on some other way of distributing gifts, as the first plan of handing them while the boys were still in the hall had to be dropped. The only way left to them was to carry the gifts secretly to a landing beyond the doors at the entrance to the hall, and have Julia and Nota hand them to each of their little friends as they passed out. As soon as the carol was finished Mr. Hendon asked the boys to be all very quiet while he showed them the prize boy with his present, lifting on his shoulder Little-Liberty-Alley, holding a beautiful Christmas horn larger than himself.

"Three cheers for Liberty-Alley," resounded through the hall. Hats were waved and swung around the heads of the owners, hundreds of hands were clapped and one round after another of applause showed the popularity of the tiny comrade, who perched on Mr. Hendon's shoulder bowed and smiled mischievously to the right and left, and descending from his height proudly took a seat on the stage, slyly giving signs for "order" behind Mr. Hendon who spoke a few parting words, begging the boys to never forget the first Christmas Eve of all, as well as the first they had spent together; and hoping to see them all on many yet to come, in the mane of the ladies wished them all a "Merry Christmas!"

"SAME TO YOU!" came in a concerted shout—while boxes were once more strapped to young shoulders, unsold papers were gathered from under seats and ragged slouches were drawn out from under jackets.

O, it was a picture well to see! The thin old clothes, the bright little faces, the holiday look of the room, the festival air from lights and evergreens, over all; every one happy without knowing why!

The closing carol was sung. Once more the boys were at their best. Through the hall swept the simple melody with the words:

> "To-night I heard the children,
> Going on their homeward way.
> Singing 'Carol, carol, Christians,'
> A song for Christmas-day."[23]

Each little guest was in his place, waiting for the final word from Mr. Hendon, when Julia and Nota started quietly down a side aisle to reach the entrance doors in time to give the presents.

"There goes the ladies!" called out a little "pardner."

In an instant, the boys with one accord turned in the same direction. Nota suddenly found herself lifted from the floor and about to be carried with the crowd.

"Oh boys!" she called under her breath, thoroughly frightened.

The little ones neither saw nor heard. But Terry, a bootblack, taller than the others, saw and heard.

"I'll see whether y'll hurt 'er," he cried at the top of his voice and sparring to the right and left, with strong arms well bent at the elbow he reached the place where she was hedged and made a space in which she regained her footing.

Realizing it all in a moment, the boys stood transfixed wherever they chanced to be, looking anxiously toward her, the happy faces changed with perplexity and penitence.

"Will it be safe for me to start again?" she asked.

From over the room came cries of: "Oh! yes"; "'deed it will!" "Go on, Miss Nota"; "it's all right now."

"And will you take care of me?" she continued.

With much valiant promising they kept a space cleared for her all the way as she moved to the exit of the hall and, joined by Julia and Mr. Hendon beyond the doors, gave to each one as he came out his packages and gifts with plenty of fruit, nuts and sweetmeats and a "Merry Christmas!" greeting; receiving in response a joyful *Same to you!* as down the stairs into the cold streets the little fellows plunged, hugging tight the precious bundles that were to bring to many a home the only joy it was to have at Christmas.

When the two ladies returned to the hall, they were surprised to find a group of boys standing under the tree; Julia came towards them saying:

"So, boys, you are not ready to go yet?"

"No, not yet," one of them responded, looking up into the tree, continuing: "Say, can't I hev' one o' them?" pointing to a fairy with a tiny gilt star on her forehead and holding a silvered wand.

"An' say," pleaded another, "won't ye gi'me that doll?"

"An' me a star?" begged the third.

"Why, boys," the ladies exclaimed, "what will you do with a fairy or a doll?"

"Got sisters," was the quick answer

from one while another emphasized:

"I've got a sister, please gi'me a doll—
Say won't cher?"

Now this was a revelation to Julia and Nota, who had given much thought to what might please a *boy*. Had they known the boys longer they would have learned that a love for the beautiful was strong within them and that something from the tree meant more than all the rest. But most of all they would have realized the close bond of caretaking the little children of the poor feel towards each other.

"Come," said Julia, "look up into the tree and take your choice."

The little fellow did not stir; hands in pockets he looked wistfully up into her face, saying:

"Y' ain't stuffin' me, is yer?"

"Stuffing?" asked Julia, not yet understanding the newsboys' vocabulary.

"Foolin' me, is yer?"

She answered gently: "No, I am not fooling you, what will you have?" at the same time bending a laden branch within his touch.

His look wandered over the branches; the many colored shining things; the little banners; the bright sugar fruits, his eyes were full of delight—but stood on tiptoe until he reached a little doll and pointing to it, asked for that:

"My sister ain't been yere," he said simply, reaching out both hands for it.

The doll, a dainty one in soft clothes and laced with a wreath of tiny rosebuds on her flaxen head, was handed him and with a quick "good-night," he ran out of the hall as fast as the rough shoes he wore could get over the floor, calling out: "Oh, *thank* ye!" as he reached the door.

Alone in the hall stood Julia with Nota and William Hendon:

"Good-night," he said, extending a hand to each, "My work waits for me and must take what remains of Christmas Eve to the dawn—but we have heard the Angels from Judea's Hills to-night," he added earnestly, a fine light speaking in his eyes.

As he passed down the streets a little newsgirl, the only one then in Baltimore, looked up from the curbstone where she stood waiting, and said softly: "Good-night"; he passed his hands before his eyes for a moment, then he bent low to say gently: "Good-night," and hurriedly closed after him the door of his office as he stepped within for a whole night of work.

In the hall one by one the lights went out and soon it was dark and empty. But all through the night something like a white wing seemed to move among the garlands and stir the branches of the Christmas Tree.

Now and then the pine above the windows dropped a spicy leaf upon the floor; through the silence distant voices breathed and left an echo in the holly boughs; the late moon looking in through a high window sent a shaft of light here and there along the walls, resting among the texts the children had been spelling out, until it lifted into sudden light:

"Peace on earth,
Good-will to men."

In his cot in a miserable loft, Pilkey turned and turned but could not sleep.

"Say, Dick," he called softly, "it's all over 'til nex' yere, ain't it?"

Dick slept on by his side. But Pilkey's eyes were wide as he turned towards the small, high window looking out upon the roofs and chimneys of the poor houses across the narrow street.

"Say, Dick," with another awakening punch, "y're got yer or'nge in bed wif yer? I hev."

Slowly Sleep came down and brought with her a beautiful room in which she placed Pilkey under a lighted Christmas tree full of stars and angels; and each angel carried a silver trumpet and under the tree were bright-colored fruits and many good things; and in among the branches he saw in dancing letters: "Merrie Christmas, Pilkey!"

"SAME TO YOU!" he cried, sitting straight up in his cot as the bells rang out the dawn of

CHRISTMAS DAY.

Lucy Meacham Thruston (1862–1938)

"I often feel that history often throws light on the facts of today, and that the present day in turn can throw light on the facts of history." —Lucy Meacham Thruston

History, and more specifically Southern history, occupied Thruston throughout her writing career. All of her novels are grounded in the historical South, and a large number are set in Virginia, where she was born and raised. She moved to Baltimore at the age of twelve,[1] but never forgot her southern roots. While living in Baltimore, Thruston indulged her passion for history by adopting the genre of historical fiction.

Her first publication, *Songs of the Chesapeake* (1900), was quickly followed by her best-known novel, a colonial romance titled *Mistress Brent: A Story of Lord Baltimore's Colony in 1638* (1901), which brought together Maryland history and myth. According to a *Baltimore Sun* reviewer, the novel helped to "reanimate" the reputation of Margaret Brent as an influential figure in colonial Maryland.[2] Brent, who emigrated from England to the colonies with her family in 1638, was actively involved in colonial governance and was an independent landowner who was not afraid to speak her mind. Women were legally prohibited from speaking in the Maryland legislature, but she became the first to do so.

Thruston's interest in the South and her pride in being a Southern woman was reflected in her other publications, which include: *Jack and His Island: A Boy's Adventures along the Chesapeake in the War of 1812* (1902), *A Girl of Virginia* (1902), *Where the Tide Comes In* (1904), *Called to the Field: A Story of Virginia in the Civil War* (1906), and *Jenifer* (1907), which takes place in the Carolina mountains. Although she writes about Southern womanhood and Confederate soldiers, the *Sun* reviewer averred that she sympathizes with family and the "devastation" of war more than picking a side—and that she focused her attention of the growth and change in women by "keeping up with the times."[3]

Her beautiful language and evocative descriptions can be seen in the following pages. One can also see the strength she grants her female characters, both real and fictional. In *Mistress Brent*, Thruston promotes colonial southern womanhood by showcasing the strong voice of Margaret Brent as she made her case to the state. Both the natural beauty of the Chesapeake region and colonial Maryland society and history take on new life through Thruston's writings. —M. Hultberg

Songs of the Chesapeake (1905)

Through My Window

The breeze comes in at my window
And brings me a breath of the sea;
A taste of the salt, and the perfume
Of blossoming bush and tree.
A mocking-bird swings in the cherry
And sings his varying song:
The catkins are on the mulberry
And the days are bright and long.

The quince, and the pear and the lilac
Bloom out by the garden walk;
The jonquil and while narcissus
Have opened their lips for a talk.

Oh the wind is strong and glorious
As it rushes on its way!
It blows the wave—Victorious—
Far down the Mobjack bay.[4]
The river runs in the chapel,
—Naught now but a flashing thread—
And the sands are bare and barren
Where once the waters spread.
A boat on its bosom is flying,
The spray dashes over her bows;
The sea-gulls and wild ducks are crying,
And skimming the waters low.
Oh the world is aglow and a-ringing
With the sun, and the wind and the Spring!
And the breeze from the ocean is bringing
The youth of the year on its wing.

Margaret M. Piggot, artist; A. Hoen and Co., lithographers; pages from *Songs of the Chesapeake* (1905). Special Collections and University Archives, University of Maryland Libraries.

High Tide

The waves are moving in rhythmic dance
    Down the Mobjack bay:
As the sunshine strikes with sparkling lance,
They shoreward turn and all advance
    To a rippling roundelay.

The pines trees stand—a dark green hand—
    Round the Mobjack bay:
The wild plum blooms on every hand
The waters seem running all over the land
    As the tide makes strong headway.
Into ditches and creeks the salt flood pours
    From out the Mobjack bay:
Flows through the bay bush, over green floors,
Creeps through the grass to the very doors
    Of the people who live by the bay.
The west wind blows, and the sea gulls scream
    Over the Mobjack bay:
The wild ducks cry where their black heads gleam
On the top of the wave as they float with the stream
    Or dive 'neath the crest for their prey.

ꜽ

The sun's in the West, and the tide is low;
    Way out on the beach doth stand
Our tiny boat with the wave at her bow
    And her keel stuck fast in the sand.
The jolt of the row locks, the splash of the oar,
    The race of the drops 'long the blade;
And the swish of the wave as it breaks 'neath our boat
    Is the sweetest music, e'er made.

See the swallows are twittering about their nests
    And telling their tales of love
On the yellow clay cliff where the thin wheat grows
    And the pines stand guard above.

At the mouth of the creek a pungy[5] waits
    The ride of the morning, to sail;

Her captain is lazily smoking his pipe
    And watching the faint blue trail.
Beyond the bar, where the current is deep
    And the tall green rushes grow
Where the scarlet cactus blooms on the sleep
    And the gulls flit to and fro:

There let us rest. Doth know my love
    How sweet is the evening calm
With the joy of thy radiant presence so near
    And the touch of thy soft warm palm.

           ❧

Under the old gray wharf
    The waters ebb and flow;
And the jellied nettles, with milk white tentacles
Pulse, and curl, and beat the barnacles
    On the wave-worn piles below.
There's a low swift hush,
    And a short crisp rush
Where the gray blue streak, with the wind at its heel,
Runs with the rippling and dark curled wave;till we feel
    Our boat and our sails are a-flush.

So ho swing wide the sail
    Where lasts this feathery gale!—
With toss and turn, with quiver and strain, and rushing sound
Of music made by waters cleft, filling the air around
    So ho, we sail! We sail!

See, through the misty flow,
    Green and blue, the bright rainbow
Curves at our keel. The cloud is past: with shimmering haze
Now runs the stream like molten silver 'neath the rays
    Of the sun strong his glow.

The sail hangs loose against the mast
    There's not a breath: so fast
Sped wind and wave together. Peacefully now we rest
With rock and lurch, soft cradled on the river's breast—
    The tide has turned at last.

Borne homeward by the tide
     And splashing oar along our side
We reach the wharf—Quick, slip the mast,
And seek that cool green shade betwixt the piles.—How fast
     The ripples form and break and float away at last—
Now listen to their song—

It is the eternal flow
     Of waves that ever go
Running to the sea.
It has an under moan
     That touches the deepest tone
In the heart of you and me.

Calm

The bay spreads out to yonder mighty shore
     Without a ripple on her breast,
Nor flash of white cap 'long the tidal flow,
     Nor curling wave with snow white crest:
But silver streaks, and darker breaths
     Of blue; and here and there a gleam,
As if the sparkling sun flashed back
     From jewels bosomed in the stream.
Across the sweep of blue lie boats becalmed;
     Their white sails mirrored in the deep
Shine in the distance like the wings
     Of giant butterflies a-sleep.

Down by the line where sea and sky are one,
     Thin curling clouds close huddled lie:
As if the Master painter—whites and grays all done—
     Had lightly drawn his brush across the sky.

Myrtle

O the myrtle grows on the river's bank
And spreads its foliage dark
     O'er the shining sand
          And the pebbly land
Where the sea has left his mark.

And the myrtle grows in the forest cool,
And hides, with its thick small boughs,
    The flower at its foot,
        And the pale green shoot,
Of the moss that bends and blows.
But the myrtle's own love is the sandy shore
Where the wind and the wave are at home;
    And the strong salt breeze
        Bends the trunks of the trees
And sprinkles them briny with foam.

When the wind and the storm have spent their might
To crush and to bruise and destroy:
    It fills the air
        With a perfume rare—
An incense of strength and of joy.

From *Mistress Brent* (1901)

Margaret Brent emigrated from England to the settlement of St. Mary's City with her sister Mary and brothers Giles and William in 1638. She and Mary effectively managed their property, which they called "Sisters' Freehold," and became prominent land-owners in the colony. In 1647, Margaret was made executrix for Leonard Calvert, the colonial governor, on his deathbed. Her appointment was opposed by Leonard's brother Cecil, proprietor of the colony, and her request to be included in the Maryland General Assembly as a voting member was subsequently denied on the basis of her sex. In this excerpt near the end of the novel, she returns to the Assembly to demand her right to vote. Although she was denied and eventually returned to England, she established herself as an early proponent of women's rights.

The morning of that January day was bitter cold. Mistress Margaret, her morning meal finished at Mistress Hawley's board, shivered as the icy blasts howled about the house and blew the flickering flames far out on the hearth, and bent and curled the red light of the pine torches stuck in the mantel-shelf to aid the sullen light of early dawn. Mistress Hawley herself made a little exclamation of dismay at the howling blast.

"There is storm and snow abroad, Margaret," she said; "thank God we can bide indoors to-day."

Mistress Margaret was silent; and Katharine, who had learned much of her moods, knew from her darkened face there was some warfare and strife within.

"Margaret," she protested, as Margaret pushed away her plate, the food scarce touched, "thou hast scarce eaten a mouthful; surely thou hast not finished? This venison is tender and toothsome, or there is cold capon within the kitchen."

"Nay, thy fare is of the best"; she pushed back her chair absent-mindedly and went over to the window-pane and breathed upon the ice fronds and wiped them away with her handkerchief of lace. Outside, the stiffened rose-bush rattled against the casement; the snow drifted over the door-yard; down the street, gray and ghastly in the early morning light, the fierce wind whirled the powdered snow in clouds. About the coffeehouse it had blown in great drifts, and the close shut door made it seem a house deserted; but as she looked the door was thrown open; she could see the red light shine out in the snow, and men, wrapped in long cloaks close drawn about their faces, their wide hats pulled low, came hurriedly out. There was Thomas Gerard, stately and soldierly; there was Thomas Wair from the Potomac; there was that rank, disaffected Hammond; there was Richard Preston from his new claimed manor on the Patuxent; there was Giles, she knew his quick, firm walk, and straight, slender figure; there was her brother-in-law, Rogers.[6] She rubbed a bigger space with her hot palm on the pane and watched them around the curve. She well knew where they were going. The sunrise gun had sounded and the gun for the half hour afterward, though the morning was too dull to know the sunrise save by the hour. They wended their way to the fort, in which they would hold the day's session of the Assembly.

But yesterday she had sat amongst them, their honored head; to-day, to give full edge to her bitterness, a heavy step came crunch-ing beneath the window. Jock, foreman and holder of property upon her estate, was bound thither likewise; he, now, had a right to sit in the sessions and add his voice to the vote. She crushed her thumbs to the palms of her hands as she turned about.

Mistress Hawley was gone from the board; through the open door she could see her, as one in mental disquiet will see and note each detail they gaze on, unknowing how clearly it is for all time imprinted on their minds; she saw Katharine's tall figure at the kitchen fire, the haunch of venison on the spit, the cook but newly brought from overseas gazing stolidly at her mistress as she cautioned her as to the basting and browning of it. Margaret, too, gazing at her face, noted with a shock of surprise how slender the figure had grown, how thin the outline of the cheek, how big and bright the deep blue eyes. Then, as if each detail were never to be forgot, she saw the sanded floor, the rough bench near the fire where the servants rested in the eventide, and caught the scarlet gleam from the loops of pepper overhead and the silvery sheen of the ropes of onions.

Yet the long look was but for a moment. Mistress Hawley reached for a leaf of sage and a sprig of savory from the low rafters overhead, and Mistress Brent turned and went quickly to her chamber in the attic. There on a wooden peg behind the door hung her rich fur cloak; here were heavy boots. She slipped her feet from her slippers; they were icy cold from the draughts along the floor, but she heeded it not, though the corn-cob coals were red upon the hearth, and fastened the thongs of her heavy boots. She looked quickly at her dress; the brown paduasoy, short of skirt and slashed about the bodice with scarlet, would serve her purpose well. She thrust her arms into the warm thickness of her cloak and drew the hood about her resolute face.

Down the stair and out the hall she made her way with word to none. Outside the icy wind caught her and fair whirled her off her feet, but Mistress Brent threw back her head and smiled at the wintry touch. She was bent on contest, and contest with the storms but whetted her humor. She noted with keen eyes every drift and curious whirl of snow along her way, and saw how heavy the smoke hung over the wide chimneys of the coffee-house; saw the rift which came in the clouds toward the east and the long rays of the sun showing fanwise through it, and the crows flocking overhead, and thought on the Indian saying that augured from such,—windy weather and a clearing sky ere nightfall.

By the governor's house she made her way and noted its deserted look, for Deborah kept to her kitchen, and save for the servants it was untenanted. How heavy the snow drifted against closeshut door and window, on shrubbery, tree, and vine! but the path by it and down to the fort where the Assembly-men met was well trodden. The creek was still and mute beneath the icy coat that could have borne the huntsman to the snow-covered forest beyond an he had not been busy in the meeting at the fort.

She put her hand upon the buttoned door and without a moment's thought was within; nor did she look to right or left or heed any curious glances as she undid the fastenings from her cloak and slipped the hood from her dark, roughened hair. That done she looked about her steadily: one had been speaking who made pause at her entry, and in the mute astonishment of the Assembly resumed his seat. This was the time for the utterance of those flaming sentences which had burned within her all night.

"Gentlemen," she said firmly, and there was no sound in the room save her fresh, clear voice and the howling of the wind outside,—"Gentlemen, I come to claim a vote in this Assembly."

The newly appointed governor moved anxiously in his chair, and Giles, after one shrewd glance from face to face, turned his keen gaze upon the glowing logs at the far end of the room, whose heat scarce took the edge from the bitter air, so that the Assembly-men sat for the most part with their cloaks about them.

The silence grew painful, until Gerard rose courteously. "Mistress Brent," he said, slowly, "'tis against the terms of the charter of Maryland."

"And wherein is this stated?" she asked, quickly.

Gerard hesitated for a moment, but another, in quick, raucous tones, was answering for him.

"'Tis so expressly stated in the laws of the Assembly."

Mistress Brent's gray eyes flashed full on Captain Rogers's face ere he sat down.

"The laws of the Assembly," she said scornfully to herself, but she dared voice no contempt for such here.

"What would my Lord of Baltimore say to such?" asked Rogers, from his seat.

"My Lord of Baltimore, Captain Rogers," she said, quietly turning to the speaker,—it was not the first time she had heard his voice in combat,—"my Lord of Baltimore is a lover of justice; think you he would grant manorial privileges to one to whom he was unwilling to give a voice in the Assembly likewise?"

"To what woman," called the same raucous voice, "hath he granted that privilege save his kinswoman?"

Mistress Brent turned upon her brother-in-law one flash of her great, dark eyes; she would husband her anger and not show it now.

"How many women," she asked steadily, "are within the provinces tending their own affairs peaceably and sturdily and might serve as ensample for many?"

There was a note of keen delighted joy in Captain Rogers's voice as he sprang to his feet and fair shouted, "Aye, but amongst the first laws made in this Assembly was the one that no woman should hold property in this colony, and should she inherit it, and at the end of seven years be still obstinately unmarried, that property would be confiscate. Why hath that law been neglected because the governor—"

"Shame! shame!" came the cry from many quarters.

The flush died from Mistress Brent's cheek, though her voice was clear enough. "Such law touches me not," she declared proudly; "I hold special privileges from my cousin of Baltimore, and I thank God," she went on, her voice rising somewhat, "that the papers conveying such intelligence to the governor were not amongst those destroyed in the fire of St. John's Manor, but are e'en now in my own possession. Concerning the last," she drew the bit of lace she held crumpled in her hand across her mouth that trembled slightly, "*obstinately*

unmarried, I need not speak."

Giles looked about him quickly once more. There were few faces in the room but showed some feeling, but feeling was not conviction.

Mistress Margaret went on rapidly:

"Gentlemen, well may ye ask why in all the years I have been amongst ye I never thought on such step. I thought not on it. I have been content to go my way. One, I knew, was at the head whose wisdom would remember each one of us. I had ventured amongst ye, and no man in the colony ventured more, for I staked all I had, and whether I have succeeded or lost I leave ye to judge. Then by one great loss the questions of your government were forced upon me. How have I met them? Is there a man amongst ye, God knows I say it not boastingly, could have done aught more? Did I not find the province shaken? Had not my Lord Baltimore's authority been disregarded and the laws ye yourselves made set aside for nigh two years? Who amongst ye favored the invader 'tis not for me to say.

"Did I not find chaos, rents unpaid, accounts unkept, invasion of savages threatened, and menacing soldiers within the town? Ye have seen my accounts, how stand they? What did ye say in the letters ye writ my Lord Baltimore yesterday? Did ye not say in such words, no man of all would so have wrought it? And yet, because I am a woman, forsooth, to-day I must stand idly by and have not e'en a voice in the framing of your laws, a voice in the making of those regulations which shall govern one who is amongst the largest of your landowners.

"Is this justice? I ask in the name of years yet to come. Ye have prided yourselves on being the only colony within the New World which grants to every man the right of worshipping his God as he wisheth; ye boast of your liberty and freedom and are proud that ye lead the way in the right, lead it in this likewise, build wisely, grant us justice, and let the woman who hath equal risks with ye in this new province have an equal voice in the government, else is your boast as empty wind."

She made impressive pause, and Gerard, who fain would have seen her success, moved in the next breath that the Assembly should vote on this question which Mistress Brent had raised.

Yet when the question had been put to such test she stood defeated. Giles and Gerard moved toward her, but she put aside all sympathy and drew herself proudly erect. "Then," she cried in clear, ringing tones, "I do hereby protest against all this present Assembly and all its doings, unless I may be present and have voice as aforesaid."

Emily Emerson Lantz (1862-1931)

Emily Emerson Lantz, an honorary member of the Women's Literary Club of Baltimore, dedicated almost all of her writing to the local. A lifelong contributor to *The Baltimore Sun,* Lantz published a number of columns that delved, with extraordinary detail and accuracy, into local lore. Her Maryland Heraldry series compiled the genealogical histories of many of the state's most eminent families.[1] Another series, Do You Know the Street on Which You Live?, ran weekly for much of 1923 and 1924, depicting the histories of twenty-seven of Baltimore's most significant thoroughfares. Lantz's interests were not contained within the city limits, but encompassed the entire state of Maryland. She compiled a history of each of Maryland's counties in her 1929 volume *The Spirit of Maryland,* which her obituary names "her chief monument," and her series Suburban Baltimore displayed a distinct interest in the areas surrounding Baltimore's urban heart. In these columns, she focused both on the planned suburban neighborhoods of the Roland Park Company, as well as county communities including Catonsville and Towson.[2]

The poetic style Lantz developed in her literary pursuits often shines through in her journalism. "Finding Five-Cent Christmas Opportunities" captures the reader's attention with its lighthearted charm as Lantz describes some of Baltimore's historical and recreational attractions. Lantz's thirty years of historical writing for the *Sun* opened the eyes of Baltimoreans up to the uniquely rich history of the city they inhabited. Perhaps it can do the same today. —H. Flynn and N. Day

Suburban Baltimore: Charles Street (1905)

There is a tide in the affairs of men
Which, taken at the flood, leads on to
*   fortune.*[3]

It may be said concerning the development of cities and their surroundings, as in the lives of individuals, that there is a tide in the course of their upbuilding which, taken at its full, leads to unusual social and financial development; or the opportunity offered by the hour neglected, the reverse of good fortune results.

Charles Street and the avenue which extends its length almost to Towson is an example of the most fortunate town and county development. If a city Street can be said to have a horoscope, Charles Street, with its right kingly appellation, must surely have been laid out under a lucky grouping of stars. As a promenade and drive of fashion its career of social precedence began with the building of Old St. Paul's Church[4] and the stately homes that were sheltered beneath the eaves of that sanctuary.

The beauty and real estate value of the street increased with the erection of Washington's Monument[5] and the parking of Mount Vernon Place, and the final crown of the social glory was set upon it by the erection of magnificent residences along the line of its country extension and the establishment of the clubhouse of the Elkridge Fox Hunting Club[6] at its northern limits. Here the annual Horse Show is held, and Charles Street Avenue is the setting each year in the "merrie month of May"[7] during Horse Show week for such a pageant of beautiful women, athletic and fashionable men and up-to-date equipages as few cities can rival. The Madison Square Horse Show in New York boasts of the rich costumes worn by the women who attend it, but the Maryland hunting clubs boast of the beauty of the daughters of the State who grace the Elkridge Horse Show and also demand blue ribbons for the fetching gowns they wear.

Someone has truthfully said that the land where city and country meet is rarely beautiful, nature and man each withdrawing their best work jealously to the heart of the country or the center of the city, but between Charles Street and Charles Street Avenue there has been no such antagonism. The city residences continue in uninterrupted elegance to the northernmost boundary line of Baltimore and there suddenly melt away into the soft green of a country road bordered with picturesque dells, through which ripples a wayside brook.

The secret of this unusual harmony in the meeting of town and country lies in the extent and value of the estates lying directly north of the Monument and the fact that they have largely been kept intact as the permanent residences of wealthy owners. The property lying north of Charles Street and bounded on the east by York Road and on the west by Roland Park has enjoyed the facilities of two electric lines and one railroad line to connect them with the city, and they also enjoy the conveniences of excellent water supplies, electric lighting and telephone service. With these city comforts the section has become a permanent winter and summer residence section. Some of the estates fronting on Charles Street Avenue extend to the York road or to Roland Park and are intersected with pretty avenues that afford quick communication between these neighborhoods with Druid Hill Park and with Mount Washington.

The educational advantages of the locality are unusual now, and with the establishment of the Johns Hopkins University at Homewood will be infinitely greater.[8]

There is already the Boys' Country School,[9] just south of Merryman's lane; the College of Notre Dame of Maryland[10] crowns a hill just a mile or so beyond. There are also the public schools of Govanstown, Roland Park and Mount Washington, and the convent school of Mount St. Agnes,[11] at the latter place. Thus a wide choice of secular, parochial and public instruction is afforded. Govanstown has elected Mrs. George M. Lamb,[12] a lady of great culture, as one of its three public school trustees, the other two being Mr. W. S. Norris and Mr. H. D. Everding, of Baltimore County.

The altitude of Charles Street Avenue and the adjacent region, the beauty of the forest land surrounding it and its social importance from a neighborhood standpoint have long made its further development the dream of many. A public park where Wyman Park is destined to be was long discussed before the recent definite action was taken concerning it, and the Maryland State Agricultural Society once held its fairs on ground through which Charles Street Avenue now extends.

The Charles Street Avenue Association, incorporated in 1854, was the first organization to open the way for future suburban development. The association was granted the privilege of extending Charles Street from its northern termination in an avenue 66 feet wide northward to the powder mill on the York road. The way lay through Clover Hill, the property of Mr. Joseph Merryman and others, through Guilford, the estate of Lieutenant-Colonel William McDonald, who commanded the Sixth Regiment Maryland Infantry at the Battle of North Point, across the land of Jeremiah Tille to Cold Spring road and thence through or between the properties of David S. Wilson, Emanuel Croker, William Broadbent, Dr. Benjamin W. Woods, the estate of the Orphans' Home, the late David M. Perine, Daniel Alder, W.C. Wilson, Ann Price, David Holt, Mathew T. Gosnell, Augustine W. Bradford, I. McKim Marriott, John Beatty, Edward Sweeny, and thence to the powder mill. At the present time much of the land mentioned has passed into other hands, the four hundred acres comprising Homeland, the David M. Perine estate, being probably the only land not a foot of which has been sold since the death of its owner. But if the properties have changed hands, most of them have not been cut up or diminished, and Charles Street Avenue stretches cool, green and reposeful between miles of woodland that give small hint of the beautiful residences that are reached by long driveways beneath forest trees or that are set like English manor houses in the midst of finely cultivated farms.

Admission to the avenue is guarded by an old-fashioned toll gate, which usually stands hospitably open, and within sight of it is the fine old Colonial residence built at Homewood in 1803 by Charles Carroll of Carrollton[13] for his son, Charles Carroll, Jr., who brought to it his young wife, Harriet Chew, daughter of Hon. Benjamin Chew, Chief Justice of Pennsylvania. It is a long low building, a story and a half high, modeled, it is said, after Doughoregan Manor,[14] as it is also Brooklandwood,[15] in the Green Spring Valley, which was also built by Charles Carroll of Carrollton.

The brick walls of the mansion at Homewood are double, with air passages between, and the cellars are built with the massive solidity of a fortress. A flight of stone steps, wide and low, leads to an imposing doorway that grants admission to an enormous entrance hall, with a spacious apartment on either side. A smaller hall crosses the great hall transversely and leads to the wings of the house. On one side there is what was formerly the chapel, and in the hall, without the chapel door, a narrow stairway winds to a room concealed in the ceiling of the hall, where were kept the priests' vestments. The floors of the house were laid in hardwood and the walls paneled in wood, with cornices so exquisitely carved as to delight the eye. There are deep fireplaces for glowing logs, and the high mantel shelves are symphonies in wood carving. In ancient days the wood was all painted a colonial white, except the dining room, where it was blue, to match the walls.

The ancient window panes were engraved with the initials C.C. and the same letters are carved on many of the trees surrounding the mansion. The chapel windows were the only ones protected with iron bars in addition to the heavy wooden shutters that distinguish the rest of the house, and this safeguard to the consecrated vessels kept in the chapel is said to have led to many curious rumors in after days, when their reason for being was no longer understood. A brick bathhouse was formerly sunken at one side of the residence, which was supplied with water from a pump. The building of the stately home is said to have cost $60,000. At that time the estate included what is now Charles Street Avenue, and the grounds were entered from Merryman's lane. A winding avenue led to the house and the ravine was spanned by a beautiful bridge, now in ruins. After the death of his son, Charles Carroll, Jr., Charles Carroll of Carrollton sold the estate, but bought it back again at a later date. At the present time the youth of Baltimore attending the county school enjoy the privilege of daily association with one of the most beautiful and unique specimens of the architecture of Maryland in colonial days.

In those days the near neighbors of the owners of Homewood were Jerome Bonaparte and his wife of a brief year, Elizabeth Patterson;[16] the Robert Oliver family, who resided at their handsome place, Greenmount, and Colonel Nicholas Rogers, of Druid Hill.

Among the many stately homes along Charles Street Avenue Evergreen, the estate of Mrs. T. Harrison Garrett and the home of Mr. John W. Garrett,[17] of the United States Legation at The Hague, is one of the most beautiful. It includes sixty-four acres of magnificent woodland, abounding in oak, chestnut, spruce, pine, sugar maple and the evergreens from which it takes its name. The residence rivals in architectural beauty the most imposing dwellings of Newport, and the grounds are adorned in keeping with its elegance. To the beauties of nature common to this climate have been added a wealth of fern and flora collected from all parts of the world. Twenty thousand feet of glass protect the greenhouses, that, under the care of Mr. Charles Uffler, of Alsace, probably rival any other private greenhouses in the United States. There are hothouses for orchids alone that have blossomed with over one thousand rare and curious flowers at one time, including the wonderful orchids that sway like elfin pitchers from a delicate stem or peep forth, facsimiles of Cinderella's slippers, from enfolding leaves. The violet beds in February stretch for fifty feet a carpet of purple fragrance, and in Japan three hundred years ago was begun the growth of some of the rare plants that adorn the conservatory. The terraced Italian garden is lined with standard rose trees and tulip begonias, and in spring the ground blossoms forth in the delicate pink of magnolia trees, azaleas and rhododendrons like the very breaking of rosy dawn.

Mrs. Horatio W. Garrett's residence adjoins that of Mrs. T. Harrison Garrett, and is built of stone finished with cement and dark wood after the design of Holland architecture. It is also furnished in the quaint fashion of that country to harmonize with that architecture.

The estate of the late David M. Perine covers four hundred acres that extend from Charles Street Avenue to the York Road and from Homeland to Melrose Avenues. The place is called Homeland, and in 1799 Mr. David M. Perine, when but three years of age, came to live there with his mother. At her death it became his own and grew from 150 acres to 400 acres, which descended to his heirs. The property extended upon both sides of the avenue, and a frame house about the center of the estate was the homestead. This building Mr. Perine replaced upon the same site by a stone mansion designed architecturally like that of the Washington residence at Mount Vernon. This house was destroyed by fire, and again a stone house was erected which is now occu-

pied by Mr. E. Glenn Perine, son of the former owner. The residence is approached from both Charles Street avenue and York Road by driveways passing beneath forest trees, the approach from the York road extending half a mile. All the trees on the estate, except those of the virgin forest, were planted by Mr. David M. Perine, and the dining room of the mansion is adorned with beautiful furniture and a handsome dining table made from apple wood cut from the estate.

Suburban Baltimore: Roland Park (1905)

The "season of mists" beloved of the poet Keats is round about us; the "happy autumn fields," immortalized by Tennyson, stretch in sunlit restfulness beyond the city gates, while from humble altars heaped with withered leaves rises the pungent incense of oak and maple and beech.[18] The smoke of these altar fires ascends, delicately gray, against the blue November sky and bespeaks the silent passing of the summer months. It is a beautiful pageant, this procession of autumn days, but only those enjoy its beauty to the full who live apart from the tower and town. Luckily, through the energy and progression of a few far-sighted men in developing the rolling, picturesque, and richly wooded country surrounding Baltimore city, residents of the latter who love Nature in all her changing moods need no longer sigh for opportunity stands at their very doors and knocks, and many wise ones have already followed gladly this happy summonsing.

Someone has truly said that once grown accustomed to the luxuries of life mankind can more easily dispense with the necessities of life than do without these luxuries. Hence the ideal country life is that which offers the beauty, freedom, and healthfulness of rural life combined with the twentieth-century civilization. The intelligently developed suburb presents this admirable combination, and perhaps comparatively few Baltimoreans are aware that in Roland Park they possess what is generally recognized throughout the country as one of the most representative suburbs in the United States. The place possesses all the elements essential to fine suburban development, and the practical and artistic have been so happily united as to have secured exceptional results. Newport, Rhode Island is noted for the beauty of its surroundings, and to those familiar with both places there is much in Roland Park to suggest the famous island colony. Newport is not exclusively the abode of kings of finance and queens of fashion; there are many cottage homes. Roland Park boasts of most stately residences and homelike and artistic cottages, and both places are maintained in a degree of order and perfection that makes their environment acceptable to the cultivated eye and life there truly worth the living.

The tract of land now known as Roland Park was formerly two estates—Woodland, owned by Mr. Richard J. Capron,[19] and Oakland, possessed by Mrs. W. C. Pennington, formerly Miss Emily Harper.[20] The first tract lay chiefly upon what is now the east side of Roland Avenue, while the second extended west of the avenue and included a ridge of land that overlooked one of the fairest bits of valley landscape in Baltimore County. To these tracts was added a few smaller sections of land, the most important of which was owned by the Misses Armat. The whole included about 550 acres, which has since increased about 200 acres through the purchase of the estate of Mr. Charles O'Donnell Lee and other smaller pieces of property. An additional 85 acres belonging to the John W. Garrett[21] estate has just been purchased by the Roland Park Company, which lies between the improved portion of Roland Park and Baltimore city. It extends upon both sides of the boulevard now in course of construction, and will connect Roland Park directly with Homewood, the future site of the Johns Hopkins University, the Wyman estate and the picturesque drives that will be included in the much-talked-of chain of parks.[22]

In 1801 several who were making American investments for some English capitalists induced the latter to purchase a controlling interest in the Roland Park Company, then being formed and of which Mr. Edward H. Bouton was made manager and vice-president. About two and a half years ago a local syndicate was formed by Mr. Bouton which bought out the English interests, so that the affairs of Roland Park are now almost wholly controlled by Baltimore people. The officers are: Mr. Edward H. Bouton, president; Mr. George Miller, first vice-president; Mr. Robert J. W. Hamill, second vice-president, and Mr. Richard W. Marchant, Jr., secretary and treasurer.

The plateau upon which Roland Park is located is nearly four hundred feet above the City Hall of Baltimore, yet only four miles from the city's center. Its name was chosen from the chief avenue that divides it and which terminates at Lake Roland, a few miles beyond. At the date when the company was formed the only means of communication with Baltimore was over what is now the Pennsylvania and Maryland railroad. Rapid and reasonable access to the city was the first essential to be secured and this was done by the building of the Lake Roland Electric railway, often spoken of as the "elevated road," which, without change of cars, conveyed the residents of Roland Park to the City Hall, where the line terminated.[23] The railway was subsequently sold to the City and Suburban line, and now forms part of the United Railways and Electric Company system.

The excellent electric-car service maintained between the suburb and the business and shopping districts of Baltimore has been manifestly influential in the rapid upbuilding of Roland Park.[24] Whereas the residents of many fashionable suburbs in various parts of the country must content themselves with a fifteen-minute schedule, discontinued altogether after midnight, persons living at Roland Park pay but a single fare and have the benefit of a four-minute schedule throughout the day, with the great advantage of all-night car service.

The promoters of Roland Park organized with a capital of $1,000,000, and fully $2,000,000, has been spent in improvements. From the beginning the management kept two vital truths constantly in mind—first, that what was worth doing at all was worth doing well; and, second, that the practical and beautiful can be made to harmonize perfectly in all things, provided sufficient knowledge and thought be brought to bear upon the subject.

The suburb was laid off after designs prepared by Mr. Olmsted,[25] who is identified with the plans for the chain of parks, and its healthfulness was secured by a sanitary sewage system designed and superintended by the late Colonel George E. Waring, Jr., formerly street commissioner of New York City. All houses are connected with this system, the lines of which are flushed automatically twice within every twenty-four hours.

The water supply for the park is drawn from eight artesian wells and various springs and the plant is a gravity system, insuring continuous and uniform pressure from a centrally located water tower seventy feet in height. This is supplemented by several reservoirs.

It is said that the latest fad in luxurious living is multiplicity of bathrooms. Whereas the man of wealth used to excite the envy of his associates by lavishing jewels upon members of his household, he now expends his money in fitting his home with lavatories, and the extent of his wealth is estimated by the number of doors he can fling open disclosing tiled floors, porcelain tubs and shining spigots. In Roland Park the bathroom proclivities of house owners is limited only by their incomes, since there is a daily water capacity of 320,000 gallons with a consumption of but 125,000 gallons, and most of the residents boast at least two bathrooms.

In the first development of Roland Park nearly one-fourth of the original area was sacrificed to roadways and lanes. Over

$76,000 was expended in grading and half as much again in providing granolithic sidewalks, stone gutters and under-drains. The original tracts were for the most part well wooded, but along the winding roads many trees were planted, while no forest trees were sacrificed in the clearing of the ground for building where it could possibly be avoided. Roland Avenue, the one portion of the park through which the trolley passes, is, notwithstanding, this electrical necessity, a beautiful and imposing driveway. Unsightly rails are hidden by luxuriant hedges of green, and upon each side of these are wide driveways beautified with rows of trees and flagstone walks bordered with velvet sod. The park restrictions prohibit the building on this avenue of any house costing less than $5,000 or the erection of any dwelling representing an investment of less than $3,000 on any of the other roadways.[26] The company stipulates that its officers may be privileged to pass judgment upon the plans of any and all structures proposed to be erected in the park and has built primarily upon its own responsibility and under the supervision of its own officials more than two-thirds of all the dwellings in the park. This involved expenditure of nearly $850,000, but the property holder is under no obligation to have plans prepared for his prospective residence by the architect employed by the company nor to entrust to the latter of the erection of his dwelling. He is obligated, however, to provide plans that will meet the approval of the administrative officials of the park. The object of this supervision is to insure architectural harmony to as great a degree

as possible, and the good results obtained have justified the precaution.

Queen Anne and English cottages are numerous, and there are also many representations of Colonial architecture and a combination of Colonial and Dutch styles. Domestic Gothic designs are frequent, and while few pure types of architecture are found, the modifications and combinations adopted prove exceedingly effective. Many of the houses are entirely shingled, the treatment being frequently unique. The residential sites in Roland Park range from fifty feet front to one acre in extent, the average being seventy-five feet front.[27] The houses are constructed chiefly of frame at an average cost of $3,500, although a number of the more imposing residences represent investments ranging from $18,000 to $25,000. The houses have, without exception, cemented cellars, all modern conveniences of electric light, telephones, etc., and are heated by steam, hot water, hot air or gas. Few of the houses have less than twelve or fourteen rooms.

The extent of Roland Park is sufficiently large to protect the place from unwelcome neighborhood intrusion. The roadways are chiefly macadam and range from forty to sixty feet in width, while the lots run back to twenty-foot-wide service lanes. Before each property is the twelve-foot parkway mentioned above, which includes the stone sidewalks, ranging from three and one-half to five feet in width, that are screened from too vivid sunshine by long rows of trees. Each portion of the suburb possesses its own individual attraction, and a walk or drive through the place affords only pictures to delight the eye.

The roads wind here and there, presenting now a vista of distant hills, now a glimpse of ruddy sunset between tall trees or again penetrates the seclusion of some woodsy dell, where drifted leaves rustle beneath the feet and squirrels scamper unafraid.

Saloons and shops are effectually barred from this community,[28] and in order to maintain the strictly suburban character of the park the few stores necessary to the comfort of the residents are confined to one block, where picturesque Flemish architecture has been employed in the erection of these places of business. The group of buildings is set back on a line with the residences and looks upon a well-kept lawn surrounded with a high hedge. Here is the headquarters for telegraph, postal delivery, a drug store, the offices of the company and such other lines of trade as are necessary.

A special "tax-for-the-maintenance" is paid to the land company in lieu of a general municipal tax. It cannot exceed twenty-five cents for each front foot property during any single year, and its disposition is entirely to defray the expense of all items properly amenable to classification under maintenance. This embraces repairs to sidewalks and roads, lighting up avenues and roads, collection of garbage, ashes and rubbish, and disposition of sewage. No part of this administration fund is used for improvements or new construction.

One of the most unique features of Roland Park is that private stables are permitted only under exceptional circumstances and when such buildings cannot prove any annoyance to property holders in the vicinity.[29] As a substitute for the individual stables the company has erected at a cost of

$14,000 an apartment stable, conveniently located. Each section of this building provides accommodation for two horses and carriages, with quarters for a coachman.

In addition to its universally well-kept lawns and decorative shrubbery, one of the features of Roland Park is its charming gardens. Mr. and Mrs. William M. Ellicott have transformed an acre or more of ground that overhangs the ridge and commands a westward view of several miles into a formal garden that produces a truly picturesque setting for their handsome and artistic residence. The grounds of the Baltimore Country Club,[30] at Roland Park, are also terraced and beautified so as to render the hours spent in them a delight, and there are the most alluring English gardens encircling several of the homes. These are grouped about the Country Club and Club Road and are protected from inquisitive eyes by high brick walls surmounted with paling fences overrun by riotous vines. The homes of Mr. and Mrs. Allan MacSherry, of Mr. and Mrs. Ralph Robinson and others on Club Road are delightful examples of these gardens, and the roadway itself, thus screened from neighborhood view, is reposeful and secluded—a pleasant thoroughfare that carries the mind back to days of Continental travel. And then there are the flower gardens where flowers riot in a veritable wealth of beauty and color. Scarce a house exists in Roland Park whose doorway in June is not wreathed in roses or honeysuckle, but there are other gardens where flowers bloom from March until December. The perennial garden spot of the park, perhaps, is that surrounding the home of Mr. and Mrs. John Morrow Adams, whose grounds of 165 by 82 feet, corner of Woodlawn Road and Cold Spring Lane, were supervised in the planting of flowers by Beatrice Jones[31] of Boston and garden fame. A hedge of crimson rambler roses extends along the north side of the lawn, while sweetbrier roses entwine in a thick hedge along the terraced front. Honeysuckles bound the south and western sides and fling the sweetness of their blossoms to bee and passerby. Throughout the year in an old-fashioned "hardy garden" bed 140 feet long bloom those plants so dear to the heart—the pansy, mignonette and pinks. Purple flags herald the spring and chrysanthemums crown with the gold and sunset tints the closing year. For these latter flowers Mrs. Adams, the genius of the garden, has taken prizes at the annual exhibit in Baltimore of the Gardeners' Club, while almost until snowfall roses blossom in profusion. Mr. Luther Jackson, of Hawthorn Road, is noted for the beauty of his chrysanthemum beds, and the garden of Mr. J. H. Straw, corner of Hawthorn and Wyndhurst Roads, is equally picturesque. Several roads of the park pass through what was once the orchard of the Woodlawn estate, and in early spring cherry trees in exquisite bloom shower their delicately tinted petals over lawns and cottage roofs.

In the matter of education Roland Park has exceptional advantages. The public school is an artistic building of brick and stucco, planned in conformity to the most scientific designs for light, ventilation, etc., and the laying out of the grounds along landscape gardening lines has been undertaken by members of the Woman's Club of Roland Park, who will begin their labor of love for the children of the community as soon as certain vexed questions of boundaries are adjusted.[32] Notre Dame College,[33] on Charles Street Avenue, is but a brisk ten minutes' walk from Roland Park, and coaches daily carry groups of laughing children to and fro between the suburb and the school. There is also the Country School for Girls,[34] conducted by Miss Bertha Chapman, on Roland Avenue, and St. Mary's Female Orphan Asylum[35] on Cold Spring Lane, which, under the care of the Sisters of Charity, is an educational institution as well. St. Mary's embraces a group of imposing buildings surrounded by extensive grounds and lends dignity to the vicinity.

An exceedingly beautiful stone church has been erected on Roland Avenue by the Presbyterian congregation of which Reverend J. W. Douglas is pastor. There is also an attractive Methodist church, under the pastorate of Reverend W. V. Mallalieu. Many residents of the park worship at the quaint old Protestant Episcopal Church of St. Mary's, south of Roland Park, of which Reverend F. Ward Denys is rector, and for those who possess carriages the Church of the Redeemer, on Charles Street avenue, is a short and pleasant drive. St. Thomas' Catholic Church at Woodberry, and the Catholic church near Notre Dame Convent, are also accessible.

Socially the needs of Roland Park, and of many residents of Baltimore as well, have been met by the establishment of a country club, which has a perfectly appointed clubhouse, extensive athletic grounds, golf links, tennis courts and every facility for out and indoor amusement. While designed primarily for the enjoyment of residents of the place where it is located the membership of the club includes many fashionable residents of Baltimore, and debutantes' balls, formal receptions and the like are frequently held in the pleasant ballroom of the clubhouse.

Dinners are served until late in the autumn on the wide verandas of the building, with lighter refreshments served on the several terraces beneath the trees.

The Woman's Club of Roland Park has also been an important element in the social life of the neighborhood. This was organized by thirty ladies, residents of Roland Park, during the winter of 1896. The first meeting was held at the home of Mrs. Isabelle Parlett and Mrs. Charles Chapin Heath was elected first president of the club. Mrs. Edward H. Bouton, who is still on the board of governors, was one of the first vice-presidents. The club prospered as everything else associated with this successful suburb seems to have done, and in 1903 the club members purchased grounds 125 by 250 feet at the corner of Roland Avenue and Ridgewood Road, where an ideal woman's clubhouse was erected. The building is colonial in architecture, with a wide porch across the front, which has arched ends and is supported by Colonial columns. The assembly room, which is also a beautiful ballroom, has a seating capacity of 250 persons, and there are cozy committee and tea rooms on the same floor. The clubhouse is a center of social and educational activity and the building is open each afternoon for the informal serving of tea and to give club members opportunity for meeting for pleasant conversation.

The present officers of the club are: President, Mrs. B. W. Cockran; vice-presidents, Mrs. James H. Van Sickle and Mrs. Emory Morgan; recording secretary, Mrs. E. W. Davison; corresponding secretary, Mrs. Charles Reutlinger; treasurer, Mrs. W. C. Van Sant; governors, Mrs. William H. Appold, Mrs. E. A. Robbins, Mrs. Angus Cameron, Mrs. David Clark, Mrs. E. H. Bouton, Mrs. Edwin Griffith, Mrs. John R. Cary and Mrs. George Cochran.

The most important advantage recently gained by Roland Park, second only to the establishment of trolley service between that suburb and the city, is the opening of the boulevard from St. Paul Street, through Merryman's Lane, to Roland Park and the development of the Wyman estate in connection with the chain of parks. The boulevard will give Roland Park what it has always needed—a direct and splendid drive to Baltimore's leading thoroughfare—Charles Street—while the drive through the Wyman estate is romantically beautiful, and the picturesque windings of the driveway a triumph of successful roadmaking.[36]

Finding Five-Cent Christmas Opportunities (1915)

It all came about from the Optimist meeting a stranger in the taproom of a Baltimore tavern, remarking that the spirit of approaching Christmas and Christmas adventure seemed already in the air.

The stranger, whose mood was pessimistic, rejoined that it was difficult to cherish a Christmas spirit without a pocketful of money.

"Here am I," he said, "ready for adventure at any season of the year, desirous of many things. I want to drive and have no carriage to ride and have no horse. I want amusements and cannot afford them. I want to visit historic places and must stay at home. I want athletic sports and cannot afford to belong to clubs. I want to eat, drink and be merry and—I possess a jitney[37] income!"

He slapped a nickel scornfully upon the table and fell to studying with resentful eyes the buffalo calmly grazing thereon.

The Optimist laughed.

"The nickel income is not wholly to be despised," he said. "Of course, whether or not you be merry is an individual matter, but a nickel will afford you a few of the pleasures you crave. You want to ride, you say? Well ride. Take a United Railways car at Electric Park, journey by way of Mount Washington to Overlea, and you will have ridden sixteen miles. You exclaim, like King Richard III, 'A horse, a horse!' At any merry-go-round you will find a perfectly safe mount and can gallop withal to an accompaniment of music."

The Pessimist laughed in spite of himself. "Wouldn't I look like Don Quixote or Sancho Panza, with my long legs adjusted to the stirrups of a wooden horse," he protested.

"You said a horse—you did not specify a blue grass race horse or a horse show high stepper," retorted his companion, "and while we are considering motor problems, there is the jitney bus—a luxurious vehicle that will take you swiftly by the swellest route in town from *The Sun* office to Homewood at University Parkway. Or if your tastes are more democratic, there

is another line that will transfer you from Howard street to Highlandtown."[38]

"And walk back, I suppose," sneered the Pessimist.

"Oh, borrow an angel's wings or hire an aeroplane!" Responded the Optimist. "I am only telling you what you can do once. You will have to look after the encores yourself.

"Amusements you want? What is the matter with moving-picture shows? Can you not see all the kingdoms of the earth and all the countries thereof through the medium of films? Kings on their thrones, Sarah Bernhardt, Raymond Hitchcock[39]—all for a nickel at the 'movies.'

"Then, too, there is the pleasure of the public bath. The Romans regarded the bath as the height of luxury and pleasure. What prevents your patronizing the municipal bathhouse, where a spray bath, two towels and a cake of soap are yours in exchange for fine pennies? Or, if you wish to combine amusement with sociability, try pool at the nearest pool-room, where a nickel will provide entertainment for yourself and friend."

"If you long for athletic sports, a jitney will take you to Druid Hill Park,[40] where tennis courts are free to the earliest comer. If you wish to develop your chest, you can row on the lake for five cents, or should your tastes be aquatic there are divers city swimming pools in summer, such as the one at Patterson Park,[41] said to be the finest open-air pool in the world, or the river swimming at Fort McHenry, where five cents will provide you with bath suit and towels. In winter a car fare will take you to either Druid Hill or Patterson Parks, where there is free skating upon lakes, the ice of which is guaranteed to bear your weight."

"If it is sightseeing you are yearning for, one of the prettiest and most comprehensive views obtainable can be enjoyed by taking a street car over the elevated road from the Post Office to Preston Street. Here you see both the freight and the passenger terminals of the Northern Central Railway, the City Hall, the Post Office; you can compare the old and the new methods of street paving; can see the notable McShane bell foundry,[42] which the Christ Church chimes and many other historic bells, including the bell for the Jamestown Exposition,[43] were cast. You glimpse the gilded dome of the Cathedral and the towering height of the Washington Monument;[44] also Loyola College and several sky-scraping office buildings. Many churches and homes of wealth and culture are seen to the west of the elevated road, and the Penitentiary and City Jail are seen to the east. Baltimore packing industries are grouped here, and Mercy Hospital is sighted. The new Fallsway is seen, that not only indicates the engineering and architectural development of Baltimore, but local art as well, in the splendid fountain designed by the Baltimore sculptor, Hans Schuler.[45]

"You would 'eat, drink and be merry,' you say? What hungry man would refuse a baked apple for five cents, or a sandwich—ham, tongue, cheese or minced chicken or minced ham—any one of them for the same price; or a slice of pie—mince, apple, pumpkin, sweet potato—each five cents; or, in lighter refreshments, a slice of cake or ice-cream (small order)—good cream, too—for five cents; or two ice-cream cones for a nickel? Enjoy one yourself and treat your girl."

"If it is drink you crave, refresh yourself for five cents at a soda fountain or invest in some bottles soft drink—strawberry, sarsaparilla, root beer—pay your nickel and take your choice. If you are pro-German and disdain any other than the national beverage of the Fatherland, you can always get a glass of beer for five cents and frequently with one hard-boiled egg, one fried oyster or one wienerwurst thrown in, or, without liquid refreshment, you can feast upon one crab cake, one deviled crab or two fried oysters for the same modest sum."

"As for visiting historical places, a single carfare will carry you to Fort McHenry, one of the most perfect examples of the five star forts in existence and made sacred to the American people because 'The Star-Spangled Banner' proudly waved there defying an invading enemy amid a baptism of fire, a sight so inspiring it moved a Maryland poet to write a great national hymn.[46]

"Or you can take a street car to Mount Clare, the oldest house in Baltimore, built in 1754, and once the Colonial manor of Charles Carroll, barrister, who wrote the Bill of Rights.[47] The home of a gentleman and a patriot, and from the picturesque terraces of this ancient estate, now known as Carroll Park, you can look down upon the old Washington Road[48] often traveled by the Father of Our Country, by the French soldier Lafayette and other worthies of Revolutionary days."

"Go to Old St. Paul's burying ground, corner Lombard and Fremont streets, where rests the honored dust of Samuel Chase,[49] Signer of the Declaration of Independence. Lieut.-Col. Tench Tilghman, who carried in hot haste the official news of Cornwallis' surrender at Yorktown and of liberty to the National Assembly at

Philadelphia. Here also rest the bodies of Daniel Dulany;[50] of John Eager Howard[51] and of Colonel George Armistead, who defended the Star-Spangled Banner and Fort McHenry against British foes."

"In Westminster Churchyard lies buried the poet, Edgar Allan Poe, and General Samuel Smith, who commanded the Maryland land forces in the War of 1812."

"Rembrandt Peale's Museum,[52] built in 1813 and the first building in Baltimore to be illumined by gas, is still in use as one of the City Hall annexes. Or stand upon the southwest corner of Liberty and Baltimore streets and realize that here, in 1777, once stood Congress Hall, where Washington was made dictator of the Revolutionary Army. Walk down the east side of Charles Street, near German, and know you are passing where Commodore Joshua Barney[53] once lived and entertained Jerome Bonaparte.[54] Or take a street car to Homeland, between Waverly and Clifton, where William Patterson once lived and where Betsy Patterson dreamed of love and her Corsican lover.

"Or stroll along Front Street near Gay and invoke a vision of old Front Street Theatre,[55] where Jenny Lind[56] once sang and Edgar Allan Poe's mother played in her brief dramatic day. Five cents will take you to any of these memorable spots.

"Have a heart! Have a heart!" protested the Pessimist. "I feel like the princes of East Indian folklore, transported breathlessly from place to place on a magic carpet. I'll be a tottering old man, like Oliver Wendell Holmes' 'Last Leaf,' before I have lived long enough to take in all the five-cent sights of Baltimore! Have done, have done!"

But the Optimist has still a word to say.

"Go to Lexington Market,[57] one of the three great markets of the world, and the spirit of Christmas will enter your heart, though your heart had been asleep for eons. Buy a Christmas trumpet, or a branch of mistletoe, or a Christmas angel to deck a Christmas tree, or a Yule candle to set in your window upon the blessed Christmas Eve to guide the Christ Child through the snow. Any of these inspiring things may be yours for five cents. Or drop a nickel into the gypsy kettle of the Salvation Army Santa Claus and you will not only have your heart warmed by entering into the spirit of giving that makes the Christmas tide beautiful, but you will be laying up treasures in the world to come. It was Joaquin Miller, you remember, who said, so truly and poetically, that all we can hold in our cold, dead hand is what we have given away."[58]

"I will remember the gypsy kettle," said the Pessimist, softly, as he paid his score and rose to take his departure.

Do You Know the Street on Which You Live? Calvert Street (1923)

Calvert Street possesses the distinction of bearing the family name of the Lords Baltimore,[59] and was indicated, but not yet christened, when the first plat of the original Baltimore Town was made, in 1729.

The only public wharf that Baltimore knew up to 1783 was at Calvert Street, and ancestors of men now resident of this city knew the street well when Baltimore Town was surrounded by a stockade, or at least a stout board fence. The latter had two carriage gates and one pedestrian gate, and was designed as a protection against Indian attack.

First Courthouse

The first difficulty to be surmounted in Calvert Street's struggle for existence was the turbulent waters of Jones' Falls.[60]

Those who catch occasional glimpses of that chastened and diminished stream that in latter days has hidden itself beneath the stone masonry of the arched Fallsway, scarcely can conceive of its lusty current, when vessels of considerable burden were built and launched in tidewater, where the City Spring long flowed, surrounded by tall elm trees and which is now the site of Mercy Hospital.[61] At Lexington and Calvert Streets ships anchored, men were drowned and boys rejoiced in swimming.[62]

What is now the bed of Calvert Street was then deep water.

At Fayette and Calvert Streets, where the Battle Monument[63] now stands, there was then what historians of early Baltimore called "a precipice," fifty or sixty feet high, which overhung Jones' Falls. Upon this hill, in 1767, was built the first courthouse Baltimore knew.

This was a two-story brick building surmounted by a cupola, which continued to stand there until 1808. The location was called "Court House Hill"; and the falls, when swollen by heavy rains, swept about the base of the hill in stormy violence.

Battle Monument Built

This building took the place of the ancient county seat at Joppa; and, after a season, an engineer, Leonard Harbough,[64] to satisfy the demands of pedestrians for more direct passage to upper Calvert Street, performed the then difficult task of tunneling beneath the courthouse and

arching the tunnel, thus giving wayfarers a direct route to their destinations.

Hipped-roof houses clustered about the base of "Court House Hill"—wooden houses, most of them, painted blue, white or yellow, with here and there mansions built of brick with court yards. Locust trees abounded, making fragrant the days of spring.

Later, when the Battle Monument was erected, in 1814, to commemorate the Battle of North Point and the defense of Fort McHenry, the hill had been leveled to the street bed and the plaza became known as Monument Square.

Water Supply Aided

When Calvert Street was graded in 1809-1810 the course of Jones' Falls had been diverted. The lot occupied by the City Spring was purchased by the City Council; and under direction of Peter Hoffman and Jesse Hollingsworth, buildings were erected and the grounds improved at a cost of $27,000.

It was then called North Fountain, and five springs of peculiarly pure water gushed from this source. Being municipal property, its water was free to all, and in a niche in the keeper's house, behind the spring, was a small monument in memory of Colonel George Armistead, who so gallantly defended Fort McHenry during the bombardment by the British fleet in 1814.

Calvert Street assisted in overcoming the problem of abundant water in Baltimore. In addition to North Fountain, the waters of Jones' Falls were taken from that stream, a short distance north of the jail, and brought in an open canal to the southeast corner of Calvert and Centre Streets.

Nucleus of Academy

From there it was elevated by waterpower to a reservoir at Franklin and Cathedral Streets, 94 feet above tide. A second reservoir, 200 feet square and 16 feet deep, was built at Calvert and Madison Streets, supplied with water brought from Keller and Foreman's Mills, about one-half mile distant. The water company owned works and extensive grounds in the neighborhood.

Baltimore Museum once stood at Calvert and Baltimore Streets, where the Emerson Hotel[65] is now.

The museum owed its existence to the untiring efforts of a member of the Peale family. A lottery broker named John Clark built the museum in 1829, and in 1830 the Peales rented the upper portion of the building to exhibit pictures and art treasures and also interesting specimens of natural history.

This museum was the nucleus from which there developed the Maryland Academy of Sciences.[66]

Railroad Used Site

P. T. Barnum, the notable showman, purchased the Baltimore Museum from Edmund Penle, who had become the owner, in 1845; and, after conducting it for a season, sold it to Albert N. Hann, until it finally became the possession of the actor, John E. Owens,[67] in 1850.

Henry C. Jarrett and George Zieglef owned it in turn, and Charles Getz, a scene painter, purchased it last. Its natural wonders were distributed by him to different educational institutions, but the building had a remarkable and brilliant history both as a the-

ater and Baltimore's first gallery of fine arts.

The administration building of the Baltimore and Ohio Railroad next occupied the site of the old Baltimore Museum and continued a landmark of which Baltimore was justly proud until the conflagration of 1904, when that portion of the city was swept to its destruction in the elemental splendor of smoke and flame.

Churches were built early on Calvert Street, with Ebenezer Baptist Church, between Lexington and Saratoga Streets; the New Universalist Church—now St. Francis' Xavier Catholic Church (colored)—at Pleasant and Calvert; St. Ignatius' Catholic Church, at Madison; the First Reformed Church, near Read, and the New Jerusalem Church, above Chase.

Loyola College was opened on Calvert Street, near Madison, September 15, 1852, but already it has outgrown its location and is prepared for removal to Evergreen, Jr.[68]

"The Elegant Depot"

Calvert Station was noted in 1852 as "the elegant depot of the Baltimore and Susquehanna Railroad Company, where "the gentleman having charge of it politely permit strangers to examine it at any time." It cost about $45,000.[69]

Calvert was a busy street as early as 1833. The American Tract Society,[70] instituted in 1816, had its depository corner Calvert Street and Lovely Lane. Carroll Hall, a large and costly building erected by a private subscription, stood on the northeast corner of Baltimore and Calvert, just across from the Baltimore Museum.

The Farmers and Merchants' Bank was

at Calvert Street and Bank Lane, with Nicholas Brice as president and J. Duer, cashier. The Mechanics' Bank stood at Calvert and Fayette Streets, with George Brown as president and W. H. Murray, cashier.

This was before the Baltimore and Ohio had had its fine administration building and the offices of the railroad were in the basement of the Mechanics' Bank and P.E. Thomas was president.

Basement Post Office[71]

The post office was then in the basement of the City Hotel, at the northwest corner of Calvert Street and Bank lane, with J. S. Skinner[72] as postmaster.

It was a "happy-go-lucky" mail station, concerning which it was placidly stated that "Owing to the change of seasons and other causes, no permanent time can be specified for the arrival and departure of the mails." The office was supposed to be open week days "from 7 a.m. until dark, or after the arrival of the Eastern mail." Sundays it was open from 7 until 8 a.m. and in the afternoon for the delivery of Eastern mail.

The street was a newspaper center then, as afterward. The *American Farmer*, a weekly paper, was published there, and the *Temperance Herald* had its office at the intersection of Baltimore and Calvert Streets.[73]

Barnum's, or the City Hotel—that hostelry where Charles Dickens said he had been more comfortable than in any hotel in America, and where Jennie Lind found cordial entertainment in 1850—was built by David Barnum in 1825.[74] It was 120 feet front,[75] six stories high and 213 feet deep. It was the most fashionable place of entertainment for strangers and a winter resort for Baltimoreans living in country seats near the city.

Pike, Henry & Ward, importers of cutlery, conducted their business at 21 South Calvert Street. Others on that street were Foy & Whitelock, hardware dealers, at 68 1/2 South Calvert; Charles B. Austin, general agent for the Union Glass Company, of Philadelphia, at No. 36, and William Tileston, agent for the Providence Flint Glass Company, at No. 49.

Dorman & Amos, grocers and commission merchants, were at 73 South Calvert, and White & Son, grocers and wine dealers, at No. 67 South Calvert. L.G. Cox & Moir, commission and grain merchants, were at Pratt and Calvert Streets.

Exchange and Printing

John Clark had one of three lottery and exchange offices corner Calvert and Baltimore Streets, and Isaac Brooks, iron merchant, was at 74 South Calvert. Ward Sears was agent for the sale of Thompsonian medicines at South Calvert, and D. N. Neilson, a dental surgeon, was found corner Calvert and Pleasant Streets.

Books and job printing found favor on Calvert Street. John W. Wood was No. 1 North Calvert. He carried books and did job printing. E. J. Cole & Co., importers of foreign books, were at 4 North Calvert, opposite the City Hotel; the Depository of Maryland Sunday Union School was at 15 South Calvert, and Houghton & Johnson, paper dealers, were at 47 South Calvert.

Thomas B. and C. Deford, tanners, were at 44 South Calvert. and William Wilson, also in the leather business, was at 39 South Calvert.

Other Business

Jacob Balderston, interested in sheet iron and copper, was at 60 South Calvert Street and his neighbors in the same line were Jacob Stahl and William Wallace, on Calvert Street, opposite Water Street.

Robert Skinner conducted a last-finding store, corner Calvert and Water Streets; A. Marye conducted a wholesale and retail establishment at 17 South Calvert; Samuel Hunt, merchant tailor and draper, was at 14 South Calvert; John Barker and Son, iron foundries, were on North Calvert, and George McGregor manufactured patent locks on South Calvert Street.

J. Irvine Hitchcock had an agricultural and horticultural establishment at 16 South Calvert in connection with a stock and experimental farm, garden and nursery, in the vicinity of Baltimore.

Jesse Comegys was interested in bread stuffs near the City Spring, and hat stores or manufactories were conducted by Clap & Cole, at 5 South Calvert Street, and Elder & Boston, at 8 South Calvert. James Sloan conducted a boot and shoe business in the basement of the City Hotel.

St. Clair Hotel, Guy's Hotel and the Gilmor Hotel were places of public entertainment associated with Calvert Street.

A Social Center

About Battle Monument clustered the homes of most representative families.

Reverdy Johnson regarded the monument from his drawing room windows, and near him were the residences of the Gilmors, the Swans, the Nelsons, the Smiths, Didiers, Whites, Taylors, the Greenways, the Cohens, the Merediths, Beatys, Williams and Wilsons.

About Monument Square, indeed, began the fashionable social life of Baltimore, while, later, the elite of the city had homes on Calvert Street in the vicinity of Calvert Station.

In 1741, Mr. Edward Fottrell, a gentleman from Ireland, imported the materials and erected the first brick house of Baltimore with freestone corners and the first which was two stories without a hipped roof. It stood near the northwest corner of Calvert and Fayette Streets, on or near the lot later occupied by Reverdy Johnson's mansion opposite Barnum's Hotel. Mr. Fottrell lived there until just before the Revolution, when he returned to Ireland.

Among the few old homes still standing, as of old, is that long occupied by the Metropolitan Savings Bank, which purchased it of Thomas Wilson.

Belvedere, the magnificent estate of Colonel John Eager Howard,[76] included what is now Calvert Street and his mansion stood upon what is now the bed of Calvert Street, at its intersection with Chase Street. In 1852 the mansion was owned and occupied by John S. McKim. From Belvedere, onward, North Street was called Belvedere Street, and from the point where it was crossed by Preston, citizens using Belvedere Bridge crossed diagonally over Jones' Falls valley to just opposite the entrance of Greenmount Cemetery at Oliver Street.

From the bridge a picturesque view was obtained of the valley and one of the reservoirs of the Baltimore Water Company. This dam was swept away in a flood of July 14, 1837, which did enormous damage along Calvert Street in that portion known as the Meadows. The Belvedere Bridge was removed prior to 1874.

Shop of Image Maker

Many familiar with Lower Calvert Street in olden days will recall an old Italian image maker—Furechici—who had a workshop on Calvert Street between Lexington and Saratoga Streets. The children who attended Dr. Nathan Brown's Baltimore Female College on St. Paul Street (chiefly patronized by Southern girls) loved to be admitted to the workshop, which was as interesting as a street in some foreign country.

Here the image maker modeled madonnas wrapped with blue mantles, and "plaster saints" such as those whose virtues were the despair of Kipling's British soldier.[77] He carried them about the streets for sale, and at the Christmastide added to them quaint plaster churches, with tall steeples and colored glass windows. With a lighted candle inside they shone beautifully beneath fragrant Christmas trees.

Old Furechici once modeled for Dr. Jacob W. Houck, a prominent physician of Baltimore, a portrait bust of Dr. Christopher Johnston that was the admiration of the latter's medical friends until it was destroyed by fire.

Two Mayors' Homes

Two mayors of Baltimore, Robert T. Banks and Joshua Vansant, resided on Calvert Street, and Mrs. Emmett Banks of R. W. still resides in the home, 803 North Calvert Street, where her honored father-in-law lived and died.

Goldsborough Griffith, identified for many years with the Prisoners' Aid work in Baltimore,[78] was her neighbor. In the 600 block were the Farbers, the Kings, the Marstons, the Maetiers, the Pinkneys, Mr. William George Reed, Hugh Sisson and his family, Dr. Robert Robinson (whose drug store was a landmark opposite of Calvert Station), Miss Mary Talbott, Miss Hannah Leitel and others. Mrs. John E. Owens, widow of the actor, lived at a corner of Madison and Calvert Streets after she gave up her country home at Towson.

The Torrance family, General Anderson and old Mr. Hance, also Miss Helen Kirk, all lived in that vicinity, as well as the Tarrs, the Cunninghams, the Delorays and Professor Curlander, long associated with the musical life of Baltimore.

Homes of Beauty

The late banker, John B. Ramsey, and his sisters lived on Calvert Street: and in a handsome house with a garden in the 900 block lived Samuel Appold and his sons and daughters. On the opposite side Mr. William F. Lucas, Jr., still occupies the residence of the Lucas family and continues to keep the property in the beautiful order peculiar to a past regime.

Belvedere Terrace is a section of representative and fashionable Baltimore homes. In the 1000 block lived for many years I. Freeman Rasin, long associated with the political affairs of the Democratic party. His next neighbor was Mrs. John C. Wrenshall,[79] for many years president of the Woman's Literary Club of Baltimore. Professor Basil Gildersleeve still is a resident of that block.

Above Belvedere Terrace, Calvert Street continues a handsome residence section, and having reached Mount Royal Avenue, the street leaps by bridge still farther, then cuts its way through the grounds of the Baltimore Polytechnic Institute,[80] and follows its own sweet will to the educational heights of the Johns Hopkins University.

Elizabeth Lester Mullin (c. 1874-1952)

Elizabeth Lester Mullin may not have held many titles as an unmarried woman and stay-at-home daughter in 1900, but today she might be described under the titles of historian, translator, and storyteller. Her father, Michael A. Mullin, was a well-known lawyer and politician, a member of the Maryland state legislature, the Baltimore city council, and president of the Baltimore City Bar association. Her mother, Elizabeth C. Mullin, was a prominent member of the Catholic church to which the family belonged, as was her father. As a result, Mullin was deeply involved in Maryland society and history. She was an active member of the Maryland Historical Society and served as the secretary of the Edgar Allan Poe Memorial Association. She also served as treasurer of the Women's Literary Club of Baltimore.

"Mistress Brent's Bluff" was the winner of a short story contest sponsored by the *Baltimore Sun* in 1915, and recounts the tale of Margaret Brent, a prominent woman in colonial Maryland history (Lucy Meacham Thruston's novel *Mistress Brent*, excerpted in this volume, also features Brent as its central character). Brent was the first woman to appear before the Maryland state assembly, and she demanded that her voice be heard. Her story sends a plainly feminist message: that women ought to be viewed as equal to their male counterparts. Mullin's choice to chronicle this woman reveals something of her character that is mostly lost to history, a belief in women's rights and the right for women to have a political voice. —K. Shiber

Mistress Brent's Bluff (1915)

For an infant settlement St. Mary's was precocious. It soon learned to talk, and the first thing it said was, "The Governor is in love with Mistress Margaret Brent."

To be sure, Leonard Calvert, the brother of the Proprietary,[1] "Deputy Governor of the Province, Lieutenant-General, Chancellor, Admiral, Chief, Captain, Magistrate and Commander as well by sea as by land," fenced in by his many titles and wrapped in his unapproachable dignity, never for an instant supposed that the public made grist of his private affairs.

Yet by 1643 the report was so common that when the Governor one bright April day stepped down to the landing to take a seat in his pinnace two men standing by wagered that when he reached the river he would turn south as far as the "Sister's Freehold," and a certain bright-eyed maiden peering over the bluff went home and made this entry in her diary:

> The Governor is gone a-wooing. Mistress is not so yonge as she onct was. Warm daies she waits his Cuming under St. Adauctus Tree, where there be a Bench and they do take Councell together concerning the business of the Province. The Idea!

Whether or not St. Adauctus was the special patron of spinsters the calendar fails to announce, but true it is that at the southeastern extremity of the lands allotted to her sister and herself at a point overlooking the river there rose a great tree marked "St. Adauctus," and beneath its shelter Mistress Brent sat and waited.[2] Nor had she long to wait.

The Governor came and brought with him a letter he had received that morning from England.

As Mistress Brent held out her hand for the letter she asked: "Does Lord Baltimore fix the date of his coming?"

"On the contrary, he writes for me to return to England."

"England!"

The Governor was completely taken aback. Her exclamation was short and sharp, while the hand she held out for the letter trembled. He had never known her to betray any emotion. Now he watched the blood flood into her cheeks, then fade away again, and he felt the effort she made to regain her self-control.

Mistress Brent read the letter: then her hands dropped into her lap and her eyes wandered out over the water to where a ship rode at anchor.

She took in the whole sweep of the harbor. Nothing escaped her. Neither grassy slope nor jutting headland, the little town as it nestled for protection between the two arms of the river or the forest which stood a menace in the background. Finally she spoke:

"We evidently miscalculated. From Lord Baltimore's last letter we thought he was making preparations to come to the province."

"Others seem to have thought so too," replied the Governor. "The master of that ship tells me that the day he sailed it was rumored in England that Lord Baltimore was to be cited before the Lords and bonded not to leave the kingdom."

"How soon do you go?" she asked.

"Go?" said he. "It is out of the ques-

tion. Cecelius[3] does not understand the situation over here or he would not suggest my return."

"The situation over here is evidently worse than he is willing to admit. Who will help him?"

Her question pricked. The Governor became irritated. "My going is not to be considered. I could not leave the province in its present plight. You know that the Indians have risen. Virginia refuses to join us against them, Claiborne[4] is at his old game, the Assembly is divided"—He stopped short. He has a queer feeling that he was talking to himself.

Mistress Brent was silent. She knew him too well to argue with him.

The Governor lowered his voice and said in a more persuasive tone: "What I want you to do is to advise me about tomorrow. You have heard that the Assembly has been called for tomorrow and, knowing the temper of the crowd as I do, I am afraid that the recommendations the Proprietary makes in this letter will not be allowed to pass."

"But they must pass," proclaimed Mistress Brent with vehemence. "It would ruin Lord Baltimore's chances at this crisis if the news reached Parliament that he had lost the confidence of his own province."

"Exactly," agreed the Governor. "But what can we do?"

Mistress Brent thought for a minute. "Pack the Assembly," she suggested.

The Governor shook his head. "I have no majority to work upon."

"Then unpack it."

"What!"

"Get rid of the opposition," she explained.

"Impossible." he argued. "If you were a

man now, you would understand—"

Mistress Brent interrupted him. "Would you rather I were a man?"

The way in which the question was put brought the conversation back upon a personal basis.

The Governor laughed. "You are delicious! At the very height of the argument you always drop back upon your femininity."

"Femininity or not, I am tempted to show you how to run an Assembly."

Such a speech from another might have been considered as *lese majeste*, but the Governor was far too enamored to take exception to the audacity of Mistress Brent. He simply smiled and demanded:

"Where would you begin?"

"Whom do you fear?" she inquired.

"Your brother Giles, with his seventy-three proxies, and Cornwallis, whose eloquence sways every Burgess in the House from the Sheriff down to Tom Tottle."

"Leave them to me," said Mistress Brent coolly.

"What do you mean to do with them?"

Instead of answering his question, Mistress Brent made this proposition: "If I hold the opposition in hand for a couple of hours tomorrow morning, could you convene the Assembly at the usual time, read the Proprietary's letter and have the unthinking multitude pass upon those few recommendations before the mischief-makers have a chance to do harm?"

"It is well worth trying," he responded.

"And if I succeed," she continued, "will you do what I ask?"

"Certainly," he granted. "provided, if you fail, you will do what I ask."

Mistress Brent hesitated.

The Governor rose to leave. "It is a fair compact," said he. "Win all, lose all."

Still Mistress Brent stood irresolute. Once again her eyes wandered over the water to where the ship rode at anchor.

"It is a fair compact." she repeated mechanically.

The Governor made his adieu, but he looked back and asked with a laugh: "Would I rather you were a man?"

⁙

Just before the Assembly convened the next morning Mr. Secretary Lewger[5] said to the Governor: "Mistress Brent came to me half an hour ago and asked me to make her brother's excuses. He has been unexpectedly called to Kent Manor,[6] but he has left these proxies, which she asks that I hand to Cornwallis."

The Governor's only comment was: "Do I understand that Mistress Brent brought them herself? Which way did she go?"

Had he but known, Mistress Brent at that early hour threaded an Indian trail through the Proprietary's forest. She rode cautiously—not that she was afraid.

Danger served as a tonic to a nature such as hers. Adventure was in her blood, a spirit of mischief possessed her and in the exhilaration of the moment she laughed. "Were I married," said she to herself, "this would not be allowed."

When she reached a point where two trails crossed she stopped and listened. Immediately a drum beat.

"There is the second drum!" she exclaimed. "If it is true that Cornwallis went on a reconnoitering expedition at dawn, he should return to town this way."

Five, ten, fifteen minutes dragged by.

Mistress Brent began to have misgivings. Suddenly her horse lifted its ears. Soon she heard voices; then Cornwallis approached, followed by two other riders in Indian file, while the Sheriff brought up the rear.

Cornwallis pressed forward. "Mistress Brent," said he, "alone in the forest?"

"I am on the warpath," she explained. "Can you direct me to the lands owned by one Thomas Tottle?"

"His lands lie back by the creek, but here is Tottle himself."

As he spoke Cornwallis moved aside and a heavy square-jawed man doffed his cap and faced Mistress Brent. She looked at him. Then she looked over his shoulder and recognized the next who rode in file was a man known in the community as "Miser Smith."

"My good man," Mistress deigned to address Tottle, "a white bull of mine, one of the Lord Proprietary's stock is missing, and I understand it is on your place."

"I have never seen it," was the blunt reply.

"Then allow me to show it to you." And Mistress Brent made a movement as though she would pass on.

Tottle grew very red. "I am no Indian to steal cattle."

"Had I believed you had stolen it, sir, I would have had the Sheriff here to put you in prison."

"Oh, Mistress Brent!" exclaimed the Sheriff. "There is no prison but my hands."

"Then come, Mr. Sheriff, and take my 'bull by the horns.'"

Cornwallis thought it was time to intervene. "Do not stop us, Mistress Brent. We are on our way to the Assembly. This little matter can be adjusted later. As for

my friend Tottle, I would be willing to wager a hundred pounds of tobacco that he has no cattle on his place but his own."

Mistress Brent was too true a sport to be on a surety. However, Cornwallis had to be punished. She turned to the miser.

"Mr. Smith," she said in a dulcet tone, "I am sure you will champion my cause. Take up this bet—"

"Lady! Lady!" cried the miser in alarm, "a hundred pounds of tobacco—"

"Thank you, Mr. Smith."

"But lady! lady! I did not—"

The Sheriff interrupted him. "There is the third drumbeat. The Assembly meets. We will be late."

"We will be fined," groaned Smith.

"Pay your fine out of your hundred pounds," suggested Mistress Brent, as she again moved forward.

But Cornwallis barred her way. He spoke with authority. "Mistress Brent, you must return with us to St. Mary's. The Indians have risen and the forest is unsafe. I cannot allow you to proceed alone."

"Then," quoth Mistress Brent, "I will hunt me a knight in war paint and feathers." And quick as a flash she turned her horse and dashed along another trail into the very heart of the forest.

Cornwallis, taken completely by surprise, swore he would never be outwitted by a woman and, turning to the others, gave the command:

"Follow!"

It was a reckless chase. Mistress Brent had the best horse. Swift and sure-footed, the little steed sped over the tracks beaten by red men's feet. Primeval trees arched overhead, occasionally a fallen timber served as a hurdle across the narrow path; tiny rills made the way slippery and the possibility of an arrow shot by an unseen hand added zest to the adventure. Mistress Brent was willful enough to make many a detour to prolong the ride until she reached the edge of the woods where the creek spread before her and she drew rein on Tottle's ground.

As they were at his very door, Tottle insisted that they should search for the white bull. They dismounted and he led them over his pastures. Sheep and kine he had in plenty. Bulls black, dun and spotted, but none that was white. Cornwallis laughed. He felt himself a hundred pounds richer. The miser wrung his hands in despair, while the sheriff asked in official tone:

"Has this ox of your any mark by which we may know it?"

"On its left hind hoof," Mistress Brent assured him.

The search was fruitless. They were about to return to their horses when a low bellow came to them from over a fallow field. They hurried in that direction, and there stood the white bull a prisoner—tied by a long halter to a tree which grew near the banks of a deep pool.

"White, but not innocent," commented Cornwallis, as he eyed the animal standing with lowered horns.

Meanwhile the Sheriff, unobserved by the others, had stolen behind the bull to examine its hoof. The animal, conscious that it was approached, veered suddenly and with a loud roar raised its front feet ready to charge.

The Sheriff had to choose between the bull and the pond, and he took to the water. But the water was deep, the water was cold

and the Sheriff, being a man of considerable weight in the community, sank from sight.

Cornwallis tore off his coat and plunged in to the rescue. Tottle swore, the miser trembled and Mistress Brent, conscience-stricken, shrieked aloud.

Midst the general excitement the bull tore loose from its halter and at the very moment that Cornwallis and the Sheriff rose like dripping naiads from the stream the bull, with a parting roar, shook the dust of Tottle's field from off its hoofs.

༄

"What I do not understand," said the Governor to Mistress Brent that afternoon, "is who tied that bull in Tottle's field?"

"That," replied she, "is a leading question and not admitted in the testimony."

The Governor smiled. "You have done all you undertook to do. And," said he, "I have come to redeem my promise."

Mistress Brent grew suddenly pale.

He observed her agitation. "Don't be afraid," he urged gently. "Had I won, you know very well what I meant to claim."

Still the words refused to come.

The Governor tried to take her hand. "Do you think," he asked tenderly, "that I could refuse you anything?"

Her white lips faltered. "Go back to England and help Lord Baltimore."

"Margaret!"

Staggered, hurt, humiliated, Leonard Calvert awoke to the realization that he stood only as a younger brother in the eyes of the woman he loved.

Annie Leakin Sioussat (1856-1942)

Annie Middleton Leakin Sioussat was born in the Georgetown neighborhood of Washington, DC and was an author, historian, and reformer. Her book *Old Manors in the Colony of Maryland* (1913) traced the establishment of wealthy estates in Maryland on indigenous lands, while in *Old Baltimore* (1931), Sioussat vividly depicted the relationship between one of Baltimore's most storied women, Elizabeth Patterson, and her husband Jérôme Bonaparte, brother of Napoleon Bonaparte. In the excerpt included here, she provides a comprehensive view of the social scene in Baltimore among military leaders and their wives. Sioussat's anecdotal quotes from Elizabeth Patterson throughout *Old Baltimore* highlight the wit and self-possession with which she stood up to men like Napoleon.

Sioussat was one of the founding members of the Women's Literary Club of Baltimore, and led the women in conversation and in organizing meetings and other activities. Though she has a prominent voice throughout the Club minutes, she held a leadership position for just a single year, 1892-1893, where she served as Vice President.

In addition to her work for the WLCB, Sioussat was a prominent member of the Maryland Society of the Colonial Dames of America, a society that advocated for the publication for genealogical discovery and raised funds to preserve historical landmarks both locally and nationally. Many of her notes and letters contain information on her avid interest in the American Historical Association, the English-Speaking Union,

Civil Service Reform, and the Maryland Forestry Association.[1] Her historical works provide a holistic view of colonial Maryland and Baltimore culture of the eighteenth century. —J. Flink and M. Pikus

From *Old Baltimore* (1931)

In this excerpt, Sioussat tells the story of Elizabeth ("Betsy") Patterson Bonaparte, an almost mythical figure in Baltimore lore. Elizabeth's father William Patterson immigrated to America from Ireland before the American Revolutionary War, was a signer of the Declaration of Independence, and became the second wealthiest man in Maryland after Charles Carroll of Carrollton. Elizabeth married Jérôme Bonaparte in 1803, but Bonaparte later joined the French Navy and took another wife, the German princess Catharina of Württemberg. After the dissolution of their marriage, Elizabeth returned to Baltimore with her son, "Bo" Bonaparte, and spent the rest of her life in her home city.

Not only had the constant intercourse with the West Indies, and with Brazil and other points in South America, brought great wealth to the coffers of Baltimore merchant princes, but it had other far-reaching consequences. It had long been the means through which many valuable additions to our city had been received. In 1766 William Patterson had come from Donegal[2] to Philadelphia. Having entered the shipping business, in 1775 he sent two vessels to France, one of which returned in March, 1776, with gunpowder and arms, at a time when, Mr. Patterson declared later, it was said that General Washington had not powder sufficient to fire a salute. On his own journey from Europe Mr. Patterson tarried a while at St. Eustatius,[3] but finding that the Dutch government could not protect Americans against the English in their trade, he went to Martinique. Finally arriving at Baltimore Town in 1778, in the thick of the Revolutionary conflict, Mr. Patterson established himself in business there and prospered greatly.

Lieutenant Barney[4] had first saluted the Dutch flag of the quay of St. Eustatius and received their return. Thus came the first recognition accorded the continental flag, which cost the flourishing little community dear, in the loss of their homes, the roofless houses testifying to the vengeance of the English for this rash indulgence of premature courtesy. Young Barney, while in the service of the French navy, had many such adventures, and it was in one of these daring expeditions that he met the brother of the First Consul, the dashing young Lieutenant Jérôme Bonaparte,[5] the spoiled child of an otherwise Spartan mother, who ruled her model home so well that it was said to be like a convent in its systematic conduct. For the earlier part of his life Jérôme was regarded by his august brother with tolerant amusement,—"petit mauvais sujet."[6] The boy of fifteen who had been refused permission to make the Italian campaign with the army had no word of welcome for the Conqueror on his return, and actually won by his petty and willful conduct a promise to hive him whatever he might ask. "The sword of Marengo"[7] was the modest demand, and to him it

came. The acquisition at this early date of a travelling case with silver fittings, mother of pearl and ivory mountings, with razor and every appurtenance for a "whiskered pard,"[8] aroused Napoleon. "So it is you, Sir, then, who indulge in travelling cases costing 10,000 francs." "Oh!" made answer the incipient warrior, "I am always like that, I only care for beautiful things!"

A commission in the army was short-lived. A duel with a fellow officer, the mark of which Jérôme bore to his grave, led the First Consul to change his career to that of the growing navy of the Republic, for which, as Brittania was vigorously making good her traditional right to "rule the seas", a great need was felt. Forwarded to the rear admiral on the flagship *Indivisible,* at Brest, he bore order: "I send you, citizen general, Citizen Jérôme Bonaparte to serve his apprenticeship in the navy. You know that he needs to be treated strictly, and to make up for lost time. Insist on his carrying out exactly all the duties of his profession."

The capture of the *Swiftsure,* an English 74 gunship, gave Jérôme his first honorable mention. He received the sword of the captain, notwithstanding the orders, and really to the delight, of the First Consul. "Let me be told that you are active as a very cabin-boy . . . . Seek every chance of distinguishing yourself," and the Tuileries soon received him into the height of the festivities then in progress.

The seventeen-year-old midshipman was ordered to the West Indies, where Le Clerc, his brother-in-law, was in charge of the French possessions, and had with difficulty persuaded the fair Pauline to share what she considered a fearful exile. It was not a long one, however, for sent to quiet the islands after the massacre of San Domingo,[9] LeClerc died there of yellow fever, and Jérôme was transferred subsequently to *L'Epervier* under young Halgan, commander. But after reaching Martinique and St. Lucia, illness, which was the nemesis of this expedition, at last overtook Jérôme.

Toussaint L'Ouverture,[10] sacrificed to the imperial will, a mistake which later harassed Napoleon at St. Helena, had said: "Moi, je compte sur la Providence,"[11] and the hospital called by that name was filled to repletion. As soon as Jérôme was sufficiently recovered, the course was continued. St. Pierre[12] was sighted. In leaving this port, they hailed a merchantman to whom Jérôme endeavored to speak, and conveyed his desire by a shot across her bow. She proved to be an English vessel and an officer was sent abroad her with his apologies. This virtual act of war moved the commander Villaret Joyeuse[13] to frenzy and he insisted that the First Consul should hear of this complication from Jérôme himself. The lieutenant declined to risk a French vessel from his return and waited for a neutral craft. So *L'Épervier* sailed out and was promptly taken by the English, who were overjoyed at their supposed capture of the brother of the First Consul.

Meanwhile lured by the interesting stories of the new nation which had been in so many ways allied with France, Jérôme at the moment of his supposed capture was sailing up the Chesapeake Bay to the port of Norfolk accompanied by Meyronnet, went at once to his brother officer from *L'Épervier*; Lecamus, a Creole; his former secretary, Reubel, whole people had been active in the French Revolution; and his

physician. Meyronnet went at once to Philadelphia to charter a vessel, while the two others repaired to the seat of government to look up the French Commissaire Pichon.

Suitable accommodations had to be provided for the very unexpected guest and Pichon hearkened gladly to the plans for departure from Philadelphia, imploring Jérôme meanwhile to conceal his identity. But an invitation from his former acquaintance Joshua Barney,[14] whom he had known in the French service, completely mollified all the endeavors of the anxious Pichon, whose troubled were only now the beginning. In a few days the guest from the French Republic was writing, "My name is no longer a mystery in Baltimore. This has not caused me to alter my plans nor my manner of life."

Pichon continued his endeavors to persuade Jérôme that "the very unhealthy town of Baltimore" was undesirable for him and urged a northern tour, but Jérôme could not have been expected to relinquish this, his first chance to play the prince. So no slurs as to the health of Baltimore or the reputation of his friend Barney moved him other than to reply that he had discerned enough to choose his own society.

All doors were quickly open to him. The adoration inspired by the First Consul[15] was at its height, and that a Bonaparte should be in our midst meant much not only to those who, like Jefferson and his friends the Smiths, General Sam and Robert his brother,[16] had worshipped at the shrine, with many others who had been in constant contact with France, but as well to all men. Society was never more brilliant in Baltimore, current events on both sides the water never more exciting, and the group of lovely girls who has attended Madame La Comte's pension,—Mary Chase, Maria Martin, Marcia Burns, and Henrietta Pascault (one of the refugees from San Domingo, only awaiting the arrival of her lover Reubel),—made a circle of friends at once who have their verdict on Elizabeth Patterson, the beautiful creature who was the center of their circle.[17] Jérôme had bewailed the fact that he must necessity make a *marriage de convenance*, but he was assured by her devoted friends that Elizabeth Patterson combined all the qualities which he could desire, and was in addition "the most beautiful woman in the world." So that by the time an opportunity came for a meeting, he had already given her the title of *ma belle femme*.[18]

At the September races, for which a new course had been opened on Whetstone Point[19] near the fort, when Mr. Harrison's horse Hamlet had won the four-mile, Lieutenant Bonaparte saw for the first time Miss Patterson. Her buff-colored silk dress, her hat with long ostrich plumes, her pure Grecian contours, her exquisitely shaped head, her large dark eyes, a peculiarly dainty mouth and chin, the soft bloom of her complexion, beautifully rounded shoulders and tapering arms, all combined to form one of the loveliest types of womanhood. The handsome young Frenchman drew about him the young men of the place—Barney, John Comegys[20] and others, while the usual festas were inaugurated. So that with such a setting one can fully realize that neither threats nor coaxing were sufficient to move Jérôme in the direction of his native land.

At Judge Chase's ball[21] her gold chain caught in the buttons of his uniform and seemed only the outward sign of her willing capacity, although it is said that she gave but haughty reception to the man who had thus come into her happy girlhood. All the world looked on with breathless interest at this love affair of two continents and it was not long before her hand was desired by the Marquis d'Yrujo, who having won his own beautiful American wife, was very well affected to this courtship. Dinners, balls, dances were in order, and Baltimore was at her gayest. Not until October did Jérôme pay his much delayed devoirs to President Jefferson, and asked his good offices in the approaching marriage. The President was so good as to pardon him with the sentiment that no apology was needed from one so far as the family was concerned, the invitations were issued and the unhappy Pichon was disconsolate at his own future prospects. He had reasoned and threatened and quoted French law, but to no purpose.

Letters flew hither and yon. Mr. Patterson called a halt and withdrew his consent; and although the cards reached both ministers, French and Spanish, for the marriage on November 7th, there were complications enough and to spare, and finally Jérôme wrote Pichon that the affair was off. Elizabeth had departed for a visit in Virginia.

So again the representative of France endeavored to get the brother of his ruler on a French frigate lying at the Baltimore, but *Le Pursuivante* did not have that honor. Jérôme preferred the royal reception which he had in New York. Talleyrand had been notified that the day was saved, and upon Jérôme's return to Baltimore on December 1st, M. Pichon, overjoyed at the felicitation, advanced a sum of money from his consolation fund, and all seemed well. On December 24th, however, another advance was made, just in time for the trifling expenses incident to the marriage ceremony of which the formal notice accompanied the receipt for the money, when Lecamus wrote: "Sir, I have the honour to inform you on behalf of M. Jérôme Bonaparte that his marriage with Miss Patterson was celebrated yesterday evening. He charges me also to tell you that he is awaiting with impatience the 4000 dollars which you are sending him. His engagements are becoming pressing and his household will soon be in need. He begs you, therefore, to be so good as to dispatch this sum to him as soon as possible."

So it was: the wedding had taken place in the stately old Patterson house on South and Gay Streets, with all the pomp and solemnities of the Roman Catholic Church. They were married by the Right Reverend John Carroll, Bishop of Baltimore, Primate of the Church in America. The mayor and all the polite world were present, Lecamus and Sotin, who had succeeded d'Hébécourt at Baltimore, and other dignitaries. Descriptions of the costumed of the contracting parties were carefully preserved. Indeed the groom's wedding suit was kept by his wife to the day of her death,—a purple coat of satin, skirt lined with white satin reaching to his heels, with knee buckles and with diamond buckles on his shoes. In such an array and with his powdered hair he must have presented a rare and gallant sight.

Madame, the bride, wore a gown that had done service before, for she wished, to use her own words, "to avoid a vulgar display"; and "truth to say," she writes, "there was little as possible of any gown at all, dress in that day being chiefly an aid to setting off charms to advantage." It was, for the information of those interested, one of those exquisitely embroidered French robes, so dainty and so light that one of the guests averred he could have put the costume in his coat pocket. The wedding certificates were all duly signed and sealed by the contracting parties, with the proper witnesses. To her family it had been a matter of great concern, and every obstacle had been thrown in her way. So that when later the Emperor of the French saw fit to write to His Holiness the Pope that everything had been done in the most surreptitious way, that the ceremony had been performed by an obscure Spanish priest, the documents were ready in rebuttal.

President Jefferson had written Chancellor Livingston, then minister of Paris: "Mr. Patterson is the President of the Bank of Baltimore, the wealthiest man in Maryland, perhaps in the United States, except Mr. Carroll;[22] a man of great virtue and respectability; the mother is the sister of the lady of General Samuel Smith," which seemed final. It is usually supposed that there were no attendants for the bride or groom, but through the courtesy of Mrs. Henry Rogers, a letter[23] was sent the writer from the family archives of Miss Comegys, then regent of the Mount Vernon Association. This was a letter from John Comegys, descended from Augustin Herrman and the brilliant circle of families of which he was the center. Mr. Comegys wrote his brother in March, 1804: that in December he was called on to attend at the marriage of Mr. Jérôme Bonaparte as "right hand" man, and as it was a very high compliment, he could not refuse, although not very convenient. Dinners and evening parties had followed as Mr. Patterson, whose daughter Mr. Jérôme Bonaparte married, was the head of one of the most notable families in this city. He also attended the wedding of Mr. Patterson (this was Robert), a good friend of his, with all the patties given them, concluding with a dinner with the President of the United States.

The journey to Washington was made by coach, and as not infrequently happened, there was a runaway. No damage was done, as the bride chose an opportune moment to land in a snowdrift.

Turreau was then minister of France. The wrath of the First Consul had fallen heavily on Sotin, but Turreau entertained them in Georgetown in January 1804, consoling himself by letters to M. le Marquis de Périgord-Talleyrand, while Robert Patterson went abroad to place matters clearly before the First Consul. He found the family urbane, but the First Consul was implacable, and in April Jérôme was otified that no money would be forthcoming. He was to return at once to France and all transportation was to be forbidden to the brief. It was difficult for them to realize Napoleon could not be softened by the sight of "the most beautiful woman in the world." So the ensuing time was spent delightfully in and about Washington and Baltimore. A tour to the north was equally a royal progress and the departure of the French vessel without him did not trouble the lieutenant.

A start was finally made for the *Didin,* then, with the *Cybèle,* in the port of New York, and they embarked. War between England and France having been declared meanwhile, it was found that the British frigates *Cambrian* and *Boston,* with a sloop, were at the mouth of the Hudson. On remonstrance from our Government, they moved to Sandy Hook, but it was evident there was no escape, so the couple disembarked and visited Niagara.

If the news of the events of May 18th, when Napoleon was proclaimed Emperor, had not accompanied the next order, Jérôme might have been willing to become, as had been contemplated, an American citizen. Or if they had not missed General Armstrong, who has going out to replace Chancellor Livingston, Madame Bonaparte might have entered France as a member of the family of the American minister, and so would have seen Napoleon. But in their next venture took place a wreck off the coast of Delaware, when by her own order she was thrown into the lifeboat. This, however, only seemed to bring out her fine courage, though she scandalized her aunt when she discovered food for fun in the plight in which they found themselves, arrayed in motley costume, seated in a cabin near the shore, having lost their all and four thousand dollars to boot. Her sedate relative upbraided her with the fact that when she should have been on her knees, giving thanks to a kind Providence, she was devouring roast goose and apple sauce, with mirthful accompaniment.

The wealth of Mr. Patterson was utilized and the *Erin* was fitted out suitably for their journey to Lisbon. Jérôme had already been visibly affected by events in France and was longing "for the flesh pots of Egypt." In his letter to Du Cres, he writes: "I beg you to be so kind as to give my brother the enclosed letter. I explain to him my situation in this country, which daily becomes more cruel and I urgently ask for orders to leave it. You have yourself been long in this part of the world, and can, best of all people, explain to him how out of place my life is here. . . . The great events which today occupy the world's attention do not prevent my brother, I suppose, to send me news of himself and of my family, as soon as I could wish."

During a reception on board the *Didin* he had been addressed as "Your Imperial Highness." This concluded the American sojourn. Arrived at Lisbon, the full measure of the Emperor's wrath and vengeance was made apparent. No mercy was to be shown Jérôme unless he absolutely abandoned and repudiated his wife. Madame Bonaparte had with her, her brother, Mr. Patterson, and her physician. She saw that Jérôme's journey without her was inevitable and they made their plans accordingly. Their farewells were spoken, as they both thought for a little while, but in reality forever. She only saw him once again and they never exchanged another word. That the lieutenant was sincere in his intention to return for her, his visit to Madame Junot[24] proves; for meeting them at an inn on the road to Lisbon he breakfasted with the party and in leaving said with tears: [The Emperor] "is kind—he is just, Even admitting that I had committed a fault in marrying Miss Patterson without his consent, is this the moment for inflicting punishment? And upon whose head will that punishment light? Upon that of my innocent wide? No, no; surely my brother will

not outrage the feeling of one of the most respectable families in the United States; and inflict at the same time a mortal wound upon a creature who is as amiable as she is beautiful." Taking from his breast a golden miniature, he showed therein the ravishing face of Elizabeth, so strangely resembling, as Madame Junot said, his sister Pauline, but with more fire and animation. He comforted himself, too, that after much contention in the family, Christina, the first wife of Lucien, was finally greatly loved by Napoleon. When ordered by Napoleon to give up his wife, Lucien had written, "Rather than descend to such infamy, I would be capable of immolating my son and daughter with my own hand. If you order it so, I will quit Europe, but I will never leave my wife and children until I lose my life"; and Jérôme averred "I am determined not to yield." Alas, Napoleon would take no risks in seeing Elizabeth, nor would he receive Jérôme until he should promise unconditional submission.

It took only twelve days to end the drama, and the uncertain glitter of a crown in the distant future outweighed the honor of a man. This was the turning point. He had never a chance to redeem himself.

Meanwhile the *Erin*, good ship of the American Republic, was having strange and unfriendly experiences in the Texel Roads.[25] She was placed under guard of a French man-of-war, although peace reigned between the nations, and her clearance papers showed her to be a neutral vessel. Sylvanus Bourne, the consul at Amsterdam, soon relieved the situation, and after Madame Bonaparte had looked into the muzzle of the French guns for a week, the ship set sail for England, where through the good offices of Lord Hawksbury and the promise of a suitable guard from William Pitt to protect her from the curious mob gathered to see her land, she finally reached "the haven where she should be." She spent a while in peace and quiet, waiting for the summons that never came, but comforted by the arrival of her son, Jérôme, who made his appearance on the stage July 7th, 1805. All the ceremonies attending the birth of a prince were observed to testify to the event, and at the first possible moment the baptism took place with a right royal lot of sponsors—the Very Right Reverend John Carroll of Baltimore, the Reverend G. Beeston, Rector of St. Peter's Church, and Mary Caton; while the witnesses were Eliza Bonaparte,[26] Elizabeth Caton, Louisa Caton,[27] Margaretta Patterson.

Meanwhile letters galore from Jérôme assured her of his undying devotion. She was to refuse nothing to the Emperor, who lamented that she should have tarried in London. "For," said the potentate, "Miss Patterson has been in London and caused great excitement among the English—from which she has rendered herself more culpable." One laughs when one thinks how impotent he was to control such a woman. But later came the formal request that the marriage should be annulled. The adverse decision of his Holiness, the Pope, stands out in bold relief against the ages. Napoleon, however, found a bishop who was more pliable, but as those learned in the law remarked, it was only by an act of political complaisance that the King of Westphalia[28] and the Emperor of Russia were persuaded that Jérôme Bonaparte was free to contract another marriage. At all events he espoused, on August 12th, 1807, the Princess Frederica Catherine of Württemberg,[29] and in the month of December of the same year was crowned King of Westphalia. In the following year he made demand for his son. He writes: "Chère Eliza," that events will never efface her from his memory. She is to count on a happy future and be assured that nothing will ever make him forget the tie which binds her to him, etc., etc.

Naturally Madame Bonaparte declined to commit her son to Lecamus, envoy of the King of Westphalia, and in her grief and dismay lest they should be parted, she made known to the Emperor her desires for herself and her son Jérôme. But for this the king reproached her and revealed his plan for her happy future. He offered to her the principality of Schmalkalden,[30] with a dower of two hundred thousand francs, and the title of Princess of Schmalkalden for herself and Prince for her son. One delights at this distant date in her amiable reply: "Westphalia is not large enough for two queens, and as to the annuity, she preferred to be sheltered under the wing of an eagle rather than to be suspended on the bill of a goose"; and in her well known answer to Napoleon's proposition in giving her the 60,000 francs a year on condition that she should relinquish all claim to the name, "that she would never consent to barter a name which had been made so famous." This quite won the Emperor to the appreciation of so much *bel esprit*, and his last offer was to know what he could do for her, with the promise of the title of Duchess, which signified her willingness to accept, but which was soon lost in the ensuing years.

Madame Bonaparte, however, realized that it was time she should dispose of her rights and ties, to which the King of Westphalia so feelingly attested from time to time. Accordingly, she applied for a divorce according to the law of her own country, and in 1813, six years after Jérôme's second marriage, such a decree was passed by special act of the Maryland Assembly, "a vinculo matrimonii,"[31] with reservations for her rights and the rights of her son.

Here, sheltered among her own people, she watched with interest the victorious career of the man who so nearly owned the whole world. Her son Jérôme charmed his father's family by his keen appreciation of his wonderful sagacity for so young a boy. To these qualities he added a delightful manner and geniality. It was fortunate that she had so protected herself, for it was not long before the one-time Emperor was pacing his forsaken beat on the lonely island, while the King of Westphalia found himself a bankrupt "king without a kingdom." Indeed the day came, when even the family name of which he had so cruelly attempted to deprive her was proscribed in his own land and the Compte du Survilliers and the Compte de Montfort were the only titles borne by these kings in exile.

It is interesting for us in our survey of Old Baltimore to have the story told through the Colonel King one of the beautiful Eastern Shore houses had already been fitted up in preparation to receive the former Emperor in the ship which, so the legend goes, Stephen Girard[32] had sent to La Rochelle for him. But his degeneration was swift, he lacked the power to use his once overwhelming will. "He sits and reads" all the time. St. Helena was waiting for him.

The visits of Madame Bonaparte across the water were frequent, and wherever she went she had a little court of her own about her. Her beauty and wit captivated all.

Mr. Patterson's will revealed the fact that he had made some change in his disposition of his estate, giving signal proof that he considered this alliance as anything but an honor. Strange to say, the property he left to Elizabeth appreciated in value, and with her own accumulations from her frugality, she gathered a fortune quite royal. On the day that she met Jérôme in Florence with the queen and small Mathilde his daughter, she recognized the man who had been her husband by his likeness to their son, Jérôme of Baltimore, and simply laid her cloak open so that he might see how gently time had dealt with her beautiful figure; the queen having but little shape of which to speak. She saw him no more. At her home Madame Patterson Bonaparte had in her circle all the notable people of the day, such as Albert Gallatin and Daniel Webster, and abroad the Prince of Gortchakoff, the Russian minister of Florence, afterward prime minister, the Princess Galitzin, Madame Récamier, the Duchess d'Abrantès and hosts of others. While in Italy, she met members of the Bonaparte family, Pauline, Madame Mère[33] and the different generations. As we have seen, the Junot's had insisted that Madame Patterson Bonaparte was the double of Pauline in figure and face. In the case of her son Jérôme, the resemblance was positive. So late as in 1867, John P. Kennedy[34] was our commissioner to the Paris Exposition, when he wrote that he saw Prince Napoleon, who bore the most extraordinary resemblance to his half-brother in Baltimore, not only in feature and expression, but also in gesture and manner. When seated at the table with him, he could scarcely avoid addressing him as an old friend. Young Jérôme preferred his own land, and while the proposed marriage with his cousin Charlotte, daughter of Joseph, who living in New Jersey for quite a while, had the sanction of all the family, he had made his choice from his own country-women. Madame Bonaparte would have never been satisfied if her son has made a foreign alliance, but before her death she must have rejoiced that he had so chosen.

Her loyalty to Napoleon was unswerving. She realized she had been sacrificed to political considerations, and when her presence was desired at the court of Louis XVIII, who had expressed sympathy for her treatment at the hands of the Corsican usurper, her pride made her answer that she declined to pass as the victim of imperial tyranny, that she had accepted the kindness of the Emperor and that ingratitude was not one of her vices.

Born to rule, imperious from her girlhood, fate and destiny gave her the desire of her heart. That the man of her choice was faint of will and infirm of purpose may perhaps be now forgiven him since the overpowering will of the First Consul had overshadowed everything within reach. Looking back over her life, one can only believe that she was more fortunate as the uncrowned queen of Jérôme's first and best affection, than she would have been amid the uncertainties of the kingdom of Westphalia, the ephemeral dynasty so insecurely founded.

For us in old Baltimore, there is only reason to felicitate ourselves on our heritage,—that no entangling alliances or rococo wills interfered with the development of a type which gathered up all the best of the virtues of Madame Mère with the stern integrity of William Patterson, that our Bonapartes were not dependent on a foreign country for their fame, but were known the world over as American citizens pure and simple, without fear and without reproach.

The Voyagers

While the women of the Woman's Literary Club of Baltimore were undoubtedly concerned with the city that brought them all together, many writers of the club were just as fascinated with life outside of Baltimore and the United States. Many club women were both wealthy and well-educated, which afforded them unique opportunities to learn about and experience foreign lands. The Club had several committees in place that strove to shed light on foreign customs and cultures, such as the Committee on Translations as well as the Committee on Foreign Languages. Though this anthology does not provide a glimpse into meetings hosted by such committees, the published works of certain Club women reiterate and recognize the desire to transcend American culture through literature.

Some women, such as Florence McIntyre Tyson, dedicated their lives to translation; Tyson herself spoke five languages and was successful in her literary pursuits. She translated many short stories and had several published. We have chosen to include two, "Waiting" and "Two Men and a Women." Another writer who demonstrates the importance and beauty of translation is Elizabeth Lester Mullin. Though raised in Baltimore, Mullin used her nuanced knowledge of the French language to translate works and transport her fellow Club members and the American public to a country very unlike their own. Her translations of "The Codicil" and "Missa Solemnis" are included in pages to come.

Others cultivated an intense fascination with exquisitely external cultures, such as Francese Litchfield Turnbull. Turnbull, one of the Club's founders, who was well-known for her novels that depicted wholly fictional, but historically-influenced, accounts of Italian elites. We truly hope you enjoy the excerpts from *The Royal Pawn of Venice* we have chosen to include. [***Include info on Latimer here (?)]

In addition to fictional accounts of life abroad, several Club women wrote personal accounts of their travels to foreign countries. An example is Letitia Humphreys Yonge Wrenshall's "Traveling in the Radiant Old Mediterranean." The name of the essay speaks for itself, and

Wrenshall's writing depicts a sea-journey along the Mediterranean coast, speckled with visits into sleepy, sunny towns. Similarly, Adaline Vanderpoel's article "Bermuda Past and Present" serves to illuminate Americans on the beauty and history of Bermuda; Vanderpoel turns to personal experience, established historical research, and accounts of fellow travelers to communicate her impression of the island.

It is our greatest desire that this section of our anthology will adequately articulate the fact that the writers of the Woman's Literary Club of Baltimore were more than wives, mothers, club members, and even writers. They were, in fact, world travelers, aspiring to gain an ampler world-view. Thankfully, this intense interest became tangible in the works of these women, and their works live on today. In a time when it was hard to be seen as anything more than a woman, these writers pushed against societal expectations in order to produce enlightening, fascinating, and timeless works centered around life outside of the United States.

Elizabeth Wormeley Latimer (1822-1904)

Elizabeth Latimer traversed nations, centuries, and genres in her writing. Originally from London, Latimer moved to New England for schooling, where her love of literature flourished. She eventually became a Baltimore resident upon marrying Randolph Brandt Latimer. Latimer was an honorary member of the Club; her membership brought great esteem to the Club due to the approbation her work received both in America and England.

Latimer was perhaps best known for her weighty series on nineteenth-century European history, including *France in the Nineteenth Century* and *England in the Nineteenth Century*. These works gave equal play to both men and women, princes and princesses. The excerpt from *England in the Nineteenth Century,* for example, recasts Queen Victoria at the time of her jubilee as being a mother as much as a ruler of empire.

Latimer also published prolifically in magazines and wrote several novels, including *Princess Amélie: A Fragment of Autobiography*, *Amabel: A Family History*, and *The Prince Incognito*. These works frequently depict women navigating conflicting gender roles—sometimes, as we see in *The Prince Incognito,* literally disguising or transforming themselves to conform to societal expectations. Not all of her works concerned women, however. She was inspired, for example, by Richard Johnson's *Seven Champions of Christendom* (1596-97), which she recast in modern English and narrative verse. We include her retelling of the story of St. Anthony of Italy in this volume. In *Europe in Africa in the Nineteenth Century*, Latimer admitted that her aim was never to provide a historically detailed depiction, but rather, to write of the people, places, and subjects that interested her most. —E. Roussel

From *Princess Amélie: A Fragment of Autobiography* (1883)

In this fictional "fragment of autobiography," Amélie, born to Alsatian nobility, recalls her experiences with the feudal marriage market before her life is upended by the French Revolution. Of the book, the reviewer for the Critic declared, "The dignity and sweetness of the young patrician heroine, who, clever enough to see that many marriages made for love turn out very unhappily, accepts not only with resignation but with willingness the noblesse oblige of a lofty but loveless marriage."

Chapter VII

The Marriage Ceremony

That bride must be much preoccupied and very miserable who takes no interest in her wedding-dress upon her wedding-day. Though my misgivings about my bridegroom were like the constant consciousness of a dull pain which we carry about us even when we forget it for a few moments of activity, I venture, old and gray as I am now, to own that I felt both pride and pleasure in the successful efforts of Mademoiselle Bertin.

The *tablier*[1] of my robe was of mechlin lace made up over white silk. It had, as was etiquette for court toilettes in that day, an enormous *panier*.[2] The train was of white silk, trimmed also with mechlin, myrtle, orange-flowers, and *rouleaux*[3] of white satin. My hair was dressed high, powdered, of course, with two long curls upon my shoulders. Interwoven with this structure, which made me about six feet tall, were strings of large pure pearls and an *aigrette*[4]

of diamonds. From my myrtle-wreath—worn in compliment to the German custom—hung a veil of lace to match my dress, enveloping my charms, as Vernouillet said afterward, "like those of Venus, in a mysterious cloud." I wish I had all that lace to leave you now, *ma bru*,[5] but the French burnt it in 1792. when they destroyed everything. As I stood before the great mirror in my chamber, and gazed at the picture it reflected back to me, my heart thrilled with the thought, "He cannot but approve the bride bestowed on him by his good fortune; he cannot but be pleased with me."

My dears, your costumes in 1833 do not seem to aim, as dress did in my day, at heightening all gifts of loveliness in face and figure. My toilette was, I think (even *now* I dare to think), almost perfection. My mother's pearls were on my neck; upon my arms I wore no bracelet but the portrait of my bridegroom.

I felt like caressing my own beauty. The Princess-Abbess came out to greet me in her own semi-ecclesiastical habit, with the cross of St. Romaric upon her breast, and the scarf of blue and red, with silver edges, tied in a large bow under her left arm. The cross at her closely-covered throat was blazing with precious stones belonging to Remiremont. She was charmed with my appearance, and very proud of me. All our ladies and the women flattered and reassured me, bending to adjust my silken folds, in wonder at the richness of my lace, a triumph from the workrooms of Mechlin,— a composition of rosebuds, I remember, worked with exquisite delicacy!

It was very sweet to my girlishness to receive flatteries in which I could not but recognize real satisfaction and approval.

At a little before eight we were summoned by the court chamberlain. Leaning on the arm of the Princess-Abbess, with the little Duc d'Enghien, gallant in uniform, with his new little sword by his side, holding his aunt's left hand, we entered the room, where, formed and waiting for us, we found the marriage procession.

The highest gentleman of the court, the cousin and heir presumptive of its Prince, the husband of Marie Hélène, Count Philippe of Schomberg-Kissingen, was there to take charge of the little Duc d'Enghien. The French ambassador gave the Princess his arm. My uncle, the Bailli, came forward to escort me in the gorgeous white gala costume of his order,—an order of which one of the chief duties was never to spare expense on any occasion. His uniform was red turned up and lined with white; his vest and small clothes of white cloth with gold lace,—nay, even with *gold* buttons; his sword-hilt was magnificent; his ruffles of the deepest Valenciennes; a scarlet cloak hung from his left shoulder; and although not himself a man of imposing person, the splendor that surrounded him seemed to give him dignity.

In another moment we all entered the great hall, bright with a thousand wax lights for the occasion. It was noisy with the hum of voices, gay with the many-tinted brocades and gauzes of the female guests, and brilliant with a great variety of French and German uniforms.

My head whirled for a moment, as I suppose that of a new actress does when she first faces an expectant audience. I was too dazzled, too frightened, too self-conscious to cast my eyes around me at the first mo-

ment and try to recognize my prince, when suddenly I found beside me a boy not as tall as I was by a head, even without my towering hair, dressed in an absurd blue and silver uniform, with a plumed hat much too large for him, and too long a sword. His face was cut and scarred. In spite of paint and powder and gummed silk, it was bleeding in many places, swelled with crying, sullen, downcast, and tear-stained.

"I present his Highness the Prince Charles Antoine to Mademoiselle the Princess Amélie de Montbarrey," said some one near me.

I curtsied low, and made a little motion of advancing my right hand. The Prince put both his hands behind his back. I then perceived that he had hidden them behind his hat because they were disabled,—the right one being covered with a thick glove, the other done up in a black silk bandage.

I pitied him; he must be suffering pain. What should I do for him or say to him? Was he the victim of some recent accident or of some terrible malady?

A gentleman in an ecclesiastical dress leaned over him and whispered in his ear. The Prince scowled at him.

Madame the Duchess-Regent stood near me, dressed with expense, but without taste, fidgeting and nervous, from time to time smoothing with a restless hand some fold in her unruly drapery.

At that moment the Duc d'Enghien pulled my dress, and whispered, pointing in the direction of the dependents who had crowded in at the lower end of the apartment, "There is that peasant woman; I will go and ask her what became of her poor boy."

"Qu'est qu'il vous fait, ce garçon? What's that boy to you?" growled my bridegroom through his teeth.

"Mon prince," I whispered deprecatingly, "Monseigneur the Duc d'Enghien is but a child."

At this moment there came a hush upon the company. In a minute more it would have been evident that the Prince, with his hands behind his back, was reluctant to lead me up to the lawyers at the great table, which was covered with parchments, when Philippe, Count of Kissingen, with dignity and grace, stepped up to me, and held out his hand. I put mine into it. He led me to the table, while, half pushed, half dragged by the ecclesiastic I have mentioned, and by another gentleman, grave, military, but in a strange drab costume, with his gray hair un-powdered hanging on his back, my bridegroom was made to follow me so close that few of the persons present probably perceived that he had failed in etiquette, and that his cousin was leading me.

Men of the robe—"all rascals," the Bailli told me afterward—stood behind the table covered with fringed green cloth, and proceeded to read the contract of marriage.

I heard none of it. I was absorbed in my own nervous sensations,—in purposes that were not real purposes, only imaginings of the imaginary. I felt that time was passing, that in a few moments my fate would be beyond my own control. The sands of possibility were running from my glass. If I did not take advantage of the five minutes, four minutes, three minutes, one minute that remained, escape would be forever impossible. Should I turn and run away? Should I create a scandal, and cry out that I could not—would not—wed a boy so reluctant to accept me? Just then my glance fell upon M. de Champfleury, and seeing a look of amused amazement in his eyes as he fixed them on my bridegroom, the truth flashed upon me.

He was the child imprisoned in the torture chamber to subdue his contumacy! It was his frantic effort to escape his fate that had put his life in jeopardy, disabled his hands, and scarred his features!

A great throb of sympathy and fellow feeling rose within me. Before I had time to act, the reading ceased, the inevitable had come.

I turned and saw my bridegroom's sullen face. I heard a harsh voice hiss into his ear. My senses were preternaturally acute under the impulse of excitement. "Do what is demanded of you, monseigneur, or we shall not stop at trifles. You have already suffered imprisonment and the rod; worse is in store for you."

The boy raised fierce, indignant eyes. In sympathy with the flush upon his cheeks, I too blushed deeply. At that moment the white-haired gentleman, in a quaint dress but seldom seen in courts, stepped up, and Count Philippe took from behind his cousin's back his gloved right hand; standing behind the Prince, he guided the pen for him. The signature was affixed to the parchment, "Charles Antoine of Schomberg-Kissingen;" the titles had been written in below.

A new pen, ornamented for the occasion, was then handed me by Count Philippe.

"I cannot write," I said.

There was a moment's consternation. I believe they thought my convent education had not included the accomplishment of writing.

"Sign, my niece; let there be no follies upon *your* part," said the Bailli, bending down to me.

I caught a glance in Von Zwei-Brücken's eyes, as if my hesitation inspired him with hope. That nerved me. I took the pen and signed myself boldly:

"MAXIMILIENNE AMÉLIE PRINCESSE DE MONTBARREY DE SAINT MAURICE."

Then I threw down the pen, which left a black blot on the vellum.

Sobs rose in my throat; I choked them down. Was it for me to show my weakness?— to exhibit to those beneath me my unwillingness to meet the demands of my position?

I spoke just now of actresses. Princesses stand equally before the footlights, and owe equally to the public the duty of crushing natural feelings out of sight. Some of us grow to feel at last that the public is our friend, and give it confidences; but not until bereavement has made us try—and fail—to stand alone.

The sentiment that nerved me was that of obligation to my House. I saw pity on some faces, and I scorned it. Of all things I dreaded pity. Was the Princesse de Montbarrey, very young, very rich, and very beautiful, to be vulgarly compassionated by a mixed assemblage?

I stood aside. Others came up and signed as witnesses. The Duchess-Regent, mother of Prince Charles Antoine, was of course the first to append her signature. She was a small woman, singularly and incongruously dressed, her draperies having always a tendency to drop and droop about her. She was still young, with handsome hair, very rarely dressed with care, though it was always powdered. She had a little snub nose, rather a wide mouth, good teeth, and an expression which tempted you to fancy she was not so insignificant and manageable as at the first *abord⁶* you might have fancied her. It seemed to indicate ... However, let me draw a veil over the failings of this woman, remembering that I was never in a position to judge her impartially. If you need to know more of her,—of the scandals of her life, of her insatiate love of play, of her capricious management of her only son,—you may consult such *chroniques scandaleuses* as are preserved in memoirs, travels, and books that record the history of the last twenty-five years of the principality of Schomberg-Kissingen.

The Princesse de Condé and the little Duc d'Enghien signed as the next witnesses. The latter, superintended by M. l'Abbé Millot, wrote "Philippe Louis" in round hand, with childish pleasure. M. le Bailli, Count Philippe and his wife, Von Zwei-Brücken, De Vernouillet, and a crowd of other witnesses of local consequence followed with their signatures. Among the signers I observed the strangely dressed, benevolent tall gentleman of whom I have already spoken.

Then began endless presentations.

My bridegroom stood about two yards away from me, looking sullen, defiant, and ill at ease, but subdued into a sort of compliance with the necessities of his position. His ungraciousness made me feel the necessity of forcing my own part. I had to throw myself into it like an actress; all became utterly unreal with me.

The duty of self-control—of self-effacement—is the first lesson taught by what is called "high breeding." I recalled all I could remember of the demeanor of the young Dauphine at Strasbourg. I smiled gayly, I curtsied gracefully. I could feel that my new subjects praised me and were proud of me. As for the others, De Vernouillet I snubbed for his hateful verses; while Von Zwei-Brücken leaned over me, pretending I had driven him to desperation, and disparaging my bridegroom, who had slipped away from me.

"All the room is talking," he said, "of a certain incident. A feather shows the way the wind blows. Observing Monseigneur d'Enghien amusing himself with a book of prints, *le petit rustre*[7] your Highness deigns to call your husband leaned over to look with him. The picture he was examining was one of a marriage. 'Shut it up! quick, shut it up!' cried Charles Antoine. "'It sickens me to see that *grosse blonde*,[8] the *mariée*![9] She reminds me . . . '"

"*Grand merci*, M. de Zwei-Brücken," I said; "do me the favor to recollect that *un galant homme*[10] never disparages husband to wife or wife to husband."

"And where did you learn that?"

"By an instinct of good feeling."

"Bah! This marriage is mere folly. Suppose to-morrow you decline to ratify it by the religious ceremony—"

I turned from him, and overwhelmed by gracious attentions a little woman of the *haute bourgeoisie* who was standing near me. All ranks of people were admitted to Schloss Kissingen on that occasion; there were even said to be Jews.

The worst trial was to come. The hall was cleared for dancing. I must walk the first minuet with my bridegroom. Again I saw that hard-faced man with the malignant eyes bend over and address him; again Count Philippe was at hand and led him towards me.

I took his gloved hand, given with reluctance, and at the head of the room we two alone prepared to perform this public duty. As we passed a group of servants who had been admitted with the rest on this family occasion, a peasant woman in a clean starched coif, a red petticoat gathered between her shoulder-blades, and a string of chased gold beads about her neck, addressed some words of affection to my partner. I thought, too, that she scowled at me. The Prince made her no answer.

In perfect silence as to speech, but to the music of a well-trained band, we walked that dismal minuet. I would have put on smiles, having been taught to do so when I danced, but my smiles would have been too much in contrast with the downcast, mortified, and tear-swelled face of my boy partner.

I believe a minuet has been said to represent the courtship of noble personages,—the formal introduction, the gradual approaches, the final union, the dancers ending with hands clasped, at length made one. Ah! but it was the gay *gavotte*[11] of married happiness that my heart longed for. I had dreamed of comradeship and natural gayety with my young bridegroom,—a life well likened to a *gavotte*,—that dance of frolic, joyousness, and *abandon*.

There was no *gavotte* to follow our minuet, either in fact or metaphor. The minuet of etiquette was all that could be expected of a prince and princess whose families had married them for reasons of ambition. What business had we to ask for happiness? I should obtain my sovereign rights, and he my father's money.

How I began to hate the Schomberg-Kissingeners *en masse!*—the sole exceptions being Count Philippe, Marie Hélène, and the benevolent old man with the white hair, whose simplicity attracted me and took my fancy; nor did I altogether hate my prince. I would have gladly taken him under my protection, have made common cause with him and comforted him. But oh! what a dreary prospect to have him for my husband!

When our minuet was finished, Count Philippe, advancing, led me to Marie Hélène, who was seated in an obscure corner. My unhappy partner shrank away as soon as our dance was over.

Then with the old friend of my school life I exchanged confidences. Had they had any proper ideas of etiquette at Schomberg-Kissingen, they would never have allowed me to retire from public view.

She was beginning to address me with the usual courtesies; but I cut her short,—

"Nonsense, Marie Hélène; we may have only a few quiet moments. Tell me, I implore you, many things. Is the Prince that unhappy boy they shut up in that dreadful chamber? How did he escape? Who dared to put him there? Tell me all quickly."

"Yes, you are right," she said; "he dropped into the moat, which is now dry, and was so hurt he could not get up again.

There M. le Capitaine Parrot and my Philippe found him. He had one leg bent under him. You noticed doubtless that he limped a little in the dance, and that he has torn his face and hands. But they persuaded him to be reasonable. Is it very dreadful, my poor Amélie? But Philippe says that these unconsummated marriages often do not come to anything in the end . . . "

"Was that the view which he presented to the Prince my husband?" I replied, more piqued than I had been before. "Am I to be dragged through publicity and disgrace, only to be repudiated when the Prince is his own master?"

"I do not know what Philippe said to him," she answered. "Philippe can persuade—can comfort anybody. Oh! Amélie, it is happiness beyond all I ever could have dreamed of at Remiremont to be the wife of such a man,—to know that his love and tenderness will never fail me, to feel myself growing as the little flowers grow in warmth and sunshine, to be able to lavish all the best I have on one who will appreciate the offering,—to respond to his tenderness, to yearn for his caresses . . . "

"Don't tell me of such things," I said hurriedly; "I have no Philippe. Who is that dreadful man who dares to beat and imprison the young Prince?"

"Which dreadful man?—for there are two of them, the Marquis della Villa Reale, and his creature, a Spanish Dominican. The Marquis came here, I believe, because he had quarrelled with the Court of Spain. Every one who has had trouble with his own court finds refuge in the courts of our Rhineland and Alsatian princes. The Marquis has risen high in favor with the Duchess-Regent, too high, some say . . . Ah! Amélie, Philippe would blame me if he heard my tongue run on . . . "

"No matter," I said; "I understand you. I am convent-bred, no doubt, but I have Heinzel; I know more, perhaps, than you think I do. Tell me."

"After her husband died, the Duchess-Regent's life was divided between her ambition and her pleasures. The young Prince was brought up in the cabin of a peasant woman in the Vosges till he was seven years old. The woman Paulina, his foster-mother, is now here. I can point her out to you . . . "

"Yes, yes. He came to court?"

"Where he at first was spoiled; but he missed the freedom of his peasant life, and was very miserable. He could not bend himself to courtiers' ways. The only creature whom he loved was Philippe. Philippe had lived upon the mountains and had known his foster-mother. At her cottage he had visited him. Philippe was then a boy. He is now only twenty; but he could always guide the Prince with a word. Their management has angered him and made his will too strong, and he has picked up new ideas and catch-words, such as liberty, brotherhood, equality,— not fit for the mouths of princes. About the time he was learning these revolutionary sentiments, Villa Reale came here. With the Court he is very unpopular. The Regent wished to give him some office that would keep him near her person, and she made him her son's governor. He and the boy hate each other. Villa Reale

knows only Spanish discipline; he is stern and severe. The Regent is never long of one mind; but she likes well to remain Regent, and is not anxious to awaken her son's ambition. I do not know that I quite believe the worst scandals about her life, but she is devoted to play, and sometimes loses very heavily. They say Villa Reale had to leave the Spanish Court because he showed too much skill in games, and was guilty of irregularities. Here he plays high and wins nightly. He planned the Prince's marriage,—he and his Spanish follower, a Dominican with learning but no heart, whom he has appointed tutor to Prince Charles Antoine."

"Oh, Marie Hélène!" I cried, "what intrigues seem to under-lie and over-lap court life in this vile place! How shall I learn to steer my way amongst them?"

"Ah!" she replied, "I am a happy woman; I have Philippe's experience and good sense to guide me. He keeps me . . . "

"Marie Hélène! do not torment me with your Philippe—I have no Philippe," I said with a sudden cry.

"Ah, dearest! I wish you had one," she said, softly; "only not mine . . . "

"Tell me," I resumed, "who is that strange old gentleman, *militaire et gentilhomme*[12] by his looks, with the plain coat and the white hair?"

"A monsieur from America," she said, "named Captain Parrot. I have heard that his name means *perroquet*. Many strange people, as I told you, find themselves at our little courts for various reasons. *Le Capitaine* Parrot is from the same American city as that admirable M. Franklin, *le bonhomme Richard*.[13] Here M. le Capitaine does all he can to assist the cause of the Americans, only he will not fight,—not that he lacks the courage, but from religious scruples.[14] He wears no sword; nor would he draw in self-defence, or even to defend his country. He was at Bremen when the war broke out in America. He is often in Paris, where they say he negotiates loans and stimulates the enthusiastic sympathy of the young nobility. This court, however, is his home. Here we all love him and confide in him; and he can be *des plus amusants!*[15] He has made many voyages to India; has seen tigers and Gentoos and poisonous snakes of every kind. He belonged to the American marine—I mean that navy which engages only in peaceful traffic. Dupleix and Lally Tollendal loved and esteemed him. He thinks that Tollendal was a martyr, and that Dupleix was unjustly used. He hates the English,—that is, if one so good and holy as he is can hate anything. He is a heretic, of course—some sort of a strange heretic. He wears that odd plain dress because of his religion. He gives no titles to those he may address, and we all have to put up with his *tutoiement*.[16] They say that the King Jacques of England loved his sect, and that his people have always been on good terms with the true religion."

Chapter VIII

Escape Refused

O miserable evening! I look back upon it with a sob rising in my throat, prompted by self-pity.

In spite of my resolve to act my part, my spirit flagged. I could not keep up that deceptive unconsciousness which alone could make me mistress of the humiliating situation.

A blight, too, fell upon the wedding guests. They shunned a bride dishonored and *délaissée*.[17] As the evening advanced, I believe even the Spaniards gave up their vain attempts to coerce my bridegroom into good behavior. He slipped out of my sight. After some time I saw him in a corner beside a little girl of his own age. His persecutors had left him unmolested; they feared fresh scandals in the public eye.

But there was one guest present who stood and gazed at me till all my recollections of that night's distress are associated with a remembrance of his eyes. It was Prince Max von Zwei-Brücken. The man had a good figure, a somewhat brutish, jolly, dissipated face, and a very conspicuous and handsome uniform. Looking back upon that night, and impersonally upon the poor young bride who played her part in it,—not as myself, I mean, but as if she were a friend from whom I have been parted more than half a century—I may venture to say that I believe whatever manhood had been left in him by dissipation was really in love with me. Alas! one of the penalties of such a life as he had led is that it withers all the sanctities of the heart, leaving the man who experiences the passion of love, no power to rise above its animalism. Of love I was completely ignorant; I had not so much as learned the first rules of its grammar. I had read neither verse nor romance. No one had ever spoken the word "love" to me; but I had instincts, I suppose, which caused the gleam of those red eyes of Zwei-Brücken's to make me blush whenever I saw them fastened on me.

I knew that I was beautiful; *et pourquoi pas?*[18] Why should not a young girl who fears her God rejoice in her own loveliness?

That Zwei-Brücken thought me beautiful I could see without experiences; he was my first lover, and I loathed him. How rapidly I was acquiring objective knowledge, though the heart within me had not yet quickened with a first faint throb!

Count Philippe I often looked for, but he was not to be seen. Marie Hélène had retired early. I saw Captain Parrot's beautiful kind face looking at me benignantly.

The company divided. One group gathered round the Regent; another round my passive self and Madame Louise de Condé. The *haute bourgeoisie* of Kissingen, which had been invited to this wedding as a state peace-offering, drew apart at the lower end of the hall,—whilst the great ladies protected themselves carefully from any social contact with the wives of men guilty of honest industry and of earning their own living.

By an hour after midnight the guests had separated. There had been little dancing. Before two o'clock I had smiled my last forced smile, made my last weary curtsy,[19] and taken leave of the Duchess-Regent, who, as I approached her, glanced round, in search, I fancied, of the Prince, my bridegroom. Not seeing him at hand, she made no effort to find him.

Leaning upon Madame de Condé's arm, and preceded by servants carrying lights, I went to my apartment.

Taking me in her arms, the Princess kissed me on my lips and brow and eyes, as soon as we were alone; and then she passed into her own chamber, leaving me to enter mine, where Heinzel and my other women awaited me.

I walked in to them cold and calm. I stood like a marble image while they unlaced and unbusked me. They unfastened my lace veil and wreath of myrtle; they laid away my priceless robe of mechlin. Then I made a sign to Heinzel, and we two were left alone.

This time even the red grogram[20] was forgotten by my old nurse. I flung myself unreproved upon her kindly breast, a great wave of desolation breaking over me. I seized her hard hands in my trembling ones; my misery found voice, and a cry burst from my bosom:

"Oh, Heinzel, stay with me—always stay with me! I did not think it would have been so bad. Oh, Heinzel, must I live here all alone in this cold, wicked, cruel court? Oh, Heinzel, they must let you stay with me, or I shall die!"

"My lamb, my treasure!" murmured the good woman, tears running down her cheeks and chin, "it is very hard for thee; I could have stamped on some of those who chose to laugh at thinking thou shouldst have been so taken in by all their Spanish craft as to marry such a bridegroom. And that old witch, Paulina, who was crying because her boy was to be thrown away against his will on one too old for him! I could have seized her with these teeth and these old hands. I could have made her face as soft as dough for her! But, my darling, have patience; thou wilt reign over them all; thou wilt send that Duchess-Regent to a convent, or back where she belongs to her own people; thou wilt be everything,—as it is thy place to be,—she nothing. Then thou wilt purge this court—*quelle canaille!*[21] what mixing up of classes! what confusion! Holy St. Romaric! what would *he* say to see a princess from his house receiving such vile people? And their dresses! I dare swear some of their old robes, court suits, and carriages have not so much as seen the light for fifty years. My lamb, thou wert just like a heavenly angel come to teach them how to dress themselves! All will come right yet. Remember it is a great marriage for our house. The Prince thy father left thee honors and wealth, the *entrées* and the *tabouret*,[22] and now thou art numbered amongst sovereign princes. All will come right—put faith in time. But tell me,—for I did not rightly understand when *ce gros monsieur*,[23] in his lawyer's gown, read out that contract,—is thine own fortune safe from the long claws of that Madame la Régente, who, they say, would damn her soul for a good hand at écarté?[24] They say she games like twenty thousand devils, and loses sums of money to the Spaniard that would bristle up the hairs on the hide of a Jew. Indeed they say she had to ask Jews here from the Jewry this very night, and to show them my own best one in her wreath of myrtle, because she owes already to their tribe such piles of money."

"Hush, Heinzel!" I said; "don't tell such things to me. Doubtless M. le Bailli has foreseen all and provided rightly. But oh, Heinzel, keep thou near me. I shall soon have no one. They must not send thee away from me, as they did Madame la Dauphine's old nurse when she reached Strasbourg. They will not do that, will they? I am not so great a lady as the wife of the heir of France, and may surely keep my nurse with me. Oh, what griefs royalty must learn to bear! I will not stay here if you leave me."

Just then a tap came at the door of my chamber. Heinzel answered it. To my astonishment it was M. le Bailli, looking flushed, and, as it seemed to me, embarrassed, as he addressed me.

"This is well. You have not yet entirely undressed, my niece," he said. "Throw on your powdering robe and come with me into the salon."

I obeyed; I was so stunned and so bewildered by the day's events, that I hardly wondered at his summons. "Anything," I thought, "may happen to me now."

I found Madame Louise de Condé, pale and agitated, seated in a chair in the centre of the salon. She had not changed her dress, and was still blazing with the jewels of St. Romaric. She rose as I came in, and embraced me; then, putting her arm around me, she stood supporting me, as if we were two women against all the world. There was silence a few moments, then she prompted M. le Bailli by saying:

"The child has come."

"My niece," the Bailli said,—his voice was hoarse and his words trembled,—"unusual though it be for guardians or parents to confer upon matters of marriage with their wards or children, Madame de Condé thinks it best that I should not dissemble from you my regret and disappointment at that which now appears to have been an unforeseen and painful error. I had not comprehended the state of things that we have found to-day in Kissingen. The marriage is a brilliant one, no doubt, combining many advantages. You have obeyed me with docility. You have not failed in respect to your own house nor in the modesty becoming

a very young woman. You have supported the dignity of Montbarrey; you have
not recoiled, her Highness tells me, from
commendable self-sacrifices. But I see ob-
jections to this marriage which I did not
see before to-night. Now tell me, since
Madame de Condé, who honors you by
acting as your mother, desires I should ask
you, shall I at any cost—dwell on those
words, my niece—*at any cost*, before the
religious ceremony completes the contract, break off this marriage?"

I fell down on my knees at my uncle's
feet. Here was deliverance when I lay
bound upon the altar to be sacrificed,—
deliverance as unexpected as it was welcome to me. I grasped his hands and
kissed them.

"Oh, uncle, yes!" I cried. "Let me go
back to dear Remiremont with Madame
la Princesse. I have done my best; but
oh, even pride, I think, will not carry me
much further."

The Princess shook her head.

"Remiremont can no longer be your
shelter, my child," she said. "I am a vassal
of the Holy Roman Empire. The family of
Schomberg-Kissingen would lose no time
in making their complaints before the
Emperor,—complaints which, if listened
to, might involve the interests and dignity
of my Abbey. I must not, Amélie, even for
your sake, draw down on us the interference of the Emperor. I may not shelter you
at Remiremont. Already your position as
chanoinesse[25] of our order is forfeited by
this half marriage. This evening, for the
first time since your babyhood, you have
ceased to wear our colors. The rupture of
your alliance with this poor young Prince

will create a scandal which will flutter
these little courts of Rhineland. If your
contract be broken it must be by a *grand
coup*, and you will be safe only under the
powerful protection of Versailles."

I listened in amazement. How could I
call on the great Court of France to shelter
and uphold me?

"Here, Amélie," resumed my uncle,
"is the alternative. You can escape the
marriage, you dislike if you accept another suitor. Prince Max von Zwei-Brück-
en holds his duchy under the King of
France. In France he is known as Duc de
Deux-Ponts. He offers you his hand and
his protection. You must decide for him
here, this moment, on the spot. You must
ride with him to-night along the road you
travelled to-day. You must throw yourselves on the hospitality and protection of
the Prince-Cardinal at Saverne. I will ride
with you. With good horses we may reach
the Palace of the Prince a few hours after sunrise. I anticipate that he, who loves
an *escapade*, will at once unite you. The
contract may be afterward drawn out and
signed. Madame de Condé meanwhile
charges herself with the task of representing all the circumstances at the Court
of Versailles. The *enlèvement*[26] of a lady
of high rank is an offence that demands
death by the French code; but the good
King is well inclined to your family, and is
highly favorable to the Prince Max, whose
debts he has twice paid. A few months in
the Bastille or at Vincennes will probably
be his punishment; then all is over, and
Prince Max will have secured the wealthiest bride in all these Eastern Provinces. He
professes a romantic love for you. You will

have sovereign rank in virtue of his duchy, and be *grande dame* at the French Court. The match is even more honorable to our house than an alliance with this family. Shall I call in Prince Max, who waits impatiently without, having made his needful preparations?"

"No—no, uncle!" I cried, again kneeling at his feet, from whence during his speech I had risen; "anything but that! I cannot marry Prince Max von Zwei-Brücken. If you knew the horror with which his gaze inspires me! Oh, uncle, anything you please but that!"

And clinging to his hand, I turned my frightened eyes to Madame de Condé.

"There is no third course that I can see," she said slowly.

"Then," I cried, rising to my feet, "I hold fast to my present troth-plight. I accept my fate, whatever it may prove, with this boy of Schomberg-Kissingen. Prince Max von Zwei-Brücken is a bad man. I have heard that he is bad, I feel that he is bad. I will never marry him..."

"Mademoiselle," said my uncle, "for a young girl convent-bred you have too decided views upon gentlemen's morals."

"Madame," I cried, throwing my arms round Madame de Condé, "he looks at me with evil eyes!"

"The child may possibly have decided for the best," the Princess said, turning to my uncle.

"Just Heaven!" he thundered, "what folly have I not been guilty of?—to have paid attention to the whims of a spoilt child, who after all prefers a boy who hates her to a man who is really in love with her!"

He took two or three distracted turns up and down the salon. These the Princess pretended not to see. She pressed me in her arms and kissed me.

"How am I to meet Von Zwei-Brücken, who is waiting for me?" my uncle cried. "He will never believe me: I gave him my promise; I was to show him where to find her. I had no notion, Madame la Princesse, you would ask me to leave the decision of her fate to a young girl! He has his men and horses ready in the town; he has bribed the warder of the Schloss. Who would have supposed my niece would have so little courage, so little romance, so little spirit? What am I to tell him?"

"Call him in here, M. le Bailli," the Princesse de Condé said, "and tell him the truth. Amélie to-night shall share my bed. We will retire to my chamber."

But long after we were locked in there I heard voices in the salon, sometimes loud, often fierce, and oaths of the camp and of the stable.

I trembled so that I could not stand. A great chill came over me and faintness. It would have been physically impossible that I should have attempted to ride all night, even had I been willing to escape with Von Zwei-Brücken.

The Princess and her ladies and my Heinzel were engaged in ministering to me all night; but the Princess did not wish to provoke gossip by summoning a physician. At last my limbs grew warm again; the shuddering ceased; I fell asleep, and awoke only in time to be dressed for my marriage, which was to take place at the Dom Kirche of Kissingen at midday.

Saint Anthony
A Christmas Eve Ballad (1891)

I

More than eight hundred years ago—
    How changed is the world since then!
Man's nature remains the same, we know,
Man's joys and sorrows, man's weal and woe.
    But how changed are the ways of men!
Who cared in those days for the weak or the poor.
    For the patient dumb beast or the child?
For the wretches whose work-day worth was o'er.
    Or the leper sin-defiled?
Not Baron or Burgher. Our Mother the Church
    Was sole friend to the poor and the old;
She stretched out her arms from the convent gates;
    She gathered them into her fold.

It was Christmas Eve; a snow-storm passed
    O'er the hills o'ertop Vienne.
The flakes fell fast, and a furious blast
Swept over the landscape, while gathering fast
Rose a mist that obscured the hills, and cast
    Deep gloom over gorge and glen.

The women and girls in the low-built town
Watched the flakes as they hovered down.
    "Our Lady," said they, "is spinning to-day,
And the fluffs of her wool fly over our land.
Catch one, and should it not melt in your hand,
    It may bring you luck," they say.

But not long lasted so gay a mood:
For, "Where is my child?" shrieked a mother, aloud.
    "And where is my child?" "And mine?"
Were echoed in chorus by all the crowd
For each had some loved one in mist and cloud
    Herding the goats or tending the swine.

Soon the church was filled with mothers and wives
Wrestling in prayer for the precious lives
    Bound up in the bundle of life with theirs.
Oh, blessed are prayers when love would fain
Bring solace to sorrow or soothing to pain!
For it is when all human efforts seem vain
    That God strengthens our weakness and answers our prayers.

By-and-by came dropping in
    The dear ones for whom they prayed,
And many a fond caress was given,
And many thanksgivings went up to Heaven
    For rescued man and maid.
Not so many thanks as there had been prayers:
We think lightly of blessings, but magnify cares.

All who had been prayed for were housed and safe
    Ere the curfew rang its call—
All who had been prayed for—not all—for yet
Out on the mountain-side, cold and wet,
Frightened, bewildered, and shivering, sat
Two orphan children—little Linette
    And her younger brother Paul.

II

Deep in a cave the little ones hid, weeping;
    Their swine close huddled near them in a crowd.
Paul, into Linette's sheltering bosom creeping,
    Bewailed his hunger and the cold aloud.

"Look up! take heart, dear Paul!" she answered, brightly.
    "Erelong I'm sure we'll safely reach the town."
And here she chafed his aching feet, and tightly
    Wrapped them more closely in her tattered gown.

"And listen, Paul (for I must keep on praying),
    For the far tinkle or the convent bell.
I heard one day a Reverend Father saying
    That good Saint Anthony loves swine-herds well,

"That all his life he cherished living creatures.
    He sent his holy relics to our town.
You know, Paul, how he looks, how kind his features,
    And how the pig peeps out beneath his gown.

"Take courage! I am here. Keep close beside me.
    Dear God, take pity upon Paul and me!
Paul has but me to save or help him. Guide me!
    For we are orphans. We have only Thee."

So she knelt, praying—praying, but still trying
    With words of love Paul's courage to uphold,
Who all the while she spoke sat softly crying,
    And growing drowsier in the biting cold.

"Paul, it is Christmas Eve, I now remember;
    Perhaps our pigs may speak to us," she said.
"They say beasts talk on this night in December,
    When Jesus lay a babe in cattle shed.

"Oh Paul suppose it's true! Our swine might tell us
    How to Saint Anthony's to find our way.
We'll tell the Reverend Fathers what befell us;
    I know they will not turn Christ's waifs away.

"Father—our only Father; we've no other—
    Hear us and help us. Other help we've none.
Be good to us, because we have no mother.
    Save Paul! save me! I can't leave Paul alone."

And so she prayed, most piteously calling
    For help to Him who she believed could save;
But as she prayed, faster the flakes kept falling,
    And dark, dark night closed round them in the cave.

Her voice grew faint. It rallied, then grew weaker,
    But the brave heart to the last moment prayed;
When little Paul grew drowsier and the speaker
    Grew the more earnest as she grew afraid.
At last she ceased. Were both the children sleeping

That sleep to which no work-day walking comes?
Would they awake still orphans spent with weeping?
    Or, angel tended, awake in heavenly homes?

Nay, suddenly the cave grew brighter, larger;
    Their tearful, wondering eyes grew fixed and big.
Five creatures entered it—a gallant charger,
    Two lions, and a raven, and a pig.

They had no fear of lions, for Paul thought them
    Great, warm , soft cats. He seized their mighty paws,
Lifted their tawny manes, and smiling, caught them
    By the huge beards dependent from their jaws.

The lions stooped and licked the children's faces,
    The life returned that had so nearly fled;
And when revived by warmth, with queer grimaces,
    The raven dropped on them a loaf of bread.

They ate. Soft smiles lit up Linette's pale features;
    She thanked the God who sent them help in need;
And at His holy name the reverent creatures
    Bowed their proud crests and thus outspake the steed:

"Leave every hundred years," he said, "is given
    To us one hour on Christmas Eve to speak,
And do, in honor of our saint in heaven,
    One deed of kindness to the poor or weak.

"Mount on my back. The bells will soon give warning
    We must depart. Our moments fleet away.
All children should be happy Christmas morning;
    The Saviour's Birthday is the Children's Day.

"Paul, take this little pig—'tis lame and weakly—
    And hug it close; its warmth may warm you too.
Remember how the marble saint smiles meekly
    Down on his pig and think he smiles on you."

III

Down the steep hill, half frightened still,
The children rode the horse;
The raven fluttered the flakes away;
The lions slowly broke the way
Down to the rocky gorge where lay
Saint Anthony's Convent, lone and gray;
But a struggling moonbeam cast a ray
Of light on its tower cross,
And lit up its gold till it shone afar,
And Linette thought it Bethlehem star.

It was Christmas Eve, as I said, and late
When they reached St. Anthony's Convent gate.
Within the chapel was warmth and light
Such as befitted a Christmas night;
But every Brother was in his cell
Waiting the sound of the midnight bell.
Not one of them guessed, we may well believe.
How their chapel was filled on that Christmas Eve.

Over the altar, clear and bright,
Saint Anthony stood in the Christmas light.
With hand outstretched he signed the cross
O'er children and lions, pig, raven, and horse;
And then he slowly faded away,
Like the lingering light of a dying day.

IV

The gallant charger raised his head,
And with a faltering voice he said:
"Patient in hardship and trusty in need,
I was Sir Anthony's own steed
When forth he went a Christian Knight,
For God and honor and truth to fight—
One of the world's great Champions Seven,
Whose swords were consecrate to Heaven.

"Living creatures, great or small,
Feathered or furred, he loved them all.
A wondrous faculty of speech
God gave him too, that he might preach
His will to birds and beasts and fish,
What each should do, what each might wish.

For he believed that to each beast
Is given a germ-soul at the least—
A something that can make us thrill
With joy in God. Albeit still
Much that man knows of good and ill
Is hidden from us by God's will.

"He told us of a coming day
When God would wipe all tears away
From human eyes. 'And,' said he, 'then
You too shall share the joys of men;
That day will bring your own release
From servile fears. Your toil shall cease,
Lions and lambs lie down in peace.—
    The Gospel that I here proclaim
    In the babe of Bethlehem's name—
    He who, when a tender stranger,
    Shared with ox and ass His manger—
    Is a message of salvation
    Not alone to every nation,
    But to God's world-wide creation.'
"My master, Sir Anthony, rode on me
All the days that he fought so valiantly
For the honor and glory of Italy.
Me it was that he bestrode
When to that tournament he rode[27]
Where all the warriors of the East
He challenged at the Emperor's feast.

"There, in bright steel and housing blue,
I and my master overthrew
Seven Grecian Knights, who came
Honor at our hands to claim;

And from the rising of the lark
We held the lists till the day grew dark.

"Some impulse, all unknown to me,
Prompted Sir Anthony suddenly
To cross the seas to that strange land
That lies half buried under sand,

Where Earth the first faint glimmer saw
Of both the Gospel and the Law;
Where the first the infant Moses smiled.
And where first spake the Holier Child.[28]
There, following some inward call,
We went in search of aged Paul,[29]
An anchorite who many a year,
In penitence, with fasts austere,
Had dwelt in solitude severe.
Not mine my master's will to cross—
What was I but his faithful horse?
But it has always seemed to me
That God's good purpose it must be
That in a world He once called good,
Every created being should
Be just as happy as it could."

Here his voice failed. His lips were closed,
And the hoarse raven interposed:

V

"I was soaring high in the air
O'er the sands of the desert bare,
When a fallen Knight I spied
Stretched on the earth by his horse's side.
Down I flew, with glad surprise,
Whetting my beak to pick out their eyes.

"As my shadow fell across
The dying Knight and his dead horse,
He frayed me away with a feeble hand.

And spake in words I could understand:
"'Avaunt, Thou cruel bird of prey!
Spare my horse—my gallant gray.
Never Knight had steed so good.
I charge thee, by the Holy Rood,[30]
With which I sign thee, touch him not.
But to-morrow to this spot
Hasten back, and thou mayst dine,
Not on his eyes, but on mine.'

"As he spoke thus, in my breast
Something stirred. I went in quest
Of a little stream not far away—
I had flown over it twice that day.
I dipped my black wings in the pool;
I drenched myself in the water cool.

I fluttered over him where he lay;
I sprinkled his face with the cooling spray,
Till he rose refreshed, as from trance or dream;
And I guided his steps to the healing stream.
That night a sand-storm buried the corse
Of his gallant comrade, the good gray horse."

VI

Here the lions, interrupting, took the story up, and cried:
"We too helped the saintly champion after Paul the Hermit died.
We could tell how, when the raven succor in his weakness gave,
How on foot he crossed the sand hills to the aged hermit's cave;
How he cast aside his armor and the sword and lance he bore;
How he girded him with sackcloth; how a sheepskin cloak he wore;
How he, tender as a woman, waited on the aged Paul,
O'er whose eyes the mist of blindness day by day began to fall;
How life's lowest, humblest duties he accepted cheerfully—
He, Sir Anthony the Champion! he, the Knight of Italy!
Wrestling with foul visions sent him by the tempter of mankind,
Weeping, watching, fasting, praying, we were sure the Saint to find.
Till one night when we were prowling o'er the sands in search of prey,
Ere the dawning gave us warning 'twas the hour to steal away.

Lo! we heard the Champion praying— 'Heavenly Father to this cave
Send me some one who may help me dig Thine aged servant's grave!'
Soon we scooped the grave he needed. In it holy Paul he laid.
And the sign of man's redemption over him and us he made
Then we stole away and left him, as beside the grave he prayed."

VII

Said little Paul, the small white pig caressing,
    As close he hugged it fondly to his breast:
"What did you do to bring the Saint a blessing?
    They say he loved you more than all the rest."

"Nay," said the pig, "I only gave him pleasure.
    What did you think a little pig could do?
I was his link to earth, his one sole treasure,
    And that he loved me best of all is true.

"'Tis what we *are*, not what we *do* for others,
    That makes us dear to those with whom we live;
And that is nature's reason why fond mothers
    Raptures of love to helpless infants give.

"The good Saint found me one day almost dying
    Upon the burning sands. He picked me up;
He bore me home, in his own bosom lying;
    I shared his food, his shelter, and his cup.

"I never grew, was always lame and ailing;
    For this he loved me more I could discern.
And how I loved him! Words are unavailing
    To tell the love I gave to him in return.

"His last caress to me was faintly given;
    For I was closely nestled at his side.
Then his worn hands he clasped in prayer to Heaven.
    The angels came from him. And so he died.

"Men came. They found us. Me they cast forth roughly;
    Called me unclean, unholy and abhorred

Said it was shame to see me there and gruffly
　　Chased me away from my dear friend and lord.

"They buried him close of day. They cleft him
　　A tomb in solid rock and rolled a stone
Before it. Then they went away and left him
　　Alone with God. But I was all alone.

"I crept back to the cruel stone which shut me
　　From the dear friend I had forever lost,
For those cold-hearted men refused to let me
　　Lie by his side, a few brief hours at most.

"As I lay dying, ere my life departed.
　　A voice that with sweet music seemed to blend
Spake thus to me: 'Thou shalt no more be parted,
　　Fond, faithful creature, from thy saintly friend.

"'Know that in art thou shalt be found forever
　　(Whether the artist work in stone or paint)
Beside Saint Anthony. No hand shall sever
　　His faithful pig from the dumb creatures' Saint.'"

VIII

Here the pig broke off his story.
　　Over town and glen and hill
Rang the Christmas bells out. Glory!
　　Glory! Glory! Peace—good-will!

And the monks, in long procession,
　　Torches waving, banners spread,
Filled into the Convent chapel
　　With their Abbot at their head.

As he neared the light altar,
　　"What is here?" the Abbot cried;
For he saw two lonely children
　　Sleeping softly side by side.

And he added as the others
    Gathered round Linette and Paul:
"They are Christmas gifts, my brothers,
    That our Saint has sent us all.

In a vision late I saw him,
    And he said: 'Whilst I approve
All your zeal, one thing is lacking,
    Some frail living thing to love.

Such a gift, bestowed by Heaven,
    Will your Convent soon receive.
Look for it before the altar
    In your chapel Christmas Eve!"

"Glory! glory!" sang the Fathers.
    "Blessed children, they shall be
No more orphans. We will call them
    Children of Saint Anthony!"
"Glory! glory!" sang the children.
    "Glory!" heavenly angels sang.
Glory! glory! from each belfry
    Christmas bells in chorus rang.
Glory! Glory! Let all creatures
    Join in hope the Christmas strain,
Longing for that glorious Easter
    When the Lord will come again;
For which, till then, all creation
    Travaileth awhile in pain.

From *France in the Nineteenth Century* (1893)

From Chapter IX

The Emperor's Marriage

A *plébiscite*[31]—Louis Napoleon's political panacea—was ordered Dec. 20, 1851, two weeks after the *coup d'état*, to say if the people of France approved or disapproved the usurpation of the prince president. The national approval as expressed in this *plebiscite* was overwhelming. Each peasant and artisan seemed to fancy he was voting to revive the past glories of France, when expressing his approval of a Prince Napoleon. The more thoughtful voters, like M. de Montalembert,[32] considered that the *coup d'état* was a crushing blow struck at Red Republicanism, Communism, the International Society, and disorder generally.

For a while the prince president governed by decrees; then a new legislative body was assembled. Its first duty was to revise the constitution. The republican constitution of 1850 was in the main re-adopted, but with one important alteration. The prince president was to be turned into the Emperor Napoleon III, and the throne was to be hereditary in his family.

After the passage of this measure it was submitted by another *plébiscite* to the people. The *plébiscite* is a universal suffrage vote of yes or no, in answer to some question put by the Government to the nation. The question this time was: Shall the prince president become emperor? There were 7,800,000 ayes, and 224,000 noes.

When the news of this overwhelming success reached the Elysée, Louis Napoleon sat so still and unmoved, smoking his cigar, that his cousin, Madame Baiocchi, rushing up to him, shook him, and exclaimed: "Is it possible that you are made of stone?"

Having thus secured his elevation by the almost universal consent of Frenchmen, the new emperor's next step was to insure his dynasty by a marriage that might probably give heirs to the throne. He chose the title Napoleon III because the son of the Great Napoleon had been Napoleon II for a few days after his father's abdication at Fontainebleau in 1814. The next heir to the imperial dignities (Lucien Bonaparte having refused anything of the kind for himself or for his family) was Jérôme Napoleon, familiarly called Plon-Plon. He was the only son of Jérôme Bonaparte and the Princess Catherine of Würtemberg.[33] But Prince Napoleon, though clever, was wilful and eccentric, and made a boast of being a Red Republican; moreover, his father's Baltimore marriage had made his legitimacy more than doubtful,—at any rate, Louis Napoleon was by no means desirous of passing on to him the succession to the empire; and being now forty-four years old, he was desirous of marrying as soon as possible.

When a boy, it had been proposed to marry him to his cousin Mathilde, and something like an attachment had sprung up between them; but after his fiasco at Strasburg he was no longer considered an eligible suitor either for Princess Mathilde or another cousin who had been named for him, a princess of Baden. Princess Mathilde was married to the Russian banker, Prince Demidorff; but when Louis Napoleon became prince president, he requested her to preside at the Élysée.

The new emperor, or his advisers, looked round at the various marriageable princesses belonging to the smaller courts of Germany. The sister of that Prince Leopold of Hohenzollern whose selection for the throne of Spain led afterwards to the Franco-Prussian war, was spoken of; but the lady most seriously considered was the Princess Adélaïde of Hohenlohe. She was daughter of Queen Victoria's half-sister Feodora; and to Queen Victoria and Prince Albert, as heads of the

family, the matter was referred. A recent memoir-writer tells us of seeing the queen at Windsor when the matter was under discussion. The queen and her husband were apparently not averse to the alliance, hesitating only on the grounds of religion and morals; but it is doubtful how far the new emperor went personally in the affair. His inclination had for some time pointed to the reigning beauty of Paris, Mademoiselle Eugénie de Montijo.

This young lady's grandfather was Captain Fitzpatrick, of a good old Scottish family, which had in past times married with the Stuarts. Captain Fitzpatrick had been American consul at a port in southern Spain. He had a particularly charming daughter, who made a brilliant Spanish marriage, her husband being the Count de Teba (or Marquis de Montijo, for he bore both titles). The Montijos were connected with the grandest ducal families in Spain and Portugal, and even with the royal families of those nations.

The Count de Teba died while his two daughters were young, and they were left under the guardianship of their very charming mother. The elder married the Duke of Alva; the younger became the Empress Eugénie.

Eugénie was for some time at school in England at Clifton. She was described by those who knew her there as a pretty, sprightly little girl, much given to independence, and something of a tomboy,—a character there is reason to think she preserved until it was modified by the exigencies of her position.

Mr. George Ticknor, of Boston, frequently mentioned Madame de Teba to his friends as a singularly charming woman. In 1818 he wrote home to a friend in America:

"I knew Madame de Teba in Madrid, and from what I saw of her there and at Malaga, I do not doubt she is the most cultivated and interesting woman in Spain. Young, beautiful, educated strictly by her mother, a Scotchwoman,—who for this purpose carried her to London and kept her there six or seven years,—possessing extraordinary talents, and giving an air of originality to all she says and does, she unites in a most bewitching manner the Andalusian grace and frankness to a French facility in her manners and a genuine English thoroughness in her knowledge and accomplishments. She knows the chief modern languages well, and feels their different characters, and estimates their literature aright. She has the foreign accomplishments of singing, painting, playing, etc., joined to the natural one of dancing, in a high degree. In conversation she is brilliant and original, yet with all this she is a true Spaniard, and as full of Spanish feelings as she is of talent and culture."[34]

Washington Irving, in 1853, thirty-five years later, writing to his nephew, speaks in equal praise of Madame de Teba.

"I believe I told you," he says, "that I knew the grandfather of the empress, old Mr. Fitzpatrick. In 1827 I was in the house of his son-in-law, Count Teba, at Granada, a gallant, intelligent gentleman, much cut up in the wars, having lost an eye and been maimed in a leg and hand. Some years after, in Madrid, I was invited to the house of his widow, Madame de Montijo, one of the leaders of *ton*. She received me with the warmth and eagerness of an old friend. She claimed me as the friend of her late husband. She subsequently introduced me to the little girls I had known in Granada, *now* fashionable belles in Madrid."[35]

In some lines of Walter Savage Landor, Madame de Montijo was addressed as a "lode-star of her sex."[36]

The Marquis de Montijo had been an adherent of Joseph Bonaparte while the latter was king of Spain, and his eye had been put out at the battle of Salamanca. He was a liberal in politics, and his house was always open to cultivated men.

Such was the ancestry of the beautiful young lady who, tall, fair, and graceful, with hair like one of Titian's[37] beauties, was travelling with her mother from capital to capital, after the marriage of her sister to the Duke of Alva, and who spent the winters of 1850, 1851, and 1852 in the French capital. Mademoiselle Eugénie had conceived a romantic admiration for the young prince who at Strasburg and Boulogne had been so unfortunate. Her father had been a stanch adherent of Bonaparte, and she is said to have pleaded with her mother at one time to visit the prisoner at Ham and to place her fortune at his disposal.

This circumstance, when confided to the prince president, disposed him to be interested in the young lady. She and her mother were often at the Élysée, at Fontainebleau, and at Compiègne. Mademoiselle de Montijo was a superb horsewoman, and riding was the emperor's especial personal accomplishment. On one occasion they got lost together in the forest at Compiègne, and then society began to make remarks upon their intimacy.

The emperor was indeed most seriously in love with Mademoiselle de Montijo. It is said, on the authority of M. de Goncourt,[38] that in one of their rides he asked her, with strange frankness, if she had ever been in love with any man. She answered with equal frankness, "I may have had fancies, sire, but I have never forgotten that I was Mademoiselle de Montijo."

Such a project of marriage was not approved by the emperor's family, it was not favored by his ministers, and the ladies of his court were all astir.

At a ball given on New Year's Day, 1853, by the emperor at the Tuileries, the wife of a cabinet minister was rude and insulting to Mademoiselle de Montijo. Seeing that she looked troubled, the emperor inquired the cause; and when he knew it, he said quietly: "To-morrow no one will dare to insult you again." There is also a story, which seems to rest on good authority, that a few weeks before this, at Compiègne, he had placed a crown of oak-leaves on her head, saying: "I hope soon to replace it with a better one."[39] Like the Empress Josephine, she had had it prophesied to her in her girlhood that she should one day wear a crown.

The day after the occurrence at the ball at the Tuileries, the Duc de Morny waited on Madame de Montijo with a letter from the emperor, formally requesting her daughter's hand.

The ladies, after this, removed to the Elysée, which was given to them, and preparations for the marriage went on apace.

In less than a month afterwards Eugénie de Montijo was empress of France.

Here is the emperor's own official announcement of his intended marriage:—

"I accede to the wish so often manifested by my people in announcing my marriage to you. The union which I am about to contract is not in harmony with old political traditions, and in this lies its advantage. France, by her successive revolutions, has been widely sundered from the rest of Europe. A wise Government should so rule as to bring her back within the circle of ancient monarchies. But this result will be more readily obtained by a frank and straightforward policy, by a loyal intercourse, than by royal alliances, which often create false security, and subordinate national to family interests. Moreover, past examples have left superstitious beliefs in the popular mind. The people have not forgotten that for sixty years foreign princesses have mounted the steps of the throne only to see their race scattered and proscribed, either by war or revolution. One woman alone appears to have brought with her good fortune, and lives, more than the rest, in the memory of the people; and this woman, the wife of General Bonaparte, was not of royal blood. We must admit this much, however. In 1810 the marriage of Napoleon I with Marie Louise was a great event. It was a bond for the future, and a real gratification to the national pride. . . . But when, in the face of ancient Europe, one is carried by the force of a new principle to the level of the old dynasties, it is not by affecting an ancient descent and endeavoring at any price to enter the family of kings, that one compels recognition. It is rather by remembering one's origin; it is by preserving one's own character, and assuming frankly towards Europe the position of a *parvenu*,—a glorious title when one rises by the suffrages of a great people. Thus impelled, as I have been, to part from the precedents that have been hitherto followed, my marriage is only a private matter. It remained for me to choose my wife. She who has become the object of my choice is of lofty birth, French in heart and education and by the memory of the blood shed by her father in the cause of the Empire. She has, as a Spaniard, the advantage of not having a family in France to whom it would be necessary to give honors and dignities. Gifted with every quality of the heart, she will be the ornament of the throne, as in the hour of danger she would be one of its most courageous defenders. A pious Catholic, she will address one prayer with me to Heaven for the happiness of France. Kindly and good, she will show in the same position, I firmly believe, the virtues of the Empress Josephine."[40]

The State coaches of the First Empire were regilded for the occasion, the crown diamonds were drawn from the hiding-place where they had lain since Louis Philippe's time, and were reset for the lady who was to wear them, while her apartments at the Tuileries were rapidly prepared.

The emperor was radiant. He had followed his inclination, and now that his choice was made, it seemed to receive universal approval. The *London Times* said: "Mademoiselle de Montijo knows better the character of France than any princess who could have been fetched from a German principality. She combines by her birth the energy of the Scottish and Spanish races, and if the opinion we hold of her be correct, she is, as Napoleon says, made not only to adorn the throne, but to defend it in the hour of danger."

The Municipal Council of Paris voted six hundred thousand francs to buy her a diamond necklace as a wedding present. Very gracefully she declined the necklace, but accepted the money, with which she endowed an orphan asylum.

The wedding day was January 29, 1853. Crowds lined the streets as the bride and her *cortège* drove to the Tuileries, where they were received by the Grand Chamberlain and other court dignitaries, who conducted the bride to the first *salon*. There she was received by Prince Napoleon and his sister, the Princess Mathilde, who introduced her into the *salon*, where the emperor, with his uncle, King Jérôme, surrounded by a glittering throng of cardinals, marshals, admirals, and great officers of State, stood ready to receive her. Thence, at nine o'clock, she was led by the emperor to the Salle des Maréchaux and seated beside him on a raised throne. The marriage contract was then read, and signed by the bride and bridegroom and by all the princes and princesses present.

The bride wore a marvellous dress of Alençon point lace, clasped with a diamond and sapphire girdle made for the Empress Marie Louise, and she looked, said a beholder, "the imperial beauty of a poet's vision." The emperor was in a general's uniform. He wore the collar of the Legion of Honor which his uncle the Great Emperor used to wear. He wore also the collar of the Golden Fleece that had once belonged to the Emperor Charles V.

The civil marriage being concluded, the imperial pair and the wedding guests passed into the theater, where a *cantata*, composed by Auber for the occasion, was sung. The empress, robed in lace and glittering in jewels, seemed, says an eye-witness, to realize the picture presented of herself in the composer's words:—

"Espagne bien aimée,
Où le del est vermeil,
C'est toi qui l'as formée
D'un rayon de soleil."[41]

When the *cantata* had been sung, the Grand Master of the Ceremonies conducted the bride, as yet only half married, back to the Elysée.

The next morning all Paris was astir to see the wedding procession pass to the cathedral of Notre Dame. Early in the morning the emperor had repaired to the Élysée, where, in the chapel, he and the empress had heard mass, and after making their confession, had partaken of the Holy Communion. There were two hundred thousand sightseers in Paris that day, in addition to the usual population.

The empress wore upon her golden hair the crown that the First Napoleon had placed upon the head of Marie Louise. The body of the church was filled with men,—ambassadors, military and naval officers, and high officials. Their wives were in the galleries. As the great doors of the cathedral were opened to admit the bridal procession, a broad path of light gleamed from the door up to the altar, adding additional brilliancy to the glittering scene. Up the long aisle the emperor led his bride, flashing with the light of jewels, among them the unlucky regent diamond, which glittered on her bosom. After the Spanish fashion, she crossed her brow, her lips, her heart, her thumb, as she knelt for the nuptial benediction. The ceremony over, the archbishop conducted the married pair to the porch of the cathedral, and they drove along the Quai to the Tuileries.

The first favor the empress asked of her husband was the pardon of more than four thousand unfortunate persons still exiled or imprisoned for their share in the risings that succeeded the *coup d'état*.

When Washington Irving heard of the marriage, he wrote: "Louis Napoleon and Eugénie de Montijo,—Emperor and Empress of France! He whom I received as an exile at my cottage on the Hudson, she whom at Granada I have dandled on my knee! The last I saw of Eugénie de Montijo, she and her gay circle had swept away a charming young girl, beautiful and accomplished, my dear young friend, into their career of fashionable dissipation. Now Eugénie is on a throne, and the other a voluntary recluse in a convent of one of the most rigorous Orders."[42] This convent is near Biarritz, where the nuns take vows of silence like the monks of La Trappe. The empress when at Biarritz never failed to visit her former friend, who was permitted to converse with her.

The beautiful woman thus raised to the imperial throne was a mixed character,—not so perfect as some have represented her, but entirely to be acquitted of those grave faults that envy or disappointed expectations have attributed to her. Her character united kind-heartedness with inconsideration, imprudence with austerity, ardent feeling with great practical common-sense. Probably the emperor understood her very little at the time of his marriage, and that she long remained to him an enigma may have been one of her charms. With the impetuosity of her disposition and the intrepidity that had characterized her girlhood, she found it hard to submit to the restraints of her position, and the emperor had occasion frequently to remonstrate with her on her indifference to etiquette and public opinion. It was not until after her visit to Windsor in 1855 that she could be induced to establish court rules at the Tuileries, and to prescribe for herself and others, in public, a strict system of etiquette. But in her private hours, among her early friends, in the circle of ladies admitted to her intimacy, the empress was less discreet. Her impressions were apt to run into extremes; she indulged in whims like other pretty women; yet she was never carried by her romantic feelings or her enthusiasm beyond her power of self-control. Though careless of etiquette in private life, whenever a great occasion came, she could act with imperial dignity.

Although she often experienced ingratitude, she was always generous. She was as ready to solicit favors and pardons as was the Empress Josephine. Sometimes she was even sorely embarrassed to find arguments in favor of her *protegés*. "*Ah, mon Dieu!*" she cried once, when pleading for the pardon of a workman, "how could he be guilty? He has a wife and five children to support; he could have had no time for conspiracy!"

As a wife she was devoted, not only to the public interests of her husband, but to his personal welfare. She was constantly anxious lest he should suffer from overwork; and her little select evening parties, which some people found fault with, were instituted by her with the chief object of amusing him.

Ben Jonson makes it a reproach against a lady of the sixteenth century that she would not "suffer herself to be admired."[43] No such reproach could be addressed to the Empress Eugénie. Few women conscious of their power to charm will fail to exercise it. In the case of an empress,—young, lively, of an independent and adventurous spirit, and very beautiful,—all who approached her thought better of themselves from her apparent appreciation of their claims to consideration; and, indeed, in her position was it not the duty of the successor of Josephine to be gracious and charming to everybody?

Unfortunately the ladies who most enjoyed the intimacy of the Empress Eugénie were foreigners. She seems to have felt a certain distrust of Frenchwomen; and considering the ingratitude she often met with from those she served, it is hardly surprising that she preferred the intimacy of women who could not look to her for favors.

One of the ladies most intimate with the empress was the wife of Prince Richard Metternich, the Austrian ambassador. This lady seems to have had personal and political ends in view, and to have succeeded in inducing the empress to adopt and further them. That she was a dangerous and false friend may be judged from a speech she made when remonstrated with for countenancing and encouraging a project, favored by the empress, of making a promenade in the forest of Fontainebleau with her courtladies in skirts which, like those in the old Scotch ballad, should be "kilted up to the knee."

"You would not have advised your own empress," it was said to her, "to appear in such a garb."

"Of course not," replied the ambassadress; "but *my* empress is of royal birth,—a real empress; while yours, *ma chère*, was Mademoiselle de Montijo!"

Brought up in private life, not early trained to the self-abnegation demanded of princesses, the Empress Eugénie did not bring into her new sphere all the *aplomb* and seriousness about little things which are early inculcated on ladies brought up to the profession of royalty. The career for which she had formed herself was that of a very charming woman; and one secret of her fascination was the sincerity of the interest she took in those around her. She loved to study character, to see into men's souls. She loved to be adored, while irresponsively she received men's homage. She especially liked the society of famous men, and when she was to meet them, she took pains to inform herself on the subjects about which they were most likely to converse.

That Queen Victoria loves her as a sister and a friend, is a testimony to her dignity and goodness; and we have her husband's own opinion of her, published on her fête-day, December 15, 1868, after nearly sixteen years of marriage. The emperor had under his control a monthly magazine called *Le Dix Décembre*, in which he often inserted articles from his own pen. The manuscript of this, in his own handwriting, was found in 1870 in the sack of the Tuileries. He omits all mention of his wife's Scotch ancestry, neither does he allude to her school-days in England. He speaks of her as a member of one of the most distinguished families in Spain, extols her father's attachment to the house of Bonaparte, and tells how she and her sister were placed at the Sacre Coeur, near Paris, declaring that "she acquired, we may say, the French before the Spanish language." He goes on to speak of her, not as the leader of a giddy circle of fashion in Madrid, as Washington Irving describes her, but as the thoughtful, studious young girl, with a precocious taste for social problems and for the society of men of letters; and he adds that after her marriage her simple, natural tastes did not disappear. "After her visit to the cholera patients at Amiens," he says, "nothing seemed to surprise her more than the applause that everywhere celebrated her courage. She seemed at last distressed by it. . . . At Compiègne," he also tells us, "nothing can be more attractive than five o'clock tea à *l'impératrice*;[44] though," he adds slyly, "sometimes she is a little too fond of argument."

Assuredly she filled a difficult place, and filled it well; but the court of the Second

Empire was all spangles and tinsel. It was composed of men and women all more or less adventurers. It was the court of the *nouveaux riches* and of a mushroom aristocracy. There were prizes to be won and pleasures to be enjoyed, and it was "like as it was in the days of Noah,[45] until the flood came, and swept them all away."[46]

In the midst of the crowd that composed this court the emperor and the empress shine out as the best. Both wanted to do their duty, as they understood it, to France. Whether it was the emperor's fault or his misfortune, is still undecided; but, with one or two exceptions, he was able to attach to himself only keen-witted adventurers and mediocre men. Among the women, not one who was really superior rose above the crowd. The empress led a giddy circle of married women, as in her youth, according to Washington Irving, she had led a giddy circle of young girls.

From *England in the Nineteenth Century* (1894)

From Chapter XVI

Queen Victoria's Jubilee and Her Family

After the Prince Consort's death the Queen secluded herself for many years from court ceremonials, thereby greatly disappointing her subjects; she has worn black all the days of her widowhood, unless on exceptional public occasions. During these years her companionship and intimacy has been with her own family, or, for a brief period, with Lord Beaconsfield. Her health, considered frail in her girlhood, has, on the whole, been excellent. When, on the day of her Jubilee,

she drove in state to Westminster Abbey, she was attended by a gallant *cortège* of sons and sons-in-law. The papers at that time published sheets containing portraits of all her descendants,—her children, her grandchildren, and two great-grandchildren, her sons-in-law and daughters-in-law. Among all these there is not one who has openly dishonored his or her high lineage. There have been among them many sorrows, but some have been distinguished among the good and great of their generation for noble womanly and manly qualities. All the women, whether connected with the Queen by birth or marriage, have been ladies of exceptional ability and virtue.

The day of the Jubilee, Tuesday, June 21, 1887, was very warm. The sun shone with a fierce brightness he seldom does in England. The chief desire of those who planned the ceremonies was to make them, like those of the Coronation, a source of interest and rejoicing to the people,—who were to witness the splendors of a procession formed largely of princes and high dignitaries, while a solemn religious service took place in the Abbey.

Seats and windows sold at prices higher than those upon the Coronation Day, all along the line of the procession from Buckingham Palace to Westminster Abbey. The crowd was dense, but pleased, and in good humor.

Under a red and fawn-color striped awning all, except royal personages, who had tickets for the religious services had to pass to enter the Abbey. Along this covered way streamed by eight o'clock in the morning—ladies in superb toilets, gentlemen in cocked hats and black velvet court costumes, generals and general officers in brilliant scarlet, naval men in uniforms of blue and white and gold.

Among the earliest of the royal family to arrive were three young girls, daughters of the Duke of Edinburgh, their pretty fair hair floating down their backs, with flapping hats of Tuscan straw shading them from the sun. Princess Frederica of Hanover, wife of the Freiherr von Pawel-Rammingen, who had been for many years her blind father's secretary, was there, dressed all in white, looking pale, but very princely. The Duchess of Teck (Princess Mary of Cambridge), always a favorite with the people, and her daughter, Princess May, were loudly cheered. Then came the crowned heads who were not to follow the Queen in the procession, the royalties of Greece and Denmark, and the King and Queen of the Belgians. There were Indian Princes all wrapped round with shawls and stuffs of rich dark colors, stolid and stately, indifferent alike to plaudits and to the rays of a burning sun which made their jewels flash and sparkle. Queen Emma of Hawaii[47] was among the crowned heads, and Princess Liliuokalani,[48]—since dethroned, who will never have a Jubilee. There was an Indian Mahranee,[49] distinguished by her Eastern grace and quiet dignity; and a Prince of Japan, looking pleased and amused, in a queer white helmet-like cap, adorned with feathers and magenta ribbons.

It was half an hour after midday when the Queen's procession reached the Abbey. In the state carriage with the Queen sat the Princess of Wales and the Crown-Princess of Prussia.

In carriages that followed were other Princesses: the three daughters of the Prince of Wales, their carriage looking like a bower of tulle and whiteness; Princess Irene, the daughter of Princess Alice, was there, and their aunts,—the Princess Christian, Princess Louise, Princess Beatrice, and the Duchess of Edinburgh.

The Queen, in place of the black bonnet which for twenty-six years had saddened the eyes of her people, wore a coronet-shaped bonnet of white lace, bedecked with diamonds, which made her look ten years younger. It was remarked that she seemed pleased, and was smiling. Pleased and interested, too, seemed the Crown-Princess of Prussia,—little forecasting that within a year she would be both an Empress and a widow, though her husband had taken advantage of his journey to England to consult Dr. Mackenzie as to his throat, which was already becoming a cause of anxiety.[50] The Crown-Princess wore a superb gray silk, and a white bonnet, with strings of olive green. The Duchess of Albany was there, still in slight mourning. She was always a favorite, and was loudly cheered.

The most interesting part of the procession was the escort that immediately followed the Queen's carriage,—her three sons riding abreast, and her five sons-in-law; conspicuous among these last was the splendid figure of the Crown-Prince of Prussia. The only *contretemps* during the day was that the horse of the Marquis of Lorne threw him, just as the procession was about to start.

The services in the Abbey were solemn and beautiful. There is a service in the English Prayer-book for the anniversary of the succession of a sovereign. The archbishops officiated, and many bishops and high ecclesiastical dignitaries assisted in the chancel. Judges in their wigs and robes were there; groups of Indians, in gorgeous costumes and jewels, came to do honor to the Empress of India; sheriffs from the fifty-two counties of England and Wales, and mayors from the principal cities.

The next day, Wednesday, June 22, a great feast was given to all the charity-school children of London in Hyde Park, which the Queen and all the royal personages attended; and in the evening of that day all London was illuminated. "I think," says a writer in the "Monthly Packet," "that for once the English were not taking their pleasure sadly, but were delighted, interested, and amused with wondrous little. Dense as were the crowds, good humor and a certain order prevailed 'everywhere."[51]

The Queen has had nine children, of whom, in 1894, seven are still living,—Victoria Adelaide Mary Louisa, Princess Royal, now the widowed Empress Frederick, born in 1840; Albert Edward, Prince of Wales, born in 1841; Alice Maud Mary, Grand-Duchess of Hesse-Darmstadt, born in 1843; Alfred Ernest Albert, Duke of Edinburgh and Duke of Saxe-Coburg-Gotha, born in 1844; Helena Augusta, Princess Christian, born in 1846; Louise Caroline Alberta, Marchioness of Lorne, born in 1848; Arthur William Patrick Albert, Duke of Connaught, born in 1850; Leopold George Duncan Albert, Duke of Albany, born in 1853; Beatrice Mary Victoria Feodora, married Prince Henry of Battenberg, born in 1857.

Very briefly I propose to tell the history of these Princes and Princesses. We begin with Victoria, the Princess-Royal, born shortly after her parents were twenty-one, and probably the most highly intellectual member of her family.

She was born November 21, 1840. "A plump, healthy, beautiful princess," says the Court Chronicle,[52] who began her life by protesting vehemently against being inspected by the Lords of the Council and other dignitaries, who, according to court etiquette, were stationed for that purpose in the next chamber.

She was a very pretty young girl at the time of her marriage, and was always her father's especial delight. Baron Stockmar[53] was also very fond and proud of her. Before she was four years old she spoke French as well as she could speak English, and her mother records in her Journal several remarkable instances of her early understanding and self-control.

On Mrs. Bancroft's[54] first visit to Windsor, as wife of the American Ambassador, when she went to take leave of the Queen, who was in the picture-gallery, Her Majesty said, "Oh, but you have not seen the children! I will go and bring them." She soon returned, carrying the baby, Alice, and followed by the Princess-Royal and the Prince of Wales, the latter shrinking behind his sister. "It is always so," said the Queen. "They are devoted to each other. She is afraid of nothing. He is shy, and always wants her to speak for him."

The Princess-Royal was her father's constant companion, and that of her mother as much as possible. When she was three or four years old, the Queen laments in her Journal that her unavoidable occupations and engagements prevented her from nightly hearing her children say their prayers.

The Princess was an excellent artist, making illustrations for the books she loved, especially for the *Idyls of the King*,[55] which greatly pleased her father.

As the children grew older, the Queen purchased Osborne House, in the Isle of Wight, as a seaside residence, and rejoiced over her new acquisition, "as it will give us," she says to her uncle, "a home of our own."

The children had their little gardens at Osborne, and a charming Swiss cottage, where they played at housekeeping; cooked, dusted, swept, and, once in a while, guests staying with their parents were invited to luncheon, which the children cooked and served with their own hands.

Princess Alice, in after years, writes to her mother: "We always say to each other that no children were ever made so happy with the comforts and enjoyments that children would wish for, as we were."[56]

Then, too, by the time the Princess-Royal was ten years old they acquired the beloved Highland residence of Balmoral. The Queen's account of their family life in the Highlands is full of anecdotes of "Vicky," the extremely uncouth name by which the Princess-Royal was known in her family circle.

When the Queen visited Ireland, in 1849, she took with her her four children. The party landed in the Cove of Cork, at a spot thence called Queenstown. The Princess-Royal and Princess Alice afterwards went with their parents to Edinburgh. The Queen records that on reaching Holyrood she went out with her two girls, without rest, to explore the ruined Abbey. The Scottish scenes awakened the enthusiasm of the elder Princess, the daily companion of her father, who had been, as it were, brought up by his grandmothers on Walter Scott's writings, one of them having been in the habit of telling the stories of the Waverley novels before bed-time to the two eager little grandsons at her knee.[57]

Prince Albert took great pains to instruct his clever little daughter in the course of public events, and to give her ideas of politics and political economy. On one occasion he made her translate a profound German pamphlet, on the future policy of Germany, which he wanted to show to the Prime Minister.

During the Crimean War the Queen and her daughters took an intense interest in the work of Miss Nightingale;[58] and when, after the war, that lady came on a visit to Balmoral, the young Princesses hung upon her words, learning lessons they were so nobly to put in practice in the wars of 1866 and 1870.

It was immediately after the Crimean War that Prince Frederick William, son of the Crown-Prince of Prussia, then heir-presumptive to the Prussian throne, came to Balmoral, and there, with a sprig of white heather, the emblem of good fortune, wooed the Princess-Royal in true lover fashion on a Scottish hillside; but she was so young that her parents endeavored to insist that two years must pass before the marriage. It took place, however, January 25, 1858, in London. I cannot but think that a few extracts from the Queen's own Diary will have more interest than any mere abridgment into another's words.

"The wedding-presents," she writes, "were all set out in the great drawing-room [of Buckingham Palace] the evening before,—Mamma's and ours on one table, Fritz's and his family's, and Uncle Leopold's and others, on another. Fritz's pearls were the largest I have ever seen,—one row. We brought in Fritz and Vicky. She was in ecstasies,—quite startled; Fritz delighted."

Again:—

"Dear Vicky gave me a brooch, a very pretty one, before church, with her hair; and, clasping me in her arms, said, 'I hope to be worthy to be your child.'"

On the Wedding-day the Queen writes also:—

"While I was dressing, Vicky came to me, looking well and composed, and in a fine, quiet frame of mind. Then came the time to go; the sun was shining brightly. Thousands had been out since early dawn, shouting, bells ringing, etc. The two eldest boys went first, then the three girls in pink satin, trimmed with Newport lace; Alice with a wreath, and the two others with bouquets only. . . . Our darling flower looked very touching and lovely, with such an innocent, confiding, serious expression, her veil hanging over her shoulders, walking between her beloved father and dearest Uncle Leopold."

While Princess Alice wore roses and white heather, the Princesses Louise and Helena wore cornflowers, in memory of the bridegroom's grandmother, Queen Louise of Prussia. It was her favorite flower, and ever since has been cherished by her descendants.

The Queen continues:—

"It was beautiful to see our darling kneeling with Fritz, their hands joined, her eight bridesmaids in white tulle, with roses and white heather, looking like a cloud hovering over her."

But very sorrowful was the parting on the snowy February day when the Princess departed to her new people and her new home.

Then Germany was proud to receive an English bride; *then* all was hope, and welcome, and enthusiasm; *then* Germany was not puffed up with national pride. Bismarck,[59] indeed, had objected to the alliance, and some of the old court party were ready to cavil at the free and easy ways of a Princess bred in a court where all was homelike, affectionate, and natural; but the population of Berlin went wild with welcome, and it required persistent efforts of foes in her own household, backed by the powerful Chancellor, to make the sweet young bride "unpopular." Her father had said of her, "She has the heart of a child, with a man's head"; and, "Unquestionably she will turn out a very superior woman, whom Prussia will have cause to bless, I write to her every Wednesday by the courier, and receive her answer by the same messenger on the Monday following. We discourse in this manner upon general topics, while she writes to her mother daily, giving her the details of her every-day life."

A few weeks after her marriage her wise father warned her not to be disappointed if her people, having been rapturous at first, should become critical. I remember hearing it said at the time that when the German court ladies found her trousseau included a dozen pairs of stout walking-shoes, they sneered at a Princess who had so carefully provided for keeping up her English ways. There had never been a Queen of Prussia who was not a German; and the Prussian court people considered English manners foreign, and good sense an invasion of time-honored etiquette.

However, these things were but the little cloud at first, "like a man's hand." Prince Albert, writing confidentially to Stockmar, tells him that a visit which he paid to the young people not long after their marriage had afforded him complete satisfaction. "The harmony between the young couple," he says, "is perfect"; and in a hundred ways we find this judgment confirmed.

At the time of the marriage, the father of Prince Fritz (the future Emperor William) was Regent of Prussia, his brother, King Frederick William, having become imbecile.

The Princess had a long and dangerous period of suffering before the birth of her first child. A lady, resident in Berlin at the time, states that she saw the father of Prince Fritz spring into a cab in the twilight, and drive furiously to his son's residence, where he remained until, after some hours of suspense. Marshal von Wrangel came out upon the balcony, and announced to the crowd waiting for tidings: "All is well, my children! 'Tis as sturdy a little recruit as heart could wish to see." The "sturdy little recruit" was a delicate child, nevertheless, born with his left hand and arm imperfect. From his earliest months, however, he was taught to manage this defect, and he has so far overcome it as to be a skilful swordsman and rider. There is something pathetic in the entries in the Queen's Journal concerning this child, when we remember that he lived (at least at one period of his life) to flout his grandmother, and to weigh down

his mother's heart in her widowhood with sorrow that seems greater than any mother or widow in common life is called to bear.

"Such a little love!" writes his grandmother. "He came walking in at his nurse's hand, in a little white dress, with black bows; and so good. . . . He is a fine, fat child, with a beautiful white, soft skin, very fine shoulders and limbs, and a very dear face. . . . So intelligent, and pretty, and good, and affectionate,—such a darling!"

As the year 1861 opened, the old King of Prussia died, and the future Emperor of Germany became King in his stead. Prince Fritz and his wife then became Crown-Prince and Crown-Princess of Prussia. At this time all testimonies agree with that of Lord Clarendon,[60] who writes to Prince Albert that he is not astonished, but very much pleased, to find how thoroughly appreciated and very much beloved is Her Royal Highness; and adds that he has been more than ever astonished at the statesman-like and comprehensive views she takes of Prussia's affairs, both internal and foreign, and of the duties of a constitutional king.

Unhappily, these duties were differently understood by the Crown Prince and Princess on the one part, and by the King and Count Bismarck on the other, whose idea was that a king should be as little constitutional as was consistent with retaining popularity.

Before Christmas of that sad year, Prince Albert died. The Crown-Princess hastened to her mother in her great sorrow. Her visit was the drop of comfort in the bitter cup the Queen was drinking in those days.

Both the Crown-Prince and his wife were fond of travelling. Besides visiting all parts of their own country, they were frequently in Switzerland and Italy, travelling incognito, and associating on pleasant terms with such interesting people as they met.

The Crown Prince and Princess had eight children,—

William, the Emperor William II of (Germany; Charlotte, who married the Prince of Saxe-Meiningen; Henry, who married his cousin, Princess Irene of Hesse-Darmstadt; Sigismund, who died before he was two years old; Victoria, who married His Serene Highness Prince Adolphe of Schaumburg-Lippe; Waldemar, who died at eleven years of age; Sophia Dorothea, who married the Prince of Sparta; Margaret, who married Prince Frederick of Hesse-Cassel.

It was just as the Seven Weeks' War of 1866[61] was breaking out that the Crown-Prince's little son Sigismund died of diphtheria. At the battle of Sadowa, or Königgrätz, the success of the Prussians was largely due to the generalship of the Crown-Prince; and that the war came so speedily to a close was owing in a measure to his statesmanship. "But ah!" he cries, in his Diary, "victories cannot compensate me for the loss of a son!"

In the next section, omitted here, Latimer describess the Crown-Prince's ascension to emperor, his brief term, and finally the controversial medical care surrounding his death.

The next child of Queen Victoria was the Prince of Wales. It is difficult to speak of him; for he has come prominently before the public in only two characters,—the maker of public speeches on public occasions, and the fast young man, known in the gay capitals of Europe as one whose notice and attentions have been injurious to the reputations of women. Enough, and more than enough, has reached the public ear upon this subject, and on that of baccarat. There are other things, of a very different kind, that can be said about the Prince of Wales.

He has occupied for fifty years a very difficult position, and in some respects he has filled it with very remarkable prudence and ability. Can any situation be more trying than that of an English heir-apparent? Any more liable to unjust misrepresentations and to cruel disappointments? The heir of the monarchy to-day is *nothing*; to-morrow may be *everything*. He must efface himself. He must conceal his preferences and his predilections, for fear of exciting false hopes or creating dangerous jealousies. He must endeavor to shine, without absorbing other people's light; and the years slip by him without giving him the opportunity to assert his value or his manhood. Under these circumstances, some heirs-apparent have been driven into becoming men of pleasure, some into becoming men of intrigue, many into becoming both.

No Prince of Wales since Henry VIII has been without blame, if he had come of age during his father's lifetime. The quarrels of parents with their eldest sons, all through the Hanoverian dynasty, are matters of history. If public opinion reproaches Albert Edward, Prince of Wales, with a license foreign to the character of his admirable father, it must be conceded to him that he has ever been a dutiful subject, a hard worker, a man capable of rare self-control, a prince who has borne himself with dignity in a very difficult position.

In one of his first public speeches, he told his hearers that, being forbidden by his birth to take any part in politics, he hoped to devote himself to works of national utility and philanthropy. In politics, he has had the courage and the constancy to remain so absolutely neutral that no one knows what his political predilections are. For fifty years he had, in general, superb good health, a gay genial disposition, a wonderful capacity for work, and a power of endurance and activity which, even among young Englishmen, was considered amazing.

He visited Canada and the United States in the days of President Buchanan; and, immediately after his father's death, he went to the Holy Land. He was accompanied to the East by a suite of gentlemen, among whom was Dean Stanley.[62] The Dean published, on his return, a volume containing the sermons he had preached before the Prince, during their journey, on the spots where Biblical events had taken place; and in the appendix was a very interesting account of the Samaritan Passover, and of the visit they paid to Hebron and the Cave of Machpelah, where they were, by an especial fireman from the Sultan, permitted to enter the mosque built over the cave, and view the shrines of Sarah, Abraham, Isaac and Rebekah, Jacob and Leah, which no Christian had been allowed to do for six hundred years. As the gates of the shrine of Abraham were thrown open, the guardians groaned aloud, and the chief said: "The princes of any other nation should have passed over my dead body sooner than enter; but to the eldest son of the Queen of England we are willing to accord even this privilege." Then, turning to the shrine, he cried: "O Abraham, Friend of God! forgive this intrusion."

Into the real cave they were not permitted to descend, but were suffered to bend over an aperture left open, that the holy air from it, coming up into the mosque, might be sniffed by devout worshippers.

Even before the Prince Consort's death the Princess Alexandra of Denmark had been thought of as the Prince of Wales's bride. Her father, Prince Christian of Schleswig-Holstein-Sonderberg-Glücksberg, was only a distant relative of the childless King of Denmark when selected by him as his heir-presumptive. Even as heir-presumptive his revenues did not exceed $4,500[63] a year; but his children have been all advanced to high positions. The Princess Alexandra may probably be Queen of England; Princess Dagmar is Empress of Russia; Prince George is King of Greece; Princess Thyra married the Duke of Cumberland, the dispossessed King of Hanover; Prince Waldemar has married the great-granddaughter of Louis Philippe, the rich and beautiful Princess Marie, daughter of the Duc de Chartres.

The Princess of Wales has always shown exquisite taste in dress. She and her sisters, in their days of princely poverty, are said to have been their own dressmakers and milliners. The accomplishment that in her girlhood most distinguished her was music: she is an admirable pianist. But she is sadly deaf,—which may be very inconvenient to her when she reaches the throne. The Queen and all her husband's family have been always very fond of her, and she is extremely popular with the English people. I think they are thankful that she is not a German bride.

On March 7, 1863, "the sea-king's daughter from over the sea" landed at Gravesend, and was met there by the Prince of Wales and his mother's cousin, the Duke of Cambridge. A magnificent pageant escorted her through London, and she then proceeded to Windsor, where the Queen (too recently a widow to take part in a public fete) met and welcomed her. Three days later she was married.

The Prince of Wales's country residence is at Sandringham, in Norfolk. It is said that Prince Albert selected it for his son because, being quite off the route of travelers, it is one of the quietest places in England. Here the family leads a country life, greatly beloved by its neighbors, tenants, and the villagers. The Prince and his guests hunt with the neighboring gentry, and entertain them in a country-neighborly way. Sandringham, instead of being a center of intrigue, such as has too often clustered round an heir-apparent, is a real home, where the Prince (in spite of his crop of wild oats) is a most affectionate husband and father, surrounding himself with literary men and artists, noblemen of refined tastes, and distinguished foreigners.

Eight years after his marriage the Prince of Wales was taken desperately ill with typhoid fever. He contracted it at a friend's hunting-lodge, from imperfect drainage. All England was filled with anxiety, and the Queen and his sisters hastened to his sick bed.

"I shall never resist illness," said Prince Albert once to the Queen. "You would struggle, but I should succumb." The Prince of Wales, as his mother would have done, fought hard for his life. But great as his vitality was, the doctors despaired of saving him. Nothing they could do would make him sleep. At this crisis an old woman presented herself at the gate of Sandringham with a hop pillow. If it might be put under his head, she was sure it would be of service to him. The hop pillow was used accordingly; the Prince slept, and recovered.

There is a white marble slab in the parish church at Sandringham, recording in simple beautiful words the thankfulness of his wife for his recovery. When the fever left him, she rose in the early morning from beside his bed, and, with one of her ladies, walked across the fields to early morning service, that in God's house she might return thanks that her husband was spared to her.

It is said that the general feeling in England, on the day when the Prince went to St. Paul's to return public thanks for his recovery, produced a deep impression upon foreigners.

When he was thirty-four, and in the prime of life, he went to India on a species of embassy,—the representative to the natives of India of her who a few months later would be proclaimed their Empress-Queen. He arrived there accompanied by men of tried experience and ability, and nothing was neglected that could add brilliancy to his reception. He enjoyed everything like the most eager of tourists, but at the same time, in all that concerned official life and public affairs he showed the tact, earnestness, and dignity which befitted his position.

He has, like his mother, a beautiful voice, when reading or speaking. In India his activity, energy, curiosity to observe, and powers of endurance, surprised everybody. He knocked up his suite repeatedly, but he himself was always on the alert, and ready for everything.

Yet, though genial, easy, and kindly in all social intercourse, the Prince of Wales never permits any one to presume upon his kindliness, or to forget good manners. *Then* his dignity at once asserts itself.

He has four living children. One died in infancy; and his eldest son, Albert Victor, Duke of Clarence and Avondale, died January 14, 1892, on the eve of his marriage. His brother, George Frederick, the Duke of York, married, eighteen months later, Princess May of Teck, his intended bride, and he and his infant son, Prince Edward, are now in the line of succession. The Prince of Wales's eldest daughter, Princess Louise, married, in 1889, the Duke of Fife, and has two daughters. The Princesses Victoria and Maud are still unmarried. The health of the latter is delicate.

In 1884 the two young Princes, Eddy (for that is the name by which Prince Albert Victor was known in his family) and George, were sent in an English warship to visit Australia; during their long voyage their mornings were to be passed in studies bearing on Australia and the colonies. Here is an extract from one of Prince George's letters, giving an account of a visit they paid to an Australian proprietor:

"Some of us," he writes, "went on horseback, some in carriages. The first night we slept nine in one room. In the first half hour after reaching our destination Eddy killed two kangaroos, and I three. These creatures are so numerous that, though their fur would be valuable, hunters only cut off their tails, which make admirable soup, and which are sold for a few pence. Kangaroos have great difficulty in turning round; for this reason they never try to shun those who attack them, but rush upon them; and in this way many make their escape through the broken ranks of the hunters. They devour the grass needed for the sheep. On the estate where we were (about twenty-five thousand acres) four thousand were killed last year. We took one alive, and a baby kangaroo from its mother's pocket. When not at full speed, they use their tails as a lever. There are other animals of the same species, smaller, and using their tails differently from the kangaroo."

The next child of the Queen was the one who was most beloved by the English nation, Princess Alice Maud Mary, Grand-Duchess of Hesse-Darmstadt. From her earliest childhood she enjoyed popularity even greater than that bestowed on other members of her royal house; and after the death of her father she was invested in English eyes with even a more tender interest. She was with her father in his latest hours; she comforted and supported her mother in the first dark days of her affliction; and she watched beside her brother's sick-bed even when she had husband and children of her own. Her Life and Letters, published in German, and translated by her sister, the Princess Helena, is a book to touch all hearts, and was read eagerly when it came out, in 1884.

Alice herself, speaking of the day of the Duchess of Kent's death, writes to her mother:—

"From that day dated the commencement of so much grief, so much sorrow; but in those days you had one, dearest mamma, whose first and deepest thought was to comfort and help you, and I saw and understood only then how he watched over you! I see his dear face, so tearful and so pale, when he led me to you early that morning, and said, 'Comfort mamma;' as if these words were a presage of what was to come. In those days I think he knew how deep my love was for you, and that as long as I was left in my home, my first and only thought should be you and you alone. This I held as my holiest and dearest duty, till I had to leave you, my beloved mother. But that bond of love, though I can no longer be near you, is as strong as ever."[64]

For the first few days after her father's death Princess Alice took everything into her own hands, to save the Queen even communications with the Government and the household. "She is our Angel in the House," wrote one of the ladies-in-waiting.

She had been engaged some months before her father's death to Prince Louis of Hesse, the future Grand-Duke of Darmstadt. The marriage was celebrated quietly at Osborne July 1, 1862.

The world never learned to regard Prince Louis with entire admiration, but his wife adored him. "You tell me to speak of my happiness—*our* happiness," she writes to the Queen. "If I say I love my dear husband, that is scarcely enough. It is a love and esteem which increases daily. What was life before, to what it has become to me now?"[65]

There is no need to dwell upon the life she found so happy. The young people were very poor for their position, and Princess Alice's life was a combination of the Princess and the house-mother who pulls hard at both ends of her income to make them meet. She was interested in art, in literature, and in learned men. At one time Strauss almost led her away from the faith of her girlhood; but she was saved by fresh experience of her need of a personal God and Saviour, in hours of anxiety and sorrow. Her especial mission she considered to be the improvement of the condition of women. Sanitary matters also claimed her attention. Alas! that her cares had not extended in this matter to the Ducal Palace at Darmstadt.

In the Prusso-Austrian war of 1866, and in the Franco-Prussian war of 1870, she founded the Woman's Union, to assist in nursing and relieving soldiers in time of war, and in peace to train nurses and assist in hospitals. All sorts of other benevolent institutions she established,—schools for idiots, kindergartens, societies for the employment of women. She went herself among the poor in their own houses, and she was the most devoted and untiring of mothers. She did too much, for she was rarely well. It pains us to hear her say: " I have made all the summer outwalking dresses, seven in number,—not embroidered, but made from beginning to end; likewise the new necessary flannel shawls for the expected. I manage all the nursery accounts and everything myself, which gives me plenty to do."[66]

In the war of 1866 Prince Louis served with the Austrian army against Prussia. In 1870 he was on the Prussian side in the army corps of his wife's brother-in-law.

A terrible sorrow to Princess Alice was

the fall out of a window in June, 1873, of her little boy Fritz, while looking at a military procession. The child's death took place, as it were, in his mother's presence. In reference to it she quotes some lines from a German poet.

"Now unto you the Lord has done
That which we wished to do;
We would have trained you up,—
and now 'tis we are trained by you.

"With grief and tears, O children,
Do you your parents train,
And lure us on and up to you,
To meet in Heaven again."[67]

The loss of little Fritz was terribly felt by Ernest, his next brother. Their mother writes to their grandmother:—

"Yesterday Ernie was telling his nurse that I was going to plant some Spanish chestnuts, and she said, 'Oh, I shall be dead and gone before they are big' Ernie burst out crying, and said, 'No! you must not die alone; I don't like people to die alone We must all die together.' It is the remaining behind the loss, the missing of the dear ones, that is the cruel thing to bear. Only time can teach one *that*, and resignation to a higher will."

They came near all fulfilling little Ernie's wish, and dying together. Prince Louis became Grand-Duke of Darmstadt, and the Grand-Ducal Palace, like most medieval buildings, was ill-drained. The children and their father sickened with diphtheria. The mother nursed them with unresting devotion. One little darling died. The mother in her agony kissed the face of her dying child, and took the in-

fection. She was too run down by nursing and hard work to recover. She died December 14, 1878,—the anniversary of her father's death, seventeen years before.

The Queen has considered herself the mother of her orphaned children, and has arranged their marriages. Ernest has succeeded his father as Grand-Duke, and is unmarried. The eldest daughter, Princess Victoria, has married her morganatic cousin, Prince Louis of Battenberg. Princess Elizabeth has married the Grand-Duke Sergius of Russia, and is beloved by the imperial family, and unhappy in her husband. Princess Irene, the third sister, has married Prince Henry of Prussia; and Princess Alix is not yet married.

Queen Victoria's fourth child was Prince Alfred, the Duke of Edinburgh, who, on the recent death of his uncle, his father's brother, became the reigning Duke of Saxe-Coburg-Gotha. In England he is Admiral of the Fleet. He must be a man of courage, for in 1883 he was conspicuous at the dangerous ceremony of the coronation of the Emperor Alexander III of Russia. He had married the Grand-Duchess Marie, sister of the Emperor, and only daughter of Alexander H.; for English law permits the marriage of one of the royal family with a member of the Greek Church, though not with a Roman Catholic. The Prince is said to have great skill as a musician; but he and his sister, the Princess Christian, seem to be less known to the public than any of their family. He and his wife have one son and four daughters,—Prince Alfred, now twenty years old; Princess Marie, wife to Prince Ferdinand, heir-presumptive to the throne of Roumania; Princess Victoria Melita, married recently to a Prince of Hohenzollern-Sigmaringen; and Princesses Alexandra and Beatrice, who are still in the schoolroom. Their mother, the Grand-Duchess, is said to care little for gayety, but to be stately, reserved, and melancholy,—which is not surprising in a member of the Russian imperial family, for all her relations walk in dread of dynamite. Nor is she exempt from danger. A few years since, the Russian consul at Malta, an unsuspected Nihilist, was instrumental in putting an explosive into her box at the opera.

Princess Helena—or, as she is now called, Princess Christian—is an admirable translator, and must be a very sensible woman, judging by what she writes, which is always in the best taste possible. She is evidently the darling of her sisters, and was her mother's secretary, companion, and daughter at home after the departure of the Princess Alice. Rumor says that Prince Christian was brought to the Queen's notice by her seeing him much affected at the unveiling of a statue of the Prince Consort, and that this led to her thinking of him as a suitor for her daughter; besides, she wanted a husband for her Helena ("Lenchen" her family call her) who would not take her from England. The Prince of Wales opposed the marriage, one of his reasons being that Prince Christian was of the branch of the royal family of Denmark opposed to that of the reigning family, to which Princess Alexandra belongs. Princess Christian is a somewhat elderly man, and has never been a great favorite in England, though the

ready good-nature of his wife makes her extremely popular. She presides at numberless fancy bazaars and other charitable associations. They were married in 1866, and have two sons and two daughters; one of the latter, Princess Louise, was married in 1891 to Prince Aribert of Anhalt.

Princess Louise, the next daughter of Queen Victoria, was married in March, 1871, to John, Marquis of Lorne, eldest son of the Duke of Argyll. The Queen was very fond of the Duchess of Argyll, and it is said that the two mothers planned the match when the Marquis and the Princess were both children. In the Queen's book on their family life in the Highlands she relates the courtship, and "how Louise came and told her of her engagement, and of Lorne's expressions of devotion to her." The match was immensely popular in England. Archibald Forbes relates how, when he rode into Paris after the siege in 1871, the first question of all the English he met was, "Is the Princess Louise married?"

The marriage has been childless; nor does the Marquis (heir to the most distinguished name in Scotland) seem to have fulfilled the extravagant expectations some people had formed of him. He and the Princess went out to Canada, the Marquis being appointed Governor-General. But his administration was not successful; nor does the Princess seem to have adapted herself to Canadian ways.

The Princess Louise is an especial patroness of art needlework and the South Kensington Museum. Her face is distinguished by its fine intellectual profile, and her figure for its graceful pose. "The Princess is exceedingly sympathetic, merry, and light-hearted," writes Mr. Motley in 1877. "She has decided artistic talents,—draws, paints, and models, and does your likeness in a few sittings very successfully. Nobody could be a kinder or more graceful hostess."[68]

Prince Arthur William Patrick, Duke of Connaught, was "a dear, bright little fellow" in his baby days, and godson and namesake of the Duke of Wellington,—as charming a compliment as ever was paid to a subject by a sovereign. He is a general in the English army, and has been in command of the camp at Aldershot. He married the Princess Louise Marguerite, daughter of Prince Frederick Charles of Prussia,—the Red Prince, who won renown next to Von Moltke in the Seven Weeks' War and the Franco-Prussian campaigns. They were married in 1879, and have three children. The Prince's name and title led to the conclusion that it was hoped to associate him with the government and pacification of Ireland; but the post has proved too difficult, and the design too hopeless, for any administration to put the lord-lieutenancy into his hands.

In 1882, the Duke was in Egypt with General Sir Garnet Wolseley, and at the battle of Tel-el-Kebir fought against Arabi Pasha, heading a brigade of the Guards in the night march and assault on a very strong position.

The Queen, who was at Balmoral, knew the battle was impending, and she wrote in her Journal:—

"How anxious we felt I cannot say, but we tried not to give way. I prayed earnestly for my darling child, and longed for the morrow to arrive. Read Körner's beautiful 'Prayer before the Battle,'—'Father, I call

on Thee.' My beloved husband used to sing it often. My thoughts were entirely fixed on Egypt and the coming battle. My nerves were strained to such a pitch by the intensity of my anxiety and suspense that they seemed to feel as if they were all alive."

At last came a telegram announcing the victory, with a postscript from Sir Garnet:—

"Duke of Connaught is well. Behaved admirably, leading his brigade to the attack."

"I carried it," says the Queen, "to Beatrice, where Louischen [the Duchess of Connaught] was, and I showed it to her, embracing her warmly, saying what joy and pride and sense of thankfulness it was to know our darling safe, and so much praised."

Queen Victoria's eighth child was Prince Leopold, on whom was conferred the ever-unlucky title of Duke of Albany. He was delicate from his birth, in a manner that made the smallest wound or scratch a serious matter. He lived almost entirely under the care of Colonel Grey, and the English public believed that in disposition and turn of thought he was the one of the Queen's sons who most resembled his father.

At one time there was some talk of his taking orders. He was known to the public by his excellent speeches, and he was frequently called upon to make them on occasions of public interest.

He went to Oxford, though his health had prevented his going, as he wished, to Eton. He was forever cut off from the sports and athletic exercises of other young men, in which he took great interest, and of which he seemed extremely fond. During all his short life he associated as much as possible with "great men,— men of renown." Mr. Ruskin[69] was fond of him; and Prince Leopold said that he had "never looked up with such reverence to any man as he did to Ruskin."

In 1879, he moved his personal establishment to Claremont, a house always associated with sorrow. He was a loving brother to his sisters, and a tender uncle to his orphaned nieces at Darmstadt. In 1882, he married Princess Helen of Waldeck, a lady gentle, good, and gracious, who since her own widowhood has filled the place of a daughter to the widowed Queen.

Prince Leopold had been somewhat out of health in 1884, and went to Cannes, a place he was fond of, to recover. At Cannes, in his boyhood, he had had a strange psychological experience, and it is probable that this was repeated, for a friend says:—

"The Duke, two days before his death, *would* talk to me of death, and said he would like a military funeral. In fact, I had great difficulty in getting him off that subject. At last I asked him why he talked on this matter. He was interrupted at the moment, but said: 'I will tell you later.' I never saw him to speak to again, but he finished his answer to me to another lady. 'For two nights,' he said, 'Princess Alice has appeared to me in my dreams, and says she is quite happy, and wants me to come and join her. That is what makes me so thoughtful.'"[70]

He went out that night alone, without, as usual, a gentleman in attendance. Returning, he stumbled on the marble steps of the hotel, owing, it is believed, to vertigo or apoplexy, and fell, injuring his head.

He died in a few hours.

He left a little daughter, and had a posthumous son.

The youngest of the Queen's children is Princess Beatrice, now thirty-seven years of age. Her face is full of character. "Baby" they long called her in her home circle, and the family letters and journals are full of her sweet baby ways and little accomplishments.

She grew up to be her mother's especial companion, absorbed in all the joys, cares, and sorrows of the Queen. The world said there was an attachment between Princess Beatrice and the Prince Imperial, and the story appears to have some color, from entries concerning the sad tragedy of his death in her mother's Journal. It was also said that the Queen was anxious that Princess Beatrice should be the second wife of the widowed husband of Princess Alice; and with that view used her personal influence to get the bill permitting marriage with a deceased wife's sister to pass through Parliament. Meantime the Duke of Darmstadt had formed other views; he desired to contract a morganatic marriage with Madame Kolémine, the divorced wife of a Russian diplomatist. This marriage the Queen broke off, considering it an insult to the memory of her daughter; and, although the Grand Duke had been married to Madame Kolémine, he was divorced from her in the Hessian courts.

Princess Beatrice is a charming artist, and once published a beautiful birthday book, illustrated by her own drawings. She loves bric-à-brac, old lace, and such matters, and says of herself she could find it in her heart to have as many gowns as Queen Elizabeth. Some one who saw her with her mother a few years since in the little church at Aix said that her care of that dear mother made a pretty picture. "She seemed to be listening, watching, breathing for the Queen; not in a fussy, irritating manner; but with the most genuine consideration she would steal her hand into that of her mother, hand her a fan, pull up her shawl, give her a cordial little smile."[71]

Princess Beatrice has married Prince Henry of Battenberg, who is handsome and well educated. Before his marriage he was an officer in a Prussian regiment, with only slender pay. But the marriage was celebrated with much pomp in July, 1885, the young Princesses of Wales then making their first appearance in public as their aunt's bridesmaids; together with Princess Irene of Hesse, who has since married Prince Henry of Prussia. By the way, there must be considerable fraternal affection between this Prussian Prince and his eccentric brother the Emperor, for the Prince, when his first child was born at Kiel, held him up at once to the telephone, that his voice might be heard at Potsdam by his imperial uncle.

Princess Beatrice and Prince Henry of Battenberg have three sons and a daughter. The Princess and the widowed Duchess of Albany take turns in living with the Queen.

At the Jubilee on June 21, 1887, the Queen, as she sat in regal state to receive the homage of her children and grandchildren on that spot where she assumed her royal robes fifty years before, must have been a touching sight to all beholders. Long and blameless has been her reign, marked on her own part by rare tact and self-denial.

Queen Victoria alone of English queens regnant has been a mother and a queen at the same time. Elizabeth, Mary Tudor, and the second Mary were childless. Queen Anne had had the misfortune to lose all her children before she ascended the throne.

From *The Prince Incognito* (1902)

Rinaldo, a Catholic nobleman, and the Protestant narrator, Antoinine, fall in love; due to prohibitions against mixed marriages in France, they are secretly married. They resolve to escape to the New World, where they hope to find greater religious tolerance. Antoinine disguises herself as a young man and convinces the captain of the Sainte Luce, which is headed for the Caribbean, to take her on as his cabin boy.

Chapter IX

Only a Plank Between Death and Paradise

We were a week at sea, tossing cruelly in the Bay of Biscay, and the captain kept his unwelcome passenger closely confined in her cabin. What account he gave of me to his sailors I do not know. With me he was distant, shy, and silent, refusing to let me render him any services, and apparently avoiding me. Finally we made the harbor of La Rochelle, with its lighthouses and its long mole.

Hardly had the brig anchored before, through a porthole of the stateroom, in which I may say the captain kept me confined, I saw a boat approaching. Two persons, apparently men of quality, were in the stern sheets. One—oh, rapture!—was my husband, well, free, and debonair; the other was my honored father, looking careworn and severe. I turned from the porthole, and was about to rush into the cabin and thence up on deck, when I found myself intercepted by the Scotch captain.

"I see him! I see my husband, the Comte de Tarnaud; I see my father with him," I cried; "they are coming on board. Captain, I must meet them!"

He stopped me. "For many reasons—for every reason, madame—I cannot suffer you to go on deck," he said. "Allowing that you have been married with your father's consent, as you say, by a Protestant ceremony, do you not know that that consent entails, according to the King's edict of May, 1725, the penalty of death upon the parent who gave it to you? This being so in any ordinary case of a forbidden marriage, I know not what it might be in yours. It would probably involve all concerned in it—nay, even myself, if I aided and abetted it—in pains, penalties, and imprisonment. In any event, the scandal must be great. You will suffer for your fault, and I fear that others may suffer too. You must remain in the stateroom that I have given up to you, until I take' the pleasure of these gentlemen and know more than I do."

"Then give the Comte de Tarnaud," I said, "this ring, and tell him that the person to whom he sent it is waiting for him in this cabin."

Oh, minutes that seemed years! I had wrapped myself in my cloak. I could not bear that they should see me in the dress I wore, even though my own mother had so disguised herself in order that she might the more safely rejoin her husband. But every thought of myself, of my dress, of what impression I might make in it vanished when I heard a hurried step on the companion ladder. The door of the cabin was opened quickly, yet as quickly closed. Rinaldo stood before me. Running to him, I threw my arms about his neck. It was the first time I had embraced him. He pressed me passionately to his heart. But even in that moment of exquisite happiness, he took the precaution of drawing me back into my stateroom.

"My brave, brave Antoinine! My wife! my love! my treasure!" No words but incoherencies of love and longing would come.

At last I said, "My father is with you; I must go to him."

"Hush, hush!" he said; "not for the world. Your appearance would compromise him and would send me to the Bastille. He is safe, and is going on a mission to his people in England and Holland. He has secured the favor of the King. Your appearance would ruin him. Be easy, Antoinine, about your father. My brave, brave Antoinine, who has not shrunk even from this disguise to join her husband! And how lovely she looks, my sailor-boy, with her short, golden-brown curls! What shall I call her? Antoine?"

"I shipped as Antoine Rhodez," I replied. "O husband, now I must tell you everything!"

"Not now," he cried. "I shall come on board to-night, and we shall have whole days and nights of sweetest intercourse during our long voyage. I was dreading its dreariness. I hardly hoped—and now all will be the fulfilment of our dreams. We shall land on our Enchanted Island—but farewell! Keep close within your stateroom until the ship sails, when I shall join you. Beware that your father does not see you."

"O Rinaldo!" I exclaimed, "ask him, at least, to send me his paternal blessing.

Give him, I entreat you, his daughter's fondest love."

"No, sweet, for I want all her love myself. But I will do anything she can in reason ask of me." I need not tell how his kisses were pressed with frantic warmth upon my lips, and hands, and forehead. He was gone, and I was left with a beating heart to wait for his return.

Soon I saw the boat put back again to the shore; the boat that carried all I loved. Joy was sparkling in the eyes of my Rinaldo. They had gone ashore to make some final preparations. When the last moment came and they were ready to depart, the good woman, proprietress of the rooms in which they had had their lodging, asked what was to be done with the furniture. "I had forgotten all about it," said my husband. "Keep it. Keep it to remember me by."

My father saw his charge mount up the side of the *Sainte Luce*, and felt that his responsibility was at an end. He saw the brig weigh anchor, little guessing with what willingness the Comte de Tarnaud was going into exile, or who was his companion. By morning we were some miles out to sea, and we calculated that my father must be several leagues upon the road to Sceaux, whither he would be hastening to make a satisfactory report to the Duc de Penthièvre. Then the cabin of the little brig *Sainte Luce* became to us a floating paradise. My husband, and the presence of my father, had in some way satisfied the scruples of the captain. The Count may have shown him the marriage contract which, I forgot to say, had been drawn up on the night of our betrothal, in the presence of M. Théophile and the old hosier of Montauban, with Martin and Justine as additional witnesses. "Ye are married sure enough by good Scots law, and by a minister of the Gospel," said the good man; "but what the French King and his Papist Court may say of it I do not know. The edicts which I keep in my locker here, that I may not run foul of them, seeing as how I am myself a Protestant, are very strict and explicit about Protestant marriages. And yours is an aggravated case, as you cannot but know. What I fear may come of it, my lord, to one or both of you, I would not care to say."

Though evidently not at ease concerning us, he may have felt that he could not interfere further. We were left to do what we pleased, except that he insisted that no suspicion of my sex should reach his crew. He stipulated that I must maintain my character as a cabin boy whom he had engaged at Bordeaux to wait upon the expected passenger.

I acquiesced with great reluctance, but my husband only laughed, saying that in any dress I was beautiful, but that he looked forward to days when he would see me in satins and jewels, a great lady, admired by all eyes.

"Oh no, Rinaldo," I replied, "I only wish to live with you under cottonwoods and palm trees, and to spend my life in waiting upon you!"

And yet there were moments—for I was a woman—when my vision of the future changed, and, gazing down upon my hateful dress, I complacently imagined myself Madame la Comtesse, clad in rich raiment, doing honor to my husband by receiving admiration and laying at his feet all tributes paid by other men to my beauty and grace. Ah, how different from the prospect that opened before me on that now far-off night, when I contemplated my fate as the servile adopted daughter of the old hosier at Montauban! A thrill of gratitude passed through me, awakening new love in my heart, as I thought what I had been saved from by the man who had so generously stooped to love me and exalt me. Oh, days of early love, when every joy shone with a double brightness; when self—love was no longer selfishness, but had become a keen appreciation of myself because I had become so dear and priceless to my husband—the husband whose praise was worth more to me than that of the whole world besides!

Those weeks on board the *Sainte Luce* were to me—to both of us, I think—that time of entire enjoyment which, even if brief, must form some part of love. All the experiences of life were as new to me as love itself; and my husband had not fully ripened into manhood. In all those glorious days of unmarred contentment there was growing more and more in both our hearts the feeling that he was mine, and I was his—body, soul, and heart; his in mind, will, hopes, and aspirations. Men are so masterful; women are so happy to resign everything in the rapture of knowing themselves to be beloved! Happiness seemed to enfold us in those days. We lived only in the present. The past and the future lay beyond our horizon. Sometimes we sat in silence, with full hearts beating in unison. Sometimes we quoted Tasso, and applied his descriptions to the island paradise in which we meant to dwell. Sometimes he was boyish, playful, witty, gay. Mere nothings would breed mirth, because we were so happy. With what pleasure I rendered him small services, under pretense that they served to keep up my disguise! Most often, however, we talked of our Enchanted Island, which the *Sainte Luce* was nearing day by day. It was an isle to which he who has quitted it longs ever to return. At least, Rinaldo told me that that was implied in the name given to it by its earlier inhabitants. We talked of its sweet air and its green hills and green valleys, in happy contrast with the close, dark cabin where we were stowed most of our time. We pictured years to come, in our home, as we conceived it, with its tender ties. "I for thee, and thou for me," he said, "and all things that surround us will be parts of ourselves, of our love, and of each other."

There was only one disappointment, but my husband assured me it was not material. The captain one day told us that he could not land us on any Protestant island to obtain the ratification of our desert marriage. "And even if your marriage were so ratified," he said, in his Scotch French, "it would only expose you, if you were imprudent enough to assert it, to the most terrible penalties of the French law." Here he pulled out from his locker his copy of the King's edicts of May, 1724.

"This paper begins," he said, "with preachers. 'All Protestant preachers are guilty of death. Every man or woman who may hear them preach, harbor them, or hold any communication with them, goes—if a man, to the galleys for life; if a woman, for the rest of her days to Aigues Morte, where is a castle on the seacoast set apart for the punishment of Huguenot women. Children are to be baptized and educated as Roman Catholics. If not, the penalties for the parents are the same. Sick persons who refuse the Catholic sacraments are to be prosecuted if they recover. No Protestant can be a physician, surgeon, apothecary, midwife, bookseller, or counsellor-at-law,' *et cetera*. Ah! here we come to it. Here is what His Most Christian Majesty has to say on marriage: 'We forbid all our subjects, of any condition or quality whatsoever, to consent or approve that their children, or any who may have been placed under their ward or guardianship, shall marry a Protestant in foreign parts, without obtaining our permission, under any pretext whatsoever. The penalty in such cases is the galleys, or imprisonment, and confiscation of half the estate of such parent or guardian.' This ordinance, you will observe, may be put in operation even in Martinique, which is part of the French King's dominions. You, madame, by living in strict seclusion and concealing your sex carefully, may escape. But the time must come when his lordship will return to his hereditary duties—"

"No, no!" I cried, "we will always cling to each other!"

"Be it then at your peril," said the captain. "But it is my duty to inform you that there are no Protestant islands at the present time on which I could land you. England is leagued with Austria, and is at war with the French King."

The captain was not always stern and silent. The geniality of my husband awoke in him the genial nature of a sailor. Often he would sit beside us and talk. He told us chiefly of his own adventures, or stories of adventure he had picked up as he sailed from port to port on his trading voyages. In this way we came one day to talk of the Dutch settlement on the island of Manhattan, and of the Dutch West India Company, which had been very powerful at one time in the western seas.

"People, when I was there ten years ago," he said, "were still talking of the wonderful escape of a young Bohemian gentleman, whose family had shared the fortunes of Elizabeth Stuart and the King of Bohemia, her husband, when they were driven into exile in 1620, and were followed by thirty thousand Protestants, their subjects of all classes, who chose expatriation rather than submit to Popish rule. This gentleman, Augustine Herman, was born in exile. He early entered into the service of the Dutch West India Company. He acquired considerable property upon Manhattan Island, and was a prosperous man, when he mortally offended Peter Stuyvesant, the one-legged Governor, by refusing to give him up a noble Barbary horse which he had rescued from a Spanish troop ship that went ashore in Delaware Bay. The fury of the Governor was great when Herman went over into the rival province of Maryland and became a close friend of the Lord Proprietary, who gave him a large tract of land, which he named Bohemia Manor.

"The Lord Proprietary of Maryland, having occasion to send a confidential agent to Manhattan, selected Augustine Herman for that mission, disregarding his outlawry by the irate old Governor, who ruled over the small city then called Nieuw Amsterdam. But the Governor's wrath burned fiercely against Herman, and no sooner had he got his enemy into his power than he clapped him into an underground dungeon, erected a scaffold on the parade ground of the fort, and appointed the next day for his execution. That morning, however, the Governor received news which obliged him to take all his boats, and as many men as could be spared from the fort garrison, down the bay, to avert a threatened danger. The wife of the tyrannical old Governor was a kind, good woman. She had known Herman in his prosperous days upon the island. She sent him food and wine from her own table, and a message, earnestly asking if there was any kindness she could do for him.

"Herman had drawn his table under a slit high up in the wall of his dungeon, which let in light and air, and standing upon it, his eyes were on a level with the turf of the parade ground. Thence he watched his noble horse, which was being led round the inclosure for exercise. When the message of the Governor's wife reached him, he said: 'Do you think that generous lady could grant me permission to mount my horse and ride round the inclosure of the fort and look upon the sunlight? Ask her. But if she grant this request I hope not to bring on her the displeasure of her husband.' Half an hour afterwards Herman was led out from his prison. He mounted his gallant Barb, who rubbed his nose against his master's hand. But I am making this a long story," said the captain.

"No, no; go on; you interest us," I cried. "I dearly love a noble horse. It is one of my enthusiasms."

"Well then: From a window the Governor's wife and her maidens were looking out on the parade ground and silently weep-

ing. At first Augustine Herman rode slowly round the inclosure. The Dutch sentries at the sally port and the turnstile, and the soldiers off duty in the castle yard, stood and gazed upon his horsemanship. On either side the fort flowed a swift river— the East River on one side, on the other the Mauritius, or North River. The earthworks that surrounded the inclosure were too high for a man on foot to see over. Herman rode round the open space five times. It was not large, only three hundred feet each way. Then he put his horse into a gallop. He saw the lady of the Governor at her window, but he would not lift his hat to her.

"Suddenly there were shrieks from the women, a stir, a rush amongst the soldiers. The very sentries left their posts and ran together to one side of the courtyard. Where were Augustine Herman and his noble horse? They had flown—literally flown— over the earth wall, at a spot where Herman had perceived that the hoofs of his horse, after his desperate leap, would find the safest footing. If they fell, no one in the inclosure saw them fall. They were up and away before any spectator reached the ramparts; before the first pursuer was out of the gate the gallant horse was breasting the North River."

"What then?" I cried.

"There is little more to tell," the captain answered. "The guns of the fort summoned back the Governor, who arrived full of apprehension. He fancied Indians had attacked the fort and were massacring his garrison. He lost no time, however, in pursuing the fugitive, and hoped to head him off at a ferry which crossed the Delaware River. But Herman from a high knoll caught sight of the ferry boat drawn up on a bank, where it was guarded by Dutch soldiers. The river was smooth; the danger in crossing lay in its great breadth. Herman and his horse were half across before they were perceived by the pursuers. But the breath of the gallant horse was coming with effort and labor. His nostrils were blood-red, his eyes were blood-shot; even his delicate ears were drooping, from distress. With every word of affection Herman could think of he encouraged his brave steed.

"Two Indians pursued them in a boat. One sent an arrow whizzing on their track. It struck the gallant horse upon the neck and made a bloody furrow; but it acted as a spur to revive his drooping courage. Never had he known a goad or a whip before. Shaking his head, he roused himself to efforts which made his rider fear he might burst his gallant heart from overstrained exertion. But friends had gathered on the Maryland bank, and shots were fired at the red men, who pulled out of range. Then Herman and his horse were left to contend only with the danger of perishing from exhaustion. "Near the shore they found a current which carried them down stream, but through the instinct of the horse and the presence of mind of his rider, they crossed it obliquely, and found footing on the opposite shore. Many hands were held out to help them up the bank. When they reached the turf man and horse dropped, equally exhausted. Those on the bank, with flasks of Hollands and Jamaica rum, endeavored to revive them, but their first care was for the good horse. They washed the blood that trickled from his nostrils, and bound the wound made by the Indian's arrow. These cares seemed a forlorn hope,

yet the people persisted. After a long time the horse shivered, shook himself, and rose slowly from the grass, to be embraced with transport by his master.

"Herman was himself no mean artist. He had two pictures painted of his gallant horse lying exhausted on the shore after crossing the Delaware, and I have been told that they are now in the possession of members of his family. But," added the good captain, "has not my long yarn tired you?"

"Oh no!" I cried; and after that, as we sat together on the deck, when the sea was calm, he never wearied of telling us other tales that he had stored away in the recesses of his memory.

Chapter X

We Land on Our Enchanted Island

There came a day when the brig *Sainte Luce* lay helpless and becalmed, after we reached the tropics; a fierce and cruel sun heat down upon her; the pitch softened in her deck seams. We spent two choking, weary nights, with clear stars shining overhead, reflected out of a cloudless sky into a sea as calm, that lay below. By day the water looked stagnant; by night it sparkled with phosphorescent gleams. My head throbbed, and my soul sickened. But I had no time to think about myself; my husband was stricken down by fever. There we lay motionless, and far from help. There was no help but such as I would give him in my ignorance, or such as could be rendered by the captain, with kindly zeal, from the ship's medicine chest. No help! For had I not forgotten God? Had I left Him any place in my dreams of earthly happiness? Had I any right in my distress to plead with Him for mercy? I had all my life been bewildered by religious controversies. I had clung fast to the Protestant cause, not so much for conscience' sake as to satisfy my honor. My loyalty to my parents seemed to demand my allegiance to the faith for which they had been persecuted. I would have accepted martyrdom for Protestantism, but not, I think, in the spirit of one that dies for the Christ who died for him; it would rather have been with the enthusiasm of an obstinate patriot who will not disown his flag or adopt the cause of his enemy. And then one night there came to me the thought of the people who brought their sick to Jesus. They· asked nothing for themselves, only for those they cared for, and He healed them. Under the inspiration of this thought I prayed the first real prayer, I think, that I had ever prayed; I said aloud, beside my husband, who was lying in his berth, the Paternoster, that he might hear familiar words, in which his heart could join with mine: "Our Father Who art in Heaven,"—the Father who had all a father's feelings, and irresistible power besides! These words sank into my heart. There and then I gained my first vague glimpse of the fatherhood of God.

I had not much time for reflection. All I did and thought was by instinct and intuition. I could only cling to that idea of fatherhood, with an energy like his of old who cried : "I will not let Thee go except Thou bless me."[72] Such prayer is always answered, I believe, though not always in the way that our self-will and short-sightedness would prescribe to our Father. But since that time, when reviewing those days of pain and dread, I have realized that above Protestantism and above Catholicism lies the Christian plane, where, holding fast three cardinal ideas, true Christian hearts may always meet each other; may say together the Paternoster, the Credo, the Te Deum, and the Gloria in Excelsis. There God is, as the apostle calls Him, "the Father of all"; there Christ is the hope of all; and there the Holy Spirit is God's good gift to "all who love the Lord Jesus Christ in sincerity."

Well, what I thought in those dark days I hope has borne its fruit. Meantime the dead calm ceased; a blessed wind came floating through the shrouds. We hoisted sail. My husband revived, and after a day or two I had the happiness of attending him on deck, where I found our relation to each other changed: he was weak and dependent; I had that lot that Heaven has pointed out as the most blessed upon earth, the lot of those who serve in love. Then I appreciated why men are apt to love helpless and dependent women. Is not a sense of the dependence of the thing or person loved a part of protecting love? Has not the babe's helplessness something to do with the strong maternal passion? I anticipated my husband's every want; I hung upon his looks; his feebleness drew us closer and closer together.

We were now in latitudes where the sea becomes a wondrous blue, and Old Ocean, with his great, long, heaving swells, seems as if he were asleep and breathing peacefully. Before long we were among islands, keeping a sharp lookout for any English cruisers that might lie in wait for us upon our way. Soon we were called on deck to catch a first view of Martinique, with its long ridge of violet-tinted mountains, the backbone of the island, running its whole length from west to east, until at last its base seemed to dip into the ocean. Those peaks were hooded with clouds, but the landscape, as we approached, was one glory of greenness. There were two sharp promontories sticking out into the sea. A little village, very dark, with a tall yellow church steeple, was nestled at the foot of the hills, and long lines of surf were breaking on the beach.

"A dangerous coast," the captain said to my husband.

"Is yonder town our landing place?" we asked; and at sight of land Rinaldo seemed to have recovered his vigor and animation.

"No, my lord," (the captain always called him so; it was an English custom to acknowledge the title). "No, my lord, no ship can land her cargo on this coast; no boat of any size could live among those breakers. We are making for St. Pierre, on the other side of the island. Pray God we may fall in with no English cruisers!"

At this moment we saw a small and rough canoe pushed by two men through long lines and lines of surf. When they got it beyond the breakers, the swimmers sprang into it and came off to our vessel. The men were all but naked; their wet limbs gleamed, my husband said, like glorious antique statues of bronze. In their small boat they had fruit and vegetables. My husband bought these and distributed them to our crew. Then he threw two gold pieces into the sea, and the men dived for them. My heart trembled for terror. They came up breathless, but radiant with pride and satisfaction, holding the gold in their beautiful, gleaming white teeth.

The captain, who could speak the *patois* of the island better than pure French, questioned them. They told him that an English frigate was lying in the offing, watching for any vessel that might try to enter the harbor of St. Pierre, but they believed that we could avoid her by standing out to sea and then running, by good luck, into the Port au France, called Fort Royal, for it was the residence of the Governor of the Windward Isles, and considerable fortifications had been erected there. Guided by the information we had received from the statuesque bronze natives of Martinique, (who remained on board, apparently unconcerned by the fact that they had brought no clothes with them), we proceeded cautiously to round the northern portion of the island, keeping closely under the shadow of giant cliffs until nightfall. Dominica, an English island, was frequently visible upon our right;—to starboard, the captain called it;—but while a passenger on the *Sainte Luce* I had not familiarized myself with nautical terms. He and his crew, together with the men from Martinique, were on deck as darkness suddenly came down upon us like a dropped veil. It was the captain's purpose to weather the northern point of the island, to give St. Pierre a wide berth, and to lie off the land, out of sight of the English cruiser, until the next night, when, under protection of the darkness, he would run in for Fort Royal. By morning we were well out to sea. The peaks of Martinique, now bluish gray, lay low on the horizon; but the captain was uneasy. "Mont Pelé," he said, pointing to what seemed to be the highest peak of the long mountain range, "has taken off his nightcap. There are no clouds upon his crest. When he doffs his bonnet, we may look out for a squall."

Sure enough, the next morning, when the sun, long after dawn, climbed over the peak of Mont Pelé, gilding the long range of his attendant hills, an angry wind was rising. It was blowing, it seemed to me, from all parts of the heavens at once. Instead of the usual long, lazy swell of these tropical seas, the waves became short and irregular. At last the gale made up its mind from what quarter it would attack us; it came howling out of the northwest with a sudden squall of rain, and a rattling accompaniment of distant thunder. Wind and rain soon beat the waves down flat, but there was still a heavy swell.

We were ordered below at once. Before we could get down the companion, the course was changed. The waves once more rose high. The brig was on her beam ends. She righted, however, and was then driven before the gale straight back on the island of Martinique. There was no fear now of the English cruiser; our thoughts were occupied with our fight against the wind and the sea. In such a gale, with the wind in our enemy's teeth, we knew she would not dare to chase or capture us.

Once or twice my husband, impatient at being sent below, made his way up the companion stairs, opened the door a little way, and looked out. He saw the captain, with his speaking trumpet in one hand while with the other he clung to a stanchion, blinded by the spray and unable to move because of the excessive roll of the vessel; and all around, as far as the eye could reach, there was a wild, white sea. In order to right

the brig, when she fell into a trough between two waves, they had had to cut away one of her masts, and she was now driving before the gale under a solitary foresail.

"We have run past both St. Pierre and Fort Royal," the captain said, when, during a momentary lull, he came down into the cabin, shaking his cap and wringing his wet hair.

I had made ready a stiff glass of grog for the captain. Such little services I had taken on myself, as well as all the duties of a valet to my husband, in order to keep up my disguise. I brought him the glass, steadying myself against the cleated table, but as the captain took it from my hand, a roll of the ship sent me spinning across the cabin. Our lamps went out, and as the sailors had long before put in the dead lights, we were in total darkness. My husband picked me up, and I lay passive in his arms.

"Keep here. Don't think of trying to look out; you could see nothing," said the captain. "Both sea and sky are all white scud and spray. We have man ropes across the deck, without which even the oldest sailor could not keep his sea legs." And then he added reverently, "While we men do men's work, do you, madame, do that of a woman. You may do more for us than we for you. Pray."

As he spoke we heard the swash of a great wave as it broke over the brig's bows, carrying everything before it. The captain returned quickly to his post. In spite of his prohibition, my husband, before long, grew impatient of the darkness. We could not find the tinder box, which in some lurch of the ship had rolled away. Rinaldo could not resist the impulse to look again on Heaven's light and watch the contest between seamanship and the sea. He crept cautiously up the companion stairs, and I, holding fast with one hand to the skirts of his coat, crept up after him.

The sea seemed white, it was so full of scud. Far as the eye could reach the gleaming crests of the waves were rising and falling. As we looked, a heavy sea took the brig right on her side, or, as sailors call it, on her quarter, and then came a rush of water which poured down upon us; and, though my husband, with all his strength, hastened to close the door which opened from the deck, I thought for a moment that we should have been drowned together in the cabin. The wave had washed a boat into the sea. We caught sight of it for a moment, floating keel upwards, driven before the storm. All this time we had been running in upon the land, and now the southern point of Martinique, the Cap du Rochet, lay about three miles away. Either we must drive before the gale right on the rocks that there rose out of deep water, or we must try to weather that high point of land.

My husband grew too anxious to be controlled. Again he went up the companion. Again, too, I crept after him. The captain stood just under the poop deck, his white hair blowing forward, his trumpet to his lips, one hand over his eyes. He was giving orders to make a last attempt to spread more sail. The ship, I heard them say, was leaking in many places; we heard water swashing furiously in her hold. The noises of the ship were as terrible to me as the motion or the tempest—the groaning of her timbers, the creaking of her cordage, the swish of the water deep down in her bowels, combined with the rhythmic

uproar made by the bursting of the surf upon the rocky shore. But there was little or no sound of human voices; the sense of danger, the nearness of approaching death, kept the men silent.

I cannot describe all that was done to avert our fate. I saw little of what passed on deck, and had I seen all I should not have been able to understand it. We weathered Cap du Rochet, thanks to the captain's seamanship; but then the wind suddenly changed. We had hoped that, blowing from the northwest, its force might have been broken by the intervening range of high hills; but just as we were round the cape it seemed to have gone half round the compass, and was now blowing a steady southerly gale. The brig, almost water-logged, would not obey her helm; she drove along furiously, speeding to her doom; no efforts could now keep her from running straight upon the long black beach that stretched between the cape they called Croche Mort and the Pointe du Rochet.

All impressions of the perils we had safely passed seemed wiped out from our memory, as we contemplated our fate, which was now inevitable. The only thing that could be done was to maneuver, so that the brig should go ashore sideways (if I may so express myself), thereby leaving some chance that expert swimmers through the surf might have the advantage, for a few strokes at least, of being under her lee. All the land before us was in shadow. The sun speedily would disappear over the crest of the hills. Did I say that our last mast went overboard as we rounded Cap du Rochet, and that the bowsprit had broken short off at the bows? All that could be done had been done. We had now only to await the final shock. Ever since rounding the Pointe du Rochet we had seen people running along the beach to watch what would happen to the *Sainte Luce*; for to help us was impossible. Each wave seemed literally to bear down upon us high and steep, green as a hill in spring-time. Long rollers followed each other in swift succession, breaking with hiss and roar along the beach. Seven were the lines of foam, each succeeding another.

We struck where the second roller lifted its crest, and there were five other rollers between us and the shore. The brig had cleared the first one, quivering until the stumps of her masts seemed as if they would shake themselves out of her. She hung trembling on the verge of the second wave, then the water toppled over. She was borne down, and struck, the shock sending every man on deck off his feet, and flinging us, who were in the companion way, back into the cabin. The next wave seemed to lift up the brig's stern for a moment, then she pounded down a second time, happily not on rocks, but on a sandy bottom. The breakers rolled higher, it seemed to us, than where the main yard would have been, had any yards been spared to us, casting their green shadow over our deck, then breaking and bursting over our brig when she was helpless, no longer able to get out of their way. She began to go to pieces.

My husband and I clung to each other. There, full in sight, but with death and all eternity between ourselves and it, lay the Enchanted Island of our dreams, its slopes ascending to the clouds and bright with the shimmering green of its cane fields, its feathered palms, its mango trees, its cocoa-nuts and silk cottonwoods; while between all this and us lay, as I said, five roaring ridges of white surf, lashed into fury by the storm, breaking in foam upon the beach, which was like a sharp black line drawn between the green of the fields ashore and the terrible white breakers. Overhead the clouds were breaking up into fleecy white masses, with blue patches of sky between them; while in the distance the sea lay blue as indigo, with foamy whitecaps sparkling and tossing on its higher ridges.

I noted all these things in what I believed would be my last long sight of God's good sea and earth and sky, while I clung to my husband's breast, my arms around his neck, my head upon his shoulder. At this supreme moment came to him a reminiscence of the first days of our young affection. He whispered in my ear, "Sofronia and Olindo,"[73] and repeated in Italian:

> "Thus closely linked, pressd face to face we stand.
> Thus, and not thus, I hoped—"

Here a great wave surged over us. He never finished the quotation. Yes, we stood helpless, clinging to each other. Again I was a woman though still in my boy's dress. We were husband and wife for yet a few moments, at the last. If any of the crew now chanced to notice us, what did it matter? When we should be washed up on the beach all men would know our secret. All earthly anxieties had dropped away from me; I was waiting for the end that was at hand.

Suddenly I saw black objects bobbing in the surf. They were the heads of our two

Martinique swimmers. They had slipped off the brig's bow into the surf, carrying a line between them. It was glorious to see them dive straight through a breaker, then rise, whirled round and buffeted, but still holding fast to the rope that was to save our lives; doing battle with the sea as best they might, and after every struggle ready to repeat it with another mighty wave. One—two! They rose on the crest of the third sea, which, running forward toward the shore, and toppling over, seemed to discharge them like a burden on the beach; but ah! as if repenting of having aided their deliverance, quickly it tried to draw them back as it retreated to the sea. No! Mighty as Old Ocean has too often proved himself in his contentions with men for mastery, those gallant swimmers, half amphibious from boyhood, inferior, it may be, to men of other races except in such a struggle, did what the bravest European seaman perhaps could not have done: they mastered the wild surf; they disappointed the hungry breakers. Their friends stood watching them upon the land, with beating hearts, no doubt, but hearts that beat with hope, while we on board the floundering wreck felt scarcely any hope, but only sickening fear. The fourth breaker was shot through, and then the fifth. Then the men's feet touched the sandy bottom. Hands were held out to them, and in a few moments they stood on dry land.

A long line of islanders, women as well as men, impetuously seized the rope and hauled it up the beach to where a cluster of great palms lifted their tall plumed heads. To the stoutest of these they made it fast. Hand over hand they then drew in the slack. Our sailors paid out the brig's cable. Would it be

long enough to reach the shore? Would it be strong enough to bear the strain? Yes, thank God; the cable stretched to the black beach. Like the line, it was run up to the great palm tree, and there belayed. It stretched over the lines of roaring breakers.

A whip and a basket were rigged quickly. There was no time to be lost; the ship's timbers seemed to us to be giving way under our feet. My husband, being the passenger, went first, and I as his page and faithful servant, was clasped tightly in his arms. There was a moment's hesitation about this. The sailors tried to take me from him, fearing the frail makeshift might not bear our double weight, but he would not let them touch me. A sailor had gone astride over the rope, bearing a line. By it those on shore were drawing us along the cable. We hung over the dreadful deep. I shut my eyes. The cable trembled. I could not bear the sight of that horrible white sea.

We were safe. Many hands received us as we reached the beach. We could not understand the chatter of the gold-colored, bronze, or sable people who surrounded us. But soon a French voice welcomed us; it was that of a creole planter who had come down to the shore from a neighboring estate to lend assistance. By my husband's dress and bearing he knew him to be a man of consideration and quality. Though we knew he was speaking French, we could hardly hear his words for the loud booming of the breakers. He pointed to a light carriage, drawn by mules, and before we had collected our scattered senses we were lifted into it.

We turned our heads as the carriage started, and saw the crew of the *Sainte Luce* coming ashore, each man clinging to the cable, which sagged and swayed fearfully, but still held firm. "O my God!" cried my heart, "may it hold firm until the end! O Father in Heaven, help them to get all safe on shore!" They hung—oh! it was horrible to see them—they hung over the surf. Every wave seemed to be running after them; to be trying to catch them by the legs and drag them from the swinging cable. But by God's grace the captain the last man to quit the wreck—had but one breaker more to cross, when the ship, smitten by a wave longer than the rest, broke up with a crash that we could hear even above the general uproar. He sank into the sea, and loosened his hold upon the cable, but six or seven naked swimmers on the beach sprang into the surf, and, buffeting the waves, rescued him, just as he was being drawn back into the breakers. We saw them bringing him on shore, whether dead or alive we did not know, for the mules were by that time ascending a mountain road at a quick pace, their faces being turned to their own home.

"And I have not a louis left with which to reward our gallant deliverers," were my husband's first words. "All is lost! My papers, my money, my very identity is gone!"

"What matter? What matter?" I cried, soothing him. "It is far better than we could have hoped. We have our lives. We have our Island. We shall live here unknown and in safety. And as to the reward that you wish to give those men, I have a few gold pieces sewed in my clothes; take them, and let the men who have delivered us know that we are grateful."

Chapter XI
The Fatal Blunder

We reached the planter's house. It was five hundred feet above the sea, they told us afterwards, upon the side of the mountain; but I had no strength left to think of houses, trees, courtyards, fountains, or grand views. All that I was conscious of was the coolness of the matted hall, and the kindness of the welcome. I heard my husband desire that his page might attend him in his own chamber. There we found it hard to get rid of the various attendants who swarmed about our path and about our beds; they were men and women of all shades and tints, from glowing gold to dark bronze. The women wore colored kerchiefs for headdresses, in which yellow predominated; their dress was only a chemise, with a skirt of printed cotton. So persistent were they in their services that it seemed as if no white man on the island was expected to use his hands. As my husband said afterwards, if a man wished to commit suicide in Martinique, he would apparently be expected to allow a servant to do it for him. At last we got rid of them, even of the children, and, taking off our clothes, stiff with brine, we put on gay cotton garments called *douillettes*, familiar to me, because they owe their origin to Provence. In Martinique they are used by the whites while taking the siesta. The garment is common to both men and women, and I rejoiced to find myself enveloped in anything so feminine. As I laid aside my sailor dress, I made an exclamation implying that I would never wear it again.

"*Ma chérie*," said my husband, taking me in his arms, with tender kisses, "you must remember our situation. It is now very precarious. Be guided by me in all things; accept my counsel; be ruled by my instructions. Our position has become very difficult; it is not now as it was on the "Sainte Luce." I see dangers ahead."

"Oh, Rinaldo, now that we are safe on our own Island?" I said, as, hiding my face, I burst into tears.

"Do not weep, my wife, my treasure, my darling, the only jewel I have rescued from our wreck!" he cried. "See now; be reasonable; compose yourself. I will go with the rest as soon as supper is announced, for they have brought me some of our host's clothes. I shall then know how to be guided by circumstances. I shall see, as our good captain would say, 'the lay of the land.'"

He left me, therefore, soon after, nor did he come back till it was almost midnight. They had brought me wine and fruit. I lay on a small bed, in an immense matted room, with little furniture, but what there was was of the native satinwood, and beautifully carved. The great bed, shaped like a barge, and intended for my master, was especially elaborate in its ornamentation. On the walls of the room were engravings in carved frames, all on sacred subjects, and in one corner was a shrine, before which, as it grew dark, a servant lit a lamp and rearranged some flowers.

When my husband came back to our room I was lying awake. He seemed to me a little flushed, and in unusually high spirits; I felt aggrieved that he could be so buoyant when he knew that I had good cause to be depressed.

"*Ma chérie*," he said, as, looking round the chamber, his eyes fell on the pictures, the shrine, the flowers, and the lamp, "Martinique, it appears to me, is the most Catholic portion of His Most Christian Majesty's dominions. It is peopled with Jesuits, Dominicans, and Ursuline nuns. White fathers and black fathers have splendid convents, and own sugar estates all over the island. The people are as submissive to them as their domestic animals. This is a great missionary station for all the French West India islands. There is no persecution here because there are no heretics. There is only one Protestant besides yourself in the whole island, and he is tolerated because of his great skill in refining sugar; for the Dominican Superior who has the care of his Order's sugar estates is reported to have said that he did not care whether his sugar was Lutheran or Catholic, provided it was whiter than that made by the Jesuits. It is positively certain, my darling, that we must keep our sentiments concerning your religion to ourselves. You must bow to every shrine you pass, and not wound the prejudices of the people by showing disrespect to them."

"I can do that without hurting my conscience," I replied. "I never see on a crucifix the figure of the agonized Redeemer, without wanting to pay it some sign of reverence. But, Rinaldo, do I not act falsely when I try to lead people to believe me that which I am not—which I can never be?"

He laughed. "My dear little Rhodez, are we in any respect that which we try to seem? I am not. And still less, meseems, are you. No, little one, keep tranquil. Let us 'stand by,' as sailors say, and be ready for what next may happen. Then we will decide upon our course of action. Till then be still and silent." The next morning was bright, clear, beautiful, a radiant day. Rinaldo waked me with a kiss, and, pointing to my sailor's dress, which had been washed and dried, said persuasively:

"A little longer, dearest page."

"Oh, Rinaldo, till how long?"

"Till we find means to elude the English cruiser and can run over to one of the English islands, Curaçao, Dominica, or St. Eustache. Then I will bring back my beautiful bride to Martinique in triumph, with her hair dressed as high as Mont Pele, and her panniers, her high heels, her jewels, and her rich gowns. I shall say she is an English lady of high birth, or an Italian princess. No one will recognize in Madame la Comtesse de Tarnaud the little sailor page, who gave up his own fondest wishes to aid and pleasure his admiring master."

I did as he wished, of course, and after the morning coffee had been brought to us in our chamber, and his hair had been dressed and powdered by my hands, I followed him, at his desire, out on to the wide veranda, where he was received with almost open arms by the planter and his family. That gentleman's name was Duval Ferol. He had some small employment under Government, but was principally engaged in sugar-planting. His wife and daughters seemed to be amiable but languid ladies. Oh, how I longed to speak to one of them as one of their own sex, to receive from some other woman the advice and countenance of a friend! I was struck, struck painfully, by the high-bred ease with which my husband adapted himself at once to this refined society. Hitherto I had never seen him among those who could be con-sidered socially his equals. Could my poor attractions retain his affection now?

I sat apart, while he conversed gaily, gallantly, wittily, with the planter and his ladies, exchanging badinage and compliments as if in some Paris salon. We learned that the *Sainte Luce* had gone totally to pieces; that the whole population of the village (they called it Grande Anse) was abroad upon the beach, gathering such wreckage as might come on shore, especially provisions; for the island, which depended upon foreign ports for its supplies, was very short of food, owing to the strict blockade of its only good port, St. Pierre. Our captain and his crew, they said, had been kindly cared for in the village. The captain was in bed, having received some severe cuts and bruises.

As the day advanced, and the planter and his servants, who had been down on the beach, returned, there began to be much whispering in the family circle. Looks of curiosity followed my husband. He was treated with oppressive deference. The services of the colored servants, too importunate before, were more and more pressed upon both of us. Then they began to question me; but I could not understand their French creole *patois*. They called a white boy who spoke French, and through him they asked me a multitude of questions. They had heard, they said, from the sailors, that my master was some great personage and very rich; so rich and so generous that he had flung gold louis into the sea for Louison and Marcel to dive for. He had bought up their whole boat-load of fish and fruit, and had given it away, a free gift to the sailors. Who was he? Madame

Ferol had credit for being a genealogist. She had been searching in her memory, but in vain, for reminiscences connected with the Comte de Tarnaud. All I could tell them was that my master's father was a Field-Marshal in the allied armies of Spain and France, now serving in Italy; that he himself had served in Spain and France in the war still going on, the War of the Succession; and, when they asked me about myself, all I could answer was,—no doubt with blushing cheeks, but they did not look for blushes on a page's face,—that I was a poor sailor boy, whom the Count had met on board the ship and had taken into his service. But soon I found that every particular known about us by the crew had been told by the sailors to those who questioned them, and the result was a general conviction that the island had secured a prize in Monsieur le Comte de Tarnaud, and that his dignity and influence must be very great. I saw very little that day of my husband. I sat, to be sure, at the same table with him, but no opportunity offered itself for any private speech, and I felt lonely and unhappy. After dinner he found a moment to seize me by both hands and to exclaim: "Darling, be true to me. Be tranquil, and be silent. We are getting every moment into deeper waters, and I am not yet sure where we may land. M. Ferol tells me that, as a servant of the Government, it is his duty to report our arrival to Monsieur Nadua, his superior, a planter who lives about three leagues further into the interior. He asked me, as far as his politeness would admit, for explanations concerning myself, to be forwarded to this official. I made my answers as vague as possible; and as to what may happen to us next, we can only repeat the French saying, 'We shall see what we may see.'"

And now I was in our tropical Island. I looked down upon verdant slopes, and upward to the cloud-capped peaks of the great range. Below me was the black beach;—beyond it the white breakers, and the sea, blue as lapis lazuli. A fountain of cool waters sparkled in the courtyard; great tropical trees cast their shade over the garden; exquisite creeping plants hung like drapery from every rock; magnificent tree ferns attracted my attention; luscious fruits, to me unknown, hung from overladen branches; strange birds, insects, and reptiles were forever coming into sight, and then like lightning disappearing from my view among grass and foliage. And yet here, where I had dreamed of lifelong bliss, I found only disappointment. He who was the light of my eyes, he whose words and whose caresses were to me the breath of life, was no longer mine only. He belonged to social life, to the obligations of his position, to the people around him; whilst I, placed socially on an equality with him by marriage, I, gently born, and gently bred in the old castle in Provence, was compelled to stand aside and to look on, despised and disregarded, a menial, though relieved in part from the obligations of servitude by the customs of the place, which assigned a species of equality to all white men. I was miserable; yes, miserable. I had no one to turn to. Even God seemed very far off. I found myself weeping, as I thought with a softened heart of all those whom I had left behind me with no pangs of regret at our parting. Had any one seen me weep, which, happily, I trust that no one did, and had I been asked what I was crying for, I should have answered, "For longing to hear the voice of old Justine." Her harsh voice calling, "Mam'zelle Antoinine!" would have sounded like music. I dare say that there were kind hearts among these creole people, but their jabber I could not understand.

That evening a light carriage arrived, accompanied by two running footmen. It had been sent from the plantation of M. Nadua, the great man on the part of the island where we had landed, he being Commandant of the Valley of the Anse Marine. The footman presented a letter to my husband, addressed to him as Monsieur le Comte de Tarnaud, requesting him to change his quarters to the Commandant's house, where he would find a cordial reception. The request was a command in our position. No packing had to he done, for we had nothing. My husband, however, accepted the gift of necessary clothes and linen from M. Feral, not forgetting the douillettes of bright Indienne, in which we had been wrapped on our arrival. Then, getting into the carriage, with very kindly farewells to the family of Duval Feral, we set off for new quarters, and for new perplexities, but with no prescience of the things that were to befall us there. Circumstances had wrenched us away from all that had been second nature to us in the past. The future we could not even picture to ourselves; it was wrapped in an impenetrable mist. We did not know then that that mist would turn into a thunder cloud.

We drove away into the hills, with the two mulatto footmen running by the door of our carriage, in addition to whom M. Ferol had sent one of his own servants, who was to bring him word if the journey was accomplished in safety. We drove almost in silence, being too closely attended for much speech, each of us keeping guard over the secret thoughts whose expression might have pained the other.

The road lead us over grassy slopes, or savannas, and many times through mountain streams, for five small rivers flow down from the hills into the Grande Anse Valley; and it wound up the mountain side, which we ascended slowly. Innumerable were the little roadside shrines, with plaster images, and almost childlike offerings. We met women whose graceful walk and rounded limbs roused the admiration of my husband. They carried wooden trays upon their heads, and stepped along firmly and swiftly.

"Monsieur Ferol told me last night," my husband said, "that all commerce is conducted by these women, who are called *marchannes*. Indeed it must have been so everywhere in old times, for do not our very words *marchand* and *marchandise* come from *marcher*, to walk? These women carry weights upon their heads heavier than I could lift, and journey immense distances through these rough mountains."

Up and up we went, until we came to a lovely level plain, shut in by a primeval forest and the mountains. There stood a stately stone house, with walls of extraordinary thickness, and a long, broad piazza, supported by pillars of stone. Here we were hospitably received by Nadua, who told the Comte de Tarnaud that he had asked some friends to meet him at dinner, which would be ready after he had taken his siesta. What pleased me most was to see that the little children came up to us to be caressed, without forwardness or shyness. "With these," I thought, "I may find sympathy, or at least, companionship."

After getting rid of the servants, and having refreshed ourselves with cooling drinks, preparatory to the still more grateful refreshment of the bath and the siesta, we were disturbed by a knocking at the door of our apartment. It was the servant who had accompanied us from M. Ferol's. Being about to return to the Anse Marine, he desired to know if M. le Comte had any message for his master. The Count interpreted this to mean that the negro hoped for a gratuity from the rich gentleman, whose generosity was being vaunted in the village. He received it, and at the same time was desired to wait, while the Count, half undressed, and in haste, penned a brief note to his master. The note was a very simple one, merely thanking M. Ferol and his family for their kindness; but on it hung our fates. We little thought, as my husband put his name to it, what consequences were hanging on the words traced by his pen.

Chapter XII

An Unwelcome Welcome

The guests of M. Nadua, the Commandant, began to arrive. They were sugar planters from neighboring estates, with their daughters and their wives. They had pleasant voices, cordial manners, and that air of aristocratic ease which comes from a habit of command combined with habitual acceptance of service from inferiors.

A seat was assigned me at the lower end of the table, the custom of the island being that all white persons should eat together at one board. My husband was seated beside Madame Nadua, in the place of honor. As we were about to sit down, I observed that my husband looked about him for something that was missing. My eyes, indeed, were always fixed on him. I remembered at once that he had left his handkerchief upon the table when he had written his brief note to M. Ferol, and in my capacity as his page I believed it to be my duty to go and fetch it for him. I was absent but for a moment; but when I returned, all faces, white, yellow, and black, turned toward me in astonishment. Their deference to the personage on whom a white guest had waited was increased. I could not understand it at the time, but afterwards I learned that it was contrary to the customs of Martinique that one white person should wait upon another, and that my action had greatly confirmed the general impression that the distinguished-looking stranger wrecked upon their coast was some great personage. His account of himself was so vague and so mysterious that the whole province of Anse Marine was lost in conjectures as to who he could be. He was surely a man of rank; he was evidently a man of accomplishments and education. It was suspected that he had been sent out to the colony in some high official position.

The dinner went on. What we ate I do not know; the viands made little impression upon me. By and by the ladies left the table; I remained, not knowing what I ought to do, and fearing if I absented myself that I might compromise my husband, or that he might need me. The gentlemen drew round the punch bowl; the jokes became less choice, and the gayety grew noisier. It may have been a scene far more decorous than a Colonial convivial gathering of Englishmen at that period, but it shocked and disgusted me, a French girl, bred in Puritanism, and in decorum. What business, I asked myself, had I to be masquerading as a young man, when I should be an honored wife, one who deserved at least the respect due to a woman? How could my husband hereafter dare to introduce me as his wife and his countess, to all these men, who had seen me in my humiliation? How could I look them in the face when dressed as became my station? and how run the risk of dire discovery?

My husband was in high spirits, enjoying and promoting the general gaiety. It seemed to me that he could hardly remember my existence. I rose up silently at last, and left the table; he was talking with vivacity, and did not miss me. I went back into our bedchamber, threw myself face downward on my bed, and stifled my sobs, lest they should be heard in the veranda. My husband came in by and by, and seemed astonished to find me there, so miserable. I was thoroughly aroused to a sense of my situation. Its humiliation had suddenly burst upon me, together with the knowledge that I had only one straw or rope to cling to, and if that should fail me—if I should ever lose my husband's respect and love—

"I cannot hear it!" I said. "I cannot hear it! All the womanhood left in me cries out against this degradation. O Rinaldo, how could you expose your own wife to such jests, such ribaldry? I shall never feel that my mind is clean again. I cannot keep up this character; I cannot act this part. And if

I could, what would hereafter be the consequences? Set me free from the obligation of obedience; do something to deliver me; tell these people that I am your wife; that persecution in France drives faithful wives to these disguises. Or let me die! I am not fit to bear humiliation. I say again, set me free; do something to deliver me!"

"Then I shall walk straight into the Bastille. Dear Antoinine, be reasonable. We are in an exceptional situation, and we must both put up with exceptional things. Our position is even more exceptional and difficult than you are aware of. You will ruin me if you invite investigation. This outbreak of yours surprises me; I thought you were all patience, and submission, and devotion. My dear wife, I believed that your first thought in everything was for me, but I find you wholly occupied with interests of your own. I was mistaken."

"O Rinaldo," I cried, "my interests are your interests; wife and husband are one. What injures my honor impairs yours. Will it be for your credit if these men look scorn on me when you present me as your wife, or that their wives should draw their skirts aside when they pass by me? A woman must, in virtue of her womanhood, at all risks defend her honor; and her husband should defend it too, for it is his.

O Rinaldo, do not ask me to keep up this disguise, to go as a man among men any more for your sake. I wish I could die now; I have had my days of happiness; I think that they may never come again. Nothing can efface the pain of the last few hours."

He seemed annoyed, rather than moved, by my complaints. I had failed to awaken his pity; he was embarrassed by my behavior, and for the first time I saw him angry. He said something about making scenes; whereat I burst into fresh floods of tears, and this still further annoyed him, for he feared lest the family of M. Nadua should hear our quarrel.

All this time things that we knew not of were happening upon another plantation. About two hours after dinner a servant arrived, sent by M. Ferol, with a letter to the Commandant, to the following purpose: "You wish for information relative to the French or Italian gentleman I received into my house after the wreck; his signature will furnish more than I am able to give you. I inclose you a letter I have just received from him, and which he wrote on arriving at your plantation." My husband's letter of thanks for M. Ferol's hospitality and kindness, written in haste, was signed H. R. d'Esté, and not Comte de Tarnaud.

Immediately on receiving M. Ferol's note and its inclosure M. Nadua led aside the most trusted of his friends and consulted him as to the possible rank of his young guest, as disclosed by such a signature. The friend hastily took horse and repaired to the plantation of the Marquis d'Eragny, which was at some distance. The Marquis, with a party of guests, was still at table. The conversation was very lively when the Commandant's messenger entered the room. Each man was relating some new anecdote, fact, or conjecture concerning the young man who so strangely interested them. M. Nadua's friend lost no time in mentioning the matter of the signature. M. le Marquis d'Eragny, who prided himself on his knowledge of family genealogy, produced an almanac containing a list of the names and alliances in all royal and princely families, and in a few minutes the company ascertained that the young man in question was no other than Ercole Rinaldo d'Esté (in French, Hercule Renaud d'Esté), Hereditary Prince of Modena, born November 27, 1727; cousin, through his mother, the daughter of Philippe, the Regent Duke of Orleans, to the kings of France and Spain, and brother-in-law to the Duc de Penthièvre, the largest landed proprietor in the island.

"I have seen the Prince in Spain and Italy," cried out Captain Bois-Ferme, a connection of the Commandant, M. Nadua. "I saw him on his father's staff, not a year ago."

"And I too," said another officer. "I was in Venice when his insubordination and his mad pranks, and his adoption of ultra-revolutionary opinions were talked about by everybody. They said the Council requested him to leave the city." "Let us ride to the Commandant's house and take a look at him. A Prince incognito and revolutionary must be worth seeing," exclaimed one of the party.

"By all means," cried the others.

They mounted their horses, and reached M. Nadua's sugar plantation as we were sitting down to supper; for my husband had soothed me into compliance with his wishes, and I was with the rest of them. My husband had assured me that he would on some pretext send me away when the punch bowl made its appearance; and thus it happened that vanquished, distressed, humiliated, and miserable, I was seated again at M. Nadua's table.

The moment Captain Bois-Ferme, a redfaced, rollicking, rough soldier, was introduced to the Comte de Tarnaud he made a sign to M. Nadua, who was watching him, and another to his black servant, La Plume, whose cue it was to support any assertion of his master's, however preposterous or incredible; but he also received a nod of affirmation from the Lieutenant, who had said that he knew by sight the Prince of Modena. The new comers then sat down with us to supper.

My husband did not notice all these winks and signs, though I did, but I could not comprehend what was meant by them. The supper, which was gay before the sudden coming of these guests, was now constrained and silent.

It seemed to me as if some of the party were on the watch for something. Suddenly there came from the courtyard a blare of bugles, with an accompaniment of hideous negro drums. There was a small detachment of French soldiers stationed in these hills, and they had been ordered out by a message from their captain, sent them by La Plume. The bugles were blown by Frenchmen; the drums were barbaric instruments thumped by slaves from the plantations.

When the charivari ceased, all the officers rose from their seats, with wine cups in their hands, and so did M. Nadua. With a shout that seemed to me to rend the air, they drank to His Highness Hercule Renaud d'Esté, Hereditary Prince of Modena! The cheer was taken up by those outside. More than a hundred voices shouted welcome to the cousin of the kings of France and Spain, the Heir Apparent to the Grand Duchy of Modena.

My husband started up. His face was pale at first, then it flushed with anger. "Gentlemen," he cried, "this is an indiscretion. What business has any one in Martinique to assume to be acquainted with more of my private history than I am willing to disclose? If I wish to appear upon your island as the Comte de Tarnaud, what right has any one to tell me to my face that I am any other man? I have thus far received nothing but kindness and hospitality since I arrived among you. I owe you thanks, and your conduct toward me emboldens me to entreat that I may hear no more of this vague suspicion, but that you will be willing to accept me as Renaud, Comte de Tarnaud." So saying, he bowed and quitted the table, leaving the Marquis d'Eragny, M. Nadua, and the other guests bewildered and confounded.

The negroes and mulattoes were still cheering in the courtyard; the drums and the bugles still made their hideous uproar, nor was this silenced by our retirement from the table. The people of Martinique, having obtained a Prince, the possible future ruler of a sovereign state, a personage connected with half the royal families of Europe, were not to be defrauded of the distinction of possessing such a prize. Whether they might address His Highness by the titles that belonged to him or not, they had him on their island; they would make him their medium of communication with the court of France; he would redress the grievances of the islanders! So the roaring and the cheering, the drumming and the bugling, went on for half the night, while in the Prince's bedchamber reigned anger and consternation.

"The fools!" he cried, "the fools! And I

too-what a fool!" For he held in his hand his own letter to M. Ferol, with its hurried signature. "So premature, so ill-advised a welcome! It was not for that I came here. Why could they not have respected my incognito? Has any man a right to tear away the fictions with which a Prince has veiled his secrets? Now I suppose, unless I find some means to help myself, I cannot escape a *lettre de cachet*. I passed my word to the Duc de Penthièvre to preserve a strict incognito."

He was so much moved that at first he took no notice of my presence. I stood silent. I shed no tears. I was too thunder-stricken for emotion. Suddenly, with irritation in his manner and his voice, he came straight up to me. "You too," he said, "embarrass me. You would assist my ruin. You importune me—"

"Rinaldo," I said, "you are in fault toward me; you have deceived me. I know now that our marriage, imperfect as it always was under the cruel laws of France, is absolutely a thing impossible. How can a subject, were she ten times a Catholic, and the daughter of a Duke, lawfully marry a Prince of the Blood Royal without the King's permission? Obscure, we might have lived in exile, like other married Huguenots; but now—"

"Antoinine," he cried, "do not, in such a strait as this, bring your wrongs to embarrass me. Accept the situation. I swear to you that I was honest, that I told you but the truth. I meant to live unknown upon this or some other island, but these fools have now made it impossible for me to keep up my incognito. I had renounced my hereditary rights, my relatives and my family. My father, in his white wrath, had renounced me: he told me to go where I would, to take what name I pleased, to be whom I chose. He said he washed his hands of me; that I could never come to any good. He denounced me for my philosophy, for my renegade opinions, and he said he was weary of my pranks. He expelled me from his staff; he put me to shame; he dismissed me from the army. I had already engaged passage on the 'Sainte Luce,'—he ordered her not to touch at the point where I expected her, but to proceed upon her voyage. In an open boat I and my poor Victor, having escaped the sentinels by night, made our way to land where we were beyond his reach, and thence into the mountains. There is an organization of banditti in the Apennines. I made promises to its leader; he sent us on. We passed through Savoy, we tarried some weeks among the Vaudois; then, by way of Avignon and southern France, we were pushing on to join the Sainte Luce when she should put into Bordeaux. You know the rest. I felt myself free. I had no idea that the King of France was going to step in between my father and myself, as head of our family. I was on my way to embark for Martinique as a private adventurer, when accident brought us to your retreat. Accident, Antoinine, left us a few days in the society of each other. I loved you, Antoinine! You know how much I love you. I thought our marriage, such as it was, would satisfy your father, would be as safe—as legal—as any Protestant French marriage could be. You could not make in France any marriage that would hold good in law; neither can I; we united our disabilities. Here, incognito, under a new name in Martinique, forgotten by the world, forgetting ourselves, I thought we might be happy. But—these fools! These selfish fools! So proud of having secured a Prince among them! My secret was known only to our good Scotch captain, who thought I was flying from the Inquisition; he never betrayed my rank and birth even to you."

I hid my face and moaned.

"Ah, forgive me, my wife! Do not forsake me. We have gone too far for you to draw back now. It is cruel, I know, for you; but, Antoinine, hard as are the laws of court etiquette, they give privileges to women beloved, *par amours*, by Princes."

"Comte de Tarnaud!"

"No no. I did not suggest it. They cannot force me to be the hereditary Prince of Modena against my will. We will be Comte and Comtesse de Tarnaud. But you must conform to the Religion of the Island for my sake. We shall find some priest to marry us. I will take the consequences of the displeasure this may draw on me from my royal cousin. We will escape to the mainland, and live happy upon English soil, but in exile. I will brave everything for your sake, and in return I only ask your silence and forbearance; that no foolish reluctance to conform to the religious feeling of this place shall stand between us and happiness. Say yes, Antoinine, and I will boldly deny that I am he whose name those fools have given me. If any man shall dare to recognize me as the Hereditary Prince of Modena I will stop his mouth by two inches of my sword blade."

He tried to fold me in his arms, but I escaped from him.

"Rinaldo," I said, "I am only a woman. I have suffered for some days shock after shock; my head is all confused, and I see nothing plainly. In some things, such as paying reverence to the shrines put up along the waysides by these poor babes in Christian faith and knowledge, I am willing to please you; but to go through another illegal marriage ceremony would be to involve myself in deeper falsehood. When in the sight of God and in the presence of my father and our pastors and our brethren I made my marriage vows, I did so with my whole heart, in truth and sincerity. My father had consented to our union, and a marriage contract had been written. Such marriages are the custom among our people. I had no thought that ours could be any more irregular than that of my own father and mother—that of all persecuted Protestants. If those of our religion sin in this, the guilt must lie upon the heads of men who enact and enforce ungodly laws. But now that I know that your rank and condition make it impossible that you ever should acknowledge me, even before Protestants, as your wife, the case is changed. My fault thus far has been involuntary. I can ask God to forgive my having been led astray—for having loved you—loved you as a true wife loves her husband. But were I to remain here as your wife, I should be only what I cannot name. O Rinaldo, is this the end of all our happiness?"

"My dearest Antoinine, I feel for you. Believe me that in those hills of the Gévaudan I never thought of wronging you. I never dreamed of bringing on you trouble and disgrace. But for the discovery of my scattered papers in the hills, which the military commander sent to Paris, and for the prying and precipitancy of these fools, and for my own slip of the pen when I signed in haste my note to M. Ferol, we might both have remained happy in exile and obscurity. Dear wife! my treasure! we have not made this situation for ourselves. If we call the accidents that have brought us into it sent by the hand of Providence, we surely may accept it without sin; or, as you say, the sin forced on us is not our own sin, but the sin of others. Do not forsake me, Antoinine. Stay with me, all my life be my good angel. In all save in the cruel eyes of the French law, you are my wife. Think of our happy days on board the poor 'Sainte Luce,' whose planks are being now tossed up on the black beach of the Anse Marine."

"Don't—don't recall the wreck," I cried. "My life is wrecked, even as that poor brig is,—so glorious only a few hours since, so proud and happy, with the sunlight on her sails, coming into sight of our Enchanted Island,—and now, all gone to pieces, broken up forever!"

"My darling, I love you; you have given me your love; all is not wreck. A little compliance upon your part, and we shall ride safe through the breakers."

"Whose hand bore us safe along that slender rope?" I cried. "It was God's hand! It will not he stretched out to save me, if I wilfully, with open eyes, despise His laws and do His name dishonor."

"Oh! puritanism!" he said, and drew apart from me, and sat down by himself, with his face in his hands. "And if you withdraw yourself from my protection, whom are you to appeal to? What can you do?" he said. "And as for me, when through you my cousin, the King of France, knows of my escapade, what punishment may he not inflict on me!"

At that moment M. Nadua knocked on the chamber door, saying that he had come to present his company's apologies, and to request Monsieur le Comte de Tarnaud to return to their supper table. My husband went with the Commandant. His last words were still ringing in my ears; more and more I grew afraid of fate.

I went out into the night. I sat down beside the fountain in the courtyard and prayed. I prayed God in my misery to cut the knot of my troubles—to take me to Himself, before worse should happen to me or to him whom I still called my husband. And I pitied myself, which is weakness. Poor Antoinine! so rich in love and happiness not many hours before, now with her crown of glory cast down to the earth—her wifehood gone, her womanhood dishonored! And my own heart was treacherous. My loneliness, my unprotectedness, laid me open to any fate. I loved him, oh, I loved him! Whom had I to turn to but him whom I had followed across the ocean as my husband? Where could I go? Yes, indeed, he had said the truth; if I withdrew from his protection, what could I do? To whom could I turn? I had no money, no way to make any. I was a stranger in a strange land, among a people of strange speech who had been cradled in superstitions that were not mine. I had not even my sex, which among men of honor might have procured me pity; I was not entitled to be looked upon with Christian charity; I was a living lie, and must remain so, for, for his sake, I must still conceal the truth that I had believed myself a married woman, and if I revealed my sex, every one would look upon me as a fallen creature.

There came a bitter thought with the words, "Put not your trust in Princes, nor in any child of man, for there is no help in them."[74] What hope had I except in death? For I could see that if I did not leave my husband, his persuasions and my habit of obedience might overcome my resolution. "Lead me not into temptation," said my heart, "lead me not into dishonor." What hope had I except in death? For I could see that he did not mean to give me up. He had attempted already to drive more than one entering wedge into my resolution. I had but one Friend, and of late I had neglected Him; One who could help me, and I had rarely asked Him to lift His arm to save me. My only Friend, my father's and my mother's Friend, the Friend of our people, was the good God. If I asked His help, I must in honesty endeavor to obey His laws. My marriage vows had been made in ignorance, but in all sincerity, and I had followed my husband, braving ill report. Now my eyes had been forced open. That marriage could be no marriage which must be made void as soon as it should be avowed. And—and—he had said the words himself—my claims and my importunities might embarrass his future career.

One must not, I knew, make bargains with God Almighty, yet my heart said, "O Father in Heaven, stand by me, and I will stand by Thy commandments. I will give him up because it is Thy will that I should part from him. But let me die. Or if Thou wilt not, supply me with the strength to do Thy will; open some door by which Thou canst deliver me."

I have wondered, since that time, what becomes of people in sore trouble, if they cannot turn to God in their distress. How horrible it must be to be utterly alone!

Elizabeth Lester Mullin (c. 1874-1952)

(See Mullin's biography in the Local Favorites section for additional information.)

Elizabeth Lester Mullin was fluent in French and translated numerous works by writers including Paul Ferrier, Adolphe Ribaux, Paul Gaulot, and Édouard Rod. Through translation, Mullin brought to English speakers the stories and experiences of foreign lands, stories that expressed her own values and beliefs as well as those of their original authors. "Missa Solemnis," by French writer Adolphe Ribanx, communicates the power of music and companionship. "The Codicil," by dramatist and librettist Paul Ferrier, depicts a romance that runs deeper than material gain or social advantage.

Translation is often viewed as a lesser or purely derivative form of literary work, and has often been relegated to women. Yet Mullin's translations allowed these works to be disseminated to new audiences while also revealing her beliefs and values to modern readers. —K. Shiber

Missa Solemnis—A Christmas Story (1901)

Translated from the French of Adolphe Ribaux

Little by little shadows encroached upon the Gothic Cathedral—a masterpiece of an unknown architect in which extreme grace and delicacy of detail formed the basis of a severe though imposing whole. A flood of light seemed to amplify the gigantic windows, where the figures of Christ, the Virgin, and the Saints stood amidst symbolic lilies emblazoned in scarlet, gold, rubies, and chrysolites; while above the main entrance a glorious rose-window was set in the organ-case. Everything foretold that the sunset would be followed by a speedy twilight. Already the lower end was plunged in obscurity and the shadows mounted and spread with a sepulchral damp over the immense structure, sparred in stone.

Two persons occupied the organ-loft.

"Well, Master, are you satisfied?" Anxiously Christian turned towards his judge.

He waited an instant before answering, then measuring his words so as to give each its proper value, said: "More than that, my child; as far as technique goes you have nothing more to learn and your interpretation is excellent. Your two years at the Conservatory have not been lost, and I see that even under the direction of the celebrities of Leipzig you have remembered the advice of Conrad Waldmann. You are a virtuoso; you are more; you are an artist. Without fear I can intrust this dear old organ to you. Love it as I have loved it, never put it to any but the highest uses. Our organ is like myself, worn out and decrepit. It is seriously in need of repairs. You know arrangements have been made with Nisch, the celebrated manufacturer of Nuremburg. He has signed a contract with the burgomaster and will soon arrive with his staff and ap-paratus. Nisch thinks that to do the work satisfactorily it will take from six weeks to two months. By the middle of December, perhaps sooner, you will be able to make your debut. My task is done; yours begins. Pluck up courage, Christian."

For fifty-eight years Conrad Waldmann had held the post of organist in the cathedral of the little town of B——, capital of the principality of K——. The position was poorly remunerated and Conrad was not worth a farthing, so he had to look out for scholars. He had never failed to get them, but they in turn brought little, so, materially speaking, he had remained in moderate circumstances. Otherwise he had few wants. Shunning society, his only recreation consisted in long walks in the fields and woods.

Into this life, apparently so peaceful and uniform, some asserted without the least foundation that romance found place—a virginal ideal tragically ended. Conrad Waldman gave lessons to the only daughter of the reigning prince. Fresh as a spray of white lilacs, with the grace and mystic charm of one of Hemling's saints, she sang with a splendid voice. Conrad, they said, was passionately enamored of her, and she did not disdain his love. They had been seen walking together in the palace gardens, the French gardens copied after those of Versailles, planted with box and trimmed yew trees, and dotted with sheets of water and mythological statues. It was these very walks that had betrayed them, for a light burned in their eyes that none could mistake. Then it was suddenly understood that the physicians had ordered the Princess Elsa to go south on a pretense of illness. One day a great coach with armorial bearings departed, and behind the panes the young girl's charming face was seen bathed in tears. The Princess accompanied her, and their absence lasted three years. At the end of the time a marriage was announced that sealed a reconciliation between the older and younger branches of the family and assured the succession to the throne.

But eighteen months later the flag was hoisted at half-mast over the principal tower and the palace was put in mourning; Hemling's little Saint had taken another voyage towards a country where state affairs cannot thwart the inclinations of the heart. She left behind her a little daughter in the cradle, who was to be sole heir to the principality, for the reigning prince was no longer of an age to marry and he had no other children.

Since then especially, Conrad Waldmann had become taciturn, never going out except for lessons, for his duties as organist, or at intervals for one of those long walks when he never proposed to any one to accompany him. Nor had a word ever escaped him that could give substance to the village tattle. If he had really loved the Princess Elsa, his secret was well preserved as a relic in the depths of an inviolable sanctuary. The little Princess grew with years. To have her taught music they had recourse to an outside master, and that seemed to confirm persons in their suppositions. Then other years passed by, and they thought no more about it. In the meantime, the father and mother of the Princess Elsa died and her daughter ascended the throne.

II

Invariably Conrad spent his evenings at home in reading, meditating, constructing periods and setting them to music. That was

his requital. Those hours when with doors and windows closed he could abandon himself to inspiration and gather in the divine things that murmured in his ear. What delightful perplexity, what blissful feverishness, and also what dejections! Occasionally the struggle was equal to that of Jacob and the archangel. But still it was a joy. His temples at times throbbed as if they would burst; a fire ran through his veins; victoriously he broke loose from reality.

Thus Conrad composed many things,— songs, sonatas, symphonies, and a whole series of pieces for the organ. Two or three timid overtures to editors hard by, made him understand that an unpretentious organist like himself, who gave private lessons in a small town, had no chance of success. With patronage, intrigue, platitude perhaps, he might have succeeded—by his sole merit—what folly! Conrad was proud; when you are rich, pride in the eyes of the world is called dignity and becomes a virtue. If you are poor, it is named presumption and is the worst of faults. Conrad did as Sebastian Bach did,[1] be buried his manuscripts in the depths of a chest, not without continuing to compose, but sacrificing once and for all his hopes of fame. His great work was his solemn high mass for Christmas, a mass for orchestra, choir, soloists, and a leading part for the organ. He had consecrated twenty years to this work. Never satisfied with himself, and often seized with a frightful despair and ready to throw it in the fire, he became a martyr to an over-sincere soul when he compared his dream to the realization that he could give in. Nevertheless, amidst these interior combats that sometimes dampened Conrad's brow with the sweat of agony, but which he would not have exchanged for any voluptuousness, the Mass was completed. One evening he recognized that all his science and all his convictions were condensed within it, and with a trembling hand he wrote the word "finis" at the bottom of the last leaf, and the enormous bundle of scored paper went to join its predecessors in the depths of the "death chest" where it slept for the next twenty years.

Besides the author, only two other beings knew of it—Mephistopheles,[2] Conrad's cat, black as Erebus,[3] which he had picked up in the streets, starved, mangy and pitiful, but which, when well cared-for, had become a superb animal, with a glossy coat as soft as velvet. While Waldmann worked, Mephistopheles had the habit of placing himself opposite to him on the table, and he had been the first to hear Conrad's voice try the motives of the "Missa Solemnis." The other privileged being, more capable of enjoying it, was Christian Hofer, the favorite pupil of his maestro, an urchin of the town. This Christian was the son of a humble blacksmith.

Conrad Waldmann found again in Christian all his former illusions, all his enthusiasm, all his devotion for art, added to a steady application, so that he seemed to re-live his youth. For eight years he lavished upon him all his care, inculcating in him a love of the Masters, guiding him step by step, with the solicitude of a father and the disinterestedness of a great heart, along the paths of Art towards the highest summits. The child himself was remarkably gifted, passionately fond of study, and threw himself with delight into the terrors of counterpoint, to which Conrad piteously forced him. In addition to all

this, he was a true little man, grateful and affectionate, and Conrad would sometimes say, "If I had a son, that is how I should wish him."

In his modesty Conrad had seldom spoken to Christian of his compositions. At long intervals he had played a fragment of a sonata, a motet, or an andante cantabile, each of which increased the scholar's ardent admiration for his professor. Only upon the day that Christian had returned from Leipzig with the first prize in harmony, while drinking the laureate's health in a bottle of Johannsberg,[4] which had been presented to him long before and forgotten, Conrad Waldmann could not refrain from taking out of the famous chest the manuscript of the "Missa Solemnis," and then dragging Christian to the cathedral made him listen to it from beginning to end. The young man remained astounded at that ignored work, sparkling with supreme beauty. He could find nothing to say, nothing but that incapability of expressing the least eulogy which was the best of eulogies. They spent the entire evening in Conrad's room, Christian never tiring of reading and re-reading the score, ever discovering new treasures in it. Alas, its long sojourn in the damp chest had terribly yellowed the paper; in some places the ink had become almost imperceptible, mice had nibbled several leaves, though fortunately only the margins.

Alarmed at the thought that such slight causes might in a few years finish the work of destruction, Christian refused to leave until his Master allowed him to take the manuscript that he might make a new copy on indestructible parchment and in India ink. The old man finally consented, saying all the while, "What is the use?" A month later, Christian brought him the copy, also a masterpiece of its kind. Waldmann in his quiet way admired the solidity and flexibility of the vellum and the faithful minutia, then, turning to the young man, said: "Let us talk about yourself: I am worn out and need repose. Tomorrow my resignation will be sent in and you ought to succeed me. It is not a brilliant post, but I look upon it as only your first halting-place while awaiting something better. Are you willing?"

"Oh, Master, how can I ever repay you the hundredth part of all you have done for me?"

"As for the heart, remain as you have been up to the present, but, in art, continue to study and improve. That is the recompense I want. Tomorrow my resignation will be sent in, Christian, or rather I will hand it in myself to the five town-counsellors who hold a meeting at five o'clock. They take me for a bear; but I have always done my duty, so they may wish me well all the same. At six o'clock I will be at your father's house with a formal promise of your nomination."

And so Christian Hofer was about to fill old Waldmann's place.

III

"Ah, my dear, dear child, is that you,— at last? Yes, at last, because it has been several weeks since you found a minute to devote to me, and I had begun, even knowing your good heart, to wonder if that miserable weed of oblivion was going to spring up so soon. Better late than never; sit down, I am glad to see you." And Conrad Wald-

mann indicated to Christian a place by his side near the small latticed window.

"Forget you, Master? Oh, you could not have believed that," rejoined Christian.

"Water flows towards the river and youth goes with youth. Nothing more natural than your preferring in your leisure an excursion, or a stein of beer with some friends, (you ought to be very much sought after)—to this gloomy room and the conversation of a dull old man."

"That would be on my part vile ingratitude, and I should despise myself for it. The truth is, Master, that I have been very, very busy. You know that Nisch arrived last month with his gang of workmen. The repairs have been conscientiously done. They followed your advice in everything."

"And is it all right? The great organ?"

"Like thunder."

"The recitatif?"[5]

"Sensible to the least shade."

"The 'vox humana'?"[6]

"It could fool you."

With each of these answers Conrad Waldmann seemed to revive; he straightened up, his eyes sparkled. His organ, ah, he would always love it.

"Then the instrument is as good as new?"

"Exactly."

"Do you know I want to go to hear you on Sunday?"

The young man was confused for the moment, but regained his composure, and in the most natural tone said, "Not Sunday, Master; I will not play. The idea came to me to wait until Christmas and then make my debut under the best possible conditions. Yes, at the midnight Mass.

I have drummed up a choir and we work together assiduously studying a great Mass. The cathedral is not far from your house; wrap up well and you will run no risk of catching cold. I am affecting a fine debut, and I count upon your presence to help me through. Forsooth, it is no small matter to be your successor."

"And what work have you chosen?"

"Oh, you may be sure that I do not select anything mediocre. Therefore, what I have chosen is not only a piece, but a masterpiece. Don't ask me for details. I cannot give them to you because it is now after half-past seven, and we rehearse at eight, and I must go. I have just come to say that when the Princess deigned to call me to the palace to congratulate me upon my prize, I went so far as to lay before her my plans; she immediately interested herself, and thanks to her the vocal quartette and the orchestra from the theatre will lend their co-operation."

"Then it will be a real solemnity?"

"I hope so. Promise me you will come."

"True, it is not far to the cathedral, but from living a hermit I have become so chilly."

"I will send a carriage to take Odile and yourself. You promise?"

"Could I refuse my Christian?"

"Just see how happy I am!"

"Shall I not see you between now and then? Will you not stop in between rehearsals to tell me all about it?"

"I am afraid not; I shall have too much to do. But I shall think of you, Master, oh, every day. As to forgetting you, never say that again!"

The old man remained alone in the little room lighted by a bijou lamp, its four branches of beaten copper suspended from the ceiling. His hands on his knees, his head thrown back on his arm chair, he gave himself up to musing. As long as be retained his position, his will—a little pride, too, that pride which had never faltered a day in his long life—sustained him. Besides, he wished Christian to succeed him. To have retired before the young man had taken his degree would have been to hand the place over to another. Conrad held out. His duties abandoned, a great lassitude came over him, and age bore down upon him with all its weight.

IV

The cathedral was already crowded; there were hundreds of wax lights bursting in luminous clusters from the pillars. The main altar was dazzling, while the carved altar-screen displayed its pathetic "Descent from the Cross," dating from the fifteenth century.

Conrad Waldmann had never contemplated that marvel without emotion. It shone with the sublime sincerity of the artists of former times. The man who carved the hard oak with his patient chisel surely never dreamed of gaining money or renown. His soul spoke in the wood, and after four centuries it was still admired. More than once Conrad had come to seek in that masterpiece an example of artistic probity and humility.

"This way, Mr. Waldmann," said the beadle; "they told me to save two chairs for you." And he conducted the old man and Odile to their places on the left of the altar. They finished lighting the candles. The church blazed. Persons were continually arriving, not leaving a single corner empty.

A stir was produced when the Princess, preceded by ushers in laced coats, made her entry amid the dignitaries of the Court. She was very young, blonde like her mother, as frail and as enchanting. At the right of the altar other seats had been reserved, where the Princess installed herself with her suite. Immediately the clergy appeared, in splendid vestments, escorted by the altar boys swinging the censer. In an instant the cathedral was perfumed with the odor of myrrh, and the candles through the thin veil of blue smoke had the appearance of stars on a hazy night.

The archbishop had mounted the steps of the choir. There was a sudden silence. Old Conrad Waldmann was greatly affected. His eyes were eagerly fixed on the organ loft, following every movement of his young friend, the son of his heart. Christian, the soloists, and the leader of the orchestra exchanged some final comments, and then silence reigned also in the gallery.

"My God! What will he do?" Conrad repeated for the hundredth time. "Will he be able to maintain his composure so that all will go well?"

The leader of the orchestra raised his baton. Conrad, breathing with difficulty, bowed his head in his hands and waited. The organ pealed forth in full majestic chords. Like a great stream of harmony it flowed slowly through the classic lines. Only twenty or thirty measures, but majestic, and bearing the stamp of genius.

At the first sounds the old man raised his head and became white as the altar linen.

"Do I hear aright? It is impossible."

The thrilling prelude continued. Solemnity fell from the organ and spread across the church, the stream widened, until it became a sea of powerful waves.

"*Kyrie, Kyrie eleison*."[7] To the voice of the officiating priest the choir responded, sustained by the organ and orchestra. "Kyrie eleison, Christie eleison." Each note was like an act of faith. The whole had the beauty of things eternal, and Conrad Waldmann, his head fallen again into his hands, wept, overcome with surprise, fear, and joy.

He had recognized his Christmas Mass!

The execution was faultless. In its least details the gigantic work had been thoroughly studied, and searched into. Not one of the author's intentions had escaped. The orchestra, the choir, the soloists, vied in their zeal to render his ideas with integrity. The part for the organ was played in a masterly manner, not only at the melodious sanctus, in the ecstatic trio. at the Agnus Dei,[8] at the sweet benedictus accompanied by the string instruments, and above all at the elevation when the kingly instrument sang alone, a hymn over-flowing with candid joy, with infinite love; then in accents of beatitude, with a heart enraptured, prostrated before the Divine cradle, when the agrestic flute and the pastoral horn of the shepherds responded alternately to the viols of the Cherubim. All were spellbound, there was not a dry eye in that immense crowd. As for the old man, he wept continuously. A stream of tears rolled down his emaciated cheeks between his fingers, all cramped with rheumatism. But the dew of May on the calyx of a rosebud was never so sweet as were those tears; without them Conrad's heart would have burst.

His dearest, his most secret dream, one he had never hoped to see realized, had by a miracle become a vivid reality. It had been granted to him to hear his Mass, the great agony, the great delight of his life, magnificently rendered. And modest though he was, he felt that his labor had not been lost, that the work itself was beautiful, and in it he should live. Happier than his Master Bach, while yet alive he entered into the Promised Land.

"Ah, that noble child," he thought of Christian. "It was he who conceived the idea of all this, contrived it all, brought it all about. And I accused him of neglect when he had not a single thought but of me."

The Mass ended with an Alleluia, which could almost be compared to that of the Messiah. In a colossal fugue the organ, the orchestra, and the choir ran up and down the scales bounding like a torrent, reverberating as thunder. The prodigious edifice of that Mass had a crowning worthy of it—in the confusion of notes, regulated into supreme order, in the blare of those enormous pipes, blown to their full, in those two hundred voices and sixty instruments, the entire cathedral vibrated, while a tremor passed over the multitude.

Then all was hushed, and for several minutes you could have heard a pin drop.

"Ah, Master, Master, I cannot wait to embrace you."

It was Christian, who had descended in haste from the gallery tingling with electricity to the tips of his fingers.

Incapable of articulating a syllable, Waldmann opened his arms and clasped the young man to his bosom.

"Come, Master, the Princess wishes to see you."

Through the immense crowd which respectfully made way for them they slowly passed. The beautiful, young girl, radiant as Spring, advanced towards Conrad.

"This is a happy day for us all," she said. "In the name of our city I thank you." Then, in a lower tone, "You knew my mother, I believe."

Had an echo of the old story reached her? Probably. However, it seemed to Conrad she intended in that word to show that with the evening's success she wished to associate the dead. In vain Conrad tried to answer. But the Princess offered him her delicate hand, which he bent to kiss, and over those patrician fingers circled with gems his long white locks flowed like a silver stream.

Masters, musicians, critics, amateurs, had come from Leipzig, Munich, Weimar, and Dresden. Christian pronounced their names and titles, and at the mention of each a greater amazement spread over Conrad's features.

What! come on his account—all these celebrated people wishing to be presented to him, surrounding him, and congratulating him? The old man could not believe his eyes and threw by turns looks of astonishment towards the radiant Princess and towards Christian, who was in the seventh heaven.

Ah! the young man had bestirred himself indeed to reach this result. He had applied to both friends and acquaintances, using every means, writing, soliciting, putting to profit all his influence, warming the coldest with his enthusiasm, and moreover supported by the leader of the orchestra, who in his turn was enraptured with the "Missa Solemnis," and by the

Princess, to whom he went every week to report the progress of the rehearsals. The result at least came up to his expectations.

"Master, I have taken it upon myself to conclude a contract with the house of Holler and Son, of Munich, to publish your work. Mr. Holler was anxious to come himself to present you with the first copy." A portly little man smilingly advanced towards Conrad, bent in an automatic bow, and offered the old man a superb volume in octavo, on which these words, "Missa Solemnis," and his name, "Conrad Waldmann," shone in gold letters amid Gothic gauffering.[9]

The candles were about to be put out. At a sign from the master of ceremonies, the ushers of the Court made the people stand aside for the Princess's departure. She, with an exquisite grace, offered her arm to the old man who was trembling like a leaf and escorted him as far as the main entrance; the dignitaries of the Court, the strangers assembled for the fête and Christian, charged with that precious volume, walking behind. The people passing out through the side doors, the square became a human surge. In the center, holding lighted torches and fluttering banners, the students of the university formed a double line, and when the old artist appeared, still on the arm of their adorable Princess, the plaudits, restrained with difficulty in the cathedral, broke forth like a tempest.

"What is it now?" thought Conrad. "I am surely dreaming." But already strong arms had seized him, lifted him, and Conrad, notwithstanding his protestations, saw himself carried off in triumph. The night was unusually mild, the sky strewn with stars, while in the center of the flags and torches, amidst the songs and huzzahs of the flower of the town's youth, Conrad was borne home. He looked at the windows everywhere illuminated, the flare of the torches reflected on their facades, and then at the dense crowd preceding and following. He heard the refrains, the bravos, saw hands held towards him and hats waved, and more and more it all seemed to him a dream.

They reached his cottage. On the threshold, lamp in hand, stood Odile swelling with pride.

"Well, Master," said Christian, "they need never say again that there is no more fire in young hearts."

"My child, my dear child, you will thank them for me, will you not? As for me—I cannot, I cannot."

Staggering like a drunkard he entered the house, preceded by Odile, who was saying to herself: "My God! My God, what a night!" The door was closed. But the students remained awhile under the windows singing in honor of the old man. Then two o'clock struck from the cathedral, with a last formidable hoch[10] the crowd dispersed.

It was a lovely night, a perfect Christmas night. The frost glistened in fantastic girandoles on the trees and shrubs, necklaces of pearls and strings of diamonds hung from every branch. The snow, too, seemed luminous, and in the sky there was an exceptional transparency, where myriads of stars seemed to mark the route of the Seraphim[11]—the bearers of Glad Tidings.

"You will sleep late in the morning," said Odile to Conrad Waldmann on leaving him.

"I do not believe I will close my eyes; I am too happy!"

As the clock struck ten, not having heard him stir, she entered his room. He was seated before his table, his hands stretched out, and his head resting on the volume with the gauffers in gold.

"He did not even go to bed," murmured Odile. She called him without obtaining an answer. She approached and shook him by the shoulder. Never a stir. His eyelids were lowered and he smiled the smile of an old Simeon singing Nunc Dimittis.[12]

That immobility astonished Odile. She felt his hands and found them cold and rigid. Death in his clemency had not wished Conrad Waldmann to survive his apotheosis. As the reaper rests on his sheaf of wheat, so he had fallen asleep in the height of his triumph, passing without transition from the immortal music of his "Missa Solemnis" to the ineffable concerts of the Angels.

The Codicil
A Comedy in One Act (1908)

Translated from the French of Paul Ferrier

Characters

Marie De Chantenay, a widow.
Gaston De Morières, her lover.
Pitou, a gardener.
Pontgouin, a notary.

Scene: Château de Chantenay,[13] *Poitou, France. Time: The present.*

Scene I

(*A drawing-room. Enter Pontgouin and Marie De Chantenay*)

Marie: Why do I remain a widow? Because men are so conceited, so absolutely selfish that marriage has become nothing more than a speculation. Beauty, wit, and heart count as nothing in their estimation and cannot balance the weight of a dowry.[14] There is not one among them, not a single one, I say, who has love, generosity, or chivalry enough to encumber himself with a wife without a fortune.

Pontgouin: A Malabar widow—through misanthropy.

Marie: Malabar—minus the funeral pile.

Pontgouin: You are a dreadful sceptic.

Marie: Whose fault is it? The fitful changes of life have in a few years allowed me to go through a double experience. As a young girl in sad need of a dowry I ran the risk of becoming an old maid. But as a widow, endowed with the fortune M. de Chantenay has left me, that is quite another thing. I personally have worked out the rule and now see it verified. What a contrast! This time the suitors fairly spring out of the ground and I cannot take a step without stumbling over a proposal.

Pontgouin: Who assures you that they are all so interested?

Marie: Who assures me? A test, whimsical, perhaps, but conclusive, by which I regularly try each of my lovers!

Pontgouin: And that test?

Marie: You are not in the ranks, my friend, so I can tell you. M. de Chantenay by his will bequeathed me his fortune absolutely, but I have imagined a codicil that will deprive me of it. You understand— this is the game! He proposes. Usual formula. I reply in an incredulous tone.—"Yes, you may swear that you love me, yet how am I to know that you love none but me?" (He), "I love any but you! What woman could contend against such charms, such grace, such fascination?"—Then I become more explicit. "If I could feel sure that you love me for myself alone"—(He), "I not love you for yourself, Madame, I who adore your every feature. Your beauty, your hair, your brow, your soul that reflects—" I sigh. "Then I need no longer fear to make you a revelation that might cool a less ardent devotion."—(He), "You have a revelation to make me?"—Here the voice of the lover trembles, though love plays small part in that tremor. I hasten to explain—"Oh, reassure yourself, that revelation has nothing to do with my honor, nor with anything you love in me. It only refers to some miserable financial details." The countenance of the adorer darkens. I continue—"By his will M. de Chantenay left me his fortune uncondi-tionally."—Unconditionally, at that word the lover's brow regains its serenity—"But there is a codicil attached, a codicil which reads"—Clouds gather once more—"In case Madame de Chantenay should con-tract a second marriage my will becomes null and void and my property in its entirety shall revert to my nephew, my sole natural heir."—Then the face of my wooer expresses stupor in its most aggra-

vated form—"But you love me for myself, my hair, my brow, my every feature." Oh, how ridiculous they appear protesting, stammering, and finally beating a retreat. And they never come back again. Never! Wretched men! It is such a farce. But you are not laughing—?

Pontgouin: I am thinking of a case that might present itself.

Marie: Let's have it.

Pontgouin: If you chanced to meet a man, a paladin, who would come out of the test triumphant—

Marie: He will never be met.

Pontgouin: Still admit the hypothesis.

Marie: He would not be of this century and that very circumstance might less-en the desirability of the match.

Pontgouin: Not necessarily.

Marie: He would have to be an Arcadian Shepherd.

Pontgouin: But you would marry him?

Marie: You lay great stress upon my marrying.

Pontgouin: I am greatly in favor of it.

Marie: What did I ever do to you?

Enter Pitou.

Pitou: Madame de Chantenay, the Sub-Prefect[15] asks for you.
Pontgouin: One of your admirers?

Marie: Yes, for a week he has been beating about the bush. Will you bet on him?

Pontgouin: Oh, no.

Marie: You are prudent. However, you need not go far. He will not be long.

Pontgouin: A farce?

Marie: Always the same with the invariable conclusion.

(*Exit.*)

Scene II

(*Pontgouin, Pitou.*)

Pontgouin: I would not bet on the Sub-Prefect, but I would bet on Gaston de Morières (he hesitates), I will bet— hey!—hey! Should I bet? Gaston is a noble fellow and generous too, yet to see an income of thirty thousand francs suddenly vanish under your very eyes is enough to knock the breath out of you. You are taken unawares and feel the full strength of the blow. (*He is struck with an idea.*) I will bet on a certainty. A word to the wise is sufficient. I will warn Gaston. (*He writes*) Courage, my friend, go ahead and propose. That story of the codicil is all an invention. Don't you believe it. There is no codicil. Only feign to believe it and victory is yours.

Pitou: (*advances*) M. Pontgouin, since you are here you had better take a look at the espaliers.[16]

Pontgouin: Why should I, Pitou? I am not a gardener.

Pitou: Quite true, sir, but you are a law-

yer, and can tell if a neighbor has any right to let his wall tumble down on Madame de Chantenay's fruit.

Pontgouin: Always something the matter with your neighbors' wall.

Pitou: M. Pontgouin, you know M. de Morières and could persuade him to have his wall repaired. If Madame de Chantenay would only listen to me she would sue him.

Pontgouin: I would not think of doing that, Pitou, until I had tried conciliatory measures first.

Pitou: You hope to conciliate?

Pontgouin: It was with just such a hope that I had written to M. de Morières. Will you take the letter to him?

Pitou: (*taking the letter*) Did you put in it that only last night two rocks fell down and crushed seventeen fine Duchess pears?

Pontgouin: Yes, I told him what he had to expect.

Pitou: A marmalade of seventeen pears! Pshaw! If he knows what's right he'll have his old wall fixed up.

(Exit.)

Scene III

Pontgouin: I have an idea that he will arrange to have it pulled down so as to unite the two estates. Then this will be the finest tract of land in Poitou. Ah! Well, since he is in love with Madame de Chantenay he can act the Arcadian Shepherd and maybe she will marry him. Here she comes. She is laughing.

The government official has evidently been ousted.

(*Marie enters laughing.*)

Marie: *E finita* la commedia![17]

Pontgouin: The Sub-Prefect?

Marie: He has flown as fast as he could. You will see that he asks to be transferred.

Pontgouin: *(seeing Pitou enter)* Pitou, already? (He makes a sign, says in an undertone), Sh,—You have not delivered my letter?

Pitou: On the contrary, I put it into M. de Morières own hand. I met him coming here.

Pontgouin: *(aside)* Good for me! I was just in time. We will clear the field. Come along, Pitou. (*Perceiving that Marie is watching them*) Yes, Madame, we are thinking of bringing action against your neighbor. Show me the way, Pitou, and let us have a look into these damages.

(*Exeunt.*)

Scene IV

Marie: A suit against M. de Morières? Oh, Pitou is such a savage! M. de Morières, the only one of my neighbors who has never courted me. Never. Is it indifference or timidity? It would be ridiculous for him to do it now after so many others. After the Sub-Prefect, for instance. (*She laughs.*)

(*Gaston enters.*)

Gaston: You are in a gay mood to-day.

Marie: M. de Morières! I am glad to see you.

Gaston: Are you not going to laugh any more?

Marie: No, it is all over.

Gaston: So much the worse. Your laugh is clear and sweet as any chime. I love to hear you laugh.

Marie: Then it is a question of sound?

Gaston: Have you begun to tease already?

Marie: No, but you spoke as a lover of music.

Gaston: That is because I dare not tell you that I am a lover of another kind.

Marie: Now, my friend, no nonsense.

Gaston: I know you do not like it. Yet, you ought to be particularly indulgent to a— neighbor who has come to say farewell.

Marie: Farewell? Are you going away?

Gaston: This evening.

Marie: That means you are off on a hunt?

Gaston: Yes, to the jungles of India, after the tiger.

Marie: You are not serious?

Gaston: About the tiger? Certainly. Also of my plans. I have often spoken to you of Roger de Montluel.

Marie: Your friend who has been three

times around the world?

Gaston: Yes, and this time he has taken it into his head to have me go with him.

Marie: Ah! If that is the case, it is time I should stop laughing.

Gaston: Really?

Marie: Am I not going to lose a friend?

Gaston: Yes, a—friend.

Marie: You don't seem to be any too sure.

Gaston: Of course I am.

Marie: Are you, indeed! Let me see. You are my country neighbor. In the country it is quite the proper thing for neighbors to go to law. The occasion is not lacking, M. de Morières.

Gaston: It is a clear fact that that beastly drain of yours—

Marie: I advise you to complain, you whose boundary walls are daily tumbling down upon my espaliers.

Gaston: I shall leave orders to have them repaired. You say it is the proper thing for neighbors to go to law?

Marie: That does not apply to a case like ours where difficulties can be solved by friendship.

Gaston: Nothing else?

Marie: Nothing else.

Gaston: You see no other alternative?

Marie: Say rather that I wish to see none.

Gaston: Very well! But as far as I can see these neighborly relations need not exclude an attachment of a deeper and more intimate nature than mere friendship.

Marie: Again? M. de Morières, I have never known you as disagreeable as you are to-day.

Gaston: I have not had the chance so far, but I had promised myself to be more than agreeable.

Marie: So as to add keenness to my regrets at parting? You were unkind to make such a resolution.

Gaston: I was about to observe—

Marie: You were about to observe— Come, come, M. de Morières, we have had enough of nonsense, let us speak plainly. Ever since my arrival at Chantenay, a year ago—

Gaston: A year already!

Marie: Oh, spare me such exclamations. For a year, then, we have kept up these neighborly relations under the semblance of friendship.

Gaston: The resemblance is indeed striking. My chateau is within two gunshots of yours and your grounds run into mine. I am very thankful for this proximity and am indebted to it for the water that your drain continually backs into my cellars.

Marie: And I to your crumbling walls for the stones that crush my finest fruits. But our object is not to discuss the annoyances arising from bordering estates. Allow me to continue.

Gaston: I am all attention.

Marie: In consequence of some interchange of seeds, principally for the kitchen garden—

Gaston: Those white melon seeds! I will never forget them as long as I live.

Marie: In consequence of the interchange of some melon seeds—

Gaston: White. They were white melon seeds.

Marie: Well, then, white melon seeds, you paid me a visit.

Gaston: Ha, ha! I can still see myself, how I brought you, first, buds from my rose bushes, then roses from my buds—so you might judge for yourself.

Marie: And I accepted those roses and buds and later a basket of game.

Gaston: A hare, three pheasants, and seven quails.

Marie: I remember it.

Gaston: I shall remember it eternally.

Marie: Then followed other seeds, other roses, other baskets of game, and a number of calls.

Gaston: A hundred and eleven.
Marie: A hundred and eleven!

Gaston: I kept count of them. It seems quite a number in a year. Yet between neighbors in the country—

Marie: In short, by degrees we became inseparable. I found you frank and a genial comrade. Certainly nothing in your manner or conversation warranted me in doubting the sincerity of a friendship which I naturally returned.

Gaston: Oh, I see what you are driving at now.

Marie: Ah, indeed!

Gaston: Yes. Would you like me to finish it for you? "You came as a friend, you were received as a friend. If you change your role—"

Marie: In that case, my friend—But why discuss it when you are leaving for the Indies?

Gaston: Yes, I am glad to say that I am going to the Indies, although the Indies are scarcely far enough to suit me. To remain here and continue this role of friendship would be utterly impossible. For three months I have struggled to throw off the mask, but refrained through fear of displeasing you. The emotion of parting has at least given me courage to speak.

Marie: Stop, M. de Morières. Not another word. You are going too far.

Gaston: Is it going too far to say that I love you?

Marie: And he too!

Gaston: Yes, I love you, and whatever comes of it I congratulate myself for having dared to tell you so. Now you may dismiss me, prohibit my coming, withdraw your friendship, etc., etc. I will barely add that I am thirty, in sound health, and can offer you a spotless name and an ample fortune. There is nothing in my proposal to offend, even if, alas, there is nothing to flatter you. Only allow me to call you Madame de Morières and I promise you on my honor never to cause a shadow of sadness to darken those bright features that I so dearly love.

Marie: *(aside)* Behold! Still another plunges in.

Gaston: Have you nothing to say to me?

Marie: I do not doubt your sincerity, M. de Morières, and I will tell you candidly that your proposal surprises but in no sense offends me. I am a widow, my own mistress, therefore you come directly to me to ask for my hand. I would not be a woman if I took offense at a sincere love sincerely expressed.

Gaston: You were not shocked at my abruptness?

Marie: Not at all. It is your nature and I do not dislike men of your nature. However, to be absolutely true, I must confess there is a tinge of resentment to my surprise. You see, I was accustomed to view you solely as a friend, now your proposal changes the aspect of things and I find myself somewhat confused. You had never courted me and consequently I never questioned myself about you. Things have taken a grave turn, M. de Morières, and I must ask a few days for consideration.

Gaston: Do not refuse immediately. I will withdraw, already feeling less despondent than when I came.

Marie: One moment! I believe in your sincerity. I am sure that you love me and that you love none but me.

Gaston: You, you alone. Your beauty, your grace, your distinction.

Marie: *(aside)* Naturally! (*Aloud.*) Then, I fear no longer to make you a revelation that might cool a less passionate devotion.

Gaston: You have a revelation to make me?

Marie: *(aside)* His voice trembles.

Gaston: *(aside)* Could M. de Chantenay have imposed any conditions?

Marie: Reassure yourself. The revelation has nothing to do with my honor nor with my dignity nor with anything you love in me.

Gaston: I could have vouched for that.

Marie: It only refers to some miserable financial details. (*Aside*) His brow does not even darken.

Gaston: Miserable, indeed! But we will not bother about them. That's a lawyer's business, as the saying is.

Marie: *(aside)* Such disinterestedness!

Gaston: You certainly cannot do me the injustice to think that your fortune could influence my suit?

Marie: *(aside)* He affects the brave.

Gaston: On my honor, if you had no lands, nor stocks, nor even a jewel, it would make no difference, I should love you all the better.

Marie: Surely you would not wish me to be—

Gaston: Penniless. Rudely speaking, then, I might have some chance.

Marie: Well, my friend, you have your wish.

Gaston: Indeed!

Marie: (*aside*) He didn't even wince!
Gaston: And your fortune?

Marie: I possess wholly through M. de Chantenay.

Gaston: The family, I suppose, intend to contest the will?

Marie: Not at all. It is incontestable.
Gaston: Well, what then?

Marie: There is a codicil.

Gaston: Oh, I can guess the contents of the codicil. In case of second marriage?

Marie: M. de Chantenay wished to leave that opening for the benefit of his collateral heirs.

Gaston: What will you lose by marrying again?

Marie: An income of thirty thousand francs.

Gaston: I have fifty. I do not intend to boast of the difference, yet inasmuch as it does away with all fear of impoverishing you I feel warranted in pleading that you consent to an exchange which, unless objectionable to you, would assure my happiness.

Marie: You persist?

Gaston: I persist without any misgivings of the future. In the first place, you will have to make the same sacrifice for whomsoever you choose. Proud indeed should I be if you would make me the man, and I think I may pretend to be as worthy as a good many others.

Marie: You, my friend, you are the best of men, the most generous.

Gaston: That will do, that will do. Don't offer me sugar-coated pills. Only take to heart this one truth, that I love you. Think it over. Marry me. Leave Chantenay for Morières. You have but a step to take, but a little stream to cross. A propos of that stream, we will greet the new incumbents of Chantenay with a lawsuit as soon as they take possession. Be compassionate, Madame, reflect upon my proposal and decide as soon as possible. Then dispatch me word to Morières, where I now go in a fever of anxiety to await your answer.

Marie: Why are you in such a hurry?

Gaston: Why? Because the sooner you begin to reflect the sooner you will come to some decision.

Marie: I can think just as well in your presence. Unless you are afraid it might augment your fever, I would offer you some dinner.

Gaston: I will be poor company, but most happy to accept.

Marie: I will give the necessary orders.

You need not worry. There will be no extra preparations, for it is known that lovers live on little.

Gaston: Do not mock me. It is true that I love you with all my heart and only ask the chance to prove it.

(*Marie gives him her hand as she leaves the stage. He gladly siezes it and detains her. They exchange glasses.*)

Marie: (*aside*) Ah! Indeed, I should have been truly grieved if he had not proved better than the others.

(*Exit.*)

Scene V

Gaston: (*sighs*) Heavens! how I sigh. Yet, there is no sin in sighing. I sigh because I am in love and I love like a—no—I do not want to say, like a fool, on her account. I love, let me see, I love like a man of thirty who knows the charms and deceptions of life, and who says to himself when he meets the woman in the world who realizes his fondest dreams, 'Now, then, now, then, if I should not displease Madame de Chantenay, Madame de Chantenay would suit me marvelously.' No romantic introduction, no sudden emotion, no electric thrills. Talk to me rather of love that is founded on congenial tastes and fortune. Such a love is warranted not to fade with time. It does not blaze up as ignited straw only to end in a handful of ashes. It has its gradations, first Madame de Chantenay pleased me, then she charmed me, and finally bewitched me—yes, bewitched me. And to think that for three months I concealed my love under the guise of friendship. Ah, I

was right to screw my up courage! A courage that took me by surprise. Upon my honor I came here intending to do nothing more than say good by. I was half off to India and maybe farther for all I know. Now, I think of it, what did I do with Pontgouin's letter? We have a common notary. He will draw up the contract. (*Finding a letter*) No, that is Roger's. By the way, Roger is expecting me and I had forgotten all about him. (*He looks at his watch*) Five o'clock, I have barely time to run home and send a telegram to let my traveling companion know that I have given up the trip—detained by a—hope.

(*Exit.*)

Scene VI

(*Marie, Pontgouin.*)

Marie: No, no, M. Pontgouin, that will do, I beg of you.

Pontgouin: But Madame de Chantenay—

Marie: It is useless. I do not blame you. You thought that friendship would justify such perfidy. That excuses you in some degree, but as for M. de Morières, do not try to defend him.

Pontgouin: You make it seem worse than it actually is.

Marie: Perhaps it is because I held him in such esteem that his fall seems all the greater. I was foolishly taken in by his protests of chivalry. I am angry with him for two reasons, for having assumed the role of Don Quixote[18] and for having played it so cheaply.

Pontgouin: You make me bitterly regret—

Marie: Regret what? Having doubted his disinterestedness so far as to put him on his guard, or for having confessed to me your treason? The latter absolves you from the former.

Pontgouin: But the latter was involuntary. You forced my admission so dexterously—

Marie: Merely by chance. If it had not been for Pitou's indiscretion, who, in his innocence, informed me that he had just delivered a letter from you to M. de Morières.

Pontgouin: Pitou is an idiot! But didn't you allege what was false in order to get the truth out of me?

Marie: That was fair play.

Pontgouin: Yes, in a criminal prosecution against a felon, but against an inoffensive notary. "That was a clever ruse of yours," you said, "to have warned your friend. He has loyally confessed the whole affair and shown me your letter," and you were laughing as you said it, so that I fell into your trap. Awkward fool! When I had made my confession, you stopped laughing, and then I realized that through my stupidity I had ruined poor de Morières.

Marie: Console yourself, you have saved me.

Pontgouin: Saved?

Marie: Yes, from the greatest misery. From the misfortune of having to regard with contempt the man I should have married. Here he comes. Will you leave us, M. Pontgouin?

Pontgouin: What, you are going to make him undergo—

Marie: A cross-examination.

Pontgouin: And if he should deny?

Marie: Do you think he will deny to the end?

Pontgouin: No. But I think there is a gap in our judicial system. Women ought to be made prosecuting attorneys.

(*Exit.*)

Scene VII

(*Marie, Gaston.*)

Marie: Well, Neighbor, are you still here?

Gaston: Still?

Marie: I thought you had gone.

Gaston: I went home for a minute to send a dispatch to Montluel.

Marie: Your traveling companion?

Gaston: My ex-companion. Think of my forsaking him.

Marie: Why, have you given up your trip round the world?

Gaston: Am I not right to believe that there is no longer any reason why I should take such a journey?

Marie: Are you quite sure?

Gaston: You encouraged me to hope—

Marie: To hope for little—

Gaston: Yes; But—

Marie: You will admit there was no engagement?

Gaston: No, I asked you to consider—

Marie: And I have considered.

Gaston: Why, how strangely you say that?

Marie: I have thought it out to its bitter end.

Gaston: I beg of you—

Marie: I came to the conclusion, if you will allow me to be frank, that there was a little too much lightness in your character, a carelessness about your own interests, and a scorn for the material things of life that I should be distressed to encounter in my future husband.

Gaston: I do not quite understand—

Marie: At least, I thought that this levity, this indifference, this great disdain must come from some secret cause I knew nothing about.

Gaston: I am still in the dark.

Marie: Nevertheless, it is very clear, M.de Morières, and my reflections have brought me to the conclusion that you are either frightfully light or even more artful.

Gaston: If these little quarrels have no other end than to test my disposition,

quarrel away, Madame, you will find me as gentle as a lamb.

Marie: Yes, I understand you are armed against all tests.

Gaston: I am armed?

Marie: In full armor. Against which the news of my poverty made not a dint of impression.

Gaston: Very natural, was it not?

Marie: On the contrary, it was very astonishing. As if it were of no importance, as if you could have foreseen—

Gaston: As if it were of no importance. Certainly.

Marie: That you had not foreseen.

Gaston: No.

Marie: For which you were not at all prepared?

Gaston: Why, how could I have been?

Marie: Such innocence! You know my notary, M. Pontgouin?

Gaston: Very well. He is a great friend of mine.

Marie: Against such a friend you would not commit the least indiscretion?

Gaston: What do you mean?

Marie: I mean this. M. de Chantenay's will was deposited in the care of M. Pontgouin. Did he never in his conversation with you allude to the clauses of that will or to the codicil?

Gaston: Pontgouin has never spoken of it.

Marie: Nor written?

Gaston: Still less.

Marie: Now I have made up my mind, M. de Morières, that it is not carelessness you are guilty of, but dissimulation.

Gaston: Pray, what does this mean?

Marie: Oh! Do not inquire, do not feign to inquire. You have deceived me. It is easy to make a show of generosity when the display costs you so little. Happily, Providence intervened at the right moment to expose the imposture which was unworthy of a gentleman.

Gaston: Great heavens, Madame! I am led into a maze of astonishment, I swear that I am. Pray, be explicit.

Marie: You wish it? Very well, I will then tell you that I know everything. Do you understand? Everything.

Gaston: It is an advantage you have over me, for I know nothing—will you understand? Nothing.

Marie: Nothing? You do not know what was in that letter of M. Pontgouin's that my gardener just delivered to you?

Gaston: Pontgouin's letter. I never even looked at it.

Marie: (quickly changes her voice) Truly.

(He takes the letter from his pocket and holds it towards her. She seizes it with both hands.)

Gaston: No, I thought it was about those boundary walls, you know. Pitou handed it to me with such a triumphant smile and said: "Maybe M. de Morières will stop crushing Duchess pears."

Marie: You have never opened this letter.

Gaston: Remember, I had other troubles at heart. But since it has aroused your suspicions, it is very easy. (He takes it to break the seal.)

Marie: No, no, don't open it. I beg of you.

Gaston: Why not? I am curious to know what you accuse me of.

Marie: I accuse you no longer.

Gaston: Then my innocence is established?

Marie: On the contrary, I ask your pardon for having for a moment doubted your loyalty, your nobleness, your—

Gaston: Yes, you doubted me. I am entitled to a very great compensation, Madame.

Marie: Do you think it is in my power to give it to you?

Gaston: It requires only your good will.

Marie: We will discuss it later. Come, give me your arm.

Gaston: For dinner?

Marie: Yes, M. Pontgouin awaits us in the dining-room.

Gaston: Pontgouin! Is he there?

Marie: I retained him, thinking he would confound you.

Gaston: In reference to that letter? What could it have contained?

Marie: He will tell you. It is within his province.

Gaston: We will go, but, if it is just the same to him, he had better come to-morrow.

Marie: Will his presence annoy you?

Gaston: Oh, bother! He will rob me of my tête à tête.[19]

Marie: Not at all. Not at all, you shall have it before the notary.

(*Curtain.*)

Adaline Vanderpoel (1830-1912)

A retiring Club member but well-traveled, Adaline Elizabeth Van Schaack was born and raised in New York and married Aaron John Vanderpoel in 1852. The couple had seven children, three of whom died before the age of six, and two grandchildren.[1] Vanderpoel moved to Baltimore later in her life and joined the Woman's Literary Club of Baltimore. Her membership lasted a decade, from 1900-1910, but she rarely appears in the Club minutes. She did, however, read "Bermuda Past and Present" to the Club on more than one occasion. After she left the Club in 1910, she moved abroad, and died in London in 1912.[2]

"Bermuda Past and Present" is Vanderpoel's attempt to capture the history, sights, and spirit of Bermuda. In 1902, she had the essay published privately. The work begins with a section showcasing serious historical research about the "discovery" and colonization of Bermuda, followed by accounts of several well-known sites and their historical significance. This research is interspersed with observations about the lifestyle and temperament of the native people of Bermuda. Though her writing describes Bermuda as a charming getaway destination for wealthy white travelers like herself, Vanderpoel's work is rooted in her careful observation of the life and history of the island. —C. Love

Bermuda: Past and Present (1902)

It has been said that the Bermuda Islands are the most isolated inhabited land on the face of the earth, still it is difficult for any one who sees them in their present beauty to realize that for nearly a century after they were discovered they were regarded with terror by all mariners. They were known as "The Devil's Islands," full of bad weather, storms and evil spirits; a land in which it was impossible for human beings to live.

But in 1609, the *Sea Adventurer*, one of a small fleet sent from England to the new colony of Virginia, was separated from the other ships during a violent storm and wrecked on the coral reefs that surround the islands. The vessel was lost, but all on board, one hundred and fifty in number, reached the land in safety and also succeeded in saving the ship's rigging and stores.

The sailors were amazed at finding neither gnomes nor pixies on the island. Wild hogs, good for food, roamed in the cedar woods; fish were plentiful in the water close to the shore and the climate was so delightful, many wished to remain in a country that had proved so attractive. But Sir George Somers,[3] the commander of the expedition, felt that they ought to carry out the orders given to them when they left England, and go to Virginia.

Two small vessels were built of the cedar wood in which the islands abound, and nine months after the shipwreck the whole party sailed for Virginia. On arriving there they found the colony destroyed, and Sir George and his men at once returned to Bermuda, intending to form a new colony on the Island of St. George, which had been named for him. But he was no longer a young man, and the fatigue and exposures and disappointments of the repeated voyages proved too exhausting, and he died soon after landing. His discouraged men returned to England, taking his body with them; but his heart, at his own request, was buried on the island that still bears his name.

The stories told by the sailors on their return roused the interest of the English government, and, in 1611, a shipload of emigrants was sent out, under the charge of Sir Richard Moore, to take formal possession of the islands.

The story of the quarrels among the early colonists and the sufferings they endured from the depredations of the Spanish buccaneers would be too long for me to tell, and although they grew and prospered there is nothing of special interest to Americans in that part of their history until the time of our Revolutionary War. Then their sympathy for us was shown in a most practical way, for when General Washington,[4] before the evacuation of Boston, heard that a quantity of ammunition was stored in a remote part of the islands, he wrote to some prominent Bermudians telling of his great need and his wish to purchase the powder; they replied that he should have it, and the powder came in time, but so secretly that how it was brought to this country was known only to those actually engaged in the transfer. In later times Congress granted the right to export provision to Bermuda in return for this act of kindness to the colonies in their struggle for independence.

In 1804, Tom Moore, the Irish poet, was appointed Registrar of the Court of Vice Admiralty in Bermuda. He was delighted with the honor and supposed that the salary would be large. Great was his disappointment, on arriving at his post, to find that his perquisites depended principally on war, and that in times of peace his revenue would be very small. He wrote to his mother that even a war with Spain would not make it worth his while to stay in such a primitive country, and he soon returned to England. But he felt the charm of the wonderful Bermudian coloring and the climate with its aromatic breath of the cedars, and some of the best descriptions of the islands are to be found in his odes and letters. His warm, genial nature made many friends, and his memory was so cherished that on the one hundredth anniversary of his birth the town flag was raised at St. George in memory of his connection with the islands, and some of his stanzas describing their beauty were posted on the flag staff and read by the passers by with great interest.

In these days few tourists go to Bermuda who do not visit his home at Walsingham and the old Calabash tree of which he so often wrote. The chimney of his room, with its blue tiles, is unchanged and the cedar doors and casement are blackened by time. Even his peculiarities are still remembered. Among others, his dislike to mice that almost amounted to fear. He had another foible which men are fond of saying belongs exclusively to women, but my observation in life has convinced me that it is masculine as well as feminine. He was exceedingly inquisitive. A lady at whose house he was a frequent visitor, one day, when she was expecting him to call, in a spirit of mischief placed a mouse in her work box and turned the key but left it in the lock. When the poet entered he took his seat by the table on which the box stood and soon began to play with the key. The temptation was irresistible; he turned the key and raised the lid, when, to his great disgust, the mouse jumped into his lap.

It is said that he never forgave the lady for her mischievous trick, and to her were addressed the familiar lines,

> "When I loved you, I can't but allow,
> I had many an exquisite minute,
> But the scorn that I feel for you now
> Hath even more luxury in it!
> Thus whether we're on or we're off
> Some witchery seems to await you.
> To love you is pleasant enough
> And oh! tis delicious to hate you."[5]

Moore only remained in Bermuda for four months, but he continued to draw his salary for forty years, and then was removed from the office on the ground of "continued non-residence."

Could the poet return to Bermuda at the present time, he would wonder at the changes that have taken place. A massive causeway nearly two miles in length now connects the island of St. George with the larger island of Bermuda, and the town of St. George, which was the principal place of business in 1804 and also the center of military and naval life, is now quite superseded by Hamilton, with its more central location, better business facilities and fine hotels. The seat of government was removed there in 1815 from St. George by Governor Hamilton, whose name was given to the new city. The Parliament House there and the Post Office would be considered fine buildings in any country.

Ireland Island has one of the largest and best dockyards in the world. There are forts on every point and red coats and marines are seen everywhere.

At first, a stranger wonders why these small islands are so well fortified, for they rank next to Gibraltar[6] in England's strong fortifications. But they are the rendezvous for the British fleet in the Atlantic Ocean, and, with Halifax[7] in the north. Englishmen feel that the whole Atlantic coast of the United States is under their surveillance. But we feel sure that this is only in a spirit of true friendliness, for during the last twenty years these lovely islands have been a winter home to many Americans who are warmly welcomed by the residents. And the change from our cold winters to a land of sunshine and flowers is most welcome.

The flora of Bermuda is wonderful, though not indigenous to the soil. One of the English governors, in the early part of the eighteenth century, sent to the West Indies for a variety of tropical plants, which have grown and flourished in their new home, and it is said there is not a poisonous plant in the islands.

The hedges of oleander, sometimes twelve feet high, are beautiful with their great clusters of red, white and pink flowers. The poinsettia is much prized in northern greenhouses for the large red flowers at the extreme end of its green stalk, but in Bermuda, the stems, leaves and blossoms are all a brilliant red and make a bright spot in the landscape. Scarlet geraniums and lantanas grow everywhere and the rose geranium is equally common, but is usually called "the graveyard geranium," as pillows are made of its fragrant leaves to place under the head of those who are resting in their "last dreamless sleep."

All are familiar with pictures of the large fields of Bermuda lilies, but it may not be generally known that onions are often cultivated in the same field and are called "Bermuda violets." We are told that "a rose by any other name will smell as sweet," and I am equally sure that an onion whether it is called violet, mignonette or snow-drop will still retain the peculiar odor by which it is recognized in all lands.

There are many interesting churches in Bermuda. The old Devonshire church dates back to 1719 and is still standing, though no longer used, for the walls have been pronounced unsafe. At one end of the church is a cedar tree, the oldest in the islands, from whose topmost branch the bell was hung that for more than a century called the congregation together for daily and weekly services. It is dead now, but in its hollow trunk is a vigorous young tree growing up as if determined to carry on the good work begun by its ancestor.

The Mother Church in the islands is St. Peter's[8] in the town of St. George. The present walls were built in 1713, and at first the roof was thatched, but in 1765 this was replaced by one of stone, which still remains. The massive silver communion service given by King William III is still in constant use. But the service most frequented on Sunday morning by strangers is held in what is called the Garrison Church, near the barracks at Prospect. It is a lovely drive from Hamilton, and not a long walk for good pedestrians. A large West Indian regiment is now stationed there, and the contrast between their shining ebony faces and sleeveless red coats worn over full white shirts was very picturesque as they marched in and took their places. I have heard the *Te Deum*[9] in some of the finest churches in Italy, but it has seldom seemed to me more impressive than in that barn-like building, used as a gymnasium six days in the week, with a temporary altar at one end and the walls covered with ropes and swings and ladders and bars. The voices of the men were so full and strong, led by their own band, which is said to be one of the finest in the British Army. After service the band usually plays for an hour on the green near the church, and the music is good even if not strictly devotional.

The colored race in Bermuda seemed to me much superior to that in our own country. Better looking, better mannered, and far more efficient as house servants. But, oh suffering housekeepers of this southern land, "ye must possess your souls in patience,"[10] for slavery was abolished in these islands in 1834, and if nearly three-score years and ten are required to make good servants of freed blacks, I fear that few of you who are now struggling with the great problem will live to see it solved.

The Boer prisoners[11] excite a good deal of interest in modern Bermuda. Last December two thousand were confined on two of the islands. They are housed in Bell tents with plank floors and are as well fed as the soldiers in the English army. Their meat alone costs the British government a thousand dollars a day, and last summer, while the drought prevailed in Bermuda, water was carried to them from St. George's at one hundred dollars a day. I was told on good authority that the meat and groceries and vegetables furnished them were of the best. England knows that the whole civilized world is watching to see how these prisoners are treated, and even if she were not influenced by the higher motive of humanity, she would care justly for them. The only work required of them is to prepare their own food and take care of their own quarters, but if they wish to work there are trees to be cut on the islands they occupy, and some fertile spots to be cultivated. If they choose to do this work they are well paid for doing it, but it is optional with them. Many employ their time in making children's toys out of the red cedar wood or in carving brooches or other trinkets out of bones. There is a shop on one of the principal streets where these things are sold at a good price, only a small percentage being allowed to the saleswomen and the rest of the money goes to the prisoners. The day

that the steamer sails for New York the shop is almost emptied of its contents, for most tourists wish to take away some memento of such a strange people. Many of them are living more comfortably than they have ever done before, but they are captives and captivity is always hard to bear. The islands they occupy are protected by many straight rows of barbed wire which are crossed and recrossed by the same material so many times it would seem impossible for any one to get away, yet one man contrived to escape and went up to New York on a steamer as a stoker. His fellow stokers knew that he was an escaped prisoner, but no one betrayed him, and on reaching New York, he was feasted and feted by many who sympathized with his cause.

Two young English officers sat smoking one day, and were idly watching rather a large box that seemed tossed back and forth on the water, when one of them sprang to his feet and exclaimed, "There's something wrong about that box, for it is steadily making its way against the tide!" A boat was sent out, and a Boer was found under the box. When asked how he could expect to escape in that way, he said he hoped to get into the interior for he knew he could take care of himself if he could only get there. The poor fellow did not realize that there is no interior in Bermuda. At no point is the largest island more than three miles in width, and although there is a great growth of cedar woods on the island yet those woods are crossed at short intervals by roads broad enough for three horses to go abreast. I often wondered if being on an island did not add to the bitterness of exile, for many of the prisoners had never seen a river or lake or any body of water until they were taken to Durban to embark on their long voyage.

What matters it to them that the Bermuda Islands are three hundred and sixty-five in number when they can see but few of them, and the water all around is less attractive to them than the broad velts[12] of their own land? But to us who were free to go and come as we pleased that water was always beautiful, and we found the good roads on all parts of the islands a great pleasure. These roads were cut by the convicts when Boaz Island was used by England as a penal station, through the coral rock of which the islands are formed, and whether they lead through cedar woods or through walls of rock fifteen feet high or on a level, with nothing to obstruct the view of the sparkling ocean on one side and the sound studded with islands on the other, they are always hard and smooth. There are many beautiful drives on the islands and the excursions by water even more numerous. The sky and water are so blue and bright there is everything in Bermuda to make life out of doors delightful and health giving.

Have any of you bronchial tubes that refuse to do their work? Go to Bermuda; the soft air will bring healing strength. Have any of you rheumatic twinges? The place is a panacea for those woes. Are any of you haunted by that dreadful "something still undone that waits and will not go away?" Go to Bermuda. The soothing Spanish "Mariana" must have crept across the water from Mexico for Bermudians are never hurried. If a thing is not finished today, it can be done tomorrow or the day after or the next day—there is time enough. And that is a lesson good for wearied nerves to learn. And lest I should be considered too enthusiastic about these beautiful islands, I will close this paper with the even more positive words of another:

"Nowhere can be found within the compass of nineteen square miles so much that is novel, beautiful and interesting with such air and such sunshine and such peace as can be found in Bermuda."[13]

Florence McIntyre Tyson (1854-1926)

Born in Hanover, Delaware in 1854, Florence McIntyre Tyson was intelligent and worldly. She was a member of the Woman's Literary Club of Baltimore from 1893 until the 1909-1910 season, when she resigned due to her frequent absences from Baltimore. Tyson served as the chairman of several committees while involved with the Club, including the Committee on Foreign Languages and the Committee on Translations.

A woman of many languages, including French, Italian, German, and Spanish, Tyson turned translation into art. Her most notable published work is her translation of *Russia*, by Théophile Gautier, from French to English. This volume was warmly received by critics, the public, and the Club itself. In addition to *Russia*, Tyson translated short stories from several foreign luminaries, including Nobel Prize recipient Grazia Deledda. The works of Italian author Deledda and French author Jean Madeline included in this anthology encapsulate life in foreign lands through contemplation of grand European landscapes and the recurring theme of temporal love, which Tyson beautifully conveys in the English language. Tyson's translations make it possible for her readers to travel the world through print. —J. Fury and C. McElduff

Waiting (1903)

Translated from the French of Jean Madeline[1]

"Well, it is decided—you are to go?"
"Yes, Suzanne; it is my destiny that demands it."

She fixed her great, lovely eyes upon him sadly.

"You know it is not my fault—I would have been only too proud and happy to be your wife—but since that is not possible, go, my love. We must each 'dree our own weird.' You must go into a new world; lead a brilliant and full existence. You will be admired and sought for, and, I hope, very happy,— I shall grow old amid the narrow life of a little town, a little road illumined by a little lamp—I shall always be a provincial, like those you make fun of in your books—I shall keep on wearing hoops, and shall look ridiculously. In the evening, after my pupils have gone to bed, sitting in the chimney-corner, I shall read your books and find my happiness in following the progress of your success, in seeing your name, your portrait in the papers, in hearing from a distance the sound of your triumphs. So I shall fasten to my existence a leaf from your laurel-wreath, which will enrich my humble, quiet life. Of course, like all girls, I have had my dream, which was that we should travel in

the same compartment, to use one of your images, Sir Novelist; and I used to love to fancy that our road would always be the same, and that together we would go to the end, in the same corner of the car, where fate had placed us, without troubling ourselves about the stations called out along the way. But apparently you must change cars and here we separate. You get out—I remain in—" Then, seeing some one approach, she gave him the delicious smile of a saleswoman, for sweet charity's sake, and offering him a flower: "See, Monsieur Gerbaud, pray buy these pinks—for the sake of the poor."

All around them, the 'charity bazaar' had stirred into unusual life, the chilly classrooms, whose bare walls were now garlanded with evergreens, among which the young girls, full of delight at finding themselves shopkeepers, were doing a thriving business.

In the halls, even in the gloomy courtyard, charming, coquettish little aprons were flashing about, while amid the universal gaiety, and offering of flowers and various trifles, many an opportunity was seized for a handclasp or whispered word—thus gathering a petal from the sad rose of Love.

❧

It had begun as a little love affair, when they were children at school. She was the daughter of Madame Lantelme—

School for Young Ladies—who were dubbed "the little blue girls," on account of their uniform. On Thursdays, and Sunday afternoons, when the "little blue girls" walked in pairs around the boulevard, under the drowsy plantain trees, they were always followed by a crowd of young wretches. Each one had his sweetheart; it was the fashion at the college. His had always been this slight, pale girl, with great, dark eyes, who walked behind the rest with her mother, with a seriousness and precocity beyond her years. She had stirred his youthful heart, whence sprung up a vague tenderness. And, too, on her side there awoke a certain agitation and trembling sympathy for that look that never failed to seek hers.

By degrees these uncertain impressions were crystallized into definite form, quite free from the usual coquetries and sillinesses usual in such cases, and simple nosegays of violets gravely offered and as gravely received, alone shed their fragrance over the birth of this love. When, grown up, she became the assistant of her mother in the school, and, he was no longer a schoolboy, with ink-stained fingers, but a handsome young man, whose gaze began to catch glimpses of life, the seeds placed in the furrows of their hearts had burst into abundant bloom, and their love, already of long standing, seemed each to date from that hour in which, in the long ago, they had felt that they loved.

Then one day, Pierre Gerbaud, whose nature was sensitive and open to impressions and feelings, which, whirling through

his soul with irresistible force, united in the formation of his 'ego,' felt awaken within him new needs, new desires. Walking among the narrow streets of his little native town, he was seized with a feeling of suffocation, an intense, desire for a larger horizon, new faces, new things.

Whenever he went out he would come across those excellent, fat shopkeepers, standing placidly before their doors, their expressionless eyes fixed intently upon the opposite wall. Their ideas were choked under a mass of flabby flesh, nor had they any thought of the world beyond, nor that men were created for aught else, than to sell shoes or to buy them. And, above all else, it was these sanctimonious personifications of a narrow life, that drove Pierre Gerbaud to desperation. Their limited horizon their existence, turning ceaselessly within the same circle of occupations and ideas with the meagre and resigned lassitude of horses in a treadmill, filled him with repulsion against which all that was his of youth and hope and aspiration revolted.

He recalled a memory of his childhood, when, during vacation, he would go by rail to pay a visit to a neighboring village. On the opposite side towards the North, the road lay straight amid its shining rails: then, turning, was lost in the distance, and at this point there was a great disc. And to this little boy, who had never gone beyond, this disc closed in the known world. When he thought of mysterious, far-away lands, especially when he thought of Paris, he at once in fancy beheld the disc, and although he knew it was far away, he would picture to himself all that lay beyond for once plunged into the unknown, all notion of space would disappear.

And now that the world beyond was drawing him with irresistible force, this disc once more showed itself as the termination of all his dreams, becoming the definite end of his efforts and desires, till life appeared to him but under these two aspects—the shopkeepers or the disc. And by degrees there arose within him an intense longing to write, to create. He became one of those unfortunates, burned by an inward fire, who, instead of enjoying in peace their visions and emotions, are pursued by the desire of seizing them all palpitating with life, to enclose them in written words, whose insufficiency brings to them an ever-present discontent.

One of his greatest happinesses was to linger for hours before the bookshops where the last new books displayed their titles temptingly under the gas jets. Over the harvest of little yellow books, filling the window, Pierre intoxicated himself with the fragrance of the freshly-cut leaves, and to turn with the tips of his fingers their still damp pages, filled him with strange delight. Then, choosing a volume, he would tear along the streets till people turned to look, and reaching the solitude of his own little room, he would immerse his trembling hands in its pages. But his especial joy was to loiter at the library of the railroad station where the portly goddess, who presided over the spot, would gaze from her corner curiously at the boy, who was always ready to stop among the books. For there he found united, the beverages that quenched but to augment his thirst—the intoxication of new books, and the stirring life of the station. In the midst of the clanging of bells, the shrieks of locomotives, the bustle of travelers, bringing with them the fascination of the unknown, he would console himself by fancying that to him, too, might sometime come the happiness of going away.

For a long time Pierre hesitated. For Madame Lantelme's daughter, whose humble livelihood was assured by "the little Blues," did not dare to even think of going. Her life rose before her colorless and straight, readymade without anything of mystery or the unforeseen. To help her mother, then to take her place educating little girls, who would leave her to enter life, become mammas, then grandmammas, while their children and grandchildren took their places in the bare classrooms; till gradually she would reach old age, cloistered within the same narrow horizon, the monotony of days each exactly like its predecessor.

But she accepted it all with the resignation of a nun. And when Pierre begged her to place her hand in his and together to face the unknown, she replied with a sad smile: "No, mon ami, it may not be. The Good Lord has not granted me a permit of travel."

Pierre came very near unpacking and settling down; for he loved tenderly and truly this frail maiden, whose sad, dark eyes showed sorrow born in silence and alone. And for a while he struggled against the fever that was consuming him. But it was of no avail, and at last he determined to go.

The train reached the disc, then passed it. Pierre felt this was the turning point of his life, and that he had indeed left the past far behind him. He looked eagerly about. Paris was not yet there—but already Suzanne had disappeared.

᪥

A man descended from the railroad carriage. His hair was white and his eyes those of an old man. The porters approached: "Hotel de Luxembourg, m'sieur?" He shook his head, and standing with bent head and hands crossed, behind him, looked about that station which his youth had quitted—to which his old age had returned. He turned towards the avenue. The bare branches of the trees shivered painfully under the chill of the violet sky, while the houses on each side assumed unwonted proportions in the misty November evening. He turned up the collar of his overcoat and, his hands still crossed behind him, he turned into the avenue.

He met very few people. Some servants who were hastening homeward after having filled their pitchers at the fountain. Once a hack, whose driver was whistling, passed. A sentinel, in front of the prefecture, had fallen asleep, and enveloped in his great military cloak, he looked like a pile of clothing. The traveler threw away his cigar.

On the other side of the avenue, they were lighting the lamps in front of a café; their brilliancy turned the twilight into darkness. The delicious dreaminess of this charming hour, into which but the outlines of things are apparent, was shaken by a crude reality, which brought a feeling of actual suffering to the lonely wayfarer.

Crossing the street, he stopped at the café. He read "Café de France," and saying to himself: "I don't know this: it must be something new," he went in.

A dozen people were seated at the tables, leaning their heads on their hands. The heads promptly were raised. Then they began to whisper, to move their chairs and evince a surprise full of curiosity at the entrance of a stranger. Then every one was still, but finally began to talk and form into parties to play dominoes.

He was seated on a bench with a glass of hot punch. As he looked unhappy and the collar of his coat was lined with fur, the host approached and addressed him: "Good evening! have you just arrived?" He replied "Yes," and raised the glass to his lips.

The host remained standing before him, his eyes fixed upon him. The other asked: "This café has just been opened?"

The man burst into a loud laugh. "Well, hardly! It is a matter of twenty-five years' standing." The traveler exclaimed in amazement: "Twenty-five years!" Then, bowing his head: "True! true!" And the image of his absence rose suddenly and took possession of him, till he seemed to perceive at a distance, as if at the end of a long tunnel, this little town the day he had left it. He remembered it was more than thirty years ago. He saw himself forgotten, a stranger to all that was around him, in which, indeed, he had no part. Then he seized his hat and went out, leaving his glass but half empty. The lamps of the esplanade were shining on the bare branches of the trees. In a corner a pile of chairs, used for the music in summer, was covered with a thick awning. The empty pathways re-echoed to every step.

But on the boulevard on the other side, the fronts of the houses were alight with the charm of the life of night. Not the night of the country, which erects a wall each side of the road, beyond which lie the silent sleeping fields; nor the dusty, chilly life of the suburbs. But the warm, soft night of the boulevards, through which pass exquisite toilettes, and fur mantles, and luxurious flashes from brilliant windows. Carriages returning from afternoon visits; charming figures in front of the shop windows, admiring the beautiful things there exposed, and leaving with smiles.

The man continued his way, more and more oppressed with the feeling that once he had been a part of it all, and that now he was nothing. Till this idea assumed within him a sensation of actual physical pain, among the trees and houses and passing people, each eager for his own elbow room, and especial portion of air. It was the unhealthy sensation of a broken, tossed-about creature, whose nerves are over-excited by his sufferings, with whom the slightest sensation assumes the keenness of pain.

So this poignant feeling drove him to quit the boulevard, where there were too many people, and to choose a deserted street, a poor country lane, lighted by but a single lamp.

There suddenly this feeling that was breaking his heart, melted into a vague, sweet sadness which at first he was unable to explain. But it brought him great consolation, as if, on the edge of this shadowy silence, all the agitation of his life, his unhappiness, the wretchedness of his evil days, had disappeared amid the tenderness of familiar objects in this street so well known in the long ago.

And suddenly he understood.

He stopped before a two-story house. On the door was written:

SCHOOL FOR YOUNG LADIES, MADAME LANTELME.

As he stood before the stone steps, the emotions of his childhood returned. His heart beat so violently, he could almost hear it across the distance of thirty years.

And once more he saw himself before this door a lad in short trousers, and later a young man, his heart full with his beautiful love. And then, for the first time in his life, he asked himself why, when this door was open, and a kiss was awaiting him behind it, he had not entered, seized it and kept it forever.

Before his weary eyes, there passed a vision of a smile given under the evening lamp, of a cozy, warm fireside. And he groaned in the cold, dark street, this poor victim of a bad life, who, after having struggled and broken his nails, had returned wounded and suffering with infinite weariness. Brusquely there arose before him the cold rigidity of the END, this immutable barrier, that shuts in our horizon. This sensation of the irretrievable fell upon him heavily, overwhelming him with despair.

He went onward.

After taking several steps he stopped and hesitated. Then returned drawn by an irresistible force. Once more the door was before him, and he rung the bell.

He waited and was on the point of leaving when he heard footsteps descending the stairs. The door opened.

A little old lady appeared, the strings of her cap falling each side of her face. She was very thin with that meagerness of an old maid who has never known the development of maternity. She held in her hand a lamp raised high in order to see more clearly. Seen thus, she made one think of a little life shriveled up, then wrinkled, then bent, then—silence.

He asked: "Pardon, Madame. Madame Lantelme and her daughter once lived here—Would you perhaps know—Could you tell me——?"

The tiny old lady bent forward anxiously.

"I am Suzanne Lantelme, Monsieur."

She raised the lamp a little higher.

"You do not know me?" asked the man. She shook her head: "No, no."

"Good-evening," he replied. And without another word he turned and was swallowed up by the darkness.

She mounted the stairs slowly, full of anxiety over this inexplicable, late visit.

Once upstairs, she opened the window to assure herself that the unknown man was not wandering about the house. But the little street was empty, cold and dark.

Then she seated herself once more in her little, solitary chamber, which was the sanctuary of a modest, tender, never-forgotten love. And, as happened every evening, the poor little, loving old lady resumed her knitting of mittens for him for whom she had been waiting thirty years, for whom she would wait until the end, and whom she did not know, when he came.

Two Men and a Woman (1903)

Translated from the Italian of Grazia Deledda

Among the prisoners who arrived at the Penitentiary on the 23rd of March, as the setting sun was flooding with crimson its cold, grim walls, was a young man of distinguished appearance; he was dressed in gray, and the folds of his large, soft gray hat, adorned with a knot of gray ribbon, quite hid his pale, thin face, with its aquiline nose and carefully kept pointed beard. During the journey he had not spoken once, but sat with bent head and knitted brows, his eyes intently fastened upon his thin, nervous hands with their long, polished nails, enclosed in the shining bands of the steel handcuffs. On reaching the Penitentiary he had for an instant raised his head and fixed his shining, burning eyes upon the countenance of the Direttore,[2] who on his side returned the gaze coldly and at length. By a queer coincidence, the prisoner and the Direttore had the same name—Cassio Longino! And they both knew it; and the prisoner, who in his distant country across the sea where "Cassio" means "a white petticoat," had often been the subject of many a caricature, experienced now a sort of bitter satisfaction, on seeing himself on that account sought by the cold, scornful glance of the Signore Direttore. With the first glance, the two men hated each other. The Direttore was approaching middle life, was small and stooped a little. His feet and hands were small, and the latter were always plunged in the pockets of his long, black overcoat. His clean-shaven face bore the marks of physical suffering, which was accentuated in deep lines about the pale, thin lips; his eyes were small and green and full of an almost cruel indifference; his hair was blond and short, and his ears large and prominent. For all these reasons, but chiefly because he was the commandant of the prison, he was exceedingly displeasing to No. 245; and No. 245 was displeasing to the commandant on account of his haughty manner, the fiery look with which he observed him, and especially on account of his vigorous, superb youth.

While the prisoners were being consigned to their quarters, the Direttore did not open his mouth, and for several days, Cassio, shut up in a private cell, did not again see him. His cell faced the east, and through the tiny aperture pierced in the great stone rampart, he could see the distant Apennines,[3] still covered with snow, and the Tuscan landscape, over which the early spring was scattering a vivid green sward, and the pale, tender coloring of bursting twig and blossom. In the Penitentiary garden, which was cultivated by prisoners clad in white linen suits and red caps, Cassio, who by especial permission of the Government retained his gentleman's clothes, watched the peach trees burst into a glory of intensest pink, and the apple trees toss their delicate bloom in rich masses through the balmy, fragrant air.

A prey to keen anguish and despair, he never wandered far from his cell. The long, silent evenings overwhelmed him with despair; often he did not sleep at night, but tossed feverishly upon his hard straw pallet. When, in the morning, the guard, a great, tall fellow, whose red head brushed against the ceiling of the cell, would come in to make up the bed, Cassio was always dressed and standing before his tiny, barred window.

Outside the swallows were wheeling and fluttering about, their wings and breasts flashing in the sunshine. The prisoner did not deign to speak a word to the guard, nor did he take the slightest notice of the continual complaints, whistles, or gestures of his neighbor on the right; but when the exercise hour arrived and he was allowed to walk in the courtyard, he paced in haughty indifference, without even a glance at his companions, up and down the sad, dew-covered pavement.

The rumor spread through the prison that he was a very rich lord from Sardinia, a relation of the Direttore, and since the Direttore was feared and hated (though none of the prisoners knew the reason of this hate and fear, for the poor man had never done them any evil, except with his look of icy indifference), No. 245 within a week after his arrival, was hated, and strange to say, was feared.

Having requested permission to write, the first of April he was sent for into the office; through the barred window there penetrated a ray of pale sunshine, in whose light danced the shadows of a distant treetop. The Direttore, bent more than usual, was working at a gray table; he neither moved nor spoke for a long time, during which Cassio, standing upright and stiff, his eyes fixed on the branches trembling in the sunshine, grew hot with humiliation.

Ah! in the presence of the others, of that crowd of criminals, and the vile guards, he could at least give himself the satisfaction of taking refuge in a certain, scornful dignity; he was stronger than those who bound him, greater than those whom he would not even deign to call companions in misfortune, but in the presence of this little man, so ill and full of disdain, he must bow, must reply, must humiliate himself.

"You," said the Direttore brusquely, turning around but not rising, "are condemned to three years of simple detention for forgery; and you may write only once a month."

His voice was rather weary, but the tone was pure Tuscan.

"I know it," replied Cassio, "but I have

not asked to be allowed to write to my own home, but on my own account, in my own cell."

"It is not possible. Why do you not ask to be placed in the office of the clerks?"

"Is there chance of being allowed to do so?"

"Yes, there is every chance."

That very day Cassio proffered his request, and on the next was placed in the office, where a great quantity of work was badly executed by three other prisoners. The room, which was next to that of the Direttore, was even more desolate and gloomy, and the three clerks, the first, fat and bald, with small, bleared eyes; the second, fair, pale, and with a transparent look, and the third, a tall muscular young man, with black curly hair, and the face of a Roman emperor, made a bad impression on the new arrival.

They appeared resigned to, and even contented with, their melancholy fate. Cassio, on the other hand, experienced a profound disgust, which was but accentuated by the stupid resignation of his companions in misfortune—a very anguish of impotent desperation, and regretted his request. Better to have remained alone in his cell, with his hands clasping the bars of the little window, and before him the distant Apennines, that brought to him memories of his own native mountains, resounding with the neighing of his black charger, dashing in pursuit of the straying sheep—alone with his sentence and his sorrow!

He of the curly head, bolder than the other two, who contented themselves with casting stealthy glances at him, sought promptly, though respectfully, to make his acquaintance. (They knew that he had the same name as the Direttore, and so it was told among the other prisoners.)

"Are you a Sardinian?"

"Yes;" replied he coldly.

"Since Fate has sent you to this place, allow me—"

"A beautiful Fate!" interrupted Cassio bitterly, and cut off sharply the compliment the unfortunate man was about to present to the presumed great Sardinian signore. But he said nothing more himself, nor asked anything of the others.

Three days later, there arrived for him from Sardinia a letter bearing an air of indefinable elegance. The handwriting was large and firm, while a delicious, almost imperceptible fragrance escaped from the sheets.

The Direttore opened it, and read it with a certain hesitation and half feeling that he had been expecting it.

After all, he was a man who was still young; he had suffered much and loved much, and if his own sufferings had produced that profound indifference which passed for cruelty among the unhappiness it was his fate to control, there still remained in his heart something of sympathy and compassion. Had No. 245 been a poor devil, like almost all the other prisoners, instead of a most interesting personality, the Direttore, after the first day, would never have given him another thought. But this handsome young stranger, with his haughty, distinguished air, who had arrived surrounded by a romantic mystery, had attracted the attention of everyone, as well as his own.

The queer stories current in the gloomy cells and dark corridors had also reached his ears.

The thought that there might be something of truth in them, had even begun to pierce his customary indifference with a faint interest, which was augmented as he perused the letter.

Not that it contained anything of especial interest. It was written by a half-sister of Cassio.

An intense affection manifested itself through all the four sheets, a certain nameless sweetness, and exquisite suggestion of comfort and resignation.

"Have courage, Cassio, do not despair nor suffer too much; remember that we two are alone in the world, alone to love and believe in one another. The time will pass, and when God reunites us, I will know how to recompense thee for the immense sacrifice thou hast made for me. Do not feel humiliated nor cast down; the good know that thy fault was an act of heroism—"

"Indeed," thought the Direttore, "prisoners are always innocent, generally are victims, but that they should be heroes!"

This letter, so different from the vulgar epistles that were accustomed to come to the Penitentiary; so good, delicate, and loving, gave him food for reflection.

A sort of morbid curiosity took possession of him, against which he struggled in vain, to find out, to know everything. So that in spite of himself, though not contrary to the regulations of the establishment, which he scrupulously observed, he sent for No. 245, and on his arrival, he opened the conversation by explaining some difficult work to be done in the office, and then fixing a look of close scrutiny upon him, said:

"Here is a letter for you."

Cassio proffered never a word, but raised his head, and his face turned red to the tips of his ears.

And for the second time a wonderful thing happened. The Direttore of the Penitentiary envied his prisoner. For to the prisoner in his profound wretchedness, had come a voice of comfort and affection, illuminating his dark horizon with a glory that was mirrored on his countenance, and to him, free and powerful, alone and lost in the infinite sadness of deep suffering, there never came one word of tenderness, one ray of light.

In spite of his emotion, Cassio perceived something abnormal was passing in the mind of the Direttore, and astute Sardinian that he was, he took advantage to ask eagerly if he might not have the letter at once and read it there in the office.

Better there, under the badly concealed indifference of the little, green eyes, than in the repulsive surroundings of his workroom, subject to the vulgar curiosity of the three clerks.

From that day, he became more sociable, more resigned, and the Signore Direttore showed him a certain deference which did not escape the eyes of the others, and but confirmed the report of an assumed relationship.

But still he did not receive permission to write until he had been there a month, though on the very day he was given two sheets. And his letter was not less affectionate than had been his sister's, though less sweet and delicate; in every line was displayed the agony of helplessness.

"I have been here but a month, though it seems thirty years. I am beginning to be more resigned. They have put me in the clerk's office, with three terrible strangers (this the Direttore erased), the work is hard, but it helps to pass the time. At first I could not accustom myself to it, now I am less desperate. The Signore Direttore is very kind to me. Yes, I know the time will pass somehow or other, but still I feel as if my sentence would be eternal; that the 987 days yet remaining are as boundless as the waves; but most of all do I suffer when I think of thee; and yet the thought brings me much comfort. Thou art so good. Please do not forget me and get married while I am away! But I am ashamed, my dear Paola, such a thing I well know is impossible. How could a good sister forget her unhappy brother? But all the same, when I am tossing sleeplessly on my narrow bed, the thought fills me with terror. Who could believe such a thing possible?

"Though I am now resigned to all, I did once believe in the justice of men. But what have they done to me? Write very soon and do not forget me. If that were to happen I would soon find a termination to my sufferings."

Not a word nor thought for anyone else, only for her! The answer arrived by return of mail, together with clothes, books, and money.

The Signore Direttore, felt anew the strange fascination of envy and longing, as he read the delightful, tender letter of Paola. She had not a word of reproach for the lack of confidence the unhappy man had shown in her, but said how grieved she was that he should be so sad, and assured him she would never marry until his return. She had, too, a good word for the Signore Direttore. "Love and respect him; he can do much for thee; can be like a father to thee" ["a brother, young lady," thought the Direttore]. "I pray for thee and for him."

"Thanks," he murmured rather bitterly.

In the third letter, Cassio having asked what she was doing and how she passed the days:

"The days pass sadly in thy absence. I look after my affairs as well as I can, and often go into the country with my foster-parents. Poor things, they are a great comfort to me! We go on horseback, and these trips are my only diversion. In the house nothing new has happened. I am embroidering the tapestry I began at school, when my dreams were so different from the present reality. I am working into it certain rich Sardinian embroideries ferreted out by the foster-mother.

"I never see anyone, but am always thinking of thee and counting the days."

"Why in the world do not these people, who seem rich and cultivated, think of asking for a pardon," the Direttore asked himself, and, rising, he went into the garden, where the Tuscan spring was rioting amid a very glory of roses—crimson, white, and yellow; while gleaming among the deep green of the shrubbery, like brilliant butterflies, moved about the little red caps of the prisoner gardeners, and fell into a strangely sweet strain of thought of which the tender, strong sister of No. 245 was the subject. In fancy he saw her, tall and dark, like her brother, with the pallor and distinguished appearance so marked in the prisoner; or bending patiently over her embroidery; or else trotting on her little Sardinian horse, her eyes half closed as she faced the ardent beams of the midday sun. Then, lost in wonder, he took himself to task for such boyish romance, till he worked himself into quite a frenzy of anger at his foolishness, which left him exhausted and more indifferent even than was his wont.

And so the months rolled by, bringing three or four more letters from Paola. In the last she promised to send her picture, if Cassio was quite sure he would be allowed to receive it.

"It is allowed," wrote the Direttore at the bottom of the page before sending it to the prisoner.

For one, two, three weeks, in that great pile, under the overarching blue sky and ardent sunshine that turned it into a very furnace, two souls were awaiting with passionate eagerness, though under different aspects, that picture of a woman.

The waiting of Cassio was sweet and full of peace, amid the passive resignation that habit and hope had begun to plant in his heart. The pleasure of anticipation brought him almost a sentiment of happiness; he would rise up early in the morning with the thought that perhaps to-day he would receive it, and as he waited for the guard who came to conduct him to the office, he would turn to his little window and reach out his hands as if striving to gather in some of the freshness of the morning; and he was always thinking of the picture.

Outside the swallows were flitting and wheeling as they sang, their wings and tails gleaming in the sunshine; the yellow corn surrounded with its golden glory the shining green of the distant vineyards, while farther away, the watching Apen-

nines shone in the luminous morning air. The prisoner called to mind the crimson dawns of his native mountains, brilliant with flowering yellow broom, then his thoughts turned to the expected picture, till he felt a vague feeling that was almost happiness.

The Direttore quitted his bed with a face even paler than was its wont, and he, too, thought of the picture; but his waiting was made up of a strange mingling of restlessness, bitterness and anger against himself, because he could not overcome his foolish curiosity, his foolish sentimentalism, the foolish interest "these people" awakened in him.

He went into the garden, and then into his bureau, and did his duty, performing all his tiresome work, and with cold eyes, and hands in his pockets, inspected those men clad in their prison garb of shame, but all the time he was waiting for the picture. In the bottom of his heart, under his anger and cruel indifference, there glimmered a spark of joy, from which a tiny ray sprang into his eyes and stayed there. And this spark, this hidden ray of light, burst into brilliant flame on the arrival of the picture, so instinct with life and loveliness and charm. She was not in the least as his fancy had pictured her; for hers was a blond and delicate loveliness. The beautiful dark eyes, in the delicately curved lips and dimpled chin were suffused with an infinite sweetness. It was the same ineffable sweetness as filled her letters, a fragrance exhaled from every word, and this mysterious and suggestive fascination it was which had conquered the soul of this silent man, who was thought cruel and was feared and hated only because he was a poor dreamer.

The letter accompanying the photograph was, as usual, full of sweetness and charm.

"I was thinking of thee and smiling when the picture was taken; may it bring thee a little joy and comfort in hoping for better days. Read in my eyes all that I would fain say to thee."

Just here, the Direttore, too, looked into the eyes of the picture, then finished reading the letter, only to return to gaze on the picture, turning it so the full light should fall upon it, until the face seemed to assume a sort of reality, the lovely eyes to shine, the lips to smile.

"Oh, Dio!⁴ What a fool I am!" said Signor Longino to himself; but in his heart he was thinking, "How would this exquisite creature write to her lover, if she writes thus to her brother!" And then he fell to thinking sadly, that he was small, ugly, almost old, hated and feared by all those unfortunates whom his cold eyes dominated.

Once more he read the letter and gazed at the glowing picture, and—and that day neither the one nor the other were given to the prisoner.

That night the Signore Direttore had a queer dream; he thought a mutiny had broken out among the prisoners and they yelled and shook their chains and rushed upon him. He held Paola's picture in his hands and could neither move nor defend himself, for then the picture would fall to the ground and No. 245 would know that he had stolen it. But just as he was about to be killed by the prisoners, Cassio threw himself between, crying: "Leave him alone, for he is to marry my sister, and then he

will become good because she is so good!"

He waked up bathed in perspiration, and passed the rest of the night sleeplessly tossing about his bed.

Cassio, in the meanwhile, was waiting patiently, though as the days passed a vague anxiety disposed his new-found repose. A week went by and still no picture came, and he had waited so long! so long! What could be happening over yonder, beyond the sunlit sea among the purple solitudes of the fragrant thyme-scented mountains? Paola must be ill—or had she forgotten him? Cassio fell back into the agonized despair of his first days. He asked, but was refused permission to telegraph. With difficulty he got permission to write two days sooner than his allotted month.

His letter was so sad and full of despair, that the Direttore felt more than ever ashamed of his deed; for two weeks he had lived in torment, and while he seemed more cruel and hard then ever, his little, green eyes fell sadly upon the prisoners, for at last he understood how, against his will, a man might be led into crime. As he read the sad letter of No. 245, he murmured again: "But why do not they ask for pardon?" And he became aware that with the new-found pity awakened for No. 245 mingled a certain egotism of hope, that then he could speak frankly to the prisoner—one no longer—and say: "Signore, I may be a fool, but all the same I have fallen desperately in love with your sister, whom I have never seen. Will you give her to me for my wife?"

Paola telegraphed at once that she had sent another photograph by registered mail. In the eagerness for the peace of her poor prisoner, she pretended she had not sent a picture, and had been unable to write on account of a lot of reasons, which she detailed at length, principally she had been unable to be photographed before.

"How good she is!" thought the Direttore in admiration, and he felt inclined to write and tell her everything.

But of course he did not do so. "She will think I am mad,and will fear for her brother."

And so the summer passed and autumn approached; prisoners came and went. In the office the three clerks were not only resigned, but even happy, but showed an ill-concealed dislike for the haughty Sardinian, who, to an extent, was himself resigned. Only amid the sweetness of the autumn, when the dawn flooded the pure sky with crimson and gold or the setting sun threw his red beams on the sad walls, he was tortured with longing for freedom and home; and he fretted like a horse taken from his free pastures and shut up in confinement; but he was learning to control these rebellions and to immerse himself to the lips in hope and dreams of the future, till the present seemed scarcely a reality. But when winter came and the Apennines were black with storm clouds, and the angry rain pelted incessantly the grim fortress, Cassio felt his nerves snap like cords stretched too far. During the day the three heads of the clerks, pinched with cold, the blear blue eyes, the transparent profile, the head like the Roman emperor, appeared to him as in some tortured vision, awakening within him a brutal desire to seize some object and crush them to pieces. This desire increased from day to day,

and was at times so intense that Cassio experienced the strange sensation of having realized it. Once in his cell he would come to himself and understand that he hated the three unfortunate clerks because they represented during those terrible winter days all the human power that was torturing him, against which his inmost soul revolted. His nights were almost sleepless. Outside the wind was roaring with a suggestion of distant torrents. Amid the darkness and roar of elements Cassio lost all perception of time, and as he tossed on his narrow bed, blessed visions came at last to his storm-tossed heart. The sighing of the wind in his distant well-loved mountains; the prints of the wild boar among the green ferns; the noisy stream bounding from rock to rock; the partridges flitting among the flowering oleanders; the joyful neighing of his black horse, and above all else, the smile of Paola.

But with the gray dawn, the sweetness of dreams was turned into bitter reality, and no one knows what might have happened to the three clerks had he not been one day providentially summoned to the Direttore's office.

The Signore Direttore deigned to ask a favor. He had been sent a little fragrant plant with a few slender, dry branches; it had come from Sardinia, and he wanted to know if the prisoner could tell him anything about it.

Cassio took the slender branches in his long, delicate hands, and inhaled its fragrance with closed eyes. The perfume brought him a vision of the green mountains of Gennargentu.[5] An intense homesickness thrilled him.

"It is the tirtillo."

"The tirtillo. I thought so. The precious secret of the Sardinian shepherds, that gives its especial aroma to the Sardinian cheese."

Cassio bowed in assent.

"The famous tirtillo," continued the Direttore, "the new cure for épizoötic."

"In Sardinia it has been used for centuries," replied Cassio humbly. "Many things that on the continent pass for discoveries are well known on the island."

The Direttore did not reply, but turned his back and resumed his writing, and apparently all was over, when suddenly turning around, he addressed Cassio without looking at him.

"Has a pardon been asked for you?"

"Yes; after the sentence in the Court of Cassation I appealed in the Giudiziarie[6] of Cagliari."

"To whom did you appeal?"

"To the Ministry."

"That was unfortunate. The Ministry when appealed to never decides. Often the prisoner has finished his term before they arrive at any conclusion."

Cassio looked very grave.

"It would be better to send your request to the Queen; it would sooner be obtained."

"Pardon me," returned Cassio, bowing his head, "but is there a chance that it would be obtained?"

"If the request should be made by your sister, it would be granted," answered the other brusquely, and again he turned his back so that he should not see the prisoner's emotion, and the latter should not see the Direttore's confusion.

This time the conversation was really over, and Cassio was reconducted to his office. But he was really another man; the presence of his three unhappy companions aroused his compassion, but no longer his hatred. Around his thin fingers still lingered the fragrance of the tirtillo, and raising them to his mouth, he inhaled the fresh sweetness of his distant meadows.

And probably for the first time, the Direttore was sincerely loved by one of his prisoners.

Cassio wrote to Paola begging her to ask the Queen for a
pardon.

"You can make the request for yourself, without having recourse to the formal process of the law. Explain things as they are. I hope and bless him who has counseled it."

And so the winter passed. In the limpid dawn of a February day, Cassio was standing before his grated window; his face was pale and bloodless, but his eyes were shining with hope. From the Apennines which raised their lofty, white crests into the crystal azure of the sky, there came a delicious odor of snow; long strips of vivid green were scattered over the valley, and already in the garden the apricot trees were displaying their rosy blossoms.

Cassio felt his blood dance through his veins with the mysterious expectation of coming happiness; all the glories of the opening spring seemed reflected in his soul.

Another man, free, in his cold and melancholy rooms, felt the same tumultuous, though sweet sensation; his green eyes reflected the tender splendor of the budding season, his heart inclosed a precious shrine.

There came a day when the inquiry of the Ministry into the conduct of the prisoner, Cassio Longino fu Isidoro, reached him. The Direttore's reply was of the best. He did not know why No. 245 had been guilty of forgery, but he believed him to be an honest young man, of fine morals and excellent education. By the same mail he also sent to an intimate in the Bureau a letter that, coming from such a person as Signor Longino, could not fail of effect.

Whether it was instrumental in bringing about the result or not, the decree of pardon and order for freedom arrived very soon after—when Cassio had been there just a year.

Once more he was summoned to the Direttore's office.

Outside, the air was balmy and fragrant, and the sky of deepest blue. Inside, the shadows of distant branches trembled in the sunshine that poured in through the barred window. The Direttore was seated at his table, but this time he rose as Cassio entered. The youth noticed it, but did not dare to give words to the wild hope that sprung up within him, but he felt his heart beat with a violence that well-nigh choked him.

"The decree has arrived," said the Direttore, and he was holding something in his hand.

"The decree?"

"The decree of pardon."

"For whom?" asked Cassio eagerly.

The Direttore began to lose patience.

"For whom but for you?" And he rejoiced in the deep emotion shown by the young man. So much the better; if the thing was so great as to seem impossible, so much the greater would be his grati-

tude. But then he thought sadly, "Suppose his efforts should result in failure! If in the excess of his gratitude Cassio should give him false hopes!"

"For me! for me!" stammered the poor youth. "For me! For how long?"

"For all the rest of your sentence. You are free—that is, not at once, but after a few formalities, in a week at most."

Gradually Cassio pulled himself together. At first he had gazed at the Direttore without seeing him. Now he began to look at him. He observed his pale face was flushed, that the air of physical suffering had disappeared, that the small, green eyes were shining.

He, on the other hand, was trembling violently, his face was ashy, his hands cold, and a mist floated before his eyes.

"This man is fine, when he is rejoicing in the happiness of another. How I have misjudged him," he thought. Then he asked himself, "But why did he do it?"

He was to know very soon.

The Direttore begged him to be seated; he showed him the decree, and profited by the moment in which Cassio was looking at the King's signature to begin:

"Now, I have something else to tell you. Listen and do not judge hastily. I have long been awaiting this moment and the thing seemed easy, but now I see I need great courage and you great indulgence if we are to understand each other."

He smiled sadly, and the old expression of suffering returned once more.

Cassio looked at him stupidly, still confused with the weight of his happiness, but beginning to gain his self-control. The other understood that his opportunity was slipping away and hastened to speak though, in spite of every effort, his voice trembled.

"I scarcely know how to express myself so you may understand everything; but I have confidence in your intelligence. Listen. I have done everything in my power to obtain that piece of paper there"—and he pointed to the decree, and Cassio, following his gesture, sat gazing at the sheet—"and above all, I did so because I felt you deserved it." ("Does he know my story?" Cassio asked himself, feeling that his deserts in prison had been very few.) "I do not ask for gratitude, indeed I will be thankful, if you will not allow that sentiment to influence you at all. I wish to speak to you as one gentleman to another." ("Heavens! does he think me a gran Signore and wish to ask me for money?" thought Cassio. "I am not ungrateful, but what *can* he want of me?") "Now you are free and are at liberty to act as seems good to you."

"Speak," returned the other, with a sad impatience, "whatever lies in my power—"

"I do not know if it lies in your power."

"Speak! Speak!"

"Listen, but do not ill-judge me, nor think me insane. While reading your sister's letters, I have learned to appreciate so good and noble a soul, and—" ("Oh, Dio mio![7] he has fallen in love with her!" cried Cassio to himself, and the world grew suddenly dark.) "I have learned to love her. Do not laugh at me. I am still young!"

But Cassio felt small inclination to laugh.

"Have you written to her?" he asked brusquely.

"No, certainly not. Pray do not be offended. I have not

allowed myself so great a privilege. Only to you—"

"But it is impossible, not to be thought of—impossible!" interrupted Cassio, striking as he spoke the paper which was laying on his knees, till it rustled.

"It seems impossible, but it is true; and though it may be strange, it is not the first time it has happened. My demand is serious, Signor Longino. Can your sister accept it?"

"What demand?"

The other thought a moment— "This young man is laboring under too much excitement, I was wrong to speak to him so suddenly. He is not in a state to hear it."

"My proposal of marriage."

Cassio did not reply at once. By a terrible effort he controlled himself. When the mist cleared from his eyes he turned and looked at the Direttore and beheld him as in the past, pale, suffering, and ugly, and into his terrible pain there fell one drop of comfort—she would not accept him—he felt sure.

"But," he asked, "have you reflected what you are doing? Have you written to my country and obtained information? In such cases—"

"I have not written. What would be the good? I know your sister, that she is good and noble, I desire nothing more. I, too, am all alone."

"You are too good. I do not know how to properly express my gratitude. Do not fear you are not understood. I both understand and admire you. I feel myself greatly honored by your offer, and if it remained with me—but let me assure you I will do all in my power. Do not despair."

He rose and rolled up the pardon, looking at it with ill-concealed bitterness as he towered over the small person of the Direttore, who approached with extended hand to express his thanks. He asked permission to return to his cell and unroll his bed. Everything was granted him. As he threw himself on his comfortless cot he groaned in agony. Paola was not his sister, but his fiancée. For her he had soiled his honor, compromised his future and broken with his family. She alone remained to him. She had feigned to be his sister in order that she might write to him. And must he lose her now? That other possessed a splendid position, was good and noble. Had he a right to snatch such a brilliant future from Paola? He had sacrificed to her his honor and well-nigh two years of liberty, but she had not asked the sacrifice of him, and was it right that in exchange he should ask for her whole life? In any case she must decide for herself, and at the bottom of his heart he felt secure of her—but it made him wretched to think he had deceived and was still deceiving so noble and excellent a man.

"I will tell him everything, come what may," he decided after an hour of anxious thought, then uncertainty took possession of him once more. "No, I will say nothing. After all he has no right to know, and I will write when I reach home. After all he did it only because he wanted to on his own account. His cat-like eyes fill me with distrust; perhaps he would do me some harm."

Later he grew ashamed of his distrust and cried out loud in his lonely cell, "Am I indeed vile?"

Approaching the grating he stood gazing at the white, diaphanous clouds piled up on the horizon; they had assumed the shape and coloring of an alabaster staircase whose luminous steps disappeared into the unsealed heights. Cassio, as he looked, was overwhelmed with an intense homesickness and suddenly he felt good and pure, as if he had indeed mounted to the last step of those silver stairs and caught from that height a glimpse of his beloved native land. He murmured:

"Had it not been for him I should have languished here for yet a weary time. I might have died or committed some madness. I will tell everything, let the result be what it may."

He waited anxiously the hour when it would be possible for him to see the Direttore, then addressed him in clear tones:

"See, Signore Direttore, I have been thinking of what you were good enough to tell me this morning."

"Very well," answered the other, though he feared for the result.

"Before entering upon the subject, please allow me to tell you in a few words of the strange circumstances of my condemnation, for," he added, smiling sadly, "I am bold enough to believe you do not think me guilty."

The other man said never a word.

"Listen. For ten years I have loved a maiden of my own country. She was rich, but an orphan living with her guardian. I was sent away to college and was absent many years. On my return I learned that the poor girl, although she had attained her majority, was kept in subjection and badly treated by her guardian, who had possessed himself of all her property. He gave her nothing, but kept her shut up and frightened with terrible threats. I succeeded in communicating with her and, finding that she loved me, I vowed to free her and restore her property. 'Let us be married.' she said, 'and I will fly with you.' But as my intentions might involve me in many difficulties, I would not accept her offer. I assisted her to take refuge with friends, and when she was in safety, I began my operations.

"And can you guess what I did? I almost think so. I forged the name of her guardian, and since he was very rich and well known at home and abroad and his credit was illimitable, I obtained a good deal of money. I placed all in the name of the young girl and waited. When the notes fell due, all became known. I had foolishly hoped I should be considered a hero. Instead I was seized, villified, condemned. My little property was taken, my family disowned me. She, alone of all the world, remains to me and she, Signore Direttore, is Paola."

The Signore Direttore remained absolutely silent. What, indeed, could he say? He only felt that Cassio's story and his own seemed impossible, though he knew but too well it was but too true. Cassio understood him perfectly.

"It is strange, impossible, is it not? Had I been told it, I would not have believed it."

"Life is strange," said the other at last, and he clenched his hands till the nails penetrated the flesh. The ways of destiny are indeed mysterious."

"He is resigned," thought Cassio, and he hazarded another remark.

"Life is often a terrible romance." But looking the Direttore in the face he saw an expression of such agony imprinted as caused him to retract his thought of a moment before.

"But see," he continued, "in spite of everything I will do all in my power to prove my gratitude."

"What do you mean?"

"Let me speak. It was my duty to let you know the exact truth, but you have been so good to me that I give you my word of honor, as a gentleman, that I will do everything—"

"What are you saying? What are you saying?" repeated the other in a strange tone, as if he were listening to distant voices, and not to Cassio's words. "After all, Paola alone can decide. I will tell her everything, as if I were indeed her brother and nothing more."

"Oh, no! No! What are you saying?"

"Nay, if you will allow it I will write this very day and we will await her reply. Perhaps when it comes I will not need to return to my own country."

"What are you saying?" repeated the Direttore; but now his voice had regained its strength and, raising his eyes, he looked Cassio full in the face. "You must not write, but return at once to your home where, I prophesy, every happiness awaits you. From the bottom of my heart I hope so. And yet, who would ever have imagined it! You are right, Life is a terrible romance."

"But," Cassio persisted, "let me write. I beg it of you as a personal favor. You will see the debt I owe you can never be canceled, and duty should be stronger than love. Paola will be much more fortunate with the Direttore than with me, and above all things I desire her happiness and well-being."

The other listened patiently; once his eyes flashed with a vivid light, but he remained immovable.

"See," he concluded, after having expressed his appreciation of Cassio's generosity, "if your duty is to prove yourself grateful and generous toward the signorina,[8] her duty is no less to make you happy and recompense you for all you have suffered."

"But—" interrupted Cassio.

"One moment—let me finish, please. If the signorina were to act otherwise, she would not be the noble, lofty being I have imagined her, and then my offer would no longer exist. Do you understand? Am I not right?"

But Cassio answered never a word and the Direttore turned toward the window. And the soul of each was full to overflowing.

Cassio thought but of his happiness, and the Direttore reminded himself with bitterness that in any case his dream was lost to him forever.

Letitia Humphreys Yonge Wrenshall (1845-1924)

Letitia Humphreys Yonge Wrenshall was the president of the Woman's Literary Club of Baltimore for seventeen years, elected in May of 1898 and unanimously re-elected each year until 1915. Wrenshall was the center of activity in the literary sphere of the Club and was endowed with the gift of organization and administration. She had the faculty of creation and the power to inspire and guide the energy of others. She was a leader in many organizations including the Maryland Folk Lore Society and the Audubon Society.[1] She was also the organizer of the Edgar Allan Poe Memorial Association in 1907 and its only president. Dividing her time between the US and England, she also was a member of the Royal Asiatic Society of London and contributed her writing to its journal.

Wrenshall was born in 1845 and was raised in Georgia. She married John C. Wrenshall, an engineer for the Confederate Army during the Civil War, with whom she relocated to Baltimore following the end of the war.

Wrenshall loved travel and in the early twentieth century, she toured the United States, giving lectures of her travels to Europe that were accompanied by hand-colored photographic slides taken by her daughter, Katharine H. Wrenshall and displayed on a device known as a "magic lantern." In "Traveling in the Radiant Old Mediterranean," Wrenshall employs evocative language that allows readers to travel with her. In this and her other travel writing, Wrenshall paints images of the places she experienced and the people she met, providing readers who may never get the chance to walk its shores, a vivid experience of Italy. —J. Morgan

Traveling in the Radiant Old Mediterranean (1908)

Gibraltar,[2] March 20.—Gray skies and grayer water, dull leaden color o'er all the world save far off to the south, where light falls through rifts in the clouds, warming the waves to sparkling life. A rippling line where the bay flows into the sea, and where we soon will pass with the promise of the careless joy of the wanderer.

'Tis the moment long waited for, rush, bustle, disturbance, hoarse cries of the seamen, haste of belated passengers, good-bye being said, handkerchiefs commencing to wave and drawn back surreptitiously on finding the ropes are not yet cast off. At last the gangplank is up and silently, quietly, the great ship moves slowly forward. There are some wet eyes, but the skies are responsible for most of the dampness, it is drizzling finely, but it does not cool the ardor of those on the lower decks who are singing manfully.

There are many hundreds down there, Italians, Portuguese and Sicilians, going home for the winter, with a comfortable bank account, accumulated through the nine months of work in America, on railroads, in mills and iron works, and heavy stone cutting.

With great propriety their first song is one of farewell to the land they are leaving, but it soon passes into a joyous greeting to Italy. They sing well, as with one voice, and with much spirit the Italian national anthem.

Later they are quiet, very quiet, with no appetite for their macaroni,[3] for deep water is soon reached sailing from New York. After three or four days, however, they are all back on their decks and happily settled with their lotto,[4] which they played unceasingly through the voyage.

Third Class Not Immigrants

At first we called them emigrants, but were sternly corrected by the Italian doctor, who explained the difference between the third-class passenger and the aforesaid emigrant. The emigrant has his passage paid for him by his government, the third-class passenger pays his own, quite independently, and is entitled to corresponding privileges.

The Italian government, however, exercises a paternal care over its citizens, and requires all ships carrying over 500 third-class passengers to have an Italian doctor in addition to the ship's doctor. As there were nearly 3,000 third-class passengers aboard (a not unusual number), it will be seen this is a wise provision.

Each ship also carries an Italian commissioner, appointed from the royal navy, whose duty is to inspect the food served three times daily, and keep a strict watch over the welfare of his people. This gentleman was so quiet and unobtrusive that his full importance as a ship's officer was perhaps not fully appreciated until a day later[5] on the voyage, when a game of shuffle board was interrupted by a delegation of his countrymen, who suddenly appeared at the head of the small steps leading from the deck below, loudly vociferating and showing their tin basins of macaroni and tomatoes, together with a small can of coffee each carried.

They were an excited company and looked very fierce; evidently their macaroni had not been cooked sufficiently, and their coffee did not please them. The shuffle-board players startled, at first by the invaders waving their weapons frantically to and from as they talked. But the two jolly tars[6] in charge of the upper deck quickly assisted the irate ones down the steps just ascended, a second look showed the shining weapons to be only the cook's huge spoons, the commissioner quickly appeared, and an immediate calm closed the episode.

Altogether, the third-class passengers seemed a very happy, good-natured crowd; their songs and dances and their mock auctions, with peculiar features, were very entertaining in an uneventful voyage.

But there were some unhappy ones among them, for it is stated on good authority that a very large percentage of Portuguese and Italians return unsuccessful from America; this is to be attributed to their not speaking English as well as their unwillingness to leave the large cities. Disappointed in securing work, they return to their native countries.

On the afternoon of the seventh day after leaving New York after long days of rain, with decks shut in by tarpaulins, the clouds lifted, melting in golden mist before the welcome sunlight. To the north a purple horizon line lay in graceful slopes against the blue sky, fairy mountains, every moment growing closer and not less beautiful, in the knowledge that it was a land, the first sight of Europe, the Province of Portugal, the Islands of the Azores.

Flores Looks Like Mummy

All the afternoon we were running among them. Flores, the first passed, is a long hill, the outline of which has the appearance of an elongated mummy in its case. The head is quite perfect, with the tall body and the turned up toes added by a square-like box of a rocky islet, that only at close approach is seen to be a detached mass. The fields are quite green, there appear to be but few uncultivated, and no sign of winter is apparent.

Closely adjacent is the Island of Pico,[7] which has some lofty heights; these, too, presently fade away, darkness falls, and we can see no more: our ship makes good time, and we have passed the greater part of the 400 miles of latitude occupied by the Azores, when the dawn finds us anchored off St. Michael, the largest of the group.

Later the ship steams into the harbor, but not within the protecting Mole,[8] some nautical etiquette with another steamer preventing. The Portuguese third-class passengers are impatient, for they have reached their island home, they have brushed up astonishingly, and are quite clean as well as happy as they scramble down into the boats which take several hundred off the ship.

The first-class passengers are also in a state of excitement, gay with the prospect of landing for a few hours in the pretty town of Ponta Delgada,[9] which seems to very close. All are ready and boats, broad and strong, each manned by several rowers, have put out from shore.

Alas, the wind has risen and the waves with it, white caps appear on the suddenly dark waters, the big ship itself is not quite steady, and the boats bringing out passengers for Naples pitch and toss. The first two to board are young Portuguese soldiers, bright-eyed and rosy, scarcely more than boys; they have come on some business of the Port, and soon re-embark.

We watch the process and speculate, but think we can manage it. Another boat arrives with several ladies in it, trunks and piles of small luggage and—delight of the eyes—enormous bouquets of red and white camellias. Our boats are waiting at the foot of the gangway; the fruit boats with their loads of pineapples and tropical flowers are alluring, and the town itself looks beautiful with its rows of pink and green and snowy-white and yellow and blue houses.

We are impatient to be off to gather roses, violets and camellias in December. All are ready, when suddenly, as the crack of doom comes the fiat, "no first-class passengers to land, seas too rough, squalls threatening."

The next few moments are not quiet, and the tempers of the first-class do not compare favorably with those gentlemen whose macaroni was not acceptable. Some eager ones desire to assume all responsibility in landing, and waive claims to damages from the steamship company should their shoes be spoiled or their clothing spotted with the salt water.

But all requests are refused, the disappointed passengers are obliged to accept the situation and sit for four hours on the deck watching the town, the water front, the streets and the people on them. In the meantime the wind is going down and the water quieting, but it is now too late.

A passenger, looking back through life to find consolation in an analogous environment, recalls one instance, that of a fond father, who, loving his little girl, and wishing to teach her self-denial, bought a stick of candy which he unwrapped and showed to her on Sundays. The candy was kept indefinitely.

The child survived and so did we, but the four hours were long, though slightly brightened by the quantities bought and eaten of pineapples and oranges, fresh from the plucking, till the decks of the third-class and the water were thickly covered with the golden rinds.

The December day was lovely, like that of an English May. Ponta Delgada, which we had the pleasure of contemplating so long, must be a land of perpetual summer, with little changes of temperature, tropical fruits growing out of doors. Only the pineapples are under acres of glass.

Land of Perpetual Summer

The gardens showed magnificent evergreens, the fine foliage of the camphor tree, palms, and tree ferns. Noting two very handsome trees, new to all, and asking their names of one of the Portuguese ladies who had come on the ship en route to Naples, we were told that one was the maugoba, the other the enona; both were natives of Brazil, but, like other vegetation transplanted to the Azores, had thriven and spread.

Town on Water's Edge

It was a very pretty picture. The surf upon the beach, the town rising directly from the water's edge, the vari-colored pastel tints of the houses, some built directly on the gray sea wall; others set in the luxuriant growth of the gardens against the background of sharp-pointed and serrated hills close about the little city that looked so gay in the sunshine.

The houses are small, two-storied, and mostly with flat roofs and no chimney visible; only two or three could be counted in all the town. The building material is the coarse volcanic rock of the island, covered with stucco, which is colored in these rainbow contrasts.

They rise beyond and above each other on the hillside, all overtopped by the tall white tower of the cathedral church, with its pretty Renaissance façade.

It is an enterprising little city. Windmills on the crest of the hills supply water. The pineapple industry, for which the island is justly noted, is very extensive. The apples are small, but of delightful flavor and sweet as sugar. There is a respectably sized furnace for the making of iron and bronze, extensive barracks, which at first sight might be supposed a hotel; a coal depot, which has its sign in English, and an agricultural college, with many other indications of a wide-awake community.

The Mole, which was being repaired, is an object lesson by which larger cities might profit, built on this isolated bit of land remote from the path of travel. It is between thirty-five and fifty[10] feet in height, a little engine running along its broad top with materials to add to its twenty-four arches. The round arch is used in the Mole, as in the sea wall and other buildings, and is supposed to add to its strength in these volcanic regions.

From our posts of observation we could see the people passing up the narrow streets leading from the waterfront and recognized the national cloak, previously seen in pictures; it is of dark blue cloth and fits over the top of the head quite smoothly. It has a crescent-shaped front and is turned up at the sides, and a cape attached hangs over the shoulders, ending in an embroidered point.

The women we saw had handkerchiefs tied over their heads, and a huge cloak, also of dark blue, and their shoes, of many colors, being the only part of their costume that escaped the guardianship of the long wide cloak.

The Portuguese lady already mentioned told us much that was interesting of the island and its history. She had been educated in England and spoke English well; also French and Italian. She was a lady of many names, with "de" between each one, as we discovered when receiving the address, to which we promised to send some American papers. She was devoted to the King and Queen, and was much pleased when remined of the descent of King Carlos III from King Charles I of England. Her lovely gray-blue eyes shone brightly with interest as she talked and when reference was made to the surprise of their color, where we only expected sparkling black or melting brown, she said: "Blue eyes are frequent among us. The ladies of the Azores are called the daughters of the sea, so we must wear her colors."

Two days later our disappointment at not landing at the Azores (so infrequently visited) was somewhat forgotten in a visit to Gibraltar.

Gibraltar at Dawn

In entering the Mediterranean on a former visit fortune favored us by giving the sunset hour for the passing, and it made a scene of unequaled natural splendor, never to be forgotten. This time we came with the dawn, cold and dark, at 6:20, on the hurricane deck.

Outlines of the shores of Spain and Africa were just discernible through the mist, faint indications of color in the East showing the approach of day. Mount Leone loomed up splendidly, a band of cloud encircling its girth below the summit, which was black against the gray sky.

To the left Gibraltar grew more distinct with each moment, the rising sun's struggle with the mist throwing marvelous phantasmagoria on sea and sky, a rich cerise against the background of deepening blue the key to the color scheme.

Carthage and Rome, with other countries, left their mark in the record of Gibraltar, but none so deep as Jebel's, until the British had clasped it tightly, when a few of her red-coated soldiers climbed the narrow steps up the cliff, surprised the garrison and won this bit of Spain, which now hold from five to six thousand men in permanent encampment.

Gibraltar's past is interesting, but the present calls loudest, and the tender at last arriving, a few more moments found us in the strange old town.

Has Modern Exterior

The first impression is not of ancient, but of modern military engineering. The Mole is wide and strong, as of the living rock. Further on there is a large warehouse for luggage and freight. We see many queer-looking packages through the open doors. Queerer-looking vehicles just beyond at once proclaim the Spanish characteristics of the English town.

At the wide gate, guarded by bronze-faced "Tommies,"[11] the sad intelligence was received that to enter the fortifications one must be not only a British subject, but be English born. So tightly have the rules been drawn within the last few months.

Calling up all our equanimity and recognizing the propriety of the rule, we again accepted disappointment and drove on into the strange scenes beyond the gates.

Narrow streets, filled with every variety of the genus *homo*: scarlet and khaki *mantillas* and French hats (who wears a bonnet nowadays?); gabardines and English frock coats, an Anglican parson amidst Moors, barelegged and yellow-slippered, *burnous*, *fez*, and stovepipe;[12] water-carriers, vendors of charcoal; donkeys, loaded with huge grass panniers, piled high with loads of merchandise covered with boughs, upon it all sitting the placid owner; turkeys in flocks, driven by men wearing broad-brimmed Spanish hats and guiding the birds with long sticks; enterprise, undoubtedly, in every form, especially in postal cards and paper fans depicting gorgeous bullfights; all this you see and more.

An Englishman canters past, mounted on his tall hunter, an Arab guide rushes out of a hotel and claims the acquaintance of an American, shaking hands in English fashion with this lamb, whose wool well-sheared has made comfortable this desert chief.

Yet over this meeting-ground of Eastern apathy, vociferation of Southern Europe and British stolidity, a certain calm appears to brood, the Orient working its spell as the strange assemblage goes daily on its way.

A touching spot in Gibraltar is the tiny God's Acre. At the foot of the mighty overshadowing cliff, simple stones bear witness to lives of honor by those who here sleep well beneath the waving boughs of acacia and palm. The December roses drop their fragrant petals upon these soldiers' graves. We think of our own heroes, some beneath the blue sea that we turn to dreamily gaze upon, remembering the gray shaft that bears Herndon's[13] name at Annapolis, where

> The flowering Almond casts her rosy
>   bloom
> 'Round the dark shaft that bears the
>   Horn's name,

So his brave deed illumined his
country's gloom
And marked him with imperishable
fame.

Further are the Alameda Gardens,[14] flowers and trees of all kinds happily transplanted to this favored spot. Dacturas hang their heavy white heads in fragrant somnolence, borders of crimson cacti mingle with the heliotrope's purple; sturdy firs rear their lofty tops; buttercups shed gold on the general green of the grass. Then, glory of glories! we are greeted by the dear, homely wild flower of cornfields and wayside thickets, for whom no better name could be devised than the "morning glory." A whole pergola of them, fragrantless, fading with touch of human hand. Frailness and strength, the Rock of Gibraltar and springing from it the airiest film e'er spun by Mother Nature.

On the way to the north face of the rock the Moorish market is well worth a visit. The imperturbable Moor! There is no invitation to buy. If you want their goods you can have them, but not a word.

The snowy eggs are attractive in their wire baskets; hardly so, the turkeys, which are being plucked while the customers wait; rabbits and hares are hung up as in other markets, whilst a flock of turkeys, as yet unplucked, wait outside the iron fence, their fate in the balance with the arrival of new customers.

The vendors are all Moors, of every shade of complexion, their costumes varying in degree, not fashion—a long loose gown of cloth, dark blue, the favorite color, long snowy white stockings, the inevitable yellow slippers and turbans of thin muslin wound around a crimson *fez*. The poorer class wear the coarse brown gown, no stockings, but are quite clean— remarkably so, when the character of the occupation be remembered—that of killing and plucking the turkeys.

The center of attraction is the letter-writer, a portly Othello, who sits in a high chair, his feet upon a footstool, reading in a tiny book. His customers also are slow in coming, but he is as calm as a statue, and very, very fat. His robe is disposed imposingly around him, his turban is in innumerable folds, his long, crooked horn of ink is on a bench beside him. Several wooden tablets rest upon his knees. He realizes that he is an important man and it is not for him to show impatience.

Though we could not enter the galleries within the rock, we could, and did, drive along the base of the west and north sides. Breath seems to come with difficulty when looking up at that overwhelming height of fortification. Line above line of openings in the rock indicate the level of the passages and the rows of guns within.

The lowest is far above our heads. It is the face of the lion, overlooking the low, sandy isthmus, the neutral ground between the British possessions and Spain.

The point of view from which the grand rock is seen alters its aspect, the west side smiling with vegetation, rows of bright-colored houses and pretty villas; the east frowning and bare, with many caves, in which dwell the apes of Tarshish.[15] The north is majestic and terrible, for we known that a word or sign would transform its broad expanse into a sheet of destroying flame.

The height of Gibraltar is best realized after passing the strait and looking back at its rising from the level of the sea; sailing away, the lines soften into mysterious shadows; these, too, presently fade, leaving us only the vivid impressions of the morning and the determination to return another day to the ancient rock of Calpe.[16]

Along the Two Gulfs of Naples and Salerno (1908)[17]

In so crowded a story as that of the shores of "The Two Gulfs" it is only possible to glance from point to point, as through individual interest or opportunity, the light falls strongest. This especially applies to that bold headland, the Peninsula of Sorrento.[18]

In journeying through the magnificent scenery of this coast, a two or three days' drive from Cava, or Amalfi, to Sorrento or Castellammare is considered indispensable. It is better to extend the time several days longer, and among other things include the drive through the beautiful "Valle de Pompeii," or, better still, commence it at Naples for Cava.

Deciding on the latter, the first few miles give an excellent idea of the crowded population and the occupations of the people. The villages run into each other and there are always exquisite views of sea and mountain.

At Portici the horizon line shows Naples, and its heights and the mountains of Ischia, Capri and Sorrento. The round is completed in the blue lights of sky and water, which invest the scene with its own incomparable fascination. There is here an agricultural school of the Italian government, where many experiments are made preparatory to introducing new forms of growth. Among these tobacco has proved a success. It attains large size, the ground yielding four crops—as of many other products—yearly.

Buried Herculaneum

Beyond Portici is Resina, beneath which is Herculaneum, still a buried town, forty feet below the present surface. There is much to see, but a visit to Pompeii is far more agreeable and satisfactory.

All through this part of the drive lava is in evidence, but, with the fatalism that underlies the gayety of the Southern Italians, the people disregard the repeated warnings of earthquake and fire and continue polishing the coral which the men bring home from the fisheries.

Near Pompeii a beautiful charity exists in an industrial school for the sons of prisoners, who, without means or friends, are received, educated, taught trades and go hence prepared to become respectable citizens.

From Pompeii to Cava dei Tirreni is the long and beautiful Valle di Pompeii, entered immediately on leaving the ruined city. At first it is quite wide and it remains so until Vesuvius is left behind.

The road leads through a straggling village, picturesque but dirty. The people sit at their doors sewing and working at leather for harness. A curious sound comes from some little distance ahead; it seems familiar, and presently the light from within the doorless shed shows the village smithy. It is "an anvil chorus" from the beating of the heated bar by six men, who, with perfect rhythm, keep a swinging measure.

Poverty is apparent, but no real need. The people do not look hungry, and they cannot be cold in this equable climate, where during two-thirds of the year they sleep on the flat roofs of their small square houses.

Lamps Before the Shrines

The staircases are all outside, and lamps are often burning before the shrines that frequently adorn the front walls of these tiny homes. The religious paintings, mostly under glass, are sometimes really pretty, and in one we noticed the surrounding wreath of roses and carnations frescoed on the coarse stucco would not have been out of place in a city mansion.

Over the door of the same house was a precaution to secure good fortune in an ox horn projecting above the lintel. Oak branches above other doors proclaimed the Osteria, with wine for sale within. Of these the wary are grateful, for there is an old saying in Italy, "As a beautiful girl does not need finery, so good wine does not need the oak branch."

Beyond the houses to the right and left of the road are perfectly kept market gardens, stretching as far as can be seen—a green plush carpet, varying in shade with the vegetables planted. Orange and lemon trees are in abundance, glowing with the golden fruit, and where the soil is recently tilled it looks like powdered chocolate, rich for indefinite yielding.

After passing the town of Angri the valley narrows, the mountains come closer, their volcanic origin always indicated in their sharp outline, their sides and crests affording commanding positions for a few convents and ancient strongholds, while in the valley the orange groves are, if possible, in fuller bearing, the ground beneath them covered with the close green of another crop. The fertility is exceptional.

High up on the mountain an artificial plateau has been hewn. Upon it is a villa of purest white marble, its terrace planted with flowers and trees. The arched windows of the noble front are wide and long. A palace in these wilds, far removed from every disturbing influence—what a place for dreams! And what a view from those windows!

A Magnificent Estate

It is the chateau of the d'Angri family,[19] and as seen from the road "is fit for a prince." The great estate is well cared for and must bring in large revenues. Prosperity is apparent, as it is in Angri, which is a busy place with linen factories. The industries of Italy offer constant surprises, and the universal use and masterly adaptation of electricity make up not the least among these.

At Pagani, another flourishing little city, the characteristics of the valley are accentuated. It is narrower and the mountains wilder. Those who sought the protection of their inaccessibility—nobles, robber chiefs, stately abbess or jolly abbot—were secure in their medieval eyries.

At Nocera, remembered as the birthplace of the great Knight Templar, Hugo de Pagani,[20] the founder of the order, we had expected to find a forlorn hamlet, but another surprise waited us in the factories and extensive electrical works, looked down upon from the twelfth-century castle on Anjon. The gardens in Nocera were full of roses, the trellises covered with the yellow varieties, rivaling the orange trees, and this in midwinter.

Further on is a fine old church, massive and square towered, where all passing should stop a few moments. Its thirty-two columns of peacock marble with rich capitals date from some faraway period before the church was built, and it has stood there for fifteen centuries.

Now the horses pull harder, for the way is steep and shadowed by the mountains. It is but a pass through them.

A Lofty Monastery

From the loftiest peak of a monastery looks cheerfully down upon the world below. On one side there is a sheer fall, a fierce glissade of bare rock; on the other side gigantic teeth line the backbone of the approach. The mountain's name scarcely appropriate, for it is called St. Angelo.

For a long, long way back on the left of the road we had noticed the strangest of stone ways, thirty feet wide, and the walls on its sides from eight to twelve feet high. Enormous steps within it keep the level of the rising grade of the road. A puzzling structure, resolving itself under skilled eyes into a surface aquaduct for receiving the mountain torrents of spring and autumn, the steps preventing washouts under the pressure of the swollen streams.

Twilight falls as we drive through Cava dei Tirreni in the heart of the hills. In summer it is a gay town. There are arcades in its half mile of streets and a public garden where the band plays under the pine trees.

At last the tired horses draw up in the garden of the Hotel de Londres, where bright fires, cheery greetings and the best of dinners await visitors. Dainties of Southern Italy are in generous profusion.

One, an entire novelty, came with the dessert. Little packages three inches square and wrapped in grape leaves, unfolded yielding raisins full of rich juice. They resembled the fresh raisins of California, but were tenderer and more luscious.

When the fruit is prepared too late to secure intense summer sunshine the oven is resorted to.

The Pope's Cross

But all the comfort within the hotel cannot keep us from the windows and the outside galleries, drawn there by the unusual view which the perfectly clear night does not conceal, but rather enhances.

The sharp-pointed mountains hem in the circular valley, the ground only broken where the road comes through on which we entered today, and just opposite, where we will pass through on our way to Paestum. On the highest mountain of all, straight up above us, a gilded cross is alight from a flame burning before it. It is the Pope's cross, one of the many which it was his beautiful thought to have erected on similar mount peaks throughout Italy to commemorate the coming in of the twentieth century.

Fine as was the night, the morning lights upon the hills brought even more marvelous effects. The sunrise was a riot of color above the greenery of the hotel garden, where some carved slabs in a corner had attracted our attention, together with the fact that a section of the garden had been cut lower than the main part.

In answer to questions, the manager of the hotel, himself an archaeologist, told us that in digging a reservoir for rain water a number of tombs had been discovered about twenty-one feet below the surface. The gracefully designed slabs had formed some of the white terra-cotta sarcophagi, and in each tomb had been found a little pot holding just one bronze nail and also a lamp, the wick of cotton still strong within it.

From the World's Childhood

From the large number of tombs it is thought that a great necropolis lies beneath the gardens, and indications point to its very ancient use. One of these is the layer of volcanic deposit dug through, which belongs to a very old page in the history of Vesuvius,[21] when that treacherous mountain destroyed a Greek settlement, a city mayhap as beautiful as its later victim, Roman Pompeii, but antedating the latter by long geological time.

Within easy driving distance of Cava dei Tirreni are many temptations to linger, but even for those who do not travel in wild haste hours count, and today has been waited for through the years in the first visit to Paestum's wondrous temples.

The Drive Down to Amalfi[22]

From Cava to Paestum the distance is too great to permit of driving. The country is highly malarious, and the people reserve their best manners for well-armed gendarmes. Thus we reluctantly exchanged our comfortable traveling carriage for the crowded local train.

Running due south, the Gulf of Salerno is soon reached. The attention is always held by new and striking interest; now, beside the sea, we are passing a convict station, which, like all government property, is painted red; close beside it are cement works, the enormous blocks of concrete drying in the sun, cubes of about five feet the average size, grooved in the sides for keying or for the ropes in lifting; again, high up on the mountain side are arched viaducts and green terraces, betokening fine engineering and prodigious labor.

A Fearsome Population

The sudden cessation of all these signs of busy life was very marked with the passing of the line of the dread malaria. Here, as far as the eye could see, were only vast stretches of uncultivated ground. A few flocks of sheep and herds of horses grazed on the coarse semi-marsh grass or rested beneath the tall eucalyptus trees planted by the government and private bounty, their water-feeding roots having already lessened the percentage of fever in this region.

Halfway to Paestum we changed cars. This involved a stop of twenty minutes and afforded an opportunity to see a contingent of the population. There were several huntsmen with snowy white pointers (the game hares and pheasants); there were many peasants, herdsmen and shepherds; poor sickly-looking creatures with sheepskins thrown over their shoulders, and a few mountaineers dressed in holiday costumes of bright colors, gold rings in the ears of both men and women, and yellow silk handkerchiefs and gay caps on their heads; the countenances of all none too amiable.

It was quite the setting for "Fra Diavolo,"[23] and we were looking up to the rocks which were the scenes of his last exploits. The soldiers, also, were not lacking, a large force being on the train as well as on the station platform. They were bright-looking fellows, acting as military police, well dressed and well armed. Their round cloaks, occasionally falling back, showed a short magazine rifle, with a hinged bayonet, a cartridge box, a sword and a revolver on the hip, with a holster buckled, but open at both ends. Their uniforms were beautifully clean and well-fitting, the rifles slung by white leather straps. They were quite dandies in their way, as well as walking arsenals, ready for action.

In View of the Sea

Nearing Paestum the sea again came into view, the Appennines far to the left, the wide plain yielding undisturbed sight of the most perfect of the remaining monuments of Magna Grecia.[24]

Majestic, inscrutable, their story lost, they stand in the desolate Campagna, outlined against the intense blue of sea and sky, honoring Neptune, Ceres and two other unknown gods in the third and oldest temple, all divinities of the city that once surrounded these Cyclopean[25] structures.

The city wall still encloses the ancient site. Through its gates roads lead to the three temples, to which all hasten, eager to view them closer. The blocks used in building are of great size, and the methods employed for raising those composing the architrave[26] awake discussion. The stone is travertine, in which the structure of sea weeds and coral is clearly shown. Coarse and fine are mingled, and the secrets of the sea under which the limestone was made are read.

Time has beautified them with soft fungous colors and weathered tints, while Ceres has done her part in planting the flowers that cover the ground and spring from crevices in the mighty columns and lofty frieze.

Familiar flowers they are—sweet alyssum and rosy-tipped daisies, gathered in the temples of the gods of 2,500 years ago. "Life everlasting" springs up between the vast blocks of pavement upon which we stand, and the pink bloom of the wild geranium droops from the capitals of the columns between which we look across the sea to Capri.

The Hills of Cava

As we discontentedly walked away, dissatisfied with our short two hours, we left the road and went through the deep grass, where remains of what was once a populous city are scattered over and imbedded in the ground. Marbles and potsherds, and at the gate a cart passed laden with great amphorae for daily use, their shape the same as those of the broken pottery of the ruins. Fashions do not change quickly in southern Italy.

Another night among the solemn hills of Cava in all their solitude. The early morning found us with bags and bundles, lunch baskets, rugs and all the impedimenta of travel packed closely with us in our landau,[27] on the way to Salerno, where the celebrated coast road begins.

The latter city possesses a wonderful old cathedral, only to be reached through a narrow street, too narrow and too steep for driving. It is entered through an atrium with no less than twenty-eight magnificent columns taken from the ruins of Paestum. Within are treasures of mosaic and bronze, with the rarest of ivory carvings and precious marbles.

A service was being held, and the church was quite full. Chairs were placed at the right and the left of the choir for those unable to obtain seats elsewhere. Two of the chairs were occupied by an old peasant and her cat. Be it remembered that the woman had paid a soldo[28] for the one on which the pussy was seated, as well as a soldo for her own. Standing not far away was a boy with a little dog in his arms, which was as well behaved as the dignified feline. The Italians love their pets and take them everywhere. This laxity never brings trouble or annoyance to either owner or bystander.

An Earnest Preacher

It was a strange picture—the old cathedral of pronounced Byzantine type, the congregation representing every strata of the people, the clergy in their garments of silk and lace and the archbishop on his splendid throne, all intent upon the words of the monk who was preaching.

He was a poor Cappucini,[29] in his brown robe, rope girdle and sandaled feet, and he was eloquently and earnestly declaiming in his soft and sonorous language.

The sun was overhead as we entered on the most wonderful road in the world. It was the one to Amalfi, and a day further on to Sorrento. It is hewn in the side of the rocky cliffs, winding through and over innumerable ravines, on viaducts of massive masonry, through lemon groves and vineyards on terraces. The clouds often drifted and concealed the heights. Forty-two terraces were frequently counted upon a mountain side, the lemons protected by trellises covered with oak branches and sometimes by the hardier grapevines.

Sometimes towns and villages lined the way, and then again there was no sign of habitation. Little fishing hamlets were half hidden in the bottoms of the deep ravines or perched along their sides, with boats drawn up on the shingly bank. We crossed a rushing river that had cut its way deep in the rocks in tearing madly down to the sea. Ruined castles were on the cliffs and watch towers on the miniature headlands close to the water level, and every village had its church and spire.

A Magnificent Highway

The road is as smooth as a floor and guarded by a low wall. It leads us safely over noble heights and profound depths, and as far as the vision carries we look upon the sea. The sunshine is delicious, the air is invigorating, and our three horses, harnessed abreast, take us gayly onward into Amalfi, which we greet with a sigh that such a day is over.

We need not have felt regret, however, for the evening on the terrace of the old convent was a revelation of the beauty earth can give. The moon was at it full, the strip of orange trees behind the Pergola was golden in its light, and the sea, more than 200 feet below, was a sheet of silver.

Before sunrise we were awake to welcome the day. The cloudless sky changed from crimson to gold; a splendid headland to the left, crowned with its round tower, was painted in lilac against the dark blue of the mountains beyond; lights twinkled from the houses, where the fishers were making ready for their busy day. Nets were to be mended and boats caulked, and the women were to dry the wheat on the beach, from which they were to make their best macaroni.[30]

Our breakfast is in the refectory of the old convent, which is now the hotel. The floor is of stone, and just over our heads is a great white cross in relief against the ceiling.

Otherwise it is like a city hotel—"all modern comforts." Even the little boy, just twelve, who waits on us wears a dress suit. He is a beautiful child, and his dignity is superhuman. After breakfast, as he escorts us by a new way to the Pergola, we venture to ask his name. It is Michaele, and he wishes to go to America.

Over Fair Amalfi

From the Pergola we climb to Bellevue. Many of the terraces are eight to ten feet high and covered with vegetables—clean, rich growth. At first the way is a series of steps (land is too valuable for treading), but soon we have passed the perpendicular and strike a wooded path. Flowers are everywhere—orchids and lilies in bud, holly and oak among the pines.

As we still look up there suddenly appears upon a slope of not less than forty-five degrees a woman cutting grass and making it into a bundle. It is as big as a cartload, but she ties it together, slips her curved knife into her belt at her back, swings the bundle on her head and walks lightly down the mountain side, somewhat as a fly might.

There is a walled spur to our left. She stoops there, unlocks a door and goes through, managing to squeeze her rebellious bundle with her. We follow, but in the moment the woman has disappeared.

Bellevue absorbs our attention. There are olive and locust trees and an old well with a circular curb. There are stone seats, and the huge capital of an ancient column is a table. How such a bulk of marble was gotten here or the water found in the solid rock to fill the well would be questions were it not that in Italy one soon learns to accept, enjoy and abandon the interrogation mark.[31]

A low parapet gives safety to look over. The town of Amalfi is in the narrow ravine 1,000 feet below us. The cathedral front, rich with mosaic and frescoes, faces us; the bell is ringing in the open Campanile, and far down the purple coast is Paestum. We look and look, but turn to rest. There is our grass-cutter; she is sitting on a bank fanning herself and taking off her stockings. They are red and have soles a half-inch thick, doubtless aiding her perilous walking. We are mutually interested and the few words we exchange (mostly nouns) carry us a long way in acquaintance.

Country Hospitality

She poses for her picture, her hazel eyes shining like chrysoprase;[32] a lira promotes geniality. Leaning over the parapet, we see a flat-roofed stone hut on a ledge of the precipice, just as wide as it is. Further conversation in gestures follows, and we accept her invitation to visit her in her residence.

This is reached by some perilous steps, down which she skips like a squirrel. With silent prayers for safety, we follow and are in her little home. There is not an article of furniture in it, except one, and that a ladder. How happy she is! There is nothing to be dusted or broken.

Two old guns rest against the wall, and some traps for wild creatures are on the floor. A bundle of bedding is rolled tightly up in a corner, and a few garments hang above it. The place is not untidy nor unclean, but there are no means for cooking. From the rafters hang grapes drying and bunches of the red Indian fig. She shows us the working of the traps and the guns. We admire the drying fruit, and in an instant she places the ladder, mounts it, breaks loose and brings down generous handfuls of the grapes and figs.

We shudder, but we eat. The broad windowsill is a table, and where else could such a picture be hung above a feast as that which is beyond the opening in the wall.

A Feast of Figs

Our Contadina[33] draws her knife from her pocket. It is a murderous-looking weapon, and we think of the traps, but with nice, natural instinct she wipes and polishes it on a grape leaf, adroitly peels the thorny figs, and without touching them with her hands, gives them to us in turn. Another lira, and we part friends for life. Surely no hospitality was ever more graciously offered than that of this lonely princess of the hills in her realm of grassy slopes and jagged rocks and sea and sky.

Another day finds us on Ravello's Heights, and still another in Sorrento's smiling orange groves; then Capri, and we are back in Naples.

Each place has individual features of natural beauty, and the daily incidents give us insight into the nature and life of the people, leaving delightful memories of sunshiny days and of the genial courtesy of the southern Italians.

Katharine Humphreys Wrenshall (c. 1880–?)

Katharine Wrenshall's life is shrouded in uncertainty. The daughter of John C. Wrenshall, a Confederate Army engineer, and longtime Women's Literary Club of Baltimore president Letitia Wrenshall, Katharine followed her mother in both literary pursuits and passion for travel. Club documents frequently refer to her as "Mrs. Wrenshall Markland" after her marriage to Fletcher Gerard Markland of California in 1901. However, the marriage ended in divorce by 1905. It is perhaps for this reason—the shame of divorce—that so little is known about Katharine Wrenshall's life, including her exact birth and death dates. What we *do* know is that she, like her mother, loved to travel, and this theme appears in nearly all of her written work—not only in her travel-related writings, but in works of fiction as well.

"The Parson and the Pick-Pocket" was published in the *Smart Set* magazine in 1909, two years before fellow Baltimorean H. L. Mencken became editor. The story takes place almost entirely upon a ship from Liverpool bound for New York City. This setting upon the ocean serves a symbolic function: it evokes a world that is neither England nor quite America, where the laws of either country can be called into question; perhaps, the perfect place for romance, religious conversion, or—petty crime.

Wrenshall, in writing and in life, was quite the entertainer. For years, she served as her mother's photographer and assistant during her magic lantern shows, which were designed to simulate the experience of travel for their audiences and were a popular precursor to vacation slideshows, the educational filmstrip, and travel documentaries. As a photographer and painter of slides, Katharine Wrenshall saw travel as more than just a pastime; she dedicated her life and writing to sharing her experiences abroad. Wrenshall shared her love of culture and art with the WLCB, following in her mother's footsteps. —H. Flynn

The Parson and the Pick-Pocket (1910)

It was the second day out from Liverpool. The tarpaulins stretched along the dripping nails crackled with the wind; the big ship plunging through the waves rose and rolled; the girders creaked and moaned; the water gurgled in the scuppers; but the Widow sat in her deck chair absorbed in her book.

A fellow passenger standing near was watching her profile, unconscious that he was being studied closely by the Parson, until turning, he met the old man's kind blue eyes.

"She is charming," he said.

The Reverend Mr. Goodheart smiled. "Yes, blessed with the power to make all the world love her. No, not I," he hastily deprecated; "I am too old for that, but I have found her a sympathetic listener to my anxiety over my daughter, who is desperately ill in New York."

"What is the nature of your daughter's illness?"

"I do not know. The cable said: 'Come; desperately ill,' and I took this steamer, fortunately a moderately fast one." Doctor Mervin relighted his cigarette, leading the conversation to other things to distract Mr. Goodheart's thoughts, until the sound of their voices penetrated the Widow's abstraction, and she looked up with a smile.

The men, approaching, drew chairs close to hers.

"You are a veritable sea witch, Mrs. Patterson. It is so rough and stormy that everyone is ill but the Doctor, you, and myself."

"Here comes another not ill," and she glanced at a man lighting his cigar in the shelter of the tarpaulin.

"I heard that his name was Craig when I was in the smoking room last night."

"You spoke as if you did not like him, Doctor Mervin."

"No," decidedly answered the Doctor, "no, I do not. He scrutinized everyone in the smoking room and especially their watches." The Widow laughed, but Mr. Goodheart clapped his hand to his watch pocket. "Doctor Mervin, you make me quite nervous; it would grieve me to lose mine."

"A good opportunity, Mr. Goodheart, for you to make a convert. Surely you could bring him to a state of grace by the time we reach New York."

The Widow was laughing, but the Parson shook his head in gentle reproof. "Do not jest, my child, upon such a subject. But your thought is excellent, though given so lightly and frivolously. I will act upon it."

The three watched Craig stroll toward them. The man was not unpleasing in appearance, but the Widow looked out to sea and the Parson was busy with his cufflinks when the Doctor supplied the match Craig asked for. Craig having walked on some distance, the two looked at the Widow, whose pale cheeks were flaming.

"I never was so rude in my life to anyone; I am ashamed."

"It was your prerogative, my dear Mrs. Patterson, not to speak," soothed the Parson.

"I don't care; I was rude, and it was

your fault." She turned stormy eyes upon the Doctor, who smiled aggravatingly, she considered. "I have half a mind to make you go and talk to him and then introduce him to me."

"I will, instead." The Parson rose and left the two, who from the first had seemed to fancy each other.

The ship passing out of the gale-swept Irish sea, the sick passengers emerged, and the three had no further uninterrupted conversation. Doctor Mervin and the Widow had become absorbed in each other, and Mr. Goodheart did not appear to seek any opportunity to talk to them, though his mild glance would reprove their evident amusement when he passed with Craig, his boon companion of the trip, while at the same moment he would furtively clutch his watch fob to show them he still had his cherished possession.

The last night before landing the usual coast fog wrapped the decks, but the Doctor and the Widow sat in their favorite corner, with chairs drawn close, and the Captain smoking near smiled at the insistent tones of Doctor Mervin.

"Dearest, don't you think you could say 'Yes' before we leave the dear old ship?"

The Captain did not hear her answer. Mr. Goodheart's voice drifted through the fog.

"I will hope to meet you again, my dear young friend, for the hours we have spent together have been delightful. Indeed, I feel I have learned so much from you, for you have a rare and unusual knowledge for one so young. My card? Surely; and yours? Thank you; I will place it in my Bible, for it has been a privilege to meet one with so much insight and knowledge combined with the rare respect you have manifested for all for all things sacred, a delight to one traveling through the forests of earthly indifference. Good night; we shall meet tomorrow for an hour."

"Good night, Mr. Goodheart." Henry Craig's silky voice caressed the words, and the Doctor's hand tightened on the Widow's, as he murmured: "That is surely the voice of a scamp." As he spoke the Parson appeared on the deck, still smiling. He hastened to the corner where he knew the two were.

"Ah, Doctor, such an estimable young man! And you two have jested."

"No, no, Mr. Goodheart."

"Yes, you have, my little lady, you both—" He suddenly gasped and rocked where he stood, his hand on his watch pocket, and the Doctor cried out: "It is gone!" But the Widow, flinging her rug aside, had left her chair. For one second her slim figure was silhouetted against the lighted doorway: the next the two astonished men could hear her talking to Craig. Striding to the porthole, they could see her standing between Craig and the staircase, her furs slipping from her shoulders, falling half across the top step; and surmising that she would hold him from going below with his spoil, Doctor Mervin turned to consult with the Parson on the surest way to recover the watch. But he was talking with the Captain.

"You say you have been all evening with this man, your close companion of the trip?"

"Yes, Captain." Mr. Goodheart's pleasant affability was broken with ripples of agitation.

The Captain looked sharply at his benign and gentle face, then at the Doctor standing near. "Where is Mrs. Patterson?" he demanded.

"Holding Craig at the head of the companionway," answered the Doctor, and in spite of his vexation, the Captain smiled as he looked through the porthole before he joined the couple within.

"We shall be at the wharf very early, Mrs. Patterson. Are your trunks ready?"

"No, indeed; I am going now to finish my packing." She moved to the door with a parting bow to Craig.

"Allow me to fold your rugs," exclaimed Craig, hastening forward, as though he divined the trap closing upon him.

"The Doctor is on deck, Mr. Craig; he will fold Mrs. Patterson's rugs," interrupted the Captain in a stern voice. "And I wish to speak to you for a moment."

Craig looked desperately at the open door, but he submitted to the officer's detaining hand on his arm.

"I have had a conversation, Mr. Craig, that has annoyed me greatly. An accusation has been made against one of my passengers; perhaps you can aid me." The Captain spoke low and persuasively, but Craig looked steadily at the letter rack.

"I regret I do not catch the drift of your words, Captain—but I was always a dull fellow."

"I will be clearer, Mr. Craig. I am due on the bridge shortly, and I should like to know how many minutes I have for my cigar before going up." Drawing one from its case and a match from his pocket, he waited.

"I will not light this if I cannot smoke it to the end. I am sure—I am sure that you must have a—watch."

The last word was jerked out by the Captain as though he found it most distasteful, and Craig started nervously, for simultaneously the Parson appeared in the doorway.

"Come in, Mr. Goodheart; Mr. Craig is just going to give me the time."

The Parson assented, his gentle face lighted with eagerness.

"Here it is," slowly muttered Craig and he held out the old watch, the dull silver shining under the electric lights. The Captain silently handed it to the Parson, who clasping his beloved trinket, faced Craig.

"I regret that I cannot at this moment find sufficient grace to thank you for returning my watch, or wish to continue our acquaintance. Good evening." And turning, he went immediately to the Doctor and the Widow waiting on the deck.

"I am so agitated," he moaned. "Do strike a match, Doctor; I wish to look at my loved possession. Alas, that old as I am, my soul should still hold such earthly feelings!"

Under the flaring match the watch was turned to and fro; then Mr. Goodheart turned to the Widow.

"How am I ever to express to you my appreciation for your wit and courage?"

"Don't try," she laughed; "but sit down here and rest." The Parson placed his watch in his pocket, tucked in the fob and sank back in the offered chair with an exhausted sigh. The two looked at him curiously, but the Widow retrained her desire to tease, and the Doctor laid his hand quietly on the Parson's, expecting the rapid pulse that raced beneath his fingers.

"Pray, allow me to give you something tonight. I never offer to prescribe, but you seem to feel this affair so keenly that I think it my duty to advise your talking a very mild sedative."

"Yes, do take what the Doctor offers you," urged the Widow.

"Are you going to take *all* his doses, my little lady?"

"Yes, surely, if I decide to have him for my physician." Mr. Goodheart looked at the Doctor, but his eyes were on the demure face beside him.

"May I offer my warmest congratulations and wishes, my friends?"

"Thank you, sir." The Doctor spoke heartily, but the Widow, laying her hand lightly in the Parson's clasp, rose and slipped away. Mr. Goodheart immediately reverted to Craig.

"I am so shocked and grieved over this affair; Craig had impressed me favorably. And such a habit!"

Doctor Mervin's eyebrows went up at the added word, and the other explained.

"I cannot call it a vice; it must be a habit. Indeed, I did wrong to feel such displeasure. I must endeavor to repair it."

"He has probably gone down now to his stateroom, but you will have time tomorrow and then again on the wharf. Don't worry; he is a scamp. Be glad you have your watch safe. Certainly you were most restrained in what would have been natural anger when he gave it up."

"I am glad you think so, Doctor, but I fear I am acquiring an irritable manner in my old age."

"Not so, Mr. Goodheart, not so; come down now. See that flashlight out there on the coast! It is spelling: 'Buffalo, Chicago, and all points West.'"

Mr. Goodheart walked slowly to the door, and the Doctor, gathering up the rugs, leisurely followed, when glancing through the porthole, he saw the Parson and Craig talking, the former protesting with mild vigor:

"I cannot believe it, I will not believe it, that you are a professional thief, with such intelligence, a good education, and"—Mr. Goodheart hesitated—"with such excellent respect for the church."

"But it takes a man with some wit to steal and not be caught," growled Craig.

"My boy, I cannot think it to be a confirmed evil with you; indeed, I refuse to— no, not if you took my watch again! Surely, it is an unfortunate—ahem! Did you ever have brain fever?"

"No," laughed Craig.

"How sad! And you really acknowledge this—ahem—lamentable tendency of yours to be frequent?"

"Very frequent, Mr. Goodheart." And Craig laughed again. The old man clasped his hands and almost wrung them at the other's levity, but he spoke mildly.

"I am a poor man, Mr. Craig, yet I will gladly give you a temporary loan to start you if you will cease this wickedness."

"Can't promise that, Mr. Goodheart; temptation might prove too strong—but by gosh, sir, you must have a mighty trusting disposition to offer me a loan."

"My disposition has nothing to do with the matter, young man; I would save you if I could."

"You mean you would save your watch—in short, buy me off."

The old Parson stepped back, looking doubtful and sadly at Craig.

"Respect my sacred calling, if you do not my gray hair," he said sternly, and after a moment Craig apologized.

"Forgive my seeming disrespect, Mr. Goodheart."

"Oh, my boy, I do forgive most truly, for it grieves me deeply to think of your future; let me, I beseech you, have the humble gratification of knowing that I have influenced your conduct. Think of how you must answer for all these delinquencies, and pray for strength to combat such tendencies. Here is a little pamphlet, my son; you will see I have marked it for my own benefit during this voyage to my daughter's deathbed. Take it; perhaps there may come a moment when you would like to look at it."

Mr. Goodheart, putting the pamphlet into Craig's hand, turned to the door. "Are you coming, Doctor?" And the Doctor emerging from the gloom, they went down the companionway together.

As the liner entered New York harbor the waters were shining in the sunlight, and the Doctor and the Widow leaning over the rail watched the ships and the tug that, having brought the customs officials, screeched itself hoarse and departed; then the two seated themselves in their favorite corner, looking after the Parson where he strolled along the decks.

That the Widow was still uncertain in her answer was evidenced by the pucker between the Doctor's brows, and Parson and Pickpocket faded from his mind as he looked at her. Her cheeks were pink with the sea air, and happiness possibly had added the smiling brilliance to her eyes, but she sat silent until suddenly she exclaimed, "Look!" and the Doctor turning, saw Mr. Goodheart and Craig at the gangway. The latter was shaking hands effusively with the Parson, for at the old man's earnest request no charges had been proffered, and Henry Craig was the first passenger ashore, the pamphlet sticking out of

his pocket. Doctor Mervin, pointing it out, told his companion of the last incident of the previous evening, and she laughed, but her eyes suddenly filled with tears, and the Doctor took them as an evil omen for his hopes, his heart sinking lower and lower as later he waited near when her trunks were examined on the wharf.

She seemed absolutely shy of him, until at a sudden crowding on the wharf she retreated hastily to his side. A police wagon had been driven through the gates and the crowd ordered back.

"What is the matter?"

"Some poor devil caught breaking some laws, I expect."

"I hope it is no one from our ship," she breathed.

"They're arrestin' a first-class passenger," yelled an immigrant from the decks of the liner.

"Yah! Yah!" Yells and hisses filled the air, and a policeman waving his baton hurried up the gangway. "Shut up," he cried, and as he stepped on the deck he added, "Get back."

The immigrants laughed, but someone on the wharf protested loudly, while a woman's voice cried out: "Poor dear gentleman, what an indignity!"

"It's a mistake I tell you," shouted a man and the Doctor swung the Widow up onto a dry goods box. Once she could see over the crowd, she scrambled down panting. "Oh Bob, we must go to him!" and she vanished through the crowd, followed by the Doctor.

In the center of a small space kept open by the police was a marshal, a warrant in his hand; to one side waited a silent, motionless prisoner between the two officers.

Instinctively understanding, though not formulating his surmise, the Doctor stepped hastily into the circle of police surrounding the marshal and his prisoner.

"I will go his bail, marshal," he said authoritatively. The officer shook his head, but at the Doctor's look of protest he silently passed his hand into his inner vest pocket. For one brief second the Doctor and the Widow saw a sickeningly familiar old silver watch. A spring threw the back open; the works were out, and a mass of diamonds glittered in their place.

"It must be a cruel mistake," she protested. The police smiled at her faith, but the marshal answered sternly:

"He is the greatest diamond thief in the world, madam."

"But he asked the Captain to let Henry Craig go after he had taken his horrid old watch from him," Mrs. Patterson expostulated.

"Henry Craig knew what was in the watch, Madam, but the prisoner was the cleverer of the two and the more daring. He must have known that Craig was on his track, and to rid himself of him he allowed him to first steal the watch."

With a despairing little gesture Mrs. Patterson accepted the marshal's words and the Doctor led her away. As she paused at her trunks to receive the checks for them from the waiting baggage agent, she raised her head and dabbed angrily at her tears.

"How could anyone know if the minister was really a true one?"

"Oh, I know one who is very real, dearest, both as man and minister—one I can vouch for, as he is my own brother living here in New York. We will go by way of his rectory."

The Widow declared she would not, but she stepped into the carriage that Doctor called.

Francese Litchfield Turnbull (1845-1927)

The Woman's Literary Club of Baltimore was not Francese Hubbard Litchfield Turnbull's idea. (That belonged to Hester Crawford Dorsey and Louisa C. Osborne Haughton, also included in this anthology). Nevertheless, she was elected as the Club's first president, a post to which she was re-elected five times. Turnbull's sister, Grace Denio Litchfield, also participated in the Club as an honorary member; the two often presented each other's work.

In April 1890, in her first address as president, Turnbull declared that the goal of the Club was "formed to encourage exact and noble thinking among our women; hoping to prove that added strength will cultivate larger grace of speech and man-

ner, keener instincts of pure womanhood, a deeper appreciation of the precious opportunities of the home life, with a truer comprehension of its responsibilities—a broader, and not less loving and believing heart." In subsequent years, she firmly guided the Club toward these aims of aesthetic appreciation, literary cultivation, and intellectual pursuits in lieu of social reform and philanthropy. As president, Turnbull was a frequent presenter, by which she asserted her involvement as well as her authority within the Club. She helped create an environment in which both successful and fledgling writers flourished.

Turnbull, who was educated privately in both the United States and Europe, married Baltimore attorney Lawrence Turnbull in 1871. They were admirers and friends of Southern poet Sidney Lanier, and were instrumental in his attainment of a position at the Johns Hopkins University as a lecturer on poetry. Following the deaths of Lanier in 1881 and their son Percy in 1887, they established the Percy Turnbull Lectures in Poetry in 1889, bringing such figures as T. S. Eliot and W. H. Auden to Baltimore for well over a century.

Turnbull's first publication was a narrative poem, *Marguerite's Vow* (1882), but the remainder of her writing was prose: historical fiction and several pieces of literary criticism, much of which were initially presented at Club meetings. Her first novel, *The Catholic Man* (1890), centers on a character based on Lanier, a Confederate officer (as Lanier was), who is taken in by a Northern family during his convalescence and imbues them with his poetic "soul," thus effecting a reconciliation of sorts between North and South. In subsequent novels, she reached back in time and toward more distant realms: Napoleonic France in *Val-Maria* (1901), and Renaissance Italy in *The Golden Book of Venice* (1909).

Female characters appear in all her work, gradually transforming from domestic paragons and admirers of male authority figures to leaders in their own right. *The Royal Pawn of Venice* (1911) is based on the life of Caterina Cornaro (1454-1510), Queen of Cyprus. A reviewer for the *Dial* wrote that Cornaro "is pictured for us with a penetrative sympathy that makes her . . . nothing less than a real woman of pure and exalted ideals, whose tragic destiny we may not contemplate unmoved."[1] —J. Fury

From *The Royal Pawn of Venice: A Romance of Cyprus* (1911)

During the fifteenth century, the rulers, or Signoria, of Venice sought to take over the wealthy and beautiful island nation of Cyprus. They scheme to do so by arranging a marriage between Caterina Cornaro, a young fourteen-year-old Venetian maiden, and the island's young king, Janus.

Chapter II

They had just told her a thing most strange—a secret that made her childish heart stand still with wonder, then beat with a sort of frightened excitement, all unbefitting the new dignity to which she was called; for she was still enough a child to feel the glamour of it through all the strangeness, and she had stolen out upon the balcony, high over the Canal, to say over to herself the words that had been confided to her—the little maid Caterina.

She dropped the title softly down to the water below, and started at the echo of her own trembling voice.

Caterina Queen of Cyprus: Caterina— Regina!

A swaying figure in a passing gondola glanced up to the balcony of the old Palazzo Cornaro[2] and the young girl hastily fled, not pausing until she had reached her own little chamber, looking on an inner court—the only sanctuary that she could call her own, in all this great ancestral palace, she, the future Queen of Cyprus.

Had any one heard her murmur those words? Would the Senate know that some one in a gondola had caught the new title from her own lips? And so—perchance—

to punish the indiscretion—for the Senate was masterful, never-to-be-disobeyed, and the matter was not to be known until it should be declared by that solemn body of world-rulers. And if the gondoliero had carried her word to the Palazzo San Marco—What if he had been sent there by the Senate itself to watch and see if she were already woman enough to be trusted? Then there would be an end to the golden dream—no coronation—no splendid ceremony of adoption. For there was more. Before she should be made queen of that distant island she was to be formally acknowledged "The Daughter of the Republic—" She was to be made a real Princess of Venice!

What wonder that the heart of this young Venetian maid quivered with the excitement of these visions of splendor, for by all the traditions of her ancestors she measured the unwonted honor that was being decreed for her—no one had yet been adopted "Daughter of the Republic"—the title was to be created that she might wear a crown, to the further honor of Venice! For her, who had never worn a jewel, nor a robe of state, nor taken part in any but the simplest fête,[3] who had never left the walls of her ancestral palace, save under closest veil and guard—this sudden vision of freedom and empire was intoxicating.

If she had known of those wonderful tales of the "Arabian Nights,"[4] these things that were happening to her would have seemed more wonderful still: but her young mind was free of similes—a sensitive blank whereon the Senate might duly inscribe whatever tendencies seem judicious; and after the Betrothal there would be much time.

Caterina had taken courage again and stolen back to the balcony that opened upon the Canal Grande from the vast upper salon, impelled by her longing for freedom and light. The ripple of the water to the plash of passing gondolas took on the note of distance and soothed her like a lullaby, as the charming maid yielded herself to the golden day-dream—the soft breezes lifting the bright rings of hair that clustered about her dainty head, while the wonderful light of the skies of Venice smiled down upon her like a caress. The strangeness slipped away from the new facts she had been repeating to herself, for she had already begun to take pride in them; and the other questions that had troubled her for a moment, were forgotten. All kings were to her youthful imagination great and noble when they were the friend of the Republic, and Janus was the close ally of Venice. In this stately patrician household she had suddenly risen to first—not only as all maids are wont to be on the eve of their betrothal, with much circumstance of laces and brocade and gifts and jewels—but she was to bring new honor to their ancient house—honor even upon Venice, for her father had declared that the Senators, the Councillors, all the great men of the Republic—the Serenissimo himself—would bring her homage. It was a dizzying dream of glory—beautiful, child-hearted and fancy-free, she could dream of no more golden vision than the Signoria[5] were preparing for her.

So many generations of Cornari had gone forth from their palaces scattered through the great places of Venice, as ambassadors on momentous missions, or as Senators or Savii,[6] had instilled the lesson of the glory of service to Venice; and more than once the mighty Lion of San Marco[7] had set his imperial seal above their portal, and she, Caterina, was to lead them all in the honor she was bring upon her country! If her own estimate of the part she was to play was a foolish one, only a Venetian patrician maid could comprehend the glamour that overlay this vision of Caterina's—the royal delivery from bondage—the unknown delights it must open to her!

"Thou art sent for, *carina*, to the crimson salon; thy Father would speak with thee."

It was the Lady Fiorenza,[8] who seemed always a little sad to Caterina—too sad for all the state that surrounded her; too grave to suit the splendor of her silken robes and gleaming jewels; too weak to cope with the masterful ways of her lord, the Senator Marco Cornaro.[9] Her mother's hand almost crushed hers in the strenuous clasp which, strangely to Caterina, seemed to convey a passionate message of sympathy; yet surely, at this radiant moment, there was nothing to regret! She met the love in her mother's eyes with the smile of a satisfied child, though she would have liked them all to rejoice with her.

The curtain that hung before the door of the crimson salon was raised by the page who stood in waiting. Her stately father rose to greet her—which he had never done before in all her little life. She felt with a sudden vague discomfort, that the world was changing for her.

"My daughter," he said, with a gravity of demeanor that befitted the importance of his message, "thou bringest honor, not alone to the Casa Cornaro, but also to the Republic. I have this day received from the island of Cyprus—of which thou shalt be Queen—" and he bent his knee, in courtly fashion before his child, as though he would be first to bring her homage, "by the hand of the ambassador Mastachelli, this portrait of thy Lord, Janus, the King; and these Eastern pearls—a royal gift."

He kissed the little hand which Caterina eagerly stretched out for the casket; but her mother covered her face with her hands, almost in an attitude of prayer.

The miniature was blazing with diamonds, and the pearls were more lustrous than any that had ever been seen in Venice—for Cyprus was even beyond Venetia in luxury; and Caterina called to her mother, with a note of triumph, to clasp them about her childish throat.

"I must learn to *look* a Queen!" she said with a little, playful, regal air: and then she dropped her eyes upon the beautiful, laughing face of the royal lover who was to open paradise to her. Her father watched her furtively; while her mother, over her child's shoulder, studied the picture closely, feeling that it was too beautiful to trust.

"He is charming!" the girl cried in pleased surprise. She had not known what his face would be like; she had scarcely had time to think of it since the strange news had been brought her, a few hours before.

"He will be kind to thee," the mother said at length with conviction, yet with a sigh, as if dissatisfied.

Caterina meanwhile, in the simple straight blue robe of a young Venetian maiden, her dimpled throat encircled with the pearls that had been the ransom of a kingdom, stood turning her miniature from side to side, catching the sunlight on the jewels and the face, with the pleasure of a child in a new and splendid toy—for it was all beautiful together.

"He is charming—charming, my King!" she repeated.

But a shadow had crept into her mother's eyes. "It is a face that an artist might paint for his pleasure," she said with hesitation, as if seeking expression for some vague fear that haunted her; "I pray that he may make thee happy, *carina*; that he may be good and—and—noble."

"Noble!" cried Marco Cornaro, scornfully; "what seekest more? Is Cyprus not enough for thy nobility? Is there another mother in Venice who doth not envy thee thy fortune! Go to thy tire-women[10] and consult with them, for the Betrothal will be soon, by order of the Senate, and there is small time to waste in regrets that somewhat more to thy liking hath not befallen thee. See to it that the robing of Caterina be fit for that other kingdom thou wouldst, perchance, have chosen for her."

"If he be noble—truly noble," the Lady Fiorenza said with unwonted persistence—for something moved her to assert herself, "I ask no more."

But the Senator permitted her the questionable honor of unanswered speech, as he turned with a scowl and left her. For her word had rankled: since it was known, in the innermost circle of the Council and there discussed in strictest secrecy, that had Janus been born in Venice, the law would have excluded him for its *Libro d'Oro*,[11] and no patrician father would have sought him for his daughter. But Cyprus lay far away beyond the sea which washed the borders of Venetia, and many of Oriental race had peopled its shores—the ideals of Venice might be no law for Cyprus.

Chapter III

These things took place in the spring of 1468; nor was it long before the ceremonial had been prescribed and the pageant had been made ready for the betrothal of the youthful Caterina; for the Senate could be as prompt in action as far-seeing in judgment when haste seemed wise; and other rulers were looking with no disfavor on the King of Cyprus in this matter of an alliance, for it was known that overtures had already been offered by the Court of Naples and His Holiness of Rome for one of his own family who had claim to his protection.

While Venice was plunged in a turmoil of preparation, the Casa Cornaro gathered from all its palaces and surged up and down the grand stairway of the Marco Cornari, bringing counsel, gifts and glorification; the dowagers to the remotest branches, were much in evidence, refurbished, and coming in solemn state to testify their approval of an alliance so honorable to their house, with many wise worldly maxims and pious thanks to the Madonna.

There was no quiet anywhere within the palazzo, save deep down in the heart of the Lady Fiorenza, who had never been one with her family in worldly ambitions; and far below the giddy current of the day's happenings ran the ceaseless flow of the mother's wordless prayer, enfolding her child— pleading that that which was to come to her should make and keep her noble.

Resistance would have been vain, if only because she stood alone in her family circle; but the decision of the Senate was supreme— unquestionable and irrevocable; she stood alone indeed with only prayer to help her, and a great faith that because of it her child would be saved in the path of danger from which her love might not hold her feet. And so the day of the Betrothal dawned.

Ah, how the bells were ringing—*Madre Beata!*[12] For such a *festa*[13] as never had been in Venice! The hearts of the happy people throbbed to their rhythm, while each gave something to the splendor of the day— were it but the color of a mantle, or the grace of a jubilant motion, or the radiance of a beaming face—there was no *festa* in Venice of which the people had not its part.

They had been gathering since earliest dawn in the Piazza San Marco, arriving breathlessly in gondolas from the nearer points, in fishing boats with painted sails from the distant islands—hastening from their unsold wares in the market stalls near the wooden bridge of the Rialto to wait long hours for the pageant that no Venetian might miss. For never had there been such another, and there was not too much space where one might stand to see the glory and the beauty of it! *Dio!*[14] But it was good to be born in Venice, where life was a *festa!*

Along the Riva their radiant, dark faces gleamed in the sunshine, where they stood in serried ranks, picturesque in all the brilliant coloring that their rustic wardrobes held in store for these days of *festa;* silken shawls that were heir-looms—strings of coral and amber and great Venetian beads of every tint, or an edge of old lace on the gala *fazzuolo*[15] that many a noble lady might be proud to wear; everywhere there was color against the background of festive garlands and brilliant rugs decking the balconies of the palaces—a dazzling picture in the sunshine, under the blue of the Venetian sky.

Every window in the Piazza and the Piazzetta was thronged with spectators in gala robes, while under the arcades that stretched from San Marco to the ancient church of San Giminiano across the square, the people surged crowding and jubilant; climbing to the roofs and ledges of every building, the campanile, the churches, the columned palaces, leaving not a space where a man might stand save the avenue through the crowd which the soldiers kept free for the procession.

The bells were beginning to ring— *Santa Maria!* All the bells—a true jubilee!

Messer San Marco and San Tadoro were good to them to-day; how their golden images flashed in the sunshine on the columns! and the four great golden horses, in the dancing sunlight, seemed to quiver and prance among the frost-work of the arches of San Marco, while the gold and blue and scarlet of frieze and archivolt made a picture of delight.

The little ones shouted and babbled, were lifted high on their fathers' shoulders, or clamored with disappointed half-sobs down in the crowd which shut out all vision, beside the weary, expostulating mothers whose arms were filled with wee things who could not stand, and who had come early in the day—so early—in hope of a treat for the *bambini.*

They had carried them around the Piazza when they came in the early morning before the crowd—"Santa Vergine— wasn't that enough for them! To get a sight of all the grand balconies where the *nobili* were to be, with the garlands and the tapestries and the curtains of velvet and brocade, and the beautiful paintings, and the banners of San Marco, and the great golden horses in the Piazza—the wonderful golden horses—up so high, thou knowest, eh, Battista? What dost thou want more. *Pazienza!*"

There was a commotion on the Piazzetta; the first barge, heading the long procession from the Palazzo Cornaro in San Cassiano far up the Canal Grande, was coming in sight, bearing the brilliant *Compagnia della Calza*, the noble youths of the Company of the Hose, whose gilded duty it was to appear at State Ceremonials in all the extravagance of fantastic elegance with which Venice had decreed their costumes. A laughing, dainty company, they sprang ashore at the landing of the Piazzetta, doffing their jewelled caps to the admiring crowd with capricious grace and whimsical motions, like a flock of birds of paradise, in doublets of velvet and cloth of gold, with hair floating loose about their throats; with devices of fabulous birds—of stars flashing light—of mystic arabesques and hieroglyphs embroidered on their silken hose, in pearls and gold and precious stones:—truly a gay and frivolous company to be under the grave control of the Ten!

The people shouted with delight as they took their stand at the steps of the Piazzetta to receive the oncoming barges, for the "Calza" were the very darlings of their eyes, and never had they been more brilliant. With true Venetian comradery the crowd tossed them light banter on the names of their divisions, with pantomimic interpretation, in response to their sweeping salutations.

"*Cortesi!* saw one ever such courtesy!"

"San Marco keep you *Immortali,* for the grace of you!"

Sempiterni!—everlasting—ay, to be young like that, with so much pleasure in life—*Cielo!*"[16]

"And the *gondolieri* of the *Sempiterni*—do they live also forever? Signori Nobili, have you need of *gondolieri*?"

But it needed only a whimsical motion of the Calza to fasten all eyes on the Canal Grande, where to the gracious rhythm of countless strings and flutes, the barges of state were nearing the steps of the Piazzetta, bearing the standards of Venice and Cyprus—their prows garlanded with roses, their rowers wreathed with myrtle—banners and draperies of snow and silver floating in the breeze.

Far up the Canal Grande the gondolas of the nobles, waiting before their palaces, had glided into position as the procession swept down toward the Piazza—each gondola showing the colors of its *casa*, each fluttering a silken streamer in honor of Cyprus, each bearing its freight of crimson-garbed senators and ladies in festal array.

A murmur of intense satisfaction broke from the excited crowd along the Riva, as the barges which bore the youthful bride and her newly-appointed suite floated nearer; the great festal barges carved with bas-reliefs from classic story, were all of white and silver, their sails of satin, plumed with roses, and from each prow the figure of a glorified swan flashed rosy light from eyes of ruby: and every rower in white and silver plying his silver oar, wore the arms Cornaro blazoned on his sleeve, with a sash of the colors of Cyprus.

An opal light played over the group of

the dainty maids of honor, yet each showed, for her only color, the arms of her ancient Venetian house wrought large upon the creamy fabric of her tunic, the threads of gold and gleam of jewels half lost within its folds as she walked: but the people looked for the heraldic devices and named them eagerly as, two by two, the maidens stepped on shore—Mocenigo—Giustiniani—Morosini—Dandolo—Contarini—a new name for every sweet young face—the King of Cyprus could add none fairer, nor no more noble arms to the court of his youthful Queen. The Senate had outdone itself in luxury of imagination.

"Ecco!"[17] The low long-drawn sound of delight swept through the expectant throng like the rustle of the wind among the rushes, for here, at last, was La Caterina! and a very child she seemed as she stood surrounded by the escort of noble Matrons of Honor most sumptuously clad, whom Venice had appointed to act as sponsors in the ceremonial of the Adoption. She was like a snow-drop in a garden of exotics—so pale and fair and young, in her robes of filmy lace from the cushions of Burano—the great pearls of Janus rising and falling with the frightened throbbing of her breast. Her mother only stood beside her under the canopy—her hand clasping that of her child with a pressure which gradually steadied her to forget herself and to do her part mechanically, as she might be instructed: for, deep in the heart of the Lady Fiorenza that ceaseless prayer upheld her with a rare and noble dignity—it brought her calm for the drama she had not willed, and faith that for her child all would be well. She had pleaded

with the Senate that on this day of deep import the barge of Caterina should not be without the benediction of its tutelary saint, since every gondola was wont to have its shrine; and behind them under the canopy, from a mass of roses on an altar of alabaster, rose a noble Madonna by Bellini, painted with exquisite grace—the votive picture which later kept within the Chapel of the Lady Fiorenza in the Palazzo Cornaro, the memory of this day.

The little ones cried and struggled down among the crowd, seeing nothing, and conscious from the chorus of ecstatic exclamations that they were missing a golden moment.

"*Pace!*[18] Yes, they are coming: she is there—the Regina. Every one of you shall see—every one. *Pazienza!* Some one will hold the *bimbo* who sleeps? Then I could lift Tonino and Maria. *Mille Grazie!*"[19]

A dozen sympathetic arms had instantly offered in response to this appeal, for the good-natured Venetian crowd adored *festas*—they also—and it would be a pity of pities that the bambini should miss it, and this one was like heaven!

"Ah, but she is beautiful, the bride—beautiful as an angel: and young—young like my Teresina! And to be a queen—Santa Marie!—she who was like the other daughters of the nobili on the Canal Grande! Ah, but life is wonderful for them—the nobili—but Messer San Marco is gentile to make this *festa* for Venice!" The recollection of their own little part in the festa came with a patient sigh.

"It is our Caro Maestro Giovanni Bellini who hath fashioned it all they say—the garlands, the barges—the costumes—he talked with their Excellencies, the Signoria."

The rumor went round, for the Maestro was the honest pride of Venice.

"It is he, verily, who hath painted our Blessed Lady for the *barca*[20] of the Lady Caterina; for Madonna Fiorenza is almost a saint—and *devote*—! She hath the heart of a *carità*[21] within her."

"They come now from the *palazzo* of the Cornaro," cried the little peasant-mother eagerly. "Hearest thou, my *bimbo?*" She moved the restless hands to and fro, the round eyes following the motion. "Clap thy hands for the Regina—thou too, give thy greeting; thou wilt remember it when thou art old. May the holy Madonna bless her!"

The shouts to which Caterina landed were deafening: the children screamed for very ecstasy.

The lagoon, from the Riva far out toward the islands was a dense mass of floating craft of the poorer sort, for below the Piazza there had been no restriction, and the waters were crowded with islanders—old people grateful for this nearness to the pageant, with a chance of separation from the standing, jostling crowd, and proud of lending the color of their pennons and painted sails for their share of the glory of the day. If one could see nothing, it was good to be there to hear the shouting—one would understand the better when Tonio should be taking his bit of supper and free to talk—for he was no good to his old mother now, with watching the tacking and the people. And one might as well be dead as to stay far off the Burano on a day like this! *Cielo*, but the bells and the shouting were divine! It made one young again.

"A *king*, thou sayest? Who is the king that the child is going to marry? What is he like, Tonio? I cannot see so far."

"*Not there?* Holy Mother, but it is a strange wedding! There would have been the gossip of all the islands to answer if there hadn't been two to a wedding when I was young. But the Signori Nobili must have everything after their own new fashions. And to miss his own *spozalizio!*[22] San Marco is not good to him—he'll never see another half so fine. Is she so young as they say—like Maria, there?"

"Ah, to be Signori just for to-day!" sighed the little peasant-mother in the crowd, as the dazzling cortège passed out of sight into the golden glooms of San Marco. "To go with the *nobili* into the Duomo where one may behold the Pala d'Oro and the wonderful golden candlesticks which the Serenissimo hath given—to *see* the Serenissimo take her for the Daughter of the Republic—wonder of wonders! And then to the Palazzo Ducale for the Betrothal—*Pazienza*, one must wait; they will come again later, my *bambini*. Ah, but the beauty of it!" For the brave little woman was weary, and there was nothing like enthusiasm for keeping up one's courage, "and Heaven alone knew where Zorzi was with the *barca!*"

The crowd relaxed and grew restless, losing some of the gaiety of its temper when a weary neighbor settled back a little too roughly on a fellow-shoulder, or the babies who had been put down on the ground to rest lost the last sweet morsels they had been munching and clamored in vain for more—too much excited by the unusual noises and happenings to deign to notice the brothers of the next size who were busily turning somersaults in their behalf.

But it would not be long before the procession came again; for the last of the sumptuous nobles who made this holiday for the people had disappeared under the portico of San Marco.

The bells were chiming now in soft low undertones, a very ripple of sound—like the breath of the summer-breeze upon the sea—stilling the shrill voices of the people in the Piazza, calming the exuberance of their motions. For it was a signal. They knew that within the Duomo, before the great altar where slept their patron-saint, ablaze now with lights and the marvel of the Pala d'Oro which was not for the sight of the eyes save on days of a *festa* like this, the child of the Cornaro was waiting to be made the Daughter of Venice.

And now—for the bells were silent—in the magnificent storied chamber of the Gran Consiglio, where so many momentous questions of state had been discussed, in the presence of the Serenissimo, the Signoria, the Senate and the Forty Noble Matrons, a new leaf was to be added to the story of the Republic, and thither the feeble old Doge led the Daughter of Venice with the brilliant assemblage who had witnessed the ceremony of the Adoption in the Duomo.

Caterina had moved through the splendid pageant of the morning as in a dream, still too much a child to comprehend the responsibilities it portended—too much in awe of the distinguished company assembled to do her honor to be conscious of any feeling but unwonted timidity. But the tottering footsteps of the old man who held her hand as he led her through the Porta della Carta into the Ducal Palace, awoke her inborn sense of pity, and it was she who upheld him with her strong, young, vital clasp, recovering her own perfect poise in the act of giving help.

The Ambassador Mastachelli was waiting with his suite, and the signing of the parchment which bore the seals of Venice and Cyprus was the trifle of a moment. A circlet of rubies—the sign of the promise—had been consecrated by the saintly Patriarch, Lorenzo Giustiniani, and the Lady Fiorenza took comfort from the look in his noble face as he bent over Caterina to give the benediction. She would seek his aid in the training of the young betrothed for her life on that distant island.

But now—at last—the hour was the people's once more, for the Serenissimo stood on the balcony above the portal of San Marco, between the great golden horses, with the Daughter of Venice beside him—the sunlight irradiating her white robes and beautiful, girlish face.

"Caterina—Regina—*Figlia di Venezia—Nostra Venezia!*"[23] A great cry rent the air; it came from thousands of hearts and thrilled her own to its core, and the first, great emotion of her young life swept through her, transforming and wholly possessing her.

A mist swam before her and her heart throbbed as if it would break: she dimly saw innumerable faces leaning to her from roofs and balconies and windows, and below in the great Piazza, the dense mass of the people with faces offering love and homage, lifting their children to clap their tiny hands for her—it was wonderful—beautiful—had the Madonna, indeed, given her so much!

The mist cleared before her eyes and each face, to the remotest corners of the Piazza stood out individualized, while a sudden great love of humanity was born within her. "She would pray to make her people happy—she would be something to the poor and suffering ones of her distant land of Cyprus—the Holy Mother would teach her—"

It was the supreme moment that does not come to all, yet when it comes holds the making or the marring of a life—as the lightning gleams for an instant only through a rift of cloud, awe-inspiring and too luminous to be forgotten. To Caterina, on the verge of womanhood, it came with the force of a prophetic vision, giving her sight of the tie between a queen and her people—it was like the strong mother-love of a great woman—all-embracing; the splendor of the pageant, the personal homage had no longer part in the exaltation of that great moment—it was the *real* beneath it all that stirred her soul. She lost herself in the emotion, seeking only for expression; she opened her arms wide to them as if she would embrace them all, turning on every side to smile her heart out to them—tossing kisses to the children who clapped their eager hands for her—scattering sunshine with that rare magnetic power which is the most wondrous gift the Heaven can bestow.

"*Simpatica!*" the responsive people cried with glowing faces. "*Angiola!—Tanto Simpatica!*"[24]

The Lady Fiorenza standing where she could see the face of her child gave thanks for the vision with joyful tears.

"This hast thou granted her, *Madonna mia Beatissima,*[25] for a wedding gift!"

Chapter IV

Now that the brilliant pageant of the Betrothal had taken place life went on serenely in the Palazzo Cornaro in San Cassan, while the seasons came and went and Caterina developed into a charming maiden of seventeen—expanding in the gracious atmosphere and the wonderful new joys that it brought her, as a rose matures to its most radiant perfection in the sunshine. Her eager mind which had hitherto known only the meager culture bestowed upon young Venetian maids of her time and estate, awoke with ardent response, growing with leaps and bounds to meet the new demands—yet always deepening because the spring of her will had its impulse in noble emotions.

Her thin, restricted life had suddenly overflowed with interests: the boundaries of her vision had opened far beyond the narrow confines of the lagoons of Venice and the Euganean hills, as the consciousness dawned upon her of a world that had been rich in beauty and vital memories before Venice began to be. Life was beginning to pulsate tumultuously in her veins; her heart was awaking. All the fulness and delight of this germinal spring-time she owed to the lord and lover who was waiting for her across the shimmering, beckoning sea. What wonder that her maiden heart should cling to him with a passionate trust, while all her sweet self grew in shy loveliness out of the dream that she was fashioning, and the deepening currents of her being flowed purely about this vision of her betrothed, enthroning her love with her religion in one center.

The mimic court in the Palazzo Cornaro, under the supervision of her monitors of Venice, was already attracting distinguished strangers—for the element of romance in her position made the salon of the future Queen of Cyprus the feature of Venetian social life; and long hours of eager study with masters of the many tongues spoken in the Cyprian court—alternating with the teachings of her mother's noble friend, the Patriarch, as he sought to familiarize her with the early Christian story of her distant island, proved the quick grasp of her mind—giving dangerous hints of strength which, if disregarded, might thwart the moulding purpose of the Signoria. So it seemed wise to forestall her questionings with such historic glimpses as should fascinate her with her realm to be, while Venice was silently smoothing out the crumples of that distant Cyprian shore; and it was fitting that the bride of Janus should make acquaintance with the literary and legendary treasures of this fabled isle of poets, for the house of Lusignan had been known for its taste in literature. But of a certain proverb current in Cyprus in the days of the Lusignans, the watchful Senate took care that she should be left in ignorance, *Ce n'est pas Minerve qui est née en Chypre!*[26] and that Chief of the Ten whose difficult duty it had become to supervise the education of Caterina was giving peremptory instruction to the newly-created Historical Secretary to the Queen-elect:

"Begin with thy narration far back in the days of the Greek myths—she hath much poetry in her soul. Take her carefully over the early Christian traditions—she doth most seriously incline to venerate the Church:—there is food in these matters to consume much time."

"And then, *Eccellentissimo*, one may venture to tell the story of the House of Lusignan?"

The research of the learned Secretary had brought him in contact with Cyprus, but it had not inclined him to make fancy pictures of its kings.

"Of Guy—the founder—and of the Crusades; it is a tale a maid may hear," the Capo[27] responded grimly. "Of gleanings, now and again, through the pages of the chronicle, as it may be wise. She hath not the judgment to endure it all, being yet scarce more than a child—and with leanings rather toward Church than State, being over-much under the influence of the Lady Fiorenza—*over-much.*"

The words came with pauses which lent them force, and the new Secretary, being Senate-trained, lost none of their significance.

"Thine office doth demand discretion," the Chief continued, fixing the other with his piercing gaze. "One should choose the tale that may best please—that she may go glad-hearted and with a maiden's fancy."

"Aye, your Excellency—for maids and women are not as men; and facts not over-gentle may be best untold."

"Nay—not that—not that: but there is time—much time—and for the present the care shall be to delight."

"It is the office of a courtier, *Eccellentissimo*; it befools a scholar," the Historical Secretary exclaimed with indignation. "There be poets and romancers who would do it honor, rather than I—who have spent long years among the records searching for truth, that I may leave a chronicle to trust."

"And most unworthily, Signor Segretario, if thou hast found no least trace of the great philosopher Zeno in the ancient city of Cition that was his birthplace; nor of Homer, that maker of literature, who hath, perchance, won space enough in the estimate of mankind to be worthy the brief thought of a child—even of thine—a scholar seeking for truth—he being the pride of Salamis.

"But the Signoria have never learned the backward step that they should withdraw an appointment which conferreth unwilling honor," the Chief concluded coldly. "Thou shalt find some beauty in the legends of the Cinyradae, or the myths of Aphrodite, in this land of Cyprus where the goddess rose from the foam of the sea!"

"Were not substance better than froth to train a maid to rule, your Excellency?"

"Nay, but to *obey*; to *rule* needeth not teaching."

"Signore, foam shall suffice to teach obedience—thou hast heard the most gracious will of the Senate."

The eyes of the scholar who loved truth better than fortune dropped baffled; for he could not afford to surrender the favor of the Senate which promised him means to achieve in his own special field; and he groaned in spirit while the wide halls of the Frari,[28] with their treasure of ancient manuscripts rose before his mental vision as the most tempting spot on earth, with his own *magnum opus* lying there unfinished, yet far toward completion. And for one who had meant to chronicle the complete history of

a *movement*, who had sought ever to weigh and sift in the interests of truth alone, to surrender the freedom of his mind to the Senate—to come down to the teaching of a child—to be commanded what he should speak—it was maddening!

"My own work," he murmured in a last appeal:—"I have so little time."

"The time of a Venetian is his best gift to the State," the Capo made answer icily.

There was a pause during which the unwilling Secretary *felt* the eyes of the Capo upon him, forcing him to lift his own. For an instant he met the strange fixed gaze which conveyed to him without words that what had passed between them was to be held inviolate; then, with a courteous salute, the man of power spoke:

"The interview is dismissed." And the Segretario Reale went out from the presence, his soul revolting at the absolutism that forced him to accept; and he despised himself.

Meanwhile the soul of the maiden was thrilling to the Patriarch's tales of early Christian conquests in her islands—at Paphos—at Salamis—of the miracles of the great Paulus, saint and bishop and leader—as her eyes followed along the red-lettered parchment page of the rare volume which the holy man brought from the treasures of the "Marciana"[29] for her teaching—translating the story from the Greek, which was yet hard for her, into her own softer tongue.

Cyprus had indeed been a favored land in those early days; for the Holy Spirit had commanded by a revelation that Barnabas and Paulus should set sail for Cyprus to preach the new faith at Salamis;[30] and they had taken with them Marcus—their own San Marco!—it was so written in this strange, old book.

"Tell me about him!" Caterina cried, clasping her hands eagerly: "what did he do in my land?"

Every Venetian was familiar with the Patron-Saint of Venice in his symbolic guise, with his terrible, flashing jewelled eyes—as a power who would guard them and confound the paw of the fierce Venetian lion rested always on the open gospel-page. But to hear of him as a man, before he was known as saint—young—'sister's son to Barnabas,' setting forth on this mission to Cyprus, made him strangely real to the young Venetian girl; it even brought Cyprus nearer with a tender home claim, to hear of the wanderings of San Marco among those temples of Aphrodite; and his scorn of the unholy worship kindled her soul as the Patriarch told how the young Evangelist had not feared to curse the godless Cyprian city for its idolatry—of the tumult that had been raised by his followers, as they hurled the images of the pagan gods from their pedestals, ruining portions of the huge, unholy structure as they fell and killing some of those who were taking part in the games. She would visit these vast ruins in the ancient grove of Aphrodite, where giant-trees had grown among the fallen columns, and wonderful vases of gold and silver and alabaster, wrought like finest cameos, had been disinterred from mounds of rubbish to decorate the palaces of patricians.

Of these, antique goblets, some flashing with an indescribable rainbow luster, delicate as an opal, had already been sent her among the rich gifts of Janus. And so

life took on new color for her—historic memories and trifles of the day crossing each other at many points, linking the old to the new, in unsuspected continuity.

"Our San Marco was a hero even then!" she cried; "an early Crusader fighting for his faith!"

"Aye, daughter—as thou and I must fight," the Patriarch answered her with tender approval in his eyes, a shadow of apprehension dimming them before he withdrew his gaze—for of such tender stuff had martyrs been made. "The story of those early days is for our guidance. If trials should come," he added, "cleave but to thy faith and Heaven shall show thee a way."

"I never thought before that one might *love* San Marco!" Caterina said, as she turned her glowing face frankly to the old man: "he was never a person, but just a grotesque image to me."

"Symbols are for our race in its childhood, for with primitive peoples imagination dominates reason," he answered her: "later we weave a more enduring fabric out of the truth of history—still cherishing the myth—the earlier impulse."

But it was Barnabas who was the true hero-saint of Cyprus; for he had owned estates in his native island and had sold them and given all for the propagation of the new faith; and when, after his cruel martyrdom the fierce spirit of persecution had cooled, and his remains were found interred in a grotto near the city—the divine revelation of St. Peter clasped to his breast—the possession of so sacred a relic sufficed to win great privileges among the hierarchy for the island of Cyprus, in perpetuity—the proud title of Archbishop of

Salamis—the imperial staff with the gold apple at top—the cap with the red cross, and many other honors and immunities. It was a long way from the primitive simplicity of the fruitful ministration of José Barnabas, the Son of Consolation, as he had fought for souls in the splendid vigor of his youth and consecration!

"I am glad of these sacred bonds between my two homes!" the young girl exclaimed with a little wistful sigh.

"There are yet other links in the history of our Church; for Sant' Elenà, the Mother of Constantine—whose tomb thou knowest on our fair island of Sant' Elenà—hath enriched thy favored land of Cyprus with its most sacred relic, bestowing there the portions of the Holy Cross which she had brought from Orient, and thou shalt find them still revered in the Chapel of Santa Croce on the Mountain of the Troödos."

"Thou perchance, most Reverend Father, wilt come some day in pilgrimage to this blessed shrine in my new land!" Caterina cried hopefully.

"Nay, dear daughter; for my work lieth in Venice. But thou seest that where our Holy Church hath planted her banner, one may call no land strange."

It was partly with this thought that the Patriarch had striven to interest Caterina in these incidents of early Christianity; and partly from his undefined dread as to what the future might hold for her, with the wish to keep the Church and its teachings uppermost in her mind, that she might lean upon them in need. She had been deeply interested and again and again had turned the talk upon this theme—a docile pupil, growing in grace

and strength from the teachings he gathered for her from that quaint old volume so little known by the women of her time. It was his gift to fit her for the unknown life to which she was going, and it gave him an opportunity for many helpful words which if scarcely understood at the time came back to her later; yet he darkened her bright visions with no fears, thinking that hope and joy and faith would suffice for strength in trial.

After several years of such education, Venice sends Caterina off with great fanfare to become the consort of Janus, King of Cyprus. Her marriage is a happy one, but within a year Janus dies and leaves her regent for their soon-to-be-born child. Caterina learns of an earlier power struggle for the throne between Janus and his half-sister Carlotta, and worries about the legitimacy of her position as Queen. Two of her advisers, Chamberlain Aluisi and Lady Beata, discuss what is to be done.

Chapter XIII

"*Madre Mia!*" he said with deep tenderness, "I think it is not possible to hold the knowledge from her longer. It must be told to-night."

They were in the loggia overlooking the splendid stretch of terraced gardens, now flooded with moonlight; they had been standing there, quiet silent, for a long time, each feeling that there was something to be spoken and suffered—each praying to defer the moment.

"Oh, Aluisi—no!"

Her tone was an entreaty: but he only put out his hand and laid it tenderly upon hers: the beautiful, tapering fingers trembled under his touch, then slowly quieted, for there was a rare sympathy between them.

"I have done everything," he continued in a low voice, without looking at her, "but they will not wait—matters of State, they say, to be passed upon—a Queen must give her signature when it is needed."

He came closer, suddenly turning upon her a gaze which compelled her startled comprehension. "They would be quite willing to pass the measure *without* her signature," he added, in a still lower tone. "It has come to that—we must think of her rights and protect her *against her Councillors!*"

"She has had so much to bear, poor child—so young—and her heart is broken already with sorrow for her husband. For she had faith in him. And now!—Have they no feeling for her?"

"*Madre, carissima*, thou knowest not Rizzo; he is the most powerful among them, and the most ill-disposed. 'Let her take the Prince of Naples,' he hath said openly before the Councillors, 'and give us a man to reign over us.'"

"And Janus but two weeks dead!" The Lady Beata gave an involuntary cry of horror. "But Fabrici, the Archbishop?" she asked after a moment, "may he not influence them to be more gentle with her—having a brother in the Council?"

Aluisi shook his head sorrowfully. "Nay, Mother—I know not which is worse. Venice, at his election, would have prevented it, but could not, because he represented this intriguing power of Naples which hath not ceased from effort to have its will of Cyprus, since the betrothal of Caterina—which also it sought to overthrow."

"How knowest thou?"

He laid his finger on his lips—"If we were yet in Venice, I might not answer thee; but here—and it is for me and thee alone—it was I upon whom the Signoria laid the task of drawing up their monitory letter to Janus to hold him to his contract."

"Oh, if thou hadst not done it! I would rather thou hadst not written it!" she said with a low moan.

"Aye—Mother: and I—even then I knew that it must be happier for the child if that contract might be broken. Though if I had dreamed of *this* I could not have doomed one of our Casa Cornaro to such suffering and dishonor. But thou knowest the pride of Venice: if not *my* hand, another's would have written it: and I then—we should not have been here to shield her."

"But the Archbishop Fabrici cannot hold malice against Caterina. He hath all the church of Cyprus in his command; he *must* be friendly to the Queen."

But Aluisi's face gave her no hope, as she turned to him.

"Fabrici, for another cause, holdeth the queen in deep disfavor," he said, "for that he, having been sent by Janus on some embassy of marriage for the child Zarla, came into the Chamber of Counts of the Kingdom—not many days since—and with much grossness of speech would have discussed the matter at length in that presence; which we, of her household—she being in the first grief of her young widowhood—prevented, through members of the Queen's Council, better disposed."

"It was well, Aluisi: it seemeth even now too soon—too cruel—to add this shadow to her grief: and but for thee, she must have known thereof that day. For she seeketh already to take up the burden of the State and questioneth daily of the secretary of the King of that which passeth in the Council. 'That I may rule my people,' she sayeth sadly, 'and those who loved the King will help me!' With what a tender grace she sayeth *my people!*"

"*Madre mia*, thou who lovest her and art so wise—shall I leave this parchment with thee? Thou best canst spare her in what must be told. I have had made this copy of certain clauses of the Will of Janus, which may not longer wait official reading before the Council in the Chamber of the Counts and in presence of the Queen. Thinkest thou not it would be too hard for her to learn first of its provisions before them all?"

"Thou art right, Aluisi—always right. But her faith in him is deep; how shall I make her believe?"

"I know not," he answered with a groan, and crushing the parchment in his hand. Then he smoothed it out remorsefully and gave it to her. "It is a faithful copy; there is no other argument. Thou wilt go to her now—for it *must* be."

With bowed head he led her to the door of the Queen's ante-chamber. "I am here," he said, "if need should be."

She hesitated. "It may be long, for I know not how to tell her."

"Thank Heaven that she hath one like thee to care for her," he answered, gently forcing her through the doorway as he held her hand. "For I do think the Council would willingly have her away."

In the ante-chamber scattered groups of court-ladies in deepest mourning, were talking in low tones. They all rose as the Lady Beata entered: but she, with only an inclination of her head, passed on hastily into the inner chamber which was the private boudoir of the Queen.

Caterina was quite alone, lying back on a low couch near an open window, through which the moonlight streamed in long pale rays; while many soft lights of perfumed oils, burning low in lamps of ivory, made only moonlight within the chamber. She held the miniature of Janus pressed against her cheek, and as the Lady Beata came towards her she tried to welcome her with a quivering smile.

"I sent them all away, *Zia mia*: sometimes it seems less hard to bear when I am quite alone."

The Lady Beata bent over her, stroking her hair caressingly, striving for courage to break the silence.

"Caterina *mia*," she said at last, "it is needful to give some thought to matters of government—the Council will not wait. Hast thou the strength?"

"I *must* have strength," she answered with instant resolution, rising and laying aside the miniature with a lingering look. "Wilt thou call Aluisi? He ever maketh me understand. It is so new to me," she pleaded feebly, as the Lady Beata did not move.

"Carina, it will be best alone; Aluisi hath asked me to speak with thee. If—if thou wilt read this parchment"—the Lady Beata held it out to her—"it is the Will of the late King; Aluisi hath bidden me give it thee."

"There is no need," Caterina answered listlessly, as the Lady Beata opened it and put it into her hand, "the provisions have been told me."

But the other persisted. "To-morrow—for the Council say that they will not longer wait; it will be read before the Counts of the Chamber, and they would have the Queen take oath of fealty to Cyprus."

"I shall have the strength when to-morrow cometh," Caterina answered wearily, and making a motion to return the parchment.

"There are other clauses; Aluisi thought it might be better to read them here—alone—before—before—" Her face was blanched and pained, and her words came with difficulty.

The young Queen looked at her in surprise, then, after a moment's indecision, dropped her eyes upon the page and read the short clauses through; then once more—as if she did not understand—then again, a scarlet flush growing as she read.

The parchment contained but three short clauses: King Janus left his kingdom to his wife Caterina, who was to reign, with their child, if there should be one; or alone, if the child should die.

He provided a Council of seven to assist her with the Government:

In the case of her death and the death of the child, the kingdom should descend to each of the three other children of Janus, in the order named. The unwedded mother of these children was not mentioned and Caterina had never dreamed of their existence.

She stood trembling—her face slowly paling to a marble whiteness. *"Mater Dolorosa!"*[31] she gasped, with a moan of pain, instantly repressed.

The Lady Beata put her arm around her to steady her: but Caterina drew herself away, standing upright.

"Call back the Chamberlain!" she cried, imperiously: and stood waiting—panting—until he entered the room.

Then she drew up her slight figure in defiance, her eyes flashing in her white, white face—her voice ringing scorn as she pointed to the document which had dropped from her hand.

"How should I believe this—this *baseness* of my husband—your King? She cried. "Who hath *dared* to fashion it?"

"Beloved Sovereign Lady"—he answered her, and for very pity could say no more.

She turned from one to the other with an impatient, questioning, imperious gesture.

They came nearer—slowly—silently turning upon her such faces of love and sorrow and comprehension that the fire in her eyes died in anguish.

A quiver shot through her, but she struggled to stand, motioning them away again when they would have helped her—she must drink this cup of bitterness alone. "How should I believe it?" she repeated brokenly, still studying their faces.—"How *should* I believe it—ye are not faithless to him—to me—?"

There was no need to answer her: again they looked their unspeakable compassion.

But as Caterina's eyes rested upon the parchment once more, a sudden hope came to her. "The will of the King was written in his own hand," she cried eagerly. "Thou hast said it, Aluisi; this is not the writing of the king!"

"Nay, beloved Sovereign Lady," the Chamberlain made answer, as he picked it up, and held it before her; "this is but a memorandum made for your Majesty's convenience, but attested under the seal of the kingdom. The original will is in the keeping of the Lord of the Privy Seals, awaiting your command. It was thought that your Majesty would wish to see it before the Council should be assembled."

She understood and bowed her head in silence, while all hope died out of her face.

Aluisi advisedly used the ceremonious form by which he was accustomed to address the Queen in public, hoping to hint to her of some necessary preparation to control the meeting of the Council that could not, in any event, be long deferred.

They lingered wistfully, seeking vainly for words that might not hurt her; but Caterina looked at them beseechingly, with dim eyes—her lips moving without sound.

The Lady Beata understood.

"I go now to pray the dear Christ for thee—the Man of Sorrows," she said with inexpressible tenderness. "And later—*Carinissima*—I will come again, and thou wilt rest."

So young—so sorely stricken—she knelt in the cold moonlight alone—her hands clasped in passionate repression on her throbbing heart—"*Mater Dei!*" she moaned: "Death—and then *this!*—If but it need not have been told me! If I might but have kept the *memory* of my happiness!"

Only the stars and pitying angels looked down on the fierce conflict of grief and love and disillusion with which her desolate young soul wrestled alone through the long, midnight vigil. How should she separate these two beautiful faiths which had been enthroned as one

in the happy depths of her guileless heart, without perilling her very trust in God!

Yet, as the sad day dawned over the hills and sea, she knew that God was still in His Heaven, behind the clouds—while she clung as a drowning mariner—the more desperately for her weakness—to the spar of this faith in the wreck of her happiness, though the love to which her whole being had moved in rhythmic content was as a lost star, glimmering uncertainly behind the mists.

But through the desolate night-watches the Lady of the Bernardini in the ante-chamber of the Queen had been agonizing in prayer for her until thought was spent; and now she had moved out upon the loggia and stood there waiting for the dawn that seemed long-deferred, in a half-conscious wonder that there were no sorrows great enough to stay Nature's punctual recurrences—that to-day and tomorrow there would still be dawns and sunsets, whatever happened to the souls of men.

In the silver line that etched the dark mountain crests against the pale monotone of the sky, single firs stood forth saliently, while dim in the distance, vast shapes, clothed in perpetual snows, held wraith-like watch over the smiling plains below, where life and bloom were possible.

Athwart the low, confused twittering of bird-notes which had infused the solemn silence with a vague hint of life, strident sounds grew dominant—a crow calling to his mate from tree to tree—a short, sharp symphony of swallows—a cock announcing the coming of the dawn.

Then motion broke in upon the majesty; hurried rushes of flight across the sky—beatings of wings—pulsings and ecstasies and tri-umphs of bird-life—and the Day was new.

Faint twitterings in the copses deepened to melody—to canticles of rejoicing; tints of turquoise and opal crept into the shad-ows and gold into the greens: the night-dews gleamed upon the firs and grasses, while a luminous haze dimmed the dark glint of the waters to pearly gray, softened the grimness of the mountain-faces and wrapped them—sea and mountains, as soul and body in a vision of mystery, a pre-lude to the blaze of golden glory that was suddenly outpoured on land and sea.

Yet the heavenly splendor was but for a moment; it faded in sudden gloom, as a bell from the inner chamber called the Lady of the Bernardini to attend the Queen.

When at early morning, the Cham-berlain was summoned to the Queen's presence, the change in her beautiful face smote him to the heart: every line had been chiselled by pain—ennobled by a high resolve—by a strong new-born will, rendered selfless; and in her eyes a soul—tried by fire and suddenly grown to a great height—looked forth, luminous.

Instinctively, he dropped his eyes and fell upon his knees, as if in the presence of some heavenly spirit, his hot tears falling upon the fragile hand she held out to him, which he clasped, unconsciously, in both his own, with a grasp so like a vise that it would have smitten her with sharp pain had she been capable at that moment of any physical emotion.

"Beloved Cousin and Queen!" he cried, when he could find his voice, "we love and revere you; we would give our *lives* to help you!"

She made an effort to speak, but no words came; she could only bow her head to accept his homage, while his asseverations of loyalty and love and impotent help came crowding upon his first utterance—the immoderate outpouring of a deep, knightly soul, unused to confess itself—the barriers of reserve once over-come by the stinging sense of the irrepara-ble wrong of which the revelation to this guileless, confiding girlish nature had sud-denly wrenched every memory that once had been happiness, out of her young life—yet, in the very immensity of her an-guish, had searched to the inmost truth of her woman's fiber and, in the fierce un-folding, had found it wholly noble.

As he knelt, still protesting, yet out of his great reverence, using no word to wound her—the more compassionate be-cause he might not denounce the one who had wronged her—it was as if he were looking up to a beloved daughter, immea-surably above him, who yet had need of his knightly protection. He did not know that he was speaking—he did not know what passed—only that deep in his soul he prayed to comfort her.

Slowly, with expression, the hot passion melted into a softer mood; his grasp re-laxed and she withdrew her hand, seamed and marred with red lines where he had unconsciously tortured it; yet in her mis-ery she was grateful to be reached across the awful gulf of loneliness that separated her from the world by a sense that such loyalty yet remained to her.

She laid her hand lightly on his head, the fingers moving for a moment—half in ca-ress—half in benediction, while he felt her almost imperceptible gesture dismissing this unusual audience where soul had faced soul on the brink of a great catastrophe; and he rose to meet the strange, luminous, unsmiling gaze of the great dark eyes which yesterday had been almost the eyes of a child.

She pointed to the loggia, where the morning breeze came freshly laden with the fragrance of myriad blossoms that were just opening to the gladness of the sunrise—a sunrise over the beautiful, fabled slopes of Cyprus—while shadows still lay on the flower-gemmed plains that stretched between them and the sea. Ah, yes, the cool, blue, restless sea stretched far between her island realm and the proud Venetian home from whence she had sailed a happy girl—one little year before—to meet her radiant visions of the future; and now, in all the splendor of the morning, for her the light of life had died forever on the hills of hope.

It was to this loggia that Janus had first led her when he brought her to this summer palace of Potamia, that she might see what a vision of beauty he had prepared for his bride—the far-reaching terraced gardens with their brilliancy of exotics, rivalling the plumage of the peacocks that proudly flaunted their jewelled eyes among them—the pergolas of precious marbles from which the vines flung out a wealth of bloom, luring the birds to a perpetual feast of song; and behind them, spreading up to the deep groves of varied greens upon the hillsides, the snow of countless blossoms lay whiter than the wings of the swans, floating at leisure in silver pools among the beds of color. It was here that Janus had spoken words she

had dreamed eternally and sacredly her own: Mother of Consolation, she must remember them no more!

She had not thought of this when the sense of suffocation had impelled her to seek the air, to rush where it might blow over her and through her, lift her hair about her throbbing temples and help her to forget. Oh God—Omnipotent and Merciful—can one never forget!

A sob broke in her throat, but she made no sound, as she turned to re-enter her audience-chamber—the sumptuous audience-chamber where she might feel herself less a woman and more a queen.

But Aluisi, obeying her slight motion, had already passed between the marble columns of the portico, out into the sunshine, and stood confronting her—her friend, her cousin, and a Councillor of her realm.

The thought gave her courage, and after a moment's struggle, she grew calm again, listening gravely to the question of State he had wished to open to her before it should be discussed in full Council.

He spoke at first with averted gaze, feigning to be attracted by the beauty of the morning, that he might give her time to recover herself; but as he turned his face to hers for her reply, she put the matter aside with an imperious gesture.

"Today, Auisi, I have graver matter to command my thought: the Council shall *wait* until I give orders for its assembling—thou, meanwhile, using all courtesy in its delay and the enforcement of—of my command—the Queen's command—so only that it be enforced. These methods are new to me," she added, with a sudden softened appeal in her tone; "thou wilt know the way to compass it—for my sake—for it must be done."

"It shall be done," he assented uncompromisingly; but in surprise, knowing only too well the imperious methods of the Council appointed to assist her in her government and the temper of the men who composed that body—for Janus had not been great in his knowledge of men; and possibly the only one of the seven who had been strictly devoted to the King, had died shortly after his appointment, and the place had been filled with one less favorable to the present rule of Cyprus. Fabrici was known to be in sympathy with Naples; Rizzo, Chief of Council, strong, domineering, unscrupulous, was perhaps the creature of Ferdinand, King of Naples. "It shall be done," he said again, having vowed to help her.

"For, until I have had speech with the holiest man among the priests that may be found in all this kingdom of Cyprus," she said with a decision that amazed him, "I will treat of no matter of State, however urgent. Nay, Aluisi—my cousin"—as she noted his start of surprise—"to thee alone—who must be my counsellor in days of desolation—pray Heaven more dark than thou shalt ever dream of—I will confide that out of this night of vigil hath come this resolution which I dare not break. Seek thou the man."

He had already turned to fulfil her quest which might be long in the doing—and these impatient Councillors would be hard to hold; yet he had no thought of parleying with this girl-queen, so suddenly grown to a full stature.

But her voice, even and low, arrested him. "He must be Greek in birth," she said, "and of the Greek Church, which my people love. But above all—*he must be a man to trust.*"

He turned when he had crossed the great audience-chamber, under the entrance colonnade of huge porphyry columns, wrought with barbaric symbols of earlier dynasties and guarded by colossal Assyrian bulls—she seemed so young and tender to leave, even for a day, in those surroundings unguarded, at the mercy of that Council of Seven whom he had reason to distrust—in her kingdom seamed with dissensions of which she had, as yet, small comprehension; of which, perhaps, she did not even dream—with her shattered happiness behind her and loneliness before, and this great responsibility pressing its leaden weight upon her fair young head.

He longed to throw her a last reassuring glance—to leave with her the absolute faith that with every power of his being he would uphold and steady her in the rough and desolate way.

For since he came from Venice he had not ceased his vigilant study of the complications of Cyprus, that when her need came he might be ready.

He never forgot the vision of the girl-queen in her sweeping widow's robes, across the great space between them, in the sunshine of the loggia—her hand extended as if to hasten or to bless him—a wonderful, unearthly light and strength in her face; and, for one moment as she met his gaze and understood the full depth of his devotion, the ghost of a smile—as if it had been granted him to bring her in this hour of martyrdom one little ray of human comfort.

Chapter XIV

Hagios Johannes, the holiest man in Cyprus, stood waiting in the vast, empty presence-chamber of the young Queen; for, since the sudden death of Janus, there had been no court-life in this palace of Potamia, and the gloom hung most heavily over the more sumptuous halls of ceremony.

Hagios Johannes—*the holy John*—they called this prior of the House of Priests from Troödos—the Mountain of the Holy Cross—after the name of the earlier Saint who had made the spot famous for the holiness of his living, for his boundless charity and the wisdom of his judgments, so that the people had gone to him in ceaseless procession with their sins and woes in the days of primitive Christianity in Cyprus, and had returned to their peasant homes the stronger to endure and to renounce. Johannes the Lesser, this one called himself—being truly great and devout of heart, so that his vision was wise and true as that of Hagios Johannes the Greater.

A curtain at the further end of the audience-chamber parted to admit a stately figure in mourning-robes, as the Lady Beata of the Bernardini advanced to meet him, bringing the message that the Queen would receive him in an inner cabinet.

"She is very worn and tired, most Reverend Father, and in years so near to childhood that the nobility and strength of her resolve are marvellous. And the comfort that she seeketh of thee she doth most sorely need."

The eyes of this strong and faithful friend gleamed with unshed tears as she turned them upon the prior, in tender appeal.

But to Hagios Johannes all courts were strange; the life of his mountain overflowed with possibilities of ministration which busied all his powers, and it was the first time that he had ever entered any of the palaces of the luxurious Kings of Cyprus—of which, perhaps, this summer palace of Potamia was the most sumptuous. The long corridors of precious marbles, with intricate carvings and gleamings of gold and mosaic displeased him, though he had no knowledge of their worth or beauty; but he stood aghast at the magnificence of the audience-chamber, and the huge Assyrian bulls which guarded the entrance gave a hint of the pagan power and oppression which instantly angered him.

The appeal of the gracious Lady Beata but roused his indignation.

He was a stern, wild figure with his flowing beard, his long hair falling straight and unkempt about his brown throat; and his sombre monk's garment was wrought on breast and shoulders with a salient cross of natural thorns—the symbol of those monks of Troödos—the Mountain of the Holy Cross; and the Lady Beata trembled for the interview that was to be, as he answered her rudely:

"The dwellers in palaces of ivory have naught to do with wild men of the mountains who live close to nature and care only for suffering humanity. I have Christ's work to do; let others bring her rose-leaves and honeyed words."

She laid a gentle, detaining hand upon him as he thrust aside the curtain of the inner chamber.

"Most Reverend Father, are not the words of our Lord and Saviour, as well for those who suffer in palaces, as for the wanderers and poor upon the earth?

"Are not the wounds of the spirit as deep in anguish as those of the physical man?

"May not the burdens of rulers be greater than those of the ruled?—Have compassion upon our Queen!"

"Christ knoweth not kings," he answered her, as he shook off her light touch—"save only those who bow to Him: and the mighty among men—aye—even he who calleth himself His Vicar upon earth—are puffed up with pride and know in their hearts no virtue in this—His sacred symbol." He pressed his rough hand hard against the thorns upon his breast as he spoke. "Hath not he—this false and sumptuous Vicar—but now asserted that we, of the Holy Greek Church have no part in the Communion of the Holy Catholic Church on earth? Did Christ call the Latins only?" he ended fiercely.

It was a grievance that rankled: and Hagios Johannes had not learned the gracious art of self-control, being accustomed to feel that whatever he thought or wished was good—his hatred as well as that which appealed to him—since he honestly sought nothing for himself, despising riches and station from the depths of his soul, with an open scorn for the great ones of earth and imperious assertion of his own methods and judgments which he would have denounced in any earthly ruler, however wise. He never dreamed himself an autocrat over that continuous stream of pilgrims who made their way into the House of Priests on Troödos: they were chiefly peasants, rude in ways and understanding, whose accustomedness to absolute methods and short words made their obedience the swifter; and the few more learned ones who came to consult him knew that in his heart he was faithful and seldom treasured the offense against him—though they may have decried his wisdom. But these came more rarely as his absolutism grew upon him, and the prophet of the mountains came down to the cities of the plains only to see the luxury of them—the sin and godliness of them, and to denounce them, in unmeasured words.

Within his soul, although he did not confess it to himself, the generations of men were separated by a wide impassable gulf—the rich and ruling class, the godless, on one side; the poor, the suffering and lowly—the to-be-saved,—on the other, and none ever passed across the deep abyss. He would have challenged any man who counted *him, Father Johannes,* in his hempen garment studded with thorns, among the rulers of men!

The youthful Queen, weary and worn indeed from the perplexities and struggle of the two long nights and days that had elapsed since she had sent her Councillor on his quest of "the holiest man in Cyprus," rose from her couch as the prior entered and advanced to meet him with a gracious reverence.

But he, unconscious of any rudeness, spoke at once, without turning his eyes upon her, and offering no homage.

"I am a plain man from the Mountain of the Holy Cross, your Majesty; I know naught of the ways of courts. The matter should be great that calleth me from my work. Let it be presented, that I may be dismissed."

She was almost too weak to stand, and the rebuff smote her to the quick; her lip trembled slightly, but she only stretched out her hand to her beloved friend, drawing her close and leaning lightly upon her shoulder, that she might feel the support of loving companionship in her great need.

Father Johannes had been vaguely conscious of some movement in the chamber and involuntarily he turned towards this royal lady whom, as yet, he had never seen, but whose urgent summons had roused his indignation.

She looked so young and fair and simple in her heavy fold of mourning—so worn from vigil, with the lines of anguish and of a strange strength written in her white girl-face—that she might have been the vision of some youthful saint, wearing the rough cross of Troödos upon her breast, beneath her robe: and for a moment, the holy man was startled—did such heavenly visions, in truth, visit the palaces of the great?

There was a moment of stillness in which his wonder grew.

The breeze blew faintly in through the great arched openings, behind which rose the mountain chain that led to his own Troödos; there were the groves of pine, darkly green, below the hills, with their deep solitudes for prayer and meditation between the vast gnarled trunks; and the group of the two noble women before him—severely simple—was a vision of love and womanly grace and spiritual need; the younger one, all pleading and pain, clinging to the elder

who closely enfolded her, her face strong in the strength of love. It was not like any life that he had ever seen—this holy man, whose personal life had been solitary and whose knowledge of human love, as it is known in happy homes, had died long years ago with the passing of the mother who had borne him in her heart. It might be that he needed such a vision to redeem his spirit from the harshness which sin and pride in high places, and want and crime and poverty of spirit among ignoble ones, had made him grow to think the whole of life!

He was very weary and his vision was not clear; for the previous day had been a solemn fast, and he had walked far and long since the early morning, that he might be the less delayed. He felt like kneeling where he stood—if perchance it should be a vision!—But he only bowed his head and waited—and his weakness passed.

The younger one—the maiden with that strange mystery of pain and strength in her white face, was coming towards him.

"Father," she said, "hath none offered thee refreshment? Thou must indeed be weary, for the way is long. *Zia*, let us be served here—in sight of the great forest that will seem like home to our good Padre."

"Nay, nay," he interposed quickly, with an effort to shake off this incomprehensible spell and return to his wonted mood of protest, "for I have never banqueted in the palace of a Queen—your Majesty."

"Let it be brought," Caterina said, turning to the Lady Beata, "a simple meal; for I myself have need, having tasted nothing since the long vigil of the night—being too sore from my great perplexity." For she divined that she must be alone with the prior to melt his mood, which grieved her; but she had not the less faith in his judgment for his hatred of royalty, and at all costs she had the grace to crave the truth in the questions she would ask of him.

"My Father," she said with winning gentleness when they were alone, "we will speak together as father and daughter— it will be better so, for I was not born to Majesty, and I have sent to ask of thee thy counsel, for life is difficult. And for my hospitality—is it not offered to the pilgrim in the House of Priests of the Troödista? Hath not our Lord Himself commanded the giving of the cup of water?"

He was startled at her learning: surely it was rare that women out of holy orders had such knowledge of Christian traditions. He looked at her reverently, still wondering, and would have spoken to excuse his rough speech, but that he knew not how to frame a thought so strange and new.

She motioned him to a seat where a table had been spread under the deep arches that looked toward the forest. There wines and fruits in tempting chalices of rainbow glass and low baskets of ivory and chiselled silver, cooling with snow from the mountain; figs from Lefcara; *caistas*, golden and delicious, emitting a fragrance of glorified nectarine that rivalled the perfume of the wine itself; pomegranates—the gift of a goddess to the thirsty Cyprian land, planted, as was well known, by the royal hand of Aphrodite herself, each fruit holding a fair refreshment for a torrid Cyprian day in its sparkling, semilucent, ruby pulp: ortolans from the sea-coast, steeped in wine.

The table was a slab of oriental alabaster, polished like a jewel, upheld by griffins with outthrust tongues curiously contorted and entwined. But beyond the silken curtains of the palace-windows the forest and the hills, with a wandering breath of coolness from the mountain-breeze, drew and welcomed him, with some faint, new perception of the oneness of God's earth.

She had banished with a glance the maiden who stood waiting with her lute to give the customary accompaniment to the meal, and they were quite alone.

He crumbled his bread and swallowed his wine like a hungry man, drawing the wild, purple figs nearer, unconscious of the dainties which she did not press upon him, while he tasted the familiar food— the food which his Lord Christ had blessed to man's uses. So, also, the luxury of the service passed unnoticed, as he fixed his eyes on the distant darks of his own forest, with the "Troödista" rising on a peak far, far away—that haven of distressed souls to whom he was a father of consolation. Her fingers toyed with the fruit that lay untasted before her, while the difficulty of speech struggled within her. Yet he felt, subtly, as he kept his eyes upon the hills, that he was in sight of the shadow of a soul in pain, and he waited—for once, oblivious of the distance between a palace and a convent.

"Thou art born a Greek, my Father?" she questioned. "Thou art a priest of the Greek Church—which my people love?"

The commanding habit of a lifetime was strong upon him and again his resentment rose to quench the softer mood which was possessing him, and of which he was afraid.

"I knew not that I had been summoned

from my work for Christ to answer of myself," he said sternly. "If thou hast need of counsel, tell it quickly."

Again her lip quivered at the hurt, but she put it aside bravely, as she rose and moved backward for a pace further into the shadow. "I ask it for my people's sake—I being their Queen," she said, "and knowing that my people are rather Greek in feeling, I would do naught to hurt them."

How tenderly the words "my people" fell from the lips of this young, Venetian woman, who seemed almost a child—had their imperious Grecian Queen, Elenà Paléologue, ever so uttered them? Had she not named a boy to the highest See in the gift of their church—with no thought of fitness—but solely that he might be put aside lest he come between her and her greed of domination? Had she not plotted murder and whatever else might lie between her and the accomplishment of her will? His heart melted within him, and he rose and followed Caterina into the chamber.

"The most Holy Father of Rome hath of late been prejudiced against the King—my husband—and I sought for one who might give me counsel, unprejudiced."

If she had been a wily diplomat she could not better have wielded the prior's mood than by this unconscious utterance.

"So help me God, I will strive to help thee in counsel," he answered fervently. "But are there not men, set apart as Councillors for the realm, to aid one so young in ruling her kingdom?"

"Aye, Father," she admitted sadly, "but it is to steady mine own judgment *to judge of theirs*—that I have sent for thee. The question is not for Court Councillors, but for one who hath no part nor lot in this matter—who is often in meditation on holy matters, and hath won wisdom."

He made a motion of deprecation, but she went on speaking in her clear, even voice, still questioning: "Thou knowest well the history of the kings of Lusignan?"

He bowed his head in assent.

"And the history of the life of the King—my husband?" She dwelt on the word with inexpressible tenderness—the slight pause that followed it was like unuttered music.

Did she know? Was it possible that she knew? he asked himself.

"And for the provisions of his will—for myself and for—for others?" A wave of color had flushed her cheek and brow.

He looked at her searchingly, seeking for words that might best comfort. "I know them," he said, "the provisions of the will having been told me by your Majesty's messenger: and I, being a Greek, and the friend of the people, the sins of the race descend from father to son, and are in the blood; and there hath been no loving care of holy women about his childhood—which should be remembered and win forgiveness."

"It is no question of forgiveness," she answered proudly, "of which I would speak with thee—*that* lieth between our Holy Mother in Heaven and the souls of those who suffer." She seemed to dismiss the subject with an imperious wave of her slight hand. "It is a question of human judgment in which that of a holy man may avail, but in which this knowledge is necessary—else had it not been spoken of."

She paused for a moment to gather strength, while the old man watched her in growing wonder—so young—so wronged—so tender—so brave—so strong to endure!

Hagios Johannes the elder had been known through the long years of his canonization as *Lampadisti*, the *illumined:* and as the prior listened, he prayed with fervor that the wisdom of his sainted predecessor might descend upon his soul.

"My Father," she resumed with a great effort, "I knew not of this history of the last of our Kings of Cyprus, until my marriage had been made. . . . I knew not of any right of Carlotta, being o*wn* daughter to the King, the father of my husband"—again that tremulous pause of unuttered music—"to contest the crown with him, until I learned it in Cyprus, these few weeks past."

Her head drooped lower, but she went on resolutely. "I knew not, until I came to Cyprus—for they who knew and should have told me, held the knowledge from me—that any might question the right of Janus—my husband—to this kingdom of Cyprus—he being only son to the King. For I knew not that his mother was *not* the Queen, until I came hither."

She paused again to gather strength, lifting her guileless great eyes to his, in agonized appeal, while he watched her dumbly.

"And now, my Father," she said, throwing back her head with sudden vigor, and with the dignity of a great resolve, "this is my question, which hath come to me in the watches of the night and will not be denied, and for which I have summoned thee. I—being wife to Janus, who hath been crowned King of this people—and I, with him, crowned Queen; and by his will left Queen of Cyprus—with Council, appointed by him, to help me rule; shall I, a Christian woman—a Venetian and not a Cyprian—his widow—*hold this kingdom against Carlotta,* who is daughter to the King, the father of my husband—and to the rightful Queen, Elenà—his father's lawful wife?"

He was dumbfounded and could not answer her at once; but while he sought for words he bowed his head in mute reverence.

"My daughter," he said at length, "hath this question been put to thee by any men of Cyprus?"

"Nay, Father; but it hath come to me in these sad nights, because I fain would do the *right*—that which is well for my people: and life is very difficult."

"My people," again uttered with the accent of a mother who folds her child to her heart—it was a revelation; but he must probe more deeply before he could answer her.

"And this palace—and all the palaces of this estate?" he asked slowly, as if he could not comprehend her. "Thou wouldst renounce this splendor when none hath asked it of thee?"

"I would even bear the weight of it, if it be *right*," she said, "though rest were sweeter."

"Thou wouldst be free, perchance, to seek thy home in Venice?"

"Nay, nay!" she exclaimed, shrinking from him—"never Venice again—since she hath sent me hither, knowing all, and told me not. I cannot go back to Venice!"

He pondered gravely.

"Then what is thy will, my daughter?"

"To do the right!" she cried vehemently; "out of my own great sorrow to expiate the wrong! May it not be, my Father, if I shrink not from the right at any cost?"

"I will consider," he said, "since thy will is strong for this sacrifice."

"Sacrifice!" she cried, in her amazement breaking all reserve. "Oh, Father! To call *this* 'sacrifice,' when the very light of life is gone from me! He was so beautiful and gracious—with such a light in his eyes—and I thought—oh, I *thought* we were so happy! And now—oh, God, it breaks my heart—I loved him!"

"Daughter—"

"May not the suffering of one atone for another's sin?" she questioned feverishly.

"Nay—leave that thought, it is too heavy for thee: and not revealed to men, that they may declare it."

"Pray for him, Father! Thou wilt pray for him—thou and all those who come to thee. There will be many, many prayers and God will hear. For his people loved him—none could stay from loving him, he was so winsome. Mother of Mercies, thou wilt take my anguish for his atonement!—*Oh I suffer!*"

The words came in a low moan, wrung from her unaware. Father Johannes caught the small hands which she had flung out before her clenched, in her passionate struggle for control, and with faltering motions of unaccustomed gentleness, he soothed her until she had grown quieter and he could unclasp them. Then he spoke strange words, out of a great compassion:

"Christ knoweth; for He is Love—and He will save!"

"There is more," she gasped with her spent voice—"but I dare not name it—the thought of it is torture. But it is not true; *Madonna mia*! it *is not* true!"

The strong man could bear no more; he groaned in spirit and ground his hands against his breast—his lip curling with scorn at the pain of his own torn flesh. "Tell it!" he commanded; "it *cannot* be true."

She looked at him, hope dawning in her stricken face. "The words they speak—they who are his enemies—that he had forsworn his faith: it is not true."

"It is the very machination of the Evil One!" he thundered. "I know the slander and the man who fathered it, for spite. And may Heaven forgive its maker—for he hath need—standing high in the holy place of Earth. I *know* it is not true!"

He looked his faith into her eyes until he had banished her terror, and she put out her wan hand, grateful, for his assurance.

Then he turned from her abruptly and wandered away to weigh her question, looking into the depths of the great forest while he pondered and prayed to be enlightened. He must have sight of his own solitudes if he would keep his judgment free, and though she called to him, timidly, thinking he had forgotten her, he made no answer, being not yet ready. Surely, it could not be God's will that so fine a spirit should resign her claim to their uneasy crown!

It was long before he returned to her side, for the shadows were lengthening and a crimson light flamed in the West.

"Daughter," he said with deep solemnity, "it hath come to me with full light in answer to thy question, that thou, being crowned Queen and consecrated in the

Duomo of Nikosia, together with King Janus, thy husband—whom this people loved—and decreed by him to hold this realm, which—for the first time in many years, and by his hand, is now united under one sovereign, that thy duty biddeth thee hold and rule it against all other claimants—were it even Carlotta who hath once been called its Queen.

"Rule thou this people with the fear of Heaven in thy true heart—so God shall make thee wise!"

She came slowly, as to a heavy task, and knelt before him with clasped hands, kissing the crucifix which he held out to her; the red light streamed through the arches with a fierce illumination.

"Father—and Janus!" she cried—"hear my vow!

"To do for my people as Heaven and the Madonna shall teach me: to bear them in my heart and seek their happiness; to live for them alone! And if harm hath been—oh God, if harm hath been done—to nerve me to the more strenuous duty, that wrong may be forgiven!"

Caterina's son is born and during the baptism festivities she connects with the people of Cyprus who embrace her and her son as their ruler. A faction of the noble class, fearing Caterina as ruler would be a pawn of Venice, attempt to overthrow and replace her with prince of Naples, but are thwarted with the assistance of Venice. Before his first birthday, Caterina's son, the prince, dies. She is devastated but rallies to rule Cyprus and moves her court to Nikosia to take control of the country.

Chapter XXXVI

An Embassy from Venice was expected upon important affairs of state, and there was an unusual radiance in the face of the Queen, for it had been announced that the Illustrissimo, the Signor Zorzi Cornaro, brother to Caterina, was chief of the Commission, and it was long since one of her very own had been with her.

"*Zia mia,*" she said eagerly to the elder Lady of the Bernardini. "Thou wilt see that no courtesy of reception shall be omitted—it is to welcome one of my very own!"

She dwelt on the phrase with a pathetic accent of delight, returning to it again as she discussed some details of the welcome that should be offered to her brother, whom, for years she had not seen.

Never had an ambassador been received with higher honors in the Court of Nikosia, or with such glad faces by all the attendant circle—for was not His Excellency of the Queen's own household?—and it had been rare to see such a light of happiness in her beloved eyes.

And well did the Cornaro seem to carry the honors due to his house—being very noble in bearing, as befitted the brother of the Queen; and so eloquent in speech that already before the first day had passed, the scholarly men of the Court were exchanging glances of admiration at the skill with which he parried their compliments; while Caterina, noting their courtesy and the deftness with which he had won them, grew more than ever radiant, with a certain look of restfulness and of heart-satisfaction which, since the death of the child, those who loved had scarcely seen her wear.

But Aluisi Bernardini grew somewhat

graver than his wont, as the banquet proceeded, while he watched his cousin, the newly-arrived Ambassador, less graciously, his lady thought, than he need have done on this first evening when all were hastening to shower honors upon him.

"What cometh," he said to his wife, as they rose at last from the brilliant tables and passed out upon the terraces at the invitation of the Queen; "whatever cometh, leave her not alone with him though she should urge thee; use thy sweet insistance—as thou knowest how—to keep other about them for this first evening."

"What meanest thou, Aluisi?" she asked in alarm, and moving quickly aside, as the gay company swept by, that he might explain himself. "Surely she might wish to speak with him alone; she is more happy in his presence that she hath been for years. Seest thou not?"

"Aye, my very dear one, I see it well. It is that I would hold this rare happiness for her so long as may be; and there is that in the manner of my cousin, the Cornaro, which pleaseth me not. I would not have him unfold to her the matter of his Embassy, if it may be a little deferred."

"It hath been told thee, already?"

"Not more than to thee. But in all the grace of him I see his head above his heart—a certain quality of his father, the 'Magnifico, Marco Cornaro'—as he was known in Venice. Yet one who standeth watching, somewhat apart, may note a hint of displeasure at the splendor of his welcome and the loyalty of the court for the Queen: and the ready wit with which he answereth concealeth under its sparkle a certain persistent measuring of some purpose which he hath much at heart—as if he were studying meanwhile how best to compass his end."

She laid her hand entreatingly on his arm. "For once, my Aluisi, it may be thou dost o'er-reach thyself. Is he not her brother?"

He smiled at her, unconvinced.

"I have watched so long," he said, "and the life of our Queen-Cousin hath been so sadly thwarted that it may well be my fear for her taketh flame too lightly. But she hath set such store upon his coming, and with such gracious scheming for his pleasure, that if he leave her time she may soften any hard intent. San Marco grant that I have misjudged him, for he is of our house."

"Thou hast much weight with her," the Dama Margherita answered very low. "Stay near me, that we may guard her."

But scarcely had they reached the terraces where all the Court were scattered, than they found the Queen pleading with her brother.

"Not to-night, Zorzi *mio*! For this one night let us take the pleasure of thy coming as a brother to my home. Thou must know our customs and our people and let them offer thee glad welcome. I have music and song planned for thee:—and our Cyprian gardens—with their delights!— Let us stroll awhile."

He mad a gesture of dissent.

"The banquet hath been long enough," he said, "nor lacking for sweets. There is meat of stronger quality to digest. Not for feasting I came, but upon an embassy the matter of which we must discuss."

"And *now?*" she asked, still unwilling.

"Said I not 'now'?" he answered resolutely, advancing toward the arches which admitted to the palace.

But Bernardini stood in his way, arresting his quick pace.

"My cousin, thy 'now' must wait upon the Queen's good pleasure," he said, with due deference. Then more lightly, "It is the way of our Court in Cyprus—which would do thee honor. Her Majesty hath ordered some festive trifle of music, or other entertainment, which our music-maidens, skilled upon the lute, would fain begin."

At a signal from the Lady Margherita, they came floating out upon the terrace: but the Cornaro turned frowning from them and signed with his hand that his cousin, the Bernardini, should let him pass.

At a glance from the Queen, Bernardini moved courteously aside, but Caterina did not follow: she waited for a moment before she spoke—as if to weigh her speech.

"If it be for matter of the Embassy which may not be delayed," she said, "I will bid our Chamberlain advise our Council of the Realm, that we may receive it with all honor befitting the Court of Venice, so soon as they shall be gathered in the audience-chamber. Though the hour be strange, it is of thy choosing; and thou art our dear guest—as, also, our honored Ambassador from the Republic."

The Cornaro stood for a moment as if uncertain what part to play; then, making light of it all, he dismissed his frown and with a whimsical laugh and graceful deprecatory motions, he turned to his sister and offered his hand to lead her in.

"Nay, nay, my sister; I spoke of no formal session of state to receive my Embassy; rather of a friendly talk between us two, touching the matter upon which the Republic hath sent me hither—that we may better understand each other before it be laid before the Council. With thy leave, my cousin."

He passed with a friendly nod and some jesting word, which the Bernardini returned more gravely:

"Thou dost verily surround thyself with state, Caterina!" her brother exclaimed in a tone of stern displeasure, when she had indicated a chamber where they might be alone, and he had carefully assured himself that the quaint Eastern draperies concealed no guards—the while she watched him in amazement.

"It is better for thee that there be no listeners," he said, as he placed a seat before her and sat down, fixing her with his gaze.

"Hearken without speech until I have spoken." His tone was threatening.

She turned white and red, half starting up, but cowed by his manner, fell back into her seat again.

"Is this my brother," she asked, "or is it the Ambassador?"

"Nay; leave tragedy, Caterina; I am come to bring thee word of great opportunity."

"For my people?—For Cyprus?" she responded with instant interest.

He laughed, a curious, unmirthful laugh.

"Aye—for 'thy people'—'for Cyprus,' verily. Listen! Thou hast it in thy power, at this moment, to bestow a gift upon the Republic—thou who art the Daughter of Venice—that shall make thee memorable throughout the ages."

She was taken unaware; yet suddenly the happenings of all the past years seemed to converge in her, as their central point, binding her hand and foot so that she might not free herself: an icy bolt shot through her: "I—I fail to understand," she answered faintly, for there was somewhat in his look that interpreted the meaning she would fain have missed.

"Aye: it *is* hard to understand—that thou, who art one of our Casa Cornaro—a woman—upon whom Venice hath bestowed such fatherly and unceasing care—should have it in thy power so to reward the Republic, who might have seized the throne of Cyprus, without waiting for thy gift! Yet, of her grace, the Serenissima Republica doth verily ask it of thee, as a favor—thou who art Daughter to Venice. Thou mayest well find it hard to understand!"

She rose, indignantly.

"Hath the Signoria of Venice broken faith with her ally of Cyprus? Is she not content to wait for the sovereignty of this realm until my death—knowing that by my will Venice hath been created heir to this throne—that she should wish to deprive me now of that which hath come to me through so great sorrow, by the will of my husband, the King?"

He watched her curiously, while the color came and went with her tumultuous emotions, and her troubled breathing; and he changed his tone—being subtle.

"I said that the Signoria would have thanked thee for thy gift of the realm; and that the ages should have decreed thee great honor for thy queenly giving: but it would have been more of their courtesy than of

thine. For thou dost verily hold too great a matter this little kingdom of Cyprus—forgetting the nets that have many times been spread for thee; and the disfavor of those Cyprian nobles who would have a man to rule over them and not a woman—young and without power—unless Venice be her ally and defender! Even now, thou mightest have been a slave in the land of the Turk, were it not for thy faithful upholding by the galleys of Venice, which came between thee and the devastators. Where is the generous response of a woman who, without them, were nothing?—I thought thee more noble!"

She was bewildered, and he had cut her to the quick.

"Nay, Zorzi: thou dost not comprehend. A Queen must first be faithful to her people."

"Aye—'to her people!'" he retorted scornfully. "And are thy people of Venice, of or Cyprus?—that thou mayest be faithful neither to one nor to the other! Wilt thou show thy faith to Cyprus by turning thine only helpers and defenders from thee, that thine enemies of the coasts may have free entrance to thine unprotected harbors, while the galleys of Venice no longer waste upon thine ingratitude their unrequited care?"

"It is not true!" she cried; "they would not thus desert me."

"It is like a woman to build a belief without foundation," he answered her—calmly, as one who makes a study at his ease.

"And this is verily thy mission from Venice—*and to me?*"

"I have spoken," he said, "but the time is short: thou mayest not delay to reply—

Venice hath so decreed."

"My people love me," she pleaded, with a gasp. "I have only them to live for!"

"Thou hast only them, if thou wilt perforce give up thine own," he answered readily; "it is of thine own choice."

"What meanest thou?" she questioned, grasping his arm in terror: "Zorzi!"

He shook off her touch and answered her unmoved. "The choice will be thine, between thy people of Cyprus—who love thee, thou sayest—and the Signoria, whom thou wilt offend and who have spent themselves upon thee. *They will leave thee to thine own devices, withdrawing every galley from thy Cyprian coasts.*"

She gave a low moan, pressing her trembling hands to her brow, as if brain-weary from perplexity; then she turned to her brother again with the exclamation:

"How shouldst thou so utterly desert me, Zorzi—*thou*, and my people whom I love!'

"The mercy of the Republic is at an end," he assured her uncompromisingly, "and for the Casa Cornaro—thou dost mistake, which seemeth easy for thee; it is rather thou who wilt disgrace me—thy brother, with his honorable pride in his house and his most noble country. For him and his children there will no longer be honors, nor any favor of the Senate: upon thy brother, who doth so faithfully counsel thee and from his heart, will fall the enmity of the Republic who hath *forbidden him to fail* in his mission. And what is left for a patrician who hath suffered exile and confiscation, but death and the extinction of his house? This will be thy doing."

She sprang up, attempting to reach a silken cord that swung upon the wall near her; but Cornaro raised his hand above her and lightly tossed it aside.

"No one shall come between us until I have thy promise: it lieth between me and thee."

"I need some one to help me," she implored; "and Aluisi is of our Casa Cornaro,—he would understand."

"Two are enough," he said,—"nay, too much; for where the matter is urgent, one sufficeth."

She sat on mutely, wrestling with her problem.

From the time that she had first known of her royal destiny, problems of rights of governments had never been put before her in unpartisan, clear-cut lines of white and black—as right and wrong: her judgment had been intentionally befogged by those who should have been her teachers, until she found herself Queen by coronation and inheritance, consecrated in her right by the awful seal of the great High-Priest Death—before whose inviolable silence questions cease, and the scroll of the closed life is no longer searched, save with eyes that blur the lines through overflowing mercy.

It had been easy for Venice to retain her ascendency over Caterina by intensifying her dependence, by fostering the distinctively feminine and predominant side of her nature—by insisting upon abnormal claims to her duty, her obedience, her love, her gratitude.

When the eyes of the Queen had finally been opened to see the danger of these claims of Venice, it was already too late, for the freedom of her realm had been inextricably tangled in the toils of Venice. Since then she had struggled with all her soul to govern her recalcitrant people by the only power that she believed in or possessed—the power of love. But it was love with little knowledge of the problems of nations or the measures needful to cope with the disaffected nobles who were numerous enough to create an influence and who cared rather for their own pleasure, than for any duty that they owed to enhance the unity or moral splendor of their land.

"My husband left me Queen," she said at last, raising her troubled eyes to his. "It was by his will that I rule. Have I the right to yield this power?"

"POWER!"

She recoiled from the irony of the tone.

"They are my people—they love me," she persisted, "and thou canst not know how the care for them doth fill my life. Have I the right to give them to any other?"

He laughed again. "Thou hast a veritable talent for creating problems wherewith to vex thyself, my sister, conscience-tossed! Hath one a right to *give* that which he can no longer hold? Art thou the first who could not rule, to *abdicate* in favor of a stronger scepter?"

"We must ask these questions," she said struggling to be firm, "for duty is not easy to find."

"Nor fortune," he answered coldly. "And one must be wise indeed to know when 'one may grasp it by the hair'—as thou hast the chance with this most gracious proffer of the Signoria before thee to reject."

She turned her away that he might not read her thoughts, while she dwelt upon the full meaning of the cruel word he had spoken so easily—*to abdicate:* it meant the disgrace of rulers, the acknowledgment of supreme weakness—unless to the greater power belonged the supreme right.

Was this supreme Right vested with Venice, that she might bow without question? The word smote upon her like a touch of ice and her heart quailed.

Meanwhile Cornaro was watching, urging her decision with further arguments. The Signoria would provide for her; she should retain her title; she should still be styled '*Caterina, Regina*'; she should live in royal state.—But—*if she did not yield*—our Lord himself in heaven would be displeased with her, hating no sin so much for any Christian as base ingratitude—with much more, to which she made no answer.

And thus the night wore on.

At last she rose, weary and heart-broken.

"My brother," she said in trembling tones, "none of thine arguments move me: yet thou knowest I should grieve if thou, because of me, shouldst suffer exile and disgrace, or thy children be held from any honor they might win. But even for this I could not yield. Thy happiness and mine must be as naught in this great crisis, against the welfare of my people. Them only I must consider."

A torrent of imprecation rose to his lips, but he left it unuttered. For as he turned his angry glance upon her and saw her face pallid and distraught by the anguish of her struggle, with the strange gleam of unearthly strength in her sorrowing eyes—it would have seemed like cursing a spirit. He crossed himself unconsciously, drawing a little apart from her, and waited impatiently.

There was a motion of her lips, as if she had more to say: but her strength was spent, so that her voice would not come with her first effort. Cornaro was conscious as he watched her of his fear lest it should fail her utterly before she found her speech. He knew what he had to expect if he did not succeed in his mission, and for him the moment was crucial; others, for a far less bitter thwarting of the will of the Signoria, had suffered death—which had been hinted to him. He had meant to offer this as his supreme argument when all others had failed to coerce her: but instinctively he held it back, fearing to anger her to the point of stubborn refusal, for there was some unexpected power of resistance within the soul of this slight woman.

Just as he was beginning to assure himself that, at all costs he must use further persuasion, her voice came—far away and colorless:

"And if I yield—?"

He went nearer, almost abject in the joy of this sudden reaction, promising her with glowing visions, state, glory, luxury, honor, favor of the Senate, ease, everything that his vivid imagination could seize upon to tempt the fancy of a woman; but she waved her hand impatiently to arrest his quick flow of words.

"Not for myself—but for my people—what for them?"

"Everything!" he answered undaunted; "security, prosperity; they shall be ruled as Venice rules her provinces—ever more wisely than the people rule themselves. Thou knowest that, because of this, foreign states have come to plead that Venice would accept their submission."

She knew that this was true; but her heart was like lead within her as she raised her impotent clasped hands with a sudden, sharp cry of pain. "My God! my God! I am not faithless to my vow—Thou knowest. I must choose their welfare, though my heart should break!"

As the Cornaro gave his hand to lead her to her chamber in the light of the early dawn, she turned to him pitifully imploring his comprehension of her motive: "The Holy Mother knoweth that I am not faithless to my people—since with the favor of the Republic turned from me, I might neither serve nor guard them.—My lot is bitter!"

But the day had dawned for him, if not for her.

"Nay; trust me, sweet Sister and Queen, thou hast chosen wisely," he answered with easy gallantry, as he kissed her hand and would have left her where the Lady Margherita stood waiting with troubled eyes and heightened color to receive her—scarcely condescending to notice the Cornaro's homage or his gay, parting words—"your fair Queen hath done this night an act that shall send her name down through coming ages, wreathed with glory."

For words came easily to him, and he had been too well content with his own triumph and escape to weigh the effect of its cost upon Caterina. But now, after the mockery of his conventional salutation—which none knew better than he to make an expression of profound deference—as he turned his bright gaze upon her, the strained pallor of her face with its deep lines of suffering smote upon her, and he addressed Dama Margherita again with some assumption of concern for his sister's welfare.

"I fear she is overwearied: but the long discussion upon business of the Senate hath been needful. Yet now there is only rest before her, and I may leave her, in confidence, in your gracious care."

But the Lady Margherita had turned impatiently from him to busy herself with the Queen before he had finished his speech: then she flashed him a glance which he found it hard to meet.

"We who love her need not your counsel, my Lord, to strive to undo your doing of this night. These are the apartments of Her Majesty. We need to be alone."

Chapter XXXVII

Was Venice insatiable in requirement?

"It is enough," Caterina pleaded impotently. "Venice cannot ask more!"

"Nay, it is little," the Cornaro answered, "and only that which shall bring thee further honor. The Provveditori[32] will charge themselves with the details of the Royal progress—as the Signoria hath directed."

"Let me but sign the parchment, as it may please them," she urged, "for the last time with the Royal Seal of Cyprus—but spare me more! I would fain withdraw into the Holy House of St. Francis and be at rest."

But this might by no means be permitted; and the Ambassador of the Republic was ready with his threadbare argument of ingratitude, with much other reasoning of which he was scarcely less proud.

"One giveth not a regal gift with the downcast air of compulsion—else were it base in him who receiveth. Bethink thee ever of thine honor and of that of Venice," he admonished his sister many times during the weeks of preparation that followed upon the Queen's decision; whatever the detail under consideration—and few escaped his vigilance—he was inflexible, and her opposition could not go beyond his announcement: *"It is the will of Venice."*

Where were the nobles of this country tossed hither and thither like a shuttle-cock at the will of the strongest, that they would not arm for resistance—nay—wrapped themselves in sullen silence in the seclusion of their estates, or gathered in great companies to plunge into the forests and forget their vexations in the comradery and excitement of the chase, while for Caterina the slow days passed in agonized entreaty that some miracle might yet chance to save the realm for Cyprus?

Sometimes a wild hope came to her that this extremity might stimulate them to an uprising to save the integrity of their land: but a few words with those of the Council most devoted to Cyprus convinced her that the hope was futile. The days of national ambition were over for this people of many races: their luxuries sufficed for their content and lulled them into a lethargy which had so deadened their perceptions that the gradual encroachments of Venetian power could reach this climax without arousing them to action.

Even the burghers who had so valiantly defended their Queen in earlier days looked on in mournful inertia while preparations for the royal progress went forward, knowing that if Venice thus joyfully accepted the 'resignation' of their Queen—for thus had the act been freely translated to the Cyprian people—they were themselves powerless; and the day of farewell dawned at last, when the royal cortège passed out from the palace-gates to the grand Piazza of Nikosia, where the formal act of renunciation was to be made.

It was a long and ceremonious procession—the high officials of the realm were there in splendid vestments, with many Venetian functionaries in crimson dignity among them—with a numerous escort of guards in full armor—with companies of cavalry and men-at-arms, while, in their midst the Queen, in regal velvet and pearls, rode surrounded by the knights and ladies of her court. But the color of her robe was black, as were also the garments of her maids of honor—of satin, soft and lustrous, reflecting the lights from their jewels as they gleamed in the sunshine,—yet, to the Embassy of Venice the sombre choice was displeasing, as an unpermissible expression of the Queen's sentiments.

"Hath Venice also concerned herself with sumptuary laws for the ladies of my household?" Caterina asked with ineffable disdain when remonstrance had been made. And they, having gained so much, feared to press her further.

After the solemn mass in the Duomo, the magnificent chords of a jubilant *Te Deum*[33] filled the Piazza with harmonies—it was the music of a Triumph indeed:—the soldiers, the knights, the high functionaries of state, the priests and chanting choirs were all there; but the central figure under the golden baldachino, upheld by the barons of the realm surrounded with royal honors, was not the Conqueror—but the victim—the prey—the sacrifice. It was rather they—the leaders of this pageant, in their crimson robes of office with the shadow of the banner of San Marco above them, who rode proudly, sure of the honors and emoluments that awaited them when Venice should echo to them the Roman cry of victory—*"Io Triumphe!"*[34]

And now the Queen pronounced the speech that Venice had decreed, wherein she claimed the love that her simple people had lavished upon her—

"For Venice—to whom we have freely yielded our right."

The words were strange upon her lips, and she spoke them stonily, as if she knew not that they had a meaning; and thus tortured from her, it may well be questioned whether the Recording Angel ever noted them in his book—yet they were her answer to the *popolo* who thronged about her with tears and blessings, as she journeyed from city to city to repeat the mournful ceremony of farewell; and the people heard them with sobs and groans.

In every city, as one for whom life had died and speech had lost its soul—she uttered these words which Venice had decreed; in every city she looked on mutely from under her royal canopy—she who was so powerless—while the flag of the island of Cyprus was supplanted by the banner of San Marco, and the sculptured marble tablet with the winged lions guarding its triumphant inscription, was placed as a record of a kingdom too weak to rule.

Fran. De Priuli Venetae Class.
Imper. Divi Marci Vess.
Cypri Feliciter Erectum Est.
No. MCCCCLXXXVII. 28 Febru.

How dreary the passage across those wide waters to the shores of the smiling Adriatic for the desolate woman who had left them in the first flush of her youth, with hopes as brilliant as the skies of Venice, and with a promise as fair—to return to them lonely, despoiled, heart-broken, craving rest! The gray light of the storm-clouds by the banks of the Lido and the moan of the rising winds which threatened to engulf the Bucintoro[35] and the fleet of attendant barges coming in state to meet the deposed Queen, were typical of the change.

Not caring for the splendor of her equipage, though the Doge himself was her escort—not deceived by the pageant of welcome that Venice offered, Caterina—very beautiful and pale and still, with the sense of the motive power broken within her—passed up the long length of the Canal Grande by the side of the Serenissimo, receiving the glad homage of the people of Venice.

"Caterina Veneta! Caterina Regina!"

Venice was outdoing herself in triumph, showering regal honors upon her: the bells of all the *campanili*[36] were ringing a jubilee: music greeted her from the shores as they glided by—the portals wreathed with festal garlands, the beautiful city a glory of light and color; for the storm of the evening had passed and the morning had dawned in sunshine, and along the Riva the people were thronging to welcome her—the Queen who had bestowed the gift of her kingdom upon Venice!

Yet how had the Republic kept faith with Cyprus? Step by step, through the years, drawing the velvet clasp closer—closer—until there was scarce life left—smiling the while: gathering in the revenues of the rich land amply, with no care to spend them on the welfare of the island, or for its increase: slowly, strenuously, with deft insinuations of filial duty, striving to dominate the young Queen's moral judgments and press the claims which were of Venice's own creation—jealously watching lest she become too popular, and hampering her action through the very officers sent in guise of help—lest through freedom she should in truth grow strong to rule: Year by year—

stealthily—smiling under a cloak of splendor which the Cyprians loved, Venice had grasped at power—a little more, and a little more—until resistance was impossible.

Was it meet to receive her thus? Could she find smiles for the people to-day with the memories of her bridal pageant greeting her at every turn—a woman despoiled of hope—a widowed wife—a childless mother—a queen without kingdom or power?

Before the Palazzo Corner Regina, the long procession came to pause, and with the ceremonies that were meet, Zorzi Cornaro, brother to Caterina, knelt down bareheaded before the Doge and was knighted for his prowess in persuasion—since without his eloquence it might well have been that the Queen of Cyprus would not have given that complete and absolute surrender which was so graciously announced to all the allies of Venice as *"of the full and free determination* of our most serene and most beloved daughter, Caterina Cornaro."

For the grace of Venice—when her smiling mood was on her, as for the fear of her life-crushing frown, men did her bidding without question, and never *dared* to fail.

But Venice still claimed a final act of gift and submission, where the Venetian people be her witnesses: and when the domes of San Marco flashed in the sunset light, the procession entered in solemn state—the Senate and Signoria and all the Ducal Court, in full attendance—and once more Caterina knelt before the altar and repeated her hard lesson, taught by that imperious ruler who knew how to hold the sea "in true and perpetual dominion," and who would not suffer "his beloved daughter" to fail in one jot or tittle of her act of renunciation.

The homecoming of the Daughter of

Venice was over.

Then, at last, came rest, and the sylvan-shades of Asolo—vine-crowned among the hills, with the sea spreading far below—blue, shimmering, laughing—as if she laved but the shore of content, under happy skies.

Whatever of good there remained for Caterina to do in this petty domain which the munificence of the Signoria had bestowed in exchange for Cyprus, she did with a gracious and queenly hand, so that her realm was wider than her territory, for she had won the love of the people wherever she had passed, and in the years of her tried and chequered life, no evil was ever spoken of her. Yet often the gentle Queen slipped away from the modest festivities she had devised for the pleasure of her slender mimic court—the music tourneys—the recitations—the fanciful quibbles in words—which could have had for her great weariness of empty hands but a pale moonlight charm—to the lovely gardens of her hillside castle, to woo sad memories—and sweet as sad—of the far-off terraces of Potamia which Janus had prepared for his girl-bride.

Then once again Venice decreed a pageant for the gentle Lady of Asolo.

It was night, and the skies had clothed themselves in gloom; out on the lagoon the lights in the shipping scarce pierced the mists, and the rain fell in flurries, drifting in gusts under the arcades of the Ducal Palace, and lifting the cloaks of the senators and councillors who sought shelter there while the procession was forming. But none turned back for the wildness of the night, for the order of the Senate was imperative that all the state officials and all the embassies must do her honor; and the time had been appointed by a king who bows to no mortal will and brooks no delay. Across the Piazza, down through the palace court-yards and through the *calle* the people were flocking—dark groups over which the lights of the torches flared fitfully: the nobles were waiting in their gondolas—each at his palace portal to take his place—there were no sounds but the wind and the rain—footsteps plashing over the wet pavements—a whispered order.

And now to strange, solemn music,—the sobbing of the cellos, the tenderer melancholy of the flute—the long procession was moving up the Canal Grande—the ducal barge and the gondola of the Patriarch not keeping decorous line, for the roughness of the waters. From the portals of the Palazzo Corner Regina a bridge of boats had been thrown across the Canal Grande to the mouth of the Rio of San Cassan, and out of the blackness of the great Cornaro Palace the bearers met them, bringing in reverent state the form of the gracious Queen for whom all earthly problems were solved—who might never again answer their devotion with smiles or benediction.

Silently each noble stepped up from his gondola, crossing himself devoutly and bowing his head as he joined the long, never-ending procession: like a phantom vision it swept through the mists—each dark figure bearing its torch—*as if it were the soul of him above his head,* casting a ghostly reflection, in lessening rays, down through the blackness—gliding in air across the water, over the arch of the bridge which was all but invisible in the darkness—and down through the narrow *rio* to the Church of the Sant' Apostolli—the weird harmonies of the songs of the dead echoing faintly back through the windings of the *rio*, like half-heard whispers from the spirit land.

When the solemn music of the midnight mass had been chanted over the noble company in the Church of the Sant' Apostolli, they left her lying in state before the altar of the Cappella Cornaro, while in the church, outside the chapel, the Ducal guards kept watch. Very still and pale she was in the light of the tall wax candles burning about her and the torches flaring from the funeral pyre, and strange to look upon the coarse brown cape and cowl of the habit of St. Francis, with a hempen cord for girdle. But the Lady Margherita had tenderly folded the hood away from the beautiful face and head, and in the pale patrician hands a rose lay lightly clasped, and a wealth of floral tributes heaped her bier—which was crowned with the royal crown of Cyprus.

Now that the gentle Sovereign had put aside forever her robes of royalty and donned for her last vestment the symbol of service and humility, how should Venice fear the unconfessed rivalry of her rare spirit,—a mere woman—conquered by the power of the State and stricken by death?

Now that the slight hands, folded nerveless over the quiet breast, might never more thrill to her emotions of large motherliness, and scatter gladness with gracious flutterings, in swift response to a too-adoring populace—now that the sleeping eyes might never again unclose to smile her loving soul out to her people—the Signoria could be magnanimous in homage: and through the days that the proud city mourned for her, the sable hatchments on church and palace bore the arms of Venice and of Cyprus.

The Singers

There is beauty in nature, people and life. Moments pass by before we take them in; things happen that suddenly make us see life differently. Experiences are hard to capture, but as Alice Emma Sauerwein Lord shows us, they can sing in harmony when they are repeated and articulated. Words flow from a pen and fingers work away at a typewriter to create a strand of poetic language to express itself to a reader.

The melody of everyday experiences takes on new light with every poem. Sunsets, sunrises, flowers, birds, the wind in trees—all speak through the poet, who brings them to life by giving them voice. Alice Emma Sauerwein Lord conveys the power and musicality of the sea and the seasons in her *Symphony in Dreamland*; Marguerite E. Easter's onomatopoeia places you in a soothing setting listening to the animals, who, personified, communicate their own outlook on life in, beside, and under the trees. Clara Newman Turner's reflections on nature, in contrast, leave us to think on the passage of time.

Odes, not only to nature, but to history and memory: each poet in this section crafts stories and images that touch those who read. Their opinions and thoughts flow with ease, one line to the next. Family histories, life histories, color the pages with sentiment, as we can see in poems like Lucy Randolph Cautley's "Betrayal."

Ella Morrow Sollenberger writes of wartime, when people fear everything. Young men leave and may never return. Sollenberger reminisces about her sons and comments on the transience of life. Her somber tone, juxtaposed with playful memories, stirs the emotions. Even decades later, words can place a person into a moment in time and make them feel as though they were there. To be immortal is to be documented in the written word, whether yours or another's words about you. Language is magic that cannot be matched.

People forget that poetry originated in the lyric tradition, sung by traveling troubadors. So please, let these voices sing. Let the words of these poets transport you, telling stories of times long since passed and experiences that will resonate in your bones.

Alice Emma Sauerwein Lord (1848-1930)

Alice Emma Sauerwein Lord was a prominent figure in the Woman's Literary Club of Baltimore. A member from its earliest years through at least 1917, she served on the Board of Managers and was longtime chair of the committees on essays and travel. She was one of the Club's most active members, frequently presenting her works and the works of others to the Club, and she was decisive and opinionated when organizational matters came to the floor.

Lord was born in 1848 into a family headed by Peter G. Sauerwein, a notable figure in Baltimore commerce and civil society. She married Massachusetts native Charles W. Lord when she was in her early thirties and was his second wife. Lord was also involved in the Woman's Club of Roland Park and the Lend-a-Hand Club of Mount Washington, which was founded by fellow WLCB member and author Elizabeth Turner Graham.

Lord was a published poet, novelist, and playwright. Several poems, including "Rubinstein's Ocean Symphony" from her collection *A Symphony in Dreamland* (1899), were featured in George C. Perine's *The Poets and Verse-Writers of Maryland* (1896), and her historical novel *The Days of Lamb and Coleridge* (1893) was positively reviewed in the *Baltimore Sun*. Perine noted that the bulk of Lord's writings were published following her marriage, underscoring the seriousness with which she undertook her literary pursuits and, perhaps, implying her husband's support of her activities. Lord, in fact, dedicated *A Symphony in Dreamland* to her husband, whose "tender counsels bade me hope and work."[1] —J. L. Cole

From *A Symphony in Dreamland* (1882)

Allegro-Maestro

Dreamland

There is a land where I can go
   And none may know;
Where skies are brighter, far, than ours;
   Where sweetest flowers
Bloom ever; where no winter's blast
   Need ever cast
Its touch of death. This happy land
   Is close at hand,
And I can reach it by a thought;
   Yet there is nought
To guide another to its shore;
   There is no door,
Nor road, nor boat, that we can show.
   Each one must go
Alone, and in his separate way.
   Still, any day
'Tis open to each soul that longs
   To hear its songs.
It is a land where we can lay
   Our dead away—
Dead loves, dead hopes, dead selves, dead friends,
   Yet here death ends;—
They live again to greet us here
   When we draw near.
It is a land that steals each grief,
   And gives relief;
The homesick heart finds here a home
   In which to roam;
The childless ones have nurselings here
   That are as dear
As clinging babes to mothers' hearts;

And all the smarts
Of yearning love, misunderstood,
    Can hither brood
And flutter and again grow calm:
        For here is balm.
Thank God! for dreamland! For this rest
        To hearts oppressed!
That 'mid earth's incompleteness, meet
        Some joys, complete.

Symphonies

A symphony, what *is* a symphony?
In music, 'tis the perfect harmony
Of many parts—each in itself complete,
Yet each a part of all—wherein we meet
The self-same theme, wove like a silver thread
Through all the pattern. Each in different
    tone
Of grave or sad or gay; yet is there thrown
The image on each part of that same dream,
Like heaven mirrored in the wandering
    stream.
In symphony, are thoughts and music wed.

Methinks a Summer day, with azure sky,
And brave green trees that lift their arms
    on high
To throw the nestling shadows o'er the grass;
The golden grain that waves as breezes pass;
The luscious scent of clover on the air,
And thousand mingled sweets that hover
    there;
The happy bird-notes ringing through
    the drone
Of insect-harper's pulsing, drowsy tone,—
Methinks all this is *Nature's Symphony.*
The clouds may gather fast, and spread
    on high
Their leaden veil to catch the golden showers
The sunbeams fling on grass and trees
    and flowers;

Perchance the rain may fall in silvery lines,
And drive its arrows through the oaks
    and pines,
And o'er the meads and fields send little rills,
And swell to rivers, streams among the hills;
'Tis the *Adagio,* weird and grave and gray,
To the *Allegro* of the summer's day.[2]

Then if the theme, the golden, flashing sun
Shine through the drops ere yet the day
    be done,
And quiver o'er the weeping grass and grain,
Paint sunset clouds with rose and gold again,
To Nature's *Larga-Allegretto,*[3] shall
The moon and constellations write—*Finale.*

So Beauty, in God's noblest work, to me
Seems shaped upon the model, Sympho-
    ny—
The handsome features, stately form and
    grace,
Calm eyes, and winning smile of charm-
    ing face.
Each lovely part is needed for the whole,
And faultless body needs a noble soul.
Else does the Symphony fail of its end;
For man may mar what God doth nobly
    blend.

Thus have I dared use Nature as my guide
To lure my fledglings through the empy-
    rean, wide.
If we would soar at all, we must be bold;
Though broken flights scarce reach the
    goal, we hold:
With Dreamland for a theme, I can pursue,
Through many a field, the heights that lie
    in view;
And, loving Nature, follow close her lead,
Though failing oft—at last I may succeed.

My Home

There's a wee little nest
    Where the world's staring eye,
In search of gaudy treasures,
    Would pass the plain thing by;
Full of sunshine and flowers,
    And the work of tasty hands;
But the secret I'll not tell you
    Where my bonny cottage stands.

In my wee little nest
    Are true, loving hearts,
Replete with every blessing
    That trusting love imparts;
Little faces at the door,
    Little birds in the nest,—
With love-light and with sunlight,
    My bonny home is blest.

But a cloud rolls along,
    Passing over my sun,
And my dear little home
    Lies a wreck and all undone;
Only one heart is left,
    Mourning love and love's sweet home;
They say 'twas but a day-dream,
    And still homeless I must roam.

Maiden-Faith

Somewhere, in this world of sorrow,
    Midst its turmoil and despair,
Waits for me a quiet comer,
    Peaceful refuge from all care;
Warmed with love and tender friendship
    Barred to other touch than mine,
Only waiting till I enter
    To unfold its joys divine.

Somewhere, midst the world of wanderers,

Each on his life's scheme intent,
Waits *one* life, that for completion
    Needs my strength to bring content;
Needs my might of love and friendship
    Counsel, prayers, and sympathy,
E'en as I need his, to perfect
    What there is of good in me.

Somewhere is he waiting for me,
    Even as for him I wait:
Little matter if he's near me,
    Or if he come soon or late.
Each may find some soul's ideal,
    Ere each meets the other one,
Still our souls will know each other
    When the waiting time is done.

Somewhere he is looking for me
    Though he knows not it is I;
While I'm busy, working, dreaming,
    Waiting for him, silently.
And I'll know him when I meet him;
    He is wise, and good, and true,
Tender, earnest in his manhood,
    He will read my spirit through.

Somewhere, when a life is brightened
    By prosperity and peace;
Somewhere, when a heart is shadowed
    By life's conflicts and distress,
When God's own good time has reached us,
    I those joys and griefs shall share,
In his heart rest my disquiet,
    Find and bring contentment there.

Les Chateaux en Espagne

Beneath the maples, arched o'erhead,
    With sunbeams dripping through
    their green,

A maiden sits, with golden hair—
    Gold as the sunlight's dancing sheen.

'Neath sunny hair, her violet eyes
    Are gazing dreamily into space,
And heeding not the twittering birds,
    And flowers that nod before her face.

She never heeds the snowy clouds,
    That float like boats o'er azure skies;
Or beauty spread around her feet,—
    A far-off look is in her eyes.

Awaken, dreamer, from your dreams;
    You're chasing phantoms of the wind,
You're losing youth's sweet morning time;
    And leaving *real* delights behind.

Your visions are but luring dreams
    Of noble knights on fiery steeds,
Of dazzling castles in the air,
    Of chivalry and valorous deeds.

Come back, come back, O little maid!
    Those dreams will lead you to a land
Where all is vague, and weird, and dark,
    Where none can take you by the hand.

Who wander in that elfin land
    Where winged arrows strike the eyes
Henceforth are blind to earthly joys,—
    They view old scenes with sad surprise.

Come back, I pray you, little one,
    And see what beauties round you spread:
Come back, ere it has grown too late,
    And hope's fair sunshine fades o'erhead.

A mother's arms will clasp more close
    Than any knight's in elfin land

(And mothers may not always stay);
    Beware how you let go her hand!

The future that you paint so bright
    Comes never to a human life:
The now, the here, is all we have;
    All else with tears and snares is rife.

Sabbath Bells

Hark! I hear the murmuring of bells—
    Distant bells that pulse the city's heart!
Silvery throb from hill to hill that tells,
    What their wordless messages impart!
        Murmuring Bells!

List! The many voices rise and fall
    With a resonance that fills all space,
Many-toned, yet blending, each with all,
    Till sonorous echoes reach this place.
        Chiming Bells!

Wherefore should my heart respond so fast
    To this far-off music of the bells?
Is it that they whisper of the past?
    Can it be hope's voice that still foretells?
        O ye Bells!

The Wanderer

One morning, when all earth was bright,
A boy set out in glad delight
To find the road to wealth and fame,
And on earth's records set his name.
On either side an Angel stood:
One whispered evil, one was good.
One lured him down each flowery track,
The other gently led him back.
For in the road his feet must take
Lay rocks and briers; and many a break
Showed two paths leading to his goal—

One bright to tempt his doubting soul.

Hope beckoned on, and oft he flew
To reach yon temple, just in view;
But streams and mountains intervened,
And sudden turns the palace screened.

He grew perplexed: "Which path was
    straight?"
His tempter whispered: "Stop and wait;
Why plod and climb the weary steep?
'Tis pleasant here, come rest and sleep."

His face has lost its radiant smile;
Deep lines of suffering and guile
Are furrowed on his weary brow;
Where is the better Angel now?

Far back, where he had turned astray,
The patient Angel, in dismay,
Unheeded, scorned, called: "I will wait;
Return, ere it has grown too late."

At night the wanderer reached the gate
And knocked; but he had come too late,
Too worn and soiled to claim his place;
He crouched below, and hid his face.

And while he stood, in mute despair—
His tempter following even there,—
Death beckoned.   Then the wanderer cried:
"Come, patient Angel, to my side!"
"Forgive my wasted life and powers,
My cold neglect, my idle hours!
Lead me to heaven!" And from his clay,
The Angel bore his soul away.

Heimweh[4]

I know a home, a sunny home,

Where I can wander as I will,
From room to room, upstairs and down;
    For I am mistress of it still.

Sweet quiet reigns within its walls,
    For only those I love are there;
No strangers haunt each room and door,
    No stranger's foot is on the stair.

My loved one greets me gaily here,
    Within these sacred walls of home:
No curious eyes can question us,
    No careless step can hither roam.

I know a home, with curtains drawn
    Enfolded round the warmth and light;
The glow of summer noon is there,
    Though outside there are snow and night.

I know each picture on the walls,
    Each gem in bronze or bisque or brass;
The dainty chairs, the carpets bright,
    I greet as friends whene'er I pass.

Oh, bonny home! oh, dreamland home!
    My heart yearns for you night and day;
What cruel fate has barred your door,
    And forced my steps another way?

Adagio

La Tristesse[5]

The snow lies white and soft across the hills,
And rugged steeps and jagged valleys fills;
It spreads rough knots and black impurities
With seamless mask, that fair and level lies.
The bare, brown earth with ghostly
    shroud is spread,
Marred by no mark, save rabbit's dim-
    pled tread;

And snowy-powdered twig and branch of pine,
Form lovely lace-work where they intertwine.

And yet, methinks the Earth this beauty wears
As a disguise, to hide the scars she bears,
When summer charm and freshness,
  dying, left
Our earth in widow's weeds, like one bereft.

The thought is sad to me; so like our hearts
That try to mask their gloom when joy departs!
We wear a surface of gay smiles, to hide
The shadowed cares and bitterness inside.

Aye! it is well to veil, with careless grace,
Our deeper selves from this world's star-
  ing face;
Our precedent from Nature's self we bring,
Who rounds her angles with soft covering.
And like the snows, our masks oft melt away
And show scarred features to the eye of day.
Fall on, bright flakes, and pile up, white
  and deep.
Smile on, sad eyes, 'tis better than to weep!

Lost Treasures

A mother kneeled before her babe,
  With tender love-light in her face:
"God keep thee pure and true, my child!
  God give thee every Christian grace!"

     ☙

The years roll on. That baby face
  Now wears the look of morning skies;
Whose smiles, like sunbeams, come and go,
  'Neath misty veil of sweet surprise.

"Thou hast thy fourteen years, dear child
  The second stage of life on earth,—
'Tis time thou shouldst thy jewels wear

That came as heirlooms at thy birth.

"These gems are thine," the mother said,
  "To bind upon thy neck and brow;
I pray thee, guard them day by day,
  To keep them just as pure as now."

"This emerald, hope; yon ruby, love;
  The topaz, joy (imprisoned sun)
Are for thy bosom; for thy brow
  This pearl of truth—a precious one!

"Ambition's diamond brightly gleams—
  I'd have thee use this gem with care;
This purple amethyst of pride,
  Thou couldst, best, of thy jewels, spare.

"The sapphire, blue as summer skies,
  Is faith, the bond, the central clasp."
"And must I wear them all?" she cried;
  And pressed them with a timid grasp.

     ☙

The years glide on, as time will go;
  The child has grown a woman now;
She roams the cedars' freckled shade
  With drooping head and pensive brow.
"Gone! all gone!" she sadly moans;
  "I dropped them on life's tangled way.
Those gems my mother held so dear
  Were lost, like stars before the day.
"The topaz was the first to go,—
  For joy can but to childhood cling;
And next the bright green emerald fell,
  Hope, too, seems only for the spring.
"Soon, soon my pearl of truth grew dark
  In noxious vapors which I breathed;
I, somehow, lost it from my brow,
  That since, with shadows, has been
  wreathed.

"The ruby, lost and found again,
    Lies hidden now beneath the sea;
And since I dropped that from my heart,
    Life has not been the same to me.

"I grasped my diamond closer, then
    Ambition's voice I would obey;
'Twas flawed—my aims had soared too
    high,—
    In pain I flung it far away.

"The amethyst alone is left.
    Would God that I had lost that too!
For pride is full of bitter pain,
    When life is hedged and friends are few!"

Marah[6]

Can it be true,
That life is poisoned at its very source,
    That bitter dew
Must fall into each fountain-head perforce?

Can it be so,
That when each life begins a demon waits—
    A deadly foe—
To drop into the soul its chrism of hates?

Can it be thus,
That every hope and every joy is crossed,
    For some of us,
By bitter taste of sweets we've had and lost?

Can it be just,
That through all life, from cradle to the
    grave,
    All falls to dust,
That we can grasp, or touch, or love, or
    crave?

Ultimatum

Whether our lives be sad or gay,
Whether we learn to doubt or pray,
Whether we smile or weep alway,
It will all end alike one day.

Whether the road be short or long,
Whether our steps be weak or strong,
Lonely or set amid life's throng,
Still to one goal we haste along.

Whether in brown-stone front we live,
Whether we board, or spend, or give;
Whether in reeking dens we stay,
There's but one end to all, some day.

Wealth cannot save the millionaire,
Nor gold bring one more hour to spare;
For cushioned ease and famine's fast,
There's but one bed for all at last.

Sometimes

Sometimes, in God's glad sunshine
    We make a darkness round us with
    our fears,
As sullen clouds obscure the sun,
    And shut his bright beams out, until
    it clears.

Sometimes, God waits to answer prayer
    Until our hearts are ready to receive;
Yet while we wait for Him to bless,
    We are too weak to trust Him and
    believe.
Sometimes, we thrust our needs at Him
    And cry: "Give me this thing to fill
    my heart,
That I may better serve the Lord."
    Does He not know the best what
    gifts to impart?

We think we wish to serve the Lord,
  And yet 'tis oft to serve ourselves we
    pray;
And if He shows another path,
  Shall we not teach our feet to go His
    way?

Sometimes we are afraid to take
  Some longed-for good that lies with-
    in our reach,
Fearing the gap when it is gone;—
  Mistrust, life's disappointments often
    teach.

Sometimes we leave all fears behind,
  And faith and love our earth-born
    clouds dispel;
Then, in a burst of song, we say:
  "He leadeth me"; "He doeth all
    things well."[7]

Violets

Rich, royal violet,
Crimson and blue are knit
Into the hue of it;
Love's stamp lies true on it;
Blue, as of summer sky,
  Mingled with sunset flush;
Blue as a maiden's eye,
  Lit by her warmest blush!

Sweets that intoxicate
In its breath lie in wait,
Through the room percolate,
My senses satiate.
What is the fragrant spell
  Thrown o'er me by its breath?
Memories I dare not tell
  Rise, when I prayed their death.

What dainty, subtle sense
Do its perfumes condense,
Thus to recall events,
Memories and joys intense?
Thoughts I had banished
  Out of my memory,
Hopes that have vanished
  Come back to torment me.

Ruined Castles

Ah, the woods, the sylvan shades!
Dark and cool, and fresh and green!
With waving tree-tops interlaced,
And dancing sun-spots in between;
With rich old moss and matted grass,
And the spicy earthen scents that pass.

How the cedar essence brings
Subtle thoughts of long ago!
And dreaming visions charm my brain,
As the opium-eater's fancies grow;
I give my soul to the witching spell
That is thrown by the scent I love so well.

Ah, those visions, proud and fair!
Dreams, bright dreams! from which I woke
And found my life's realities!
My chateaux[8] were but clouds of smoke;
But the fragrant woods are lovely yet,
Recalling dreams I would not forget.

Picture of the Good Shepherd

Sweet picture of the Shepherd with the
  Lamb!
I look at thy sad Christ-face and grow calm;
For as He bore our sorrows, healed our grief,
So in His love our troubles find relief.

Oh, weary head that had no place to rest!
And arms that clasp a weak lamb to Thy

breast!
Thy look of love and sorrow makes me
    weep;
It says: "I lay My life down for My sheep!"
Aye! though we oftentimes stand cold
    and dumb,
Thou waitest yet, dear Lord, for us to come.
Oh, by Thy griefs and sorrows borne for me,
Help me to leave the herd and follow Thee!

Thou saidest: "None shall pluck thee
    from My hand."
Thus, in Thy love my fainting faith shall
    stand;
Thus, on Thy bosom shall I rest my care,
And, like a helpless lamb, lie nestled there.

Hammock Sketches

Pendulous between two trees,
Nodding to the summer breeze,
In my hammock gently swinging,
With sweet bird-notes round me ringing,
I would paint this lovely scene;
Yet my words are dead, I ween,
Colorless for nature's tinting,
Light and shade, and sunbeam's glinting.

One long vista stretches down
To the steepled, distant town;
Hills and valleys, quick succeeding,
Grow more blue in their receding
Back, until the blue horizon
Their far mist-veiled summit lies on.
Near me slopes a deep ravine,
Bordered by a tiny stream,
Gurgling on and softly plashing,
Often through the sunbeams flashing;
And the cows wind down the dell
To the music of their bell.
Close around me, swelling high,

On the hills stretched toward the sky,
Pretty homes, like nests, are builded
Where the far-off trees seem gilded.
Here a field of golden grain
Rounds off to a grassy plain;
There a garden terraced down
Meets a clover-field, new mown.

Over hill and dell and wood
Sunbeams pour a golden flood,
Through the oaks and maples straying,
On the mosses gently playing,
Dripping through my leafy bower,
Golden sun-flecks gently shower:
And the nodding, tasselled grasses
Bow to each soft wind that passes.

Pictures, Three

I

The lake, with fragrant morning breath
    Not yet lifted from its breast,
Blue of water, air, and sky,
    Distant hills in mist-veils dressed.

Green the forest on the shore;
    Ferns and vines hang o'er the brink,
Mirrored downward in the lake,
    Where the birds skim down to drink.
All the rippling, blue expanse
    Sends back diamond sparks of light,
And along the pebbly beach
    Waves chase waves in mad delight.
All my sunny morning scene,
    With the glad birds on the wing,
Pictures *"Hope and Buoyancy,"*—
    Nature's time to laugh and sing.

II

Ashen, this picture,
　　With cloud piled on cloud;
The lake, like the sky,
　　Purple-gray, heavy-browed.
The winds lash the waters
　　Till white-caps dash in;
And the spray is tossed high
　　With a hiss and wild din.

The forests fling wildly
　　Their arms to the sky,
As the trees swaying back
　　Turn white faces on high.
The grain-fields are rolling
　　Great billows of gold;
And the town in the distance
　　Stands out, white and cold.

Yon fast-riding schooner
　　Is stripped of its shrouds;
And frightened birds sail off,
　　Like specks on the clouds.
Aye! if I could paint
　　The wild sounds in the air,
You'd know that this picture
　　Means "*Restless Despair.*"

III

Waters gold as golden sky;
Golden boats sail, double, by;
Crimson splendor in the west,
Crimson path on lakelet's breast!

Woodlands gay in autumn dyes,
Stealing hues from sunset skies;
Maple, walnut, oak, and pine,
Scarlet, gold, and green combine.

Here a cornfield's bound-up shocks

Gaudy-tinted foliage mocks;
O'er yon trees, a sloping plain,
Decked with stacks of hay or grain.

Fruitful earth has ceased to bear,
Rest is painted on the air;
Hope fulfilled, with glory crowned,—
Vanishing as soon as found.

Windows in yon little town,
Send their sunset flashes down;
Bells from yonder spires disclose
That this picture means "*Repose.*"

The Two Little Angels

A little cradle swinging low,
And rocking gently to and fro;
A new-born soul lies nestled there,
A new-born heart, to learn despair.

Another life has wakened here,
To love or hate, to hope or fear;
And o'er that cradle angels bend—
The spirits that each life attend.

God's Angel waits to help and bless;
But Evil, closer, tries to press;
For strife commences at our birth,—
'Tis but the heritage of earth.

Sleep! little baby, while you may;
For sleep may flag, perchance, some day.
O mother! pray that Good prevail,
That Evil's wily schemes may fail!

The sleeping baby smiles to hear
God's Angel whispering in its ear.
The other Angel comes anear,
And baby's face is crossed by fear.

の

"I bind Truth on thy brow, dear child,
To make thee earnest, honest, mild."
"And I will teach thee cunning speech
When truth thy purpose cannot reach."

"I give thee Love, to comfort thee;
I promise friends and sympathy;
If Evil's bane shall mar thy life,
Love's ministry shall soothe its strife."

"And I shall show thee love grown cold,
Friends treacherous, and hearts grown old;
I'll prove that friendship's but a name,
And love, a quickly burned-out flame."

"I offer Heaven, and peace, and rest,
If thou wilt live and love thy best.
Cling close to Christ, with steadfast trust,
And Evil cannot harm the just."

∽

At rest! and closed the weary eyes!
No more can sin or grief surprise!
What reeks it, did he laugh or weep?
"God giveth His beloved sleep"!

Larghetto[9]

Rubinstein's Ocean Symphony[10]

Allegro-Maestro

Thou art so grand, so wonderful, O Sea!
In all thy depths and whispering mystery;
Forever chafing 'gainst thy destiny,
Forever telling o'er thy tale to me!
Thou art the pulsing, throbbing heart of
    earth—
Throbbing in chaos, ere the world had birth;
Still art thou heaving, surging 'gainst her
    girth
With yearning throes, till dimpled o'er

by mirth.

When morning's sun pours forth his
    shimmering light
Thy waves leap up and dance in mad
    delight;
Then croonest songs so softly, gay and
    bright,
My heart, too, sings, forgetting there is
    night.

A change! a cloud! A storm is brewing fast!
How moan the winds! Thy joyous mood
    is past,
Thy fury thunders, and the howling blast
Hurls helpless ships beneath thy waters, vast.

Adagio

Alas! that storms must come,
    And skies grow dull and gray!
There is no gladness but shall die,
    All joys will fade away.
Ah, woe to hearts that love!—
    So soon does love seem cold;
Ah, woe to hearts that hope!
    Hope lives not to grow old!
Pale sky and moaning sea!
    Art calmer grown, to-day?
So spirits, too, shall rest;
    Life will not last alway.
As on thy storm-tossed breast
    Sweet peace dwells once again,
So hearts shall calmer grow,
    After long days of pain.

Allegro

Away with gloom and pain and fears;
    Away with tears!
Our God is Lord of Earth and Heaven:
    By Him are given

All storms, all calms. And in His hand
    Lie sea and land.
Bright waters circling 'round the sphere
    Sing loud and clear.
Stretch golden arms to golden sky;
    God draweth nigh.

Go, wrap the shore in swift embrace
    With shining face;
Go, steal a kiss, and hie thee back,
    Nor leave thy track.
"Thus far, no farther shalt thou go"[11]
    In ebb and flow.

Adagio-Allegro

Roll on, O sea, till time shall be no more!
Beat on thy crags, and woo th'unyielding
    shore!
Black clouds may frown, and hide the
    sun's bright smile,
We know his glory is but veiled awhile.
Let all within thee sing a rapturous psalm
To Him who holds them in His hollow palm.
Let winds and waves their voices lift on high,
The Universe, its King shall glorify.
Ah, heart! my heart, wilt thou alone be
    dumb?
Have these few tempests left thee cold
    and numb?
Behold yon radiant, rosy sunset-flush,
Where sea and sky respond with con-
    scious blush;
'Tis Love that folds them in his warm
    embrace,
And Love is giving thee a resting-place.
"Let the floods clap their hands, the hills
    rejoice."
"Let the sea lift to God its mighty voice."
"Let the round world and all that dwell
    therein,"[12]

To serve the Lord with gladness, now begin.

My Diamond

    Imprisoned ray
Of scintillating light!
That caught the arrows bright
    Of earth's first day,
    And held them fast—
Ray burning ray, till grown
A miracle in stone!
    Breath of the past!

    How then art thou,
We know not; how the light
Congealed through primal night,
    Till glittering now
    A sunbeam's ice!
Swift flashing back the rays
Lent by those earliest days—
    Imprisoned twice!

    Sealed in the earth,
Or 'neath some limpid stream,
Thy sheathed, piercing beam
    Awaited birth;
    And till man bid
Thy spirit break the spell
That locked thy frosted shell,
    Thy light was hid!

    Resplendent stone!
Flinging out rainbow tints,
And living light, and hints
    Of cycles gone!
    Would I could read
Thy tales of other times,
Of other men and climes,
    Since thou wast freed!

Requiem For De Long and His Comrades[13]

Plodding through limitless ice-fields,
　　Famished and fainting and cold;
Ice-needles pricking their vitals,
　　Snow lying fold upon fold,
Gaunt Famine beckons and mocks them,
　　Brave hearts! despairing, yet bold!

Lost! in that blank, sterile region!
　　Lost! 'mid the ice and the snow!
Vistas of glaciers before them!
　　Rivers congeal as they flow.
Tombed in their graves while still living!
　　No hand to soften their woe!

Dying alone! where the tempests,
　　Cruel and cutting, have birth!
Dying! where piercing winds, howling,
　　Send the last greeting of Earth!
Death reigns supreme o'er this desert,
　　Throned in its silence and dearth!
Dead! in this land that is changeless!
　　Dead! with the pole star o'erhead!
Dead! from the pathway of duty
　　Brave spirits sunward have fled!
Ah, woe! to the homes that are empty!
　　And the hearts that are weeping their
　　dead!

Prince Louis Napoleon's Requiem[14]

Toll! toll! all ye English bells!
　　In England's cause a prince is slain!
Toll! like a sob that swells and swells,
　　Our sighs shall echo the refrain!
Toll! toll! for a son is gone—
　　A widow's son,—like him of old,
Cut down amidst life's rosy dawn,
　　Her vanished past's last link of gold!

Toll! toll! for the fair, young life
　　Ambition sacrificed to fame;
'Twas valor thirsting for the strife,
　　Nor martyr's crown, nor conscience's
　　claim!

Toll! toll! for in him has died
　　The hope of France's greatest name—
The star that twice beamed far and wide,
　　And twice set, 'neath dark clouds of
　　shame!

Toll! for in this adopted son
　　Would Britain heal the blow she gave;
That he whose life she had undone
　　Might find redress e'en in his grave!

Toll! toll! 'midst our honored dead
　　Our foster-child's remains we lay;
In England's cause he fought and bled,
　　And England shall this tribute pay!

Was It a Dream?

I had a dream last night, a troubled dream:
Methought I sailed and drifted down a
　　stream
That bore me to the sea; my little craft,
With all my treasures filled, both fore and aft,
Sailed on. It dipped and dipped, like
　　fluttering bird
O'er dancing waters tipped with foamy
　　curd.
I was so happy that I sang with glee;
For I had her I loved, and all I owned,
　　with me.
And skies were calm, and summer airs
　　were sweet,
All life was joy, all happiness complete.
On, on we sailed, my dearest love and I;
We left Past behind. Beyond lay Destiny,

Far in the blue expanse,—a "promised
    land,"
Where summer never wanes, by south
    winds fanned,
Where flowers bloom ever, and where no
    decay
Steals o'er the forests till they fade away.
We knew no fear, we left behind all pain,
One steered my barque,[15] whose help is
    ne'er in vain,
And skilfully I sailed my bonny boat.
But suddenly a squall arose and smote
And lashed my skiff, as if in angry fray.
She strained and plunged like an affright-
    ed steed,
Whose fright to bit and bridle gives no heed.
I furled my sail and grasped my clinging
    wife,
How helpless now to save that precious life!
Yet, as we tossed and sank through piled-
    up waves,
I cried: "I have Him at the helm, who saves;
And this, a trusty craft, though weighted
    now
With all our treasures, from the stern to
    bow."
I flung them one by one into the sea,—
Our household gods! Oh! what were they
    to me
Compared with life; compared with that
    dear love
That still was mine? Was pride, was hope
    above
Our lives? Were wisdom and philosophy,
Or e'en ideals worth our lives, that I
Should freight our bark with them, and
    with them sink?
So, ruthlessly I flung away each link
That fettered. And the One who held the
    helm

(Though fiercest billows threatened to
    o'erwhelm)
Guided us safe, from rocks that would
    have wrecked.
The storm abated, and the sea was flecked
With foam,—like spotted serpent writh-
    ing still.
We had escaped—we were not saved, until
We flung out all we fixed our hearts
    upon—
All that our future days seemed builded on.
They were the lawful treasures of our hearts,
That we had culled and earned in worldly
    marts;
Yet, they had weighted us, and clogged us
fast; But, yielding them, our Helmsman
    saved at last.

Ocean Phases

A quiet sea, all studded o'er
    With golden gems from the morning
    sun,
Whose deep blue depths, with mystic
    whisper,
    Breathe the tale that is never done.
A placid sea, all dimpled o'er
    With dents where the soft south
    breezes play,
All glowing bright, in the noontide light,
    And sprinkling high thy frothy spray.

A plashing sea, where white-caps dance
    And crest the waves, like snowy birds;
Now stealing tints from the sunset glow,
    Now curling in, like milky curds.
And swelling waves that, leaping over,
    Send silvery foam o'er satin sands,
Whose opal hues are bright or hidden,
    As ebb or flow of tide demands.

An angry sea, that wider, higher,
Its black, impatient, water throws,
Whose dashing billows heave and toss—
The tone a maddening roar now grows!

Till wind and wave, with fearful might,
Combat, and hiss, and writhe for power;
The winds hurl back the angry waves,
That seethe, and boil, and lash the shore.

Then calm again, O changeful sea!
Each ripple tipped with lucent light;
While o'er thy breast a shining path
Illumes the darkness of the night.

De Profundis[16]

Father, we know not why the way is dark.
We slip and fall;
We lose our all;
And life seems drifting, like a helmless bark.
Be Thou our stay!
Turn night to day!
And light our darkness with a heavenly spark!

Father, we know not, ofttimes, right from
wrong.
Show us Thy way;
Help us to say:
"Thy will be done." Lead us along!
Cheer every heart!
Bid fears depart!
And help us turn our sorrows into song!

The Seven Last Words[17]

The hour is come!
Christ prays alone upon the mountain top,
Whilst they who love him sleep. And,
drop by drop,
Great beads of agony roll down upon the
sod—

The human nature wrestling with the God.
"Father, if possible, remove this cup;
Yet, if thy purpose bid me drink it up,
Thy will be done!"

From judgment-hall
To Calvary, the Son of Man is led;
A crown of plaited thorns upon his head.
They scourge, revile, and crucify our Lord;
Yet, at their buffetings he speaks no word—
When mocked by Roman, spit upon by
Jew—
Save: *"Lord, forgive; they know not what*
they do!"
This prayer is all.

Nailed to the tree,
Our Saviour hangs between two com-
mon thieves;
And one, touched by his love, repents,
believes,
Reproves his fellow for his blasphemy,
And humbly prays: "O Lord, remember me!"
The suffering Saviour turns his pitying eyes
On him, and says: *"This day, in Paradise,*
Shalt thou meet me!"

With fear oppressed,
'Mid jeering soldiers and blaspheming crowd,
The friends that love him, near his cross
are bowed.
Christ sees his mother's heart pierced by
his woe,
And John, the loved one, shrinking at
each throe;
Commits her as a sacred charge to John,
And to his mother cries: *"Behold thy Son!—"*
Love's last bequest.

Then on his soul

Falls the world's sin, and man's disgrace,—
Foul cataclysm that hides the Father's face!
Alone, his human heart must bear the
    weight,
And curse, and guilt his sufferings expiate.
"My God, my God, hast thou forsaken me!"
His human nature cries, in agony,
        While thunders roll.

        Like patient lamb
On Jewish altar laid for sacrifice,
He pays his life-blood—our sins' awful price.
Through all the pains that rack his tor-
    tured frame,
No groan escapes. And when the wounds
    inflame,
No murmur, no complaint, till the heart
    burst,
And his first cry of suffering comes: *"I thirst!"*
        Then he is calm.

        Behold! 'Tis done!
Back to the Godhead, from the sacrifice,
Divinity, the conqueror, shall rise,
With human body deified. The Son
Shall reign with Father, Spirit, three in One:
"'Tis finished, in thy hands my spirit take!"
Earth trembles, darkness falls, the dead
    awake.
        Pardon is won!

Scherzo-Allegro-Vivace[18]

Why I Love Her

My ladye is faire wi bonnie blue eyes—
    As blue as ye skies above her,
With never a cloud in their sunny
    depths;—
    But this is not why I love her.

My ladye has haire like a web of golde,
    Where ye sunbeams love to hovere;
My hearte in its meshes is tangled
    faste;—
    But this is not why I love her.

My ladye has lips, like a dewy bud
    Whose petals enfolde and covere;
And chekes, like a fragrant, blushing
    rose;—
    But this is not why I love her.

My ladye's voice is so winning and sweet,
    That all who heare it, discovere
Her hearte is as tender and pure and true;
    And this is just why I love her.

Midsummer Day Song

Thank the Lord for a day so sweet,
    And for skies so clear and blue!
For breezes that chase the whispering wheat,
    And rumple the hay-fields, new!

Thank the Lord for a day so fine,
    While the cherries hang ripe and red!
My soul is drunken as with new wine,
    And the birds are mad, o'erhead!

Thank the Lord for a day so bright,
    In the midst of the summer's glare;
When butterflies pause in their zigzag flight
    To sip from the flowers, fair!

Thank the Lord for the honeyed scent
    Of clover and grape and pine!
The lily and rose for the rich are meant;
    But the wild-wood flowers are mine!

A Summer Wind

I sail the piles of fleecy cloud,

O'er azure seas of ether;
I scatter them, like flecks of foam,
    Or drift them close together;
I spread them into gauzy veils
    To hide the sun's bright glances,
And toss them in fantastic shapes
    To please my idle fancies.

I rock the tops of stately trees,
    And set their branches swaying;
I glide and creep, like hide-and-seek,
    Till every leaf is playing;
I sweep the willow's drooping plumes;
    I make the aspens quiver,
The oak-leaves shake the sunbeams through,
    And maples gently shiver.
And when I've left each bush and tree
    In gently waving motion,
I bring the flowers a cooling breath
    I gathered from old Ocean;
I kiss the rose's blushing cheek,
    And fan her perfumed sisters,
And bear away their fragrant breath,
    Whilst they nod to my whispers.

I wander over sunny plains,
    And swing the tasselled grasses;
I linger o'er sweet clover-fields;
    I climb dark mountain passes;
I set great fields of bearded grain
    In undulating quiver,
Till, in the sun they seem to be
    A rippling, golden river.

And then I leave the scented fields,
    And out of very pity
I waft a purer atmosphere
    O'er dusty, crowded city;
The fragrance borne from bud and flower
    Is lost in reeking alleys;

But still I bear a purer air
    To hut as well as palace.

To many a weary, restless one
    I bring refreshing slumber;
As ministering spirit, go
    To sick-beds without number;
And then to roll a bursting cloud,
    I gather all my powers,
And thirsty fields and dusty streets
    I bathe with summer showers.

To Somebody

I love thee, Dearest!
    Let my heart speak out,
And ring the happy utterance of my love
    Full free, without a doubt.

I love thee, Dearest!
    And my woman's heart
Tums to thee as a flower turns to the sun,
    That doth her warmth impart.

I love thee, Dearest!
    And that love has filled
The empty shrine, left desolate enough
    By love long stilled.

I love thee, Dearest!
    With whole-hearted love,
That puts thee first, in thought and act,—
    All else, above.

I love thee, Dearest!
    Will thy love hold true?
In sweetest pain, I trust my heart again
    To love, to hope, to you.

Modern Philosophy

Mid all the philosophies, labelled as Truth

There's one it were well to impress,
  As a motto for sages, for youth, and for age;
'Tis this: "Nothing succeeds but success."

It seems paradoxical, thus to assert,
  That merit is useless, unless
There be stamped on its face the applause
    of the hour,
Which is needed to give it success.

See the struggles to rise of some poor *inconnu,*
  Waiting vainly for fortune to bless;
We grant he has genius, but fate does not
    smile;
For "Naught can succeed but success."
He may be an Artist, with vision inspired,
  Whose brush Nature's charms can express;
We gaze and admire, but his pictures,
    unsold,
Prove that "Nothing succeeds but success."

Perhaps a Musician, with heaven-lit fire,
  Pours out his full heart. We confess
That his music is fine; but we wait to applaud
Till fashion shall grant him success.

Perchance 'tis an Author who draws from
    his soul
  Deep thoughts that he aims to impress,
Or sweet, subtle fancies, or dreams of the
    heart;
Yet, somehow, he fails of success.

While some fair *dilettante*[19] has made a
    great stir
  By her froth of wit, love, and distress,
She's the furore[20] to-day—though
    to-morrow, forgot,—
For "Nothing succeeds like success."

Believe me, all ye who are tempted to soar
  By genius, your fate you can guess;
For "*vox populi, vox Dei,*"[21] in truth,
And, "Nothing succeeds but success."

Finale-Allegro

A Happy Voyage Symphony

On the Ocean—Allegro

O heaving Sea! our boat on thee
  Skims on, like flying arrow;
She flits and darts, whilst happy hearts
  Scarce know the decks are narrow.

Against the keel, and on the wheel,
  The sea, unceasing, splashes,
In dulcet tones, or restless moans,
  As on the vessel dashes.

Folk-Song—Allegretto[22]

  Our Hearts are gay,
  As day by day
We near the distant haven,
  Whilst love and song
  To us belong,
And joys on memory graven.

  Come, watch with me
  The sparkling sea,
With myriad mermaids, dancing
  To Triton's horn.
  Bright gems adorn
Their brows, in sunlight glancing.

Love Song—Adagio

O restless Sea! O golden Sea!
  My Love doth read thy depths with me.
As gaily as thy ripples play,

So my Love's heart is blithe and gay!

As deep as Ocean's waters roll,
    So lie the depths within her soul!
As restless waters kiss and blend,
    Our hearts and lives together tend.
Fear not, dear Love, to trust to me
    The gem thou guard'st so tenderly;
These arms shall shield thee from all harm,
    My Love surround thee like a charm.

Land! Ho!—Allegro-vivace

What, ho! that call? How hasten all
    To gaze on the horizon!
Against the sky, we can descry
    A spot to rest the eyes on.

'Tis land, at last—the voyage, past,—
    The birds fly out to meet us.
'Tis "home, sweet home,"—no more to roam;
    There dear ones wait to greet us.

Oratorio of "Israel in Egypt"

I heard the singing of a mighty throng;
Methought I stood 'midst Israel when
    their song
Of glad, exultant freedom swelled and tossed,
Like surgings of that sea they had just crossed.
The Lord had saved them by His mighty
    arm,
Had gone before and shielded them from
    harm.
Their bondage o'er, their cruel tyrants slain,
They sang with streaming eyes: "The
    Lord shall reign."
Above them hung the monument of
    cloud;
The women danced; the hoary men were
    bowed;

Behind them lay their slavery and their past,
Before them hope was beckoning at last.
The Lord had led them with His own
    right hand,
And He would guide them to their
    "Promised Land."
Triumphantly they sang the grand re-
    frain—
Moses and all the hosts:—"The Lord
    shall reign."
They sang in rapturous chorus "how the
    Lord
Had triumphed gloriously, how His word
Sent dole and plagues on Egypt, till the king
Bade them depart; and how the Lord did
    bring
His children through the depths of the
    Red Sea,
Whose waters swallowed up the enemy,
When he had dared pursue." And yet again
The hosts of Israel sang: "The Lord shall
    reign."
Methought I stood with them and heard
    their song,
And heart and thought were swiftly
    borne along.
Could these "redeemed and chosen of the
    Lord"
Murmur and fear so soon, and doubt His
    word?
And cry: "We thirst," and "Wilt Thou
    starve us yet?"
And look to Egypt's flesh-pots with regret,
Scarcely one Sabbath after? And in vain
Moses reminded them: "The Lord shall
    reign."
Oh, faithless human hearts whom God
    hath blest,
So ready to sink doubting and oppressed!
What wonder that our wilderness is long,

And weary wanderings to our lives belong?
One burst of rapture for some answered
    prayer,
Then is forgot our Red Sea and His care.
We need, like Moses, tell our souls again,
The Lord hath led us out: "The Lord
    shall reign."

Oratorio of "The Messiah"[23]

An Angel came, and whispering to the Seer,
Bade him heed well the voices of his soul,
Attuned to measures whose sonorous roll,
Chaotic, waited his attentive ear.
"Write, whatsoe'er thy genius bids thee hear,
In tender cadences and swelling tones."
Then Music, such as brings high heaven
    near,
With sighs and prayers, and paeans and
    sad moans,
Burst on his ravished consciousness, and
    taught
His pen t' inscribe these symphonies
    intense,—
For music is the soul's sweet utterance.
The rhythmic thoughts embodied he,
    and wrought
Messiah's story through each thrilling strain,
Till homesick souls hear their own
    tongue again.

Treasure-Trove

A leaflet came fluttering earthward,—
    Amber, with carmine wings;
Nature's death-angel, the hoar frost,
    Droves of these wanderers brings.

A feather came drifting toward me
    A flake from the azure sky,
That a bluebird returning southward,
    Dropped as it flitted by.

I wandered along where the sea-drift
    Scallops the tawny sand;
A shell, like an ocean rose-leaf,
    Lay on the pearly strand.

A thought came hurrying by me,
    Lured by my treasure-trove,
I grasped it ere it had vanished—
    So swiftly these spirits rove.

As leaflet and feather and sea-shell
    Trace what has come and passed,
Naught but our works and our bounties,
    These transient lives, outlast.

Frühlingslied[24]

Joyous Spring has come again,
Spreading verdure o'er the plain;
Golden sunbeams waken earth
To her glorious new-birth.

Through the budding woods we hear
Easter carols, loud and clear;
Merry songsters chirp and sing,
Heraldings of early Spring.

Dainty wild flowers show their heads,
Peeping from their mossy beds
Tiny gems to deck earth's breast,
Till in living green she's dressed.

Ferns their plumy crests unroll,
Opening, like folded scroll:
Nodding to the wild flowers fair,
Chivalrous and debonair.
Fruit-trees, bare awhile ago,
Look like drifted, scented snow;
Cherry, peach, and apple bloom
Fill the air with sweet perfume.

Grass each day becomes more green,
Giving earth an emerald sheen;
And the streamlets flow along;
With a merry, rippling song.

Folded into tiny buds,
Bathed in sunbeams' golden floods,
Forest trees their leaves unclose,
Gently as a blooming rose.

Every leaflet, folded down,
Droops like fuchsias, newly blown;
Till the sun and winds have given
Strength to tum their heads toward heaven.

Then the sun-rays filter through
To the beds of violets, blue;
Rest in flitting, golden spots
On the shy forget-me-nots.

Autumn

How glow the hills with yellow light,
    Through all these Autumn days!
The sunlight drops, like molten gold,
    Through mellow, lucent haze.

It turns the gaily colored woods
    To red and orange flame,
And sets their gorgeous tinting off,
    Like pictures in a frame.

The fringed gentian nods its head
    To scarlet cardinal;
And blue lobelia scarcely peeps
    At golden-rod, so tall.
The living green of Summer time
    Has ripened with decay,
And decks the toil-worn, weary earth
    With this last bright bouquet.

The oak's carbuncle glow is set
    Beside the hickory's gold;
And scarlet sumac, chestnuts brown
    Round crimson dog-wood fold.
I ofttimes think the Autumn glow
    That dying forests wear
Is like the smile dead faces have,
    When freed from life's de pair.

Indian Summer's Aftermath

O dreamy days that linger
    With trace of Summer yet;
So soft, so mild, so mellow,
    Though breathing a regret!
Ye come, like farewell kisses,
    When love must soon grow strange;
That cling with painful fervor,
    And bode the bitter change.

Ye come, with added glory
    Of red and amber sheen—
The Summer's ripened beauty,—
    To supplement her green.
Ye pour this glory on us,
    In these sweet days of rest,
That our regret may deepen
    To find the last, the best.

O peaceful days, and golden!
    Ye call back Summer flowers;
For daisies and red clover
    Peep out to count your hours.
'Midst golden-rod and asters
    They wander, wondering
To see the Autumn banners
    Beneath the skies of Spring.

So into hearts well ripened
    Spring joys may bloom again,
And tangled cares and losses

Find hope amid their pain.
That clover is the sweetest
   Which blushes in the Fall;
That happiness, completest,
   Which comes the last of all.

November

Summer leaves all scattered lie,
Under the cold, white, wintry sky,
Shriveled and brown, like the empty
   shells
That butterflies leave for sunny dells.
Heaped in the hollows by the blast,
Like phantom spirits of the Past.

Trees of Summer glory stripped,
Living green with sunbeams tipped,
Ye toss your gaunt, bare arms around,
With hideous creaking, whistling sound;
Whilst piercing winds sweep howling by,
With wailings like a lost soul's cry.

Hushed is cricket's blithesome chirp,
Katydid, and tree-frog's quirp;
And all the droning harmony
That thrilled the soul on Summer-day
Now is stilled; nor voice of bird
In all the lonely wood is heard.

Brown of earth and gray of sky
Chill the heart, oppress the eye,
Speak of gloom and death and dearth,
Of fading hopes and change on earth.
Sad, we turn from Nature's sadness,
Looking now within for gladness.
Now the ruddy, glowing coals
Warm our bodies, thaw our souls,
Till with talk, a book, or sewing—
Whilst cold winds without are blowing—

We find comfort, hearts grow lighter
By the contrast, homes seem brighter.

The Christmas Bells

Oh the gladsome bells of Christmas,
   Ringing through the frosty air!
Chiming, ringing, singing, rhyming!
   Driving out all thought of care!

Merry Christmas bells! proclaiming
   Joyful news of "Peace on Earth,"
Swelling on the air, and telling
   Tidings of a Saviour's birth.

Prayerful bells of Christmas morning!
   Making spirits upward soar,
Winging prayers, and heavenward bringing
   Hearts that thought to pray no more.

Joyful bells! that ring a paean
   To our resurrected King,
Pealing gladly, while we, kneeling,
   All our adoration bring.

Meer-Schaum[25]

Fit emblem art thou of our life, O Sea!
O restless, changeful, calm, tempestuous
   Sea!
Now swelling high with angry, fretful surge;
Now singing, gay; now moaning a sad dirge.

Life with its changes and vicissitudes!
Life with its calms, its storms, its angry
   moods!
The throb of life is in each pulsing wave,
As, rolling in and out, thy sands they lave.
On thy impressive surface glow the hues
That thy surroundings shed, like gentle
   dews:

The green and gold of hope; the blue of
    peace;
The "couleur rose,"[26] when clouds and
    tempests cease.

When clouds, like a dark Providence, collect,
Thy chafing breast their gloom will soon
    reflect;
As hearts, despairing, throb and cry aloud,
Thy ashen surface fronts the dripping
    cloud.

As though thou wert earth's mighty,
    pulsing heart,
Whose veins and currents permeate each
    part,
Our restless hearts find prototype in thee,
And in thy ceaseless plaint, find sympa-
    thy.

The Fairies' Revel

'Twas New Year's Eve, the last of the old
    year,
When fairy folk and brownies do appear;
The earth was decked in robes of bridal
    white,
And the young moon hung out her
    silvery light;
Old Boreas proclaimed throughout the
    land
A summons to collect the fairy band.

From hill and glade they came with elfin
    glee,
To elfish frolic and gay revelry;
They flew in myriads down the North
    Wind's path;
They spread o'er earth, like Autumn's
    aftermath;
Their errand was to hide each wintry trace

With flashing spangles, and 'neath crystal
    lace.
They hung each bush and tree with spar-
    kling gems,
Till all the branches looked like diadems;
The crystal-coated boughs and sprays,
    entwined,
Cathedrals seemed, with dome and spire
    combined;
The roadside weeds, that erst were brown
    and bare,
They hung with frozen dew-drops, pure
    and fair.

The golden-rod, shorn of its summer
    glow,
That nodded ragged heads above the
    snow,
By magic wands transformed, is standing
    now,
Rich jewel-plumed, fit for a monarch's brow;
And naked stalks, where shriveled asters
    hung,
Are crystal wands, with flashing stars among.

Wild carrot flowers, dried to tiny nests,
They filled with snow. And on the fences
    rests
A fringe of icicles, wove by these sprites,
That gleams beneath the moon, like
    diamond lights.
The withered heads of sumac, on bare stems,
They turn to scepters, crested with bright
    gems.

At midnight, when Time ushered in his
    bride,
The earth was radiant, and far and wide
The trumpet tones of Boreas rang out:
"Come, fays and sprites! come, dance

and sing and shout!
Come, with your frolics make the welkin
    ring!
A glad New Year to one and all I bring!"

The morning came-the sun sent gleams
    and glints
Into each crystal, and gay rainbow tints
Flashed out from bush and foliage and
    fence;

But all the fairy folk had vanished
    thence,
Leaving their gems to prove they had
    been here
To welcome in another glad New Year.

Marguerite E. Easter (1840-1894)

Marguerite E. Easter was born in Virginia in 1840, but made Baltimore her home.[1] Easter was a founding member of the Club and presented several of her pieces at meetings. Her poems were published in journals including *Southern Magazine* and *Eclectic Magazine*. Two years before her death, she collected her poetry into the book *Clytie and Other Poems*. Easter's work was well-regarded by the regional literary establishment throughout her lifetime. Several articles about her appeared in the *Baltimore Sun* and she was included in several anthologies and encyclopedias of Southern writers. Her obituary noted that while Easter was "not as prolific as many of [the] verse-makers of the day, her work was far superior in quality and finish, in character and motive, to much and has attained far wider celebrity."[2]

The poems included in *Parole Femine* highlight the lyrical nature of Easter's poetry. Her references to nature and mythological allusions deepen the emotional impact of her observations and her interactions with others. She also experimented with a variety of poetic forms, including the sonnet, roundelay, and alexandrine.

During the time period in which Easter was writing, women wrote poetry that embodied their sense of sexuality and the suffering that came along with being a woman. According to Yopie Prins, "'*the poetry of woman*' is both the performance and the perpetuation of that suffering."[3] —S. Johnson

Selene[4]

Selene, thou art
As fair to-night, as erst of old, when men
Adorèd thee with mystic rite in glen
And temple grove. Lo! thou dost fill my heart
With such enthrallment that the blood doth start
Renewed from it; the ecstasy of ten,
Aye, twenty votaries are in me when
Thou glid'st to my sight.

                              Thy serene eyes
Connect me ever with another life
Than this. I feel that a two-edged knife
Cuts t'wixt the two and bares my scant disguise
To all; for I am one held by the ties
Of the ideal world with old myths rife,
And glory in its great heroic strife
As in thy light.

                          Selene, I knew thee
In that golden life, methinks; and for the sake
Of thee and Crete, my hand will never break
A flower's stem, or wound a shrub or tree;
They are the Dryad's own, or it may be
Themselves that unwittingly I should wake
To tears again. Coy Syrinx,[5] I might take
For a mere reed that any Pan could blow,
With it, lure Echo from her haunts, and slay
Narcissus while the nymph was far away I
Ah, what might I not do!

                          To-day doth grow
A laurel by the brook; how do I know
But it is another young Daphne! Nay,
I know nothing, therefor, dear Light, I may
Believe all things; and do indeed. To-night
Thy radiance fell on a hill-top nigh;
So calm it was! so white! I clomb up high
And enraptured laid me down. O right
In the refulgent sweetness of thy sight,
Laid me down and listened for thy sigh.
So, on Latmos[6] steep did Endymion lie,
And that he might ne'er miss what then he had
Desired death.

                          And waiting thus,
I heard From some far wood the plaining of a bird,
'Twas Philomela's[7] voice divinely sad,
Or that of Orpheus—divinely mad
From Hebrus[8] borne; and while my soul was stirred,

Pan piped in the vale, and thou did'st gird
Thy draperies and flee.

                              Selene, thou art
As fair to-night, as erst of old, when men
Adored thee with mystic rite in glen
And temple grove. Lo! thou dost fill my heart
With such enthrallment that the blood doth start.
Renewed from it; the ecstacy of ten,
Aye, twenty votaries, are in me when
Thou glid'st to my sight.

The Vine Will Planted

"And these?" I asked, "these flowering vines.
    That climb this southern wall?
    I stand here, marvelling
    To see such blossoms fall,
    From where instead should cling
Trumpet-creepers, and homely briar vines."

"He was my only son," answer she made;
    "My sailor boy, my Will,
    The youngest of them all,
    My last sweet babe: and still
    I often hear him call
Me in my troubled sleep," she slowly said.

"And often feel upon my wasted breast
    His soft warm lips. O God!
    They were so soft! They were
    So warm! Thou knowest, God,
    How soft and warm they were,
Those baby lips upon their mother's breast!

"He was a brave and handsome boy,—my boy!
    But he must sail the deep;
    For him nor farm, nor inn;
    He could not calmly sleep
    On land, he missed the din
And dash of billows, and the 'Ship-a-hoy!'

He brought to me the seeds of this same vine
    From sunny foreign lands;
    Just here he planted them,
    My Will, with his own hands.
    It has a slender stem,
This vine—and yet it lives—this fragile vine,—

And he is gone. His ship went down, they say,
    Upon a summer's morn,
    And all the men were lost
    But one, and he was worn
    With years and had been toss't
By life, as by the cruel waves, they say.

"But Will was young and gay and loved still
    His life, and sweetheart, too;
    ("And was she constant?" Nay!
    But mothers' hearts are true.)
Ruth wept—and wed that day
Twelve month; and yet, I think she loved poor Will.
"We must not judge, lest we misjudge the dead—
    And passion flowers
    Above Ruth's gravestone twine;
    More than all these bowers
    Of roses, she prized the vine
Will planted; and one blooms above her head.

"We must not judge," she said, and gently drew
    The pendant buds to her.
    Her scant tears fell on them;—
    Their petals seemed to stir
    At her embrace: "This stem
Is but a fragile stem," she said, "and still 'tis true—

"That it doth live, and he—and he is gone.
    I do not understand
    How this should be, and yet
    The waves were in Thy hand,—
Dear Lord, I will not fret though Will is gone."

Then rising, she led the way to where
　　Thickest the garlands clung,
　　To the rude trellis; there
　　Pausing, from the vines that hung
　　Low down, she pluckèd rare
Blue blooms for me; and then, I left her there—

Herself and Memory; and after took
　　And pressed the flowers
　　And wrote these few sad lines:—
　　"More than all these bowers
　　Of roses, she prized the vines
Will planted,"—beneath them in my book.

Mistress Betty's Pitcher

*Lines to my Great-grandmother's Pitcher—now in my
Possession.*

The pitcher white and blue, bring from the shelf,
　　And move this modern bric-á-brac aside.
Place, *faience*, for this dear old piece of delf,[9]
　　That knew my great-grandfather and his bride.

Pitcher, your swelling bowl was made to hold
　　A satisfying draught, and held it, too!
Things had their uses in those days, I'm told,
　　And men,—was it not so, old white and blue?

Pray make yourself at home, you have the air
　　Of being quite one of the family.
Methinks this snow-bound night suits well a pair
　　Of gossips, such as we propose to be.

With candles lit, and fire brightly burning,
　　We'll journey back into the days of dips.
Into the days when great dames did the churning,
　　Then held assemblies, dressed in satin slips.

Again, a youthful pitcher, you will grace
　　The dresser, grandmamma's special pride.

Or, with cider filled, will hold your place
      And flank the roast, grandpapa's place beside.

You'll hear them talk about the king—perhaps
      Of Washington; and later on, the ire
Of freemen will blaze forth, and in the gaps
      Between the growls of rage, you'll hear the fire

Roar up the mighty chimney, and a shout
      From woods near by, as if the very blast
Was revolutionary!—and without
      One cherished memory of the past.

The changeless wind! O hark! dear pitcher, hark!
      It howls the same to-night, as when men dared
      To fight for conscience sake!—but never lark
That sang in field colonial cared

Less for such things than we do now, yet still
      We like to hear the story when well told.
Proceed. Were all the men of doughty will?
      Were all the women brave, in days of old?

And were they always clad in dignity—
      As see each formal portrait in its frame?
And did my great-grandsire in Arcady,
      "Mistress Betty," always call my great-grand-
         dame?

And did he wear a blue brocaded coat
      With flying skirt, and vest of peach bloom hue?
Three Flemish ells of lawn[10] about his throat,
      Ailes de pigeon[11] puffs, and ribboned queue?

And I should like to know, dear White and Blue,
      About your double, that was wont to stand
By Mistress Betty's salver, and never knew
      The touch of any other mistress' hand.

(Ah, I feel that you are somewhere sighing)
      The maiden at the cottage door looks sad,

(Pitchers like mortals must sometime be dying)
    She's very old and so must be the lad

In lengthy hose and bulgy roundabout,
    Who talks to her beneath the thatched roof.
They have stood there years and years, nor grown stout
    Or thin; most else has changed, death stands aloof

From them and you, and from the castle wall,
    The farmer and his span, the chestnut-trees,
The wind-mill and the fence that gently falls
    To south of them, to one and all of these—

That 'tween the border of primroses, wait
    With an immovable tranquility
The menace of a sometime certain fate,—
    He seems to grant a strange immunity

Pitcher, when others sit before my fire,
    Bethink you how, in former days, I came
And talked to you, about my great-grandsire,
    And Mistress Betty, and, then name. My name

Among the dames and grand dames of my race,
    And in some kindred mind, dear White and Blue,
As in your comer cupboard, make a place
    For me, Pitcher, I leave it all to you.

The Face of Rafaeta

It is a winter's night without, and shriller, fiercer wind
Ne'er blew from Arctic coast than in these mountain fastness' find
A lurking place; but in my chamber curtained close, I hear
No sound of raging storm or vengeful blast brigading near,
For far remote I roam to-night 'neath Southern sapphire skies,
And tranced gaze into the rapt responseful dreamful eyes
Of Rafaeta:—aye, many thousand miles am I away,
Who sit before this ashwood fire and write this roundelay![12]

Aye! many thousand miles away, the broad and black lagoon,
Upon a pulseless breast reflects the crimson tropic moon,

And on the sloping hills of Caliente,[13] and on the white
Dismantled towers of Cartago I view her dazzling light.
Beyond, the Cordillera shows a background dimly dark,
But its peaks unnoted are,—I only think to mark
The subtly odored lilies—the lilies ruby red
That burn amid the dusky braids upon Rafaeta's head.

And bending down to stir the embers, in their depths I see
Not the flickering flames- but lilies holding up to me,
Chalices of sentient sweetness that silently unfold,
And lo! the face of Rafaeta enshrined in lambent gold!
And lo! the face of Rafaeta, with wistful weary gaze
Turns to the place I sit, and as the ashwood's leaping blaze
Dies out, so disappears into the distant realms of space
Rafaeta's lovelit, languid, weary, wistful, twilight face.

Dawn

A whirr! as the wings of the birds were unfolding
    Simultaneous; a prolonged interlude
    In which the faint chirp of a cricket traverses
    The silence; a solo; and the whole solitude
    Bursts into song—vibrate and shrill—overpowering
    From big-trunked trees the monotonous sighing
    Of Dryads, whom light is devoting to darkness
    Again; and the voice of the buds, that are crying
    From the garden:—"Kiss us, Daybreak, O breathe thy
     breath
    Into these chilled bosoms, that through the long night
    Dreamt of thy coming, and now, O grieving with tears,
    Waken to find still absent thy life-giving light."
A rustling of leaves, and a glad leaping of rills,
And the first streak of dawn gilds the somnolent hills.

Dusk

Now almost unseen in the gloaming, is speeding
    A belated bird, whose tremulous swelling throat,
    E'er he shadows his nest in the gloom of the night,
    Essays love's signalling impassioned note
    Of approach:—"I come, sweet, I come! lift up thy wing
    And let me lie close, O close to thy soft downy breast;

I am spent with my flight, and chill with the dew,
And I long, Sweet, I long! O for thee, and for rest."
Now among the green leaves with the deepening dusk
A faint love-in-idleness languor is creeping,
Born of the breathing of roses—enamored
Of the Adonis—Night,[14] who from their pink, sleeping
Bosoms is kissing their hearts, unheeding the fall
Of envious dews, or the gnome-owl's forboding call,—
Or the sting of marauding bees—those fierce rovers
On the sea of sweet-scents, those brigands of blushes—
Romans, that would rob any land of her virgins;
Take the humming-birds' nectar, and the bloom that the thrushes
Sing madrigals to.[15] Now crickets from each lapping leaf
Emerge—fays of the field, brown-doubleted and grey,
To waken drowsy dragon flies, and Dryads hasten
From Thracian[16] valleys where their happy footsteps stray
From dreaming dawn to closing day,—alas, that these
Should only have the crickets' chirp, and tree-frogs' call,
And modish modern-elves, in place of fleeting fauns and Pan,
And possibly a god in masquerade, and all
The classic joys the old-timer knew! Now fire-flies gleam,
Bull-bats[17] wheel low, and daylight seems a faded dream.

A March Day

Grey sky, rigid as a prison's blank stone wall
That has no ray of hope or sunshine piercing thro'.
Winds that have slipped the leash and with hoarse bay pur-
sue
Winter's wan wraith o'er frost-held fen; or yapping fall
On Spring's fresh trail. Suddenly the atmosphere all
Blurred with asteroids of snow, that hither flew
And yon, and instantaneous to tears and view
Dissolved. A sun-burst! and heaven's prison wall
Succumb'd to light!—as that of earth will yet succumb.
A strip of azure sky, and the tweet of wax-wings
In the cedars nigh, and the Arcadian[18] hum
Of bees in maple boughs; then a sunset that brings
Back of the mountain ridge a yellow line of light
That ushers in a starlit moonlit tranquil night.

A Summer Blow

Hast seen the greenwood in a summer's blow?
How the long limbs twist and dip and dangle
And twirl themselves into a tangle,
Thro' which the startled birds dart to and fro,
The while the ragged wind clouds come and go;
And the golden sun keeps shining, shining
On the quivering leaves, their shapes defining
In flick'ring shadows on the ground below.
Hast heard the greenwood in a summer blow?
'Tis like a tilt in tourney, like the clash
Of women's voices, and the merry splash
Of swimmers in the surf; and doth bestow
Upon the agitated air refrains
That have in them—*the drip of former rains.*

Summer's-Farewells

(Local name in Virginia for late wild-wood flowers of Aster genus.)

Unto the complaining woods suddenly they came,
To the fields so desolate but the day before,
To the unsmiling paths and to the hills that wore
Such sullen looks; there was no further need to blame
Nature's improvidence, for lo, where pin oaks flame,
And large leafed yellow hickories sprout with more
Than Spring's abundance seemingly, they bloomed o'er
Her lately bereaved breast. I asked their name—
That suddenly to wood and path and meadow came—
And that on warm upland slopes were white in hue,
But in hollows, where I had thought but shadows grew,
Were purple-petaled, with calyxes the same
As ragged-robins have, and stamens that became
Golden or red, as by chance of birth they knew
Of sunlit clearings, or of depths where pines renew
Themselves perpetually. I asked their name.

"'Summer's-farewells,' we call them here." Summer's farewells!
They are the final gift of sentiment to sight.
O certainly, the earth should be contented quite
To be remembered so.—"We call them here 'Farewells.'"

O love, I am the field, the wood, the path, the hill
Before these come. Alas, I bide thy coming still—

Who have been gone so long, so long. E'en summer days
Send back greeting to the earth they loved of late,
But thou abidest in silence, and I must await
Thy recognition. Hateful clime! whose woodland ways
No Summer's-farewells have;—I am that clime that stays
Wrapt in November's loneliness, my woods debate
Their dolor, my falling leaves deplore their fate,—
There are no Summer's-farewells to my Autumn days.

"'Summer's-farewells,' we call them here." Summer'sfarewells!
They are the final gift of sentiment to sight.
O certainly, the earth should be contented quite
To be remembered so.—"We call them here 'Farewells.'"
O love, I am the field, the wood, the path, the hill
Before these came. Alas, I bide thy coming still.

A Steady Rain

They say, "It is a steady rain." Aye! faith, I own
It seems indeed to have the gift of constancy.
For days its fogs have hid the purple hills from me;
Hither and yon, like fugitives, its winds have blown
The roses that were my lingering guests, and thrown
Into a prone helplessness that grieves the sight
The grass and tall stalk'd growths. Another weeping night
Is drawing nigh, and the despairing sky hath shown
No sign of clearing up; the earth hath sadder grown
Perceptibly, in these last days of steady rain.
A subtle something 's gone, that will not come again
This year;—in Nature as in man so have I known
All storms to work. Good-night, the fog creeps slowly down,
Obscures the vale, and shuts from view the mountain town.

Oracles Ye Were—And Are!

Oracles ye were,—and are! In mid-air to-day
Flocks of wild geese, whose spreading wings were set
On the blue bosom of the sky, with loud honks met.
Cried "Comrades, good cheer! we head for Bressay Bay!"[19]
Then flapped their wings and with loud honks hove away.

One that lagged—preening her plumage of the fret
Of travel—dropt a cygnet feather, which I set
Within the pillow that beneath my head I lay.
Oracles ye were,—and are! The feather your breast
Had shed in flight, wafted to earth, was augury
Propitious the Sibyls taught,—on this faith I rest,
Assurèd that some gracious day will bring to me
That which my heart desires most; till then I let
Myself: remain content,—the gods will not forget!

Other, Other Days

Other, other days will come; other days—
        But not for me.
And laverocks[20] will pipe their tuneful lays,
And roses flaunt their white and scarlet rays—
        For thee, for thee.

Instead of which the autumn leaves pertain
        To me, to me.
I feel myself one of their countless train,
Swept by the wind across a barren plain,
        Away from thee.

Other, other days will come; other days—
        But not for me.
And thou perhaps wilt seek the purple haze
Of other eyes, and let their depths erase
        My memory.

But do not quite forget the heart that gave
        Itself to thee
Before those other days. In my lone grave
I could not sleep, if I should fail to save
        One hour to me.

One hour from out the other, other days
        That are for thee;
Wherein thou'lt see nor bud, nor hear the lays
Of bird, but give thy yearning backward gaze
        O love, to me.

The Nights are Best

The nights are best; aye, better than the days;
It is with joy I lay me on my bed;
Dispose my pillow so, and with my arm
        Beneath my head—

Welcome the sweetest thoughts I ever have,
(From which all knowledge of the day has fled)—
And fancies of them born, and with my arm
        Beneath my head—

Sink—dreamful, dreaming to my nightly rest—
Whereto, sometime, methinks I shall be wed
For aye, upon my pillow so, and with my arm
        Beneath my head.

I would have it thus,—the red dawn shining
On my face; without a good-bye—dead—
(Good-byes are useless sorrows) and with my arm
        Beneath my head.

Clara Badger Newman Turner (1844-1920)

The literary world has long praised the poet Emily Dickinson. The works of her cousin, Clara Turner, however, have remained in the dark until now. Born Clarissa Badger Newman, Clara was orphaned at a young age and raised in Amherst, Massachusetts by her uncle Edward Dickinson and his wife, alongside their daughter Emily. In 1869, Newman married Sidney Turner of Connecticut. The couple had no children and divided their time between Norwich, Connecticut and Baltimore.

Turner joined the Woman's Literary Club of Baltimore in 1893 and remained a loyal member for over twenty years. She appeared in programs hosted by a variety of committees, including the Committee on Art, the Committee on Essays and Essayists, and the Committee on Modern Poetry. According to the November 1983 Club meeting minutes, Turner produced her own "Personal Recollections of Emily Dickinson," and brought before the club "the life and personality of the author, with vivid and affectionate interest and regard."

Turner's only known publication is a book of poetry titled, fittingly enough, *Mail from Nowhere*. Small in size but wide-ranging in subject matter, it appears to have been privately published in the late-nineteenth century. Like her more famous cousin's fascicles, the book may have been circulated only to close friends; a single copy is held in Harvard's Houghton Library.

The familial connection with Dickinson inevitably invites comparisons between the two poets' work. Like Dickinson, Turner uses simple language and direct address in the treatment of her subjects. Turner, however, conveys a deep contentment with domestic life as well as an abiding faith in God wholly absent from Dickinson's work. While Turner's words have been available to few until now, we invite you to indulge in the poetry of this special club member. Within the poems that follow, you'll find that Turner was a pious woman, a celebrator of nature, and a romantic with a sense of humor. —J. Fury

From *Mail from Nowhere* (1900)

From what station the mixed train of thought contained in these pages leaves, I cannot tell. I only know that nearly all these little verses have arrived at the depot of my own mind in my soundest sleep, so disturbing me by their command to be recorded that, with almost closed eyes, I have written them down on any piece of paper at hand, and gone back to immediate sleep again. Very rarely have I changed a word, and it is to know why these little messages have so come that I send them out to my friends for answer.

– The Author

Revelation

I saw a Summer Sunset,
　　A comma in the sky
In dashing, daring colors
　　No brush would ever try.
A five-lined bar of color
　　At one side—a little way—

With opals running up and down
Like angels at their play.
A flash-light from the West
Lighted all the circle round;
The mountain-tops the couriers.
　　Could grander way be found
To carry glory messages
From Heaven's golden light?
　　The words—a Summer Sunset
On a simple Summer night?

Reverie

O, Moon! Are there realms beyond thy
　　light?
Secrets we do not know?
Could we reach to your lips and listen to hear,
Would you whisper, sweet and low,
Of beautiful things we long for so,
And have missed,—since God has willed it
　　so?

We wish we *dared* to wish we knew.
Has earth a bribe we can offer you?
But then would Honor be gone from thy
　　light!
And dishonored moon would be darkness of light,
And Night would be always—Night!

Motherhood

It had a gift to give, nor could
　　It live to give again—
The gift of Love, in setting sore of pain,
　　A Child to earth!
The boundless mother-love of Heaven
　　Returned—the priced to pay
Of such a gift—the sacrifice again
　　Of Love to Birth!

The New Year

Thou hast opened thine eyes to a new, strange thing;
Thou hast opened thine ears to hear bells ring
    To the birth—to the birth of a year.
Thou hast opened thine heart with those who pray;
The dear old year is a yesterday;
    A new, strange thing is here.

To-morrows are all bound close together,
With their varied suns, and winds, and weather.
    Can any one—any one know?
We sometimes wish, "If we only knew!"
We only say, "Happy year to you!"
    And pray it may be so.

A New Lesson

I used to *expect* what I wanted to come,
    And look for it by Life's way.
I walked with a thought of the thing as done,
    And turned my head some other way
That the thing I expected might surprise.
    I viewed that Hope-future with my own hopes's eyes.

But now it is changed—I have learned to reject;
    I have met a strange master in school.
Have learned *not* to look for what I expect;
    Learned to guard my own heart by a new-found rule
Of loving and living in the same old way,
    But expectant-wish to put away.

There is no less love in my heart, I know,
    In this new-found rule for avoiding pain,
It is just because I do love so
    That I fear to meet disappointment again,
And have learned *not* to wait for what I expect,
    To find greater calmness of heart the effect.

The Introduction

Good morning, young! Good morning, old!
I bring you warmth in place of cold.
  The Winter is gone,
  Summer is won;
  I am leading her gently,
  Blushingly on,
 Her beautiful story to tell.

I'm only a hyphen between these two;
  By the sweet name Spring I am
 known to you.
  I am not very long,
  I am young, I am green;
  When summer is come
  I'm no longer seen;
 But I love her,—so it is well.

Widowhood

I am seeking, ever seeking.
 Seeking? Seeking what?
I am roaming, ever roaming.
 Where? I answer not.
I am catching at the cloudlets,
 I question of the wind,
I strain my eyes to see,
 And, fearing, I am blind.
There is a great love somewhere,
 And it encircled me;
There's a mighty mystery,
 A realm I fain would see.
I am seeking, ever seeking.
 You ask me, seeking what?
Yet I must e'er be seeking,
 Though this world hold it not.

Outside My Window

I wonder what people are thinking about
 That go around looking so queer;
I sometimes wish they would tell me,
 And sometimes I 'most think I hear.
With some I suppose it is money,
 And with some it is dinner and tea;
And some look so dreadfully worried
 I know great woe must befall;
And some are so flustered and flurried,
 I feel they can't think at all;
And the girls are thinking about the boys,
 And the boys of the girls, I suppose.
And so I imagine sorrows and joys,
 And the end is—nobody knows.

To A Bridegroom

According to arithmetic,
 One and one are two.
But I've a little secret
 I'm going to tell you.

Cupid hated mathematics,
 And called it stupid prose;
And out of this dislike
 A new equation rose.

I do not understand it,
 But sure it is, when done
By Cupid's calculations—
 That one and one are one!

The Bible too, on Cupid's side,
 Asserts that this is true.
Accept congratulations
 That this truth is for you.

After the Valentine

He says that he loves me,
    And I but smile.
He says he must love me
    All life's while.
'Tis sweet as the sunshine,
    Bracing as wine,
Conquest without battle,
    To know he is mine.
And yet—do I love him?
    Ah! there is the pain,
For the gift of a heart
    Craves a heart back again.

So what shall I do?
This is not for me,
And yet has been given
    For Eternity.
Is it Cupid's mistake,
Or his—or my own?
Any answer is sorrow,
    How to atone!

January the Second

January First promised to protect me.
January First has gone away and left me;
Me—January Second, at the head of all
    this train!
Indeed you'll never catch me in such a
    scrape again!
I can't live many hours; "I feel it in my bones,"
The sad responsibility of all these other ones
Tugging at my heels as tho' their lives
    depended
On their getting right along as soon as
    mine was ended.

It's the way with lots of things—They're
    sort of in the way
If they claim a single minute beyond
    their little day.
You're January Second till the Third
    comes up apace.
And then you just step down and the
    next one takes your place.

We all just have to face it, and have our
    little day,
Without a single question as to any other
    way.
We're on the top a little while, and peo-
    ple read us through,
And then we're gone, and laid aside, the
    best that we can do.

Petition

Father! An enemy is at hand,
Following closely through the land,
    Everywhere I go:
Prompting to evil instead of good;
Leading astray—when oft I would
    Do the best I know.
Father—O Father—guard me!
Guard me from myself!

Strengthen the purpose to do right;
Help me to conquer in Thy might,
    When I would go wrong.
Help me to turn from self to Thee,
From sweet temptation swift to flee;
    I to Thee belong!
Father—O Father—guard me!
Guard me from myself!

Lucy Randolph Cautley (1854-1937)

Cautley was beloved by the community of the Woman's Club of Baltimore. Her name pops up in discussions throughout the recorded minutes of WLCB meetings, where she shares writing of her own or other members, or contributes to the discussion. Cautley made a point of bringing minor poets, especially woman poets, to the attention of the Club. In "A Plea for Small Poets," which she presented to the Club in 1894, she argued that "all singers can not be nightingales. And the nightingale sings only one month in the year, must all the other birds keep silence, all the year round because they are not nightingales? Must we walk through the woods with our ears stopped with cotton wool, and see spring flowers, but not hear the spring songs? . . . we can let the little birds sing."[1]

Cautley herself was a "small poet." She shared many poems with fellow Club members, but only a single poem of hers has been recovered in the publication record. Yet as she argues, her work is not insignificant even though she was less prolifically published than her peers. "Betrayal" is a sentimental poem about young love and bitter betrayal told through the personified voices of a young woman's emotions. Cautley's poem embodies the central themes of sentimental literature, which Joanne Dobson describes as a "cultural discourse" that drew strength from human connection in a dehumanized world and focused on the emotional connection and intimacy between individuals and communities. "Betrayal" focuses on both of these intimate relationships.

Cautley published several essays and opinion pieces in religious periodicals. She was also an aspiring playwright, with at least three plays registered with the US Copyright Office. Scenes from one of them, an adaptation of William Makepeace Thackeray's novel *Henry Esmond*, was performed for members of the Club by Cautley and fellow member and playwright, Louise Malloy during the 1901-1902 season. —T. Brooky and F. D'Aloia

Betrayal (1901)

One day Love came to her: no virgin flame
Blazoned her cheek; for pride and maiden shame
Held o'er her heart's dear secret fast control,
And shuttered all the windows of her soul.
And no one guessed her happy hidden weakness,
Through lowered eyelids and pure front of meekness.
But once she sang, when Joy arose and wove
Into the strain a telltale Song of Love.
And all the little world around her smiled,
By memories of their own fair youth beguiled.
For in her happiness, as in a glass,
They saw their own loves delicately pass.

One day Love went, and none her anguish guessed;
For still she laughed and jested with the rest.
Her fair proud forehead faced the world about,
And every prying peeper put to rout.
Until she sang. Then Sorrow burst his bounds,
And passion's chord broke off in jarring sounds.
All turned and gazed, drawn by a piteous crying,
And saw a broken heart, in her bared bosom, dying.

Ella Morrow Sollenberger (1876-1951)

Ella Morrow Sollenberger was born in Newville, Pennsylvania and later moved to Baltimore with her husband, Lawrence Randall Sollenberger, with whom she had three sons. Inspired by the world around her and her personal relationships, her poems echo her life and experiences. Recaps of the Women's Literary Club meetings in the *Baltimore Sun* and her numerous publications in other magazines and newspapers display both her interest in literature and her wide influence. Her poem "Heritage" was published and reprinted in newspapers across the country, including the *Philadelphia Inquirer* and the *Oshkosh Northwestern*.[1] Her best-known work, however, is "Knitting."

"Knitting" was published during World War I, which had a profound impact on family dynamics as well as world politics. "Knitting" eloquently describes the war's rippling effects on the American home front. This poem struck a chord, appearing in many notable publications, including the *New York Times*.[2] The repetition of the words "knitting" and "thinking" in the poem sets the scene of a woman's agency and role during wartime. The second stanza's evocation of the "spilling" of blood on the battlefields of World War I connects to stanza three's repetition of "killing." In the final stanza, she brings the reader's attention back to the little agency women have during wartime, and their "futile" struggle against anything happening abroad. Ultimately, Sollenberger's word choice and use of repetition in "Knitting" brings the honesty and weight of the poem to the forefront of the reader's attention.

Driftwood and Other Verse, which includes "Knitting," appears to have been published in the 1930s as a compendium of poems that Sollenberger wrote throughout her life. Several others also reveal her sentiments toward war, while others underscore her love of family, especially her children. The collection includes several free verse poems—the only such poems included in this volume—and a few directly address the poetic impulse in ways that show that Sollenberger did not consider herself a *female* poet, but rather a poet without qualifications. —S. Barrett & M. Hultberg

From *Driftwood and Other Verse* (1930s)

Driftwood

On the margin of the deep
With its restlessness, I keep
Tossing, sobbing ceaselessly.

At swelling of the tide,
To thy bosom calm and wide,
Take me to thyself, oh Sea!
Or upon the barren shore
Cast me lifeless—evermore,
Dead and feelingless to be.

Sympathy

Amidst a peopled loneliness,
The burning prescience I possess,
Life sudden sun in greyness drear,
Ere floodgates of the soul arise
In cognizance of meeting eyes.
To thee, released and unafraid,
The thought goes forth but half essayed,
Anticipated in its flight,
To greet in turn with keen delight,
Thy rare unfettered subtlety,
Bestowed without excuse or plea
From hidden place of mind or mood,
Accredited and understood,
For what thy heart or nature wills
The tenor of my own fulfills
And alien judgments cannot mar—
I know—thou—what we are.

Creation

An overpowering, primal fierce desire;
Plasmatic shapes, conceived in holy fire
Of hot unrest in impregnating brain;
A drear, uncertain struggle to attain
While quick, elusive, half formed fancies fill

Long futile days and sleepless nights—until,
In swift, blest travail of the soul,
The poem live—a breathing, perfect whole.

Genius

A chosen few—those who the God-mark
    know,
From starry heights to lowest depths may go
And from the darkness and the creature
    slime,
Pearl laden, rise again to heights sublime.

Pioneers

Strong men, brave men,
You men who blazed the way,
Whose sharpened axes swung,
And notched here and there a tree
Throughout the tangled wilderness,
Stripping it of clinging vines—
Tenacious, opiate faiths,
That caught and held
Halting, stumbling feet.
Men of spirit and of brain,
You who bore, each upon his brow,
A single, steady ray,
Let me follow in your steps
To the trail's end,
Take from your light and try,
Though lonely with your loneliness,
To penetrate a little farther on
Into the dark forest.

Reality

Forth from the Vale of Dreams come he,
Dear face and form seen mistily
Yet all his presence a caress.
Enfolded by his tenderness,
Sweet, unregarded hours are spent
In an ineffable content,
Until the nightmare of the day

Sets free once more upon my way
Ghosts of reality—and then—
To sleep, to dream, to live, again.

Resurrection

Mere mockery, that first fair Spring
    With joyous resurrection rife,
Whose sweet, bright newness could not bring
    Our severed blossom back to life.
A timeless winter, then from sleep
    The floweret, each hid long ago,
Grew into faith and love so deep
    As only deep ploughed hearts can know.

Heritage

My sweet, why do I love thee so?
    Since of my being thou wast part?
For such mere way of nature, no,
    But that so like to him thou art.

Thou hast his form, his face, his hair,
    Like his, the color of thine eyes.
And thy wee rose-bud lips do bear
    His charm of laughter, baby wise.
I cannot think of him away
    Nor feel, as one bereaved, alone,
In thee, he lives again each day
    And thus I have you both, my own.

Renunciation

Ah, Dear, I hold you very dear,
For all the bitterness we bear,
Each day returning.

'Tis just that two so far apart,
Yet bound together, keep the heart
Forever burning.

For love of all we could not know
I would in gladness, bid you go
While deeply yearning.

Yet hold me close nor let me miss
The long expiatory kiss,
Our freedom earning.

It Does Not Hurt to Die

It does not hurt to die—
The long excruciating pain we dread,
Is life—an ebb tide sigh,
A gentle slipping back—and we are dead.

The Joy Killer

Life so full of wonderful things,
    Light and love and laughter sweet,
Holding yet, with shafts and stings,
    Killer of joy, by chance we meet.

Turn we dumbly out of his way
    Covering brightness till he is past;
Hastener of death, his own decay,
    Bearing the brand of his lonely cast.

To—A Friend

A genius for friendship?
You too, my friend—
Because we know
What friendship means
When comes an end
To dreams
And life can show,
Here and there,
A few who care.
But only one or two,
Tenderly platonic,
May mend brokenly

The dream's rent fabric.
Just one or two—
I, maybe,
And you.

Love's Child

At hand, the longed-for, dreaded, fright-
    ened hour,
Two white clad forms, alert and undistressed,
A woman, summoning all her power,
Unflinchingly to meet the world old test.

Man's quick drawn breath in sympathetic pain;
Fierce, impotent desire to share the strife;
At length, the small, free cry that lifts the
    strain,

Then meeting lips in speechless ecstasy,
Fond answering eyes, released from fear:
"How could you, Love, endure all this
    for me?"
"For *you*, believe, 'twas truly nothing, Dear."

The Man with Jonquils

This bleak March day, who rings my bell,
    Old clothes to buy, new brooms to sell?
A hasty "No" lips form to say
    The bargainer to drive away.

The door is opened smallest space,
    Then flung to meet the smiling face
Of man with jonquils, come to town
    In faded hat and suit of brown.

"Jonquils today for twenty cents?
    They grow beside our garden fence."
"Just twenty cents?" "Oh yes, you see
    They're no expense at all to me."

Oh, man with jonquils, what could pay
For glimpse of spring and *you* today!

Rosamond

With last perfect petal in beauty unfurled,
Grown fair for the King—sweet Rose of
    the World.

His Poem to the Sea

Brave plunger in the deep
Thy courage I adore,
Though the tides may sweep
Thee farther from my shore.
Yet never shall be stilled
Your voice from out the sea,
Since strangely thou hast willed
To leave its song with me.

Italy

A living, achieving present
    Rising out of the mold of the past,
Beauty and truth and tawdry sham,
    All into one crucible cast.

Anger and laughter and singing,
    Drear poverty, gorgeous display,
Dignified pride in ancient fame
    And carefree life of each day.

Dear paradox land of sunlight
    Where citrons look up at the snow,
Where littered street or Virgins sweet
    Are all in the charm that we know.

The dream in the mist, Perugia,
    The dance of the lads at Capri,
The lure of old Pisa and Roma
    Will call me again—Italy.

England, 1924

Between the sea and shifting clouds
    Grey gulls wheel in leisured flight
And rest upon the wave worn shelves
    Of chalk cliffs, towering softly white.[3]

From grassy nest, a tiny form
    Goes soaring upward to the sky;
A lark's sweet rapture, trilling down,
    Is caught in rapture where we lie.

With silent sheep, in wattled fold,
    Our world the sweeping Sussex Down.[4]
We feel the poppies' dreamy breath
    And peace in England is our own.

Campane[5]

God cannot be
So far away
When thrice a day
We stop to pray.

At dawn we wake
As slowly swell
The limpid tones
Of matin[6] bell.

The Angelus[7]
Brings pause at noon,
As heads are bowed
And thoughts attune.

L'Ave Maria,[8]

The day is done
And rest and peace
Our benison.

The Stranger Within Our Gate

We Flag-born ones, with our blood-writ-
    ten creed,
    Should welcome give to every pilgrim
    band.
The privilege ours, whose brave fore-fa-
    thers freed,
    for all oppressed, this wide and gen-
    erous land.

Should foreigner, just come within our gate,
    Meet fraud and sneering names of
    "Kike" and "Wop"[9]
With jeers that turn his ready love to heat
    And kill a generation builded hope?

Is it a strange thing that he should rant
    Against such hospitality and scheme,
In secret meeting place, revenge to take,
    With strike and bomb, for every
    shattered dream.

As hosts, 'tis our noblesse oblige[10] to greet
    The stranger at our door with out-
    stretched hand,
To help him see how all we have is his—
    And soon his eager soul will understand.

Bethlehem

So fair he was, the Holy Child
That shepherds stood by mystified
And beasts were still in wonder mild.
One, brooding by the manger side,
Thought it but mete that men should kneel
And lay their priceless treasure there
But in her heart did she not feel
The hurt of thorns[11] that he must bear?

The Empty Stocking Club

A thousand names on tickets
     To give to each seat
Inside the dear old Play House
     Which holds the Christmas treat.

A thousand little children
     Who wait the great surprise
Are led in happy singing
     Before the curtains rise.

A thousand, thousand blessings
     On guests and givers fall
For once a year, 'tis surely here,
     The Christ Child comes to all.

To Maryland Legislators

Good men of boasted chivalry:
Forego thine ancient sophistry,
Of homage and of service fine,
While yet politely ye decline
To lend an ear to honest claim.
Honor would best deserve the name
And prove a vaunted manhood true
That freely grants a rightful due.
Dost fear that such concession might
Deprive you of your tend'rest right,
Protection of the strong right arm,
And bring the fair ones all to scorn?
Displace the creature of your dream,
Unsexed and monstrous as they seem,
Champions brave, and simply note
That womanly women want the vote.

Knitting

Knitting and knitting;
Jacket and helmet,
Mittens and muffler,
Into the mesh of them
Thinking and thinking.

Monarchies crumbling,
Democracies shaking,
The blood of our manhood
Spilling and spilling.
Sorrow and sacrifice,
Fatherless children,
Desolate womanhood
Drudgingly living.

Wanton destruction
That centuries builded.
Nothing is sacred.
Killing and killing.
Passions unbridled,
Lust and despoiling.
What does it matter?
There is no tomorrow.

Crowned heads and statesmen
Round green baize and carving,
For greed and aggression
Precipitate horror.
May the Hell they've let loose
Take their souls in its keeping!

So little, so futile
This work of our fingers
Yet we keep knitting;
Jacket and helmet,
Mittens and muffler,
Into the mesh of them
Thinking and thinking.

The Cross

They bear the sacrificial sign—
Those valiant dead in far flung line—
For lives they gave.
A myriad cross to amplify
The Cross of Him who chose to die
The world to save.

Though once through darkness rang his cry,
"Eli Lama Sabachthani!"[12]
His life he gave.
Today too shall live who there have died
The world to save.

The Lawn—University of Virginia

Leaves falling in gentle shower,
Crimson and gold;
Five minutes to the hour,
The Bell's release from storied room;
Leisurely across the grass,
Students go from class to class,
By colonnade and brick arcade,
Drinking in Autumn's glory;
Beautiful, until a night of snow
Brings beauty new
To roof and bough,
Ephemeral beauty, soon to turn,
In icy sheathes a gracious sheen
In Southern sun.
Then halcyon days;
Magnolia scent;
Maples bursting, feathery red;
Carpet of velvet green
From Rotunda to the Hall;[13]
Cool shade in June;
Long line of black gowned men.
Beloved Lawn!
Always we shall recall
Your ever changing loveliness—
A memory, lingering in the heart,
To soften stress
Of Life's grim fight
In bank or bar or mart.

Blessings

Hand prints on the bath room towel,
   Mud upon the clean white steps,
Buttons off and jagged tears,
   Tossed up rugs and puppy yelps;

Skates and bats about the hall,
   Pillows soiled in bedtime fight,
Pictures crooked on the wall—
   And the boys safe home at night.

Sons

By my sunny bedroom window
   Every afternoon I sew
Waiting for three busy children
   Presently to come and go.
Soon I hear the front door banging
   And a scuffle on the stair,
Calls for shoulder pads and helmets,
   Cries of "Mother, are you there?"

"Look, you see, I've won my Letter.
   "Aren't you glad as you can be?
"Sew it quickly on my sweater,
   "Practice game at half past three."

Here and gone again to field games
   And I'm left alone to sew,
Left a happy, happy woman
   With three sons to come and go.

Inheritance

Why do I fear the wayward turn,
Collapse of will and thoughts that burn
Towards the forbidden, luring thing
For sake of pure adventuring?

Because your mind and temperament
Have from my own, received their bent.
If I have kept the narrow way
It is that you shall never pay
For what I've done with blush of shame—
My son, for me, will do the same.

My Little Son

I begged him hard, in foolish mother play,
Not to grow up but, just for me, to stay
A little, little boy.

The seasons swiftly sped, he would grow tall;
In summer, camp; the gridiron in the fall:
A strong, ungainly lad.

His life choice in a West Point training lay
Yet soon beneath the gold and spotless grey,
I sensed a bitter youth.

Stern years until the day they set him free
And, khaki clad, they send back to me—
A hard, commending man.

Home late, he comes. He's down beside
    my bed
In hollow of my arm, I find his head.
With one free hand, I smooth and
    smooth his hair.
I hear his whisper, "Mother, mother, dear."
"Oh, little, little son."

Ordinary Seaman

I watched my boy go out to sea.
He was so young and fair, could he,
Unhurt and clean, come back to me?

My boy's come back, come back to me.
He's changed—but in clear eyes, I see
The same dear look that went from me,
The day his boat put out to sea.

Spring

In the country where my aunt lives,
    Sweet blossoms scent the breeze;
Out in the fields are little lambs
    And blue birds in the trees.

On the city block where I live,
    "Strawbe'es!" hucksters cry,
And an organ man and monkey,
    Each afternoon, come by.

The Open Fire

Of all the things about our house,
    There's nothing that is quite
So pleasant as the open fire,
    We light each winter night.

As it grows darker out of doors,
    The only things we see
Are just the rising, yellow flames
    And on the couch, us three.
I snuggle close to mother's side.
    Her other arm's round Sue.
She tells the nicest fairy tales
    And Bible stories too.

The time is up at eight o'clock
    And then our prayers are said
And oh, so warm and sleepy
    We hurry off to bed.

Engaged

This is the day he told me.
And so the girl has won?
She's taken only what was hers.
She cannot take—my son.

The Nest

Daily care for helpless need;
Clamoring, hungry mouths to feed;
Aiding strong, young wings to fly;
Last wee speck against the sky—
Now rest but what care I for rest
Within a silent, empty nest!

Crusaders and Critics

Unlike many women's clubs of the time, the Woman's Literary Club of Baltimore did not actively engage in philanthropy or social reform. Individual members, however, certainly did. While well-to-do women were expected to confine themselves to the domestic sphere, within those boundaries they were granted moral authority, and the women of the Club thus spoke out regarding what they perceived to be the moral failings of the era.

Club members also defended women's rights to education, intellectual development, and professional careers. Florence Trail and Mary Noyes Colvin, both largely privately educated, showed themselves to be on par with male scholars in history, literature, and music. Christine Ladd-Franklin was the first woman to complete doctoral coursework in mathematics at the Johns Hopkins University and became a faculty member at Columbia University. Louise Malloy, Emily Emerson Lantz, and Margaret Sutton Briscoe became professional journalists and editors and made a point of representing women's concerns and reporting on women's accomplishments—while also, at times, making fun of them.

Malloy and others also used literary forms including fiction, poetry, and drama as vehicles for addressing societal issues. Katharine Pearson Woods's novels—one of which, *The Mark of the Beast* (1890), we include in its entirety here—offered visions of a socialist utopia that would eradicate economic inequality and promote Christian values.

The works included in this section show that the members of the Woman's Literary Club of Baltimore were both very much a part of and ahead of their times. Many Club members defended traditional domestic values, but they did so with a critical eye. Some lived by example, pursuing independent careers, remaining unmarried, or leading organizations. Still others spoke out boldly in favor of suffrage and women's rights. The range of attitudes offered by Club members is a testament to the diversity of views held by women at the time, and to the Club itself for providing a place to express them. —J. L. Cole and K. Kazmierski

Florence Trail (1854-1944)

Florence Trail appears almost destined to have been an intellectual. She was born into a prominent Maryland family, affording her opportunities not available to most women in her day. She attended the Frederick Female Seminary, the Mount Vernon Institute, and the Peabody Conservatory. In addition to her formal education, Trail was an avid reader. Interestingly, her mother approved everything that she read until the age of thirty-seven, burning the books she did not find appropriate.[1] At a young age, Trail became interested in Italian literature, leading to the publication of one of her most respected works, *A History of Italian Literature*, which King Victor Emmanuel III and his wife Queen Elena of Italy personally praised. She also wrote—voluminously—on the subjects of history, European literature of all kinds, and music.

Trail was a public supporter of the women's vote. She attended suffrage conventions and wrote essays arguing for the vote.[2] Trail cared deeply about the improvement of women. She seemed driven to write and publish critical essays at a time when women were frequently excluded from intellectual discourse.[3] Indeed, an 1888 review in *The Times Democrat* from New Orleans, negatively referred to Trail's writing as "hasty and feminine." Despite this criticism, she continued to do what she loved, exploring and writing about music, history, and literature.

In "History in Literature," and "The Purposes of Music," Trail displays a style unexpected from a female writer in this time: erudite, exhibiting a wide range of reference, and paying careful attention to

historical accuracy. In doing so, Trail combated gender stereotypes. She was capable of a historian's objectivity while also using an American woman's view of the world. She proved, in spite of critics misunderstanding of her, that she was capable of the same intellectual level as men.

Under the Second Renaissance, in contrast, is an excerpt from a novel. Theater in Trail's day was a place where attitudes toward women were transforming. Women became spectacles on the stage, portraying passion and unapologetically drawing attention to themselves, breaking away from the traditional roles that expected women to be quiet and submissive.[4] Trail's novel explores the complexity of navigating the changing roles of women while also providing a fascinating glimpse into the demimonde of the theatrical world of the *fin de siècle*. Alma, Trail's protagonist, is seen as an object of beauty instead of an intellectual, autonomous person, but insists on her artistic vision, moral standing, and theatrical ability. —M. Fazio and A. Hughes

From "History in Literature" (1888)

"Literature and history," Trail writes, "are so reciprocally related that the one is valueless without the other." In this essay, Trail argues that great literature is produced at significant moments in human history. As she puts it, literature "is the exquisite adaptation of the language to the subject matter, not as the work of individual genius, but from the political history necessarily involved in both

the language and the subject." The bulk of the essay traces the historical roots of literature in the classical and early modern periods, beginning with Horace and ending with Voltaire, Diderot, and Rousseau.

Such, of course, is the barest outline of the study of history in literature,[5] and it may not be inapposite to ask, what are the practical results of such a study?

First of all, I would answer myself, were the labor involved in it the only profit to be reaped this in itself would be an immeasurable compensation. Happiness is incompatible with the torpor of the faculties. All work is ennobling, but in the work of the intellect this process is as much more direct as the powers of the mind are infinitely more noble, and its enjoyments incomparably more exquisite than those which the capacities of the body can under any conditions permit. It is in transforming the curse of labor into a blessing a miracle which Divine Power is perpetually performing that men discover the negative character of evil, that without our acquiescence nothing is evil in itself, that there is nothing which cannot be made subservient to higher ends, nothing which cannot be made a stepping stone towards attaining "the measure of the stature of a perfect man."[6] Again, it is by means of labor that man finds his nearest approximation to creative power. And it is in intellectual labor that consciousness, or the power to connect the acts of the mind with the mind itself, is developed. And it is in developed consciousness that men refuse to hold cheap the meaning of their own lives, for, as George Eliot says, "The fuller nature desires to be an agent, to create and not merely to look

on; strong love hungers to bless and not merely to behold blessing. And while there is warmth enough in the sun to feed an energetic life, there will still be men to feel, 'I am lord of this moment's change and will charge it with my soul.'"[7]

But it is not only as a means that such a study is available. "Classical studies are beyond comparison," says Cousin, "the most essential of all, conducing, as they do, to the knowledge of our humanity which they consider under all its mighty aspects and relations; here in the language of the literature of nations who have left behind them a memorable trace of their passage upon earth; there in the pregnant vicissitudes of history which continually renovate and improve society: and finally in philosophy which reveals to us the simple elements and the more uniform organization of that wondrous being, which history, literature, and languages successively clothe in forms the most diversified and yet always relative to some more or less important part of its internal constitution. Classical studies maintain the sacred traditions of the intellectual and moral life of our humanity. To enfeeble them would, in my eyes, be an act of barbarity, an attempt against true civilization, and in a certain sort, the crime of lèse-humanity."[8]

The consolations of literature are inexhaustible. The world's misinterpretation of our best actions, the power of circumstances to thwart our cherished schemes, the irony we see in our own destiny could not be borne with equanimity were it not for the more than refuge to be found in the pleasures of the intellect. Nor is intellectual labor barren of relief for those deeper and more mysterious sufferings of the soul. That men do not yet discern the true significance of the intellect is indisputable. But if, as the revered Wayland taught, "knowledge of every kind has in its very nature a tendency to devotion," it is manifest that in refusing to cultivate the intellect we throw away a priceless means toward accomplishing the end of our creation.

That intellectual labor has been abused affords no ground for argument. There is nothing in the compass of man's capacity that he will not abuse. Look at its influence in individual lives. Where books and ideas are not discussed, personal character in all its length and breadth becomes the subject of conversation. Irrespective of the moral deterioration that is here inevitable, this has a most unhappy effect on the nervous system: it is irritating, it destroys serenity of mind, it takes a large amount of happiness out of life. And, conversely, what if the intellect should be chief among the probationary elements of our present existence? If the victories over the animal propensities of the body are great and affect the development of what we call character, the conflict between the moral nature and the subtleties of human reason must be as intensified in meaning, as it is in suffering. If of those to whom much is given much is to be required, does it not immediately follow that the feeblest consciousness of intellect assumes the character of moral obligation? And as its abuse awaits a fearful punishment, so will not its true and lawful exercise bring with it a pure and bountiful reward?

But it is especially in such a study as the one we have sketched that the larger intellectual influences that affect our status as human beings are found. To aver, as I have done, that literary master-pieces attain their celebrity through the political history involved in both the language and the subject seems to annihilate personal responsibility and ignore individuality. But, in truth, no study can more forcibly demonstrate human accountability. If there is history in literature, it may lessen the burden that is generally thrown on the individual author, but it is to assign the portion due to the individual reader. That time, place and universal culture enter into the composition of every great work, no one familiar with English literature can fail to notice. Froude, in his fascinating history, speaking of Shakespeare says: "Such greatness is never more than the highest degree of an excellence which prevails widely round it and forms the environment in which it grows. No single mind in single contact with the facts of nature could have created a Lear: such a vast conception is the growth of ages, the creation of a nation's spirit: and the poet filled with the power of that spirit has but given it form and nothing more than form. Nor would the form itself have been attainable by an isolated talent. No genius can dispense with experience: the aberrations of power, unguided or ill guided are ever in proportion to its intensity, and life is not long enough to recover from inevitable mistakes. No great general ever arose out of a nation of cowards, no great statesman or philosopher out of a nation of materialists, no great dramatist except when the drama was the passion of the people."[9] Cannot any child see that unless those who read are educated the learned few can play as many jokes on them as they choose, and, as the children say, never be found out? The history of English-speaking people is full of generations which have been either the dupes of erratic genius, or the obstacles to true individual and national glory. And there never was a time when this danger was more imminent than it is today. For the tendency of our civilization to equalize all classes of society takes power more and more out of the hands of the individual, and while his importance diminishes, that of the masses constantly increases. Hence to wield any kind of power, the individual must put forth an energy that is almost desperate; his expressed opinions must be ten-fold as pronounced as his inward convictions. While he thus arrests the attention of the people, they cannot be expected to pause and see through the exaggeration, and the flaw that is ingrained in this advocacy disgusts the practical few, imposes on the unlearned many, and tends to produce morbid melancholy in the two or three who understand and sympathize with the author.

There is no surer sign of the times than the current literature of any given period. When the enthusiastic crowd carried Voltaire in its arms through the streets of Paris and suffocated him with roses, the French Revolution was virtually accomplished. Literature says, "See how wicked a man Voltaire was!" but history says, "Look at the condition of society that could welcome such writings as those of Voltaire!" I ask which of the two is the more just judgment? The whole testimony of History is for virtue and against vice. Whatever literature may boast of her own realm; history constantly declares that the standard of morals is the standard of taste. And while it is true that the great revolving wheel of time must crush and overwhelm all that thwarts the purposes of its revolutions, yet this same record of its mighty cycles is impartial enough to show that often in individual cases the judgment of posterity is far harsher than is strictly just, and that where we stigmatize, we might often weep.

It is with a perfect realization of the expanded scope and magnificent import of history that Buckle in his incomparable "History of Civilization" has said: "To solve the great problem of affairs; to detect those hidden circumstances which determine the march and destiny of nations, and to find in the events of the past a key to the proceedings of the future is nothing less than to unite into a single science all the laws of the moral and physical world."[10] The sublimity of such a glorious, conception is full of awe and solemnity. What self-denials and sufferings are too great if we can but emerge from the basilar instincts that claim us to materialism! Who that is capable of a noble thought can hesitate to rejoice that his fellow-man has given it an utterance to which his faltering tongue and trembling hand were too weak even to aspire? It is a subject of daily, of hourly, rejoicing that such men have lived to unravel the web of events and bring forth from the chaos of unutterable longing and vain strivings, shrouded in a more than midnight darkness, the exalted idea of progress, to be the guiding star of our race, as it is already the hope of noble souls in the long and laborious pilgrimage of humanity toward the unknown end which Providence has marked out for it. Then

> "Heureux qui jusqu' au temps du
> terme de sa vie,
> Des beaux-arts amoureux, peut culti-
> ver leurs fruits!

Il brave l'injustice, il calme ses
    ennuis;
Il pardonne aux humains, il rit de
    leur délire,
Et de sa main mourant il touche
    encore sa lyre."[11]

From *Under the Second Renaissance* (1894)

Against the wishes of her family and the man who loves her, Paul Vandeveer, Alma Macdannald leaves her Southern home to seek a career as an actress in the great city of "Petronius" (likely a stand-in for New York City). After attaining a phenomenal success in a dramatic adaptation of Richard Wagner's opera Tristan and Isolde, *she learns of the severe illness of her younger brother, Frank, and decides to break her contract and return home.*

Chapter IV

Reunion

"Serene will be our days and bright,
And happy will our nature be,
When love is an unerring light,
And joy its own security."
—*Wordsworth.*[12]

Pleasant walks, drives, talks and readings whiled the weeks away. And now the whole family began to breathe freely again, buoyed up by the hope that Alma had forever abjured the hateful stage. Grace, turning over in her own mind what she ought to do if Alma resumed her old place in the family, one day started to say:

"Uncle, perhaps Alma—"

"Intends to stay, my dear," interrupted the old gentleman at full speed. "Well, what if she does? So much the better for us all. Wouldn't any man rather have two beautiful daughters than one? Ha! Ha! As if I couldn't supply all your little fancies!" and, having chucked her under the chin, the kind-hearted man walked away, charmed by the prospect of being once more within the sacred circle of the conventionalities.

In all ages the village community is found to be a profoundly interesting study; for it is only prehistoric in the sense that there is a prehistoric stratum running through the upheavals of every civilization. It is not defined by numbers, since there are enormous towns covering their square miles and numbering their hundreds of thousands, which yet bear its most distinguishing characteristics. It is not even to be estimated as such by its amount of culture. Wealth, and all the opportunities it gives, may abound in such societies. But a colossal indifference to any and every interest which does not pertain to its own self-interest is the grand feature of the village community, and among the consequences of this mental attitude, may be mentioned *en passant*, that slavery to precedent, that idolatry of custom, which acts as a drag on the wheels of the whole caravan of national progress.[13]

Gattie Cloman was in, but not of, the village. Left an orphan at an early age, she had been educated for a teacher, and her strong self-reliance almost marred the beauty of her expressive features. For, of the three friends, she undoubtedly carried off the palm for beauty. With dusky hair and steel grey eyes, the fairness of her complexion only heightened the charm of the regular features which physiognomists say indicate a well-balanced mind, and which, in her case, were cast in an heroic mold, and by common consent dubbed Napoleonic, so indisputably did the expression recall portraits of the First Consul.

Hers was the only heart at all troubled by Alma's recreant inertia. As the weeks passed and not one word was said of Alma's return to the city, Gattie felt that she must assume the burden of responsibility if no one else would, and at last deliberately greeted Alma with:

"What! not here yet? I should think you would be taking your flight at any moment now."

"Oh," rejoined Alma, more impetuously than was her wont, "I could not think of going until—"

"Paul is not in town, Alma."

"He will come."

"Well, do as you think best, of course. But consider the precious time you are wasting—in the height of the season, too!"

Just then the door flew open and Grace came dancing in with beaming face, exclaiming:

"O girls! I have had such a charming walk with Paul Vanderveer. He will be back in a few minutes to take tea and spend the evening. And Alma, you will come into the parlor, won't you? I know you and Paul were always sparring at each other, but I never knew him to be in the mood he is in to-night. He will atone for all his past rudeness, I am sure. I looked into the parlor as I came on up-stairs, and found such a lovely fire on the hearth. Everything is propitious for a good time."

"Will there be others in to-night?" asked Alma quietly.

"Oh, yes, very likely," and Grace broke into a merry laugh as she added, "but they won't count."

Gattie's eyes met Alma's for a moment, and the new idea that flitted through each mind was reflected in the troubled glance they gave each other.

But there was no time for further conversation, and after due preparation, Alma, dressed in her prettiest gown of crimson cashmere, with dainty white lace at throat and wrists, ran down-stairs and entered the parlor by one door just as Paul Vanderveer entered in the opposite direction by another.

Grace was right. Everything was propitious for a pleasant evening. Every log in the spacious fireplace seemed to aspire to send out more than its prescribed portion of light and heat, and the beautiful red and gold glow would have heightened the charm of costlier pictures than the pretty Psyche Returning from the Inferno which covered the wall above the mantel.[14] The comfortable easy chairs—just shabby enough to be thoroughly comfortable—never looked more inviting, and a huge bunch of violets in the window sent forth an odor suggesting fairy-land. To crown it all, Paul's unusually fine form and handsome face never appeared to better advantage than as he came forward saying:

"This is the pleasantest surprise of my life."

This was such a departure from his habitual reserve and wonted sarcasm that it took him almost as long to recover himself as it took Alma.

"Yes," she said as quickly as possible, "it

is a surprise to everybody. But I have not been home for two whole years, and then you may remember, only for a week," and she succeeded in assuming the self-possession she longed to feel.

The young man standing in front of her was very handsome. Tall, supple and nonchalant, he was one of the blondes who outgrow all save negative signs of their blonde boyhood. A bronzed complexion, rather light brown hair and an expressive mouth were irradiated to a rare degree by a pair of dark, magnetic, blue eyes, whose gaze was steady, intense and penetrating. It is not easy to meet such eyes with indifference even when one does not feel interest of a peculiar kind.

Paul, on the other hand, had just emerged from the gossip that was running high in the town as to the cause of Alma's coming, and it was with difficulty that he stifled the questions on his lips, and talked about the speed at which he had ridden and the obstacles in his course.

Alma had only time to say, in response to his inquiry about the time of her arrival, "Yes, I have been here six weeks to-day," when one after another of the family came in to greet Paul, whom they had not seen now for many months, and then supper was announced.

All the girlish love of coquetry came back to Alma as she abandoned herself to the enjoyment of the hour. She had been on stilts so long; *always* in the presence of a dreaded public; for the very fact that she was not forced to support herself through the whole weight of her undertaking on her talent, and at every step of the way she was compelled to reassert herself.

Now it was all just as entrancing as she had pictured. Not a feather's weight of care rested on her shoulders. How charming it was to see that her every word was of importance; how delicious to find that she could make Paul wince by the merest references. That sense of power for a few minutes compensated her for her lost position on the stage.

The conversation at table was not of a very connected character. When it turned upon beauty and little Winifred rashly said:

"I never could see how sister Alma could go on the stage. She isn't pretty enough,"— and Alma drew herself up haughtily as she retorted:

"Oh, my dear child, the histrionic art cares nothing for the vulgar beauty of the drawing-room. Charlotte Cushman was not what you would call pretty. I am not on the stage for the display of my person,"—

There was an embarrassing pause, and again, when Mr. Macdannald ventured to remark:

"Literature is such an interesting calling, from the fact that the author is permitted to live in private."

Alma felt obliged to say:

"O, no, Papa, there is no more public, exposed arena in our modern civilization than that afforded by the literary profession. On the stage one only has to recite the thoughts and feelings of another. In literature you tear away the veil from your own heart, and must be prepared to have it transfixed by as many arrows as the critics care to let fly."

Still, with these exceptions, there was very skillful dodging of the proscribed theme, and, on returning to the parlor, freer and more genial intercourse could be enjoyed, for they found Will Gray, a particular friend of Frank's, with Rob Grimthorpe, the reporter, and Hugh Delancy, who both sang in the church choir with Grace, waiting to increase their numbers. Mr. Grimthorpe came to meet them, breaking out in his easy, cavalier-like way with,

"Well, here you come, all filing over into the same room! I never saw such a devoted family. And this is—?"

"My daughter, sir, my eldest daughter," and good, stout Mr. Macdannald put his arm around his queenly daughter's waist with more than ordinary paternal pride, as he turned and added for the general benefit, "whose coming has given us all such unexpected pleasure. Alma, I am sure you will be glad to meet your sister's friends."

"Why, Frank, you seem to be all right again," said Will Gray, coming up and bending over the lounge on which the semi-invalid had at once thrown himself.

"Oh, I am, now that Alma is here. Hers is no misnomer. She *is* life, soul, spirit. I don't know how we ever existed without her. This last illness of mine has been a real success."

"Ah! Frank has been making me read Schiller with him, that is the explanation of his partiality," and Alma laughed gaily as she responded to Mr. Gray's inquiring look.

"And you are Die Jungfrau, her very self," remarked Will, half-meditatively.

"Oh, not a bit of it," and Frank threw back his head and laughed long and heartily as he ejaculated, "Alma the *zarten, weichen Jungfrau!*[15] O, no, no, no! I Why, Johanna had visions, to be be sure," he

continued more soberly, "and they were of her own glory, too, that's a fact! But then at the last she's utterly swamped by her emotions. Now Alma's lived twenty-four years in the world without any emotions, and it's not very likely she'll succumb after this. Come, Paul, you have known Alma for some time, did you ever know a person with less sentiment? Why, she doesn't care for anybody!"

Paul was very glad that Mr. Grimthorpe then and there insisted upon having a rehearsal of the chorus "Great and Marvelous," from the new Cantata of A. R. Gaul, thereby necessitating a general movement towards the piano.[16] But he watched Alma's face with new interest as Grace, on her way to resume her seat after playing the accompaniment, stopped to speak to her *sotto voce*.[17]

A face has its compass just as a voice has, and Alma's extraordinary range of expression touched the sensibilities of intellectual people just as vocal music commonly effects the emotional mind. Pretty she was not, as Winifred had declared, in the ordinary acceptation of the word. Her brown eyes, slightly upturned nose and rather large mouth were not remarkable in any way. And even her wealth of rich brown hair and her well-marked eyebrows (perhaps the predominating characteristic of an attractive face) might not have excited attention. But the rare animation of which her whole countenance was capable alternated with a dreamy, poetic sadness, and while the one expression opened new avenues of thought and feeling, the other baffled the keenest scrutiny.

Now her flushed face was suffused with a light that seemed to spring from some unknown source, "far, far from the sphere of our sorrow." She looked up at Grace standing in front of her, laughed, seemed about to say something, then changed her mind, laughed again and shook her head.

Neither of the girls gave Paul credit for much intuition, but he understood the pantomime perfectly, and knew that Grace was chiding Alma for her indifference to his entertainment.

Grace did not know that they were at that stage of affairs when words are all unnecessary. Paul, indeed, had now but one thought, one desire,—*not* to find out how long Alma meant to stay; or any of her plans—what had brought her, or what would take her away. So he chatted in a friendly way with Grace; allowed Mr. Macdannald to talk politics to him *ad nauseam*, and answered as many questions in History, Geography and Natural Philosophy as the wary Winifred took the opportunity to propound to him, though Frank rather cruelly interrupted the little enthusiast by saying,

"I wish now, Winnie, that while you're getting an education, you'd get a memory."

Paul, however, continued imperturbable, and replied very graciously to Mrs. Macdannald's kind inquiries after his gouty father, his pompous mother and the haughty Misses Vanderveer, all of whom, he knew, looked down upon the Macdannalds from untold heights of family, wealth and learning.

But Grace, thinking this kind of thing had gone on long enough, ran to the low window opening on the veranda, threw it up and called,

"Oh, you must all come out and see the stars, they are perfectly magnificent!"

It required no manoeuvering on any-

one's part for Paul and Alma to find themselves alone at one end of the piazza, and with a desperate effort to overcome his dreamy moodiness, Paul laughed a little nervously and said:

"The pleasure of seeing you again seems to deprive me of the power of speech. But I suppose you are bored by this necessitated visit."

"It was not necessitated."

Paul, taken off his guard by his surprise, exclaimed instantly,

"What! You came because you wished to?" but hastened cautiously to add:

"What a change this sleepy little town must be to the active life around you in the great city!"

"Yes," retorted Alma, half gaily, half indignantly, "it is a perfect Bedlam there. I do not see why you think it strange that I should want to see this tranquil spot, my home, my own people, my old friends."

"'Far from the madding crowd's ignoble strife.'" quoted Paul, apparently more absent-minded than ever. Then, trying to realize that he ought to take advantage of this fine opportunity, he blurted out,

"You think, perhaps, of—ahem!—Ah!—abandoning the—your—ah, I mean, will you be here long?"

"Oh, I don't know anything about it. I have been through so much lately, living in a whirl, that now I feel entitled to take a little time to get my breath. It is good to fling all care to the winds, sometimes. What are you doing with yourself now?"

"How can you ask? You know I never do anything. None of us do anything down here but stagnate. Besides, in my own case, my life has lost its inspiration."

Paul bent forward to catch Alma's reply, but Frank's voice drowned it, jarring harshly on the still night air with,

"Look here, now, you two must be coming in. You've had time to name every constellation in the heavens. We've gone the rounds now and Alma is the only one who hasn't given us any music.

Of course there could be no hesitation about responding to this demand, and Alma walked directly to the piano.

All were gratified and highly delighted by her selection of a simple little English song, taking this (as the unthinking world always takes it) to be an act of deference to the popular judgment, which declares sententiously that 'Nature is always superior to Art.' No one present had the faintest conception of the laborious training which the fair singer had undergone before she could so affect them with the words:

O whither, whither, speed the stars
    When silent night is o'er,
Ah! tell me, do they journey far
    To light some distant shore?
"Oh, no, my love," the mother
    said—
"The sun's more glorious ray
Still quells the light of starbeams
    bright
    At dawning of the day."
"And thus, my child, on youth's fair
    stream
Bright starry lights may play,
And softly glide the glancing tide
    'Mid buds and blossoms gay.
But youth's bright day must pass
    away,
Then, after sorrow's night,
The heart more blest will gladly rest
    In Heaven's more perfect light."

Mr. and Mrs. Macdannald, indeed, accepted this little effusion as a kind of vaguely, though subtly, conveyed guarantee that Alma had returned to private life, and the younger people felt that it drew them to her level. But, though differently affected, all felt that the charming song had brought to a fitting close an evening which would long linger in their memories, and it conveyed an undefined, yet delightful, impression that this evening constituted a kind of pause in the remorseless course of time, and that the new chapter about to be opened in the book of fate was going to be the inauguration of a brighter order of things.

Chapter V

"There is a vision in the heart of each,
Of justice, mercy, wisdom, tenderness
To wrong and pain, and knowledge of their
    cure;
And these embodied in a woman's form
What best transmits them pure, as first
    received
From God above her, to mankind below!"
—*Robert Browning.*[18]

Paul Vanderveer left the Macdannald's in a very hopeful mood. He had loved Alma from the time that they were boy and girl together. He knew and loved all that was in her except what he called, with set teeth, "her accursed ambition." It was not that he did not wish her to excel, for he well knew that he was drawn to her through her intellectual gifts. But the stage! Ah! there was indeed the rub! To his aristocratic sensibilities the actor's profession was simply despicable. Devoted to the Law from babyhood by his father, a lawyer before him, he had inherited and imbibed the legal traditions which class actors with rogues, vagabonds and sturdy beggars, and would have had them caught and "whipped until their bodies be bloudye" for no other offence than the actual one that they were actors.

His thoughtful, earnest mind brooded over the undignified character of a life of mimicry, the vulgarity of its associations, its risks of life and honor, the pettiness of the Art itself. He was not ungenerous enough to wish that a woman should not pursue the only profession in the world commanding fame and fortune which men have left open to her for two centuries. But his very generosity tortured him with the bitter regret that Alma should seem to accept this challenge of a weak and selfish world, which applauds woman when she spends her life for its pleasure, and taunts her when she devotes it to its good.

On returning to the hotel in his buoyant frame of mind, and strolling into the office to look around, smoke and read a line or two before retiring, his attention was arrested by a lively young man, talking now to this person, now to that one, and no sooner had Paul appeared than he, too, was accosted, and to his surprise with:

"I hear the Macdannalds live in this place, and that the pretty little actress, Alma Macdannald, is here now. Do you know her?"

Paul's curt affirmative monosyllable did not in the least check the young man's vivacity, and he continued,

"I know her too. Fine young woman, by George. Never had a better time in my life than in the Détour Theatre with her. She did me such a favor. D' you ever see her on the stage? No? Well, that's drôle! I saw her act some time before I met her. She's awfully jolly on the stage—something worth seeing, I can tell you. Didn't know her for the same person when I met her off it. She was in disgrace, though, when she left the city. What's she doing down here anyhow? 'S that member of her family dead yet?"

The fellow's insolence fascinated Paul, and held him so spellbound that he was conscious of doing violence to himself in turning squarely around and compelling himself to walk directly to his own room.

What could it all mean? Could it be possible that this brute, this impudent puppy, really knew Alma personally? What nonsense! He scorned himself for believing the rascal for a moment.

But as he began to walk up and down his room he found that, try as he would, he could not quiet his fears, vague and shapeless as they were. He must nerve himself to the point of determining to make Alma look him in the face and tell him positively whether she knew this man or not, and it was long before sleep came to his rescue even after his mental wrestling had brought him this decision.

Next morning it was very easy to find out from everybody's conversation that the young man was a Mr. Ernest Driscol, who was making a musical tour through the Southern cities and was here for the purpose of giving a piano recital in a day or two.

Paul meant to go to the Macdannald's that night anyhow, for he knew they were all such church people that they would be sure to go to the Wednesday night lecture, and he wanted to go with them,—and with Alma specially, half curious to see whether she would still conduct herself unaffectedly and naturally under such circumstances.

All seemed very glad to see him, as he came in a few minutes before it was time to start. And to his intense relief Frank asked him almost at once whether he had heard anything down town about the Mr. Ernest Driscol who was to play on Thursday night. Alma did not betray the slightest interest in the musician, and the way seemed well paved for Paul to say, as soon as she had taken his arm on the sidewalk,

"Did you ever meet this Mr. Driscol, Alma?"

"No, indeed," was her quick, positive reply, as she turned her face up to his.

He looked into the strong, pure, resolute, innocent face, and felt like Christian when the burden of sin fell from his shoulders.

They walked on very happily, recalling many past experiences in this home of their childhood, proud (as very young persons usually are) that they had a past to dwell upon.

Being thoroughly familiar with the service, they needed a Prayer-book only for the Psalter, and Alma offered hers to Paul for their mutual accommodation. As he took the book from her, on the reading of the last sentence, and her fingers relaxed their hold, its leaves fell apart and a card fell out and over into the pew in front of them. Paul stooped to pick it up and could not avoid seeing, as he did so, the very legibly written name which almost covered the one side. He gave a perceptible start as he read:

MR. ERNEST DRISCOL.

The blood surged to his head, he felt his face bum, and for a few moments neither saw nor heard anything.

On recovering himself he sat wondering whether Alma had seen the card and his confusion. Had she told him a downright falsehood? What could be the explanation of this mystery? Was she actress indeed, all the way through, down to the ground-work of her heart—with no sincerity, no trustworthiness about her?

By the time the lecture was over and they were walking out of church, he felt that a dull, hopeless kind of misery was taking possession of him, and that whatever this misunderstanding was, it would never be cleared away.

But a new shock was in store for him. What was his unbounded surprise to see the young man who had become so hateful to him standing at the church door, and half-deferentially, half-familiarly raising his hat to Alma as she came nearer and happened to look in that direction. But bewilderment, surprise, confusion were all swallowed up in a vortex of rage as he saw Alma deliberately leave his side, extend her hand and cordially shake that of the young man, while her pleased expression fully justified the impression that she was greeting an old friend.

When Alma turned to rejoin Paul, she found that he had gone on with Grace, and Frank was waiting for her.

"Who was your friend, Alma?" he

asked sharply as soon as they had fairly started homeward.

"Why, really, now that I come to think of it, I do not know his name. I met him at the theater just after receiving the news of your illness. That and the bustle and hurry of getting off must account for my absent-mindedness."

"Well, all I want to say is—that you cannot expect to keep in Vanderveer's good graces if you make friends of men like that; the fellow was, evidently, intoxicated."

"For pity's sake, Frank, do you imagine that I would accept Paul Vanderveer's friendship on conditions!—much less compromise my most sacred convictions for it?"

"Pshaw! Alma, that's all stuff and nonsense; it's impossible that you can have any sacred convictions about a man like that. We were all in hopes that you had given up your 'sacred convictions' about the stage. But here we are at the gate. Shall we go in or walk on? I think I ought to have a serious talk with you."

While standing here a moment, undecided as to what course they would pursue, Paul came out of the house and almost fell over them in his efforts to disappear as quickly as possible. Frank called out after him:

"I say, old fellow, what on earth's the matter with you that you can't stay and spend the evening with us? You're getting entirely too pious, just coming to go to church with us and then skedaddling in this style!"

Paul muttered something about "Imperative engagement," never looked at Alma, and was soon out of sight.

As soon as Alma entered the house Grace came running to her, exclaiming:

"So you know Mr. Ernest Driscol!"

A vivid realization of the whole state of affairs flashed through Alma's mind like lightning, and she replied scornfully,

"So it seems!" adding more deliberately, "I have invited him to call to-morrow."

"O Alma! What will uncle say? Paul does not consider him at all nice."

"Well, fortunately, Paul's dictum is not universally accepted in this house. Papa has perfect confidence in me," and hastily pushing Grace aside, Alma ran up to her own room, locked the door and began to walk up and down excitedly as she said to herself:

"Paul distrusts me in my character of actress!" and indignation sent the hot blood through her veins, as she clenched her hands and teeth.

In a few seconds, however, the rattling of the door-knob stopped her rapid walk, and drying a few bitter tears, she turned the key and asked who was there.

It was Gattie Cloman on her way home from church, saying she had stopped in to get Alma to play her something "*fur ein guten nacht*," as the German lovers always do on parting.[19]

"But what's the matter?" she began abruptly, as she came in and the two girls took seats facing each other.

"I am very much disappointed in Paul Vanderveer," said Alma, sternly and laconically.

"Why? What has he been doing?"

"Oh, it is not worth while to enter into details."

"Ah, yes, he always was a dreamy, vague, unpractical sort of fellow; a frank and undisguised trifler, in fact. The idea of a man of twenty-five or six idling away his life as he is doing! I wonder, as I've told you before, how you can devote a thought to him. He is incapable of appreciating your motives and aims in life. Were you really influenced by a desire to know him better in your coming home this time?"

"Oh, Gattie, you can hardly imagine the trials we are subjected to in our life on the stage. Our very existence seems at times to be a grand sensational farce. You have never seen this scrap about me, I believe," and Alma took out of her pocket-book the slip of newspaper which spoke of her as one well known to the theatre-loving public, dwelt upon her impersonation of "Isolte," her manner, her dress, but especially and above all, her person, after the prevailing and disgusting fashion of the era. When Gattie handed it back to her, she continued:

"No, Paul is not so contemptible as you think him. We girls at Ronconi's get to know so many, many men, and—"

"And they take horrid liberties with you."

"No, indeed. Did any man ever take a liberty with you?"

"Oh, *no*. But—"

"Exactly so. And a bad man always wants to get out of the way of a good woman. ·But I was going to say we have so many offers, and sometimes I am tempted to make a grand sensational match and end all my difficulties of head and heart. Yes, I have a persistent lover, and I felt that I must come home and see Paul once more and know how much he could affect me before I said the last word to Signor Cetti."[20]

"But he has utterly failed to stir you up in the right direction."

"No, not utterly," and Alma threw her head back against the rocking-chair, looked up to the ceiling and sighed deeply as she added:

"How I wish I had been born in the good old quiet times when nothing was expected of a woman!"

"You forget that whatever else our age may ask, it does not demand that you shall marry," retorted Gattie, rather dryly; "there is nothing that it so applauds and approves as the celibacy of superior women."

"That is too personal a question to be settled by the exigencies of the age," replied Alma energetically. "Besides, this is just where we come to the parting of the ways. Your profession freely absolves you from all thought of that, while mine lashes me into thinking of it every day of my life."

"Well, come down now and play to me, for I must be going. If this episode with Paul only makes you more determined than ever to carry out your cherished schemes, I am sure you will be glad it ever happened."

Alma was, indeed, being consciously strengthened in her old heroic determinations and resolves. And when Mr. Ernest Driscol appeared the next morning, she met him with a sweet, womanly graciousness that not only put him at his ease, but made him wish and strive to be far more of a gentleman than he as yet knew how to be.

"Come to the piano," Alma said at once. "I know you will enjoy talking there more than anywhere else in the room, its very presence must give you a delightful consciousness of power. What do you think of our town?"

After chatting commonplaces for a

while, they began looking over music, playing passages of favorite compositions for each other, then played a number of duets, and finally drifted into "talking music" to the total exclusion of all other thoughts and interests.

Sitting thus on the stools before the piano, their elbows resting on the instrument, they did not notice that the door opened and some one was looking in on them. Mr. Driscol had his back to the door and could not well turn around, and Alma just lifted her eyes—drawn upward as if by magnetic compulsion—in time to recognize Paul's retreating figure.

It was Paul, who, thoroughly ashamed of his lack of self-control and unjust suspicions, had come around as soon as he could get off, penitently disposed to accuse himself of all that was base and excuse Alma for all shortcomings.

His look into the parlor was indeed inauspicious. He gave one glance and then the door was slammed with a violence which seemed to shake the house to its very foundations.

Mr. Driscol gave a "Hallo! what was that?" and ran to the window in time to see Paul dashing around the corner, while Frank, Winifred and Mr. Macdannald all came running into the room from different directions to ask what had happened.

Alma alone remained calm, self-possessed, unagitated, and when Mr. Driscol came back and said he thought Mr. Vanderveer had just been in the house, and Mr. Macdannald exclaimed: "How abominably rude, to run into the house, slam the door and run out of it again!"

Alma gently ventured to apologize for him on the ground that "A door often slips from one's grasp and seems possessed of an evil determination to slam in spite of one's best efforts." She was sure, she went on to say, that if it had been Paul, he was called away suddenly by some recollection of duty. He had much to occupy his time when in town.

The excitement having subsided in a measure, and the others having left the room, Mr. Driscol broke out with:

"Who is this purse-proud Vanderveer, anyhow?

He seems to lord it over everybody at the hotel, and, in fact, over the town—on the strength of his good looks and his money, I suppose."

"Oh, you must not say anything against him, he is one of my oldest friends. He is a member of the best known and most influential family in the county."

"Oh, no offence, no offence, I assure you. He isn't musical, and I shan't mind anything so long as you don't talk music with him," and as the young man noticed Alma's heightened color and strained, tired expression, a faint idea that she was making some kind of sacrifice for him began to steal into his mind.

He did not dream, of course, at what a cost to herself she had entertained him all that morning, but now a vague feeling of compunction moved him to bring his lengthy call to a close, and after a hurried exchange of their city addresses, he was off and Alma once more at leisure.

Everyone in the house seemed to be pretty well engrossed in individual concerns during the afternoon and Alma managed to slip down town quietly and unnoticeably, though she seldom transacted business of any kind in the town, finding it too painful to be the cynosure of all eyes and the subject of so many invidious remarks.

But that night, after all had retired except her father who was down stairs shutting up the house, Alma, throwing a shawl over her night-dress, hurried over into her mother's room, exclaiming,

"I could not go, Mamma, without saying good-bye to you. I am off for Petronius to-morrow morning long before any of you are up."

"O Alma! O my child! This is such a blow, such a terrible disappointment!" and poor Mrs. Macdannald sank in a chair and covered her face with her hands.

Alma threw herself on her knees by her mother's side, pulled away her hands and clasped her own arms around her mother's neck tenderly, saying,

"O no, Mamma dear; you can bear it for my sake, can't you? You have Grace and May and Winnie. You can spare me. You believe in me, don't you, dearest mother?"

Mrs. Macdannald's only response was to bow her head on her daughter's shoulder while she wept freely and almost passionately.

Alma strained her to her breast, smoothed her silky hair and kissed her again, until her mother lifted her face and said,

"This blow is worse than that of your first going. Then we trusted that it was only a freak, but now—" and she burst into tears again.

"You ask me—to trust you—my child," she began brokenly, "about this strange life of acting—. I'm afraid you are unwilling to trust your own mother with the things near-

est to your heart, the most important step you can take in life. Tell me, Alma, if you want me to trust you, has Paul Vanderveer anything to do with this sudden decision? And O, my child, how can I acquiesce in your association with that strange young man who was here this morning!"

The fire flashed from Alma's dark eyes, her cheeks crimsoned, and so long had she lived in reserve, self-reliance and the strictest reticence, that for a moment she thought of evading an inquiry which gave her so much pain.

The sight of her mother's unfeigned sorrow and apprehension, however, carried away all opposition and she replied, after a little hesitation,

"Paul has never asked me to be his wife."

"But you know that he loves you. Oh, Alma, why can't you—"

"Oh, well, if he loves me, it will come out all right in the end. Here comes Papa. Don't say a word to *anyone* about my going till to-morrow. I have arranged about my trunk and luncheon. Good, *good* by!" and with one more strong embrace Alma turned and ran across the hall, imparting a degree of strength to her mother by her brave example even as she fled.

Great was the consternation, of course, the next morning, when Alma's non-appearance had to be accounted for. Frank was taken with a severe headache and Mrs. Macdannald found herself too depressed and agitated to rise.

Grace sent off for Gattie Cloman, and her cheerful view of the case did much to comfort the family. But she could only stop a few minutes, and was on her way out of the front door, when, on opening it, she was confronted by Paul Vanderveer, just about to ring the bell.

"Why, come in, Mr. Vanderveer, though, upon second thought, I'm afraid you won't find anyone to entertain you. I suppose you do not know that Alma has gone," and Gattie gave utterance to this last piece of information with a tiny bit of malicious pleasure.

"Gone! Gone where?" stammered Paul, with an almost savage indignation.

"Back to Petronius, of course, as she always intended."

Paul grew a shade paler and seemed obliged to lean against the door for support.

For the first time Gattie was touched with a little sympathy for him. "Come in and sit down a minute," she said as carelessly as she could, and led the way into the parlor.

For some minutes the two sat silent and absorbed in thought. Then Paul, as though coming back to the present after a long, long, journey, and wishing to test the identity of his companion, began in an interrogative tone,

"Miss Cloman?"

"Well?"

"Will you do me a favor?"

"That depends. I never let my imagination run away with me. What is it?"

"Be my friend."

"Are you in such dire need of one just now?"

Paul had been greatly spoiled at home, where his every word was law, and this coolness on the part of Miss Cloman roused a feeling of resentment strongly inclining him to end the conversation then and there.

But there was something so restful, helpful and sustaining about Gattie's very presence that he felt too great a longing to be consoled by her to give up the battle, and came out bravely with:

"You certainly must know what a severe disappointment it is to me not to see Miss Alma again?"

"Oh, I thought you had given up your interest in her now that she is so undeniably devoted to the stage."

"I am glad you know of my aversion to the stage. But I can think of her apart from her profession."

"Do you really think yourself worthy of her regard?" and Gattie smiled just enough to take the edge from the keenness of her question.

"I think myself ten thousand times more worthy of it than that lunatic who was here yesterday," replied Paul, spiritedly. "Seriously, Miss Cloman, what do you suppose can account for Miss Macdannald's fancy for that scamp? Is there insanity on either side of the Macdannald family?"

Gattie laughed so heartily at this that it was some time before she could recover herself enough to say,

"Of course there isn't. But that brings me back again to my question. It seems to me that you are incapable of understanding Alma's aims in life, and by the side of her I think you cut rather a sorry figure."

"Really, Miss Cloman, I am not accustomed to such extremely uncomplimentary remarks. I had no idea, either, that you entertained such a poor opinion of me. What have I done to incur such disapprobation?"

"I am afraid it is what you have not done,

rather than what you have done. Have you, in fact, ever done anything at all? I doubt whether you even have any well-defined theory of life. Well, perhaps it is because you are a man. We girls are accustomed to consider the deepest moral questions from our babyhood. You do not seem able to understand Alma's heroism in renouncing home, ease, affection,—everything that a girl loves—to show by example, *not* precept, that she believes in the law of service. Her kindness to Mr. Driscol is an illustration of her cardinal doctrine. She is on the stage for the express purpose of taking by the hand all who are despised for their profession. She knows that it is only by sharing this public scorn that she can ever understand how to avert it."

"You have given me some new ideas, Miss Cloman," remarked Paul, as Gattie paused to take breath, and he began to walk up and down the room. "But isn't all this a little visionary?

"Visionary! Is the train that's carrying Alma back to Petronius visionary? Hasn't she ever talked to you about these things? I really thought you knew all this and then were incorrigible. Perhaps I shall think better of you for your ignorance. But I was on my way out when you came in and must not stay longer. Good-by. I am glad I have left you something to think about."

"Yes, I thank you a good deal for this talk, Well, if I'm not to see anyone here, I may as well go with you."

The clicking of the gate brought Grace to the upstairs window, and she called out instantly, "O Frank, what can be going to happen? Here are Gattie Cloman and Paul Vanderveer walking away together in the most friendly style!"

Frank rose from the lounge and joined Grace at the window, silently sharing her astonishment.

Chapter VI
Fatality

"If all the crowns of earth must wound,
If saddest sighs swell sweetest sound,
What say ye unto this? refuse
This baptism in salt water? choose
Calm breasts, mute lips and labour loose?
Or, oh, ye gifted givers! ye

Who give your liberal hearts to me
To make the world this harmony,
Are ye resigned that they be spent
To such world's help?
The spirits bent
Their awful brows and said, 'Content.'"
—*E. B. Browning.*[21]

Was God unjust when He made woman? It may seem so in acrimonious moods, but different points of view are afforded by reflection. What if she alone, of all his creatures, does bear the *stürm und drang* of passions and emotions?[22] What if she is maimed and worsted in the battle of life through her affections? She has one hour of triumph which eclipses many of defeat.

While a man remains in painful doubt and vexatious perplexity as to whether he is loved or not, a woman's clearer intuition gives her absolute certainty in the only case she cares anything about,—when she is beloved.

As village and town, field and forest succeeded one another from the car-window, and the shadows of a long day at last commenced to lengthen, Alma began to realize that she was being carried back to the scene of former labours with a heart that was heavy enough, perhaps, but not altogether miserable. After all, had not Paul made himself utterly ridiculous for her sake? What greater proof did she need that she could bring him to her feet whenever she felt inclined? Ah! she experienced a new consciousness of power; and, better still, a sense of exhilaration in discovering that her profession was so dear to her that it stood the test of being pitted against her warmest feeling.

The journey over, the energetic girl began to wend her way to her old lodgings. The jostling crowd was annoying in the extreme, for to her surprise a blinding snow-storm had set in and she was all unprepared for it. But was not that a familiar form? Another moment, and Alma raised her voice and called out, "Mr. Battou!"

The Master turned, met his pupil's upturned face—eye to eye,—but not a shadow of recognition passed over his stony countenance.

In an instant the surging crowd had swept the two apart in opposite directions.

What did it mean? Surely it must be a mistake!

Abruptly facing about, Alma made a dash forward with an impetuosity which ennabled her to clutch Mr. Battou's coat-sleeve, and while all around seemed to be in a conspiracy to pull them asunder, she gasped,

"Don't you know me?"

The thundering "No I do not!" that came from her old friend, as he snatched away his arm and strode forward, sent Alma reeling against the nearest street-stand, and when she was able to walk on, it was with a feebleness that was new to her.

She kept up bravely, however, until she reached the flat. The janitor gave her the key to her apartments and she turned it with a new sense of loneliness and desertion. She had expected dreariness, for in her sudden departure she had not thought of notifying the maid and companion who had lived with her since she had been on the stage. But O this dreariness! this desolation! It was beyond her wildest fancy.

The magnificent flowers which had graced her triumph on the last night she played "Isolte" now filled the room with a fetid and intolerable odor. Her gown of cloth of gold was lying on the bed covered with a thick layer of dust. The universal disorder, the empty, draughty grate, the bitter cold of the long-untenanted room, all combined to chill her to the very heart; and with a sudden realization of the desperate character of her situation, she fell into a seat and let the big bitter tears roll down her face in abject spiritlessness.

A noise at the door compelled her to look up. The janitor handed in a telegram. Hastily tearing it open, she read:

"Did you leave town with Ernest Driscol? Answer at once"—Paul Vanderveer.

A sudden shock will often restore one's nerves, strengthen the heart and clear the intellect. All had seemed dark and dreadful enough before. But now Alma felt there might be unfathomable depths of trouble yet to be encountered in her life. A new kind of despair took the place of the dreary, disappointed feeling she had just had.

"Answer at once"! Indignation deepened into fury as she dwelt upon the distrust, the insolence, the suspicion embodied in the demand. She would like to see herself comply with any such request! Rage gave her an artificial energy, and she at once

set about restoring the old order of things in her establishment, telephoning to the different employés, going out, herself, to find Mrs. Hendricks, her companion, and dusting, arranging and rearranging her rooms far into the night.

The morning's return found her far too ill to rise, and the days that followed only chronicled a rapidly increasing illness.

The unfortunate telegram had had its origin in a series of very natural blunders. Mr. Driscol had left the town on the train with Alma, though neither was aware of the other's intention or of the fact itself. It happened, however, that Mr. Grimthorpe, the ubiquitous Reporter, had seen the two meet at the church door, and walk home together, gained information of the morning call from the young man himself, and then been present when the two started forth on the same journey. What more natural than his eager clutch at the fact as an item for the *Evening News?"* Under the head of "Brief Personalities," he inserted a neat little paragraph, stating that: "Alma Macdannald, the Petronius Actress, and Mr. Ernest Driscol, a noted Pianist, left Ambleton for Petronius on the 7:20 train, there being a rumor of an approaching marriage in theatrical circles."

That night the mortification and chagrin of the Macdannald family reached a climax. The idea of questioning the veracity of the Reporter or his statement never entered their minds. They simply thought it was his duty and privilege to "bar the gates of mercy on mankind," and a dull, unspeakable wretchedness took possession of the entire household.

Paul Vanderveer, too, had seen the Paper. As he still clung to the hope that there might be some explanation of Alma's apparent untruthfulness, so now he caught at the idea of finding a way out of this horrible suspicion; and, without pausing a moment to think it over, rushed to the Telegraph Office and sent his message.

As he was returning to the Hotel, he felt a strange sense of relief and restfulness on seeing Gattie Cloman a few yards in front of him. Managing to quicken his usually languid gait, he overtook her and said with warmth,

"You have no idea how glad I am to see you!"

"What! is the novelty of being scolded such a pleasant one?" asked Gattie laughingly.

"I suppose so. But I was thinking how distressed the Macdannalds must be over the item in to-day's paper,—and I thought,—perhaps, you might be able to throw some light on it."

"Oh! yes, I am. But I can hardly believe they can be so easily befogged and befooled as to be worried by such outrageous nonsense."

Paul felt so amazed and overwhelmed by Gattie's unshaken faith in Alma and so intensely small in his own eyes, that he did not dare to utter a word for some time, lest he should betray himself. At last, after trying in vain to concoct an enigmatical sentence, he ventured to say,

"To what, then, do you attribute such a report?"

"Oh, to a mere happening; the accident of their getting on the same train."

"Miss Alma knew this man before she met him here, did she not?"

"Perhaps by sight, hardly by name."

"Then how could he persuade her to leave so abruptly?"

"He did not persuade her."

"Why he talked with her all one morning and the next day she left!"

"I admire the force of your logic. Perhaps if you apply it to your own case, you will find the way out of your difficulty. But we've reached the Seminary and I must say Good-night."

"You are being a friend to me, in spite of yourself," said Paul, his tall slender figure towering above the compact little body at his side, as he raised his hat and held out his hand. "Aren't you going to ask me to come in?"

"No, indeed, I couldn't think of such a thing. That's against all my principles."

"Well, in the face of such discouragement, I am going to ask another favor, anyhow. Will you let me know when you hear from Miss Alma?"

"Oh, I'm entirely safe in agreeing to that—I shall not hear from her for a long time—we're too good friends to be scribbling to each other all the time—and by that time you will have heard from her from other sources, so I'll not have to keep my promise at all." And with a careless nod Gattie ran up the steps, and Paul turned away, baffled, and yet diverted, by this novel treatment.

And now another wave in the advancing flood of time seemed to roll up and obliterate all trace of the impressions but lately deemed so ineffaceable.

Paul returned to his suburban home, a briefless barrister, to wait for inherited fortune. Grace and Frank resumed their interest in the town life, and Gattie became more engrossed than ever in her absorbing profession. They felt that Alma had renounced them, and they saw no reason why they should not renounce her. To be sure, they were taking things as they came, and she was laboring to make them as they should be; but they felt it was their bounden duty to challenge her to prove that her game was worth the candle. In the course of a month or two they had ascertained from Alma's brief notes that she had not left town with Mr. Driscol, that she was in her old quarters, and that she was somewhat under the weather with a cold, and, Pythian priestess as she was to them, they accounted themselves true diviners and concluded that all was going on just as usual with her.

Lonely and miserable as she was, Alma did not dream of letting them know anything of the desperate straits to which she was reduced:—that she was too ill to get out of bed, that she had been shunned and avoided by her old master and was without any prospect of employment, while her carefully hoarded money was disappearing rapidly day by day.

The statement of her probable elopement with Mr. Driscol had been very generally copied in the northern papers. Nothing could so play into the hands of Mr. Battou as this abominable scandal. It answered his every purpose, and little did Alma know that when she confronted the world again, it must be with a damaged reputation.

This indeed was the explanation of the neglect she was now suffering at the hands of former friends. Notes, messages, entreaties failed to bring anyone near her, and each morning she would ask wearily:

"What *shall* I do?"

Her sister-actresses had either left town, or were too much occupied in supplying the inexhaustible demand for entertainment to pay her any attention. For neither Lent, fashion, weather nor hard times availed to suppress the cravers for amusement.

When at last, a few old friends had a moment to give her, they would rush in, tell her excitedly and incoherently of the changes that had taken place at Ronconi's in her absence, of Signor Cetti's return to Italy, of Mr. Battou's new protegés, of the petty triumphs and trials in each one's private history, until poor Alma felt nothing but unmitigated relief when abandoned once more to the solitude of the sick-room.

Worry, uncertainty and suspense greatly retarded her recovery, and the shadows of the spring were lengthening into those of "the long, long summer days" when still weak and tottering, she felt able to venture out into the streets again to look after her own affairs.

Knowing that it would be useless to attack either Mr. Battou or Mr. Sims, Alma had written to Mr. Herbert, but received no reply.

Now she determined to walk in on the assembled club in Mr. Herbert's rooms and openly demand an explanation of this cruel treatment. She remembered that there were two or three young men in the club who had always acted towards her with chivalric deference, and in the smallest details claimed to be her champions. And tho' she had been too much exalted by her success to notice them at the time (so immeasurably superior had her rank and remuneration as actor been to theirs as author), she turned instinctively to this recollection for support in this hour of necessity.

It was a memorable moment when the gentle, high-bred actress appeared, framed in the door-way of the dull, smoky rooms.

There was hemming and hawing, the throwing away of cigarettes, the removal of obstructions, and the vacating of seats while Alma made her way to Mr. Herbert.

He received her with a calm coldness, chilling her in the greeting, offered her a seat and indicated a bare willingness to hear what she had to say.

But just as she was about to speak, to her surprise she heard Mr. Battou's familiar voice proceeding from some invisible corner and startling her with,

"Beefore you speak onyt(h)ing, tell us vat becomes of zat scoundrel moosician. Are you married to heem or not?"

The disgust depicted on Alma's countenance was too genuine to be doubted for an instant, and with the explosive force of a pistol the young men broke into an irrepressible shout.

It would have been a trying moment for one less versed in self-possession, but while Mr. Harvey endeavored to call her attention to the paper containing the insinuating statement, Alma, anticipating the questions about to be hurled at her, brushed it aside, and with the *savoir faire* bred of successful contact with the world and the subtle charm born only of the "gentle life," reached over and picked up the MS. on Mr. Herbert's desk, quietly saying,

"A truce to nonsense! What are you at work on now?" Oh, an episode of Eastern life! Then you understand the Renaissance!"[23]

This was too much for Mr. Herbert. Captivated by the compliment, he exclaimed eagerly,

"I should be very glad to know your interpretation of the movement."

"O, we are going to make the past live again for the benefit of the present. We realize our wealth and are bringing home our argosy. You heralded it yourself in your beautiful "Isolte.""

"Yes, but we took that rather boldly from the Wagner opera."

"Because it was dramatic and not lyric in its character, affording scope for acting, not for singing. Only in the drama can we possess all human nature, and we want to have the representative man and woman, in any and every age, show us that human nature under the pressure of real, not artificial, circumstances. We want to see that Sakoontala is just as human and as lovable as Juliet."[24]

"You would not exclude all flights of fancy, imaginary situations and modern sentiment?"

"No, no, of course not. But Shakespeare covers every hero of the past with the mask of his own age. And certainly three hundred years have made a mask of their own. We have a right to look at everything from the standpoint of our own age, or, in other words, we have a right to our Americanism. But the Renaissance when it treats of the Present must treat of the ideal. It brings too much good, solid, substantial proof of ideality from the archives of the Past to be less than buoyant over the El Dorado of the Future."

In the discussion of the absorbing theme, Alma had almost forgotten her exasperation over Mr. Battou's repeated insults, but the thought of paving the way for her own appeal never left her for a moment, and now rallying all her forces, she was just about to turn the tide of the con-

versation, when a disturbance at the door arrested general attention, and the next moment general consternation, as Mr. Ernest Driscol walked into the room.

"Found you at last! Ha, Ha! Come to give you back your money. By Jove, I meant no harm, but the fact is, forgot all about your confounded old arrangement. Couldn't recollect what 'twas you wanted me to do. Why, here's the actress now!"

Mr. Battou sprang from his seat and would have collared the musician then and there, but Salisbury pushed him aside, saying,

"Sit down and behave yourself. Remember there is a lady here."

Blows were thus avoided, but one violently abusive epithet demanded another, and the altercation bade fair to be interminable.

Alma could not help seeing, as the strange tale un raveled itself, how greatly Driscol was to be censured, that he had been utterly faithless to his engagement— injuring her even more than he injured the club, that he was, every moment he stood there, rendering himself more and more contemptible to them and sinking in his own esteem. And, woman-like, her sympathies rushed, *en masse*, right over to his side.

Sick with disappointment and physically ill, hating to leave without one crumb of hope for the future, and hating still more to forfeit the good-will of the few men who were yet friendly to her here, the conflict in her mind was for a few minutes sharp and merciless.

Was the man sober? Was he ever entirely so? Why not let him go out into the world again with a few more of his fel-low-men's hands against him? She thought of Frank—then of Paul. Oh, this flippant fellow had doubly injured her!

But with that rush of feeling came the bracing recollection of her very *raison d'être* as an actress, and without a mo-ment's hesitation, she jumped up and said,

"I am going home, Mr. Driscol, and should be very glad to have you walk down town with me."[25]

He was at her side in an instant, and as they started out on the bright, gay streets, he looked into her eyes and said with a gentleness that surprised her:

"You are my good angel."

"Let me be, in earnest," she replied with a seriousness that rendered further talk impossible, and the silence was not broken until they reached the door of Al-ma's lodgings.

Then as she told him he might call to see her, he wrung her hand and said:

"You're the first and only friend I've ever had." And as the door closed on his retreating figure, and Alma stumbled up the steps and fell into her room, she was amazed at the state of mind in which she found herself.

All her despair seemed to have van-ished. Worse off than she had been before, she yet felt almost cheerful.

She was too weary, too utterly fagged out to analyze her thoughts, but as she threw herself on the bed, something bet-ter than physical relief came to her aid; for she saw that she had touched one of the great realities which underlie all human existence.

The Purposes of Music (1918)

Great was my astonishment, I must naïvely confess, when I found that the Neth-erlanders were the founders of the science of music. During the Middle Ages there was no written music. Popular airs were hand-ed down from generation to generation in a traditional style, by means of mimicry and imitation. Instrumental music was at its lowest ebb. Of course there were occa-sions in the nascent civilization of Europe when music was as much in demand as it is at present. Festive, social, martial, mournful, ecclesiastical purposes were found then, as now, in these rude, unpolished strains. But when we ask for the cause which changed these sounds into a science, I believe we can find it solely in the ritual of the Roman Catholic Church. In endeavoring to outvie the imperial and worldly claims of Constan-tinople and Ravenna,[26] Rome hit upon the expedient of an elaborate Church ceremo-nial. The part played by music in the Jewish ritual, with the divine sanction, suggested the employment of it in the Christian form of worship. To fill the papal choir, fine voices were selected from all parts of Europe. The stipend was high, life in Italy was indolent and easy, and with no great difficulty cho-risters were induced to come and sing. Boys and men of all ages were wanted, and when parents refused to give up their children, the agents of the Church did not hesitate to steal them, as in the case of Orlando di Lasso.[27]

We are not only surprised, but startled, upon learning that the Netherland com-posers who first undertook to formulate rules for part singing, i.e. to invent coun-terpoint, were largely influenced in their modes and methods by the Schoolmen.[28]

In a life of study I believe no discovery has ever given me more pleasure than this: I have always taken an unbounded delight in the Schoolmen, believing in the appeal to the intellect, the practical applications of metaphysics, the grandeur of theology as a science, and the aristocracy of learning. And now to find that in addition to all we have long recognized as their work, we also owe to their subtleties all that we now call music is, indeed, a glorious confirmation of our faith in those old doctors.

During the fourteenth century every province of European thought was dominated by the scholastic philosophy: and—as far as anyone can ever know—but for the metaphysical hair-splitting of Albertus Magnus, Duns Scotus and William of Occam, musical science would never have had a beginning.[29] For the great desideratum of the times was a mechanical invention. We may laugh until the tears run down our faces when we hear of the contrapuntal jugglery of these early Flemish composers, but unless they had exhausted the capacities of the *cantus firmus* (or plain song) there would have been nothing for subsequent composers to build on. And so they took this plain song and wrote it backward, then they reversed each interval, later still, they doubled the value of the intervals, and finally, of course, tried to see how small they could be made. That they took a true scholastic delight in these ingenious contrivances is a fact to which the bulk of their compositions still testifies, for a considerable collection of them is yet in existence. And of course it is easy to see in the entire perversion of the purpose of music. It is difficult, indeed, to as-sociate these tone-feats with music. There was absolutely no thought here of art. Everything that posed under the name of music was a pure mathematical problem.

Meanwhile the *people* kept up their folk songs for secular occasions. But the entire attention of *composers* was given to ecclesiastical music. The subject of their works were almost as peculiar as their treatment, for we find that the genealogy of the first chapter of St. Matthew was frequently set to music.[30] Whether there was a popular revolt against this we are not told, but the next striking fact is the conglomeration of the folk song and the Church music. "L'Homme Armé" was a popular song in the fourteenth century, and as the people seemed determined not to give it up, the composers arranged pieces in which the leading voice sang "L'Homme Armé" while at the very same time the chorus was singing an Agnus Dei.[31]

When we are told in very general terms that Palestrina effected a revolution in church-music we have no idea what it means.[32] But when we have followed out the above line of thought and fully realize the degradation music had suffered, the name of Giovanni Pierluigi da Palestrina takes on a new luster.

It is, indeed, a name which should be tenderly cherished by musicians; for it is to this one man that we owe the genesis and being of music as an art. Volumes have been written to explain the greatness of Palestrina and wherein he differed from or surpassed the famous Fleming, Lasso. But I believe it may all be summed up in this one sentence: he made music an art. Under the magic spell of Palestrina's genius music for the first time responded to both the intellectual and emotional cravings of the soul. Beauty was impressed on his creations and genuine dignity was brought to light. Great indeed is the name of Palestrina. It helps us to understand the colossal character of the Italian genius. In painting, in sculpture, in literature and in music the Italians have been creators. Italy's men of genius have appeared at critical moments in the world's history to turn the arts in a new direction. The purposes of music were ably vindicated by Palestrina, for he openly taught that it was not only intended to cheer, but to guide and control the minds of men. It was his avowed object to demonstrate the separation of sacred from secular music, and this will always be considered the crowning glory of his life.

We may well ask now how it was faring at this time with the Northern form of the art. The first important fact seems to be that the scientific counterpoint originated and formulated by the Netherlanders was handed over intact to a family of Germans by the name Bach. The high order of talent existing in this family in the sixteenth century was transmitted from generation to generation for two hundred fifty years, only dying out in 1845. It culminated, however, as everyone knows in the genius of Johann Sebastian Bach, who lived from 1685 to 1749.

The name of the great Bach will always be a synonym for scientific music at its best. But to understand this music as an exposition of the true purposes of the science one must study the conditions of German life at the close of the seventeenth century. Reduced to dire poverty and almost denationalized by the Thirty Years' War, these humble people of Thurungia found in music a compensation for the loss of earthly good.[33] Their music was no joyous burst of gratitude, no lively gush of sentiment, but an imploring, upward cry for help from above. This severity and spiritual earnestness gave the impetus to German music; and when we know that it was developed in the instrumental line, and by means of the organ, and in the service of the Protestant Church, we gain a clue to the comprehension of its lofty character. And just as Johann Sebastian Bach, himself, could not depart from the pre-determined course marked out for him by his ancestors, so the later Germans were compelled by the peculiarity of national conditions to follow in the wake of Bach.

In Bach's day, however, and for some time after, the Italians were still looked upon as the masters of music. Bach was a zealous student of Italian chamber music. Haydn studied under Porpora in Vienna.[34] Mozart's Italian journey,—or, rather, triumphal progress,—gave rise to his many Italian operas, written strictly in the florid style of that country. Beethoven openly emulated the aristocratic coldness of Cherubini. Handel entered into the happiest kind of rivalry with Domenico Scarlatti in Rome, and the English demanded Handel's presence in England that he might initiate them into the mysteries of Italian, not German, art.[35] Even Gluck, whose glory resides in his open and exultant departure from the well-trodden road of the Italians, served a long apprenticeship as a pupil of Sammartini, and spent the best years of his life in writing the music for Metastasio's librettos.[36] All of this is, of course, very amusing to us of to-day. It is evident that the Germans were not aware of their own supremacy. How was it, then, that they so completely wrested the scepter from their rivals?

This strange turn of fate can probably be best accounted for by a consideration of the purposes of music. The very word, purpose, gathers psychical force as we contemplate it. We cannot divest it of a moral value. It lifts our thoughts to the design of our Creator in endowing us with this means of expressing our delight, our consolation, our enlightenment; our comfort, exaltation, self-abasement and rapture. It leads our destiny out of the narrow limits of the sectarian religionist and equally as well out of the barren domain of the pedant and the worldling. Music is the indelible divine seal set upon the intellectual and the emotional, as well as upon the spiritual, capacities of man. Hence the only explanation anyone can offer is that the triumph of the Germans was due to a virility of purpose,—a stronger national aspiration, a deeper aesthetic conviction, a higher moral aim,—all of which were set in the framework of the divine arrangement which brought the individual and the state into equilibrium at this time.

This dictum will gain in impressiveness by applying it to the Spanish people. Passionate lovers of music and constant patrons of foreign talent, the Spanish have never been able to produce a single counterpointist. Now to explain this we have only to deny them what we affirm of the Germans.

It would be interesting, though it would be presumably unnecessary in this connection, to trace the unfolding of spiritual purpose in the successive masterpieces of the great Germans. It is enough now to concentrate our thoughts on the teleological explanation of the art as such, wherever we find it. For scientific and metaphysical explanations of the worth of music are often offered, but seldom or never do we hear anything of its purposes, i.e., its teleological value.

There are those who think that the purpose of music is to fill the mind with images. They speak of the objects called up by the hearing of good music, describing the clouds, the storms, the Alpine peaks, the cataracts, villages, vine-clad bowers and what not thus presented to the inward eye. Ingersoll's famous speech in praise of Seidl was wholly of this character.[37] To me it seemed a confession of inability to grasp the subject. If music were dominated by the sense of sight, painting ought to suggest the concord of sweet sounds. One process would be just as logical as the other. But allowing that there is an inferior kind of music which openly aims to be of an imitative character, simulating brooks, birds, cataracts, mill-wheels, etc., even this does not claim to suggest pictures, and most certainly this is not the kind of music that Seidl produced. It cannot be said too often that the highest purpose of music is to express the soul of the man. Modern counterpoint has learned that it must not exist for itself, but for an ulterior purpose,—to reveal the divine spark which makes man truly great. There are those who think all music pernicious, and they are scarcely more amusing than the class that thinks all music elevating. In remonstrating with this latter class, one meets the rejoinder, "But music is music, is it not?"—as though music either composed or performed by a human being could be devoid of a human element! On other occasions man does not regard himself as a machine or something worse than a machine, and there is not more reason why there should not be discrimination in music than in literature and gastronomy. But one may ask, "Can a true music-lover condemn true music as immoral?" Most certainly. The case of Gounod's *Faust* has been pointed out to me.[38] It is exceedingly beautiful. But as it was composed to set forth immoral actions, it cannot do less than partake of the nature of those actions. And, indeed, in nearly all the old operas the undue value placed upon sexuality, as it gives a lopsided, distorted form to the character of the personalities portrayed, also gives a pernicious bias to the music as music. The operas make no secret of exciting and sustaining the passions, the lowest part of our nature. A thoughtful person will take them in small doses. After the stage of mental infancy, almost everyone is aware of the limitations and exigencies of artistic expression, that it must emphasize and exaggerate a project in order to effectuate it. Applying this, it can hardly be said that the opera is taken seriously by any one, and this must deprive it of any real influence, relegating it entirely to the dominion of pure pastime. But this also makes it clear that opera music is not suitable in church service or upon serious occasions.

Of course it is not possible to pass over the mighty name of Richard Wagner in this connection.[39] Wagner's music is so intensely serious and so avowedly a purposeful music, that this characteristic obliterates every other. He demonstrated his genius by breaking with the past and initiating a new species of musical composition, so that the opera and the Wagner opera are two distinct entities. Yet the question is still an open one as to whether this music is in itself an end, or simply a means of illustration. Divested of drama, scenic effect and elaborate explanation, and studied solely as music, musicians are still asking, "Does this music satisfy the demands of an art-loving soul?"

That Wagner made a great gain for the opera when he undertook the task of writing his own librettos cannot be disputed. His works thereby attained a unity hitherto unknown. This is specifically noticeable in *Die Meistersinger*, a portrayal of the life of the cobbler-poet, Hans Sachs of Nuremburg.[40] An opera without a single melody, this is an intensely subjective work, and the music itself is in wonderful keeping with the aspirations of obscure genius and the conflict of individuality with environment.

Lohengrin and *Tannhauser* retain some features of the Italian opera, not only in glorious melodies, which have never been surpassed, but in the variety introduced by choruses, duos and quintets.[41] We will not stop, therefore, to remark upon these fascinating productions, for they can scarcely be considered exponents of Wagner's particular power. That power seems to reach its climax in *Tristan and Isolde*, where the larger theme of Fatality swallows up a simple idyll of Arthurian origin.[42] The orchestra here plays the most important role, "and up from its symphonic profundity emerge melodies which are involved, interrupted, mingled, modified, superposed, separated and lost to re-emerge."

A modern Italian, Gabrielle D'Anunzio, has analyzed this work partly to show the capacity of his own melodious language.[43] He goes on to say: "in the impetus of its chromatic progressions we see the folly of pursuing a good which flies from us while it flashes in our face. In the mutations of tone, of rhythm, of measure, in the successions of syncopations is a search without truce, an anxiety without limit, the long punishment of that desire which is forever deluded and yet never extinguished. The 'motif' of the opera is an eternal longing, now illuminating the summit of its harmonic waves, now obscuring them with a tragic shadow."

Wagner, himself, however, set his seal of approbation upon the great trilogy of the Niebelungen Ring,—*Die Walküre, Sigfried* and *Die Götterdammerung,* preceded by the prelude of *Das Rheingold,*—a Nature-myth, representing the struggles of the human will to subjugate itself to the Divine Will, or as Wagner expresses it, "to will its own undoing."[44] We are evidently in point of time too near to this masterpiece to judge of its merits. We cannot get the right perspective. But we may and do rejoice that a serious, yes, even a severe character has been imparted to the opera by Wagner.

The production of *Parsifal* in this country has occasioned so much agitation that another word is, perhaps, superfluous.[45] Certainly we have all been brought face to face with the possibility of making art too serious. We are reminded of the Horatian maxim,

"Fas atque nefas exiguo fine libidinum discernunt avidi."[46]

"Musically *Parsifal* has more sanity, balance and restraint than any other of Wagner's works except *Die Meistersinger,*" says one critic. But equally reliable is the verdict of another, who says, "The music of *Parsifal* is impotent and disappointing; it must not be judged by its music."

But if Wagner has used his musical motives to illustrate rather than express the passions, he has at least broken away from a bad precedent. The Italian school had sinned grievously not only in levity, but in pandering to emotionalism in music.

Yet in the course of literary investigation it has been a surprise to me to find that the later Italian librettists and composers worked together to delineate the leading dramatic episodes in Italian history. *Belisario, Mastin della Scala, I Lombardi, Il Trovatore, Masaniello, La Battaglia di Legnano* and *I Due Foscari* were so true both in spirit and form, that they paved the way for, or rather, suggested the possibility of, that the brilliant treatment of more burning themes in the dramatico-lyric poets of the nineteenth century.[47]

In all modern art the characteristic sin is a straining after poignancy of expression. And in music especially, this calls forth a protest from the thoughtful. And this protest, we must confess, is perennial; for of course all through the ages it is not musical composition, but musical interpretation that is the great theme of interest.

Music is the only one of the arts dependent upon an interpreter. The interpreter must have his own special purposes in assenting to, or assuming, his role. Hence it happens that a person of strong will, conspicuous position and authoritative mandate will often set the fashion of interpretation. And as it often happens also that such an individual is possessed of a very small soul, we have seasons of barren pyrotechnical display, in which flesh and spirit are alike victimized. Art becomes an exhibition of dexterity, and the artist appeals to a world gaping for marvels of musical execution rather than for music. This is well characterized as "the dosing of subjects proper to the intellect with the sensational vapors."[48]

Certainly the crowning sin, at the bottom of all musical misinterpretation, is the sentimental attitude of mind. In other arts this may go off in smoke and "leave not a wreck behind," but in music it is the fosterer and promoter of a disguised, but none the less real, form of sensualism. The degradation of music in the worship of the Church is the worst result of this attitude. Every force should be exerted for the restoration of ecclesiastical music to its true position, as a strengthener of the moral fiber, a source of awe and reverence. For social life and national character will take their cues from ecclesiastical precedent in the matter of music, as we have seen in the cases of Italy and Germany. Hence the subject addresses itself to the entire nation. No one can be permitted to feign indifference to the musical culture of his country. Was there not a grand old sage who said, "Let me make the songs of a land and I care not who may make its laws"?[49]

Hester Crawford Dorsey Richardson (1862-1933)

An anthology of the work of the Woman's Literary Club of Baltimore would surely be incomplete without the inclusion of Hester Crawford Dorsey Richardson. Dorsey Richardson co-founded the Woman's Literary Club of Baltimore in 1890. She and Louisa Courtauld Osburne Haughton recognized the need for a woman's club focused not only on reading, but also on advancing female literary pursuits, and took the initiative to create one. What resulted was the Woman's Literary Club of Baltimore, a woman's club that prided itself on being more than just a book club. Though Dorsey moved to New York shortly after the founding of the Club, she was proud of what it became, paying visits and sending letters to the Club after her departure and retaining honorary membership.

Richardson produced a diverse portfolio of work, writing poetry, essays, and several books on Maryland history and genealogy. Richardson's poem "Dethroned," about Emperor Maximilian of Austria, was graciously received by Emperor Francis Joseph of Austria, who personally thanked her for her work. Richardson was a historian of the Daughters of the American Revolution, the national historian of War Mothers of America, and a member of the Société Académique d'Histoire Internationale of Paris.

Born in 1862 to a family that traced its lineage to colonial days, Dorsey Richardson was drawn to the history and genealogy of the state of Maryland. Her most lasting work, *Side-Lights on Maryland History*, originally published serially in the *Baltimore Sun*, details an early history of the state of Maryland with sketches of early Maryland families.

Here we feature some of Richardson's earliest publications for the *American*, which have never before appeared in book form. In the years before forming the WLCB, she published several columns under the pen name "Selene" that caused a local sensation. In "What Woman Can Do," she disputes the belief that women must marry in order to find success and instead advocates for the financial independence of women. (The work of her sister Mary Virginia Dorsey, who published under the name Marion V. Dorsey, examines this problem from a different perspective later in the volume.) Yet Richardson also respected the domestic arts. In "The Lady in Society," Dorsey Richardson details the expectations of a good hostess, upholding the values of the Cult of True Womanhood, the ideology that a woman's rightful place was in the home.

Richardson lived during a transitional period in history, encapsulating both the ideals of the true woman and employing her intellect in a way many women before her did not. Whether she was, in fact, a feminist we leave up to the reader to decide. —K. Kazmierski and K. Shiber

Things Woman Can Do (1889)

Miss Juliet Corson, the talented editor of the *Household Monthly*, has asked me in a personal letter the vital question, "How can an intelligent, untrained woman earn money?" or, in other words, How can she gain a support. My sister scribe, "Ayesha,"[1] declares that matrimony is the only safe goal for a woman who is the unfortunate possessor of unlimited intelligence, without either training or money. We would immediately vote Ayesha a cynic were she alone in her opinion; but, when remembering the advice given a young lady by the thoughtful and amiable Bayard Taylor[2], we must hesitate ere condemning her suggestion as wholly without merit.

An ambitious young woman wrote to Mr. Taylor, asking him to tell her how to succeed in life. His reply was: "My young friend, get married." But to her mind matrimony and success were not necessarily synonymous; so she wrote again, this time to Mark Twain, putting the same query.

The humorist took a serious view of the question, and encouraged her to never be depressed by rebuffs, but to work on with faith and hope, and success would eventually be hers, and so it proved. Her ambition was to gain success in the world of letters, which, no doubt, explains Mr. Bayard's advice, as he likely spoke in the interest of sorely afflicted editors.

But there are really very many persons who think with Bayard Taylor and my friend "Ayesha," that a woman's marriage means her success.

For many of our girls are reared in this belief; the creed of Hymen[3] is early instilled into their minds and hearts; then, if, perchance, the blind little god passes them by, they are left desolate and helpless upon the shores of life, untrained in all save the extravagance of society, with no money to gratify their expensive tastes, and many times not enough to buy them the daily necessities.

These come under the class indicated by Miss Corson in her question quoted above. There are, however, many others included in the same category of "intelligent and untrained."

It is a deplorable condition for a woman to be in, and yet it is by no means a hopeless one, for there are women all around us who, from one cause or another, find it desirable to increase their incomes, and who, without training or experience, adopt a vocation and pursue it with invariable success.

There are such various avenues now open to women or fallen fortunes that it is not a difficult task to point out several desirable ways of earning money. Notably among these is the Woman's Industrial Exchange,[4] an organization exclusively for the benefit of ladies who are untrained in any other than the domestic accomplishments. Every city now has its industrial where the wares of the needy are sold at fair prices. All kinds of cakes and breads, pickles and jellies find ready sale at these rooms, while large cases of fancy novelties and useful articles are displayed in a way to attract the notice of the wealthy customers who patronize the exchange. All are the handiwork of intelligent, untrained women in need of money. But there are women who capabilities are not limited to brewing and baking, or even fashioning dainty articles of use and beauty; the women who cannot be tied to a rolling pin or a crochet needle, who have noth-

ing in common with recipes or worsteds. These must look for their sphere or usefulness outside of the Woman's Exchange.

If they are of an artistic turn, there is the Decorative Art Society[5] ready to receive specimens of their skill. One need not be either a finished or trained artist to successfully decorate saleable articles. There is one opening to young women in our city to which I have never seen any reference in the papers—that is the decorating department in the Chesapeake Pottery.[6] While visiting the pottery with some friends a few weeks ago, my attention was particularly drawn to the room full of well-bred looking goods, whose deft fingers gave the finishing touches to the beautiful wares turned out in such abundance from this factory. I have been told that the part done by these girls is very simple and rapidly done, as the decorative figures and patterns are stamped on the porcelain, after which the lady decorators put in the shading with mineral paints before the articles are placed in the great kilns for firing. A certain amount is paid for each piece decorated, so the receipts of the day depend largely upon the efforts of those doing the work. It seems that notwithstanding it inconvenient location, not a few girls of excellent social standing have passed many days in the decorating room here. Conspicuous among these was Miss Fanole Haynes, daughter of the owner of the pottery, who, it will be remembered designed a vase which took the hundred dollar prize at the Philadelphia Art School, resulting in the appointment of Miss Haynes to the chair of instructor in the New York Academy of Fine Arts.

The young persons who do this attractive and remunerative work are, with few exceptions, those who have had no previous training. A new means of employment for women is that of a professional shopper.

So far I have not heard of one in Baltimore, where there undoubtedly is an excellent opening awaiting some energetic woman who had not the aversion to shopping characteristic to most of her sex. The professional shopper in New York fills orders for persons residing outside of the city in any part of the country; she will also receive city orders. She attends to every detail, and charges a small commission to both the customer and the merchant. The merchants are glad enough to allow her a reduction in the goods to secure her patronage, while the party for whom she is buying is willing to pay the trifling commission for the sake of the comfort and convenience of herself. Most persons who live at a distance from the city impose this laborious task of shopping on some uncomplaining friend or relative in town, without realizing what an imposition is becomes when the orders increase and multiply, as they sometimes do. No doubt it seems a trifling request to the party off in the country who sends the list to be filled, but it does not so impress the city friend, who must tire herself out to get the things just right and in time to ship by the next boat or train, as is invariably the instruction. Let us hope, for the sake of our city cousins, that a professional shopper will soon announce herself in our midst, for she will be even more of a blessing to them than to the country friends who need her services many times a year.

These are but a few of the ways in which intelligent untrained women can earn money, for as my time draws to an end many other practical suggestions crowd into my mind, but I will have to leave them unmentioned until another day.

The Lady in Society (1890)

"You must come home and be my guest: You will give joy to me, and I will do All that is in my power to honor you."—Shelley[7]

To be convinced of the fact that modern society has largely missed the spirit of true hospitality, as expressed by Shelley in his song to Mercury, one needs but to remember Mrs. Sherwood's[8] late assertion, that in New York there are hostesses who "apparently make a party in order to show to half of their guests that they despise them." But one need not make a pilgrimage to Gotham[9] to learn that many persons who entertain have not grasped the first principles of hospitality—good nature and good manners: for the essence of hospitality is courtesy, and courtesy is consideration for the rights and feelings of others, and, as an able writer lately said, "Persons who lack that fundamental feature of good breeding have no place in the company which forms our ideal."

Many a member of the society which is now either entertaining or being entertained would readily confess that the fact of being invited to the home of another is by no means a guarantee that you will, upon entering the portal, be made to feel that "the house is yours," as does the friend or stranger who crosses the threshold of the warm-hearted Spaniard. That this gracious air of welcome is not familiar to the so-called hospitable homes of our country was exemplified in the experience of a young Baltimorean who was among the first exodus from the East to New Mexico. Upon his arrival in the quaint little town of Santa Fe he called upon the chief official with letters of introduction from personal friends. The old Spaniard received him with the salutation, "Señor, the house is yours." The young man was overcome with the generosity of the vulnerable Spaniard, supposing that he has presented him literally with his comfortable adobe house. He, however, soon learned to appreciate the genial hospitality more than he would have valued the mere walls of heartless clay.

I have heard of an old man who would invite people to his house to eat with him, and when they were seated at his board he would help himself to whatever he wanted, and proceed to eat without offering a single viand to his guests. Upon being reproved for his rudeness on one occasion, he replied that when he invited people to his house to eat they knew they were welcome to all he had, and as he had to help himself, he did not see why they could not do the same; and so they had to, if they wanted anything. His was a false, though honest, idea of hospitality, and one that could not be safely adopted by the present generation. But there are many entertainers who ask persons to their homes who pointedly slight them when they accept their invitation. These are the ones who Mrs. Sherwood describes as "the haughty hostesses who have been suddenly raised to a prominent position either by wealth or their husband's political rank, and who seem to think that the assumption

of a haughty manner will improve their positions." These are the most unpopular members of society, although their parlors are always crowded when they give an entertainment, because they can and do supply plenty to eat and drink, and, to some natures, these are the all-needful.

The haughty hostess makes a difference in the treatment of her guests: to those who are richer and more powerful socially, she is the fawning hostess; to only the less favored, she is haughty and overbearing. Imagine one who called herself a leader guilty of such ill-breeding! For, to quote once more from Mrs. Sherwood, "There is no such detestable abuse of one's privileges as to be rude on one's own ground. If a woman is rude everywhere else, she should be gracious at home. One lady noted for hospitality in one of our great cities has a national reputation for bad manners, and although she gives beautiful dinners, people are afraid to go to her house, lest she should be overtaken by a desire to be uncivil."

I know of a lady the counterpart of the one described by the social critic. She gives elegant little tea parties, her invited guests go in high spirits at the prospects of such an exclusive and charming affair: but, presto! Before the evening is half over—through some inadvertent remark, perhaps, of one of the party, or for some reason never fathomed—she who should be all graciousness, amiability and gentleness, makes her visitors realize that there is a "tempest in the teapot," and all pleasure and comfort vanish.

The same woman is a self-constituted autocrat, and in her own eyes aristocrat, and she has put forth the decree that she will meet no one but those she may be please to specify by nod of her royal head. No friend, however intimate, dare take the liberty of presenting another friend, be the latter no more aggressive a personage that a shy, modest debutante. But, on one occasion, an intimate of the autocrat, while driving out of town in the summer, bethought her of her Royal Highness, whose country seat was near at hand: so, with criminal lack of thought, she turned the pony's head thusward, her companion being the debutante referred to. As it happened, Her Highness was at home, and ready to welcome her friend until she espied the young creature with her. Immediately her manner became icy. She scarcely recognized the introduction, and addressed no remark to the girl during the call. The next night the fiancé of Her Highness called in high dudgeon and demanded to know why his niece has been so rudely treated when Mrs. Somebody took her to call. The result was a rather serious one to her autocratic highness, as it very nearly ended the engagement, which has since, terminated in a marriage. However, be it said to the credit of the unoffending niece that she has never accepted the smallest hospitality from the woman who slighted her because she did not carry her credentials of high social standing on her sleeve.

No lady at heart would decline to meet a friend of her friend: she would take for granted that on whom she would honor with her confidence would not introduce any one unworthy her acquaintance. To a woman who is blessed with the courtesy of a lady, the feelings of others are sacred, and one who enters her home will never be made to suffer mortification or rebuff at her hands, whether they are there at her own or another's invitation.

Good nature is really the basis of good manners, and "elegance comes of no breeding, but of birth."[10] But many women fail to realize this; for they conduct themselves to their relations to each other and society at large as though elegance of manner could be purchased with gold, and friends gained by snubbing and haughty bearing. The successful members of society are those who are thoughtful of others, who lose sight of their own overweening importance in the desire to put others at their ease. We have all, no doubt, heard of the hostess who, when an awkward guest dropped one of her Sevres plates, lightly picked up another like it, and smilingly broke it in two, saying, "Pray, don't be annoyed; for, see how easily they are broken." Not one woman of a hundred could have so sacrificed her china to her ideas of politeness.

True hospitality is such a different thing from so-called hospitality. The hostess who is worthy of the name is entirely incapable of such a thing as the "possibility of being overtaken by the desire to be uncivil" to the persons she has invited to her home. She is one of the women whom Emerson says: "They fill our vase with wine and roses to the brim, so that the wine runs over and fills the house with perfumes; who inspire us with courtesy; who unloose our tongues, and we speak; who anoint our eyes, and we see. We say things we never thought to have said; for once our walls of habitual reserve vanish and leave us at large."

Hospitality includes so much more than

something to eat and a warm house. "For what is it we seek in so many visits and hospitalities? Is it your draperies, pictures and decorations? Or, do we not insatiably ask, was a man in the house?" In this paragraph Emerson makes apparent that it is not the environment or wealth that constitutes hospitality; but, rather, the sympathy and presence of a human heart.

Those who entertain their friends in small congenial parties are the ones who receive and give more real pleasure by their hospitalities, than any other class of entertainers. It is not at all necessary that the chosen few at each affair should previously know each other, as it often happened that much pleasure is experienced by meeting thus intimately for the first time persons whose tastes are congenial, and whom it is desirable to know. It is generally supposed that the first object in entertaining people is to make them enjoy themselves; yet, I have read of hostesses who were thoroughly miserable if their guests seemed happy, and who would not hesitate to break up all tete-a-tetes that offended their jealous eyes. Some hostesses, after inviting their guests, pay no further heed to them, but leave them to entertain themselves as best they may. At a large gathering there is little alternative, unless music be provided, in which case there is no need for further concern on the part of the hostess.

The old idea that only the rich can dispense a pleasant hospitality has almost entirely disappeared since the introduction of the afternoon teas, as which only light refreshments are served, unless the hostess prefers a more elaborate and expensive menu, in which case, a veritable banquet is spread. There is really no more charming way to entertain than by giving a series of afternoon teas, one the same day of the week for several successive ones. Dispense with the caterer entirely. In the back part of the parlor have a brass tea-kettle swinging on its stand of twisted iron, beside a small table holding the dainty cups and spoons, decorated tea caddy and sugar bowl and tongs. On another small table, which, like the first, must be covered with a white linen cloth, embroidered with some appropriate designs—like, for example, one I saw lately done in green lotus flowers with the quotation from the "Lotus Eaters": "And they came to a laugh where it seemed always afternoon"[11]—on this table have the plates of small cakes, wafers or tiny sandwiches, three by two inches, each plate covered with a pretty little doily. Have one or two attractive girl friends to preside at each table, and if, possible, insist that they wear tea gowns of artistic cut. Several softly-shaded lamps and a moderate number of good-natured, bright people will make your affair a success. Too much to eat spoils the afternoon tea, while nothing to eat makes it a hollow mockery, and sends the guests home with an aching void, and the steaming cup of tea, dispensed by fair hands, taken with a light, but nutritious water, is just enough to prompt sociability and make your callers feel glad they came,

The teas give greater scope for originality in entertaining than any other kind of social gathering. At a reception one cannot deviate from the regulation program of paying your respects first to the host and hostess and then to the supper room, and thereafter, as soon as possible, to the coachman. At a ball the rules are equally rigid; one must dance and flirt, or the affair will have no charms. But the possibilities of the "tea" are illimitable, if the women who entertain would but realize the fact, and instead of making each a vain repetition of the other, would bestir themselves and add their individuality and their own china to their entertainment.

From *Side-Lights on Maryland History* (1913)

Chapter XXXIII

A Colonial Business Woman

Dinah Nuthead, the first seventeenth-century business woman in Maryland, and perhaps in America, received a license from the General Assembly to set up her printing press at Annapolis "to print blanks, bills, bonds, writs, warrants of attorney, letters of administration and other necessary blanks useful for the public offices of this Province." In her petition before the Assembly she had declared her willingness to forfeit her license and her bond and go out of business if she should print anything other than specified.

The Assembly having graciously granted Dinah's humble petition, she gave bond for £100 lawful money of England, with Mr. Robert Carville and William Taylard, of St. Mary's County, as her securities, and proceeded to carry on the business which had previously been established by her deceased husband, William Nuthead, public printer for the government.

Curiously enough this energetic and progressive Maryland woman, who was clever enough to conduct this important business, could not write her own name.

It is quite evident from this that Dinah had no thought of sticking type with her own fair hands. She merely supplied the money and brains, leaving the mechanical part to her more highly educated employees.

Despite the modern idea that the twentieth-century woman is a new species of woman because she has taken a more assertive part in the world's affairs, we find that in the middle of the seventeenth century, while few had the education of text books, the women of that day were endowed with executive ability and a rare natural intelligence, else the keen men of that pioneer period would not almost invariably have appointed their wives—and if unmarried their sisters—as executors of their wills.

Estates were often difficult to settle in colonial times; false claims to property were frequently set up in the absence of the rightful heirs in England or other foreign parts—a notable instance being the attempt to wrest the property of Mr. Benjamin Gill, of Charles County, from his daughter, Ann Gill Neale, and her husband, Captain James Neale, during their absence from Maryland.

As executors and administrators of estates women had the same legal right to appear in court that they have today, and, whenever it was to their interest to do so, they did not hesitate openly to defend their claims. From this fact the superficial students of those times have drawn the conclusion that the woman with the "power of attorney" vested in her was a lawyer by profession.

Thus this pretty and picturesque Portia[12] of the Maryland provincial bar is despoiled of her gown and mortar board 'neath the X-rays of historic research, and is compelled to take her rightful place with the other bright and intelligent colonial women who, by their office, appeared in the halls of justice to execute the business committed to them.

There is a unique case on record in which the jury of women was impaneled to give their verdict regarding the guilt of a woman, Judith Catchpoll, who was accused of infanticide.

The trial was held at a general provincial court in session at Patuxent, September 22, 1656.

While the jury was called upon to give a verdict only on a certain phase of the case, its decision established Judith's innocence in the eyes of the Council, of whom were present Captain William Fuller, Mr. Richard Preston, Mr. Edward Lloyd, Mr. John Pott, and Mr. Michael Brooke.

The names of the women composing the jury were Rose Smith, Mrs. Belcher, Mrs. Chaplain, Mrs. Brooke, Mrs. Battin, Mrs. Canady, Mrs. Bussey, Elizabeth Caxton, Elizabeth Potter and Dorothy Day—the number being ten, two less than the legal male jury.

Evidently women of colonial Maryland were quite as brainy as their present-day descendants, since the gentlemen of the Council recognized the fact that the opinion of ten intelligent women was equal to twelve men at any time!

A description of the Maryland girls, written in the year 1660 by one who had spent several years in the colony, says: "They are extreme bashful at first view, but after a continuance of time hath brought them acquainted, then they become discreetly familiar and are much more talkative than men. All complemental courtships, drest up in critical rarities, are meer strangers to them, plain wit comes nearest their Genius; so that he who intends to court a Maryland girle, must have something more than the tautologies of a long-winded speech to carry on his design, or else he may (for aught I know) fall under the contempt of her own frown and his own windy oration."[13]

From this we can conclude that the old-time Maryland girls were not to be taken in by pretty speeches. They must have all been belles, as some married not only once, but many times, it being no unusual thing to find a colonial dame who had been four times led to the altar. Four seems, however, to have been the limit, as there is no record so far as known, where anyone promised to obey the fifth time!

Katharine Pearson Woods (1853-1923)

Katharine Pearson Woods was a novelist, essayist, and poet born in Wheeling, Virginia to Alexander Quarrier Woods, a tobacco merchant, and Josephine Augusta (McCabe) Woods. Woods's parents promoted literature, education, and religion in the upbringing of their three daughters, and this emphasis would influence the her literary career. In 1874, at the age of twenty-one, she joined the religious organization of the All Saints Sisters of the Poor. Due to poor health, Woods withdrew from the convent, but this experience led to her philanthropic work, which formed the religious and moral basis of her writing. In addition to publishing a number of novels, Woods also was a teacher for many years. She never married or had children.

Woods published her first novel in 1889. *Metzerott, Shoemaker* was based on the principles of Christian Socialism, a nineteenth and early-twentieth century religious movement that advocated for economic reform for the benefit of the working class. Published anonymously, debates about the identity of the author briefly occupied the national media, during which critics favorably compared *Metzerott, Shoemaker* to the bestselling utopian novel *Looking Backward,* by Edward Bellamy (1888), which had inspired a political movement rooted in the principles of Christian Socialism. The success of *Metzerott* may have led the WLCB to make Woods one of its first honorary members. *The Mark of the Beast* (1890), included here, is, in many ways, a follow-on to *Metzerott, Shoemaker*. It was published in *Lippincott's* accompanied by a profile of Woods by Hester Dorsey Richardson, which is included in the "Tributes" section of this volume. Woods's other works include *Web of Gold* (1890), *From Dusk to Dawn* (1892), *John: A Tale of King Messiah* (1896), *The Son of Ingar* (1897), and *The True Story of Captain John Smith* (1901). Woods also penned nonfiction pieces such as "Queens of the Workroom, the Shop, and the Tenement," an article addressing labor conditions, which appeared in *Cosmopolitan* in 1890. —J. Morgan and J. L. Cole

The Mark of the Beast (1890)[1]

"Am I my brother's keeper?"[2]

"That no man should be able to buy or to sell, save he that hath the Mark, even the name of the Beast, or the number of his name."[3]

I

Outside, it was high noon! The round whirling globe in her voyage through space had brought the little town of Smoketon as nearly beneath the vertical rays of the sun as was possible, under existing limits of latitude. It was but natural that Smoketon took credit to itself accordingly, and from one end to the other tried to outrace and outsmoke its own record.

Factories, factories, factories! How they bustled and thumped and shook and roared! There was positively no end to them,—nail-mills, foundries, glassworks, potteries, blast-furnaces: their smoke went up night and day, and their noise entered into the ears of the Lord God of Sabaoth.[4] Cotton-, woollen-, and planing-mills, shirt-factories also; above, a dense veil between them and the soft blue heavens; beneath, a roar as of a huge insatiable monster, crushing, devouring, and breaking the residue in pieces with his teeth; producing, producing, producing, without regard for the needs or capacity of consumers, to satisfy his own illimitable greed; producing always, and sending forth every product enriched with the blood of many victims:—this was the proud little city of Smoketon.

Serpent-wise, from north to south,

with many a turning and twisting of its slender body, it trailed its grimy length along for perhaps five miles, between the fairest hills and the loveliest river—I was about to say, in the world. Smoketonians were proud of their scenery; and they felled every tree on the hills, and foully clogged their beautiful river, with royal disregard of any rights therein but theirs.

The city was half a mile wide at its widest point, just where a tiny tributary to the river had forced its way between the enclosing hills; and here a way of escape had been built for certain poor souls.

Quite around the hill it curved, this steep smooth road, with its side walk of worn and treacherous planks; but once upon the other side, one seemed to have stepped back at once fifty years at least. Primitive but peaceful, the little four-roomed or six-roomed dwellings, with their steep white steps, to which a double hand-rail was a vital necessity, their high porches covered with vines, and their tiny front gardens full of gayly-colored blossoms, first climbed as high as they dared up the hill, and sent vineyard or orchard up still higher. Land was not valuable on that side of the hill, so every man was both architect and tenant of his own house, and, though taxes were sufficiently familiar, rent-day was an unknown evil. The last of these dwellings was somewhat different from its neighbors. The site had been carefully chosen at that precise point where the hill receded a little, and the space thus left had been utilized for a thriving vegetable-garden, between which and the street ran a range of hot-houses, sparkling in the sun. The dwelling-house had neither high steps, gay garden, nor vine-clad porch; but the place of these was supplied by a little, brown, weather-stained, one-story shop, over whose low creaking door stood for sign a brown wooden angel, holding in his left hand a trumpet, while the right hand with its raised forefinger seemed about to mark the brow of all who crossed the threshold.

Within, the shop was full of golden lights and warm brown shadows, and the air was fresh with the odor of sweet-smelling wood; figures of many shapes and sizes, boxes, brackets, clock-cases, baskets, with many other articles in boxwood, pine, and cedar, stood on shelves about the room; and in the midst, just where the light from the open door fell over his left shoulder, a man of nearly eighty years sat before a low wide table, whereon lay a tray of sharp and oddly-shaped tools and a narrow block of wood about nine inches in height, which he seemed to be shaping into a rough semblance of the human form.

The costume of this old man was commonplace enough: a blouse of the blue material hitherto peculiar to workmen, but now patronized by aesthetes under the name of denim; the wide turn-over collar unfastened at the neck, the sleeves rolled above the elbow, showing the still muscular arms, and long, slender, nervous hands. His trousers were of coarse brown cloth, and his low-cut, square-toed shoes, fastened with a strap and buckle, showed gray cotton stockings evidently of home manufacture.

There were steps upon the wooden sidewalk, gay voices in talk intermixed with sweet youthful laughter. The old man raised his head from his work, and turned his face towards the two figures who stood in the open door, intercepting the sunlight. From the shadow thus formed, his head and face shone as if carved in alabaster. Abundant white locks were combed straight back from his lofty, narrow brow, and lay in heavy masses upon his shoulders; a snow-white beard flowed to his waist; his eyebrows were bushy, and black as ebony; and from the deep hollows beneath them shone two blue lake-like eyes, still, solemn, and sad as the fathomless pools that shine amid the eternal mountains.

A gleam, which was scarce a smile, fleetingly touched their surface, as the old man rose to his full grand height and came forward to meet his visitors.

"You are welcome, son and daughter," he said, kindly, in a voice from which age had taken nothing of strength or melody: "You have walked far under the burning sun, and are weary. Be seated. I will give you of my best."

He drew forward two curiously carved wooden chairs, and placed them where the soft air might sweep gently over them, while they were shaded from the burning sun.

"Of milk," he continued, "we have abundance; but the fruit of the vine is not yet ripe. Berries I can offer you, red and sweet, and the water of our well is clear and cold. Which of these will you have?"

"Strawberries and milk? Oh, there is nothing in this world I love so well."

"Nay, my daughter," said the old man, gently, "is it well to use words in jest whose earnest bears so clearly the Mark of the Beast?"

The girl looked surprised, yet half amused. She had expected to hear much of this Mark from the old man, but not quite

so soon. "I don't understand," she said.

He smiled indulgently, then sighed. "Thou dear Heaven!" he said, "when a fair young maid like this lends her sweet voice to the language of the Beast, knowing not that it is his, how very evil this world must be! Rest, my children. I will summon Elsa."

"Oh! isn't he just lovely and wonderful!" cried the girl, when he had left them. "I feel as if I had seen a real angel."

"Engel's[5] his name, and the same is his nature," replied her cousin. "But we've got to pay for all this, you know: he gives of his best, but he expects his visitors to return the compliment."

"It is a compliment to suppose that one has a best," said the girl. "But I thought he never used money?"

"He has a daughter-in-law, who very conveniently is *not* affected by the same complaint. At least, so people say. I have never been here before."

They were very like each other, these two young people, with the likeness to which their first-cousinship entitled them, but with the difference due to their widely varying individualities. Both were tall, with slight, elegant figures, and a manner of exquisite grace. Both were dark as to eyes, hair, and skin, with delicate aristocratic features; but whereas the epithet most frequently used for the one was "dainty," the *sobriquet* of the other was "Lazy Tom."

Their names were Shirley and Thomas Meredith; and the last-named personage stretched out his limbs, not ungracefully, in a wearied sort of way, and put a question to space in reply to his cousin's last utterance:

"Now, I leave it to anybody, if it isn't

bad enough to drag me here at noon of a summer's day, without forthwith requiring me to hold up my hands and deliver of my best? Take my word for it, Shirley, it is false political economy. Second-best is good enough for weekdays. As for—"

He paused abruptly and sprang to his feet as if he had been shot; for in the open door-way leading to the interior of the house stood a figure which needed few adventitious aids in the way of wings and haloes to be taken for what Shirley had called a "real angel."

She was dressed in—well, well, it was only a calico, after all, but the tiny blue dot upon the white ground was indistinguishable against the background of pure light revealed through the open door, so that a robe of the morning cloud before the rising sun has turned it to gold could hardly have been whiter or clearer.

Her hair was of the palest shade of golden, and the heavy braids, which when loosened fell to her knees, were wound round her head like a diadem. The face was pure and pale, with a low wide fore head, arched brows and lashes somewhat darker than the hair, and large, strangely beautiful eyes, which sometimes seemed almost colorless, mere fountains of white light, but which now, as she advanced into the room and stood looking from one to the other of the two, grew a soft, deep, tender blue.

Shirley's quick, vivid brown eyes glanced at her cousin with some amusement, as she saw him stand dumb and absolutely awkward for once in his life before this daughter of the people. That he was an ardent, passionate admirer of beauty she knew well, but beauty in a calico dress had not hitherto attracted him.

Then Elsa spoke; and the words and tone might have been those of "a lady," as Shirley, knowing no better, said within herself.

"My grandfather bids you share his noontide meal," she said, smiling.

The quaint, archaic flavor of the sentence took Shirley's fancy. She looked at her cousin.

"Tom," she said, appealingly, "one can't be commonplace enough to refuse!"

"The commonplace," said Tom, with a tremendous effort at his usual manner, "is relegated to an infinite distance. Of course we accept with gratitude."

"It is cooler in the arbor behind the house," said Elsa, turning to lead the way, "and when the day is fine we like to eat there, with only the living branches between us and the free heaven."

The door from the shop opened into a small hall-way, and had opposite to it another door, which, by some curve of the hill, looked down into the valley. To the right, this hall-way led to the hot-houses, while still another door opened into a room, from which a large, pleasant-looking woman came forward to greet them.

The Merediths were too well bred to permit themselves any exchange of glances; but the same conviction sparkled in each pair of brown eyes,—that the commonplace had, as usual, only waited behind the door. Tom, as if some shielding crystal had been removed from the girl, found himself able to lift back a branch which hung in Elsa's path, as they left the house, and to accompany it with one of those glances of his soft brown eyes which, it was popularly believed, no feminine heart could resist; while Shirley began to make the conventional apologies and excuses which in the white light of Elsa's sincerity had been simply impossible.

"We forgot it would be your dinner-hour," she said, "and I fear you have put yourself to trouble about us. Indeed, we ought to have come and gone early in the day; but my cousin was late at the meeting-place we had appointed,—late, as he always is."

"So?" said Frau Engel, pleasantly.

She was a woman who evidently had been handsome before she grew stout, and who had still such a kind, good-natured, placid face that one could not be blamed for admiring the commonplace, as he found it in her.

"But, *ach!* it is no trouble at all," she continued, smiling, "and the father, he will always have every one share with us who comes at meal-time. And I have seen the days when that was a trouble, for we had sometimes but a little share for each; yet, if the dinner was but cold cabbages, it troubled not the father. *Ach!* it is well to have a saint in the family!"

"Some persons find it inconvenient," said Shirley, laughing.

"So? but those are Romans,—not so? Protestant saints are different. And those who come to dinner often buy his carvings," she ended.

Shirley's pretty lips curled with amusement. "But he does not use money, does he?" she asked.

"He? no!—that means, not if he can help it. It is me; I do the buying and the selling for us all. They hate money, the two Engels: for me, I was born Kaufmann, and I find it often convenient."

Her last words brought them to the arbor, which had been formed by the natural growth of two primeval forest-trees.

Shirley's nerves were all in a quiver with the many new impressions she was receiving; she looked from the one Engel to the other, and then to the "born Kaufmann," and wondered if this indeed were "she, Shirley Meredith, eating with these common people" and feeling not ashamed. Then the old man's eyes met hers, and Shirley *did* feel ashamed—of herself.

"Is it true, Mr. Engel," she said, plunging into her subject head long just because she had felt that shame,—"is it true that you are a Socialist?"

The old man smiled.

"My daughter," he said, "men call me so, and in my youth it was sadly true. Now in my age I call not myself after any *ism*; for love and truth comprehend them all,—all, that is to say, which are founded on love and truth."

"But," said Shirley, "is Socialism so founded? for it looks to me like hatred and falsehood, root and branch."

"And so it often does," returned the old man, sadly. "But call it Brotherhood, my daughter; for that is the true meaning of the word. Then you will see that it needs but to grow, to send deeper its roots and enlarge its branches, until it shall include all the races of mankind."

"But that is Christianity?" said Shirley, interrogatively.

"And Christianity is an *ism* in my own tongue," returned the old man. "Nevertheless, in becoming the life-blood of all men it will cease to be such; and thus shall it be also with Socialism. A theory needs a name: Life has only to live."

Shirley's eyes were fixed earnestly upon his face; but as he ceased they clouded over, and she shook her head with vexation.

"I am like a girl in a fairy-tale," she said, laughing: "while you speak to me I seem to understand it quite well, but as soon as the sound of your voice ceases I am as ignorant as before. It is just like what you said to me in the shop about the Mark of the Beast. Won't you explain what you mean by that?"

"Who can explain one word that he dares to utter?" replied the old man. "How awful it is,—a word! Christ Himself could find no loftier title and just the Word of God!"

"You remind me, sir," said Tom, with a sudden impulse to show himself not quite a fool, "of some experiments I was reading about in sound-pictures. Of course the phonograph has taught all of us something about that, that this experiment was by means of a thin paste spread upon a vibrating membrane; and it was found that properly correlated sounds produced some very beautiful flower-like shapes. I believe they were not articulate sounds, though: so my analogy falls through."

"Are you sure of that?" asked the old man. "Perhaps it only goes deeper than you dream. For *our* words—nay, our articulate sounds—may be but lines and curves without beauty or living form; but the perfect language—"

"Is without consonants, perhaps," said Tom.

"Now I am reminded of the 'Little Pilgrim,' and the language that she heard in the Celestial City,"[6] said Shirley. "Of course a word of purely vowel sounds *must* be a flower; it could not help itself."

"Or a star," said Elsa. "'By the word of the Lord were the heavens made, and all the host of them by the breath of his mouth.'"[7]

"We've done it," said Shirley, under her breath, "and Tom began it! Happy Tom!—But, Mr. Engel, what sort of a picture does that word make which people say you speak so often,—the Mark of the Beast? What is the Beast, anyway, and what is his mark?"

"The Mark of the Beast," said the old man, "is in the right hand and on the foreheads of all, the small and the great, the rich and the poor, the bond and the free, so that no man is able either to buy or to sell, save he that hath the mark, even the name of the Beast, or the number of his name."

Shirley waited a moment before she replied, whereat Grandfather Engel's eyes brightened, as though this in itself were a sign of grace. And indeed it means much to a teacher when his disciple questions himself, not his master, as to the teaching, when he begins to search his own heart for his own individual pearl of truth, that he may add it to the universal chaplet.

"I don't believe that can be true," said Shirley, deliberately. "I know it's in the Bible, but all the same I don't believe it."

"But why?" asked the old man, without any of the indignation which the girl had expected.

"Because buying and selling are necessary acts."

"Well?"

"And nothing necessary *can* bear the Mark of the Beast."

"Because?"

"Because God made us and the world and governs both."

"If your proposition be a true universal, it will bear turning round," said the wood-carver, smiling. "Nothing that bears the Mark of the Beast can be necessary. Are you willing to to accept it?"

"I don't know anything about universals," said Shirley, "but it *sounds* true."

"So? Then if we find that buying and selling bears the Mark of the Beast, we prove it to be unnecessary?"

Shirley looked puzzled, but assented.

"There is an Italian proverb," said the old man,—"'The buyer needs a hundred eyes, the seller only one.' Why?"

"That's easy enough," said Shirley. "There are a hundred ways in which the seller can cheat the buyer, while he can be cheated only in one way, and that only if he sells on credit."

"My daughter," said the old man, solemnly, "why should it seem so natural to you that they who buy and sell should also cheat?"

"Why, that is the name of it," said Tom, in his debonair way. "We call it human nature to try to get the best of a bargain."

"Well, I suppose it is," said Shirley. "One does try to make money go as far as possible; one *must*; and so, as it is necessary, it cannot be wrong; *or*," she added, hastily, for those deep eyes of the old man shone full upon her, "if wrong, it isn't really necessary; though I don't see how to manage without it."

"Prove to yourself that it is wrong, and then be sure that with the temptation there is also a way of escape," said the old man. "Have you a brother?"

"I have only my mother and this cousin—Tom."

"Then between you and your mother is there any question of buying and selling?"

"Oh!" cried the girl, as if shocked.

"And if you offered to buy from or to sell to her, that would at once change the relations of love between you?"

"Stop a minute!" said the girl. "I am just beginning to understand the fifth chapter of Acts."[8]

"Ay," said Grandfather Engel, "to such love as theirs, buying and selling was impossible. They simply gave all that they had, once for all, then each took what he needed."

"And if they had bought and sold among themselves, love would have soon grown cold," said Shirley, thoughtfully.

"My daughter," said the old man, "you have found the Mark of the Beast."

"But what are you going to do about it?" asked Tom, as Shirley did not reply. Tom was much graver and more serious than his wont; he had not made a single witty remark or once turned the matter into ridicule, as he knew so well how to do. "You may call it necessary or unnecessary, as you like; but what is one to put in the place of buying and selling?" asked Tom.

"The answer to that question, my son," said the wood-carver, "is what men call Socialism."

When the cousins were ready to depart, they looked one at the other before they could express a desire for any of the old man's handiwork. At last Shirley summoned courage to ask if a certain exquisitely-carved vase were for sale.

"Nothing here is for sale to you," said the old man, gently. "If I have given you aught to-day, it was of that which is more precious than much fine gold; you shall not pay me for it with money, under any cover, no matter how kind. Nevertheless, take what you will: all is yours."

"You'll never make money that way, sir," said Tom.

"The only coins that I desire are those stamped with the image of God," returned the wood-carver. "Man is the measure of all things."

They walked home together very soberly. "He has given us a good deal to think of," said Shirley,—"of his best, indeed."

"Which would be all very well, if a fellow were allowed to return it in any way but in kind."

"I'm sure you gave of a better best than I thought was in you! How did you like it, Tom?"

"Well, and not well," said Tom, drolly. "For once in a way it isn't so bad; but whether one could breathe in that fine air as a constancy is quite another question."

"Tom," said his cousin, "I wonder if it isn't the fault of the Beast that it isn't our normal atmosphere?"

"That we don't want to wear our dress-coats in the morning?"

"A morning-coat may be best of its kind, Thomas. A clean calico is not second-best, but the extreme of poverty is to be forced to wear out one's shabby finery at home."

"A *pretty* calico," said Tom, "is fit for a queen."

Shirley glanced at him rather anxiously. "That Elsa is a beautiful girl," she said, "and they seem so well educated and refined, and all—"

"They speak far better English than we do."

"Because they have learned from books. But, Tom—"

"Don't disturb yourself, my dear," replied her cousin, coolly. "Fascinated as I confess myself, I am quite well aware that though Fräulein Elsa may be an angel she unquestionably is *not* one of ourselves."

II

In the pearly twilight of the same day, Elsa and her grandfather sat together under the forest-tree branches, the mother near them, busy with the true German hausfrau's never-ending knitting. In Elsa's lap lay a delicate fleecy fabric, such as she made by the dozen for a store up town; but the light had grown too faint for the intricate pattern, and the girl's head lay in delicious idleness against her grandfather's knee. Both were quite silent, watching the young moon slowly sink below the western hills, and the golden stars gleam fitfully through the faint haze across the summer sky.

Frau Engel's needles clicked steadily, for light was quite unnecessary to her practised fingers. She was not at all of that uncomfortable order of women to whom speech is a necessity, and the "having a saint in the family" had trained her in holy silence; but it struck her presently that she really had something to say, and she said it:

"*Ach! Grossvater*, what a sad news have I heard to-day!"

"So?" said the old man's deep, sympathetic tones, from the shadow of the arbor.

"*Ja*, so! It is the pretty miss who was here this morning. She the betrothed of a wicked man, Otho Goldsborough."

"You are sure of it, Elizabeth?"

Frau Engel laughed. "I know better

than to repeat gossip to *you*, grandfather," she said. "The day is not set for the marriage, but the betrothal is announced; even the bride's outfit is begun. It is a sore pity for so sweet a maiden."

"It is a strange thing that *his* bride should come to *me* for that which she received to-day," said the old man, thoughtfully.

Frau Engel pricked up her ears in quick curiosity, and Elsa's eyes sought his, in mute inquiry for the meaning of his tone and emphasis. The old man smiled.

"There is no reason you should not know," he said, in reply. "It is a tale belonging to my old life, when I was young, and my heart was hot and bitter against the wrong and tyranny I saw around me, not understanding why the patience of God is infinite. Part of the story you know already: how well I loved the young count, my master and foster-brother, how we studied always together, for he would have it no other wise, and how I, feeling—knowing—myself their equal, at least, in all our studies and games, bitterly resented the slights that came to me from his noble young associates. And it is ill to resent an insult, children, for that way it harms us indeed; but forgiveness robs it of all its sting to us, and of half the harm to the insulter."

"But as for the count himself, he loved me through all; and no insults came to me in his presence. We were Socialists, he and I,—or so, at least, we called ourselves; and we thought it no wrong to a just cause to use falsehood and treason in its behalf. Among those of the count's own class who professed to feel as we did, was one—ah, well, it may be that he was no deliberate traitor. It was the madness of jealousy that caused him to betray our treason. For there was a certain fair maid whom both loved, he and the count, and who preferred my dear master,—as who would not? And then arose the old cry of a plot among the students,—a just cry, too, though I doubt if the plot could have harmed any but the plotters, had it been let alone,— and there were many arrests, my master and I among them. We tasted of the fare of a German prison, children; and, though I lived until an amnesty in honor of a royal wedding opened the prison doors, my dear young master, never so strong as I, had sunk under the hardship and confinement, and was dead, only a month before my release."

"And his beloved?" asked Elsa.

"Long before married to the traitor. What would you? She had little choice, perhaps, and they told her evil tales of the young count.

Well, well, she knows the truth now! But your grandmother, my child, was made of different stuff; she was peasant-born, like me; and she waited my release, then we married and came to America together. I have learned much since then," he added, solemnly.

"To be saint as well as angel," said his daughter-in-law within herself; but aloud she only asked, "And what has all this to do with Herr Goldsborough, grandfather?"

"You know I still have friends over yonder," he answered, "who write me, from time to time, tidings of themselves and how the work goes on. And from them

I learned, years ago, that the daughter of the traitor had married an American. Otho Goldsborough is her son."

"And he is worthy of his ancestors," said Frau Engel.

"Speak not so, Elizabeth," said the old man, gently; "yet they were not to their own consciences so much to blame. Nor is he. It is the teaching of the world that each should seek his own good, not that of his brother; and in the race for wealth, none can afford to fall behind. But Otho Goldsborough believes himself an honor-worthy man."

"He grinds the faces of the poor," said Frau Engel. "The girls in his factory get not so bad wages, because he fears to refuse; they are organized, and can force him to give what they ask; but he gives out work also, and to sweaters; and that is murder,—no less than murder!"

The old man's face was very sad.

"It is murder," he said, solemnly; "but the man does not think himself a murderer. He gives out work,—well, if it did not pay these men to take it, would they do so? They in turn supply with work women who are never seen on the streets to mock them, who have no decent raiment wherein to seek work for themselves, and are glad to work for any pittance wherewith to obtain bread for their famishing bodies. On whom shall we charge the guilt of murder, when the victim drops dead from hunger and toil, while the sweater and employer grow rich on the money earned by her needle? On them alone? Nay, I tell you, but on all the race of man, who seek each one to get a living, to get

wealth, instead of casting the wealth into God's treasury and receiving their living from Him, as do the lilies of the field. Verily, if we would *so* seek first His kingdom and His righteousness, the riches of all the world should be added unto us, and not Solomon[9] in all his glory should rival the splendor of the race."

"If *all* would do it, that would be a great convenience," said Frau Engel, without intermitting her work; "but where only *one* tries, it is bad. For, see you, grandfather, you would not take money from the Junker[10] and the Fräulein this morning; and therefore have we no breakfast."

"Well, well, we can do without," began the wood-carver; but his eyes fell upon the girl at his knee, and he added, in a different tone, "None at all?"

"There is always milk, *Mütterchen*,"[11] said Elsa, brightly, "and I will try to find eggs. It is only the flour is out, grandfather, and we have no money to buy more; but we can do without bread for one morning, and I can get money to-morrow when I take home my work. Oh, it will all be well."

"Quite well," said the old man, smiling; "more than well, my child, for it is God's will."

"And this is the end of the world," said the girl, "as you have so often told me; the latter days, when the forces are gathering for the great battle of Armageddon,[12] which is to overthrow the Beast and his image, and to establish the kingdom of peace and righteousness."

"Rather, has not the conflict begun already?" he answered. "For, behold, on all sides there is a sound like the treading of a mighty host, and the clash of swords. But the dust and smoke hang low over the field, so that we know not friend from foe. Nay, what say I? For all are friends, all foes, around us; we ourselves strike blindly, sometimes, against, even against our Leader."

"Therefore we dare use but one weapon," said the girl,—"the weapon of Love, the sword of the Spirit. Grandfather, it would be a glorious conquest if that fair young maid who heard you so earnestly this morning could win for her betrothed a rescue from the Beast."

"Glorious vengeance for an ancient wrong," said the wood-carver. "We will not mourn then, daughter, for the loss of a breakfast?"

Elsa laughed joyfully for all reply; but when the old man had gone to his bed, the girl's brain still throbbed with the wonder of the words he had spoken.

The little street was as quiet as her own garden. She opened the gate and wandered on, scarce knowing whither, lost in the magic of her own thoughts, until she found herself at the head of the cross-street which led down into the city, where through a deep cut of the railroad a late train rushed suddenly, with noise and glare which broke her revery.

As she turned to retrace her steps, a man who had stood so closely in the shadow of a house that she had not perceived his presence, threw away his cigar and came forward to greet her.

"Fräulein Elsa," said Tom Meredith, "you will not require of me to let you go home alone at this hour?"

She was "not one of ourselves"; but she might have been a canonized saint, from the young man's tone.

Elsa looked at him with wondering eyes. "I am in no danger," she said, smiling; "and I require of you just nothing at all, Herr—Herr Tom. Is that right? It is so your cousin calls you."

"It is quite right," said the young man. "'Herr Tom'! I feel as if I had been made a duke."

"A duke? but that is a leader," she said, not forbidding him to walk beside her as she turned homeward.

"Ah! I shall never be a leader," he answered. "It is rather more than I can do to follow at an immense distance."

"It is the great battle that I was thinking of," she said, "the battle of Armageddon. And there is no distance there; it is a hand-to-hand conflict; and, on one side or the other, one must fight. But we may choose our weapons,—the sword of Love, or the poisoned arrows of Hatred."

"If all were like you, the battle would be won already," he said, softly.

"If all had lived with my grandfather and been taught by him as I have, there isn't one would not be far better," said the girl, so simply that he could only smile, without venturing to contradict her.

At the little gate she paused and held out her hand. "Good-night, Herr Tom," she said.

He held it closely, that large, firm, work-worn hand, feeling inarticulately enough the help and strength therein for "Lazy Tom," if he had but courage to grasp and energy to hold it.

Elsa looked up; but it was too dark to

read the meaning of his brown eyes. Then he let her fingers go. She went to her bed smiling, but not dreaming *why* she smiled; and Tom, as he sauntered homeward, drew out his cigar-case and lit another of the Havanas which burned up so much of his salary.

"It is an awful pity," he said to himself, "that when a woman is already an angel it should be so imperatively necessary that she should be also—an aristocrat."

He was at least consistent, this poor Tom. The angelhood was all very well; but the second-best was necessary for every day.

III

Colors seen by candle-light
Will not look the same by day,[13]

says Mrs. Browning; and, though star-light is not supposed to have exactly the same effect, Tom Meredith came down-stairs the next morning feeling more ashamed of himself than if he had done something absolutely wicked.

Tom's enemies—but no! he had not an enemy in the world, nor was he the enemy of any one, even of himself,—Tom's god-fathers and godmothers, then, his relatives and intimate friends, were accustomed to say of him that he was too lazy to be ab-solutely anything, even wicked. He was good-natured to a fault, they said, but be-yond that was best described by negatives. For instance, he was not dissipated, not inattentive to business, had no bad hab-its of any kind, and made no pretence of being religious, though he went to church sometimes to please his aunt.

But relations and friends are not always the best judges of a man's character; and these of Tom's scarcely gave due weight, perhaps, to the steady though silent re-sistance implied by their own negations to the numerous temptations that beset young manhood. Indolent he was, though capable of sufficient energy when once aroused; but a very positive point indeed in his character was a certain almost ul-tra refinement, a repulsion for all things unlovely or of bad report, which, in the abeyance of the higher spiritual quality of which it is the human manifestation, had done him yeoman's service. But in the severing of the bond between this earthly purity and its divine counterpart lies, as in every death, a threatening corruption; and, all unconsciously, Tom had come to a crisis in his life.

He was late for breakfast, of course, for this was his holiday fort night, which he was spending at home,—he *said*, because it was too much trouble to go away, but partly at least because the absence of his fortnight's board would have made a seri-ous hole in his aunt's house-keeping purse, and he had not the money to travel in the princely style which was the only one he knew, and also pay his expenses at home.

Mrs. Meredith was awaiting his com-ing behind her coffee-pot, when he de-scended the stairs which led from his bed-room door down into the dining-room itself; but Shirley had enthroned herself in a great arm-chair on the tiny porch out-side, where she was diligently basting the waist of a dress of white India linen, so called for euphony, perhaps, as it was of American make.

It was a quaint old house in which these two women struggled *for* a living, and *with* the pupils who under their charge were supposed to acquire the elements of a thorough education. It was very old,—as old as any house could be in Smoketon,—and had been added to, perhaps incongruously, at various times. There was a wide, cool hall running from the front door to the main school-room, with doors to the right and left, opening into a smaller recitation-room and a parlor. Beyond the parlor was the kitchen, with its windows opening upon the same street as the more aristocratic apartment; and behind both ran the long, narrow dining-room, which had in all probability once been the entrance-hall. On the other side of the modern entrance, beyond the recitation-room referred to, was the cloak-room, with a door opening upon a side-street,—so that, as Tom said, there were plenty of exits in case of fire; but, as they had unfortunately never had a fire, the multiplicity of doors served only to strike terror to the soul of the stranger within the gates. For at his own first visit to the mansion, having rashly descended from the upper regions without a guide, and trusting solely to the light of nature, Tom was sure that he had opened at least two dozen doors, surprising a bevy of giggling girls, and an irate teacher, behind each one. The second floor—there was no third—he characterized as a "congeries of desolation." "It is the coolest house in winter, and the warmest in summer, that I ever inhabited," said Tom. "The landlord ought to be prosecuted for breach of promise, or assault and battery, or something."

"I suppose they think it is a free country and we can move out whenever we like," replied Shirley. "But that is just their mistake, Thomas: it is just because it's a free country that we *cannot* move out."

"Well, we *have* got so much freedom as individuals that collectively we crowd each other," said Tom. "Where did you get it, Shirley?"

"Get what?"

"Your treatise on Socialism."

Shirley laughed, and owned to having demanded the latest work upon that subject at the public library the evening before, and to having sat up far into the night to read it.

"I suppose you supplied yourself with an automatic fan?"

"Several hundreds of them, and all calling me 'cousin, cousin,' in the most affectionate manner."

"Zeal, indeed! I wish Grandfather Engel joy of his proselyte," said Tom, lazily; for this was on the morning which we have already reached.

"I don't know what in the world Shirley is thinking about, to read such books," said Mrs. Meredith: "I am sure Mr. Goldsborough will disapprove."

She was a woman whose still pretty face bore tokens of her life-long struggle to make both ends meet,—a struggle which had warped her parts of speech, while her actions remained true to an unperverted instinct. As she spoke she looked very anxiously at Shirley, with a mixture of feelings which she could by no means have explained.

Shirley pressed her red lips close together in silence, and the word was taken up by Mary, the cook, who brought in at the moment a plate of hot biscuit.

"Do you know Grandfather Engel, Mr. Tom?" asked Mary, delightedly. It was one of Mary's peculiarities to be always delighted or else in the depths of woe: she wept when the wash was large and the weather unpropitious; and her pride in the snowy, foamy biscuit of the present was doubly radiant because of the remembrance of past failures, for it was usually an even chance whether her cookery turned out delicious or uneatable.

She set the plate upon the table, and the backs of her large red hands upon her capacious hips, with a conscious smile. "I kept 'em back yet, because I know you are late a'ready," said Mary; "and how they are good! Mr. Tom, do you know Grandfather Engel yet?"

"I had the pleasure of making his acquaintance yesterday," said Tom, leisurely breaking open a biscuit. "By George, these *are* good, Mary! You'll be an honor to your country and a terror to the foe, if you'll only do it all the time."

"My country? I don't be a-cooking for the President, nor the poor-house, Mr. Tom."

"Nay, but in the home of the aristocratically poor," said Tom.—"Mark that, Shirley: she has no ideal of a country anywhere between those two extremes. Mary, I fear you're not a Socialist."

"Not in this country," said Mary, with a toss of her head.

"Sociable! they don't know what Socialism is a'ready."

"Mary went to a picnic yesterday, and was disgusted with their unsocial proceedings," said Mrs. Meredith, her anxious eyes sparkling with fun.

"And did you have a pleasant time?" asked Tom, politely.

"Time!" said Mary, her broad red face strongly expressive of scorn; "more time than I'll ever give 'em again, Mr. Tom. I don't know so very many people in this neighborhood. Only last Sunday, Miss Cowan she says to me after church, 'Mary,' she says, 'why don't you come to the picnic?' she says, 'for there's lots of handsome fellers,' she says."

"I thought better of Mrs. Cowan," returned Tom, gravely, "than to be putting such ideas into your young mind."

"I ain't so young but I can talk to the fellers a'ready," said Mary; "but not one of 'em come near me the whole day, Mr. Tom."

"You don't say so!"

"Not one of 'em; and my new shoes was too tight to walk yet, and I didn't know nobody: so I sat under a tree, and got grass-stain all over my dress, and broke my parasol leaning on it when I tried to get up, and I think next time I'll climb up on top of the house and look at the picnic."

This was too much for Tom; he threw down his knife and fork and screamed with laughter. Mary was flattered, and laughed also at her own wit so unrestrainedly that she was obliged to sink into the nearest chair. "*Mein Gott!*[14] how I am funny this day!" said she.

"But where was Mrs. Cowan?" asked Tom.

"Oh! Miss Cowan she pass me by, and she say, 'How you are, Mary? why you don't go have some fun with the young folks?' And I say, 'Miss Cowan—'"

"Well?"

"Well, I didn't say no more," said Mary. "I couldn't think of nothing to say."

"Dear me! I wish I were like you,

Mary," said Shirley, wiping her eyes on her new dress; "for then my tongue would get me into fewer scrapes than it does."

"That's just what Miss Cowan used to say," cried Mary, delightedly. "When I lived with her, she said every day, 'Mary, I wish I was like you, Mary,' she says. And one day she sent me to the crocery-store for some molasses, and the crocery-man he took the pitcher into the whare-room to fill it, and I think he gave a little too less. So I told Miss Cowan, and she says, 'I wish I was as sharp as you, Mary,' she says. And Grandfather Engel he says—"

"Oh! so you know Grandfather Engel, do you?" asked Shirley.

"My mother's own uncle was his cousin in Germany," replied Mary, smiling broadly. "Frau Engel she's a nice lady too; and Elsa,—oh! she uses such fine language! Do you know Elsa, Miss Shirley? She's my cousin."

"Cousin-German," murmured Tom under his moustache, while Shirley replied, "I have seen her, Mary."

"Well, she and me is both one age," said Mary. "The fellers don't run after Elsa much, neither. But her father he was a engineer on the railroad. My father he thinks the rich people ought to divide with us poor ones. You wouldn't like that, Mr. Tom."

"Mary," said Tom, "I assure you that at the demand of the people I would gladly surrender all the railroad-bonds and bank-stock in my possession, and be a thousandfold happier afterwards."

"That's just like Mr. Cowan," said Mary, clapping her great hands in ecstasy: "he failed in business when I lived with

them, and he was teetotally ruined, but he laughed yet."

"Well, I never imagined that the Cowans had a 'divide,'" said Shirley, when Mary had with difficulty been relegated to her kitchen: "to my sorrow, I know they had a wedding in the family, and everything else has happened to them that has ever befallen us; but when it came to a 'divide' I did think we were safe."

"A little of Mary's conversation is rather amusing, but after a bit it certainly palls upon one," said Tom.

"And she never knows when she passes the boundary-line," returned his cousin. "How odd that she should be related to that beautiful, *spirituelle* girl!"

"Oh, as to that, we are all related through Adam," answered Tom, wearily. "By George! a holiday is pretty hard work. I think I'll take a walk."

"I never expected to hear Tom complain of a holiday," said Mrs. Meredith, looking after him. "Did you finish the skirt of that dress yesterday, Shirley?"

"Very nearly, mamma."

"Then if we work on it together we can finish the dress for you to wear when you take your drive with Mr. Goldsborough this afternoon."

She came close to the girl and laid her arm across the pretty shoulders.

"It is a great happiness to me, Shirley, to think how soon you are to be rid of the burden of poverty," she said. "Yet I would not for anything have you marry him if I did not believe him to be a really good man."

"If he is as good to you as he promises to be, it is all I ask of him, mamma."

"Oh, don't think of me, my child: all that I wish is to see you happy; and I am sure you ought to be. You will have all that heart could wish, and a good kind husband besides."

"All the modern conveniences, and the Decalogue[15] thrown in," said the girl. "I say, mamma, do you think these darts are perfectly straight? *I don't.*"

Tom, meanwhile, had wandered out into the highways,—and very high some of them were,—disconsolate and ashamed, though he would have been puzzled to explain his own feelings. He had been in love in a mild sort of way several times in his life, but anything like the feeling inspired by Elsa Engel was altogether outside of his experience, for which reason he was not at all prepared to admit that he *was* in love. It was simply a sense of glaring incongruity, he said to himself, that made him so very cross about her being Mary's cousin, no matter how distant.

"Hello, Tom!"

Now, Tom strenuously objected to being tapped on the shoulder; but on this occasion he was rather glad to see the tapper, a young journalist of his acquaintance, who was very fond of airing in conversation views which as to print were limited in expression by the necessities of the counting-room.

"Hello, Hopkins," said Tom, "is this you?"

"Why, it *yoused* to be," said Hopkins; "but we are changing all that so fast that I don't feel sure of it."

"Change your puns, and you may hope to improve our glorious Constitution," said Tom. "By George, Hopkins, I should think the spread eagle would blush for shame."

"Oh, you let the eagle scream; he's all right: you've got more cheek than he has, any day. What's the matter with you?"

"Social distinctions," said Tom. "You'll never do away with them, Hopkins."

"They don't bother me much," returned the other. "I know a girl whose grandmother was a cook, and she's as pretty and refined a little thing as you'll find anywhere."

"So she may be; but how about the relations?"

"What are her relations to me? I'm not going to marry her,—worse luck!"

"Suppose you were?"

"Oh, is *that* it?" said Hopkins, doubling over with amusement. "Only think of it! caught at last, are you, my King Cophetua?"[16]

"Nonsense! nothing of the sort!" cried Tom, growing very red. "I am discussing the matter impersonally, you idiot."

"Oh! are you? Well, then, I should say that a fellow with any snap to him would personally take the girl, and impersonally let the relations go to the mischief."

"And a girl with any snap to her wouldn't send her relations to the mischief," said Tom.

"Well, if she can stand 'em you can, I should think."

"I tell you, I'm speaking impersonally."

"So I see. Well, I've got to interview a man in here; so I wish you an impersonal adieu. And I say, Tommy the fastidious, don't worry over trifles, or quarrel with your bread-and-butter. See? If she's the right sort of girl, you freeze to her—impersonally, of course. Ta ta!"

Tom felt very uncomfortable indeed, when he had parted with the vivid young journalist. Of course Hopkins was an idiot, and he, Tom, had no idea of marrying any one; it was simply that he found it uncomfortable to look down and up at the same moment of time. He strolled idly along, scarcely knowing whither, until he found himself standing before a stone-cutter's yard. The master himself was at the gate, and invited him in with a pleasant smile.

"Anything I can do for you this morning, sir?" he said.

"Not that I know of," replied Tom. "I've got a holiday, and don't very well know what to do with it."

"Ah! I've been that way myself," said the stone-cutter, sympathetically. "Won't you come in, sir? I'm always glad to have gentlemen call on me in a cheerful sort of way. Monuments and tombstones, you see; and when you come to think about it, it ain't as cheerful a business as it might be, nor it don't bring me cheerful society, as a rule."

He led Tom through the sheds, chatting pleasantly and intelligently, though with a free use of very colloquial English.

"Now, here's a monument I've just finished," he said, at last; "and, by the bye, they say the poor woman's husband is engaged to be married again. I know he has nearly hurried the head off me: so I suppose he wants to be entirely off with the old love before he is on with the new. And *that* man left directions in his will to have this sentence cut on his tombstone."

Tom stooped to read it:

"For we shall all stand before the judgment-seat of God."

"Was he a Socialist?" asked Tom.

"Not that I know of; though, Lord! everybody's a Socialist now. You can't throw a stone in any direction without striking one. Yes, sir; there's where you do get your social equality."

"It doesn't make things at all less unequal on this earth, though."

"Well, maybe it would if you could get the right focus," said the stone-cutter. "Ever been to Rome, sir?"

"Not yet," said Tom.

"Ah! Well, I have. My poor old father thought I was going to be a great genius, like Michelangelo, or any of those fellows, and he stinted himself—poor old man!— to give me a fair show. Well, it wasn't exactly my fault if I disappointed him; for I certainly did work the worst way; and I'm about as good a stone-cutter as you'll find in America, if I ain't a sculptor, exactly. So I don't believe I regret the trip, at all. But what I want to say is this. There's a place there called St. Peter's Church,[17] and you can stand up in the dome of it and see the people walking on the pavement below, and, I give you my word, sir, they look no bigger than flies. You may not believe me, sir, but that is the actual truth."

"I haven't a doubt of it," said Tom, gravely.

"Yes, sir; and, what's more, there ain't as much difference between a tall man and a short one, or even a man and a child, as you might suppose. Everybody looks pretty much about the same size. And so when I hear people talking about social distinctions and classes, and so on, I say to myself, 'Why in thunder don't they get the right focus?'"

"There's a good deal in that," said Tom. "Well, good-morning. Much obliged for your kindness in showing me your place."

"Don't mention it, sir: I enjoy a talk with people who are not in grief. If you ever want anything in my line,—though I hope you never may—"

"Never is long word," said Tom. "It's what we've all got to come to. You may grave on my tombstone, 'He tried to find the right focus.'"

"Hope you may, sir," said the stone-cutter, heartily.

Tom went home so tired with his morning's walk as to fall asleep the instant he sat down. He dreamed that he stood in the dome of St. Peter's and watched the multitude below, all ages and every rank mingled indistinguishably. Suddenly he found himself among them, and the place was no longer St. Peter's, but the judgment-seat of God. Beside him was Mary the cook, and between them was thorough equality, for all there were rated not by what was theirs, but by what they were. Tom felt that the case was going against him,—when suddenly came a cry from the girl beside him, who reached out her arms towards a great white angel who, with folded wings and the face of Elsa Engel, stood beside the Throne.

"I'm her cousin," cried Mary; and therewith he awoke.

He sat up erect in his chair and wiped the perspiration from his brow.

"By George," he said, "if she'd said she was cousin to Victoria R.,[18] how we should have toadied to her! Well, it's a poor rule that won't work both ways, and a very bad social staircase that won't grade down as well as up. Thomas, I believe you have got the right focus. Mary, I respect you; you have angelic blood in your veins; you are Elsa's cousin."

IV

Shirley was ready, in her white frock, and with her pretty face bright and smiling, when Mr. Goldsborough drove up to the door. He was a man of about thirty-five, who might have been of any age within ten years on either side of it; rather above the medium height, with a strong, squarely-made, muscular figure, a quiet, smooth-shaven, sensible-looking face, squarely cut as to brow and chin, with thick, straight, light-brown hair and clear, alert blue eyes. No one could have been less romantic in appearance, yet he did not seem at all unsuited to his bride, as they drove off together. But as a matter of fact it would have been hard to find two people who understood each other less.

Otho Goldsborough was an only child; and he had been educated with a single eye to the advantage he might gain thereby, not that he might add to the world's knowledge, far less return to humanity any of the benefits procured for him by the age-long struggles and triumphs of the race. He had lived much abroad, a quiet, scholarly life, without any excesses either of learning or of pleasure,—such a life as a man of average intelligence and ample means can live in a European university town. From this he had been summoned home at his father's death, to find his affairs rather in disorder, which he had set himself to remedy with all the energy that was in him. It had required hard work, close economy, and strict attention to details, wherein he had not always had the hearty co-operation and sympathy of his workers. But these, indeed, he did not expect from them, as why should he? Certainly co-operation and sympathy on his side were conspicuous by their absence. And yet he did not rate himself as a hard master; it was simply a question of conflicting interests, and he had no more doubt that his own interests ought to carry the day than he had of his ability to guide and check the spirited horses he drove, or the spirited bride he had chosen.

Shirley, on the other hand, had as yet scarcely realized how largely her yielding to his not over-passionate wooing had been influenced by the wealth and luxury he was in a position to offer her. Of course she was fond of him; she liked his quiet, undemonstrative manner; his conversational powers, though not brilliant, were easy, and his choice of subjects excellent. Moreover, it was flattering to be chosen by a man of his age, position, and weight of character; and the thought of passing her life at his side was thoroughly pleasant to her. She had told him frankly that she was not "in love" with him; and he had answered, as men do, that that made no difference at all,— he was quite willing to marry her and let the love come afterwards; which willingness upon his part, Shirley considered, made it all quite right, and completely removed the burden of responsibility from her shoulders. Girls will still argue in this way, all unknowing that the argument is as obsolete as their grandmother's gig-top bonnet, and, like that, absurd and unnatural even when most fashionable.

"You will like to attend vespers at the convent, Shirley," said her lover, as they turned from the streets into the smooth though hilly turnpike. "The music there is wonderful; and to-day, you know, is a great occasion."

"I don't mind," said Shirley; "though mamma won't like it very well. She has always been afraid to let me go inside a convent since once in the East, when I was perfectly fascinated and wanted to become a nun, then and there."

"Why, I should rather object myself to such a result of this visit," he said, laughing; "but, fortunately, there is no danger."

"Well, I don't know," said Shirley,—a little perversely, it must be confessed. "There's a wonderful charm about conventual life, I think."

"I have heard it stated as an axiom that the first impulse of an uncorrupted mind is always towards the cloister," said Mr. Goldsborough; "but I must say—tell it not in Gath, Shirley!—that it seems to me rather a morbid impulse."

"Do you think so?" asked Shirley, thoughtfully. "Now, it seems to me that when a girl—or a man—begins to understand what money is, and how this question of buying and selling destroys all real brotherhood among men, it is very natural to take refuge in a convent, unless they know better and turn Socialists."

"Eh? Socialists? What do you know of Socialism?" asked Mr. Goldsborough, amusedly.

"Not much," replied Shirley, modestly, "for I have only just begun to study the subject, you know."

She had never seen her *fiancé* laugh so heartily as he did at this; and perhaps he had some excuse; she looked so pretty, so young, and so innocent, that it was hard for him to think seriously of her studying anything more abstruse than the language of flowers; and so he said, when he found that his amusement vexed her.

But Shirley was not propitiated by the compliment, as he considered it.

"I am not silly or sentimental," she said, with dignity, "and the language of flowers is certainly both. You forget, Otho, that I have had my own living to earn, and it hasn't been easy work: so that makes me realize what a great thing Socialism would be for the country."

"There ought to be one in every family, no doubt," he said, with renewed merriment; "but your struggles are all over now, my darling."

"Other people's are not, though."

"No, and never will be. You cannot make over the world, my dear; and why should you spend your strength in trying or even wishing to do so?"

"Because I don't wish to be like the man in the rhyme, Otho:

Of all my mother's children
I love myself the best,
And when I am provided for
I care not for the rest.

You say I must do the religion for both of us; and Socialism is nothing else but religion, it seems to me."

"Then, indeed, you must do the Socialism for both of us, too," said the rich man, laughing. "I suppose this is the result of your visit to Grandfather Engel yesterday."

"He's a saint," said the girl, fervently.

"Or a precious old hypocrite, I have never been able to determine which. Well, well, don't look so indignant: I dare say he's all you think him. And I do not at all mind your studying Socialism, or Theosophy, or any other nonsense you like, my dear. It is very pretty and sweet of you to feel for the miseries of others, and, for any practical assistance that you can give them, my purse is always at your service."

"I'm not of enough importance to be worth disagreeing with," said Shirley, still annoyed.

"Your importance to me, personally, is so great that I can't afford to disagree with you," he replied, good-humoredly. "There! that, I always think, is the very prettiest view of the convent."

He drew up his horses at the brow of a hill, and pointed with his whip across the valley into which they were about to descend.

St. Agnes' Convent in itself was not a building of any especial architectural merit. It was large, square, and roomy, with—for beauty, though not for sanitation—rather an over-supply of windows, and an occasional feeble turret; but its situation half-way up one of the lesser hills, at the foot of which the swift little mountain-brook was crossed by a picturesque red bridge, and the brownish gray to which its painted bricks had faded, against the blue-green background, made it attractive and beautiful.

The chapel was upon the ground-floor, and of the height of two stories, its roof arched with oaken rafters, and every remaining inch of wall and ceiling covered with vivid frescos. In the slanting rays of the evening sun, which shone through the stained glass of the western windows and filled the place with rainbow light, it sparkled like a gem.

Shirley drew a deep breath as they were shown softly to a seat by one of the still-faced, black-veiled nuns; her eyes lighted up.

Mr. Goldsborough glanced at her with a smile. "One enthusiasm drives out another," he thought. It gave a very pleasant fillip to his own emotions, that vivid face beside him: indeed, Shirley's capacity for enjoying everything had been her chief attraction in his eyes.

It was the first vespers of a feast; and the high altar was brilliant with lights, and covered with many flowers. Soft and clear, the sweet voices of the nuns chanted the holy words; then the tender strain was taken up in tones richer, deeper, but not less sweet, by the richly-robed priest at the altar.

Shirley did not try to understand; she did not attempt to follow the words; she simply surrendered her senses to the glory of the place, the sweetness of the enchanting melody, and the penetrating fragrance of the curling wreaths of incense.

When it was all over she heaved a deep sigh. "Oh, I wish I could stay here forever!" she said.

The Sister who had received them, and who had come again to their side, smiled, well pleased.

"You must come again, when you can see the house," she said, kindly. "It is too late now, and against our rule; but I can show you the grounds, if you like."

"I like anything that will keep me here half an hour longer," said Shirley.

There were winding paths in the garden, here encircling the image of a saint, there ending at a niche in the high brick wall, containing the glass-enclosed figures of the Madonna and Child.

Shirley arranged with Sister Ursula to come out by rail on the following day and spend several hours, Mr. Goldsborough undertaking to drive out for her in the afternoon. "She's not such a promising convert, though, as she looks," he said, laughing: "her ardor soon evaporates, Sister Ursula."

"It is scientific zeal," returned Shirley. "I am interested in studying the possibility of living without money."

Mr. Goldsborough laughed rather significantly: he was more of a Roman Catholic than of anything else, in a religious way, and had had practical experience that if the Sisters tried to live without money they certainly did not succeed.

"As individuals," said Sister Ursula, gently, "we have no use for money; and you are quite right, my dear, in supposing voluntary poverty to be good for one's soul."

V

It was rather a misfortune that Mr. Goldsborough did not understand the true significance of Shirley's study of Socialism. There have been periods in the world's history ere now when some truth, hitherto overlaid and obscured by the traditions of men, has started out upon the palimpsest of history with such youthful freshness and vigor as to be appropriately called a renaissance, or new birth. This new birth comes to one individual at a time: *then* suddenly it is found to be a part of the conscience of the race: so that it has been said that in every reform there are three stages: in the first people say, "It is absurd"; in the second, "It is irreligious"; in the third, "Everybody knows *that!*"

Mr. Goldsborough had not advanced beyond the point of believing Socialism too absurd to be worthy of serious consideration; but to Shirley it was indeed a renaissance. She had been brought up, it must be said, in an excellent school for it. Mrs. Meredith had been the daughter of a naval officer, who, as naval officers will, had lived fully up to his salary; she had married the clergyman of a fashionable church, and had led the life demanded by his wealthy flock, until, when Shirley was but four years old, his death left her a widow, with no inheritance except very expensive tastes and habits.

Of course his parishioners "would not see her suffer,"—or said so: they started her at once with a little school, and when Shirley was of an age to be benefited by them, all the advantages of the diocesan school were open to her without money and without price.

But, in some way or other, Mrs. Meredith's income never quite held out. It was like trying to sleep under a baby's blanket,—pull it up one way, it comes short another; and so if Mrs. Meredith's rent was covered, the coal-bill went bare; if she paid her grocer, the cook must wait for her wages. Shirley was quite inured from childhood to wearing fewer and plainer frocks than her companions; sometimes her eyes looked wistful over it, but she soon forgot it. But attending a free church with no money to put in the plate was undoubtedly a cross; and as for Sunday-school, when she had found that the

pennies contributed by each child were noted in a book, Shirley decided that Sunday-school was not in her line, and that, whether or not it was expected of her as clergyman's daughter, she did not propose to go again. But for her sweet and wholesome nature, Shirley might have been seriously injured by these and innumerable other petty vexations and mortifications, the chief antidote to which was the teaching she received at home,—quite opposite to the practical effect of the Sunday-school contributions,—that her poverty was the will of God, and in His sight a higher state than riches. To be sure, she heard this at church too, and very earnestly preached; but as a matter of every-day experience it seemed rather easier for a rich man to enter by *that* gate of the kingdom than for a poor man to go through a needle's eye.[19] Shirley quite appreciated the need of money to pay clerical salaries and provide candles, flowers, etc., for the altar; she did not see how the condition of affairs could be materially altered or improved; for, though it seemed that the times were out of joint, she had been taught to look upon inequalities of fortune as disagreeable necessities, like earthquakes and thunder-storms.

What would a hope of one day controlling the earthquake and guiding the thunder-cloud be to a votary of science? Such was to Shirley the new radiance that shone from the study she had "only just begun." It was not merely the solution of the mysteries that had perplexed her, and hope for the world; it was justifying the ways of God to men, the establishment of His claims as their King, the setting right in the eyes of all men of His power, love, mercy, justice, and truth.

There was not a nerve of her spiritual being which did not thrill with the new life, not a well-known object about her, not a thought, however old, but seemed new in the new light that fell upon it. "The former things had passed away; all things were become new."[20] That her first impulse should have been to share her joy with her betrothed, is surely not wonderful; and Otho Goldsborough was far— very far—from any intention of being unkind. Shirley's enthusiasm was, in her, very sweet and pretty, but he could not help feeling amused at ideas so extremely unpractical. "But just for that reason they were the very ideas to fascinate women," he said, and he was not at all afraid of their gaining ground enough to become troublesome. So he let Shirley take her own way,—"gave her her head," as he expressed it, until the first fervor of a new convert should have had time to evaporate; fully convinced that the new interests and duties which married life would bring would be more than sufficient to obviate all that was *prononcé* in her opinions.

The girl was fond of him; but her heart had been thrown back upon itself; she felt chilled and wounded. Her marriage had been fixed for the end of the summer vacation, but Shirley positively declined to let it take place at that time.

"I am not sure of myself," she said. "Besides, I must get my successor into training."

For Mr. Goldsborough had advised that Mrs. Meredith should keep up her school, a task from which Shirley had hoped to be able to release her.

"She will be much happier so," he had said. "Of course I shall pay the salary of whoever takes your place; that is only fair and right; and you may help her in other ways as much as you like; but, believe me, she will be far happier in a position of usefulness, where she is respected and esteemed, than she could possibly be as a dependent upon you."

"There has never been any question of dependence on my side," said Shirley, rather indignantly: "we have just had a common purse, and what was hers has been mine, as mine was hers."

"But now that what is yours is mine and mine yours, it would hardly be reasonable to wish to include her in the bargain," said Mr. Goldsborough, smiling.

Shirley felt that her own dignity as well as her mother's would be compromised if the argument were pushed farther.

"What's his is mine, indeed!" she said to herself, bitterly. "That's the worst lie in the whole marriage service. I wonder why they put it in?"

જી

She went very often to the wood-carver's cottage: it was like a little piece of heaven, and rested her, she said. For Shirley, as is the way of women, had gone to the heart of the subject at once: she had had no battles to fight with social prejudices, no difficulty in finding the right focus, as had been the case with Tom. That Elsa Engel should be even distantly related to their own absurd Mary, with her trusty heart and unreliable head, was simply comical to Shirley, who from the vantage-ground of genteel poverty had always viewed classes more on a level than is possible to most people; but those who see classes on a level are more easily able than others to note the varying heights of individuals: so there was no sense of social inequality to vex Shirley's intercourse with the wood-carver's family. But of that consciousness of inequality which lies at the root of hero-worship and justifies it—that is, makes it righteous— Shirley had her due proportion; and it was a constant delight to her, and source of refreshment, that the world held those whom she able to love and reverence as heartily as she did Grandfather Engel and Elsa.

She found her way to the little cottage one September afternoon, when the woods were just gaining their first touch of red. There was a crispness in the air and a faint haze over the distant hills that told of the near October, and Shirley was not sorry to meet Elsa at the gate, in her out-of-door dress, with a basket on her arm, and a shining tin can in the other hand.

"Going out? How nice!—that is, if I may go with you," she said. "It is such a perfect day, that it seems a sin to be shut up within four walls."

"Ah! so!" replied Elsa, with a soft sigh. "You may gladly go with me, dear friend; but there are sad sights to be seen on such a day as this."

"But they will not last long, Elsa: in the beautiful time coming, we shall all be happy."

Elsa smiled, and yet sadly shook her head. "For many, for most, of these," she said, "no deliverance will come in this world but death. And, someway, I cannot be sorry, my Shirley, when one of them seeks out that deliverance for herself. It is wrong,—yes! but to the dear Father above it is but as the impatience of an angry child who throws himself against the door of the closet wherein he has been locked."

"But the child has done wrong, Elsa, before being locked up; and most of these poor sufferers are good. It is the wicked ones who are well, rich, and happy."

"I do not know," said Elsa; "some say there is no poverty or pain without some fault; but I am sure it is not always the fault of the individual sufferer. We do not know, Shirley; but God knows."

They had by this time reached the point where the steep street led downward into the town. Shirley paused for a long look over the beautiful panorama of hill and valley they were leaving.

"I rather wish we were going in *that* direction," she said, wistfully; "but of course wherever you go is right, dear Elsa."

"Let us carry the beauty and the glory in our hearts," returned Elsa, "for they need it where we go."

There were no tenement-houses in Smoketon, but there was something immeasurably worse,—the private house used as a tenement. From a dingy street the two girls turned into a filthy alley, where piles of garbage lay rotting in the gutters. There was scarcely room to walk, between the broken curb and the low, once white wooden steps that cropped up every two or three yards, as it seemed; and what foot way there was, was rendered unsafe by the broken pavement. Scores of children of all ages, some with hair bleached by the sun till it was by far the whitest thing about them, others grimed from hair to heel until it was hard to say if they were white or black by nature, announced themselves as literal cumberers of the earth, which, in spite of the great hills and the wide deep valleys around, had apparently no place for them upon her bosom except under the feet of the passer-by.

The houses were but two stories in height, which at first thought might be considered a gain; but the population of each was such as six stories could not have sheltered with comfort and decency. Each dwelling, however, had its cellar-way, politely termed its basement entrance; and into one of these Elsa made her way, closely followed by Shirley.

The room they entered was evidently a kitchen; for a huge cooking-stove stood nearly in the middle of it, and between that and the one low window, considerably below the level of the pavement, a tall, stalwart-looking German woman stood at her ironing-board.

She nodded pleasantly to Elsa and fixed a curious gaze on Shirley as the two girls entered the open door without the ceremony of knocking and passed through to a back room, whence sounded the whir of a sewing-machine and the peevish wail of a young child. This room was smaller and darker than the front one; its one window was quite high in the wall, and under it, stood the machine they had heard.

Before it, bending over it, her motions as regular and unvarying as if she herself formed part of the machinery, sat a woman who ought to have been young. Her long black hair hung tangled and dusty over her shoulders,—though she had evidently tried to fasten it up with a broken comb. Her dress was a tattered and filthy calico which once been black and white, but now could scarcely be called either; and there was plenty of evidence through the numerous rents that she wore very little besides.

On a small chair in the corner sat boy of perhaps seven years,—sat, because he was unable to stand; for his form was bent and distorted, and his poor little face was the face of a malicious fairy. On the floor lay a baby of two years, thin and wizened, clad—for there is no other word to take the place of the misnomer—in what had been a flannel skirt of its mother's. The binding was pinned around its neck, and the poor little arms were thrust through holes that had been torn for the purpose. The arms themselves were covered with what upon further examination proved to be the legs of a pair of worn-out knitted yarn stockings. Both children, the room, and the mother herself were rather more than dirty; and upon each side of the machine lay, as if in mocking contrast to the attire of the inmates, upon a newspaper spread to prevent their contact with the filthy floor, a pile of light-colored fall wraps, dainty in cut and delicate of hue, in which the mother was rapidly stitching the seams. At the cry of delight which broke from both children, this woman did not pause or turn her head.

"Good-day, Marie," said Elsa.

Shirley wondered how she dared use the words in such a place as that; certainly she got no answer; but she did not wait for one. She had already the baby in her arms, and was feeling her feverish hands and poor little hot cheeks.

"No, no," cried the little cripple, peevishly; "put Minne down, Elsa, and take me in your lap. I am so tired of this chair!"

"Minne is ill, Friedel," said Elsa, gently; while Shirley mutely held out her arms to the child, who pushed her crossly away and covered his face with his poor sleeve. "Marie, you know that she is ill?"

"And what good if I do?" replied Marie Wahman, as she dropped a garment upon the pile at her left and caught up another from the right. "Have I time to stop and nurse her? Besides, if the good God take her to Himself that will be best of all. She will be a woman if she lives; and there are worse things in this world than starvation, for a woman."

"I have brought some milk," said Elsa: "that will be good for her, and also for Friedel. Where is Teresa?"

"Gone! She did not come home last night. I know why. Do not dare to blame her, Elsa."

Mein Gott!" said the girl, with a look of terror; "and she but barely fifteen!"

The mother gave a short, hard laugh, more expressive and more terrible than words. "Teresa will not long be young," she said. "Elsa, you see my hair, how it is thick and long? When they have told me to cut it off and sell it, I have said, 'Ah, no! if I should take to the streets at last, I should need my hair.' And I ought to have done it, Elsa, but I was a coward; I could not give myself to such a life; I thought starvation better: therefore Teresa has gone instead. Elsa, I could have saved my child, and I did not."

She spoke in shrill, hard, tuneless voice, without pausing, or raising her eyes from her work.

Shirley leaned against the grimy wall, white and trembling. Elsa had lifted the baby to her lap, and was holding to the little parched lips a glass of cool sweet milk, which it drank greedily. She motioned to Shirley to do the same for the boy; meanwhile little Minne nestled her head against the kind breast that supported her, and fell into a soft and sudden sleep.

"There is little amiss with her: she will soon be well," said Elsa, tenderly.

"*Gott bewahre!* she had better die," said the mother.

"So I think," said Friedel, sagely. "She does nothing this day and but lie on the floor and cry, so that she makes my head ache; and she will not pick up my spools when I drop them," showing a long string of the only playthings he possessed. "Yes, yes, she had better die."

"Do you not love your little sister?" asked Shirley, gently.

"If she dies there will be her share of bread for me," said the boy, shrewdly.

At the sound of a strange voice Marie Wahman turned for the first time; then she pushed back her chair, rose swiftly to her feet, and confronted the intruder. She was deadly pale,—Shirley had never seen anyone so utterly bloodless,—and her face was worn not merely into furrows, but, as it seemed, into chasms, from amid which her large black eyes shone, fierce, wolfish, terrible. Her dress was so nearly reduced to ribbons, as Shirley now saw, that it could only with difficulty be kept about her; it slipped from her shoulder with the rough abruptness of her motion, and she held it across her wasted bosom with one hand, while with the other she threatened her uninvited guest.

"You!" she cried, wildly. "How dare you come here and be pretty, and happy, and young, and good also? What is it to you if we live or die? Go home and send your mother to me! Does she love you better than I love my child? No; but she has more money; and therefore you live safe and honored and happy; and when you die there is your place in heaven ready for you; while *my* child has only hell before her,—hell here, and hell hereafter. And you think that Jesus Christ is your Saviour? I tell you, no! What saves you is money!—money!—money!"

Shirley could not speak; she held up her hands as one begging for mercy. Elsa would have interposed to shield her, but, before she could speak, a wild shrill laugh was heard outside, and the form of a girl rushed into the room. She had her mother's black eyes and abundant dark hair; the paint on her pale cheeks was smirched and smeared over her whole face; the tawdry finery which she had, as was afterwards understood, borrowed for the occasion, was torn and disordered. She threw a roll of bank-notes at her mother's feet, caught up Friedel from his chair, and kissed him. "Friedel," she cried, "you shall have a little carriage to ride about the streets, and a blue coat with brass buttons. And you, mother, no more work for the sweaters! you shall live like a lady. There's the money, and plenty more where it came from."

The woman stood for a moment looking from the money on the floor to her daughter's face. The room,—malodorous enough before, heaven knows!—was redolent with the fumes of whiskey. She did not need to ask why Teresa had not come home earlier.

Suddenly the ghastly face flushed crimson, her eyes filled with blood; she rushed forward and tried to snatch the sleeping baby from Elsa's arms.

"Give her to me!" she cried, furiously; "let me dash out her brains against the wall and send her home to God, before the devil gets his grip of her also!"

There was a short, fierce struggle, then a fall, and Marie Wahman lay upon the floor, with the red life-blood pouring from her lips.

When they took her up, she was quite dead.

"Could you not have helped her? Could you not have saved that poor girl?" asked Shirley, passionately, of the German woman who had stood ironing in the outer room, and who ran hastily in at the outcry.

The woman looked at her curiously, then shrugged her broad shoulders. "Help her!" she said. "Do you suppose I did not help her when I could? But what is the good of helping one or saving one, when there are so many others? They are like flies: kill one, and a hundred come to the funeral; and so save one of these girls, make her able to earn an honest living, and, while you do it, a fall in wages throws a hundred into the sweaters' hands, or on the streets. No one can help them but the dear Lord God; and sometimes it seems as if He would not try."

☙

"What is a sweater?" asked Shirley, as they went home together.

"A sweater," replied Elsa, "is one who takes large quantities of work from a clothing-house and puts it out again to women who undertake to do it for him. The difference between what he receives and what he pays for the work is, of course, his profit."

"Then he does none of the work himself?"

"None at all."

"And the clothing-houses know that when they give it to him?"

"I suppose; but *ach*, no! they *cannot* realize it!"

"It is cruel, wicked, of them!" cried Shirley; "it is murder,—murder!"

Her eyes grew suddenly large with dread and horror.

"Elsa," she whispered, "tell me, does Mr. Golds—I mean, do you know what house Marie Wahman's work came from?"

"Shirley," said Elsa, solemnly, "I did not take you there to show you, but it is best you should know; only, remember, it is always true that they know not what they do. Smoketon is but a little place, and in it is only one house where work is done like that which lay on the floor yonder,— the floor too foul for those fine coats, but clean enough for a human child. And that one house is—Goldsborough Brothers."

VI

In spite of her poverty, Shirley's life had been a sheltered one; she knew little of the world, little of business customs and code of morals; nothing of the cesspool of infamy that poisons in secret our whole social life, except vaguely and indistinctly, as of "something not nice to talk about." Such innocence is a beautiful thing. Would to God it were possible for every young maid! would to God there were no cesspool at hand to swallow up a sister before her eyes, and to turn herself sick and faint with the fumes of its horrible iniquity!

Elsa Engel had lived her sweet life close to the knowledge of evil, all untainted and unsmirched thereby; for hers was the purity of the diamond, a purity possible to but a few stainless souls; yet even Elsa had not foreseen the effect of so sudden a revelation upon a mind so ignorant, yet so quick of apprehension, and a heart so loving and tender, coming also, as it did, just upon the joy of the new faith that had dawned upon her spirit.

She went home, pale, wide-eyed, and silent, and sank into a chair dumbly despairing. Were her feelings morbid and exaggerated? Perhaps; but to Shirley even her own poor luxuries rose up in judgment against her, as though she had no right to cleanliness and comfort, to a roof over her head and bread to eat, while for the lack of these things girls not as old as herself were—

She trembled from head to foot, her teeth chattered as if with an ague-fit, her eyes swam, her heart beat faintly.

What was that flash upon her toilette-table? There! it was gone; no, there it came again; now it burned like a spark of prismatic flame. Her eyes grew clearer, her brain steadied itself: she understood that the afternoon sun had found out a crevice in the closed green shutters and had sent a long ray like a finger to point out to her a dainty pin, set with a single diamond,— Mr. Goldsborough's last gift.

Goldsborough Brothers!

She sprang to her feet; she threw her arms wildly into the air. "I cannot see him! I will never see him again! I will never, *never* marry him!" cried Shirley, aloud.

૬૩

Mr. Goldsborough came as usual that evening; but Shirley was in bed with a headache, he was told—quite truly.

"She was out all the afternoon with that Engel girl, dear knows in what sorts of places," said Mrs. Meredith, "and this is the consequence. She is too much upset to tell me what happened, except that some woman burst a blood-vessel, or something, and died in her very presence."

"It is outrageous that she should be exposed to such sights," said Mr. Goldsborough, indignantly; "and really, Mrs. Meredith, if you don't put a stop to it, I will."

"Indeed, I wish you would," replied the widow, sincerely. The rich man meditated. "I'll tell you what to do," he said. "Find out from the Engel girl exactly what happened; and if the people are poor, let me know how much money you want for them. That will cheer up Shirley and show her that you sympathize with her on general principles, and that you object simply to allowing her to kill herself. She has been just a little *tête exaltée*[21] ever since the unfortunate day when she made the acquaintance of that hoary old humbug, and needs to be handled with gloves on."

"Why, you know *who* those Engels *are*," said Mrs. Meredith, with scornful emphasis,—"cousins of our Mary in the kitchen!"

"Don't depreciate them to Shirley, though," said her future son-in-law, smiling: "remember, there are more ways of killing a cat than choking her with cream; better ways, too. Good-night."

"As if I did not know how to manage my own daughter!" said Mrs. Meredith, looking after him.

But she took good care to follow his advice; and the "points" which she readily obtained from Elsa and confided to Mr. Goldsborough made them both more determined than ever to separate the two girls.

"I am very sorry for the poor souls, and quite understand how Shirley, in her ignorance of business, holds me responsible," said the rich man, thoughtfully, when a day or two had passed and Shirley still refused to see him.

"I will write to him when I get stronger," the girl said, "but I pray God never to see him again. I hate him."

The message reached her *fiancé* in a much modified form; yet he grew a little pale over it, and bit his lip before he could answer calmly, as recorded above.

Mrs. Meredith was as ignorant of business as Shirley, and almost as unversed in the world's wickedness; moreover, her sympathies had been deeply moved. "I don't wonder her heart broke,—poor mother!" she had said; and now she ventured to intermeddle, timidly enough, on behalf of other mothers and daughters.

"Mr. Goldsborough," she asked, diffidently, "is that sweating system really necessary? Would it not be possible to abolish the middleman?"

Mr. Goldsborough shrugged his shoulders. "My dear madam," he said, "all things are possible, but most things are very inconvenient. The middleman—who, by the way, is often a middlewoman—is eminently a labor-saving machine to the manufacturer: we give him a fair price for the work he undertakes to have done; and what he pays the women is his affair and theirs, not ours."

"But you know that he makes his profit out of their necessities?"

"I know that everybody preys on everybody else, in our modern society; but I don't see what I am going to do about it."

"If you were to give the work directly to the women themselves—"

"These particular women would be

rather worse than better off, my dear Mrs. Meredith; for neither I nor any one at the factory has an idea the most remote of their names or local habitations; and you may be very sure the sweaters wouldn't tell: so the practical result of that move would be to take away even the little that they have."

"You could trace most of them, I should think."

"I doubt it; besides, I have certainly not the time to plough around in alleys."

"Then why not advertise?"

The man laughed aloud with amusement. "How many of those poor devils—begging your pardon for the word—have time or money to spend on a newspaper?" he asked.

"Why, they are as completely slaves as if they lived in a dungeon!" said Mrs. Meredith.

Mr. Goldsborough shrugged his shoulders again. "I did not make the system," he said, "but, finding it made to my hand, I don't propose to scatter my brains against it in the effort to break it down. That's all."

"By the way," said Mrs. Meredith, who did not venture to pursue the subject further, "Shirley is very anxious to leave home for a while."

"Perhaps it might be the best plan," said Mr. Goldsborough; "though you may tell her, from me, that I will not try to see her until she sends for me. Her nerves have had a shock, and must have time to recover, I quite understand that,—poor child! Where does she wish to go?"

"Well, at first she wanted to go to stay with the Engels; but of course I vetoed that at once."

"I should say so!"

"Then she spoke of the convent."

"St. Agnes'? Hum! I don't know—well, yes, certainly; just the place for her," cried Mr. Goldsborough, as an idea suddenly occurred to him. "Quiet, country air, regular hours, no nonsense,—nothing could be better. If you like, I will see Mother Ignatia myself, and give her an idea of the situation and the sort of treatment required."

"You speak as if we were sending her to a lunatic asylum! Shirley isn't crazy," said the mother, with some indignation.

"She is morbid," replied the man, "and morbidness may lead to anything. Do you suppose I should take her treatment of me so quietly, if I considered her fully responsible?"

"Perhaps you are right," said Mrs. Meredith, with a sigh. "If the rest of us felt these things as deeply as Shirley does—"

"It would be a world of maniacs."

"No; the cause of *her mania*, as you call it, would be very speedily annihilated," answered Mrs. Meredith.

VII

"I must see Elsa before I go," said Shirley, so vehemently that Mrs. Meredith, whose sympathies were on one side, while her inherited opinions remained on the other, did not think best to oppose her. This was on Sunday afternoon, the very day succeeding the conversation described in our last, and Tom was therefore free to offer his escort; indeed, he was as glad to do so as Shirley was to accept it.

For Tom's acquaintance with Elsa had not made much progress since we last had leisure to observe it. He had few excuses for seeking her society, not feeling free to do so openly and avowedly for its own sake, as Shirley did. And in some mysterious way the girl's white soul held him in awe: he felt that an interview obtained by a false excuse would not profit him in the least. He could not look into her pure pale face, or meet the still radiance of her lovely eyes, and feel that he had wronged her even by a shadow of deceit. Other women might be wooed by means of "innocent falsehoods," as they are called; not Elsa Engel; second-best might be good enough for every day, it was not good enough for her; and Tom had come to understand that for him also only the best would suffice,—Elsa herself. The knowledge elevated, purified his whole being; he felt in some dim manner that the one way to make her truly his was to tune his heart and soul to accord with hers; and, though the very effort taught him their dissonance, their lack of accord with the harmony of the universe, even here his easy temper and hopeful spirit stood him in excellent stead, and made him cheerily patient.

"We needs must love the highest when we see it," said Tom to himself, "and it ain't a bad sign that one *can* see it."

He walked along very silently at Shirley's side, this Sunday afternoon, very observant, though, of her paleness and the dark shadows which her brief illness had left under her pretty eyes, and very careful of her at crossings and such-like, with that tender courtesy in which he had always been such a proficient.

Both of them were in rather a mood for silence, and were distinctly sorry when at a cross-street they encountered the vivacious Hopkins.

"Now, it's not possible you are going to old Engel's!" said Hopkins, immediately. "You are? Then, 'Tommy, make room for your uncle!' I'm going there too, and you're the very people to introduce me."

"What are you going to distort out of all possibility of recognition, now, in your wretched paper?" asked Tom, rather crossly.

"Oh, go away!" retorted Hopkins, humorously. "I only want a few funeral baked meats; that's all."[22]

Shirley mentally finished the quotation, applied it to her own marriage, and shuddered.

"Cold?" asked Hopkins, sympathetically.

"She has not been well," said Tom. "Take my arm, Shirley: the hill is steep just here."

"I heard you were laid up," said Hopkins. "Must have been an awful shock for you, and that's a fact. I suppose you didn't get to the funeral this morning?"

"I didn't suppose the poor woman would be honored with one."

"Why, I understood your mother came down very handsomely towards the expenses?"

"She did not mention it to me," replied the girl.

"No?" said the newspaper-man, with apparent surprise, while within himself he added, "I thought it was a case of 'alias Goldsborough.'"

"Yes," he said, aloud, "they had all the trappings and the suits of woe; but I could not find out what was to become of the young ones, and that is what I'm here for. I say, Miss Meredith, if you see an article or so in my paper soon, defending the poor, and doing a little spread eagle about vampire plutocrats and all that, you won't lay it up against me, will you? I ain't malicious: it's only a question of—"

"Most probably I shall not see anything of it," replied Shirley, coldly. "I am going to the country to-morrow or next day for my health, and may not see a paper until I return."

"Then there's an apology clean throwed away," said Hopkins. "Never mind: keep it in camphor seven years, and you'll find use for it at last." But to himself he said, "Goldsborough, my boy, I don't believe you'll make a trade with this party. The bargain's off, or I'm a bigger fool than I know."

The evening was almost too cool for supper to be served under the forest-tree arbor, as Shirley had hoped; but in the door-way which led from the little passage between house and shop, into the conservatory, sat Grandfather Engel in his Sunday coat, and beside him the crippled boy whom Marie Wahman's death had left motherless, whom the old man was amusing by drawing quaint and beautiful designs on scraps of paper. Through the open door into the garden were visible the forms of the two girls, slowly walking back and forth upon the level part of the path, Teresa carrying in her arms the little Minne.

"Is it possible that you have them here?" asked Tom, when, with a thrill of disapprobation, he had seen his cousin, after a greeting to the old man, hasten into the garden to join the others.

"No other refuge was open to them," said the wood-carver, quietly. "Poor children! they suffer for the sins of others."

Friedel's eyes were keen and watchful, and the conversation was rather constrained until Frau Engel came in to carry him off to bed.

Then Hopkins said, "You'll find some difficulty, I fear, sir, in getting these children anything to do; and I understand you are opposed to charity?"

"I?" said the old man, smiling. "Not to charity, my son, but to alms-giving. Yes, it will be hard to find a safe place for Teresa, poor girl, outside of these walls."

"Well, I mean to write up the case pretty thoroughly," said Hopkins: "it's a point where our present infamous system of production is peculiarly open to attack, and Goldsborough is our paper's political enemy anyhow, so it is killing two birds with one stone, you see. Oh, yes; the sweater has got to go, and there's all about it."

"All that is evil has got to go, in the end; righteousness will finally triumph, my son."

"But why are you opposed to alms-giving?" asked Tom. "The Bible recommends it, and it is preached in the churches loudly enough, Lord knows."

"Can you give of that which is not yours?" asked the old man. "It is preached indeed loudly in the churches, that a man should give; scarce loud enough, that he has lawfully nothing of his own that he *can* give."

"Nothing?"

"Nothing, except himself. For example:

a man has money invested in railway-stock, which pays him a yearly dividend. Does he earn that money? It is earned by the train-men and the engineers. Nay, even these could not have earned it but for James Watt, George Stephenson, and a long line of other inventors, upon the fruit of whose genius every child of the race has surely an equal claim. My son, when the Lord Christ said that it was harder for a rich man to en-ter the kingdom of heaven than for camel to go through a needle's eye, what did He mean, think you?"

"Well, sir," said Tom, "that is some-thing that has always puzzled me. I sup-pose it isn't figurative?" he added, dubi-ously.

"That the Scriptures contain figura-tive expressions is a discovery of tremen-dous practical convenience," returned the wood-carver. "Is it also figurative to say that no robber or murderer hath eternal life abiding in him?"[23]

"I'm afraid that is a cold fact."

"And if private property, beyond the limits of a man's personal needs, *is* rob-bery, and involves the murder, body and soul, of the dispossessed?"

"I see what you mean," said Tom, con-scious in every nerve that Elsa was ap-proaching the door, "and I agree with my friend Hopkins that the vampire plutocrat has got to be enjoined; the sweater must go; but I don't see how we are going to manage it."

He did not quite know what he was saying, but it sounded more coherent than he had dared to hope. He took Elsa's hand in his for a moment, found a chair for her,

and seated himself on the step down into the hot-house, just where he could see her face. Teresa, with the sleeping child in her arms, had been attracted by his last words, and paused in the opposite door-way to hear what should follow.

Clothed and in her right mind, Teresa was a somewhat stunted and sullen-look-ing girl, with coarse, dark skin, heavy fea-tures, fierce black eyes, and a quantity of coarse hair to match. She was not at all an attractive-looking girl, but of just the sort whom one finds in reformatories and is not surprised to hear of there as the difficult subjects. Yet she held the child very carefully in her arms, and hushed her softly, with her face against the innocent cheek.

"It *could* be managed, if the wom-en were organized," said Hopkins. "By George, what a scheme that would be!" he added. "If we had a missionary, now, to go around and find out who they are, first of all,—for that is the hardest point to overcome,—then get them into the Assembly which the regular workers have already formed."

"Dues!" said Tom; "you don't suppose they've got any spare change to pay dues, do you?"

"Bah! I'll collect enough money in a day to pay all the dues they'll need for six months!"

"And then?" broke in Teresa, without moving from the door-way. Her great eyes burned; but the flame was not a holy one.

"Then strike!" said Hopkins; "that's all. The whole Assembly, you know, demand to receive work and wages from the factory direct, with no intervention of middlemen, and no discrimination between in-door and out-door workers; though that's hardly fair, either, for the outs furnish their own light, power, and heat, and so ought to receive more."

The color had faded quite out of Teresa's dark cheek; her face was like that of the dead; but her eyes were dreadful. "So easy as that!" she said. "If I had known it a month ago—Will you do it?" with suppressed vehemence.

"Will I do what?" asked the man, uneasily.

"Will you raise the money? *I* will do the rest."

"By George, I believe you could," he said.

"Teresa, dear child, Minne is waking," said Elsa, softly. "Come, let us take her away."

"You see, my son," said the old man, when Teresa had silently yielded to the gentle hand on her shoulder, and had disappeared into the house,—"you see that the child is in great danger, even here. I am sorry such a thought should have come to her; it will be hard to banish from her mind."

"But why should it be banished? She is the very one for such a work; her history will arouse sympathy; and we should kill the sweating system in Smoketon at a blow."

"At the cost of the girl's own soul," said the wood-carver, solemnly. "My son, would you try to serve God by the help of the devil? Would you overcome evil with evil?"

"Why, I never thought of it exactly in that light, don't you know?" replied Hopkins, with some embarrassment. "But let me understand your point of view: do you disapprove of strikes in general, or only this one?"

"There may have been strikes, as there may have been wars," said the old man, "untainted by malice or revenge, and righteous throughout. But, at best, strikes are but war measures, and war is of the devil."

"Then you hold, with Tolstoy, that any active resistance, even to the most cruel wrong and oppression, is sinful?"[24]

"I hold," said the old man, "that love, not discord, unity, not strife, is the law of this world. I hold that the growth of the race has been from the physical to the mental plane, and thence to the spiritual. I hold that good is stronger than evil, spirit than body: therefore, in resisting force with force we are using a weak weapon, which may at any moment break, or be turned against ourselves, while in opposing good to evil, love to oppression, we wield the sword of the Spirit,[25] which cannot but conquer at last."

"At the long last, perhaps," said Hopkins, with a grimace. "Then you would stand by and see any wrong worked upon the innocent, without raising a finger to help?"

"Not so," said the old man. "For which is worst off, the murderer or his victim? Doubtless the murderer: therefore it is right to hinder a wicked deed even by physical force, though the hindering be at my own proper peril."

"Why so?"

"The man of violence moves only upon the physical plane; if I meet him there, I lay myself open to all the temptations of that plane,—wrath, strife, envyings, and such-like. Nevertheless, to do so may be a clear duty."

"Well," said Hopkins, rising, "if those are your views, I guess I'd better take myself off before Miss Teresa comes back, for I must say that my sympathies are with her—Tom, you don't want to walk a bit with me, do you? I'll send him back safe against you want him, Miss Shirley."

When they had gone some little distance quite in silence, Hopkins laid a hand upon Tom's shoulder, and recited, funereally,—

> "There was a man named Ferguson,
> He lived in Market Street,
> He had a speckled Thomas-cat—"

"Confound your impudence! what do you mean?" cried Tom, breaking away from him.

"Don't swear, Tommy: it isn't pretty for little boys. I merely wish to remind you how one ambitious Thomas was 'busted in the back,' and to remark, in a general way, that if Elsa Engel is the young lady you were impersonally doubtful about marrying, you've got cheek enough for Jonah's whale."[26]

Tom's first impulse was to knock him off the bridge, which they had just reached; but nobody ever got angry with Hopkins, so he only said, "Tell me something I don't know. It's as clear as daylight that she don't care a snap for me."

"Well, by George, what if she don't?" replied the other, unexpectedly: "it's a privilege just to sit and look at a girl like that,—makes a fellow a better man, and so on, don't you know? And as for the grandfather,—by George, I had to leave instan-

ter, or he'd have had me on the mourners' bench[27] in less than no time. By gracious, Tom, I didn't know there were such people," said Hopkins, leaning his back against the bridge-railing, with his hands in his pockets, and his hat on the back of his head, and gazing sentimentally at the moon. "It makes a fellow understand, you know, how a little leaven leavens the whole lump, and that, don't you see?"

"I don't see," said Tom, "what has produced this effect. She scarcely said a word while you were there."

"Jealous?" said Hopkins, interrogatively, closing one eye and turning the other on his friend. "No: he don't look it, and perhaps even he is not quite such a fool. It's not what any of them *did*, Tommy, it's what they are; the whole moral atmosphere. To see that girl with her hand on the shoulder of that poor weak child—ah! Your cousin is a very good little girl, no doubt; but Elsa Engel don't go to bed on account of the wrong and suffering in the world, any more than any of the other angels."

Hopkins's ecstasies left Tom in rather a depressed state of mind: he retraced his steps slowly and disconsolately to the wood-carver's cottage, to find that Shirley had persuaded Elsa to walk home with her.

"For I don't know when I shall see you again," she had said, and Elsa had yielded.

Even Tom had quite forgotten Mary, who opened the door in answer to their ring, grinned all over her honest face at the sight of them, and grinned still more when she saw Tom start off to see Elsa home.

"Are they keeping company? Is he her fellow?" demanded Mary, looking after them.

"Nonsense!" Said Shirley, with severity: "Elsa is not that sort of a girl, Mary. She came home with *me*, and of course Mr. Tom is polite to her."

"He's polite to me a'ready, but he don't look at me so lovin' as that," murmured Mary, unconvinced.

Her fellow! Poor Mary, who had never had a sweetheart! "I'll see him when he comes in, though," she said, with that wistful determination to share, if ever so little, and the joy of others, that is known only to the unattractive and neglected ones.

She drew a chair to the window which commanded a view of the gate, put up her feet on another chair, and laid her head against the window-frame. But, alas! poor Mary was a sleepy-head by nature, and the next thing she was conscious of was a hand upon her shoulder, and a requisition from Mrs. Meredith to know the meaning of this.

It was two o'clock in the morning.

"Where is Mr. Tom?" asked Mary, starting wildly to her feet.

"Mr. Tom? In bed, of course, where he should be at this hour! What business have you with Mr. Tom? And the kitchen gas blazing so high that the reflection on the pavement outside my window waked me out of a sound sleep!" said Mrs. Meredith. "Go to your room at once, and don't let this happen again."

With a burst of tears, Mary obeyed.

But while she had slept, and missed even her poor share of the romance, the glamour of the moonlight had been very strong upon the two who had walked home under its rays. Yet they had said very little to each other; but there had been something in the touch of her hand upon his arm which had comforted Tom. So when they reached the gate he took her hand in his, and looked down into her face,—not very far down, however, for she was nearly as tall as himself.

"Elsa," he said, "I have wished to see you so often, and have had no excuse to come. May I come without an excuse?"

"Yes," she said, softly.

He laid his left hand over hers.

"I'm a poor sort of a fellow," he said, "but at least knowing you has taught me what I ought to be, and perhaps I can grow better, nobler, less unworthy to know you. Will you help me?"

She did not reply in words; she only raised her eyes to his, in the brilliant moonlight. There was no coquetry in that glance; if I dared to define love, I should say there was no love in it. It was as if she had opened to him the depths of her pure soul and let him read there all that he was able to comprehend.

Tom went home as lightly as if he trod upon air; but his slumbers that night were somewhat broken, while Elsa slept the sleep of a tired child.

VIII

It was upon that very Sunday afternoon, and almost at the precise moment when Tom and Shirley set out upon their walk, that Otho Goldsborough drove up to the gate of St. Agnes' Convent.

His business there was to arrange for Shirley to be received as a boarder for a fortnight, or longer if she chose to stay,—the necessity of giving a *quid pro quo* for the nuns' hospitality had not occurred to Shirley, nor did her lover mean that it should,—and also to come to a little private understanding with Mother Ignatia, the Superior of the convent, a tall stately woman whose sixty winters had not robbed her of her erect carriage and grand air; a woman about whom her serge habit hung as if it had been a queen's coronation-robe; with strongly marked features and dark, deeply set eyes that could flash as keenly as diamonds, but, unlike these, could melt to tenderness and pity.

But as she listened to Mr. Goldsborough, Mother Ignatia's eyes were simply clear, intelligent, and business-like; for what he had to say "told itself," as the French have it, and demanded no very strong effort to take it in.

"The poor child is completely under the influence of these crazy Socialists," said Mr. Goldsborough. "I believe they have convinced her that it is her duty to break off her engagement to me, if she breaks her heart in the process. Meanwhile, she refuses even to see me; so that my hands are completely tied; but, as coming out here was her own suggestion, she will be receptive to the influences of the place. And if you can make a Catholic of her, reverend mother, I confess that I should not be sorry: you know I come myself of a Catholic family on my mother's side, and was baptized by a priest, though I have never made a communion."

"It is a duty you should not neglect any longer, I think," said the Mother, gravely; "but as for Miss Meredith, it will be easy to show her how all that is true or beautiful in Socialism has already a place in the Church."

"If you will remember that she has re-

ally had a great nervous shock. Fancy seeing a woman drop dead at one's feet!"

"I see. Yes, that was terrible for her. What she wants, then, is quiet and rest, when I should hope the other matter would right itself."

"Under Catholic influence," said the rich man, smiling.

Neither of the participants had any more notion of considering this conference a conspiracy than had Hopkins and Teresa in planning to "enjoin the oppressor." After all, what *is* a conspiracy? It is not the making a definite plan to reach a definite object, for all of us do that, and get other people to help us, as often as we can; nor is it even the element of secrecy, for there is no law, moral or otherwise, that obliges us to discuss our private affairs until we are ready and willing to do so. Is not the essential feature of a conspiracy that we plan the accomplishment of an object, which in itself may be either good or bad, by *means* the righteousness of which is not altogether above suspicion?

Shirley abandoned herself to the peace of the convent, as a frightened child to the security of its mother's arms. Her tiny room was plain and bare enough to spare her all sense of luxury; and the stillness of the place, the sweet, calm faces about her, the concentration of all the beauty, glory, and melody within the walls about the tiny chapel, satisfied her sense of right and soothed her jarring nerves and troubled spirit. For several days she was left to go and come exactly as she pleased; then—she hardly knew how it happened; there was nothing to fret her, no atmosphere of controversy to arouse and agitate her,—but Shirley found herself reading,—reading, too, stories of lives so pure, so noble, that it filled her with strange sweet gladness to know that they had ever been lived; lives of St. Francis d'Assisi, the "Gray Friar," whose bride was holy poverty; of Père Lacordaire, the Dominican artist; of the noble army of martyrs who planted the cross along the banks of the St. Lawrence, the Lakes, and the upper Mississippi. Of these men and their doings, Mother Ignatia was ready to talk to her; that was natural enough; but it was rather a surprise to Shirley to find her so willing to discuss the principles of Socialism, the essential justice of which she was quite prepared to admit.

Shirley did not feel more nearly drawn to Otho Goldsborough by such conversations as these. She compared him, now, not merely with the lofty enthusiasm of Grandfather Engel, but with the heroes of whom she read; and more and more, as her ideal of her own possible life grew clearer and purer, did she feel the utter lack of any sympathy or comprehension from her betrothed husband.

So the fortnight had not ended before she wrote her promised letter to Otho Goldsborough: "I told you from the first that I did not love you; I never promised to do more than try; and now I find that our views of life are so unlike, that if I were to succeed in caring for you it would be a great misfortune to us both. I do not hope to bring you over to my way of thinking, and sincerely trust that I may never adopt yours."

That the mother should be vexed and disappointed was but natural; but she was very kind, as Shirley always said.

Mr. Goldsborough wrote a short, prompt, and business-like acceptance of her decision. Whether his heart had turned from her, or whether his acquiescence were merely a strategic move, Mrs. Meredith did not know; as for Shirley, the doubt never occurred to her. To regret her decision as soon as it was made would have been weak; therefore Shirley did not regret it, she was quite positive on that point; but a great interest had gone out of her life, and she missed her lover more than she would have believed possible.

The Wahman family were still at Grandfather Engel's; and Mrs. Meredith had "put her foot down," as she expressed it, that Shirley should not be "mixed up with such a girl as Teresa."

"If you were married, it might be different," she said; "but, as you have settled that for yourself, remember that a woman who has her own living to earn, especially as a teacher, cannot afford disreputable associates."

Shirley yielded, for the bread-and-butter argument is the strongest that can be brought to bear upon any subject; but time hung very heavy upon her hands, with the excitement of preparing for her marriage gone out of her life, and her place in the school filled by the substitute whose first quarter's salary Mr. Goldsborough had paid in advance. Shirley often wondered what was be done about the rest of it, and how that already advanced was to be repaid to her ex-*fiancé*. It was a minor matter, perhaps, but it helped to make his utter silence the most wearing form of revenge he could have chosen.

She had been at home nearly three weeks, when, one day, as she returned from a very welcome errand up-town, which had helped her to feel as though she were still of some slight use in her day, and generation, she became suddenly conscious of a very wide smile approaching to meet her, which smile, later, took on the physical semblance of the journalistic Hopkins.

"Well met by moonlight,[28] Miss Meredith!" said Hopkins. "Not that it's really moonlight, you know, but Shakespeare says so, and Shakespeare's sure to be right. That's a fundamental principle of all criticism."

"Well, moonlight may be the name of it," said Shirley, smiling, "but it looks to me very like Scotch mist."[29]

"Is that so?" he asked, in apparent surprise, turning to walk beside her. "I'm glad not to have *missed* you, at all events. Have you seen your friend Miss Engel lately?"

"As well as I can remember, after such a pun, I don't think I have," replied Shirley; and at that very moment, as she smiled brightly into Hopkins's ugly face, Otho Goldsborough turned the corner and met them, touched his hat, and passed without a word.

Shirley whitened as though he had struck her.

"He despises me!" she thought.

Hopkins glanced at her sympathetically. "It does make a fellow sorry even for a Goldsborough, who has lost a girl like that," he thought; "but why should she seem to care more than he does?"

In a moment more they reached the store for which Elsa worked; and here Shirley paused.

"I wonder whether Elsa may not be here now," she said: "it is her day for bringing home work. Good-morning, Mr. Hopkins: I shall go in and see."

She was as flushed now as she had been pale, sparkling and brilliant, her pretty mouth dimpled with smiles. "Rum critters is women," soliloquized Hopkins, as he walked off alone, fairly puzzled for once in his life.

Elsa was not in the store,—had not been there, the proprietress said, but would surely be in during the course of the day. Could she deliver any message? Shirley had answered no, and was turning away, when Teresa Wahman entered.

Her fierce black eyes brightened at sight of Shirley. "Stop," she said; "I want to speak to you;" and, as Shirley hesitated, "I have a message from Elsa."

The girl sat down to wait and listen, while Teresa transacted her business as Elsa's ambassador.

"She wants more material, this time," said Teresa; "for she has taught me to knit those pretty little silk socks in the leaf-pattern. She said you could always find sale for them."

"So I can: they're unique," said the proprietress. "Elsa is real good to you, ain't she?"

"Well, I should smile!" replied Teresa, fervently. "Not that it's any credit to her, though," she added: "it comes as easy to her to be good as it does to a cat to climb a fence. It's her nature."

She turned abruptly to Shirley.

"I'm ready. Come on," she said.

Shirley hesitated. "Cannot you tell me here?" she asked; for indeed the bold ways and loud harsh voice of the poor child were very painful to this daughter of centuries of culture and refinement.

"You don't want to be seen on the street with me!" cried the girl, with a hoarse laugh.

The proprietress stepped forward quickly. "Of course she don't, Teresa," she said; "nor you can't blame the young lady. Just step into my little parlor here, miss: if she has a message from Elsa, it won't hurt you to hear that; but as to being seen on the street with her, you are perfectly right. She don't understand the difference between her and a young lady like you."

"Don't I?" said the girl, sullenly, when they were alone in the little parlor referred to. "I don't know why I don't, then. Your mother had time to look after you and teach you to be a lady; mine,—you saw for yourself how we lived and how she died. When I was only four years old, I could sew on buttons as well as you can now, and I was kep' at it, too, sometimes fourteen hours a day. Nor that wasn't the worst, neither; they was lots of things I never knew was bad till Elsa told me. Fact is, I don't see how we could have done no different, livin' ten of us, men, boys, and women, in the one room."

"Ten in one room!" cried Shirley.

"Not the one you saw us in," said the girl: "we'd just moved into that one, which come cheaper on account of bein' a cellar. There was only one more family in that one besides us, and they was a woman and two daughters. They worked in an artificial flower factory, them three, and that was why they wasn't at home when you was there. The youngest daughter died just before I went to the bad. Doctor said it was arsenic as they uses in the green leaves, you know; and the others won't

be long behind. You just ought to see the sores on their faces and hands."

"How horrible! I have read of such things."

"Yes; readin' about it is one thing, and seein' of it is another," said the girl. "Doctor said there was other dyes could be used to make just as pretty a green, but arsenic come cheaper; and o' course the boss don't care how many women die, 's long's they's plenty others to take their place."

"There ought to be a law," said Shirley, "forbidding the use of arsenic in manufactures of any kind."

"And then another law, to say as they should mind that one," said Teresa. "No, miss, laws ain't no good. What we want is to organize, to demand justice and resist oppression."

"You must have been talking to Mr. Hopkins."

"Maybe I have, and maybe I haven't," said the girl, cautiously. "Tell me, miss; is it true that you ain't a-goin' to marry Otho Goldsborough?"

Shirley drew herself up haughtily. "I really don't see how my private affairs can possibly interest you," she replied.

"That's the second time you've reminded me as I'm no better than the dirt under your feet," said the girl, low and vindictively,—"you as would have been worser than me if you'd a' been brought up as I was."

"Teresa," cried Shirley, catching the girl by her poor dress, as she flung away angrily, "oh, can't you understand?—but no! of course you cannot! that is the very misery of it! we cannot even understand each other!"

"Elsa understands me," replied the girl,

sullenly; "nor she ain't ashamed to be seen on the street with me, neither; and she's enough better than what you are."

"Indeed she is," said Shirley, humbly. "Did you say you had a message from her?"

"I said so, but it was a lie," returned the girl, calmly. "I knew you'd never stay without it; but I wish now I'd let you gone; 'tain't no use to expect nothin' from none o' you aristocrats. If 'twasn't for Elsa, I'd go back on the streets,—I would; there's nothin' in the world *but* that except hard work; and if I don't get no credit nor respect by bein' good, I might as well have a good time."

With a look and shiver of horrible repulsion, Shirley swept past her, and was gone before Teresa had fully realized the situation, very fortunately for all concerned, as the poor girl immediately rushed after her in a fury, and was with difficulty checked by the proprietress.

"Now, you go home," said that worthy person. "Don't get excited, you know; because there's nothing to excite you."

"I'll tear her eyes out and strangle her!" cried Teresa.

"No, you won't; you only think you will," said the proprietress.

"She's a poor lost thing that Elsa Engel is trying to save," she explained to a customer, when Teresa had finally been persuaded to depart in peace.

"Elsa Engel! oh!" said the customer.

"Yes; you know *her!*" said the proprietress. "And she says to me, Elsa says, 'I can't keep the poor child a prisoner, Mrs. Long,' she says, and 'if I let her come after my work, it's a risk; but if you're willing

to help me save one of them little ones for whom Christ died,' she says,—and I interrupted her right there. 'Elsa Engel,' I says, 'willing is a long word,' I says, 'but if you'll send her, so do; and if she makes a disturbance in my store it's my loss; but if she trades off the bundle for liquor, or drops it in the gutter, we'll share the damage,' I says."

"Elsa Engel is as good as her name," said the customer.

"Just so; and if there is any reform *in* that girl she'll bring it out. You see, she's so far above all that sort of thing, Elsa is, that she don't feel it as we do; but there's no denyin' that to ordinary Christians Teresa is a trial," said Mrs. Long.

The house was very quiet when Shirley reached home. She went in by the dining-room door,—which, as we have seen, opened on the side-yard,—up the dining-room staircase, and into her own room, so quietly that Mary, who was, as Shirley at first glance supposed, tidying the wash-stand, did not hear her.

A second glance, and Shirley stood quite still, gazing intently. Was it—could it be? No,—yes,—oh, impossible!—YES! Mary was brushing her teeth with Shirley's own tooth-brush!

"Mary!"

The girl whirled suddenly around, brush in hand and open mouth full of pink lather. "Throw that thing out of the window!" commanded Shirley, pointing with rigid finger, like Macbeth at the air-drawn dagger.[30] "Throw it out, I say!" her voice rising to a shriek, "and the tooth-soap, *too!* Do you suppose I'll ever use it again?"

Then, suddenly overwhelmed by the

comic aspect of the case, as Mary stood staring, choking, and utterly uncomprehending, Shirley dropped into a chair and laughed and cried hysterically, which, setting Mary off at the same upon a grander scale, brought Mrs. Meredith and a detachment of irrepressibles from the school-room, to find out the cause of the disturbance.

"I didn't mean no harm," sobbed Mary, when she had been piloted out of the room and partially quieted; "I never seen nobody brush their teeth till I come here a'ready; and when Miss Shirley was sick yet, and I handed her the tooth-brush and soap, I thought it must feel so nice."

"And have you ever used any one's tooth-brush until to-day?" asked Mrs. Meredith, with Shirley's horror in a milder form.

"Never, never," asserted the girl; "but at Cowan's they had only one tooth-brush yet, for all of us to use. Oh! Miss Cowan she was a nice lady!"

"Yes, she must have been," said Mrs. Meredith, mentally resolving to throw away all brushes then in use and lay in a supply of new ones that very day. "You'll never do it again, Mary?"

"*Ach! nimmer, nimmermehr!*"[31] cried the girl. "I didn't know it was no harm; but Miss Shirley she went on so, it must have been awful!"

"Oh, well," said Shirley, with a sigh, when she was able to discuss the subject calmly, "it's hard for us to realize, but I don't believe she *did* know there was anything out of the way in it. A tooth-brush, like many other things, is a question of education. Sometimes I wish I were less fastidious."

"No, don't do that," said Mrs. Mere-

dith. "These minor morals, Shirley, are the guardians of one's real modesty; and we cannot afford to part with one of them."

"But if they make us careless and unsympathetic?" said Shirley, thinking of Teresa.

"Perhaps," said Tom, "it is like a dream I had once, a mere question of focus. Some people see their own image so large in their mental camera that there is no room for any one else's feelings."

"Tom!" said Shirley.

IX

Otho Goldsborough, having seen Shirley tremble and grow pale at sight of him, went on his way triumphant. "She is already penitent," he thought: "it is time for my next move."

So he went to see her the very next morning, as one who knew that her mornings were now free; and when she came into the room, he held her hand for a moment without speaking.

"You will think me a poor-spirited wretch," he said, at last, "but I cannot stop loving you, Shirley. Are you tired of your freak? Will you come back to me? There! I never expected to ask you!"

"No; I never thought you would," she said.

"Come, sit here and tell me all about it," he went on. "I could not understand that crazy letter."

"You have never understood me," said Shirley, quietly.

He frowned, for he had hoped to carry his point by storm, before she could gather strength to oppose him. Perhaps he should succeed better on another tack;

for Mr. Goldsborough was thoroughly convinced that a woman ought to be conquered, not deserved. "Then I am to believe that you have deceived me all this while, when you professed to love me?"

"When did I profess that?" she asked. "From the first, I have said that I did *not* love you, though I liked you very much; and you said that was quite enough."

"As I say still," he replied. "Your liking is all I ask; and who else has a right to complain?"

"I," said Shirley.

He gave his sudden short laugh.

"You?" he said. "Well, you *are* an exacting little beauty. With plenty of money, and an adoring husband to gratify every wish, what else would you have?"

"A *little* love on *my* side," she replied.

"Why, you own that you love me a little!"

"No; I am fond of you, I like to talk to you; but—oh, leave it there, Mr. Goldsborough: don't make me say anything rude."

"Be as rude as you like," he answered, roughly: "I *will* get to the bottom of this business. What sort of a husband do you want, if I don't suit you?"

"I never expect to have any," she answered; "but, if I do, he must first of all be a man whom I can thoroughly respect. There! I said I should be rude."

"Go on," he said, with a forced smile. "What have you found out, or imagined, about me, that has cost me your respect? I should like to clear myself if I can."

"I have found out nothing; but what I already know has appeared to me in a different light. If we were put into this world to live just to and for ourselves, Mr. Goldsborough, you would rank as a good man, and I might be able to love you; that is, if any one could love in such a world as that."

He drew a quick, short breath through his set teeth. "I need not ask further," he said: "it is evident that you love me passionately. But tell me one thing more. Who is back of all this? Who is it that you *do* love?"

"No one at all," said Shirley; with her brown eyes looking full into his.

"You wrote that letter entirely of your own impulse, without the advice or counsel of any one?"

"I wrote it," she said, "entirely of my own impulse: I am not so weak and unable to stand alone as you seem to imagine."

"And yet," he said, sneeringly, "as a mere matter of detail, won't you tell me the name of my happy successor? That ape Hopkins, perhaps?"

"I will not tell you anything," she answered, steadily; she was very pale, and her eyes shone; "and, so far as know now, I shall never marry any one; certainly no one who looks upon me so entirely as a mere plaything that my feelings towards him are a matter of supreme indifference, provided I submit to be loved *by* him."

He put out his hand as he rose to leave, took hers, and wrung it hard before he let it go. "Oh, you are fond of me," he said, bitterly; "you are very fond of me, Shirley. If I sooner realized just how fond, it would have spared us both some trouble, perhaps. Good-by."

"Good-by," said Shirley, coldly; but there was a strange weight at her heart when he was quite gone.

"I *had* to speak plainly," she said excusingly to herself: "he would not understand. Besides, his attitude was quite as if I had only been waiting for him to hold out his finger; and a woman has a right to resent a slight to her own dignity."

But Tom's words on the evening before persisted in coming back her: "Some people see their own image large that there is no room in the camera for any one else's feelings."

"I really do *not* know what has come over Tom," said Shirley.

X

Perhaps the course of our story would have been different, and the story of the world trifle less tragic, had Shirley's fastidiousness been upon a rather higher plane; for Teresa had had something of genuine importance to tell her, and was fully minded to do so. And the solidarity, the independence, of mankind is a solemn and terrible fact, which, with its consequences, is, like death, rendered only more awful by shirking the thought of it. No word, no action, of ours is without its effect upon those around us, to react upon ourselves and spread the influence in widening circles throughout the globe; thus returning upon us, touching us at every angle, every point of our being, so that

The trials that beset us,
The sorrows that we endure,

are the work of our own hands and of the hands of our forefathers, in which way also the sins of the fathers return again to visit the children.

Teresa had grasped the hope of a possible revenge upon the system which had murdered her mother, with the tenacity upon which even the astute Hopkins had not reckoned when he threw out carelessly the words which had so influenced her. Indeed, as a journalist, Hopkins was rather accustomed to abuse the existing state of things without producing much visible effect; it was decidedly a surprise to him, therefore, to find himself taken *au grand sérieux*[32] and expected to live up to his professions.

Teresa waited for him to come again to the house where she had found shelter; but when two or three days had passed without bringing him, she sought him out in his office, which she found in some manner known only to herself, and reminded him of what he had said. Thus assailed, Hopkins was forced to consider the practicability of the proposed scheme.

"The money is all right," he said: "as I tell you, I can get hold of plenty for such a purpose is that. But we want to keep awfully quiet about this, Teresa, because, if you like to be indicted for conspiracy, I don't; and some of the best measures for in joining tyrants have been viewed in that light, at times, by the unregenerate mind. See?"

"I don't know what all those fine words mean," said the girl, spicing her sentence with an oath or so,—she felt at liberty to swear in Hopkins's presence,—"but I see what you are driving at."

"Just so," said Hopkins, politely.

They concerted a plan of action, into the details of which it is not necessary to go. It was indispensable to act with and through the already existent Assembly, to which all the operatives employed in the factory itself of Goldsborough Brothers already belonged, and those in authority proved to be at first in conservative frame of mind; but as the measures progressed, and applications for membership poured in, they agreed with enthusiasm that to wipe out the sweating-system in Smoketon would be feat worthy of the Order.

"If it can be done," said one of them; "for you know, Mr. Hopkins, an unsuccessful strike is worse than none; and women—well, women are not tough enough to fight it out, generally speaking."

"Don't you worry over that," said Teresa, roughly. "This strike is going right straight through."

"The fact of the matter is," said Hopkins, "it ought to be done by legislation. That's how they are trying to do it in England. First make your factory-laws very stringent, then extend them to every house, tenement or otherwise, in which the manufacture is carried on."

"Yes, I've heard of that plan," said the Authority, dryly. "Legislation is a good thing in its place, Mr. Hopkins, and I don't deny that its place is factories. Far from it. But there's just this about it: if a woman can't make enough to starve on, *by* living sixteen to the dozen, working eighteen hours or so, and never taking time to clean up, what *is* she going to do about it, if you enforce all sorts of regulations?"

"She couldn't live, of course, on her previous wages,—that she couldn't exist: therefore wages would inevitably rise."

"And so would rent," said the other. "Mr. Hopkins, legislation is no good when it's in advance of public opinion. Why, not long ago there was some abuse in—," he named a certain city, "that wanted straightening out; and the people undertook to straighten it. And when they looked over the statute-books, there was the very law they wanted, passed years ago, never enforced, and forgotten: why? because public opinion didn't insist upon it."

"I don't understand what you mean by public opinion," said Teresa, with the usual embroidery; "but if any adjective policeman had come botherin' the life out of my poor mother as to the way she lived, and how long she worked, I'd have chucked him out the winder and broke his blank neck for him, so I would!"

"There you are, you see," said the Authority. "Besides, how would you reach the farmers' daughters, Mr. Hopkins?"

"Farmers' daughters?"

"Just so; also wives. Don't you know that a good deal of this work goes to the country? and while that's so, you may legislate till you're black in the face, but town wages won't go up. Why, I know one girl—father's pretty poor,—you know how farmers are,—plenty to eat when strawberries turn out well and the peach-crop's good; when they *ain't*, times are hard. So this girl makes shirts at two cents apiece and works eighteen hours a day."

"It's a shame! it's murder!" said Hopkins.

"Yass," said the Authority, dryly, "that's about what it is; and this girl says she's bound to have a black lace dress, if she kills herself."

"Pshaw!"

"Well," said the Authority, "if you were

a girl, Mr. Hopkins, you might like to have a black lace dress yourself. Personally I prefer a white what-you-call-um—muslin, I guess; but black lace ain't ugly. But you see that nothing—nobody—can remedy this thing but organization, don't you?

"Well, ain't we organizin'?" asked Teresa.

"That's a fine girl spoilt, Mr. Hopkins," said the Authority, meditatively, when Teresa had left them.

"Well, yes," said Hopkins; "spoilt about two hundred years ago."

"Not so long as that," said the Authority, smiling. "You see, I knew her mother, who was as fine a woman as God ever made; no coarseness or roughness about her, but all pluck and stubborn endurance right down to the ground. I didn't know what had become of her until I heard of her death; for I was out of town for several years, and meanwhile she kept going down, down, as wages fell, until—well, you know how it turned out."

"Hadn't she a husband?"

"Of course; painter; and, equally of course, painter's paralysis. Lost the use of his right arm when Teresa was a baby; but he lived long enough to give her two more children to take care of—living ones, that is; there were several who died, Teresa tells me before he finally gave up and died too. He was a queer sort of a fellow, Wahman; first-rate workman; put him to work, and he'd go like a machine; there never was any difference in the quality of his work; you were always sure he would do the best he knew how. But there wasn't a fragment of originality about him, and once out of his groove he was perfectly lost; never attempted another stroke of work, even so

much as making a pot of tea, to save his wife's time; just lounged around, spending her hard earnings in tobacco and beer, until at last he took to whiskey, and that finished him."

"So that was how it happened?" said Hopkins. "Well, I'm glad to know all about it, and how Teresa came to be spoilt, as you express it; for while I try to look upon her altogether in a scientific light, as a product of our social system, I confess that she is apt to jar my nerves. She strikes me as a girl who would have gone wrong under almost any circumstances; and that she will ever be a credit to Fräulein Elsa's teaching, I fear I don't quite believe."

"Well, well, there's no knowing," said the other: "she's young enough to outgrow some of the poison, and strong enough to make herself anything she pleases."

Hopkins's conscience was not quite easy when he thought of Grandfather Engel's words, that they might win the battle at the cost of Teresa's soul, but he consoled himself by reflecting that the old man could not possibly have known what he was talking about, and that souls were obsolete anyhow; while nothing could be more elevating to the character than a struggle for oppressed womanhood.

Teresa, however, cared little enough for womanhood; but she longed fiercely, passionately, for revenge; revenge upon the system that had murdered her mother. It is, however, difficult to hate a system without hating the upholders thereof; and Teresa did not try to do so; to her, the system was Otho Goldsborough.

Elsa found her a heavy charge, given to mysterious absences which made the hearts of her protectors sink with fear; absences of which she would give absolutely no account, while any restraint on her liberty was met with bursts of wild fury, and sometimes of actual violence. Yet at other times she showed an affection for those around her as fierce as her anger; she would kiss them passionately, and assure them that she would try to do right,—she *was* trying; she meant no harm, and had done none; only she must have her liberty.

It was not long before they suspected something of what was going on; and it must be confessed that the suspicion was a relief, as being less evil than they had dreaded.

Yet the thought troubled the old man. "I cannot work against them, for their object is great and good," he said. "How can I help the good in themselves without strengthening the evil?"

XI

If the heart of Otho Goldsborough had been hot and bitter when he entered Shirley's presence, what was it when he left her? It had been said of him that he was a man who grew white and cold when he was most angry; and there is no anger like such anger as that. Yet he was not angry with Shirley: it seemed to him that he had never loved her so well; after so long separation from her, all her little tricks of manner and gesture, the turn of her head, the flash of her brown eyes, the quiver of her small, restless fingers, the play of the dimples about her mouth,—all these had for him a double fascination. Even her outspoken condemnation, although it wounded, did not rankle: one of her attractions in his eyes had always been her

simplicity and unworldliness; and he felt now that these had been used to turn her against him. And that there was an element of justice in her criticism he readily admitted: he had never pretended to be more than a thorough business-man,—which, as every one knows, does not constitute a claim to saintship. The business of a man of the world is to make money; it is the wife's affair to supply the softening element in his life and to keep him from quite forgetting that there is another world than this. Upon one point, however, he felt that he had been severely misjudged: he was not at all the man to be content with less than his wife's whole heart; but a little coyness in his betrothed had not displeased him, as he had been confident that she loved him better than she cared to show.

But he remembered that there had been a change in her from the day of her first visit to Grandfather Engel; and therewith Mr. Goldsborough breathed a fervent curse through his teeth, with the full conviction that he had reached the root of the matter at last. This crazy Socialist theory had gone deeper than he had understood; that was all. Poor little girl! he had wronged her in supposing some other man—that is, young man—to have caused her defection. Well, maybe he'd never get even with that hoary old rascal, but he rather thought he should try, some day.

It was the very next morning that he received a message that Ludovic Engel would like to speak with him, and sent him word to come to his office at twelve o'clock.

This office was a shabby little den on the ground-floor and at the rear of the great building which he called his factory. The rear of the building looked upon a blank wall across a very narrow alley, and was consequently very dark; and just outside the proprietor's office the elevator rose from the cellar, its sides entirely unprotected, and leaving behind it an awful chasm in the floor, yawning like the mouth of the pit for the destruction of the unwary. There had, however, never been an accident there, as those who passed it were nearly all *habitués*[33] of the building, and the few strangers who came there were apt, on their first visit, to be warned just in time, and to get such a thorough fright as never after to forget the location of the pitfall.

As the old man entered the dingy little office, Mr. Goldsborough raised his eyes from his letter for a second, then nodded carelessly, and went on writing.

"I'll talk to you presently," he said, without concerning himself that his visitor remained standing. His manner was as cool and composed as ever, but his heart was a volcano of rage. Grandfather Engel's hat was in his hand when Mr. Goldsborough next looked up; and his posture was rather that of a soldier on guard than of a suppliant kept standing to await the convenience of a superior. If anything could have infuriated the man before him to a higher point than he had already attained, it would have been the stately picturesqueness of this figure, with the white hair upon his shoulders, the abundant beard gleaming like silver upon his breast, and the deep eyes looking so kindly out of their dark hollows. No wonder Shirley's imagination had been taken captive!

"I understood," said Mr. Goldsborough, "that you wished to see me. State your business."

"I have come hither on my Master's business," said the old man; "for One is my Master, even Christ."

"There is no business of that kind transacted in this office," said Mr. Goldsborough, roughly. "Suppose you take yourself off."

"When my task is accomplished," said the old man, tranquilly.

Mr. Goldsborough eyed him for a moment, as though measuring his strength; but an undignified struggle was the last thing he could stoop to.

"Well, well," he said, "say your say, you old hypocrite, and be quick about it. My time is precious."

"Ah! thou dear Heaven! *how* precious!" said the old man, solemnly.

"Once for all," said Otho Goldsborough, "I want none of your infernal piety. Do you hear? Now come; you see this button? I give you just five minutes to deliver your pure soul of whatever confounded humbug you have filled yourself up with; at the end of that time I ring for a policeman." He laid his watch on the table as he spoke, and surveyed the intruder with a cold sneer.

"Verily," said the old man, sadly, "the sins of the father of your innocent mother are visited this day upon you, Otho Goldsborough."

"Did you come here to talk about my grandfather?"

"I came to plead with you, if yet while there is time you will turn and repent, blessing both yourself and the poor helpless ones."

"And what am I to repent of?" said Otho Goldsborough.

"Has not the finger of Heaven already made it plain to you? Was not a victim of your oppression—yours, because you permit the system to exist under which such oppression is possible,—was she not struck down in the very presence of the woman you love——"

"By ——, if you say another word I'll—I'll strangle you!" said the rich man. He was lividly pale; the sweat stood in great beads upon his forehead; he clinched his rigid fingers upon the arms of his chair.

"My message seems hopeless," said the old man, sadly; "yet it is not mine, but His, and I needs must speak it. Otho Goldsborough, grandson of Otho von H., the workers beneath your roof have resolved that the system upon which work is given outside is unfair and unrighteous and must be done away. They are banded together to resist you; a committee of them is to wait upon you in a few days. I have come before them as a messenger of peace. In this paper are contained their demands; read it; grant them, for the love of God and your brother; or—"

"Or?"

"Nay, I mean no threat," said the old man, gently: "it is but that, if you refuse, many a struggle must come, and many souls be confirmed in the service of the Beast, whether the just cause win or lose."

Otho Goldsborough laughed. "It is the wildest scheme that ever was hatched," he said; "not worth vexing one's self about. What is to hinder me from discharging the whole crew and hiring others?"

"The place is not a large one," said Grandfather Engel; "nor, though poverty is on the increase, owing to the sweaters, are there many, outside their present victims, who will work for what they give. And these few are known; they will be watched and guarded; nor, if this were not so, could they alone supply the needs of your factory."

"Time's up," said the rich man. "Shall I ring? or will you go peaceably?"

"I came in peace, in peace do I depart," said the old man. "May God soften your heart, Otho Goldsborough, that you may no more serve the Beast and his image, adding coin to coin, according to the number of his name. Behold it!" he cried, as one inspired, and tracing upon the grimy walls with red chalk, in huge characters,

.666+

"Six *hundred* and *sixty* and *six*," he said,—"an infinite decimal, increasing to everlastingness by growing less, and less, and less. O friend, put a stop, while you may, to the unholy growth, by the symbol of the Lamb,[34] the sign of the Cross!"

"I'll put a stop to your preaching first of all," said Mr. Goldsborough, rising. "Did you or did you not understand me, just now? I refuse even to read this paper, and you may tell those who sent you to strike, boycott, do whatever they like. We shall see who conquers. Now go!"

The door of his office stood wide open; the way lay straight forward to the outer door. A second glance assured him that the elevator was above that floor, that the mouth of the pit yawned undefended. He uttered no warning, although the old man had paused upon the very verge of the shaft, unconscious of his danger, to make one last effort for the soul of the man who now leaned forward to watch the result, with a smile of cold, cruel, devilish hatred and curiosity.

"Shall we indeed see who conquers?" he said. "In the battle of Armageddon, Otho Goldsborough, there can be but One Victor. Here or there His forces may seem to be routed; but conquerors they are, though, like Him, it may be by their death. May He be merciful to you, *not* as you are merciful to others."

He turned away.

Even then, had his eyes been clear, he could have escaped the fate that threatened him; but they were full of pitiful tears for the man who sat watching him with that awful smile upon his lips.

And so—

A crash, a terrible dull thud,—and Otho Goldsborough rushed forward with wide eyes and that smile frozen upon his lips by the horror of the moment.

"I have killed him!" he cried. "Oh, my God! I am a murderer!"

Had he not murdered others with a worse death than this?

Feeble women, ground under his iron heel, had been driven many times to shame or a swifter suicide; but he had called it "business," and had heard no voice of the crying of their blood from the ground.

"Am I my brother's keeper?"

Otho Goldsborough had answered that question at last.

XII

But, after that first cry, Otho Goldsborough gave no sign of what was working within him. Clear-headed and cool as ever, he gave directions to the army of helpers who, as if by magic, assembled around him; for there is plenty of sympathy, and help also, for that which happens only rarely. It is the usual, the frequent, the daily living death of the thousands and hundreds of thousands who spend their lives to buy the necessities and luxuries that make our life possible, whose "bones we grind to make us bread,"—it is these things whereof we think not merely little, but absolutely nothing at all. What fair lady with her flower-wreathed bonnet thinks of the poisonous dyes which, in a time *averaging less than two years*, destroy the life of the flower-maker? What gallant gentleman, with his cigarette between his lips, remembers the maker, poisoned with nicotine? May God be merciful to us— MURDERERS!

Grandfather Engel was lifted once more into the light of day, white, insensible, seemingly quite dead.

But the old man was not dead, said the physician. It was concussion of the brain, how severe could not yet be determined. They must hope for the best, he added, cheerfully; though to Mr. Goldsborough he said, apart, that the old man was past eighty, and, though a wonder of health and vigor for that age, it was quite certain he would never again be the same man, even if he recovered at all, which was more than doubtful.

"Do what you can for him, doctor,"

said the rich man. "Spare no expense at all. I'll make it right with you."

"That's all right," said the doctor, "but it shows very good feeling on your part. However, I understand that as it happened on your premises, and all, you feel responsible. And, by the bye, if I were you I'd have that demon of a hole guarded in some way; a light fence, for example, with a gate wide enough to roll a wheelbarrow through— Of course I only throw out the suggestion."

"It shall be done," said Mr. Goldsborough, "in some way or other. We have never had an accident here, and it has never seemed necessary; but it shall be done."

No one suspected that the old man's injury had been more than an accident, but Mr. Goldsborough was considered to show, as the doctor had said, a great deal of very good feeling.

Good feeling! Otho Goldsborough wondered why the brand of Cain[35] upon his brow was not as visible to other eyes as to his own; and yet he tried to hide it even from himself, and, in a sort of bravado, found his way late that evening to the wood-carver's cottage. It was overflowing with guests,—hard-handed workingmen, poorly-dressed women with their aprons to their eyes, children clinging to their mothers' skirts, all hushed and still with the awe of a great calamity.

They stood aside or drew together in groups as the rich man entered whom most of them knew by sight, but no one came forward to welcome him. There was no hostility on their faces, and very little interest; only a wondering curiosity looked out from some eyes as to what this man, who had hitherto let their joys

and sorrows severely alone, had to do with them now, in the hour of their deep affliction.

"I should like," said the rich man, "to see Miss Engel."

They looked one at the other, and then one of them said that she was with her grandfather, and another volunteered to call her. But still he stood among them solitary amid the crowd, an alien to his own mother's children, a stranger to the brethren of his blood.

"Can any of you give me news of the old man?" he asked. "How is he?"

"He is about the same," said one.

"Has not revived at all?"

"No, not at all."

Ah! how hotly the brand burned into his brow!

At that moment there was another movement in the crowd, and, turning, he saw that Shirley Meredith had just come into the room, flushed and tearful, her pretty hair all disordered, thinking evidently of nothing less than of her own appearance.

Ah! Shirley was quite innocent of the old man's blood; she had no need to preserve an outward calmness.

"Oh, how is he? tell me he is better!" cried Shirley. Then her eyes fell on Mr. Goldsborough. "You here!" she said: "is it true that it happened at your office?"

"Yes," he said, "it happened at my office."

She came closer to him and put out her small hand with a gesture of sympathy. "I am very sorry for you," she said. "I know how terrible it is, a shock of that kind."

He bowed and turned away: he did not

dare touch her pure hand while his own seemed dripping with blood.

Shirley's eyes followed him wistfully. "How he feels it!" she thought. "He looks ten years older, poor fellow!"

At that moment he was speaking to Elsa, who had come into the room quietly, her beautiful face calm but very sorrowful. "He has not spoken; it may be that he will never speak again," she said, and, lifting her eyes to Otho Goldsborough's face, "it may be, sir, that you heard the last words from his lips!"

Oh, loving, tender words! oh, lips forever silent!

The strong man's pride was utterly broken down. Otho Goldsborough cried out aloud in his great agony: "I saw his danger, and should have warned him! I am his murderer!" he cried. Then he turned from them all, and hid his eyes and branded forehead in his guilty hands.

For a moment there was utter silence, then a soft stir. He had thought never again to feel either pain or joy, after those awful words; but his heart gave a great throb, as a soft little hand was laid on his, and, looking down, his eyes met those, so soft and brown, of Shirley Meredith. He was crushed and humbled now out of all semblance of pride; he fell on his knees beside her, and Shirley gathered the once haughty head in her arms, and laid her cool sweet lips to his burning brow.

"Don't be hard on him," she said, entreatingly; "he has suffered so much,—so very much!"

"Ah, no!" said Elsa, smiling, though the tears rained fast over her pale cheeks; "we will not be hard upon him, friends. Do we grudge the life of even our best and dearest, if it can save a soul? Shall we not rather rejoice? for this our brother was dead, and is alive again; he was lost, and is found."

☙

"And you love me again, Shirley?" he asked her, when, not many hours later, they stood alone together. "Is it possible that you love me again?—that you who forsook me in the days of my prosperity return to me now when I am a despised outcast?"

"Not quite that, I think," said Shirley: "you have done nothing worse, you see, in the eyes of these people, than you have done all your life, or than hundreds of others do every day. Oh, I did not mean to hurt you."

"If you love me, *nothing* can hurt me," he said; "but how can you love one of whom you think so very ill?"

"Because you need me," she said. "And I believe, Otho, I always loved you better than I myself understood; and now,—oh, you are so strong, so true! you will be so very, very good, now that your eyes are open, and— anyway—I love you, because—well, I suppose, because I love you; that's all!"

XIII

During the days of watching and anxiety that followed, Tom Meredith was often at the wood-carver's cottage. It was a strange bond that had grown up between him and Elsa; there had no word of love or marriage passed between them, yet each one knew that they belonged only to each other. Tom was much improved, every one said,—less lazy, more sober and sedate; in short, more reliable, though quite as merry and good-natured as ever.

Elsa would have found it hard to understand these criticisms; for to her the soul of the young man was pure and free from stain as her own,—one of the very few quite untouched by the Mark of the Beast. And it may be that Elsa was more nearly right than the young man's less kindly critics: the sweetest souls breathe less freely away from the air of the high countries; they care little for the aims and objects of this present world, and suffer its rewards to slip carelessly from their grasp. Not always do they themselves know what is lacking; but they are convinced that the highest is unattainable, and often consent to dwarf their own natures by contenting their souls with that which they recognize as second-best to something, though they know not exactly what. In the coming days, when the victory over Mammon shall have been won, such souls as these will attain their full development, and blossom into a beauty little dreamed of by those who say of them now, "Ah! he is a man one cannot help loving,—poor fellow!"

Grandfather Engel fulfilled that which had been said of him: his last words were those which were heard by Otho Goldsborough. But just at the last there was a flutter of the eyelids, a smile upon the grandly silent lips; then the eyes opened wide, and their glance fell on that fierce dark countenance with which Teresa crouched near the foot of the bed.

The girl had not been present when Otho Goldsborough confessed himself to the world the murderer which she had always called him; she had not felt the power of Elsa's forgiveness; but she knew the facts, and, even as she watched the dying man, had brooded on thoughts of revenge. The dying eyes drew her closer and closer; they seemed to burn into her very soul; she hid her face from their awful power.

"I won't hurt him! I promise to forgive him!" cried Teresa. "I'll never try to get even with any one again. Oh, grandfather, grandfather!"

The eyelids fell, the face settled once more into the marble stillness it had worn in these last days. His daughter and grand-daughter came hastily into the room at the girl's cry; it was the first time since the accident that both of them had left him at the same time; and now—

"He is quite gone from us," said Frau Engel, as she laid down the mirror which she had held to his lips.

"And no look, no smile, for me!" cried Elsa. "Why did I leave him? who should look last into his eyes but me?"

"She who needed the look," said Tom, softly. He had followed them into the room, and now took Elsa's hand and laid it on the head of the shivering, sobbing Teresa. "Once," said Tom, "I grudged this child to breathe the same air with you, my beautiful darling. Now, the better I love you, the more do I wish you to be to all others the strong sweet angel that you have been to me."

And Elsa put her arms about the weeping girl, and laid the wild dark head upon her pure and tender heart.

"Oh, Elsa, Elsa," cried the girl, "am I so very wicked? Oh, help me to be good, like you."

"God will help us all, dear Teresa," said Elsa, gently.

XIV

They laid the old man to rest without many tears or loud and bitter wailing, which even those who loved him best, and most would miss his presence and his counsel, felt would be unsuited to the life he had lived and the death that he had died. So, very silently, the long, long train followed his mortal frame to its waiting open grave, round which stood the solemn winter trees, draped each in his mantle of snow fringed with icicles. The hills also were white to the very tops, and the valleys seemed wrapped in one vast winding-sheet.

"That suits the grandfather very well," said Frau Engel, as she looked around, "very well indeed,—this beautiful whiteness. Ah, I hear sometimes people say it is not convenient to be so very good; but for me, I think it is beautiful to have a saint in the family."

"But I cannot find out what the old man ever did, that people should care so much about him," said Mrs. Meredith. "Of course I know he was a good old soul; but if he lived more than eighty years without doing anything but carve clock-cases and candlesticks, I don't see why his death should move people so."

"It is *because* he lived," said Tom, to whom she spoke.

"But if he had been a great reformer—" said the lady.

"The greatest reformer," said Tom, "is he who so reforms his own life that it purifies and ennobles every life that touches it. Of what use will it be if we reform the body of society without touching the soul? Yet there are outward reforms that must be made; but he who overcomes the Beast, the Mammon of greed and selfishness, must do so by the sword which proceedeth out of his own mouth, by the breath of the life that is in him."

❧

Otho Goldsborough had not been among the train of mourners at the old man's funeral. "It would be a mockery," he had said: "there is no place there for the murderer." But it was not often that the pain within him found voice in such words as these. Stern, silent, self-contained as ever, few but Shirley suspected the depth of his remorseful repentance; but in her the comprehension of his sore distress wrought a passion of sympathetic tenderness of which she had not believed herself capable. And on his part also the sympathy she had once craved was poured out in overflowing measure; and, though reforms which he had once scorned he now furthered chiefly to satisfy his restless conscience, one cannot do brotherly acts without awakening in one's self the feeling of brotherhood.

❧

For the rest who remain, they are very happy. Not free from trouble and sorrow; for Tom and Elsa, in particular, have many things to endure: without, sneers and scoffs; within, the jar of differing tastes and habits. But of these matters they have learned the exact value; they love each other, too, so well that each tries to be the readiest to make concessions, and between them they are in a fair way to rediscover the original fount and source of all domestic and social etiquette, which source and fountain, indeed, is but sincerity and love. Of worldly goods they have enough to live upon, and they ask no more.

Mr. Goldsborough and Shirley have, perhaps, rather more to bear than Tom and Elsa in the way of the world's contumely; for there are what people call "very ugly rumors" afloat concerning the share of the rich man in the death of Ludovic Engel. It has been proved, by the testimony of an employee who saw the fall, too far off to prevent it, that Otho Goldsborough could have been merely a passive agent in the matter; and there is no law on our statute-books to require that each man warn his brother of possible pitfalls. In this respect the race-conscience is better than the law.

Those, therefore, who give least heed to the welfare of their brothers and sisters in other matters are most glad to prove to themselves that there are some things they would not do, by condemning Otho Goldsborough. He bears his partial ostracism very patiently; while Shirley professes to be rather glad of it than otherwise.

"For if we are not expected to go out, or to entertain very much, we can live in a small house and as we like. Besides, if they didn't send us to Coventry,[36] I'm afraid we should send them, heartless plutocrats that they are," says Shirley.

There is no such thing now in Smoketon as a sweater; and though the high wages paid in the factory of Goldsborough Brothers both to in-door and out-door workers, and the care taken to insure the well-being of the employees, no doubt keep down the owner's profits, the zeal of the workers, and the reputation which the factory deservedly enjoys among those who have at heart the cause of the oppressed, create steady demand for its products which places its business as far as possible in these present days above the ebb and flow of competition.

Teresa Wahman is a forewoman, and, as may be imagined, grudges neither time nor trouble to insure that the work which passes though her hands is done by those to whom she entrusts it and is not sublet on any terms. Friedel's lameness is much improved, and he has developed talent for wood-carving. He has the old man's tools and models; but it is a strange contrast, his shrunken body and wizened face, in the little brown shop once lightened by that white hair and stately figure. Minne is growing into a very sweet little maiden; and to both of them Teresa is a kind and tender guardian; but her passion is for the sinful and the outcasts of her own sex, among whom she labors untiringly, and with all her old fierce vehemence, compelling them as by actual violence to turn and repent.

"For I've tried both," says Teresa; "and it pays better to live respectable, if people will only fix things so you can."

And very often there are pilgrimages to the cemetery on the hill, where the angel in brown wood blesses the grave of Grandfather Engel.

So, in their several ways, one and all fight valiantly in the great conflict, the battle of Armageddon, which, heed it or not as we will, is at this very moment raging around us; the battle of Him whose name is Faithful and True,[37] against Mammon, greed, and the lust of gain,—against the spirit which says, "Each man for himself! Am I my brother's keeper?"

Sometimes they grow weary in the conflict. Sometimes even to Tom, with his cheerful philosophy, which makes the best of what now is, to Shirley's hopeful spirit, and to her husband's steady courage, the hour of victory seems to tarry overlong. Then it is Elsa who revives them,—Elsa who nerves heart and hand again for the deadly struggle—Elsa, with the white glow of inspiration upon her beautiful face, who unveils to them the legions of guarding angels, and the glow of the dawning victory upon the eastern hills.

For in this battle our weapon is the sword of the Spirit, which kills by making alive, and the Banner over us is Love:[38] therefore a foe that is vanquished is a friend forever gained, and every recruit counts *two*.

And the Day of the Lord at hand.

Queens of the Shop, the Workroom and the Tenement (1890)

"Queens you must always be; queens to your lovers, queens to your husbands and your sons; queens of higher mystery to the world beyond, which bows itself, and will forever bow, before the myrtle crown and stainless scepter of womanhood."—Ruskin[39]

"As the unwise, inequitable and defective features of our present economic conditions inevitably tend to reduce all who live by their own labor to debasing poverty and dependence, and as the suffering and degradation resulting from this system bear most heavily upon women who support themselves by their own labor. . . . We have formed the Working Women's Society, believing that relief and rescue for those women now oppressed and wronged cannot come without their united effort and mutual association."—Preamble to the Constitution of the Working Women's Society.

To enumerate the different trades by which women in New York are endeavoring—not to live—that for many of them is as utterly unattainable a goal as the end of the rainbow—but simply to postpone as long as possible their appearance at the morgue or the cemetery—to attempt to do this would be useless. Briefly they may be divided into certain broad classes, such as medicine, literature, education, manufactures and domestic service. Under medicine we include the lady doctor and the unskilled hired nurse; under literature we shade down from the editor or fashionable lioness, through typewriters, stenographers and compositors to the book stitchers and folders and the gold-leaf girl; while manufactures covers everything from silk weaving to buttonhole making. Now in all these trades or professions it remains emphatically true that there is "room at the top." The women of exceptional ability, who knows her niche in life and climbs upward to it with unflinching courage and unswerving will, usually attains it, though often at the price of treading under her more feeble sisters. The editor of a popular paper or magazine does not often quarrel with her salary; the fashionable milliner or dressmaker can command her own price; the lady professor has her own work and her own reward.

But queens?

Which is correct, Ruskin or the Working Women's Society?

To the credit of the noble profession of letters let it be spoken, it knows no distinction of sex. "There is neither Jew nor Greek, bond nor free, male nor female,"[40] when one comes within the sound of a printing press, chiefly because what is wanted is work of a certain kind and grade; and also, in the lower ranks of the profession, because of the intelligence and strong organization of the Typographical Union,[41] which admits women upon exactly the same footing as men. Compositors receive on an average twelve dollars a week; their work is piece work entirely, their hours are comparatively short, and the wages in almost every instance sure.

Stenographers and typewriters have often a hard struggle to secure a foothold; they have unions, but they are rather social clubs than trades-unions; their wages run from six or eight dollars a week up to twelve and even eighteen; their success usually depends upon their own business ability; and they receive in all but the rarest instances all that their employers agreed to pay them.

Education is considered the peculiar business of women; perhaps for that very reason it is one of the worst-paid businesses in the world; the salaries of men who engage in it are double those of the women, who do better work and more of it.

Into the servant-girl question we shall not go at present; it would in itself require a volume; and there remains therefore the one department of manufactures.

Among these there are four trades which are not injurious-that is a war word—but murderous to women. These are artificial flower making, cigar or cigarette making, working on ostrich feathers, and sewing in all its forms. I may also mention the girls who work in soap factories, and whose business it is to wrap the separate cakes, while hot, in paper. The caustic soda used in the manufacture first turns their nails yellow, then eats away the ends of their fingers. There seems no way to help this, as the deftness of touch required would be of course impossible if the workers wore gloves. It is indeed only possible to any given set of workers for a very short time; but there are always plenty to take their places when they drop out, and though one wonders sometimes what becomes of them there does not seem to be any answer. A machine which should wrap the soap and save their fingers would also throw the majority of them out of employment, and they would probably bitterly oppose its introduction.

The arsenic used in making artificial flowers is, in about two years, almost invariably fatal to the workers, who exhibit all the symptoms of arsenical poisoning— sores on the face and hands, swelling of the limbs, finally nausea and convulsions. Arsenic is, however, about the cheapest dye that can be used.

Workers in tobacco suffer from nicotine poisoning, which kills in a less repulsive manner but no less surely; and the feather workers suffer also from poisonous dyes used in the manufacture; the slightest prick of a finger with the needle allows the dye to mingle with the blood.

The mention of the needle, that ancient emblem of womanhood, brings us to sewing women of all grades: cloak makers, shirt makers, everything makers. At first glance this trade seems healthful enough, and so indeed, in itself, it is. And it is so pleasant, so thoroughly womanly, to sew; there are so many bright fancies stitched into the work or evolved by the whir of the sewing machine.

It seems inhumanly cruel, therefore, to make this special trade the means of the most grinding oppression that can be or is practiced upon woman.

But why should one trouble to write about this class of workers, or indeed, any class? What good does it do?

"Yes," said one woman with whom I spoke, "there was a lady around here about three years ago asking them same questions, but it didn't help nobody."

"No, I suppose not," I said.

"Then why do they ask them?" she returned, with absolute justice. This woman was out of work, but better off than some, inasmuch as she had neither husband nor children to support. She has worked hard all her life and is now past middle age, thin and worn, with a face of quiet hopelessness and long, thin, pathetic hands.

She is a very fair specimen of the American working woman, the development of the girl who comes to the city full of hope and energy to "get work." She has been told that industry and economy are the high road to wealth, but she does not aim at wealth, only to lay by a little against a rainy day. So she hires a furnished room and does her own cooking—Heaven save the mark!—a cup of very strong tea and baker's bread! Upon this, with sometimes a "relish," she makes two meals a day, and she works twelve, fourteen, sixteen, eigh-

teen hours. Consequently, when youth leaves her, which it does very speedily, health goes with it; she has no reserve force of vitality to draw upon, for overwork and underfeeding have exhausted that as she went along; she drops out of the ranks and goes—where? God knows; may He help her!

The woman of whom I have spoken is or was a cloak maker. "I make the cloak," she said, "all but the machine stitching and pressing; yes ma'am, buttonholes and all. If I'm kep' busy all the time, and no delays, I can make six dollars a week, but there's a many delays. The boss he says, 'Now, I'll give you a dollar and forty cents or a dollar and fifty cents for that jacket,' he says, 'or that plush coat,' and that doesn't sound bad. But when I baste it together and send it to be stitched, the stitcher's work is ahead of mine, and I must wait half an hour or an hour to get it back again, for I've no other coat to work on between whiles. Then when I've done it all there's maybe no more work ready, and I wait—I've waited as much as three days to get some more, and then been told there was no more for me. And the forelady, she can be very ugly when she likes; if she has a spite on you she gives you work you don't like, and if you name it to her, 'You can go,' she says. It's them Eyetalians that spoils everything," she went on; "they come over here and they'll work for next to no wages at all; an Eyetalian can live on ten cents a day, and no American can't do that, and they can run the machine faster than a woman."

"Them Eyetalians" and Polish Jews seem to be the bane of the clothing trade from the worker's side. In the department of ladies' cloaks as of men's clothing they reign supreme, and male foreigners are taking the places of American women because they work cheaper or, by reason of their greater muscular strength, more rapidly. There are 1200 women tailors in New York working on men's clothing. These work from 5:00 or 5:30 a.m. until 7:00 and 8:00 o'clock. The male worker receives eighteen dollars a week, and is expected to stitch up from twelve to fourteen coats a day; the woman finishes the same number and receives six dollars a week. That limit of six dollars is one which it seems almost impossible to overpass. She who can count upon it is considered fairly well off; nine dollars for the very few who attain it is absolute wealth.

Dressmaking is also a favorite industry with Italians. Almost any morning upon Broadway one may see one or two Italian women, bowed, miserable and filthy, each of whom carries upon her head a bundle about ten feet long, four or five broad, and of the same thickness. My own first impression regarding this sight was, "What a big bundle of rags!" But they are costly rags. She has received them from a fashionable clothing house, and she is carrying them home to the tenement where she resides. Here, amid filth and vermin inconceivable they are made into robes of the latest style, returned to the factory to be draped, and then may be seen behind the plate-glass windows of uptown stores. Some idea of the risk run by this method of manufacture may perhaps be gained from the fact that foremen and "foreladies" who come in contact with these workers bring home living remembranc-

ers to their uptown boarding houses.

Shirt-making has had a bad name as an industry since Hood wrote his Song of the Shirt;[42] nor does the invention of the sewing machine appear to have benefited the worker. In this trade the average earnings are about four dollars a week; some make even less, others more. About five years ago, I am told, the average wages were about eight dollars; but within five months there were three reductions. The first the workers—at least those in one particular factory—took without rebelling, at the second they murmured, at the third they struck. "We were not organized," one of them said to me, "but we struck all the same, and organized afterward. Well, they held out for awhile then they gave us one-half; the other half we got in August without asking."

"And yet wages have steadily gone down," I said.

"Because they broke up our organization," was the reply. "The next August they closed their factory on purpose, and the girls being thrown out of work drifted off in various directions. The employers did it to break up our organization."

"What can women get who make shirts that retail at fifty cents?" I said.

"Oh! those are made in reformatories," was the reply. "The House of the Good Shepherd, the Westchester Protectory and others do this sort of work so cheap that business firms can't compete with them.[43] Why, when we were on strike that time the House of the Good Shepherd worked straight along. The others all stopped, but that held straight on. They claimed it didn't interfere with us."

Let us be just. Perhaps it did not; perhaps the House of the Good Shepherd was then working on a special line of goods which did not compete with the strikers. Let us make every excuse possible. But oh! false shepherds unworthily called good, who foul the waters with your feet so that the flock cannot drink thereof; who take from the streets girls who have been driven there by poverty, and use them as instruments to beat down wages, to tread down their struggling sisters into the mire from which they have been temporarily lifted. Only temporarily; for of what avail is it if you wash and clothe a girl and fill her mind with new thoughts and purer hopes; if you accustom her to greater comfort in the way of shelter, food and clothing than she ever dreamed was possible; or if you create in her new wants of flowers, books, and pictures? All these things are good, if you do them; but how shall they profit her, if with them you teach her a trade that she cannot live by? which you have taken pains to ruin for her. Find her a place in a factory and leave her. At the first cut in wages—even sooner perhaps—she will remember that she already knows a trade far more lucrative. We try to be just; but does it not seem as though the saintly ministrants in these reformatories were as anxious to lay up treasures in heaven as are worldlings to do so upon earth, and so took pains to secure a perennial supply of the raw material?

All counters of cheap underwear are supplied from reformatories. Not long ago Mrs. L. M. Barry,[44] well known as a Knight of Labor and defender of woman, found such preternatural bargains at Wanamaker's[45] in Philadelphia that she determined to find out how he came by them. She obtained employment from him as a machine hand, and soon found out from the wages paid that the cheap goods were not of home manufacture. Further inquiry satisfied her that they, as usual, came from reformatories. Now, there is no reason for prejudice against prison or reformatory work as such, for in respect of cleanliness and good sanitary conditions it is preferable to much made outside. That to which the unions object is the low rate at which the work is contracted for, which injures those within the prison equally with those without.

Shopgirls, or salesladies, as they prefer to be called! Here the great evils are excessive hours, working overtime without extra pay, unwholesome sanitary conditions and excessive fines. Just here it may not be amiss to speak of the Working Women's Protective Union, No. 19 Clinton Place,[46] whose special mission it is to collect wages which the worker cannot collect for herself. It has been in operation for twenty-seven years, and has collected in that time thousands of dollars' worth of wages due without one cent of cost to the person wronged. But fines are beyond the reach of even this Union; from them there seems no redress—though upon what principle a woman who receives seven dollars a week is fined thirty cents for ten minutes' tardiness I confess myself unable to see. Seven dollars is by no means the usual wages per week, which range from two to eighteen dollars, the latter to a girl with a good figure who can show off cloaks in the cloak department. In one store the fines in one year amounted to $3,000, which was divided between the superintendent and the timekeeper, and the former was heard to charge the latter with lack of strictness. So much for the slave-drivers! The owners also have their pick at the bones of the slave; for in many houses employees are expected to take from two to three weeks holiday in the dull season at their own expense. This on a salary of, say, three dollars a week!

Is it possible to live pure, upright lives under such conditions? Thank God! it is possible, as is attested by the thousands who maintain their integrity in spite of all hindrances; but it is more than hard. It has been well said that, while men's wages cannot fall below the starvation line women's can, since the paths of shame are always open to her. This is a terrible factor in our political economy.

Why write of these things? Where is the remedy? God help us if we cannot find one! For the souls of the coming generation lie in the hands of these women; and we shall never be the people we should and might be until we have learned that it is the first and most important business of a nation to protect its women, not by any pulling sentimentality of queenship, chivalry or angelhood, but by making it possible for them to earn an honest living.

For this, the only method is union among women, the best hope is in the women themselves. For men, hard as they have been to women workers, are now being driven by the pressure of their competition, by the effect which women's low rate of wages has had upon theirs, to see that their own interest demands her enfranchisement and elevation. The unions are opening to her, she has long been "free of the guild" among the Knights of Labor, whose preamble sets forth among the things to be accomplished by organization: "Equal wages for equal work, without regard to sex." The newly formed clothing unions are ready to welcome her; but woman shrinks back from organization, Heaven knows why! It is perhaps because in organization one finds the truest freedom, and woman has been a slave too long to know what freedom means. Then, too, we are so hard upon each other, we women; it is so difficult to make us trust one another, to bind us together, to create in us a feeling of real sisterhood. And our weakest point is just where our strongest should be; it is in those women workers who have found or made a standing-place for themselves and who by no means wish to be classed as working women. What could not the educated workers of New York do for their struggling sisters—teachers, writers, stenographers, and such like? It would have been amusing to a student of human nature had it not been so infinitely sad, to watch the look of scorn which rose to the surface at the question, "Can you give me any points about your business? I am studying the working women of New York—"

"I know nothing about working women," came the quick, short answer.

Some of the things that might be done are shown to us by the two societies already quoted. The Working Women's Society aims to organize women, to teach them the strength and self-respect that organization brings.

Among its remaining aims as set forth in the preamble are to enforce existing laws for the protection of women and children in factories, to investigate and protest against all violations of these laws, and to promote further legislation on this subject, to found a labor bureau, and to secure for both sexes equal pay for equal work.

On May 6, 1890, a mass meeting was held at Chickering Hall under the auspices of this society and over one hundred clergymen. "A Report on the condition of Women and Children in the New York retail stores" was read, which ought to have caused the very stones to cry out. A preamble and resolutions were adopted, and it was attempted to start a consumer's league, the members of which should pledge themselves to buy at only such stores as should be included in a white list, to be prepared by a committee. To this white list—the obverse of a boycott—there could be no possible objection, provided a sufficient number of stores could be found where employees are treated fairly well; but will it be possible to find consumers enough to found the league?

Wealthy women of New York, attention! This is your business. Will you give up your bargain counter—for it is the wealthy who seek bargain counters—for the sake of your suffering, starving sisters?

The work of the Protective Union, as already explained, is very different, but equally needful. It would seem that small as the wages are, it is a mere matter of course that the workers should receive them when they are due; but whether this be so or not the books of the Union abundantly testify. Some methods of defrauding an employee it has almost broken up, such, for example, as taking girls on trial without wages to learn a business, and when they asked to be paid, turning them off and taking on a new set. The union has taught the workers to demand a written contract, the keeping of which it stands ready to enforce. Against other wrongs it is powerless, but this of violation of contract it sets straight with all its might; its scope is limited, but it does well all that it attempts without money and without price. No officer is allowed to receive any salary; the lawyer has given his services gratis for twenty-three years; each case is carefully and impartially investigated, and if the money is due payment is enforced if there is any property to levy upon. If not, the offender may be imprisoned for fifteen days if a man; if a woman there is no redress—a bit of chivalry on the part of the law which appears, after the facts we have been considering, exceedingly ill-timed, when taken in connection with the fact that your most arrant and barefaced defrauder of her working people is your high-class, fashionable dressmaker.

A small attempt on the part of the workers to help themselves is the Coöperative Shirtmakers, 770 Third Avenue. It was a little pathetic to hear from them that they have been together five years, "longer than most cooperative things hold together." They are thoroughly bright, intelligent women, large-hearted and large-minded, with full sympathy and sisterly love for their sex. Not all of their members work together; of those who do, no one receives more than her regular wages; the profits, if any, are divided between a sinking fund to increase the business and a benefit fund for sick members.

I have not tried to exhaust this subject, in fact it is inexhaustible; only to say such things as may perhaps open the eyes of some one person to the lives that are being lived through around us. And yet, what good will it do? But God help us all unless we change this state of things, and that right speedily!

Christine Ladd-Franklin (1848-1930)

Christine Ladd-Franklin was nothing if not a crusader. Born in Windsor, Connecticut, Ladd-Franklin sought an education from an early age. She attended the Johns Hopkins University and was the first woman to complete the requirements for a PhD in mathematics, in 1882. Unfortunately, she was not awarded her degree until 1926 due to discrimination she faced based on her gender, but that did not stop her from continuing her scientific work. Ladd-Franklin was a member of the faculty at Johns Hopkins and later at Columbia University in New York City. Ladd-Franklin's main academic focus was visual perception and color theory, but she also studied logic and psychology.

Ladd-Franklin published articles in various journals including *Science* and the *American Journal of Psychology*. Here, we feature a few short op-eds and letters to the editor she wrote, rather than her scientific work. These pieces offer critical commentary of the society in which she lived: one takes aim at the discrepancies in pay of teachers; another advocates for working-girls clubs. And the piece entitled, "A Logic Poem," shows the bridge between her scientific work and her literary interests, which was also manifest in the comments and contributions she made to the Woman's Literary Club of Baltimore. An early member of the Club, Ladd-Franklin was a frequent contributor to Club programs and discussions regardless of subject, offering frank opinions that underscore her fearless assertion of female intellect in all areas of her life. —S. Johnson

The Convention of Working-Girls' Clubs (1890)

The full report of the convention of working-girls' clubs, lately held in this city,[1] is a volume which may well give ground for thought. There is nothing which invites so much to oppression on the part of the strong as a dejected spirit on the part of the weak; and if the poor sewing-woman, whose name has hitherto been a synonym for the crushed and the down-trodden, has come to hiring halls and making speeches in her own behalf, it may well be believed that a better era is setting in for her.

The term workingman calls up at the present moment a picture of something firm and self-reliant—discontented, perhaps, and more or less unreasonable, but conscious that he is not altogether without power to affect his own circumstances, and hence conscious that he is a man. There is no reason why the term working-woman should not carry with it a similar connotation. In this country there are few workingwomen who do not at least earn enough to buy themselves sufficient food; and, short of insufficient food, there is no reason why a workingwoman should not, if she orders her life well, have that spirit and energy and hopefulness which, after all, are the inmost secret of the happiness of all of us, and which are enough to prevent any class of people from being regarded, or from regarding themselves, as a pitiable portion of the human race.

The proper objects of working-girls' clubs are, it seems to us, two in number: (1) to teach the working-girl not to waste the means of happiness which are now within her reach, and (2) to give her that feeling of solidarity, of mutual trustfulness, of confidence in the power of concerted action, which will enable her, as occasion presents itself, to make effectual claim to a larger and larger share of the products of her labor. Existing clubs seem to have done little as yet towards organizing strikes. There is no necessity for having that object distinctly in view, but neither is there any doubt that the strong feeling for the common good which club life not of the frivolous kind tends to promote, will furnish the standing ground from which to force, either directly or indirectly, better terms from employers. A beginning in this direction has been made by the association of stenographers of Phil-

adelphia.[2] Its members pledge themselves not to accept less than a fixed standard of work. Last year this association held the first banquet ever given by workingwomen to themselves.[3]

The other object—that of securing a greater amount of happiness out of their present earnings—is a simpler matter. Happiness, for all of us, is at bottom very little a matter of the richness of our surrounding; it is much more intimately connected with their cleanliness, refinement, and good taste. Mr. Stanton Coit,[4] after an intimate acquaintance with the very poor, said that the chief respect in which the rich differed from them was in the use of the tooth-brush. But habits of personal cleanliness are readily learned when quick-witted girls see of what vital consequence they are to the ladies who attend their clubs. Pleasing surroundings are easily in reach of girls in their clubrooms, if not in their homes. The most interesting report in this book is that which describes the way in which the Hartford working-girls are engages in furnishing their summer home. Old packing-boxes are converted by muslin into washstands and tables, or by paint into book cases and cabinets. Pictures cut out of art newspapers are mounted on seasoned pine boards with a margin painted in gold and silver and finished with a row of picture-screws. All the bed-linen and table-linen is marked with a pansy, in different colors for the different rooms; hammock pillows are made of bits of newspaper torn fine; the hangings and sofa-covers for the parlor, which is to be in Dresden-china colors, are made of blue denim embroidered in white, and this embroidery is kept at the rooms of the United Workers,[5] and worked upon by any one who has a few moments to spare.

Does not all this give a far more pleasing picture of summer rest, though it be only for a week or two for each worker, than the denizen of the crowded summer boarding-house is not looking forward to? Will all the monotonous fancy work which is to be executed upon the piazzas of sea-side hotels this summer give half the pleasure which is being got by these girls out of their blue denim embroidered in white? Separate pleasures are not in the reach of working-girls, but, by putting their small means together, pleasures in common may be had by them to an almost unlimited degree.

If we should ask ourselves what would be the source of our most poignant suffering, were we suddenly be forced to live among the very poor, the answer would probably be (after the loss of good air and cleanliness) the lack of a courteous and considerate behavior on the part of our associates. Scolding mothers, ill-tempered fathers, quarrelsome brothers and sisters—these are things much more productive of unhappiness than poor food, hard beds, or long hours of work. The association of working-girls with the ladies who aid them in their clubs has a marvellous effect in quieting their manners and teaching them gentleness and forbearance. What the people who are most to be envied have reason to pride themselves upon more than all their possessions, is the subtle charm with which they know how to invest human intercourse. This is, in its

perfection, the product of generations of culture, but its beginnings are not difficult to catch by girls who have the training in quickness which the sewing-machine brings with it. Their wealth the rich are not very likely to share with the poor, but the outward forms of respect which they show each other may not impossibly penetrate further and further into the lower strata of society, until virtuous poverty is robbed of no small portion of its hardness.

Clubs may easily be of so much advantage to working-girls that it is hard to see how any benevolent ladies who are not already overwhelmed with work for others can help doing something to start them, one after another, in large numbers, and to help them to become, as soon as possible, independent of outside aid. There is no doubt that the New York Convention[6] will be productive of great enthusiasm among both of the necessary parties to the working-girls' club.

The Poor Pay of Teachers (1905)

There is a dearth of teachers for the country schools this year. The thorough training which teachers are now required by law to be in possession of can only be obtained by those who have been through college or normal school,[7] or teachers' training classes, and for such the remuneration at present offered is an indignity. What is to happen? Are the highly trained teachers to swallow their pride and to accept salaries that were intended for the untrained, or are the salaries, which were pitifully meagre in any case, to be raised? It is upon such occasions as this that labor gets its innings,—that the financial level of a class of workers becomes (or fails to become) permanently raised. But another condition is essential if the outcome is to be the desirable one,—it is that the workers concerned should have strength of mind to hold out for higher wage which they have a right to demand. This fall, therefore, every woman who accepts a mean salary when her preparation fits her for receiving a decent one should feel that she is a traitor to the interests of her class. It is true that women frequently have members of their family dependent upon them; but then male workers are almost universally responsible for the subsistence of wife and children, and yet they can make sacrifices for the good of their class.

Society Women (1908)

To the Editor of *The Nation*:

Sir: is it not time to make a concerted effort against allowing that most vulgar phrase, "society woman" (or man), to creep into the English language? Incredible as it may seem, it has appeared now and again in quarters that are otherwise above reproach, and when once as indefensible phrase passes beyond the region of newspaper slang, where it had its birth, nothing but distinct and conscious effort can arrest it. Frivolous society is not the same thing as society. It is the social intercourse of *les intellectuels* which constitutes the really important part of society, and to devote the term, unmodified, to describing its noisy froth and foam is to throw away a most honorable and a most useful word to no purpose. Debasing the coinage in speech is (as George Eliot has ardently pointed out) a crime.

There is not the least necessity for the use of the term in this restricted sense. The English language furnishes plenty of good descriptive phrases for the people whom it is sought to characterize. They may be called the "ultra-rich," the "ultra-idle," the "fashionable," the "smart," or the "worldly." It might even be possible to bring back that good old English word, "worldlings." Any of these terms would do, but "the worldly" is probably the best—*les mondaines* is the word devoted to this use by the French; and Esperanto warns us to put our languages into harmony, where we can actually gain by doing so. Of course, if one goes far enough back, the same objection held originally to considering that the ultra-rich constitute the world, as holds now to considering that they constitute society, but the signification of worldly is so ingrained in the English language that it would be foolish to take exception to it now. The "smart" is a good term in England, but in this country it has acquired a bad connotation.

Collectively, the group in question could be called "the gay world," or "the fashionable world," or "the idle world" (or, with Veblen,[8] "the world of ostentatious expenditure"); while the other and more important group would naturally be called "the grave world," "the serious world," "the weighty world" ("the better world" has been, unfortunately, preempted for another sense),—or—here, again, the French have given us the right model—simply "the intellectuals." The word has as good ground for its use as has, for instance, the noun, "the criminal."

It is to be hoped that a word of warning will be sufficient for those who belong to the class in which good English prevails.

Christine Ladd-Franklin[9]
Baltimore, Md., October 18.

A Logic Poem (1926)

What is logic? Are not the following examples cases of logic? The first is a poem developed out of a well-known Irish distich.

(1) It goes thus:

Unless the kettle boiling be
They labor in vain who make the tea;
Unless the tea be properly made
My guest will not like it, I am afraid;
Unless my guest contented be
She'll never again come visiting me.

Consequently:

Unless the kettle boiling be
She'll never again come visiting me.

(2) Are the two following sentences logically equivalent or are they not? "Not unless it rains do I take my umbrella," "Not unless I do not take an umbrella does it not rain."

(3) A child of four, sitting at the dinner table, was making the interesting experiment of eating her soup with a fork. Her mother said to her: "Nobody eats soup with a fork, Emily," and Emily replied, "*But* I do, and I am somebody."

This last is an antilogism—a form of reasoning which is has been proposed to substitute for the syllogism. It is the argument of rebuttal, the conversational argument, and it doubtless arose earlier, in the development of the human race, than the argument of drawing conclusions. It is certainly fully as easy, as is proved (if proof were necessary) by its having been used, in exactly this form, by a very young child. Here is another example of it, expressed in terms of the logician's favorite *s, m* and *p:*

"If no priests are martyrs and there are no saints who are non-martyrs, then it-is-impossible-that any saints should be priests." Here it will be noticed that the common term of the first two premises is martyrs and non-martyrs, *i.e.,* a positive and a negative term. Common logic, however, insists upon it that the term common to two premises must be absolutely and exactly the same; nevertheless, this argument would appear, to the untrained logician, to have a certain degree of validity; what is the trouble? Senator N. said: "*It-cannot-be-that* any of these measures are idiotic, *for* they are all necessary, and nothing that is necessary is idiotic." This is not common logic. What, then, is it? What *is* logic?

Margaret Sutton Briscoe (1864-1941)

A beacon of traditional values, Margaret Sutton Briscoe played an influential role as an honorary member of the Woman's Literary Club of Baltimore. Briscoe was born in Baltimore but made her career in New York City, where she became an editor and frequent contributor at the popular magazine *Harper's Bazaar*. As an honorary member of the WLCB, her name recognition added prestige and recognition to the Club. But unlike many of the Club's honorary members who did not actually participate in Club activities, Briscoe attended meetings on occasion, and she also maintained Baltimore connections. At a meeting in 1892, she read an essay depicting the homeless population in Baltimore which may have been an early version of "The Tramp Problem in Baltimore." It was published on the eve of the Depression of 1893, which rocked the nation.

Briscoe assumed the duties expected of influential society women. As a counselor and professor at Amherst College,[1] she influenced numerous students, one of whom wrote a poem dedicated to Briscoe. Her desire to help others led her to be a counselor for troubled youth at Amherst College. Her presence as a lady and intellectual influenced her professional work. In addition to her work at *Harper's Bazar,* she published short fiction, essays and novels in the domestic vein in *Harper's, Scribner's, Outlook*, and elsewhere.

Briscoe's adherence to traditional values influenced her opinion on social issues. More crusader than critic, Briscoe understood social issues from a genteel, antebellum mindset. While she fought for social reform, her efforts fell short of fighting for equality. Briscoe was a typical figure of the Progressive Era, taking up social justice issues that promoted and perpetuated traditional, Victorian ideals. Briscoe considered herself a Southern woman and opposed female suffrage. She walked the tightrope between professional woman and Southern belle, framing her works through traditional ideology. —M. Malouf

The Tramp Problem in Baltimore (1892)

Much lies among us convulsively, nigh desperately, struggling to be born. —Carlyle[2]

"Charity is centralized; offices are hired; societies founded, with secretaries, paid or unpaid. The hunt of the deserving poor goes merrily forward,"[3] says Robert Louis Stevenson. The sheep and the goats are separated with an abundant care, and then—what of the goats? The Bishop of Maryland, in a late address to his clergy, has asked this question with some sternness.

Those who have been busy throwing out life-lines into the sea of sinking humanity, and in organizing life-saving stations, are sometimes startled on realizing that close by their feet, and within reach of their very arms, hands have emerged from the depths of depravity, and are, without aid from above, finding a way to the light.

A few steps off from one of the most crowded thoroughfares of Baltimore City there has been such an uplifting of hands for two years, almost alone and unrecognized. There, in what is called the "Fayette Street Narrows," stands an old church which for many years sheltered a large and influential congregation. As the dwellings around it gradually changed into warehouses, the bustle of trade rose higher and higher, until the church and the chapel beside it were reduced to silence and closed. When the chapel opened again, it was to admit a widely different assembly. Dives went out and Lazarus came in, and worse and Lazarus; for his sores were confined to his body.

A curious and pitiful sight awaited

those who looked into the hall of this chapel on any cold night in the past winter. A huddled mass of sleeping humanity lay on the bare boards of the floor, with arms, heads, and legs in what seemed an entanglement so hopeless as to make it difficult to realize that this was not an awful monstrosity of aggregate flesh and blood. Yet they were all separate beings with separate souls, and, alas! Separate responsibilities, to be parted with the morning; each bedfellow (if the term be not mockery) moving on in his own individual path, upward or downward as it might be, and according as the efforts of those who labor among them bore fruit. For this is now the headquarters of "The Free Sunday Breakfast and Rescue Association," the purpose of which is told in its charter, granted February, 1892: "Incorporated for religious and charitable purposes; and its aim will be to secure food, clothing, shelter, and employment for the poor and unfortunate, and to aid and elevate and save the fallen by means of the Gospel; and it shall be absolutely undenominational and unsectarian."

In the hall of this chapel as many as two hundred men have been fed, taught, and sheltered in a night. The average attendance has been about a hundred. Lodging was not a part of the original plan. That, and indeed the whole Association, has been an evolution, meeting needs as they arose. The cellar was first pressed into service as a shelter, and, despite its large stove, makes about the order of sleeping quarters that might be expected underground—damp and impure, though scrupulously clean.

In the emergency of a stormy night, when the cellar was full, and the tramps still came pouring in from the cold street, pleading for refuge, the floor of the hall was offered them; and the precedent established thus became a nightly custom. Here collects the tramp element of the city, and the precedent established thus became a nightly custom. Here collects the tramp element of the city, and here their bodily and moral needs are met as far as is possible by the officers of the Association and their assistants, who are all unsalaried laborers, animated only by a great enthusiasm for humanity.

The work depends wholly on the voluntary contributions of these workers, and on what they can collect from outside. On this Apostolic basis the Association rests, for it is but little known by those in a position to assist financially. Yet, undoubtedly, in that very circumstance has lain the power of growth.

From the people themselves striving upward this movement has had its origin, and it is the expression of a heavenly sympathy for the erring on the part of those who have themselves known the bitterness of such a life. The reformed have become the reformers. The raw material is wrought into the image of a self-respecting man by those to whom every inch of the process is a personal experience.

To the effort of one man, now Superintendent, the Association owes its direct birth, and he founded it literally on faith. Walking home one night from a meeting at a mission station in the lower part of the city, he paused before this silent church, and stood looking at it regretfully.

To use his own words, "As I stood there I suddenly heard a voice say, 'Bill! You open up this place.'"

And he was not disobedient. The next day he presented himself at the door of a bank whose president he knew through some mutual mission interest. There, without backing of any description, he asked the loan of one hundred dollars.

"For what purpose?"

"For the Free Sunday Breakfast Association."

"What is that?"

As it was then nothing but a name, naturally the request was not granted.

"Lend me ten dollars, then, on my own account, and let me see what I can do," was the next proposition, which was acceded to.

Bread, ham, and coffee were given by others to the same unassociated Association. Those in power granted the use of the chapel building, free of charge, until it might rent to a more profitable tenant. Thus, on Sunday morning, November 16, 1890, the "Free Sunday Breakfast Association" opened.

The first effort was disappointing. The table was set for the guests from the waysides and hedges, but only five of those bidden appeared, and the sandwiches and coffee which the superintendent had spent half the night in preparing where in a large part wasted. But from this beginning the Association has reached its present point of progress. It is now open every night for supper, teaching, and shelter. Its reading room stands open all day, and a separate room has been fitted up with comfortable beds for individual cases.

The methods of work are extremely simple and fundamental. Prominent among the texts and inscriptions hanging on the walls of the hall is one which gives the system in a nutshell. It stands thus:

Soap

Soup

Salvation

Bath-tubs and facilities for washing clothes are freely provided to such as wish to avail themselves of them; then follows the supper in the hall, consisting of a roll and a cup of coffee served by the workers—an inexpensive entertainment, which yet forms a platform enabling the workers to get alongside of the men, and, as they frankly admit, attracting many who might not come at all otherwise; but once there, they are often taken hold of and rescued from the mire.

At one of the meetings a nicely dressed young man was heard speaking to a worker aside:

"You don't remember me, sir?"

"No; have I seen you before?"

"I was a Free Breakfast man. I have work now."

"And you are doing nicely? Well, I am glad that I was not able to recognize you."

The evening ends with prayer and exhortation; those who have been "picked up" are seated on the platform at the end of the room, and rise one by one to testify to their change of life in the face of an inscription which reads: "Testimonies short, sharp, and to the point." One rises who had not wandered far away when rescued. He was on the downward path chiefly because it seemed the only way open to him. Another speaks from the platform of a "body full of whisky, and no coat on his back," when he struggled into the hall and safety. "I was as low as the lowest among you," he says simply, and you look around the strange assembly of faces, all more or less degraded, many repulsive, expecting to see offense expressed, but you find only interest.

The exhortations are earnest and direct. Men speak as only men who know can speak. Driven upward themselves by the implacable gadfly of a desire for good, they have proven their possession of a spark of the divine, else the gadfly might have stung in vain; and it is on their belief in this birth-right in others that they base their efforts.

The language is rough at times, and a spade is always a spade, but it is the speech that is understood by the listeners. You feel sure that no silver-tongued orator could touch these ears so delicately. They listen, and nudge one another when hard hit; some only half liking it, some enjoying it, with a callous lack of self-consciousness, and a few of the younger men distinctly sheepish. All are interested in one way or another, and the attention is held. The people seem to know the secret of reaching the people as no political economist could have taught them. There is a pulse of life felt indescribably throughout.

As the workers mingle with the crowd, and as one or another gives them reason to think that his heart is touched and his dead aspirations quickened, they keep him in sight, and when the benches are piled up on the platform in preparation for the night, he is withdrawn from the human scramble on the floor, and given a bed in the separate room before mentioned: his first upward step. There he lodges till he can be returned to his home, or be respectably settled elsewhere with work. It may be that he has been drinking for days, and is rum-soaked to the core. In that case the key is quietly turned in the lock, and the poor besotted carcass nursed from the brute into manhood again. When he can once more eat and sleep and reason, his choice is given him. There is the sty, if he will return to it; and here is a coat for his back, and decency of life.

The money expended for the passage home, for the decent clothing that made seeking and securing work a possibility, or for the new start in life, has not always found its limit. Again and again these sums, refunded with scrupulous care, come back to aid the next poor stumbler. Some of the "cures" are passed on to the church or mission to which they belong, but many still linger about the spot where they first looked up to a different existence, and become the more efficient workers among the new-comers.

Although the Association is now a proven factor for good, there must of necessity come times of discouragement, when its workers, were they hirelings, might be tempted to leave all and "go a-fishing." Case after case arises that could only have been treated successfully through the father's fathers. The sour grapes have been eaten.

"What is your percentage[4] of success?" one of the workers was asked.

"It is small; we work with the lowest grade of material, and the percentage in product, as every practical man knows, must be low in consequence. With a higher grade of material comes a higher percentage of product."

Another slum worker has said: "We cannot expect garbage-picking to pay well."

That the results in this case have been what they are is, as has been stated, undoubtedly due to the fact that the Association has been let alone to work out its own way to the light. That they are comparatively unknown, and that they do not themselves appreciate the advantage of this, is proven by a clipping from their monthly bulletin, which states with some feeling that ten dollars expended in sending out to the various churches appeals for aid met a return of three dollars and twenty-five cents. Those who have tested the liberality of the same churches know that, when properly approached, the response has been widely different.

But with the growth of the Association, with the necessity for music at the meetings, with the opening of the reading-room and Bible classes, has arisen a serious question. New workers were called, and among them came men of a different culture and wider knowledge. With rare tact and far-seeing self-control, they have taken the position of subordinates and assistants only, but they are in touch with another world, where "organized charity" has wisely taught that, for all that is given, the take of bricks must be exacted in one form or another. The very name of "Free Breakfast" smacks of pay without work in ears thus educated. In a natural line of growth, a wholesome fear of pauperizing has been aroused in the Association, and the need of providing work for the men who come for shelter and food is now recognized. But this involves a different home, and one of less uncertain tenure; and lodgings, if worked for, must rise above a standard which, in spite of cleanliness, just escapes a charge of lack of decency.

Growth calls for nourishment, which, calling in turn for the wherewithal, must inevitably bring into touch with the Association a social element hitherto almost excluded. With the difficulty of saying in the same breath "Give plenteously" and "Hands off," and with the danger of weakening which lies in any other policy, opens a new and equally interesting chapter of this social experiment.

Mary Noyes Colvin (1850-1926)

In 1888, Mary Noyes Colvin became the first woman in the history of the University of Zurich to earn a PhD. She remained in Europe, continuing her study of language, and in 1893, she published a new edition of William Caxton's historical work, *Godeffroy of Boloyne; The Siege and Conqueste of Jerusalem,* accompanying the original text with an extraordinarily detailed introduction, notes, index, and vocabulary. Colvin's edition has remained authoritative. The page images we include here provide a glimpse of Colvin's deep erudition.

In the introduction to the volume, Colvin noted that her translation painstakingly compared the ten extant copies of the volume published by William Caxton in 1481, held in libraries throughout Europe, along with manuscript materials in English, Latin, and French, and translations of Caxton's work into other languages, including Italian and Spanish. It is to be assumed the she herself traveled to all of these locations and devoted time studying each of these copies in creating her edition.

Though Colvin was only a member of the WLCB during its earliest years, from about 1890-92, during that time she spearheaded an effort by a Club committee to investigate gender equity in Baltimore schools. Her criticisms were taken seriously by the school superintendent and resulted in changes that made girls' education more equal to that of boys; female grammar schools "were raised to the curriculum of male grammar schools," noted the *Baltimore Sun* at the time. She also set the stage for female high schools to provide college preparation for girls at the same level as male high schools.[1]

Colvin was recognized as someone extraordinary in her day. When she was appointed a professor of romance languages at Western Reserve University in Cleveland, newspapers around the country noted her achievement. In one letter of reference, Colvin is called "a lady of more than ordinary ability and teaching power" who is "as valuable in society as she is forcible in the class-room."[2] —K. Kazmierski

Godeffroy of Boloyne,

OR

The Siege and Conqueste of Jerusalem,

BY

WILLIAM, ARCHBISHOP OF TYRE.

TRANSLATED FROM THE FRENCH BY

William Caxton,

AND PRINTED BY HIM IN 1481.

———

EDITED FROM THE COPY IN THE BRITISH MUSEUM, WITH INTRODUCTION,
NOTES, VOCABULARY, AND INDEXES,

BY

MARY NOYES COLVIN, Ph.D.

LONDON:
PUBLISHED FOR THE EARLY ENGLISH TEXT SOCIETY
BY KEGAN PAUL, TRENCH, TRÜBNER & CO.,
PATERNOSTER HOUSE, CHARING CROSS ROAD.
1893.

Title page of Godeffroy of Boloyne: The Siege and Conqueste of Jerusalem by William Caxton (1481), translated and edited by Mary Noyes Colvin.

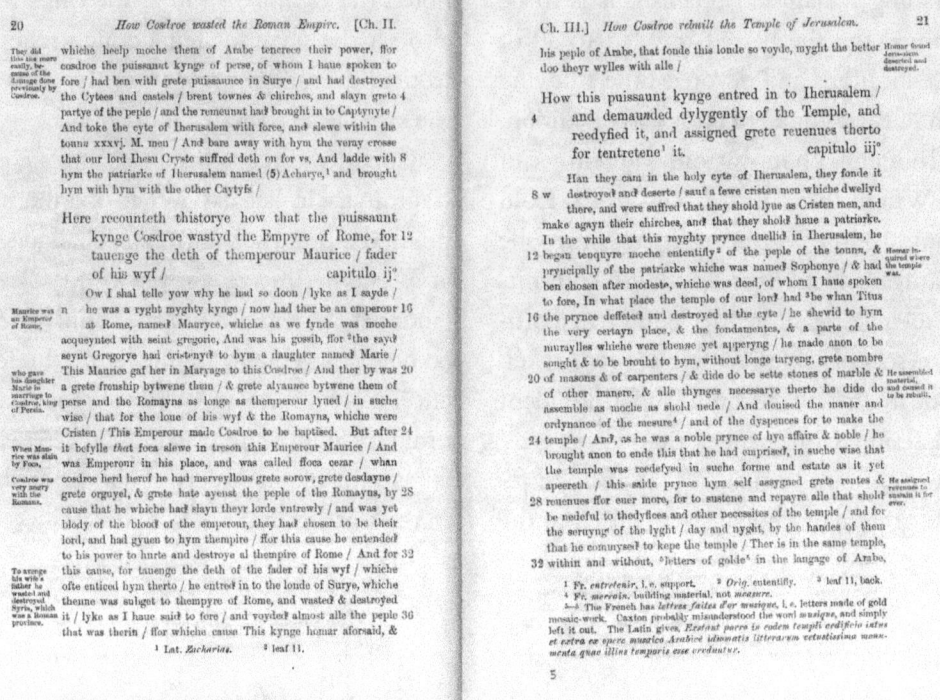

Representative pages from Mary Noyes Colvin's translation of William Caxton's medieval history, Godeffroy of Boloyne, showing her extensive marginal annotations.

Louise Malloy (1858-1947)

As Baltimore's first woman journalist and as a playwright, Louise Malloy was one of the most influential crusaders in the Woman's Literary Club of Baltimore. Malloy was a reporter and columnist for the *Baltimore American* for more than three decades, beginning in the mid-1880s. During her long journalistic career, she wrote and edited material for the children's page, and she also wrote reviews of plays and editorials.[1] For over twenty years, she also wrote and edited the daily humor column for the *American* under the pseudonym Josh Wink. "Josh Wink" was not Malloy's invention—the pseudonym had been invented by Wilbur D. Nesbit, who edited the humor column from 1899-1902. But the persona became wholly hers: during her tenure, she published literally *thousands* of jokes and poems as Josh Wink. Malloy was a serious advocate for social and municipal reform during her lifetime, but she was also very funny. And it's that quality of her writing that we choose to highlight here.

While expressing progressive views in her writing, Malloy is not known to have actively participated in suffrage or women's rights movements. Her reticence may have been due to her devout Catholicism. Yet her sense of humor made readers stop and think about the treatment of women in a male-dominated society. Even though many of her jokes are made at the expense of other women, by taking offense to Malloy's comedy, women may have turned a critical eye on their own lives.

Malloy was an admirer of William Shakespeare, as we can see in her romantic comedy *The Player Maid*. Malloy wrote the play in 1905 and first presented it at the Academy of Music in Baltimore. It centers on the offstage love triangle of the actors in David Garrick's production of Shakespeare's *Romeo and Juliet*. Malloy uses the wit of the title character, Eleanor Hallam, to satirize what real women experienced during this time.

Newspaper accounts relate that *The Player Maid* delighted those who saw it. The *Baltimore Sun* even reported that the play, which received a single performance on Broadway, "took New York by storm." It also toured small theaters located throughout the South in the early years of the twentieth century. —K. Kutch and F. D'Aloia

Jokes and Verse by "Josh Wink" (1903-1917)

Jokes

A Change (May 12, 1903)

Doctor—You must have a change, with complete rest and quiet.
Patient—Oh, Doctor, do you mean to say that I'll have to be taken away in this condition?
Doctor—No, Indeed. I'll have your wife sent away.

Lucky Dogs (May 12, 1903)

Night—My business has gone to the dogs.
Day—That's nothing, old man. My wife's affections went to dogs long ago.

A Hero (July 9, 1905)

Recent Arrival—Why do all the people cheer every time that man comes on the beach?
Regular Resident—He made a rescue yesterday which taxed to the limit his unselfishness and heroism.
Recent Arrival—What did he do?
Regular Resident—He swam out and rescued his mother-in-law.

Unbreakable (July 9, 1905)

Peters—Do you think the court will succeed in breaking the will?
Parr—It's doubtful; it was made by a woman.

A New Version (July 9, 1905)

Apostle Reed Smoot[2] (senator-elect from Utah)—What is the meaning of those letters W. C. T. U.,[3] used by those women whom I see are going to object to me taking my seat?
Another Mormon (meditatively)—From the way the women are acting it looks like they might mean Women Can't Trust Us.

At 11:59 P.M. (May 10, 1903)

Irate Father—What do you mean by calling on my daughter at this hour?
Young Man—I pressed her-
Irate Father—W-h-a-t's that ! ! !
Young Man—Pressed her for an answer to my proposal, and she asked for an extension of time.

He Was Slow (May 10, 1903)

Ethel—How did you feel when he asked
    you to marry him?
May—Felt like shaking him for not hav-
    ing done it sooner!

Good Example (May 14, 1903)

"How is it your parrot talks so incessantly?"
"I bought him from the janitor of a
    woman's club."

Half Truths (May 14, 1903)

The most exclusive fashion is comfort.
Life's leading testimonial is a happy person.
Love is a precious currency, but it has a
    poor circulation.
If you have a conviction, live it first and
    preach it afterwards.
Real beauty is a rare gift; If you doubt set
    your ideal and go search for it.
We have only two friends in life—the
    friend that makes us laugh and the
    friend that makes us think.
The way to a woman's heart may be
    slightly strenuous, but the road com-
    ing from it is the hardest to travel.

Heard at the Horse Show (May 15, 1903)

Ethel—That Miss Van Lipp and Charles
    Dasher don't seem nearly so devoted
    to each other as they used to be.
Clara—Of course not. Haven't you
    heard? They're engaged.

A Fruitful Quarrel (Sept. 21, 1905)

"Oh, I know you depend on your pull,"
    said the Grape to the Peach, "but
    there's always lots of pluck about me."
"I don't know about that," retorted the
Peach. "I notice you are apt to give a
    wine when you are hard pressed."

The First One (Oct. 9, 1905)

"I am the original kid-napper," whispered
    the cradle as it rocked the baby to sleep.

The Youthful Diplomat (June 9, 1906)

Visitor—Willie, tell your mamma that I
    have come to call on her.
Willie—Mamma's not at home.
Visitor (shocked)—Why, Willie I'm sure
    I saw her looking from the parlor
    window as I came up the street.
Willie (stoutly)—No you didn't, neither.
    That was Sis peeking through the
    parlor blinds. Mom saw you coming
    from upstairs.

Diplomacy (May 10, 1909)

"Am I the only *girl* you ever made love to?"
"Now if you were how on earth could I
    know how far superior you are to all
    other girls by comparison?"

Her Merits (Nov. 18, 1910)

"I wonder why Mrs. Luckett is so popu-
    lar in society? She is as deaf as a post
    and as blind as a bat."
"Can't you see, man, she makes an ideal
    chaperon."

Poems

A Sea Tale (Sept. 18, 1905)

The sea swells embraced the summer girl,
The surf was her bounden slave;
The whitecaps e'en at her feet went broke,
For her cheer did the ocean wave.
The sea urchins ran at her beck and call,

The boats were manned for her joy;
But she fooled them all, for this summer girl
Eloped with the harbor buoy.

With Apologies to Poe (E.A.) (Sept. 20, 1905)

The voters were quiet and sober
The polls they were busy all day,
The polls they had doing's all day;
The primaries were hard on October,
So 'twas fall time for some on the way,
For public opinion was prober
On the problem of how the land lay,
The public was prophet and prober
Of just how the losing land lay.

Here early through brass-buttoned bunches
Of coppers, I roamed with A. P.
Of coppers, with Arthur G. P.[4]
They were hours when my heart beat in
    bunches
As the breaches that roll from the sea,
As the breakers that roar in the sea.
And the lion who has bloody prey crunches
Felt not more ferocious than me—
The beast that carnivorous crunches
Was never more maddened than me.

And Arthur, his finger uplifting
Said, "sadly these pills I mistrust.
These ballots I strangely mistrust!
They're straight ones! Oh, let us not linger,
I'm fly—so we'll fly—for we must."
In terror he spoke, for though tinker,
His mending was crumbling to dust;
In agony sobbed, for as tinker,
His prestige was tailed in the dust.

But I pacified A. G. with cheering,
And tried hard to lighten his gloom—

His Garland-bred, gathering gloom,
Till we passed to the end of a clearing,
But were stopped by the door of a tomb,
By the door of a legended tomb.
And I said, "What is written that's bearing
On the vote, on the door of this tomb?"
And he said, "Woe is me! Poe's Amend-
    ment!"
'Tis this grave of my loved and lost
    boom!"

At the Wedding (Sept. 23, 1905)

What she said.

"How did the bride and the bridegroom
    look
As they came down the church's aisle?"
"Oh, the bride was too sweet for any-
    thing!
And her dress was in such style.
'Twas a peau de soie of ivory white,
Thick-weaved and soft and rich,
Cut square in the neck with real Val
    lace—
Yards if there was a stitch—
Filling it up, and a deep wide fall
On the elbow sleeves. Such fit!
I declare it looked as she were boiled down
And poured right into it.
Long train, of course, the skirt well flared.
Her veil—'twas old family lace;
It touched the train and all around,
Coming well down on her face.
The orange blossoms caught it down
On her hair, dressed high, you know.
Her bouquet, Bride roses—a white-
    bound book
In her other hand for show.
I tell you, her diamonds sparkled and
    flashed—
The necklace, he gave, they say—

The sunburst that caught her corsage lace
Shone like a rainbow ray.
The bridegroom looked grand in his full-
    dress suit;
It fitted him like a glove;
He wore white kids, and his boutonniere
Of white was a perfect love!

What he said.

"How did the bride and the bridegroom
    look
As they walked down the church's aisle?"
"Well, the bride was covered with blushes red,
And the groom wore a happy smile."

Traveling in Russia (Oct. 26, 1905)

*(News Dispatch: Railroad travel in Russia is
practically tied up.)*

At running trains in Russia now,
    The strikers all do balksky,
So if you want to travel there,
    You'll have to take a walksky.
This season, too, is hard on foot;
    The prospect does appallsky,
And you never travelled in the times
    They had no trains at allsky.

Perhaps if you some millions have,
    You can employ a sledgesky;
Your chattels and your family,
    And food all in a wedgesky,
It won't seem like a parlor car;
    You'll find a many rubsky,
And maybe packs of hungry wolves,
    Who try to eat you upsky.

A blizzard you may chance to meet
    That makes our own jokesky,
Or Kansas cyclones put to sleep
    As for the ring too pokesky;

And miles and miles must stretch between
    The points where you feel frisky,
And where, for bracing sore in need,
    You can come to where there's whiskey.

The walking there is very bad
    Besides these trials hardsky,
And Russia is a few miles square,
    So listen to this bardsky.
If through its palaces and towns
    You feel desire to roamsky,
You'd better take a fool's advice,
    And just now stay at homesky.

Her Choice (Nov. 2, 1905)

In vain the iceman wooed her,
    She did not think him nice;
And all his summer's profits
    With her could cut no ice.

The carpenter she sent off;
    She found he was no good
Because he wouldn't keep still
    And go on sawing wood.

The gas man she detested
    Although he loved her long,
Because he wrote her poems
    And got the meter wrong.
She couldn't love the printer—
    She didn't like his type.
The plumber she rejected
    Because he "hit the pipe."

The gay young electrician
    Vainly sung her beauty's praise;
She wouldn't have a husband
    Who had such shocking ways.
As vain to catch her fancy
    The architect did plan;

She said she'd never marry
    Such a base designing man.

The merchant fared no better;
    She knew he had a way
He'd keep up after marriage
    Of dictating all she'd say.

She feared to wed the poet,
    Though he wrote poems by the ton,
Lest the burden of their life song
    Might be, "Owed to everyone."

At last she took a blind man,
    Who no fault in her could see,
And, deaf and dumb, lived with her
    In silent ecstasy.

The Victim (Jan 5, 1906)

Who makes us quiet as a mouse?
Whose anger any glim can douse?
Who is real head of the house?
    The cooklady.

Who turns the whole house upside down,
And makes it tremble at her frown?
Who retails gossip of the town?
    The washlady.
Who makes life with discomfort rhyme?
Who gets the household out of chime,
By never getting there on time?
    The scrublady.

Who haughty works out by the day
Just as a favor—not for pay—
And on all subjects has her say?
    The charlady.

Who looks with calm, superior face
On luckless customers, with grace,

And puts them in their proper place?
    The saleslady.

Who pays the freight for all of these?
Who dares not least advantage seize?
Who has to mind her "q's" and "p's"?[5]
    The poor snubbed woman.

The Modern Writer (Jan. 9, 1906)

If you want to be an author of the up-to-
    datest type
    And find your work among the six
    best sellers,
You must take an altogether melancholic
    view of life
    And top gloom's notch past other
    fiction-tellers.
You must get your local color from the
    jaundice and the blues,
    And select a phase of life that's very
    yellow,
Or otherwise you cannot teach a moral
    lesson great,
    Or have your books like very hot
    cakes sell, oh!

Don't let a gleam of humor or a healthy
    human throb
    Of any kind get in your style of writing;
Don't picture men and women who are
    neither rakes nor snobs;
    From your love tales take out all that
    is inviting.
Remember, love and cheerfulness and
    wholesomeness of taste
    Are deadly sins in modern story-telling,
For the epicurean palate of the reading
    public now
    There must be a taint to help along
    the selling.

Avoid romance as you would fly a
    plague—it isn't style;
    Dissect society—or vivisect it, rather;
'Tis the only life worth noticing in this
    big world of ours—
    The only field in which real life to gather.
Avoid the light and flowers—seek the
    gloom and gather weeds;
    If life is clean and happy, never tell it.
Both are most inartistic, and the artist's
    touch you need
    In your novel—or, my dear, you'll
    never sell it!

The Real Expert (Mar. 9, 1907)

(The University of Chicago wants a college established to teach courtship.)

    Now they're talking of a college
    Where they'll teach much useful
    knowledge,
All about romance and marriage and of
    love's alluring arts.
    They'll bring learning quite terrific
    To make courtship scientific,
And will give all graduates high degree of
    Bachelors of Hearts.
    Well, perhaps they'll get some mummies,
    Or a lot of freaks and dummies
To take collegiate courses at this fount of
    wisdom's brim;
    But never man or woman,
    Who's alive and really human;
They might as well establish schools to
    teach ducks how to swim.

    They needn't try to tell, oh,
    Any businesslike young fellow
How to pick his teacher when he starts to
    learn of love's sweet love.
    You won't find him an addresser

    Of a cranky old professor,
When he wants to add for reasons to his
    sentimental store.

    No; he takes a teacher girly,
    Who has hair that's long and curly,
Bright eyes, witching, dancing dimples
    and a dainty figure trim;
    Pouting, flirting, frowning, smiling,
    Now coquetting, now beguiling,
Sweet and pretty as a picture—that's the
    teacher picked for him.

    Schools of courtship, when one wishes—
    O ye gods and little fishes!
When it comes to teaching men to love
    some mite of a slim girl—
    Can take all the world's professors,
    All of learning's greatest guessers,
And give them points enough to make
    their learned noodles curl!

The Place for Her (Apr. 19, 1907)

Oh, she was a woman of fighting blood
    Of a pure Milesian[6] strain;
People might try to oppose her once,
    But they never did it again.
She bossed her social and ran her club,
Once at a debate she called Browning[7] a
    "dub"!
And against her everyone feared to rub,
    For she argued with might and main.

At home she was always in a spat,
    And life was a constant fray;
She bullied her husband, poor cowed man,
    Afraid just one word to say;
Her voice was like a horn in a fog,
She could scold like rolling off of a log,
She spanked the baby and beat the dog—
    E'en the tax man she drove away.

What could be done with this warlike dame
    Was the problem, early and late.
Why, she had even terrorized the cook,
    Till she dared not break a plate.
The neighbors they wanted some rest
    from the strife,
They wanted to snatch some quiet from life.
So they sent her off with flag, drum and fife,
    To be a peace delegate.[8]

The Smile Feminine (June 24, 1908)

(A Democratic club in Tennessee has put itself on record by flaming resolutions against female participation in politics, and denounces the exercise of feminine blandishments in the way of charms, smiles and sandwiches ns bribery in no wise better than the direct bribery by money of professional politicians.)

They are down on lady bribers,
    Down in Tennessee;
They allege some reasons divers
    Down in Tennessee.
Why the Indies fair—God bless 'em—
For the men's votes shouldn't press 'em,
Feed, or flatter or caress 'em,
    Down in Tennessee.

For the woman's smile, they hold it
    Down in Tennessee,
When for ballots she has sold it
    Down in Tennessee,
Is as bad a "smile" corruption
As the kind that raise 'ruction
In the way of liquid suction,
    Down in Tennessee.

And as all bribes are pernicious
    Down in Tennessee,
This enticing is real vicious
    Down in Tennessee.

For the men to do their voting
While the ladies charms they're noting,
Which is wrong—we're only quoting
    What they say in Tennessee.

House Cleaning Time (May 20, 1909)

Come, masters of the city come, men in
    places high.
The times are getting ticklish, for a sharp
    reform they cry;
So disdain not from the women, take a
    hint of what to do.
Adopt a plan authentic, and one that's
    tired and true.
Just about this time the women start a
    plan which twice a year
They put in practice with the vim to
    womanhood most dear;
No small detail of labor in its thorough-
    ness they shirk,
But never stop their cleaning up when
    once they get to work.

They search each nook and corner with a
    sharp and eagle eye.
There's not a hidden cobweb but out its
    place they spy;
They pull up rugs and carpets to see what
    is beneath,
No things so hidden from them but they
    drag from its sheath.
Water floods each inch of house room,
    cleaning soap is everywhere.
Mop and broom and brush and duster
    flourish strenuous in the air;
Every object is examined be it great or be
    it small.
Yeah, the way this cleaning's managed
    doth the male mind much appall.

Yet a regular house-cleaning on this com-
    prehensive plan,
To take in each department and miss no
    single man
Would be a first rate model for the peo-
    ple to install
And keep in working with the City Hall.
There might be dirty corners and neglect-
    ed spots, 'tis true,
But the half-year overhauling would
    bring them out to view.
And no chance would be given these big
    scandals to carouse,
If the city followed housewives thorough
    way of cleaning house.

Her Soliloquy (Feb. 10, 1910)

I'll put all my gay clothes away,
    And dress in most sober of tints,
The contrast will have more effect,
    When I get back to fine Paris "hints";
I'll give up my parties and balls,
    And become on church-going intent.
As there I meet most of my set,
    And 'tis fashionable now to keep Lent.

I'll pay only decorous calls,
    Where talk intellectual I find,
And promptly join some Browning club
    For the sake of improving my mind.
It will be very stupid, I know,
    For Browning I don't care a cent,
But 'tis one's sole chance to flirt,
    When one's keeping a fashionable Lent.
But still, I'm not sorry 'tis come,
    For the season has quite tired me out;
It has been so unusually gay,
    I feel I have been put to rout.
The rest—it will tone up my nerves,
    And to freshen—here's some comfort
        sent—

Complexions, they say there is naught
    So good as a fashionable Lent.

Ideals. Danger. (Oct. 4, 1910)

*(Cooking dainties is now the fashionable fad
in New York society.)*

It is talked of in the parlors,
    It is whispered in the clubs,
It is written in the papers,
    It is gossiped o'er the tubs.
Other topics for the moment
    Are forgotten or forsook,
As the news flies to all quarters,
    Social queens will learn to cook.

Loud is housewives' scornful laughter,
    Joy of fuddists[9] is intense;
Pride of "womanly" idealists
    In the project is immense;
Chefs are swearing mad about it,
    But the husbands—ah, the look
On their faces, when they find out
    That their wives will learn to cook.

Home will now be place of terrors,
    For dyspepsia looms on high;
Days of loathed food, nights of anguish,
    For the victims who can't fly,
But some hurried trips on business,
    Many happy homes forsook,
Will result, till fad is over
    For the social queens to cook.

The Woman Question (Feb. 27, 1911)

Must I be a pro or anti?
    Both to me with force appeal;
The arguments of each side
    Make me quite strongly feel.
Must I, to protect my sisters,
    And my own rights, claim a vote?

Or by equal rights asserting,
    Fame of womanhood demote?

Shall I be a pro or anti?
    Shall I, as the antis say,
Lose my charm and my influence
    And what they call my sway?
Or claim an equal balance
    In the making of the laws
If I bring more logic bearing
    Than the ancient one, "Because?"

Must it be a pro or anti?
    Must I be content to live
'Neath the laws I have no say in,
    Take the rights they please to give?
Or declare for home and woman
    Laws must recognize their right?
For upon that sacred issue
    Will turn the real, true fight.

A Monosyllabic Tragedy (Aug. 8, 1911)

Girl
    Sweet,
Nice,
    Neat.
Bright
    Eye,
Cute,
    Shy.
Man,
    Brave,
Tall,
    Grave;
Looks
    Seem,
Girl's
    Dream.

'Nuff
    Said:
They're
    Wed.
With
    Ties,
Love
    Flies.

L'envoi.

Life's
    Gall;
That's
    All.

The Picket's Cry (Aug. 20, 1917)

I want to be a picket,
And guard the white house gate,
With banners most insulting
Which on the loyal grate;
I want to rouse mob feeling
Our hats and flags to muss,
So we'll complain as injured,
And create quite a fuss.

I want to be arrested
And carted off to jail,
So I can be a martyr
And at the police rail,
To tell how I'm ill-treated,
With criminals to be:
Since is that way I'm bound to
Get much publically.

The cause I may be hurting,
As many people may,
But that to me is nothing,
If I can get my way,
I'll leave my home and children

For this fate glorious—
For this, my aim and object—
To be notorious.

The Player Maid (1905)

A Comedy

Characters

Maurice Beaufort—Earl of Roxbury.
Lord Canning—Uncle of Lady Dorothy.
Charles Barry—An Actor.
David Garrick[10]—A Manager.
Thomas Sheridan }
Samuel Foote[11] } His Friends.
Duggett—Servant to Lady Dorothy.
Boy—At the Theater.
Eleanor Hallam—A young Actress.
Kitty Hayden—Her Friend; also an Actress.
Lady Dorothy Hastings—A young Heiress.
Mrs. Pendarves—Lady Dorothy's Aunt.
Sally—Eleanor's Maid.
Maid—Lady Dorothy's Maid.

Act I

Scene—Dressing room in London theater. Kitty discovered dressed as the nurse in "Romeo and Juliet," is taking off her head gear. Noise of cheers, clapping, etc. apparently in front of house. Kitty stops to listen, works at head, stops again, smiles, turns to glass again.

Kitty: They're fairly going wild over her— what is the matter with this wig?—and I never saw her act better—I'll never get the thing off! Mistress Woffington,[12] you'll have to look to your laurels with Eleanor Hallam contesting them—is this wig bewitched! Sally! Where is that girl? Sally, come here this instant!

(Enter Sally)

Kitty: What do you mean, running off in this way when I need you?

Sally: I bega parding, Miss 'Ayden, but Hi was honly a-peepin' through a 'old at Miss Helnor a-hactin'. Her do hact Julyet just diwine.

Kitty: You're right, Sally. But come and help me with my wig.

Sally: Lor, Miss, wouldn't Hi like to be you hon the styge with 'er, hand 'ave 'er a coaxin' hand a-'uggin of me! Don't hit make you feel proud-like, Miss?

Kitty: She's a dear creature to act with, Sally, for she doesn't grudge your share of applause—a little easier there!

Sally: Her did look so lovely to-night, didn't her, Miss?

Kitty: (*Enthusiastically*) She was like a poet's dream when she looked so sweetly at Romeo—(*Sally gestures ecstatically and unconsciously begins to pull off wig in gestures*) and softly breathed—Wow! Am I to be scalped like a red Indian?

Sally: (*Startled*) Lor, Miss! Did her say that to Romyo?

Kitty: No— I'm saying it to you. I'll Romeo you if you try to pull my head off like that again!

Sally: (*Laying wig on table*) Hit's hoff, Miss.

(Enter David Garrick, Thomas Sheridan and Samuel Foote.)

Garrick: May we come in here, Mistress

Hayden? We have been driven out of the green room by Mistress Hallam's admirers, waiting there to catch a glimpse of her.

Kitty: Possession's better than politeness, Mr. Garrick. If you turn your eye to my glass, you'll see you're in already.

Garrick: You did fine to-night, Kitty. You're the best Nurse I've ever had on my stage—she certain is.

(*He turns to the others.*)

Kitty: Who wouldn't be good when they're near Eleanor Hallam?

Foote: Egad, she's hit it! That girl's just overflowing with vitality and spirit. She's the best thing you've done for the stage, Davy.

Garrick: Yes, I'm a bit proud of her discovery, but from the minute I saw her in a little Irish provincial theater, her big bright eyes just snapping with mischief, her dimples dancing with merriment, and her whole talking as much as another woman's tongue, I knew London would go wild over her.

Sheridan: So it has. Why, she makes 'em cry and laugh as she pleases. And how she changes in a minute! Who could suppose with all her wild Irish humor, she could so play Juliet as to stir one's very heart strings?

Garrick: Talking of that same Irish humor we've a wager here, Tom and I, that you can't stand up against it, Sam, though 'tis believed, I'll admit, you

have a pretty nimble with of your own.

Foote: Not too nimble that it will run away from a girl in her teens.

Kitty: Don't be so confident, Mr. Foote; wit is not a thing like wine to improve with age.

Foote: Ho, ho! You've caught some of Mistress Eleanor's pertness, have you?

Kitty: Try her, Mr. Cocksure; she has a-plenty left.

Foote: Which of you has done me the honor to lay on my ability to outwit the lady?

Garrick: Faith, the gentleman who has had the least experience of the lady's tongue, and that's not myself.

Sheridan: I'm not frightened, Sam, for I laid on the quality, not the quantity, of the talk; otherwise, I'd have backed the lady.

Garrick: But, Davy, have you no fear that this beautiful prize of yours will succumb some day to the plague of matrimony?

Garrick: Matrimony! Why, the girl has all the beaux of fashion at her feet, and could put a coronet on her head to-morrow—but she laughs at all of them.

Kitty: She says that to exchange all the years of one's life for one man, seems like giving so much to get so little—that taking a man on trust is too much like paying down for a dress before one has seen it, and then having to wear it whether it fits one or not, and that she never could abide an unbecoming gown.

Sheridan: What terrible views of matrimony for a young woman! Do you think she'll stick to 'em?

Kitty: Certainly—as long as she's heart-free.

Foote: You know your sex, Mistress Kitty.

Kitty: Yes, and I know yours; and 'tis precious few of you that can make Eleanor Hallam think good enough for her—now any of the danglers in yonder greenroom. And as for coronets—'tis what *is* in a man's head, not what's on it, that will interest her.

Garrick: Well, may the Prince Charmings keep away from my house as long as—

Foote: Mistress Eleanor brings sovereigns into it, hey, Davy?

(*Sound of loud applause from without.*)

Kitty: Run, Sally, and see if the curtain is down.

(*Sally runs out.*)

Kitty: Just listen! They seem frantic!

Sheridan: They say Barry is extremely anxious to play the role of Romeo in private life as well as on the stage. Doesn't that worry you, Davy? He's a handsome young dog.

Garrick: Worry me? Humph! He acts all the better of it.

Foote: And forgets to ask for more salary.

Kitty: He has a nasty temper; he'll get too ugly for Eleanor to manage if she isn't careful.

(*Sally rushes in, excited.*)

Sally: The curting has went down this minit, hand 'er's a-comin', hand the people 'as been bonbasin' 'er with buckets o' flowers, hand them's a-screechin', "Braver! braver! 'Allam! 'Allam! Braver—

Foote: (*Putting fingers in ears*) Mr. Garrick, will you choke that girl?

Kitty: Sally, are you crazy? Hold your tongue!

Sally: (*Subsiding*) Hain't hit 'evingly!

(*Enter Eleanor, followed by Barry, scowling, his arms full of flowers.*)

Eleanor: (*Beckoning to Kitty*) Come hither, Nurse. What are these gentlemen?

Garrick: The greenroom was so full of your lovers, Mistress Eleanor, that we were fairly blown out by the torrent of their sighs, and fled here for refuge. Besides, I would like you and Barry to try that embrace once more—I'm not altogether satisfied.

Eleanor: (*Mischievously*) My ears have not yet drunk a hundred words of that utterance, yet I know the sound. Art thou not Garrick and a manager? (*Bowing to others with sweeping curtsy*) Mr. Sheridan, Mr. Foote, your humble servant.

Sheridan: (*Also bowing*) Your most obedient.

Foote: (*Ditto*) May I kiss your hand?

Eleanor: (*Holding out hand*) Yes, for I'm thinking lip service is all I'll ever get out of you, Mr. Foote. Charles, don't stand there like a human flower-pot.

Barry: (*Sullenly*) Where shall I put the flowers?

Eleanor: (*Carelessly*) On the floor. Help him Kitty, won't you? Here, let me give the gentlemen some first. Mr. Sheridan, allow me—these lilies, they toil not, but just litter up valuable space in the theater. 'Tis a bad habit that like some others they have fallen into. Mr. Foote, these violets will just suit you—the violet is such a shrinking, modest little flower. Mr. Garrick, will you accept these forget-me-nots? (*Pensively*) To-morrow is salary day.

Foote: (*Laughing*) A new language of flowers?

Eleanor: (*Sweetly*) I hope you find the translation accurate. Dear me, Charles, what are you scowling at there? Won't you take a seat and help me to entertain these gentlemen?

Barry: I think, Mistress Hallam, you are quite equal to that task without my poor assistance. I have some friends in the greenroom.

(*He throws the flowers on the table before Kitty and exits angrily.*)

Eleanor: (*Innocently*) What is the matter with Charles to-night?

Garrick: (*Calling after him*) Barry, that embrace—he's gone!

Foote: I rather suspect that one of the friends he is going to meet, or who has met him, is the green-eyed monster,[13] hey, Mistress Eleanor?

Eleanor: Charles jealous? How foolish your wits can be sometimes, Mr. Foote.

Foote: And why am I foolish in supposing that, Mistress Eleanor?

Eleanor: Because your meaning doth appear in this: that Charles is jealous of *you*.

Foote: (*With a bow*) Thanks for the compliment. My wit was too modest to see at once the folly of poor Barry's jealousy of me.

Eleanor: Indeed, Mr. Foote, if modesty is fatal, you'll live to die of old age.

Sheridan: Now you've a chance to save me some guineas, Sam.

Foote: Old age has its terrors, Mistress Eleanor, but wit has one advantage over beauty—it does not lose its complexion with its years.

Eleanor: And beauty has this advantage over wit; it can be good-natured as well as striking. I'd rather make people love me than frighten them. Your wits do that—but so do scarecrows.

Foote: You do make people love you; that's why they call you a coquette and coquettes soon get to be shunned by the knowing.

Eleanor: By people who are too old and sharp for them to cope with—yes, I know they are. Coquettes like the excitement of the chase, so they prefer young game; the old ones are too eager to be caught.

Sheridan: Come, come, this won't do, Sam.

Garrick: I'm sorry for you, Tom.

Foote: Have you then been trying all kind of fools, Mistress Eleanor?

Eleanor: No; all kinds have been trying me, and any kind of a fool is very trying.

Foote: Oh, then, the wise ones shun you.

Eleanor: (*Demurely*) You are here, Mr. Foote; to say that wise men shun me would be manners.

Garrick: Neatly trapped, Sam.

Foote: Suppose I was to admit I was a fool and try to out-talk a woman?

Eleanor: Such an admission would do more credit to your penetration than to your politeness. If I were you I wouldn't make it.

Foote: Faith, Mistress Eleanor, when you marry, if your husband be not fond, as Will Shakespeare hath it, of my Lady Tongue, he had best set his wedding bells a-tolling.

Eleanor: If he be not better master of my Lady Tongue than you, Mr. Foote, I promise you he will never ring this Nell.[14]

Foote: Tom, have I not proved my friendship and Mr. Garrick's right to your guineas?

Sheridan: I do confess that you have been as badly routed on your tongue as you routed poor Macklin on his memory.

Kitty: How was that?

Sheridan: Why, Macklin was boasting he could memorize any lines no matter what, he had once heard, and Foote here rattled him off some nonsense lines that paralyzed poor Macklin so that he forgot his whole part that evening.

Kitty: What were they?

Foote: I put so little connection in them that I have forgotten them myself.

Eleanor: I heard you read them off to Mr. Macklin, and I wager you I could repeat them.

Foote: I know you could not.

Eleanor: Twenty guineas if I do? 'Tis only fair after your laying bets on me.

Foote: Twenty guineas if you do. Stay—I forgot. I have the paper I scribbled them on here in my pocket. Here, Sheridan, see how much my Lady Tongue owes to her memory and how much to her imagination.

Eleanor: My imagination never ran such a crazy riot among words, Mr. Nonsense-Maker. Here are your lines. "So she went into the garden to cut a cabbage leaf to make an apple-pie; and at the same moment, a great she-bear, coming up the street, pops its head into the shop. What! no soap? So he died, and she very imprudently married the barber; and there were present the Pickaninnies and the Joblilies and the Garynlies and the Grand Panjandrum himself with the little round button at the top; and they all fell to playing the game of catch-as-catch-can till the gunpowder ran out of the heels of their boots."[15]

Kitty: (*Faintly*) You're making me dizzy!

Sheridan: You owe Mistress Eleanor twenty guineas, Sam. Devil take me if she missed a single word.

Foote: It is hard to lose forty guineas and two bets in ten minutes.

Eleanor: It is even harder, gentlemen, to lose such agreeable company at its height and such pleasant conversation in its flow. It grieves me that you *must* go. Good night and fair dreams to make it better.

Foote: Damme, Mistress Eleanor, but that sounds like an infernally polite way of saying, "Get out."

Eleanor: You are so quick, Mr. Foote, you read one's very thoughts.

(*All three rise with great dignity.*)

Sheridan: (*Ceremoniously*) It is useless to press us more, Mistress Hallam.

(*All three bow with the utmost gravity, saying in solemn unity:*)

All three: Good-night, Mistress Hallam.

Eleanor: (*With sweeping curtsy*) Good-night, gentlemen.

Three: (*Turning to Kitty*) Good-night, Mistress Hayden.

Kitty: (*Curtseying*) Good-night, gentlemen.

Sally: (*Fervently*) Haint hit grand-like to see 'em a-bowin' hand scrapin' to she! Just like King Sollerman rambuctious hin hall 'is glory a-scrapin' to the Queend o' Shebar!

Three: (*With low bow*) Good-night, Mistress Sally.

Sally: (*Taken aback*) O lor! Them is a-bowin' to Hi! Good-night, gemmen!

(*She tries to imitate the curtsey of the others, almost falling over in the awkward attempt.*)

(*Exeunt Sheridan and Foote.*)

Garrick: Barry, that embrace—he's gone!

(*Exit Garrick, hastily.*)

Eleanor: Now, Kitty, we can have a quiet chat together. Men are so tiresome— Oh, dear!

(*Knock at door. Sally opens it; enter Charles Barry.*)

Barry: Mr. Garrick desired me to come and wait for him here to rehearse that embrace. I heard you desired no visitors, Mistress Eleanor, but if you wish to indulge a favored one, I would remind you that it is but a short time now till the curtain is up, and if there is no Juliet ready in her bower, the people will laugh at our tragedy.

Eleanor: Further visitors are unwelcome tonight, Master Barry, including yourself— how dare you talk so? When did I forget my duty to listen to gallant flatteries? I am tired enough of them as it is.

Barry: You are skillful in concealing your weariness.

Eleanor: And you are so bold in exposing your rudeness. Faith, when my manners want mending, I'll not come to you for the tinker.

Kitty: Fie, Charles! You are so green with jealousy that the leaves of the flowers here are turning pale beside you.

Barry: I am not jealous, Mistress Kitty. I am grieved to see Mistress Eleanor so slight her work for a pack of worthless macaronies—But I am not jealous.

(*Knock at door. Sally opens it, showing boy with large bouquet.*)

Boy: For Mistress Hallam, and there's a note, Sally; don't forget to show her the note.

Sally: 'Ere be more flowers, Mistress Helnor, hand another note.

(*Eleanor takes note and smiles.*)

Barry: (*Furiously*) More flowers and another note! How many more fools are you going to let dangle after you?

Eleanor: Why should you care, Charles, dear! You know you are not jealous.

Barry: Of course, I'm not jealous! Why should I be jealous?

Eleanor: Why, indeed? For sure, I never gave you the slightest right to be.

Barry: I never asked it.

Eleanor: Kitty, Mr. Garrick will have to look me out another Romeo. Mr. Barry has lost his memory.

Barry: You're a coquette, madam!

Eleanor: I'm nothing of the sort, sir!

Barry: Then give me those flowers to send back to the fool who else will plume himself vastly on your keeping them, and boast of your favors to half London to-morrow.

(*Eleanor flings them at his head.*)

Eleanor: Take them! I only wish they were as heavy as your own wits!

Kitty: (*Laughing*) Fie, fie, you bad children! What would the audience say if they could see Romeo and Juliet now, quarrelling like a pair of spitting pussycats?

Eleanor: (*Passionately*) I tell you once more for all, Charles Barry, I will not be plagued with your jealous fits and your masterful airs. If you could only keep your temper as I do mine when you undertake to advise me—but instead of being kind and gentle as I always am to you, you bluster and rage and storm, and I won't stand it—(*Raising her voice angrily*) I won't stand it!

Barry: Very kind and gentle you can be! Look at her, Mistress Kitty!

Eleanor: Because the gentlemen of London admire me and pay me respectful compliments, am I to blame for that? Am I to blame if I am young and pretty, or because men admire pretty women? Shall I turn nun, good Mr. Turk, tell my looking-glass it is lying every time I look in it, and shun all men—except Mr. Charles Barry of Drury Lane,[16] who plays Othello off the stage vastly better than he can play Romeo on it—as if they had the plague?

(*Barry flings the flowers in corner of the room.*)

Barry: Oh, I know there are other Romeos far better fitted to Mistress Hallam's transcendent Juliet than my poor self—but pray, do not speak of shunning all men. There are yet some whom you have no need to shun, so fast they fly the other way.

Eleanor: (*With pretended indifference*) Indeed, Mr. Barry! You are too kind to call my attention to them—I had not noticed them.

Barry: Only yesterday, my friend, Sir Harry Holland, told me that the Earl of Roxbury, who is such a figure in London society, declined the honor of being introduced to you. He said—but perhaps 'tis best left unsaid, 'tis so uncivil a speech for a lady to hear of herself.

Eleanor: Oh, I am not at all anxious to hear what the Earl said—not at all. 'Tis of no moment to me what the Earl said. Sally, you careless girl, where is that wreath for my hair?

Sally: Lord, Miss, you're a-holdin of it your hand tight.

(*Eleanor looks with start at wreath, then proceeds to adjust it.*)

Eleanor: I suppose we can allow the Earl of Roxbury to think as he pleases—it harms nobody!

Barry: He said he had no taste for popular actresses, part of whose stock in trade are the fools they make; that he had not the slightest desire to meet Mistress Hallam personally, and that even if he did, you were not the style of woman whom his associations and taste would ever permit to capture his fancy.

Eleanor: The Earl of Roxbury is vastly polite, but we must do our best to survive his refusal to meet us, though 'tis a crushing blow. Ha! ha! ha! how vastly amusing!

Kitty: Now don't get angry, Eleanor. Don't you see that is what Charles wants?

Eleanor: I am not angry—why should I care for what the Earl of Roxbury thinks? I am as cool and unruffled as a sleeping babe. Where is my fan? You dolt, you idiot, where are you always hiding that fan? Get it for me—do you hear me? (*Seizes the bewildered Sally and shakes her*) Get that fan this instant!

Sally: (*Half-crying*)i hain't -'idin' hof hit, Miss. Hit's pinned onto your gownd, Miss.

(*Eleanor sees it, takes it up and fans vigorously.*)

Eleanor: Well, Mr. Barry, can you think of other ways of making yourself agreeable, except the only real way?

Barry: I would not attempt so hard a task as to please you, Mistress Eleanor.

Eleanor: I am sorry, for you could do it so easily by going away. I am sure you did not come in the first place because you were asked.

Barry: Oh, as to that, there are places where I am welcome without forcing my company.

(*Turns to go in great wrath; at door collides with Garrick.*)

Garrick: Glad I found you here. Just run over that parting in Juliet's chamber in the next act. You're a bit stiff in that, Barry.

Barry: (*Sullenly*) Didn't we go over it to-day enough to satisfy you?

Garrick: Just once more, to make sure. Have you been quarrelling again?

Eleanor: Indeed, Mr. Garrick. His temper is past all bearing.

Barry: I'll leave it to you, Mr. Garrick—

Garrick: (*Impatiently*) Come, come, the scene. Begin, Juliet. "Then, window—"

(*They throw themselves into impassioned attitudes.*)

Eleanor: "Then, window, let day in and let life out."

Barry: "Farewell, farewell! One kiss, and I'll descend."

(*They embrace.*)

Garrick: A little more ardor there, Barry—Mistress Hallam, put a bit more passion in your expression just before Romeo catches you in his arms.

Eleanor: (*Angrily*) How can I when he clutches me like I was a broomstick?

Mr. Garrick, can't he practice embracing Sally here, till he can do it without clawing me like a tiger-cat? (*Maliciously*) I'll raise her wages.

Barry: Perhaps I could do it better if you would keep the points of that confounded wreath out of my eyes.

(*Eleanor pulls up a leaf in the wreath to stand it upright.*)

Garrick: Come—the embrace.

Barry: "One kiss and I'll descend."

(*They embrace with most loving looks.*)

Garrick: That's better. Now, don't forget to-night.

Eleanor: That's over, thank heaven! Please take him away, Mr. Garrick.

Barry: I need no urging to go. At your service, Mr. Garrick.

(*Exeunt Barry and Garrick.*)

Eleanor: Charles is becoming insufferable. He acts as though I belonged to him.

Kitty: You irritate him too much, Eleanor. You had best be careful—he has a sullen and revengeful temper, and he's jealous of every man that comes near you.

Eleanor: Nonsense! Charles Barry is nothing to me that I should humor his silly tempers. To think that he dreamed he could annoy me with his horrid Earl of Roxbury's opinion of me! But, come; there are other things of which I wish to chat with you.

(*Knock at door*)

Eleanor: Who is that? No peace for us to-night!

(*Sally opens door; enter boy.*)

Boy: A lady won't say who she is, begs Mistress Hallam to let her see her here.

Eleanor: Go back and say I receive no visitors to-night, particularly strangers.

Boy: I did tell 'er, ma'am, that she couldn't come here, but she begged so hard and said it was so important for her to see you, and to ask you to let her come in only for a few minutes.

Kitty: Some curiosity-monger. Don't let her in, Eleanor.

Eleanor: I like the scent of mystery here. Bring the lady in.

(*Exit boy*)

Eleanor: Perhaps it is a lovelorn maid who has fallen a victim to Charles' charms. Would not that be rare sport?

(*Enter boy, conducting Lady Dorothy Hastings, veiled*)

Eleanor: (*As Lady Dorothy hesitates*) Come in, madam. You wished to speak with me?

Lady Dorothy: (*Still hesitates*) Yes— but alone, if you will so favor me.

Eleanor: Go, Sally.

Sally: Lor, but wouldn't Hi like to stay! Hit's just like a real live novel.

(*Exit Sally*)

Eleanor: As for my friend here, madam, she is my other self. I share every confidence with her, so what you say to me, you may say before her. She will be as secret as myself.

(*Lady Dorothy throws up her veil.*)

Lady Dorothy: I come on a strange mission, but I am in sore trouble, too young to know the world or where to go for advice, and I have heard so much of your kindness and talent, that I determined to come to you and ask assistance to help me at the crisis of my life.

Eleanor: Have you no friends that you come to a stranger at such a moment?

Lady Dorothy: None that could or would help me. Will you hear me?

Eleanor: If you will be brief.

Lady Dorothy: I am Lady Dorothy Hastings, the niece and ward of Lord Canning. I am an orphan and heiress to a large estate in Devonshire. I have been in France at school, where my uncle put me in my childhood, and now I am of age, he hath sent for me to come home.

Eleanor: I see no need to ask my help in this story, madam.

Lady Dorothy: Oh, I am in extremity of need. My uncle hath betrothed me to a husband of his choosing, a man I have never seen and can never love, for, Mistress Hallam, I am in love already and I will not wed none but the man of my heart.

Eleanor: Then why not tell your uncle so?

Lady Dorothy: Oh, I dare not! He is a terrible man—everybody is afraid of him. He would shut me up if he but dreamed I would oppose him.

Eleanor: And you wish me to oppose this terrible uncle for you?

Lady Dorothy: No, no! I am expected this week at my home. I am secretly come to London with a trusted friend; my betrothed will meet me and make arrangements for our marriage. But this he cannot do at once, so he will take me to his mother, who approves our love, and I will stay with her until I can marry.

Eleanor: As yet I cannot see wherein I can aid you.

Lady Dorothy: The heiress of Gloster Park must be there at the date my uncle hath set. You are so wonderful an actress you can deceive anybody. I want you to go to Gloster Park in my place—to be Lady Dorothy Hastings until I am safely married.

Eleanor: (*Amazed*) Who put such a wild idea into your silly head, my child?

Lady Dorothy: Oh, help us, sweet Mistress Hallam! Do not refuse us! I thought it all out myself—it seemed such a beautiful plan, and I told it to no one.

Eleanor: That I guess from your being here. But it is impossible.

Lady Dorothy: Why? It will not be for long.

Eleanor: Even were I to consent to so crazy a device, how could I pass for you in your own home for one day without detection?

Lady Dorothy: (*Sadly*) Easily, alas! There is none in my own home who knows me.

Eleanor: Your uncle and guardian?

Lady Dorothy: He hath not seen me since I was twelve. He hath not taken interest enough in me even to visit me, and he would not know me if he came in here this minute. The had to send to him to tell him that I was of age and must leave school; he had forgotten me. I think this marriage he hath arranged is partly to get rid of me.

Eleanor: But have you no other relatives at your home?

Lady Dorothy: An aunt, who knows no more of me than he. Neither one cares for me. The servants have not seen me since I was a child. Ah, do not desert me!

Eleanor: 'Tis easy to see you are what you say, for only a foolish child's brain, just out of school, and knowing nothing of the world, full of romantic fancies and silly novels, could have concocted such a scheme. It cannot be, my child.

Kitty: Mistress Hallam must be at the theater playing, Lady Dorothy.

Lady Dorothy: I know that Mistress Hallam is a great enough actress to do as she pleases about that. Does she not take holidays, too?

Eleanor: The little minx is shrewd for all her ignorance. But, child, sorry as I am to disappoint you, I cannot undertake so mad a scheme.

Lady Dorothy: (*Bursting into tears*) Then my uncle will find me out, and I must give up my Robert, and my guardian will make me go to Gloster Park and marry the Earl of Roxbury!

Eleanor: (*Starting*) The Earl of Roxbury!

Lady Dorothy: Yes; 'tis he they want to marry me to.

Eleanor: The Earl of Roxbury!

Kitty: (*Warningly*) Eleanor, do not let that madcap brain of yours—

Eleanor: The Earl of Roxbury!

Lady Dorothy: You will help us? You are so good!

Eleanor: What sort of man is your uncle?

Lady Dorothy: A very tyrannical old man, with a terrible temper, they say. He makes everybody tremble before him.

Eleanor: And your aunt?

Lady Dorothy: Her letters make her out a very stern and pious person; she is always writing me sermons.

Eleanor: And they are your only relatives?

Lady Dorothy: The only two.

Eleanor: None of the neighbors or family friends know you?

Lady Dorothy: None. I come to my own home the greatest stranger that ever entered its walls.

Eleanor: I will help you as you ask, my child.

Lady Dorothy: (*Joyfully*) I knew you would!

Eleanor: Make all arrangements to go home at the time set. I will be there in your place. But what is the matter? You look suddenly troubled.

Lady Dorothy: Do you think you could so play my part as to have no one suspect? It would be terrible to have us discovered.

Eleanor: Isn't that just like a woman, Kitty? She is full of her plan and thinks of nothing else, and will not be denied, though she beg with tears. Then the moment she hath her wish, she begins to doubt and tremble.

Lady Dorothy: (*Faintly*) It seemed all right at first, and now I feel afraid!

Eleanor: It will be all right, never fear. Who is your betrothed—your own choice, I mean?

Lady Dorothy: Sir Robert Estcourt.

Eleanor: Sir Robert Estcourt! (*Turns on her suddenly*) Sir Robert Estcourt, did you say?

Lady Dorothy: (*Astonished*) Yes—do you know him?

Eleanor: And has told you he loves you— he is going to marry you?

Lady Dorothy: Yes, but why—

Eleanor: Then he is a villain!

Lady Dorothy: A villain! Robert!

Eleanor: One of the worst villains that

ever cursed the earth! Girl, the man you say you are going to marry is the man I love—the man who loves me— or so hath sworn a thousand times!— the man I will give up to no woman living—for villain though he be, I love him—I love him—I love him!

Kitty: Good heavens! What's this, Eleanor?

Lady Dorothy: (*Beginning to cry*) Oh, heavens! Can I be so deceived!

Eleanor: I have loved him long and faithfully, I believed his vows that I was the only woman he ever loved, and now— Oh, Robert, Robert! How can I bear this blow—and from his hand!

(*Throws herself down in passionate burst. Lady Dorothy looks miserable and half defiant. Kitty goes to Eleanor.*)

Kitty: And you never told me this, Eleanor?

Eleanor: Forgive me, Kitty, but I told no one; I was so happy with my secret—we seemed to belong to each other when no one but ourselves knew. (*Springs up suddenly*) I dreamed only of him—all my triumphs were for him—his praise was my reward—I lived only in the thought of him! (*Springs passionately on Lady Dorothy and seizes her*) And you shall not take him from me—you little white-faced chit—he does not care for you—it is a passing folly—but he loves me—me—do you hear?—me! You shall never have him! He belongs to me! (*Lady Dorothy shrinks back frightened*) I'll never give him up! You dare to dream you shall come between us? I will

kill you first and myself—Oh, Robert, Robert!

Lady Dorothy: Let me go—I never dreamed of this! How could he so deceive me! Let me go!

Eleanor: (*Detaining her*) Not yet, Lady Dorothy. I don't want your Robert.

Lady Dorothy: You do not!

Eleanor: No; I do not even know the gentleman; but as you seemed to doubt my powers of acting, I merely wanted to prove to you that I can deceive whenever I wish to. Come; do forgive me for frightening you?

Kitty: Of all your tricks this is the worst! Eleanor Hallam, you deceived *me*!

Eleanor: Thanks. Now, Lady Dorothy, come to my lodgings to-morrow, and we will discuss the details of our plan, and you shall give me further instructions. I have little more time

to-night to bestow on you.

Lady Dorothy: How can I thank you?

Eleanor: (*Calling*) Sally! (*Enter Sally*) Take this lady out quietly and tell her how to find my lodgings.

(*Exeunt Sally and Lady Dorothy.*)

Kitty: Eleanor, do you really mean to carry out this mad prank?

Eleanor: That I do. What a glorious chance I will have to pay back the Earl of Roxbury for his insolence! I will make him fall in love with me, Kitty, and when the masquerade is over, I will pay back his insults with interest. I am not the style of woman to capture his fancy—the aristocratic Earl will not condescend to the popular actress—we shall see.

Kitty: So you will really go?

Eleanor: I really will. (*Suddenly*) And you shall go with me.

Kitty: But the theater—Mr. Garrick—

Eleanor: Leave that to me. Kitty, revenge is a sweeter thing than love, and if ever a man was madly in love with a woman, only to be her laughing stock, that man shall be the most noble Earl of Roxbury with Eleanor Hallam.

(*Call outside; "Third Act."*)

Kitty: It is dangerous sport, Eleanor.

(*Eleanor goes to door, her face bright and smiling. She stops at door and looks back.*)

Eleanor: This will be the best farce I ever played, Kitty. A farce for me, but the tragedy of his life for his lordship, the Earl of Roxbury!

(*Curtain.*)

Act II

Scene I

Scene—Drawing room at Gloster Park. Sally is seated with an air of great consequence in one of the armchairs. Maid, Butler are standing near, regarding her with deference.

Maid: What a pretty lady our new mistress is! Have you been long with her, Mistress Sally?

Sally: 'Er maid what come hover from France with 'er, a dark slip hof a thing what talked that houtlandish nobuddy knew what 'er meant, was took sick in Lon'on, hand has my cousin fust removed was hown lady's made to Lord Cannin's sister, Hi was hengaged, bein' used to survise hin the hupper ranks. (*Aside*) Hif honly Mistress Helnor could a yeard me sayin' that stright!

Butler: Lady Dorothy seems werry lively like—I remember as a child she were werry shy and timid.

Sally: Shy! Mis—my lydy? Not 'er! That's forin' heddication, Mr. Doggett.

Maid: Is Mistress Hayden, her friend, goin' to stay here long?

Sally: (*Energetically*) Hi 'opes so! My lydy'd die if 'er were shut up halone with your 'orrid hold Mrs. Pendarves.

Butler: (*Warningly*) Sh! (*Looks around uneasily*) How do you like Gloster Park, Mistress Sally?

Sally: Werry fine, but hit hain't Lon'on.

Maid: Lon'on be a fine place, Mistress Sally, they say.

Butler: Of course it is, of course it is, girl. When I was there with my Lord Granby—(*With a sigh*) But I dessay things is not as smart now as in them days!

Sally: Oh, yes, they his, Mr. Doggett, things is smart there just the same— turble smart.

Maid: (*Whispering to Sally*) He hain't never been to Lon'on no more'n I have; he just puts on.

Butler: Is the ladies and gentlemen still so dressy and fine? What a gay life I did lead with my Lord Granby, to be sure! Is they still as gay?

Sally: Lor, yes, indeed! They dress-es hin silks an' welwets hall the time, an' sometimes the gentlemen gives the lydies flowers, hand sometimes they gives 'em di'mans—hit seems to be all the same to 'em whichever hit is, an' they drives habout his ker-ridges made hall hout hof pure gold, an' hif they don't 'ave four cream-colored 'osses a pullin' hof 'em, the little boys hin the street 'oller hat 'em.

Maid: (*Much impressed*) Deary me! Mustn't it be grand!

Butler: (*Superciliously*) Yes, Mistress Sally, 'twas so in my time.

Sally: Hit's that grand you can't think! Hand then the ply—you hought to go to Lon'on to see the ply!

Maid: (*Deferentially*) I suppose you went werry of'en to the play, Mistress Sally.

Sally: Lor bless you, Hi were a-goin' hall the time. "Romyo hand Jewlelyett" his the best.

Butler: Yes, yes, they played that in my time, and many a hearty laugh I had over it. 'Tis a fine comedy.

Maid: What's it all about, Mistress Sally?

Sally: They're hin love, you know, hand Romyo 'e's that 'andsome you can't think, hand 'is legs his just grand! Jewelyett, 'er ma gives a ball, an' 'er's dressed him white satting, hand Romyo comes to the ball, hand 'im's got a mass hon 'is face—

Maid: Mass of what?

Sally: (*Impatiently*) A black piece to 'ide 'is face, you know.

Butler: Of course. Don't be so iggerent, Walker.

Maid: (*Humbly*) I didn't know. Will you go on, Mistress Sally?

Sally: Jewlyett's pa wants to kill Romyo, but you see—

Maid: Gracious me! What for?

Sally: Hi don't know persackly, but Hi thinks hit's to make the ply go hon. Hafter the ball, Romyo he comes hover the garden wall, hand there's Jewelyett a-sittin' hin 'er bal-cove, a-talkin' hout loud about 'im. Then 'e calls hup to 'er, and 'er hasks hif 'e's romyo, hand 'e says yes, hand then 'er speaks up hand sez hiy hor git hout—'er hain't goin' to 'ave no triflin'.

Maid: (*Mournfully*) That's the way to talk to 'em. That Jewelyett's got sense. There was a young feller trifled all last summer with me, and just as I was thinkin' of given no-tice fer the weddin', he walks off with the laundress—he wasn't no time courtin' her. What do Romyo say?

Sally: He says yes, hand then Jewelyett she sez they'd better git married next day.

Maid: Lor, but that's sudden! Why couldn't she wait?

Sally: (*Doubtfully*) Hi spect 'er thought 'er 'ad better make sure hof 'em afore 'e 'ad time to change 'is mind. But hit's lovely the way they talk! 'Er sez, "a thousan' times good-night!" hand kisses 'er 'and like this— (*Strikes attitude*) hand 'im kisses 'is hand like this— (*Ditto business*).

Butler: Yes, they played it that same way when I went with my Lord Granby.

Maid: (*Deeply interested*) Do they get married?

Sally: Yes, hon the sly, hand then Romyo kills somebuddy, hand 'e 'as to run haway, hand hof hall the 'uggin' hand kissin'— lor! hit do make your mouth water to see 'em! Then Jewelyett her drinks somethink to meke 'er like 'er's dead, hand gits scared, hand hit's hawful to see 'er!

Maid: (*Breathlessly*) What do she do?

Sally: 'er do like this (*Begins attitudinizing in grotesque imitation of business in potion scene*) 'Er don't like bein' put hin the vault hand maybe goin' crazy, playin' with the dead men's bones, hand a-seein' ghosts—then she sees the man Romyo killed comin' hin to got hafter Romyo, hand 'er lets hout a yell like this—

(*Shrieks and imitates what she has seen Eleanor do in scene. Maid screams. Eleanor and Kitty appear in door. Sally is absorbed; Maid is tremblingly intent on Sally; Butler looks on disturbed. Kitty laughs—Eleanor frowns.*)

Butler: It don't seem to be as comic as they plyed it when I went with my Lord Granby.

(*Eleanor and Kitty advance.*)

Eleanor: What on earth is the matter with you, Sally? Have you got another fit?

(*All start.*)

Butler: (*Recovering*) She had the hysterics, and we was tryin' to quiet her, my lady.

Eleanor: Hysterics! You were gossiping here instead of attending to your duties. Leave the room. (*They turn to go*) Come back, Sally. (*Exeunt others*) What have you been talking about to these people?

Sally: Habout the ply, ma'am—

Eleanor: Didn't I forbid you in the strictest way, to mention my name or give a hint—

Sally: (*Eagerly*) But Hi didn't, ma'am; Hi were just a-tellin' habout Romyo hand Jewelyett—

Eleanor: Don't you mention a word to them about the theater in any way, for you will be sure to let something slip. Now remember, Sally, if you do let slip one word, I'll discharge you and send you straight back to London. Do you hear?

Sally: (*Faltering*) Yes, ma'am.

Eleanor: Now go.

(*Exit Sally.*)

Kitty: You were foolish to bring that girl, Nell.

Eleanor: Wouldn't I have been more foolish to leave her in London for Mr. Garrick and Charles Barry and all the rest of them to cross-examine about my plans? Sally's a faithful creature, but she hasn't an intellect that could stand a vigorous attack. I wonder what they are saying in London about my disappearance, and how many parties are out after me.

Kitty: It was a mad thing to come here, Eleanor.

Eleanor: That is exactly why I did it. Life would be very monotonous if we never did any but sensible things.

Kitty: But how can we keep it up?

Eleanor: Oh, Kitty, after all our successes on the London stage?

Kitty: But it will take more than acting to keep up the deception.

Eleanor: Only a bit of the Irish wit that was all my poor father left me, barring his debts and his blessings.

Kitty: But what do you propose to do?

Eleanor: First, to pay back that old Pendarves cat and that miserable old Lord Canning for their treatment of Lady Dorothy. Kitty, I am going to make them so sore at her very name that they will be glad for shame's sake, to let her marry whom she will. So much will I do for Lady Dorothy for the charity of it. Then I am going to make the Earl of Roxbury fall in love with me. So much will I do for myself for the fun of it.

Kitty: Why are you so submissive and demure with Mrs. Pendarves?

Eleanor: The better to beguile. She will report to Lord Canning that I am everything that is meek and prim and spiritless, and I want to give the dear old creatures a pleasant surprise. And Mrs. Pendarves shall have hers, too, don't fear. The woman's a hypocrite. She takes to pious devotion to make people fear her, because she hasn't any money enough to be influential nor brain enough to be smart. I hate to see such people putting goodness around them as a cloak to be put off as soon as they get home to themselves. 'Tis as repulsive as the string of diamonds you see around the yellow and wrinkled necks of skinny old dowagers.

Kitty: Eleanor, do be careful with these people.

Eleanor: Why, Kitty, how can they harm me? Even if we are discovered, 'twill be nothing more with the world than one of that madcap Eleanor Hallam's wild Irish pranks. These people hurt me! Why, I can make them the laughing stock of England.

(*Enter Mrs. Pendarves.*)

Mrs. Pendarves: Dorothy, child.

Eleanor: (*Demurely*) Yes, dear aunt.

Mrs. Pendarves: Your uncle and guardian, Lord Canning, is coming to the Park to-day and 'tis likely that your betrothed, the Earl of Roxbury, will accompany him or follow very shortly. I hope you are prepared to meet your uncle in a spirit of dutiful obedience.

Eleanor: Yes, dear aunt.

Mrs. Pendarves: I hope you have imbibed none of these shocking ideas of a woman's independence, and are ready to receive with proper gratitude the very excellent choice of husband his lordship has made for you—that you have not allowed any foolish fancies as to love and romance interfere with your duty to him?

Eleanor: No, dear aunt, the very thought of a girl's selecting a husband to please herself when she has relatives to do for her, is positively shocking to all ideas of female decorum.

Mrs. Pendarves: I confess you surprise me agreeably with your prudence and docility.

Eleanor: (*Reproachfully*) Oh, ma'am, how could I be otherwise with your letters to guide and direct me? Have you not constantly pointed out to me the path from which the feet of a virtuous young female should never stray? (*She clasps her hands*) Oh, that I may be found worthy of so discerning a monitor!

(*Kitty chokes with suppressed laughter. Mrs. Pendarves turns and looks at her with stern rebuke, Eleanor with mild and reproachful surprise.*)

Mrs. Pendarves: I fear your friend does not share your excellent sentiments, Dorothy.

Eleanor: My friend, I fear, is rather worldly, ma'am, but I hope by argument and entreaty to win her to more serious pursuits.

Mrs. Pendarves: 'Tis a generous thought, but you are young, Dorothy, and Mistress Hayden is not the best friend for you. I think Lord Canning will disapprove of her companionship for you.

Eleanor: In that case, ma'am, I will part instantly from her, deeply though it grieves me.

Kitty: The consummate little liar!

Mrs. Pendarves: How have you been employing your time this morning, Dorothy?

Eleanor: I mediated long and deeply on the uncertainties of life and the vanity of the young in pursuing pleasure instead of serious duty. I also reflected with much sadness on the woeful want of respect with which the youth of the day treats its elders; it troubles me much to think of the homage the world pays passing youth and shallow beauty, while slighting the wisdom and experience of age. Ah, aunt, it must be truly painful when one has passed the gay and giddy period of life to find how little use men have for the intrinsic merits of character and mind which have neither youth nor the perishable attractions of looks.

Mrs. Pendarves: (*Trying to conceal annoyance*) These are good thoughts to occupy your mind, child; but did you spend the whole time in meditation?

Eleanor: No, ma'am; as is my daily custom, I perused some of your letters, and was affected to tears by the good advice and affection they expressed. I was looking over one in particular which I remember showing to the other girls at school; they were wicked enough to say that if my relatives cared at all for me they would come once in a while to see me. It was so full of affection—and then the girls asked me what you looked like. (*Mrs. Pendarves looks uneasily at her*) I must confess, my dear aunt, that I was somewhat disturbed that I could not tell them. Of course, while I had the beautiful image of your soul in the letters, *I* did not mind, but it did look queer to the girls that I didn't know what you looked like.

Mrs. Pendarves: 'Tis time for your morning walk, child.

Eleanor: With your permission, ma'am, I will take this letter, (*She draws it from her pocket*) and read it to my friend to wean her from worldly thoughts. Come, Kitty. (*To Kitty*) I have rubbed the old cat's fur the wrong way, and she's afraid to use her claws.

Kitty: Oh, Nell!

(*Exeunt Eleanor and Kitty.*)

Mrs. Pendarves: Hm! I don't know that these foreign schools are good for our girls, after all.

(*Enter Butler.*)

Butler: Lord Canning has arrived, ma'am.

Mrs. Pendarves: Show him at once, Doggett. (*Looks towards garden with air of being perturbed, smooths down dress, betrays nervousness.*)

(*Enter Lord Canning.*)

Mrs. Pendarves: Ah, so your lordship has come at last to greet your ward.

Lord Canning: At last! Why do you say, "at last," madam? Do you expect me to run my legs off and break my neck for the sake of a chit of a girl as though she were his majesty's gracious consort? I've come at my own convenience, and that's soon enough for her. Where is she?

Mrs. Pendarves: Doggett, send some one to fetch Lady Dorothy hither. She went out this moment into the garden for her daily walk.

Lord Canning: What's the girl like— what's the girl like? A pert foolish miss like the rest of 'em, with an empty head full of lovers and fine dress?

Mrs. Pendarves: On the contrary, she is most timid and retiring in her manner, and as submissive as one could wish, with her mind given to serious things—

Lord Canning: Serious fiddlesticks! Who ever heard of a girl's mind in a serious frame? Women are born fools, all of 'em. If the girl's docile, she's well enough.

Mrs. Pendarves: Oh, I'll answer that she's quiet and docile—

(*Enter Eleanor and Kitty.*)

Eleanor: You sent for me, aunt?

Mrs. Pendarves: This is your uncle and guardian, Lord Canning, who has come to see you, child.

Eleanor: (*Dropping a curtsy*) Lord Canning, my uncle and guardian, who has come to see me for the first time in ten years, your most obedient. (*Truculently*) But why come now?

Mrs. Pendarves: (*Astounded*) Dorothy!

Lord Canning: Bless my soul!

Eleanor: (*To Mrs. Pendarves*) Don't Dorothy me! (*To Lord Canning*) Yes, why now? Why did you leave me all these years for the other girls to jeer at, and wonder if I had any relations? Why did you so mortify and neglect me? Why don't you answer me? (*She bangs with her fist on the table*) Do you hear? Why don't you answer me?

Mrs. Pendarves: Did I ever!

Lord Canning: Is the girl crazy? Is this the docile and quiet girl you told me of, madam? How dare you be so insolent, miss—

Eleanor: Don't you say dare to me! I won't stand it! I am Lady Dorothy Hastings of Gloster Park, I am of age and mistress here, and uncle or not, if you try to bully me, I'll order my servants to turn you out of the house.

Lord Canning: (*Gasping*) Turn me out of the house!

Mrs. Pendarves: Dorothy, do you dare to talk so to Lord Canning?

Eleanor: Sit you down and wait your turn. I have plenty to say to you. Sit down, I tell you! (*She advances with threatening gesture. Mrs. Pendarves, astonished and frightened, sinks down in chair, eyes and mouth open in dismay.*) Don't interrupt me again. (*To Lord Canning*) A nice uncle and guardian you've been—Oh, I made up my mind to have it out with you as soon as I saw you. Why was I left in such neglect? And why am I to be married off in such a hurry as soon as I come home? Who is this man to whom I am to be handed over with your compliments and the family plate?

Lord Canning: (*Choking with rage*) Take care, miss, take care! I'll soon tame that ugly temper of yours!

Eleanor: 'Tis the family temper as good and strong as your own. Tame that first and then try mine!

Lord Canning: You saucy baggage, I'll lock you up till I've tamed you, and you'll marry the Earl of Roxbury as soon as I say so.

Eleanor: I'll do nothing of the kind. If it pleases me to marry the Earl of Roxbury I'll do it, and if it doesn't please me, I won't!

Lord Canning: You will—

Eleanor: (*Almost shrieking in her rage*) I won't! I won't! I won't!

Mrs. Pendarves: Oh, dear! Oh, dear! (*Appealing to Kitty*) Can't you quiet her?

Kitty: Dear Dorothy—

Eleanor: Don't speak to me! Lock me up! In my own house, too! Oh, I wish I were a man! I'd teach you to bully and oppress me, you bad, you ugly old man!

Lord Canning: Is it this spitfire you told me was so meek and so submissive? By gad, ma'am—

Mrs. Pendarves: (*Crying*) Oh, the little hypocrite! She took me in completely!

Eleanor: Yes, and I'll put you out in pieces if you don't take care how you use me. Hypocrite, indeed! Why, that woman who has been sending me long sermons at school, and living on my substance at home, is false to the core. Her tongue is false, her heart is false, her religion is false, even her hair and teeth are false. (*She snatches off Mrs. Pendarves' wig; the latter covers her mouth*) The only real and solid thing about her is her appetite! Oh!!!

(*Folds her hands and begins to pace up and down, working herself up into violent passion.*)

Lord Canning: Go to your room, miss, and you will not leave it until you humble yourself to this worthy lady and myself for your outrageous conduct. Go this instant.

Eleanor: Ordered to my room to be locked in like a naughty child! I won't endure to be treated so! I won't! I tell you, I won't!

(*She seizes a vase, throws it down, and seemingly blind with passion, begins throwing down and breaking everything in her way. Lord Canning rushes forward to catch her by the hands.*)

Lord Canning: You impudent hussy, I'll teach you to be such a spitfire!

Eleanor: Don't come near me! (*She seizes the tongs*) Don't you lay a hand on me, you wicked old man! How do I know what you have been doing with my fortune all these years you had me bundled away in France? (*Lord Canning starts*) How do I know what she (*Pointing to Mrs. Pendarves*) has been helping herself to all the time she has been ruling in my house and writing me sanctimonious letters? I'll have my accounts seen to, if you threaten me any more, and maybe there'll be more locking up than you have a fancy for, my Lord Canning!

Lord Canning: You dare suspect—

Eleanor: I dare to do anything I've a mind to. And I won't be threatened, and I won't be preached to, and I won't be married, and I won't be locked up. Do you hear me? Oh, I wish I could say all I think of you—but you had better let me alone—you had better let me alone— (*Makes a dash at Lord Canning, brandishing the tongs. Kitty, who has been mutely appealing to her, snatches her around the waist and pulls her backward.*

Eleanor struggles) Let me get at him once—let me get at him— (*Kitty drags her off, Eleanor still struggling and brandishing the tongs fiercely at Lord Canning*).

Lord Canning: What did you mean, ma'am, by telling me such a lot of nonsense about this girl's meekness and decorum?

Mrs. Pendarves: Indeed, my lord, she simply paralyzed me! These few days she hath been as meek and mild as a child, and pretended the utmost docility and respect for me—now, I see, all a pretense. I was deceived as completely as yourself.

Lord Canning: You did not deceive her so completely, egad, ma'am.

Mrs. Pendarves: She slandered me cruelly. My teeth are as good as her own, and my hair—that was illness. Now if she goes to remarking on your lordship's person—

Lord Canning: (*Hastily*) Well, well, we'll marry her off soon, and then she'll give no more trouble, for Lord Roxbury is a man that hates the hint of scandal in his affairs, and he'll keep her quiet for the sake of his own peace.

(*Enter Butler.*)

Butler: The Earl of Roxbury.

Mrs. Pendarves: Show him in. (*In awestruck tones*) Shall we tell him?

Lord Canning: It would be better to prepare him.

(*Enter Lord Roxbury.*)

Mrs. Pendarves: Welcome, Lord Roxbury, to Gloster Park.

Lord Roxbury: Thanks, Madam. (*Kisses her hand*) Lord Canning, my deepest respects. I hastened after your lordship at the earliest moment to pay my duty to my bride.

Lord Canning: She is a bride who will do you credit, Lord Roxbury, and she will bring you a magnificent dowry. But I must tell you frankly—

Lord Roxbury: (*Easily*) Then you have some unpleasant news about my bride, for when people tell you they are going to be frank, they always mean they are going to be disagreeable.

Mrs. Pendarves: (*Hastily*) Only this, Lord Roxbury. The girl has been spoiled at school, and is a bit high-tempered and willful. She needs curbing.

Lord Canning: (*Angrily*) Yes, sharp curbing. She needs a master hand to hold the rein and use the whip. She has a hard mouth and she'll bolt at every chance.

Lord Roxbury: (*Smiling*) Then she must have no chance. This rather pleases me, for to control a wife will give me some amusement—life is at times so wearying. Of course, I make no pretense to love and that sort of thing, no more than I expect it from my bride. I am ready to by the family bargain that joined our hands—as for hearts—pouf!—ill-bred things, interestingly only to footboys, ladies' maids and surgeons. But may I see the lady?

Mrs. Pendarves: Ahem!

(*Looks at Lord Canning.*)

Lord Canning: Since you are betrothed, Lord Roxbury, Mrs. Pendarves and I will waive a point and let you see Lady Dorothy alone. She is somewhere about the grounds. Mrs. Pendarves, will you send for her? We will discuss the settlements later, Lord Roxbury.

Lord Roxbury: (*Calmly*) Settlements may wait, your lordship. They should not interrupt the raptures of two such ardent young lovers as Lady Dorothy and myself.

Lord Canning: Remember—the curb and tight. Damn the minx!

(Exeunt Lord Canning and Mrs. Pendarves. Lord Roxbury throws himself into a chair in deep thought. Enter Eleanor, cautiously. Looks about, perceives and the Earl whose back is towards her; holds up a hand warningly, as though forbidding Kitty to enter. Advances, surveys him critically, nods her head as though in approval, comes lightly a step or two forward, and shakes her fist at him. Then towards the door and calls loudly while she motions Kitty not to come in.)

Eleanor: Kitty! Kitty! (*Lord Roxbury starts up. He turns about, perceives Eleanor, who also starts and stands in apparent great embarrassment. A short silence, he looking admiringly, she in great confusion.*) Pardon!—I did not know any one was here—I beg—(*Going.*)

Lord Roxbury: (*Starting forward*) Do not go, I beg.

Eleanor: You are come to visit my aunt, Mrs. Pendarves? I will tell her—

Lord Roxbury: Your aunt? Then I have the honor of addressing Lady Dorothy Hastings?

Eleanor: (*In confusion*) Why, yes—

Lord Roxbury: Then do not go, Lady Dorothy, for I have the permission of Mrs. Pendarves and Lord Canning to see you alone—in fact, they have sent to find you to tell you of my arrival.

Eleanor: (*Shyly*) Then you are—Lord Roxbury?

Lord Roxbury: I have come to pay my deepest respects to my betrothed, Lady Dorothy. The ship and spur for this dainty creature!

Eleanor: You have their permission to see me alone? Then we can arrange everything!

Lord Roxbury: (*Surprised*) Arrange everything?

Eleanor: Yes. I have thought it all out, and I have a beautiful plan to make everything right. Now, Lord Roxbury, you and I were betrothed by a family compact, as I understand it, when I was a mere child and you, a boy at school, and neither of us was asked what we thought about it, now were we?

(*She looks coquettishly at him. He looks at her with increased admiration.*)

Lord Roxbury: No, we were not, but it is

not always wise to disturb these family compacts, you know.

Eleanor: (*Admiringly*) How generous you are, Lord Roxbury. But I do not see why we should both be sacrificed to old cut and dried family traditions—

Lord Roxbury: Sacrificed!

Eleanor: Yes; that is what it is. They are forcing me on you as a wife, and you on me as a husband. Now we don't know each other, and I am sure you have seen some beautiful great lady whom you would rather have in my place. You are a great lord and used to the court and its ways, and I am only a simple little girl just from school, unfitted for so grand a position as that of the Countess of Roxbury—

Lord Roxbury: You underrate yourself, Lady Dorothy.

Eleanor: Oh, it is kind of you to say that, but you must have given your heart elsewhere long ere this.

Lord Roxbury: No, no.

Eleanor: You are so good to a simple maiden like me.

Lord Roxbury: You mistake—

Eleanor: (*Pensively*) I know you will help me. I am not fitted to be a lady of fashion—I need love—and—and— (*Breaks off, seeming much confused*)

Lord Roxbury: You mean you are already in love?

(*Eleanor with downcast eyes, plays with her ribbons.*)

Eleanor: Oh, Lord Roxbury, how can you say such a thing? I am too young— love! La, what should a poor little school girl like me know of love?

Lord Roxbury: No one has ever made love to you, Lady Dorothy?

Eleanor: (*Very conscious*) No-o—that is— why, certainly not, Lord Roxbury! They wouldn't have allowed it.

Lord Roxbury: (*Sternly*) Now, tell me truly, Lady Dorothy, did he ever make love to you?

Eleanor: Why, how did you know—Oh, no, no! Who?

Lord Roxbury: Never mind who. You know whom I mean. Answer me, Lady Dorothy. I am your betrothed, remember. I have a right to know.

Eleanor: (*Defiantly*) Well, he only sent me some flowers.
Lord Roxbury: And no meetings?

Eleanor: Good heavens, no! Why, the bulldogs there ate up a man that once climbed over the wall.

Lord Roxbury: And he never sent you notes?

Eleanor: Only a few. And I burned them—I read them first, though.

Lord Roxbury: (*Aside*) A perfect child— and what a lovely one! I feel it my duty to tell your guardian of this.

Eleanor: (*In pretended alarm*) You wouldn't tell Lord Canning? Oh, he's a dreadful old man! He would make me marry you to-morrow!

Lord Roxbury: (*Resentfully*) Is that such a dreadful prospect?

Eleanor: (*Innocently*) Oh, yes! To marry a strange man I have never seen before? But (*Looking at him shyly*) you do not seem strange, Lord Roxbury. Now, you won't tell on me to my uncle, will you? You wouldn't so use a poor forlorn little girl who trusted you— (*Softly coming nearer*) would you, Lord Roxbury?

Lord Roxbury: I would not play the traitor, Lady Dorothy. But this man—

Eleanor: (*Innocently*) What man?

Lord Roxbury: The man who sent you flowers and notes.

Eleanor: (*Playing with ribbons*) Oh!

Lord Roxbury: Who is he?

Eleanor: Oh, I mustn't tell. But, listen what a beautiful plan I have. We must pretend to be betrothed for a while— (*Anxiously*) you could do that, couldn't you?

Lord Roxbury: (*Fervently*) Yes, I could do that.

Eleanor: (*Clapping her hands*) I knew you could. Then we will quarrel dreadfully, and you must go to Lord Canning and tell him I have such a bad temper—oh, I have a dreadful temper!—that you could not think of marrying me. But you must let him break it off for me. I couldn't think of appearing in the world for the first time as a jilted maid— you wouldn't ask that, Lord Roxbury, now would you? (*In pretended alarm.*)

Lord Roxbury: (*Softly*) I would ask nothing that would give you pain, Lady Dorothy.

Eleanor: How good you are! Then it is all arranged, and soon we will both be free.

Lord Roxbury: Free! Does that give you such joy, Lady Dorothy?

Eleanor: (*Pouting*) You have not thanked me, Lord Roxbury, for freeing you.

Lord Roxbury: You have not asked me if I wished to be free.

Eleanor: (*Gayly*) No, for then if you spoke truly, you would have to say yes, and that would pain you to be so discourteous to a lady, for I see you are a true gentleman, Lord Roxbury. How am I to thank you for being so good to me? (*She impulsively holds out her hands, which he takes eagerly in his own and kisses*) And how noble to show no sign of joy at being rid of me, which I know you must feel.

Lord Roxbury: Rid of you—

Eleanor: You will not hurt me by thanking me, but I understand. Now we are friends.

Lord Roxbury: Friends!

Eleanor: (*Laughing as though relieved*) Now we can be good friends, and what a fine time we shall have with my aunt and uncle, playing at being lovers. (*She glances at him archly*) For we must play it out bravely, and you must make love to me—oh, so ardently, and sigh and smile, and I must smile, too, and be coy and abashed— (*Laughing*) Oh, Lord

Roxbury, what a great joke we will make of it!

Lord Roxbury: (*With attempt to echo laugh*) Yes, it will be vastly amusing.

Eleanor: Now you must be tired from your journey. (*She rings*) We will meet again. Can you imitate a lover's raptures before my Aunt Pendarves and my Uncle Canning? There—would you like to kiss my hand by way of practice?

(*She stretches out her hand with a coquettish look. Lord Roxbury seizes it and kisses it. Eleanor smiles at Kitty in the garden.*)

Oh—this is only practice, my lord. You need not press it quite so lard.

(*Enter Butler*)

Doggett, conduct the Earl of Roxbury to his room.

(*Exeunt Butler and Lord Roxbury. Eleanor watches him out of room, then leans back luxuriously in chair.*)

An easy prey!

(*Smiles to herself. A figure enters from garden, approaches chair in which she is lying, looks down on her a moment, then speaks.*)

Figure: A fair good day, Mistress Eleanor Hallam!

(*Eleanor starts up with cry—sees Figure and sinks back horrified. Kitty appears with gesture of alarm in window.*)

Eleanor: Charles Barry!

(*Curtain.*)

Scene II

Scene—Same as previous one. Eleanor is pacing up and down, apparently deep in thought. She goes outside on balcony over-looking garden and calls.

Eleanor: Kitty! Kitty! are you there?

Kitty: Yes, Nell, I'm watching.

Eleanor: Oh, stop watching—'tis no good—and come up here with me. Was ever fate so contrary! (*Enter Kitty*) 'Tis of no use being on the watch, Kitty. Charles will come when it pleases him, and I'm sure that will be soon.

Kitty: (*Gloomily*) He has been here now for a week.

Eleanor: Yes, and I cannot keep him off much longer. We must try some other plan, Kitty. I have exhausted my ingenuity in keeping him from seeing people here, and he cannot come thus secretly to see me without soon being discovered. I wonder that discovery hath not already taken place.

Kitty: Nell, why not give it all up and go back to town?

Eleanor: My promise to Lady Dorothy.

Kitty: She surely is safely married by this time. Indeed, it is best, as Charles urges, to go back to London.

Eleanor: I cannot go back just yet, Kitty, indeed I cannot.

Kitty: And why not?

Eleanor: (*Hastily*) I cannot explain, but there are reasons—

Kitty: Only one, that I can see. And I'll admit 'tis a handsome reason, with gallant ways and monstrous fine clothes, and a still more wondrous fondness for the society of Lady Dorothy Hastings.

Eleanor: Kitty Hayden, you talk in riddles. You're past my wit to find out what you mean.

Kitty: Then your wit has grown monstrous dull at Gloster Park; 'twas sharp enough in London. Plainly, I mean your reason is—the Earl of Roxbury.

Eleanor: Nonsense, Kitty. Truth, I have a score against him which my pride would care a bit to see settled.

Kitty: Your pride! I wish it were no more. Have a care, Eleanor. You are playing with fire, and you will yet burn your own fingers.

Eleanor: What a wise Kitty! What a Kitty come to judgement!

Kitty: Eleanor, be sensible—

Eleanor: Not yet, Kitty, dear. I'm too young, and there is too much joy and sport in life that you sensible people, always looking out for consequences, miss. No, no, don't preach to me, Kitty. How do you suppose Charles found us out?

Kitty: Do you expect me to follow the traces of the sharpened wits of a jealous man? The boy at the theater who let Lady Dorothy in your room—the

maid who came with her—Sally's stupidity—-how does it matter how he learned? The main fact is that he is here. The question is not how he came, but how to get rid of him.

Eleanor: Talk of angels—only this one hath such terribly green feathers in his wings! Don't let him see you, Kitty, but keep near.

(*Kitty hides. Enter Barry from the garden with stealthy air. Eleanor pretends to be musing; Barry advances; she gives a start as though completely taken by surprise.*)

Charles! And back so soon! What of your promises, sir?

Barry: I made no promises, and I am tired of yours. How much longer do you expect me to skulk about this place, avoiding notice as though I were a poacher or a thief?

Eleanor: If you are tired of Gloster Park, Charles, why not go back to London?

Barry: I will go back when you go with me.

Eleanor: Charles, listen to reason. Your visits cannot be kept secret with all the sharp eyes hereabouts, and if it is discovered, as it must be, that Lady Dorothy Hastings is holding clandestine meetings with a strange man in her gardens, don't you see how we shall compromise the poor girl?

Barry: Oh, I shall clear Lady Dorothy. I shall simply tell—and I think, today—that you are not only she, only a masquerader in her place.

Eleanor: Would you throw such shame on me, Charles? Would you see these people drive me as an imposter from the Park in disgrace? And yet you say you love me!

Barry: (*Gloomily*) Sometimes I think I hate you!

Eleanor: Oh, Charles, how can you say such a dreadful thing? Hate me! (*Softly*) How that would grieve me if I thought you meant it!

Barry: (*Eagerly to her*) Would it grieve you?

Eleanor: Of course, it would. To have one you are fond of, hate you—

Barry: (*Bitterly*) Fond of!

Eleanor: (*Insinuatingly*) Yes. For I am fond of you, Charles; you are one of my dearest friends.

Barry: Friend!

Eleanor: Well, if you would have me more, are you taking the right way to make me fonder? I am tired out with work, I take a little rest, I come down here to help out a girl like myself, in distress, and to amuse myself a little with a harmless game, and, lo! here you follow me to be a spoil-sport and to compromise me. (*She looks at him reproachfully*) Now, Charles, how could you do it?

Barry: (*Obstinately*) It is a duty I owe these people you are deceiving to tell them the truth.

Eleanor: Now, Charles, you have used me badly—but if I ask you like a dear, good friend, not to interfere with my sport just yet, you wouldn't do it? (*She comes nearer and looks up pleadingly in his face*) And I do ask it, Charles, dear. (*Barry looks a trifle uneasy and irresolute*) You always do whatever I ask you—you will do this? (*Coaxingly*) Won't you do this, Charles?

(*She slips her hand into his—he turns away. She gently forces him around and looks up into his face, smiling coquettishly. He tries hard to preserve his air of offended sternness.*)

For me? Don't be angry with me just for having a bit of sport. Come, be friends, Charles—be friends with me again.

Barry: If it were only sport—

Eleanor: (*Eagerly*) Only that, I assure you.

Barry: But this Lord Roxbury—he is in love with you.

Eleanor: (*Laughing*) Oh, you silly boy! He has known me only a week.

Barry: (*Savagely*) I have seen you do more mischief in less time, Mistress Eleanor.

Eleanor: The Earl is not in love with me—indeed, he is not, Charles.

Barry: He is, and you are in love with him!

Eleanor: Indeed, then, I'm not! I've more spirit than to fall in love with my-lord-in-love-with-himself.

Barry: But the way you look at him!

Eleanor: How do I look at him? Like this? (*Gives a languishing look into Barry's eyes*) Oh, Charles, how can you be so hard, so ugly to me? I never thought I would have to beg so hard for so simple a favor. You have made me so unhappy! (*She pretends to weep*) And yet you say you love me!

(*She sobs*)

Barry: If I didn't, would I be willing to make such a fool of myself? (*Uneasily*) But there—don't weep, Eleanor. If I were only sure about this fancy earl—

Eleanor: Then be sure. Suppose that if I were to tell you while I amuse myself with many, there is only one man in the world for me—there, there now— (*He makes eager motion towards her*) You must not expect me to betray my secrets.

(*She smiles meaningfully in his face*)

Barry: Eleanor, are you playing with me?

Eleanor: I am playing with the Earl of Roxbury to help poor Lady Dorothy; for why should I not feel for another in love, when I myself am—am—(*She breaks off in apparent confusion.*)

Barry: In love? With whom, Mistress Eleanor?

Eleanor: (*Saucily*) There's none so blind as he that will not see. But I promise you I'm in love with no one that doth not care to please me.

Barry: Would I not give my life to please you, Eleanor?

Eleanor: Why, yes. Odd that I never saw it before! You interfere with my harmless trick to help poor Lady Dorothy, you compromise me with secret meetings, you threaten my disgrace from exposure to these people—all this pleases me mightily! And the keenest part of my pleasure is that you should so distrust me.

Barry: What would you have me to do?

Eleanor: Trust me—love me—go back to London.

Barry: And leave you here for that popinjay of an earl to make love to?

Eleanor: He makes love to me as Dorothy Hastings. Be sure, I come back to London— (*She pauses*) and friends as Eleanor Hallam, and soon. The play is nearly played out.

Barry: Is it, in truth?

Eleanor: In truth. Charles, dear Charles, will you not do this for my sake? Are you really jealous of this man whose insults I am but repaying in kind? Will you, my friend, betray me? You cannot—I see it in your face. Here is my hand—yes, you may pledge your secrecy upon it.

Barry: Only your hand.

Eleanor: My lips shall thank you when yours can tell me of the pledge fulfilled. You will go?

Barry: I will go, but I will look for that pledge next week in London.

Eleanor: Next week—in London—it shall be yours.

Barry: Then 'tis farewell for a week.

Eleanor: For a week—a long week.

(*He snatches her hand, kisses it and exit. She regards her hand.*)

Eleanor: You had to go to his lips, but I would have rather laid you—and soundly, too—about his ears! The jealous fool!

Kitty: (*Coming forward*) Eleanor, are you doing well to play so with Charles Barry? Or is it right?

Eleanor: Sure, Kitty, the law allows you to kill a man in self-defense—then why is it wrong to make love to one for the same purpose? Faith, it's got to be done, and it's pleasanter for them—while it lasts.

Kitty: It is not right, Eleanor, for at least he loves you.

Eleanor: Loves me! He loves his own will, his own fancy. Oh, Kitty, love is not the harsh, domineering, jealous and revengeful feeling that Charles Barry has for me. I am his fruit, to be plucked at his pleasure, which he will not endure to see another touch, because it is his property. Did he really love me, I would be a star in the heaven of his hopes whom he would have all other men worship. I feel no remorse in deceiving a love that is so hard to me,

and seeks so to hurt me with its jealous passion. Real love seeks not itself, but its beloved; it cherishes, it protects, it trusts; it is strong and it is gentle; it will bear any sorrow, dare any danger, before it will let harm come to the one it loves. That is love—the love I could feel—the love I would have felt for me!

Kitty: Eleanor! You do not mean—

Eleanor: Nothing, except I am not heartless in trifling with Charles, and that love is such a good thing to make pretty speeches of, and that I'll get a good round of applause when I put that one in my next play.

Kitty: Eleanor, you were in earnest.

Eleanor: Kitty, I never was in earnest in my life. I must be sentimental every night in my work; do let me jest on my holiday.

Kitty: But you have promised Charles to fulfill your pledge to him in London next week.

Eleanor: And so I will if he fulfills his own. But I doubt him, Kitty. If he comes here again, and breaks his word, then I'll not coax him again—I'll force him.

Kitty: How?

Eleanor: That, my dear, is part of the farce. He may not return, but there is no way of meeting an emergency like being prepared for it. (*She rings bell*) Now you shall see. (*Rings bell*) Now you shall see.

(*Enter Sally*)

Eleanor: Sally, go tell my Aunt Pendarves to attend me here; I wish to speak to her on a matter of great importance.

Sally: Mistress—my lady, I'm afeard o' she. 'Er's a horful hold 'ag!

Eleanor: Do as I bid you, Sally, or I'll box your ears. I'm a lady of the aristocracy now, and must behave like one. Tell her not to keep me waiting.

Sally: Then sh'll box my hears, sure!

Eleanor: If she shows any signs of doing it, run, Sally, as soon as you've delivered your message, and try to knock over a chair or something on her as you do it.

(*Exit Sally, grinning*)

What do you say, Kitty, to having Mrs. Pendarves send Charles about his business for us the next time, if he breaks his word and comes again?

Kitty: What mad trick are you plotting now?

Eleanor: Oh, 'tis a mad one, sure. But I have not yet told you my greatest secret.

Kitty: No more secrets, Nell, if you love me, lest I faint under the number if not the weight of them.

Eleanor: But this is one you must know. I had a letter from Lady Dorothy this morning, and she is safely married and wants me to arrange her coming home.

Kitty: When?

Eleanor: She leaves that to me. Sh! (*Enter Mrs. Pendarves*) See how meekly the old cat obeys my summons. Oh, but she's a miserable creature of her tribe! She is too mad to purr, and too afraid to scratch.

Mrs. Pendarves: I came to look for you, niece Dorothy, to complain of your maid for bringing me a rude message.

Eleanor: Sally's manners are not courtly, but from your presence here, I judge she delivered the message aright.

Mrs. Pendarves: (*Plaintively*) Indeed, Dorothy, my dear, cannot you come to me when you wish to speak with me?

Eleanor: Oh, yes, I can, but I won't. Why should I come to you? Am I not the mistress of Gloster Park? Those in it who like not my ways are welcome to leave.

Mrs. Pendarves: (*Hastily*) Oh, I did not mind coming down here, my dear; I wished, in fact, to take the air.

Eleanor: The air, madam is one of the few things at Gloster Park which it is safe for one to take without fear of its being missed.

Mrs. Pendarves: (*Feebly*) You will make a joke of everything, Dorothy.

Eleanor: There is no joke in what I am about to tell you. Now listen calmly and don't get frightened.

Mrs. Pendarves: (*Alarmed*) For goodness sake, what is it?

Eleanor: I cannot tell you if you agitate yourself, and yet you must be told. We are in great danger!

Mrs. Pendarves: The Lord help us!

Eleanor: There is a murderous maniac,

who has probably escaped from some asylum, prowling about here.

Mrs. Pendarves: (*Shrieking*) A maniac! We'll all be murdered in our beds!

Eleanor: He has been here, but ran off before I could get help. We must notify the servants to be on watch.

Mrs. Pendarves: Oh, at once, at once, and tell them to give the alarm!

Eleanor: If he makes his way into the house before the men can be summoned, as he did this morning, there is only one way to keep him from doing us harm until help comes.

Mrs. Pendarves: What is that? Tell me, for pity's sake!

Eleanor: (*Solemnly*) Humor him. He must be humored. He hath strange fancies, but we must agree to him.

Mrs. Pendarves: What fancies?

Kitty: O wicked Nell! A mad trick, in trust!

Eleanor: He fancies I am an actress he has seen in London, and calls me by some name I cannot recall now. He ordered me this morning to act. He vows that Kitty here is his nurse, that Lord Canning is a bishop, and that you—Oh, how can I say what he takes you for!

Mrs. Pendarves: (*In agony of fear*) What does he think me?

Eleanor: A dancing girl.

Mrs. Pendarves: A dancing girl!

Eleanor: Yes—a pretty, slim, graceful sylph of a dancing girl. You can tell by that how mad the man is.

Mrs. Pendarves: What shall we do?

Eleanor: Tell the men to be on the watch about the grounds to catch the maniac if he returns. Then let them be prepared to give assistance if he makes his way into the house. Tell Lord Canning of this, and warn him if the man takes us unawares, we must all humor him, and act out what he thinks us to be till help arrives, and, above all, take care not to contradict him, but agree with all he says. Lord Canning must preach, I must act, you must dance, and Kitty here must soothe and pet him. Remember, as you value our lives.

Mrs. Pendarves: I will! I will! Oh, that the men will catch and secure him!

(*Exit Mrs. Pendarves.*)

Kitty: A nice part in this ridiculous farce you have assigned me, Mistress Eleanor. Your plot is madder than I thought.

Eleanor: The case is desperate, Kitty; I have no chance against exposure but to turn Charles' weapons against himself. And as you plead his cause so warmly, I thought it only proper to let you do his soothing.

Kitty: I wish I could be as angry with you as you deserve, Nell; And poor Lord Canning and Mrs. Pendarves! Why do you treat them so? 'Tis a mean trick.

Eleanor: Since it must be done, it might as well be amusing. (*Suddenly.*) Kitty, if you would like a stroll in the garden, you needn't stay here with me.

(*Kitty looks at her narrowly.*)

Kitty: Suppose you come, too.

Eleanor: I am so tired, I would rather sit here and admire the garden in comfort.

Kitty: (*seating herself*) So would I.

Eleanor: I forgot, Kitty, all about the lovely gowns that came down from London yesterday for Lady Dorothy. Don't you want to look at them in my room?

Kitty: To-night will do as well.

Eleanor: (*suddenly*) You need not miss your ride because I am too tired to go. I will order the horses.

Kitty: I am better satisfied as I am.

Eleanor: (*laughing*) Oh, you provoking Kitty!

(*She shakes Kitty.*)

Don't you see I want to get rid of you before HE comes?

Kitty: (*calmly*) Now, how did you dream I could suspect it? (*Seriously.*) Was Charles right, Eleanor?

Eleanor: Nonsense. 'Tis all in the play.

Kitty: (*taking Eleanor's hand*) They are pretty little fingers. 'Twould be a thousand pities to burn them.

(*Laughs and runs off.*)

Eleanor: Am I playing with fire?

(*Sits down in deep thought. Lord Roxbury enters and comes towards her. She does not see him; he gazes at her a moment, then softly advances.*)

Lord Roxbury: Lady Dorothy!

Eleanor: Lord Roxbury!

(*She starts up and is confused at sight of him.*)

Lord Roxbury: Must we still be so formal? We are yet engaged, and I have made love so faithfully at your behest this week, I should have some reward.

Eleanor: What reward could you have, my lord?

Lord Roxbury: Call me Maurice.

Eleanor: 'Tis a small reward for so great a sacrifice, is it not? And Maurice— (*She lingers a little over the name*) hath a pleasant sound.

Lord Roxbury: Is there any other name that rings sweeter in your heart—Dor-othy?

Eleanor: My heart? What a question! How should I know what is in my heart? I never thought of looking.

Lord Roxbury: Then look now and tell me.

Eleanor: Nay, I am sure I shall find nothing worth the telling.

Lord Roxbury: If I thought there was another name that could make your heart throb where mine started no thrill, I would—

Eleanor: What would you do—Maurice?

Lord Roxbury: I would leave this place to-morrow, and never set eyes on your face again.

Eleanor: (*innocently*) What mean you by that? Why should you go away? Would that make you angry?

Lord Roxbury: It would make me miserable.

Eleanor: I do not understand. Are you not playing so bravely at love-making that I may have my freedom?

Lord Roxbury: Playing! What passion is left for earnest if men play at love as I have done? Dorothy, is there yet too much of the child about you for you to know that this play means to me life itself? Are your eyes yet too young in their innocent ignorance to read the passion in a man's?

Eleanor: Oh hush! You don't know what you are saying, Lord Roxbury!

Lord Roxbury: I love you, Dorothy.

Eleanor: Oh, no—no!

Lord Roxbury: Have I frightened you? And yet, child as you are, you must have felt that it was not all play.

Eleanor: You have known me but a week—

Lord Roxbury: And that week hath been a lifetime to me, sweetheart—a new, a better, a sweeter life than I dreamed existed on this earth. But a week? Till this week I have never lived!

Eleanor: (*faintly*) You but think so. You have known so many grand and beautiful women—your equals—I am only a simple unlearned girl—

Lord Roxbury: That is your charm to me, dearest. Listen to me, Dorothy. I have grown up in the midst of the world where women courted me for my rank and wealth till I despised them all. I saw only selfishness and hollowness and unwomanly eagerness to sell hearts for position and riches, and I scorned such hearts as not worth the buying. Then I met you—and I found what a woman could be. Nay, hear me out, Dorothy. My title, my wealth, were nothing to you. Young, fresh, inexperienced as you were, unknowing the world or yourself, I saw that nothing could buy your heart but the only thing that a king might envy a beggar for—love.

Eleanor: I know not myself, Lord Roxbury, I—

Lord Roxbury: This love hath made another man of me. Dorothy, you are too young, too innocent, to know what deceit, what sham are in the world. Not one of these grand and beautiful women you speak of is true. And you are all truth, all sincerity. In you, I could find that truth I sought when I believed men to be as they appeared, and which may later years taught me to cease seeking in the hearts of those around me.

Eleanor: (*faintly*) Then you could never forgive deceit in the one you loved?

Lord Roxbury: Love cannot deceive, Dorothy; not such a thing as I feel love to be now. Love and deceive! As soon seek sunlight in the night.

Eleanor: Then you could not forgive deceit?

Lord Roxbury: Had you experienced as much of it as I, you would not ask. Why, the women who play nightly on the London stage do not so assume to be what they are not, as the women that one meets in the world, and who act not so open and honest a lie. But sweetheart, have you no answer?

Eleanor: (*hastily*) Not now—not now! But tell me—these women of the stage—you have seen them? You know this Mistress Hallam, of whom we have heard even in our far-off school for her wonderful powers?

Lord Roxbury: Do you call me off so? 'Tis not of Mistress Hallam but of Lady Dorothy I would speak.

Eleanor: Nay, but I am curious, indeed. Tell me of her.

Lord Roxbury: There's naught to tell save that she is a woman who belongs to the public as no man cares for the women of his love to do—stared at nightly, talked of daily, with a string of young fools and oldrakes for her retinue, her name bandied about London, the property of every tongue, be it base or noble—I know her not, for I refused to join the train bending before the puppet queen of the hour. But why talk of her? What is there in common with the tinsel idol of London, tarnished with every idle touch, and the pure gold of a fresh young heart, unspoiled by the taint of the world? No more of her. But this engagement of ours, Dorothy? Can you not find it in your heart to let me woo you in earnest? Let me but woo you—none other shall win you.

Eleanor: I cannot answer—I cannot think—Let me go, Lord Roxbury, let me go!

(*She breaks from him and exits hastily. Roxbury starts after her, then stands still, looking after her.*)

Lord Roxbury: Poor little girl. I startled her. I must be more gentle with her. But I'll win her.

(*Enter Barry from garden, showing signs of anger and irritation.*)

Barry: Lord Roxbury!

Lord Roxbury: (*astonished*) Who are you?

Barry: (*with harsh laugh*) That is a question you might better ask of some others here, my lord. For instance, of the lady to whom you were so gallant here a moment ago.

Lord Roxbury: (*haughtily*) You speak of Lady Dorothy, fellow—

Barry: Lady Dorothy, indeed! 'Tis plain you know naught of Lady Dorothy Hastings, if you take the woman you have been making love to here for her.

Lord Roxbury: Once for all, fellow, tell me who you are, and what you mean by such wild talk as this.

Barry: Have you ever heard your friend, Sir Harry Holland, in London, speak of Charles Barry of Drury Lane?

Lord Roxbury: Yes, often; but what—

Barry: Well, Lord Roxbury, I am he. And have you ever heard your friend, Sir

Harry, speak of Mistress Eleanor Hallam, the famous actress, also of Drury Lane, to whom he wished to present you, and whose acquaintance you did refuse?

Lord Roxbury: Yes, but—

Barry: Well, Lord Roxbury, that lady you had with you but a moment ago, is she.

Lord Roxbury: You are mad!

Barry: Saner than you, my lord, for she hath juggled your very senses from you. I came here from London to track her. That woman within there, masquerading here as Lady Dorothy Hastings, of Gloster Park, is Mistress Eleanor Hallam, of Drury Lane Theater.

Lord Roxbury: You expect me to believe so wild a tale as this?

Barry: Oh, I have proofs. Here are letters from Sir Harry Holland—you know his hand?

(*He hands him letters.*)

Lord Roxbury: (*bewildered, taking them*) 'Tis his hand.

Barry: In them he doth tell of seeing Lady Dorothy, who he met in France but a year ago, in London, where she hath privy married Sir Robert Estcourt this last week.

Lord Roxbury: Stop, man, for God's sake!

Barry: (*bitterly*) Aye, I see you are in the toils where many a man hath been before you.

Lord Roxbury: But if this tale of yours be true, why this masquerade?

Barry: Eleanor Hallam is noted in London for the tricks of her blood. She knew of your rejection of her acquaintance, and when Lady Dorothy came to her secretly and begged her to personate her here till she was safely married to Sir Robert Estcourt, Mistress Hallam vowed it was too rare a chance to let slip for your proper punishment. I have been skulking about here for a thief for a week; but she begged me so hard not to betray her, promising to end all and go back to London, that I yielded. But I felt she was playing me false, and when I saw her with you here—you kissing her hand—she smiling on you—

(*He stops, choked with passion. The Earl has grown very grave, and is regarding him keenly.*)

Barry: (*suddenly*) I got the story from Lady Dorothy's maid—I bribed the girl to come here—she is easily produced; she can give you the whole story— where you may find Lady Dorothy in London now.

Lord Roxbury: I see!

Barry: You believe me, my lord, do you not?

Lord Roxbury: Yes, I believe you. I see that in your passion which verifies your words.

Barry: She hath played with us both, but I will expose her and revenge—

Lord Roxbury: Mr. Barry, you have

opened my eyes, and I thank you. Will you be guided by me in this matter?

Barry: What do you propose?

Lord Roxbury: Leave this place at once, and give this matter into my hands. Let her not have the slightest hint that her plot hath been discovered. 'Tis a rare good play—'twould be a thousand pities to finish it so soon. Suppose we carry it on?

Barry: To turn Mistress Nell's weapons against herself—that would be a fine revenge, indeed!

Lord Roxbury: But you must go away, or she will suspect.

Barry: I am content to have it so.

Lord Roxbury: Will you take to London for me a letter to Sir Harry, bearing on this matter of Lady Dorothy's marriage?

Barry: Willingly.

Lord Roxbury: I will not be long writing it. In the meantime, be careful that you are not seen. Down there, in the shrubbery, past the fountain, I will come to you with the latter.

(*Exit Lord Roxbury.*)

Barry: So you thought, Mistress Nell, I was safely off, and you could amuse yourself in peace with the love-making of this sprig of rank and fashion.

(*Enter Mrs. Pendarves in nervous agitation.*)

Mrs. Pendarves: Dorothy, are the ser- vants—Where is she? (*sees Barry. She jumps.*) I wonder who that is?

Barry: I'll make her dance to my tune!

Mrs. Pendarves: (*screams*) Oh, the maniac himself! Good Lord, what shall I do!

(*Barry turns at scream and advances. Bows.*)

Barry: Pardon me, madam—

(*Mrs. Pendarves in great terror, begins to dance. Barry looks at her in amazement.*)

Barry: Is the woman crazy?

Mrs. Pendarves: How he glares at me! (*Keeps on dancing vigorously.*) Lord Canning! Lord Canning! Come quick- ly! (*To Barry, almost breathless as she dances.*) I'm calling the Bishop—he will be pleased to know you are here—Oh, I can't keep this up!

(*Enter Lord Canning.*)

Lord Canning: What is it, Mrs. Pendarves? (*Sees Barry.*) Who is this?

(*Mrs. Pendarves pauses and wipes her face.*)

Mrs. Pendarves: The maniac! As you value your life, preach!

Lord Canning: I'll call the men—

Mrs. Pendarves: Don't leave me—for heaven's sake, don't leave me! He's look- ing at us—preach—preach!

Barry: What are they whispering about? Is the old lady a lunatic, and that her keeper? Sir, will you relive my mind by speaking—

Lord Canning: (*gesturing*) Dearly beloved, I exhort you to a good end—man's life is but grass—Solomon, in all his glory could not paint the lily—how the devil can I preach,—I don't even know the texts!

Mrs. Pendarves: (*feverishly*) Say anything to keep him quiet!

Barry: Madam—Yes, yes—do you like this better?

(*Goes off into a livelier step.*)

Barry: Sir—

Lord Canning: And thirdly, I wish to impress upon you the point the prognostication of evil as foretold, and the residuum of earthly vanity, and the errant sensibilities of man's peccant nature that availeth not against destruction—

Barry: The keeper is as crazy as his patient! Has Lady Dorothy a crazy family?

Mrs. Pendarves: Just a minute, if you please, for breath! I am not tired—oh, no, only for breath! (*Calling.*) Dorothy! Mistress Hayden! Sally! Walker! Doggett!

Barry: I must humor them. You dance admirably, madam. One would not expect such agility from your years. Sir, you excellent exhortations I shall lay to heart. Now, I must, with your leave—

(*Enter Eleanor, Kitty and Sally.*)

Sally: Lor, Mistress—my lydy, hif hit haint Mr. Barry!

Eleanor: Hush! Run and tell the men to come here. Tell them the crazy man is in the drawing-room.

Sally: (*screams*) The crazy—Oh, Lor!

(*She runs off.*)

Eleanor: Why, who is this?

Barry: (*enraged*) You know well enough. Come away from these insane people before more harm is done!

Eleanor: Lord Canning and Mrs. Pendarves insane! What is the man thinking of?

Barry: Lord Canning! Mrs. Pendarves! Now I will tell them!

Mrs. Pendarves: Dorothy, for the love of heaven, don't irritate him! Have you sent Sally for the men?

Eleanor: Yes—they must be here soon.

Barry: This is not your niece, Lady Dorothy Hastings—'tis Mistress Eleanor Hallam, an actress of Drury Lane Theater, in London.

Mrs. Pendarves: Yes, yes, we know she is Mistress Hallam.

Lord Canning: To be sure she is Mistress Hallam.

Barry: (*amazed*) You know that?

Both: Of course, we know it.

Barry: You know Lady Dorothy is in London, married?

Mrs. Pendarves: Certainly Lady Dorothy is in London—who says she is not?

(*Barry, discomfited and astounded, looks from one to the other. Kitty comes up to him, smooths his head.*)

Kitty: There, there, Charles, they know everything. Come now, be quiet.

(*He turns savagely to Eleanor.*)

Barry: Have you bewitched them, too?

Mrs. Pendarves: Act, Dorothy, for the Lord's sake, act!

(*Barry turns suddenly to Mrs. Pendarves. She begins again to dance. He looks at Lord Canning, who raises his hand, and in sonorous tones says:*)

Lord Canning: "Mend thy ways, for the day of retribution cometh, my brethren."

(*Barry turns in bewilderment to the others; Kitty pats him, smooths his forehead, and in dumb show, begs him to be calm. He shakes her off angrily. Eleanor strikes attitude. As she delivers the speech, which she does with a view to taunting him, he gets more and more angry.*)

Eleanor: "Oh, what a noble mind is here o'er thrown!
   The courtier's, soldier's scholar's, eye, tongue, sword,
   The expectancy and rose of the fair state,
   The glass of fashion and the mold of form,
   The observed of all observers—"[17]

Barry: Now I know what it all means. You—

Mrs. Pendarves: Go on, Dorothy, go on—distract his attention any way till the men come!

(*Barry, infuriated, tries to reach Eleanor, but is restrained by Kitty, whom he cannot throw off, and who soothes him, pets him, pats him in an exaggerated way. Whenever he looks at Mrs. Pendarves, she begins to dance; when he looks at Lord Canning, the latter gestures solemnly and mumbles oratorically.*)

Barry: I tell you, that girl is playing on all of you, and leading you like a flock of sheep!

Lord Canning: (*conciliatory*) To be sure she is—to be sure she is.

Mrs. Pendarves: (*out of breath*) Yes—yes—lead—flock—sheep—

Eleanor: (*courtesying*) Good day, fair sir; you thought to befool a poor maiden, to take her unawares, like a noble gentleman, a gallant gentleman, a kind, a loving gentleman—and, faith! 'tis so comical how fate has turned your point 'gainst yourself, I must laugh—laugh—laugh—ha! ha! ha!

(*She bursts into a fit of laughter, pointing her finger at Barry, who stands staring at her; she goes on laughing convulsively, the laugh trailing off into a sob. Kitty looks at her curiously.*)

Barry: I'm damned if I stay here to be made a fool of any longer! Or have you all lost your own wits! Let me go!

(*He struggles with Kitty, wrenches himself free, and takes a step forward. Mrs.*

Pendarves screams, Lord Canning rushes out of his way, Kitty wrings her hands, Eleanor breaks out into another peal of hysterical laughter. Just then the men rush in and throw themselves upon Barry. He fights furiously, but they overpower him and drag him off.)

Mrs. Pendarves: The wretch! Oh, he has killed me!

(*She falls fainting; Lord Canning rushes to pick her up.*)

Eleanor: Help him, Kitty, to take Mrs. Pendarves inside. If I touch the old cat I'd pinch her before I could stop myself at all!

(*Lord Canning, with Kitty's support, assists Mrs. Pendarves, who moans and wails, half-conscious, as they take her off. Enter Lord Roxbury from opposite direction from others. He has a letter in his hand, which, on seeing Eleanor, he slips into his pocket.*)

Eleanor: Why did you not come sooner to help us with the madman?

Lord Roxbury: (*apparently surprised*) I heard no madman. You mean to say one was here?

Eleanor: Yes, but they have taken him off. Aunt Pendarves is having hysterics comfortably in her own room, Uncle Canning is soothing his feelings with my best wine, and so we are—alone.

(*She pauses a little on the last word.*)

Lord Roxbury: Alone—with you and love, Dorothy? O love, how can you bid me go from you!

Eleanor: You frighten me, Lord Roxbury—let me go!

Lord Roxbury: Dorothy, dearest, shall I swear again how I love you?—that I must win you, my darling, for my own—my queen, my wife?

Eleanor: (*seriously*) You really love me, Lord Roxbury?

Lord Roxbury: Can you doubt it, sweetheart? Ah, Dorothy, you do not know what the love of a man like me, deceived from his childhood, never loving before, can be. I love your truth, your innocence, your perfect freedom from guile—they are so dear to me, Dorothy; they are jewels I have sought for so long, and which I would be prouder to wear than my coronet.

Eleanor: I cannot answer you yet, Lord Roxbury; there are reasons—

Lord Roxbury: What reasons have found lodging in that dear little simple brain of yours?

Eleanor: Say it is my whim, my caprice— but urge me not. You know, I shortly give my grand ball— (*Faltering*) my first ball. I will answer your question then, if you choose again to ask it.

Lord Roxbury: If I choose! What choice have I when love drives me with a goading spur? But you will answer me at the ball, sweet?

Eleanor: (*extending her hand*) At the ball—Maurice!

(He kisses her hand and goes out. As he goes, he fixes on her a peculiar look, smiles meaningfully and disappears. Eleanor begins to pace the room nervously.)

Eleanor: Oh, if I have never begun it! If I had never begun it!

(Enter Kitty.)

Kitty: Eleanor, what a peril your wit overcame. Charles was wild—poor Charles!

Eleanor: Oh Kitty, I am a wicked, wicked girl! I have gained my point—Lord Roxbury is in love with me, but such a manly, honest love! He hath told me how all deceived him, and he looks for happiness in the heart of a young innocent girl, fresh, unspoiled, unlike those—oh, how he will suffer when he knows I have so cruelly, so heartlessly deceived him!—made such a noble heart my plaything! He has bared his soul to me! But how could I know it was like this!

Kitty: Eleanor, is it all pity for Lord Roxbury that makes you so repentant and so miserable? You are not the merry, mischievous girl who came as Lady Dorothy to Gloster Park. *(Tenderly.)* What is it, Nell?

Eleanor: I have trifled shamefully with him, I have been thoughtless, wicked— but that is not the worst. Oh, Kitty, I love him—I love him—I love him!

(She bursts into tears and flings herself into Kitty's arms.)

(Curtain.)

Act III

Scene—Anteroom to drawing room at Gloster Park. Ball is in progress. Lord Roxbury and Eleanor enter from ball room and come down.

Lord Roxbury: You promised if I asked a question at the ball, you would answer it, Dorothy.

(Eleanor plays nervously with her fan.)

Eleanor: But before you ask it, Lord Roxbury, I must tell you something. I—I—have deceived you.

Lord Roxbury: *(laughing)* Deceived me! Little Dorothy deceived me! Why, that were too good a jest. But in what wise, sweet lady, am I the victim of your guile?

Eleanor: Suppose, Lord Roxbury, I am not the simple girl you take me to be—

Lord Roxbury: I have no doubt you think yourself so wise that Solomon himself would be but a simpleton beside you. But come—this terrible deceit you have practiced upon me?

Eleanor: He makes it too hard!

Lord Roxbury: Well, sweetheart, I am waiting for your confession.

Eleanor: I did not know it would be so hard as this!

Lord Roxbury: Then do not spoil your ball, my child. Heaven only knows what thought has come into your brain that you have tricked me, but I do not fear the secrets of your white soul, dear heart. Keep your deceit and your confession; they have no terrors for me, though to your innocent, true mind they may seem matters of awful weight. Consider your confession made, forgiven, and think no more on't.

Eleanor: No, no, 'tis no such sight a thing as that.

Lord Roxbury: Do you think, Dorothy, I could treat so lightly your scruples did I not know how fantastic they are? You are truth itself; I do not fear the airy troubles that some girlish indiscretions are making in your mind, for I know that indeed are simple and innocent, my little flower, whose maidenly bloom the world's coarse touch hath never profaned.

Eleanor: Nay, now you *must* listen to me, Lord Roxbury—

(*Enter Mrs. Pendarves*)

Mrs. Pendarves: Lord Roxbury, your aunt, the Duchess of Suxton, has arrived, and wishes you to attend her.

Lord Roxbury: By all means, let us attend the Duchess. Dorothy, I go with Mrs. Pendarves, but my soul, my heart, I leave with you.

(*He goes off with Mrs. Pendarves. Kitty comes in to Eleanor.*)

Kitty: Eleanor, remember watchful eyes are on you. You will betray yourself.

Eleanor: Betray myself! Kitty, I tried just now to tell him—he laughs at me; I could not go on. He believes me but a silly school girl with fantastic scru-

ples. My hints of deceit and confession amused him. Oh, Kitty, what shall I do?

Kitty: Hush, Nell, you must go on with it now.

Eleanor: If he did not love[18] me it would be easy. But I love him—and it is torture!

Kitty: Poor Nelly! You have found out at last that you have a heart.

Eleanor: I will brave it out. Lady Dorothy is here, Kitty.

Kitty: Here!

Eleanor: Yes; I have arranged it so that she and Sir Robert Estcourt will be announced shortly. My mind is changed, Kitty. I shall tell of my deceit publicly, and shall laugh it off as a fine jest. I could not tell him now—and you will help me to laugh it off—you will, Kitty, for heaven's sake, you will? (*She seizes Kitty's hands convulsively*) Let him think me what he will, let him hate me for playing him so vile a trick—but let him never know— Oh, let him never know—

Kitty: Eleanor, Eleanor, you will betray yourself!

(*Mrs. Pendarves comes in very excitedly with Lord Canning.*)

Mrs. Pendarves: Dorothy, who do you think is here with the guests—heaven only knows how he got it!

Eleanor: (*with horror*) Not the crazy man!

Mrs. Pendarves: Yes, the crazy man. He must have got out of the madhouse again, and only think! if he makes us dance and preach as he did—and before all these people—I shall die of shame!

Lord Canning: I must summon the men at once and have him taken out.

Eleanor: You will do nothing of the sort, Lord Canning.

Lord Canning: Is the girl mad, too?

Eleanor: Understand me, Lord Canning. I am mistress here, and if you have that man put out by the servants, out you go with him.

Lord Canning: (*gasping*) Turn me out!

Eleanor: Mortify me before my guests, and I will humiliate you before them.

Mrs. Pendarves: (*nervously*) Don't irritate her, Lord Canning; she hath a most vile and revengeful temper. She will do terrible things if you anger her.

Eleanor: The man is not a maniac. Lord Canning, Mrs. Pendarves would speak to our guests and wishes your arm.

(*Mrs. Pendarves clutches at it and Lord Canning, with angry looks, allows himself to be drawn away.*)

Kitty: Oh, Nell, how you have made those two fear you.

Eleanor: 'Tis their guilty consciences. Ah, Kitty, there is nothing so troublesome as a bad conscience when it thinks it is going to be found out. But, Kitty, go, and if Charles is here, bring him to me.

Kitty: Eleanor, suppose he makes a scene?

Eleanor: I think he will not when he finds that I leave Gloster Park tonight.

Kitty: To-night!

Eleanor: I could not sleep under its roof again. There is a cottage near here where we can pass the night, and to-morrow we'll to London. Go, find Charles.

(*Kitty turns to go, take a few steps. Barry appears and comes to meet them; stands smiling maliciously.*)

Kitty: Nell, he is here!

Eleanor: (*calmly*) Ah, Mr. Barry, so you have done us the honor to attend our ball.

Barry: Yes; even overlooking the fact that I was neither invited nor wanted.

Eleanor: You always were such a sweet-tempered, forgiving, obliging creature, Charles, dear.

Barry: (*furiously*) Don't drive me too far, Mistress Eleanor. That trick you played me the other day when you had me dragged from here as a madman—

Eleanor: I thought I was rid of a spy.

Barry: A spy!

Eleanor: I can find harsher names if you care to hear them.

Barry: I know your tongue too well to doubt that. But I am not to be driven off this time by names. I had too much trouble in persuading the officers into hands your men gave me, to let me go.

Eleanor: What do you mean to do?

Barry: (*with malicious smile*) Nothing.

Eleanor: (*astonished*) Nothing!

Barry: I am come to witness your triumph.

Eleanor: Charles, you are here for no good purpose. What is it?

Barry: I told my purposes too freely before. You have made me wiser.

Eleanor: You mean a public exposure before all my guests?

Barry: If there is such an exposure, I will not be the one to make it. But I have not come here for naught. Rely on that, Mistress Eleanor.

(*Exit Barry.*)

Eleanor: Kitty, Charles means mischief, and I cannot fathom what it is. But he is sure of revenge. I saw it in his eyes.

Kitty: I wish the evening were well over!

Eleanor: I will forestall him. I will send for Lady Dorothy. Then I will tell the tale of our adventure as a great jest.

(*Exit Eleanor.*)

Kitty: Poor Nell! This jest hath turned out sad earnest for her!

(*Lord Roxbury enters.*)

Lord Roxbury: Was not Lady Dorothy but just now with you?

Kitty: Yes, Lord Roxbury; she is gone to prepare a great surprise for her guests.

Lord Roxbury: Are you so sure it will be a surprise to *all* of her guests? (*Kitty looks alarmed.*) What so meet as a merry plot against the lady of the revels at her own betrothal ball?

Kitty: I do not understand you, my lord.

(*Exit Kitty.*)

Lord Roxbury: A merry plot! 'Twill be earnest before it ends—and yet—how she made me love her!—and, damn her! I love her still!

(*Enter Barry.*)

Lord Roxbury: You here? Did you not give me your word to go to London and leave this in my hands?

Barry: I must be assured first that she shall be punished for the trick she hath played.

Lord Roxbury: *Must*, sir?

Barry: (*peremptorily*) What are you going to do?

Lord Roxbury: (*haughtily*) The matter lies between Mistress Hallam and myself. 'Tis no affair of yours.

Barry: (*passionately*) It is, my Lord Roxbury, and if you do naught to humiliate her, I will make her and you—yes, you, too—the laughing stock of London.

Lord Roxbury: Dare attempt it, and there will be a reckoning you will remember to the last day of your life.

Barry: Oh, I'll meet you, my lord—

Lord Roxbury: Meet me! Think I would cross swords with you? I will not fight you—no—but I will flog you as I would a dog. Now go. Or must I—(*Imperatively.*) Go.

Barry: I will go, not for fear of you, but to London, where lies revenge on you both.

(*He rushes out.*)

(*Enter Eleanor.*)

Eleanor: Kitty! Ah, Lord Roxbury, I was about to seek you. I have so good a jest with which to astonish and amuse you all—

Lord Roxbury: So Mistress Hayden hath been telling me. I am all on fire with curiosity to know this merry jest.

Eleanor: You shall know soon, and 'tis so good that when you find how cleverly and merrily you have been tricked, your would-be frowns will be chased away by the laughter of the thing.

Lord Roxbury: Why should I wish to frown, Lady Dorothy?

Eleanor: Why, because some do not like a trick which hath fooled them, though it be but a merry one and played in all goodness of heart.

Lord Roxbury: Play your merry jests, if it please you, sweetheart. Only be true to me in things too deep for laughter.

Eleanor: (*with a gasp*) Come.

(*Enter others and Lady Dorothy and Sir Robert Estcourt.*)

Eleanor: Let me present my guests of honor for whom, indeed, this ball was given—Sir Robert and Lady Estcourt.

(*Sir Robert and Lady Estcourt bow, the former proudly, the latter timidly.*)

Lord Roxbury: (*to Eleanor*) Excellently done—a merry jest, in truth. So the real Lady Dorothy hath come into her own.

Eleanor: (*horrified*) *You know*!

Lord Roxbury: (*bowing*) Oh, I have known for some time of the entertaining comedy Mistress Eleanor Hallam hath been playing at Gloster Park, and I flatter myself she will give me some slight credit as an actor, too, though new to the boards.

Eleanor: You knew it all along?

Lord Roxbury: Long enough to help along the play.

Eleanor: Charles Barry?

Lord Roxbury: Yes.

Eleanor: How much do you know?

Lord Roxbury: That I will tell in a toast. (*He takes a glass as Doggett serves all with wine.*) Before our ball begins, let me toast our fair hostess—our queen of the feast. Let us worldlings drink to a fair young girl, a fresh young heart, with the freedom of her youth upon her face and the innocence of her school days in her heart. Drink to her ignorance of the world, to the sincerity which would honor a man's love, to the simplicity that would shrink from playing with his heart, to the truth that would never think of turning, like the puppets of the theater, all life and emotion into a painted comedy—I drink to the maidenly modesty which is so rare in these days of tricks and guile—that could never deceive nor lure by the trust placed in her—a bumper to the health of the mistress of Gloster Park.

Lady Dorothy: (*timidly*) A pretty toast, my lord.

Sir Robert: But bitter, too, Lord Roxbury.

Lord Roxbury: I could tell you of a man so deceived and beguiled, so fooled by the appearance of this sweet, maidenly sincerity—so led and lured by practiced coquetry under the guise of girlish truth, that man of the world as he was—

All: (*starting forward*) Well?

Lord Roxbury: A very dear friend of mine.

Eleanor: Let me finish the toast, my lord, and drink to the art which hath deceived all here, to the art that made a comedy, indeed, to help the real Lady of Gloster Park to the happiness you all would have denied her; for Lady Estcourt is the real Lady Dorothy Hastings.

All: Lady Dorothy Hastings!

Lord Canning: (*violently*) And who are you, then, who hath so imposed upon us?

(*Eleanor makes a sweeping curtsy.*)

Eleanor: Mistress Eleanor Hallam, indifferently well known to the fashion of London as the leading actress of the popular theater there, and who hath this fortnight played her best part in the comedy of her life.

(*Great astonishment. Mrs. Pendarves gasps in a vain effort to say something. Lord Canning sinks astounded and staring, on a seat. In the general astonishment, Lord Roxbury comes up close to Eleanor.*)

Lord Roxbury: And the end of it all has come for you—and for me.

(*He goes out.*)

Eleanor: The end!

Lord Canning: The impudent jade!

Mrs. Pendarves: And so it is but a common actress, a player woman who paints her face and makes herself a public show upon the stage, who has been intruding herself as our equal, who has been passing herself off as a lady of quality—

Sir Robert: Madam, please you, Mistress Hallam is the friend and honored guest of my wife, who, I beg you to remember, is the mistress of Gloster Park, and who welcomes none more heartily than Mistress Hallam within its walls.

Lady Dorothy: Yes, dear Mistress Hallam—

Mrs. Pendarves: (*vindictively*) Then, as she is to stay, will she not do something to justify her presence? Let her be the show here that she is paid to make herself in London, and use her trade to amuse the guests whom she hath befooled into thinking herself a person of birth and quality like themselves.

Lord Canning: Yes, a good idea, faith, and we will pay her as we do the other servants to our diversion.

Sir Robert: (*indignantly*) Mistress Hallam is the friend of my wife. No insults shall be offered her here—

Eleanor: Nay, Sir Robert, I thank your courtesy, but I am not ashamed of my trade, as Mrs. Pendarves hath it. (*To the others.*)

As Lady Dorothy Hastings, you all accepted me as your equal. As Eleanor Hallam, I am a creature not fit to mingle with you. But what are all you of the world but actors? What is the man who makes use of his position and standing in the esteem of the world, to rob the orphan committed to his care, but an actor? (*Lord Canning winces.*) What is the woman who hides vindictiveness and neglect of all honest duty under sanctimonious cant, but an actress? (*Mrs. Pendarves glares at her.*) Are such unknown among you? We actors of the stage show all that is good in virtue, all that is hideous and dangerous in vice. But you actors of the world trample down virtue and uplift vice; your acting is not for the moment, but 'tis to last, and in the end to drag down lives and hearts and souls with the fall of the curtain.

Mrs. Pendarves: You dare to say we are no better than play actors?

Eleanor: No, I had no such meaning. I mean that actors of your stamp are the worse.

Lord Canning: Your presence, madam—

Eleanor: My presence here need disturb none a moment longer. I came to play

my comedy—it is played out. I have no desire to stay.

Lady Dorothy: You will stay as my guest, Mistress Hallam?

Sir Robert: As our honored guest, Mistress Hallam.

Eleanor: Take my place, Lady Dorothy—your place—and lead the guests in the dance.

(*Lady Dorothy makes a gesture of appeal, but Eleanor with a decided shake of the head, points to the ball room. They go off, leaving Eleanor and Kitty.*)

Eleanor: Kitty, will you tell Sally to get together our belongings? I must leave here to-night.

Kitty: Poor Nell!

(*Exit Kitty.*)

(*As Eleanor goes up, dejected and drooping, Lord Roxbury comes in with cloak and hat, and confronts her.*)

Eleanor: You!

Lord Roxbury: I could not go.

Eleanor: You know—

Lord Roxbury: Yes. I know that I love you now as when we sat on the terrace—I, too, have played out my play and found it earnest.

Eleanor: Earnest!

Lord Roxbury: I knew my heart was gone even when I tried to call it back. Sweetheart, only be true to me, and play whatever other part you will.

Eleanor: But it was Lady Dorothy you
wooed—

Lord Roxbury: No matter, since 'tis Eleanor Hallam I love.

Eleanor: Then you forgive—

Lord Roxbury: Forgive! It is you that
must forgive that I wounded you. But I
had learned too well to love you.

Eleanor: But we are so apart.

Lord Roxbury: (*gayly*) In truth, we are.
We should be no further apart than
heart to heart!

(*He flings down his cloak and hat and
catches her in his arms.*)

(*Curtain.*)

Emily Emerson Lantz (1862-1931)

Emily Emerson Lantz, an honorary
member of the Women's Literary Club
of Baltimore, contributed her talents to
local news sources, such as the *Baltimore
Sun* and *Herald,* for much of her adult
life. Though she was born in Lancaster,
Pennsylvania, she was widely recognized
for her knowledge of Maryland—and especially, Baltimore—history. (Her profiles
of the environs of Roland Park and north
Charles Street are featured in the Local
Favorites section of the anthology.)

But Lantz wasn't just a booster of Baltimore. She also took progressive positions on
societal issues and made sure that they were
covered in the local press. She wrote about
women in the workplace, women writers,
and female business leaders and activists,
revealing her to be one of the most liberal
members of the WLCB. Lantz was one of the
Baltimore Sun's first female reporters. Later in
life, Lantz went blind, though she remained

dedicated to journalism and she continued to
write by dictating to her sister.

This section features three of Lantz's social commentaries, all of which were originally published in the *Baltimore Sun*. The
first work, "The 'Registered Nurse,'" details
the extensive training and role of the profession, crediting women in the position
for their public service. The second, "Baltimore's Effort for Healthier Babies Through
Bureau of Child Hygiene," emphasizes the
importance of registering births, and taking efforts to ensure safe practices for children. Finally, "Her Centenary Sees Susan
B. Anthony's Cause Near to Success" celebrates the woman Lantz terms "the greatest leader in the cause of equal suffrage the
United States has known," showing her
dedication to female trailblazers. All three
pieces demonstrate that, through her compelling literary achievements, Lantz was
both a critic of her society, and a crusad-

er of her time, who sought to improve the life of all people, especially women, in the city, state, and country she knew and loved.
—H. Flynn and N. Day

The "Registered Nurse" (1906)

The reason firm, the temperate will,
Endurance, foresight, strength and skill;
A perfect woman, nobly plann'd,
To warn, to comfort, and command;
And yet a Spirit still, and bright
With something of an angel light.
—*William Wordsworth*[1]

The month of June is pre-eminently the season for changing or bestowal of titles and the conferring of academic degrees indicative of proficiency in some art or science. It is due to the multiplicity of June weddings that one has to suddenly adjust their mental faculties to the unaccustomed addressing of some Lady Kitty Bristol as Mrs. William Ashe,[2] and to the conferring of scholastic degrees that one must remember to introduce a college chum by the august title of doctor of philosophy or medicine.

Such titles, to be legal, must be sanctioned by the authority of the state, and the present season of June marks in Baltimore the state's recognition of a professional title that has been adopted by only four states in the Union and for which the same professional class in England is still asking recognition of the British government. This is the title "registered nurse," expressed by the abbreviation R. N., which carries with it assurance to the professional world and the public that the

woman privileged to bear this title has pursued a course of professional training in the care of the sick for a specified length of time in a nurses' training school qualified to give an intellectual course of study and a practical course of nursing adapted to the most successful ministration to the sick. The appellation "registered nurse" indicates that those bearing it have attained, by proficiency in the care of the sick, a diploma of graduation from one or more recognized training schools and have stood the final test of examination by a board of examiners appointed by the state. Thus persons so registered enter upon their public service of nursing bearing, like the coin of the realm, the government stamp and guarantee of professional fitness for the duties they assume.

Hitherto the term "trained nurse" has indicated that the person calling herself such has had some training under training-school auspices in attendance upon the sick, but the degree of excellence of that training was known only to professional medical circles acquainted with the standing of the training school where the instruction was received.

State registration and the establishment of a standard of fitness gives a definite legal status to the professional nurse and effectually prevents incompetent and unskillful persons from occupying this status or pretending to have it. Such registration in no wise interferes with anyone pursuing the profession of nursing, but it effectually distinguishes between those who have given several years of their life to preparatory training, intellectual and practical, and others who have not done so.

New York, New Jersey, Virginia, and North Carolina have adopted state registration of nurses on the principle that both nurse and invalid benefit thereby. State registration, to whatever profession applied, stands for the safeguarding of everyone affected by it. Both lawyer and public receive by state registration protection against the shyster; the physician and public benefit by protection against the charlatan; the clergyman is officially ordained that church and public may be protected from frauds practiced under a cloak of sanctity. Thus wherever vital interests are concerned the government should, and generally does, guard against inexperienced, careless or fraudulent methods.

One writer has said in regard to trained nursing: "It is unique in being perhaps the only profession unreservedly assigned to women—in which their pre-eminent fitness is not disputed, and in which they occupy all the higher positions. In other lines of life women either struggle in ineffectual competition with men or occupy the subordinate or less well-paid posts."

Through the American Federation of Nurses, the nursing profession of the United States is admitted to the National Council of Women.

Since the establishment, thirty years ago, of a system of trained nursing in the United States, the field of usefulness for experienced nurses has constantly broadened, until at the present time the trained nurse is one of the most important factors in municipal life, and her sphere has been extended along lines that a few years ago were wholly undreamed of.

When the first training schools were established, beyond a few positions in hospitals, private nursing was the only career open to the nurse who had spent two years at a hospital. Until about twelve years ago, according to the best authorities, private nursing continued to occupy more than three-fourths of the nurses. Fifteen years ago there were thirty-five training schools for nurses organized, where there are now 867. A remarkable increase in the number of hospitals in the United States—the latest reports show about 1,500 hospitals—together with these training schools, opened a large and important province for nurses in institutions.

Supply and Demand

In this case, the supply has created a demand. Here is offered a body of disciplined women, women educated in head and hand, whose motto, like that of the Prince of Wales, is, "I serve." The world has always need of the helpful man or woman, and the helpfulness of the trained nurse has become quickly apparent. Experimental district nursing has rapidly grown to be a municipal necessity, and the one or two district nursing associations established have increased in number to 220, employing between 500 and 600 nurses. The trend of modern development in medicine and surgery and the keen and complicated warfare of science against disease have opened up long-protracted battles between the powers of life and death, where physicians are the commanding officers and nurses the soldiers on vigilant watch and in active fight.

The visiting nurse has become an almost indispensable factor in the administration of a large city, in that she can discover and report to health boards unsanitary conditions of living unknown to official inspectors who lack her opportunity for daily observation in the very heart of things. "As a server of the community rather than the individual her work has expanded from the narrow limits of private charity into the broad lines of public service."[3]

In large hospitals the supervision and control of all nursing is vested in the superintendent of nurses, and frequently the supervision and control of domestic affairs as well. In smaller hospitals a nurse is often the chief executive officer of the entire institution, and not the least of her duties is that of instruction by lecture and in classrooms. The complexity and variety of these demands upon her capabilities have produced in the trained nurse a definite demand for the highly qualified woman with some gift for imparting knowledge—one who is not only mistress in the art of nursing, but can transit her knowledge to others.

Instructors of nursing are now a recognized feature of some of the best training schools for nursing, and this has opened still another province in training-school work. Statistics show for the past year about 2,200 pupils in training in the nursing schools of this country, and the high ideals of the woman guiding and directing this great educational and ministering work is shown in the report of one superintendent of nurses, who says concerning this instructive branch:

"Every one of these pupils should be from the time she enters the school under the teaching and guidance of the most able, skillful nurse instructors which we can produce, just as truly as they should be under the influence and inspiration of women of intellect, of education and culture and the noblest personal character."[4]

The hospital and training school for nurses are interdependent upon one another. The hospital experience is indispensable as supplying the field for the practical instruction of the nurses' training, and the establishment of a training school for nurses in connection with the hospital is proved to be the least expensive method of caring for the sick. In the most representative schools the nurses neither receive wages nor pay any tuition fees, the service rendered by them being regarded as equal to the value of their education, while the hospital gains in the fact that a group of scholars feel greater enthusiasm in their work than paid servitors, and also in the fact that the class of young women presenting themselves as candidates for instruction in nursing is higher when financial remuneration is not an incentive to their undertaking the work.

The demand for nurses in private cases or for special attendance upon patients during hospital treatment has also greatly increased, due probably to the advanced prosperity of the country and individual ability to pay for such a luxury and due, most of all, to the real satisfaction and comfort afforded by the attendance during sickness of a nurse conscientious and capable in the discharge of her duties. Protracted cases of nervous or mental disorder are largely dependent upon intelligent nursing for the recovery of the patient. Saving of valuable time to the physician is another important result of securing experience and judgment in a nurse, since the physician knows such a one can be depended upon either to notify him if a serious change in the condition of his patient occurs or to act intelligently herself in an emergency.

The trained nurse is now found in the social settlement, the public schools, the inspection of tenements, the control and relief of tuberculosis, the army corps, in district nursing in rural communities, in the nursing of Pasteur patients, and such a trust reposed in the individual requires some guarantee that the latter has been proved both in character and attainments worthy of the confidence she inspired.

It was felt that a nurse to represent worthily the profession of nursing must have been instructed not merely in one, but every department of surgery and medicine. If a patient suffering from a broken limb develops pneumonia or typhoid fever, the nurse must be as well qualified to attend one class of illness as the other. This determination to bring the standard of nursing instruction to a definite status of proved ability led to the successful effort of the Maryland State Association of Graduate Nurses to have a bill providing for the State registration of nurses passed by the General Assembly of Maryland.

Sets a Definite Standard

The bill is regarded as peculiarly happy in its framing since it sets a definite standard for registered nurses, without in the smallest way interfering with either voluntary or paid nursing by others.

The bill provides that the Maryland State Association of Graduate Nurses, which includes nurses from all the most representative training schools of the state, shall nominate for examiners twelve of its members of not less than five years' experience in their profession. From among these the governor of the state shall appoint five members for differing terms of service, upon whom shall rest the responsibility of deciding the acceptance or otherwise of candidates for the degree of registered nurse. This board of examiners shall meet at specified times, and it will include in its duties the prosecution of any persons violating the provisions of the act. The requirements for securing registration after the first of the present month are that the applicant shall furnish satisfactory evidence that he or she is twenty-three years of age, is of good moral character, has received the equivalent of a high-school education, and has been graduated from the training school connected with a general hospital, where three years of training with a systematic course of instruction is given in the hospital or has been graduated from the training school in connection with a hospital of good standing supplying a systematic three years' training corresponding to the above standard, which training may be obtained in two or more hospitals. Special provision for registration is made in the act for nurses who were graduated before a three years' course was introduced and who have been pursuing their vocation since that time in private or public capacity. Beginning with this month, it is unlawful for any person to practice professional nursing as a registered nurse without a certificate in this state. A nurse who has received his or her certificate according to the provisions of this act shall be styled and known as a "registered nurse." No other person shall assume such title or use the abbreviation "R. N." or any other letters or figures to indicate registration. It is, however, definitely stated that the act shall not be construed to affect or apply to the gratuitous nursing by friends or members of the family, nor to any person nursing the sick for hire who does not in any way assume to be a registered nurse.

Baltimore as a center for training in professional nursing has been in the lead of almost every progressive development of this advanced line of woman's work. The Johns Hopkins Hospital, starting with a magnificent hospital endowment, established in 1889 its training school for nurses, with exceptionally gifted women at the helm and a board of trustees wise in stimulating and supporting progressive work, intellectually evolved and practically carried out. The training school started upon an exceedingly high plane of excellence—far in advance of its day and generation—and beginning with a group of forty or fifty pupils, the training school has increased to the number of one hundred forty. The school was organized by Miss Isabel Hampton[5] (now Mrs. Hunter Robb, of Cleveland), as superintendent. Miss Hampton came from the Bellevue Hospital,[6] New York, which had opened a training school in May, 1873. The departments of the Hopkins training school were admirably organized, its standard of work high, and it became from the first one of the leading schools of the country. Upon the marriage of Miss Hampton,

the duties of superintendent devolved in 1894 upon the latter's assistant, Miss N. Adelaide Nutting,[7] who has by her unusual ability guided the school to its present enviable position among the educational institutions of the world. Miss Nutting resigned her position as superintendent of nurses and principal of the Johns Hopkins training school for nurses within the past few days to accept the chair of institutional management at Columbia Teachers' College, New York. Her resignation is a distinct loss not only to the institution with which she has been so long associated, but to the state of Maryland as well.

Baltimore Training Schools

The University of Maryland Hospital Infirmary,[8] under the supervision of the Sisters of Mercy, had organized a system of nurses' training in connection with the infirmary as early as 1838, but their present admirable training school for nurses was organized December 14, 1889, by Miss Laura Parsons. The latter was a graduate of St. Thomas' Hospital, London, England, where, after the Crimean War, Miss Florence Nightingale organized the first English training school. Miss Parsons had also served as head nurse for six months at the Johns Hopkins Hospital. The mantle of Florence Nightingale, angel of the European battlefields, had fallen in some measure upon Miss Parson's shoulders, since she also had seen nursing service in foreign wars, and she brought to the training school of the Maryland University Hospital a little feminine heritage from her battlefield experiences which is especially treasured by graduates of the school. This is the nurses' cap they wear, which is a duplicate of the cap worn by Florence Nightingale in his ministry to wounded and dying soldiers. Trained nurses were for the first time officially engaged by the United States government during the recent Spanish-American War,[9] and the nurses of the Maryland University Hospital Training School were among the first to volunteer their services and to go forth, wearing the white emblem of their battlefield nursing ancestress, to the same mission of healing.

The length and course of study and practical instruction in the representative training schools of Baltimore are practically the same and render their graduates equally eligible for the degree of registered nurse.

The Johns Hopkins Training School is an integral part of the Johns Hopkins Hospital and under the same government. The school buildings are within the hospital grounds but separate from the hospital buildings. They are large, comfortable, well heated, lighted and ventilated, supplied with class and lecture rooms equipped with facilities for teaching and with access to an excellent reference library.

The 360 beds of the hospital offer great opportunity for thorough and varied practical experience in surgical, medical, gynecological, and obstetrical wards. Teaching is also given in the operating room, the dispensary, and at orthopedic and other clinics. Instruction in the properties and preparations of food and in their application to the needs of the sick is given in a model kitchen equipped for teaching purposes.

Applicants for admission to the training school must not be under twenty-three years of age nor over thirty-five, and of good health and moral character. They must have gradu-ated from a high school or received the equivalent for such a degree of education, and women of superior education and cultivation receive preference for the spring term in February and March and for the autumn term in August and September. The full course of instruction occupies three years, and students are not accepted for a shorter period.

An entrance fee of $50 is required from all students to cover the additional cost of preparatory instruction, but no other charges are made for tuition, and they receive board, lodging and a reasonable amount of laundry work from date of entrance. During the period of probation they provide their own dresses, but on entering the wards are required when on duty to wear the uniform supplied by the hospital. They are also provided with text-books.

Eight scholarships of the value of $100 each have been established that are awarded by the authorities of the hospital annually to such members of the junior and intermediate classes as have shown exceptional merit and are need of pecuniary assistance to enable them to continue their studies. A single scholarship of the value of $480 is awarded at the graduating exercise at the close of the third year to the student whose work has been of the highest excellence and who desires to pursue post-graduate study and special work in the school.

Before entering upon definite instruction in nursing, applicants of the Johns Hopkins training school must pass through a probationary period of instruction in a school of dietetics and household economy. This includes theoretical and practical instruction in everything that pertains to food, to marketing, to the care, preservation and cooking of foods, to the care of kitchens, pantries, refrigerators and the attractive serving of foods both for the sick and well. Especial attention is given to the relation existing between general cookery and cooking for the sick and convalescent. In the household economy department instruction is given the student in maintenance and administration of the household, the relative values of materials and their care, furnishing of bedrooms, ventilation, plumbing, drainage, laundries and linen rooms. Here the student receives also instruction in the preparation of all surgical supplies, sterilization, disinfection, and in the outside clinic in the preparation of patients for examination, treatment and application of surgical appliances; also, of solutions, their preparation and use.

This department of the school is a most valuable one, not only in the profession of nursing, but in any department of life for women. It has been adopted by all the representative schools to a greater or less degree in connection with the probationary period of their student instruction. Such department of housekeeping and domestic and institutional administration is very similar to the housekeeping schools of Switzerland, except that it is conducted upon a scientific basis, with the general trend of every detail tending to the comfort of the invalid and the prevention or cure of disease. The leading training schools throughout the United States are in constant receipt of applications for trained administrative women not only in connection with hospitals, but in large schools and institutions of every sort, and this housekeeping training is invaluable in connection with such work.

A Dream of the Future

It is a future dream of the superintendents of most training schools for nurses that in time such preparatory training of pupils will be conducted at a preparatory central school, whose relation to the hospital training school shall be that of the secondary school to the college. One large school of this sort in each city co-operating with all the training schools, but independent of them, would relieve the superintendents of nurses of an immense responsibility in preparing the totally inexperienced person to be even a help rather than a hindrance in the sick room.

The high standard of discipline and thoroughness set by Miss Parsons for the University of Maryland Training School for Nurses has been upheld by her successors, and the size and importance of the hospital and the eminent ability of its medical and surgical staff have given to the nurses associated with it the most advanced and thorough mental instruction and the broadest practical experience.

The course of training is three years, under conditions approved by the highest authorities upon professional nursing, and the social relations between the nurses of the training school and the ladies who compose the woman's board of the hospital are peculiarly intimate and pleasant. The latter have been untiring in providing for the nursing staff comforts of surroundings and diversion of mind as well. Miss Flanagan is at present superintendent of nurses, and the student nurses are fifty-four in number. The training in orthopedic surgery for the hospital course is given at the Hospital for Crippled Children.[10]

The Maryland Homeopathic Hospital is "an house set upon a hill"[11]—a breezy hill, with terraced lawns sloping downward, and the administration building is a hospitable, roomy, old-fashioned mansion, overshadowed with trees. Other buildings are erected upon the lawn. The training school, established in 1891, gives the full course of instruction required for the Maryland state registration of nurses, and is also registered in New York state. Its nurses have the advantage of instruction in both homeopathic and allopathic methods, so that the services of graduates of the school are equally sought by physicians of both schools of medicine. Pupils are admitted only for a three years' course of training and must pass a mental examination and three months' probation before being formally accepted as student nurses. Dresses, aprons, caps, sleeves, and shoes are supplied by the hospital, but no remuneration is given, as the education and training are considered sufficient return. The hours for duty are from 7 a.m. to 7 p.m., with two hours off duty for rest, study and exercise. An afternoon each week and part of Sunday are given each nurse for her own time. The hours for night nursing are the same as for day, beginning at 7 p.m. and ending at the same hour in the morning. A vacation of fifteen days is allowed each year. The training school includes twenty nurses, and their home is removed from the hospital building, thereby insuring quiet and restful environment. The school has an alumnae association, and sixty graduates have completed the course of instruction. Miss Mary J. Putts,[12] the present super-intendent of nurses, is a graduate of the school; one of the graduates in the United States Army Nursing Corps, and a number have been called to responsible positions in other hospitals.

Thorough System of Instruction

The Baltimore City Hospital Training School for Nurses was organized during the Spanish-American War, when many of the religieux of the institution, whose special mission was nursing, were called from their hospital duties to minister to the sick of the army. The school is nonsectarian, Sisters of Mercy and young women of the outside world of whatever religion receiving the same course of instruction. The requirements for admission are the highest moral standing, intelligence, good education, and health, and pupils are admitted from the age of twenty-two to thirty-five years. The course comprises three years of theory and practice. After two months' probation, candidates, if they possess the necessary qualifications, are admitted to the training school proper. A small allowance is made them to procure uniforms, text-books, etc., and laundry is provided by the institution. The education received is regarded as compensation for the services rendered. The hours of duty are from 7 a.m. to 7 p.m. and the free time one hour daily, one afternoon from 2 p.m. each week and two weeks' annual vacation. The school is under the supervision of one of the Sisters of the order. The course of instruction includes lectures by members of the faculty of the hospital upon anatomy, hygiene, physiology, medicine, surgery, obstetrics, fevers, contagious, nervous and mental diseases, gynecology, diseases of children, orthopedics and other lines of medical work.

The 300 beds of the City Hospital[13] and the fact of its location in the heart of Baltimore and near the railroads give to the nurses in training there an especially wide field of experience in accident and emergency cases. The Pasteur department of the City Hospital also gives to the nurses associated with it an opportunity for instruction in this department of nursing not included in the other training school courses of the city. The City Hospital department for the preventive treatment of hydrophobia is modeled after the Institut Pasteur,[14] of Paris, and identical with the latter.

The Union Protestant Infirmary School for Nurses[15] was established in 1891 and is in connection with that admirable hospital. The superintendent of nurses is Miss Susan Shrive, and the student staff of the training school numbers thirty-six nurses. The course of training is three years, which includes a full course of obstetrical training at the Johns Hopkins Hospital. The age for the admission of nurses is from twenty-three to thirty-five years, and the requirements, privileges and course of instruction of the school are the same as in other institutions whose graduate nurses are eligible for the degree of registered nurse. The infirmary has one of the most beautiful children's wards in the city, and the hospital itself is an attractive one, with pleasant nurses' apartments.

The above-mentioned training schools are only a few of the many excellent ones in the city too numerous to include in a short sketch. A great many of them have equally high standards of nurses' training, but the necessity of this all-around training of a nurse if an official degree is desired cannot help but have an immediate effect in raising the instructive standards of smaller schools. It will also conduce to the co-operation of hospitals in sharing one with another any special facilities for training which may be lacking in individual schools, and it is hoped by many who are deeply interested in nursing as one of the higher professions open to women that some of the philanthropists who so generously endow hospitals will in future regard the training school for nurses as an opportunity for the bestowal of similar gifts.

Baltimore's Effort for Healthier Babies Through Bureau of Child Hygiene (1919)

The Baltimore genealogist of today seeking to trace a Maryland family's lineage to colonial days often finds the road to accurate birth and death records a thorny and faintly outlined path. Tradition lacks authority; family Bibles are not always available; scattered parish records, the land grant, the will, the tombstone inscription, must be depended upon for piecing together the uncertain family tree and occasionally an ancient gravestone bears the words "legitimate son of," etc., showing that even in pioneer days men felt the importance of handing down to posterity proof of the lawful right of descendants to bear their name and inherit their possessions.

The recent drafting of thousands of men, Americans, for military service, emphasized the necessity for more complete birth registration than has hither to prevailed. It is always important, and sometimes absolutely necessary, that a man shall be able to prove his age and citizenship; his right to avail himself of public school facilities; his right to go to work at the age that the law allows; his right to an inheritance, his right to marry without consent of parents or guardians, his right to hold office, to secure passports for foreign travel and to prove his mother's right to a widow's pension if she is eligible for such emolument.

Another thing, medical examination necessitated in mustering the masculine youth of the United States into military service during the recent war, proved that this country had eight million men between the ages of eighteen and forty-five years who were physically sub-standard and unfit to fight for their country in a modern war. This discovery through army medical examiners, greatly emphasizes the vital necessity of a new, systematic and permanent plan of public health education under municipal direction to obtain accurate information regarding what is literally a life-and-death matter and to conserve and build up the physical fitness of the American people.

All Births Now Registered

The Baltimore genealogist of the future will have a less arduous task than his predecessors. The law, in fact, now requires that a baby's birth be reported by physician, nurse or whoever is in attendance, to the health officer or town clerk who reports it to the State Board of Health. The parents then receive, from the Health Department of Baltimore,[16] a birth receipt card stating that the birth of the child has been officially registered. If this receipt card is not promptly received, the parents may know that the law in regard to the registration of their child's birth has not been complied with, and should hasten to report the birth themselves.

Again the present law of Maryland has safeguarded the welfare of the new-born child by making it unlawful for a mother to be separated from her infant either voluntarily or by compulsion, until six months after the child's birth.

The Babies' Own Bureau

But Baltimore is doing still more to establish the identity of the child, to educate parents to the proper care of it, and to safeguard its condition up to its tenth year, when the public school system in a way becomes every child's municipal guardian.

This was done by the organization within the past year of the Bureau of Child Hygiene, under the Health Department of the city of Baltimore. Of this Dr. Mary Sherwood[17] is the chief and Dr. Mary Cook Willis her assistant, and they are aided in their work by a staff of twelve experienced nurses.

The establishment of the bureau was due primarily to the very evident need in Baltimore of such a department of municipal work and to the interest and co-operation of Dr. William Travis Howard of the School of Hygiene and Public Health. Dr. Raymond Pearl,[18] also of the School of Hygiene and Public Health of Johns Hopkins University, has been untiring in efforts to devise simple yet comprehensive card codes that minimize the labor of registering official data, yet which include all essential details of information. As soon as a birth is registered at the Health Department and the certificate of birth made out, such certificate before filing is passed on to the desk of Dr. Sherwood, who assigns further research and duty pertaining to that child to the nurse in charge of the district in which the birth occurs.

As soon as possible, this nurse then pays a visit both official and friendly to the mother of the child. Upon a little code card she jots down, not only all the essential facts concerning the birth and sex of the baby, its parentage, their ages, occupation, etc., of the parents, but also enough of the family history and nationality to make a most valuable record. Housing conditions are stated, light, space, air, and whether the child is breast fed, or fed upon cow's milk or canned milk and what the results of the nourishment given. If death occurs, the nurse ascertains the cause. She also notes any congenital defects, malformations, or accidents of birth. Her advice and interest may become a most potent factor in the life of both mother and child because having classified the home as belonging to one of several groups, she endeavors to improve the condition of such as need her supervising care. In touch with the Instructive Visiting Nurse Association, the Babies' Milk Fund Association, the Henry Watson Children's Aid Society, the Hebrew Children's Bureau, the Mount Wilson Sanatorium, the Johns Hopkins University of Maryland, Maryland General and Hebrew Hospitals, and other agencies for public welfare, she can do much to make the baby's journey in life begin under the happiest possible auspices.

Standardize Boarding Homes

One important feature of the work under the special supervision of Dr. Mary Cook Willis is the standardization of all boarding places licensed to take babies and young children to board. These must measure up to hygienic standard in the matter of sanitation, air, space, cleanliness, correct appliances for taking care of babies, suitable cribs, beds, porches, outdoor space. All these essential things are considered, and when it is realized that the license has this year been revoked of a baby caretaker who crowded fourteen children into one room of ten by nine feet, it will be realized how essential such supervision, with power to act, is to the health of the city.

The bureau has inaugurated a most important educational health work in the establishment of several small prenatal clinics where mothers may go before children are born, to advise with the physician concerning care of themselves and preparation for the coming of the little stranger, whose future health and happiness is so dependent upon the mother's physical condition. Here they are taught the vital importance to the baby of being fed with milk from the mother's breast, since out of 195 babies that died in Baltimore during last July, only eleven were breast fed. Modified cow's milk is regarded by the bureau as the best substitute for mother's milk, as it most resembles mother's milk in composition and contains the vitamins which are essential to child growth and development. Condensed milk and substitute foods are not recommended. These, it is considered, do not promote the best growth and development of the child.

Mothers are encouraged to bring their babies regularly, whether sick or well, to clinics established by the Bureau of Child Hygiene or to the welfare stations of the Babies' Milk Fund that they may be weighed and their physical condition intelligently watched over.

The bureau intended to start a welfare center in Northwest Baltimore during the past summer but found it absolutely impossible to find a house suitable for specific needs. There is now a small clinic established at McCulloh and Baker streets, another at Locust Point, and a small pre-natal clinic in South Baltimore General Hospital, with a resident woman physician in charge who several times weekly conducts the clinics and also attends women in confinement at their homes.

Since the bureau was established on February 1, 1919, and up to November 1, 12,921 babies, born within the year in Baltimore City, have been visited by the physicians or nurses of the bureau. The largest number of deaths, occurring in children under two years of age, are from congenital debility, premature birth, and from acute gastro-intestinal affections, while under four years of age the greatest number die of acute bronchitis and pneumonia and acute gastro-intestinal diseases. Fewer of the negro race are found to die of gastro enteritis and more colored babies are naturally nursed. However, more colored than white babies die of bronchial pneumonia. The death rate among the children of American parents is not so high as among the foreign-born. Gastro enteritis is the cause of death among many children of foreign nationalities.

Personnel of Bureau

Dr. Mary Sherwood, chief of the Bureau of Child Hygiene, has long been identified with the municipal affairs of Baltimore, and, because of her interest in and experience with child welfare and her untiring efforts for better obstetrics in this city, is peculiarly qualified to develop the department of which she is the head. She is a graduate of Vassar College and of the medical school of the University of Zurich, Switzerland. Dr. Sherwood has for years been the physician to Bryn Mawr School and has served on many municipal boards. She was appointed by Mayor Hooper, one of the trustees of the poor, and by Mayor Hayes upon the Public Bath Commission,[19] where she still serves. She is on the board of Mount Wilson Sanatorium[20] and a member of the Babies' Milk Fund Association. She was also one of the original members of the Child Hygiene Association.

Dr. Mary Cook Willis is a Baltimore physician of wide experience and unusual executive ability. She is a graduate of the Woman's Medical College of Baltimore[21] and was resident physician of the Good Samaritan Hospital. She was resident physician of the Barre Street Dispensary and for four years physician of the Florence Crittenden Home,[22] also of the Northwest City Medical Agency, and she is now physician to the Maryland Industrial School for Girls.[23]

Ten efficient nurses are the links between babies and the chief of the Bureau of Child Hygiene and her assistant. They are nurses carefully chosen because of their experience and suitability for the work, and most of them have a saving sense of humor that enables them to pursue with cheerfulness an exceedingly arduous vocation. Some unofficial item of humorous nature usually enlivens official reports at the conclusion of the day's work, as, when securing data in a suburban district, a nurse ran frequently across such startling information as this:

"Occupation of father—invalid.

"Occupation of mother—spinster."

Time and again the word spinster occurred, and the worker thought a wave of immorality was gripping the locality, until she discovered that the mothers were married women, employed in cotton mills at spinning, which is occupationally designated as "spinster."

Another nurse, warning a mother against a food she was substituting for her baby in place of breast feeding or modified cow's milk, received from the mother the indignant response: "Why, I have fed ten babies on that food and only lost eight of them."

A nurse striving to make a wan mother and her infant comfortable observed that the children were hilariously rolling a loaf of bread from end to end of the adjoining kitchen floor. She asked permission to stop them, which was granted, with the weary remark: "But what better can you expect on wash day?"

A visiting nurse praised a little Italian baby. "You lik-a dat babee?" asked the mother, and without waiting for an answer, thrust it into the nurse's arms, saying: "You tak-a dat baby. Gotta nine!"

"You know we just love Mutt and Jeff[24] in the comic page of the *Sun*," said one young mother joyously, "so we have named the baby Cicero."

The Bureau has devised a code that most specially classifies female occupations both for women whose work is entirely at home and who receive, or do not receive, money compensation for their services and wage-earning women who work away from home. This code recognizes the housewife as a woman with a distinctive vocation. She is not classed, formerly, as a woman, "without occupation," but as a woman with a most engrossing occupation, that of housekeeping.

Dr. Sherwood has recently called a meeting of physicians and heads of benevolent agencies in Baltimore to confer in regard to the standardizing of boarding homes for babies and children and will shortly call a meeting of representatives of institutions in which babies and children are received with reference to the co-operation of the Bureau of Child Hygiene in reference to foundlings and children under three years of age who are committed to them.

Her Centenary Sees Susan B. Anthony's Cause Near to Success (Feb. 15, 1920)

Today is the one hundredth anniversary of the birthday of Susan B. Anthony, American reformer and the greatest leader in the cause of equal suffrage the United States has known. Born of Quaker parentage February 15, 1820, in Adams, Massachusetts, Miss Anthony taught school from the year she was fifteen until she was thirty years of age. She was an ardent advocate of antislavery, prohibition and woman suffrage and spent her life in eloquent speaking and working along these lines.

On her one hundredth anniversary the ideals she believed in have prevailed. Slavery is long since a nightmare of the past, the United States is a prohibition country and but two more state ratifications are needed to win the cause of equal suffrage in these United States. Miss Anthony's death occurred in 1906, and her last public utterance in behalf of the cause to which she devoted her life was made at the Lyric, in Baltimore.[25]

Dr. Mark Recalls Her

Perhaps among Baltimoreans who knew and revered Miss Susan B. Anthony, none can boast an acquaintance dating further back than Dr. Nellie V. Mark,[26] of this city, who was for years a member and an officer of the Association for the Advancement of Women and personally acquainted with the galaxy of brilliant women who were pioneers in the equal suffrage movement. Dr. Mark said yesterday:

"It was thirty-nine years ago, when I was a young girl reading medicine with a Philadelphia physician, that I first saw Miss Anthony. The physician was well acquainted with Phoebe Cousins, then a beautiful young woman and an ardent suffrage speaker. The three of us had gone to some suburban meeting at which Phoebe spoke upon the equal rights of women, but not returned together to the city because some

gentlemen had invited Phoebe, after the meeting, to go sledding and we returned to the city without her. It was quite late the following afternoon when the door of the doctor's office opened and a tall, slender, angular middle-aged woman entered, and, after depositing her traveling bag upon the floor, abruptly demanded:

"Has anyone seen Phoebe Cousins? She was to speak with me tonight at Chadd's Ford and I can't come up with her anywhere."

"It was explained that the last seen of her, Phoebe had been whirled off amid tinkling sleigh bells along a broad, white way of snow-covered road.

"Miss Anthony groaned. 'If Phoebe has a man in tow I foresee that I'll have to run that Chadd's Ford meeting alone, and I am belated now through searching for her.'

"But before hurrying off, the pioneer suffragist turned kindly to me asking: 'Who is this little lady?' and upon my being introduced she said: 'I hope you believe in equal suffrage, my dear,' to which I made answer that I believed I had been born a suffragist, since I had always wanted to be a physician, and was then working to attain that goal.

"It transpired that Miss Anthony was mistaken in supposing Miss Cousins had deserted her, because Phoebe was already at Chadd's Ford when the much-behind-time elder woman reached there.

"Later while pursuing my medical studies in Boston I now and again saw Miss Anthony, and I recall attending a yearly meeting of the National American Woman Suffrage organization at Washington when Miss Anthony was presiding.

My mother and Mrs. William H. Appold accompanied me to the convention and the latter had purchased a photograph of Miss Anthony and was exceedingly anxious to obtain the autograph of the original. As we sat at luncheon at the Riggs Hotel[27]—the Washington headquarters for suffragists—I saw Miss Anthony pass the window. On the impulse of the moment I ran out and asked if she would not come in and meet my friend and write her name on the picture, which she did with the utmost cheerfulness.

A Tombstone Inscription

"Again I recall her meeting with Baltimore suffragists at Heptasophs' Hall, and because all women are instinctively inclined toward matrimonial gossip there had been some talk of the possibility of Miss Anthony marrying a gentleman of much distinction, who believed heartily in suffrage. I do not suppose either Miss Anthony, or he, had ever thought of such a thing, but they were very good friends and there was some speculation on the subject, and so I asked Miss Anthony if there was any truth in the report.

"'What report?' she asked, and when I explained that people thought she might marry, she replied: 'Never! Susan B. Anthony will be inscribed on my tombstone.'

"Well, I replied, you might inscribe Susan B. Anthony with the addition of a married name. To which she emphatically answered that no man's name should supplement her own upon her memorial stone. As Susan B. Anthony she had lived: as such she would die.

"The last time I saw her was in 1906, when the National American Woman Suffrage Association met at the Lyric[28] in Baltimore. Miss Anthony and Mrs. Julia Ward Howe were at that time the guests of Miss Mary Garrett[29] at her residence, corner Monument and Cathedral streets. Because of the latter's great gift of the medical school to the Johns Hopkins Hospital the faculty of university and hospital attended the night meeting, and the large reception given by Miss Garrett at her home in honor of her distinguished guests was a brilliant social affair. But Miss Anthony was not well before she came to Baltimore and both she and Mrs. Howe were very aged, and the former had expressed a premonition that the Baltimore convention would be the last she would attend. The strain told upon her, and unfortunately on the occasion of the reception the drawing room was too cool and the location of the receiving party drafty, and both Mrs. Howe and Miss Anthony took cold. Mrs. Howe had tonsillitis and, having been her physician previously, I was able to prescribe immediately what she needed and she recovered. But Miss Anthony was never well again and shortly after died.

Fine Presiding Office

"Whether Miss Anthony was blond or brunette I do not know. She was gray haired upon the occasion of our first meeting. In looks she much resembled her friend Louisa M. Alcott,[30] both being tall and angular. Miss Anthony was a typical Yankee in appearance. Her face was very fine, severe in line, but softened by a most kindly smile that atoned for a certain abruptness of manner. Elizabeth Cady Stanton, Miss Anthony's intimate friend, possessed the suavity and graciousness that Miss Anthony lacked, yet Miss Octavia

Williams Bates,[31] whom Baltimoreans will recall as a delegate to the International Council of Women held in London, said that in England Miss Anthony was always the central figure of interest among Americans attending that council and that English women singled her out to honor. As a presiding officer she was without an equal among women interested in suffrage."[32]

Dr. Shaw Recalls Convention

The late Rev. Dr. Anna Howard Shaw, in her book, "The Story of a Pioneer,"[33] speaks of Miss Anthony's last public appearance in this city. Dr. Shaw writes:

"In 1906, when the date of the annual convention of the National American Woman Suffrage Association in Baltimore was drawing near, she (Miss Anthony) became convinced it would be her last convention. She was right. She showed a passionate eagerness to make it one of the greatest conventions ever held in the history of the movement, and we, who loved her and saw that the flame of her life was burning low, also bent all our energies to the task of realizing her hopes. In November preceding the convention she visited me and her niece. Miss Lucy Anthony, in our home in Mount Airy, Philadelphia, and it was clear that her anxiety over the convention was weighing heavily upon her. She visibly lost strength from day to day. One morning she said abruptly, 'Anna, let's go and call on President M. Carey Thomas,[34] Of Bryn Mawr.'

"I wrote a note to Miss Thomas telling her of Miss Anthony's desire to see her and received an immediate reply, inviting us to luncheon the following day. We found Miss Thomas deep in the work connected with her new college buildings, over which she showed us with much pride. Miss Anthony, of course, gloried in the splendid results Miss Thomas had achieved, but she was, for her, strangely silent and preoccupied. At luncheon she said:

"'Miss Thomas, your buildings are beautiful; your new library is a marvel; but they are not the cause of our presence here.'

"'No.' Miss Thomas said, 'I know you have something on your mind. I am waiting for you to tell me what it is.'

'We want your co-operation and that of Miss Garrett,' began Miss Anthony promptly, 'to make our Baltimore convention a success. We want you to persuade the Arundell Club,[35] of Baltimore, the most fashionable club in the city, to give a reception to the delegates and we want you to arrange a "College Night" on the program—a great college night with the best college speakers ever brought together.'

"These were large commissions for two extremely busy women, but both Miss Thomas and Miss Garrett—realizing Miss Anthony's intense earnestness—promised to think over the suggestion and see what they could do. The next morning we received a telegram from them stating that Miss Thomas would arrange the college meeting and that Miss Garrett would reopen her Baltimore home, which she had closed, during the convention. She also invited Miss Anthony and me to be her guests there, and added that she would try to arrange the reception by the Arundell Club.

"'Aunt Susan' was overjoyed. I have never seen her happier than she was over the receipt of that telegram. She knew that whatever Miss Thomas and Miss Garrett undertook would be accomplished, and she rightly regarded the success of the convention as already assured. Her expectations were more than realized. The college evening was undoubtedly the most brilliant occasion of its kind ever arranged for a convention. President Ira Remsen[36] of Johns Hopkins University, presided, and addresses were made by President Mary E. Wooley, of Mount Holyoke; Prof. Lucy Salmon of Vassar; Prof. Mary Jordan of Smith; President Thomas herself and many others.[37]

"From beginning to end the convention was probably the most notable held in our history. Julia Ward Howe and her daughter, Florence Howe Hall, were also guests of Miss Garrett, who, moreover, entertained all the speakers of College Night. Miss Anthony, now eighty-six, arrived in Baltimore quite ill, and Mrs. Howe, who was ninety, was taken ill soon after she reached there. The two great women made a dramatic exchange on the program, for on the first night, when Miss Anthony was unable to speak. Mrs. Howe took her place, and on the second night, when Mrs. Howe had succumbed, Miss Anthony had recovered sufficiently to appear for her. Clara Barton was also an honored figure at the convention and Miss Anthony's joy in the presence of all these old and dear friends was overflowing. With them, too, were the younger women, ready to take up and carry on the work the old leaders were laying down; and 'Aunt Susan,' as she surveyed them all, felt like a general whose superb army is passing before him.

"At the close of the college program and when the final address had been made by Miss Thomas, Miss Anthony rose and in a few words expressed her feeling that her life work was done, and her consciousness of the near approach of the end."

The Leader's Last Review

Of the death of the great spirited leader in the woman's cause Dr. Shaw writes:

"On the last afternoon of her life, when she had lain quiet for hours, she suddenly began to utter the names of the women who had worked with her as if in a final roll call. Many of them had preceded her into the next world; others were still splendidly active in the work she was laying down. But young or old, living or dead, they all seemed to file past her dying eyes that day in an endless, shadowy review and as they went by she spoke to each of them."

Chroniclers of the Homefront

The significance of the home in late nineteenth and early twenti- eth- century women's fiction cannot be overstated, and it serves as the setting of most of the works collected in this section. We define "home" and broadly to include not only matters of domesticity, but also matters of intimacy, identity formation, and social change and transformation.

The women whose works we have collected in this section were working in a genre that has been referred to, sometimes disparagingly, as "domestic" or, more commonly, "sentimental" literature. But like any genre, sentimental literature has its own well-established motifs and conventions, and these conventions serve both ideological and artistic purposes. As Joanne Dobson writes, it is "premised on an emo- tional and philosophical ethos that celebrates human connection, both personal and communal, and acknowledges the shared devastation of affectional loss."[1] One of the most interesting aspects of the genre is how it depicts internal spaces, whether they are literal or figurative.

The works of Mary Spear Tiernan typify the sentimental impulse. A true chronicler of the "home front," Tiernan's sense of the home was intricately tied to the South, and by implication, the Confedera- cy. Tiernan makes Virginia during the Civil War the backdrop to her short stories "A Widow, Indeed!" and "The Two Negatives." But Tier- nan was not as concerned with the war itself as she was with the lives of women navigating romantic relationships at home and the price exacted by the war on relationships and families.

Ellen Duvall likewise wrote stories focusing on women and their relationships with men in the South. One might assume that senti- mental fiction depicts a world in which women rule over a domestic space. Duvall's short stories prove that this is not so. Her female pro- tagonists contest male dominion, and risk ostracization and isolation in preserving individual freedom.

This section includes two works by Club co-founder Louise C. O. Haughton—a short story, "The Ever-Ready Edgar," and a short play, "The Decision." "The Ever-Ready Edgar," culminates in the revenge of four women against a womanizing man, while "The Decision," subtitled "The Vacillations of Amelia," uses its single act to lay bare the conflicting desires of its eponymous protagonist.

Harriet Lummis Smith's work operated within a realm more overtly domestic. Her stories provide windows into the gender dynamics of the household, depicting with meticulous and revealing detail the lives of women in the domestic sphere. And in her writings, Marian V. Dorsey, sister of Club co-founder Hester Dorsey Richardson, wrote about her own domestic spaces and learned to use them to provide a living for herself.

The heroism displayed by the women in these stories looks a bit different from that of their male counterparts. Nevertheless, they prove themselves clever, determined, and at times, surprisingly brave.

Mary Spear Nicholas Tiernan (c. 1836-1891)

Mary Spear Tiernan shared many commonalities with other women writers of her generation. She had genteel origins: her father had a long career as the United States District Attorney of Virginia, her grandfather was a judge, and her great-grandfather served as state treasurer of Virginia. As a native Virginian, she and her family were aligned with the Confederacy during the American Civil War. She was employed in the Confederate treasury department in Richmond, while two of her brothers were Confederate soldiers, eventually perishing in the hostilities of the war. In 1873, she married Baltimorean Charles Tiernan and subsequently moved to Maryland, where she became one of the founding members of the Woman's Literary Club of Baltimore.[1]

Tiernan was held in high regard by her fellow members. Unfortunately, her tenure was short lived; she died in 1891, during the first year of the club's existence. Nevertheless, her influence proved long-lasting. Club members held a memorial meeting in honor of Tiernan, and they also showed their respect by embellishing her grave with decorations.[2] Eventually, they extended this tradition to other Maryland authors, decorating their graves every year on All Saints' Day. A death announcement in the *Baltimore Sun* called her a woman of wit, and stated that it "brought to bear upon her literary work the advantages of a scholarly education."[3]

Tiernan's writing focuses on strong-willed women who face romantic difficulties that reflect struggles women of her era faced in the domestic sphere, including courtship and mourning. Interestingly, these stories are not era-specific; they parallel domestic struggles faced by women today. Ignoring marriage proposals to avoid the rudeness of an outright rejection, and feeling jealousy over misunderstood relationships could be plot points taken from a prime-time sitcom.

Although the Civil War is not the primary focus of these stories, it is still quite prominent in her writing. While it's unclear if she was a Southern sympathizer after the war ended, she was certainly involved with the Confederacy during it. Some critics argue that her novels *Homoselle* and *Jack Horner* play into the romantic notions of slavery emphasized by Lost Cause ideology, which used romantic portrayals of slavery and appeals to sympathy to perpetuate the ideals of the Confederacy by making it look more attractive and acceptable to readers.[4] Others maintain that Tiernan is unique among other Southern postbellum writers because she avoids the brazen flag-waving characteristic of proponents of Lost Cause ideology. They claim *Homoselle*'s depiction of slaves' acute yearning for freedom and her dramatization of an actual slave rebellion separates her from other Virginian writers. And they claim that black characterization in *Jack Horner* departs significantly from conventional stereotypes.[5] However, traditional postbellum Southern literature tropes and themes are not wholly absent from either novel. Tiernan's writing remains controversial.

Tiernan's works includes the use of dialect and racial slurs which may be offensive to some readers. Nevertheless, Tiernan was a woman of wit and humor as well. Her writing provides a fascinating glimpse into the mind of an unapologetically Southern woman. —M. Fazio and S. Barrett

A Widow, Indeed! (1887)

I

We were nothing but girls, Lottie Linley and I, and up to all sorts of mischief. Lottie was nineteen and I a year younger, but she was smaller and not so sensible as I thought at that time. We had come to spend the summer in the country in Virginia with an aunt of mine, Mrs. Page Brinton. Lottie was not related to my aunt, but had been invited as my friend. So I played hostess, as well as superior intelligence.

"Aunt," I said, almost as soon as we arrived, for I thought I saw signs of previous occupation. "Who is here, besides Lottie and me?"

My aunt laughed as my precipitancy.

"Nobody but our old friend, Mr. Power, and a new one, Mrs. Mossom."

"Mrs. Mossom? Who is she?"

"A young widow we met traveling in Florida last winter."

Lottie and I exchanged glances.

We did not like young widows. St. Paul declared that young widows should stay at home; and even if he had not done so, our unassisted wisdom would have arrived at the same conclusion. On more than one occasion we had found them dangerous.

"A young widow! How old is she?"

"Thirty, or thereabout."

"Thirty!" I exclaimed, looking down from the proud eminence of eighteen, "Why, I consider that quite aged; and what a horrid name—Mossom!"

"I don't think so," said Lottie, decidedly. "It is such a nice rhyme for blossom."

Lottie wrote things she called poetry, and was on the lookout for nice rhymes.

"Why not 'possum?'" I snapped.

"You will find Mrs. Mossom a very nice person," said my aunt, leaving us to do our unpacking.

"I don't think we need to bother our heads about the widow if she is thirty," I said, unlocking my trunk and taking out one of my second-best gowns for Mrs. Mossom's benefit. Our most becoming things we kept for especial favorites. Lottie and I had spent the previous summer in this same house, and, among the young men in the neighborhood, we each had a particular—well, we called him friend, as covering the ground, present or prospective. Lottie's admirer was a Mr. Archer Cullen, and mine a Mr. John Bryan, commonly called Jack.

Mr. Power did not count for much, being a confirmed bachelor of about forty, good-looking, well-to-do, but exceedingly shy and a little eccentric.

"I hardly think Mrs. Mossom will be dangerous if she is thirty, eh, Lottie?" I repeated, brushing out my frizzes at one glass, while my friend brushed out hers at another.

"We shall see," said Lottie, oracularly.

"I wonder how Mr. Power gets on with her?" I said, after awhile.

"The same way he gets on with me, I suppose—by letting her alone."

"But widows don't put up with that kind of thing," I suggested.

"Nobody can make anything of Mr. Power."

"How do you know?"

"I have tried it," said my friend, frankly.

At dinner Mrs. Mossom was the last to make her appearance. I was a little taken aback when she came into the room, she was so different from what I had imagined. Without being exactly pretty, she was very elegant, her greatest charm being a sweet gravity of countenance, indicating a character the very opposite of that which I had endowed her. She was a person whose entrance into a room made itself distinctly felt. My uncle's face brightened; Mr. Power turned a shade redder than usual, and my aunt pointed with a caressing gesture to the chair nearest herself, saying, "Here is your seat, dear."

The widow's dress was black and sombre, but a gleam of transparent white frills around her throat and wrists reminded me of "the cloud's silver-lining."

Upstairs, brushing out my bang at the glass, I had thought I was not a bad-looking girl; but Mrs. Mossom's finished elegance, some how, made me feel as raw and green as a cabbage beside a delicate garden-flower.

Lottie's wishful eyes showed that she, too, was impressed by the stranger.

We looked at each other again, as in that silent interchange of glances we concluded a defensive alliance.

Mrs. Mossom greeted us politely when we were introduced, and I fancied her eyes rested kindly for a moment on Lottie's pretty face, most persons' did; but she did not seem interested in us, beyond what courtesy required.

She and my aunt soon fell to discussing plans for relieving a destitute family in the neighborhood, while my uncle and Mr. Power talked politics, as usual. Lottie and I, finding it impossible to confine our gay, young thoughts to either poverty or politics, talked of the pleasures we were anticipating—a repetition of the drives, rides and parties we had found so delightful the summer before.

"By the by, girls," said my uncle, catching the drift of our conversation. "There is to be a party in the neighborhood next week, to which we are all invited; and as it is given to the bride, Mrs. Sherwood, I think everybody ought to go. You, too, Mrs. Mossom."

My aunt gave him a deprecating glance in vain. Uncle Brinton was one of those healthy, jovial natures, whose wounds, physical and spiritual, lose no time in getting healed.

Devoted as he was to my aunt, I am sure that, once she was fairly dead and buried, he would have considered it a Christian duty to get comforted as soon as possible and to look out for somebody to take her place. As to Mrs. Mossom not going to a party on account of mourning, when her husband had been dead two full years, he never could have been made to understand such nonsense.

Mrs. Mossom was too well bred to appear scandalized by his kindly-meant proposition. She did not seem half as much disturbed as my aunt.

She answered pleasantly, although her face flushed a little and her eyes were bent on her plate as she said, "I do not go to parties, Mr. Brinton."

My uncle could not, for the life of him, understand the full significance of her manner, but I noticed he never asked her to go to a party again.

After dinner Lottie and I, walking up and down the front portico, our heads full of the Sherwood party, did not see—

at least, I did not—Mrs. Mossom, partly shaded by curtains, sitting at one of the windows that we passed and repassed in our promenade.

"Did you notice how uncle put his foot into it? '*I do not go to parties, Mr. Britton,*'" I said, mimicking the widow's voice and caricaturing her manner by lowering my eyes and drawing up the corners of my mouth. To my surprise, Lottie did not laugh at my fine powers of mimicry as usual, but turned furiously red and pinched my arm. Following the direction of her eyes, I perceived Mrs. Mossom, who had both seen and heard me.

My cheeks turned redder than my companion's, as I caught the lady's glance. I ought to have made an apology, but I was too much embarrassed to do the proper thing.

Instead of being sorry for my incivility, I was unreasonably angry that my attempt at ridicule had recoiled on myself. I quickened my steps, dragging Lottie with me. When we reached the end of the portico I did not turn and resume my walk with her, but jumped into the garden below, landing, with my best slippers, in the middle of a damp bed of scarlet geraniums. I hurried on in no dignified way, for I was obliged to skip over flower-beds and tall box borders until I reached the main walk, which, fortunately, was shaded with trees and screened from the house. The remembrance of Mrs. Mossom's amused glance piqued me.

Instead of being glad that she was good-natured enough to smile at all, I fancied her look expressed an intention to take up the gauntlet. I worked myself into a state of indignation, like the wolf who complained of the lamb muddying the stream.[6]

As I walked along the dim, cool avenue, my vexation changed suddenly to gladness. My heart throbbed with delight as I recognized a well-remembered form leaning over the gate at the end of the walk, and a pair of dark eyes, that danced with pleasure at my approach. It was Jack Bryan, who had heard of my arrival and had lost no time in assuring himself of the fact.

"What a fine color and what muddy shoes somebody has! Have you been running a hurdle race?" he asked, letting himself in the gate and warmly shaking my outstretched hand.

"Something very like it," I said, with quickened breath, from my late exercise over the box-borders.

When we had expressed our mutual satisfaction at seeing each other again, Jack and I resumed our acquaintance where we had left off the previous summer, and began walking up and down the avenue just as if a whole year had not elapsed since our last meeting there.

Jack liked me and he was my beau-ideal of a man.

People said he would never set the river on fire,[7] but that did not trouble me. When a man is handsome, good-tempered and brave there is no need for him to set the river on fire. Besides, if the necessity for such a conflagration should ever arise, I felt that I was quite equal to the task; and, in the wise economy of nature, it would not have done for both to possess the capability.

I do not know if Jack would have ap-peared so handsome in a city. His great, strong figure, his ruddy complexion and simple, unstudied ways seemed suited to the country. I am inclined to think that nature, with the background of the ever-lasting hills, was the proper setting for his manly beauty.

How glad I was to see him again! My feet seemed scarcely to touch the ground; my light dress, fluttering in the breeze, made me feel like a winged creature, and my heart, with its weight of eighteen summers, was like thistle down.

"You have not told me yet what all this excitement is about," he said, looking on my still glowing cheeks with frankly approving eyes.

"Oh! My tongue, of course. It is always getting me into mischief."

But it is a clever, little tongue; could it not get you out again?"

"Yes, it might, but there is my temper, you see."

"Tongue and temper, both?"

"Yes. They are like the Siamese twins—they always go together. I am afraid you will think I am a dreadful girl."

"I would not have you changed," he said, in a low voice.

Oh! My friend, you could not set the river on fire, but—you knew how to kindle a fire in my poor heart.

"It will not be as pleasant here this summer as last," I said, after a pause.

"Why such gloomy forebodings?" smiling at my serious face.

"There is a young widow staying here."

"A widow!" he exclaimed in his deep, tender voice. "Poor thing, what harm can she do us?"

I was silenced with compunction. If I thought the late Mr. Mossom was anything like Jack, his widow might as well be called "poor thing."

I hastened to change the subject.

"Are you going to Sherwood's?" I asked.

"If you will go with me. That is why I came so soon. I wanted to get ahead of the other fellows."

Some time was required—or we imagined so—to talk over the party, and we lingered in the shade of the lindens until the sun went down behind the mountains.

When I returned, alone, to the house, the family were on the portico taking tea, and watching the golden sunset.

I, with all my nerves atremble, too happy to take tea, or talk about clouds, seated myself on the steps below the rest of the company, and, clasping my knees with my hands, looked up into the sky and dreamed of—the Sherwood party.

II

Our little company soon ranged themselves. Lottie and I, with our young visitors, formed the gay portion of the household. My uncle and aunt with Mr. Power and Mrs. Mossom were more quiet in their enjoyments.

Mr. Power, indeed, usually kept company with himself. He seemed to have plenty to say to my uncle, but when the ladies made their appearance, he had always an excuse for leaving. He would either go and smoke a solitary cigar on the back portico or bury his nose in a newspaper. Mrs. Mossom had the most remarkable effect on his nerves. He had become, in a measure, accustomed to Lottie and me in

the summer before, and bore our entrance into a room where he was with tolerable equanimity; but at the sight of Mrs. Mossom, he would turn red, stammer, and look uncomfortable until he made his escape. The lady, herself, seemed not to notice his painful shyness, but it was great fun to us girls. Mrs. Mossom had a fine talent for not seeing what she did not wish to see, or she could scarcely have so completely ignored our ill-concealed amusement whenever she and Mr. Power were in the same room. We watched them narrowly, exchanged glances, turned red with suppressed laughter, in fact behaved in a very school-girlish way, but she seemed severely unconscious of our bad manners.

One of Mr. Power's habits we found particularly amusing. He and the widow were great pedestrians, taking their five miles constitutional every day in the cool of the evening; but he was so fearful lest they should meet in their rambles, that he never set out until he had ascertained what road she had taken, and then he turned his steps in the opposite direction so that there would be no possibility of meeting, unless, indeed, they each walked half round the world and met on the other side of the globe.

The evening after our walk in the linden avenue Jack Bryan came again accompanied by Archie Cullen. They were great friends, these two, although utterly unlike. Indeed their points of difference seemed their strongest bond of union. Archie was small and not handsome; but he had plenty of brains. In a fight Jack could have knocked the breath out of his body in five minutes; in an argument he tripped

Jack up in less time than that. But there was never any rivalry between the two, although Lottie and I sometimes squabbled over their respective merits. She affected intellect; I admired form, grace, color and had a profound respect for muscle.

When we got down stairs to the gentlemen, who had been waiting a few minutes while we added some touches to our toilet, were discussing a lady who was in the parlor when they arrived but soon after left the room.

As soon as the first greetings were over Archie asked Lottie, "who is the lady in the black dress with the beautiful white hands? Such hands! On her bombazine lap they looked like a flower-de-luce on a field sable."

Lottie, who was poetically inclined, admired Archie's flights of fancy when addressed to herself; inspired by another they were not so effective. She answered without enthusiasm.

"Mrs. Mossom, I suppose."

"What do *you* think of her?" I asked, turning eagerly to Jack.

"The same as Cullen," he said with delightful indifference to the widow.

"Oh! That is impossible," said Lottie.

"How so?" he asked.

"I don't believe you know what a flower-de-luce and a field-sable are."

The dimples in Lottie's face gave her an immunity for saying what she pleased.

"That is so. I haven't an idea," said Jack laughing. "But there goes the lady now."

Following the direction of his eyes we saw through the open window Mrs. Mossom, with parasol and shade hat starting off on her afternoon walk. This time, her elegant figure and graceful movements came in for Archie's commendation.

"She walks like Juno! Doesn't she, Jack?"

"Yes, she walks like—like everything." Jack was not fluent.

We looked after her retreating figure with its undulating flow of black drapery, until she was lost to sight on the road that, a few miles south of my uncle's house, ended in a bosky dell, one of the most beautiful and romantic spots in the neighborhood.

When she had been gone quite long enough for us to have forgotten the incident, we were reminded of it by seeing Mr. Power, armed with a stout walking stick, come out of the house to take his constitutional, and as Mrs. Mossom had gone south he turned his face due north.

As this oft repeated little comedy was re-enacted under our eyes, Lottie burst out into a tinkle of laughter that excited Archie's curiosity.

She explained to him that Mr. Power, being dreadfully shy, was always running away from Mrs. Mossom; and then went on, in a grandmotherly kind of way, to express her interest in the two and how nice it would be for them to make a match. When upon Archie intimated that, as the lady had already made one match for herself, she might be trusted to manage her own affairs in regard to a second, and that Lottie had better be looking after her own admirers. Lottie admitted that there was sense in what he said, and took occasion to carry out his suggestion by going off with him to the summer house.

III

The Sherwood entertainment came off and Lottie and I enjoyed it as much as we had anticipated, which is saying a great deal. Jack was very attentive to me, so devoted indeed as to excite comment. I thought, myself, that he was on the point of saying something very particular, under the stairs after supper; but another couple found us there, and the words I was expecting were not spoken.

The next morning Lottie and I, with my aunt and Mrs. Mossom, were talking over the party in the dining-room after breakfast. We were all engaged in some flimsy summer work. Mrs. Mossom was knitting a cloud in pink wool for Lottie.

It is true that Lottie amused herself making impossible matches for the widow behind her back, but she was very sweet and friendly when they were together and Mrs. Mossom liked her.

Mr. Power, who had come in to read the morning news, finding such a feminine array, had gathered up the papers and hurried out again. When he was gone he fell, naturally, under discussion.

"I do wish Mr. Power was not so shy," said my aunt, "he has so much sense and is so thoroughly good, it is a pity for him to hide his light under a bushel of modesty."

"He ought to get married," said Lottie gravely.

"I quite agree with you," said my aunt, "But how is it to be done? How could he ever screw up his courage to make a proposal when he is afraid to look at a woman?"

"He might do as the children do when they take medicine; shut his eyes and open his mouth," I suggested.

"Yes," said Lottie, seconding my motion with animation, "that would do. I have noticed that when he does open his mouth he speaks to the purpose. Couldn't somebody blindfold him?"

Mrs. Mossom, who had been counting stitches, looked up and gave Lottie one of the rare, bright smiles with which she sometimes rewarded friend's light-hearted nonsense. It inspired Lottie to speak more freely.

"I have a match in my mind for him," she said earnestly.

Everybody laughed. The absurdity of a little creature like Lottie mapping out a man's destiny was irresistible.

She was not disconcerted.

"I wish he would let me do his courting for him," she continued. "He would be married before the year is out."

"Why don't you make a match for your friend, Mr. Cullen?" said Mrs. Mossom, without a shadow of a smile that Lottie or I could detect. My friend, cogitating as to whether the widow meant more than met the ear, was silent for a longer time than usual.

"If you were thirty," said my aunt; addressing me. "I should advise you to set your cap for Mr. Power. He *does* say a word to you now and then."

I bridled, although I knew the words he said to me were, for the most part, about the weather. Perhaps this conversation, or the natural depravity of youth, prompted Lottie and me to try and bring about meetings with a view to making a match between Mr. Power and Mrs. Mossom.

I remember well our first experiment and its result.

One morning I had purposely left the newspapers in the parlor with the understanding that Lottie was to decoy Mrs. Mossom thither on the pretext of arranging flowers and then leave her.

I stationed myself in the dining-room, knowing that Mr. Power would be along presently to look over the papers as was his habit every morning when he thought the coast was clear of ladies. He was not long in making his appearance.

"I beg pardon, but do you know where the papers are?" he stammered after an ineffectual search.

"Yes, I was so thoughtless as to leave them in the parlor, wait a moment and I will get them for you," I said, making a motion to go.

"By no means, I will get them myself," he said energetically, moving off. At the door he turned back, looking a little flurried. "Is anybody in the parlor?" he asked.

"Nobody was there when I left," I answered, turning to the window to hide my guilty face. He went off nothing doubting.

Lottie and I, like boys who wait round the corner to see the effect of their firecrackers, waited in the hall to see the result of the meeting he had brought about. Never were conspirators more completely foiled.

Mr. Power, having reached the middle of the room before he perceived Mrs. Mossom, whose back was turned, halted with an explanation of dismay. The lady, busy with her flowers, glanced hastily over her shoulder, startled by the sound. At this moment, Lottie and I, on tiptoe, full of expectation for the next move, were brought to confusion by the entrance,

through another door, of my aunt, whom we had imagined safe for an hour with her housekeeper.

"My! My! Who has been littering the room with newspapers?" she exclaimed.

The spell was broken, Mr. Power recovered himself and escaped. Lottie and I were slinking away, when Mrs. Mossom with heightened color and impatient step came out of the room.

She gave Lottie and me, huddled together near the door, a searching glance, and I knew by the reflection of my feelings in my friend's face that we were a miserably guilty-looking pair.

IV

The very day of our discomfiture an incident occurred which convinced me how desirable it was that Mrs. Mossom should become interested in Mr. Power, or some other suitable person.

That evening Lottie and I, with several visitors, among whom were our friends Mr. Bryan and Mr. Cullen, were sitting together at one end of the portico. Quite at the other end, forty or fifty feet away, Mrs. Mossom, in a low rocking-chair, was swaying gently back and forth, knitting on Lottie's pink cloud. Her pale, high-bred face and the rhythmic motion of her graceful figure in widow's weeds were very pleasant to look upon, and attracted the attention of more than one pair of eyes in our party.

I was feeling very happy with Jack on the steps at my feet although, in the general conversation going on, we had not much to say to each other. He never remained long when I had other company, so I was not surprised when he rose to go.

He had lifted his hat in bidding us good-bye and in another moment would have been gone, but just then a ball of pink worsted fell from Mrs. Mossom's lap and, rolling the length of the portico, came to a stop not far from where he stood.

He darted forward to pick it up and I watched him as he returned it to the owner with the deferential inclination which made a bow from Jack such a compliment. The lady's beautiful smile of thanks was more than a reward for his slight service. He paused a moment to say a few words before leaving, but the few words grew presently to be many. Finally he took his seat beside her and as he leaned forward, watching the movement of her knitting-needles, I could hear their pleasant voices in an uninterrupted flow of conversation. I am afraid I appeared *distraite* to the man who was trying to entertain me. I know my eyes often wandered to where those two were sitting, their figures outlined in beautiful relief against the glowing western sky.

"Had it not been for that odious, little pink ball," I mused, "he would have been half way home by this time."

His horse stood impatiently stamping and champing at the gate, but still he lingered. He seemed so much interested that he might have remained there until now, but presently she dismissed him by rising, "I must go in now, it is getting chilly," she said, wrapping the pink cloud around her head and shoulders in a wonderful, becoming way.

I suspect that Lottie was secretly amused at my gravity that evening. I know that when our company was gone, she made herself very merry over Jack and Mrs. Mossom.

"I have heard of 'beauty drawing with a single red hair,' but never with a strand of pink worsted," she said, laughing.

Her cheerfulness annoyed me. She could afford to be cheerful, Archie Cullen had eyes and ears for nobody but herself.

After tea I was standing alone on the portico, troubled with vague discontent, gazing sadly at the stars, when a most unusual thing occurred. I heard the crunching of a heavy step on the gravel walk.

My heart beat quick with expectation as a figure emerged from leafy shadows into the light, that streamed softly from the hall lamp. My excitement subsided when I found that it was Mr. Power. I remember being half amused to see that he carried a bunch of roses, for I had never seen him with a flower before. He smiled when he saw me star-gazing alone in the dusk, and coming up the steps, to where I stood, gave me his roses. Had the stars above fallen at my feet I could not have been more astonished.

"I gathered these for you," he said, in his grave, shy way, and passed into the house before I had sufficiently recovered from my surprise to thank him.

What was the meaning of this? Did Mr. Power feel more than a friendly interest in me? The remembrance of Aunt Brinton's playful words flashed over me. The idea was absurd, and yet there came, quick as thought, the desire to make Jack feel the twinge of jealousy I was suffering. I returned to the house, my nose buried in the roses, my head full of dreams and fancies.

My forebodings with regard to Jack proved correct. The acquaintance with Mrs. Mossom ripened, on his part, into undisguised admiration. He became as attentive to the lady as she would permit him to be. It was impossible not to see that my empire was divided. Day by day I felt my happiness slipping away from me. This state of things became apparent to those who looked on. One afternoon, Mop, the colored girl supposed to perform the duties of lady's maid to Lottie and me, was pretending to brush one of my dresses but, in fact, was amusing herself looking out of the window. Suddenly she exclaimed, "La! Miss, dar go Mr. Bryan a-walkin wid Miss Mossom. He ain't yo bo no mo, is he?"

My cup of humiliation was full.

My attempt to play off Mr. Power succeeded indifferently. His attentions were sporadic and not to be relied on, and Jack did not seem a bit jealous.

Lottie was a trial to me in those days. She was so light-hearted and secure in Archie Cullen's loyalty. But her bad quarter of an hour came. One day Mrs. Mossom returned from her woodland rambles, her hands so full of ferns, mosses and vines, that two young men she picked up on her way insisted on helping to bring them home. She would not trust her treasures to their masculine hands, but graciously permitted them to hold up the vines that on either side trailed on the ground. Lottie and I were in the avenue when the party entered the gate; Mrs. Mossom, with her stately tread, coming up the walk looked like a conqueror bringing captives in her train. That is, it required no great stretch of the imagination for Lottie and me to regard it in that light, for the young men she held in chains were Jack Bryan and Archie Cullen.

Mrs. Mossom, her face glowing with exercise, her garments fragrant with the breath of the woods, paused when she reached Lottie and me and generously offered us some of her prettiest ferns.

"No, I thank you, I hate ferns," said Lottie with unusual asperity.

"That is because you are young," said Mrs. Mossom with an indulgent smile. "Young people like flowers better, they are so much gayer than ferns."

"I am sorry you hate them Miss Linley," said Archie, "I was about to propose that you and I would go fern-hunting some day in the woods."

Lottie looked like a blank at having thrown away such an opportunity, and her countenance indicated a willingness to be converted to ferns.

"It seems a charming, *companionable* occupation, eh Jack?" continued Archie, his face beaming with a hidden meaning that roused my suspicions.

Could he have found Mrs. Mossom and Jack fern-hunting together?

I glanced from the lady, who colored slightly, to Jack who laughed uneasily as he replied, "I am sure I don't know, I never have tried it."

I wondered, with a pain at my heart, if he was getting to be deceitful.

Mrs. Mossom and her attendants passed on to the house where she dismissed them.

"Much obliged," we heard her say, "I am going in now. You will find it pleasant in the avenue with the young ladies."

She was actually turning them over to us.

V

Mrs. Mossom was one of those women to whom—without effort, apparently without a wish on her part—all men pay homage of some kind. Even shy Mr. Power paid her the tribute of being shyer than ever in her presence, while Archie Cullen yielded to the charm of her personal influence as readily as Jack Bryan. Lottie was destined to go through the discomfort I was suffering, but she bore it more patiently. I was very proud and scornful, although on one occasion my curiosity got the better of my pride. Jack and I were on horseback, walking our horses through a green lane after a brisk gallop on the road. Some ferns growing in a shaded hollow reminded me of Archie's innuendo.

"Will you tell me something?" I asked inconsequently in the middle of a discussion on the relative constancy of men and women. Jack, who had removed his hat the better to enjoy the breeze that ruffled the leaves overhead, answered gravely:

"Anything in my power."

"Oh, don't be so serious about it. It is a very small matter, only that I should like to know what Mr. Cullen meant by saying that fern-hunting was a *companionable* occupation."

"Because he thought so, I dare say."

"One would have imagined from the way he appealed to you that he had seen you fern-hunting with some one," I said, whipping the leaves from low, overhanging boughs.

"But I said I never had been," answered Jack warmly, turning his honest eyes on my averted face.

"So you did; I beg your pardon," I said, ashamed of having suspected him of an untruth. "But," I continued, whipping the boughs more vigorously, "didn't Mr. Cullen mean something more than what he said?"

"Well, yes," returned Jack, evidently surprised at my interest in the matter.

"Then tell me, please," I asked, blushing at my own pertinacity.

Jack looked at me for a moment, then reining in his horse, pointed with his whip to a domestic fowl that ran cackling across the road.

"Do you know what that is?" he asked gravely.

"That?" I repeated, puzzled to see the connection. "Why, yes; that is a goose."

"And so are you," he replied, in a tone that made me happier to be called a goose by him than a wit by another.

That was all the information I got.

Not long after this Aunt Brinton decided to give us a party. It was to be a large affair. Everybody was to be invited. The lawn and gardens were to be illuminated; we were to have music and dancing, and everything that could make a country party delightful. The house was turned upside down, for the dining-room was to be the dancing room, and the supper was to be upstairs.

Mrs. Mossom was helpful about everything. I don't know what my aunt would have done without her. It is true that she had an able and intelligent co-worker in Archie Cullen, who had only to hear a suggestion to understand and obey. What prodigies of work he and Mrs. Mossom performed for that ball. Lottie did not enjoy these preparations as much as I did.

Archie followed Mrs. Mossom like her shadow. Under her supervision he devoted himself to house decoration with an ardor of which, I am sure, he had never until now believed himself capable.

I was enchanted that Jack was a clumsy fellow about some things. He could manage a horse, an oar, or a bat, but tacks and tack-hammers, paste-pot and scissors were as impossible to his hands as a needle and thread. Archie had it all his own way in the decoration business.

One rainy day in the middle of our preparations, when there was not a place to sit down, I found Mr. Power in the dining-room, the picture of discomfort, but with an unusually cheerful countenance, mounted on top of a step-ladder, smoking a pipe.

"What are you doing, perched up there?" I asked, gathering my skirts around me, and picking my way through rubbish and litter, in search of a book I had left somewhere.

"Where else can a fellow sit? I am like Noah on Ararat; this is the only dry spot to be found."

Mr. Power must have felt very safe, out of harm's way in his elevated position. I had never known him to be facetious before.

"You are not a bit like Noah," I replied; "he took the whole family with him, and you have your Ararat all to yourself."

"Glad to share my seat with you, if you don't mind smoke," he said, making a place for me with an airiness of which I had not believed him capable.

"You should always sit on a step-ladder, Mr. Power, the situation seems to agree with you; I never knew you to speak so much to the point. Thank you, no. I do not wish to sit down."

While I was speaking, Lottie, looking heated and vexed, came in, fanning herself vigorously with a newspaper.

"Oh, dear! Oh, dear!" she was saying, "I wonder why some things were ever made except to bother other things?"

"What are you talking about?" I asked.

"Flies," she said, slapping at one ineffectually, "and," setting her teeth, "widows!" bringing out the last word so vehemently that Mr. Power nearly toppled from his seat.

"How do you like widows, Mr. Power?" I asked maliciously.

"Widows! Widows!" he repeated, stammering and reddening, "If I had my way there would not be one in the house." A remark which, from any one else, would have sounded ambiguous.

Lottie and I had one consolation. We were at least to be queens of our own ball.

Mrs. Mossom declined to be present on account of her black dress, and made arrangements to spend the night at the house of a friend in the neighborhood. Mr. Power, too, backed out on the plea of not having brought a dress-coat to the country.

I think I never looked so well as on the night of our party. My dress was so great a success that, when I entered the dancing-room, I wondered who the tall, handsome girl opposite to me could be, and blushed to find that it was myself reflected in a mirror. Partners for the dance crowded me, and repeated in many a word and glance what the mirror had already told me. I began the evening in the gayest spirits, but Jack, who had driven Mrs. Mossom to the house where she was to spend the night, did not come early, and my eyes often wandered anxiously toward the door. I saved several dances for him, but he did not come to claim them. Could Mrs. Mossom have kept him? I tried not to be uncharitable to her. I wished her no worse harm than that the late Mr. Mossom had not died and left her a widow.

The music and dancing went on, but they began to lose their charms for me. The tender speeches, which at first seemed such fun, grew painfully insipid as I waited and watched for Jack. When at last he came, just before supper, I would not look at him. As soon as he arrived he crossed the room to speak to me, but I pretended to be too deeply interested in my companion to see him. He turned on his heel and went away. I rejoiced in the belief that he was hurt. When the party was over I went to bed and cried myself to sleep.

The next day was as bright as though there was no aching hearts in the world. It was the day on which Mrs. Mossom was to leave for her home in the South. Our company was breaking up. The day following, Mr. Power was going back to his home in the North; he and the widow, to the last, going to opposite points of the compass.

When Mrs. Mossom, equipped for traveling, went round, bidding everyone good-bye, I was disposed to hold back resentfully, I don't know for what, unless for her fascinations, which I dare say she could not help, but she seemed not to notice my childishness.

"Good-bye, girls," she said to Lottie and me very affectionately and with so sweet a smile that the impulsive Lottie threw her arms around her and kissed her, a proceeding I thought entirely unnecessary.

Mine were probably the only dry eyes in the group that waved her adieu as my uncle drove her to the station.

The morning after Mr. Power's departure Lottie and I came down late to breakfast. We had scarcely taken our places, when my aunt began, "Girls," she said, breaking an egg with the deftness of daily practice, "I have something to tell you."

We were all attention. She looked as if her news might be interesting.

"A lady has asked me to tell you of her engagement."

"An engagement! Any of those spooney couples who were at the party the other night?" asked Lottie.

"No, this couple were not at the party, but you know the lady very well, Mrs. Mossom."

Lottie and I looked at each other, this time in speechless amazement.

"Mrs. Mossom?" I gasped, "to whom?"

"Mr. Power."

"How? When? Where?" asked Lottie in a breath.

I think from the way my uncle laughed that he never enjoyed a comedy as much as the expression of our faces at this announcement.

My aunt, with laudable effort to tell what she had to tell with becoming dignity, was shaken by his uproarious merriment. It was sometime before she could answer Lottie's comprehensive question.

"As to *how* the engagement took place, I don't know; the usual way, I suppose. But I do know *when* it occurred, for the lady told me; it was the very day before our party."

"And that is the reason he looked such a smiling idiot on top of the step-ladder that day!" I exclaimed.

"Possibly. *Where* it all happened, I can only conjecture, was among the ferns."

"And his running away from Mrs. Mossom was all bosh?" said Lottie.

"All bosh," said my aunt, wiping her eyes.

"To deceive us, I suppose?" said I.

"Well, to turn your attention from her affairs. You know you two were disposed to make fun of Mr. Power and the widow when you first came."

"So she turned the tables and made fun of us," I said bitterly, seeing with a flash of enlightenment how she had used Jack and Archie as a blind, and had probably put Mr. Power up to giving me a rose.

"And the courting and the engagement," laughed Lottie, whose temper was more facile than mine, "took place under our very noses, and we did not suspect!"

"Just so," said my uncle.

I began to understand why Jack would not tell me about the fern hunting. He and Archie had probably seen this engaged couple so employed, and felt it a point of honor not to tell.

"We will not tilt against a young widow again, will we?" said Lottie, who had entirely recovered her good humor.

"No," I said savagely, "for in 'the ways that are dark' they are worse than the heathen Chinee."[8]

"Come, now; you know she let us off very easily, considering how impertinent we were."

There was no gainsaying this, but I never quite forgave the widow until I had entirely made up with Jack.

As to Archie Cullen, I do not know what explanation he made to my friend of his temporary defection, but I do know that she took him back and seemed very glad to get him.

Two Negatives (1889)

I

Her Letter

By a change, which in the order of evolution seems natural, the feminine portion of the Confederate States Treasury Department at Richmond was lodged in a building which had served originally as a fashionable dry-goods store. There exists, in men's minds at least, and indissoluble connection between women and dry goods. One cynical husband of the period was known to say that the irony of fate decreed that where women used to spend good money for worthless rags they were now converting good rags into worthless money.

The fifth and uppermost story of the old dry-goods store was occupied by the aristocracy of the Department. For there, as elsewhere, there was an aristocracy. In every community, as in every pan of unskimmed milk, there are elements which detach themselves from the rest and rise to the top. The cream of the Treasury consisted of a score of pretty girls who, high up under the roof, signed their names to bits of blue paper[9] and made money at the rate of a million dollars a day. Ask any old Treasury clerk of the sterner sex—they are all old fellows now—what name was given the room in which those slim-fingered girls forged the sinews of war. Ten to one his eyes will flash with the light of other days as he answers, "Angels' Retreat."

Now "Angels' Retreat" was a dusty, cob-webby attic, bare of furniture, except for a lining of shelves, which gave evidence of its former use in storing purple and fine linen, and rough writing-tables adapted to its present purpose. The lodgment was poor enough, but there was no question about the angels. They were as good as can be made. The Retreat during working-hours had the appearance nothing so much as a young ladies' school at writing-time. Twenty girls bending over desks and twenty pens scratching in unison. Absence of school discipline was indicated by twenty tongues often talking at once. The sun coming in through dormer windows on two sides of the room shone on the usual medley of fair and brown types, only that in this instance the types were unusually fine. Among them was of course a beauty par excellence; likewise a vivacious girl they dubbed chief speaker, and a lovable one they called the favorite of the Retreat. Beauty answered to the name of Rose Chandler. The chief speaker was one Norah Grattan; while the favorite, Madge Dillon, an enthusiastic young Carolinian who had gained the sobriquet of "Palmetto,"[10] her companions, with the superlative speech of feminine youth, declared to be "the nicest girl in the world."

Rose Chandler's supremacy in the matter of looks did not admit of doubt. She was a beauty of the loveliest type, with a fabulous number of "Lee's miserable" at her feet.

Norah Grattan would have been plain but for a clever, satirical mouth and a pair of keen, gray eyes. Palmetto, a tall, slender brunette, was ordinarily not pretty, but capable of great illumination on occasions.

The Confederate Treasury hours were from 9 a.m. to 4 p.m., and within that time the clerks signed from two to four thousand notes, according to their ability. Palmetto's signature, "M. Dillon," being short, and her writing being rapid, she was able to put in the larger number every day without troubling herself to be punctual, so she rarely made her appearance before ten o'clock. This in another would have been a finable breach of the Treasury rules. Palmetto, the angels complained, was in some incomprehensible way independent of rules. But this is not an altogether haphazard world, and the people who seem independent of rules balance the account somewhere, and are, for the most part, exceptional people who do better without rules than others with them. Palmetto's work, clean, swift, and clerkly, was the best in the Treasury. Why should she bother about rules? She was the poorest and of necessity the proudest of the angels. She did not explain what household drudgery she had to do at home before she came to the Department, and her unruffled countenance and her neat dress did not betray her.

One cold morning early in December she entered the Retreat at ten o'clock, as was her custom, and her appearance was greeted with a gust of exclamation.

"Well, here you are at last! We have been waiting for you."

The stir created by her entrance every

morning would have led one to suppose that she ranked her fellow-angels as an archangel, but this big unanimous breath of welcome was even more emphatic than usual.

"What is it now?" she asked, disposing of her wraps and her lunch basket on one of the old dry-goods shelves and trying to thaw her fingers at an ineffectual stove.

Palmetto posed well as archangel. Besides overtopping her companions in the matter of height, she had a distinguished air of her own. She was large-natured in every way, and was everybody's friend, with a decided leaning towards the underdog.

In her companions' estimation there was nothing she could not do, from the tying of a shoulder-knot to the pacification of a feminine feud. Certainly there were few things she had not been called upon to do since she became a Treasury clerk.

"Oh yes," she said when once questioned on the subject, "there are some things I have not done for the girls. They have never asked me to buy or sell horses."

"What is it now?" she repeated on this particular morning when her presence was hailed with so much interest. She stood before her desk, the tips of her slender fingers resting on it as though it was a keyboard, and with head thrown slightly back, looked round on the fresh-faced pen-drivers for explanation.

The direct question reduced the chorus of voices to a titter. Everybody looked to somebody else to explain. The angels addressed themselves to the note-signing with vigor. That is, all except the beauty, Rose

Chandler, who sat biting her pen-handle with a deprecating expression, as if she wished to say something but did not know how. She looked as rosy and beautiful as the dawn, but withal a little silly, as though the dawn was ashamed of itself.

"Well!" said Palmetto, taking her seat and arranging her things preparatory to writing her name four thousand times. "Can't some of you tell me what it's all about?"

"Help wanted—female," said Norah Grattan with a dry smile, fishing a superfluous hair out of her inkstand. "Your peculiar talents are invoked to assist a lady out of a tight place. There's Rose Chandler now—"

"Rose?" exclaimed Palmetto, arching her eyebrows. It was something new for Miss Chandler to want assistance. "What can she want with help, female or otherwise, having a good part of the army at her back?"

"Now, Palmetto," remonstrated Rose, still nibbling her pen, "you know that's an exaggeration; besides, those army fellows are the very people who give one trouble."

"They don't bother me"—with delightful frankness.

"Because you have a talent for keeping men straight," said Rose, politely, knowing that Palmetto had few admirers. "But I haven't; I can't even sign these old notes straight."

"Perhaps if you were to devote more attention to the other end of your pen you would do better," suggested Norah.

Whereupon Rose, amid a general smile, left off nibbling, and began scrawling her name. Note-signing, it may be remarked, is an occupation charmingly adapted to women, being compatible equally with want of thought and endless conversation.

"You see, Palmetto," resumed Rose, "I want somebody to write a very particular letter for me. I asked Norah and she wouldn't, and all the girls said they were sure you would."

"All the girls are very kind to offer my services"—with a circular bow to the company; "but I should thing that writing your own letter would be more satisfactory to your correspondent."

"But you see I don't know what to say."

"I am equally at a loss," began Palmetto, intending to be satirical, when her satire was nipped in the bud by the entrance of one of the men clerks bringing in her package of notes, which he proceeded to count in her presence before delivering. He was a good-looking young fellow, well calculated under normal circumstances to create a flutter in a dovecote like the Retreat, but men clerks were not in repute during the war, women acting severely on the principle that none but the brave deserve the fair. Poor Waller counted his notes in chilling silence. The angels did not even take the trouble to look their best, but pulled long faces and looked their worst. Only Rose's beautiful blue eyes gave him one soft glance as instinctive as the extension of pussy's velvet paw at sight of a mouse, and then she called herself to order and remembered that in spite of his broad shoulders and shapely limbs he was nothing but a man clerk.

When he was gone the subject of her letter was resumed. The matter was pressing and she was in earnest. It may be said in explanation that Rose, whose reputation as beauty and belle was co-extensive with the Confederacy, had no secrets from her companions. She talked with them of her admirers as openly and artlessly as another would talk of her bonnets—or lack of bonnets, as was more apt to be the case during the war.

"Now, Palmetto, I'm not jesting," she said. "I want you to write a letter right away. My—my friend says there is to be a battle soon, and he wants an answer before he goes into it."

"What is the answer to be—yes, or no?" asked Palmetto, gravely.

"Why, no, of course. I know how to say yes. But when you refuse a person I suppose you must let them down 'easy,' and that is what I don't know how to do."

Palmetto's face flushed. She took things more seriously.

"You are a heartless little monkey, Rose. You don't mind disappointing the man, but you shirk the trouble to yourself. No, you must do your own refusing. I don't know how to do it. I never refused a man in my life."

"Neither did I."

"Oh, oh!" from all parts of the room.

"It's true," said Rose, stoutly.

"Then what *do* you do with all your 'captains, colonels, and commanders-in-chief?'" asked Norah.

"I—I—"

"It isn't possible that you accept them all?"

"It's less trouble."

"Oh, you dreadful girl! And what becomes of them after you accept them?"

"I don't know; I suppose they just—dangle."

"I see," said Norah, "like fish. Recipe:

you first angle, then entangle, then dangle them."

"That sounds very fine, but I never angle"—with dignity.

"Oh, no! I dare say you never steal soft looks at them."

"Pooh!" blushing, and looking prettier than ever. "I can wear goggles, or a blind bridle."

"Rose," said Palmetto, interrupting this side skirmish, "what makes you refuse this one? Why not let him dangle with the rest?"

"He won't dangle; I wish he would. He is the most distinguished of all. But he says he must have an answer at once. It's very hard,"

"He won't dangle?" said Norah. "Upon my word, I am delighted to hear it. He is the only man among them. What's his name?"

"It's—it's a French name"—nibbling again.

"You don't mean that handsome creole, Major Rodrigue?"

"Major Rodrigue," assented Rose.

"Then I won't do it. You can't expect me to do for you what I would not do for myself," said Palmetto, warmly. And all the angels fell to laughing at the vehemence of her confession.

Rose opened wide her blue eyes. She was not insensible to the spur of the rivalry. "You mean you would not refuse Major Rodrigue? I did not know you knew him."

"Nor do I, except by reputation," said Palmetto with heightened color. "What I mean is that I should never let him or any man ask me if I could only refuse him."

Rose put up her lip discontentedly. "You don't know what you would do if—"

"If I were a belle?" interrupted Palmetto, good-humoredly. "That is so."

"Not that, but if you were me."

"If I were you I suppose I should do as you do."

"Being Palmetto, you will do like a dear, good girl and write the letter for me."

In the end Palmetto was persuaded, against her judgment, to write the letter. But her sympathies were all with the Major. She could not understand his devotion to a flimsy coquette like Rose; but then women never understand men's taste in the matter of women, and she felt sorry for him.

His letter, which Rose gave her to answer, touched her deeply.

Written on the eve of battle, it laid bare his heart, full of manly and tender love. To Palmetto it was desecration that it should be seen by other eyes than those for which it was intended. Her face tingled with shame that she should be reading the secrets of a brave man's soul.

Rose's flippancy had made the affair a bit of commonplace; the Major's simplicity translated it into poetry, and inspired Palmetto to write a worthy answer. It was the only amend she could make. Never perhaps has a woman's refusal been expressed more generously and sympathetically, nor pair a higher tribute to the man. It was written in the heat of the moment after her notes were signed, in the brief space before the Department was closed, and was all the better because she had no time to spend on calligraphy or the polishing of phrases. It was far beyond the capabilities of the girl in whose name it was being sent. Rose's sugared little platitudes were to Palmetto's breathing words as the ticking of a lady's watch to the beating of a heart.

"How will this do?" cried Palmetto, flushed with guilty consciousness that she was in a way deceiving the Major, and excited by the unusual task of refusing a man who had never proposed to her.

Standing with her bonnet and shawl on, ready to depart as soon as she got through, she read the document aloud for Rose's approval, while the angels put down their pens to listen.

Rose's request had been greeted with laughter. Palmetto's way of granting it made them serious, not to say solemn.

Rose hung her head.

"O Palmetto!" she said presently, "I'm so much obliged to you. I could never have written like that."

"I should think not," said Norah.

"There!" cried Palmetto, tossing the letter to Rose. "It is written shockingly and on shabby paper; so be sure to copy it before you send it, and never let me hear of it again. I had much rather try to trade a horse for you that do the like another time."

"All right," said Rose, wondering if, after all, she was wise in refusing Rodrigue. "Anyhow," she reflected, "he will give me credit for a beautiful letter."

It was Saturday afternoon. The Treasury clerks would not meet again until Monday, so Palmetto threw her companions a kiss as she called out, "Goodbye, girls!" A flight of kisses and a hubbub of girlish voices followed her with an affectionate, "Goodbye, Palmetto!"

Late that evening, while Rose was in close conversation with one of her epauletted danglers, she was startled by an energetic pull at the house-bell, followed by Palmetto's abrupt entrance into the parlor, where Rose was winding up one of her little affairs.

"O Palmetto!" she cried, rising and covering the gentleman's confusion by more than ordinary effusiveness. "So glad to see you! Let me introduce Captain Dalrymple; Captain Dalrymple, my friend Miss Dillon."

The Captain, who in the meantime had made a dive under the sofa in the search of his hat, acknowledged the introduction with a very red face.

But Palmetto was too preoccupied to notice the gentleman's heat or the lady's coolness.

"Thank you, Rose; I can't sit down. Haven't a moment to stay. I came on a little private business. Can't you come into the hall with me? Captain Dalrymple, you will excuse us; I won't keep Miss Chandler."

"What is it?" asked Rose, her curiosity excited to the highest point by Palmetto's eagerness.

"Have you sent that letter?"

"That letter?"—bewildered. Dalrymple had for the moment obscured Rodrigue. "Oh, yes. Why, long ago"—laughing, and relieved to find it nothing worse. "An orderly was waiting for it while you wrote. The Major was to leave town at four o'clock."

"Rose, did you copy the letter before you sent it?"—anxiously.

Rose changed color. Palmetto's intensity was discomposing.

"To tell you the truth," she began.

"Rose, don't you say you sent the letter without copying it."

"What difference does it make? *I* don't mind the bad writing. He will think it was because I was agitated."

"Pooh! Didn't you even *look* at it before you sent it?"

Rose was obliged to confess that she was so pressed for time that she had thrust it in an envelope and sent it without looking at it.

"Do you know what you have done?" cried Palmetto. "You have sent it signed with my name."

"You don't mean it," gasped Rose, to whom this intelligence was anything but agreeable. "What made you put your name?"

"I did it mechanically, of course, and unconsciously. How could I help is, having just signed my name four thousand times? When I got home I thought about it, and I know I put 'M. Dillon;' and oh!" cried Palmetto with burning cheeks, "it serves me right for having written the letter at all. My sin has found me out."

A little cough from Captain Dalrymple within reminded Rose of his existence, which she had forgotten in her dismay on learning that Major Rodrigue by this time knew that she had betrayed his confidence and employed another girl to reject him, and she would not even get the credit of having written the beautiful letter!

It was a horrible contretemps. Palmetto worked off some of her feeling on the house door, while Rose made it no easier for the Captain.

II

His Letter

On the Sunday which intervened before the Treasury clerks met again a great battle was fought, as so often happened on Sunday with dearly bought victory on the Confederate side. Late the night before the engagement, Major Rodrigue, a young artillery officer, having placed his guns on the height where they were to do effective work in the morning, and having seen to the minutest detail of preparation for the attack rightly anticipated at dawn, drew from his bosom, to read once more, the letter he had received from Rose Chandler. He had already read it many times, and each time with a modification of feeling. As he opened it now, for the last time, he remembered, with a sort of self-pity, the thrill of joy with which he had recognized her writing address and the ardor with he had pressed it to his lips. Then, how on opening the envelope he had been chilled and puzzled by the unfamiliar hand within, and, as he read, how he had forgotten the writing in the words—so kind, so gentle; treating love so reverently, and himself with such tender regret that she could not make his happiness. It had dawned upon him then that he had not given Rose credit for so much feeling. Her rejection seemed more akin to love than any kindness she had shown him. His heart glowed within his breast again. Then when he turned the page and saw the signature, "M. Dillon," he started as if he had been shot. The hot indignant blood mounted to his face. He had been betrayed.

Reading it now for the last time by the

light of his campfire he felt that he had forgiven Rose Chandler, and forgiveness was more painful than resentment. In the last few hours he had learned the value of a woman who could encourage a man's honest love and reject him with a practical joke. The letter had destroyed for him more than could the enemy's guns. And yet he read it again. Some words in it had, for a moment, warmed his heart, and he lingered over them with the bitter reflection that they were only words.

"Pshaw!" he said at last, holding the letter over the fire until it crumbled to ashes. He buttoned up his overcoat and walked up and down in the shadow of a long line of breastworks overlooking the enemy's camp.

The night was clear and cold, a full moon hung high in the heavens, and her brilliance was reflected in the glitter of a light fall of snow which covered the earth and encrusted the blue and the gray of two sleeping armies.

"I wonder," mused Rodrigue with a thought for the sleepers on each side of the breastworks, "how many of those poor fellows lying there are dreaming of a woman. Tomorrow's shot and shell will waken you more gently than I have been wakened tonight. Who can 'M. Dillon' be?" he thought, his quick French blood boiling again. "Can it be a man,"—with his hand upon his sword-hilt,— "a rival who has put this insult upon me? One of the Treasury canaille?[11] The writing was clerkly enough, but the sentiment was more like a woman's. Bah! The whole thing is a comedy."

Then he put away love, and lighting his pipe went to look at his guns again and cover his horse with his overcoat.

In the great battle which took place the following day, Rodrigue, who had the good fortune to occupy a position well adapted to show his ability, so covered himself with glory as to be commended for gallantry and recommended for promotion by the great Stonewall[12] himself. His praise came to be in everybody's, especially every woman's, mouth; for, besides being a brilliant soldier, he was a handsome fellow, and had been severely wounded—three qualifications anyone of which would have commended him to feminine favor. Possessing all, nothing was left undone that could express woman's admiration.

His room in a hospital near Richmond was a conservatory of flowers, and his table was supplied with every delicacy that versatile Confederate mind could achieve from limited Confederate material. Colonel Rodrigue was the hero of the hour.

One morning, when he was coming back to life from the effects of wounds which had carried him into weeks of unconsciousness and to the borders of another world, a note was brought to him.

He was lying in bed, pale and emaciated, but smiling with the blissful languor of convalescence. The receipt of another note increased his cheerfulness to hilarity. The thing was getting to be amusing. He had already received a snowstorm of notes, little white-winged messengers of congratulation, admiration, friendship, and what not. But when he saw the superscription of this last he became grave. His great dark eyes, all the greater and darker for the pallor and emaciation of the rest of his face, opened wide with astonishment, and a faint color overspread his wan cheeks. Was it possible that here was another communication from Rose Chandler?

The unexpectedness of the thing made him dizzy. He closed his eyes and threw back his head on the pillow to think—to think, after a long, delicious rest of not thinking.

The sight of Rose's writing brought back the pain he had suffered the night before the battle—months—years—he did not know, nor did it matter, how long ago. He had been told and did not remember. But he remembered very vividly how her other letter had made him wish that a bullet would put an end so him—how it had made him so reckless and daring in battle that friends and enemies were now talking of his valor, and he had been within a hairbreadth of his desire. The enemy's bullet—in fact several of the enemy's bullets—had come and very nearly put an end to him, and (strange inconsistency) now that his pulses were beginning to throb with new life he was unreasonably glad to be alive. Rose's letter had done its work more effectually. It had put an end to his love beyond surgery, beyond medicine, beyond resurrection.

Rodrigue sighed over the lost illusion, and his hand trembled a little as he took up the note again. It was a pretty little plea for forgiveness, and as ingenious as pretty. It said that when the former communication was sent the writer had not the heart to say no to Colonel Rodrigue, who had insisted upon an immediate answer, and she was not then sufficiently sure of herself to say yes. In her dilemma she had asked a friend, cleverer than herself, to express in words what she felt but did not know how

to say. She knew now that it was wrong to have entrusted so delicate a mission to another, but at the time she was anxious only to do what was right. Colonel Rodrigue's dangerous illness had opened her eyes to many things. She hoped he would forgive her, and be her friend as before. If he only knew how wretched she had been while his life was in danger, he would write at once and tell her that she was pardoned.

Rodrigue, having read this effusion, was lying back among his pillows exhausted, wishing, with the intensity known only to convalescents, for something to eat, when the hospital surgeon came in on one of his flying visits.

"What's all this about?" he asked, with his fingers on Rodrigue's wrist. "Pulse accelerated, and not so well as yesterday. Been seeing too much company this morning, eh?"

Rodrigue shook his head. "I want some writing materials," he said stoutly, as if he expected denial.

"Writing materials! I'd as lief give writing materials to a baby. How do you think writing would agree with that lame arm of yours? Bless the women, I wonder if they know how much of my work they undo with their messes and letters and things! Come, don't look sulky. I can't have you getting a setback. You must put off your letters until you can eat a beefsteak."

Rodrigue's eyes brightened. Beefsteak! The word thrilled him more than sentiment. "Indeed, Moreton, I must write a few words and then I will eat a beefsteak, and—and anything else I can get."

"No," returned the other, pulling out his prescription book and pencil. "I will do the writing—I hope your correspondent is not particular about stationery—and you will do the eating. Now what is it? I am secret as the grave."

There was no help for it. Rodrigue was too weak to resist even mentally, and Moreton saw that the writing was on the patient's mind and had better be dispatched at once.

Rodrigue closed his eyes and contracted his brows. Composing a letter now required more effort than storming a breach yesterday. He was afraid that writing vicariously would appear to Miss Chandler as if he intended giving her a Roland for her Oliver.[13] But what was he to do with her desire for an immediate answer and his superior officer standing over him in this way? He told Moreton with all delicacy that he wished to send a lady, who had asked for it, his forgiveness for a small unkindness, to say that he had accepted her decision with regard to his suit as final, and that he was proud to be assured of her continued friendship. He left all the honors of the field with the lady. Having thus delivered himself he heaved a deep sigh, relieved to have it over. Then he looked keenly at the clock to see if it was not dinner-time.

Moreton, with a ward full of sick and wounded waiting for him, carried out his patient's instructions with medical brevity. His words reduced to their lowest equation amounted to: forgiveness; friendship; adieu.

Rodrigue's dinner coming in just as the letter was enclosed and directed, Moreton went off to look after mutilated legs and arms without another thought for this little affair of the heart.

And so it came to pass that quite unin-tentionally, and yet by a sort of poetic justice, Rodrigue's letter to Rose, as hers to him, was written by a third person, and, like hers, it was fatal to any hopes the recipient may have previously entertained.

III

The Result

Several months had elapsed and it was now spring. The Treasury clerks were still hard at work manufacturing money; in fact, harder than ever, for as the notes decreased in value they increased in volume.

About this time the joke was made that whereas at the beginning of the war one marketed with a pocketbook for money and a basket for food, the order was now reversed.

Angels' Retreat presented much the same appearance as when Palmetto acted as amanuensis for Rose Chandler, except that recent battles had clothed many of its occupants in mourning and the strain of increasing anxiety and privation was apparent in the countenances of all, except Rose Chandler, who belonged to the class of women upon whom, without effort of their own, the good things of life are lavished. She was plump, rosy, and as beautiful as ever. Palmetto was perceptibly thinner and more poorly clad. Her homespun dress hung loosely round her too slender figure, and the suave, round contour of her face had given place to the pathetic sharpness of ill-fed youth. But there was no diminution of spirit. She did her work, helped her friends, and was as proud and dauntless as before.

It was a breezy day in April when we meet her again. She has come late to the Department as of old, and without her lunch basket. She had for some time ceased to have occasion for one. The slice of bread, which was all that could be spared from home and served for her principal meal, could easily be carried in a small parcel in her hand, and she maintained that she was glad not to have the trouble of a basket. So many things had happened since writing Rodrigue's letter of rejection that she never thought of it now, unless his name was mentioned, as often happened, in connection with some brilliant military achievement, and then she remembered with an uncomfortable glow that her name was appended to the missive. Rose Chandler, too, had not a few regretful thoughts on the subject. Rodrigue, the only man who had ever touched her heart, and whose subsequent career had touched her more sensitive ambition, she had let slip through her fingers. She had not met him again. She believed if she could only see him, or, more properly speaking, if he could only see her once more, all would be right. It was easy to believe that a sight of her would influence a man's judgment. A suspicion that had it not been for Madge Dillon's name, Madge Dillon's words would have kept Rodrigue bound made her bitterly repent not having copied the letter.

To have lost a hero by such an oversight was exasperating. Added to this, a later event gave her a distaste for writing by proxy from which she never recovered.

On this April morning her desk was decorated as usual with a bunch of spring flowers, and the shabby old room was sweet and fresh with delicate odors. Where they came from nobody was supposed to know, but everybody suspected that Waller, the man clerk, could tell. The truth was, so slight a thing as a soft glance repeated every day had forged a chain strong enough to bind poor Waller hand and foot. He had come to live on the soft glance. His waking thoughts were occupied in remembering and looking forward to it.

The angels believed he spent half his salary in flowers for Rose, and were disposed to make fun of the matter. They were treating her to a deal of satire on having added a civilian to her list of admirers when Palmetto raised her hand.

"Hush! What is that?"

Her manner commanded attention. The angels stopped work and listened eagerly. It was a time of intense but subdued excitement, and everybody was on the *qui vive*[14] for news of victory or of defeat. The far-off, tumultuous noise that reached them now was unlike anything they had ever heard. It had not a note of the soul-inspiring cheers with which good news is proclaimed, nor of the angry violence of brawling men. It was a wild, unearthly wail of discontent. The angels huddled together with blanched cheeks.

"Heavens!" cried Norah. "It sounds like an army of wildcats."

"Don't, Norah, don't!" said Rose, cowering behind her. "It's more like the cry of lost spirits."

"I've never heard *them*," answered Norah, excitedly.

The tumult came on and on, like a tempest of shrieking winds.

"It has an awful, hungry sound," whispered Palmetto, interpreting the cry through her own sensations.

Just then the door opened and Waller, very white and trying not to look scared, entered.

"Ladies," he stammered, "you are requested by the Secretary of the Treasury not to go near the windows."

"What is it?" gasped Rose, forgetting her soft glance.

"It—it's a woman's bread riot."[15]

"I knew it was something hungry," cried Palmetto, clasping her hands.

"Hun—hundreds of women," chattered Waller, talking very fast after he got started, "armed with stones and whatever they can lay hands on, are coming to attack the Treasury, smash windows, break open doors, and get the money if they can."

"Poor things! They must be starving," said Palmetto.

"Poor things, indeed!" sobbed Rose. "It is we that are the poor things if we get killed."

"What are we going to do?" asked Norah.

"Stand a siege, I suppose," said Waller, trying to laugh.

Meanwhile the mob of women had been advancing. It was not long before they were in front of the Treasury doors, yelling like a pack of famished wolves. Knowing what one discontented woman can do in the way of vocalization, it is possible to imagine the clamor multiplied by hundreds.

The noise was so blood-curdling that Palmetto covered her ears.

"But this is terrible," she cried. "Can't we do something?"

"I entreat you ladies to come into the passage, where there are no windows," pleaded Waller.

"You will be safe there!" Rose Chandler screamed.

"Bread riot! I call it an ill-bred riot," sniffed Norah.

"I have it!" cried Palmetto, flying to her desk and gulping down her hunger as she took out her one slice of bread. Her companions looked on as if she had suddenly become insane.

"Come, girls!" she cried, snatching her shawl and spreading it on the floor; "empty your lunch baskets."

Surprise, excitement, and the force of Palmetto's will made them obey.

In a twinkling the lunch baskets, some of them bountifully filled, were thrown upon her piece of bread. Then she caught up the shawl and made for the door, her companions following pell-mell.

"Ladies, I entreat you. The Secretary—" shouted Waller.

But they heeded not. Palmetto with the angels at her heels—that is, all except Rose, who preferred that Waller should find her a place of safety—flew down the steep stairs from floor to floor and through the long aisles between the desks like a tongue of flame, kindling everybody with her enthusiasm, and gathering up the midday meals of the not too well fed Treasury clerks. More than a hundred baskets were emptied into the shawls caught up in the angels' flight. And all this without an idea of what Palmetto intended to do. But Palmetto knew. She hurried to the front door, which the chief clerk had ordered to be locked and barricaded, and before anyone could prevent her-the men about the place being occupied in securing the rest of the building—flung it open.

It was the maddest thing to do. There did not seem to be a chance for her life with a shower of stones and brickbats falling about her. Her companions fell back huddling together, trembling at the sight presented.

An American woman's riot is a mild affair compared with the mobs of brawny, bearded *pétroleuses*[16] that once in a while make Paris hideous. The American variety is to the Parisian as water unto whisky. But a crowd of howling women maddened by hunger is at best formidable, and it sometimes happens that innocence and inexperience rush in where wisdom gives pause.

The opening of the Treasury doors certainly quelled the storm for a moment. The mob looked to see what would come next.

Palmetto stood in the doorway, slim and straight as the tree whose name she bore. Her face, too pale and thin for material beauty, was illuminated by a pair of courageous eyes that scanned the rioters without flinching, as she extended her hands with a wheaten roll in each. The draught through the open door caught her draperies, which, floating back from her slender figure, gave her the appearance of a winged creature sent to feed the hungry multitude. At sight of her the uproar ceased and missiles were held at rest.

It was one of Palmetto's moments of illumination. She had forgotten self, and her face seemed only the reflection of a beautiful and intrepid spirit. Her countenance, with its innocent mouth and fearless eyes, was a model of heroic maidenhood.

At least this was the impression it made on a young officer on the pavement, who, finding it impossible to extricate himself from the crowd, stood, with folded arms, patiently looking on. He was dark and handsome, with fine intelligent eyes that took in a situation at a glance.

His slightly foreign face indicated not only appreciation of a fine act, but keen enjoyment of dramatic and artistic values. His temperament, not wholly American, made it not only possible but imperative that his enjoyment should find expression.

His countenance was radiant, although his body was more or less buffeted by the restless mob. He watched Palmetto with hawk-like vigilance. He trembled for her safety, he admired her high-bred face, he adored her courage, he compared her to Jeanne d'Arc.[17]

Meanwhile she was feeding some children, who at sight of bread broke from their mothers and were pressing up the Treasury steps. The act was unpremeditated, but it was like oil on water. Nothing could have so soothed the rioters as seeing the children eat. It was for their sakes that mothers had taken the war-path.

"D'ye think ye are goin' to worrk a miracle wid yer penny'orth o' bread and all these folk?" asked a gaunt Irishwoman in the forefront of the crowd.

"It looks like it," said Palmetto, good-humoredly. "My store began with a slice of bread, and see how it has increased"—moving aside that the angels with their supply might be seen.

"We ain't got nothin' agin you girls," said another, taking a potato (the angels were dealing out their provisions now).

"We knowed the women folks was all right. But we want to get hold of them white-handed, white-livered men clerks who is doin' woman's work while our husbands is dyin' in the trenches."

While Palmetto parleyed with the feeble insurgents the men clerks managed to get a squad of militiamen on the scene, and a proclamation was made that if the crowd dispersed quietly double rations would be issued to all who applied at the Commissary Department. The crowd of wretched women, as of one mind, began to disperse at this announcement. They were tired and hoarse, and double rations were even more satisfactory than the blood of men clerks.

The Irishwoman set up a cheer on her own account for the young lady who was the first person in the town to "lend a hand." Hoarse as the poor rioters were, Biddy's cheer spread like wildfire, and Palmetto, conscious of herself for the first time, stood blushing like a school girl. The officer on the sidewalk, whose heart echoed the mob's involuntary tribute, uncovered his head, and, pressing his hat to his bosom, breathed inarticulate adoration as Palmetto escaped into the Treasury.

"But, Dalrymple," he said to a comrade who had been suppressing anathemas against the hags who pressed him close in the crowd-"but, Dalrymple, did you say you knew her?"

"No, Rodrigue," he answered, still out of humor. "I said I had met her once."

"Will you, my friend, have the goodness to tell me all about it? "

"There is nothing to tell," said Dalrymple, abruptly, the reminiscence not being a pleasant one, "except that I was making a visit to Miss Chandler on one occasion and Miss Dillon came into the room for a moment."

"Chandler—Dillon!" exclaimed Rodrigue, remembering with a flash the connection in his mind between these two names. "Dillon! But did you say Dillon?"

"I said Dillon. Is there anything remarkable about the name?"

"No," he said, calming himself. "Not the name, but the lady, I find altogether remarkable."

"She does not seem afraid of brickbats, certainly."

"Brickbats, indeed! She has quelled a mob. I do not believe she has fear of anything. But are you sure of her name?"

"No; she may have changed it."

"Impossible!"

"I don't know. It is four months since I saw her, and it takes about seven minutes to get a woman's name changed."

"You have timed it?"

"I have."

"Bah, Dalrymple! You have no enthusiasms."

"I am not so young as I was."

"Adieu."

"Goodbye."

That evening Rodrigue, in town for a few days on official business, attended a dinner given by a prominent member of the Cabinet. The invitation had been to "pea soup."

Discontent among the lower classes was ripe in Richmond at this time. Women and children, whose natural protectors were in the field, were starving at home, and much ill feeling existed towards men who remained in the capital in what were called bomb-proof offices. To make matters worse, the lower classes believed that government officials fared sumptuously every day. Rumors of banquets where turtle and champagne played parts created great indignation. To counteract, so far as might be, this impression, it became the fashion among government officials to request the pleasure of one's company to "pea soup."

Rodrigue had, with the simplicity of a soldier, accepted the invitation in good faith, and went to the Secretary's prepared to dine on the specified menu. He was genuinely surprised to find a dinner, very luxurious for the times, which he enjoyed with a soldier's appetite.

The bread riot of the morning was naturally one of the chief topics of conversation. By some it was considered an important indication of popular feeling. Others pooh-poohed it as a trifling ebullition of feminine discontent.

Rodrigue's right-hand neighbor remarked to him during dessert, "Apropos of the bread riot, I wish I could manage to get my share of these good things to a girl who lives next door to me."

"Indeed!" said Rodrigue, politely, his thoughts being occupied with a young woman he had seen in the morning.

"Yes. Her family are very poor. I am sure they do not have enough to eat. Indeed, the girl fainted today for want of food. She is a clerk in the Treasury,"—Rodrigue turned his eyes, brilliant with new-born interest, on the speaker—"and today this same bread riot created such excitement at the Department that my young friend remained after office hours without her dinner to finish her work."

Rodrigue's eyes grew bigger with every word. "Well?" he said eagerly, his neighbor pausing to crack a nut.

"Nothing, except that her father came to borrow money of me to buy food, and all these good things made me think of the contrast."

Rodrigue pushed away his plate. How could he eat, knowing a being like that was suffering from hunger? There were many Treasury clerks, but he felt sure that this was his Jeanne d'Arc.

"Would it be indiscreet to ask the young woman's name?" he asked, very modestly.

"Not at all. Her name is Dillon—Miss Madge Dillon."

"Aha!—'M. Dillon.' I have seen a note with her signature. It is a good signature. I thought it was a man's. I should like to make her acquaintance."

"Nothing easier, Colonel. The name of Rodrigue is a passport to every lady's favor, and I shall be delighted to present you."

"You are very good. But we must be quick about it. My time here is short."

"Ah, well, come and take tea with me tomorrow evening. Miss Dillon is a friend of my wife, and sometimes comes in to tea. We will invite her for tomorrow."

"I shall be engaged tomorrow until too late for tea. But if you will permit me to come afterwards?"

"At your convenience, Colonel."

"Will you promise me something?"

"Almost anything."

"You are too good. But you will not mention that I am coming. I have a reason."

"Certainly, if you wish it; but I had intended using your name as an inducement—my trump card, in fact."

Rodrigue shrugged his shoulders. "But you are wrong. I am not sure that Miss Dillon would take tea with you if she thought I was to be there."

"I think I could arrange it so that she would."

"But you will promise?"

"I promise."

"Strange," mused Rodrigue over his cigar that night, "that I should meet 'M. Dillon' for the first time today, and hear of her again tonight. Things have a tendency to run in lines."

Next day Rodrigue, finding it would be impossible to keep his engagement for that evening, went to inform his friend of the fact, and to thank him for his kind intention, which he hoped would be carried out on a future occasion.

The tendency of things to run in lines, or some other occult influence, led him to stumble into the wrong house. He rang the bell at the door adjoining his friend's, and upon asking if the master of the house was at home was answered in the affirmative and ushered into the parlor. There, in the middle of the room, ready for flight, stood Palmetto. The unexpectedness of the meeting was like an electric shock to Rodrigue. He trembled from head to foot, but nobody would have guessed it. To Palmetto it was only the pleasing surprise occasioned by the advent of a handsome stranger. She was still pale from the in-disposition which kept her from the Department, but she flushed prettily when Rodrigue entered. She introduced herself as Miss Dillon, and, having heard the dialogue at the front door, asked if he wished to see her father.

"I beg pardon, Miss Dillon," said Rodrigue, with the profound and flattering obeisance of which no purely Anglo-Saxon back is capable, "but I find myself here by a mistake. I intended to call on your next-door neighbor, who had promised me the honor of an introduction to you. Since I am here by accident permit me to introduce myself—Colonel Rodrigue."

It was Palmetto's turn to be electrified; and not being used to shocks, she turned furiously red.

It must be confessed that Rodrigue enjoyed her confusion. He owed "M. Dillon" a turn, and then a blush was the one thing needed to make her face beautiful.

"Oh, oh!" she stammered. "I am so sorry. I—I hoped you would never see me."

"You are too late for that, Miss Dillon; I have had the pleasure before."

Palmetto opened her eyes. "I can't imagine where; and I don't know why you should want to know me, I am sure."

"On the contrary, there is every reason why I should. You once did me the honor to write to me, and I have never had an opportunity to reply."

"You know I did not want a reply."

"And yet it was the most momentous letter I ever received."

"I hope you have forgiven me."

"I had nothing to forgive. You did what you could to soften a severe blow."

"Won't you sit down? I am glad you

felt that the writer was sorry to say 'no.'"

"I felt it, and it made me love the writer," said Rodrigue, gravely.

"I mean—I mean," stammered Palmetto "that I thought Rose Chandler owed you that much."

"It seems Miss Chandler thought she owed me nothing. My heart went out to her who thought I deserved something."

"But it—it was to be supposed that Rose was the writer."

"For a moment I did suppose so, and had we not been on the eve of battle, that moment would have brought me back to her. You see fate has brought me to her who really did pity me."

"I ought not to have meddled," said Palmetto, distressed by the directness there was no evading. "I suppose it really was conceit that made me consent to write for Rose. She does not take things so seriously as I, and I thought that—that—"

"That you could disappoint a man more kindly."

"You see Rose is so used to that kind of thing—"

"That one man more or less does not count."

Rodrigue's manner, grave, courteous, and direct, coupled with the unusual circumstances of their meeting, was every moment deepening the favorable impression already made by his appearance and reputation. As he went on, his voice trembled with the restraint laid upon him not to startle his listener. Trembling is contagious, and Palmetto was stirred with vague uneasiness as Rodrigue attempted to state his proposition calmly.

"You know, Miss Dillon, that these are stirring times—times of sudden meetings and partings, of strange friendships and stranger loves. Your letter to me"—Palmetto hung her head—"was one of the strange things which would scarcely have happened in ordinary times. It made a deep impression upon me. The impression has grown to be something more, and I have a favor to ask you."

Palmetto looked up. She tried to emulate Rodrigue's calmness, but his glance was more discomposing than hurtling brickbats. She succeeded in being stilled. Conventionality and decorum stood like a wall between them. Silence, in which only their breathing could be heard, fell upon them, and their eyes sought the floor. After a moment Palmetto said stiffly, "You have a right to ask any favor that will make amends for my reading your letter."

"Ah, that letter!" exclaimed Rodrigue. "It is of that I would speak. It was written the day before Fredericksburg,[18] and you answered it for Miss Chandler in the negative, and I took that 'no' into battle with me. Now we are looking for another fight, and I am going back to my command. May I—may I take with me—another answer from you, and for yourself?"

"Do you mean—" gasped Palmetto.

"I mean will you give me permission to ask you for yourself if I come out alive?"

Palmetto could not speak. She closed her eyes. In a moment there flashed through her mind—as in other great crises—everything that could be thought. The brilliant soldier suing for *her*. She knew that if she lived a hundred years she would never see another whom she could so love, whom—strange, incredible incident of war—she believed she did love. Then came pride to forbid this hasty wooing and winning. She opened her eyes.

"No," she said; and then, seeing him stand before her handsome and sorrowful on the eve of battle, made a plunge as into cold water and murmured "Yes."

His face became radiant, and hers suffused with blushes as he raised her fingers to his lips.

Just then the silence was broken by the heavy, booming sound so familiar in the beleaguered city, shaking the walls and setting all the air a-tremble. Palmetto started violently. Rodrigue changed color.

Hostilities had begun again.

"I must go," said Rodrigue, with his hand upon the door. "Remember, if I come back."

"If—if you come back!" faltered Palmetto, pale as death.

"Boom, boom, boom!" roared the guns again. Ah, how quickly they shook down the walls of conventionality! Palmetto extended her hands. Rodrigue caught her in his arms, and then, pressing a kiss on her flushed and innocent cheek, was gone into the night.

Ellen Duvall (1855-1944)

Ellen Duvall, though born in Delaware, spent most of her life in Maryland. She was an active member of the WLCB from 1894 until 1915. Throughout her membership, she served as the chair for the Committee on Current Criticism and the Committee on Fiction. A public lecturer and educator, she often led meetings, shared her work, or read the work of others—such as Shakespeare, of whom she was an avid fan and critic.

Duvall was published in respected magazines like *Harper's Weekly, the Atlantic Monthly,* and *Woman's Home Companion.* She was reviewed by the *Baltimore Sun,* where she was praised for her "entertaining fiction" and "rich literary style."[1] Her short stories evoke the sentimental tradition, exploring romantic relationships and a woman's agency within them. However, she strays from this in stories like "Estelle," where the heroine experiences a personal awakening and discovers that she is better off alone than in a relationship with a man who does not understand her. This story may be based on her own experience; Duvall never married and lived with her parents, siblings, and other relatives her entire life.

Duvall held some problematic views in addition to her more progressive ones. In the 1899-1900 Club meeting minutes, for example, she presented a review on a book called "What Constitutes the Superiority of the Anglo Saxon Race," stating its argument was one of "sweet reasonableness." Duvall's inconsistent ideologies and writings exemplify the dichotomy of many of the Club's members: the constant push and pull between the progressive New Woman and the True Woman of the past. —K. Kazmierski and M. Nolan

Estelle (1907)

Count Zoffsky and his friend D'Auvillières quitted the afternoon reception late, and walked away together. Washington is at its best in the golden-green twilight of April, and as they reached the square both involuntarily paused and looked about for a seat. It had showered in the afternoon, and the air, somewhat warm and languid, was full of the odor of hyacinths mingled with those fainter, rarer tree-scents which spring evokes. They sat down near a huge flowering Chinese magnolia guarded by a spruce.

"It recalls Paris," said D'Auvillières with a long, satisfied sigh. The evening star, lone warder of the sky and of the relucent air, hung low in the west, and beneath it still lingered a hint of greenish amber filmed with rose; while the soothing quietude, emphasized not marred by distant, echoing footsteps, was like an earnest of rest.

Denizens of the world, at home in every capital of Europe, Zoffsky and D'Auvillières could only be called foreign because of the fullness of life which both so admirably suggested. The two friends spoke French, of course, that language which lends itself so well to allusion and which enfolds with meaning as with an atmosphere. D'Auvillières was a short, dark, phlegmatic Frenchman, gestureless, apparently motionless, but with a glance and an inflection of voice that could signify anything.

"It's composite, a marvelous composite; every time I return I am more and more impressed by the spectacle. But a type will eventually emerge; I wonder what it will be like. The American nation—not yet a people—to be unified by an ideal—if they can hold to it, and live up to it. Well—"

D'Auvillières broke off, and lighted a cigar. "I am sorry not to have seen your fiancée. When are you to be married?" He spoke in a deliberate, colorless way.

"Early in June, but the date is not yet set," said Zoffsky. Then after a pause, "Am I wise?"

D'Auvillières regarded him thoughtfully. "Prudent, at all events. Marriage is a necessity. Nature and social law decree that a man cannot have everything. And they get most out of life, perhaps, who accept necessity gracefully and make the best of it. Doubtless, on the domestic side of life your success will be as marked as on every other. You ought to marry, *mon brave*.[2] Beauty is nature's only essential right, and good looks such as yours should not be wasted. May your daughters inherit your beauty with the added charm of femininity."

Zoffsky smiled good-humoredly. "Won't you let me have something for myself, Henri? Your view of matrimony has always seemed rather flat and meager."

"I said *necessity*. A wise man accepts necessity, and—reduces it to a minimum. You are young at heart, kindly, amenable to the emotions; therefore—marry."

"But may I not be a little in love? Ought not the pill to be gilded?"

"Certainly, as little or as much as you please. It is the emotions, in reason, that give taste to life. Why eat a peach if you cannot discriminate between it and a mudball? But do not over-season life's banquet. If, to the necessity of marriage, one can add the free grace of affection, one does well. You care, then, for the lady? I shall be glad to hear that you do.

There is nothing I admire more than the emotions; they keep one young, elastic, resilient." His glance was interested.

Zoffsky sighed and smiled. "Oh, I am thirty-six; one's heart takes on a complexity, life is woven of more and more threads, and the pattern becomes more and more difficult to follow. If Madame Barry was not young, beautiful, rich, independent—well, if everything was not unexceptionable—" His shrug and smile were sufficient.

"A redistribution of *ifs* would upset the order of the universe," returned D'Auvillières; then, after a short silence in which he quietly scrutinized his friend, he said, "If your feeling accords with nature rather than with the novelists, you are probably safe and sane."

"I don't follow," said Zoffsky, laughing.

D'Auvillières changed his position. "The novelists over-emphasize the emotions, so that a young man, having filled his mind and fancy with emotional literature—oh, I did it once!—is quite unable to distinguish between his own proper feelings and those factitious ones superinduced by the novels. He imagines himself, emotionally, all the heroes he has ever mooned over. But one pays, one pays."

"What of Balzac?" asked Zoffsky carelessly.

"A doubtful guide," returned D'Auvillières coolly. "Fancy Balzac and Sainte-Beuve being of the same race! Both were geniuses; but only one was a gentleman. I hope you don't take even Balzac too seriously, Boris."[3]

Zoffsky leaned toward the magnolia, and inhaled the wandering breeze. "You think then that the novelists, by extolling one passion at the expense of all the others, have done as much harm as good?"

"Precisely; they have wrested the truth, and have given a twist to civilized man's emotional thinking which it takes all the years after thirty to correct."

Zoffsky was silent for a moment, then ventured, "It seems to me that the emotions fill a large part of life, Henri. I may not philosophize as you do, my feelings certainly do not crystallize so rapidly into thought. But those feelings you rather underestimate lie at the base of too much not to command attention. For instance, I wished to speak to you tonight of-Estelle." His voice softened on the name, and he turned his face fully toward D'Auvillières.

"Ah, yes; how old is she now?"

"In her tenth year."

D'Auvillières was silent.

"I should like to keep her," pursued Zoffsky, hesitating; "I mean I should like her to be brought up in my family, under my eye."

"She is agreeable to you then?"

"She is charming!" cried Zoffsky with enthusiasm.

D'Auvillières nodded a guarded approval. "There nature speaks—the father. Such matters are sometimes awkward, but they can generally be arranged. You are uncertain of Madame Barry?"

"I suppose so," said Zoffsky.

"And why?" demanded D'Auvillières, with a shade of acrimony. "Simply because of the extravagant fiction you have cloyed your mind with, because of a certain supposed racial attitude towards certain phases of human life. The Anglo-Saxons understand things without saying; while we both say and understand—is that it?"

"Perhaps."

"You are in a quandary? You don't know how Madame Barry would accept the fact of Estelle *after* your marriage, nor how she would accept the voicing of such a fact *before?*"

"Precisely. What shall I do—wait, or speak now? I wish to be just to Madame Barry; I wish to be kind to little Estelle; I wish to make no unpleasantness for myself. That ought to be clear enough, even to please you."

"I do not know madame," said D'Auvillières thoughtfully; then quickly, seeing Zoffsky hesitate, "if you love her, don't attempt to describe her-women beloved are all alike. But if you can give me any idea of her disposition—"

"We are good comrades," said the young man. "She has traveled—"

"That's nothing," said D'Auvillières, filling up the other's pause. "The stupidest people I have known have been all round the world, and have seen everything. To know one human being, even superficially, goes farther towards a liberal education. Does she idealize you?"

"I think not," said Zoffsky candidly. "Oh, of course, if I were not Count Boris Zoffsky, promising, distinguished, fairly well off, no glaring vices-As I said, everything is most suitable."

"There is no woman living who does not ask the impossible from life—that is, from the man she loves, or who she thinks ought to love her."

"Henri, don't wreak your vertiginous paradoxes on me; my Russian brain won't carry them."

"You mean your Russian heart," said D'Auvillières gently, and his smile was charming. "Well, is your heart very much set upon this marriage?"

"My mind is, at all events."

"In asking, or in giving advice one betrays the boundaries and extent of one's emotional experience. How do you really stand towards Madame Barry?"

Zoffsky reflected. "We are friends," he said at last, with confidence.

D'Auvillières regarded him with ironic pity. "Then tell her. It will be a test of her capacity for friendship, something rarer than love, beauty, genius, in the creature feminine. Moreover," and his voice changed, "if you really wish to keep the little girl, it is best that your fiancée should know beforehand; otherwise she might object. And," he added, with a certain nobleness of expression, "if there is anything which might cause Madame Barry to pause, or to draw back, it is only fair that she should know. We all win women under false pretense, but—there is a limit to allowable pretense."

The friends parted at the corner, and, because of the charm of the approaching night, Zoffsky made a detour and passed slowly on to his betrothed's. He could afford to be leisurely. The lady was won, or rather, their mutual understanding of benefits and combined suitability was perfect, so that there was no cause for a ripple of anxiety any more than for a thrill of joy. He half-smiled, half-sighed. As D'Auvillières had once said: Certainty is a foe to zest. But he was still young at heart, the future was still a golden haze, colorful, if indistinct. He had ambition rather than ambitions, yet he meant to rise high, to leave an impress, to set Russia forward in the march of the nations. Marcia Barry could and would strengthen his career, and he could open to her doors that did not exist at home.

The uptown streets were comparatively empty, and as he passed along and the delicate tree-shadows cast by the electric lights quivered over him he felt an agreeable sense of possession, as if he had laid hold upon space, upon the power and tranquility of the night. When he stood at last in Mrs. Barry's small inner drawing-room a glow of satisfaction, the warmest feeling he had for the lady, came over him. Yes, he was sincerely proud of his fiancée. He knew that she could "hold her own"—was not that the blunt American phrase?—or rather *his* own, which was more to the purpose anywhere. About her and her belongings there was no declamatory, oppressive opulence of the newly rich. For herself and her surroundings she had achieved completeness with simplicity.

Mrs. Barry came in presently, unhurried, and gave him her soft hand. She had a height and carriage which agreeably matched his, though now, as they faced each other, and he raised that soft, cool, firm hand to his lips, she appeared somewhat small; but Zoffsky was an unusually tall man. As he looked into her fine clear eyes, he was reminded of that sky, for these eyes, too, were of a greenish amber, and above them arose the sweep of pale bronze hair.

"You were not at the Ambassador's this afternoon—I missed you," he said gently.

"I was prevented at the last moment. My sister-in-law, an impulsive young person, sent her two children here with their nurse, a new one, while she hurried on to New York to meet her husband's ship. The children are great mother-babies, and insisted on clinging to me for want of better; and I have not long since disposed of them—in bed."

She had a beautiful voice, and spoke with a full, round articulation. Her reply relieved and encouraged him. How opportune and unexpected an opening! What luck, he would have said, and how needless to have racked his brain in seeking to devise a proper, and seemingly fortuitous, approach to the subject of Estelle.

"You like children, then?" he asked quickly, and there was something in his voice she had never heard before.

"Oh, no more than reason," she returned lightly. Then, noting his change of expression, she added less carelessly, "I suppose I like children as well as do the generality of women. But what it would be if I had the real care and responsibility of them I don't know."

"Balzac says it is easier to be a good wife than a good mother," said Zoffsky, hesitating, yet serious.

"Naturally; for a woman stands as Providence to her child, but she takes her husband, perforce, as she finds him—as some other woman—his mother, perhaps—has made him."

The opening was not so easy after all.

"D'Auvillières says that women expect the impossible from life."

She laughed. "But what is the impossible to one is the mere commonplace to another. By-the-bye, I'm sorry to have missed your friend D'Auvillières."

"Oh, you might not like him—women

seldom do—he won't let them." Zoffsky spoke hastily, as if he wished to get his friend out of the way.

"Then somewhere, at some time, he has been hurt," said Mrs. Barry gently.

"Yes," said Zoffsky gravely, "he has been hurt. He was obliged to sacrifice the woman who loved him to a point of honor."

Mrs. Barry lifted her dark brows.

"But, according to a Frenchman, does a woman ever mind being sacrificed except to another woman?"

Zoffsky looked rather at a loss. He made no reply, but regarded his fiancée speculatively. She smiled at his questioning regard. "What is it? You evidently have something on your mind."

Zoffsky made no immediate answer. He pulled at his thick, blond mustache, and bent forward his small, solid-looking head, the closer to scrutinize his lady. "Marcia, don't you think we are very much alike?"

"Very; my brother says we evidently pull just about the same stroke." It was true. In their leisurely, drifting life, their reach of feeling and of thought was apparently the same.

"That is what attracted me from the first; our *entente cordiale,* our good understanding. But, Marcia, we really know very little of each other. D'Auvillières says that the reason why matrimonial courage exceeds all others is that it takes so much for granted."

"And takes for granted always the pleasant things," said Mrs. Barry quietly, with a steady gaze upon him.

He drew his breath for a moment, and held it. "How much right has a wife over her husband's life?" he asked presently.

"As much as he accords her—no more," was the unexpected answer.

"But that is hardly according to law—any law," he returned, surprised.

"I spoke according to stem reality, rather than according to superficial law." Then, being a rapid thinker, she added, "You can never eliminate generosity, magnanimity—call it what you will—from the relationship."

"But," he persisted, "granting some right, where does it begin? Has she any right to his past?"

"Only in so far as the past has moulded him; she therein reckons with it, you know. The past *is* the present, and the present necessarily forecasts the future. You can't separate a man from his past, can you, any more than from his shadow? Although," she added after a slight pause, "in the high noon of a woman's affection, to her there would be no shadow; the man would stand sufficient in himself, all in all."

Zoffsky's brow contracted a little, and he drew back. "Not that," he said quickly and involuntarily, "I should not care for that. Worship demands too much."

"You have had it, then?" she asked gently.

"I have had it."

There fell a significant silence, in which Mrs. Barry looked away from her betrothed. She had no air of expectancy, still less of desire, yet her manner was so sympathetic that the young man felt his opportune moment had come. Presently, not without effort, he said:

"I was very young. She was a year or

two older, yet she always seemed much younger, so small, white, appealing. She was the wife, but more forlorn than the widow, of a man years older than herself, a man who was an exi—a—politically dead. The pathetic part of it is that then it seemed everything; now it seems less than nothing, except for the little-little—Estelle. The mother died when the child was a few months old. She is on one of the estates in southern Russia. At first she was delicate. Of course I am under no obligations, I made no promises. But—but—Estelle is lovely; she has her mother's sensitiveness, and—and—large, mournful eyes. I should like the little thing to be happy, to belong to my own class, to be a member of the family. And I was in hopes that the lady who should honor me by taking my name would also consent to my keeping Estelle."

After all, he felt that it was rather well done, that it was gracefully said. He made no appeal, he spoke as friend to friend, as equal to equal. And despite the frankness of his admission, Mrs. Barry appreciated the delicacy of a feeling that would not let her commit herself to something from which, if forewarned, she might possibly see fit to draw back. She was a good woman, with the latent, *vis inertiae*[4] goodness that comes from good inheritance, but which is not yet individualized and made active. She felt suddenly called upon to be herself. What was that self? Engaged to be married, she never perceived till now how superficial and conventional all her intercourse with her betrothed had been. But here was a passage from life vivid to the sense as flame. What should she say, what should she do? Unconscious of Zoffsky's questioning gaze upon her she regarded him steadily, so handsome, so self-sufficient, so mundanely capable. Could she strike hands with him and go on? Or was there really for such a man any going on? She began to divine that perhaps this was the best part of him, this touch of fatherliness for Estelle. Yet is there not an old saying about the good being sometimes the enemy of the best? His attitude was obvious; it was one of generosity, of magnanimity, merely. There was no thought of responsibility, no conception of a right.

He never dreamed that Estelle had any claim upon him; there was no ideal. And an ideal is to an individual what the atmosphere is to—the earth-there is no real life possible without it. Was this, then, the be-all and the end-all here? Could she marry him? She had never liked him more, nor loved him less, than at this moment, never conceived of comprehending him so fully. She sat mechanically folding and unfolding her fan, gazing straight before her; rapt in an intense inward vision. Never had she had so complete a revelation of the world within, that world with which in comparison the world without, in all its splendor, is but a darkling cave.

A slight movement on his part roused her. She looked at him consciously, with a new expression in her face, but with a hesitation of manner he had not seen before. Her relatives and friends were enthusiastic over her engagement. They averred that she and Zoffsky were wonderfully fitting counterparts. Was it true—and the truth seemed sinister—was this delightful worldling her real counterpart?

"Boris," she began, somewhat lamely, yet with a shade of tenderness he had not before received. "Boris, count, I hope you understand how fully I—I—value your confidence. I like you the better for it, think more highly of you. I believe men judge differently about these things, but--how should *you* like to be such a child, an Ishmael,[5] without claim or warrant, an absolute dependent on generosity and good-humored tolerance?" The question had leaped forth, not so much of her intention as of her instinct.

Zoffsky regarded her blankly.

"Oh—a—the case is not so unusual. It was not a vulgar affair. It created no scandal. We were most discreet. My mother and sister never really blamed me. Estelle is very affectionate, facile, charming; she will repay regard. I have seen her at intervals. Of course, she would never conflict with, any—any—other ties, any admitted obligations. All would be understood, you know. She would, of course, pass as my ward. There would never be any difficulty for you. I only wished her to be a member of the family, and that you would be so good as to supervise her upbringing. Young girls in Russia are much like young girls here."

Mrs. Barry was looking at her fiancée direct, with a large, enfolding gaze, but his physical presence was for the time being forgotten and she did not speak. It seemed as if thought was flashing upon her in waves of light, and her one fear was lest she should lose some of the effect of that auroral illumination. The things she saw by it, the things she felt, the indications, the contrasts, the inferences—could she hold them all? Her father rose up before her, quiet, modest as a woman, the reverse of brilliant, with a life as open as a sun-swept, close-sheared field. He seemed a starting point for considerations that involved all of life. But again Zoffsky moved or spoke, and her thoughts vanished.

"Count, your little Estelle appeals to me wonderfully, pathetically; a helpless child, without lawful right or claim, yet with all a child's needs and desires! I would, of course, take her gladly, would gladly help you to do a father's part by her; but—that is—I— we are not, after all, enough alike. You have had a marvelous effect on me—I never knew myself before, never knew I had a self. I'm just the average woman; if the day is fine, the music excellent, the sermon brief, I go to church. But that's nothing. Life is more, and demands more, than I realized. And I think I ought to give more to, and ask more from, the man I marry. I—I—should not suit you. I—shrink from the thought of tacit understandings, significant silences, subterranean passages of feeling and thought. We didn't really choose each other—did we?—we just drifted together. Yet it is choice only that makes us truly individuals, that cuts us sharply off from the floating human mass. I—pardon me—want things open in the sight of all men, the—the- freedom of self-control. What can you ever justly expect of Estelle, you who have given her mere life, shorn of all its dues? Father, mother, child—why, they ought to be a sacred three, a trinity whose strength cannot be broken. And marriage ought to be something more than ours would be; something finer than the mere coalition of two social units, each giving and asking the *quid pro quo*."

Zoffsky stared at her in amazement and consternation. "But if you do not object to Estelle, then why, why? We are perfectly suited, suited in every way."

Mrs. Barry shook her head. "I doubt whether we are suited at all," she said gently, and then was silent.

She recognized that what she had said was not only beyond his ken, but was indeed outside of his horizon. With a thrill she perceived that she was on a height above him. How had she gained it? She could not tell; one thing she knew—that being there, the obligation was laid upon her to act accordingly. But she could not make *him* see, she could not take him with her. That is the eternal tragedy of life, she thought, that two so near see nothing of the same vision. A breath of love—the first she had ever felt, that divine love which seeks to create, to give, to serve—stole in upon her. She hesitated. Could she take him and Estelle together to her heart, and strive over them? No, that was beyond her province. She must leave him to the same Power which had stirred her. She turned to him with distress in her eyes, and with quivering lips.

"Oh, if you only *saw!*" she exclaimed brokenly, and again was silent.

The count looked thoroughly nonplused and chagrined.

"Ah, dear madame, this is more than even American independence warrants! To draw back at the last moment! Surely you divined that, had you not done me the honor to signify a disposition to listen, I would have made no proposals."

"Fully, count. I exonerate you entirely; it is all my fault, all a question of ide-

als. I thought I had none, and you have convinced me to the contrary. You have done me an inestimable service, and I do you one in-forbearing to marry you. We should never agree. That would be terrible and might have an unhappy effect upon your career. For one who cannot perceive with you, cannot walk with you, each acts as dead weight to the other."

Zoffsky rose as she did. They stood gazing at each other in silence. He looked mystified and indignant. Mrs. Barry was pale, but showed an elation and certainty in her face which the count saw merely to wonder at.

"You do not object to Estelle, and yet you do object to *me!* Was there ever anything so contradictory, so incredible?"

The blood rushed to his face, his mortification was intense, and Mrs. Barry saw with regret that she had administered a sharp wound to his self-esteem.

"Dear count," she said eagerly and sweetly, "I—I—can't explain. Think me *bourgeoise, bornée*[6]—what you will—the very fact that you do *not* understand shows how far we are apart. We are not within the same plane of mental—or, perhaps, spiritual—horizon."

But Count Zoffsky had recovered himself. "D'Auvillières was right," he said gravely; "friendship with women is impossible."

She gave him a slow, wistful look. "Yes, if life has but the material side, friendship is impossible."

He was silent. Pride was uppermost on his part; on hers a pathetic longing to quicken, if but for one instant, his inner vision. But perhaps there was no inner vision. Arrowy words that seemed to cleave to the very soul of understanding came back to her: "If the light that is in thee be darkness—"[7]

She went with him to the very door, yearning over him. Each was dimly sensible of the gulf between them; each was desirous of speaking, and neither could say a word.

The Strategists (1910)

The occasion was obviously less that of grief than of just the proper funereal decorum. It spoke in the bowed shutters, the darkened rooms, the cautious tread and the subdued voices. Nevertheless, the goodly assemblage of relatives and friends that awaited in the parlor the coming of the immediate family of the deceased talked earnestly and freely among themselves. They had certainly observed all due ceremonies, and now, at the request of Chester Penforth, only son of the late Benjamin Penforth, they were to attend at the reading of the will—always an interesting event—and so felt agreeably at liberty to discuss character and conditions.

"Well, fourscore is a ripe old age," said Judge Erneshaw, breathing lightly on his glasses and polishing them with his handkerchief. "He died with all his faculties intact. But then such case-hardened men generally do," he added whimsically. "They come into life well preserved, and go out as they came in."

"It was a mercifully brief passage at the last," said Dr. Brand, the family physician.

"I'm glad, for Eunice's sake, he didn't suffer much," said Mrs. Brand, who was sitting next to Erneshaw.

"But Eunice is worn out, though," remarked the Doctor quickly. "All these years of serving an adaptation have surely told upon her. The old fellow wouldn't even have a nurse till I threatened to take Eunice away altogether—said he was too old-fashioned to have a 'female attendant' about him. I told him Eunice wasn't too old-fashioned to break down or die from overstrain and want of sleep, and then he grudgingly yielded."

Erneshaw's smile—he was a spare, elderly man, himself—had a certain impish quality. "Yes, he was one of your literal lawyers, mighty in the letter, yet never able to grasp the informing spirit. But, as the oldest member of the bar in Gloucester, and an honor to the profession, he'll be missed. That's why I'm officially here."

"No mortal man was ever more 'sot in his ways' than Benjamin Penforth," said Mrs. Brand tersely. "Eunice has been the best of daughters."

"She ought to have an aureole of extra circumference hereafter for all she has undergone here," said the Doctor grimly. "Deliver me from your domestic tyrants! And yet the old man wasn't mean, either."

"But could never conceive of any opinions or ways other than his own," said Erneshaw briskly. "Upright and honorable, yet almost impossible to work with. Such a stickler for trifles! While you were groping for the sense of a thing, he was all for crossing 't's' and dotting 'i's' and keeping up custom and precedent." Erneshaw adjusted his glasses, and his vivid blue eyes flashed over the assembled group and about the room.

"Repression, suppression, oppression—these three words compass the whole of Eunice Penforth's forty-five years of life," said Mrs. Brand with emphasis.

Erneshaw turned to her with a quickness that had somewhat the effect of a pounce. "Bless me, was it as bad as that? Such a nice little mousey woman! Couldn't she have cut loose from the old curmudgeon?"

"Why, Judge Erneshaw—Rob—Eunice isn't little! She's rather above the middle height," protested Mrs. Brand in surprise, while the Doctor laughed softly.

"Well, that must have been the general effect on my retina and mind," said Erneshaw carelessly. "Suppose I've never really noticed her, though I must have been coming here off and on for years. Only came to the house formally, at long intervals, you know, and I fancy she must have been in the background."

"Yes; her father scared away suitors when she was young, and he always thought that women, like children, should be seen rather than heard; so Eunice has always been more or less in the background. Her mother instilled into her a strong sense of duty, of which her father has reaped a usurious benefit. Nine-tenths of what is held up as woman's duty and virtue is apt to be man's convenience," added Mrs. Brand softly, but with unmistakable edge.

Erneshaw laughed. "Are you trying to get a rise out of me? I'm not going to respond now; but you interest me in the lady. I suppose old Penforth has divided his property equally between his two children, eh?"

This afforded conversational entrance to Mrs. Josiah Cray, who had been seeking an opportunity. "Indeed, Judge Erneshaw, we all hope he has left poor Eunice everything. It's as little as he could do after the way she has devoted her whole life to him. And Chester doesn't need it; he's rich—to say nothing of his wife, who has plenty of money."

Erneshaw lifted his brows. "I hope he may, my dear madam, but, from my knowledge of old Benjamin Penforth, I doubt it. Two children would to him mean naturally a division—unless some crotchet should have induced him to leave his property to charity. He was curiously fixed in his ideas."

Mrs. Josiah raised her lorgnette, and in her turn surveyed the rooms. "'*Fixed*'!" she murmured. "There ought to be another word. Haircloth! I haven't seen it since I saw my grandmother's parlor nearly fifty years ago. And he would have neither gas nor electricity, but used candles and lamps; that meant that Eunice had to superintend the lamps. And as for heating, he insisted on open fires to the last. Why they didn't freeze to death in these huge rooms, I can't imagine."

Erneshaw glanced over the brass-studded horsehair furniture, over the India vases and ornaments, at the sets of candelabra from whose pendants a stray beam of light brought forth the prismatic colors, to the old prints and pictures on the walls. "Perfect mahogany, and some mighty good things, besides the books," he said with interest.

"Oh, the things are really precious," cried Mrs. Josiah. "But his belief in the old amounted to an—an—obsession."

"Sh! Here they come!"

Chester Penforth and his wife and the

two eldest children, boys of sixteen and fourteen, quietly entered, and were followed after a slight pause by Eunice. She mechanically put back her veil as she came in, and took the chair that someone offered. The way in which she slipped into the room and took that chair showed that she had long since formed, and had continually practiced, the habit of self-effacement. She was a slender woman, with a pale face and delicate features; her mouth was pathetic, and she had the large, hopestrained eyes of one whose own personal tastes and longings are perpetually foregone. She was followed by Mr. Curlett, the lawyer, who held several thick envelopes in one hand. Curlett was a short-legged man with a stubby walk, and a professionally intent brow. He now stubbed across the carpet to the center table, and someone partly opened a back window shutter and let in an eye cheering wedge of light. Unconsciously Eunice turned her face toward it with a little sigh of relief, and slightly dilated her nostrils, as if she inhaled hopefully the sweet waft of autumn air fraught with the pungent odor of wood smoke and dead leaves. Erneshaw eyed her critically, for people appear so differently according to the thought with which they are regarded, and he felt as if be for the first time truly saw Eunice Penforth.

Curlett unfolded deliberately one of his documents, and all prepared to listen. No one ever heard a will read without a certain thrill; and as all drew chairs a little nearer, and settled comfortably and stilly, the atmosphere was as rife with expectation as with the soft warmth of the smoldering fire.

Mr. Curlett read slowly and monotonously, and the kinsfolk and acquaintance listened perfunctorily, with eyes and thoughts fixed kindly on Eunice. Never did preambles seem longer or more unnecessary, but Curlett came finally to these words:

> And, well knowing the clinging quality of the feminine nature, and the unstable quality of the female intellect—its judgment being very prone to error—I give, bequeath, and devise all of which I die possessed to my son, Charles Chester Penforth, with the proviso that his sister, my well beloved and cherished daughter Eunice, shall always make her home with him, and that he shall in all particulars suitably provide for her as becomes the birth and circumstance of a gentlewoman—

Even the stolid Curlett paused, as if uncertain in his reading, and the telling silence was broken by Erneshaw.

"Well, I'll be—blessed! Consistent to the end!" The Judge was leaning easily against a window frame, with his thumbs in his pockets. He snatched them out and strode quickly over to Eunice, as did several others. She had half risen, and was gazing at Curlett with a piteous expression of deepening dismay. Chester Penforth was unmistakably too surprised to speak, while his wife was simply gaping in her astonishment.

"Why—why," faltered Eunice at last, "I—don't—understand! Will you please read it again—that about me?"

With a doubtful look at her, Curlett reread the ominous words, and Eunice drank them in. "But he doesn't really give me *anything!* He doesn't—Oh, he doesn't let me be free!" she gasped. Then, as a fuller realization of the curbing nature of her father's provision came to her, she uttered a smothered cry and fell to her knees, as if beaten down by an unseen hand. "My life, my life, the things I've always wanted to do—he doesn't give me my life! Always the same arrangement, somebody else to think for me and to decide! I can't! I won't! It chokes me! It's not right nor just; I'd almost rather die!" She snatched off the bonnet and veil, as though they were smothering her; she beat on the carpet with her hands, then lifted them as if to tear the prematurely gray hair. The repression of a lifetime had momentarily given way, and nature *would* assert itself, speak and be heard.

"It's hysteria," said Brand sternly, as he and Erneshaw raised her and put her back into the chair. "She has been overwrought for days, and has had far too little sleep."

One brought water, and another wine, while Mrs. Brand and Mrs. Josiah fanned her, for her condition was pitiable. The scene was very painful, and everyone looked most uncomfortably helpless, as all do before the exposed privacies of feeling and of thought. Chester Penforth seemed fairly petrified by his sister's outbreak, and tears of mortification stood in his wife's eyes, as she murmured brokenly: "Eunice, of all people—that *she* should take it so!"

They soothed and comforted her, and after a time the tearless sobs subsided, and the shaking body began to sit quietly again. And then Judge Erneshaw turned pointedly to Chester Penforth. "A very remarkable man, your father, Penforth, and in nothing so much as in his prej—convictions. But I congratulate you on having the opportunity to do a very handsome thing. For, of course, you will so arrange matters as to fall measurably in with your sister's wishes. She is neither a minor nor an imbecile, and her life ought to be independent."

Penforth perceptibly stiffened, and the expression of his face brought out the strong resemblance to his father: the prominent light eyes, the Roman nose, the long, yet rather flat and receding chin; narrowness, obstinacy, a gritty goodness—all the family traits, physical and mental, were manifest.

"I think my father's intentions and wishes should come before my sister's; and if he could trust my affection and integrity, I think my sister and the family connections may well do so."

Erneshaw's blue eyes spat fire. "An admirable reply, sir; eminently characteristic, yet hardly to the real point. It's not a question of your father's intentions, nor of your integrity, nor even of your sister's wishes. It's a question of justice. In the face of patent fact, such a will is absurd. As I said, your sister is neither a minor nor incompetent; why, then, make her a perpetual ward?"

"Sh!" whispered the Doctor; "even chivalry must be circumspect."

Penforth was anything but a dull man, nor was he slow to see an advantage. The flush on his face deepened, as he answered: "My sister's unfortunate—ebullition, shall we say?—would seem to go far to justify my father's—a—precautions. He and she have always been most closely associated; surely he may be considered the best judge of what will most conduce to her welfare and happiness."

At her brother's tone, and the word "ebullition," Eunice's white face turned, if possible, even whiter, and the look of sickening hopelessness made of her expression almost a blank. Erneshaw's speaking Irish eyes turned a jade green, like cold waters under an angry sky. "It is the paradox of life—some call it the irony or cruelty—that the selfsame facts will often bear entirely opposite constructions. There is such a thing as living beside people for a lifetime and never understanding them nor conveniently ignoring them. Some see only what they want to see, believe only what they want to believe. Do you suppose so indefinite a will can stand?"

"Oh, you're ruining everything!" moaned Mrs. Josiah softly.

Penforth's look and manner were very ugly as he returned: "Yes, Judge Erneshaw, even if my sister were capable of going to law with her only near relative—But she will not so far forget herself."

"Gentlemen, this is untimely," interposed the Doctor, determined to check the dispute.

"Rob, we love you utterly, but *do* use a little tact," whispered Mrs. Brand on the other side; and Erneshaw, quick-tempered and angry as he was, saw the folly of persisting. Penforth, too, bethought himself, especially as his wife, looking both shocked and frightened, had been making him imploring gestures to desist.

The atmosphere gradually cleared. People settled down or back into their chairs again, and Curlett was asked to proceed. The rest of the will was brief. In case of Penforth's death, the property was to be left in trust for her benefit, and at her decease

was to pass intact to the Penforth children.

The silence that followed the conclusion of the will was distinctly awkward. Everybody looked at everybody else, and waited for someone to make a definite move. Chester's mouth was one straight, hard, ugly line. Erneshaw looked contemptuously indifferent—but then everyone knew that he was a privileged character, determined to say and do just what he pleased. Mr. Josiah Cray, with what Mrs. Chester Penforth always called his "enormous social prestige," turned his back squarely upon the room and began to study intently the pictures and the prints; yet the effect of that dorsal attitude seemed, somehow, to focus upon the Chester Penforths.

Eunice, meanwhile, in the high old haircloth chair, sat limp, white, wordless, scarcely conscious of what went on around her. Some thread of hope, held to through all these unselfish years, had either snapped utterly or was no longer vibrant. People came pityingly up to her, with polite commonplaces which she did not hear nor heed, and then passed reluctantly on.

The Doctor regarded her anxiously. Presently, turning to Mrs. Penforth, he said: "Eunice must leave the house at once and go with my wife. The strain has been much too great, and the shock of surprise is too severe. She must be removed from these surroundings immediately."

"I will take her to Atlantic City with me," murmured Mrs. Penforth.

"That will hardly be change of thought," said the Doctor drily. "Put on her bonnet and get her a wrap; I'll send her home with Mrs. Brand. Later, you may come to some understanding as to what is best to be done. Now, she must be with us to be carefully watched and tended."

Penforth made a dissenting gesture. "Really, Doctor, hadn't she better go with us? Surely it would be more fitting."

"Going to be responsible for a nervous breakdown, Chester?" asked the Doctor coolly.

But Eunice herself was regaining her self-possession. She raised her head and said: "For the present I will go with Mrs. Brand, Cousin Susie. Then—I can think."

Chester and his wife were evidently both surprised and mortified. "Why, Eunice," he exclaimed, "you can surely trust me. You will always have your own way, except in those matters in which my better judgment shall supervene."

She looked at him for a moment in silence, looked him through, then said gently: "Would *you* be satisfied with such a will? You know you wouldn't. Then why ask it of me? It is not the loss of any money, nor the reflection on my capacity; it is not anything of what you think; it is the awful lack of justice, which cannot even dream what freedom means. Come, Cousin Susie, let us go." And without another word or look Eunice rose and on Mrs. Brand's arm went from the room.

That will, of course, made a great stir in Gloucester. It was the unexpected that had happened, and everybody had an opinion and a say. Various accounts of what had occurred at the reading were soon spread abroad, and, such is the gaily or tragically incalculable quality of human nature, that that little outbreak on the part of the self-contained Eunice did more to damage her cause with some than did her whole self-abnegating life to uphold it with others. To the ordinary eye it is the unusual that counts, and to the mass of men demanding that stones shall be made bread,[8] on sober second consideration the will did not seem so hard. A rich brother and rich sister-in-law, unquestionably affectionate and kindly disposed, a more than comfortable home, with more than the traditional "full and plenty"—what could a reasonable woman ask further? Perhaps old Benjamin Penforth did know best; volatile woman, changing and changeable, flighty and inconsequent in her desires, had best be properly tethered. So the townsmen rather sided with Chester, and the townswomen with Eunice. And yet they admitted that her feeling was somewhat above and beyond ordinary comprehension. What did she really want?

Meantime, her close friends, particularly the Doctor and his wife, watched over her with some anxiety and no little perplexity. This is a hard and definite world; if she wouldn't abide by the will, and wouldn't attempt to break it, what was she to do? She was certainly not prepared to dig; to beg she would be as certainly ashamed; and yet one must live. How utilize the pretty inutilities of a middle-aged gentlewoman? Mrs. Chester Penforth came every day, stayed long and talked volubly of duty, proper mourning, family affection, wall paper, Atlantic City and "dear Eunice's extraordinary notion in wanting to live alone."

"But, Fanny," interpolated Mrs. Brand at this point, "Eunice never said anything of the sort. So far as we can gather—for she puts very little concerning her feelings into words- she seems to think that it was due herself as a rational being, or due to abstract justice, that she should have been allowed to arrange her life according to her own discretion."

"But, dear me, why can't she?" cried Mrs. Chester protestingly. "She will have everything just the same, if not far more. We live delightfully; we know the best people—almost all of them; she will always go wherever I do, and not have a care or responsibility. Chester can't understand it at all. He's deeply mortified, and is becoming quite morbid. It does seem so unreasonable. One would think she would acquiesce with pleasure."

"Not one who knew Eunice," said Mrs. Brand drily. "She has always wanted to travel, for one thing, and, of course, according to her own interests and desires. She wants to see, she says, 'concrete history and art, not the written page, the photograph, the description.' Old Mr. Penforth was as non-adventurous as an oyster, and quite as much of a stay-at-home. A few weeks or days in the city now and then represent poor Eunice's hoppings beyond the family rooftree. She has never been farther North than Boston, nor farther South than Norfolk, and never West at all. And it wasn't as if they had been poor—she, with such a thirst for all that this wondrous life of ours offers!"

Mrs. Chester's large brown eyes, with their vaguely uncertain expression, fixed themselves earnestly on Mrs. Brand. "But, dear Cousin Susie, I don't suppose Chester would seriously object. We've been to Europe several times ourselves, and surely expect to go again."

Something in Mrs. Brand's look checked her. Propriety, conventionality, virtue, were to Mrs. Chester Penforth almost synonymous. The habitual vagueness of her eyes was caused not by indefiniteness of desire, but by doubt as to means. She was quite sure that her desires were laudable, all the more so that they were shared by the world at large; but she was uncertain as to resources. The Josiah Crays, for instance, called, as in duty bound, once in a year or so; but they never came to her dinners, and most infrequently to her teas and receptions. What was lacking? Yet Mrs. Chester was sure she was socially impregnable, for did she not dine late even on Sunday, instead of partaking of the simple, more primitive tea? Then as the granddaughter of a locally famous cabinetmaker, one of her unresolvable doubts was whether it was better to know a great deal about old-fashioned furniture or nothing at all. For knowledge come by elegantly, as a connoisseur, is one thing, but inherited inevitably by way of trade is quite another. And then, in her inmost soul, she could never decide whether a grand manner was the more desirable as indicating the greater exclusiveness, or—no manner or manners at all, apparently, like little Mrs. Dorsey Greaves, who, nevertheless, was tremendously followed. But now all perplexities were swallowed up in this burning question of Eunice-her strange stand and incomprehensible dissatisfaction. Mrs. Chester declared that her position was most anomalous, staying on uncertainly at the Penforth house in Gloucester, when by rights she should be at home in the city—and giving directions about Penforth belongings unhelped by so much as a syllable from Eunice.

Then at the Brands' she daily encountered Judge Erneshaw, who certainly poured no oil on the troubled waters of her doubts and surmisings. His exquisite politeness somehow made her exquisitely uncomfortable. Just enough of the Celt to have a trace of unhumanness about him, the elfin quality, whether of fairy or of imp, a spice of that malice which is not wholly averse from the caressing lick that neatly takes off the skin—his sympathy was deeply disconcerting.

"Unreasonable, my dear lady? Why, of course. But then aren't we all agreed that unreason is a feminine prerogative and charm? Leave unlovely logic to us coarser men. And if among gentlemen, you know, a lady's wishes are commands, then surely a sister's ought to be paramount. Oh, there's no compulsion, of course; just the inspiriting authority exercised by a common ideal of conduct, a common understanding. I'm awfully sorry I butted in, though—it must have been an Irish cow that kicked over its own pail of milk—but I was childishly disappointed. You see, I expected a pretty action, had set my mouth for pie, as it were, and got—this is in the bosom of the family—sawdust. There burned the fire; here lay the will; now what was to hinder Chester Penforth from picking up that will and dropping it promptly upon that fire? It would have cleared his skirts at once—so simple, immediate and direct. That was the way I romantically felt. Old Jos Cray and I were talking about it at the club, and it's curious that we should both have counted on the same thing, and should both have been disappointed. Yes, we looked for a pretty action, something to warm the blood;

the kind of thing you might not have the grace to do yourself, but would love to see done by your best friend or a brother-in-law or the husband of your first cousin, something really to brag about."

With his malignly innocent eyes fixed upon his listener, and a voice and accent not to be excelled, Erneshaw was surely making an impression.

"Pity he didn't influence his father in the other direction, though," continued the Judge blandly.

But by this time Mrs. Penforth, concerned and tormented, had found speech. "Oh, Judge Erneshaw, you don't think—people don't suppose"-She faltered and stopped.

"Dear lady," returned Erneshaw in his handsomest manner—the manner most fatal to the opposing counsel's witness—"in a strictly academic sense, historians always, and lawyers under certain conditions, are not supposed to think. They are simply to state or to present facts. But I am human and empiric enough to hold that no one can state a fact without giving it thereby an interpretation. The will gives everything to Chester. Tongues have wagged, do wag, will wag, to the end of time. You are far too socially experienced, dear madam, not to be able to put two and two together. The will gives everything to Chester. I leave to your own imagination the interpretation people put upon it."

Tears of bitter mortification stood in Mrs. Chester's eyes. "Judge Erneshaw, I do assure you Chester never dreamed of such a will. He was as surprised as anyone."

"I'm convinced of it," murmured Erneshaw soothingly, "but the world in general is not so simple and charitable as we are. Sixty or seventy thousand is a tidy little sum, and comes in handily at this time, when your good husband desires to make certain improvements in the Dorley Mills. I, as a shareholder, happen to know. It would have been so much better if he had burned—But, there, we won't speak of it further. Filial piety, and a due regard for a father's wishes are most admirable. Generally, such soul values are incalculable; but in this instance they are worth, aren't they, about seventy thousand?" His sighs, his pauses and hesitancies, were very effective. "Ah, Richter is right; we never do know any man until we divide an inheritance with him or want him to divide one with us."[9]

At this point, mystified and troubled, the lady rose to go, and Erneshaw bade her good-bye as if she were a client who had just reposed in him an unhappy confidence.

"You were almost—cruel," said Mrs. Brand, smiling reproachfully, after she had seen her visitor out.

"I must 'be cruel only to be kind,'"[10] quoted Erneshaw briskly. "She's a mighty handsome woman, but wooden as one of her grandfather's fine sideboards. It won't hurt to inoculate her with an idea which, under Providence, may take. I trust she will think it her Christian and wifely duty to repeat to Chester what I said—possibly with embellishments. It's a point of honor to separate him from half of that money. He owes it to his sister in justice, and to me in courtesy for his manner the day of the will."

But Mrs. Brand's face was grave behind its smile. "After all, it rests with Eunice. No one can take another up and support

her. She must find her own way out."

"I fancy she will," said Erneshaw confidently. "Her strong feeling will crystallize into the appropriate action. I'm beginning to feel that Eunice is exceptional. But now that Mrs. Penforth has safely turned the corner, I, too, must go."

∽

A few mornings later, when Mrs. Brand went into the large, sunny room where her kinswoman spent most of her time, she found Eunice with a more alert expression on her face, a return of the usual quietly compressed energy.

"I'm sorry to have worried you all so," she began earnestly. "No, don't excuse me, Cousin Susie, for as I look back I see I might have known. The will was perfectly consistent and characteristic, and my poor father thought he was doing it for the best. I don't question his affection. I didn't know I had hoped so strongly and deeply all these years, however—such poor little starved hopes—till I saw them all drowning like blind kittens in a water butt, the day of the will. Well, it's over. Only, I don't forgive myself for the unseemly scene I made, and for the anxiety I have caused you all." There was even a trace of the old subsurface humor now, together with the customary bravery which had faced every exigency of life with patient cheerfulness.

"Sit in that comfortable, chintz-covered chair, Cousin Susie, and listen. Don't interrupt me till I've finished, and then tell me frankly what you think. Let's dispassionately inventory Eunice Penforth, and see what she's good for." She drew a long breath, and said more gravely: "I want to be my own guardian, under God, till my life's end. I consider the desire perfectly legitimate and just. Chester and Fanny would be as fair to me as they know how, and generous. I should have purple and fine linen, the best of food and warmth, the utmost of physical comfort. I should be at liberty to run up bills, perhaps, under certain restrictions, unless Fanny, which is more likely, attended to all my clothes; but I should have scarcely a cent of spending money, and my very time would be largely mapped out for me. Shall I sell my birthright of approximate freedom—which presupposes work of some kind—for the mess of pottage?"[11]

She paused for a moment before adding: "Then, their ways and thoughts are not mine, and their plane of life is different from that I should like to occupy. But I'm forty-five, and have been bred up to nothing in particular—just a lady. I read French and German a little, can keep accounts, play the piano a little-Beethoven's waltzes and the schoolgirl things of years ago; nothing possible there, I fancy. But you know my father's—a—rigidities of opinion, how, without realizing it, he was—hard to please. Servants came and went, and I trained them all. There is nothing about a house I don't know and cannot do. If I do say it myself, I'm a perfect cook. There lies my marketable ability, my likelihood of trade. All the world's a mart, and all the men and women merely traders.[12] It depends on what you trade with and for, you'll say." She smiled, and took a rapid turn through the room. "There are places in the city, tea or lunch rooms, some of them conducted by women, where I might find an opening, subordinate at first, of

course, to learn practical details, yet with possibilities, dependent upon my business capacity, beyond—working housekeeper, managing cook, something of that sort. In this way I shall still own myself, shall still have the blessed privilege of hope, and after a time, may yet be able to see and to do some things to my own liking."

Eunice's clear, pale face had been undergoing many subtle changes of expression, as if the spirit within breathed lightly upon a delicate pane. But the changes in Mrs. Brand's countenance were far stronger and more marked; first, shocked wonder, then suspense, then an almost incredulous, repressed joy.

"Eunice, you! Would you really dare?"

Eunice regarded her with mild surprise. "Certainly it's the one thing I can do thoroughly. Why shouldn't I turn it to account? And if, to all your lifelong kindness, you will add that of getting me a place—more elegantly, securing me a position, I shall be so grateful. Not 'lady help,' mind; just the plain, everyday thing. I've thought it all out; it will be a new experience, and I rather enjoy the prospect of seeing life from a below-stairs point of view."

Mrs. Brand listened keenly to all her kinswoman had to say, but in replying she herself said very little. On leaving the room, she called up Erneshaw and asked him to come to dinner, and to come early. He came, expectant to the fingertips, as was evident when he shook hands.

"Your very voice over the 'phone intimated new developments; what is it?" he asked eagerly.

"I've been dying to tell someone all day. Frank's away. Rob, she has thought of a way out; she's going to cook!" Mrs. Brand was breathless.

"Wha-at?" gasped Erneshaw, staring.

"And if she had thought the world over she couldn't have hit upon a more perfect plan. Don't blink at me, Rob Erneshaw; grasp the situation. Eunice Penforth is going, if necessary, to cook!"

They gazed at each other in silence and presently the mundane joy of her face was matched by the impish glee of his.

"Eunice? And she thought of it herself? What a train of possibilities! Oh, the simplicity that confounds wisdom! And here we've cudgeled our brains, till I, for one, haven't any brains left. Susie, will you look me straight in the eye and swear you never offered a breath of suggestion? We began life on the same school bench together, and, from the alphabet on, you've been a subtle-minded person."

"No more than yourself. But I swear it—cross my heart; I never dreamed of such a thing. And I wouldn't have suggested it, if I had. Eunice is too high and too humble, too generous and too fine, to stoop to devices. Moreover, she is thinking kindly of her father, is justifying him to herself and to others. She has put the hard past and present disappointment behind her, and is quietly facing the future. No," continued Mrs. Brand earnestly, "I was almost afraid to speak for fear of spoiling her ingenuousness and simplicity. She's essentially young, Rob, despite her forty-five years."

"Undoubtedly, since the power of initiative means youth." Then, regarding his lifelong friend sympathetically: "But I might have known you, Susie. Thucydides[13] has a noble passage about only great hearts respecting and understanding simplicity; you, too, are fine. Yet, it's the best I ever heard. And that she should have thought of it herself! Is that thirty thousand I see before me?"—plucking an imaginary something out of the air. "Yes, I think it is."

Their two-part laughter filled the room.

"And I know the person who shall hire Miss Eunice, a person provided by destiny to fill the part," continued Erneshaw. "It's Mrs. Dillwyn. She has a cafe or lunch room for saleswomen and clerks that she's trying to run on philanthropic principles. But there's too much theory, too much sentiment and too little human nature. Her iridescent bubble is bound to burst, but meantime she wants a combination of all virtue and ability to blow it, and she has had the mischief with her employees. Dillwyn says he's kept alive by watching his wife's experiments. She weighs two hundred, and has no waist line even in fifty-dollar stays—"

"Be careful!" interpolated Mrs. Brand.

"Don't squirm before you hear. I never verbally fall overboard—

"Except the day of the will."

"Well, hardly ever. Anyhow, Mrs. Dillwyn will serve our turn. Her mind has no waist line, either; indeed, *her* mental condition is always nebulous, but full of loving heat and energy. She's more innocent than Eunice herself, and she's always mothering a person or a cause. And when she espouses a cause, oh, the momentum of it! All you have to do is to sit back and get a free ride. The explanation ought to satisfy everyone; that Eunice has too much respect for her father's memory, and too much affection for her brother, to dispute the will, but too much self-respect to accept it. How does that strike you?"

"Rob, you're an angel."

"But our unwitting silent partner will do the trick. She is our strongest card."

"Our 'silent partner'!"

"Mrs. Chester Penforth herself. Again the simple will confound the wise, the lesser motive prove mightier than the finer. Alas, for human nature! I'll engage to hoist Chester with his own wife, quite as effectually as the engineer with his own petard. Wait and you'll see what you will see."

"Sh! Here comes Eunice," said Mrs. Brand hurriedly. "Don't give us away."

ↁ

It was about three weeks after this that Mrs. Penforth, sitting at her handsomely appointed breakfast table, began slowly to open her morning's mail. The admirable Hooper, whose clean blackness was thrown into high relief by his white duck morning coat, had just presented it on the little silver tray, with the ivory paper cutter laid carefully on top. Mrs. Penforth's ample brow was not only serious, but even showed signs of care. She had been at home more than a fortnight, yet was still "in the dark," as she expressed it, concerning Eunice's possible movements. One thing seemed certain, and that was that Eunice did not intend to take up her residence either temporarily or permanently with her family. And the few affectionate short notes which she had written were as noncommittal as had been the desultory interviews.

"She evidently means to make her own arrangements, and to carry out her own ideas, whatever they may be," Mrs. Penforth would repeatedly say to her husband. "And as time goes by, I feel only the more anxious. I really think you might have tried, Chester, before you quitted Gloucester, to find out what would have satisfied her, and what it was she wanted. For people are talking; there's no doubt about that."

"Let them talk!" said Chester shortly. "There's no earthly reason why she shouldn't abide by our father's will. I'm only left the property provided I provide properly for her-which would have been done, of course, under any circumstances. But the truth is, Eunice is opinionated, like most women, and obstinate, like all the Penforths."

"I think you're mistaken," returned his wife mildly; "but, at all events, *my* peace of mind ought to be considered. You said yourself that old Jos Cray"—she had been quick to adopt Erneshaw's familiar phrase—"scarcely took a dog's notice of you now at the club; yet before this be was always perfectly civil. I'm uneasy, Chester."

"Jos Cray, pshaw! The Penforths are as good as the Crays any day, and better, too. Old fossil!" muttered Chester; but he reddened. under his golf tan—his wife made him play, and made him belong to the country club—and then added: "Erneshaw's capable of putting him up to anything."

"It's no use to fight public opinion, Chester," said his wife firmly. "And it's much better to be generous sometimes than to be merely just—I can see that."

Chester truly liked and admired his wife. She was a fine administrator; she had ten thousand a year in her own right, and she was wholesomely devoted to him and to the children. He and she were good friends, good comrades—in so far as they were capable of *camaraderie,* and he knew, as a sober and significant fact, that he had always profited by taking her suggestions and advice.

As she opened her mail he watched her with a pleased, proprietary satisfaction. She always looked well; she did things with ease and aptness; and with one plump white hand poised with the paper cutter and the other holding the open sheet over which her eyes began to glance, she was a becoming wife for any man, and not many, he thought, had the like.

"Good Lord, Fanny, what's the matter!" For as be looked, his wife turned suddenly white, with eyes staring; there was downright horror in her gaze.

"Water, Hooper! Fanny—wine, brandy! Don't stand like an idiot!" cried Chester. But by this time he was beside his wife, holding her arm and helping her up.

"Come into the library," she managed to gasp, and, helped by him, she made her way thither. "Shut the door," she cautioned briefly, then dropped into a chair and broke into tears.

"Of all wonders! Are you sick?" asked the alarmed Chester.

"Read that," she said tragically between sobs, and held up some thick note paper. The small, rather indefinite hand conveyed no idea to Chester's bewildered mind.

33 Vanderlen Place
November 12, 1908
My Dear Mrs. Penforth:

Quite as the merest, veriest, matter of formality, and at the instance of Mrs. Franklin Brand, whom I used to know and whom I greatly value, and who is, I understand, a cousin of Mr. Penforth, and therefore, of course, a cousin of his sister, Miss Eunice, in whose unusual venture Mrs. Brand is deeply interested, and to be perfectly in keeping with the lovely and exalted view that Miss Eunice takes of it—I mean, her wishing to do the thing just as any everyday person would do it-a professional cook and manager, that is—conducting the matter along what my husband calls, "strictly business lines"—do I make myself clear? I write to ask you—it seems too absurd, for I am perfectly convinced that she is wonderful— whether Miss Eunice can cook; yet I know that this note is as superfluous as the word "for" before the infinitive. However, if you will just send me a line to make the circle complete, shall we say, I suppose all formalities will be satisfied. I, at least, am most fortunate in being the one to profit by Miss Eunice's independence and delightful ability.

Very truly yours,
Jessie Barclay Dillwyn

"What's all this drivel about? What's the woman driving at? How does Eunice come in? And what in heaven's name is the matter with you, Fanny?" demanded the anxious and angry Chester, mumbling and stumbling over the words and parentheses. "I'm getting just a little sick of Eunice and her tomfoolery. I shall wash my hands of the whole affair."

But the stricken face his wife lifted stilled his irritability. For the tears were gushing down her cheeks; she could hardly speak for emotion. Never in their married life had he seen her so wrought upon and overcome.

"Chester, are you doing it on purpose, or don't you really care and see?" she wailed.

"After all these years, and the way I've honestly striven to help you in everything, and to do the best for the children, to have this happen! It's simply fiendish! She's a real lady and naturally wants to spare my feelings even if you and Eunice don't. *I* can appreciate things and people, even if you can't; and yet I never pretended that my family was anything like as good as yours. But I'm coming to the conclusion that there's such a thing as being too well born. Eunice thinks she's privileged to *do* anything, and you think you're privileged to *ignore* everything; you are both about on a par; while sensible people know there are precious few privileges coming to anybody, unless it's the privilege of making oneself ridiculous. Chester Penforth, you haven't the sense heaven gives to goslings!"

She was rapidly condescending to the vernacular now, anger being a terrible leveler; and never had the astounded Chester seen his conscientiously polite wife so thoroughly incensed.

"If you'll just tell me what it all means—" he began.

"Means! None are so blind as they who won't see! It means that your sister, Eunice Penfield, has gone out as cook-manager to Mrs. Miles Fournoy Dillwyn. And this is neither more nor less than a note to me asking for a recommendation—a recommendation! I almost wish I was dead! It means ruin! And Dorothy twelve years old, and to come out six or seven years hence, her aunt, her father's only sister, a cook, or working manager! Chester, if I could have foreseen this day, and that you and Eunice Penforth, the pair of you, would prove such abject fools, I never, never would have married you! And you can stand there and glare at me as if you hadn't good sense! Did any man ever appreciate the look of things? But I shall do something, if you don't. I'll go on my knees to Eunice, if necessary; she may have half my fortune—all, but she shall give up this—this—horror! That sickening will—your father was an old tyrant, Chester; I'm awfully sorry I named Ben after him—has turned poor Eunice's brain, and has hardened your heart. I can never hold up my head again!"

And with this her handsome head did go down into her hands, and she became fairly hysterical.

The domestic upheaval was now complete, and the dazed Chester, feeling as if his particular life were rocking to its foundations, stood helplessly silent.

In individuals and nations it is ideals alone that count. Fanny's ideal was society. The entity as she conceived it did not exist, but the conception had had, nevertheless, a strongly formative effect upon her, and had made of her a very definite person. Like most American men, Chester, of course, pooh-poohed his wife's social awes and admirations, her aspirations and imitations, her whole social "scheme of values"; but he was none the less insensibly impressed by them. No one can live intimately for eighteen years beside a mind bent consistently to one end without being strongly influenced; and her distress now affected him as with a powerful impingement. And while no married woman with ten thousand a year in her own right is ever perhaps, wholly a Griselda,[14] still, Fanny was an admirable wife. There was no gainsaying that she did her duty as she saw it, even if she believed that one of her chief duties was the placing of her husband and children at the social summit. The Penforths, she felt, had never "made enough of themselves," had never thoroughly utilized their unquestioned advantages of birth and position; but, strengthened by her energy and precision, there was no reason why the coming Penforths should not stand commandingly in the forefront. She was a somewhat slow-thinking woman, always grippingly serious, from hat trimmings to the catechism, but, granting the quality of her thinking, she was exact and coherent. She knew her social values, and Chester knew that she knew, and perceived that she was destined to succeed. If now, for the first time in a really benign and equable married life, he saw in her a temper approximating to what might vulgarly be called a tantrum, when she at last lifted her abased head she saw in him the un-Penforth grace of humility. Deeply concerned, mortified and angry, he stood staring at her, unmistakably open to suggestion, not to say ready for guidance.

But eighteen years of married life must inevitably disclose weaknesses at which an indignant wife may safely point an unerring and disconcerting finger.

"Why, you yourself simply writhed under your father's overbearing temper; you got away from him as soon as possible. Wouldn't study law to please him, but went into business on your own account. And poor Eunice, after forty-five years of it, must be tied down for the rest of her life by this ridiculous will! How she must have felt! And rather than be treated like a baby, she's willing to become a menial—has actually done it! A pretty figure you cut, Chester Penforth. But a man always expects a woman to bear what he wouldn't dream of putting up with himself. You told me yourself that your father never allowed Eunice half a chance; that, when the young men used to come to the house, he would sit in the back parlor, within earshot and full view, reading, and would sniff and snort at the little nothings that young people always talk about. Horribly impolite, almost vulgar of him, even if he was a Penforth. And yet he was one of those men who have a rather slighting opinion of a woman who doesn't marry! Thought that matrimony was a kind of gauge of a woman's ability; as if any idiot couldn't marry who hadn't sense enough to do better! But I intend to save your poor children from their father's blindness, and their aunt's madness. I'm thankful they had left for school before I opened that dreadful note."

She wiped her eyes, mechanically touched her hair and sat upright, preparing seriously to consider. Impressed, yet gloomy, Chester watched her. A woman must be tremendously incensed so to violate all her own canons; for Fanny, in her anger, had transgressed all the rules she prescribed in placidity. Fanny impolite, Fanny personal, was a wholly new woman to Chester. Moreover, she had not only been grossly personal, but her remarks had smacked of the very market place, and of raw, unsophisticated, humanity.

"Oh, I wish I hadn't taken things so for granted! I wish I had had a frank talk with Judge Erneshaw," she moaned.

"Damn Erneshaw!" cried Chester fervently. "You don't know Erneshaw, Fanny. He can shuffle human beings like cards. I shouldn't be surprised if he were somehow at the bottom of this."

But his wife regarded him with scandalized severity. "Chester, if insanity is in the Penforth family, it must be coming out now. You know perfectly well there isn't a woman in this city-worth considering—who doesn't simply gloat over having Erneshaw to dinner. He's over and above mere fashion. As somebody said—Cousin Susie, maybe—he's 'quintessential.' And you can speak of him in this common way, when you know, too, my feeling about profanity?"

"The way he cocks his eye at me makes me suspicious," growled Chester. "Oh, he's polite enough, with a vengeance! But when he wants to shunt a fellow off at the club, he talks in a strain that makes you feel as if you were standing on tiptoe and craning your neck to listen. I tell you, Erneshaw is deep."

"Pity some others are not deep, too," retorted his wife pointedly. "I repeated to you what he said."

"Yes, and the chances are that he said it for that purpose. I'm not the fool he takes me for," muttered Chester.

"Well, I intend to ask his advice, and to abide by it. He's better able than anyone else to pull us out of this hole-I mean, save the situation. I shall telephone and ask him to see me as soon as possible. But, Chester," she continued solemnly, "it must be understood that the property is to be equally divided. Then matters may be righted. And I might say that Eunice holds extreme views," she added tentatively. "Any woman who's as fond of books as Eunice is apt to have views—at least, it's taken for granted; and, really, some very nice people nowadays do make the queerest social experiments: her action might be given a look, a turn-" She spoke hopefully. "Chester, do I show—is my face—"

"No, you're all right," said her husband encouragingly; "and I give you *carte blanche*.[15] Eunice's conduct is outrageous and most unfilial, but it can't be helped. And you'll be equal to the emergency." And with a consolatory pat on the shoulder, Chester quitted the room.

Mrs. Penforth's drawing-room was soothingly delightful, warm, luxurious, rose-scented, with eye-cheering but not too effulgent lights. The lady herself, none the less handsome for a pale face and a perturbed manner, awaited nervously the coming of her rescuers, as she mentally phrased it, thinking anxiously of Judge Erneshaw's and Mrs. Brand's help. They came at last, however, pleasantly full, it seemed to poor Fanny, of everything save the Penforth coil.[16]

"Now, my dear lady," began Erneshaw, after greetings and explanations were well over, "let us clear the ground by finding out just what you do want." Mrs. Penforth regarded him earnestly, while Mrs. Brand covertly did the same. For Erneshaw himself seemed somewhat tentative and rather subdued.

"I want," said Fanny breathlessly, "to keep Eunice from ruining the family; and to do it, Chester is quite willing to divide the property."

Mrs. Brand with difficulty checked a slight exclamation, but Erneshaw's look was ingenuousness itself.

"Then you know she is at Mrs. Dillwyn's?" he asked gently.

"I had a note from Mrs. Dillwyn yesterday morning," said Fanny somberly, in a tone that spoke volumes.

"And I have come as soon as possible in obedience to your summons," returned Erneshaw. Mrs. Brand fairly studied him. If he were acting, then his histrionism—the instinctive histrionism of the Celtic strain—was far greater than even she had ever suspected. But she felt rather than perceived a new element in his expression and bearing, something that altered him, so that she could not conceive either his intention or drift.

"Oh, Judge Erneshaw, you and Cousin Susie surely must perceive what a terrible mistake it all is!" entreated Fanny, with clasped hands.

What was the change, Susan Brand kept asking herself, in Erneshaw? If it were possible for so socially assured a man, he seemed almost embarrassed. She knew that his wit was like a shield protecting the delicate sensitiveness of the imaginative; and she divined that imagi-nation, which is the true "second sight," and which in him had always so loyally and chivalrously served others, might at last be allowed to serve its possessor. He hesitated; he fumbled with his glasses; he looked speculatively at Fanny, and rather appealingly at Mrs. Brand.

"Oh," burst out Fanny, "if *you* can't help us, then we're lost!"

"Nothing so bad as that," said Erneshaw quickly. "But, to tell the truth, I had—an idea, a day or so ago, which makes me, myself, rather dissatisfied with the outcome of things."

"An idea?" asked Fanny hopefully. Again Erneshaw hesitated; yet be was evidently recovering his usual consummate self-possession.

"Or an emotion—well, what a psychologist might call a conceptual reorganization of the universe."

"What!" gasped Fanny, while Mrs. Brand stared. Erneshaw looked defensive, challenging, defiant; a fine color mustered in his wholesome, lean face. He threw up his head and drew a deep breath. "Yes, I had an idea."

"What is it?" asked both ladies together.

But Erneshaw swerved. "I don't see why it didn't dawn on me sooner, except that it's so hard to think of everything at once."

"Oh, do *you* ever feel that way? To this day I have it whenever I order a formal dinner." Fanny beamed on him from the happy level of mutual sympathy. Erneshaw eyed her. "I loathe mongrel thinking," he said mildly, "and why this didn't occur to me weeks ago I can't imagine, except that the mental habit of a lifetime must have prevented. But I've evidently been trying to interpret the universe in the mingled terms of emotion and of thought—an impossible feat, and hence have blinded my eyes and clouded my judgment. His tone was both whimsical and determined.

"But any idea of yours will be perfect," cried the delighted Fanny.

"And it's just what we should like," murmured Mrs. Brand.

Erneshaw's pause was so prolonged that both women gazed at him in wonder.

"I should like to marry Miss Eunice," he brought out at last.

There was not a sound. Fanny, speechless, could not trust auricular testimony; but Mrs. Brand, finding voice, exclaimed, "Rob, you're the joy of my heart!"

Erneshaw colored high, but stoutly maintained his mental and emotional ground.

"It seems an ideal thing to do, and also a sort of corollary, and my only regret is I didn't think of it before. But it really matters little. Throwing herself thus gallantly into life, as a good swimmer trusts himself to the sea, Miss Eunice is—well, I really think I ought to marry Eunice. We shall hit it off exactly. She early took to Shakespeare by divine instinct; so did I; so do all good Shakespeareans. But reasons are nothing. The idea simply fascinates me, and I mean to carry it out."

The stunned joy, the awed radiance of Fanny's face, was indescribable. "Erneshaw—Eunice!" she breathed fearfully, as if afraid to link the names together, lest all things might vanish away.

"Exactly," said Erneshaw quickly; "and I expect Fanny"—this with his happiest audacity—"to stand my friend."

There were tears of supreme gratitude in Fanny's eyes.

"Rob, do you love her?" asked Mrs. Brand softly. But wit, the warder, was on guard again.

"'But that I love the gentle Desdemona, I would not my unhoused, free condition'[17]—No woman ought ever to look a proposal in the mouth, not even the one to whom it's made." He eyed his friend loftily.

"And what does Eunice say?" persisted Mrs. Brand, smiling.

Erneshaw's face underwent a variety of expressions. "Why, I haven't asked her yet," he admitted presently. Fanny uttered an exclamation of fright.

"I haven't had the chance," he protested quickly.

"And suppose she won't have you?" said Mrs. Brand gravely. Fanny uttered a cry of dismay.

"Won't have me? The dickens! I never thought of that!" exclaimed Erneshaw. Then, as the suggestion took full effect: "Why, it's impossible—after all my pains, after fairly sweating my brains out! If Eunice Penforth could be so monstrous as to fly in the face of Providence, of the eternal fitness of things, and not to have me—why, she sha'n't have me, that's all!"

Mrs. Brand laughed openly. "You are all alike. A man may go down on his knees at the moment of proposal, but makes amends for it all the rest of his life by thinking he has done a kind and condescending thing. You've simply worded and witted yourself into love with her, Rob Erneshaw."

"It's not for mortals to know the ways of Eros," returned he with spirit. "Think what honor he will win for himself from a bachelor-logged creature like me. Two young things, by the pout of a lip or the length of an eyelash, he may easily net. But I'm a trophy worth showing. I expect my friends to stand by me. They'll be here presently."

"Who?"

"Mrs. Dillwyn and Miss Eunice. I suspected why Mrs. Penforth had done me the honor to send for me, so I straightway dispatched a note to Mrs. Dillwyn, asking her to bring Miss Eunice here, that I had something to say on my own account, as well as on behalf of the family. You must both back me up."

"Rob, you never in your life did things like other people," said Mrs. Brand.

"Circumstances alter cases," said Erneshaw. "Lamplight and the drawing-room will do quite as well as moonlight and a bower: it's the immortal youth of the heart that counts. At all events, I shall prove my sincerity-Here they come." And, indeed, as the door opened, Mrs. Dillwyn and Eunice entered.

After greeting Mrs. Dillwyn, Fanny folded Eunice in her arms. "Oh, my poor Eunice, if I had only understood how you felt at first, and had taken matters then into my own hands!" she murmured. Eunice smiled at her affectionately. "Chester is taking steps to divide the property, and Mr. Curlett is making out the necessary papers," continued Mrs. Penforth hurriedly. "Everything is to be arranged justly, as you and our friends would wish; half the property, including the house in Gloucester with its belongings, for there you were born," concluded Fanny firmly, with eyes fixed on Erneshaw.

"Thank you, Fanny," said Eunice simply. "I had an idea, when Judge Erneshaw asked me to come, that perhaps Chester would see the matter in this light."

"It was more for myself, though, I asked you to come," said Erneshaw softly. "I want to set myself right." He paused a moment, and, as Eunice fully faced him in a way she had, he continued, "Could you, would you, think of marrying me, Miss Eunice?" Then in the ear-thrilling silence that followed, he added: "I leave to your own heart and imagination how much the plain and open question carries."

For the moment, in her surprise and sweet confusion, Eunice's youth flowed back, and touched her cheek with rose, her eyes with fire, her brow with light. After all, thought Erneshaw, the spirit is immortal, and the real condition of immortality is youth.

"Do you—don't you—ask me from—pity?" whispered Eunice, almost inaudibly.

"Lord knows! Probably from every motive, simple and mixed, that has actuated man from the Garden of Eden till now—all focusing in me upon the one thought and hope," said Erneshaw charmingly. "I never yet belittled life, nor did other than thank God for the ineffable gift of it: it is because I know you, too, love life that I want you to share mine—that is, if, for this supreme feeling there are ever any such foolish things as reasons."

Very winning were his look, his smile, the way he held out his hand—Eunice could not but put hers into it. He drew it up into his arm, then turned his head over his shoulder, and said triumphantly to Mrs. Brand, "And you wanted to scare my life out of me beforehand! I knew she would."

"Oh, Eunice"—Fanny's rapture had no adequate expression, but she shook hands impartially, and freely used her handkerchief.

"Don't take the property unless you particularly wish it," said Erneshaw lightly. "I have much more than enough for two."

"Oh, indeed she must—more than ever now," cried Fanny quickly.

Mrs. Dillwyn, whose amplitude, and hurried breathings, and utter amazement, had till now prevented speech, exclaimed, "Why, it's ideal! Oh, Judge Erneshaw, I'm glad I live in the same world with you, for you do achieve delightful things."

"Rob," said Mrs. Brand softly, "there surely was one strategist we didn't count upon."

"Sh! Who?" asked Erneshaw, with interest.

"Your friend Eros," returned Mrs. Brand.

"Well, perhaps," admitted Erneshaw, with eyes resting happily on Eunice.

Marian V. Dorsey (1859-1947)

Marian V. Dorsey was a founding member of the Woman's Literary Club of Baltimore and sister of Club co-founder Hester Crawford Dorsey Richardson. She was born Mary Virginia Dorsey on the Maryland's Eastern shore in Dorchester County, the subject of much of her writing, but spent a significant portion of her life in Baltimore, where the Dorsey family had originally become established through trade. The Scarborough family depicted in "Telling the Time at 'Controversie'" is based on the Dorsey family history.

Dorsey published dozens of articles in newspapers and magazines, many dealing with "feminine subjects" including home decoration, cooking, household management, and etiquette. Her work appeared in national magazines including *Harper's Bazaar* and *Good Housekeeping* as well as in syndication and was also commissioned by publications including the *Philadelphia Press* and the *New York Herald*. She also wrote for publications closer to home, including the *Patriotic Marylander* and the *Baltimore American*. Several pieces in the *Baltimore Sun* appeared under the pseudonym Constance Chisholm.

Dorsey was a valued member of local historical societies and organizations including the Daughters of the American Revolution, the Maryland Folklore Society, the Edgar Allan Poe Association (founded by Club president Letitia Wrenshall), and the Edgar Allan Poe Society of Baltimore, which appointed her in 1927 to be one of a three-member committee to curate the first public exhibition of Poe memorabilia. Her research on historical subjects won the somewhat grudging respect of members of the Maryland Historical Society and other historical associations.

Dorsey was a lifelong member of the Club but shared her work on only rare occasions. When she did, she presented her historical research rather than sharing her columns on cooking, home decoration, or antiques. The pieces included here indicate that Dorsey may have sought to publish her writings only when a downturn in the family fortunes in the early years of the twentieth century, when Dorsey was in her forties, necessitated that she make a living with her pen.

Dorsey never married and was buried, along with her sister Hester, in the family plot on Church Creek in her beloved Dorchester County. —J. L. Cole

Telling the Time at "Controversie" (1908)

Perhaps there was never such an easy-going household as that inheriting the old home down in Dorset known from early colonial times by the quaintly charming name of "Ye Ende of Controversie."

Its abandonment to the feeling of don't-care is proof of that inevitable law of reaction which nature imposes as the safeguard of mental and physical equilibrium; for these "Controversie" people, though heirs of the land held in their name since 1662, were not, in this generation, born and brought up on the family acres but in the great city across the Chesapeake,[1] where, instead of watching the wheat and corn grow amid its natural environment, the breadwinning members spent the turbulent hours of day with feverish eyes upon the grain ticker which announced, not the helpful showers that presaged a good harvest, but the storms of wreck and ruin that carried under a daily contingent of those who succumbed to its stress and strain.

Needless to say, then, that when fate finally cut the Scarboroughs off from all connection with that maddening little fiend that registers the rise and fall of fortune on the Corn Exchange, they thanked Heaven for the love of the land born in

their bones, though till now latent in their own blood, and got them to their paternal homestead—so heartsick of the very sound of "puts and calls" and "how did Chicago close?" that the man with the hoe seemed a being thrice blessed of the gods.

But—as the murderer takes with him some fatal evidence of the tragedy—they carried the office clock to "Controversie." It was a severe, hexagonal disk, without embellishments of any kind. Just such a relentless looking chronometer as one might suppose had spent its life in harrowing up the souls of men who dreaded the too quick-coming hour of doom.

Yet, strange to say, this uncompromising timepiece, that had never relaxed in all its years in the grain brokers' office, was not long in proving a country convert and as keenly sensitive to environments as its owners; for, as soon as installed upon the dining-room wall, over the high mantel in the corner, it yielded to the enervating effect of old Dorset's drowsy atmosphere; becoming such a "Weary Willie" that it was despaired of as a ticker for even slow-going "Controversie."

It was an eight-day clock[2] that ran two days and a quarter, stopping anywhere along the line of march that seemed good to it.

No amount of tinkering, oiling and winding would induce it to keep the pace of its youth among the breathless brokers.

So erratic was its announcement of breakfast time that the matutinal meal came to be served so near the hour for luncheon that neighboring farmers and laborers, who came on business, were unspeakably scandalized at the "Controversie" laziness, and it soon came to pass that nobody approached the premises till mid-afternoon for any purpose whatsoever.

Finally, in its complete surrender to the delights of the rest cure,[3] it took a late morning nap that sunk it to the depths of coma, when it failed to arouse "Controversie" at any hour.

All the watches were run down and hidden away in bureau drawers, for who would take the trouble to wind watches and wear them where one felt that "time was made for slaves?"

Nay, there was nothing to set the clock by but one's ingenuity, and that, as is ever the case, was the active principle in the brain of the Little Woman.

One morning conscience, or the persistent lowing of a bereaved cow, made slumber impossible and the Little Woman went down stairs to seek her coffee and corn cakes.

Just as she entered the dining room the clock stopped at ten and happening to look out the window she saw Jack, their beloved collie, coming down the lane from a tramp abroad when he was supposed to have been guarding the premises from nocturnal foes.

All that day they were timeless except for shrewd guesses at the lengthening and shortening shadows on the lawn.

Next day, the bereaved cow-mother still lamenting her transported offspring in no modified tones, the Little Woman again aroused herself betimes and when she pulled up the dining room curtain Mr. Jack ran up the lane again.

Putting her scientific knowledge to instant practical purpose, as is ever the way with the Little Woman, she argued to herself: "Now if it was just ten o'clock yester-day morning when Jack came up the lane surely it is just ten now, judging by the fixed and regular habits of animals. In the name of Darwin, I will set the clock with a feeling of certitude,"

And she did.

Presently a machine agent stopped at the door, who was found to have the "latest New York time" among his other up-to-date offerings; and it agreed exactly with Jack's announcement—also with feminine intuition.

"Weary Willie" ran on for two days longer, when he came to a standstill again at three, while the Little Woman was dusting his face off and distractedly casting about in her mind for some other instance of animal precocity that might indicate the point of the meridian, it being quite too late in the day for Jack's homecoming to announce the hour.

Instantly a hen began to cackle under the house and the Little Woman greeted the sound with a joyous laugh—for did she not remember that yesterday at three "Singin' Polly" had run out from under there shrilly proclaiming her contribution to the riches of the world?

Ergo, it was three now, and no mistake.

So the long and short hands were whisked around and "Weary Willie" started off for another two days and an uncertain fraction.

"Go to, now," laughed the Little Woman to a mocking, incredulous member of the broker brood as she jumped down off the old Hepplewhite chair.

"Don't every Dorset oysterman know that the kingfisher descends upon the creeks here on the seventeenth of March as unerringly as St. Patrick's parade upon the city streets?

"And if birds migrate the very same day and hour, year after year, why shouldn't hens lay at the same time every day? They ought to, therefore they must."

This logic being irrefutable, even the skeptical cynic had no resource with which to combat it and revengefully determined that he would put the author of it to shame by going up to the village post office, getting the time there and proving that she had "overloaded on futures" by forty minutes.

When he came back he looked as sheepish as one of his newly sheared Southdowns. "Little Woman," he said humbly, "you hit it on the dot. If you'd take a flyer like the Singin' Polly on 'change, you'd make a fortune on 'shorts' and 'spots. You'd know how long to hold on and just the right minute to let go. I wouldn't buy a new clock for the world. Jack and Singin' Polly are good enough time keepers for me, and dear old "Weary Willie" has all the charms of the uncertain and the unexpected."

Like the rest of us, he is taking his innings now and is only temporarily overcome by the memories of other days when he hadn't the time to faint at the shock he got.

But now we need not even trouble ourselves to watch for the homecoming dog, the laying hen or the crowing rooster; for as I came along the woods road I had the good fortune to fall in with old Uncle Mose Wanky, an oracle high above even these infallible guides to Apollo's course around the heavens, and he says:

"Ef yo' wants t' be dead sartain o' de time t' set yo' clock by, wait tell yo' kin step in de middle o' yo' shadder—kin step right plum on de shadder o' yo' waist-ban'—an' den its high noon er dis sinner-man don' know catfish pie fo'm sweet pertaters an' possum."

Raising Lavender (1910)

When unfortunate investments dispossessed us of our city property and our health at "one fell swoop," then it was that the love of the land born in our bones, though until now latent in this generation, clamored to express itself in reinstating activities, and it is needless to say that we thanked Heaven that the homestead was still ours, in an Eastern shore county of Maryland.

The time had now come when life demanded something more of us than the mere summer enjoyment of our ancestral acres. It demanded that we wrest our living from the corn and wheat fields: but as a pin-money project the idea occurred to me of raising lavender, for sale in the large cities where there is always a contingent of the elect who appreciate the finer things and are willing to pay a fair price for them.

Accordingly, after we were well settled in the old home, I set about carrying out my plan.

In the spring—it may be done from the first of March to the middle of May—I filled a box, twenty-five inches square and ten inches high, with good rich garden earth, adding no fertilizer of any kind, and placed it in a sunny window of an upstairs room that had no fire in it.

In this earth I placed my finger and ran it from end to end of the box, making long shallow drills, into which the seed were shaken rather thickly, and then lightly covered by taking a handful of earth at a time and evenly sifting it between the fingers until the seed were no longer visible: after which I sprinkled them and left them to germinate.

When the top moisture had dried off, the sprinkling was renewed every few days, never allowing the earth to get dry and hard. In three weeks the seed came up, and three weeks later—six weeks from sowing—the plants, having four leaves, were ready for transplanting to the garden, where a bed from three to four feet square had been spaded-up and pulverized ready for them.

I was warned against putting stable fertilizer in this transplanting bed, as being too heating, and none was put in.

The rows were made eight inches apart, and the plants set five inches from one another in the row. This is enough space to allow for the first season, as they grow very slowly. The second spring, a neighbor sent me eleven cuttings from a large bush of true English lavender, and of these I rooted seven successfully. It was then that I learned the difference between the *vera* and the *spica*,[4] as to both bloom and length of life.

When I sent to a horticulturist for lavender seed, those sent me were *Lavandula spica*—having longer stems and shorter life than the *Lavandula vera*, or true English lavender, which, if once successfully started, persists for many years if properly transplanted every two years, dividing the roots and setting them deep in the earth each time.

After the young growth has put out on the true English lavender-bushes—

well-started ones—you may break off the tender shoots, and root them, just as you do geranium cuttings, in wet sand, and then plant them. These will produce fine bushes, in bearing, by the third year.

Also, that second spring, I had four long rows ploughed and raked, in the garden, putting them in the best condition for setting out the year-old seedlings, which were then about three inches high.

Three feet were allowed between the plants, and the rows were also three feet apart, so that a horse and small cultivator could pass both ways.

In a neighboring garden there were very large lavender-bushes that had been growing there over ten years, but the last of my fine ones, raised from cuttings, became extinct after five summers of blooming, do what I could to save them: and even the *Lavandula spica*, which is better adapted to our soil, has rarely survived the fifth year; so I found that I must sow seed every season in order to keep up a supply.

The seedsman advised sowing the seed in the fall, in cool, moist earth, and transplanting in the spring—a method which, after repeated trials, I abandoned altogether, as they did not come up well for me when sown in the autumn, though I have had them come up satisfactorily and make fine, sturdy plants when sown out in the open ground in the spring.

I kept up the box method in addition, however, in order to be sure of coaxing up plants and saving them from possible outside accidents. Both those germinated indoors and outdoors must be planted deeply: that is, the long, fibrous root must have a deep hole dug to receive it and earth pressed around the plant, clear up to the leaves.

Some of the beautiful gardens of England have division hedges of lavender, and one cannot imagine a more delightful place to ramble—for a lavender-bush will smell of lavender as long as there is a leaf or stick of it alive.

I myself keep even the dry stems from which the blossoms have been scattered, to place a handful at a time on the open fire in the great old fireplace of our living-room, where its curling smoke wafts forth a faint aromatic reminder of its summer fragrance.

As lavender was only to be a by-product of farming, I aimed to restrict my bushes to a number that I could personally care for, assisted only occasionally by a boy who ploughed the rows in the spring. My aim being to have a hundred bushes, I planted out over a hundred and fifty plants so as to allow for losses: having been told—and it is true—that lavender, like so many other desirable things, is not too easily obtained.

One who had been the mistress of a beautiful old garden for fifty years advised planting it on high, sunny, well-drained ground, as it will surely die out quickly if moisture settles around the roots.

The third year, when the lavender came into its first blooming, I had a hundred and twenty-five bushes, including the seven splendid bushes of the English lavender I had rooted.

Every other year, in the spring, about the last week of March or soon after, I changed the position of the bushes in the rows, planting them two feet from the spot they were growing in, which still kept them in rows.

The sprigs were allowed to remain on the bushes until they had flowered clear out to the ends, but not to stay till they had dried up on the stems—a mistake some people make.

When in full bloom they were cut with large shears and laid or spread on open newspapers, to save all the shed blooms. It was then dried on old sheets.

The sprigs were cut near the bottom of the bushes, making them about twenty-five inches long, and all the bloom ends placed in one direction so as to save trouble when arranging the bunches. Sometimes, when the bulk was quite large, it was laid on a sheet in the sun—out-of-doors—with papers spread over the blossom ends to prevent drying them too much before the stems cured. A couple of hours in the summer sun is ample time.

When entirely dry I made up my bunches for shipment. The bunches were five or six inches round—a fairly good handful—held together by winding a yard of very narrow lavender ribbon around them and tying the ends in a bow. To this ribbon, before rolling the bunch of lavender in half a sheet of white tissue-paper. I attached a little tag on which I wrote: "Light a sprig of lavender at the blossom end, invert, extinguish, and allow to smoulder. Will fill the sick-room—or any other—with the elusive sweetness of an old garden. An English use of it."

As every one knew the ordinary use of lavender—putting it with bed linen—I wished to disseminate this bit of aestheticism imparted by an English friend.

The ends of the tissue-paper wrappings were folded down and pinned to keep in the fragrance and the loose blossoms: for the shed blooms made delightful sachets when sewed up in little squares of organdie and bring dreams of "Araby the Blest,"[5] if slipped under one's pillow.

Louisa Courtland Osburne Haughton (1866-1951)

Louisa C. O. Haughton left her mark all over Baltimore social life. Born in Cheshire, England, she moved to the city as a girl when her father, a shipping clerk, crossed the Atlantic to try his fortune in this bustling American port. The elder Haughton's business acumen seems to have rubbed off on his daughters. Louisa and her sister, Maud, ran a successful dressmaking establishment, Haughton & Haughton, at the turn of the twentieth century.[1] Haughton is best remembered, however, for her involvement in various organizations in and around Baltimore.

A founding member and final president of the Woman's Literary Club of Baltimore, she also belonged to the National Geographic Society and Maryland Academy of Sciences. She maintained a good relationship with all the Club's members, particularly Lizette Woodworth Reese. Shortly after Reese's death, she co-founded the Lizette Woodworth Reese Memorial Association, which collected scores of materials pertaining to Reese's life and work. This collection would eventually be donated to the Enoch Pratt Free Library in Baltimore.[2]

In addition to her work for these organizations, Haughton published short fiction in leading magazines. Her short story, "The Ever-Ready Edgar," originally published in the *Ladies' Home Journal*, is quintessential Haughton. While ostensibly focused on a womanizing young man, the triumph of the story is not his, but the women who see through his wiles.

Haughton also penned and copyrighted several plays. One of them, "The Decision," published for the first time in this volume, also typifies Haughton's concern with female desire. With only one act and one major character, the play lays bare the mind of one woman and her romantic yearnings. By placing the drama's narrative within a domestic context, Haughton participates in the sentimental tradition, a tradition that uses the home as a microcosm of the external social world. It may be for this reason that the drama contains several passing references to its setting in Baltimore's Mt. Vernon neighborhood. As an exemplar of the sentimental tradition, Haughton's balanced depiction of external and internal spaces. The balance of external and internal spaces in her works makes them multifaceted representation of life on the home front. —H. Flynn

The Ever-Ready Edgar (1906)

Edgar Morris was born to trouble as the sparks fly upward, for he was one of those men who could fall in love at sight and out again while you wait. He had three strings to his bow when he met his Waterloo,[3] and it was the miscalculated attempt to add a fourth that became his everlasting confusion.

He had met the first at a graduation ball at the Naval Academy, and, being a bit bored by finding himself for once at a discount, he exerted his powers of fascination to an immoderate extent to capture the most charming young person present. The fascinating Miss Elsie Martin was in something of a pet because her particular midshipman had dared to dance twice with her most intimate friend, and in consequence the young woman had much that was caustic to say in regard to friendship in general, and the inconstancy of the Navy in particular. Edgar having been refused a dance by the friend, was in total sympathy with her.

It was a simple thing to lead his partner to one of the cozy corners, so considerately provided, to sit out a dance, and he had always found it plain sailing when he could get a woman's undivided attention in a properly-shaded light, amid suitable surroundings.

❦

He lounged gracefully beside her, fixing his gaze pensively on the farthest possible point visible. After a few minutes' silence he drew himself up with a sigh, and leaned a bit closer, caressing a ribbon about her gown, and said: "A civilian has not the ghost of a chance in this gaudy Naval splendor. No woman will look at him while there is a brass button in sight."

He was toying with a string of buttons which she wore on her sleeve, in token of all the hearts in the Navy that were beating for her.

"Still," she answered, "a girl can never be sure of any sailor: for me a civilian ev-

ery time. The uniforms are pretty, and a girl must wear some brass buttons or she is not in it at all. But sailors are all exactly alike, and only care how many girls they can get on their dance-cards."

"You are too charming a girl to put up with that sort of thing. *You* have only to choose"—looking unutterable things in her eyes. "Do you know you have the most beautiful eyes I have ever seen? Even here in this dark place they are like stars," untying the string of buttons. "May I keep these as a souvenir of this evening?"

She laughed lightly but did not resist the robbery: "I do not need a souvenir to remember you and this evening."

"All the same I will bring you one tomorrow. May I come to you before I leave for home? I could not go without seeing you again."

When she arose to meet her next partner Edgar remained behind in a contemplative attitude, indicating that all he cared for now was to go home.

He was not the man to neglect such a good lead, so bright and early next morning he appeared, and after suitable preliminaries produced a tiny gold matchbox, engraved with his coat-of-arms and monogram.

"I bring you this rather than something I might buy for you," he said. "It was given me by the Baroness X, and I prize it so much that I want you to have it."

Elsie, duly impressed, promised never to part with it.

"You see," he continued, "my arms on it will serve to remind you of me, and our initials are the same."

They talked for an hour or more, when

he rose to go. The girl looked so pretty and dainty that he stood for a minute or two silently admiring her. She raised her eyes slowly and looked into his. It was too good a chance to pass. In a moment she was in his arms, and he was covering her face with kisses. All the more wonderful and meaning, considering the vast practice he had had.

"Do you really love me? It is too good to be true."

Soon he had to tear himself away to catch his train, and he left her—to write ardent letters to her for months.

༄

The second of the trio he met at an Easter house-party. He picked out Ethel Miller as his partner—a girl with little to say, who listened to him by the hour.

"I should think you could write a fine book," she observed one day.

"I have only to put my own life into it to make it a wonderful thing," he said. "All authors do, I suppose! Listen to this!" reading from Eric Mackay's poem:

> "'And could I enter Heaven, and find therein,
> In all the wide dominions of the air,
> No trace of thee among the natives there.
> I would not bide with them—No! not to win
> A seraph's lyre—but I would sin a sin,
> And free my soul, and seek thee otherwhere!'"[4]

"How glorious I should feel if any one loved me enough to write a poem like that to me," the girl said.

"Maybe he will," answered the accommodating Edgar. "Those lovely eyes would inspire any man to great things. The violets in your gown are scarcely so blue. May I have them as a souvenir of the day?"

She looked pleased and unpinned the flowers.

"I suppose you mean the violets," she said.

"I only wish the eyes went with them," he replied. "Tomorrow I leave. May I see you before I go—I mean alone—to say good-by? I have a little souvenir for you."

That night Edgar sat long and late, cudgeling his brains for a rival poem to the immortal Eric's. At last he got it to his satisfaction, and copied it out in a fancy hand on a set of tiny gold tablets bearing his coat-of-arms on one side and "E. M." on the other. Having accomplished this mighty work he lay down to sleep the sleep of the just.

Next morning it was easy to draw the present object of his affections to a secluded corner in the rose-garden. He brought out the tiny tablets and said:

"I did my best for you, but it is not worthy of those lovely eyes." In an intense, low voice he read:

> "'Pale, passionate, purple flowers,
> With your message to me
> Of possible perfumed hours
> And eyes as blue as the sea.
>
> "'Mute, matchless, marveling eyes,
> Deep as the slumbrous sea;
> With lingering, languorous light
> You have stolen my heart from me.'"

"It is beautiful," she said softly.

"I wrote it on these little tablets, for I want you to keep them to remember our happy meeting," he said. "I prize them so much that I want you to have them. They were given me by a little Polish princess. I met her in Venice. My arms on them will serve to remind you always of the man, and our initials are the same."

She said nothing as he put them in her hand, taking hold of her fingers as he did so.

"Look at me, Ethel!" very tenderly, "will you always think of me, and today in the rose-garden?"

She let her hand rest quietly in his for in his for a moment, and looked across to the distant hills.

"Will you write to me Ethel? Tonight, so I may have it tomorrow? Ethel—do you love me a little?"

A servant appeared to announce the carriage.

※

When the chestnuts were in bloom in the Bois de Boulogne[5] Edgar was speeding along the perfect French roads in his big automobile. There was a delightful supper at "Robinson's," which was served on a platform among the branches of the trees, and there was a certain little gray-eyed American he was longing to see again. He had met her at the studio tea, where some marvelous effects in light and shade had her name to them. His thoughts were centred on "*Le vrai arbre*,"[6] and he hoped the moon would do her duty.

It all turned out as he had arranged: Eva Muse, the little artist, was there and

sat next him—laughing as the supper was drawn up in baskets to the top of the tree. The moon rose large and red, and they paused in their talk to listen to a song rising from the platform below: an exquisite tenor singing English words:

"If I love thee today it may be to
	sever!
If I love thee tomorrow 'twill per-
	chance be forever;
Shall I love thee forever, or love thee
	to sever?
Ah, love, if I'm wise, I had best love
	thee never."

Eva Muse leaned her head on her arms and gazed over the rail to the moonlit valley below.

"It is good to hear an American song again," she said. "I am longing to go home. I am thinking of the moonlight on the Chesapeake, and the purple mist over the salt marshes, and the tangled underbrush. Everything is so orderly here: everything has its hair combed and brushed, and is heavily perfumed—even the trees," and she drew a long breath of the chestnut blossoms.

A wedding party passed below, blowing through paper pigs, and impossible rams' horns, the bride and bridegroom riding in state in a hearselike carriage. Eva looked at them through the tree. "They don't even know how to love each other here!" she said.

"I thought they prided themselves on their artistic conception of that," Edgar replied.

The rest of their party clattered down to buy some of the horns as souvenirs.

"Not as I understand it," she answered slowly.

"Do you understand it?" he said softly, leaning very near (he felt he could give her some valuable points). To his surprise she burst into tears.

Edgar, in common with most men, could not bear to see a woman in tears. He smoothed her hair tenderly, and put his arms around her. She yielded to his caress and sobbed: "America is so far away, and I must stay here to finish the work I came to do."

He whispered soothingly of her talent and a great future for her. Then he spoke in glowing terms of the wonderful color-effects at a certain seaside village in the States. He told of the blue shadows in the black-green pines, with the red sunset behind them, and the violet mist rising from the salt marshes to meet the golden light overhead. These things he said she must paint when she went home.

The party below called for them to come down.

He held her closer in his arms in the bright moonlight and looked into her eyes. "Do you know you have the most beautiful eyes I have ever seen!" he said softly. "Even the tears cannot spoil them; sometimes they are gray and sometimes blue as the heavens. Eva, can you love me a little bit?"

Some one called from below: "If you don't come down we will come up." So they parted with a sigh and joined their companions.

In the automobile they soon reached Paris. Edgar stood with her at her door for a few minutes.

"It is too late for you to come in," she said.

He took a tiny fan from her and clasped her fingers.

"I am going to keep this forever as a souvenir of the happiest day of my life. Will you use this and think always of me and Bohemian Paris?"—giving her a gold cardcase. "The arms on it will serve to remind you of the man, and our initials are the same. They are so intertwined as to make you remember that I have held you in my arms. I give it to you rather than something I could buy, because I prize it so highly. It was given me by a charming little French Marquise. Good-night!"—very softly—"Beloved!"

In a few hours he was on his way to England.

☙

When October closed, Edgar sailed for America on the *Baltic*. He settled himself in his cabin and appeared only in time for dinner when they were well down the channel. At his right was seated a very handsome girl, and he felt sure of a pleasant voyage.

Of course he was not at a loss to open conversation, and when they were about three days out they knew every cozy place on the ship. When they were off Nantucket Light they felt sorry it was nearly over.

"I suppose we shall meet often this winter," he said, "as we have so many friends in common."

"I hope so," she answered. "Oh, you must come to my house-party at Christmas. I am going to have my school-friends. We have not met for three years."

Edgar, of course, promised to come.

They passed close to the lightship in the dusk of the afterglow, and as they stood a song was borne toward them on the evening breeze:

> "Beloved, I've waited for thee,
> Through the years and the loves as
> they passed."

The girl turned toward the sound.

> "For I knew that I'd see thee some day
> And meet thee and love thee at last."

Edgar stirred uneasily and looked out to sea, where the moon was making a silver pathway over the softly stirring waters. The girl leaned over the rail and sighed softly as the exquisite voice continued:

> "Ah, dear, if we'd wasted our lives
> In loving each love as it came,
> Could our hearts beat as madly as now,
> Would our happiness be just the same?"

Edgar changed his position slightly, so as to gain a better view of her face.

> "Yes, I'm glad I have waited and
> watched
> Through life's midsummer madness
> for thee,
> For I know I have found thee at last,
> And that thou hast been waiting for
> me."

She looked fixedly out to sea. He looked at her with something intangible in his eyes.

> "I am glad I have waited for thee
> Through the years and the loves as
> they passed,"

he half whispered, leaning a little closer to her.

"I hate the idea of parting with all this beauty for the bustle of the city," she said irrelevantly.

"Think of the delightful time we will have at the house-party," he said softly.

"Oh, one must not borrow happiness any more than trouble," she answered, twisting a ribbon which the breeze swiftly straightened out.

"The wind won't allow us to think about it," he said, drawing the ribbon through his fingers thoughtfully.

Suddenly Edgar threw the ribbon from him and said:

"We have built many air castles?"

"Yes," she answered, "on the quicksands of an ocean voyage."

> "'Ah, love, if we'd wasted our lives
> In loving each love as it came—'"

he hummed. "Do you remember that eight days ago we were strangers?"

"And we part tomorrow the best of friends," she answered.

"And nothing more, Eleanor?" he asked eagerly.

"Are we not the best of friends?" ignoring his use of her name, and gazing out at the moonlit water.

"I suppose we are," he muttered; "still, I can never forget these happy days. After all, what is happiness?"

"Who can say?" she answered, turning

from the rail.

"Is this good-by?" he said softly, putting his hand on her arm to detain her.

She instantly withdrew, and said in a surprised tone:

"Shall I not see you tomorrow?

"Oh, yes, when we are leaving the ship with all the rest, but that will be too poor a good-by after these happy, happy days," leaning very close as she moved father from him. "Eleanor, look at me!" (He was playing the card that usually won.) "Look at me with those glorious brown eyes— the most beautiful eyes I have ever seen." She looked steadily out to sea. "Don't you know that I love you? Can't you see I am mad about you? Eleanor—"

A woman passed them, leaving the fragrance of violets behind; as she turned to her companion, one of the officers of the ship, the moonlight caught his brass buttons, and they flashed for a moment.

"Come along!" Edgar said roughly, "this is no place for a serious talk."

"Good-night," she answered, "we have an early day tomorrow!" And for the first time in his career Edgar lost a trick.

The next day as they shook hands on the pier he pressed a tiny gold pencil into her hand as he said:

"A souvenir to remind you of the voyage. I give it to you rather than something I might buy. It was given me by an Italian countess. My arms on it will remind you of me, and our initials are the same. Write to me with it—soon—Beloved—"

Ah, the fervent letters he wrote to her for weeks! But she, being a woman of penetration, and having met other men, answered them temperately.

The sun rose on the battlefield of the Christmas house-party as it rose on the other Waterloo, and many maneuvers were developing, all unknown to this Napoleon of love. He really wanted Eleanor Morse, for he was, after all, a true sportsman, and this was the only game in his long career that had not fallen at the first shot. If a man cannot be sure where he stands with a woman after the intimacy of an ocean voyage and two months of impassioned letters, he has met with rare game indeed. Eleanor had invited the girls to come a day before the men, because there was much to be exchanged in the way of experiences, and the men would sorely interfere with these confidences.

By way of convenience in the exchange of these secrets the largest room in the house had been selected, and four narrow beds set up in a row. "Exactly like the dormitory!" they all exclaimed.

They all talked loudly and at once, for at least an hour, around a tea-table before a big log fire in the library. The conversation, put into orderly and consecutive sentences, resolved itself into this:

One had met a perfectly fascinating man at the Naval Academy Graduation Ball. He was really the handsomest man on earth, etc. He gave her a souvenir that she was crazy about and would exhibit to her friends on their return to their room.

The second had met a wonderful poet at an Easter week-end. He had read her Eric Mackay's "Love Letters of a Violinist," and then had written her a poem quite equal to them. This she would read later, when she would also show a little souvenir he had contributed to her memory of him.

The third had met an awfully nice chap in one of the studios in Paris; he was not an artist, but had a real, sympathetic appreciation. Had they exchanged souvenirs? Of course. One always does in these affairs.

The hostess was busy serving tea and cakes to the trio, thirsty with the recital of the doings of three years. For some reason, hardly formulated in her mind, she said nothing of the voyage home, except that it had been enjoyable. She listened closely, however, and found points of similarity that made her think.

It was soon time to dress for dinner, and they all tripped to the "dormitory." A maid had laid out the contents of various dressing-bags, and in a shining row now lay a gold match-box, gold tablets and a gold cardcase, each having the side with the same elaborate coat-of-arms engraved on it turned upward.

Dire confusion naturally followed this discovery, and the hostess had much difficulty in restoring order, that explanations might be made.

As her hand pressed a tiny gold pencil closer into her belt she said: "'He' seems to be one and the same in each case. May I ask what name he had to each?" The identity being proved she feigned surprise. "Edgar Morris!" she exclaimed. "Let me break it to you gently: he will be here tomorrow."

⌘

At dinner the presence of older members of the household precluded any further discussion of the all-absorbing topic, and it was with a sigh of relief that they rose to respond to the suggestion of bed, after the evening spent in the drawing room. They talked long and late over the matter.

Eva remarked pensively, "I suppose Elsie and Ethel have the most beautiful eyes he ever saw."

"Yes," answered Elsie, "and did a countess, or a princess, or a queen give him your gold souvenir? And did he prize the cardcase and the match-box?" (examining them minutely then contemplating her tablets): "'The arms will serve to remind us of the man, and our initials are the same in each case!'"

Eleanor smiled to herself; she remembered that her eyes also were "the most beautiful on earth."

"Nellie, dear, how did you happen to know Edgar?" said Eva.

"Oh, he was one of the men on board the *Baltic* coming home," she replied.

"It is a wonder you did not bring home a souvenir, too," said Ethel.

"Perhaps they gave out before he met me," laughed Eleanor, and her hand instinctively touched the pencil.

It was difficult to decide upon the plan of action, but finally Eleanor was chosen to manage the campaign, as she alone had escaped his wiles. It was agreed that each was to see the Edgar had no chance at a tête-à-tête[7] with any of them except Eleanor, who was to manage the situation as she thought best; she mentally registered an oath to make him see the error of his ways very plainly.

She had long ago learned the value of silence, and was glad again that she still had the pencil concealed. She was even more of a sportsman than Edgar, and this very chase was much to her taste. He had not touched her at any point, so she could meet him with a clear eye and steady pulse. Edgar, on the other hand, was unreasonably dazzled by his opponent.

He came—and she received him as she had all the others, with a calmly cordial greeting, while he looked unutterable things into her eyes.

The others had gone off on the motor-car. Would he walk, or come in to the fire? He decided upon the fire. He had so much to say to her that is always more comfortably said by an open fire in the twilight.

"'Beloved, I've waited for thee,'"

he whistled softly as he gazed at the flames.

She was pondering whether or not she was to prepare him for the ordeal before him. Torn between mercy and justice she glanced at him, and he looked so handsome and well-groomed that mercy lost.

"He can take care of himself," she concluded.

"I thought the house-party would never come," he said tenderly, leaning toward her. "I wish you could see your eyes in the firelight," slowly—"the most beautiful eyes on earth."

She laughed suddenly, having heard something like this before. He drew back offended.

༄

"What is there to laugh about in my remark?" he said stiffly.

"Not your remark," she answered, "so much as my own thoughts," toying with a gold pencil.

"You never wrote me a line with that pencil," he continued, mollified; "all your letters were in ink, and I wanted the think of you as using something I had given you." Leaning nearer he caressed the lace on her sleeve.

She changed her position so as to be beyond his reach. "I have some charming girls here; you must not make love to all of them. Give the other men a chance."

Edgar, for him, was somewhat abashed.

"That was rather a hard one," he said. "Have I ever given you any reason to suppose that I have even looked at any other woman! Eleanor, I love you. You must know that I love you—I have loved you, and you only, from the moment we met, and why, I do not know, for you have always treated me like a dog"—a pause—"perhaps that is why I am mad about you."

"'Ah, love, if we'd wasted our lives
In loving each love as it came,'"

she sang softly.

"'I am glad I have waited for thee,'"

he hummed, looking straight at her.

A confusion of voices arose in the hall, and the three girls came in ahead of the men. At once they struck the scent of a scene. However, they acted as if nothing had occurred.

For a moment Edgar felt the pangs of the man against the wall with a row of musket-muzzles pointed at him. Then with the instinct of self-preservation he rushed forward, shaking hands with them, and saying how delightful was the surprise Miss Morse had unwittingly prepared for him. As a forlorn hope he made his eyes say things to each one which his lips might not utter in the presence of the others. And each, woman-like, listened to her heart's delusion, unheeding the subconscious knowledge that this also was on a par with all the rest.

Miss Morse acted well the part of surprised hostess.

"Now, tell me, Mr. Morris, where did you all meet?—for we have been so scattered."

She held him on the rack of inquiry for some time, and the others, clever enough to follow her lead, kept him in agonizing dread of discovery until it was time to dress for dinner.

∽

Edgar spent the next few days in futile attempts to see each girl alone and come to an understanding. He fully appreciated the gravity of the situation, for he wanted the one woman, and the three indiscretions that confronted him would seriously obstruct his way to this end. He could not be sure of the silence of the three, for there seemed to be a sort of free-masonry among them more felt than hinted, and at the same time there was no suspicion of the truth having leaked out, for each treated him with all the cordiality possible in a crowd.

He was sitting gloomily, beside a big log-fire in the library, on the last day of the party. The others had gone out to skate, and he had pleaded letters to write, for the strain was growing too great for him to enjoy himself.

Tomorrow the house-party would be at an end, and he could not leave without doing something decisive. The short twilight of the winter evening began to be darkness, and the fire was dying down. Some one entered the adjoining music-room, and began to play softly. After a while the music shaped itself into a song.

"'Beloved, I've waited for thee,"

the musician sang softly.

He leaned forward suddenly, for it was Eleanor.

"Heavens, what a voice," he said to himself. "Like everything else about her, perfection."

Then she began Tosti's "Good-By."[8] She sang it wonderfully, and it is not an easy song to sing.

He saw every bit of it in the dying fire as a mirage—the gray sky and the seas with the black swallows silhouetted against them, above the line of white breakers. He lived it all, too, in the few minutes of the song.

"'Good-by forever!'" she sang, and he was wrought up to such a pitch of emotion that he lost the mastery of himself. He must speak to her.

He went in and leaned on the piano, looking at her in the dim light.

She did not notice him, but played on.

"Eleanor," he said—"Eleanor, beloved! Look at me! I am going tomorrow, and is it to be good-by forever? You know I love you; I want you as never in my life have I wanted anything or anybody. I want you for my own—my wife—Eleanor! And whatever has gone before no woman can say I asked her to be my wife."

She was fumbling with something on the music-rack.

"'I am glad I have waited for thee!'"

he sang softly, seating himself on the corner of the piano bench beside her. He tried to take her hand, but with a swift movement she drew it away and switched on the piano lamp. On the music-desk in a row before him were the gold matchbox, a set of gold tablets, a gold cardcase, and slowly she drew from her belt a gold pencil and placed it beside them.

"This is my answer," she said, rising.

The Decision; or, The Vacillations of Amelia (1912)

A Sketch in One Act

Persons Represented:

Amelia Maynard—A handsome woman of thirty years of age.
Anna—Her maid
A Voice

Curtain rises, disclosing Amelia's boudoir—knick-knacks about. Open fire—glass over fire-place L—divan with cushions back L at right angles to fire. Writing table R front, with elaborate furnishings and telephone instrument—chair behind table facing audience. Table R of fire-place, with tall vase. Door center back. Easy chair beside table. Amelia enters dressed in handsome ball gown—carrying evening wrap. Throws evening wrap across easy chair and takes up book from writing table—and seats herself on divan, and nearest fire, and lounges to-

ward it. Opens book and turning pages, stops and reads silently for one minute.

Amelia: (*Aloud*)
"I know not how it is with men;
For women (I am a woman now like you)
There is no good of life but love— but love!
What else looks good, is some shade flung from love;
Love gilds it, gives it worth. Be warned by me,
Never cheat yourself one instant: Love,
Give love, ask only love, and leave the rest!

(*Half closing book and leaning musingly toward fire*)

Love, give love, ask only love and leave the rest!"[9]

(*Sighs and pokes the fire*)

If only one could have some infallible test, some serum to discover if alleged love, be love indeed, or only near-love. It is so near at times that even the expert in love may be deceived, it seems to me. (*Knock at door*) Come in. (*Maid enters with half a dozen letters and notes on a tray. Amelia takes them lazily.*)

Amelia: Thank you.

(*Maid retires—Amelia looks over envelopes and drops one on floor*)

Amelia: A dinner, two teas, Annetta's wedding—(*Throwing them aside*) Ah, Margaret! what has she to say—advice—no doubt. (*Opens letter and reads*)

Washington, December 30th, 19—.

My dear Amelie:

You are the very dearest girl I ever knew, so I feel sure you will not MIND if I give you the least little bit of good advice—(*Turning to audience*)—"*Good* advice; did anyone ever hear of any kind of advice being *given* except good advice, and advice when taken always turns out to be bad." (*Resumes reading*) I saw Frederick Lane just as he was coming out of the War Department about an hour ago, and he said if he could only get leave he would be at Sophie's tomorrow night. Now, I want to implore you—not—(*Exclaims*) Oh, pooh! (*Skimming down the page and turning over—resumes reading*) You know I am only thinking of your happiness, so please don't think me brutal when I say—Fred never did really love you or he would not have given you up to marry Janie Cox, even if he was engaged to her before he met you, and I know perfectly well, and so do you, that you may be the wife of the man everyone says will be the next President if you are only a sensible woman and don't lose your head when you see Frederick Lane. Please don't be angry with me when I tell you I gave him to understand you were engaged to John Strange

as I thought it best to forestall his certain visit to you, for I am sure he will come back to make love to you now he is a widower. You know how much I care for you and I did it only for your good." (*Tears up letter and throws it into fire*)

Amelia: (*leaning on elbows and gazing into fire*) Frederick Lane a widower! (*Poking fire again and leaning closer to it, sighs*) Love, give love—ask only love—and leave the rest.

(*Telephone bell rings*)

(*Amelia does not move*)

(*Telephone bell rings*)

(*Amelia does not move*)

(*Telephone bell rings*)

(*Amelia rises and goes to instrument*)

Amelia: Yes?—This is Mt. Vernon 7781[10]—Yes—This is Amelia, Annetta—Yes, I received your wedding invitation a few minutes ago—yes—no—I have not seen him yet—I had a letter from Margaret in the last mail saying he was expected here this evening—What? One of your ushers? Best man? Oh yes, I remember, he was a great friend of Henry's—What? I am to walk with him? I thought I was to walk with William Thayer! Why on earth should I mind? You—did—WHAT?—*You—told—him—I was half engaged—to Frederick Lane!!! Don't get mad!!* (*Furiously*) I am not mad—*I'm furious*!! Not such a fool!—What do you mean?—You mean William Thayer *only* wants me because my voice will help him make a name for himself? (*Sarcastically*) You flatter me! Fred loved me? Loves me? And will *always* love me? You look ahead with an assurance that would not be wisdom for any woman to assume in regard to a man's affection!!! Someone told you they heard him say so? Now look here, Annetta, a person can HEAR almost anything they choose to invent!!!!

(*Hangs up receiver*)

Amelia: (*Walking back and forth rapidly*) Love, give love, ask only love, and leave the rest. (*With gesture of impatience*) If one could only live in a wound-proof world perhaps the wall's ears might not hear quite so much. (*Discovers letter on floor, picks it up and tearing open, reads—throws letter on floor and sinks back on divan, punching pillows vigorously*) Heaven defend us from our friends; our enemies we can take care of ourselves—*they* sleep sometimes but our *friends* are *always* on the alert for what they call *our good*! (*Picks up letter again and reads*)

Baltimore, December 31st, 19—.

Dearest Mink:

I saw John Strange last night in Washington.[11] He had just come from a cabinet meeting. He would not say one word about the situation except that he is dead against war, as the country is in no state for war—all industrial conditions being so delicately balanced at the present time that even the rumor might be sufficient to destroy returning prosperity. It has, however, leaked out that strong pressure is being brought to bear upon him to declare himself for war, or at least to remain neutral. Even the President himself, they say, cannot afford to disregard his opinions, and war would be a most popular move in certain powerful quarters. He said he would come over for the support to-night if things were settled, but that he would not leave Washington even for an hour with the question unsettled.

He asked for you and I told him you were reported to be engaged to William Thayer, and we were all rejoicing, as with William's music and your voice the world would hear from the combination.

I am awfully afraid of John Strange! O Mink dear, don't be a fool, remember those gray looks on your temples and don't be the worst kind of fool—an old fool. John knows you can help him more than any other woman of his acquaintances and you know his ambition will drive him where he would never allow his heart to lead him;—and William would always be first of all, *your lover*—(*Throws letter on divan and rising picks up a song from writing-table and reads silently*)

Amelia: I wonder who William was thinking of when he wrote these words

(*Reads aloud*)

"Ah, young Love came in merry guise
  To me, one bright Spring day;
And madly did I, gladly did I
  Bid sweet young Love to stay.
But in the bleak grey Winter time
  I saw the young Love die——
I wonder which was happier then,
  That sweet dead Love or I."

(*Pause*)

Amelia: (*Speaks*) Ask *only* love, (*Pause*)
Here are my three best friends spreading the reports broad-cast that I am
going to marry—each—a different
man—because each is absolutely certain that her choice loves me and *only*
me; which man *I* may love or hate does
not seem to matter much to any of the
three, but each is sure that her man
is *best* for my happiness, though each
seems to think I rather care for someone else.

(*Knock at door*) Come in.

(*Maid enters with huge box of roses, hands
it to Amelia and goes out. Amelia puts it
on divan and, cutting the string, opens
box, which contains letter on top of paper
folded around flowers. Amelia, examining writing on envelope, starts, opening
letter slowly, speaks*)

Amelia: From Frederick Lane. (*Reads letter, sits down on divan beside flowers, still
reading letter, turns back to beginning,
reading*)

  "Beloved:

  I saw Margaret yesterday and she
says you are going to marry John
Strange. I do not believe it—you
would have told me first of all if
it were so. I have not written you
before, for I wanted you to be free
till I could be *sure* you were waiting
for *ME*; because when you sent me
away to marry another woman, I
went with the conviction that you
loved me as much as I loved, and
do still love, and will always love
you. Do you remember that you
said something about helping me
to keep my word of honor to the
woman I had pledged myself to
before you crossed my path?—I
said I could look after my honor
myself and you replied that when
a man told a woman he loved her,
he placed his honor in her keeping
for all time and against all circumstance. The thought that my honor
was in your keeping has kept me
pretty straight in the time I have
been waiting for you, and I am
not a bit afraid of John Strange.
Now I have come back free and I
want you; with all my *soul* I want
you. Who is it that says "There is
no good of life but love?" Did you
know Janie left me a little son? He
needs you nearly as much as I do.
I have just succeeded in getting
twenty-four hours leave from 6
p.m. to-day as we are all being
detained here at head-quarters
pending the decision of the Cabinet in the matter of war. I will be
at Sophie's, but we will not have
the chance to talk things over till

very late. Wear one of the white roses I send on your heart, so I may know, the moment I see you.

Always your lover,

Fred."

"P.S.—Before leaving Manila, I was appointed on the Governor's staff and I have tied the roses with my sash because I want you to have it."

Amelia: (*Opens paper and discloses a tremendous bunch of white roses tied with a red sword sash; lifts roses from box. Clasping roses in her arms and inhaling the perfume, speaks very softly*) Do I love you, Fred—Is it love for which I have waited all these years? Or was it circumstances? (*Despairingly*) Oh, how can I tell?—How can I know? (*Rises and goes to table carrying roses. Holding roses in left arm begins to arrange one or two in vase. Knock at door*)

Amelia: Come in!

(*Maid enters with sheet of note paper, torn from back of letter, on tray—hands to Amelia*)

Maid: Mr. Thayer is in the music-room; I told him you was dressing for the party. He said not to come down but that you should listen to the new song he has just wrote. These is the words on the paper.

(*Amelia takes paper in free hand. Maid goes out. Amelia goes toward door and stands in listening attitude, still clasping roses in left arm. Voice below sings. Amelia follows words on paper—voice*

ceases. Amelia looks at paper thoughtfully; inhales perfume of roses—half recites, half reads, from paper)

Amelia:
"Soft leaves, sweet breath, red rose,
Folded with Summer they lie
Warm round thy perfumed heart
Swiftly they fade and die.

Fond eyes, fair brow, dear heart,
Where all my sweet love lie
Trembling I place it there
Last, starving it lonely dies."
(*Kisses roses*)

Amelia: (*Slowly*) Ask only love,—and leave the rest.

(*Looks at paper again*)

Lest starving it lonely dies. (*Pause*)

What is this written below? (*Reads*) "Annetta says you are engaged to Fred. Is it so? I am sending you some red roses. Wear one on your heart to-night if there is still any hope for me. With them is a little wreath they gave me at the Musical Art Concert in Chickering Hall.[12] I worked for it for you. I want you to have it. William."

(*Knock at door*)

Amelia: Come in!

(*Maid enters with huge box of roses. Amelia throws white roses on divan and takes box—places it on end of writing-table*)

Amelia: More roses! (*Opening box*) Red ones!! (*Inhaling perfume*) (*Maid retires*) How delicious. (*Lifts gold laurel wreath from box*) Ah, here is William's wreath. (*Reads inscription on blue ribbon tying wreath*) "To the best one." (*Puts wreath down on table and takes up bunch of roses from box—inhales perfume. Crosses to divan and puts bunch of red roses on divan near white ones and takes up one red one and inhales perfume thoughtfully, examines it carefully, puts red rose back on bunch, takes white one up and goes to glass over fire, holding rose thoughtfully against heart, starts to pin it on, hesitates, returns to divan, putting white rose with the others and takes up bunch of red ones, smells red roses and holds them off admiringly, puts them on divan, separates one from bunch and holds it off, looking at it thoughtfully; sits down on divan, twists rose in fingers for a moment, then drops hand listlessly. Gazes into fire with elbows on knees*)

Amelia: (*Speaks*) Love, give love, ask *only* love—(*Strips leaves from stem of red rose*)

(*Knock at door*)

Amelia: Come in!

(*Maid enters with box of violets. Amelia takes it from her*)

Amelia: Thank you. (*Maid goes out*)

(*Amelia opens box, takes up card, reads*) "Mr. John Strange."

(*Puts down card and takes violets from box*)

(*Telephone bell rings*)

(*Amelia goes to instrument carrying violets; takes off receiver*)

Amelia: Hello,—Washington wants to talk to Miss Maynard? This is Miss Maynard—Hold the line? Yes—Yes, this is Miss Maynard—Oh, how are you John—I thought you would be over for Sophie's support this evening—Could not get away? Too bad! Sent me a special delivery earlier, explaining? It ought to have been here by this time? No, it has not come—You could not get to the *telephone* before, so wrote when you could? Must say good-night and a Happy New Year? Good night—sorry you can't come. (*Hangs up receiver*)

(*Knock at door*)

Amelia: Come in!

(*Enter maid with special delivery book and letter on tray—hands it to Amelia*)

Maid: A special delivery letter, Miss Amelia.

(*Amelia takes letter and book and signs book; returns it to maid, who retires. Amelia looks at letter*)

Amelia: From John Strange. (*Opens letter and reads*) "Only a word to say I cannot leave Washington to-night. We are stopping for half an hour only and I just have time for a cup of coffee before going back to work for perhaps all night. I expected to get to Baltimore to take you to Sophie's, for I wanted to ask you to be my wife. I hoped to have it all settled to-night, so I might begin my happiness with the New Year, if you will have me. I wanted to come and ask you myself, but I see no light ahead in this business and I do not feel that I can leave, even to go to you, till I make them see reason. I am longing, starving, for a sight of you. Wear my violets anyhow and think of me at the support to-night when you stand to greet the New Year, and say to yourself as the clock strikes twelve "I will, John,' for I shall stand say with *all* my soul, 'Amelia, will you be my wife?' Send me a little letter to-night, if only a few words to say you will. John."

(*Amelia takes up violets, smells them, goes over to the divan and lays them down with the other flowers; picks up white roses*)

Amelia: Ask *only* love (*Pause*) One offers me a sword knot and, incidentally, another woman's child, (*lays down white roses*) another, his golden wreath of success—(*Takes up red rose, lays it down*) The third—(*A pause, takes up violets and smells them*) Until the world ceases to exist, men will not understand that it is not what a man *has to give*, but what he *is*, that counts with a woman.

(*Knock at door*)

Amelia: Come in!

(*Enter main with card on tray, hands it to Amelia who takes card and reads*) "Frederick Lane, U.S.A."

Maid: The gentleman says are you ready to go up to Miss Sophie's—and Mr. Thayer left word he would stop for you at nine. (*Amelia stands up and takes white rose; begins to pin it on dress,—hesitates and takes up red rose; stands a minute, considering the two*)

Amelia: Tell Mr. Lane I will be down in a minute. (*Clock strikes nine—Amelia stands apparently counting the strokes*) No, tell him I am *not* ready. (*Throws white rose down. Maid goes toward the door*) Wait a moment, Anna, tell Mr. Thayer when he comes—(*Pulls red rose to pieces*) Tell Mr. Lane—not to wait (*Throwing white rose on the floor—taking up violets and rising, goes to writing table*) I have a letter to write.

(*Maid retires. Amelia sits down at table and kisses violets; taking up pen, begins to write. Curtain.*)

Harriet Lummis Smith (?-1947)

Harriet Lummis Smith was born in Wisconsin and lived in Chicago before relocating to Baltimore. She became a member of the Woman's Literary Club of Baltimore in 1909, bringing with her a long list of previous publications in *McClure's Magazine*, the *Youth's Companion*, the *Independent*, *Lippincott's*, and other mass-market magazines. She published over ninety works, including short fiction,

novels, poems, and essays.

Smith recognized the paucity of literature written specifically for young women and girls, and she made it her mission to write exciting and thought-provoking literature specifically for them. When interviewed by the *Baltimore Sun*, she was asked, "What are girls of today reading?" to which she replied, "Why, everything their parents read and don't read."[1] She wrote for the *Pollyanna* series of girls' novels, as well as her *Friendly Terrace* series. A review in the *Sun* noted that her *Friendly Terrace* books in the Enoch Pratt Free Library were "well-thumbed."[2]

The works included here focus on ways that women shape their role within the household. "Atwater's Aunt" (1909), for example, provides a humorous look at expectations of women in courtship, while "The Footprints" (1911) showcases the complicated power dynamics associated with marriage.

During her time in Baltimore, Smith's writing was cherished not only by members of the Club, but the whole community. One *Baltimore Sun* article wrote of Smith that "in plot, in style, in treatment she shows rare originality and versatility, and Baltimore looks with pride upon the achievements of her adopted daughter."[3]
—J. Flink and T. Brooky

Blind Man's Buff (1909)

They had been talking some minutes over the phone—one of those protracted and intimate conversations in which girls delight and which drive to the point of frenzy the man who wishes to get the line in order to tell his wife that he is to take the eight o'clock train for Chicago.[4]

It was Hildegarde who broke in on her friend's account of Tuesday's german[5] with a little dismayed shriek.

"Goodness! I didn't dream it was so late. I have an engagement in five minutes and I'm not half dressed."

"Who is it? Darrell?" It was not a question for the telephone, but Irene never allowed her discretion to stand in the way of her curiosity.

"Ye-es." The hesitating answer gave Irene the impression that her friend was blushing. Darrell's adoration of Hildegarde was the season's joke. It was, however, a very suitable match. Darrell was preposterously rich and not bad-looking.

"Too bad about Jack Carr, isn't it?"

"I don't know what you mean." Hildegarde's tone was suddenly icy.

"Why, you don't mean that you haven't heard of his accident?"

"Accident! What accident?"

"Bentley Boynton told me about it last evening. I supposed, of course, you knew; you and Jack used to be such friends. Some workmen dropped a bag of lime beside him and it burst and puffed up into his eyes and blinded him. Poor, dear fellow! But he's so plucky that I dare say he'll make a joke of it."

Hildegarde rang off abruptly. Her head went down on her arms. Tremors shook her bowed figure. Hot tears rained from her hidden eyes.

Jack and Hildegarde had been good friends. The worldly wisdom which belonged to their station in life, the tacit acceptance of the theory that every girl owes it to herself to marry money if she can, alone had kept them from being more. There had been times when the glowing eyes of the young man suggested an almost irresistible temptation to set at defiance the traditions of his class, and the flutter of the girl's heart had acknowledged some uncertainty as to her own course under such circumstances.

But if Jack had kept his tongue in leash, even if his eyes had been less tractable, and had gone his way and left the field to Darrell with his millions!

And now, never again would those dear eyes woo her. Never again would she watch from her window that lithe figure swinging down the street as if it walked on air. She saw him groping his way through unending darkness, with only sad memories to keep him company. And then on the desk beside her she saw Darrell's card, which the maid had just laid there.

No one has ever given an explanation of the fact that a woman's tenderness for one man is so likely to result in cruelty to another. But owing to this peculiarity of feminine psychology, Darrell's sole reward for a year's devotion was the hasty note the maid brought down five minutes later:

I cannot see you this afternoon. And please do not come again till you are willing that I should be nothing more than your friend.

HILDEGARDE DEVRIES

"A lady to see me?" Jack Carr, sitting in his darkened room, with a shade over his eyes, betrayed no satisfaction at the prospect of companionship. "What's her name?"

"She didn't say, sir. She said to tell you that a friend would like to see you for a few moments."

"Oh, show her up. I'm not much to look at just at present; but, anyway the room's too dark for her to see." His philosophy stood by him till a swish of skirts on the stairs suggested an idea so preposterous that his heart leaped. He put up his hand as if to ward off a blow. Then a voice said, "Jack!"

"Hildegarde!" He sprang forward, stumbled over a footstool and regained his balance and his self control at the same moment. "I'm not quite used to this sort of blind man's buff," he said in a rather breathless voice. "You must find a chair, please. Awfully good of you to look me up, I'm sure."

Hildegarde was thankful that the room was dark. In the clear daylight her courage would have failed her.

"It wasn't good at all," she quavered in an uncertain voice. "I just had to see you, Jack." Her voice died away, and she regained it only by an effort. "Jack, tell me—was I mistaken in thinking that you used to care for me?"

The pause that followed seemed unendurably long. "No," Jack said at last in a voice unlike his own—"No, that was no mistake, God knows."

She breathed more freely now that the plunge was taken. Except for the dryness of her throat and her burning cheeks she felt almost at ease.

"But I was mistaken about myself, Jack. I thought I could be satisfied with a great deal of money and a good social position and all that, and what I wanted all the time was you. I have money enough for both of us, I shan't give you a chance to remember your—blindness." She hesitated at the word, but took it gallantly, like a thoroughbred. "I'll be eyes to you and sunlight—Oh, Jack. I'll make you happy in spite of everything."

He crossed the room and stood beside her. "Hildegarde!" he cried hoarsely. "You mean that you are ready to refuse Darrell and marry me?"

"Mr. Darrell means well," Hildegarde acknowledged with an air of wishing to give everyone his due. "But you're—Jack."

"You—you said something about my eyesight," stammered Jack. "Did you mean—"

Hildegarde caught his hand. "Oh, dearest, that was what opened my eyes! When I heard that you were blind, I couldn't bear it and then I knew perfectly well that I couldn't live without you."

He swept her to him, and a blissful moment followed. But the mysterious sixth sense, which belongs to love, led Hildegarde to divine disquiet in her lover. She drew away palpitating. "Jack, are you sure that you haven't got over caring for me?"

He was so reassuring on this point that the scared color came back to her cheeks. "You're not worrying because you're not rich?" she rebuked him quietly. "Why, Jack, we can get along beautifully with what I have, even if I don't come in for a share of Uncle Enoch's money!"

"It isn't that altogether, darling. You spoke about my eyes—"

She flung her arms about his neck. "My eyes are yours from now on, dear. I'll never give you a chance to know that you've lost anything."

"You are an unselfish angel," said Jack with conviction. "But the truth is, dearest, that the matter has been a little exaggerated. It's been quite painful, you know, but the doctor thinks that in three weeks I can go back to the office again."

"Oh!" Horror turned Hildegarde rigid in his arms. "And I've proposed to you without any excuse."

Jack did not answer—verbally at least—but without the aid of speech, and in an incredibly short time, Hildegarde was convinced that no excuse was needed.

Atwater's Aunt (1909)

The two friends were sophomores in college when Atwater first showed Minturn one of his aunt's letters. Minturn read it with an appreciation that was tinctured with surprise. He had aunts of his own who sent him occasional checks, and frequent budgets of advice, but their communications did not in the least resemble that of Atwater's aunt. It was a long letter but Minturn was sorry when he reached the signature.

"I say, he remarked, as he folded the letter carefully, and returned it to its envelope, "she hasn't forgotten that she was young once, has she?"

"You bet she hasn't," said the affectionate nephew, heartily, and there the matter rested for the time. But when Atwater sprained his wrist at football practice, Minturn volunteered to write his usual weekly letter to his aunt.

Atwater made such hard work of dictation that Minturn finally dispensed with his assistance, and wrote the letters himself. He received a nice note from Atwater's aunt, thanking him for his kindness, and forthwith he developed a most surprising solicitude regarding Atwater's wrist, hinting darkly at any number of dreadful consequences that were likely to result from using it before it had fully recovered. When at length he could frame no possible excuse for writing Atwater's weekly letter to his aunt, he rallied his courage to make a proposition on his own behalf.

"The friendship of an older woman,"

wrote Minturn to Atwater's aunt, "a woman like yourself, who knows life and the world, whose mind is enriched by the culture of experience, without losing sympathy with youth, is an inestimable boon to a young man like myself." It was his best sophomoric style, which had resulted in his appointment as editor-in-chief of the college paper. It proved equally effective with Atwater's aunt. She graciously agreed to his suggestion that they correspond.

It was rather singular that though their novel acquaintance soon ripened into a sort of intimacy, they did not meet. The vacation Minturn spent at Atwater's home, Atwater's aunt happened to be in Europe, and when the boys graduated she was ill and unable to be present at the commencement exercises. But the correspondence continued without a break. Minturn told Atwater's aunt a number of things he would never have thought of confiding to any one else, and she advised him in his various dilemmas with the calm confidence of one who has lived through youth's turmoil and knows the peace that lies beyond. Minturn always thought of her as a woman whose smile had in it to a certain wistfulness, on whose delicate face, under the gray hair, love and loss had left their unmistakable tracery. It was not necessary to go into tiresome details with Atwater's aunt. She always understood him.

Minturn had been in his uncle's law office nearly two years when something came up on which he felt the need of a women's counsel. Moreover, it was something he could not very well trust to paper. His uncle had said to him on several occasions that it was time he was settling down, and Marguerite Foss had intimated the same thing, not in words, it is true, but by means of sidelong glances and unnecessary blushes.

Marguerite was a pretty girl. Minturn thought it a pity that she was so plump, and had so much color. But he told himself, judicially, he might do worse. He wondered what Atwater's aunt would advise.

The legal quality of mind had not become sufficiently a second nature with Minturn to preclude an occasional impulsive act on his part. When a letter came from Atwater's aunt, saying that she had noted signs of mental perturbation in several of his recent letters, and delicately hinted at her readiness to be of service, Minturn suddenly resolved to answer it in person. He took an early train, and reached his friend's home in the golden quiet of the summer evening.

Atwater was on the porch sitting in a hammock with a girl—a very pretty girl. If the cabman had been alive to his opportunity, he might have given Minturn any change he pleased, for the young man was thinking of the girl in the hammock, and how red and clumsy and countrified Marguerite would look beside her. With an odd pang he wondered if Atwater were engaged. There had been something in the attitude of the two not unlike the affectionate confidence of acknowledged lovers.

Atwater was down the steps before Minturn had time for further reflections. "Couldn't believe my eyes, old man," he roared. "To think of you dropping down on us in this fashion!" Then he pounded Minturn on the back, and then prodded him in the ribs, all of which is the masculine equivalent for cordiality. These courtesies having received attention, he seized Minturn by the arm and dragged him up the steps to the divinity in the hammock.

The girl had risen to her feet, and was looking down with a curious air that confirmed Minturn's suspicions. He was devoured by a sudden unworthy jealousy of Atwater, who, good fellow though he was, did not deserve such lavishness on the part of capricious fortune. He suspected a dimple back of the girl's demureness and wished impatiently that she would look up that he might know the color of the eyes shaded by the curling lashes. There was a long, silent pause which might have seemed awkward to an outsider, though not to Minturn, who was sufficiently occupied.

"O, I say," cried Atwater, who had been looking from one to the other in surprise. "I forgot you'd never been introduced. Why, Minturn, this is my aunt."

The dimple was there, just as Minturn had suspected, but a sudden, uncontrollable flush drowned it.

"There's no need of looking at me with such reproach," cried Atwater's aunt, in fluttering defiance, "just because I haven't wrinkles and gray hair."

"No, she's an all-right aunt." Atwater assured him, "even though she doesn't quite look the part. She's eighteen months younger than I am, aren't you, dear little auntie?"

"But, how—" began Minturn, and then he paused uncertainly. He was trying to reconcile the worldly wisdom that had been his guide so long, with the pretty girlish confusion of her averted face. A sudden sense of relief possessed him as he realized that it would not be necessary to ask of her counsel concerning Marguerite.

When Atwater took him by the arm, Minturn turned to him almost appealingly. "See here," he said. "I want to talk things over a little with your aunt. Just clear out like a good fellow, won't you?"

"Sure," said Atwater, obligingly, and he departed. When he came back after an hour, the pair in the hammock looked at him with gentle reproach and proceeded to ignore him. Atwater went away again, and smoked his cigar on the back steps.

"Old Minturn will make a first-class little uncle," Atwater remarked, philosophically, as he blew rings of smoke up toward the stars. "And, beside, a pretty, marriageable aunt is too much of a responsibility for a young fellow like me."

The Sister of a Genius (1909)

A very fortunate girl did Frederick McNabb's sister Hannah consider herself, and for a self-evident reason. Frederick was a genius. Nearly every week one of his poems appeared in the *Grant County Republican*, and as if to prove that men of genius are above narrow partisanship, the Pikesville *Democrat* was also favored. These contributions were gratuitous; but Frederick had sold several poems elsewhere, and the circulation of the purchasing periodicals had forthwith received a noticeable impetus in Grant County, due perhaps to Frederick's habit of expending the entire sum received for each poem upon copies of the paper containing it for complimentary distribution among friends.

Frederick McNabb was a good-looking

young man, with long hair and a short memory. Hannah had proved conclusively the uselessness of trusting him with an errand to the grocer's. As a rule, one genius is enough for a whole family, and luckily, Hannah was quite an ordinary little person, alert, energetic, and very comfortable to live with. Her mind was aa practical as Frederick's was dreamy. When the roof leaked, it was Frederick who suggested boring a whole in the floor, that the water might run through, and this casual remark almost precipitated an unpleasantness between Hannah and Mrs. Dobbs, the washerwoman. But the comment which roused Hannah's ire was little enough compared to what Mrs. Dobbs said to her family after she went home.

"It may be nothing more than genius that ails him," said Mrs. Dobbs, shaking her head dubiously. "But if that's all, it's an own cousin to feeble-mindedness. That little sister is worth six of him, according to my way of thinking. Why, she watches him like a child to see that he doesn't do himself a mischief! She's so set up over his writing poetry, and yet she had to tell him if he's scorching his coat tails!"

When Frederick poured vinegar into his coffee one morning, in place of cream, Hannah knew that a poem was under way. She liked the poem on spring which had appeared in the *Democrat* much better than the ode to liberty for which the *Home Helper* had paid Frederick three dollars, but she felt for the latter poem a reverence tinctured with awe. A poem for which a flesh-and-blood editor was ready to pay cash could be nothing less than a masterpiece, and her inability to grasp the meaning of some of the

lines prompted Hannah to humility, instead of leading her to question the poet.

After the episode of the vinegar Hannah procured a clean cup, and took upon herself the responsibility of adding the proper proportions of cream and sugar to the coffee. It was rather disappointing to have Frederick push the cup away, decisively, "I can't eat!"

"Don't you feel well, Frederick?"

"For two days," Frederick declared, gloomily, "I have been in the grip of an idea. It gives me no peace. It will not leave me alone. I cannot sleep at night, and by day my food has no flavor."

"I think you ought to eat, Frederick," Hannah said firmly, "whether you feel like it or not. Literary work is so very wearing."

Frederick looked at his sister with a smile of superior melancholy. "Literary work wearing!" he repeated. "What do you know about it?"

Hannah blushed. "Why, I've noticed, Frederick, dear," she replied, "that when you are writing a poem you get so tired that you're not equal to anything." It was all true. He was not even equal to filling the wood-box. Hannah did it herself, and reflected, as she worked, that if Frederick ever found it out he would be angry. Fortunately, there did not seem much likelihood of Frederick making the startling discovery. Apparently he labored under the impression that wood-boxes filled themselves, like springs.

"The thing haunted me all night," said Frederick. "I only slept by fits and starts. I left a light candle on the chair beside the bed, so I could jot down whatever came to me."

"Oh, did you, Frederick! exclaimed Hannah, with a guilty start. Once Frederick had left a candle lighted on the chair by his bed, and then when fast asleep had thrown out his arm and overturned the candle against the window-curtain. Hannah had arrived on the scene to find the curtain in a blaze and some of the bed-clothes shriveling at the edges. And for once forgetting the serious consequences of sudden shocks to sensitive natures, she had awakened Frederick by deluging him with the contents of the water-pitcher. Now she blamed herself for not having been on her guard the evening before. It was not due to her watchfulness, she told herself reproachfully, that Frederick had not set himself on fire. Another night she must be sure not to go to sleep till the lights were out in his room.

Breakfast over, Frederick went up-stairs, while Hannah fell to work. Mrs. Dobbs was in the kitchen, ironing vigorously. By the time Hannah had the breakfast dishes finished Frederick was down-stairs.

"I'm going out," he said, abruptly. "That horrible thumping has got on my nerves. I can't stand it any longer."

"That thumping? Oh, I see!" For a person not sensitive, Hannah showed a surprising ability to comprehend the moods of the more delicately organized. She herself rather enjoyed the rhythmic thud of Mrs. Dobb's flat-iron. But then, she was not a poet, but only the sister of one.

Frederick strode out of the house, leaving the screen door open. Hannah was prepared for this. She followed close at his heels, shooed out two or three blue-bottles which had been awaiting just this opportunity, and closed the door after her brother. Then she went back to look over her accounts for the week. This problem, although it seemed nothing more than simple addition, frequently caused rather deep furrows in Hannah's smooth fore-head before she had finished. The brother and sister were orphans, with little income which only by a dint of strict economy was sufficient for their needs. Mrs. Dobbs glanced at the girlish face, frowning over the question of how to reduce the month's groceries so as to make up for an excess in Frederick's livery bill. And she pursed her mouth in sympathy.

"It's a pity," said Mrs. Dobbs, testing her flat-iron with her forefinger, "that your brother doesn't go to work."

Hannah looked up with a start. "Why, Mrs. Dobbs, he *does* work—very hard!"

"I want to know!" In her surprise, Mrs. Dobbs came near burning one of the best table napkins. "And no one ever sees him doing a lick."

"He works," said Hannah, with dignity, "very hard at his poetry,"

She returned to her accounts, and Mrs. Dobbs said, "Oh!"

At half past twelve dinner was ready. Hannah, her eye on the clock, moved saucepans to the back of the stove and set covered dishes in the oven. At quarter of one she looked anxious; at one o'clock distressed. "Frederick does hate warmed-over things!" she sighed.

Mrs. Dobbs sniffed. "Then why doesn't he come for his dinner?"

"I suppose he's forgotten all about what time it is. He'd never know meal-time if I wasn't around to tell him."

Half past one passed. The clock struck two. Hannah groaned over the spoiled dinner, put on her hat and started out to discover her brother's whereabouts. Mrs. Dobb's flat-iron thumped disapprovingly. "Thank heaven," she said to herself, "that out of my four there's not a one that shows any signs of being a poet. And if I saw it coming on I'd dose it out of him, if calomel could do it!"

Long experience had made Hannah familiar with the haunts where Frederick might reasonably be sought when the frenzy of poetic inspiration was upon him. After searching the most accessible, she turned her steps toward the river. It ran between high banks, with a stretch of rapids halfway between bridges. Frederick loved the stream, and would have gladly celebrated it in his poems had it not been encumbered with the name Jones Rover, given in honor of one of the early settlers.

Hannah reached the high bank and looked up the river. It lay blue and sparkling under the summer sun, without a craft in sight. She looked down the stream. A little white boat was being borne rapidly along by the current. In the stern sat a young man, his hands clasped behind his head, his eyes fixed upon the heavens above him. It did not need a second glance to assure her that this was Frederick.

She hurried along in the direction in which the boat was moving, and her heart began to beat hard, although not altogether because of her haste. The darker line which ran in a zigzag course across the stream, and marked the beginning of the rapids, was not very far in advance of the little boat moving swiftly down the

stream, while the abstracted master sought a fitting rime for "blithe." Hannah remembered how Jamie Richards had been drowned in these very rapids. Her heart came up into her throat, half-stifling her, as she screamed, "Frederick! O Frederick!"

The poet did not move.

"Frederick!" she cried again, and this time her voice had the shrillness of despair.

Her hurrying feet had carried her a little below the oncoming boat. She turned and waved her arms frantically. Frederick sat immovable, his hands clasped behind his head, his eyes upon the sky.

Her next impulse Hannah did not stop to weigh. The most practical people at times act without deliberation. Something must be done to attract Frederick's attention. Delay in this case would be fatal. Accordingly, Hannah poised herself for a breathless second on the edge of the bank, which just here rose almost straight from the water, shut her eyes, and jumped.

There are some things so startling as to penetrate even the atmosphere of abstraction into which a poet withdraws, and the sight of a young woman descending meteor-like from the sky is one of them.

Frederick woke up, —thrilled with the horrified realization that some one among his fellow townsmen was bent on suicide, —and seized his oars. The process of turning the boat's head to the shore was not an easy one. He had drifted into the grip of a determined current that held his little craft with vise-like clutch, Frederick suddenly realized that he was pulling to save two lives, that of a girl who had thrown herself into the river—

and his own.

He set his teeth and bent to his oars. Frederick had been wont to belittle physical exertion. No one knew the meaning of hard work, he had told Hannah, who had not tried his hand at literature.

In the next few moments he had a chance to revise that opinion. Pulling with desperate strength which the love of life puts into flabby muscles, his thoughts circled despairingly about that tragic figure which, falling from mid-air, had broken in upon his dreams. Was the girl drowning while he struggled with the relentless current?

At last the boat was moving. The stream was baffled. But Frederick, pulling, with set teeth, realized how narrow had been his escape. If he had drifted a little farther it would have been impossible for him to extricate himself. The boat would have been dashed against the hidden rocks. He himself — He pulled desperately, driving the boat ahead. For a girl was drowning.

He could hardly believe his eyes when he saw a figure seated on the narrow ledge at the base of the steep bank, —apparently watching for him, —a dripping pathetic little figure, with something curiously gripping his attention beneath the oddity of her appearance. The boat fairly flew as an idea, grotesquely unbelievable, crept into his mind and stuck there, defying dislodgement. It could not be Hannah! And yet, by some extraordinary perversity of circumstance, it could not be anybody else.

When he reached her, panting, scarlet, an agony of apprehension written on his face, Hannah's swift intuition told her of what he was thinking. "I made you look," she said, faintly, and smiled.

"Made me look?" he repeated, stupidly. "I tried to, Frederick. You were drifting down into the rapids. It would have been too late if I had waited, so I jumped."

He stared at her. "You might have been drowned," he said. His voice was very low.

Hannah laughed. "I never thought of such a thing. I can swim a little, you know. It wasn't such hard work getting out, but I hated it when the water went over my head. I guess we'd better go home, Frederick. I'm afraid your dinner is spoiled."

She swayed slightly as he helped her to her feet, and dropped over against him, a dead weight. For the first time in her life Hannah had left her brother to meet an emergency without her assistance.

Frederick did not eat any dinner that day. What with getting Hannah home, and explaining to Mrs. Dobbs that it was only a faint and not a case of drowning, and summoning the doctor, and running to the drug-store, his time was well occupied. And such vestiges of appetite as he might have had vanished after his interview with Mrs. Dobbs, who, acting on the doctor's direction, was beating up some white of egg or Hannah.

"What I can't understand," said Mrs. Dobbs, curtly, "is how it was *her* that came to get in the river. If it had been you, now—" Mrs. Dobbs left her remark unfinished, but the meaning was obvious.

Frederick explained, to the accompaniment of the egg-beater. "It was a very extraordinary thing for her to do," he ended, uncomfortably, for once or twice during his recital Mrs. Dobbs had grunted.

"Extraordinary!" cried Mrs. Dobbs. "Why, she's doing it all the time."

"Jumping into the river?" exclaimed Frederick, protestingly. "Hannah?"

"If she's not jumping into the river, she's doing something else, waiting on you and slaving for you, and skimping her own self, because you don't know the worth of money. It's all of a piece with what she does every day."

Frederick only stared.

"I've done nothing much against poetry," said Mrs. Dobbs, magnanimously, "if folks have brains enough to divide up between that and other things. But if being poets is going to make 'em blind as bats and helpless as babies, and selfish without knowing it, I say that the sooner it's dosed out of 'em the better. I'd like to see one of my four trying to write a poem! Just let him try it!" said Mrs. Dobbs, raising her voice. "That's all!"

The atmosphere of that particular day was not favorable to poetic inspiration. Frederick did more thinking in plain prose during the next twenty-four hours than he had done for many a day. And before Hannah was quite herself again Frederick was at work in the office of Mr. Peal, the real estate man.

In taking this step, Frederick felt that he was resigning the dearest of his ambitions. But in less than three weeks a poem appeared in the Grant County *Republican*, which some people considered the best thing Frederick had ever done.

It was called "Lines to a Sister," and in the scrap-book where Hannah keeps her brother's poems it is the chief treasure.

The Footprints (1911)

She had remained sleepless until late into the night, falling at last into the stupor of exhaustion, so that the dawn came upon her unawares. She started awake to find the room brilliant with sunshine, fresh with the beneficent fragrances of morning. It was inconceivable that the day had come like other days—soft-footed, scintillating—and had found her sleeping.

The second surprise was greater. As she rose and dressed she realized that her mood was apathetic, almost indifferent. After the fever of the past weeks, their hope and dread, their ecstasy and torment, after shame that scorched, and joys so poignant as to be almost pain, and doubt that kept her wide-eyed through long, wearisome nights, decision had brought with it a profound calm. She seemed to have passed beyond the storms of love and suffering and rapture, into a tranquil harbor.

Her husband was reading his paper as she came down-stairs, and he did not raise his eyes at once. That gave her a chance to look at him. The imminence of the crisis had sharpened her senses. She saw him with that clear-sightedness impossible under normal conditions between two closely associated. It is only strangers whom we see as they are. As if this had been the dawn of doomsday, the real man was revealed, and even if she had not gone beyond the turning point, the fatuous egotism of the unconscious face would have convinced her that she had chosen wisely. His armor was proof against any hurt she could give him. It was a relief to feel that in taking the irretrievable step she would leave no wretchedness behind her, nothing but the incredulous protest of injured vanity.

At the rustle of her dress her husband looked up. "Mrs. Elmslie!"

"Yes!" she said, turning. In their twelve years of married life they had never passed beyond that formal address. The joy their child brought with him and the anguish of his going had neither been sufficient to bring the man's lips a term of endearment. He had been glad in his way. He had suffered over the knowledge that there was no longer a son to hand down his name, but neither grief nor gladness had bridged the chasm between these two souls.

The woman remembered as she stood waiting, when the other man had first spoken her name. "Margaret," he had said, his deep voice touching the syllables ever so lightly, as one touches the cheek of a sleeping child. The word had been a caress and a song, both in one. Its music had kept her wakeful many a night. Nothing that he could say again would ever stir the depths like her name upon his lips for the first time.

"Mrs. Elmslie!" The paper rustled crisply as the reader thrust it aside. "I was surprised to learn last evening that you had not called Mrs. Warren."

"No!" she acknowledged, and stood looking down, like a child taken to talk. Her husband frowned.

"Most inconsiderate, amazingly so. The Warrens have been our neighbors for three months. Warren and I are closely associated in business, and it is desirable from every standpoint that our families should be on friendly terms. What excuse have you to offer?"

"None at all." Her voice was wearily indifferent.

A little perplexity showed under the frowning attention with which her husband was regarding her. He found her attitude puzzling. He looked for humility, penitence, timid excuses. As the latter were not forthcoming, he angled for them.

"You can hardly say you have no time for social courtesies. A woman with three servants and no children to require her attention."

"I have time enough," she said, with bloodless lips. For the instant her calm was gone and she hated him, all the more that his cruelty was unconscious. He did not know his taunt would wound her. He had lived with her twelve years, and did not know. The worst was less than his desert.

Mr. Elmslie consulted his watch. "Are we going to have any breakfast?" he asked, in a tone of forced self-control. "This is the third time this week that I have waited from five to fifteen minutes for my meals. If you used your leisure in disciplining your servants, there would not be such frequent occasion for criticizing your household management. In my office punctuality is insisted upon. No employee is allowed to feel—"

The summons to breakfast cut short Mr. Elmslie's eulogy of his business methods. Ensconced behind his paper, he did not notice that his wife ate nothing. She sat back of the coffee urn, gazing about with a closeness of attention that gave the effect of novelty to the most familiar object. This was her last meal at the round table where she had sat a bride, looking timidly at the man she had chosen. The high chair had stood at her right, when the boy had been big enough to come down to the dining-room. A mist that came just short of tears clouded her vision at the thought. She had broken herself of weeping because it annoyed her husband.

It had not taken the boy long to discard a high chair. All her fond clinging had not availed to keep him a baby, and his rapid growth had brought her ecstasy as well as pain. He was every inch a boy—heedless, daring, mischievous, a manly boy who told the truth without fear, even when it meant punishment, a boy with candid eyes and lips that were always smiling. To the mother, disillusioned before his birth, his inexhaustible joyousness was a miracle of divine goodness, for which she daily thanked God.

She came back from her memories with the realization that her husband was rising from the table, that he was coming toward her for the formal, meaningless kiss which was an outward sign of the beautiful perfection of their marital relations. She turned faint at his approach. The impulse to beg him to spare her was so strong that it almost overmastered her prudence. Her lips were icy like those of a dead woman, as his brushed them. He noticed neither that nor her pallor, nor the hands which gripped each other till the finger-tips left purple prints. "Good-by," he said.

"Good-by!" she repeated, mechanically, and wondered at herself that she could feel nothing but relief. It was over, the long lie, the insufferable humiliation,

the weary monotony of dragging days and endless nights. Youth was still hers. Love waited for her. Freedom was to be had for the taking. The door shut upon her husband was the closing of one life. Now she would begin to live again.

Her preparations were already made. There was no sense of flurry, to sound its discordant note. She gave her directions for the day, making out the dinner menu with usual care, cautioning Letty about the roast. The last had been overdone, and Elmslie had sulked.

"I shall not be here, Letty," Mrs. Elmslie said. "I am going into the city by the morning train, and shall not come back for dinner." Her voice was steady but her heart-beats quickened with the realization that she was committed.

The woman's broad, kindly face broke into a smile. "I am glad to hear it, Mrs. Elmslie," she said heartily. "I often say to Ella, that it's a shame for you to live the way you do. Good gracious! You're a young woman yet, and young folks need good times same as babies need milk. You just go to some funny show in the city and enjoy yourself. Don't spend all your time shopping."

"No, Letty. I mean to enjoy myself." Mrs. Elmslie spoke gently, touched by the woman's sympathy. Letty had been with her when they had brought the boy home, his eyes open, his little body dripping. She could see now that wet, zigzag trail along the rug up the stairs. Letty had sat her beside the mother as the doctors had worked over the drowned boy in the room overhead. They had worked doggedly, though hopelessly, because of the mother who waited below. It was she who, at last, had given the word to ease the torturing of the helpless body, from which the spirit had fled hours before, and then she had turned and hidden her face on Letty's broad bosom, and Letty had sobbed over her, calling her her poor lamb and darling.

Mrs. Elmslie suddenly took the work-hardened hand in both her own. "You've been very good to me, Letty. If anything should happen to me I want you to know that I shall never forget."

"Happen to you?" cried Letty, touched and half tearful. "And what should happen? You're little more than a girl. I'm old enough to be your ma. You'll live to scatter posies over my grave, bless your heart," added Letty, with determined cheerfulness. "When you come home from the city to-day you won't feel like such thoughts. You need a little change to chirk you up."

She left her good-by to the boy's room for the last. The other ties had snapped like tow. Her farewells had been the turning of the key that opened her prison door. But the room up-stairs was different. The little white bed stood as when the boy had knelt beside it every night for his evening prayer. She had knelt with him often, as pure in heart as he. It came over her with a sense of awe, that, after to-day, her presence in that still white room would be a sacrilege.

Oh, if the boy were there! She flung the thought defiantly in the face of the Almighty. If the boy had lived, she would have had the strength to meet all temptations, even the dearest. An unlawful love could never have found its way into her heart, when she knelt every night at his bedside and prayed God to keep him pure. There

would have been no sacrifice too great to keep her name untarnished had she her son's honor to guard. But he had died. God had taken him, and left her defenseless.

She looked her last about the silent room—a long, tearless scrutiny. The striking of a clock warned her that it was time to go. As she stepped into the hall the breeze blew the door to, and she wondered dully if perhaps an angel with a flaming sword kept guard on the other side. She could never open it again. Whatever joys life had for her, whatever compensation she might find in a man's devotion for the good she had missed, she would never again have the right to enter the room where her boy had lain dead.

She put on her hat hastily, took her traveling-bag, and turned to go down the stairs. Then she halted and swayed. She tore off her veil, and fell upon her knees, peering with dilated eyes, her shoulders heaving. Her shriek died in her throat, as if a hand had clutched it. White and quivering, she bent nearer the polished oak. Was she going mad? It was that, or else a miracle had been wrought for her deliverance.

The maid coming from the room where she had been dusting caught sight of the crouching form of her mistress. "Mrs. Elmslie—for the love of heaven, Letty, Letty!" She ran forward, but the other woman's uplifted hand checked her.

"See, Ella!" The shaking finger pointed to the floor, and the girl's rosy cheeks paled as her eyes followed its direction. Against the oak, mercilessly distinct in the clear light, was the print of a child's wet foot.

"They come up the stairs, ma'am." Ella was trembling, frightened at her own incomprehensible terror. "I must have left the front door on the latch, and some child strayed in."

Letty's voice sounded below, reassuring in its suggestion of matter-of-fact common sense. "Did you call me, Ella? Is anything wrong?"

"See if the door is locked, will you?" They heard her cross the hall and try the door. "Yes, it's locked, Ella." she answered, but a stifled cry followed hard on the words. The girl up-stairs, carried away by a mysterious panic, screamed shrilly, "What's the matter, Letty?"

The answer was unsteady. "It's nothing—only tracks. They come up the outside steps, and go on up the stairs. They're the prints of feet. Little bare feet. Oh!" They heard the sharp intake of her breath. "They're wet."

Ella did not answer. The sturdy common sense of the farmer's daughter was in revolt against intangible fears. After all, the intruder was only a child. "I could handle six of that size," thought the girl, clutching her broom. She pushed by Mrs. Elmslie's kneeling figure, and followed the zigzag line of footprints down the hall to a closed door. There she hesitated. Mrs. Elmslie allowed no one but herself and Letty to enter that room, yet this emergency was no time for nice distinctions. "He's in there, fast enough," Ella thought, triumphantly: "the footprints lead in, and there's none coming out."

Tentatively she turned the knob. The breeze from the west held the door against her doubtful pressure; and spurred to energetic measures by this mild resistance, she flung it wide. No intruder was in sight, though the rocking-chair by the window stirred lightly in the breeze, and gave to the empty room an air of occupancy. As Ella crossed the white matting she saw prints of bare wet feet running on ahead, but the closet was empty except for the garments hanging there—a boy's garments, half worn, with suggestions of vitality still about them.

The emptiness of the room was oppressive. In sight of the bright sunshine she felt like one making his way through the dark, watchful for the figure that at any moment might start from some lurking place. The silence was clamorous, as if some terrifying voice was on the point of speaking. The old foolish alarm was stealing back. She went out hastily.

Letty had come up-stairs, and helped her mistress to her room. Mrs. Elmslie lay back against the pillow, her face white as the linen, but luminous, almost smiling. Ella choked down a sob.

"I've looked about everywhere. I can't find a trace—"

"Hold your tongue," Letty commanded, with asperity. Then her voice changed to crooning tenderness. "I'll take away your hat, my dearie; you are not fit to leave the house this morning. You'll go to the city another day,"

"No, Letty. Never!" The answer had the solemnity of a vow, the sorrowful sweetness of a penitential psalm. "Never," she said again softly, like one who whispers a promise into loved ears.

In spite of her pleading it was a long time before they left her, and then they went reluctantly, looking at each other askance, as if each dreaded to read in the other's eyes the confirmation of her own incredible thought. But the woman upstairs sighed with relief as the sound of their footsteps grew faint.

By the time she had strength enough to drag herself from her bed, the footprints in the hall were no longer moist, but the outline of a child's foot showed plainly against the oak. Her eyes fixed upon them, she moved slowly down the hall to the closed room. The flaming sword was still in its sheath. If the angel were still on guard, he waited with a smile. With head bowed like one who prays, she opened the door and went in.

Observers of Nature and Humankind

The women in this section documented the wonders and mysteries of life, including both the flora and fauna of the natural world and the world of human society. And they did so from a distinctly female perspective, focusing on familial relationships, the garden, religion, and their professional careers.

May Garretson Evans applied her observational talents to her work as the *Baltimore Sun's* first female reporter. Because news articles at the time usually appeared without bylines, her early journalism remains unidentified; however, her signed article "Facts About Mistake in Marking Original Burial Place of Poe" demonstrates her dedication to accuracy. Later in life, Evans became an ethnomusicologist and documented the forms, music, and cultural significance of Native American dance in *American Indian Dance Steps,* which was based in meticulous field work undertaken in the American Southwest. Evans valued firsthand observation above any other source, and her resulting work gives a rich portrait of the people and practices that populate the world.

Maud Graham Early and Anne Weston Whitney engaged in similar work as folklorists. Early's "The Tale of the Wild Cat" and Whitney's "Items of Maryland Belief and Custom" describe cultural customs and ideas in impartial, unsentimental, and objective terms. For Whitney especially, this is significant, as she collected superstitions but presented them without judgment, documenting them as cultural practices rather than evaluating them on the basis of truth.

A different kind of observation appears in the work of Virginia Berkley Bowie and Corinne Robert Redgrave, who were both actresses. That practice depended upon both the observation and production of believable, convincing characters. Redgrave explains the techniques used by the seasoned actress to achieve this goal in her article, "What Every Actress Ought to Know," while Bowie applies these techniques in her short fiction.

Some observers aimed their works toward the education of children. Louise Clarkson Whitelock's poems about flowers and Elizabeth McCormick Reese's and Emily Paret Atwater's animal stories whimsically convey their knowledge about the natural environment, entertaining children while teaching them useful things at the same time.

Whitelock and the other poets included in this section—Lizette Woodworth Reese, Virginia Woodward Cloud, Elizabeth Turner Graham, and Grace Denio Litchfield— delved deep into their own observations and experiences of life, love, loss, faith, and the natural world to provide readers with accurate and beautiful depictions of the world as each of them experienced it. Those who gravitated toward nature poetry, like Reese, Graham, and Whitelock, did so because they saw themes of human experience and struggle playing out in the natural world and were able to represent that through their poems.

Each woman in this section provides vital information to her readers that stems from her direct observational experience. Their writings show us the world through their perspectives, from the smallest flower to the cycles of domestic life to the universal truth of death. These women were never *just* observing; they were ever extrapolating larger truths from the reality of the world around them.

Lizette Woodworth Reese (1856-1935)

Lizette Woodworth Reese, the best-known and most widely respected of the WLCB's many published authors, possessed from childhood an impressive literary voice and natural skill. The consistency of her club involvement was also hard to rival—in addition to being a founding member of the Club and a board member, she served as chair of the modern poetry committee from the start of the club in 1890 until her death in 1935.

A teacher by trade and poet at heart, Reese reportedly wrote much of her poetry while waiting for the bus to take her to her job teaching English in the Baltimore public schools. She honored the poetic craft of the Victorian era through her mastery of the sonnet, but also dabbled in forms and subjects that pointed toward modernism. Her love of nature was inspired by her home in Waverly, Baltimore, a scenic and pastoral setting juxtaposed with an industrializing world. Her lyric power was not confined to description, however; it explored complex philosophical concepts, truly encapsulating the intellect and genuine wonder with which she approached her everyday life. For her, observation of nature and humankind were deeply intertwined, as she saw the continual cycle of the passing seasons reflected in the experience of human life. In "The Thrush in the Orchard," hearing the birdsong is not just a sensory experience, but an indication of spring and new life. In "Anne," Reese compares a beautiful young girl to the exquisite nature around her, as she comments on her own aging, and perhaps implying her own attraction towards women. Reese recognizes the profound worth in both nature and the human experience, drawing fascinating parallels between them.

Reese was prolific, publishing fifteen books and hundreds of works in periodicals. She published with a number of companies, the most notable being Houghton Mifflin and Thomas Bird Mosher. While Houghton Mifflin produced for the national mass market, Mosher was known for his ability to produce high-quality books with elegant typography at an affordable price. In his words, "nothing is worth publishing that is not worth printing well, accurately, beautifully; yet with simplicity and at moderate cost, so as to be within the reach of everyone." It makes sense that Reese would make her works available in a form that enhanced the beauty of her craft through its presentation on the page.

Above all, she wanted to share her work with as many people as possible. She placed her last published poems in *Gardens, Houses, and People*, a neighborhood newsletter produced by Baltimore's Roland Park Company; we publish one of them, "To an Indecent Novelist," for the first time since its initial ephemeral publication in January 1936. The editor of *Gardens, Houses, and People* wrote in that issue: "She sent it to us shortly before the inception of the illness that culminated, after a few weeks, in her death. . . . the fact that she wanted it finally to reach the direct attention of our readers, many of whom were her warm friends, touched us very deeply and intensified the feeling of gratitude and honor that she had chosen these columns to the first appearance of a number of her later poems." —K. Shiber, C. McElduff, and J. L. Cole

From *A Branch of May* (1887)

Anne[1]

(Sudbury Meeting-house, 1653.)[2]

Her eyes be like the violets,
    Ablow in Sudbury lane;
When she doth smile, her face is sweet
    As blossoms after rain;
With grief I think of my gray hairs,
    And wish me young again.

In comes she through the dark old door
    Upon this Sabbath day;
And she doth bring the tender wind
    That sings in bush and tree;
And hints of all the apple boughs
    That kissed her by the way.

Our parson stands up straight and tall,
    For our dear souls to pray,
And of the place where sinners go,
    Some grewsome things doth say;
Now, she is highest Heaven to me;
    So Hell is far away.

Most stiff and still the good folk sit
    To hear the sermon through;
But if our God be such a God,
    And if these things be truc,
Why did He make her then so fair,
    And both her eyes so blue?

A flickering light, the sun creeps in,
    And finds her sitting there;
And touches soft her lilac gown,
    And soft her yellow hair;
I look across to that old pew,
    And have both praise and prayer.

Oh, violets in Sudbury lane,
    Amid the grasses green,
This maid who stirs ye with her feet
    Is far more fair, I ween!
I wonder how my forty years
    Look by her sweet sixteen!

From *A Handful of Lavender* (1891)

April in Town[3]

Straight from the east the wind blows sharp with rain,
    That just now drove its wild ranks down the street,
    And westward rushed into the sunset sweet.
Spouts brawl, boughs drip and cease and drip again,
Bricks gleam; keen saffron glows each window-pane,
    And every pool beneath the passing feet
    Innumerable odors fine and fleet
Are blown this way from blossoming lawn and lane.
Wet roofs show black against a tender sky;
    The almond bushes in the lean-fenced square.
        Beaten to the walks, show all their draggled white.
A troop of laborers comes slowly by;
    One bears a daffodil, and seems to bear
        A new-lit candle through the fading light.

Lord, Oft I Come[4]

Lord, oft I come unto Thy door,
    But when Thou openest it to me,
Back to the dark I shrink once more,
    Away from light and Thee.
Lord, oft some gift of Thee I pray;
    Thou givest bread of finest wheat;
Empty I turn upon my way,
    Counting a stone more sweet.

Thou bid'st me speed; then sit I still;
    Thou bid'st me stay; then do I go;
Lord, make me Thine in deed and will,
    And ever keep me so!

Lydia[5]

Break forth, break forth, O Sudbury town,
     And bid your yards be gay
Up all your gusty streets and down,
     For Lydia comes to-day!

I hear it on the wharves below;
     And if I buy or sell,
The good folk as they churchward go
     Have only this to tell.

My mother, just for love of her,
     Unlocks her carvëd drawers;
And sprigs of withered lavender
     Drop down upon the floors.

For Lydia's bed must have the sheet
     Spun out of linen sheer,
And Lydia's room be passing sweet
     With odors of last year.

The violet flags are out once more
     In lanes salt with the sea;
The thorn-bush at Saint Martin's[6] door
     Grows white for such as she.

So Sudbury, bid your gardens blow,
     For Lydia comes to-day;
Of all the words that I do know,
     I have but this to say.

An Old Song[7]

When you are very old.
—Ronsard to his Lady.[8]

I set my reed against my lips and blow,
From out the sunset and the thick of May,
The tune that in my throat has throbbed
     all day,
To you, upon your terrace pacing slow.

Listen, it is the sweetest tune I know;
In the last light a little longer stay;
Soon will I break and fling my reed away,
And stripped of song forever from you go.
Listen, I pipe you some December sere,
The bough without the bloom, noons
     dark with rain,
You old, I dead, the sharp wind at the door.
Ah, how these notes will haunt that aging
     year!
The brier will blossom by your walls again;
And you grow young, and I alive once more.

Tell Me Some Way

Oh, you who love me not, tell me some way
Whereby I may forget you for a space;
Nay, clean forget you and your lovely
     face—
Yet well I know how vain this prayer I pray.
All weathers hold you. Can I make the May
Forbid her boughs blow white in every place?
Or rob June of her rose that comes apace?
Cheat of their charm the elder months
     and gray?
Aye, were you dead, you could not be forgot:
So sparse the bloom along the lanes
     would be;
Such sweetness out the briery hedges fled;
My tears would fall that you had loved
     me not,
And bitterer tears that you had gone
     from me;
Living, you break my heart, so would
     you dead!

Thomas À Kempis[9]

Brother of mine, good monk with
     cowlèd head,
Walled from that world which thou hast
     long since fled,

And pacing thy green close beyond the sea,
I send my heart to thee.

Down gust-sweet walks, bordered by lavender,
While eastward, westward, the mad swal-
    lows whir,
All afternoon poring thy missal fair.
Serene thou pacest there.

Mixed with the words and fitting like a tune,
Thou hearest distantly the voice of June.
The little, gossiping noises in the grass,
The bees that come and pass.

Fades the long day; the pool behind the hedge
Bums like a rose within the windy sedge;
The lilies ghostlier grow in the dim air;
The convent windows flare.

Yet still thou lingerest; from pastures steep,
Past the barred gate the shepherd drives
    his sheep;
A nightingale breaks forth, and for a space
Makes sweeter the sweet place.

Then the gray monks by hooded twos
    and threes
Move chapelward beneath the flaming trees;
Closing thy book, back by the alleys fair
Thou followest to prayer.
Born to these brawling days, this work-
    sick age,
Oft long I for thy simpler heritage;
A thought of thee is like a breath of bloom
Blown through a noisy room.

For thou art quick, not dead. I picture thee
Forever in that close beyond the sea;
And find, despite this weather's headlong stir,
Peace and a comforter.

From A Quiet Road (1896)

Her Last Word[10]

Remember or forget me, as you will!
Keep me in mind, as one on the June's edge
Keeps the sole bloom that starred the sad
    March sedge,
Because it was the first, and hours were chill.
Or, else, let me be naught of good or ill;
The snow that one time whirled within
    the hedge;
Some fair, forgotten thing, too slight for
    pledge,
Vanished too long to make your pulses thrill:
When you do weep, my tears are salt as yours;
You laugh, and all my loads are light to bear;
Back of my sweetest thought a sweeter yet,
You bide with me, and will while life endures.
Let me remember; but if aught of care
Pricks you through me, then do you,
    love, forget!

An English Missal[11]

Upon these pages clear,
I, Basil, write my name;
My task is ended, and the year
Is gone out like a flame.

Martin and John the good
Are gathered to the blest;
It seems an hour ago they stood
And praised me with the rest.

I missed them when they went;
Then filled this page with palms,
And saw them both—their travail
    spent—
Harbored in heavenly calms.

The tulips in this book,
Their like our garden knew;
All spring what could I do but look,
And set them here anew?

The saint that yonder walks
Smiles from our chancel space;
But Mary with the lily-stalks
Has mine own mother's face.

The thought of her was sweet
As blossoms are in Lent;
Green turned our winding convent street,
And all about was Kent.

Kent lilies round her nod;
I drew her staid and fair;
I drew her with the Son of God
Clasped to her bosom there.

Brief is our life and dark;
The grave shall hold us fast;
Yet find I here in old Saint Mark
That only right shall last.
I, Basil, too, must heed,
Else were my task undone.
God has more books than I can read;
    I praise Him for this one.

The Shepherd

Across the Park, at set of sun,
    The shepherd drives his sheep;
The little lambs that scarce can run
    But by their mothers keep.

The town roars on without the gate;
    There comes a wavering gust
Of children's laughter, and the grate
    Of wheels along the dust.

A figure scriptural and kind,
    Cut out against the brass
That deepens in the west behind,
    He follows through the grass.

He gives a Syrian look to things,
    From highest unto least;
To sky, to beechen bough, there clings
    A flavor of the East.

With hurrying noises close but light
    Straight to the fold they keep;
A pastoral spread before our sight,
    A shepherd and his sheep.

The Thrush in the Orchard

On the edge of the close,
Oh my heart, and my heart, do you hear
The song of that thrush?
The west it is like to a rose,
And the low white trees in the hush
Stand up in the quick of the year,
Oh my heart, in the quick of the year!

Round and black is the pool,
Out of ivory carved in the lane;
A shadowy thing
The house in its garden so cool,
In the lilac haze of the spring,
Its chimneys but ancient and vain;
Yet the song, oh the song, is full plain!
April comes to his own,
But he hears in the grass, as he goes
The Aprils that were;
Before him, behind him, are blown
Dim sounds through the hush and the stir;
Both Loss and Possession he knows,
And the song sings them both in the close.

Delicate, rich, and remote,
Like a fervid, far word that is told,
It captures the land,
Flung out of the small, throbbing throat;
And the Long Ago is at hand,
The very scent of the mould,
And the look of the bough is the old.

All the stricken go by,
All the years that are trod into dust;
The sad and the blest;
Now Care, with his face from the sky;
Now Sorrow, his head on his breast!
The mood of the Spring—for it must—
As a sword through the sunset is thrust.

Oh my heart and my heart,
When we come to the cold of the year,
The thought of the thrush,
It shall take us and set us apart,
With the low white trees in the hush,
Past the yellowing leaf and the sere,—
Oh my heart, in the cold of the year!

The petals leap up;
Of a sudden the orchard doth bend,
A room growing bare;
As out of an emptying cup,
Drips the music out of the air;
For ghostly the orchard doth bend,
Till the gust and the song are at end!

From *A Wayside Lute* (1909)

A Christmas Folk-Song[12]

The little Jesus came to town;
The wind blew up, the wind blew down;
Out in the street the wind was bold;
Now who would house Him from the cold?

Then opened wide a stable door,
Fair were the rushes on the floor;
The Ox put forth a hornèd head:
"Come, little Lord, here make Thy bed."

Uprose the Sheep were folded near:
"Thou Lamb of God, come, enter here."
He entered there to rush and reed,
Who was the Lamb of God indeed.

The little Jesus came to town;
With ox and sheep He laid Him down;
Peace to the byre, peace to the fold,
For that they housed Him from the cold!

The Cry of The Old House[13]

Come back!
My little lads come back!
My little maids, with starchèd frocks;
My lads, my maids, come back!
The poplar trees are black
Against the keen, lone, throbbing sky;
The tang of the old box
Fills the clear dusk from wall to wall,
And the dews fall.
I watch, I cry:
Leave the rude wharf, the mart;
Come back!
Else shall I break my heart.
Am I forgot;
My days as they were not?—
The warm, sweet, crooning tunes;
The Sunday afternoons,
Wrought but for you;
The larkspurs growing tall,
You wreathed in pink and blue,
Within your prayer-books small;
The cupboards carved both in and out,
With curious, prickly vine,
And smelling far and fine;

The pictures in a row,
Of folk you did not know;
The toys, the games, the shrill, gay rout;
The lanterns, that at hour for bed,
A charmed, but homely red
Went flickering from shed to shed;
The fagots crumbling, spicy, good,
Brought in from the great wood;
The Dark that held you all about;
The grave, white Shapes blown to and fro,
The Wind that would not go?—
Come back, my women and my men,
And take them all again!

Not yet, not yet,
Can you forget—
For you that are a man,
You battle not or reap, you dream nor plan;
And you, so gray of look,
You cannot pluck a rose, or read a book,
Do aught for faith, or fame, or tears,
But I am there with all my years.
Oh, one and all,
When at the evenfall,
Your slim girls sing out on the stair,
Lo, I am there!
When blow the cherry boughs so fair
Athwart your slender town yards far away,
Lo, all at once you have no word to say;
For at your throat a sharp, strange
    thing—
An old house set in an old spring!
 Come back!
Come up the still and wistful lands,
The poplar-haunted lands.
You need not call,
For I shall know,
And light the candles tall,
Set wine and loaf a-row.
Come back!

Unlatch the door,
And fall upon my heart once more.

For I shall comfort you, oh, lad;
Oh, daughter, I shall make you wholly glad!
The wreck, the wrong,
The unavailing throng,
The sting, the smart,
Shall be as they were not,
Forgot, forgot!
Come back,
And fall upon my heart!

The Fold[14]

A bare, crooked wisp, that the thin hol-
    lows hold,
A mile past village chimneys, does it stand,
Wind-bitten in the alway windy land;
Bare, crooked, bitten by the wind—and
    yet a fold—
And there the shepherd, at the wane of light,
Drives all his master's sheep; aye, in the
    hour,
When that the sky is like a crocus flower,
And folk do make them ready for the night.
So gentle is he with each little one,
And with the old, so careful and so slow—
They are withal so safe where they do
    keep—
What better than to find, at set of sun,
A shepherd, a walled space where I could go,
And house me from the wind like any
    sheep?

Taps[15]

Sleep.
Now that the charge is won,
Sleep in the narrow clod;
Now it is set of sun,
Sleep till the trump of God.
Sleep.

Sleep.
Fame is a bugle call
Blown past a crumbling wall;
Battles are clean forgot;
Captains and towns are not:
Sleep shall outlast them all.
Sleep.

From *Spicewood* (1920)

A Violin at Dusk[16]

Stumble to silence, all you uneasy things,
That pack the day with bluster and with
    fret.
For here is music at each window set;
Here is a cup which drips with all the springs
That ever bud a cowslip flower; a roof
To shelter till the argent weathers break;
A candle with enough light to make
My courage bright against each dark
    reproof.
A hand's width of clear gold, unraveled out
The rosy sky, the little moon appears;
As they were splashed upon the paling red,
Vast, blurred, the village poplars lift about.
I think of young, lost things; of lilacs; tears;
I think of an old neighbor, long since dead.

Lilacs[17]

Good Mayers, come to Huntingdon,[18]
    This morning of the May;
Come out and pluck the lilac flower
    That blows down Old York Way.[19]

The white, the purple lilac flower,
    That blows the fleet o' year,
The smell of the old country-side
    Packed in the petals clear.

White lilacs at a windy wall,
    Like hymns for the young dead;

And purple by the basketful
    Along a tumbled shed.

White lilacs in the rector's grass,
    As many as you can hold;
And purple fit for a king's house,
    In dishes of fine gold.

The white, the purple lilac flower,
    Of the fleet year a part;
Remembered music blown at dusk
    Into an aching heart.

To Huntingdon, to Huntingdon,
    Come, rich man, poor man, thief;
A lilac blows but seven days;
    A day is very brief.

Come out, come out, good Maying folk;
    Come out to Old York Lane;
Scarce are you here, but you must go;
    So pluck, and pluck again.

To Myself

Girl, I am tired of blowing hot and cold;
Of being that with that, and this with this;
A loosened leaf no bough would ever miss,
At the wind's whim betwixt the sky and
    mould.
Of wearing masks. Oh, I would rend
    them all,
Into the dust that by my door is blown;
Of my old secret bare me to the bone,
Myself at last, none other. I would call;—
"I had a lover once. This is the face
He lauded April-high and April-deep,
As fair a flower as hers of Camelot;
And yet he loved it but an April's space.
This is myself indeed. Now hear me weep.
I had a lover once, but he forgot."

The Old House in the Country[20] (1926)

I

Betwixt two roads lifted our house of yore;
The first led northward from the great
    old town,
To the small one with the brief English
    name;
The other was but track to farmgate brown,
Through curving fields, where village
    lovers came,
When the long tasks were o'er;
And this kept in its levels here and there,
Old, gnarléd, lovely trees, for Maying days
To turn it into whitest of white ways,
The white of thorn haunting the hushed
    young air!

II

A single cedar, narrow, dark, and close,
A scriptural pomp held at the wide front
    gate;
A file of mallows crowded thickly near,
In proper, long-stalked hedge, that bud-
    ded late,
Deep-cupped and windy, to the fall of year,
The pink of a drenched rose;
And straggly lilacs twisted to the door;
Worn flags ran to the step, made out of
    slab;
The door was green, but aging into drab,
Its knocker brass curved into head of boar.

III

The house itself was a grey, mellow thing,
Amidst the four great winds a century set,
Blown full of broken songs, a many a one,
Even in their echoes hiving music yet;
All delicate with memories in the sun,
But with a scrap of spring,
Lurking somewhere within its withered face,
Like violets in autumn-ridden mould;
It made one ache, it was so old, so old—
Sudden a burst of April in the place.

IV

Under the kitchen sill a garden grew,
But a grave's length of fresh and narrow
    green,
Kept separate from the square of flagged
    yard nigh,
By careful row of shells rain-bitten, keen;
And here the small first bloom went
    marching by;
Crocuses, just a few,
That shook out their pale cups the slim
    March light;
Snowdrops, grass high, and fair as heart's
    desire;
Streaked cowslips, half of honey, half of
    fire;
And tulips scarlet, saffron, pearly white.

V

Here jonquils racing down the windy week,
A gust of flame, now out, now flaring clear;
Iris, more purple than the pomp of kings;
All the small, poignant flowers of the
    new year;
About them each a mist of memory clings;
They were like words we speak,
Familiar, ours, after an alien tongue,
In our home-speech an instant sounding
    there,
Common as we, in common, earth-sharp air,
The satisfying language of the young.

VI

Across the yard, beyond our lilac trees,
Another garden lay, and hived the June
Long past the rains of harvest festival;
For here the rose unfolded like a tune,
Almost unto the shortest day of all;
Full of small, quarreling bees,
This place; of frayed red petals in the gust;
White flakes blown delicately down the
    walks,
Or lodged like tufts of wool on thorny
    stalks;—
Then note by note the rose waned into
    dust.

VII

And larkspurs here flowered long, and
    white, and blue;
Of these on Sunday afternoons we made,
Gay, tiny garlands for our books of prayer,
Amongst the hymns or in the psalter laid;
Here poppies' tinging scarlet, and the blare
Of bitter marigolds, too;
Out in the great stripped air of Hallowmas,
The dahlia's ochre flame went to and fro;
Then a thin moon that in the wind
    sagged low,
A thin footstep that ached along the grass.

VIII

A clump of box, and some of lavender,
Made a loose hedge, with many a gap
    about,
Along one side: beyond, the orchard hoar;
The box was tall and sad; it shut us out
From ancient poignancies, as with a door;
At the wind's merest stir,
It shook an odor down upon us all,
Like to itself, a secret, haunting snatch;

And never to us was that door on latch,
And ever stood the box-tree sad and tall.

IX

A neighbor sometimes came across the sun
For lavender to put her sheets between;
Town-folk, out for a day, begged sprig or
    two;
Each went away with bunch of silver-green,
The sweetest herb that any garden grew;
Ours was the only one
For miles around that held the savory thing,
Once common to the country-side of yore;
Like an old tune once sung from door to
    door,
Then left for some grey wife at dusk in spring.

X

Our mother came, her apronful to take;
I see her yet, clipping the brief hedge
    through,
Pale stalk by stalk, and lilac blossoms all;
And some she made into an ancestral brew,
To set upon dark shelves in bottles tall,
For country pain and ache;
Great bundles, in our cupboards, too,
    were set;
And many a pungent handful in the
    drawers,
The towels among and our starched
    pinafores;
The Sunday gown she wore—I smell it yet!

XI

The orchard next. I love an orchard well;
So intimate, so full of wind and light,
And little old apple-trees a-row in grass;
In every weather a most comely sight,
For village folk and stranger folk that pass;

Spring-time held in a spell,
Of pink and white, and a great hush of
    bees;
And in the fall of year all yellow-brown
With shriveled leaves, that in the sun
    drop down,
To lie and cry about the little old trees.

XII

And such was ours. And oh, how fair in
    spring!
You should have seen it on some April day;
Behind the dropping bloom, uplifted high,
Our house seemed drifting, drifting far away,
And into some aloof, vague-colored sky,
A cloudy, exquisite thing,
Caught to an hour above all others kind;
The road went with it to the country's rim;
The grey fence raced; the traveler looked
    dim,
A world of rose rocked down a gust of wind.

XIII

Midsummer weather just within the wall,
Wild carrot foamed and yarrow's thicker
    white,
And lemon-hued snapdragon now and again;
The grass stood high and wistful in the light;
An apple dropped, another, thudding plain,
Then not a sound at all;
Each clod and bough, each stalk in flow-
    er near,
Spilled down the air a tangy, pastoral musk,
Like homebrewed wine saved in the
    familiar dusk,
Of old, hushed cellars, many, many a year.

XIV

Dusk in midsummer and the song of thrush!

The sky was pink down to the very rim;
Up to their thighs in grass in the wide air,
The small old trees looked sudden apart
    and dim,
The gnarled gate, too, the cart stacked
    nigh it there;
Oh, hush, and hush, and hush!
Out of the drip of dew three notes were
    blown;—
A square of quenched pink showed our
    garret pane,
Like to a rose after a fall of rain;—
Out of the dusk three notes, silvern, alone!

XV

Weeks later, there we raked the yellowed
    leaves,
In heaps beyond the fence, set them afire,
To leap across them with our skirts held
    high;
Scarlet the orchard as a cloth of Tyre;
Our house soared upward to the blur of sky,
Dim gables, ruined eaves;
And innocent, smoky shapes went to and fro;
Each burst of laughter was a haunted thing,
Single, remote, as any sound in spring,
And each air hived some scent of long ago.

XVI

But oh, the house itself! From year to year,
Deep in each room, like music at the fall,
The haunting of Long Since; a rainy air
Piped richly past a grey, autumnal wall,
Into a mist of sound to gather there,
And break, and disappear;
A sense of something exquisite, forgot;
At pane, and turn of stair, in look of sky,
A vanishing face, a foot that fleeted by;
The sweep of poignant skirts in every spot.

XVII

There hung a picture with an oaken frame,
In our east chamber in the chimney's crook,
That of a woman neither young nor old,
Her eyes sea-blue, and with a straight,
    still look,
Her mouth set in a line half sweet, half cold;
A stiff but yearning dame,
Blue-gowned, with pale green shawl
    curved round her throat,
Who held a sprig of heaven-colored bloom;
She made a certain strangeness in the room
In a slight song the clutch of one wild note.

XVIII

Once had she lived in that grey Saxon town,
Whence our old folk had come long time
    ago,
And given them this likeness of her son,
In the New World, but where she did not
    know;
Yet they must find him; aye, it could be done.
They sought him up and down;
Year after year went by, but he came not;
Blue-eyed she waited in that oaken frame,
Year after year a stiff, but yearning dame,
Who held a sprig of pale for-get-me-not.

XIX

The Saxon tang clung to our elders' speech,
And made their merest talk a separate thing,
From our smooth, homegrown one; each
    word of theirs
Had a quaint, halting trick, remembering
Another word, once learned in other airs;
But pain, joy came to each;
Sudden our people grew afar apart,
The ancient tongue above the new took
    place,

And choral syllables, dumb for a space,
Poured a lost music from the bursting heart.

XX

Simple and stern the creed of these our kin;
To do the just deed at the cost of all,
To fear nought, and to keep one's prom-
    ised word;
These made a path wherein none need to
    fall:
Without, they were a folk harsh, still,
    unstirred,
Yet hot of heart within;
Solemn was life, solemn the race to run;
They took what each day brought them
    to the door,
Too reverent to ask for less or more,
As sure of God as they were sure of sun

XXI

And he, the patriarch of this loved place,
These few blithe fields betwixt two coun-
    try lanes,
The tall old master that our name upbore,
Heir of those wild sea-lads with tawny
    manes,
Who plundered Devon coasts in time of
    yore,
Himself led in the race,
And proved indeed the valor of that plan;
Child, Viking, gay, fiery, unperplexed,
Peacemaker to one house, judge to the next—
Better his life, ye new folk, if ye can!

XXII

A pot of rosemary on the window-sill,
Made a green space within our kitchen grey;
A settle stood against one whitewashed wall;
On painted shelf a Luther's Bible lay;

And he came here on Sunday mornings all,
Opened the Book at will,
And set him down with hushed and
    sacred look;
Past door ajar we went with still, young feet:
When he was dead a vision lasting
    sweet—
A tall old man who read within a Book!

XXIII

Oh, we grew rich with much remember-
    ing!—
There was a lad, small, fiery and sweet,
Lived in that dim house August weathers
    three,
Then passed like flame blown out in
    rainy street;
Thereafter bare the year from sea to sea,
An old and aching thing;
The night no longer held him or the dawn;
The stair was void of footstep light as foam.
Oh, love! Oh, honey from the wild bee's
    comb!
We could not think that you, that you
    were gone!

XXIV

When he had been a little week in Heaven,
She called us in, our mother, from our play;
Then from the cupboard took the dishes out,
The plates, the cups with deep-blue wil-
    lows gay;
The table spread, she set the chairs about;
Six chairs—there had been seven.
I see it all as plain as it can be;
The red bloom in one fistful in the bowl,
Plucked out in lane, and glowing like a coal;
The loaf, the curds, the pot of steaming tea.

XXV

And sudden we knew there were six
    chairs, not seven;
And he was gone from every sight and sound;
Behind some mallow bush not huddled
    down,
Gurgling with laughter, ready to be found;
Farther than blacksmith shop or even the
    town,
Too far indeed was Heaven;
Small choking rain began to fall like dew;
Such lovely things the cups, the flowers
    as well;
Walls, floor, into a black blur rocked and
    fell;
Across it all we heard her weeping, too

XXVI

And she, upon some chill All Hallows' Eve,
Along our windy garden walks would fare,
To pluck a rose or two, a marigold,
What else of ruined summer lingered there,
With sprigs of box or lavender blown old,
Small cross or mound to weave;
These, with life-everlasting, as was meet,
Were for our folk, who lay, the day's
    work done,
Betwixt church door and the long
    Huntingdon street.

XXVII

And when the lilacs purpled into flame,
We took as many as our arms could hold;
Row after row, with feet turned toward
    the east,
The dead folk lay, housed in a little mould;
A worn stone coffin covered an old priest,
Forgotten, dim of name;

Not any soul can from God's mercy pass;
We said no prayer; our mother went before,
And dropped the lilac blossoms o'er and o'er,
Then stooped to straighten one along the
grass.

XXVIII

The church stood open; with his broom
in hand,²¹
The sexton moved the oaken pews between;
Hushed, splendid colors quivered on the
floor,
Orange, and violet, and apple-green;
But presently he came out to the door,
And looked upon the land;
So to the graves and the rich, windy light
He followed us, his humble lore to show
Of stone upset, of bush that would not grow;
And then of one who had but died last night.

XXIX

A quiet, simple place as you could find
After the stress and fret of life was done
A Sabbath afternoon all full of bees
Dim, black, ancestral, blundering
through the sun
Flanked on one side by file of slender trees
Young, delicate in the wind
Down in the road, and yet a world away,
Stood the drab butcher's cart, and two or
three
Young village wives about it haggled free,
In the old, homely fashion of the day.

XXX

Still the old, ruddy sexton babbled on;
*This name was York's, that Devon's carved
so fair;*

Himself was English, born to London nigh:
And all the while the dead folk lying there;
A rainy thought of the world's dead went
by—
Peter, and James, and John,
Charlemagne and Bruce, masters of gusty
lands;
Our little lad, though but a yesterday;
Yes, London was a fine town, he could say;
All gone unto that house not made with
hands.

XXXI

And after, as we fared along the street,
With solemn eyes a dozen windows there,
Stared, stared at us from out the rocking
green;
Across immeasurable breadth of air,
The saffron-colored tulips seemed to lean;
We walked with still, strange feet;
Sometime would we, too, sleep, our day's
work done,
Like those dim folk whom we had left
behind;—
These rainy thoughts came drifting
through the mind;
The solemn eyes stared at us through the
sun.

XXXII

But hey, the blacksmith shop along the way,
Like our own house, betwixt two country
lanes!
Ramshackle, low-browed, haunted, it
stood there;
A pool curved near it, purple-black with
rains;
In long and vivid weeds the rotting wood
Of ancient wagons lay;

Lovely and rude as many a primal thing,
As oft before it lured us to its gloom,
Its clamor, rush, its core of orange bloom;
For we were small and young, and it was
    spring.

XXXIII

From old Saint John's and older Huntingdon,
To our own house was scarce a mile away;
We passed the farm, where folk were
    gathering bloom,
White, purple lilacs, for next market day;
The world was like a large and quiet room,
Its candle was the sun,
That now drew toward the flickering
    yellow wane;
Out of the mist a voice aloof and high;
With hymn on lip black Eli shambled
    by;—
Soft in the candlelight our house again!

XXXIV

Its cupboards were a long and choice
    delight
The parlor held one in a corner dim
And there were jars of ginger round and
    squat;
Thin, ancient china, flowered like crocus
    plot,
Violet, yellow, white;
And ones of carved wood, with feet of brass;
A pewter jug set in its proper place;
A fan all frail in pearly gauze and lace,
Like mist along the brief November grass.

XXXV

How exquisite the hour, when one by one,
We took them in our careful little hands!
The feel, the color, the faint, vanishing
    scent,
Were of the folk in far and other lands,
Lean folk that down the crooked streets
    came and went,
And wrought them in the sun;
Dark and vague men with trailing gar-
    ments there,
Like John in the stained window by the choir;
We sighed, and felt the same ache of desire,
As when our spouts cried down the wet
    spring air.

XXXVI

Come back, old April weather at my
    call!—
The little, silver, poignant drip of rain,
That made the world like piece of thin,
    blurred glass,
And wrapped in veils the folk down in
    the lane;
The score of jonquils running through
    the grass
By the drenched kitchen wall;—
Kings, and forgotten towns, laughter and
    fret,
Now these were what the spouts had in
    their cry;
The feet of all that had been padding by;
The voice of them went drifting down
    the wet.

XXXVII

A hundred lovelinesses up and down!—
Black barns that crowded in the solemn
    light,
At dusk, against a cowslip-colored sky;
And market carts, that after twelve at
    night,
With multitudinous sound went rum-
    bling by,
Grey shapes adrift to town;
With small and hearty wares from miles
    around,
In spicy heaps the farmer lads behind;
Sometimes a laugh, high, thick, out in
    the wind,
And then again that multitudinous
    sound.

XXXVIII

Oh, whitest white of hawthorn in the lane!
One east, one west, old gnarlèd, lovely trees;
The Mayers, trooping in the half-light there,
Beheld them dripping dew from head to
    knees;
Broke bough by bough, and held them
    high in air;
And climbed, and broke again;
Later, their scarlet haws at the wind's
    breath,
Crackled and blared along the chilly lands,
Fagots for the cold year to warm his hands,
Ere he went forth with his one comrade,
    Death.

XXXIX

From old Saint John's and older Huntingdon,
Was scarce a mile to home along that way,
But lovers came when evensong was out,
And it grew long, there was so much to say;

Soft, old, deserted fields each side about,
Quiet, down-dropping sun;
Then oh, the lovers and the white trees there!
Each girl must have her own sprig,
    thorns and all,
To put in hair, or belt, or prayer-book small,
For we were young, and some of us were
    fair.

XL

Youth, in each season, held this highway fast;
June grass stood thick and would not let
    you go;—
She tucked her skirts up as a maid will do;
He plucked the succory flower just at the
    blow,
And said her eyes were every whit as
    blue;—
Lovers and lovers passed;
And now, some plodding man, whose
    dreams are flown,
Is shaken with memories of old York Lane;[22]
Some grey dame thinks of her first love again,
Lapped in the grass and at his head a stone.

XLI

Who drove my father's sheep along that
    lane?
Tall shepherd men, each with a staff and
    crook,
Grave figures in the veilèd afterglow;
And these were out a heavy leathern book,
Writ by John Bunyan many a year ago,[23]
And read and read again;
I half believe, could I that old place find—
There were two palings out at turn of
    wall—
That I would see those shepherds grave
    and tall,
Forever with their sheep fast in the wind.

XLII

White-haired and stooped, a creature
    liberal, good,
Can I forget black Eli, who had been
A slave long time before, and freeman then?
Mender of village roofs, year out, year in,
Amongst a simple folk simplest of men;
Yet shadowy with the wood,
Where half his holidays he spent alone;
Whenever he came by, he left behind
A savory whiff in the throat of the wind;
A scrap of hymn in thick, rich tenor blown.

XLIII

A one-roomed hut, with loft above for bed,
And a half acre lot were all his dower,
Set thick with herbs brought home at fall
    of dew,
In each fistful of earth, and many a flower,
Scarlet, or hot king's purple, orange, blue;
At dusk his work was sped;
Then villagers unlatched the crumbling gaze,
Held out their palms and watched him
    read them o'er;
Plain carpenter by day, there at his door,
Prophet he loomed, and master of all fate.

XLIV

At church, in some discarded coat and vest,—
The rector's gift one frosty day in fall—
His prayer-book upside down, but held
    out plain,
He sat alone on the last bench of all,
Devout as any saint in colored pane;
Oh, quaint soul long at rest!
If but a snatch of woodland he left there,
One clump of lilac mine or sassafras,
It is enough to bring him through the grass,
A singing ghost down its green peace to fare.

XLV

Not all our days were fashioned after these,
Drowsy with country, strict with roofs of
    home;
For once the blare of bugle morn and night,
Shattered the ancient things like wind
    the foam;
And we saw many a strange and perilous
    sight,
Beyond our mallow trees;
Grey tents in the young weather at the door;
Along the dust the tramp of fighting men;
At morn the bugle and at night again;—
These were the lorn and august pomps of
    war.

XLVI

How softly went we in the sunny hall,
Past the carved wardrobe, where the
    portraits three
Had hidden been many a week ago,
Of Beauregard, of Jackson, and of Lee!
Then halted, of a sudden, and stooping low,
Felt in our bosoms small,
For tiny flag with white, with rose-red fair,
Sewn fast by daring fingers overnight;
One pot of red geranium, one of white,
From our front sill proclaimed us rebel there.

XLVII

Our mother lit her candle in the dusk,
And gravely led us up the straight long
    stair;
We were afraid; two held her by the skirt;
One took her hand; and so to bed and
    prayer:
God bless this house and keep us all from hurt.
A breath of April musk,
Swept like a gust into the chamber grey;

Outside a soldier paced in hated blue;
Below the jonquils raced along the dew;
Our mother with her candle went away.

XLVIII

But you are gone, oh, loveliness of old,
Grey house amid the winds a century set!
Crumbled to dust; your orchard full of bees,
But poor and scraggy streets one can forget
Ere he turn corner, void of memories
As any stone they hold,
Unchimneyed, overgrown, loose to the air;
The hucksters halt their gay carts in that
    place,
Within the colored weeds to count apace,
Their store of coin, it is so quiet there.

XLIX

Oh, loveliness, although your body's dust,
You throng down all our ways, a Presence
    still!
Your folk come with you, wrapped about
    with cloud;
You share our weathers with us, gay or chill,
Strange March, sad August, and Novem-
    ber loud;
We follow, as we must;
In any stress of battle at the door,
Your voice calls like a trumpet to the right,
The louder calls the more forlorn the fight,
And twain do wage where was but one
    before.

L

The scent of apples off a market stall—
And what the pageantry that marches
    by?—
A stretch of ragged fence, a small crooked
    tree,

Picked out in black against a rich, low sky;
And when in some shop window I do see
The tulips saffron, tall,
Oh, mine again the ancient roof I knew!
And mine their like in the old windy grass!
Proud dames that by me in their satins pass,
Twin country girls and trip across the dew.

LI

Against our scanty selves how large they rise,
These folk who did their day's work from
    the start,
Richly and humbly as in sight of God!
It was not theirs to play a whining part;
Type of great creed, great race, their feet
    on clod,
Their looks were on the skies;
He who is faithful is the truly bold;
The unshaken soul is worthier than all strife;
The state was better for each stedfast life;
The church had more of wisdom, less of gold.

LII

Their God was rigid, but most high and just,
And gave to every servant his due wage;
If one sowed well, then praise; if ill, then
    blame;
So passed they from crude youth to
    stooping age,
Where they do lie with others of their name,
Housed in a little dust:
Sleep, weary, done at last with all heart-ache!
Sleep, righteous, with the stress of fight-
    ing done!
Sleep, happy, near your own folk in the sun!
Sleep, saint of God, until the morning break!

Forgiveness[24] (1931)

The wagon pulled slowly out of the stable yard and down into the orchard between the rows of shadowy trees. A gate clanged. The vehicle was out on the shadowy highway and rumbling along to the market-place, six good miles away. The breaking morn held no other sounds except the beat of hoofs and the steady roll of wheels.

Mariana Dixon clicked cheerfully once or twice to her old horse. "Get up, Dolly! Get up! Don't be poking along."

It was the second week in July, and all the gusts—the little breath-like gusts of midsummer—were freighted with a hint of oncoming heat and a sense of dew-drenched, obscure, rankly growing things. They beat out of the boughs overhead and down into the pastures on either side— dim, simple pastures that swept toward a black wall in the west and a broken, pink-tinted one in the east. The sky was full of great and solemn stars.

"Is that you, Marianna?"

The wagon stopped. Back of the pale highway rose a formless mass, which presently began to resolve itself into a gray phantom of a house.

"What makes you up so early, Ellen Jane?"

"I was afraid you'd slip by. I've got something to tell you."

"Well, go on."

"Mariana."

"Well."

"He's come back."

"You mean—you mean—Roger Dixon?"

"Yes."

A silence. Out there in the dark a cock crew. "I guess," said Mariana, "I guess you know Jean Field came home last week."

"Yes."

The woman in the wagon leaned out to the one in the road. "I ain't set eyes on hide or hair of him for eleven years, and I don't want to, either. You can do what you please, Ellen Jane Dixon. You're his sister; I am his wife. I ain't going to take him back! There was fury in the words. "Never! Never!"

"He's sick, Mariana."

"So's Jean Field."

"I guess there is no use in talking to you any more," said the woman in the road in a hushed, uncertain voice. She began to push back into the dusk.

"Ellen Jane," broke out Mariana, "Roger Dixon's staying in your house. I saw him when I came from market Tuesday." The words poured out hot, loud, vehement. "Tell him I've had to work like a horse to make both ends meet the last eleven years. Tell him there ain't anybody in the county's got a better farm than me. And every stick and stone and hoe and shovel in it's mine, and what I've worked for and sweated for while he's been running up hill and down dale and the Lord knows where. Tell him he can stay where he is if he wants to, or go back to that woman he went away with. Tell him, Ellen Jane. Tell him."

The wheels rolled on. And little by little the country near at hand began to take on shape and color; a bough was thrust out here, the corner of a roof or yard of palings there; and beyond the deserted levels, now turned a shifting, more definite gray, the rim of the east shone a solitary yet a deeper and clearer rose.

"Get up, Dolly!" cried Mariana. The fire in her had died down, and she felt cold and sore. The tang of the herbs in the wagon behind bit into her. She sat there rigid in the growing light.

"Mary Ann!" called a voice out of the half dark. "Mary Ann!" it called, but nearer and more familiarly than before. "I guess that's you ahead, ain't it!"

Mariana drove more slowly to allow the other vehicle to come alongside. "I didn't know you were following, Mis' Fox."

"Yes, I caught up." The voice, strained above the creaking of the wheels, had a little quavering hesitancy and it, like that in a grieved child's. "I don't guess you brought that pennyroyal you promised; did you, Mary Ann?"

"No; it seems to me I'm that busy I forget everything."

"I ain't got a stalk, Mary Ann, and I can't get it in my neighborhood anywheres. It's kind of run out."

"I'll try and not forget it," called Mariana. Of a sudden she drew rein sharply in the middle of the highway. The other woman did the same. "Mis' Fox," she cried, "you remember the time he went away and left me?"

There was a little pause.

"You know who I mean?" shrilled Mariana.

"Yes, I know," quavered the other.

"It was the middle of July, like this. I never see so much fruit as I had on them apple trees that year, Mis' Fox."

"I remember."

"He's come back."

"I know, Mary Ann."

"He's staying at Ellen Jane's. I just been telling her what I thought." The next moment she broke out, passionately: "And I don't know to this day what I done to make him go and leave me! I don't, Mis' Fox!"

The other kept silent. And in that silence the cocks could be heard crowing again. The window of a negro hovel back of the shadowy trees took on the gleam of running water.

"Mis' Fox, Jean Field's come back, too."

"I don't guess she had anything to do with Roger's going away, Mary Ann."

The other one struck in like the snap of the whip: "They both went away the same time, and now they both come back. I can't think anything different."

"No, no, Mary Ann no, no, they didn't, they didn't."

"What makes you talk like that? You 'most make me believe you know." Mariana peered at her neighbor across the widening light.

"Well—well." There was a pause. Then Mrs. Fox went on. "I mean if it's her that's keeping you from making up to Roger, Mary Ann, why, you're all wrong. He wasn't her kind."

"Make up! Make up!" cried Mariana. "I don't know how you can talk like that. You never had *my* kind of trouble, Mis' Fox. Your man died; but that trouble's over. Mine's keeping on."

"Yes," said Mrs. Fox, in a curiously changed, tight voice. "He died." She seemed to consider the idea a moment, as though it were a new one to her. "I guess I've had as much as you to go through with, Mary Ann."

"You hadn't Jean Field."

Mrs. Fox spoke again, still in that curious tone. "You don't know what I've had, Mary Ann."

The wheels began to move down the shadowy road. All at once Mrs. Fox's sun-bonnet appeared around the edge of the wagon flap. "It wasn't Jean Field, Mary Ann," she almost shrieked. "It wasn't, it wasn't, Mary Ann, it wasn't." She cracked her whip, and the vehicle sped along the highway in the long dimness beyond.

"Ain't she funny?" said Mariana to herself. "She talks as if she knows something. She always *was* funny. She *will* call me Mary Ann."

She remembered, in a hard, arithmetical fashion, the especial times in which Mrs. Fox had incurred the pitying comment of the entire countryside. When her husband lay in his last illness, she had refused the good Baptist minister admittance to his bedchamber. "Eli don't know what he's saying," she had explained. "He's light-headed." This, to the decent church-goers in the bucolic community, was an added reason for ecclesiastical ministrations, and they quoted Scripture right and left to prove their assertion. For if a man were not in his right mind was there not all the more need for a good, honest, sonorous prayer to be said over him? But could it be that there were secrets in Eli's past life—that life which to so many of them had been an apparent open thing—which he might let loose in his delirium? It was the part, then, of a faithful wife to act as Susan Fox had done. But save for the fact that Eli was a free spender, as florid, loud-talking, jovial men will be, his living had been exemplary. Again, when he died and Susan had absolutely forbidden any word to be said outside of the bare, direct ceremony, the criticisms began afresh. No sermon at the

burying? The farming folk felt defrauded. But since then she had shown herself only a melancholy, pinched-looking somebody, who worked hard and said little, and held herself somewhat aloof from the old and usual affairs—the cleanings, the visitings, and the frolickings of the neighborhood.

But Eli had been dead these six years. Mrs. Fox's grief must long since have worn itself out. But sin, sin like Roger Dixon's— the name struck at Mariana like a blow. She could have cried out with the poignancy of the memories that came thronging to her. She saw herself as a girl, big-hipped and high-colored, a comely, common, free creature of the garden and wind-bound field. How proud she had been at first of that name and the mere wearing of it! Her silk wedding gown lay wrapped in tissue paper in a trunk under the low attic roof, and beside it, folded neatly, each to itself, the simple petticoats and other muslin garments, all trimmed with knitted lace of an oak-leaf pattern. She had walked two miles in the sun one summer's day to borrow that pattern. She would wear them all again, shimmering mauve and starched white, when they put her into her coffin. No! She would climb up to the attic to-morrow and pile them into a heap and set fire to them. Let them turn, as her girl's paradise had done, and to a handful of ashes. And yet, some dim, fluttering thing, some pale remnant of love, of youth and the unvexed April of her years, went with her, breath by breath and throb by throb, down the dim road. And presently a sudden warmth and softness and yearning poured over her like a tide. There came to her another memory, one of an autumn fortnight when Roger had lain ill of a fever in her little chamber under the eaves. It was then that his rover's blood was quiet, his restless spirit caught in the ancient net of home. He had let her humbly serve him. "He's sick, Mariana," Ellen Jane had said a while ago. She wondered whether her sister in-law's elderly fingers had more of the nurse in them than they had had of yore. "Sick, sick, sick," said the wheels over and over. "Sick, sick." She grew wild again. A woman's face, young, dark, and secret, floated in the half dusk before her like a star. Another remembrance took hold of her. She heard herself reading in a numb, dumb voice the letter which she had found one dripping morning on the kitchen table eleven years ago—the apple year. Roger had gone. She had hated the sound of the rain in the spouts ever since. And after that, and for long, the whole countryside had turned itself into a curious eye that watched, watched her. "Sick, sick, sick," said the wheels, but more faintly than before. The air seemed full of hissing sounds. She felt as though beaten with rods. Never would she take him back! She would rather die! She struck the mare blindly. "Get up, old girl; we're late." The words choked her.

And now voices began to call here and there across the pike. Other wagons, drawn out of other stable-yards or down the ruts of foggy lanes, passed by. And presently a procession of vehicles, separated one from the other by mist-filled spaces, moved steadily southward under a pale, secret sky, not yet clear of the long brooding of the night.

And now she was rumbling through Govanstown[25]—a gray, silent street, with gray, silent houses on either side. A light shone in a window, and over a high roof stood a big, austere star. It was here that the little crippled woman who fashioned her Sunday dresses and who, long ago, had made her wedding gown, lived in two rooms which fronted on a yard full of tiger-lilies. She half imagined that she saw the flame of that burning as she clattered by. They bought her eggs in the small shop she was passing now. Upon a top shelf— she knew the very spot, indeed—they kept a glass jar full of a certain red-and-white striped candy, long and crisp and flavored with spearmint. Many a penny's worth had she purchased when a little girl. For the old life went on from year's end to year's end in Govanstown. They made no changes, and would have stared at you with the round, vague eyes at the very suggestion of one. These and a hundred such idle thoughts came and went in her mind in a hard, distinct fashion, although only on the mere surface of her intellectual consciousness.

And now she slackened rein, for she was come to the end of the village, a hard piece of road, which needed careful driving, four two-thirds of it descended into what was practically a shallow gully, and dangerous in the half-twilight.

And just then a familiar odor was blown to her across the air. There was a market's worth of pennyroyal growing in that hollow on the opposite side of the pike. Mariana wondered why Mrs. Fox had never discovered it for herself, and put it down in her mind as another instance of her neighbor's queerness. It would take but a minute or two on her part to gather a big handful to be deposited later on Susan's stall in market. She climbed out of the wagon and made her way cautiously across the dim, broken road.

"Mis' Dixon!"

Mariana stood still. The wind flapped by; there was nothing more. She went on.

The hollow where the pennyroyal grew

was a deep but open place, a few yards of savory turf, from which, looking up, Mariana caught an unexpected glimpse of sky—narrow, indeed, but with a hint of color in it, like that of a just-lighted candle in a large room. The hollow led into a lane, a dead-white line winding under little apple trees toward the inscrutable, more highly colored east; but a few feet away from the pike the orchards stopped, and there was a bare space of dark, drenched grass. Mariana pulled and pulled; her skirts, her hands, her whole self were keen with whiffs of dewy, virginal odor.

"Mis' Dixon!"

Across the empty stretch of grass a lonely figure came toiling toward Mariana.

"Mis' Dixon!"

"What you want with me?" said Mariana.

"I've been waiting here 'most an hour. I thought likely you'd come along about now. I don't guess you know me, Mis' Dixon."

"You're Mis' Field."

"I'm Jean Field's mother."

"What you want with me?" asked Mariana again.

"She told me to tell you that Mr. Dixon ain't to blame for anything that happened. He never come near her."

All the hoarded passion of years leapt up in Marianna's next words.

"Who—who was it? Who was it, Mis' Field?"

The bent figure of the other shrank back under the gloom of the orchard boughs. When she spoke, so slow, so impersonal was her voice that it was as though a ghost were speaking.

"The man who did it—if you want to know—is dead and buried. It was—Mis' Fox's husband."

Mariana opened her lips, but no sound came. She swayed back and forth, a blind, dumb thing. The odor of the pennyroyal was like a blow struck in the dark.

"Mis' Dixon." The ghost was speaking again. "She's dead, she's dead. She died last night."

The apple trees, row after row, swam away in a surging tide of mist. They swam back again, little, black, fast. The lane was bare.

"O God!" cried Mariana. "I'll take him back. I'll forgive him."

Ghosts (1934)

A book may give up ghosts;
A doubled music there—
One from the page, one from the dust—
Leaps up in the air.
Colors, and ancient sounds, and roads,
And lonely gates—these, too;
A grave at the scent of a flower,
Crash down and let one through.

To an Indecent Novelist (1936)

You measure by a ditch, and not a height,
Make life no deeper than a country bin
One keeps for apples on a winter's night,
Thence prate the immaturities of sin.
You weigh by littles, by some cracked emprise.
Why not by that one thing a man has done,
In some vast hour, beneath hot, hating eyes,
When, hard against a wall, he fought and
     won?
The spirit still outwits the lagging flesh:
Cross but one lane, and you shall find again
That righteousness is older still than lust;
Strict loveliness of living find afresh,
Sound women, too, and reasonable men,
That not yet all the gentlefolk are dust.

Louise Clarkson Whitelock (1851-1928)

From her whimsical representations of flowers, fairies, and animals to her adult works that appeal to the human spirit, Whitelock's writing and lush illustrations (a few of which we have included here) mark her as a careful observer not only of the nature that surrounded her, but also of human nature as she saw it. She published under the name L. Clarkson for more than twenty years before marrying lawyer and city politician George Whitelock in 1895, and continued to publish after her marriage. Whitelock was a talented artist and raised her daughter, Roberta, to be an illustrator in her footsteps. Her most notable works were collections of self-illustrated poems for children from the perspective of personified flowers and talking baby animals. She also wrote poems and short stories for adults, sometimes with illustrations of their own.

Whitelock's poetics focused primarily on natural imagery, evidenced by both the trio of children's poems and her more mature "Dirge" included here. However, her works also touch on religious and domestic themes. In "The Rag Fair," she describes the transience of human life at every age, and the promise and mystery of redemption. "Love's House," meanwhile, tells the story of an ideal True Woman struggling to retain her once-perfect home and marriage. In all her works, Whitelock shows masterful command of language and voice, and addresses themes that limn her perspective on both the human and natural world.

Whitelock was a Maryland native and founding member of the WLCB. A signatory on the club's constitution, which was organized in March of 1890, Whitelock remained a member of the club from its inception throughout the first decade of the twentieth century. Throughout her tenure, she chaired several committees and served as a Club officer. —C. Love and M. Nolan

The Rag Fair: A Twilight Reverie (1879)

I have read somewhere of a marvelous
    "Rag Fair"[1]
For Spiritual Garments, to be found
In some far, unknown region, on the bound
Of the angel-forsaken Eden, where
Our fall hath shamed our souls from
    standing bare
Before the god of Self, wise in their sin;
And so, for decency, we clothe them in
Vestments of Earth which Time filches away
And keeps in hiding 'till some better day.

What a wonderful collection it would be,
And how it would amaze,
If one could see in some grim place,
Gathered together for eternity,
The cast-off raiment that men's souls have
    worn
To hide their barren want; or to adorn
Their shapely fullness; or belie their ill
In the sheep's-clothing made for wolf-
    wear still!
There are tiny robes, so purely white,
Of our child-simplicity, that might
Have screened us longer from the touch
Of sin, and covered us from much
Coldness and shame, had we not thrown

Them off, in our joy, as being out-grown.
  Out-grown! O Children!
    So ready to lose
    Your likeness to angels!
      So quick to choose
The world's hard mask! Be mother-hands
  stout
To hold their infancy about
Those unsoiled hearts; for never a stain
Of passing evil rubs off again.

There are boyish frocks that were crimson
  when
We stood sturdy in them and said we
    were "men;"
But they faded to grey, and were dropt.
    And there
Is youth's many-colored cloak, once fair
As Joseph's, but dyed with the fatal stain
Of the blood of our lamb of innocence slain.
And there is the mail of a hero's pride,
Rusted and shattered and gaping wide

Louise Clarkson Whitelock, frontispiece to "The Rag Fair," in *The Rag Fair and Other Reveries* (Philadelphia: F. W. Robinson, 1878).

Where the arrows pierced; and broken
and bent
Where the hard blows fell making many
a rent.
Near by is the mantle of withered prime,
Filthy and worn with abuse and time;
It scantily clad the shivering soul
That blamed the world for each stain and
hole.

There, too, is the lover's knot of blue,
That bound us fast, and seemed as true
As God; but we watched the color fade
Into the ghostly ashen shade
Of death. And into that Fair are tossed
All those marvelous things which are lost:
Shreds of bright hopes, too early torn;
Remnants of joys too soon forlorn;
Rags of those promises we thought
Into the "silver cord" were wrought;
Draggled ambitions, remembered not;
Sack-cloths of penitence, long forgot:

Tattered bits of the brave self-trust,
Drawn round us when we sprang from
the dust
Of a confidence betrayed and cast
Under foot. And there we'll touch at last
The shroud of doubt in which, some night,
The angel, Faith, lay hid from sight;
And know how 'twas made on the loom
of sin,
Its woof—unbelief—woven out and in
With the tangled warp of bitter strife
'Gainst Him who gave our angel life.

And banished there are the locked-up
cerements
Of lost, lost loves (not as cast-off garments
Thrust into dim corners of the Fair,—

For they are more than perishing wear,)
By memory carefully laid upon shelves,
Identified only by God and ourselves,
Each tied with the harmless bit of crape
That once, to our sad eyes, seemed to drape
The whole of the beautiful, glad world:—
Perhaps, at first, we would scarcely know
The shrunken sign of our shrunken woe.

Truly 'twould be a ghostly array!
They clothed us once but were "clutched
away
By the fingers" of Fates; or rent one day
By the thorns of disaster; or flung aside
In some sharp moment of wounded pride,
When apish Envy heard their gloss
Was wearing off. Or worse, our loss
May have been but a pitiful decay,—
A dropping off—a falling away
In tatters.—So, silently, one by one
They are left, and forgot. And the Life
goes on:—
Goes on exulting towards its goal;
For the ties of the earth cannot bind the Soul.
And when the horizon grows low and wide,
And near and plain seems the other side,
Naught follows the Soul from the world
over past,
But its own swift shadow, downward cast.

How strange to stand
In that strange land,
And hold these wretched fragments in
our hand!
How we would search and linger by the
heap,
Too sore to smile, too curious to weep;—
We'd lift each one up reverently, and try
To recognize it, pass it slowly by,
Sighing as much with wonder as with pain:

So strange 'twould be to meet spent lives
    again—
To shake hands with ourselves in long
    lost places—
Feeling half stranger with our own old faces.
'Twould be like lifting up the coffin-lid
To peer at some dead neighbor, so long hid
We scarcely think it worth our being shocked,
But look,—because the casket is unlocked.

    God help us all
    As these earth-robes fall!
For we know not what vestures we shall wear
The next:—whether a purple, princely gown
Of high success; or ease, like robes of down;
Or harsh denials, like the camel's hair
The Prophet wore; or sable weeds of grief;
Or smooth white burial robes of last relief.

    We cannot know.
    We breathe below
The purer air of heavenly things made plain:
    And what we choose,
    And what we lose,
Are given or taken by hands unshaken
By mere desires; and when our souls awaken
    The next glad dawn,
    They will sing on,
Through all eternity, the wondrous strain:—
"*We are the redeemed; for we are they*
    which came out of great tribulation.
    We have washed our robes and made
    them white in the Lamb's blood."

God help us all!—He knows "our righ-
    teousness
Is but as filthy rags," yet none the less
Has promised, as through earthly mire
    we toil,
To wash us at the last from every soil.
Yet scarce we stop, as our garments drop,

To ponder on the beauty of the thought,
That, with all changing, we are never brought
To utter nakedness; even when we
Put off the passion of mortality.

Believing God will put us on the peace
Of immortality, we smooth each crease
From out our wrinkled fame; we patch
    our pride
And darn our reputation—our best side
Turned outward, but our seams and
    stains concealed
From all but Christ—to whom all is
    revealed;—
By whom our rags are purged, and we are
    healed.

So let us hope,
Through fears that grope,
Our souls, when poising on the outer brink
Of this humanity, to catch some link
Between all earthly joys and heavenly bliss,
May find in some far limbo such as this
The fairest garments they have ever worn:—
The seamless robes that cruel hands have torn;
The fadeless vestures of unchanging love,
Folded within God's care, and laid above
Our reach, where moth of jealousy, or rust
Of doubt cannot corrupt. Though gath-
    ering dust
Of long years lies upon them, we will take
Them from their shelves when we are
    risen, and shake
Earth's dimness from their shining
    threads, and press
Them 'neath the new robe of Christ's
    Righteousness;
For they no more have trailed their hems
    below,
But long ago were washed as white as snow.

Dear Little Stay-At-Home (1879)

Blue Bird:—
Little Lily of the Valley,[2]
Living up your dark green alley,
Half the flowers do not know
You are pretty. If you go
Out some morning, you will meet
Pansy, who will call you sweet;
Blue-bell, who will want to play;
Rose-bud, who will beg you stay,
Little Lily, will you come?—
  "Thank you, I will stay at home."

Little Lily of the Valley,
I will take you riding; shall I?
Home is very nice and green;
But you never can be seen.
If you'll come and fly with me
All the merry flowers will see
You have hair like gold, and eyes
Bright and blue as summer skies;
Little Lily do not fear—
  "Thank you, I am happier here."

Little Lily of the Valley,
All the flowers will have a ballet
In the moon-light, after 'while.
You are dressed in charming style;
Your short satin gown of white
Will be just the thing to-night.
All the birds will want a chance
To see so sweet a flower dance;—
I've a dew-drop for your head—
  "Thank you, but I'll be in bed."

Little Lily of the Valley,
I've no time to dilly-dally.
But you are too sweet and fair,
With your fleecy golden hair,

With your eyes of blue, to hide
In this corner. Come and ride
On my wings up to the sky;
To the very sun I'll fly;
I will take you to my nest—
  "Thank you, I like home the best."

Buttercup's Song (1881)

I'm called Little Buttercup—dear Little
    Buttercup,
S'pose everybody knows why,
It seems such a pity my friends in the city
Should call Little Buttercup shy.
So I've come up to show you I'm happy
    to know you;
I've dressed in my gay yellow gown,
And best satin bonnet, with dew-drops
    upon it,
Just fit for a visit to town.
I run the hills over, with daisies and clover;
I'm friend of the birds of the bees;
I've aunts and I've cousins, and beaux by
    the dozens;
I've plenty of fun if you please.
But call me your Buttercup,—dear Little
    Buttercup,
Roses and lilies and all:
And don't laugh at Buttercup,—poor
    Little Buttercup,
Come up to pay you a call.

Buttercup's Visit to Little Stay-At-Home (1881)

Buttercup:
"Little Lily-of-the-Valley,
Living up your dark green alley,
I've come to town this pleasant day
Just to ask you out to play.
Half the flowers do not know
Their city cousins. If you'll go

BUTTERCUP'S VISIT TO LITTLE STAY-AT-HOME.

Buttercup:—"Little Lily-of-the-Valley,
Living up your dark green alley.
I've come to town this pleasant day
Just to ask you out to play.
Half the flowers do not know
Their city cousins. If you'll go

Louise Clarkson Whitelock, *Buttercup's Visit to Little Stay-at-Home* (New York, E.P. Dutton & Company, 1881), p. 5. Courtesy of the Baldwin Library of Historical Children's Literature, Special and Area Studies Collections, George A. Smathers Libraries, University of Florida.").

Out this morning, you will see
Daisy, dancing merrily;
Blue-bell, who will nod to meet you;
Clover, who will smile to greet you;
Little Lily will you come?—
     "*Thank you, I must stay at home.*"

Pretty Lily-of-the-Valley,
I will take you riding, shall I?
Home is very nice and green,
But you never can be seen.
Meadow-lark is nearly dying
For a chance to take you flying.
I have ridden on his wings:—
Fast he flies and loud he sings.
If you'll come and fly with me
All the bonny birds can see
You have hair like gold, and eyes
Bright and blue as summer skies.
Little Lily, do not fear—
     "*Thank you, I am happier here.*"

Little Lily-of-the-Valley,
All the flowers will have a ballet
In the moon-light after 'while:
You are dressed in charming style;
Your short satin gown of white
Would be just the thing to-night.
Every one will have a chance
To see so sweet a flower dance.
Why, our gayest butterfly
Will do naught but sit and sigh,
Because you're such a stay-at-home.
Do for once be coaxed to come:
I've a moon-beam for your head—
     "*Thank you, but I'll be in bed.*"

Stupid Lily-of-the-Valley!
I've no time to dilly-dally,
Telling you that you're too fair,

With your fleecy golden hair,
With your eyes of blue to hide
In this corner.—P'raps it's pride.
P'raps you think a City Lily
Has a right to be so silly!
Please to hand my yellow bonnet;
I shall say "good-day" and don it.
Once more—will you leave your nest?
     "*Thank you, I like home the best.*"

A Dirge (1885)

Little Violet is dead!
Lilies, let your tears be shed;
Breathe the perfume of your sighs
Over her fast-shut blue eyes.
She of all was dearest, best;
Drop your tears upon her breast.

Little Violet is dead!
Never more her pretty head
Will be lifted from the grass,
Just to nod if you should pass.
Mark the spot with reverent tread;
Weep for her, for she is dead.

Little Violet is gone!
Since the early summer's dawn
She was with us on the hill;
She was with us by the rill;
Now the winter skies are wan,
And little Violet is gone.

Little Violet is dead!
Storm, ye wild clouds overhead;
Mourn, O North-Wind, all the day;
Sigh, O South-Wind, far away.
East-Wind, West-Wind, moan your pain;
She will never come again.

Grieve, ye spirits of the air;

Never more she claims your care
Never more in sun or shade
Will she greet you in the glade.
Hover round her snowy bed:
Little Violet is dead.

From "Love's House"[3] (1895)

Part I of "Love's House," not included here, begins ten years prior to Part II, as Marion Trust prepares to marry the wealthy Chester Fairfax. The two are mutually enamored of one another, and Marion tells Muriel, her cousin and foster sister, of her ideal relationship. Muriel is distraught when Marion moves into her new mansion, the House Beautiful, with her husband, but ends up moving in with the couple years later, when she is eighteen, after the death of her mother. Chester's mother, the selfish and unkind Mrs. Fairfax, plants the seed of jealousy in Marion by suggesting the folly of inviting a younger, more beautiful woman to live with them.

Part II

Summer

The Coming of the Shadow

There comes a time to each of us to stand under the zenith of our happiness, and know that for the rest of life's journey the sun of our love and joy must move towards its final setting. But Marion Fairfax was not afraid of the waning of her sun. She had been a half-score years married, and still there had passed no dimness over the face of her wedded bliss. Once Chester was struck with the uplifted look in her shining eyes.

"Dear Marion," he said, "are you so happy?" And she answered, simply, "If there is perfect happiness in this world, it is mine."

Chester Fairfax looked wistfully at his wife. Long afterwards she recalled that strange look, at the time not noticed. But presently something began to steal across the horizon which she did notice, wondering vaguely what it could portend. It was a tiny shadow, like "the cloud the size of a man's hand,"[4] which sometimes foretells fearful storms. She could not make out from the dim outline of this Shadow what might be the shape of the thing which caused it. It was not only a faint gloom which the Shadow cast, there was a chill that crept with it into the House Beautiful.[5] Chester's mother had stolen into his Eden, and whispered,—

"Muriel ought not to be here. She is too fascinating. She throws your wife into the shade. You will grow tired of Marion, who is no longer young or beautiful."

Perhaps it was the evil wish in her that fathered the thought. Perhaps she was weary of Marion's sway and her happiness. Perhaps it soured her that she was no longer first with any one, and she grudged the other woman her great content. And Muriel,—what did she whisper to Muriel?

Muriel grew pensive, distrait. Chester became awkward, absent-minded, uncomfortable. When they sat together reading, talking, even laughing, as was their wont, Marion became conscious of a constraint. Her own voice was the only one that sounded natural; and once or twice she surprised a look between her husband and Muriel for which she had no name. It was a look, shame-faced, troubled, uneasy, on her husband's part; on the young girl's it was timid, deprecating, frightened, appealing.

Muriel had been several years with them, and the intimate companionship of the three had never suggested embarrassment either to the generous mind of Marion or the innocent heart of Muriel. Chester had been frankly unconscious of any false position until his mother spoke. They had been just husband and wife, brother and sister; and nothing could have been less constrained or self-conscious than their intercourse. Yet, with the coming of that nameless Shadow which Marion Fairfax discerned, there fell a sense of estrangement upon them all. Muriel was dropping into that nervous and morbid state of health which so often overwhelms young girls without any apparent cause, excepting the over-sensitiveness of their own growing womanhood. Marion tried once or twice to win the confidence which never before had failed her; but Muriel only broke into hysterical weeping, declaring that nothing ailed her excepting nervousness. Then Marion proposed that they should go to Switzerland for a change of air and scene. Whatever ailed her two dear ones,—and in a dozen years of married life it must not be supposed they had not ailed more than once,—the invigorating Alpine atmosphere and the interest of new scenes would soon restore them. So they hired a chalet by Lake Thun, where they dreamed away the summer, and Marion fondly hoped that her husband's demeanor was losing something of its new moodiness and irritability; that the blue lines under Muriel's wistful eyes were less marked. She was conscious that the Shadow had not quite disappeared, but as yet its significance was not defined.

The woman had a loyal heart that knew not suspicion, and when the revelation came it was like a flash of lightning across a clear and cloudless sky.

One evening toward sunset, when the waters of the placid lake lay beneath the veranda of their villa, illumined by a pink glow, as though sprinkled by the gods with fire and rose leaves, Marion bethought herself, sitting there with the exquisite rapture of roseate color all about her, that she would go in search of Chester and Muriel, that they might all row into the heart of the sunset in their tiny shell boat. Entering the large living-room from the veranda, she came upon the two sitting quite still in the half-light of the room. Chester's attitude was drooping, absorbed, melancholy. His eyes were fixed introspectively upon space, and he seemed, in one of his absent-minded moods, to be taking no notice whatever of Muriel by his side. She sat quite close to him, upon a low seat of some sort, and her form leaned lightly against him, with one girlish arm thrown, as if unconsciously, across his knee. Her beautiful gray eyes, too, were fixed as if in profound thought; but there was a rapt unconsciousness of self about her that was startling. Moreover, the attitude struck Marion at once as one which she had never seen. In all the years of brotherly affection, there had never been this suggestion—Of what was it a suggestion? She stood perfectly still in the doorway, with some of the surprise she felt depicted on her frank face.

"Well," said Chester, turning his eyes slowly outward from their introspection, "what is it, Marion?"

He seemed to be rousing himself with an effort. For an instant or two Muriel did not stir. Then she rose deliberately and began to move away with a slow, reluctant sort of motion, which would have struck Marion as odd if she had not been absorbed in the grouping, as she had surprised it. She spoke quietly:

"The evening is so fine, I had thought you and Muriel—"

Her voice died away. She was watching Muriel, who seemed to be waiting before a closed door, as if to gather what was being said before she opened it.

The girl's head was turned back, and she looked fixedly at the husband and wife.

"I have not seen Muriel this afternoon," said Chester, in a dull, monotonous voice.

"Not—seen—Muriel? Why, Chester—" Marion put out her hand and caught hold of the table.—"she was here when I came in—she is here yet—"

She fastened her eyes, which had grown strained, upon the figure which seemed to return her gaze with a look at once startled and imploring. Then it quietly disappeared through the door-way.

Marion stood another second, and then her limbs tottered under her, and she collapsed into her husband's arms, who had sprung up in alarm at her altered face.

"What is it, dearest? Why do you look so? You are ill, Marion. Let me get you some water." She let him go, sitting passively in the chair which he had placed for her, trying to collect herself, trying to think.

What did it all mean?

He had not seen Muriel—Muriel who was with him in that strange attitude when she entered—who had not jumped up and run from her but had, on the contrary, removed herself with marked deliberation from the room. Could Chester have been asleep and the girl playing some trick upon him?

Her husband returned with the water, which she drank feverishly, avoiding his anxious eyes.

"What could have given you such a turn?" he asked, with tender solicitude. "Perhaps you were walking too long in the sun this morning."

"Perhaps," she answered; "but I thought I saw Muriel when I came in."

"No, she has not been here. I think she went rowing with the Vintons this afternoon."

Marion leaned her head back and closed her eyes. She must solve this mystery, but she must not let her husband know what she had seen. After awhile she excused herself, saying that she felt weary and would retire. Shut up in her own apartment, she began to think; and with the preternatural insight of an intuitive woman, the truth manifested itself to her. She knew now, in that lightning-flash from the unclouded sky of which I have spoken, the meaning of the Shadow which had come to overwhelm her. She knew now why her husband was absorbed, shame-faced, uncomfortable; why Muriel, her own little Muriel whom she so loved, was nervous, depressed, and like one pursued by a nameless fear. Her husband's mother had come between them with that dark thought of a dangerous love. He was afraid of loving Muriel. And Muriel was afraid of waking that love. The dark thought was ever with them. It might even be that a fugitive love would grow out of' that fear. Perhaps he had come to love Muriel with what would have been a high and holy love but for her presence, and he carried with him, as a haunting reproach, the constant thought of the young girl. It was the intensity of this thought which Marion had perceived with that power of metaphysical perception which was hers. She was so en rapport with her husband, that his thoughts had always been apparent to her in the ordinary methods of mind-reading, which we call being in sympathy; but never before had the thought of any human being been so materialized before her eyes, and she shrank from the terrible possibilities of such a perception as from the insidious power of some dreadful apparition.

How could she avoid this manifestation? How could she warn her husband that the secret vision of his innermost being was, by right of their hitherto perfect accord, spread out before her as a thing visible to the natural eye? He must never know what she suspected. Nay, was it not, rather, he must never suspect what she knew?

Elizabeth Turner Graham (1837-1920)

Elizabeth Turner Graham, for all her impact on Baltimore history and society, has remained unrecognized as a poet. She was called the "Mother of Women's Clubs in Maryland" by fellow club member Emily Lantz due to her longtime presidency of the Lend-a-Hand Club of Mt. Washington, the first women's club in Maryland, which combined literary and philanthropic activities. In addition to her work for the Lend-a-Hand Club, Graham was a charter member of the Woman's Literary Club of Baltimore, and remained intermittently involved with the Club's literary committees all her life.

The eldest sister of eminent artist and muralist Charles Yardley Turner, Graham exhibited her own artistic ability in her two illustrated companion volumes of poetry, *Buttercups and Daisies: Songs of a Summer* and *Holly and Mistletoe: Songs Across the Snow*. Both were published under the initials "E. T. G.," indicating Graham's desire to obscure her gender identity, perhaps, or perhaps her identity as a poet.

We include *Buttercups and Daisies* here in its entirety. Even without the accompanying illustrations, Graham's poetry stands well on its own. Alternating between children's poetry and poetry that is religious or even sexual in tone, the most constant element in her work is the observation of nature. Graham saw all the world as truly alive. In her poetry, she personifies plants and animals, the sun and the moon, as they move with the passing year. Her poetry blurs the line between humanity and nature and urges her readers to examine the outside world anew. —H. Flynn

Buttercups and Daisies: Songs of a Summer (1884)

Buttercups and Daisies,
Oh, you pretty Flowers!
Coming with the Spring time,
To tell of sunny hours!

Welcome, yellow Buttercups!
Welcome, Daisies white!
You are to my spirit
Both beautiful and bright.

Buttercups

Oh, saucy little Buttercups,
    Upon your yellow faces
I see a world of happiness,
    Which youth alone embraces.

You bring to mind a tiny elf,
    With locks of golden yellow,
And eyes of merry chestnut brown.
    A rogueish little fellow!

Again I clasp his tiny hand
    Filled full of meadow grasses,
With Daisies and forget-me-nots
    For happy lads and lassies;

And in the other, wet with dew,
    Held fast miser's treasure,
Are Buttercups, for "Mamma's" chin,
    Her love of wealth to measure.

Again I feel his dainty kiss
    And hear his shout of laughter,
When "Mamma's" chin reflects the gold
    Which shall be hers hereafter.

Poor, paltry pelf. Ah, buttercups,
    Your gold, undimmed by weeping,
Outweighs to-day all worldly wealth,
    Which sordid hearts are keeping.

You hold a charm wealth cannot buy,
    You gild this world of sorrow
With baby smiles and baby wiles,
    Though they be gone to-morrow.

What, though he is a bearded man
    With locks of tawny yellow?
From out the Past, sweet, Buttercups,
    He comes, a little fellow!

Earth's Wedding

Our sweet brown Earth is a bride to-day
    Her lover bold? Tis the Sun!
In the mighty tones of a midnight storm
    He shouted—"Make way! I come!
"
Long months have passed since with
    white lips mute,
    And pale face turned to the sky,
Her bare arms stretched to the wind and
    rain,
    She has waited his coming night.

To-day has shown her his heart of gold,
    And snapped her bonds in twain,
The brooks leap forth, and the South-wind
    cries,
    "Earth's lover has come again!"

Heralds of summer proclaim the day,
    And virgins, in snowy white,
Swing jewelled censers of rare perfume
    Along his path of light!

Plumèd singers from out the wood,
—Fair choristers in the throng—
With sweet hosannas and glad amens,
Fill the whole world with song!

There are scents and sounds of a thou-
sand things,
Which only to weddings belong,
From the first sweet breath of arbutus flowers,
To the wood-robin's cheery song!

The gnarlèd boughs of the apple trees
Fill their rosy cups with wine,
Which the breezes toss, in delirious joy,
At the feet of Father Time!

Oh, would you could see—with your
city eyes—
The robe of this fair Queen
And the garlands, woven by April showers,
Of white and pink and green!

Its shimmering folds are 'broidered o'er
With tracings of purest gold,
Bud and blossom, in full relief,
As the High Priest's was of old!

A girdle of Jonquils is round her waist,
Clasped close by violets sweet,
And fringes of Valley-Lilies swing
Their silvery bells at her feet.

A misty veil from the far off hills
Hangs over her radiant face,
Which only a lover's hand should lift,
For a lover's kiss give place!

Waking the Daisy

All hail to thee, sleepy-eyed Daisy!
The long night of Winter is gone;

'Tis only the old and the lazy
Who linger thus after the dawn!

Dame March has been shaking thy cradle,
And Bobolink calling thy name,
While Daffodil, gay in his jacket,
And Snowdrop, are doing the same.

A bevy of gentle wild flowers
Now gladden the Earth with their grace,
And April, with sweetest of showers,
Has freshened her beautiful face!

'Tis May-day! Why then dost thou tarry?
Thou surely belong'st to the Spring!
And lovers, forbidden to marry,
Their troubles to thee ever bring!

Wake up, sleepy Daisy, I pray thee!
For 'ere thou can'st fashion a dress,
Queen Rose will be out in the Garden
Thyself in her service to press.

Then loiter not Sweetest, my Daisy,
Ope' quickly thy brown golden eye;
The Meadow-Lark sings of thy coming,
And Robin makes loyal reply!

Ah, Daisy! my sleepy-eyed beauty,
'Tis well thou art waking at last,
For Tulips take ever Love's forfeit—
A kiss for the present and past!

Children of the Sun

Fling open the portals of Summer!
For, blindly groping their way,
Are myriads of flower-buds coming
To answer the call of May!

Coming to greet the sunshine,
  Coming to gladden the Earth,
A million of rose-buds and lilies
  Hurrying forward to birth!

Ringing the sweetest of changes
  On bells of a chiming so fine,
That only the angels can hear them
  With senses and feeling divine!

Groping, and climbing, and clinging,
  With fingers so close to her heart,
That Mother Earth, weary of coaxing,
  Bids all the dear children depart.

Content, so she hold but one fibre
  Safe down in her dear loving breast,
To see them turn upward their faces
  To him who has broken their rest.

His kisses lie warm on her bosom,
  She thrills with his latest caress;
Ah, Love! thou hast ever the power
  In darkest of moments to bless!

Summer Thyme and Clover

Of all bonny birds which Spring
  Calls forth with Lark and Plover,
The sweetest wake in beds of Thyme
  And blooming fields of Clover!
They mind me of a sunny spot,
  Where Maple boughs bend over,
And shake their laughing shadows down
  To dance amid the Clover!

'Twas there, with drowsy hum, the bees
  Delighted loved to hover,
Or, droning through the sultry air,
  Fell fast asleep in Clover!

Not far away a tiny brook
  Crept out from under cover,
And, glancing shyly, went its way
  With songs for Thyme and Clover!

But further on the waters grew
  Into a dashing rover,
And wooed the Lilies, tall and fair,
  As once he wooed the Clover!

Ah, bonny Brook and scented Thyme,
  A little maid and lover
Dreamed out the sweetest dreams of life
  With you among the Clover!

Sad years have come and gone since then
  And Love's young dream is over;
The Brook still woes the Lilies fair—
  But faded is the Clover!

Fair Month of June

The hills are white,
    Oh, Summer-time!
With snowy Ox-eyed Daisies,
  And Buttercup,
  With dew filled up,
Her golden vase upraises.

The year moves on,
    Oh, Summer-Time!
Life's joys are now the fleetest;
  And 'neath thy moon,
  Fair month of June,
Are lover's vows the sweetest.

Love's Message

Oh, sweet June Roses,
    Softly blow

Your breath with perfume laden,
    Across the vale,
    Where, tall and pale,
Smiles a sad love-lorn maiden.

Oh, sweet June Roses,
        Say to her,
With kisses soft and tender,
    That, though he stray,
    Love will one day
His truest homage render!

And, sweet June Roses
        For her sake,
All crimson buds, when blowing,
    Twixt you and me
    A pledge shall be
Of perfect Love's own showing.

Mid-Summer

July's sultry sun doth beat
June's sweet roses to my feet;
But the Lilies, fair and cool,
Stately stand within the pool,
Ringing all their silvery bells,
'Till the torrid ether tells,
How the harvest draweth near
Of another perfect year!

Wheat and rye and oats and corn,
Ripened, woo the reaper's horn,
Where the Clover bends its head
O'er the Daisy's grass-grown bed,
And for many a weary mile
Buttercup now fails to smile!
Only fragrant Lilies wait
At the Summer's golden gate!

August Noon

Oh, burning heat!
    No City's street
Shall tempt my feet to roam;
    Right here I'll lie,
    Cool waters by.
Though far from friends and home,
    My soul, awake,
    Its thirst shall slake,
Where Water-lilies drift,
    And hills, most fair,
    Through purest air
Their frontlets ever lift!

Waiting

How shall I know of thy coming,
    My Beautiful! My Fate!
As, adrift with the Water-Lilies,
    I idly dream and wait?

Wilt thou come to my soul, Belovèd,
    As the subtle rich perfume,
Of the passionate Water-Lilies,
    Floats to the heart of noon?

Wilt thou come, as the rhythmic pulsing
    Of a strange resistless tide?
Wilt thou tear me from the Lilies,
    And bind me to thy side?

Oh, Queen of my long fair Summer,
    My Beautiful! My Fate!
Adrift with the Water-Lilies,
    I idly dream and wait!

"Au Revoir!"

Oh, glad bright Summer! On yon hills,
    I see the Autumn flame,
And in my ear the cricket trills
    His melancholy strain!

Elizabeth Turner Graham, page spread from *Buttercups and Daisies* (Baltimore: D. W. Glass & Co., 1884). Special Collections and University Archives, University of Maryland Libraries.

The heavens have lost their tender blue,
　　The air its rich perfume,
Oh, Summer, are thy days so few,
　　Thy going hence so soon?

Thy coming brought me such delight,
　　Such tender hopes and fears.
If go thou must, flit forth at night,
　　I am too glad for tears!

Beside me blooms the Golden-rod,
　　The red, red Rose is dead;
And tired Lilies weary lie

Upon their leaf-strewn bed.

But this is what they seem to say:
　　"Sweet-heart, we'll come again,
When wintry winds have blown away
　　The dead leaves and the rain!"

So, I will watch in wait for thee,
　　And say this o'er and o'er:
"Such happy days must come again!
　　Sweet Summer, Au Revoir!"

Maud Graham Early (1842-1905)

Born in 1842, Maud Graham Early was one of the original members of the Women's Literary Club of Baltimore and served as a member of the Board of Managers during the 1904-1905 season. Her involvement in the Club subsequently led to her participation in several other clubs, including the Audubon Society and the American Folklore Society. Her association with the Folklore Society influenced some of the work that she published, including a piece included in this section, "The Tale of the Wild Cat: A Child's Game."

This piece was published in the journal *American Folklore Society* in 1897 and is a light yet educational article designed for children to draw along as the story of a man who built a house is read aloud to them; the end result should be a wildcat. Early's documentation of a game played by a mother with her child is an example of how she documents domestic practice as a form of "folklore," a cultural practice that is worthy of study.

We also include a more scholarly essay by Early, "Three Queens of Ancient Egypt," which appeared in the Washington, DC-based *Southern Literary Messenger* in June 1895. (This Messenger was a revival of the more famous magazine of the same name based in Richmond, VA in the early nineteenth century.) This work highlights the historical contributions of three women who held positions of power in Ancient Egypt—namely, Queens Nefertari, Hatasu, and Tiye. drawing connections to what Early considers to be the modern woman of 1895: a woman of faith, maternal instinct, and feminine power. Early, it should be noted, relies heavily on the research of another early female historian, Amelia Edwards, author of *Pharaohs Fellas and Explorers* (1891).

Though these two selections differ greatly in content and approach, they reflect the overarching mission of Early to educate her readers. Early served the WLCB and the general public as an observer of both humankind in the United States as well as womankind throughout time and place. "Three Queens" draws connections to how women have and have not changed through the centuries, and aims to draw a conclusion on woman's capabilities and purpose. "The Tale of the Wild Cat," meanwhile, gives insight into the perspective of a maternal figure who must observe, entertain, and educate her children through activities like drawing and play. —S. Johnson and J. Fury

Three Queens of Ancient Egypt

The date of my study of Egyptian history is 1700 BC, the 18th dynasty, about the time the patriarch Jacob came down to Egypt to meet his long lost son Joseph, and to settle in the land of Goshen.[1]

The greatest debt we owe the biographer and the novelist is the extension of our sympathies, and I have chosen this dynasty for my subject, because in it there were three Queens who are interesting as the "eternally womanly" always is, and are typical women. Let us make a short study of these women, and consider them from the standpoint of their environment, and judge them by *their* standards, very different from ours.

Aahmes[2] and his consort Nefert-Ari begin the 18th dynasty. From this time the monuments afford us clear and intelligible history. They celebrate in prose and poetry the glory and splendor of their authors.

King Aahmes defeated the foreign kings (the Hyksos), drove them out of Egypt and as far as the Phoenician town of Sherobian. He protected his frontiers and restored peace and order; he united the two kingdoms of Egypt, and at last had leisure to prove his gratitude to the gods by rebuilding and enlarging the temples, which had fallen into decay. He reopened quarries and built great temples in Thebes[3] and in Memphis.[4] The building of an Egyptian temple was the work of centuries. It is the rock tablets of Massurah that have preserved his name, and that of his wife Nefert-Ari-Aahmes. This queen lived 3600 years ago. Is it possible to bridge that time and see a real woman?

Do the patriarchs seem real to us? Do we know Abraham, the friend of God, or the blameless Isaac, or the wily Jacob? We do realize they once walked this earth, "were men of like passions" with ourselves, because we learned of them at our mother's knee. The descendants of these men, their children, and grand-children were settling themselves in Egypt while Queen Nefert-Ari lived. How strange it would have seemed to this famous queen to know that these insignificant foreigners would live and influence men's minds for thousands of years, while until the last twenty years she was "unknown to history."

It is only since the great discovery of Champollion[5] that we can read the letters on the monuments, and have learned something of this contemporary of Jacob and Joseph. In the rock chambers of the Theban Necropolis[6] the name of this queen has been found. Long after her death this great ancestress of the New Empire was honored as a manifestation of Hathor. Her image was placed beside those of Eternal Inhabitants of Heaven. She sits enthroned at the head of the Pharoahenic pairs and before all the children of her royal race, as the revered mother of the 18th dynasty. She is also represented as the chief priestess of the Tutelary God of Thebes.[7] When her husband died she was regent until her son Amenhotep I,[8] was old enough to reign. About eight years ago the mummy of this queen was found in the Rock Chamber of Dier-el-Bahari.[9] It was seen she was a middle aged woman of medium height, of a white race. During her life she was much beloved, and after her death her worship was very popular at Thebes. Queen Nefert-Ari's mummy was brought down to the Nile to Cairo with the mummies of many of her peers, and is preserved there now. Miss Edwards[10] says "Never did history more strangely repeat itself than when the mummy of Ramases[11] and other ancient sovereigns of Egypt after more than 3000 years sepulture were borne down the Nile with funeral honors to lie in state in Cairo."

Queen Hatasu,[12] great grand daughter of Nefert-Ari is my next study. Her two brothers were both named Tehutimes. The elder was able to carry on the government, and the younger, a very young child at the time of his father's death, was left to the care of his brother and sister. Tehutimes II,[13] reigned for a time in conjunction with his sister and wife. He led one campaign against the southern people, and one against his neighbors, the Shunen. His mummy, as well as his brother's is now in the Bulak Museum.[14]

There are two accounts of this famous queen, one by Miss Edwards her admirer, and one by Brugsch-Bey,[15] taken from the Monuments. Like all biographies of strong characters, they differ widely. God alone knows the inwardness of any human soul. It is probable our friends know us better than our enemies or at least understand us better, and so I believe Miss Edwards comes nearer the truth as to Hatasu than any one else. I feel drawn to Queen Hatasu; she was so loved and hated, abused and admired. I often feel sorry for this royal lady as for others, even down to our own time. That which is all-important in our lives when we are young, and to those we love *always*, the romance of love and marriage, is entirely left out of their lives. We feel for each of us, there is *one*, and only *one*, appointed to complete our lives, the lover who is to share life with us, this is not for them. They had to marry for reasons of state, (as in Hatasu's case,) a near relation, for no reason of suitability in age or taste or even personal appearance. It must have been intensely uninteresting to say the least. So Hatasu had to marry her half brother—one whom she evidently despised. She was of royal lineage, her mother was a princess, while the mother of Tehutimes II, was a lady of noble, not royal birth, and the mother of Tehutimes III[16] was a slave woman. It is not strange Hatasu assumed the position of queen regnant, not queen consort. She was, and she felt herself of more consequence than her brothers. She reigned for

twenty-one years, most of the time alone. She had a friend named Semnut,[17] he was her scribe and historian. After his death she erected a monument to him in black granite. On the left shoulder of the statue to his honor is this short but significant inscription—"His ancestors are not found in writing." Semnut always speaks of Hatasu as "he" except in the possessive pronouns, thus he says "His majesty gave the two gilded obelisks to *her* father"— Hatasu, like the monarchs of the Stuarts line has an unerring taste it art, of which many proofs yet remain. But she will be famous as having sent forth a great expedition to Punt[18] or Arabia. She was undoubtedly the first person who ever had trees transplanted. We might call her the first nursery gardener. She delighted in the wonderful plants and animals her ships brought her from this famous voyage of discovery. She sent ships out, not to conquer her enemies, but to gain knowledge, to enrich Egypt by collecting the wonderful products of other lands, not to spread death and famine among her enemies, but for pleasure and glory of all lands. If this expedition, its idea, and its fulfilment were Hatasu's only distinction it would be enough for her fame, especially when we know almost to a certainty, that she made the canal on which her ships sailed from the Nile to the Red Sea, and so she was the scientific ancestress of De Lesseps.[19] Her reign was peaceful, and all the great resources of Egypt were employed in beautifying and rebuilding the temples.

If we could stand on the banks of the Nile, and see the temple Deir-el-Bahari which is now being excavated, we would observe and enjoy the picture of this voyage to Punt. The reception of the ships by the inhabitants of Punt. There is one especially noticeable. The queen of this country looks like the fat woman of the side show at a circus. The attitude of the monkeys and panthers are natural and interesting. The incense plants in pots and tubs, and the great store of precious gums. Mr. Edward Naville[20] is now making an excavation at the south wall of this temple, where are gigantic representations of Hatasu making offerings to the god Amon. Much has been effaced by Kuen-a-ten[21] and restored by Rameses II. On this wall Mr. Naville found a history of Hatasu attributing to her divine origin, her birth, her infancy, her Ka[22] (or double) when she was attended by the Hathors, and her enthronement by her father Amenhotep I. As an infant, youth and adult, she is dressed in male attire, though all the pronouns in the inscription refer to her as a woman. In the debris of this temple, they are finding numberless glass beads with the name Semnut (Hatasu's scribe) on them. It was Hatasu who built the greatest and largest obelisk, in seven months, cutting it from the quarry and bringing it to the temple. I had an idea the coloring of Egyptians temples was very crude, only primitive colors being used, but the pictures of the pillars of this temple in the beautiful book at the Peabody[23] called "Art in Egypt" shows the most exquisite blending of pale and harmonious shades. I envied the Egyptians their atmosphere which enabled them to decorate their temples with such colors we can only use in stained glass windows.

She set up two gilded obelisks in memory of her father, between which the Sun God Ra, rose and flooded with light the land of Egypt. The greatest historical monument of this reign in this temple of Deir-el-Bahari, on the western bank of the Nile opposite Karnak.[24] It is unlike any other temple in Egypt. It was approached by a long avenue of sphinxes, two hundred in number with two great obelisks at either end. It was built in stages or terraces and the natural formation of the ground was used. It penetrated far into the hills. The sanctuary was five hundred feet above the Nile. Great flights of stone steps led from chamber to chamber. The walls of this temple even yet retain their brilliant colors. Several portraits of Hatasu have been found here, one representing her as sucking the milk of the Goddess Hathor,[25] is often copied. There are several statues of Hatasu, but as yet her mummy has not been found though many articles belonging to her have been. Her throne chair, her cabinet, and her statue are in the museum at Berlin.[26] Religion was not a prominent characteristic of Queen Hatasu. Love of nature, and of art, with a sufficient amount of respect for the priesthood and for her ancestors satisfied her. She has left many monuments which tell us even now of one who loved beauty, and by making beautiful and noble things served the God of light who had opened her eyes and her mind to see the wondrous things of his creation.

After Hatasu, succeeded her brother Tehutimes III. Miss Edwards says he married the daughter of Hatasu, and this does not look as if, as is usually supposed, Hatasu hated him. He is called "the Alexander the Great of Egyptian History;" he reigned fifty-three years. He fought thirteen campaigns, and added countless wealth to the treasures of Egypt. Like his sister Hatasu he loved Nature and Art. It is recorded he took more pleasure in the strange birds and plants he collected than in any of his war contributions. An artist was employed to record these things in imperishable stone along with the list of victories. On one of these tablets he tells that his sister Hatasu had ill treated him in his youth, that she banished him to an unhealthy marsh and hid him from his people and the temples of his gods. After this reign there came three kings of whom there are many records on the monuments, but they are of little interest except to archaeologists, until we come to Amen Hotep III,[27] who reigned many years. This king chose for his wife a woman he loved, not a princess, not even an Egyptian, but the daughter of a king of Mesopotamia.

He met this princess Thi,[28] when on a hunting expedition, fell in love with her and, regardless of conventionalities, made her his Queen. She was of a Semitic race and from her Kuen-a-ten[29] (as the king called himself) learned to worship the sun's disk.

Amenhotep III succeeded his father, but from the first part of his reign the church, that is the priesthood, opposed him because his mother's influence was known to prevail.

This change of religion introduced by the son of Queen Thi, and Kuen-a-ten was almost as great as was the reformation of the sixteenth century.[30] In making common the religion of the Priests, by representing the Sun as the source of life, she destroyed their power and their secret. As the Sun is undoubtedly the source of life, how easy to impersonate the God, (as Queen Thi did), with his brilliant disk, and the immensely long rays taking up one side of the great temple. Instead of hiding under many forms, and mysterious ceremonies, the great and beneficent Creator was represented by the glorious sun. In the picture of this temple of the Sun many of the

Rays ended by the Cru-an-santy,[31] the emblem of life. It is a woman's place to judge by her own heart, and so reveal the love of the Creator and Father. No woman ever formulated a creed, or founded a religion, but it is woman, who has made religion live.

It has been noticed that all the ancient Egyptian temples, as well as Solomon's temple,[32] were oriented so that down the long aisle from the entrance to the sanctuary, on certain days in the year the rays of the sun would fall and light up the Holy of Holies. It does seem as if our God Himself, as he gave the direction for the tabernacle, and for the temple, permitted the use of this symbol of His being.

In the late explorations in the temple of Deir-el-Bahari has been found a beautiful altar, which is strange in this temple. The altar is like those at Heliopolis[33] where the ancient worship of Amon was prevalent. Altars of this description were used by Kuen-a-ten, at Tel-el-Amarna.[34] Perhaps the change in religious worship was, (as has been conjectured) a return to a primitive form of worship.

The disaffection of the priests reached such a point that the king built himself another capital in Middle Egypt, which is called at this day Tel-el-Amarna. The king erected a splendid temple in honor of the Sun god composed of many building in hard stone, and with little of the Egyptian characters about them. Near this temple he placed the palaces of his mother, and of the princesses, his sisters. There is a beautiful pictorial description of a visit of Queen Thi to the temple of the Sun. The king and queen are represented as going forth to meet the king's mother Thi, and to conduct her to the Sun temple. The picture is designated thus, "The Queen Mother Thi beholds her Sun Shadow." After his son's death this line of Pharaohs became extinct with the females of the 18th dynasty.

The chronology of this time and of this dynasty has been approximately fixed on astronomical grounds by Dr. Mahler[35] as being about 1400 BC.

Queen Thi was a religious and spiritual woman, and had great influence in her family. The offerings in these temples of the Sun often were flowers. It was in the reign of Queen Thi the Vocal Memnon,[36] the largest temples were built—the two great temples at Thebes. In the British Museum[37] there is a vase which belonged to Thi. The pottery of this age is the finest Egyptian pottery. The vase is of a pale grey color, with a refined and elegant design.

The monuments usually represent Queen

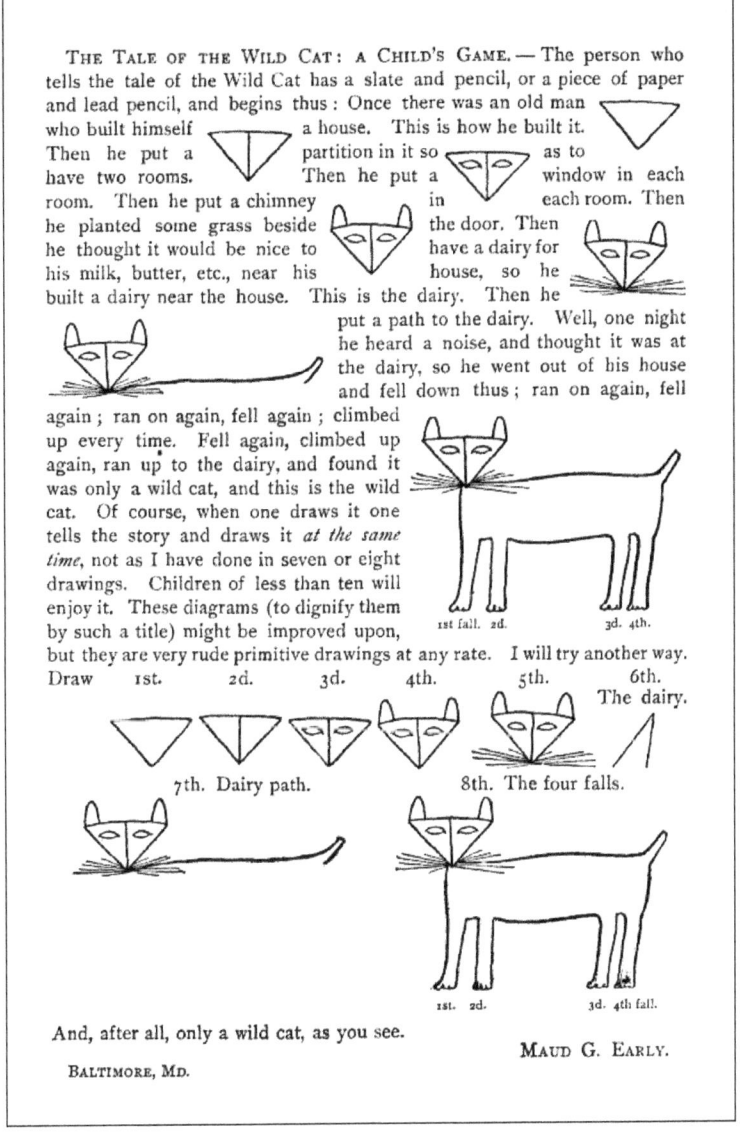

Maud Early, "The Tale of the Wild Cat," *Journal of American Folk-Lore*, Mar. 10, 1897, p. 80.

Thi as very ugly according to our ideas of beauty, and to the Egyptian standard. It is supposed they are caricatures made by her enemies. At the Peabody Library there is a magnificent book of "Art in Egypt" and in it is a portrait of Queen Thi, representing a refined and lovely woman as she probably was.

Queen Hatasu is represented as very handsome with a lovely dimple in her chin and the bright intelligent expression that she must have worn.

In these three queens we have three types of woman such as we see to this day, especially as they were women whose influence was not associated with physical charms as Cleopatra's[38] of Helen's.[39]

1st. *Queen Nefert-Ari,* the old-fashioned motherly woman always loved and remembered.

2nd. *Queen Hatasu,* the noble, genial, large hearted heroine, with courage and executive ability, as well as love of Art and Nature, and above all, of peace.

3rd. *Queen Thi,* the spiritual, loving and religious woman whose influence is eternal as it is an influence on the heart.

Nearly 3000 years ago, Queen Hatasu lived, great, good, and wise as a woman could be, before Christ came to "show a more excellent way." Her ability was recognized and appreciated, and her name is immortal, yet we talk as if it was only at the end of the nineteenth-century woman's right to rule was recognized. They have always ruled when they had the desire, or the ability, as Hatasu, or as Thi.

Grace Denio Litchfield (1849-1944)

Observation comes naturally to one with a restricted view. Grace Denio Litchfield was confined to her bed for much of her early life, and her talent for observation can be found in her poems and prose. Her chronic illness gave her a perspective on the world that few young people can grasp or even consider. She began writing in childhood and nurtured her talent into a prolific literary career.

Grace Denio Litchfield was an honorary member of the Woman's Literary Club of Baltimore, and became an active member of the Club during the season of 1914 to 1915. Born in New York City, she may have been guided to literary pursuits by her sister, Frances Litchfield Turnbull, who was

the first president of the Woman's Literary Club of Baltimore. Although Litchfield was born in the United States, she spent many years traveling in Europe, and her experience is reflected in her work. When she returned to America in 1888, she took up residence in Washington D.C. and published more than ever.

She was moved by the natural world, writing extensively on plant and animal life, but was struck too by the human experience, exploring deeply the topics of love and pain. Litchfield published six novels, several poetry collections, *and* countless works in periodicals, many of which were widely acclaimed by critics. One critic of the *New London Day* said of her 1884 novel *Only an Incident* that "the author's conceptions of character show no little keenness of observation and power of analysis," while another critic from The Academy London hailed her as, "a thoroughly original writer." Litchfield's poem "To a Hurt Child," included here, also appeared in *The Oxford Book of American Verse* alongside the work of acclaimed poets including Emily Dickinson.[1] Litchfield's varied output point to her versatile capabilities as a writer, and her popularity belies the scholarly stigma surrounding woman's poetry and sentimental fiction. It is a mystery how such a well-received author was so easily lost to history, but the recovery and dissemination of her work offer an opportunity for modern readers to understand the perspective of a nineteenth-century woman, who astutely observed and chronicled the world as it passed her by. —K. Shiber and M. Cronin

The Price I Paid for a Set of Ruskin (1884)

In days long past I bought a beautiful set of Ruskin with a book which I wrote myself. And I paid something besides,—more, I think, then any addition on earth is worth. I will put the case before you. Judge for yourselves.

My father was a widowed clergyman, with the clergyman's usual baker's dozen of children, of whom I was the oldest, so that I was wife to my father, mother to the children, and sister to all the parish, before I was well underway in my teens. As a family, our needs were naturally in the customary clerical disproportion to our means; and as to once, from our child-hood we were instructed to forgo those altogether.

"Be content with food and shelter and clothing," said my father, patting our cheeks with that gentle hand of his. "Do the robins have more?"

I felt that the robins had a great deal more. None of *us* ever looked so fresh and smart in our spring suits, or supplemented our scanty winter gleanings with scattered blessings of generous hands; while as to the roof above our heads, there was many a gallant oak-tree that warded the storms off better. However, the argument always silenced me at once, and cheered me, too, as did every word ever spoken by this dear voice; and when I looked up in my father's beautiful face and met his smile, I felt that, having him, I truly needed nothing more. Oh, how I idolized my father! Surely a braver, sweeter, lovelier soul never has been. He was now far past middle life, still working with tireless zest and unswerving devotion among the people who had summoned him to be their teacher some thirty years before. All the best days of his life, all the best powers of his mind had been given to their service; and now that he was gray and weary and spent with labor, he still had no thought of rest.

"My work is not as other men's work," he would say. "I may not take it up and lay it down at pleasure. God will take it from me when it is time."

And so he toiled on, growing every day more single-minded in purpose, more holy in character, more saint-like in expression. His life was a gospel of itself. But the strength of his soul outran that of his body, and he grew to look old and worn before his time, until at last comforts became necessaries instead of luxuries, and altogether ate up the paltry salary which from the first had been but a meager one even for our not overwealthy congregation.

"Surely, father," I suggested, "they might raise it a little now, if only in recognition of your long and faithful services."

"Nay, nay, Hester, my child," he replied, with his tender smile. "You forget that I am growing old and feeble, and am not worth as much to the parish as a younger and sprier man. It is generous of the vestry that they continue my salary the same. We should be grateful that they have not lessened it. And what should we do with more? Have we not all that we need?"

"No," I said petulantly. "You need a new coat. I can see my face all down the back of that one."

"It is a recommendation of its shabbiness, my dear, that it reflects anything so comely. I shall wear it with added pleasure now."

"And you ought to have a gig to carry you about in bad weather."

"I should but break my neck getting in and out of it. I am safer by far on my feet, my child. I am not so limber at climbing as I used to be."

"At least, then, father, you should be able to indulge in a new book or two when your heart is set on it. There is that beautiful edition of Ruskin down at Carter's, that you look at so longingly every time you pass the store."

"Hoots toots!" interrupted my father gayly. "If you come to idle wishes, not all the mints in the world could coin money fast enough for our demands, and we are better off as we are."

"But you know you do want that set of Ruskin, father."

"Ay, truly. So I would like the Bodleian Library, but that is no good reason why I should have it. I will not deny though that it is a fine set of Ruskin that Carter has,—the very handsomest edition of the work that I ever saw, and a binding that does credit to the writer. A worthy book unworthily bound is as a monarch in unseemly robes, and my simple mind prefers royalty in its pomp. Yes, it is a fine set surely. It gives me pleasure but to take up one of those books in my hand and turn over the prints, like a child with a picture primer; and Carter is very friendly, and allows me to look at it as often as I enter the store. But that is not to say I wish it were mine, my dear. Why, there are no shelves in my study fit to hold it. I should next want to be buying that little gem of a carved bookstand at Tracey's to put it in. Nay, nay, it is unsafe to begin with wishes and wants, you see, my child. There is no knowing where they would lead me to."

Nevertheless there was scarcely a day but on some pretext or other my father found his way to Carter's, to have just one peep more at that beautiful morocco-bound edition of his favorite author. How eagerly he took up one volume of it after another! how regretfully he laid each down! how lingeringly he turned away! I yearned unspeakably to make it his. His love of beautiful books amounted almost to a passion, and it was his one innocently extravagant taste. Ah, if I could but gratify it in this single instance! By degrees all my soul became absorbed in this intense desire, and by day and by night I dreamed over one by one the few arts for earning money at an ignorant woman's command. And at last I determined that I would write a book.

So these are the circumstances which made me an author; for, like many poor women who earn their living by their pen, I was by no means a writer born; and this is how that first and last book of mine was begun. I felt confident that, once started, I could tell my story well enough, and to write it would cost me no outlay save time, which I took from the night hours, that I might leave none of my day-duties undone; and if I failed, therefore I would at least lose nothing by my venture.

But I had little imagination, which was scarcely to be wondered at, for a life passed among the hard realities soon loses its frail hold on the ideal; and I could not invent a plot, try as I would, till at last, in despair, I fell back on an ended romance in my own life, a sad little story which I had lived through all unknown to anyone—even to my father— one eventful, never-to-be-forgotten summer not many years before, when I had chanced to be away from home. It seemed almost like reopening a grave, or betraying some sacred trust to write out this sorry secret of mine to lay before the world desecrating eyes. But after all, I said to myself, people will think it merely a story; no one can ever guess I wrote about myself; and at least my book must be life-like, and will run no risk of being overdrawn, if I put in it only what really happened. In all my life I had been but that once outside our city, and I knew so little therefore of any other that I preferably laid my scene where I lived, while I naturally took myself for my heroine, for how could I fit my own story to any other woman?

Yet every stroke of my pen seemed such an absolute revelation of myself, such a complete unmasking of my inmost and dearest thoughts and feelings, that my cheeks grew scarlet, and a burning shame possessed my whole soul as I wrote. What could the world think of me if it knew that I—*I*—the reserved, reticent, quiet Hester Brooks, had given away my heart's love to one so utterly unworthy it, to one so unworthy the love of any true woman living, and who had won it only to scorn it and fling it from him as a valueless toy?

But to the world it will only be a novel, a fiction, a made-up story, I said reassuringly to myself over and over again. It cannot seem true to any but myself, for no one living dreams that I ever had a lover, and not even he who trifled with me knew that he broke my heart, for all I learned to despise him through my love, and only forgave him long after, when I heard that he was dead.

And so I wrote my book, the simplest of books in very truth, and with only myself in it; for the few other characters necessary to the unfolding of the tale were all shadowy and indistinct, forming a dim background against which this one figure stood out in clear relief. A great morose-looking house which adjoined ours, and which had stood empty ever since I could remember, was the familiar home I chose for my heroine; and I described her from a fancy sketch, which, hanging in my room since childhood, seemed now almost more like my second self than could any reflection from my mirror. My story should be real throughout, I determined, and any visionary head would sit strangely on my shoulders. But this picture over my desk was as my half-sister, and it seemed not unnatural to link her features with my fate. Surely she would be willing to lend so much as that toward helping on my book, she who had watched me through so many years, witnessing with silent sympathy as sorrow hidden from all others.

So in the still hours of the night, for my dear father's sake, I sat and told my tale. My deep love for him, my passionate desire to give him pleasure, lent a strange inspiration to my pen; and if I needed further incentive, if my brain wearied or my courage failed, I would slip quietly out of the house toward dusk and go down to Carter's, and look through the window at that wonderful set of Ruskin, over which my father's spirit yearned. Several times I caught him there. He seemed unable to keep away.

"It is those books bring me here," he would say, deprecating, as I came up. "They are a magnet I cannot resist. Truly, I believe I could hardly enjoy them more were they my own."

And the recollection of the subdued longing in his face as he turned away gave wings to my midnight pen. I felt that I was writing well, and I knew that I should never write as well again. But what matters another time? I thought. It is for this once that I seek success, and I will pour all my heart into my book. I will keep back nothing of what I have to give. I will risk my all on this one venture. Ah, my poor little book, wrought in silence and secrecy, like an evil deed, yet so innocent of evil! Oh, had I but known! Had I but known!

But why dwell longer on preliminaries? My book at last was not only finished, but accepted, and in due course of time pub-lished. They told me it "took" wonderfully. I smiled to myself. It seemed whimsically odd that my heart's spoiled happiness should now make my life's success. It was like beating gold out of grief. But I experienced none of an author's repeated emotions over a first book. I thought of it only as a means to something dearer than personal fame, valuing it solely as it accomplished the end for which it was written.

Never shall I forget my dear father's amazement when the book came out. He at once locked himself into his study with it, and when he came to me afterwards, his eyes were moist and shining, and his lip trembling.

"I didn't know you had it in you, Hester," he said. "It is a wonderful book, my child. It is truer to life than life itself, but sad!—oh, my dear, sad! Were it not that I knew your life through from end to end, I could almost have believed you are telling you her own experiences, so vividly is it written. It is a great gift, Hester, and you have written a wonderful book, a very wonderful book, my dear."

Not all the praise of all the world could have touched me for nearly or satisfied me more perfectly than this praise from my father. I hid my face on his breast, and could not speak for content. Ah, I thought, when I buy him that beautiful set, when he knows why I wrote my book, surely Heaven itself cannot give me more of ecstasy than that moment!

Almost simultaneously, however, with the publication of my story, I began to notice a change in people's manners toward me. I had always been rather a favorite in the parish, and till now had had only the very pleasantest relations with my father's friends. I could not comprehend what was making the difference, yet there it surely was. Mrs. Van Anden, one of our oldest friends, who had almost brought me up with her daughter Juliet, bowed to me so strangely the first time I met her after my book had appeared, that I thought something must have happened, and ran across the street to ask if any of them were ill.

"Oh, no; oh, no. Juliet is *perfectly* well. She was never better, never happier—never in her life. Thank you *very much*," replied Mrs. Van Anden, hurrying by with such a sarcastically polite smile that I was completely dumbfounded.

And Mrs. Brownson, who lived next door to us, and whose daughter Annie—a fragile, delicate little thing—had always been a particular pet of mine, actually pretended not to see me at all at the sewing society, betraying herself by vivid blush every time I passed anywhere near her.

Even our senior warden, dear old Mr. Drake, greeted me with a positive scowl one day, when father sent me to him with some parish question. He was still at the breakfast table, and inferring that the interruption displeased him, I hurried through my errand and left as speedily as possible. His daughter followed me out to the door. Perhaps it is because she, too, is motherless, that of all my friends I have always been most drawn to Adelaide; but she is certainly a lovely girl, though sensitive and proud to a fault. She stood silently beside me as I fastened on my veil, not offering her usual assistance, and with a strange, constrained manner, which I could not help noticing.

"What is the matter, Adelaide, dear?" I asked. "Is anything wrong? Can I help you in any way?"

"No, I thank you, Hester," she replied, a slight flush tinging her cheek. "I need nothing from you."

There was the faintest possible emphasis on the you. I looked up at her quickly. She threw back her head and returned my gaze steadily. Her eyes were full of keenest reproach.

"Why, Adelaide!" I exclaimed, going to her and taking her hands, "what is the matter, dear? Why do you look at me so?"

She drew away her hands and turned aside. "Your own conscience must tell you why," she answered, with a contemptuous ring in her voice. "Surely you cannot need to be told that after this we can never be friends again."

I caught hold of her dress in despair. "Have you taken leave of your senses, Adelaide? After *this*? After what? No, you *must* tell me. After what, Adelaide?"

"After your book. Why should you pretend not to understand? You must have known when you wrote it that you were forfeiting my friendship forever."

I was speechless with astonishment.

"My book!" I gasped.

Adelaide came nearer, the scorn in her face intensifying.

"Did you suppose," she said, almost in a hiss, "that such slight alterations justify you and taking as your plot what I told you last fall in strictest confidence? I meant no one but my father ever to know my miserable history. You remember it was only by accident that you learned it. But I trusted you as I trusted myself. I thought a friend's heart was a confessional that held its secrets under seal. I told you what I would have torn out my tongue rather than have told to anyone living besides. And you—you have laid it unblushingly before all the world. It is a confidence less betrayed, when betrayed with pen instead of voice? You have played with my humiliating sorrow. You have used me as a tool. You have been false to the holiest of trusts. Hester, I *never* will forgive you! never—never—never!"

The angry words dashed over me like a torrent, taking my breath away.

"Adelaide!" I cried, when at last she paused, "what mistake are you making? *You* are not the heroine of my book. I never once thought of you when I wrote it. Don't you see that the story is altogether different? Any resemblance is purely accidental or imaginary. The story is my own, Adelaide—not yours. Why, I would no more have taken your secret for my book than I would have stolen your photograph for its frontispiece. Adelaide—let me explain—listen!"

I might as well have appealed to a marble image. The look on her proud face deepened to actual hatred, and she turned haughtily away, closing the door in my face. No explanation that I could give availed to win back her faith in me. She never fully believed in me again. I lost her friendship forever.

It was a day or two after that Mrs. Van Anden called. I was cutting out a set of aprons for Mollie, but no interruption was unwelcome that came from this friendly quarter, and I threw down my scissors and turned to her with my usual warm greeting. To my surprise, she pushed me rudely away when I would've kissed her, and sat down, facing me sternly.

"Hester," she said bluntly, "we can't go on in this way. I've made up my mind to have it out with you. That's what I've come for. Look here. Why did you do it?"

"Why did I do what?"

"Don't look so innocent. Of course you know what I mean. Why did you put my Juliet in your book?"

"Mrs. Van Anden, Juliet is *not* in my book."

"Oh, isn't she? Why, then, have you described her face, her figure, her manner even, so unmistakably that the blindness can't fail to recognize her in your heroine, in spite of the feigned name—as if that were any real disguise? You have the grace not to call her out and out Juliet Van Anden; nevertheless, there's not a soul that knows us and has read your story but believes she sat to you for her portrait, the same as if she went to be photographed when you wrote that book."

I was almost in tears. "But my heroine is entirely a fancy picture, Mrs. Van Anden," I insisted. "I didn't mean her to look like anyone I knew. There are plenty of tall girls with black hair and eyes in the world. The description would fit any other brunette just as well as Juliet, and I never meant Juliet in the very, very least. I tried to describe a sketch hanging in my room. I can show it to you there now."

"It's a most singular coincidence, then," said Mrs. Van Anden, not in the least mollified. "And you can't expect me to believe it's merely by chance that a fancy picture should so precisely resemble Juliet, that every word of your description might have been written for her, even to the identical way she wears her hair, and that loose coil in her neck. I wonder you didn't mention, too, how it is forever falling down. The poor girl is so mortified she doesn't know where to look. Here are all her brothers twitting her now on account of that fellow Goodrich, who used to hang about her last summer. Any one can see your hero is meant for him. They're as like as two peas. And of course it's taken for granted now all over town that he left Juliet in the lurch when he went off, while the fact is that she refused him up and down two and three times over, and wouldn't look at him if he were the only man in the world, though he's so dead in love with her. It's hard on the girl, I must say, to have you go and put it into people's heads that she's pining her soul out for love of him, when it's all the other way. I never would have believed you could have played us such a trick, Hester, and we always such friends!"

What could I say? What could I do? Vainly I took Mrs. Van Anden upstairs and showed her the picture above my desk, looking wistfully down at us with its deep, dark eyes, as if longing to enforce the truth with speech. She declared it did not look an atom like the girl in my book, and that my description would fit nobody she ever saw but only her daughter Juliet. There was no pacifying her. She stormed, she cried, she denounced me in the severest terms, and finally flung herself out of the house even angrier than when she had entered it.

I felt as if turned to stone. I was unable to move or think. The day dark and slowly, and I was still sitting there, helplessly idle, with my hands fallen in my lap, and the uncut aprons seeming to stare reproachfully at me out of the folded muslin, when George came in from school.

"Oh, I say, Hester," he began impetuously, throwing himself face downward on the sofa with his heels in the air, irresistibly suggesting a lizard in boots, "all the fellows are talking of your novel. You've made such a hit. There never was anything like it. Mrs. Brownson is raving distracted."

"O Georgie, don't!" I implored, putting out my hands to ward off what might be coming. "Don't speak to me of that unlucky book. It has brought me nothing but distress!"

"Now, don't you be thin-skinned!" said Georgie, contemptuously. "If you're going to put people in books, why just do it and keep your pluck up. It must be splendid fun, and you do it capitally. Why, all us fellows knew in a minute it was Mrs. Brownson's old hole of a house you meant. I declare I could draw it with my eyes shut after your description. Only your own little off when it comes to the French roof. I suppose you clapped that on as a blind."

"But I wasn't describing Mrs. Brownson's house at all, Georgie," I said, indignantly. "I meant the one on our right. That has a French roof. How stupid of you not to recognize it. It never entered my head to appropriate Mrs. Brownson's house for my heroine."

"La—la!" answered Georgie, and made an expressive, if disrespectful, gesture of disbelief. "It's all right, anyhow. The old duffer deserves a rub for being so miffy; only, you see, she says every one will suppose, from your laying the scene in her house, that you mean any by the heroine; and Annie's being so sickly and all,—just booked for a decline and so on, like your girl,—it really does look as if you were on the inside track of her story, don't you see? And Mrs. Brownson as good as told me we needn't any of us make too free about her premises any more. *I* don't care. *I* don't want any of her old cherries. They're all bird-pecked, anyway. And, oh, I say, Het, *did* you mean old Mr. Brown by Mr. Green?"

"No! no! O Georgie, what nonsense!"

"Well, he thought you did. The names are so like, you see. Both names of colors. And the old maid—what's her name? didn't you mean Miss Tibbets? It's as like! And she's as mad over it as all outdoors."

"O, Georgie, Georgie, I didn't mean *anybody*—not *anybody*!" I cried, well-nigh beside myself. "Why will you listen to such stories!"

"Oh, come now, you can't stuff *me*, you know," rejoined Georgie, with a wink. "I can see round a corner straight as most folks. But I must say your hero is an awful gump, Hester. I really don't wonder Mrs. Brownson didn't like your passing him off as Annie's beau, when he's the only beau she's likely ever to have, poor girl."

Oh, what could I do! I wrung my hands in impotent misery. Though I should proclaim the truth upon every housetop, would even that dispel all these false illusions now? There seemed no help anywhere. I tried to hold up my head and brave out the storm, conscious of my innocence; but my spirits sank day by day, as I felt more and more how completely I was in disgrace, and how impossible it was to right myself.

But when at last there came that momentous letter from my publishers, inclosing me a check, whose amount exceeded my wildest dreams, and when not only the precious volumes for whose sake I had undergone so much, but the tiny carved book-case, too, stood snugly in place in my father's study, while I waiting his coming—then for one brief moment I forgot all else, and my heart overflowed with a proud and perfect joy. After all, is not that a costlier gift that has been purchased at a sacrifice? Had I not more to give him, having bought it with such tears?

Oh, how unutterably happy I was, how my heart beat for pleasure, when I heard the dear familiar step in the hall outside! I gave a hurried glance at my treasure; it must show off at its best now; and darting to the window I hastily drew up the shade. The rays of a magnificent sunset instantly flooded all the room, and shot slanting across the red-covered books on the new shelves, lighting them up to regal splendor. That bit of brilliant coloring in the heretofore dark corner seemed to my excited fancy almost like a rival sunset. I gave it one more loving, satisfied glance, then opened the door and called my father.

He came in slowly, reluctantly, as if unwilling to answer the call. His head was bent, and his white hair fell over his forehead with a melancholy sweep unusual to him who generally stood so erect. It struck me, even, that his step faltered. Still I was too full of joy to more than notice it vaguely, as I drew him before the book-case. I could scarcely speak for gladness. My cheeks were aflame, and my foolish hands trembled as I clasped them over his arm.

"They are yours, father dear, *yours*," I stammered. "I bought them for you with my own money. It is my present to you. It is for this that I wrote my book."

My father gave a sharp cry; it sounded as much like pain as surprise; and, turning, he took me in his arms and held me close for a long, long time without speaking. "For this—for this!" He said at last, and I felt a hot tear fall on my head. "Oh, my child—my Hester!"

"Yes, father, dear, dear father," I repeated, clasping him close. "I wrote it, not for the pleasure of it—not for the stress of it—not because it was in me to write, but only, only that I might earn the money for these books. I could not bear you not to have them, and that is why I wrote the story, dear; that is why."

Again he gave that cry; it frightened me, it rang so strangely from his lips; and though he smiled at me when I looked up at him, it was a smile that cut through to my soul, for it seemed to come from a broken heart.

He saw the startled look in my eyes; and putting me gently from him, he bent over the shelves as if to examine them, and patted the books fondly, and tried to take one out; but his hand shook, and he gave it up. I stood by with a great dread stealing over me, and put my arm about his shoulders as he stooped down, suddenly conscious that he needed a support.

"Yes—yes—poor dear—poor child," he said, softly. "It is a sad price you have paid for my books; oh, a sad price, indeed; but it is God's will."

"Father, what is it?" I cried. "Oh, what is it?"

"There, there, do not you mind it too sorely, Hester," he answered brokenly. "I am glad of the books, very glad, and it was nobly done of you. Do not you mind it, dear. I am old—too old—do not you see? It is only a pretext. Perhaps it is easier so than if they had turned me away outright. Oh yes. It is much easier so."

My heart stood still. "Father," I whispered, "tell me the worst at once. Let me know."

"I will," he said, patting my hand, and trying still to smile at me. "It is best you should know it first from me. They say, dear—do not lay it to heart, my child, *we* know it is not so—but they say you could never have written the book alone; it shows too much knowledge about the people here. Some one—I—who was in the confidence of my people—I—must have helped you with it; and—O Hester, Hester! it is only an excuse, you know, only that they want a younger man; but the vestry has—has asked me—to resign! Oh, my child!"

The brave smile went suddenly all out of his face, as if an overwhelming wave of sorrow had swept up from his heart and quenched it; he staggered to the nearest chair, and, falling into it, bowed down his head upon his hands and burst into uncontrollable sobs.

I stood near him, speechless. I do not know what I did. I scarcely know what I felt. I think I was stunned beyond power of sensation, and felt absolutely nothing. My first conscious act was to bend down and draw to the little silk curtain before those beautiful red-bound books over which the heartless sun was streaming so mockingly. They blinded me.

Many years have passed, and we have a new home now, where the same books stand in a similar little study; and my father pores over them often with loving but faded eyes, and seems to take pleasure in their beauty, and tells me how glad, how very, very glad he is of them. But since that terrible day I have never touched them once; and when by chance my eye falls on them, I feel a stab like a knife-wound in my heart.

For this is the price I paid for them.

From *Mimosa Leaves*[2] (1895)

Pain Wrought

Pain, Pain, the Creator Pain
    Is making a poet of me.
He has flung my soul in the pit below
Where his furnace fires the fiercest glow.
He is feeding the flames with woe on woe
My heart must thrill with every throe
That human creature can live to know.
    I must suffer that I may sing.

Pain, Pain, the Creator Pain
    Is working his will with me.
Ashes and ruin and havoc complete
Has he wrought of all I held dear and sweet
My soul lies scarred in the scorching heat.
My thoughts run riot with blazing feet,
Like madmen through a deserted street.
    And because I suffer, I sing.

To a Hurt Child

What, are you hurt, Sweet? So am I;
    Cut to the heart;
Though I may neither moan nor cry,
    To ease the smart.

Where was it, Love? Just here! So wide
    Upon your cheek!
Oh happy pain that needs no pride,
    And may dare speak.

Lay here your pretty head. One touch
    Will heal its worst.
While I, whose wound bleeds overmuch,
    Go all unnursed.

There, Sweet. Run back now to your
    play.
    Forget your woes.
I too was sorely hurt this day;—
    But no one knows.

My Other Me[3]

Children, do you ever
    In walks by land or sea,
Meet a little maiden
    Long time lost to me?

She is gay and gladsome,
    Has a laughing face,
And a heart as sunny;
    And her name is Grace.

Naught she knows of sorrow,
    Naught of doubt or blight.
Heaven is just above her.
    All her thoughts are white.

Long time since I lost her,
    That other Me of mine.
She crossed into Time's shadow,
    Out of Youth's sunshine.

Now the darkness keeps her,
    And call her as I will,
The years that lie between us,
    Hide her from me still.

I am dull and pain-worn,
    And lonely as can be.
Oh children, if you meet her,
    Send back my other Me!

The Gift of Song

When I was born
God stood in Heaven, and asked: What
    wilt Thou, Soul?
I said: The gift of Song;
I ask no more than this—that I may sing.
God sighed, and lo, Grief fell
From out high Heaven and smote me on
    the heart.
I cried aloud for pain, and beat my breast.
But all my cries were music, and men list,
And feasted on the sweetness of my woe.
While I, I hid my face,
And knew not day from night for agony.
O God, I cried, take back thy poisoned gift,
The gift of Song!
Let me be dumb for ever, only so
My pain have ease!
Then God did hear again, and stooped
    Him down
And drew the burning arrow from my side;
And silence fell on me; my pulse stood still,
My lips closed softly, and I sang no more.
But men turned from me, saying: He is
    dead.

In My Window Seat[4]

I am sitting in my window-seat,
    An all the world is still;
On the shadows 'neath my feet
    Are creeping up the hill,
And the shadows above are stooping
    down
As if to lay o'er the sleeping town
The folded mantle, soft and brown,
    They have dropped to my window-sill.

More dim, more dense the twilight
    grows;
    A silence falls on earth

As if it waited for the throes
    Of some immortal birth.
The stars throb out with fitful light,
Like a golden pulse in the veins of night,
And across the heavens, thin and white,
    Stretches the silver girth.

Then out upon the quivering dark—
    The palpitating sky—
Athwart the gloom that seems to hark
    A decree that bids it die,
Dropped from a hand beyond our sight
There falls the glittering long moonlight,
Like a sword down-flashing through the
    night
    That it severs in passing by.

And as if wakened at the touch
    To tremulous delight,
Yet tinged with earthliness overmuch,
    Come the voices of the night,
Now sad as notes of mortals are,
Now sweet, mysterious, and far
As from seraphs poised on a distant star,
    But winged for nearer flight.

My soul, borne upward with the sweep
    Of the solemn exultant lay,
Borne on by the music grave and deep
    Is lost in the pathless grey.
Around me are living thoughts astir.
Above Truths interlace and blur.
Beneath lie shadows of things that were,
    And dreams dreamed through by day.

And as I watch, lo, over all,
    O'er sea, and hill, and wood,
A wondrous presence seems to fall
    Out of the clouds that brood—
Something immeasurably grand,

As if the shadow of God's hand
An instant lay across the land,
    And near us angels stood.

And a holy murmur fills the air,
    A strange delicious thrill,
As if men's hearts awoke in prayer
    To listen to God's will,
And listening, heard a summons sweet
Beyond compare, and ceased to beat.—
And I sit alone in my window-seat,
    And the world is very still.

From *The Moving Finger Writes*[5] (1900)

Agnes Alden is the brilliant, refined daughter of a literature scholar who falls in love with David Mulgrave, a poet. Unfortunately, David is married, and his wife, Isabel, is beautiful but intellectually little more than a child. Agnes represses her feelings for David but does not break off contact with him, instead cultivating a friendship with both David and Isabel that remains within the confines of respectable female behavior. Ideals, of course, prove difficult to uphold.

Chapter X

The Dark Bring Forth Light

David and Isabel were the two to whom the day brought the most unqualified enjoyment. It wrote itself in David's memory in blurred letters of gold,—an indistinct dream-like record of sunlight dropping brokenly through tall trees; of green shadows that lifted and fell across the slopes or lay sleepy and dim in the hollows; of cool, sweet breezes laden with a hundred different odours distilled into one intoxicating perfume; of a slow stroll, with a companion whose silence was speech, through woody spaces where the wind in the leaves was like the sighing of the sea, and where the song of the thrush repeated itself over and over in the half conscious ear like some lovely insistent thought, till there seemed for the time nothing to regret in all the past and everything to hope for from the future.

And Isabel proved the life of the occasion as Mrs. Goodwin had prophesied. Her animation infused ardour into the rest in spite of themselves, beginning with the game of croquet played by the young people, with Agnes as umpire, David meanwhile joining Dr. Kilpatrick and his host in the book-room, where the three had a congenial morning over the microscope and the classics, which went far to atone to Mr. Alden for the miseries of an all-day fête. At luncheon, it was again Isabel's gaiety that charged the atmosphere with an electric current of enjoyment to which even Mr. Alden was not insensible, though he attributed it to not yet having had more to do with Mrs. Kilpatrick than silently to shake hands with her; and afterward, when at Isabel's instigation they went on a tour through the mansion, familiar though it had long been to the most of them, it seemed an entirely new place seen in the contagion of her enthusiasms.

They had completed the round and returned to the main floor, when lagging behind the others in one of the ante-rooms, Isabel stopped abruptly before a statue of an adorable little sleeping child, and Agnes, noticing that her face suddenly trembled and changed, came back to her while the rest passed on.

"Oh, it is so like—so like!" Isabel murmured with quivering lips. "I could think it was my own little boy grown to this."

A soft colour came into the other's face.

"I did not know you had a child," she said.

Isabel's eyes were full of tears.

"I haven't any. My baby died four years ago. He was nearly ten months old. He was the dearest—the sweetest—It almost broke David's heart when he died."

"And yours," Agnes added, taking Isabel's hand with a look of immeasurable compassion.

The tears dried in Isabel's eyes.

"No, it did not," she answered in a hard voice.

"I felt horribly, of course, but—no, it did not break my heart." She turned impulsively to Agnes. Not even for fear of what others might think of her could she ever be anything but wholly outspoken, saying whatever was uppermost in her mind at the moment, less from honesty than for the relief of expression which to her ardent soul was always as immediate a necessity as air is to the suffocating.

"I was jealous of Davy," she went on. "David loved him so. He loved him better than he did me—I was sure of it—and Davy would never come to me when his father was in the room. Sometimes I almost hated the child. Of course you can't understand it, and of course it was unnatural and horrible of me. Still I felt that I had the first right to David's love, and I couldn't bear to have even our baby rob me of it. And when he died—oh, I was heartbroken until I saw how David missed him, and then I knew that if he had lived

they would have grown to be all in all to each other, and I should have been left out in the cold. I could not have borne that. I am so glad that I have never had a baby since. I was not meant to be a mother."

Agnes was surprised at herself that she was not more shocked; but as Isabel spoke, looking at her with frank, self-accusing eyes, hiding nothing, glossing nothing over, attempting no palliation, she could only be sorry for her as for an undisciplined child ignorant of what it confesses. Her hand closed more tightly round Isabel's.

"You would have felt differently if Davy had lived," she said gently. "You would have loved him with all your heart. You could not have helped it." She coloured again, still more softly, with the words. Oh, to have transmitted one's own life into another life—to have become a creative entity—a living link in a living chain reaching endlessly on down all the ages, a factor in life's farthest future,—was not that earth's one true immortality? Could Isabel be really glad not to be a mother?

"I suppose I should have loved him, of course," Isabel admitted, "for he was the sweetest thing you ever saw—such soft gold hair all in little rings, and he had David's eyes. I will show you his picture, some day. I have put it out of sight. I couldn't leave it where David would see it and keep on loving him better than me. Do you think me a monster? Or do you understand at all—in the very least—how I feel?"

"I could not feel so," Agnes replied slowly. "But you are different from anybody I know—I can't judge you yet. By and by, when I know you better, perhaps I shall understand how you could feel so."

"That is perfectly fair and just—exactly what I knew you would be," Isabel said with conviction. "I should not like it if you tried to make excuses for me. But can you like me all the same, knowing how hateful I am? You really must try to like me a little, for I like you so very, very much!"

"I could not help liking you, even if I tried to," Agnes answered with a puzzled look at her. "I don't quite know why."

"Don't try not to like me—don't try!" exclaimed Isabel well pleased. "You are a darling, and I care more about your liking me than I can tell you."

Agnes scarcely knew how to respond to such effusiveness of affection. But Isabel boldly slipped a caressing arm about her waist and drew her after the rest of the party and speedily became her sparkling self again. Later, on the outdoor ramble, she found herself between Dr. Kilpatrick and Mr. Alden, and was so charmingly vivacious and so interestingly interested, that the gallant doctor declared he had never enjoyed any walk as much. Mr. Alden, however, had an inveterate antipathy to young women matching his aversion to young men, and while no one could be more well disposed to those who came within the narrow circle of his esteem, no one was more obdurately exclusive in the choice of those so favoured, or more hopelessly disaffected toward all who remained without it. He grew increasingly bored as the walk progressed, wondering what possible attraction Matt could find in so aggressively emphatic a young person, and became completely dumb long before Mrs. Goodwin called him away to take his share of Mrs. Kilpatrick, after which time stood

altogether still for Mr. Alden, and darkness covered the face of the land.

When the late dinner was ended the party adjourned to the tower, whose summit afforded an unobstructed view of the fireworks over the entire surrounding country. There was no moon, and the dark blue dome made a superb background against which was a blaze of light,—light rising, falling, floating, breaking, changing, vanishing, reappearing,—while not a sound was to be heard even from the bursting of the nearest bombs, all taking place in seemingly as absolute a silence as does the nightly procession of the stars. It was like a pantomimic rehearsal of the whole history of the heavens from the time when God said,—Let there be Light. Suns swirled mistily into being out of the nebulous distance, and planets were born as one looked. Moons of many colours rose from every point of the horizon, dissolving into nothingness before they reached the zenith. Meteors shot dazzlingly overhead, their passage dotted with a quivering trail of sparks. Comets rushed by in furious and eccentric splendour; here and there through the flickering ether auroral lights shone out with a steadiness of deceptive promise; and the lightnings of an interstellar storm crossed and recrossed the sky in mad, zigzag flashes, followed by the bursting of golden rains whose every drop resolved into a flower that budded and bloomed and died all in one transcendent instant. It was the apotheosis of an unimaginable Transitoriness. Wherever the eye turned the glory that it saw ceased to be in the moment that it was.

Toward the close of the evening David

found himself near Agnes, who with her elbows on the balustrade and her chin on her clasped hands was standing lost in thought, looking soberly up at the fire-lit sky. In its brilliant light her face showed as clearly as by day, and David was struck afresh with the earnestness and self-unconsciousness of her expression. He felt irresistibly drawn to her, and she turned to him with a quiet relief of manner as if her thought had been awaiting his coming.

"You quoted something from Omar the first time we met, Mr. Mulgrave. You said that Heaven or Hell was in ourselves. Do you believe that?"

It was impossible to make any but a serious rejoinder to eyes that looked so straightly into his. He had always to meet her on her own ground.

"I certainly believe that it is our characters rather than our surroundings that determine our happiness or unhappiness. It is a time-old truth, and only new to each of us as we grow up to it."

Her direct frank gaze seemed to say her thought before she spoke it.

"Do we make our own miseries, then?"

There was a very friendly note in David's voice as he answered her.

"To a great extent we do. Nothing is so bad but we may make it better or worse by our attitude of mind toward it. We may not be in the least responsible for the conditions that hamper us, but we certainly are for the manner in which we meet them—don't you think so?—so that how we take our trials must be of infinitely greater importance to us than the trials themselves."

Agnes had been thinking of Isabel's confession, but as David spoke her mind reverted to herself, and her eyes shrank from his. She turned instantly away, her look changing to one of extreme reserve. But before he had time to remark it she began speaking again on an indifferent subject, and, the others joining in, the conversation became general. David, however, remained its leader, though so unconsciously and inconspicuously that none of the little circle suspected it, even when most yielding themselves to his influence. Besides the magnetism and temperamental graciousness which readily won him friends, he had a way of presupposing the general superiority of those about him which was of itself inspiring, and his searching eyes called out the best of every one upon whom they turned. Insensibly his stimulating brightness and charm diffused itself throughout the group. Mr. Alden, who during the evening's spectacle had stood abjectly at his post by Mrs. Kilpatrick, monosyllabic and unimpressed, recovered his spirits with a rebound in an alleviating forgetfulness of her presence, and entered into the talk with zest, adding an inimitable touch of drollery to whatever was said, while Mrs. Goodwin, who had been conveyed up to the tower for the occasion, surpassed herself in witticisms, and under the universal spell even Clara Dean became responsive.

A most interesting talk it was, as any conversation is bound to be in which each participant is made to feel that his own contribution is indispensable, and all were loath to break it up. But at last the evening came to an end, and the family were left to gather in the book-room and discuss the events of the day after the usual fashion of hosts.

"Do you know," observed Mrs. Goodwin, luxuriating in the comfort of unrestrained comment as if from the exchange of a ball-room costume for a dressing-gown, "that poet has a great deal more in him than his rhymes. He is infectiously June-hearted. He makes you feel that the sun is shining and that it is good to be alive. He is so delightful that I forget he is a poet."

"He is a well-informed, modest, and agreeable young man," said Mr. Alden with conservative assent. "It is a thousand pities he should waste himself on verses of his own when he has so fine a critical perception for Pindar."

"Very true," Mrs. Goodwin cordially agreed. "Only why should he waste himself on Pindar, either? As to that little wife of his—"

"I cannot imagine why he married her," interposed Mr. Alden. "She is hung on springs. The least breath sets her going, and she is instantly all chatter and flutter. The principle on which men choose their wives seems to be dissimilarity and incongruity. Just look at Matt and Mrs. Kilpatrick. Dear me, I do hope when I get to Heaven it will be easier to love those I don't like!"

"Don't mention that odious woman's name!" begged Mrs. Goodwin irritably. "She was certainly created on an eighth day along with the mosquitoes and microbes. She no sooner came in than she asked me where I got this valuable lace, and took hold of it at the precise spot where I tore it ten minutes before. She has as many eyes as a potato. She kept running that conspicuous foot of hers along the solitary threadbare spot in the drawing-room carpet the entire time we were

there, and she spoiled all Theodore Hart's satisfaction in his dudish get-up by telling him that she felt obliged to inform him, as a friend, that his coat wrinkled horribly in the back."

"Pooh—pooh," said Mr. Alden good-humouredly. "As if Theodore's coat were not always the newest wrinkle out! Surely she can do worse than that."

"That is as you look at it," returned Mrs. Goodwin with a lift of the eyebrows. "Her final remark to me as she left was that Clara Dean was the most restful of creatures, and that she hoped some day to have a daughter exactly like her. Humph! Restful! Well, yes, like a cedar-tree,—the same colour at all seasons. Ugh! That woman gives me the neuralgia. If it were not for Godfrey I would never ask her within these doors again. But Godfrey—" She looked at Agnes with an affectionate smile.

"Godfrey is a dear," Agnes replied to the smile. "I like him better than ever. And I hope he will marry Clara by and by." And then she said good-night and went away, leaving Mrs. Goodwin in doubt whether to be dis- appointed or hopeful.

ॐ

Agnes did not go to her own rooms at once. She kept on up the stairs, up, and up, and up, until she came out again on the summit of the tower. It was very late; the moonless night looked doubly dark contrasted with the flare and glow of the preceding hours, and the great flag, curling and uncurling itself around the pole at the touch of a light breeze, gave a sense of eerie companionship that heightened the solitude.

Agnes bent back her head and looked up. The stars, which had been lost in the light, were disclosed anew by the darkness, and hung over her, calm, changeless, and solemn, in that majesty of the immutable and enduring that is so infinitely beyond the utmost glory of the variable and evanescent. Agnes threw out her arms with a sudden sob.

"How am I to meet this?" she cried in a tumult of bewilderment and shame. "God help me. What shall I do?"

But the silence held no reply. All mortals must work out their life-questions by themselves; for whatever the answer, it is in the working out of its own problems that each soul's salvation lies.

Song (1901)

Were I yon star whose silver ray
   Turns dusk to day,
Lo, I would hide me till you came,
   Then burst in flame
Athwart the darkness on your sight,
   And die in light.

Were I yon rose whose fragrance rare
   Scents all the air,
I would not blossom till the day
   You passed this way,
Then pour my heart out in perfume
   And die in bloom.

Were I yon lark whose sunny song
   Sounds all day long,
Lo, I would hush me till you past,
   Then wake at last,
Spread my glad wings out toward the sky,
   Sing once, and die.

Ennui (1908)

A wide, bare field 'neath blinding skies,
Where no tree grows, no shadow lies,
Where no wind stirs, where no bee flies.
A roadway, even, blank, and white,
That swerves not left, that swerves not
   right,
That stretches, changeless, out of sight
Footprints midway adown its dust;
Two lagging, leaden feet, that just
Trail on and on, because they must.

Peace and the Sword (1926)[1]

In days that the future may sometime remorsefully remember, there lived in a land of God's loveliest making a maiden called Peace, whose sweetness and fairness were beyond the power of words to show. Her home was on a great rock that stood, majestic and precipitous, in the middle of a sparsely populated valley, over which the fame of her wondrousness was borne on the wings of every wind that blew. This rock was exceedingly difficult of ascent, but the plateau on its summit was a very garden of Paradise, and here dwelt Peace, not knowing one day from another for the equal joy of all, closely guarded by her four brothers, whose breath of life she was. So unspeakably dear was she indeed to these knights, and so extreme their dread lest any rob them of her, that each as he pursued his daily tasks carried ever an unsheathed sword in his hand, to be ready in her defense against any possible invader.

"All have heard of our Peace, and all envy us her," said the brother who loved her best. "We must watch well. To lose her were misery."

"To lose her were death!" responded the others, and looked carefully to the edges of their swords.

"Never shall I leave you willingly," said Peace. The sound of her voice was like the dropping of April rain upon a deep and quiet pool. "Here will I dwell forever in fulness of freedom and delight, lifted so near to Heaven that I all but gather its stars to my bosom. Have no fear. Who could take me from you?" And her smile was the breaking of dawn across the dark.

Before the marvel of her beauty, however, her brothers feared the more; and they held their swords high in the air, till the great blades, catching the sun, threw out east, west, north and south upon the valley long dazzling lights of warning and defiance. And they who lived below, looking up enviously at that exquisite far-off vision of Peace, saw also the gleam of those fiercely glittering swords; and none dared approach.

So passed a dateless time of happiness. Then at last one of the knights, his fears lulled by the long security, thrust back his sword into its sheath.

"How may Peace profit," he asked, "by our waving of these needless swords? The time given to their care were better spent in tending of flowers and in garnering of fruits and grains for her nourishment and delight. Why this eternal vigilance against unheralded foes? Whom need we fear?"

"The gaze of every dweller in the valley is upon us," answered the brother who loved her best. "In vigilance lies our safety. Hold high they sword, that men see it and fear. Else lose we our Peace."

"I love Peace not less than thou," protested the other, "and for her sweet sake I hate these trappings of war. Give us rather the treadle and the harrow."

So he went about his work with his untended sword swinging idly in its scabbard, till little by little its fine edge was blunted and spoiled with rust. Then, deeming it a vain encumbrance, he unbuckled it from his side and shivered it into bits. And below, in the valley, certain of the people, gazing upward with longing eyes, noted where one blade ceased to throw its dangerous lights abroad, and they ventured a little nearer.

Time came when a second knight stopped short in his work and laughed aloud.

"What fools we be!" he cried. "How needs our beloved Peace so many swords? Is not this high rock a sufficient defense, setting us beyond reach of enemies? Is not this high rock a sufficient defense, setting us beyond reach of enemies? Who should climb so far to do us harm? Our Peace is safe for ever."

"What were distance or danger to the seeker of such a prize?" returned the brother who loved her best. "Never let go they sword!"

"Nay, we are above fear of foes!" laughed the other. "Nature herself has barricaded us." And lifting his sword high in both hands, he flung it out into space with a might toss; and over the silent watchers beneath a blinding light swept in a wide arc of throbbing splendor that for a breathless instant struck craven terror to their souls. Then it was gone and all was as before, save that but two swords now blazed above in the sun. And men whispered together in the valley.

The third brother loved Peace well; but in the end, a disturbing thought took possession of his brain. At last he could grapple with it no longer.

"What right have we to guard Peace with a sword?" he demanded angrily. "Is not mankind one brotherhood? Weapons of defense are weapons of offense. Ours swords are insults flashed in the face of friends. Away with them! Reason is a better and fitter arm."

"How reason with marauders or assassins?" expostulated the brother who loved Peace best. "'Tis the fear of the sword keeps these aloof. Thy words are the very madness of ignorance."

"Nay! Nay! Weapons of war are admissions of cowardice unbecoming our altruistic age," rejoined the other. Already he had dug a deep hole in the ground, and as he spoke he plunged in his sword to the hilt, trampling the earth above its quivering blade as on a buried soul, and so stood weaponless and light-hearted, singing aloud for relief.

But the brother who loved her best was filled with bitterest forebodings. He tested his weapon anxiously, trying its mettle and sharpening its keen edge to a yet finer point, polishing and re-polishing it till it showered out light like a dissolving sun.

Nevertheless the watchers below saw that but one sword was left where he had been four to guard that beautiful Peace that all men desired, and their hearts waxed strong with courage, and in the sheltering darkness of the valley they met and schemed.

Now it was night, moonless and very still. Not a leaf stirred. Not a bird twittered. The clouds dropped drowsily. The three knights slept, with Peace in their midst smiling radiantly in some dream of mysterious rapture. Only the one brother who loved her best still kept vigil, his every sense desperately alert, watching and listening for he knew not what of ill. Then through the silence he distinguished a faint far rustling as of vines shaken by a breeze and sighing softly to the night. But there was no wind, and the leaves on the aspen above his head hung lax and motionless.

Straightway he was beside his brothers, calling in turn to each. "Wake! Wake! There are footsteps that draw near!"

They rose and listened.

"'Tis the falling of a bird's feather," they said, in scorn. "Who should draw near? The world sleeps."

But he with the sword, listening still more intently, caught a murmur like the lisp of summer waves upon the shore.

"Wake! Wake!" he cried again, still more importunate. "There are voices that whisper woe!"

Half wakened, they listened dully.

"'Tis the thunder among distant hills," they said, contemptuously. "Who should whisper woe in a world of love?"

But he stood at guard, every nerve strained to its uttermost. And he heard sounds that crept nearer and nearer— now here—now there—now on all sides at once—stealthy trailing sounds, like serpents gliding through lush grass.

"Wake! Oh, wake!" he cried in agony. "Our Peace is in peril! The enemy is upon the rock!"

"'Tis the woodpecker tapping on the tree," they muttered with fast shut eyes. "What foe could imperil our perfect Peace? Disturb us no more." And the brother who loved Peace best looked at her where she lay smiling in her dream, and his heart-beats stopped for dread.

Now all those remote and smothered sounds blended suddenly in his dazed ears to a single rushing noise like the oncoming of a wintry gale; and on every side of him—east, west, north and south—men leaped up on the rock with a derisive shout of triumph. He sprang upon them like a lion at bay. But of what worth was his one unaided arm in such dire need? Alas for those lost swords that might even now have saved them! The sleeping knights were seized and bound where they lay; and though many of the foe fell in their tracks, stricken to death by that one brave sword that held so valiantly to its post, the band pushed steadily on to where Peace, startled from her slumber, crouched terrified and wan.

"Save me, thou dearest of all! Save me!" she pleaded piteously, and the brother loved her best, striving to do alone the work of four, struck at the foe now on this side, now on that, with superhuman strength.

But already they were laying rude hands upon her. Already they had wrested her from him. Now they held her in their merciless grasp. She gave a last despairing cry that rang for ever after in her brother's tortured ears, and wrenching the sword from the faithful hand of the one who had loved her best, she thrust it through her heart, and lay dead in their midst. The place that had been a Paradise, from henceforth was a wilderness of war.

Elizabeth McCormick Reese (1848-1918)

Elizabeth ("Lizzie") McCormick Reese became a member of the WLBC in the first few years of its existence and was the longtime chair of the Committee on Fiction. She was born in Virginia in 1849 and married Percy Meredith Reese in 1872. The couple had two sons.

Percy Reese's grocery (initially Percy M. Reese, grocer, and later Percy M. Reese & Son), stood for many years at 1201 N. Charles St., one of Baltimore's main thoroughfares. The store was originally established in 1835 and was, at the time of its closing in 1913, "the oldest grocery," catering to "the best families in Baltimore." Elizabeth Reese's membership in the WLCB is notable in that she was one of a number of members who would not have been considered one of Baltimore's social elite.

A pamphlet published by the WLCB commemorating its fifth anniversary in 1895 listed nearly a dozen publications by Reese in publications including the

Youth's Companion, a highly respected family magazine of the era, the *Sower,* the *Messenger,* and the *People's Weekly.* These publications have proved difficult to locate. Here we include a facsimile reproduction of one of the publications we did find, a story published in a primary school textbook clearly intended to instruct children about the seasons, plant life, and vocabulary. Education was an area in which women were presumed to excel, given the responsibility they carried for educating their own children. It may be that Reese, prior to her marriage, also taught in schools, as a number of other Club members did. —J. L. Cole

LESSON XXVII.

A Crocus Story.

I.

"Are you awake?" whispered a little blue crocus to a white one, who had been sleeping by her side under the earth for months.

"Yes, wide awake, and warm all through. I am sure it must be spring," the little white one answered.

"Oh, yes, this is spring," whispered the blue. "Our shoots have been out a week, and all that time the sun has felt warm. Suppose we bloom; the earth will be so glad to see a flower again."

"I'm willing," said. little white crocus. "I want nothing so much as to help make the world beautiful and tell people the spring has come. Let us send round a crocus murmur to all the flower-beds, parks and gardens in the big city; then they will know it is time to wake up and bloom."

"Don't venture out yet," a tulip bulb grumbled from her earth-bed a few inches below the crocus. "March is only half gone, and you know old winter will never let him alone. There will be very cold

Elizabeth McCormick Reese, "A Crocus Story," *Johnson's Third Reader.* Richmond: B. F. Johnson, 1899.

winds before April comes. You would better stay where you are and keep warm."

"Dear! oh, dear!" sighed blue and white, "we dread the freezing winds. Perhaps, Miss Tulip, you are wrong. I am sure we ought to be out."

"Let us venture," urged a tiny pink crocus near by. "We can at least show Mr. Winter that spring has come, and that he must go away. Come, let

us do our best and not be afraid of a little cold."

So a crocus murmur went round to all the flower-beds, parks and gardens in the big city, telling the little crocus flowers to wake up and bloom. The next morning everything was made beautiful by thousands of spring messengers holding up their tiny bell-cups to the sun—some white, some yellow, some blue and a few pink. The earth was glad to hold on her breast again such beauty.

Even the people passing stopped, smiled and said,
"*Now*, spring has *really* come."

---

whispered   crocus   shoots   murmur
venture   bulb   breast   park

II.

Alas ; there was one who gave the flowers no
welcome. It was Mr. Winter. "I feel indignant,"
he said to March, "that such tiny little flowers dare
come up and make me feel uncomfortable and out
of place. Now, I suppose I must go, but before I
leave, dear March, you must let me give them a
fright and a chill."

"Oh, Mr. Winter !" begged March, shivering,
"please leave me and go away. I can't control
my winds when you keep interfering. You mix
me all up. Here you come with snow and cold
trying to kill the pretty green things that I have had
such trouble to wake out of the frozen ground."

Then Mr. Winter sent a gray snow-cloud to cover the sun, and breathed an icy air into the March wind. He laughed when a few feathery flakes settled on his nose. "Only a day more; give me just one day more, friend March," he begged. "I will then shut myself up in my big cave for a long sleep."

March agreed, and together they started like a wild express train. The whole thing was a frolic, after all. As the snow covered the flowers it whispered, "Do not fear, I will keep you folded warm until this cold wind blows Mr. Winter away."

The wind was not only merry but busy also. It blew light green into all the willows, red into the maples, a faint white into the plum and apple buds. It tore the dead leaves away from the sweet arbutus, it played a game with ladies' skirts and veils, it took off men's hats, and the noses and cheeks that came in its way were painted a deep red. By night all was over and Mr. Winter had departed. A soft breath of April filled the air. As it swept gently over the snow it said, "Melt at once; you are sadly out of place covering spring flowers."

With the morning came a perfect flood of sunshine and warmth, so the birds began to sing.

"Oh, how glad I am!" laughed the little blue crocus, "that we came out just when we did."

"I'm glad!" "And so am I glad!" "And so are we glad!" the others answered.

—*Elizabeth Meredith Reese.*

---

indignant   uncomfortable   control   icy
interfering   frozen   feathery   arbutus

Anne Weston Whitney (1849-1909)

A self-trained anthropologist, lover of folklore and what we might call the paranormal, Anne Weston Whitney was an extremely active Club member who was always eager to share her findings with the Club. Anne, or Annie, was in the Club from 1892-1908, holding office as Vice President, Corresponding Secretary, and chair of many committees, including fiction, the study of the English language, ethnology, and anthropology.

Whitney was also the secretary of the American Folklore Society, and she published several collections of Maryland folk beliefs and superstitions, including a book titled *Folklore from Maryland*, coauthored with fellow Club member Caroline Canfield Bullock. The shorter piece we include here, published originally in the *Journal of American Folklore*, has a similar format to that book. Her work demonstrates a passion for her subject, careful observation, and meticulous collection of data. However, Whitney was not especially impartial when observing other cultures. Her essays on "Negro American Dialects" portray black dialects as degraded versions of 'educated' white speech, indicating Whitney's superior attitude toward the cultures she spent so much time studying. These attitudes were not uncommon in her day, but bear noting nevertheless. —C. Love and N. Muñoz

Items of Maryland Belief and Custom (1899)

That the belief in charms as a means of preventing and curing disease is not a thing of the past, at least in Maryland, and that it is not even there confined to the Negro, has been convincingly proved recently.

One proof came in the spring when Druid Hill Park,[1] in Baltimore, was infested with moles. Through the efforts of the Park Board to get rid of them, it was discovered that a Dutchman, who was very successful in catching them, was cutting off the feet while they were alive, and thereby increasing his income; for he found ready sale for these feet among fond mothers who believe that, if worn round the neck of a child in a bag, they will prevent diseases incident to teething. In one part of the state, it is "the left hind-foot" of the mole that is used "to cut teeth on."

A charm against whooping-cough has also been brought prominently into notice lately in Maryland. It is asserted that the mother of twins has power to drive the disease away from a child by giving it a piece of bread and butter. That the efficacy of this is most firmly believed in was proved when whooping-cough broke out in Annapolis last winter. The governor's mansion was soon besieged by children who came to ask bread and butter of the governor's wife, she being the mother of twins. At first these requests were complied with, but soon the demand became so great as to be a tax upon the giver, and it was found necessary to put a stop to the whole thing.

Maryland has another cure for the same disease that is somewhat similar. This time it is a woman who has married without changing her name who "has the power," and who at any time is likely to be called on, as was the governor's wife. In this case it is said that if a child with the whooping-cough goes to her for a piece of bread and butter, and if she spreads the butter on the bread herself, and the child takes it without thanking her, "there will be no more 'whoop' to that cough."

A Cure for "Flesh Decay," or Wasting Disease, in a Baby

To cure this disease, a baby is measured by a seventh son or a seventh daughter three days in succession, before sunrise or after sunset, being passed through the measuring string each day; while, during the process, an unintelligible charm is repeated over the child. After the third measuring, the string is doubled and tied to the hinge of a door or window, and if it rots out in a certain time the baby will recover; but if the child is "foot-and-a-half gone," there is no possible cure.

To cure the same disease in Pennsylvania, the baby, wrapped in blankets, is put in the oven after bread has been taken out and the oven has cooled down. Then, with the oven door open, the baby is "baked" for one hour.

Surveyors' Custom

An interesting custom was formerly practiced by surveyors in marking out the boundaries of estates. It was usual for the surveyor, at a certain point, when surveying land, to give the smallest child in the party that followed him, whether black or white,

a severe whipping. Trees, it was claimed, might be struck by lightning or otherwise destroyed, and stones might disappear, but the child, who was likely to outlive the others present, would never forget the spot where he received the whipping. A gentleman whose childhood's home was in Calvert County writes of this custom as follows:—

"I recollect when quite a small boy, perhaps five or six years old, I was staying at my uncle's when Mr. King was sent for to survey a lot of ground." Mr. King, he explains elsewhere, was the son of a surveyor, and father and son together had not only surveyed all the land in Calvert County, but much in the counties adjoining. "He had great difficulty," he continues, "in finding the starting-point from an old deed which he had in his possession. After the starting-point was found and the compass adjusted, he told me that in his younger days, the youngest boy around was severely whipped on that spot, so that all his life he would remember where the survey began. He cut a switch from a nearby tree, and told me that he would not be hard on me, but struck me a few licks gently that I might tell the place when I grew up; but I am afraid I could not find it now, it has been so long ago."

Another gentleman, who is a surveyor, writes of the same custom as having been practiced by his father and grandfather, who were surveyors in and around Baltimore.

Why the Devil Never Wears a Hat

The Maryland collection gives many quaint and curious "reasons why" certain things are, or are believed in. Here we find out why the devil never wears a hat, as told by one of African descent:—

"De debbil, he am jes' chuck full ob fire an' steam an' brimstone, an' all dese jes' keep up a pow'ful workin' an' goin' on together; an' to keep from jes' nater'ly 'xplodin', he got a hole in de top o' he haid—a roun' hole—an' de steam an' fire jes' pour out 'n dere all de time. No cullud pusson ever see de debbil when de steam an' fire warn't rushin' out, 'n so 't warn't no use fur him to wear a hat."

Virginia Woodward Cloud (1861-1938)

Virginia Woodward Cloud published hundreds of poems and stories in magazines and anthologies such as the *Outlook, Lippincott's, Harper's,* and the *Ladies' Home Journal.* Cloud never married, instead focusing her energy on her career and assisting the other writers in the Woman's Literary Club of Baltimore to do the same. Her published work suggests she was an advocate for women's rights, and she certainly exemplified the bond of womanhood shared by the women of the Club as fellow writers.

Cloud was best known as a poet, but her short fiction is also worthy of consideration. Her stories often centered around intelligent heroines and represented a diverse range of women, from city sophisticates to farm wives, mothers and daughters, dreamy artists and suffragettes. In the Club minutes, secretary Lydia Crane wrote of Cloud's story "The Story of a Secret," that the story of "the loving heart and mind of a little girl, of the true woman's character through the means of her terror, compassion, sympathy, and heroic reticence, was traced and described with all Miss Cloud's insight and power of expression."[1]

Comments on Cloud's stories are scattered throughout the Club's meeting minutes. Club members described her fiction as bold, eloquent, and humorous. During one meeting of the Club, Crane was going to summarize one of Cloud's articles in the minutes but reverted to writing this compliment instead; "It would be both impossible and ungracious to attempt to unravel the threads of a texture so fine and rare, for realism and idealism, fact and fancy, imagination and historic truth, are here for too skillfully blended."[2]

Not only was Cloud well respected in the club, but she was also well known across North America. Her poems were published in newspapers from Ottawa to Los Angeles. "An Old Street" appeared in multiple newspapers, making its way to the desk of John Allen Carpenter, a Chicago composer who was inspired by its lyrics.[3] Cloud had the ability to precisely depict reality while conveying her own voice and ideas. Member Ellen Duvall wrote the following of Cloud; "Her prose and verse are full of this deep joy in life, this instinctive rapture in the presence of Nature and of man."[4] —T. Brooky and A. Schilke

From *A Reed by the River* (1902)

The Mother's Song

"Two women shall be grinding at
the mill; the one shall be taken and
the other left."[1]

All day and all day as I sit at my measure-
    less turning,
      They come and they go,—
The little ones down on the rocks,—and
    the sunlight is burning
      On vineyards below:
All day and all day, as I sit at my wheel
    and am ceaselessly grinding
      The almond boughs blow.

When she was here—O my first-born!—
    here, grinding and singing,
      My hand against hers.
What did I reck of the wind where the
    aloe is swinging
      And the cypress[2] vine stirs?
What of a bird to its little ones hasten-
    ing, crying and flying
      Through the dark of the firs?

When she was here—O my beautiful!—
    here by me grinding.
      I saw not the glow
Of the grape; for the bloom of her face
    that the sunlight was finding.
      And the pomegranate blow
Of her mouth, and the joy of her eyes, and
    her voice like a dove to me singing
      Made my garden agrow.

Was it I? Was it I for whom Death same
    seeking and calling
      When he found her so fair?

At the wheel, at the wheel, from dawn till
    the dew shall be falling
      I will wait for him there.
Death! (I shall cry) I am old, but yon
    shadow of plums that are purpling
      Was the hue of her hair.

Death! (I shall cry) in the sound of the
    mill ever turning.
      Till dark brings release.
Till the sun on the vineyards below me to
    crimson is burning
      There is measure of peace,
For all day and all day, with the wheel,
    are her eyes to mine turning.
But Death! (I shall call) take me hence ere
    the daylight its shadow is spurning
Hence ere the night-time can wrap me
    around with my tears and my yearn-
    ing,—
      When the grinding shall cease!

To a Poet

The pipe of one undying river reed
Borne down on myriad summers' magic
    breath
Wakes to thy playing, the immortal seed
Of Eden's rose, through gates of life and
    death,
Blooms in thy song; to make thy fragile
    mood
The loves of gods were slain and mortals
    died;
A thousand dawns are thrilling in thy
    blood,
A thousand darks are blackly multiplied
In thy despair; a thousand souls their
    tears,
Their passions pour through time to
    thine;

Thy heart is heritage of all the years
That fed upon Elysian oil and wine;—
Then with no lesser fare of love keep
    tryst,
Lest the lips starve where gods have
    warmly kist.

An Old Street[3]

The Past walks here, noiseless, unasked,
    alone;
Knockers are silent, and beside each
    stone
Grass peers, unharmed by lagging feet
    and slow
That with the dawn and dark pass to
    and fro.
The Past walks here, unseen forevermore,
Save by some heart who, in her half-
    closed door,
Looks forth and hears the great pulse
    beat afar,—
The hum and thrill and all the sounds
    that are,
And listening remembers, half in fear,
As a forgotten tune re-echoes near,
Or from some lilac bush a breath blows
    sweet
Through the unanswering dusk, the
    voiceless street,—
Looks forth and sighs,—with candle held
    above,—
"It is too late for laughter,—or for love."

Youth

Out of the heart there flew a little singing
    bird
Past the dawn and the dew, where leaves
    of morning stirred,
And the heart which followed on, said;
    "Though the bird be flown

Which sang in the dew and the dawn,
    the song is still my own."

Over the foot-worn track, over the rock
    and thorn,
The tired heart looked back to the olive
    leaves of morn,
To the fair lost fields again, and said; "I
    hear it! Oh, hark!"—
Though the bird were long since slain,
    though the song had died in the
    dark.

The Lecture (1903)[4]

    "She says they can be done without."
    "What?"
    "Men can. Be done without."
    "Why, how ever—well, go on."
    "She says they's discordant notes in
Creation's scheme—"
    "Well, I never!"
    "I wrote some things down best I
could on the margin of newspaper that
was there, so's to get 'em by heart. She says
what a woman can't do ain't worth doing.
'Curb not your powers, my sisters, with
bit and bridle like to the ox and mule,'
she says."
    "Oxes don't wear bits."
    "That's what she says, anyhow. 'Shame
not the glorious possibilities of womanhood by following like a bondswom-
an when the sovereignty of leadership is
by right yours!' I pretty near got off the
bench, and Mis' Jessup turned red in the
face and untied her bonnet-strings. The
lecture-lady went on telling how unbecoming it was for a free female to turn in
appeal to a man for everything. 'Use your
own inspired intellecks,' she says. 'Can

you name a man in this village whose mind you consider superior to one in this noble assembly of representative women? No!'"I was running them over to myself, beginning with Uncle Abe Washburn, while she talked, when Mis' Jessup spoke out like it was Experience Meeting. You know her deafness makes her lose about half, and she's always wanting to help somebody along. 'Yes'm,' she says; 'as you ask, it's my duty to speak out. Doctor's got more sense in his little finger than I got in my whole body,' she says, meaning Dr. Jessup. Her back's so wide it hid the lecture-lady all 'cepting her head. The lecture-lady smiled real polite and says:

"'Quite right, my dear madam; nothing gives such vitality to a meeting as a call for discussion. I am glad that you opened this question which is so vital to the women of our country and to the progress of the nation. I should advise an immediate consideration of the subject, an appoint this lady—'

"'Excuse me, ma'am,' says Mis' Jessup; 'that isn't just it. I was speaking about the sense of the men in this village. Now, I'll own that all of 'em, so to speak, ain't to be counted in because of one thing and another, but there's the Doctor—'

"'Yes, yes,' says the lecture-lady, real amiable; 'we shall discuss the relative values of the force masculine and the force feminine, all in good time—'I wrote this down so's not to forget it. 'I am convinced that all my sisters resent the assumed superiority of the former, and realize within themselves the voice of Freedom and individual power crying for utterance! Press on to the foreground! Let not your rights be trampled under foot! Let the banner

over you be "*Rights!*" Man is the sovereign brute of nature—'

"'Excuse me, ma'am,' says Mis' Jessup, 'but I'd say, meaning no offense, that it would go right hard to have to call the Doctor a "brute."'

"The lecture-lady smiled kind of coldly polite and said that she was speaking in abstrack—which means look at it small and it's one way, and look at it large and it's another.

"'Peas is peas, be they a peck or a bushel,' says Mis' Jessup, standing there like your dun cow that a steam whistle can't scare from those pasture bars till they're let down.

"'Your suggestions are of universal interest,' says the lecture-lady, 'and should strike to the heart of every woman whose soul cries for freedom. "Why should I be crushed beneath the wheel of Juggernaut?" should be her cry. "Down with those traditions which rob me of my birthright of liberty!"'

"We were so stirred up now that there was considerable nodding and whispering; the lecture-lady had got real powerful, and Mis' Jessup stood trying to catch every word, and she says:

"'It's a shame, ma'am, that it is!'

"'Yes, shame! shame!' cries the lecture-lady, waving her arms, 'shame, I say, my sister! Let us each avow ourselves free!' And she went on so feelingly, about the heel of man being on her neck, and so exciting about the same flag waving its stars over men and its stripes over women, that it was better than Labor Day parade, and Essie Crim waved her handkerchief.

"'I will no longer suffer in slave-like

silence!' says the lecture-lady, waving her arms, and Mis' Jessup spoke out:

"'Don't ma'am,' she says; 'as I said, it's a shame that any lady should have been treated so bad. You've come to the right place, for I think I'm speaking for all when I say that no woman appeals to us in vain for protection, and I would ask you right now to come home with me and let the Doctor advise you. Anybody can see you've been treated terrible bad by your husband, and if he's gone so far as to use his foot, as you say, ma'am, you've cause for complaint—though with most domestic quarrels there's faults on both sides, ma'am. Maybe your husband is a drinking man—'

"'*Husband!*' cries the lecture-lady, of a sudden losing hold of herself and dancing up and down. '*Me!* Me got a husband? Me put my head into the yoke of slavery? *Me* get trampled on by a *man!* she screams, slamming her books together and pinning her hat on. 'How dare you insult me? *Husband!* she panted like 'twas '*Snake!*' and she jumps off the platform, and we all got up together, and she glares at Mis' Jessup like mad. 'How dare you say "Husband!" to me? Do I look like a worm who crawls around the feet of a man? The next time you want a lecturer, send for one of your own purblind, cow-like, servile race, and not an enlightened and emancipated being!' she screams, 'a being who knows not the word "husband!" Ugh! Go home to your *husbands*, you poor, down-trod creatures, and never awaken from your ignorance!'

"And with that she pitches out the door and disappears, while we were all trying to explain that Mis' Jessup meant no harm.

"Presently Dr. Jessup drove up with his buggy-wheels all mud-splashed.

"'I wish you had got here sooner,' says Mis' Jessup, climbing in, 'to help soothe a poor creetur who was easing her mind here awhile ago.'

"The Doctor said that if it was the female he'd met on her way to the station he guessed she'd eased off pretty much all the mind she'd got, because when he picked her up she was clinging to the fence crying fit to kill herself.

"'Just like they all do,' he says. 'Something had made her mad, and when she come to she cried it out. I said to her, "Want to go to the train?" And I didn't wait, but jumped her in. She was gasping and sobbing, "Husband!" so I calculated they'd quarreled, and I says: "There, now, don't take it that way, ma'am. If your husband's gone and left you, he'll return, never fear, especially if you're a first-rate cook," I said; "all young people quarrel sometimes, and maybe you can win him back."

"'My, but she mopped her eyes and turned turkey-red as she jumped out and the whistle blew.

"''*Husband!*' says she. "I'll have you know I haven't *got* any!"

"''Well, now, is *that* it?" I said. "Then I wouldn't take it that bad, miss; *maybe you'll get one yet!*"

"'But she jumped on that train without so much as "thanky.""

Emily Paret Atwater (1873–1951)

Emily Paret Atwater took after her mother and fellow Club member, Adaline "Addie" Peck Paret Atwater,[1] finding her niche in writing educational children's stories during a time when women found a place outside the domestic sphere and within the classroom. Having written for the *New York Ledger,* the *Puritan,* and *Nickel Magazine,* she published books that focused on adventure, nature, and learning. Atwater's writing was appreciated in educational circles as it was used in textbooks and readers in New England states, and was reviewed in the *Kindergarten Review,* which specialized in child education.

One of her novels, *How Sammy Went to Coral-Land,* was reviewed in the *Tennessean,* which highlighted the novel's "useful information about marine creatures." *How Sammy Went to Coral Land* portrays both of Atwater's goals: to capture the attention of those with a love for an adventure and to intrigue those who were tired of stereotypical fairytales. These goals are mirrored within the story as the two main characters, Bob and Eleanor, are spending a month with their grandmother and claim that they are tired of fairytales and "anxious to hear about strange adventures."[2]

Trixsey's Travels captures the same balance of education and entertainment, as each chapter opens with information about a new furry character that Trixsey, a little squirrel, meets on his travels. Atwater presents scientific facts and observations, teaching children either reading or listening about their specific characteristics. Atwater includes expansive facts keeping the story interesting and educational while maintaining of the overarching plot. The reader is kept in suspense, wondering what hurdles Trixsey might encounter as he learns to live in the wild, meets other animals, and finds a way back home. In the excerpt included here, Trixsey meets up with—and learns about—his fellow rodent friends, rabbits and woodchucks.

Atwater's publisher, G. W. Jacobs, paid particular attention to the materiality of their books. *Trixsey's Travels* was no exception, as it was smartly bound and included beautiful illustrations. This reflects the greater attention that was being paid to children's literature at the time as both educational material and art. The Club minutes show that the WLCB was appreciative of the work, and the overall reception depicts the book as a useful and educational piece of literature. The reaction it garnered draws a greater appreciation for the educational mission to which Atwater committed herself. —M. Hultberg and M. Pikus

From *Trixsey's Travels* (1905)

Chapter V

Molly Cotton-Tail; the Unsociable Woodchuck; and How Bunny Wins a Race

When at the rainbow's further end
You find the pot of gold,
And you have learned where fairies
Their moonlight revels hold;
When all the seashore's yellow sand
You've gathered in your pail,
Then is the time to chase, and catch,
Miss Molly Cotton-Tail.

Bright and early the next morning, Molly Cotton-Tail was awake and stirring in her nest at the end of a long burrow, deep down in the sandy soil, under a certain young pine-tree.

Molly Cotton-Tail, you know, belongs to the large family of wood rabbits, and her name of "Cotton-Tail" is given because of the stumpy white tail which curves over her back and, when seen from the rear, looks something like a bit of white cotton.

Molly has large, round, velvety eyes, which can see very far, and very keenly; and her long ears have a most wonderful sense of hearing. Her fur is a beautiful, soft grayish-brown, which, in some members of her family, turns white in winter.

Her length is about sixteen inches, and, although her fore legs are short, her hind legs are very long and strong, and carry her forward by great leaps and bounds when she runs. A very swift runner is Molly, as you may well imagine, and few can hope to overtake her in a race.

Still, she has her foes, like all wild creatures, and the one she dreads most of all is the weasel, who is hated and feared alike by all animals.

The weasel is a small furry-coated but snaky-looking animal, with red eyes and a long, pointed nose. His color is white in winter, yellow in spring, and brown in summer, and he tracks his prey by means of his wonderful sense of smell squirrels, rabbits, partridges, field mice, and barn-yard fowls, are all hunted by him, and he is so cruel and bloodthirsty that he often kills just for the love of it. He lives on the blood and brains of his victims, and it is small wonder that they dread him as they do, and are often so terrified at the mere sight of him that they have no strength to run.

But to come back to Molly Cotton-Tail, whom we left just hopping out of her nest in the burrow. There were three soft little bundles of fur in that nest; tiny baby bunnies, all cuddled down together in the soft down which Mother Bunny had pulled from her own breast to make them a warm cradle.

It did not hurt her to do this, as some people think, for her fur is very loose when the little rabbits are born, and comes out easily.

It was because of the little rabbits that Molly Cotton-Tail was just then living by herself. The burrowing rabbits are social creatures, and generally live together in a whole colony of burrows made in sandy soil and protected by bushes and low trees. The roots of the trees protect the tunnels, and the bushes hide the entrances, or doorways.

But before her little ones arrive, Mother Bunny digs a burrow apart from the others, and at the far end of it she makes her nest and brings up her family.

None of the other rabbits are allowed inside the nursery, for, although very gentle and timid, Molly Cotton-Tail can fight fiercely for her young, and strike terrible blows with her strong hind legs.

I suspect the reason for her caution is the bad reputation of the male, or father, rabbit, who is said sometimes to kill and eat his own offspring!

But Mrs. Bunny is a watchful and devoted mother, so her little ones usually live to grow up, and are soon able to take care of themselves and have families of their own. Indeed, Mrs. Bunny is usually a mother, and sometimes a grandmother too, when she is only a year old!

This morning, Molly had left her babies sleeping safely and hopped serenely down her long, dark burrow toward its entrance, her thoughts no doubt busy with a coming breakfast. She had gone only a little way, however, when her sensitive nose warned her of a new smell in her passageway. She paused, pointed her long ears sharply forward, and, wrinkling up her large nose-pad, sniffed the air suspiciously.

Yes, it was a strange smell, that was certain, one that had no business there, but there was nothing dangerous about it. So Molly hopped boldly forward and soon came upon a small animal curled up just inside her door.

"A squirrel!" exclaimed Mrs. Bunny. "Well of all impertinent things! What are you doing in my house, I'd like to know?" and she raised her ears and looked as fierce as she knew how.

"Please don't turn me out," pleaded the squirrel. "There is a dreadful owl outside, and if I hadn't just happened to fall into this hole, I wouldn't be alive now. He carried off the end of my tail as it is." And Trixsey looked sadly at his once beautiful tail, which, sure enough, was much shorter than it should have been.

"Well, well!" said Mrs. Bunny, sympathetically, "you have had a hard time of it to be sure. And it is a lucky thing for you that my burrow was so near! And what a fortunate thing for me, too, that I stayed at home last night! Dear me! I really must go and warn the colony that there is an owl in the neighborhood. They will have to be careful about moonlight parties in the future. You can come with me, if you like. There is no danger now, for owls nev-er trouble us in the daytime."

As she spoke, Molly Cotton-Tail hopped briskly along, and Trixsey followed, glad of company and glad to be out again in the sunshine.

Many of the rabbits had already scattered to the woods and fields near by to search for their morning meal of roots and vegetables, but others were hopping busily in and out of their burrows and among the under-brush.

Some of these were young, half-grown rabbits, and they listened to Trixsey's account of his adventure, with a good deal of dismay.

"Isn't it a shame!" cried one frisky bunny. "We had planned a grand moonlight frolic to-night in a bit of cleared ground not far from here, but, of course, this news will spoil it all. You know we have great fun playing games and chasing each other in the moonlight, but we have to be careful to keep to places where the owls are not apt to come, and there hasn't been one about here for a long time. But I say," he exclaimed suddenly, "won't you tell us how you happened to wander into our settlement?"

"Yes, do tell us," cried all the other young rabbits, and they squatted eagerly around Trixsey, their funny long ears pointed at attention.

So our hero had to go over the whole story, while the young rabbits listened with the greatest interest; but, although they all had a great deal of advice to give as to what should be done, and all had seen many red squirrels, none had made the acquaintance of Pesky.

This was not encouraging, and Trixsey would no doubt have abandoned his search (of which to tell the truth he was already tired) had not one of the rabbits made a good suggestion.

"If any one in the woods can tell you what you want to know," said he, "it is Madam Jet, an old black crow who has her nest in a dead pine not far from Farmer Perkins's corn-field. I have often passed it on my way to the cabbage patch, and would be glad to show you the way. She is a great gossip, is Madam Jet, and always knows everything about her neighbors' affairs, so if any one can help you, she can."

This kind offer was very gladly accepted by Trixsey, and the two set out in the best of spirits.

Bunny was a sociable little fellow, and somewhat inquisitive, too, like all of his family. He had many questions to ask about the habits and manner of life of his companion, and many tales to tell of his own life and that of his relations.

There are about twenty different kinds

The two set out in the best of spirits.

H. S. K., "The two set out in the best of spirits," illustration for *Trixsey's Travels,* by Emily Paret Atwater (Philadelphia: George W. Jacobs, 1905).

of rabbits in North America; but only a few in South America, and none, it is said, in Australia.[3]

Hare is the proper name for those in America, but the ones which make burrows are usually called rabbits to distinguish them from the hares which live in forms, or beds of grass and leaves made in the bushes.

The rabbits are of a social nature and live in colonies, while the hares prefer a solitary life, and only take to the earth when the dogs are after them.

Then, too, the hares are much larger than their little brothers, and Bunny had truly wonderful stories to tell of the strength and swiftness of the big prairie hares, or jackrabbits, so called because of their tremendously long legs and ears. These prairie hares turn white in winter, as do some of the smaller hares and rabbits, and this white coat serves to shield them from their enemies when the snow is on the ground.

A very beautiful member of the family is the polar hare, which is pure white, with black ear tips.

Although a rodent, and therefore a cousin of the squirrel, the rabbit differs from him in a great many ways. His teeth are not so strong, for one thing; but they serve his purpose very well, since he does not care for nuts, but lives on vegetables, roots, branches, and tender stalks and bark. He has no cheek pouches, either.

Although his head is long, his ears are even longer than his head, and he has a curiously cut upper lip, and a large, sensitive nose-pad for smelling. While his fore feet are furnished with five toes, his hind feet have only four.

His large, round, full eyes (furnished with an extra eyelid at the corner)[4] are perhaps his greatest beauty, and his swiftness and great keenness of eye and ear, his greatest protection.

I am afraid that Bunny bragged a good deal of the races he had run; and Trixsey, not to be outdone, bragged of the long jumps he had made. So they passed the time pleasantly enough, for it was a long distance to Madam Jet's home.

Bunny led the way, hopping nimbly along, but stopping now and then for a nibble at a leaf or stalk, and Trixsey followed as best he could, sometimes on the ground, when they had to cross a field, and sometimes leaping from tree to tree, where he was more at home.

They met many acquaintances and friends, for all the daytime field and forest creatures were out for an airing, and once they paused intending to ask a question of an old woodchuck, who was sitting in the doorway of his burrow, under a sunny hill side.

He was an ugly looking creature, fat and flabby, with dark fur, and sharp pointed incisors[5] projecting beyond his mouth.

He eyed his approaching visitors for a minute, and then, with a shrill whistle, disappeared in his hole and although they lingered, hoping to see him reappear, the inhospitable old fellow obstinately stayed below and refused to be interviewed.

"Stupid old creature!" complained Bunny, as the two moved on again. "So silly of him to be afraid of us. But then he is a great coward, and never goes far from his hole. I suppose one reason is that his legs are short and stout, and he can make only short leaps, so he doesn't dare venture very far away. There is a decided odor about him too, so it is not hard to tell when he is at home. He is a sort of relation of ours, but he isn't fond of company, and lives such an unsociable life that he is not at all popular except with his own immediate family.

"His food is very much the same as ours: grass, clover, vegetables and the like, as well as roots, twigs, and the bark of young trees. Sometimes he will venture into a farmer's garden for a taste of his vegetables, and sometimes the farmer's boys have a woodchuck hunt, and dig him out of his hole. They think it is great fun, but I hardly think he agrees with them.

"The sunny side of a hill is one of his favorite places for digging his hole, or burrow, though he likes also to dig under the shelter of a large rock, stone wall, or ledge."

On each foot he has five toes, each one armed with very sharp claws, and with these he can dig deep and rapidly.

"The burrow is a long one, often twenty or thirty feet in length. It slants downward for a few feet, and then gradually rises until it is near the surface of the ground. Here he digs a round room, or chamber, and makes a nest for the young woodchucks.

"The young ones stay with their mother until they are five months old. After that the family separates, arid the young ones go off by themselves and begin to dig small holes for their new homes. They are not sociable, even among themselves, and prefer to lead solitary lives most of the time.

"That whistle you heard is the woodchuck's signal of danger, and he always gives it before he vanishes from sight.

"Some people call him the ground-hog, because he is so fat and flabby, but it is not his proper name. He isn't always fat either, for when he comes out of his hole in the spring (he sleeps from November to March, as a rule) he is very thin and feeble, and can hardly crawl around for a little while. But he soon picks up when he gets his regular food again.

"I suppose you have heard that old story about the woodchuck, or ground-hog, and his shadow? They say he comes out from his hole on the second day of February, and, if the sun is shining so that he can see his shadow, he is so scared that he goes back to his hole; then there are six more weeks of winter. If he does not see his shadow, he stays out, and the winter weather is over. Of course none of us believe that yarn.

"Well, we are near our journey's end now. Madam Jet's nest is in the little grove just ahead of us, and those are Farmer Perkins's fields beyond. But just hear the crows cawing! I wonder what they are making so much noise about!"

The crows certainly were making a terrible to-do. The tree-tops ahead seemed fairly black with them, and every once in a while the whole flock would. rise in the air, circle wildly around, cawing in the most excited manner, and then swoop downward as if pursuing something.

What it was all about was soon determined. Out from the bushes at one side of the grove, and just in front of our adventurers, strolling calmly along, all unmindful of the clamor over his head, appeared a large, red fox!

Catching sight of Trixsey and his companion, he paused an instant as if astonished, but in that one instant Trixsey had bounded into the branches of a dogwood tree, and thence to a near-by pine, and Bunny was speeding for life back the way he had come. How he did run! Swift and straight as an arrow he bounded, for he had no time to double, right toward the hillside he had just left, his enemy close behind. It seemed a very unequal race, for swift as the rabbit is, he is no match for the fox, and there were no friendly rabbit burrows at hand in which to take refuge.

Faster and faster bounded the terrified rabbit, leaping wildly over every stick and stone in his path, and on came the fox, gaining at every jump. Then, just as the end seemed certain, Bunny gathered all his strength for one desperate leap, and dived head first into the burrow which a certain unsociable woodchuck had made for himself in the hillside.

Chapter 6

What the Old Crow Saw; and Mr. Fox's Family

Haw! Haw! Caw! Caw! Laughed a vain old crow,
From the top of a tall pine-tree,
Though others are wise, I would have you to know,
None are equal in wisdom to me.

Mr. Fox's hopes of a fat rabbit dinner vanished with the parting glimpse of Bunny's little white tail. The strong scent about the doorway told Mr. Fox that the woodchuck was also within, but he too was safely out of reach.

Sitting down on his haunches, the fox gazed wistfully down the hole, wondering whether it would be worthwhile to try to dig out the two occupants. But the door-way was well protected by two large stones, one on each side. Moreover, it wasn't safe to linger in an open field in broad daylight; Farmer Perkins's dog might happen along. So, with another hungry sniff, he gave up the hunt, and trotting sadly away disappeared in the woods.

The flock of crows, with many jeering caws, finally flew off in another direction, leaving Trixsey crouched in the pine-tree with just one very wise-looking crow for company. She sat on a dead limb of the pine, smoothing her feathers with her beak and giving vent to what seemed like hoarse little chuckles of glee.

"Ha! Ha!" she cried, spying Trixsey just above her, "that was a splendid race. I don't know when I have enjoyed anything as much as that old rascal's disappointment. Mrs. Fox and the children will go hungry today, unless I'm much mistaken. He! He!" and she chuckled again.

"You don't seem very fond of foxes," said Trixsey, who was just beginning to recover from his fright; and he crept a little closer as he spoke.

"Fond of 'em," said Madam Jet, for so she proved to be, "I should say I am not fond of them. Every self-respecting crow hates a fox; and we always chase them and peck at them when they come out in the daytime. They have been known to catch members of our family, and there has always been bad feeling against them. But crows are only caught when they are hopping about in the snow, and cannot fly up as quickly as usual. As a rule, we are a match for any fox, and are not afraid of them either, which cannot be said of some other animals I know," and Madam

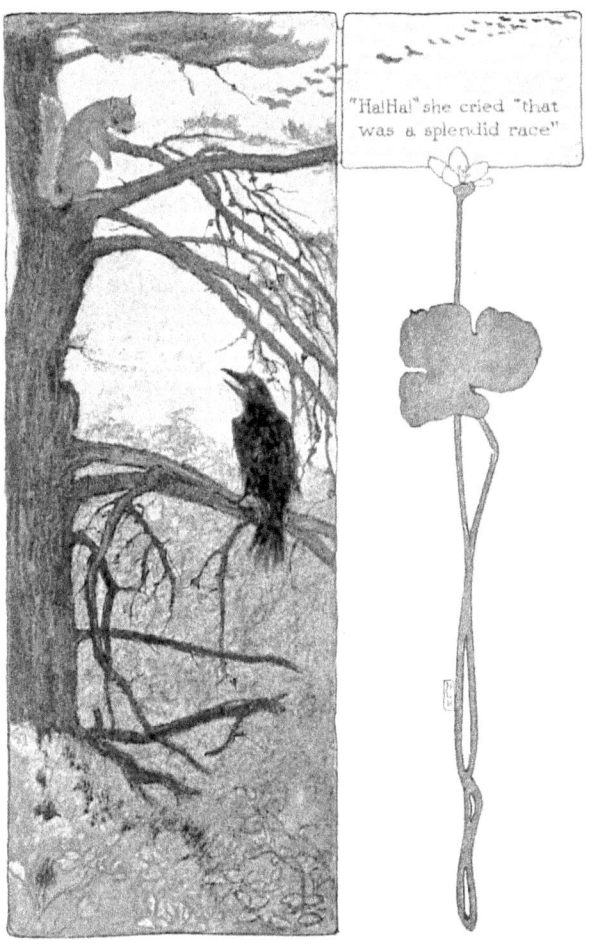

H. S. K., "Ha! Ha!" she cried, "that was a splendid race," illustration for *Trixsey's Travels*, by Emily Paret Atwater (Philadelphia: George W. Jacobs, 1905).

Jet shut one eye and looked slyly at Trixsey out of the other.

"Of course, *you* are not afraid," said Trixsey. "Neither would the rabbits and other creatures be if they could fly. It's having to live on the ground that is so dangerous. We squirrels, of course, have a better chance than some others, living as we do in the trees, but even some of our family get caught."

"Haw! Haw! Caw! Caw!" chuckled the wicked old crow. "Oh, yes, some of you get caught; red squirrels particularly! What do I mean? Oh, it's a long story, but I'll tell it, if you care to listen, though the ending is rather sad. He! He!" and Madam Jet flapped her wings and chuckled with delight.

"It all happened the other day, when a red squirrel appeared in this neighborhood. He hadn't been here an hour before he began to make trouble. There were all sorts of stories of nests robbed, young birds eaten, and goodness knows what dreadful things beside!"

"Oh, do you know what was his name?" asked Trixsey.

"No, I don't know what the squirrel's name was, but I do know that he was a dreadful thief, and was punished as he well deserved." And Madam Jet (who, like all crows, had rather a bad name herself for stealing) shook her head and looked very virtuous.

"Well, that fox you saw just now is the father of a family of five young cubs, and, of course, with so many mouths to feed, he and the mother have to be continually hunting for food.

"Their den is somewhere in the woods not far from here, and I understand that they stole it in the first place from a wood-chuck or rabbit and then enlarged it, for the fox is too lazy to dig a burrow for himself when he can get one ready-made.

"Besides his den, he has several holes ('earths' they are called). They are a good distance apart, and if the fox is chased by dogs, he has little trouble in taking to 'earth,' as the hunters say, if he wants to; but sometimes he takes the dogs a long chase to get them away from the nursery. I have heard wonderful stories of the way he cheats them by running through the bed of a brook or stream, or along the top of a rail fence, to throw them off the scent. Sometimes his tail gets very wet and draggled in this way, and that makes it hard for him to run swiftly.

"Another favorite trick of his, to throw the dogs off the scent, is to run through a ploughed field in very dry or cold weather. If the earth in the field were wet, it would hold the scent; but, being dry, it does not keep it

as well, and the dogs get very much puzzled and confused. Moisture keeps the scent and makes it stronger; this is one reason why a dog's nose is always moist when he is healthy.

"Oh! the fox is a cunning fellow! I can't help admiring him sometimes, though he is no friend of mine, I assure you. He is very dignified, too, except when some one is after him, and even then he never loses his self-possession, and usually finds a way to trick his hunters and escape. When he is actually cornered, or caught in a trap, he will often make believe he is dead, and sometimes even the most experienced hunters and dogs get completely fooled and reynard[6] escapes; I suspect he makes a good story out of it to amuse his family. Frequently, after he has successfully thrown the dogs off of his scent, he will sit down in a sheltered place where he can watch them without being seen himself, as if he thoroughly enjoyed their bewilderment, as I have no doubt he does.

"He is a famous hunter himself, but depends more on his cunning than on his courage in getting his food. He is very fond of rabbits, poultry, mice, and the like, and when he is very hungry will eat frogs and turtles. If he happens on a turtle, when he is not particularly hungry, he sometimes amuses himself by turning the poor creature over on its back, and then watching it trying vainly to struggle back into its proper position.

"He has been known to attract ducks within his reach by capering wildly about on the shore, chasing his tail, and cutting up all kinds of wild antics. The ducks usually get so curious about his strange behavior that they gradually get closer and closer to the bank and sometimes even waddle up out of the water to see what it all means. Mr. Reynard, of course, has apparently gone away by this time, but once they are safely on shore, out he rushes from his hiding-place, and the result is a nice duck dinner at the expense of the ducks.

"Although very fond of chickens and ducks, the fox will seldom rob a chicken-house or kill poultry near his own den when the little foxes are still too young to care for themselves, fearing that the dogs may track him to his home and so discover his young ones. This is particularly true of the mother fox ('vixen' they call her), who passes by many tempting henhouses near at hand, and goes to a distant farmer's to do her marketing. She is very careful, too, in teaching her young ones not to catch chickens or other poultry which may stray near their den. But the temptation is sometimes too strong for the young ones, who don't understand the real danger, and they sometimes disobey their wiser mother. When this happens, she will usually desert her den and take the willful cubs to a new home out of harm's way.

"The father, mother, and young ones are all very devoted to one another, and on summer evenings, they often come out of their den and play about in the moonlight. The cubs are very full of fun and mischief, but not particularly pretty. They are awkward, sprawling things, with gray coats, broad muzzles and short, stubby ears. As they grow older, their ears grow long and pointed, their fur takes on a ruddy tinge, and their tails become large and bushy. Their faces are very intelligent.

"Of course, there are many different kinds of foxes, but they all have the same characteristics. The Arctic fox is one of the most beautiful, and its pure white fur is very valuable. This fox makes very elaborate burrows, with different chambers and passages, and a separate chamber for the nursery. Arctic[7] foxes like to live in colonies, and make their burrows close to each other, whereas the common fox prefers to live with only his own immediate family, or perhaps entirely alone.

"Foxes who live near the seashore are very fond of fish, and watch the shores carefully after a high tide in search of any that may be thrown up on the sand. Some people say that they have been known to catch crabs by trailing their long, bushy tails over the water; when the crabs catch hold of the tail it is whisked to one side and they are tossed safely to land. But that's a fish story, and I won't vouch for the truth of it.

"But, dear me! where was I? Oh, yes! Well, on this particular morning the same fox that you just saw had been out hunting (for you know foxes will hunt by day sometimes), and I don't think he could have had much success.

"He came trotting through here just about dusk, and that saucy red squirrel I was speaking of soon saw him. Now, instead of keeping quiet as he should have had sense enough to do, he was so glad of a chance to make himself disagreeable that he ran out on the end of one of those chestnut limbs over there, and began a great barking and scolding, just to tease the fox. Of course, the limb was too far up for the fox to reach, and the saucy squirrel thought he was perfectly safe.

"Now, what do you suppose that fox did?

He sat down a minute and just looked at that silly squirrel, and then he began to race 'round and 'round that tree, faster and faster, until you could hardly see which was his head and which his tail.

"Mr. Red Squirrel was so curious to know what it all meant, that he stopped his noise, and just sat there on the limb, twisting his head this way and that to follow the fox. And, of course, the faster the fox ran, and the more the squirrel twisted his head around, the dizzier he became.

"Suddenly the fox stopped racing, and jumped up with all his weight against the tree (which was a small one), and down dropped the red squirrel! The next minute the fox had him, and was off to his den. Caw! Caw! I was sitting right here and saw the whole thing! It served the squirrel right, too, for being so stupid. I've never heard of anything but chickens being caught that way before, and they are too silly to know any better.

"Well! Well! Here I sit talking while a nestful of hungry youngsters is waiting for me; I must hurry away. Good-bye, Mr. Squirrel. Take the advice of a very old bird and go home just as fast as you can, for there is no telling when that fox will come hunting again," and with a parting chuckled Madam Jet flew away.

This seemed good advice to our friend, Trixsey, for he was a good deal sobered by hearing of the tragic fate of Pesky, and, truth to tell, only too glad of an excuse to abandon the search of which he had by this time grown rather tired. So, very carefully, and with a watchful eye on the lookout for the fox, he began to retrace his steps, never dreaming that other adventures still awaited him before he should again reach the grove.

Virginia Berkley Bowie (1880-1976)

Virginia Berkley Bowie straddled the line between society woman and actress. She attended the Bard-Avon School of Expression in 1917 and became well known for her participation in the arts as an actress.[1] As a descendant of the prominent Evensfield family of Maryland, she debuted in society when she came of age but did not marry her husband, Major Frederick Schoenfeld, until 1928, when she was in her late thirties.[2]

Bowie excelled as an actress and student of foreign languages, and had travelled with her family throughout Europe. Serving as secretary and treasurer of the Stagecraft Studios theater in Baltimore, she performed in *King Lear's Wife* and numerous other plays.[3] She served as historian for Baltimore's chapter of the Daughters of the American Revolution and donated funds to erect a marble column of Maryland at Continental Hall.[4] Admitted into the Woman's Literary Club at the end of the 1908 session, Bowie continued her membership through at least 1920, serving on the Committees of Unfamiliar Records, Colonial and Revolutionary History, and Foreign Languages. She wrote and presented essays and short stories, including "Dilemma of Patrolman Redmond" and "The

Desolation of Jean Baptiste," which were also published in the *Baltimore Sun*.

In these works, Bowie provides pointed commentary on contemporary gender roles. "Dilemma of Patrolman Redmond," for example, questions the assumed feminine virtues of temperance, obedience, female delicacy. Both pieces included here exemplify the genre of the romantic short story intended for mass consumption and entertainment. They observe middle-class society and Victorian traditions while subtly calling into question changes in gender dynamics and social norms. As an actress and author from a prominent, upper-class family, Bowie and her works provide an avenue for observing the shifting opinions regarding society during the Progressive Era. —M. Malouf

The Desolating Adventures of Jean Baptiste (1907)

I receive a letter from America offering me a position in the city of New York. My mother is inconsolable at the thought of being separated from me; my sisters weep upon my neck, fearing lest the ocean engulf me. I embrace them tenderly and depart.

Of the voyage I have no wish to speak. I find myself embarked upon an ocean, immense and sinister, which, with a terrifying motion, rises into great waves. Prostrated, I remain below in my cabin, praying for a death which does not arrive.

After many days we reach land. I am made giddy by the clamor which surrounds me on all sides. New York astonishes me.

I have never before seen such bustle, such agitated life, varied and extraordinary.

I establish myself in a pension which my employer recommends. Madame herself presides over our table at meals. I, Jean Baptiste, am seated between Jim Maddigan, professor of boxing, a man silent and powerful, and Silas Higgins, doctor of patent medicine, who converses with loquacity. There are others present, but with them I do not concern myself.

Madame is large, fat, and a little brusque, but the daughter of madame is entirely charming. She is called Mamie, and sometimes Mame. She is blond, with hair of a beautiful red, her eyes blue, her skin of an incomparable whiteness. One seeing such perfection of feature, a shape so sumptuously rounded, the poise of the head so gracious and noble, would have believed himself gazing upon Hebe. Her eyes—very blue, the blue of a periwinkle—are, at the same time, lively, caressing, thoughtful, intelligent, and good, revealing a character and a soul. Her high and rounded forehead betrays her seriousness, her elevation of intellect. She loves greatly the works of Marie Corelli, and reads continually *The Sorrows of Satan*.[5]

I adore her, as do all those in the pension, but I fear to lay my heart at her feet. Already Maddigan looks upon me with an eye of coldness, fearing lest I become a rival successful for the hand of Mame; but Higgins seeks daily more and more the honor of my presence.

To-day Mame has smiled upon me, and, in the afternoon, we go together to the park. I have then the intention of declaring my love.

Higgins has called me aside. He departs suddenly from New York to attend the funeral of his grandmother, and he begs me to accept from him this gold watch and chain, engraved with the crest of Higgins, and long an heirloom in his family, which he wishes to bestow upon me in token of his great friendship. I am deeply moved by this proof of affection, and embrace him with tears.

Accompanied by Mame, I stroll toward the park, my heart suffused with joy. We pause at a corner drug-store for the purpose of drinking a soda. Even here we find new evidences of our affinity of soul. At the same moment, we together demand an essence of strawberry.

We reach the park, and seat ourselves on a bench beneath some trees. It is a beautiful summer afternoon, full of sunshine. Everything seems touched with golden light, the clear blue sky, the heavy foliage, and even the neatly graveled walks. Little boys and girls tumble about on the grass and call to one another from a distance, while squirrels run nimbly along the ground, without fear, and eat from the hand.

I am stifled with emotion. I believe it possible for Mame to hear the palpitation of my heart. I attempt to speak but can only stammer with awkwardness.

All immediately, I gather courage to lay my devotion at her feet, to express the violence of my hidden love. I impart to her that, since, knowing her, my sun has risen and set in the heaven of her cerulean eyes, and that my life will be filed with everlasting darkness should she not consent to smile upon me. No longer will it be possible for me to live!

She replies, very modestly, that she can wed no man whose soul is not exalted above the sordid interests of modern society. A soul congenial to hers must be filled with a burning desire to benefit one's fellow creatures, and must resemble, in all respects, the heroes depicted by that great authoress, Marie Corelli.

I hasten to assure her that my character conforms to her ideal in every particular; and we linger until so late that Mame is apprehensive of the anger of madame.

On again reaching the steps of our pension, a hand is laid suddenly upon my shoulder. I find myself in the grasp of a gigantic officer of police. Behold the infamy! I am arrested, I am taken into custody, charged with larceny of the watch bestowed upon me by the generous Higgins! A gentleman has been robbed, and the thief is tracked to the pension, and, behold, I am discovered with the missing property!

I declare my innocence. I implore them with tears. I entreat them to spare me. In vain! I am torn from the arms of my adored one, and am incarcerated in a prison!

After a time, I am brought up for trial. I am overcome, and they are obliged to support me to the dock. I tremble as I look upon the man who is to decide my fate.

But fortune is with me. I behold the face of my employer, who comes to testify concerning my good character, and the face of madame, who will declare the perfidy of Higgins. I tell my story. The judge, deeply moved, conceals his visage. He believes in my innocence, as he knows familiarly the record of Higgins. That infamous man has already been many times in jail!

"You are discharged," says monsieur the judge.

I am innocent, I am free, I fly home to

my adored one; but, alas, she looks upon me with an eye of coldness! Since yesterday, she is the betrothed of Jim Maddigan!

Behold the perfidy of woman! A true coquette, she has destroyed the illusions and broken the heart of Jean Baptiste! I am desolated; I have no longer a wish to live! Unhappy one, I go to destroy myself!

To-day, I saw a beautiful blonde behind the counter of the confectionery shop. She is truly adorable, with superb hair and a dazzling complexion. Perhaps, after all, I am not entirely desolated.

Dilemma of Patrolman Redmond (1915)

Patrolman Redmond impaled a chunk of corned beef on the prongs of his fork, balanced a bit of boiled potato behind it with the accuracy of long practice, and having by means of his knife enveloped the whole with a streamer of cabbage, conveyed it to his mouth with a gesture reminiscent of a sword-swallower.

Having assimilated the last morsel with gusto, he thrust out his legs beneath the table and heaved the sigh of a contented spirit.

"Eileen," he proclaimed, magisterially, addressing his wife's graceful back, "that was all right! Yes, kid, that was pretty good!" he paused a moment to regard with approbation the little dark curls that would stray across his wide's round neck. "Every day I know you kid, I keep on wondering how you ever grew out of that roaring, rowdying bunch that was mother and father and brothers and sisters to you."

"I'm glad if you like my cooking, Redmond," Eileen responded, submissively. She still bent over her gas range in an all too apparent desire to avoid her husband's eye. Redmond remembered suddenly that since he had entered the house at noon he had missed in her those birdlike snatches of song with which she usually went about her work. He frowned a moment, seeking a cause.

"There's something troubling you, kid?" he queried. "Out with it!"

Eileen still stirred the mixture on the stove, but her lip trembled and there was a hint of tears in the Irish blue of her eyes. She spoke in a very small voice.

"Redmond, mother's back!"

Patrolman Redmond's fist smote the table with a giant whack that created consternation among the dishes and dislodged a fork. "The devil she is!" He scowled heavily at the three lithographed kittens sprawling from their blue-ribboned basket on the wall before him. "She's got to go!"

Eileen wrung her hands helplessly. "That's just what I've been telling her over and over, but she's after saying that I'm her own legal step-daughter, and that by every law of Heaven her home is here. She swears she'll not be leaving us soon again, and that if you'll be after putting her gray hairs out of the cold, Redmond, she'll shame us with the neighbors in a way we'll never forget."

Patrolman Redmond emitted a hoarse growl. "G'wan, don't you worry, kid," he vociferated. "The old rummy's not going to camp on us. I've had enough of her rough stuff since we've been married. She's going to beat it tonight!"

A heavy step on the kitchen stairway caused the patrolman to turn his head abruptly. Retribution was his! His mother-in-law stood at the twist of the narrow steps, regarding him in an irate preliminary to speech.

"Ye contimptible scut!" To the outward eye, the bellicose Mrs. Kelly drew visible breath preparatory to an outburst of speed. "I've been listening to ye, ivry worrrud! So ye'll thrun me out, will ye, your wife's old mother, wid no place to lay me gray hairs? The divil fly away wid ye, ye lowdown bog-trotter!" Her voice rose to a scream of battle. "I suppose ye're after thinking that because we've got a blue coat and all thim shiny brass buttons that I ain't good enough for ye! Well, young fella me lad, ye're wrong!"

Redmond got halfway to his feet with a denunciatory gesture, encountered the old harridan's flaming eye, and sank back, wilting visibly. He gulped down a last mouthful of coffee, twisted his neck for a glance at the clock, and rose clumsily. He slipped his arms into his coat without daring to venture a look at his wife, thrust pistol and blackjack into his hip-pocket, and jammed on his official cap. At the threshold, he shot one final glance out of the tail of his eye at his mother-in-law, and muttering something down his collar to the effect that he would attend to her later, departed hurriedly by way of the front door.

Redmond progressed gloomily toward his post, revolving the misfortunes of his position. He encountered the glances of his closest neighbors, Mrs. Shultz and Mrs. Finnigan, and detected in them a sudden curiosity and aloofness for which he was not slow to assign a cause. As he passed Hugh's place on the corner, he caught a glimpse of Hugh himself peering through his swinging wicker doors.

Hugh beckoned Redmond with a mysterious finger. "Say, Red," he communicated, in a hoarse tone meant to be confidential. "I don't want to butt into no private affairs of yours, but I guess it's only right to warn you the old woman's back again!"

Redmond regarded his informer with a dispirited gaze. "That's no news to me, Hughie; I've seen her!"

"Well, counseled Hugh, "What I mean is, Red, you oughta do something about it. I seen her going up the street about 10 o'clock this morning; and I bet it wasn't 15 minutes before she was banging at the door for a duck."

"Did she start anything?" Redmond asked, but without alacrity.

"Start anything? I should say she did! The first time she bawled me out I pacified her, but it wasn't no time before she was back with her kettle, and with that old Myers dame along with her. I gave them their pint; but an hour ago the old lady was here again, and all cooked up. She wanted to come in, but you know me, Red. I don't allow no women in my place. They've got to get their pints at the side door."

"Did you can her, Hughie?" Redmond queried, with a gleam of hope.

Hugh emitted a snort. "Can her?" I couldn't keep the old devil out. She picked up a brick and said she'd bounce it off my bean. She wanted a slug of gin, and when I wouldn't sell, she tried to bust the mirror with her brick. You gotta do something about that old woman, Red, you gotta do something!"

"I'll fix her, Hughie!" said Redmond, with a pitiful attempt at moral defiance.

"I'll fix her tonight!" He paused, ignominiously aware of the depths of cowardice into which his spirit descended at the thought. He felt a sudden need of sympathy. "It's kinder tough on us, Hughie, having that old devil back just when we'd got her a nice home down in the country. She'd promised the wife to stay and not shame her any more with the neighbors, and in less'n six months she's round here again! It's tough; that's what it is; it's tough!"

Hugh nodded feelingly, and Redmond passed on with depressed head. Tonight, he was all too aware, his domiciliary authority must be put to its final test. Either he must then forcibly eject the belligerent Mrs. Kelly or thereafter suffer her continued and disreputable presence as a third occupant of his hearth and home. At the prospect his secret soul quailed, for now be it revealed that he who was the perennial terror of small boys and the nemesis of the evildoer harbored one single, petrifying dread, and that was of his mother-in-law. Adamant to all offenders when clothed in the garb of duty, he became as the proverbial sacrificial lamb at the first lash of his amazonian relative's linguistic powers. The memory of past defeats weighed on him with doleful augury for the future. As he approached his post he saw in gloomy fancy a long succession of disturbing and disreputable days at trois spread out before him without hope and without surcease.

Redmond approached his home slowly, nerving himself for the contest. He was off duty for the night, and Eileen, and possibly Mrs. Kelly, would be waiting for him. His feet dragged a little at the

thought, but he stiffened his spine manfully and went on. He had just turned the corner into his street when a little man, salmon-pink and breathless from an over-intensity of excitement, darted up to him and seized him by the arm.

"Oh, my Gawd, officer, there's a woman gettin' killed up in that saloon! She's yellin' something awful!"

Redmond, scenting the fray with the instinct of his calling, stayed not upon the order of his going, but shaking off the grip of the little man, he broke into the police lope, a hand on his pistol pocket to insure the continued companionship of that valued weapon. His quick eye had discerned upon the instant, a block away, the motley crowd of shirt-sleeved men, excited women and enraptured children jostling and shoving each other for a vantage point at the doors and windows of Hugh's place.

Redmond shouldered his own way energetically through the shifting mass and into the saloon. In one corner, intrenched behind a table, half a dozen men had ensconced themselves in attitudes of determined neutrality, while the unhappy Hugh crouched behind the bar, an irregular broken line in the mirror showing where a rapidly-projected beer glass has just missed him. The glances of all present were focused vividly on a virago of uncertain age and general disarray of attire, who was holding the center of the stage and yelling defiance in all shades of the Irish tongue, as she strode to and fro, crunching under her feet the bits of broken glass on the floor.

Patrolman Redmond's first glance at this disturber of the peace revealed in her something sinisterly familiar. His second glance confirmed his first. By all the gods of the force, it was his mother-in-law!

Somewhere in the depths of Patrolman Redmond's soul a small still voice pealed forth in a pain of deliverance. Destiny itself had come to the rescue of his falling courage. No longer was the vociferous Mrs. Kelly a mere member of his family circle, to be dealt with according to the indeterminable ways of private right and moral suasion. She had rendered herself amenable to the law like any other evil-doer of his acquaintance, and its relentless majesty stiffened his quailing spine with an unknown resolution.

With kindling eye and hardened jaw, Redmond strode up to the offender and laid a heavy hand on her shoulder. "Come on; you're under arrest!" And then at a fresh scream of battle, "Shut up, or I'll knock your bean off!"

Mrs. Kelly regarded her son-in-law blankly with a sudden loosening of her facial muscles, her last vituperation ending in a gurgling gasp. Her fists unclenched, her arms swung limply. A tear glistened in her eye, her nose wrinkling like a baby's.

"Ye seen him to ut—ye seen him strike me." she appealed with pleading to the intrenched neutrals. "An' he's my darlin daughter's husband——me own son-in-law!"

Redmond's face was like flint. Never, oh, never again was the belligerent Mrs. Kelly to strike the same chill to his marrow as in former days! He barked sharply, "Can that guff and come along! You're pinched! I'm sending you in, see?"

A last spark of conflict flared up in the old amazon to be quenched immediately in a burst of hiccoughing tears. Redmond gripped her by the arm and propelled her through the swinging doors and down the lane respectfully parted by his curious neighbors. Followed by the inevitable crowd, he marched her to the green call-box, and rang for the wagon.

The next noon, Patrolman Redmond entered his home with the air of a man at peace with the world in general. The kiss he bestowed upon his heavy-eyed wife smacked of an unwonted assurance. He thrust his legs beneath the laden table genially.

"I guess, kid, we'll be having a little peace for the present," he proclaimed. He impaled a chunk of corned-beef neatly with a single stab. Eileen's eye held a question.

"No, she ain't dead," Redmond reassured, perceiving the inquiry. "The old woman's only locked up where she won't be any harm. Kid, I'll eat my hat if I ain't just seen the squire give her sixty days!"

Corinne Robert Redgrave (1866-1958)

Corinne Robert Redgrave used her stage presence to promote women's right to vote, performing in, directing, and organizing many suffrage plays all over the United States. In her home state of Maryland, before the Just Government League, the largest suffrage organization in Maryland, Redgrave directed part of the suffrage play *Brought Home.*[1] She also performed in *How the Vote Was Won* in 1910.[2] And as chairwoman of the pageant committee production of *The Dream of Brave Women*, she performed during the Baltimore suffrage bazaar in 1914, a nationally recognized gathering of suffrage supporters. As a member of the Vagabond Players Theater[3] group, Redgrave became integrally woven into the Baltimore theater scene.

Redgrave prided herself a thespian, yet her social responsibilities spanned beyond the theater. In 1915, she chaired the "Smoke" investigation committee for the Women's Civic League, a group devoted to the promotion of desirable living conditions in the Baltimore area.[4] This was just one of her many contributions to local organizations.

Redgrave was a member of the Woman's Literary Club of Baltimore from 1914 to 1916. Her contributions include romantic stories about women and witty, critical articles such as "What Every Amateur Actress Ought to Know." This article, which was published in the *Ladies' Home Journal* in 1913, legitimizes the status of amateur female actresses through Redgrave's comments on acting principles and her sarcastic undercutting of domestic practices. Her short-lived involvement with the WLCB may been the result of her busy acting schedule or her movement around the country as a military wife. However, it's also possible that her penchant for political and social commentary produced tensions within the Club, given that many club members avoided hot-button issues and sought to uphold traditional values. Redgrave is an important example of a Club member who unapologetically and unabashedly promoted women's rights in public. —M. J. Malouf

What Every Amateur Actress Ought to Know (1913)

If you were to come to me for help in the play you are rehearsing your first confidential whisper would be: "I feel so awkward when I am on the stage, and self-conscious; I don't understand it, because I never feel so at other times." You feel awkward because you are self-conscious, and you are self-conscious because you are uncertain of your movements; you have only an indefinite idea of what you are going to do next.

Can you remember the first time you poured tea for your mother's guests? The simple act suddenly became a serious occupation; and if any one happened to address a remark to you while you were in the act of pouring you forgot the sugar or lemon, or perhaps both. Since then you have poured tea so often that you can now pour it and serve pretty remarks along with the lemon and sugar—and it all seems as though there had never been an uncertain time.

The pouring and serving of tea stand for what we call "business" on the stage—action without lines. It is this "business" marked in your book which makes you feel awkward even though you may do that same act with perfect grace off the stage.

While at first a given stage "business" will seem to hamper your freedom of action, without it you are in a worse state: you have no definite idea of what you are going to do, and will probably not do the same thing twice. This lack of definite purpose on the part of the players is quickly conveyed across the footlights; and the audience, without analyzing, says: "Amateurish."

When the play has been selected and the parts assigned, call a reading rehearsal at some house where all can gather around a table and read the play through, each reading the part assigned. On this occasion it is well to fix upon the nights for future rehearsals, and all should agree to cancel those nights on their calendars of engagements. By having five or six rehearsals in one week more can be accomplished than by scattering the same number through a period of several weeks. A week to an act and one for the whole play is a good rule. Let the next rehearsal be in the hall where you are going to give the play. If you rehearse in a parlor you will use your parlor voice on stage, and that cannot be heard beyond the first few rows in any hall.

You will notice in your playbook directions for moving R, L, RC, etc. When you meet for your first acting rehearsal mark your floor with chalk lines into sections like the diagram above. The written directions of the book are to be read facing the audience. The expressions "Down stage" and "Up stage" originated when the stage sloped towards the footlights. Later the slope was placed in the auditorium and the stage was made level, but "up" and "down" stage has remained in use.

When you have diagrammed your floor, and have placed each article of furniture according to the directions in the playbook, then wherever doors are indicated, or the exits of an outdoor scene, place two chairs to form an opening through which to pass.

Those who are most deeply interested in their work will come to the first rehearsal with some of their lines committed to memory. In a professional company every one is required to be line-perfect at the second rehearsal. Lay aside your book as soon as possible and depend upon the prompter, and so be free to give your attention to the stage "business."

The prompter should become familiar with the lines and the stage "business," so he may know on the final night whether the actress is in need of his help of is pausing for effect or a bit of "business." The knowledge that there is a prompter behind the scenes inspires confidence though his services may not be required.

My experience has taught me that the quickest and surest method of committing lines to memory is to copy off your part from the book, reading aloud as you write, word for word, every line. Also copy any stage directions which may be printed in the book; underscore these and place in parentheses to distinguish at a glance from the lines. And copy your cues—the last two or three words preceding your lines. You have the right to insist that you be given the correct cue. Changing the lines is inexcusable, and is due to careless study. Take a short scene and rewrite it until you can dispense with the book, always repeating the words aloud.

See that the properties are at hand for all rehearsals, either the real articles or substitutes. If, for instance, you are going to enter with a suitcase something must be brought on the stage which can be laid down, so that the others in the cast may know where that suitcase is going to be even if placed for only a moment, or if it is to be disposed of immediately go through the "business" each time.

After you have had a few rehearsals, if you were to ask me to come and criticize your work, without doubt the first criticism would be: "None of you speak loud enough."

And another says: "I know positively I can't speak any louder."

To the girl with the gentle voice I say: You put too many words in one breath—that makes your voice break. Breathe often; it is the secret of much voice. Practice speaking your lines outdoors. And when you are rehearsing in the hall imagine that some one you care for, who is a little deaf, is sitting in the back row, and play to that last row.

And you who think you can't speak louder—don't try. In your effort to speak loud you have pitched your voice too high. Try a lower key—your voice will carry much farther. And do not speak so rapidly. When the lines call for an excited, rapid delivery you can produce the effect by speaking only the unimportant words rapidly, giving every word which is significant its full value. Hand me your book for a minute; I will read one of your quick lines for you. Here is an excellent practice sentence, when you rush on to tell that the bird has flown out of the window:

"I-*was*-giving-the-*bird*-its-*bath*. I-*turned* just-for-a-*minute* and-the-*bird-flew*-out-the-*window*."

Take it slowly at first, emphasizing the important words, then gradually increase the speed until it becomes an effort to articulate distinctly those same words. Words that tell the story must be heard, all words should be heard. Please, all of you, articu-late more distinctly. Clear articulation will carry even a gentle voice across the footlights. So never tire of working over your voice. Listen to its tones; make it cry, make it laugh, make it sad, make it glad—make yourself absolutely master of it.

I have criticized your voices first, and you probably thought I would find fault with the love scenes. The only way to play a love scene is at once to rid it of all sentiment by attaching no significance to the "business." If the scene calls for an "embrace" receive it or give it, at the first rehearsal, impersonally. As I said, it is usually the girl who from self-consciousness establishes the personal relation and at once embarrassment follows. To overcome this recognize this fact at the start, that each is only a means toward and end, as a "property" may be introduced to complete a scene. Always remember the viewpoint of the audience. If the mind be engrossed in producing a picture there will be no stray moment when the personal element can enter.

There is one thing which may be left until the dress rehearsal, and that is a kiss. When it is consistent with the character to kiss either the hand or the forehead the kiss should be placed; but the usual lovers' kiss need never be given on the stage. Stand so that the audience will have a side view of your faces; throw your head back, looking up into the face of the man, your head slightly inclined away from his. As his face comes down he must cover you from the audience; he will have to turn his head to appear to touch your lips, and the audience cannot see the space between.

The next criticism I must make is that when you are speaking your lines most of you show a restlessness that is disturbing. I mean that after speaking a sentence you move a few steps before speaking the next, or you shift from one foot to the other, or put your hands on the back of a chair and take them off—perhaps you cross the stage without any possible reason. All these things you would never do were you carrying on the same conversation in real life. And on the stage they are permissible only when you are representing an awkward or nervous person; in that case they help to strengthen the characterization. Here is a safe rule to follow on the stage: When you don't know what to do, do nothing. You may feel extremely awkward standing absolutely still with your hands dropped loosely by your sides, but to the audience you are the embodiment of repose; and in an emotional scene you will suggest a strong reserve force.

Let me repeat: Don't move without a purpose. And never under any circumstances start to cross the stage while somebody is speaking, unless the purpose is to show inattention and the point must be emphasized. Characters not speaking must not move during a speech. Every conscientious actress wants to work for the effect of the whole picture. When you move to a position see that you do not cover any one farther upstage.

There are a background and a foreground in every stage picture. Keep the perspective. Don't make any one speak up stage. I mean with the back directly to the audience. Adjust your positions each time, or dress the stage, technically speaking, so that the one whose scene it is, having the more important lines to speak, shall be farther up stage and so face the audience. When I say face the audience I don't wish to be misunderstood. Never, under any conditions, look at your audience. Occasionally, though not always, an "aside" must be spoken with the face to the audience. But as the "aside" is a remark to self why address the audience? When obliged to look toward the audience focus your eyes on some spot at the extreme end of the hall just above the level of your eyes.

I have reserved for the last correction the weakest point in all amateur productions: the entrances and the exits. When you make your first entrance you should convey to the audience by your manner of coming on what kind of a character you are portraying. In character work the makeup will help, but in "straight parts" the walk, the pose of the head, the tone of voice used, must suggest at once the character. The athletic girl would carry her shoulders erect, her head back, and walk with a free swing, and her voice would probably be ringing, clear cut; and we would look for a little independence of spirit too. While from the girl who is all sentiment we would expect a slower walk, a thoughtful carriage, with perhaps the head drooping the least bit. The dreamy girl would keep her hands clasped, and her eyes must often focus far off into the beyond.

There are merely suggestions how to study your role to produce effects without the aid of your lines.

If you are "discovered" on the stage when the curtain rises count six before you speak; that gives the audience sufficient time to take in the scene.

Most comedies and all farces require

quick entrances. When your stage is small take short steps to produce the effect of rapid motion.

The exits are even more important than the entrances, for a bad exit will ruin the best played scene, while a good exit often save a poorly played scene. There is just one way to a make an exit. All exits are made alike, though you may not detect the similarity until you begin to analyze. If the play is well written there will be provision for the rule. One line is intended to carry you up stage, sometimes as far as the door where you pause or come down again—another line, and you exit. There are exceptions to all rules, but note the rule: up stage, back again or pause, then off.

If you rehearse conscientiously each rehearsal will bring out some point which did not occur to you before; some new interpretation will flash over you while speaking your lines, or you will be inspired to do a bit of "business" which you never would have thought out.

May Garrettson Evans (1866-1947)

May Garrettson Evans spent her entire life breaking boundaries. She is credited as the first female reporter at the *Baltimore Sun* from 1888-1895, but this was just one of her many accomplishments.[1] She and her sister Bessie also founded the Peabody Preparatory School of music, where she also served as superintendent until her retirement in 1930.[2] Evans was an early member of the WLCB, and chaired the Committee on Fiction. Evans's professional work may have prevented her from continuing her membership after 1896. With her career in music and journalism it comes as no surprise that many of her works involved research and music.

Both "Facts about Mistake in Marking Original Burial Place of Poe" and *American Indian Dance Steps* underscore her dedication to finding out the truth, while also staying true to her musical interests. They also show the true meaning of observing humankind. In the former, Evans describes her hunt for the truth about Poe's resting place. Evans's discovery that the grave marker was in the incorrect place was instrumental in the subsequent correction of the grave marker for Poe at Westminster Churchyard in Baltimore.

The excerpt from *American Indian Dance Steps* also illuminates her desire to observe humankind. Evans and her sisters Bessie and Marion travelled to New Mexico in search of Navajo and Pueblo Indian dancers, and once there, she wrote, they "observed, questioned, and ultimately devised a system of notion to record the dancers."[3] The descriptions they present in *American Indian Dance Steps* are surprisingly progressive. Evans comments on the fact that many white people go to visit the Indians and disrespect them and blatantly disregard their wishes. She says, "Yes, lack of sympathy and of understanding on the part of the white race has, indeed, created obstacles to research."[4]
—S. Johnson and A. Hughes

Facts About Mistake in Marking Original Burial Place of Poe (1920)

Poe-loving townsman and stranger have paused reverently before this inscription on a gravestone that has stood in old Westminster Churchyard for the past eight years. But they have paused, I am convinced, in the *wrong spot*. The place where the body of Edgar Allan Poe really was first buried, and rested for twenty-six years, lies nameless and unmarked in another lot. Through some mistake, only recently discovered, the stone was set up in the lot of the late Septimus Tustin, over against the east wall, instead of in that of the poet's forebears.[5] The memorial was given by the late Orrin C. Painter, public-spirited citizen and Poe enthusiast, to mark the original grave.

How the mistake occurred no one knows. Septimus Paul Tustin, the Baltimore civil engineer and surveyor, learned a few days ago for the first time of the placement of the stone in his grandfather's lot, No. 38. "There is no tradition in our family," he says, "that the body of Poe ever lay there." S. Johnson Poe and Edgar Allan Poe, the Baltimore lawyers and kinsmen of the poet, were equally surprised to hear of the location of the memorial, as their family chronicles record explicitly that the original interment of Poe was in his grandfather's lot, No. 27. The plot of the graveyard and other old documents in the possession of the trustees also show that the Poe lot is No. 27. In this lot are the bones of Poe's grandfather, Gen. David Poe, gallant soldier of the Revolution and friend of Washington and of Lafayette. With the approval of Mr. Tustin and of the Poe family, the trustees of the graveyard have authorized the removal of the stone to the one-time grave of Poe.

As in the case of this memorial, singular mishaps have attended two other attempts to mark with enduring stone the original place of burial. It seemed as if the poet's first grave had been destined to be "nameless here forevermore."

Some years after the death of Poe, a white marble headstone was ordered for his grave, it is said, by his cousin, the late Judge Neilson Poe.[6] The tablet was standing completed in the marbleyard, which adjoined the tracks of the Northern Central Railroad. A few days before it was to be erected a freight train ran off the track, broke down the fence and smashed the first Poe monument to pieces.

The next attempt to mark the grave was made by the sexton who had helped to bury Poe, the late George W. Spence—I had it from the old man himself. In order that the exact location of the grave might be pointed out to visitors, Spence placed on it a bit of sandstone, containing the figure "80," a fragment of one of the markers used to number lots—Poe's only gravestone until 1875. When, in that year, the body was transferred to its present resting place, under the monument at the northwest corner of the cemetery, the assistant sexton, so Spence told me, took possession of the fragment of sandstone and sold it to a relic hunter for fifty cents or a dollar. Thus disappeared the second Poe "monument."

A Talk With the Sexton

My acquaintance of more than a quarter of a century ago with the sexton indirectly led to the recent discovery that the monument designed to memorialize the original grave of Poe had been wrongly placed. On my first pilgrimage to the historic graveyard I found that Spence actually lived among the graves and vaults under the chapel of Westminster Church. In Poe's day, there were no buildings in the graveyard. When, several years after his death, church and chapel were erected, the foundations were built in the form of open crypts, in order not to violate many of the ancient tombs. In a corner of a low-arched crypt Spence had set up his household gods.

"I had a nice room up town," he explained, "but I like this better. It's more quiet and independent." Certainly the living disturbed him little by day and the dead not at all by night.

He hospitably invited me into this strangest of domiciles. A few domestic comforts made the place homey, incongruous as they were in their setting. An old-time square elevated tomb, topped off with its flat marble slab, made a perfectly good table. All about us stretched the dim reaches of the crypt. Gray, crumbling headstones and solid, iron-doored vaults were but vaguely outlined in the gloom, even though the sun was shining brightly on grass and gravestones without.

We became very chummy. As we chatted together amid the tombs of Revolutionary heroes and brave pioneers, it came out that mine host had been serving in the place, man and boy, for nearly three-score years and ten.

"Oh!" I exclaimed, after a hurried calculation, "you must have been here when Poe was buried."

"Why, Miss," he answered, "I helped to bury him."

"Then tell me every single thing you can remember about it?" I begged.

Expanding in the congenial atmosphere of his own queer hearthstone, the old man dug out of the recesses of his memory bit by bit all that he knew concerning the great American literary genius.

"Mr. Poe himself used to wander about the burying ground now and then," he told me. "I remember plainly his looks and his manners as he went hunting about among the graves. He was always very quiet and thoughtful, it appeared to me. Sometimes he would stand looking at the graves of the Poes, and sometimes he would wander about among the others, examining the names and dates. Once in a while, but not often, he would ask a question about some person, or how this one was related to that one, and the like. When I met him in the streets he would sometimes say 'Good morning' or 'Good evening,' and sometimes he wouldn't.

"Well, I was mighty surprised to hear of his death. I had notice to make arrangements for the burial on October 9. It was a gloomy day; not raining, but just raw and threatening. You would have been surprised to see that funeral procession. Nobody would have thought it was some great person. There was just the hearse, with one hack coming after it. There wasn't a flower. In the hack was the preacher, Mr. Clemm, Judge Poe, Mr. Herring and another gentleman.[7] That was all—just four, besides the grave-digger and me. It didn't take long to get the work over. The preacher said the burial service and the benediction. Then the four gentlemen went away.

"Some time after this, somebody started the story in the papers that Mr. Poe had been buried like a dog. Now, that isn't true at all. The funeral was very quiet; there wasn't any show or fuss. But there wasn't anything wrong with the way the body was buried. Come, I'll show you just where the old grave was.

"This is the spot," said Spence, pointing to an expanse of ground, not far from the crypt under the chapel where the sexton had made his home. Standing there in the weeds in the quaint burying-ground, at the side of the old grave-digger, I could conjure up in fancy the unpretentious funeral train; the raw day; the six men gathered about the open grave; the benediction.

True Story of Burial

Several days afterward I learned that Spence's memory had not been at fault. I had read the widely published statement of Dr. J. J. Moran, the physician who was with Poe in his last illness, that a large concourse of distinguished folk attended his funeral. Puzzled by the discrepancy in the two accounts, I bethought me of an acquaintance, the venerable Methodist minister, the late Rev. W. T. D. Clemm, kinsman of Poe and of Virginia, his wife, the "preacher" of the sexton's story.

"There were only four or five of us at the funeral," Mr. Clemm assured me. "I had prepared a funeral oration for the occasion, but I did not deliver it."

A few days ago I came upon additional confirmation of the sexton's story, in the form of an old account of the burial by another member of the little funeral party. Henry Herring, who had married into the Poe family. "He was buried," Mr. Herring wrote, "in his grandfather's (David Poe's) lot near the center of the graveyard, wherein were buried his grandmother and several others of the family. I furnished a neat mahogany coffin, and Mr. Neilson Poe the hack and the hearse. Mr. Neilson Poe, Judge Nelson and myself, together with Mr. Charles Sutler, the undertaker, were the only persons attending the funeral."

We know, then, that Edgar Allan Poe was buried "decently and in order."

On another autumn day, twenty-six years after the burial, the sexton was called upon to assist in a very different memorial ceremony over the bones of the poet. This time there were orations, music, flowers, crowds. It was for the dedication of the new monument.[8] The body of Poe had been disinterred several days before by Spence and removed to the lot where it now rests, at the corner of Fayette and Greene streets, under the monument erected through the efforts of the late Miss Sara Sigourney Rice and other public school teachers. You can view it readily through the handsome open-work iron gate on Fayette street, the gift of Mr. Painter.

Of this occasion, too, the keeper had something to tell. "Only the skeleton was left," he said. "When the pickaxes struck against the coffin it was found that the wood was pretty well gone. We had to put the bones into another box, about two and a half feet long. When this was put into the new grave I laid all the pieces of the old coffin in the grave, too. That is, nearly all. Several big splinters got broken off, and they were kept as souvenirs by a reporter and a policeman, I think." (It must have been a *Sun* reporter, for a venerable member of the staff once showed me his mahogany penholder, which, he said, had been made from a splinter of Poe's coffin.)

"A few years before this," the sexton rambled on, "I had buried Mr. Poe's mother-in-law, Mrs. Maria Clemm, in the family lot. When the monument was put up the committee didn't want to have her body moved with Mr. Poe's. But I begged them to because she had asked me to lay her by the side of her boy. So we buried her under the new monument. Later on they brought to Baltimore the body of young Mrs. Poe and we buried it at the side of the monument."

I often ran in on the old sexton after this, and one day I took with me a friend who was an admirable amateur photographer (George O. Brown, then a fellow-worker on the staff of the *Sun*). A number of photographs were taken, including one of the sexton sitting in the arch of his crypt, and another of the first Poe grave and its surroundings.

A Startling Discovery

Revisiting recently, after many years, my old haunt in the rear of the church, I threaded my way amid the shadows of the silent crypt. It was more silent than ever. Gone was the grave-digger's cot; for old Spence had long since been gathered to his fathers. Outside, in one of the lots, a shining new headstone among the time-stained monuments caught my eye—"Original Burial Place of Edgar Allan Poe from October 9, 1849, until November 17, 1875." But it was not the place that Spence had indicated to me! Hastening home, I turned to the faded old photographs. They con-

firmed my impression that the memorial had been wrongly placed. My subsequent examination of the Poe family chronicles and of the records in the possession of the trustees of the graveyard proved to me that the sexton had pointed out the exact spot.

There is at least one man living who stood by the original grave when the body was disinterred for removal to the present grave. That man is Dr. Henry E. Shepherd, the well-known Baltimore scholar and author, who delivered a memorial address at the dedication of the monument in 1875. Dr. Shepherd, on being asked concerning the location of the original grave, said that the position indicated to me by Spence coincides more closely with his memory of the location than the lot by the East wall. At the time the tablet was erected Dr. Shepherd spoke, he said, to the late Eugene Didier, the noted Poe biographer, about this point, and Mr. Didier agreed with him in his impression, though nothing further was said about it at the time, Dr. Shepherd remembers distinctly the occasion of the disinterment of the bones of the poet—literally all that was left of the body. He recalls especially the good condition of the skull, the striking shape of the forehead and the perfection of the teeth.

Outsiders are prone to rail at what they regard as Baltimore's unmindfulness of her proprietorship in the bones of the poet. There has been much slurring talk— it crops up every now and then—about Poe's "neglected grave" and the desolate God's-acre. But to me the ancient churchyard, just as it is, has always seemed a fitting home for the mortal part of him who has been called "the greatest artist of death whom the world has ever seen." in the midst of factory and office, the clanging of car bells and the rumbling of cart and truck, it is as remote from the spirit of the bustling life about it as was Poe himself from the usual and the commonplace.

All round about, one sees the names of the brave and the gallant, inscribed on old stones with stately epitaphs of the days when one's mate was a "consort" and one's widow a "relict."

Our poet is, indeed, in a goodly fellowship in Westminster yard. Here lie the bones of General John Stricker, soldier of the Revolution and commander of the Third Brigade at the battle of North Point, in the second war with England. Of Colonel David Harris, also a hero of the Revolution, and at the age of seventy-three at the battle of North Point; or, as his epitaph reads, one of "the brave defenders of this city in its hour of peril." Of Captain Paul Bentalou, officer of the Revolution, in whose arms Count Pulaski died at the battle of Savannah. Of Gen. Samuel Smith, soldier of the Revolution, Secretary of the Navy, mayor of Baltimore, and for forty years in Congress.

Go, make your pilgrimage to old Westminster yard. Do not merely stand on the sidewalk and peer in, after the manner of the hardened sightseer. Go within the gates—they are usually locked, to be sure; but if you are persevering you will somehow manage it—and do a bit of exploring on your own account. Then you will know the poet's resting-place as another Baltimore poet, Lizette Woodworth Reese, knows it—

"Stone calls to stone, and roof to
    roof;
    Dust unto dust;
Lo, in the midst, starry, aloof—
Like white of April blown by last
    Year's stalks
            Across the gust—
A Presence walks."[9]

From *American Indian Dance Steps* (1931)

"A mere jumping up and down to the monotonous beat of a crudely fashioned drum."

In some such manner as this is the casual observer prone to dismiss the subject of American Indian dance-art; regarding it as a quite simple affair and devoid of special appeal or significance. As a matter of fact, it is far more than this. Even the briefest study of the technique and the style of Indian dancing discloses that its steps are varied and often difficult of execution, and that its mood and manner are highly expressive of a peculiar, native genius. It discloses also that the rhymes are diverse, complicated, and marked by frequent change. And, more than all this, it discloses that Indian dance-art is basically different from other forms. It is this basic difference, this distinctive expression of racial character, that makes the study of Indian dance and its accompanying song at once baffling and fascinating.

It has always been difficult for the white man to bridge the distance between himself and the North American Indian. This is due partly of course to the naturally great depth of the chasm between primitive man and civilized man; and

DOG DANCER

Po ye ge, "Dog Dancer," American Indian Dance Steps, by Bessie and May
Garrettson Evans (New York: A. S. Barnes, 1931).

partly also to the seeming impossibility of breaking down or penetrating the reserve of the Indian. His personality, indeed, is as baffling as his dance-art. So true an expression, however, of his inner self does this art appear to be, so keen is the flash of revelation it brings, that in it the soul of the Indian seems to be laid bare in a greater measure than in other phase of his personal activity. In his dance and song, he is caught, as it were, off his guard.

It is, then, important—even urgent—

that this significant American folk-art be preserved and safeguarded. Safeguarded especially from the standardizing hand of the white man; from the tragic deterioration that has been wrought in many other phases of Indian life and product. Happily, the Indian's dance and song have thus far proved to a great extent immune from the blight of the commonplace. Signs are not lacking, however, that they, too, are threatened.

There is, therefore, no time to lose. Dances of all the tribes should be accurately recorded as soon as possible, for fear that in the not distant future they may become altogether extinct; or at least may share a fate similar to that of most of the Indian music now heard on the concert stage—native melody so diluted by the admixture of vocal, instrumental, and harmonic elements supplied by the white-musicians, as to be virtually denatured. Such use of folk-music has, of course, its rightful and important place in the art of the cultured composer or performer. Its effects are, indeed, often beautiful and inspiring in the case of the free employment of Indian thematic material—however much it may tend to obscure the traditions of authentic native music.

The purely musical element of the Indian's composite art of dance and song fared better at the hands of scholars than has the element of body movement. Hundreds, thousands, of native tunes of tribes in many parts of the country have been recorded by musicians specially fitted for the task. The melodies have been transcribed by them in as accurate a form as present musical notation permits. Supplementing the work, phonograph records have been made at first-hand, by means of which not only the melodic content but the tone-quality and the style have been reproduced with absolute fidelity.

Thus a great body of pure, authentic Indian song has been preserved in permanent form. The world's debt of gratitude to these single-hearted musicians becomes the greater in view of the seemingly inevitable passing of the aboriginal American.

It is to be hoped that laborers in the field of Indian research will ultimately be moved to do as much in the case of Indian dance-art. Hitherto, efforts in this direction have been confined chiefly to the ritualistic, the symbolic, the musical, and the dramatic elements of Indian ceremonial; in which phases profound and detailed research has been made by eminent scholars.

It must be admitted that it is not easy to convey adequately by word, tune, diagram, or picture, the indefinable but distinctive mood of a dance. These aids can, nevertheless, do much to enable the student to assemble the various parts into a form that has a fair degree of fidelity to the original. Something more vivid, more dynamic, however, is needed in order to inform the substance with the spirit. There are qualities in the ceremonial dances of the Red Man that must be personally seen and heard and felt; for of them is born the elusive charm that defies analysis or description.[10] This is true of the dance-art of any race; but especially of one so-removed in thought and culture as a primitive people like the American aborigines.

Supplementing personal observation and abstract study, mechanical means are not available—or at least are rapidly being developed—that are capable of providing a very fair substitute for actual first-hand performance. Such little as has already been accomplished in this direction by moving-picture drama is at least highly suggestive of the possibilities. And this, notwithstanding the fleeting and fragmentary glimpses thus far afforded by films that are usually so speeded up that the dancers in them seem bent chiefly on scurrying out of the picture with indecent haste. With a proper application however of modern inventions for the synchronization of movement, sound, line, and color, it should soon be possible to reproduce Indian dances in complete and permanent form. With the aid also of "slow-motion photography," the technique of the art could be analyzed and thus made available to students everywhere.

It may be objected—on good grounds—that there is a very real obstacle in the way of accurate and complete recording of the ceremonials. That obstacle is the Indian's own distrust—also on good ground!—of the attitude of the white man. There is no denying the strength of this argument. Personal observation has afforded many illustrations of both sides of the case.

An instance in point: a conservative Indian of New Mexico consented to dance a secular dance of his tribe; but he flatly refused to show the steps of a beautiful ceremonial dance. Nor would he for a long while give any reason for the refusal. At last, after much persuasion, he said, through an interpreter, "It is because you will tell lies about me." His fear—a fear that probably lurks in many another Indian heart—was evidently that he would be misrepresented at Washington.

Another instance: at an impressive Pueblo ceremonial, the white folk who had been graciously allowed to attend, were informed that it was not permitted to take photographs of this particular dance.[11]

Undaunted, several in the group leveled their cameras at the dancers. No fewer than five times did the Indian Governor of the Pueblo have to leave his post in the choir to remonstrate with the recalcitrant guests. "But I got four snapshots all the same!" gleefully whispered one of the women to her companions.

Yet another instance: a curious, staring crowd of white men and women were gathered around a dignified chief, one of a group of Indians that had been taken on tour for a demonstration of Indian life and art. Suddenly one of the white women leaned forward and, in much the manner of a reporter interviewing a foreign visitor, said affable to the Indian chief: "And how do you like our country?" Our country!

Yes, lack of sympathy and of understanding on the part of the white race has, indeed, created obstacles to research. But not insuperable ones. Despite much of the Indian's experience with white folk—experience of their broken faith, of their misinterpretation of motive, of their assumption of lofty superiority as "discoverers" of America—the native good-will of the Red Man makes him still amenable to considerate treatment. Once convinced of the sincerity and friendliness and common sense of a white acquaintance, the patient aboriginal (man or woman) is generous in cooperation—as many students of Indian life can attest.

That the Indian's own attitude toward dancing is one of remarkable earnestness is manifest to the student at the outset. For example—

The Indian takes his dancing *disinterestedly*. He does not dance to earn his living; or to win applause on the stage—he is not working for curtain calls.

He takes his dancing *heroically*. And this, even to the point of self-sacrifice for a principle. "The government may send its troops to shoot us down; but we will not cease our dancing," was the answer when the United States government some years ago tried to put a stop to Indian ceremonies (as cited to the authors by Ernest Thompson Seton, who was present when the order was first issued to one of the tribes of the Southwest).

He takes his dancing *responsibly*. Night after night preceding a tribal ceremonial can the rumble of drum accompaniment be heard, making its way in somber, muffled tones from the seclusion of the meeting-place where those chosen for the forthcoming performance are assembled. There, every step, every tone, every drumbeat, every syllable, is rehearsed diligently, lest there be a flaw of omission or commission in a ceremony designed to honor and propitiate, not offend, the spirit-powers.

And he takes his dancing *reverently*. Anyone who, like the present writers, has been granted the rare privilege of attending an all-night dance-ritual in a Pueblo Indian kiva (the sacred ceremonial underground chamber of secret tribal councils, devotions, and rehearsals, where commonly the profane foot of white man or woman dare not tread); anyone who had noted there the absorbed, the rapt, expression on the faces of the dancers; anyone who has felt there the rhythm of movement and song and inexorable drumbeat, that seems to make the hard ground throb with the throbbing of the dancers, and cry out with their cry that rain be sent to a thirsty land—anyone who has been responsive to all these things can but realize that in the dance the Indian finds a channel not only for the outlet of his esthetic nature but for the inflow of spiritual power.

Though in his own worship the white man has seen fit to retain other fine arts— music, poetry, painting, sculpture, architecture—he has lost the dance-art from the service of the church (except as it may be said to linger in the processional). For centuries he has been reading reverently in the Psalms the admonition: "Let them praise his name in the dance"; but he has left it to primitive man to give heed. Not left it, though, without some little interference; for civilization has been slow to perceive that every man must be permitted to approach the things of the spirit— whether of art or of religion—by the path that is familiar and beautiful to his feet.[12]

II[13]

Some characteristic Indian dance steps are herein analyzed. A few of these steps are compared, very briefly, with dance steps of some other races or nations; including that most highly developed and elaborate dance-art of the white race—ballet, or "toe-dancing," of (notably) Italy, France, and Russia; and, through widespread adoption, of other European countries and the United States. The ballet form, in the niceties of its crystallized, traditional technique and of its exquisite though often artificial movements, probably offers the most striking contrast of all to the more natural expression of Indian dance-art—a case of the cultured versus the primitive. Since, owing to the limitations of the human frame, only a moderate number of movements are possible to it, whatever the race or the condition, there will, naturally, be found points of similarity even in these two extremes. And more especially so because of the fact that the orthodox ballet bears, in line, posture, and movement, unmistakable evidence that it too had its remote origin in a freer, more natural "out-door" style of dance—that of the ancient Greeks.

It is by no means the object, in this short, fragmentary treatise, to do more than barely touch on such comparisons and analogies; and that, merely by way of suggesting that this phase of the subject might possibly prove worthy of research in the future. The present brief—even hasty—excursion into so large and uncultivated a field can do no more than break ground at a single point. Even this slight jaunt, however, serves to show that Indian dancing is a distinctive and highly specialized form.

The three principal varieties of dancing have been concisely defined by Ethel L. Urlin (*Dancing, Ancient and Modern*) as: "(1) Dancing in which the legs are chiefly made use of, prevailing in Europe generally, and finding its most pronounced form in the orthodox ballet. (2) Dancing in which the arms and hands are chiefly used, carried to high perfection by the Javanese and also in Japan. (3) Dancing in which the muscles of the body play the chief part, as seen in Africa and Western Asia."[14]

These elements are found also in combination in many dance-forms. In Spanish dancing, for example, arms, hands, head, torso, legs, and feet are strikingly in evidence; not to speak of very characteristic facial expression.

To none of the forms described does the dancing of the North American Indian, man or woman, seem specifically to belong. There are points of similarity, yes; but withal there is found in the dance-art of the Indian a mode that is peculiar to him. The chief element in the dancing of the tribes observed consists in foot and leg movements. Arm and hand movements are made in moderation, and at times are but a reflex action of the foot rhythms. The torso is for the greater part quiet, but relaxed. There is no change of facial expression. Exceptions to the foregoing generalizations were noted chiefly in the case of dances in which there is an element of dramatic impersonations; such, for example, as the wing-like motion of the arms in the Eagle Dance, or the realistic body movements in the burlesque "horse-tail" dance, or the plastic action of the Dog Dance.[15]

In the tribes observed, the men do the greater part of the dancing, though the women also often participate. In this respect the custom of the white race in modern times is reversed, at least in so far as the dance is considered in its use as a cultural and a dramatic art-form. In its social aspect—such as in the folk-dance and the ball-room dance of the white race—both sexes are equally represented. But in the dance in the schools and on the stage, girls and women now greatly preponderate, notwithstanding the late appearance—just two hundred and fifty years ago—of the female dance in the European ballet. The Indian, in the importance he evidently attaches in his educational system to dancing by men, is but in line with some of the great nations and races of old—as witness, for example, the inclusion of dancing in the rigorous training that was given the stalwart Greek-youths, that they might the better fulfill their part in the military, the religious, and the social scheme.

Since "the gesture of a people has a more ancient and unchanging history than its speech" (J. E. Crawford Flitch: *Modern Dancing and Dancers*),[16] is it not conceivable that an exhaustive study of comparative dancing, with special reference to the art of the American Indian and other primitive races, might yield just as significant results as does the study of comparative philology?[17]

Examples of Indian Dance of the Southwest

Dog Dance

As an example of the confusion that often attends an initial effort in the study of Indian ceremonial, the writers' own experience may be cited. A friendly and artistic young Indian woman of San Ildefonso Pueblo sent word that on a certain date the tribe would give the Dog Dance.[18] The ceremony, as is usual with Indian dances, was given out-of-doors. It was a freezing day in January. The dance was done by two men whose bare legs and bodies were painted black; as were their faces also. In the right hand, each carried a decorated rattle, and in the left, a stick ornamented with a strip of gay cloth and dangling feathers. A great feather headdress extended from top to toe in the back. The dancers were accompanied

DOG DANCE

Score for Dog Dance, American Indian Dance Steps, by Bessie and May Garrettson Evans (New York: A. S. Barnes, 1931)

by a splendidly attired choir of singers and drummers. (Sometimes, it was learned, each dancer has a long sash tied to his belt and held by an Indian women, as if on a leash.)

At the close of the dance, an Indian appeared from one of the little adobe houses of the Pueblo and threw a loaf of bread to the dancers, who got down on all fours, so to speak, and grubbed on the ground after the bread with their mouths. Finally, one of them succeeded in catching the loaf securely between his teeth and carried it in this way to a singer in the choir, who relieved him of it. Another Indian came out of a house with another loaf, and the "scrap" was repeated. Then some bystanders—not Indians—threw small change; whereupon the dancers groveled again on the ground, and, after rooting about vigorously, came up with coins between their teeth and their mouths choked with the dry soil. Not an edifying spectacle, this part, however realistic.

"What does the dance mean?" one of the drummers was asked.

"Peace," he replied.

"Why, a dog-fight over a loaf of bread doesn't seem a very peaceful ending," was commented of the puzzled inquirers.

The drummer smiled his inscrutable Indian smile and said nothing.

"Why do the dogs carry the sticks with feathers?" was the next query.

"They are shields or banners," was the answer.

"Does the food belong in the ceremony?

"Yes, food belongs," said the Indian.

"Do the coins belong?"

"No," he said, "Mexicans throw coins." (That was somewhat of a relief; for the un-

pleasant coin feature seemed hardly akin to the picturesque whimsy of occasional Indian comedy.)

"What is the right name of the dance?" the Indian was asked.

"It is called Dog Dance; but it is Peace Dance," was the calm response.

Peace! There was no peace—there was only a stubborn determination to track those two dogs to their lair. At first, hopefully following the peace clue, the inquirers were heartened in their search by coming across (in the official program of a Santa Fe fiesta) a graphic description that tallied admirably with the dance given at San Ildefonso Pueblo. The ceremonial described was a "Tanoan Peace Dance—part of an ancient Peace Drama, in which two dancers, representing the chiefs of opposing forces, stage a mimic combat, and description in movement of the battle that brought peace to the tribe. It goes back to the time when war issues were often settled among the people by single combat between opposing leaders. Sometimes the wife of each chief appears, holding a cord attached to the belt of each, showing how ties of home and family life moved men to valor in battle."

Back again to the San Ildefonso tribe for further persistent questioning:

"Where did the Dog Dance come from?" one of the Indians was asked.

"It did not come from any place," was the answer. "My father said it has been dance here for years and we still dance it yet. I have seen it dance the same way as it dance now since I was a small boy.

"Are the two men who do the dance supposed to represent dogs?"

"Yes, the two man represent as dogs

while they are dancing—till it's over!"

"What does the Dog Dance mean?"

"It don't mean anything much. It's just call Dog Dance."

"Why is it called Dog Dance?"

"Because it was named it Dog Dance by the old people when they first dance it. They were painted all black and look like dogs."

"Does an Indian woman sometimes hold the dancer by a long sash tied to his belt? And what does it mean?"

"Yes, sometime the two dogs has a Indian belt tied to his belt and held by the women. They use the women same time so they can dance too. They carry the dogs around so they wouldn't run away."

"Why is the Dog Dance called also Peace Dance?"

"There is no dance here call Peace Dance. The Peace Dance is dance by the Taos Indians.[19] It is almost the same as the Dog Dance."

Back of all these conflicting versions there is probably a very ancient symbolic ceremonial whose origin is lost in the obscurity of a remote past. Research by eminent authorities show that the Dog Dance idea is widespread among tribes of the Plains Indians, and may have filtered through from them to the Pueblos of the Southwest, in one form or another. Dr. Clark Wissler, for example, describes (in his *Societies and Dance Associations of the Blackfeet Indians*) ceremonials, customs (including the food feature), and costumes of the Dog Societies of Plains Indians that would seem to establish definitely the kinship of the various "dogs" in Indian dances.[20] And Pliny Earle Goddard (in his *Dancing Societies of the Sarsi Indians*) notes that in the dances of the Dog Society, the wives of the members joined in, dancing behind their husbands; the wives of the leaders holding the ends of the long sashes as they danced.[21]

Whatever its origin, and whether the dancers represent great chieftains dancing the dance of peace, or (as is more probable) huge black dogs moving about with their lithe bodies in sinuous curves, the Dog Dance of San Ildefonso Pueblo is a remarkably effective impersonation. Not even the ensuing fight over coins mars its plastic beauty; for, happily, this feature is not introduced until the dance proper is over.

The principal movement in the dance consists in a nimble stepping forward or backward or in circles as each dancer advances toward or retreats from his opponent. The action is not difficult or peculiar in any way. It is just a continuous "soft," free stepping about—always graceful and light of foot; never jerky. Though through the greater part of the dance the two men are face to face (moving either toward each other as in Fig. 1, or away from each other as in Fig. 2), at intervals they turn away and move about in small individual circles. At certain times, the dancers advance close to each other and pause a second, while each defiantly raises his shield (or banner?) aloft with emphasis (see fig. 12c). The shield is usually held at the middle of the stick; but sometimes it is held by one end. The dance is repeated many times.

When each man is held on a leash by a woman, the latter follows the man with the same kind of step as that used by him. Each woman adorns herself for the dance according to her own fancy. She lets her hair hang loose. Besides holding the leash in one hand, she carries two feathers in each hand.

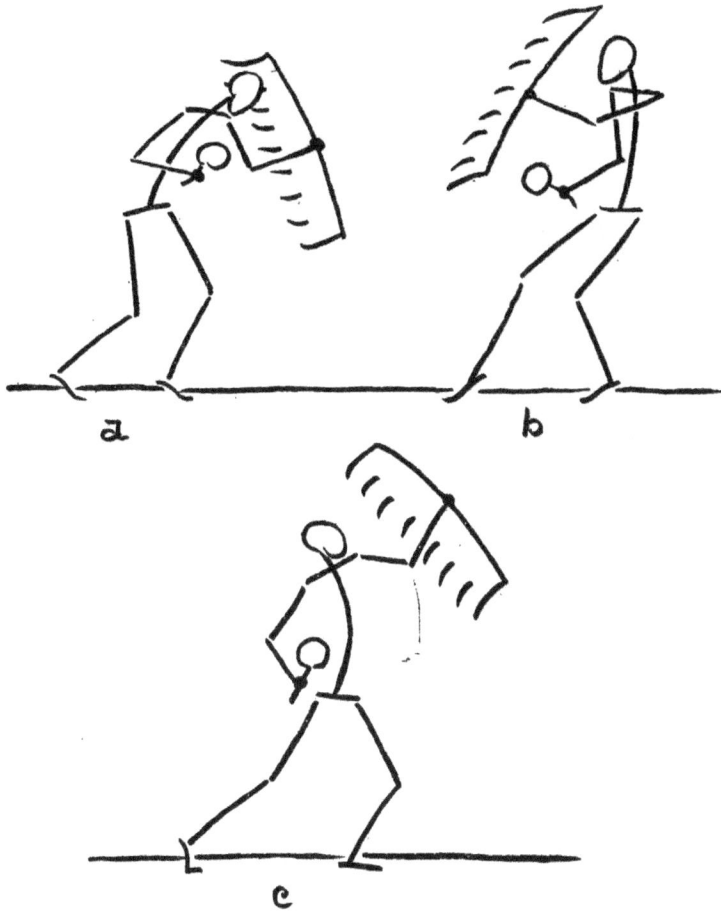

Score for Dog Dance, American Indian Dance Steps, by Bessie and May Garrettson Evans (New York: A. S. Barnes, 1931)

Dog Dance

1. Step lightly on ball of right foot.
2. Step lightly on ball of left foot.
3. Continue movements 1 and 2, with alternation, and with same time-value, a step to each quarter note (while advancing, retreating, or circling), until movement number 3 is reached.
4. Pause and hold up shield in a charging position; with the weight on the front foot.
5. and 5. Resume movements 1 and 2 (while advancing, retreating, or circling) and continue until movement 6 is reached.
6. Pause and hold up shield, as in number 3.

Tributes

The elegy, or lament for the dead, became identified with female writers during the nineteenth century. Women from the time of Mary Magdalene, after all, had been idealized as mourners, vessels for grief. Yet women writers adapted the conventions of the elegy for their own ends. Poems written in commemoration of a friend helped establish that woman's legacy for posterity and helped promote feminine virtues as culturally and perhaps historically important. The deaths of political figures or well-loved authors provided occasions for female authorship. And in the case of elegies written for other writers, the poet implicitly presents herself as an inheritor of her predecessor's genius.[1]

The women of the WLCB wrote tributes to one another and to fellow authors, male and female, in both poetry and prose. We are especially pleased to be able to present in this section the only sustained written work we have located by Lydia Crane, the Woman's Literary Club of Baltimore's longtime Recording Secretary, whose thousands of pages of handwritten minutes form the basis of our contemporary understanding of the Club. It is perhaps fitting that the writing of Crane's that has been preserved is a tribute to someone else—in this case, her sister, the best-selling author Anne Moncure Crane Seemuller, who died long before the WLCB came into existence.

In addition to celebrating female authorship and good writing, these tributes established the foundations for what would constitute, in their minds, a distinctive Southern literary tradition. Club members repeatedly returned to the image of a gothic, romantic, tragic Edgar Allan Poe as a model for the Southern author. Another model, Sidney Lanier, is celebrated for the clarity of his language and affinity with nature; his poetry is "Harmonious as the thrush's note," writes Marguerite Easter, in a harmonious poem of her own.

The model of female authorship the women present in their tributes to one another is that of intellect, moral clarity, and confidence. These are no shrinking violets; Ella Morrow Sollenberger even likens Lizette Woodworth Reese to a comet. In contrast to writers like Emily Dickinson, who describes herself as a

"Nobody," these writers asserted themselves as "Somebodies"—perhaps strengthened by the bonds they formed with one another through the WLCB.

Charles Dickens
by Alice Emma Sauerwein Lord (1882)

"Lord, keep my memory green."[2]

O man with loving heart, sleep on!
Thou hast too many friends, I ween,
To need that last sad prayer of thine:
"Lord, keep my memory green."

Thy fearless hand drew from the dark
The darker secrets hidden there,
And gave us broader views of life,
Through scenes of sorrow and despair.

Thy suffering children pictured rise—
Poor babies, thrust in dens of vice!—
So old in misery, care, and toil,
So brave, or crushed, or worldly-wise!

And pictured men with curious traits,
Some bland, or soured, or crazed, or gay;
Some warped by wrong, some spoiled by
    wealth,
Just as we know them here to-day.

Thou painted each abuse in life;
The wrongs in courts, in jails, in schools;
Religious, social, public shams,
In baby-farms[3] and poorhouse rules.

But brighter pictures thou hast drawn
Of sweet and pure domestic love,
Of cozy homes and trusting hearts,
Where peace rests like a gentle dove.

Thy mirth and whimsicalities,
Like sunbeams, steal through clouds of care;
Thy pathos conquers bitter hearts,
And melts to tears, or wins a prayer.
We bless thee for these bits of life
Portrayed with seer and artist's power!
But heartier thanks for those bright scenes
That cheer us many a lonely hour!

Thy works are monuments enough
To insure thy immortality!
Thine own the hand that wove the wreath
To keep thy memory green for aye!

Longfellow
by Alice Emma Sauerwein Lord (1882)

Longfellow sweetest singer of our land!
Cold is the heart thy music can withstand,
So full thy tone of human sympathy,
So true and hopeful thy philosophy.

In shades of evening thou hast bid us seek
Some humble poet "whose sweet thoughts
    should speak
Of beauty and of faith";[4] thyself we choose,
Whose poems ne'er their heavenly birth abuse.

Earth, heaven, viewed by thy prophetic eye
Show God's great love and nature's harmony.
Never in shadow-land dost thou abide;
But seek'st perpetual sunlight, warm and wide.

The struggles of a simple Pilgrim Band
Have grown heroic 'neath thy poet's hand;
Thy Indian idyls[5] are with beauty rife,
And ancient legends win from thee new life.
Thou throw'st a magic spell o'er everything;
Beauty springs from its grave when thou
    dost sing;

Our reverence seeks in vain a tribute meet,
We can but lay our love before thy feet.

Lit with the Sun
by Marguerite Easter, in honor of
Sidney Lanier[6] (1892)

*"But I fear not, nay, and I fear not the
    thing to be done,
I am lit with the sun."*[7]

Nay, Singer of brave songs, in days when
    naught
Was liberally thine, save thy heart's cheer
Which thou, with prodigal delight did'st
    share
With all, e'en as the thrush in tuneful thought
Pervades the vale until the air is fraught
With exhalation! Why should'st thou fear?—
Thou, lit with the sun!—whose soul (as
    purely clear
As crystal drops on vernal grasses wrought
By nature's agencies) absorbed the light
And then, with conscious radiance, beamed
It forth, yea, into the darkness of Death's
    night!—
Thou, who wert, what others *themselves*
    deemed,
Harmonious as the thrush's note, and true
As the flame that from its orb thy spirit drew.

Evangeline
by Marguerite Easter, in honor of
Henry Wadsworth Longfellow[8] (1892)

Evangeline, it was through sympathy with
    thee,
My soul, newly 'wakened, found its
    Psyche wings,
And learn'd, that as the brooklet to the
    woodland sings,

Merging all leaf tone in its rounding
    symphony,—
Thus love fills life. Which time, thy grief
    possessed me,
So that oft I went with thee, in my slum-
    berings
E'en, in quest of Gabriel; the while my
    heartstrings,
Struck by thy loneliness and fond fidelity
(As hills and dells to sighing streams
    reverberate)
Responded to the pathos of thy wanderings
In pensive strains of song, which, tho'
    inadequate,
Filled my soul with joy, being first offerings
To its ideal—thyself, Evangeline, from
    whom it took
Its keynote—as the woodland from the
    purling brook.

Author of *Metzerott, Shoemaker*
by Hester Crawford Dorsey, for
Katharine Pearson Woods (1890)

Who wrote "Metzerott"? Was the question discussed at every afternoon tea-drinking
in Baltimore last winter after Professor Richard T. Ely, of the Johns Hopkins University,
had piqued public curiosity by announcing
that the author of this much-talked-of book
was a Baltimore woman. Immediately every
girl who had wielded a pen became the possible heroine of the hour, from the maiden
who indited lines to "The Beautiful Spring"
to the professional society gossip whose most
brilliant literary effort had been the description of Mrs. Toplofty's latest gown: all shared
alike the honor of being accredited with the
authorship of the famous book of the season.

While society was thus exemplifying

its lack of perception, and the daily papers were printing lists of names any one of which might belong to the "great unknown," the latter was far from the halls of pleasure, living her creed of Christian Socialism among the working women of her city, dividing her time and energies with those whose condition in life she would better, while the petted belles of the Monumental City were dividing her honors among themselves.

But Katherine Pearson Woods cared little for the world's applause; for just when success crowned her work, and hero-worshippers were making pilgrimages to see the hero, she cast her lot with the Knights of Labor, dedicating her talents to the emancipation of the working-classes and to exposing the degrading condition of city factories.

She is a thorough convert to Mr. Bellamy's theories as set forth in *Looking Backward*.[9] Indeed, the influence of this ideal twentieth century upon Miss Woods resulted in the production of *Metzerott, Shoemaker*, which Mr. Bellamy in turn recommends to the Nationalist party as a clever exponent of his views.

It was through a letter of his to Professor Ely eulogizing *Metzerott, Shoemaker*, that the identity of the author became known; for Professor Ely, with the best interest of the modest young author at heart, entertaining for her the warmest and most sincere friendship, to the *Baltimore Sun* for publication.

This announcement caused not a little excitement in our midst. A general falling of feathers occurred among those who had been disporting themselves in borrowed plumes, while intellectual circles hastened to seek fellowship with the new light.

Miss Woods, however, with the characteristic modesty which prompted her to publish anonymously her powerful book, would not allow herself to be lionized, and decline social invitations, to become an active member of the Nationalist Club. The Economic Club, of which she was the organizer, also claims much of her time and interest. This association is largely composed of Johns Hopkins University men, and not a few progressive women, who feel it their privilege and pleasure to keep in touch with the times. Here political economy is discussed in the most parliamentary fashion. Not long since, Miss Woods took an active part in the debate on "the advisability of the government controlling natural monopolies." She is now preparing a paper on labor organizations from a Nationalist stand-point, to be read before the Nationalist Club.

The author of *Metzerott, Shoemaker* has no appearance of the revolutionist. She is of medium height, with a delicate *spirituelle* face of rare sweetness of expression. Her forehead is massive and intellectual, while her luminous gray eyes burn with the latent fire of genius. She is, however, "but yet a woman," for a curled bang of soft brown hair falls lightly, almost flippantly, over that same intellectual brow. She dresses quietly and is simple in her tastes, never indulging in extravagances.

But let us see what influences of ancestry and consanguinity tended to the development of so striking a character as that of our pioneer woman Socialist, Nationalist, and Knight of Labor.

Miss Woods comes of good old pioneer

West Virginia stock on the paternal side, men who for generations were surveyors and civil engineers, from whom she inherits her broad and analytical mind. From her maternal ancestors, the McCabes, she gets her marked literary ability.

Her great-great-grandfather, James McCabe, was one of General Montgomery's staff-officers during the French and Indian War. He was wounded at the battle of Quebec in 1759. When the American Revolution broke out, he raised and equipped a regiment at his own expense and fought on the Continental side. This large demand upon his resources bankrupted his estate, and he was compelled to sacrifice everything, including even his baby's cradle, which he declined to withhold, preferring to cut down a tree and model it into a couch for his offspring rather than deprived others of their rights.

Miss Woods's grandfather, Reverend James Dabney McCabe, was one of the most gifted members of the Virginia and Maryland diocese in his day. Although born in Wheeling, West Virginia, the author of *Metzerott, Shoemaker* passed most of her childhood in the quaint old rectory of St. James's Church on West River, Anne Arundel County, Maryland, becoming a member of her grandfather's household upon the death of her father, which occurred in Baltimore when she was but nine years of age.

Just at this time an uncle and a great-aunt who had run the blockade with their families arrived at the old parish house, bringing together under one roof eight juvenile cousins; decidedly a socialistic environment for the young genius. But the little Katharine had not yet learned the beauty of dividing her pleasures with others, much preferring solitary walks through the quiet woods to romping with the noisy brood of cousins, none of whom sympathized with her moods.

The great gloomy garret was another favorite haunt of the dreamy child. Here she would revel in the treasures of her grandfather's library, many of which had made their way up there from the overcrowded shelves of his study.

At the age of ten years this serious little girl devoured Neale's *Tales of the Early Church*, while sitting under the dusty eaves of the attic; and whenever allowed within the sacred precincts of the study, Pearson on the Creed or Lardner's *Lectures on Astronomy* was sure to claim her youthful attention, each volume being as large as herself.[10]

Wishing to secure greater educational advantages for her children, Mrs. Woods returned to Baltimore when the author of *Metzerott* was fourteen years old. Here she soon gave the first evidence of an inherited literary tendency by competing for the prize offered by the *Young Idea*, a little paper edited and published by two choristers of St. Luke's Protestant Episcopal Church.[11] The prize was for the best poem contributed to their columns within a certain time. Katharine submitted her first youthful effusion. Success met her on the very threshold of her career, and she won the coveted prize, which proved to be an engraving, cut from *Godey's Lady's Book*, of Shakespeare at the court of Queen Elizabeth!

At the age of seventeen Miss Woods was entered at the then fashionable seminary conducted by Mrs. Converse and Miss Miller, the latter a former pupil of Harriet

Beecher Stowe. She had hitherto never attended any school, her education having been entirely under the careful direction of her accomplished mother, who preferred keeping her delicate child with her. The arrival of the All Saints' Sisters from England, in 1872, materially affected Miss Woods's destiny. This order began its work at Mount Calvary Protestant Episcopal Church in Baltimore, of which she was an active member.

Becoming deeply absorbed in the mission-work, she determined to devote her life to it; and with that object in view she entered the sisterhood as a postulant, in 1874, but remained only six months, on account of failing health, the superior and her physician advising her to return to the world.

Those six months of self-denial left their lasting impress upon a character already keenly alive to the needs of suffering humanity. They did more: they helped to develop the latent spirit of Christian Socialism which is so essentially a part of Miss Woods's nature. A rule of the convent was that the postulant must eat all set before her. Many times this proved a difficult task, and she who had far more than her needs required felt an unexpressed longing to divide with those who had none,—the hundreds of wretches who were starving for bread. No environment could have been more conductive to the production of a Christian Socialist; and so it happened that the germ of this new religion, the "Universal Brotherhood," took root in the convent.

When it became necessary for Miss Woods to give up the religious life, she at once decided to substitute literature for the cloister.

In 1876 she began teaching school at Mount Washington, Maryland, but afterwards resigned to accept a position in a school at Wheeling, West Virginia.

In 1884 the *Chicago Tribune* published a series of prize stories. It was about this time that the great two years' strike occurred in Wheeling; and Miss Woods, who was much interested in the condition of affairs, wrote two stories about the lives of the nail-operatives there. Both won prizes, as did also a third, which was a love-story. Thus encouraged, she was more than ever anxious to adopt authorship as a profession. She immediately took up the study of sociology, spending much time among the German population in Wheeling, where, it will be remembered, the opening scene in *Metzerott, Shoemaker* is laid.

Miss Woods had given up teaching several years before she began her book.

She took no one into her confidence when she first began to write. Her mother and sisters had no suspicion of her secret, unless they drew their own conclusions upon occasionally discovering the amiable Katharine seated at her desk with "her head so full of big knowledges that she couldn't speak a pleasant word to anybody."

Her desk was, by the way, presented to the author of *Metzerott* by a friend, many years ago, with the admonition to "write something great here." The request has proved to be a prophecy.

Miss Woods decided quite accidentally upon the name of her book. While riding through Washington, the name of Metzerott in large letters on a sign attracted her attention just when she was casting about in her mind for a good title. This struck her fancy, and, with the suffix "Shoemaker," was at once adopted. An amusing co-incidence is that she kept her manuscript in a shoe-box, without discovering the fact until the story was completed.

Miss Woods is a most valuable member of The Woman's Literary Club of Baltimore, of which Mrs. Frances Litchfield Turnbull is president.

She is a very facile writer. *Metzerott, Shoemaker* was begun in December, 1888, and finished in July, 1889. Within the year she has also written *The Mark of the Beast*, which appears in this number of the magazine,[12] and almost completed another novel, *A Web of Gold*, which will soon go to press.

In addition to this, she has edited the Woman's Column in the Baltimore *Critic*, and contributed special articles to the *Christian Union* and other journals.

Baltimore is justly proud of her gifted daughter, whose fame is fast spreading abroad, and whose fine and earnest work marks a new period in American fiction.

In Memoriam of Mary Spear Tiernan
by Alice Emma Sauerwein Lord (1891)[13]

Nay! Azrael![14] Thou camest with the dawn,
    When the black night had burst its cerements,
And waked into a new day, gray and wan;
    Thou cam'st with icy touch of death to her—
So full of life and strength—and she is gone!

Nay! Azrael! Thou ghostly messenger!
    Angel of Death! whose fateful, icy breath
Strikes down the strongest! why didst come to her,
    Whose ripest womanhood bore noblest fruit?
And we were robbed ere the world was astir.

Azrael, Azrael! coulds't thou not have found
    Some, weary of life's burdens, for thy prey?
Some broken spirit, weary of its wound,
    That prayed for rest—and spared this earnest life,
That shed fine influence on all around?

Nay! turn thine eyes from me! Thou sayest true.
    Thou art God's messenger to His beloved.
Not only wrecks that time and sorrow strew,
    But brave, strong souls God needs at His right hand.
Heaven welcomed her ere we could say "Adieu!"

Anne Moncure Crane Seemuller
by Lydia Crane (1895)[15]

It is almost impossible to write about the people of our very own blood without the sensation of revealing sacred things, or that of indulging in a sort of egotism, especially when we find it necessary to sometimes use the first person plural, or even the first person singular. But I feel that here I am talking to my friends who will not misunderstand me in my effort to pay my long delayed tribute to the memory of my sister. It is to one whose nature seemed to me, and I believe to all who knew her, full of great promise,—promise only partially fulfilled in her earthly life of less than thirty-five years. And knowing that no one else is now living who knew her whole life well, from the day when I not more than an infant myself— was called to look upon the face of my new sister, until the one when I followed her coffin to Greenmount,[16] I must put aside personal feeling, and tell her story as best I can.

It is customary now, and I believe right, to trace every man's or woman's biography backward from his or her birth, as well as forward from it. Ancestry is supposed to make us what we are, even more than environment, though this too, especially early environment, is much dwelt upon also.

Anne Moncure Crane, daughter of William and Jean N. Crane, was born in this city of Baltimore on January 7th, 1838. Like many others in this country, and especially in this part of it, she belonged by blood to the South, and to the North,—to the States of Maryland and Virginia, of Connecticut and New Jersey.

Her father was the sixth in descent from Robert Treat, governor of the Colony of Con-necticut from 1638 to 1698—the governor who withstood Sir Edmund Andros in his effort to take away the charter of the Colony.

Her mother, whose maiden name was Jean Niven Daniel, was a Virginian by birth, and on one side by blood; on the other side she belonged to Maryland. She was the sixth in descent from William Stone, appointed in 1648 Governor of the Colony of Maryland, by the order of Cecilius Calvert, Lord Baltimore. The fourth in descent from this colonial governor was Thomas Stone, one of the four signers for Maryland, of the Declaration of Independence; and he was the great grandfather of Anne Moncure Crane.

As this is a Maryland Club, and a Woman's Club, and as Anne was a Maryland writer, I wish to tell something with regard to a piece of writing by her ancestress of 1655. It is a letter that is now in the British Museum written to Lord Baltimore, by Verlinda Stone, the wife of the colonial governor, recounting some of the early troubles of the colony. My cousin Moncure D. Conway, in London, has examined the old original manuscript, and informed me that, though of course old-fashioned, it is without fault of grammar, spelling, or punctuation, and could have gone to the printer without correction.

Of Anne's father I will let herself give her own opinion. In *Emily Chester* she gives a description of the father of her heroine, too long to quote in full, but she says, "He was an enthusiastic philanthropist and religionist. This was the form which a certain width of mind and character had taken under the bias and moulding influences of the peculiar circumstances of his early life. An innate fidelity to truth, an instinctive perception of reality which is very near akin to genius, if not itself has long since shown him the smallness and poorness of all worldly considerations. His hopes and thoughts had passed this wind and wave-tossed sea of life in which we poor worldings strive to cast anchor, and were fixed in an eternal haven of peace. But practical sense translated sentiment into action. His life was that sentence of the Lord's Prayer: "Thy Kingdom come on earth" made animate. A colony, school, or emigrant on the coast of Africa, a missionary station in India or China, were to him objects of the most intense interest, in whose service he spared neither time, pains, nor money. He was a man of powerful original mind, great love of reading, and of general information. Through his nature, generally supposed to be like granite, ran a strong view of poetic sentiment which contrast rendered only the more striking. Exquisite, emotional poetry, like Cowper's 'Address to his Mother's Picture,' or his 'Castaway,' caused the strong massive face to grow beautiful with the softened light that shone from it."

The description goes on: "The likeness between him and his daughter was strong and fundamental, but not at first sight very recognizable. She, a woman, fluent, luxurious, peculiarly open to outward influence, upon whom the claims of the body were large and imperative, however the regnant soul might control them, he, a man, who ignored the world, and disdained its pleasures,—between the two there seemed little chance for sympathy, much less for identity. And yet, the oneness was there. Agree-

ing in none of their tastes, and few of their opinions, each had a respect for the other's ideas, which on the girl's side, amounted to a species of hero worship. It suited well her stern Romanesque pride to feel that her plain old fashioned father was, for originality, strength, truth, all that makes a man mentally or morally worthy, immeasurably beyond any other man she had ever known, superior in every sense, to 'the fashion of this world which passeth away.'"

Some one asked Anne after *Emily Chester* had been published, why she did not put her mother also into it? She answered: "I despaired of doing her justice." But in her second book *Opportunity*, she did make some attempt to paint her mother; and in my own opinion, did, on the whole, fail to do her justice. Anne's mother was born in Falmouth, Virginia. Her father, John Moncure Daniel, an eminent surgeon in the United States Army, died when she was eleven years old; her mother who had been Margaret Stone, had died five years before. She was left to the care of her grandfather, Travers Daniel of Crow's Nest, and afterwards to that of an aunt; she went to school with her brothers and was rather unusually educated for the time and region in which she lived. In after years, when surrounded by children of her own, and stepchildren also, she, without neglecting their bodily or spiritual wants, or their mental training, still contrived to keep up her familiar acquaintance with the classic literature that she loved, and, to some extent, with the best authors of her own day. One of her stepdaughters said "that it would be impossible to live in the house with our mother without gaining acquaintance with books." She had begun her married life with the intention of doing much herself in the education of her children; but they were born too close together for that, and only the three eldest Fannie, Anne, and myself received much of the special teaching she had meant to give to all. But in a life so very busy as hers, so mentally and materially full, something must be left out; and what our mother did leave out was outside life and acquaintanceship.

Our father, devoted to philanthropy, business and books, cared nothing for society outside of his home. Our mother, a busy little queen in her own home, had after my birth come to Baltimore with a feeling of exile from the large circle of relations and friends she had left in Virginia—went back to it in person when she could, and always in spirit. Her own mother's family, the Stones lived not in or near Baltimore, but in Charles County;[17] and in those days when our rapid transit did not exist, communication with the county districts was much more difficult than it is now, and even now, I believe it is far more easy to go to New York than to visit some of the counties of our own state. Our young lives were full of interest and enthusiasms, but as children, we had more friends outside of Baltimore than within it.

Almost every year or two some of us were sent to make long visits to our aunt, our mother's sister, Mrs. W. Peyton Conway, living near Fredericksburg, Virginia. We had glorious times there, in the roaming over the Stafford hills and the islands of the Rappahannock River; and in the old Virginian home, with children, and grown people too, of tastes like our own:—meeting too many Virginian cousins, Daniels, Conways, Moncures, and others. Our aunt, had she lived in a city, would, I think, have been called a brilliant woman,—in a small village, she was a sort of oracle, and wonder. Her son, Moncure Daniel Conway, has inherited from her his power of expression, and many other mental qualities. At that house too, we met an uncle, then unmarried from whom by reason of his intellectual influence over herself,—Anne took the suggestion of her character of "Dr. Dan" in her book *Opportunity*.

The peculiar religious element in my sister's books, was of course to be accounted for by inheritance, early teaching and environment. I remember that the London *Saturday Review*,—the "Superfine Review," as Mr. Thackeray called it, said in a criticism of "Emily Chester," Anne's first book. "This book is that compound of Electro-Biology and the Family Bible, which is so fascinating to the American mind." Our father's religion was, as I first remember it, puritanical, with a great deal of "the fear of the Lord" in it;—our mother's was full of the love of God, everywhere and always. If, on Sunday morning we went to church, and sat with our feet hanging, wishing that the prayers or the sermon would come to an end, on Sunday afternoon we gathered around our Mother, generally on an immense old fashioned four post bedstead, and chose what she should read to us, and what we should sing. And whether the reading was of Moses, Job or Daniel, or of the parables of our Lord, it was always made charming to us. I ought to ask pardon for these details, but they went very far to make my sister what she was in after years.

Anne was a sickly child, though always a much overgrown one,—threatened with blindness in infancy; and weakness of the eyes retarded her early education. But this weakness did not destroy the brightness of her eyes in after life; though, as her sister Fannie said, "they varied all the way from lead to diamonds,—being gray or hazel, or dark or light, as the mood took her." As a child she was supposed to be a blonde, though she could not have been called so as a woman. She was something of an "enfant terrible," but as Charles Reade says, "a terrible infant, not a horrible one," never affected, nor unnatural. I remember once a member of the family brought in a flower pot containing a rare plant, with the injunction: "Don't any of you children lay a finger upon this." Anne slowly climbed down from her chair, crossed the room, and laid her small forefinger on the flower. Once, for some unusually strong assertion of her own will, she was made to sit still in a corner; when our old black cook, coming into the room, gazed at her in amazement, and then raising her hands, exclaimed "Great Britain is *tooken* at last."

When Anne did begin to study, her power of acquisition was remarkable, and her power of reading with a singular swiftness, and of yet retaining what she read, still more remarkable. Her brain was well pigeon-holed, if I may use the expression; what she had learned could be at her fingers' ends at any moment when she needed it. This quality, together with her quick mental processes and command of language, went almost as far as originality of

thought to make her conversation, in the opinion of those who remember it, something much beyond her books.

For some years Anne, and her younger brother John, were pupils in a sort of family boarding school, at Mr. Nicholas R. Merryman's in Baltimore County,—the doctor having recommended her living in the country as much as possible. Here she gained her acquaintance with "the hills and vales of pleasant Maryland," of which she speaks in the opening sentence of her book *Opportunity*.

At twelve years of age she entered the Academy of Mr. N. H. Morrison in this city, a school of high rank well remembered by many of her contemporaries. But her taste for reading always went far beyond her taste for study; and, though her rank in school was good, it was below that of her sister Fannie, who was her companion there. One strange thing was her great dislike to writing compositions on set subjects given to her. She would even come to me sometimes, after writing a single page, and say: "Give me a quotation to end off with." And if I answered: "I don't remember one," she would say: "Make one for me then! Can't you?" But, at the same time her letters, written with an untrammeled pen, were always bright and entertaining.

As a child she could sing with unusual power and expression, and she always loved good music. There are some people still left in this world who have memories of her singing and playing in after life. In *Opportunity* she speaks of the heroine's— Harvey Berney's singing as "her most perfect form of expression," and goes on to say that "she did not sing what you might hear from any one else"; that "not only her singing but her songs were attractions as essentially her own as her eyes or her smile."

I remember a visit to Cape May when Anne was sixteen, from which she took some suggestions for the visit described in *Opportunity*, especially the account of the hour spent on the wrecked ship. It is true that two men, both of whom admired Anne greatly, one of them afterwards her husband, were with us on the expedition; but neither of them was Grahame Ferguson nor yet Douglas Ferguson. At that time, under seventeen as she was, Anne appeared as a handsome, quite tall, finely developed woman, with a beautiful complexion, abundant brown hair, and the fine expressive eyes before mentioned. After she was twenty, an affliction of the liver—which was never cured—gave her face a sort of olive tint, and seemed to darken all her coloring; though she was still capable of looking handsome. I believe she never after then thought herself good looking; but sometimes said she would be content to be, in the words of Margaret Fuller, "ugly and bright."[18] Still, I once heard her say: "I don't think my appearance counts against me."

Before Anne was twenty she had been for some time writing *Emily Chester*. In *Opportunity* she says of her heroine what we who knew her heard her say of herself. "She stood gazing around her at life, with a vague wonder for what purpose she had been put into it, and yet with a strange expectant sense of waiting for some moment or event which would interpret it all. Suddenly like a revelation, the perception of that for which she was fitted, and for which all things had been preparing her, came upon her. "The angel said unto me: 'Write,'

and I wrote." It was with no irreverence, that Harvey, then and ever after, quoted St. John's words as the only explanation she could give to herself or others of her course in life. Without the slightest drill or experience in such matters, this girl sat deliberately down to write a book; and that, too undisturbed by doubt of her ability, or fear for its success when written."

Anne read her written pages before the ink was dry to her sisters, and sometimes even to one or two chosen friends; listened to their comments,—favorable or unfavorable,—and then went on writing. One summer she went to our childhood's dear old second home, our aunt Margaret Conway's house in Falmouth, on the Rappahannock; and there read her manuscript to a select company of congenial Virginian cousins. Once when this audience had been particularly critical, Anne jumped up, rolled up her papers, and walked off up stairs, saying: "It is my book: it is my man and my woman, and I will make them say and do just what I please."

When the book was finished it was laid aside; for various reasons its publication was deferred. One of these was her severe illness, a circumstance which strangely followed the completion of each one of her three books. Then the great Civil War came on; and though the book was not forgotten by its author, nor by her family and friends, it certainly seemed inexpedient to try to publish it at that time. And at last, Anne's experience with regard to the publication of her first book, was somewhat unusual. One of her friends to whom she had read her manuscript long before proved an unusually good friend. This lady was, in the year 1864, about to visit Boston, where she had formerly lived,—and I am glad to say, she is still living there now. She, entirely of her own accord, offered to take Anne's book to the publishing house of Ticknor and Fields, casually remarking that she was acquainted with one of the members of the firm. A few days after, this charming woman wrote to Anne that she had gone like Columbus, on Friday, if not into the Atlantic Ocean, into the headquarters of the *Atlantic Monthly*; that she had seen a member of the firm, not however her acquaintance, who had politely given her to understand that it was not a good time for publishing fiction. Then the letter said: "I could praise your book, Anne,—I could not have praised my own—and I did it." Mr. Fields finally said that he would take it home for his wife to read it. The enthusiastic approval of Mrs. Fields made her husband conclude that what had so much interested one woman would interest others also;—"and women," he said, "are the novel readers mainly."

In a very short time came the formal offer of Ticknor and Fields—to the author of *Emily Chester*—to buy the copyright of her book, or to give her a percentage on its sales. She took the percentage, and time proved it by far the better alternative. Anne calmly said, "I never doubted my book's success." Soon came a request from the publishers for anything else she had written of the same kind. *Emily Chester* is perhaps out of date now, and the vein struck by it has been much dug over and into since its time; but in 1864, it made a genuine sensation. I have heard that the first edition was exhausted on the day of its publication;—nine editions followed; it was published in England, and translated into German. We have the English Railway Edition, with its singular illustration on the outside cover.

Of course there was much criticism favorable and adverse. I have spoken of the London *Saturday Review*. The London *Athenaeum* hoped she would live longer, and write another book. Mr. George H. Hillard, although he called the heroine "a combination of Cleopatra, Harriet Martineau, and Florence Nightingale," also says: "From the first chapter the author seizes the attention with the strong grasp of genius, and holds it unbroken to the last." Mr. Whipple wrote that "its most notable characteristic was its originality." Gail Hamilton spoke of its theme as "new to novels, but not to life: perhaps overstated, as the motto on the title page avows, in the words of Goethe: "It is in her monstrosities that Nature discloses her secrets."

This book was published anonymously; and once or twice Anne met in print a positive denial that Miss Crane or any one else in Baltimore had written *Emily Chester*. Once she received a letter from the principal of a school in Connecticut, asking "if she was really the author of *Emily Chester*?" She simply referred him to her publishers.

Soon afterwards her correspondent wrote her an apologetic letter, telling her that one of his assistant teachers had declared herself the author of this book, and had insisted on her claim, until the publishers gave indubitable testimony to the contrary.

It has been said that the characters in *Em-*

ily Chester were taken from real life. I think only that real human beings suggested possibilities to Anne's vivid imagination. Her sister Fannie said with regard to the supposed original of the hero, Max Crampton: "He was only the *minimum* of that which Max Crampton was the *maximum*."

Some time ago, the writer who calls himself "Mark Twain," in an article on "Mental Telegraphy," related that Miss Louisa Alcott asserted that she wrote her first book, and proposed to publish it, about the same time that *Emily Chester* appeared before the world; but that she discovered that this newly published book had the same plot, and even some of the same names as her own; and that all that she could do was to alter her own book,— which failed of the success she had hoped for it. I have heard from another source that Miss Alcott said there was a woman in Baltimore who had written and published her book before she could do it herself. But my sister's book was written long before it was published; and she never heard of Miss Alcott until months after her own successful publication. Miss Alcott too, of course, knew nothing of my sister until after that publication and if the resemblance was so remarkable as she asserted it to be, it was a good illustration of what Mr. Clemens calls "Mental Telegraphy."

Early in 1865 *Emily Chester* was dramatized by Mr. George H. Miles, and was played at the Holliday Street Theatre.[19]

Anne had the usual experience of suddenly successful authors, receiving visits, letters, invitations, and applications, often prompted by real admiration and good feeling; and sometimes by impertinent curiosity or self-interest. Her circle of friends widened, and life widened out before her. There are some friends left who remember her as she was then, very busy undertaking many things. Keeping up her music, reading, visiting, etc., she also undertook to superintend the training, dressing and general education of her little sister Josephine,—to us the child or our mother's old age.

A newspaper last winter described an evening company of that time, at a well-known residence in this city, at which Miss Anne M. Crane entertained a number of her friends by reading characters from handwriting, in which she had remarkable success.

At one of his readings in Baltimore, Mr. Charles Dickens sent to my sister the little bouquet which he wore on that occasion,—and which we still preserve. One of the original members of this Club, the late Mrs. Tiernan—then Miss Mary Nicholas,—who was a good friend of Anne, came to her after the reading was over; and made a comic protest, expressing exaggerated jealousy and indignation over her having received those flowers from Mr. Dickens.

To Anne's family it has always been strange that her book, written in her youth and inexperience, seemed to foretell some events that came to pass afterwards.

Her father died, like Mr. Chester, suddenly of heart disease; in 1866. This shock naturally interfered with her literary labor. But not for long; her mind was strong and clear, so was her religious faith. As she says of one of her heroines: "Long before these years, walking through the weary land, she had sought and found the shadow of a great Rock."

In this same year Anne began her second book, *Opportunity*,—and soon became deeply interested in writing it.

Early in 1867, Anne's old friend and admirer, Mr. Augustus Seemuller, came back from Europe, where he had been living for more than two years. His family had been our near neighbors in our childhood, and he was one of the few playmates we had at that time. When Anne was ten years old, and Augustus was over sixteen, he had sent her a valentine,—which may be in existence somewhere still. He was the son of German parents, himself born in Dublin, Ireland. His father, who spoke nearly all the languages of Europe, and had lived in various parts of the world, possessed an unusually good collection of paintings and curiosities. For children like ourselves to go into that house, and to hear conversations in several different languages at once, to contemplate works of art, and to listen to music of a much higher grade than we had ever known before, was a sort of revelation to us; and was a part of our education. Augustus was, as Anne expressed it—"a mental missionary to her," and he always said she was "the brightest woman he ever met." He was a man of so much intellect, culture, and even power of expression, as to make one sometimes wonder at the smallness of his achievements in this world. His letters were extremely bright, and I know he did write in prose and verse, but do not think he ever published anything. Perhaps continual ill health and some other circumstances were hindrances to outward accomplishment, in spite of talent and excellence of mind and character. But he was successful in business and had appreciative and even enthusiastic friends. A brilliant woman in Richmond, Virginia said: "Mr. Seemuller sometimes talks too well. It stops conversation, when he sums up the whole of a subject in one sentence, and leaves nothing more to be said about it." Early in life Mr. Seemuller went to live in New York, engaging in business there; and he made long visits to Europe also. But he was again in Baltimore when the Civil War broke out; and as was the case with many others, his sympathies induced him to "go South," and join the Confederate Army. But before very long he was, on account of severe inflammatory rheumatism, released from the military service. Once, at least, he went to Europe, by way, I believe of the West Indies.

I may be pardoned for relating an incident of the War—that "now is over." Our own father was a decided, conscientious Union man; and his children were widely divided in opinion, but were required to respect each other's convictions, and were supposed to keep the peace at home. Sometimes we received mysterious letters from our near relations in Virginia; and on one occasion we were informed that they had been sent to us through the good offices of our old friend Mr. Seemuller. One evening in August 1862, one of our brothers happened to be standing at the front door, when a man looking like a rough workman came up and held out his hand. The first word he spoke revealed our old friend, who was brought in and welcomed. He declined to have the gas lighted, but told us he had come from Richmond, bringing news of our relations there. For nearly an hour, he answered questions, and gave us a large amount of entirely uncompromising, but to us, intensely interesting information. Then he rose, and said, "I have a carriage waiting for me around the corner. Of course you will not mention this visit,—or I shall be in the Fort tomorrow, Good by"—and was gone from our sight for more than four years. Quite late in the war we heard from a neighbor, accidentally, that Mr. Seemuller had been in Baltimore again, and that he had gone back to Richmond. Anne afterwards spoke of this, and our father calmly answered: "I knew it at the time." Seeing our looks of surprise, he said, "His father told me he was here; but said: "Of course you will not mention it and of course, I did not mention it." It had never once occurred to our very straight-forward father that he might have been trusted with the dangerous information on purpose to give it us,—that we might send messages to our cousins in Richmond also.

When the War ended, Mr. Seemuller concluded to establish his residence in Paris, and declared his intention of never coming back to America. Anne had never been really engaged to him, but hearing this some time afterwards, she sent him a message, to the effect, that if General Lee and Mr. Davis could give up the fight, she thought he might follow their example. Perhaps he was about coming to the same conclusion too, for, near the beginning of the year 1867, he came back to America, to Baltimore,—and to see Anne. He again fixed his residence in New York, but he came to Baltimore often during that summer. In October 1867, he and Anne became

engaged, though they were not married for nearly two years afterwards. Mr. Seemuller took deep interest in Anne's literary work, and was one of those who helped her to copy *Opportunity* for publication.

I should be glad if I could name here some other friends who are still living, whose kind criticisms and real services deserved and won her grateful appreciation. I must say at least that *Opportunity* was dedicated to Mr. Joseph M. Cushing of this city "With Gratitude."

This work, *Opportunity*, Anne's second novel, was published by Ticknor and Fields, late in 1867; and met with scarcely less success than its predecessor. Mr. Paul H. Hayne of South Carolina wrote of it, "No tale has recently appeared, North or South, which is so full of rich evidences of genuine psychological power, profound study of character,—and fervid artistic aspirations, destined to embody themselves gloriously in the future." If I may venture to give my own person opinion, I have always preferred *Opportunity* to Anne's other two books, *Emily Chester*, and *Reginald Archer*. I think the style better, the story better, more natural and truthful than theirs.

Before and after this time, Anne wrote and published in different Magazines short stories and articles in prose and verse, such as: "Little Bo Peep," "Novelists Poetry," "Private Bohemians," etc.

Anne was married to August Seemuller at her mother's house on the 23rd of September, 1869. Of those most interested in that quiet wedding, the greater part have "gone over to the majority." The bride still wore mourning for her father, and would not consent to put on a white dress for the occasion. At thirty-one, she had not, of course, the color and bloom of sixteen, but her fine, tall figure, handsome hair and eyes, and bright expression caused a French gentleman who was at the wedding to say: "She is magnificent." They left Baltimore for New York the same day, taking up their residence at the New York Hotel. As they drove off, one of our cousins from Richmond said: "Won't those two have fun!"—in allusion to their wonderful appreciation and enjoyment of the same things. Both Anne and Augustus had already some friends in New York who added much to the pleasure of their residence there. And a literary friend of ours, the late Mrs. Sarah A. Dorsey of Louisiana, had sent a letter introducing them to her friend, Mrs. Botta, formerly Miss Anne Charlotte Lynch, whose receptions were for many an institution in New York literary society. Mrs. Botta proved not only a valuable acquaintance, but a valued and true friend. I wish I could quote from Anne's letters, telling of the various "lions" she was invited to meet. In one, she speaks of having received an invitation to one of Mrs. Bigelowe's receptions, "to meet Père Hyacinthe";[20] and she says, "I thought he had blown over," but he has taken second bloom." Of her first evening at Mrs. Botta's she says: "The company was partly foreign, and wholly literary consequently both Augustus and I thoroughly enjoyed it." She tells that at that house one might meet all celebrities, from Lord Derby's grandson to the minor journalists, "from Ralph Waldo Emerson to Tom Thumb." I remember that Mr. Edmund Clarence Stedman, when I met him at the house of our President,[21] spoke to me

of having enjoyed meeting my sister when she was living in New York. But on the whole, Anne was not glad to live in New York. Even the little difference in climate was unsuitable to her; and she especially disliked the hotel and boarding house life, with which she came in contact. It was there that she began, continued, and finished *Reginald Archer*,—the most severely criticized of all her writings. Before she left Baltimore she had sent to the *Galaxy* the story she called "Little Bo Peep." After its publication, the editor of that magazine, had proposed to her to write a series of short stories founded on old rhymes and fables. She like the idea, and began a story on the theme furnished by the old nursery rhyme of the "Five Little Pigs." Living in New York, the story grew in her mind and taking the color of aroused indignation it became the novel of *Reginald Archer*.

This book was published in Boston by James R. Osgood and Company in March 1871. One of its critics called it: "The story of a rake, delicately told." Some persons have wondered how Anne came to write this book. Anne herself said that what she "had intended as a sermon, was received by most readers as a sensational novel only." She had come from a sheltered, congenial, happy—I think I may say, intellectual home,—to see an entirely different phase of life. Very happily married herself, she saw unhappy marriages,—and far worse things still. The old desire to write arose again. She had spoken of her heroine Emily Chester, as "always making Declarations of Independence on her own account." And now she herself said: "I felt that if I did not write against what I had seen and heard, the very stones of the streets would cry out against me." Possible too, her husband had seen in the older civilizations of Europe, still more of what she saw in New York, and may have added point and force to her utterances. There were unfavorable critics of course, though they spoke of the power with which "the modern phase of the Epicurean philosophy is brought out." The New York *Commercial Advertiser* said: "The doctrine of the book is sound and unimpeachable."

But of all the criticisms of *Reginald Archer*, the one I have most valued, was given in a note from my honored friend, the late Mrs. Almira Lincoln Phelps, herself a successful writer and educator; and at the time of this writing, eighty-two years of age. Having borrowed the book from Anne's mother, she wrote to her, under date of March 3rd, 1876:

"I have just finished reading *Reginald Archer*, a book of your daughter's, which I now return, powerfully impressed with a sense of her genius, and purity of character. I can understand that she might be misunderstood by some, who have not the power to appreciate her work. Had her life and health been prolonged, what might not her mature genius and knowledge of life and character have achieved."

But "*Reginald Archer* was published early in 1871; and, now, a quarter of a century after it was written, we have become much more familiar with that kind of story, and perhaps do not shrink from the plain speaking of Mrs. Sarah Grand, and others like her, any more than we do from the reports of our daily papers. Perhaps Anne was, in her third book, still more than in her first one,—in advance of her time.

Some time before finishing *Reginald Archer* Anne had suffered greatly from her old liver complaint, and rheumatism, and she spent part of the summer of 1870 at the Hot Springs in Virginia. But her old power and enthusiasm in talking was not impaired, and there were some visitors at the Springs who recognized this fact immediately. Among others, she met there General Robert E. Lee, who spoke of the interest he had taken in her company, conversation and singing.

In the spring of 1871, when Anne was very ill in New York her favorite brother John died, in Baltimore. She had known that he was ill, but it was some days after his funeral before her husband ventured to tell her of John's death. But as the warm weather came on, she rallied again, and grew better.

Mr. Seemuller's health was very poor also, and he had retired from business. He said that there is not much for an idle man to do in America, and he proposed to Anne to go to Europe for an indefinite sojourn. I am sure that Anne would have preferred to come back and live in Baltimore, but she did not say so. As they had no children and had the means to gratify their tastes, the plan proposed was carried out.

Before they sailed away, they came to Baltimore, and spent the month of September 1871, at her mother's house,—her home, as she always called it. Even if she had not been in mourning, she was too sick to make visits herself, but many of her friends came to see her, and the renewal of her former home life was a great restorative to her. Then came the parting,—to most of us at home the final one. Next came letters,—charming to the home circle she had left. She told us that travelling in England, gave one the impression of visiting one's grandparents. She saw something of Moncure Conway and his wife, then, as now again, living in London. She heard Dean Stanley preach in Westminster Abbey,—and thought the sermon little less wonderful than the Abbey itself. Then they went to Germany, and spent most of the winter of 1871-72 at Bonn. The impression had been received that the climate of that place would be suitable to their health. But they were disappointed;—that they endured cold and discomfort was evident from the letters that they tried to make cheerful and interesting. They thought the weather too cold for either of them to take the journey necessary to reach a warmer climate. That part of Germany had suffered in many ways from the Franco-Prussian War, and had not recovered from it. August said that the Rhineland, which in summer is called the Vineland, ought that winter have been called the Swineland, for the chief article of diet he saw there was pork.

Still they did improve in health, and, after two months at Bonn, Anne wrote to us to direct our next letters to Munich. Their intention was to go from there to Vienna for six weeks or more, and after visiting other German cities, to go to Paris. From there they intended to go to London, where they hoped to reside. But Anne never reached Munich, at Stuttgart, she was suddenly taken very ill, and never gained strength again; though she lived ten months longer. After February, we had from her only one letter, written to her mother, in pencil, and the be-

ginning of another one. August planned to take her to the mineral springs in Bohemia; but she was not able to go.

Before Anne left home, she made her sister Fannie promise to come to her wherever she might be, if there was need for her presence. And now the promise was exacted, and fulfilled. Fannie and our brother Ward started at two days notice, on the 3rd of July 1872; and arrived at Stuttgart, to find Anne very ill, but still trying to be at times, bright and cheerful. The brother came home again, but Fannie stayed on to the end.

Anne was living in a very pleasant *pension*, which was much patronized by English people. Before her sister's arrival, some lovely English ladies had been coming to see her, at the request of her physician, who was theirs also, and she felt that their presence, and talking to her in her native tongue, would do her good; and he was right. These ladies had recognized Anne's mental ability and power of expression even then. They also told Fannie that Mr. Seemuller ought to have a gold medal voted to him by all womankind, for his untiring, beautiful devotion to his sick wife.

The presence and ministrations of her sister also, of course did Anne good; and she seemed to grow better. She planned a course of travel, and said, "Couldn't we three have a good time,—if I was only half well?" Late in the summer it was thought best to move her out of the city of Stuttgart, to the pleasant suburban watering place of Cannstatt. She liked the change, and seemed benefitted by it, for a time. But though her mental vigor and occasional vivacity astonished her doctors, they would give no favorable opinion of her case. The pronounced her disease "the degeneration of the liver,"—that organ having been her weak point all her life.

She gradually failed, and on December 10th, 1872, after two days of unconsciousness, she died, at Cannstatt,—being not quite thirty-five years old. Her body was brought home by her husband and sister, and buried in Greenmount Cemetery, on January 10th, 1873.

Not many days before Anne died, some one was speaking in her presence of the poems of her favorite, Mrs. Browning; and the one called "The Sleep" was mentioned. Anne then repeated the last stanza.

> And friends, dear friends, when it
>   shall be,
> That this low breath is gone from me,
> And round my bier ye come to weep.
> Let One, most loving of you all,
> Say, Not a tear must o'er her fall,
> He giveth His beloved, sleep.

Then she added, "And that is what I wish too." And her husband chose that text for her tombstone.

Most of Anne's critics had said that she was capable of giving the world,—if she lived longer—far better work than anything she did accomplish. Before she was married, and before, I believe, she had thought of *Reginald Archer*, she had begun another story, of which she read a page or two in our family circle, and we were rather unusually unanimous in our warm approval, of a first reading. But she gave it no name, and did not reveal its plot.

After *Reginald Archer* had been published, in a letter to her mother dated

New York, May 30th, 1871, Anne wrote: "I am very anxious to write a story I have in my head, which I think you will like. I think of calling it: 'A Little Child Shall Lead Them.' But I have promised Augustus to put off the execution until I am strong,—and I think he is right." All of us who knew and loved her, could not help wishing that this story had been written.

Anne left no children. Mr. Seemuller lived in Baltimore after her death until the spring of 1875. His devotion to Anne's memory and his efforts to do good, silently and constantly, which he seemed to connect with that memory, were known only to those who knew and cared for him well. He had the most intense sympathy with human suffering, and the impulse always to relieve it. More than two years after Anne's death, he went again to Europe, hoping to derive benefit to his health from the waters of Carlsbad. After leaving Carlsbad, he travelled among byways and mountain districts, often writing to Anne's mother about the poor people he met. He then went to France, a country of which he was fond, and where he had formerly lived for years. He was staying alone in Paris, at the Grand Hotel, when on the morning of September 25th, 1875, he was found unconscious, and dying of heart disease. The American consul and an American physician were summoned, only to see him pass away. According to his injunctions made before leaving this country, his body was brought to Baltimore and laid by Anne's side at Greenmount.

On the first of January, 1893, Anne's much loved sister, Fannie, was laid there also. I wish that she could have written the life of our sister Anne. Near the end of *Opportunity*, Harvey's uncle Dr. Dan, asks his niece: "What essential soul-satisfying element has life every brought you?" And she answers only: "I shall be satisfied when I awake in His likeness." And believing in that awakening we can—

> "Trust that those we call the dead
> Are breathers of an ampler day
> For ever nobler ends."

From "A Sketch of the Life of Edgar Allan Poe from the Testimony of His Friends"
by Letitia Humphreys Yonge Wrenshall (1910)

In this brief excerpt from her much longer biographical profile, which was published in a volume commemorating the centennial of Edgar Allan Poe's birth, Letitia Wrenshall describes Poe's death and legacy.

According to a letter to Mrs. Clemm from Mrs. Shelton,[22] Poe spent the last evening in Richmond with the latter. She writes, "he came to take leave of me. He was very sad and complained of being sick. I felt his pulse and found he had considerable fever, and did not think it probable he would be able to start the next morning (Thursday) as he anticipated. I felt so wretched about him all that night that I went up early the next morning to enquire after him, when much to my regret he had left in the boat for Baltimore."[23]

Further accounts agree that on his walk back from Mrs. Shelton's he stopped at Dr. John Carter's office; and later "went to take a little supper across the street at Sadler's restaurant. There he met some acquaintances. . . . who accompanied him to the boat, where, as is said, they left him sober and cheerful." His last words to his friends were "He would soon be in Richmond again."

On October the 3rd, 1849, Joseph W. Walker, a compositor on the *Sun*, Baltimore, wrote Dr. J. E. Snodgrass a note which Dr. Harrison copied from the original one in the possession of Mrs. Snodgrass:

Baltimore City, October 3, 1849.

Dear Sir: There is a gentleman, rather the worse for wear, at Ryan's 4th Ward polls, who goes under the cognomen of Edgar A. Poe, and who appears in great distress, and he says he is acquainted with you, and I assure you he is in need of immediate assistance.

Yours in haste,
Joseph W. Walker.
To Dr. J. E. Snodgrass.

Dr. Snodgrass, on receipt of the note hastened to attend Poe and finding him in a dangerous state had him removed to the Washington College University Hospital. Poe was at first unconscious, then delirious, from which condition he sank into the quiet of exhaustion. In the gray dawn of Sunday morning, moving his head gently to and fro upon his pillow, he quietly said: "Lord help my poor soul," and died.

The *Sun* of October 8, 1849, announced: "We regret to learn that Edgar A. Poe, Esq., the distinguished American poet, scholar, and critic, died in this city yesterday morning, after an illness of four or five days. This announcement, coming so sudden and unexpected, will cause poignant regret among all who admire genius and have sympathies for the frailties too often attending it."

Many accounts from diverse standpoints have been written of the tragic end of Edgar Allan Poe. The evidence given by Bishop Fitzgerald strongly supports the belief that Poe was a victim of robbery and of "cooping" for political purposes—this being a common practice in Baltimore at that day—a view sustained not only by the impossibility of locating his whereabouts from Friday, September 28, to October 3, but the handsome clothing which he wore when leaving Richmond had been changed for poor and dirty garments. Testimony confirming this is given in the letter from William J. Glenn of Richmond. Mr. Glenn was Poe's fellow member in the "Sons of Temperance" and administered the obligations of total abstinence when admitting him early in July of 1849. He states: "During his stay in the city of the next three months or more there was not the slightest intimation that he had failed to live up to his obligation. In October he started to Baltimore. . . . a few days later we heard of his death at a hospital in that city, and the statement was made and too busily circulated that his death was the result of a spree commenced as soon as he reached Baltimore. We of the temperance order to which he belonged exerted ourselves to get at the facts, and consensus of opinion was that he had not been drinking, but had been drugged. A gentleman of the name of Benson, ... went to Baltimore, and as he knew Poe and felt much interest in the manner of

his death, went to the hospital at which he died, and had a talk with the doctor (J. J. Moran) who told him that Poe had not been drinking when brought to the hospital but was under the influence of a drug; he added that he suggested the use of stimulants, but that Mr. Poe positively declined taking any. Mr. Poe lived very quietly while here."

After his tired soul was at rest, Poe's magic voice still spoke in the sweetest of love ballads. *Annabel Lee*, which appeared in the *New York Tribune* October 9, 1849— the very day when his funeral cortege of six gentlemen followed him through the chill rain to his grave in the family lot at Westminster Burying Ground. In the same issue of the paper was the vindictive article by Rufus Griswold, signed "Ludwig." A month after Poe's death, the third and final version of "The Bells" was published in the November number of the *Union Magazine*, its development traced by the editor, John Sartain. A year later, October, 1850, "The Poetic Principle" appeared in the same magazine. The loveliest dream of a poet's home, "Landor's Cottage," was not given to the world until much later.

The mystery surrounding Poe's last days is long in finding solution. With his faults acknowledged by his friends, the extenuating conditions of his physical organization, heredity and disease reluctantly admitted by his enemies, prejudice sprung from malice and wilful turning from truth must disappear. All who possess the divine element of pity will unite in feeling that his sufferings were his expiation, an expiation not only in life but after death in the untruthful representations of his life and character.

Great as this has been, it has not robbed

the world of the legacy he bequeathed to literature, nor has it stilled the voices that, as one, acclaim his many fine qualities; lauding his devotion to his nearest ties and to his friends, his undaunted efforts to maintain his wife and mother when ill in body and enduring the most wearing of all pain—hope deferred, his honest and proper pride, disdaining to reproach when reproach was justifiable, his well-nigh superhuman industry and patience, his courage that refrained from lamentation and, through all and over all, the purity of his life. As these voices speak truly, their words live, for, having caught the fine ear of justice with which the people of America ever listen, they are imperishable.

Westminster Churchyard[24]
For Edgar Allan Poe
by Lizette Woodworth Reese (1910)

Stone calls to stone, and roof to roof;
Dust unto dust;—[25]
Lo, in the midst, starry, aloof—
Like white of April blown by last year's stalks
Across the gust—
A Presence walks.

It is the Shape of Song;
About it throng,
Great Others, and the first is Tears;
The ended years;
And every old and every lonely thing;
Old thirsts that to old hungers cry;
The poignancies of earth and sky;
The little sobbing of the spring.

He heeds them not;
They are forgot;
For him, behind this ancient wall,

The Best of all—
The short day sped;
A roof; a bed;
No years;
No tears.

Not his the strain
Of hill or lane;
Of orchards with their humble country
    musk,
And bent old trees,
And companies of small black bees;
Of gardens at the dusk,
Where down the hush,
A thrush
His heartbreak spills;
Of daffodils
By farmhouse doors a windy sight,
A yellow gust driven down the light.

Nor his the note
That trumpeted of war,
Of ancient creed;
Strange, innocent, remote
His reed
A wind along the hollows of an echoing
    shore:
Each day was but a pool within the grass,
A haunted space,
Where saw he as in glass.
But Wonder, with her dim, drowned face.

For Wonder was his kin.
His very twin;
Blood of his blood indeed,
And steadfast to his need;—
The ecstasies of cloud and sky;
The cry out in the dark;
The half lit spark
That lures from earth to star;

The fleeting footsteps far and far;
The trailing skirts so nigh, so nigh.
These drew he from their ghostly mesh
And made them flesh;
We reach dull hands, for we would know;
They fade; they go;
Yea, he and they together.
Into another weather.
A strange, autumnal verse;
Where griefs their griefs rehearse;
A flaw of rain within the air;
Black pools; the bough gone bare;
And red dead leaves and broken wall;
The flare of tempest driven behind them all.

Yet ever is his music such,
So rapt of touch,
It mellows all the ache.
And the heartbreak;
We cannot weep, but we stand wistful-eyed,
Like children at the eventide.
In some fast darkening spot.
Who hear their mother call, but see her not.
Oh, truest singer east or west!—
Not for the poor handful of hire.
But for the fury of the song.
The unescapable desire.
He sang his short life out, and it was best;
His wage was hunger; it was long
Betwixt the days of blame and jeers.
And that which set him with his peers;
A fragmentary song, yet dear to Art;
Its numbers hold
Enough of music for new world and old,
To shake them to the heart.

And now, many a summer's weather.
Now, many a winter's storms together.
The wind; the shower;
The blooms; the snows;

Have petaled into this brief hour.
And drop upon his dust a rose.

Roof calls to roof and stone to stone;—
Like white of April blown
The gust along—
The Shape of Song!

From *Music and Edgar Allan Poe*
by May Garrettson Evans (1939)

Poe himself, as has been cited, was keenly susceptible to music. "We are often," he cries, "made to feel, with a shivering delight, that from an earthly harp are stricken notes which cannot have been unfamiliar to the angels." There is an interesting tradition about Poe's having been so deeply moved by the singing of an anthem in church one Sunday, that, hardly conscious of his surroundings, he left the pew and advanced slowly up the aisle toward the choir—rapt, entranced. Only when the music ceased did he become aware of his strange and conspicuous actions. It is a pretty story—let us hope it is true.

It is told also of Poe that he played on the flute (some say on the piano too) and that he had a good voice—gifts which probably found their chief expression in the slight parlor pieces and sentimental ditties of the time in the American home. He was certainly not, however, a musician in any special sense of the word.

Of Poe's interest in music, Professor Killis Campbell (*The Mind of Poe*, Harvard University Press) says:[26]

He was fond of the piano and of instrumental music generally. In an early letter (written in 1835), he remarks that he has been making some off chromatic experiments by way of testing the music of some of his own lines; and elsewhere he reveals an acquaintance with technical terms in music. In certain of his essays, especially those written about 1845, he comments on the opera and on theatrical performances in New York City, which he attended from time to time.

The period in which Poe lived was, by the way, one of extraordinary musical creativeness abroad, and it must have had its influences on him, if only indirectly. The time of the birth of Poe, or shortly before or after, saw also the birth of many men destined to make musical history—Bellini (1801), Berlioz (1803), Mendelssohn (1809), Chopin (1810), Schumann (1810), Liszt (1811), Verdi (1813), Wagner (1813), and others. Compositions by the majority of these were given their first American productions in Poe's own time; not to speak of works of the musical giants of the eighteenth century.

Though the new country was of necessity preoccupied with the stress of material up building, it was nevertheless surely, if slowly, awakening to the appeal of good music. The United States had not yet become orchestra-conscious, but choral societies and other musical organizations, professional and amateur, were active in the principal cities. Opera companies and musical virtuosi, chiefly from Europe, made frequent appearances and were enthusiastically, if not always discriminatingly, received, especially in the later forties. Poe's connection with New York journals at that

time, doubtless, often gave him admission to concerts and operas which otherwise, in his poverty, he could not have attended.

Amazing Variety of Musical Forms

One expects to find vocal forms, admitting of the use of words, predominating in musical settings of literary texts. Thus it is in the case of Poe. But what one would not expect to find is the astonishing variety and number of other forms selected by composers for the treatment of Poe themes.

Even a brief listing of the modes of expression will suffice to convey some idea of their great extent—song, chant, chorus, cantata, recitation to music, opera, piano solo, chamber music, symphony, symphonic poem, incidental music, and ballet.

The first purely instrumental piece noted in the present list appeared as early as 1866. It is a piano solo, *Sleigh Bells*, based on the first stanza of "The Bells," and forms one of three *Winter Pictures* by the American church composer, Dudley Buck.[27]

A third of a century later (in 1900), a symphonic poem for grand orchestra, *The Raven*, was brought out at the Crystal Palace Symphony Concerts, London, under the direction of Sir August Manns.[28] It is the work of the British composer, Josef Holbrooke, who, by the way, has written more Poe pieces than has any other single composer, no fewer than twenty-five compositions, comprising thirty-five Poe texts, evidencing his interest in the American poet. ("Poe sings always," says Holbrooke; "and so few poets do.")[29]

Other instrumental works followed in rapid succession, both in this country and abroad. This development, which Poe himself could certainly never have foreseen, was doubtless due in part to the increasing vogue of descriptive instrumental music—"program music"—based on or inspired by a literary text or an incident or other "program." Poe's imaginative creations lend themselves readily to such depiction. In turn, they themselves find a fitting vehicle in the large instrumental forms, especially in the latest and highest development of the tone picture—the symphonic poem.

The multiform mediums chosen by composers for the musical embodiment of Poe represent no less variety in the character of the music. The compositions range from the simplest and most conventional styles of past periods in which they were popular, and the highly developed forms adhered to by followers of the "classical" school, to the restless tonality (and "atonality"), the radical departure from long-established principles, and the startling—even sometimes audacious—innovations in instrumentation characterizing the modern trends.

The compositions recorded in the bibliography represent, of course, various degrees of merit.[30] Many of the settings are the work of unquestioned genius; and of distinguished talent and originality. Most of them are products of the present century, and include many effective interpretations by rising young composers of today. Some four or five are the bubbling effusions of composers when in their long-ago boyhood days, and have a special significance for that very reason. Some of the settings are noteworthy chiefly for their antiquarian interest. But the great majority are the expressions of matured art. No attempt at evaluation of the works listed

has been made. Suffice it to say that the settings as a whole constitute a sincere and impressive contribution to music as well as a tribute to the poet. And they represent withal a highly significant phase of the belated appreciation (belated at least in his native land) accorded the bard "whose harshest idea will to melody run."[31]

Pondering on the whole remarkable development, one can but fall to musing in the old accustomed way on the irony of fate, and to speculating as to what the thoughts of struggling genius would be if only it were given to it to peer into future and take heart of courage therefrom. Perchance the prophetic soul of a creative artist does perceive somehow the things which are in store, and so goes on stubbornly with a fight that seems often a losing one. And Edgar Allan Poe, trudging the streets in bitterness of spirit, despairingly, but doggedly hawking his wares from publisher to publisher, may indeed have sensed, if dimly, what was to come—both the literary recognition of his art and the realization of the musical potentialities in which is abounds. Said he:

> In speaking of song-writing, I mean, of course, the composition of brief poems with an eye to their adaption for music. . . . In this ultimate destination of the song proper, lies its essence, its genius.

And again:

> There can be little doubt that in the union of Poetry and Music . . . we shall find the widest field for the Poetic development. The old Bards and Minnesingers had

advantages which we do not possess—and Thomas Moore, singing his own songs, was, in the most legitimate manner, perfecting them as poems.[32]

Maryland Poet Who Is Little Known in Her Own State Is Lucy Mitchell
by Emily Emerson Lantz (1921)

Have you ever motored through the Upper Gunpowder region,[33] through the beautiful wild country near the Pennsylvania boundary line? Have you glimpsed Parkton, Maryland, as you passed along and then speeded onward to Beckleysville and thence some two and a half miles farther north until you came to a little hamlet called Shamburgh? Shamburgh is something more than twenty miles beyond Towson. It lies not exactly upon the line of Baltimore's water extension, as indicated in plans of Engineer Lee, yet doubtless the river current flowing past the hamlet will eventually be included in Baltimore's water supply.

And here at Shamburgh having reached the end of a literary pilgrimage, should such be your mission, you will find a cottage environed by a garden, owned and occupied by Miss Lucy Mitchell, a poet of Maryland and a former resident of Baltimore. In childhood and the years of her youth Miss Mitchell resided at 1650 East Fayette street, just around the corner from the Church Home and Infirmary.[34] The few old neighbors who still remain in what was once a fashionable residence section opening into Broadway recall Miss Lucy Mitchell as a dark-eyed, dark-haired, somewhat reserved young woman who lived in a large house filled with valuable heirlooms and who, as a girl, used to sit and dream and write poetry at an elevated window looking eastward toward Broadway.

One by one members of Miss Mitchell's family died until she alone survives and some years ago she sold the big lonely house on Fayette street and removed to Baltimore county, where she finds solace in her garden and companionship in nature.

Contributor to Springfield Paper

Here she has written much verse, and while practically unknown in Maryland, she has been for twenty years a constant contributor to the *Springfield Republican*.[35]

While not always perfect in construction, Miss Mitchell's verse is intensely poetic in conception and treatment. Her poems have usually a tinge of melancholy resultant, doubtless, upon long years lived much alone. She possesses power to vividly visualize familiar things of life and endow them with spiritual significance. There is delicate spirituality within her lines that is both rare and beautiful. Her perception is keen and her emotional force carries her message to the heart of the reader. A certain tender wistfulness in what she writes combined with firm faith in the guardianship of God suggests the poems of Emily Dickinson.

Very lovely are the following lines:

Endymion[36]

(Rinehart's[37] Statue, Over His Grave in Greenmount Cemetery,[38] Baltimore.)

On my slow way through Green-
    mount still and fair
I paused, arrested by Endymion[39]
    couched
In slumber sweet and deep o'er
    Rhineheart's grave.
It captured sight; I could but gaze
    and gaze:
Nor did the thought, "This is a
    tomb," subdue.
As with the emerald hillocks thick
    around.
For who could pity even in death the
    hand
Which carved this almost breathing
    shape, the brain
Whence came the godlike flat, "Let
    it be!"
And lo! it was, and is and is to be
To eyes unopened yet to Beauty's
    light.

Dead? Then 'tis death between the
    zephyr breaths
Indrawn and issuing from his parted
    lips;
See! he inbreathes, and curves the
    outbreath wait.
Such is the death immortal Genius
    dies;
Yet is her thought so spiritual, 'tis
    hard
Fit form to find for its embodiment
Above her dead, whereof it may be
    said,
"Be his in lieu of time,"—but here
    'tis done.
And even so well, 'tis more than
    mortal mood—
Yea, bath rich share of immortality.

Oh if 'tis meet to look upon a grave
As warning—a memento we must
    pass—
Here may we read a deeper lesson
    still:
Man in idea perfected lives again—
Still speaks to new-born and undying
    souls!

*An additional poem, "The Departures," is
here omitted.*

Concerning her past life and literary work, Miss Mitchell said recently: "I am not, strictly speaking, a Baltimorean, although most of my life has been spent in that city. I was born in Cambridge, county seat of Dorchester, or, as the natives call it, 'Dosset' county. I was about eight years old when my family removed to Baltimore, and an elder sister, taking my hand, led me to a primary school a few blocks distant from our home. I found my own way to the grammar and high school and the public library did the rest.

"Miss E. A. Baer was the guiding mind at the helm of English literature at the time I was a pupil at the Eastern High School.[40] She was broad of mind and infinite of patience, and to such of her pupils as continued their literary studies after graduating her wide knowledge and appreciation of English letters, past and present, made her at once an invaluable guide and a sympathetic critic. Her very memory awakens my deep emotion.

"To her primarily and to Charles Goodrich Whiting, editor of the *Springfield Republican*, who seconded her work as my kind though unsparing critic. I owe the best of whatever I may be in literature. At the Eastern High School Miss Baer was succeeded by her friend, Miss Laura DeValin, the mentor and close and life-long friend of Miss Lizette Woodworth Reese. I knew and valued Miss DeValin as a friend, but she was never my teacher. Miss Reese also succeeded me at the high school, though I think she, too, felt the influence of Miss Baer. As to poetry, I have been writing for the *Springfield Republican* for considerably over twenty years."

The remainder of the article, which comprises Mitchell's recounting of her family history, is omitted.

Michael Angelo[41]
by Ella Morrow Sollenberger (1930s)

Unlovely and unloved thy destiny?
Yet god-like love and human thou hast
    known.
Else whence this rapt, exquisite ecstacy
Quickened to immortality in stone?

To Lizette Woodworth Reese
by Ella Morrow Sollenberger (1930s)?

In the wake of a comet,
Nebula, I,
Part of a flaming substance
Crossing the sky.
Though I dissolve in ether,
Mine still the flight
In the wake of a comet,
Piercing the night.

A Parting Ode

Laura De Valin (1843-1913)

Most of Laura De Valin's literary work has been lost to history—which is a shame, because De Valin dedicated her life to literature. She was an inspiring teacher, beginning her career while she was still a student at the Maryland College for Women in Lutherville, Maryland. She spent the majority of her decades-long career teaching English at Eastern High School, her alma mater, where she was also vice-principal for ten years before her retirement.

De Valin had a significant impact on her students. Some were so inspired by her teaching that they formed the De Valin Literature Club in her honor to continue their literary studies beyond their completion of her class. Lizette Woodworth Reese, one of De Valin's students at Eastern High School, followed in her footsteps and likewise became a teacher there. She and other published writers attested to De Valin's influence throughout their lives.

DeValin was an active member of WLCB, presenting articles on psychology, religion, and history. She also copyrighted several plays, but they, like the essays she wrote and presented to the Club, have subsequently been lost.

The only work of De Valin's that has been recovered is a song called "Parting Ode of 1859." De Valin was likely a student at the Maryland College for Women, more familiarly known as the Lutherville Female Seminary, when she wrote the lyrics to this heartwarming ode for commencement ceremonies that year. –K.Kazmierski

Cover and first page of "Parting Ode of 1859," by Laura De Valin; music by John F. Petri. Johns Hopkins Sheridan Libraries and University Museums.

Parting Ode
of 1859
written by
Laura De Valin
the music composed and dedicated
to the
Pupils of Lutherville Female Seminary
by
JOHN F PETRI

Parting Ode of 1859

Once more we stand together,
A happy girlish throng.
Half eager and half dreading
To sing the parting song.

Glad household bands await us
And friends whose loving eyes—
Bid hopes all bright and glowing,
Of future joys to rise.

But whilst we feel the pleasure
Today's glad meetings bring,
We feel the pain of parting,
We sorrow whilst we sing.

As children of one household,
As sisters in one band,
We've wept and laughed in union,
We've studied hand in hand.

Now some part for a season,
And some perhaps for years,
And some depart for ever,
They ask us for our tears.

Farewell our alma mater,
Farewell our studies too,
Ye loved ones, teachers, schoolmates,
A long, a fond Adieu.

Notes

Introduction

1 Emily Dickinson, in T. W. Higginson and Mabel Todd Loomis, eds., *Poems by Emily Dickinson: Second Series*. (Boston: Roberts Brothers, 1891), 21.

2 Woman's Literary Club of Baltimore meeting minutes, March 19, 1890.

3 WLCB meeting minutes, March 19, 1890.

4 WLCB Board of Management meeting minutes, Feb. 17, 1891.

5 WLCB meeting minutes, March 19, 1890; April 11, 1890; WLCB Board of Managers meeting minutes, Sept. 23, 1890. Club member Emily Lantz would write in 1915 that the Club had selected "white and lilac" as the Club colors. Emily Lantz, "Twenty-five Years Old Today," *Baltimore Sun*, Mar. 23, 1915: 7.

6 Anne Ruggles Gere, *Intimate Practices: Literacy and the Cultural Work of U.S. Women's Clubs, 1880-1920* (Urbana, IL: University of Illinois Press, 1997), 5.

7 Emily Lantz, "Twenty-Five Years Old Today." Baltimore *Sun* March 23, 1915.

8 The library appears to have been dispersed after the Club dissolved in 1941. The editors of this volume have attempted to recreate the WLCB library online at the WLCB Archive's Virtual Library, http://loyolanotredamelib.org/Aperio/WLCB/exhibits/show/virtual-library/introduction.

9 WLCB meeting minutes, Jan. 5, 1904. A Jan. 9, 1929 *Baltimore Sun* article claimed that the Club held its twenty-seventh Twelfth Night celebration that year. "Twelfth Night Is Marked," *Baltimore Sun*, Jan. 9, 1929: 3.

10 "Merry Twelfth Night: Woman's Literary Club Celebrates in Old English Style." *Baltimore Sun*, Jan. 7, 1902. According to Club minutes, the peacock also made its appearance at Twelfth Night celebrations in 1904, 1906, and 1914. Apparently the peacock underwent some difficult times. President Wrenshall reported at a Board of Managers meeting on Feb. 4, 1910 that the peacock, had been "somewhat injured," while in her possession, even though she had "kept it in camphor." She apparently hoped to bestow the beast on another Club member; finally, "Mrs. Powell offered to take it, and care for it herself."

11 This tradition of decorating the graves of Maryland writers was frequently mentioned in press coverage of the WLCB as originating with this organization, and may have inspired the "Poe Toaster," an unknown person (or persons) who decorated the grave of Edgar Allan Poe at the Westminster Burying Ground in Baltimore on the night of his birth, January 19, with a single rose and some whisky—a tradition begun in the 1940s (perhaps significantly, following the demise of the WLCB) and continuing until 2009, with sporadic revivals since that time.

12 We have, however, restricted our selections to those published by active members, meaning those who presented at least once to the Club. As a result, a number of honorary members, many of whom were invited to join to convey their status as well-known or widely published authors and frequently did not attend meetings or live in the Baltimore area, are excluded from *Parole Femine*.

13 Shivers mentions the Club a single time, calling it "the city's Women's Literary Club." *Maryland Wits and Baltimore Bards: A Literary History with Notes on Washington Writers* (Baltimore: Maclay and Associates, 1985), 248.

14 Bonnie G. Smith, "Women's History: A Retrospective View from the United States." *Signs* 35.3 (2010): 724.

15 Gere, *Intimate Practices*, 2; 8.

16 Gere, *Intimate Practices*, 44.

17 Constitution of the Woman's Literary Club of Baltimore (Baltimore: Isaac Friedenwald, c. 1891), Article IV, Section 5. This clause was later moved to the by-laws section.

18 Requardt's initial description of the collection was published as part of a bibliography of manuscript collections pertaining to women held at the Maryland Historical Society. Cynthia Horsburgh Requardt, "Women's Deeds in Women's Words: Manuscripts in the Maryland Historical Society," *Maryland Historical Magazine* 73.2 (1978): 187-204.

19 *Annals of Arundell Club of Baltimore, 1894-1925*, Baltimore: Norman Remington, 1926.

20 Gere, *Intimate Practices*, 45-46.

Local Favorites

Jane Zacharias

1 "Local Meetings and Other Notices." *Journal of American Folk-Lore* 12, no. 44 (January 1899): 147.

2 "'Miss Janie' Zacharias Dead," *Baltimore Sun*, Oct. 7, 1906, p. 7; "Lived for her 'Boys,'" *Baltimore Sun*, Oct. 10, 1906, p. 12.

3 Neighborhood in Baltimore that is home to the Washington Monument and Mount Vernon Place, which consists of four small parks that extend in all four directions from the monument. Surrounding the parks are homes, restaurants, and museums, including some fine examples of

nineteenth-century architecture.

4 Pilkey is selling Baltimore newspapers: the *Herald*, the *Sun*, and the *American*. Of these, only the *Sun* is still operating. The *Herald* was purchased by competitors in 1906, while the *American* continued publication until 1986. H. L. Mencken writes of working at the *Herald* in his memoir, *Newspaper Days* (1941).

5 The Front Street Theater, formerly known as the New Theatre and Circus, was built in 1829, but was destroyed in the Great Fire of 1904. The national Democratic convention met at the theater in 1859 to nominate Stephen A. Douglas as the Democratic candidate for President.

6 Darby & Co., fruit merchant and candy manufacturer, was located at 325 W. Baltimore Street.

7 Sutro Otto & Co. was located at 119 and 121 E. Baltimore St. (pre-1904 address) and sold a variety of musical instruments, including pianos and organs.

8 German Street, now named Redwood Street, was once the heart of Baltimore's German community but later became part of the downtown business district.

9 The central post office was spelled as one word in the city directories during this time. It occupied an entire city block on Calvert Street at Fayette.

10 Raine's Hall was located on Baltimore Street near the old city Post Office and was likely destroyed in the Great Fire of 1904.

11 The Phoenix (or Old Baltimore) Shot Tower was the tallest structure in the United States when it was constructed in 1828, at just over 234 feet. Round shot for weapons from pistols to cannons was made by dropping molten lead from a platform at the top of the tower into a tank of water, where it would harden into round shot. Annual production is estimated to have been one hundred thousand 25-pound bags of shot per year.

12 Reference to the 1st Louisiana Battalion of the Confederate Army, nicknamed the "Louisiana Tigers." They were known for the bloodcurdling yell they would issue forth as they charged, as well as their colorful and exotic Zouave-style uniforms. Like the newsboys depicted here, troops from the 1st Louisiana Battalion were recruited from the streets and wharves of New Orleans.

13 Mary N. Meigs, "There's a Wonderful Tree" (1869).

14 "Carol, Brothers" was written by W. A. Muhlenberg in 1840.

15 Wholesale produce markets congregated along Light Street and Charles Street south of Pratt well into the twentieth century (*Bodine's Baltimore: 46 Years in the Life of a City* [Baltimore: Bodine & Associates, 1973), 11.

16 Green Mount Cemetery, established in 1838, is bounded on one side by Greenmount Avenue.

17 I.e., Jesus Christ.

18 God appeared to Moses in the form of a burning bush in the book of Exodus.

19 Luke 2:14.

20 Meigs, "There's a Wonderful Tree."

21 "Wonderful Night" was written by John Frederick Meyer (1772-1848).

22 "Hark! Hark! The Sweet, Sweet Chiming" was written by Marie Mason in the 1800s.

23 "Carol, Carol, Christians" was written by Arthur Cleveland Coxe (1818-1896), Second Bishop of Western New York.

Lucy Meacham Thruston

1 "Faith of a Woman in Women of the South," *Baltimore Sun*, October 17, 1915.

2 "Mrs. Lucy Meacham Thruston," *Baltimore Sun*, April 26, 1905, Baltimore Authors sec.

3 "Faith of a Woman in Women of the South," *Baltimore Sun*, October 17, 1915.

4 Mobjack Bay, on the western shore of the Chesapeake Bay in Virginia, near Thruston's childhood home in King and Queen County, VA.

5 Large boat with sails used for harvesting oysters, developed in the Chesapeake Bay.

6 The men headed toward the Assembly feature several historical figures, including Thomas Gerard of St. Clement's, a Councillor in Maryland and Richard Preston, the "Great Quaker," whose home Preston on the Patuxent was the first provincial capital of Maryland. Giles Brent, Margaret's brother, was the Captain and Lord of Fort Kent Manor.

Emily Emerson Lantz

1 In several of *The Sun's* letters to the editor, readers from around Baltimore and across the nation asked about Lantz's genealogical work, trusting her expertise. For example, in a December 1907 letter, Robert Martin Jr. wrote from Wisconsin to inquire about the Dallam family of Maryland. In another note, an Alabama resident requested information from Lantz regarding her grandmother, Elizabeth Fuqua.

2 The Suburban Baltimore pieces constitute mini-histories of some of the nation's first suburbs. These histories also show some blind spots: for example, Lantz's piece on Roland Park makes no mention of the Roland Park Company's exclusion of people of color from living in the area. In one document, the Company announced that "at no time shall the land included in said tract or any part thereof, or any building erected thereon, be occupied by any negro or person of negro extraction. This prohibition, however, is not intended to include occupancy by a negro domestic servant." The suburb may have provided an escape

from the city's bustle and advanced twentieth century civilization, but it did not do so for everyone.

3 William Shakespeare, *Julius Caesar*, act 4, scene 3, 218-219.

4 St. Paul's Protestant Episcopal Church was founded in 1692 and is located on the southeast corner of N. Charles St. and E. Saratoga St.

5 Baltimore's Washington Monument was completed in 1829, decades before the better-known monument to George Washington that anchors the mall in Washington, DC, which began construction in 1848 but was not completed until 1884. Both monuments were designed by the same architect, Robert Mills (1781-1855).

6 The Elkridge Fox Hunting Club, now known simply as the Elkridge Club, now encompasses over one hundred acres at 6100 N. Charles St.

7 Likely a reference to English Elizabethan dramatist Thomas Decker's play *The Shoemaker's Holiday*, first performed in 1599.

8 At the time of Lantz's writing, the Johns Hopkins University was in the process of moving from its overcrowded campus in downtown Baltimore to what is now known as the Homewood campus. The grounds for the new campus were transferred to university ownership in 1902. Gilman Hall, which anchors the academic quadrangle, was completed in 1915.

9 Likely referring to the Boys' Latin School of Maryland, which was located in a downtown complex on Brevard Street, south of Merryman's Lane, until the 1950s when it was relocated to its present campus in Roland Park. It could also refer to Gliman School, which used to be located in the Homewood Mansion, now the Homewood Museum, until moving to Roland Park in 1910. The Gilman School was originally named The Country School for Boys.

10 The College of Notre Dame of Maryland was founded by the School Sisters of Notre Dame in 1873. In 1896, it became the first four-year Roman Catholic College for women in the United States. In 2011, the institution was elevated to a university and given its current title of Notre Dame University of Maryland.

11 In 1890, the Sisters of Mercy opened Mount Saint Agnes College for women in the Mount Washington neighborhood of Baltimore. The college remained open as its own degree-granting institution until 1972, but beginning in 1971, the school merged with Loyola College, which is now known as Loyola University Maryland. Loyola continues to sponsor the Mount Saint Agnes Alumnae Association today.

12 Mrs. George M. Lamb also belonged to the Neighborhood Improvement Club of Govans

(*Journal of the proceedings of the Senate of the State of Maryland*).

13 Signer of the Declaration of Independence for Maryland, politician, and US Senator.

14 From 1766-1832, Doughoregan Manor was the country home of Charles Carroll of Carrollton.

15 Historic home owned by Charles Carroll of Carrollton and eventually sold to Alexander Brown and Sons, the oldest private banking firm in North America.

16 Jérôme Napoleon was the youngest brother of Napoleon and reigned as Jerome I, King of Westphalia, from 1807–1813. He married Elizabeth Patterson, daughter of William Patterson (1752-1853), in 1803. Their sensational courtship and marriage is detailed in the excerpt from Annie Leakin Sioussat's *Old Baltimore* that we have included in this volume.

17 President of the B & O Railroad from 1858 until his death in 1884. In the generations that followed, the Garrett family was prominent in the railroad, shipping, and banking industries.

18 John Keats's "To Autumn," line 1; Alfred Lloyd Tennyson's "Tears, Idle Tears," line 4.

19 First president of the Roland Park Company, which developed Roland Park by laying out its street patterns, installing water, electric, and sewer lines, and selling property lots.

20 Granddaughter of Charles Carroll of Carrollton, who was a signer of the Declaration of Independence for Maryland, politician, and US Senator.

21 John W. Garrett was the president of the B & O Railroad from 1858 until his death in 1884. In the generations that followed, the Garrett family was prominent in the railroad, shipping, and banking industries.

22 Baltimore established its first park board in 1860, which led to the building of Druid Hill Park. In 1900, the park board expanded to include oversight of eight additional major parks: Patterson Park; Riverside Park, Federal Hill Park, Johnston Square, Madison Square, Collington Square, Caroll Park, and Clifton Park; these parks were included in a major park plan in 1904 ("History of Baltimore," City of Baltimore Department of Planning).

23 The Lake Roland Elevated railway was built in 1892-1893 and was the first electrified elevated line in the United States. The railway spanned eight blocks, having only three stops, and was the only elevated line in the city, which hosted an expansive streetcar system. The line, along Guilford Avenue, had to be elevated, since on the ground the street was already occupied by the Northern Central Railway—a subsidiary of the Pennsylvania Railroad.

24 Throughout the twentieth century, Baltimore had one of the nation's leading trolley systems, with over

440 miles of fixed rail serving us in the city and suburbs, going in all directions. Streetcars served as a major source of transportation for city residents.

25 Frederick Law Olmsted (1822-1903), pioneer of American landscape architecture and co-designer of several prominent urban parks, including New York City's Central Park and Trenton's Cadwalader Park. Olmsted was also a journalist, public administrator, and social critic.

26 This is a significantly above-average home price for 1905; in 1915 in the United States the average house cost roughly $3,200, according to census records.

27 In real estate, a "front foot" refers to the width of the property where it faces the street.

28 The Roland Park Company set in place strict community guidelines when establishing its suburbs. Covenants effected business and building rules such as those mentioned by Lantz, and required, for example, that houses cost over a set price to ensure wealthy homeowners. The codes also racially segregated the community by barring persons of color from purchasing residences.

29 In the early 1900s, in most American cities, residents mostly walked, rode bicycles, or used public transportation, such as the streetcar system in Baltimore. Typically, only wealthy residents traveled by horse drawn carriage, but throughout the following twenty years, this transportation mode decreased considerably as automobiles replaced horse-drawn vehicles.

30 The Baltimore Country Club, still in existence today, was founded in 1898 and was one of the first hundred clubs established in the United States. It currently occupies its original clubhouse in Roland Park and more expansive grounds at its Five Farms location in northern Baltimore County.

31 Beatrix Farrand (née Jones), an American landscape gardener and architect who was commissioned to design over one hundred gardens for private residences, estates and country homes, public parks, botanic gardens, college campuses, and most notably, the White House. Farrand was also one of eleven founding members of the American Society of Landscape Architects, and was the only woman to take on the position.

32 Roland Park Elementary Middle School is located at 5207 Roland Ave.

33 See "Suburban Baltimore: Charles Street," n. 4.

34 In 1894, the Roland Park Company established the Country School for Girls, which became the first fully accredited independent school for girls in Baltimore and is still open today under the name Roland Park Country School.

35 St. Mary's Female Orphan Asylum was founded in 1818 for the support and education of destitute female orphans and operated until 1960.

36 A list of over one hundred names of Roland Park residents follows and has been omitted here.

37 The word "jitney" was slang for "nickel," but eventually it was used to describe a mode of transportation that only cost a nickel, such as an automobile that carried passengers over a set route for a cheap fare or a small bus.

38 Charles Carroll of Carrollton, signer of the Declaration of Independence for Maryland, offered the Homewood Estate as a wedding present to his son. Johns Hopkins University now owns the property and runs it as a historical museum. For Highlandtown, see "Suburban Baltimore: Roland Park," n.8.

39 Bernhardt was a French stage actress in the late nineteenth century who gained widespread international fame in plays such as Jean Racine's *Phèdre* and Hugo's *Hernani*. Hitchcock was a silent film actor and stage producer involved in over thirty Broadway plays from 1898 to 1928.

40 Druid Hill Park first opened in 1860. The Mansion House, once connected to the Park, now serves as the main administration building of the Baltimore Zoo.

41 Patterson Park was established in 1827 and was named after William Patterson, who was a founder of the B&O Railroad. It is well-known for its landmark Patterson Park Pagoda, which is a uniquely-styled observatory that overlooks the park.

42 Established by Henry McShane in 1856 at Holliday and Centre Streets. By the late nineteenth century, it moved to a large factory complex on Guilford Avenue, which was known as North Street at the time. In 1979, the Foundry moved to Glen Burnie, Maryland, where it remains today as the only large Western-style bell maker in the United States. Since 1856, it has produced over 300,000 bells, including the 7,000-pound bell that hangs in the dome of Baltimore's City Hall.

43 The Jamestown Exposition was a world fair and exposition held in Norfolk, VA from April 26 to December 1, 1907. Several prominent congressmen and senators visited the fair, but it ultimately closed as a financial failure, having lost several million dollars.

44 The Washington Monument was constructed in 1815 by Robert Mills, and was America's first civic monument to pay tribute to George Washington. It is still a popular landmark, located in the historic neighborhood of Mount Vernon.

45 Prominent American sculptor and monument maker who served as the president of the Maryland Institute College of Art for several years.

46 During the War of 1812, Francis Scott Key, a resident of Frederick, Maryland, observed the 1914

British bombardment of Fort McHenry. At dawn, Key saw the American flag still flying over the fort, and was inspired to write the poem "Defence of Fort M'Henry," which he published a week later. The poem was later put to the tune of the then-popular song "To Anacreon in Heaven," and eventually became "The Star-Spangled Banner," which was officially made the national anthem by a congressional resolution in 1931.

47 Charles Carroll of Carrollton helped to write Maryland's Constitution of 1776, but he is not known as a writer of the Bill of Rights.

48 Likely referring to what is now known as Washington Boulevard.

49 Signer of the Declaration of Independence, a representative of Maryland, and an Associate Justice of the United States Supreme Court; however, he was impeached from this office after being accused of allowing partisan leanings to influence his court decisions.

50 Maryland Loyalist politician an mayor of Annapolis.

51 Howard served as Maryland governor and was eventually elected to Congress and the Senate.

52 Officially known as the Municipal Museum of the City of Baltimore, the Peale occupied the first building in the western hemisphere to be designed and built specifically as a museum. It was created by Charles Wilson Peale and his son Rembrandt Peale. In 1930-1931, the building was rebuilt and restored, and in the 1980s it went on to merge with other historical museums, houses, and sites, taking on the name of Baltimore City Life Museums. In 1997, the Peale branch, as well as other historical branches and houses, closed after running in to financial difficulties, and the collections were handed over to the Maryland Historical Society. The building is being relaunched as the Peale Center for Baltimore History and Architecture and expects to be fully reopened in 2020.

53 American Navy officer who served in the Continental Navy during the Revolutionary War. He also went on to serve in the War of 1812.

54 Youngest brother of Napoleon who reigned as Jerome I, King of Westphalia, from 1807–1813.

55 Front Street Theater was built in 1829 in the Jonestown area of Baltimore, near the central post office, and was destroyed in the Great Fire of 1904.

56 Swedish opera singer who was one of the most highly regarded performers of the nineteenth century.

57 Historical market in downtown Baltimore that opened its doors in 1782 and still stands in its original location.

58 Joaquin Miller, "Peter Cooper," line 11.

59 Lord Baltimore, otherwise known as Cecil Calvert, English nobleman who was the first Proprietor of the Province of Maryland.

60 Jones Falls is a 17.9 mile-long stream in is impounded to create Lake Roland before running through the city of Baltimore and finally emptying into the Baltimore Inner Harbor. It has a history of involvement with Baltimore transportation, as its valley carries Amtrak tracks and the Baltimore Light Rail. Baltimore's Penn Station also rests on an elevated platform in the valley.

61 Founded as Baltimore City Hospital by the Sisters of Mercy in 1874.

62 Likely referring to Baltimore's Inner Harbor, south of Lexington Street, which is a historic seaport, attraction, and landmark of the city.

63 The Battle Monument, which was built from 1815-1825, commemorates several battles in Maryland's history, such as the Battle of Baltimore with the British fleet of the Royal Navy's bombardment of Fort McHenry and the Battle of North Point. The monument is depicted on the seal of the City of Baltimore that was adopted in 1827

64 Builder, carpenter, and designer who lived in Baltimore where he built various churches, taverns, dwellings, warehouses and bridges.

65 The Emerson Hotel opened in 1911, closed in 1969, and was torn down in 1971. During its time, the 17-story hotel hosted a number of celebrities, including Charles Lindberg and Herbert Hoover, and was the election headquarters of the Maryland Democratic Party

66 The Maryland Academy of Science is one of Maryland's oldest scientific institutions. It was established on S. Charles Street in 1797 as an amateur scientific society—members met to discuss papers on astronomy, botany, zoology, and other subjects. Rembrandt and Raphael Peale, sons of painter and scientist Charles Wilson Peale, were among the distinguished early members. Near the end of World War II, the Academy relocated to the third floor of the Enoch Pratt Library, but it then outgrew the space and moved to a new location where it currently remains in the Inner Harbor. The WLCB affiliated with the Academy in 1891 as associate members, and met in the Academy's meeting room until 1921.

67 Comedian and actor who gained fame across England and America. He died in his Towson, Maryland home in 1886.

68 Nickname of the manor house built on the southern edge of the Garrett family's Evergreen estate for Horatio Garrett, who died before he and his wife Charlotte Garrett could occupy it. The Jesuits from Loyola College purchased the property, along with twenty surrounding acres, in 1921 and relocated the college's campus from the Mount Vernon neighborhood. The building now anchors the academic

quadrangle of Loyola University Maryland, which has used it for academics, as a Jesuit residence, and administrative offices. It was renamed the Knott Humanities Center in the early 1890s.

69 Calvert Street Station served railroad passengers of the Northern Central Railway in Baltimore, Maryland from 1850 until 1948. The property was sold to the *Baltimore Sun* to construct a new headquarters and printing facility. The Baltimore and Susquehanna Railroad Company was chartered by an act of the General Assembly of Maryland in 1828, as the second designated rail system in the state with authority to construct a railroad from Baltimore northeast to the Susquehanna River. The railroad competed with the renowned B&O railroad. The Baltimore & Susquehanna, York & Maryland Line, York & Cumberland, and Susquehanna Railroads eventually merged together.

70 The American Tract Society is a nonprofit, evangelical organization that was founded in 1825 to publish and disseminate Christian literature.

71 Spelled "Postoffice" in the original, reflecting the fact that the central post office was spelled as one word in the city directories during this time.

72 Lawyer, publisher, and editor who served as postmaster of Baltimore from 1816 until 1849. In 1814, as the prisoner-of-war exchange officer, he was selected with Francis Scott Key by President James Madison for a mission to release Dr. William Beanes, who was being held prisoner by the British.

73 The *American Farmer* was a successful early farm paper founded by John Stuart Skinner. It contained news on agriculture, horticulture, and livestock, market prices, and activities of agricultural societies until its end in 1897. The *Temperance Herald* was a monthly publication of the Maryland State Temperance Society.

74 Barnum's City Hotel, situated in the heart of Monument Square, was built in 1825 and was torn down around 1889. During its time, it hosted several well-known guests, including President John Quincy Adams, John Wilkes Booth, and, as Lantz notes, Charles Dickens. The hotel served as a prominent Baltimore landmark, demonstrating through its success that the city was on the rise. Jennie Lind was a highly-regarded Swedish opera singer in the nineteenth century who came to America to work with showman P. T. Barnum, performing ninety-three large-scale concerts for him, before continuing on under her own management. Lind also went on to be a singing professor for several years at the Royal College of Music in London.

75 Meaning that its frontage to the street was 120 feet—an immense building for the time.

76 American soldier and politician who was elected as governor of the Maryland in 1788 and served three one-year terms. He also was elected to Congress and the Senate.

77 English journalist, short-story writer, poet, and novelist, author of the novel *The Jungle Book*, and poems including "The White Man's Burden" and "The Young British Soldier."

78 The Prison Aid Association of Maryland was founded in 1869 and provides temporary shelter and other resources for homeless women and men in the city.

79 Letitia Humphreys Yonge Wrenshall, featured in the Voyagers section of the anthology, was elected President of the Woman's Literary Club of Baltimore in 1898. She was a gifted writer and an exceptional administrator within the Club, and served as a mentor to her peers. In addition to the WLCB, she was a key force in founding several other clubs and associations, serving as Vice President for the Maryland Folk Lore Society, the Audubon Society, and the Quardriga Club.

80 The Baltimore Polytechnic Institute, once known as the Baltimore Manual Training School, was established as an all-male manual trade school high school in 1883. Today, it is a coeducational academic institution that emphasizes sciences, technology, engineering, and mathematics.

Elizabeth Lester Mullin

1 Leonard Calvert was the first propriety governor in the state (or at the time, Province) of Maryland, and the second son of George Calvert, first Baron Baltimore, the first proprietor of Maryland. Baltimore was the name of a manor in County Longford, Ireland. Proprietary governors were granted charters by English monarchs.

2 St. Adauctus was a saint and Christian martyr who lived during the third century AD.

3 Cecelius (or Cecil) was the elder brother of Leonard Calvert and the second Lord Baltimore, following his father, George Calvert.

4 William Claiborne, pioneer, surveyor, and early settler in the Virginia and Maryland colonies.

5 Secretary John Lewger was the secretary of the province of Maryland in the 1630s.

6 Previously known as Kent Fort, this was the first English settlement and fort in colonial Virginia, and later Maryland, established by William Claireborne in 1631.

Annie Leakin Sioussat

1 Sioussat's papers are held in the Leakin-Sioussat Papers (c. 1650–c. 1960) at the Maryland Historical Society; a finding aid is available online at

www.mdhs.org/findingaid/leakin-sioussat-papers-c1650-c1960-ms-1497.

2 A county in Ireland.

3 In the Caribbean Netherlands.

4 Joshua Barney was an American Navy officer who served in the Continental Navy during the Revolutionary War.

5 Jérôme Bonaparte was a French-American military officer who served in the French army, and aided American military forces when he traveled to American soil.

6 "little scamp."

7 Napoleon used the sword of Marengo at the Battle of Marengo in 1800 to take control of northern Italy from Austria.

8 An old man.

9 Also known as the Parsley Massacre, which took place in October 1937, and was ordered by the Dominican dictator, Rafael Trujillo, who targeted Haitians living in the Dominican Republic's northwestern frontier.

10 Leader of the Haitian Independence movement during the French Revolution, as the growing resistance manifested during the Massacre of San Domingo.

11 Translates to: "I count on Providence."

12 French territory located off the coast of Newfoundland.

13 French admiral who rose in the ranks of power in the early stages of the French Revolution.

14 American navy officer who served in the continental navy during the American Revolutionary war.

15 Referring to Napoleon Bonaparte.

16 Sam Smith was a United States senator and representative from Maryland, a mayor of Baltimore, Maryland, and a general in the Maryland militia. Brother Robert was the second United States Secretary of the Navy and the sixth United States Secretary of State.

17 Mary Chase (née Dudly), wife of Samuel Chase, had a son, Jonathan Chase, who fought in the American Revolutionary War. Artist Maria Martin was a contemporary of John James Audubon and sometimes collaborated with him; both were known for their highly detailed water colors of flora and fauna. Marcia Burns was married to Honorable John P. Van Ness, a member of Congress from New York. After their marriage they lived in Washington, where they became prominent figures in the D.C. social scene.

18 Translates to "my beautiful wife."

19 Whetstone Point was named after a London park, and was established as a port of entry by the Maryland Colonial Assembly in 1706.

20 The Comegy family was prominent in Baltimore. Cornelius P. Comegys, likely John's grandfather, settled his family there, but soon moved to Little Creek, Delaware, where he became a member of the Delaware House of Representatives.

21 Samuel Chase was an Associate Justice of the United States Supreme Court and a signatory to the United States Declaration of Independence as a representative of Maryland. He was impeached by the House for letting his partisan leanings affect his court decisions but was acquitted by the Senate. He was married to Mary Chase.

22 Charles Carroll was a wealthy Maryland planter, who became a Maryland State Senator, and a signatory of the Declaration of Independence. He inherited vast agricultural estates and was regarded as the wealthiest man in the American colonies when the American Revolution commenced.

23 *Sioussat's note*: With this letter of John Comegys, who attended Jérôme Bonaparte as "right hand" man, came the following paper: In the presence of J. Carroll, Baltimore, Sottin, vice consul of France, Alex Le Camus (afterward minister of affaires entragères en Westphalia Comte de Furstenstein)Jean Comegys Josíe Barney Commodore. With the certificate of the religious ceremony read with license—I have this day united in the holy bonds of matrimony conformably to the rites of the Holy Catholic Church Jérôme Bonaparte, brother of the first consul of France, with Elizabeth Patterson, daughter of William Patterson Banker of the City of Baltimore, and of Dorcas (Spear), his wife.

24 The Duchess of Abrantès was a French writer, married to the French general Jean-Andoche Junot.

25 An island originally made up to of two islands connected by shoals, currently in the province of North Holland.

26 Napoleon Bonaparte's sister.

27 Mary, Elizabeth, and Louisa were three of John Carroll's four daughters. They were each known for their beauty, wit, and virtue.

28 Referring to Jérôme Bonaparte.

29 Historical German territory.

30 Schmalkalden is a town in the state of Thuringia, Germany.

31 Translates to "A marriage bond."

32 Native Frenchman and naturalized American, philanthropist, and banker credited with saving the US government from financial ruin during the War of 1812.

33 The "Queen Mother" of Napoleon.

34 John Pendleton Kennedy (1795-1870), novelist and politician from Baltimore. Pendleton's novels, *Swallow Barn, or A Sojournal in the Old Dominion* (1832) and *Harse-Shoe Robinson* (1835) are early examples of the novel in the United States.

The Voyagers

Elizabeth Wormley Latimer

1 Apron.

2 Literally a basket; here, hoop skirt.

3 Rolls.

4 Egret, referring to a headdress often made with egret feathers.

5 My daughter-in-law.

6 Approach.

7 The little lout.

8 Fat blonde.

9 Bride.

10 Gentleman.

11 A French dance.

12 Soldier and gentleman.

13 Reference to Benjamin Franklin and his *Poor Richard's Almanac* (1732-1758).

14 The Quaker faith advocates peace, and many members refuse to bear arms or participate in military action.

15 Very funny.

16 Informality.

17 Helpless, unloved, neglected.

18 And why not?

19 "Courtesy" in the original.

20 A coarse, stiff silk fabric.

21 That scoundrel!

22 The *entrée* and the *tabouret* are two kinds of royal privilege. Those with an *entrée* are permitted entrance to the king's rooms at certain times, while the *tabouret* was a special stool placed close to the king or queen.

23 That fat man.

24 French casino card game.

25 Canoness, a member of a women's religious community.

26 Kidnapping.

27 Richard Johnson tells this story in chapter 12, "The Tournament at Constantinople," of *Seven Champions of Christendom*.

28 The story of St. Anthony and St. Paul is normally attributed to St Anthony the Great. St Anthony (January 12, 251–January 17, 356 A.D.) is known as the Father of Monasticism in Christianity.

29 St. Paul of Thebes (227–342 A.D.), is regarded as the first Christian hermit. He is often represented with two lions and a raven.

30 A relic of the cross on which Jesus died. The Middle English word *rood* translates into pole or cross.

31 French for referendum.

32 Charles Forbes Rene de Montalembert (1810–1870), French publicist and historian.

33 Jérôme Napoléon Charles Bonaparte (1814–1847) was the son of Elizabeth Patterson and Jérôme Napoléon Bonaparte; the story of his parents' scandalous marriage is related in the excerpt from Annie Leakin Sioussat's *Old Baltimore*, included in this volume.

34 Published in Blanchard Jerrold, *The Life of Napoleon III* (London, Longmans, Green and Co, 1877), Chapter 7.

35 "The Empress Eugénie Sketched by Napoleon III," *Littell's The Living Age*, November 28, 1874.

36 Walter Savage Landor, "To the Empress" (1863), in *Heroic Idyls, with Additional Poems* (London: T. Cautley Newby), 125.

37 Titian, or Tiziano Vecelli, Venetian Renaissance painter.

38 One of the Goncourt Brothers, Edmond or Jules, who were both French writers.

39 Jerrold, *Life of Napoleon III*.

40 This passage was likely translated by Latimer from the original French.

41 Ah, beautiful Spain,/ With thy skies ever bright,/ Though has formed her for us/ From a ray of sunlight.

42 J. C., *The Empress Eugénie*.

43 The line is from Edmund Waller's poem "Go, Lovely Rose"; Latimer appears to have mistakenly attributed it to Jonson.

44 "To the Empress."

45 Spelled "Noë" in the original.

46 Matthew 24:37-39.

47 Emma Kalanikaumaka☒amano Kaleleonālani Na☒ea Rooke,(1836–1885) was consort of King Kamehameha IV from 1856 to his death in 1863.

48 Lydia Lili'u Loloku Walania Kamaka'eha (1838-1917) was the last Hawaiian soverign monarch of Hawaii, reigning from January 29, 1891 to January 17, 1893.

49 A maharani is a Hindu queen consort, the wife of a Hindu maharaja.

50 Morell Mackenzie (1837–1892) published a work on the controversy in 1888.

51 "One View of the Jubilee, 1887," in *The Monthly Packet of Evening Readings for Members of the English Church*, 14 (London: Walter Smith and Innes): 180–86.

52 May refer to the *Morning Chronicle* newspaper, also referenced in Thomas W. Handford, "The Princess Royal," in *Queen Victoria, Her Glorious Life and Illustrious Reign* (Hammond, IN: Frankli, 1901), 413-26.

53 Christian Friedrich, Baron Stockmar (1787-1863).

54 Effie Bancroft (1839-1921), English actress.

55 Alfred, Lord Tennyson, *Idylls of the King* (1859-1885).

56 Princess Alice, Grand Duchess of Hesse to Queen Victoria, Potsdam, in *Letters to Her Majesty*

the Queen (London: J. Murray, June 13, 1885), 201.

57 Sir Walter Scott (1771-1832), Scottish novelist known for his novels featuring Edward Waverley, including the eponymous *Waverley* (1814).

58 Florence Nightingale (1820-1910), English social reformer and founder of modern nursing.

59 Otto von Bismarck (1815-1898), chancellor of the German Empire.

60 Probably either George Villiers (1800-1870), fourth Earl of Clarendon, or his son, Edward.

61 The Seven Weeks' War of 1866 or the Austro-Prussian War ended in the exclusion of Austria from Germany.

62 Arthur Penrhyn Stanley (1815–1881) was Dean of Westminster from 1864 until his death.

63 $4,500 in 1894, the year in which this work was written, is worth about $130,000 today.

64 *Letters to Her Majesty the Queen*, letter dated March 19, 1869.

65 *Letters to Her Majesty the Queen*, letter dated July 24, 1862.

66 *Letters to Her Majesty the Queen*, letter dated May 3, 1866.

67 *Letters to Her Majesty the Queen*, from Princess Alice's letter dated October 31, 1874. She is quoting and translating a poem by Friedrich **Rückert** entitled "Nun hat euch Gott verliehen."

68 John Lothrop Motley to Oliver Wendell Holmes. "Wedding at Westminster Abbey," *The Correspondence of John Lothrop Motley* (New York and London: Harper and Brothers, January 30, 1900).

69 John Ruskin (1819–1900), English art critic.

70 Latimer may have sourced this quote from Myers W. H. Frederic, "Personal Recollections of the Duke of Albany," *Littell's The Living Age*, May 31, 1884.

71 Latimer may have sourced this quote from M. E. W. Sherwood, "Royal Girls and Royal Courts: Royal Girls of England," *Wide Awake*, August 1886.

72 Genesis 32:26.

73 Torquato Tasso, *Jerusalem Delivered*.

74 Psalms 146:3.

Elizabeth Lester Mullin

1 Johann Sebastian Bach (1685-1750), according to lore, hid his manuscript scores, many of which were not rediscovered for nearly a hundred years, when Félix Mendelssohn brought them to the attention of the music world. In actuality, it is likely that Bach did not hide his manuscripts but rather that his music simply became unfashionable and was forgotten.

2 One of the chief devils and the tempter of Faust, the protagonist of the German legend based on alchemist Johann Georg Faust.

3 In Greek myth, the underworld.

4 In German, this word actually spelled out as "Johannisberg." This word comes from the Schloss Johannisberg, which is a castle and winery in the village of Johannisberg in state of Hesse in the wine-growing region of Germany. This castle has been producing wine for the past nine hundred years.

5 Term used in opera for the passages of sung dialogue, indicating that the thunder is like a musical declamation.

6 The vox humana are stops on a pipe organ, so named because of their supposed resemblance to the human voice.

7 The Greek phrase for "Lord, have mercy," which is used in Greek Orthodox and Roman Catholic churches. The following line, "Christie eleison," is the Greek phrase for "Christ, have mercy."

8 A figure of a lamb bearing a cross or flag, as an emblem of Christ.

9 Frills or pleats; here, Mullin appears to indicate some kind of ornamentation.

10 An expression of salutation and approval.

11 A type of angelic being, regarded in traditional Christian angelology as belonging to the highest order of the celestial hierarchy, associated with light, ardor, and purity.

12 Song of Simeon (Luke 2:29–32), used as a canticle in Christian liturgy, especially at compline and evensong.

13 An estate located fifteen miles north of Paris.

14 Spelled "dowery" in the original.

15 A French administrative official in immediate charge of an arrondissement.

16 Fruit trees or ornamental shrubs whose branches are trained to grow flat against a wall, supported on a lattice or a framework of stakes.

17 "And the farce is finished!"

18 Don Quixote: The hero of Miguel Cervantes's novel *Don Quixote de la Mancha*, inspired by lofty and chivalrous but impractical ideals.

19 "Face to face," as in a face-to-face conversation.

Adaline Vanderpool

1 *Genealogies of the State of New York: A Record of the Achievements of Her People in the Making of a Commonwealth and the Founding of a Nation, Volume 1.* Lewis Historical Publishing Company, 1915, pp. 172.

2 Saratoga. "Adaline Elizabeth Van Schaack Vanderpoel." *FindAGrave.com*.

3 Sir George Somers of Britain, an admiral of the

Virginia Company, was the first man to explore and map Bermuda.

4 George Washington.

5 Lines from Thomas Moore (1779-1852), "When I Loved You."

6 The British territory Fort Gibraltar is located in present-day Manitoba, Canada.

7 The first permanent European settlement by the British in the Canadian province of Nova Scotia located on the Halifax Peninsula.

8 Their Majesties Chappell, St. Peter's Church, is the oldest surviving Anglican church in continuous use outside the British Isles to this day.

9 A Latin Christian hymn and a core hymn in the Ambrosian hymnal, composed in the fourth century.

10 Luke 21:19.

11 Prisoners of war from the Anglo-Boer War in South Africa were placed in camps on the Bermuda Islands.

12 The word "velt" or "veld" means field or open country, stemming from the Dutch word for field.

13 Quoted from the 1884 book *Bermuda: An Idyl of the Summer Islands* by Julia Caroline Ripley Dorr.

Florence McIntyre Tyson

1 A note in the original publication in *Short Stories* indicates that the story was translated for the magazine.

2 Italian for "Director."

3 Mountain range in Italy.

4 Italian expression meaning "Oh my God!"

5 Mountain range in central-southern Sardinia, Italy.

6 Italian for "Judiciary."

7 Italian expression meaning "my goodness!" or "My God!"

8 Italian for "young lady."

Letitia Humprheys Yonge Wrenshall

1 Wrenshall's "Incantations and Popular Healing in Maryland and Pennsylvania," for example, was published in the *Journal of American Folklore* 15, no. 59 (1902): 268-74. doi:10.2307/533200.

2 British territory on the South Coast of Spain.

3 During this time, all sorts of pasta were commonly referred to as "macaroni."

4 A form of bingo that originated in Italy.

5 "Late" in the original.

6 English term used to refer to the seaman of the Royal Navy.

7 An island in the Azores.

8 Protective beach.

9 The largest city and capital of the Azores of Portugal.

10 The actual number is unclear, as text is missing from the original.

11 Slang term for British soldiers.

12 Forms of headwear.

13 Explorer and seaman of the United States Navy, who died on board his sinking ship, and for whom many American cities and towns are named. A monument dedicated to Herndon is installed on the grounds of the US Naval Academy.

14 Botanical gardens that opened in Gibraltar in 1816.

15 The Hebrew bible notes that "once every three years the fleet of ships of Tarshish used to come bringing gold, silver, ivory, apes, and peacocks." Tarshish was likely a large region across the Dead Sea from Israel (1 Kings 10:22).

16 Peñon de Ifach, often referred to as Calpe rock or the mini Gibraltar, is an enormous geographical landmark off the coast of Calpe, Spain.

17 Published in two installments in the *Baltimore Sun,* June 28 and July 5, 1908.

18 Located in southern Italy, the Peninsula of Sorrento separates the Gulf of Naples to the north from the Gulf of Salerno.

19 The Palazzo Doria d'Angri is a historic building and monument in Naples in southern Italy commissioned by Prince Marcantonio Doria.

20 Co-founder and first Grand Master of the Knights Templar.

21 Volcano known for its eruption in 79 AD, which destroyed the Roman cities of Pompeii, Herculaneum, Oplontis and Stabiae.

22 The second installment begins here.

23 Opera by Daniel Auber set in southern Italy.

24 Name given by the Romans to the coastal areas of southern Italy.

25 In Greek and Roman mythology, the cyclops were a race of giants with a single eye in the middle of their foreheads.

26 The main beam running across the tops of the columns.

27 A four-wheeled, horse-drawn carriage with enclosed sides.

28 Soldos are a former coin currency of Italy.

29 The Order of Friars Minor Capuchin was an order within the Catholic Church.

30 At the time, the word "macaroni" was used for all kinds of pasta.

31 Interrogation mark is another name for question mark.

32 An apple-green gemstone.

33 Female peasant.

Katharine H. Wrenshall

1 William Morton Payne, "Recent Fiction," *Dial*

51.606 (Sept. 16, 1911): 201.

2 Located on the Grand Canal in Venice, Italy, the Palazzo Cornaro was the birthplace of Caterina Cornaro in 1454.

3 Party (French).

4 A collection of tales also known as *The Thousand and One Nights,* first written in the 1400s.

5 Lordship, a governing authority of the time.

6 Elders.

7 An ancient statue of a winged-lion holding a bible, located in the Piazza San Marco in Venice, Italy, as a symbol of the city.

8 Lady Fiorenza, or Fiorenza Crispo, was the mother of Caterina Cornaro.

9 Marco Cornaro was the fifty-ninth Doge or Duke of Venice (1365–1368), the chief magistrate and leader of the Republic of Venice.

10 Ladies' maids.

11 The "Golden Book" of Italian nobility, which was not actually established until 1896.

12 Blessed Mother.

13 Party.

14 God.

15 A lacy neck covering.

16 Sky.

17 Here.

18 Peace.

19 Thank you very much; literally, "a thousand thanks."

20 Boat.

21 Charity or love.

22 Wedding.

23 "Caterina!—Queen!—Daughter of Venice—Our Venice!"

24 "Wonderful!" . . . "So wonderful!"

25 "My blessed lady."

26 "It is not Minerva who was born in Cyprus!" in French.

27 chief.

28 Church in the San Polo district of Venice, Italy.

29 The Biblioteca Marciana was not actually built until the sixteenth century. Today it is known as one of the largest repositories of classical texts, and faces the Doge's palace in St. Mark's Square in Venice.

30 Salamis was the site of Paul's first missionary efforts.

31 Reference to one of the Latin titles of the Madonna, meaning "Sorrowful Mother."

32 Superintendents.

33 Latin hymn of the fourth century.

34 A phrase originating in Latin, meaning informally, "Hurrah, O Triumph!"

35 The state barge of the doges of Venice.

36 Bell towers.

Francese Litchfield Turnbull

1 Alice Emma Sauerwein Lord, *A Symphony in Dreamland* (New York: G. P. Putnam's Sons, 1882), 1.

2 A symphony is usually played by an orchestra (with strings, wind instruments, and brass) and customarily has between three and five movements that correspond to different and varied tempos. A movement designated Adagio tends to be slow and lyrical; an Allegro is lively and faster.

3 Allegretto is a moderately quick tempo noted within a music composition. Larga means grand in Italian, suggesting that the music should be played boldly and richly, but with energy.

4 German word for homesickness

5 French word meaning sadness.

6 In the Book of Exodus, the well of bitter water. Upon appealing to God, Moses is shown a piece of wood, which he throws into the water which then becomes fit to drink.

7 Titles of two popular hymns.

8 Plural of the French word chateau meaning manor, or a grand home.

9 Larghetto is a fairly slow tempo noted in a musical composition.

10 Russian composer Anton Rubinstein's Symphony No. 2 in C major, Op. 42 (1851) was known as the "Ocean" symphony.

11 Job 38:11.

12 Psalms 98:8-9.

13 George W. De Long was a Navy officer and explorer who led an expedition in 1878 to find the Open Polar Sea, an ice form that surrounds the North Pole. He and all twenty of his men starved to death in Siberia in 1881.

14 Louis Napoleon or Napoleon III (1808-1873) was the nephew of Napoleon Bonaparte.

15 An archaic French term for a sailboat.

16 Latin for "from the depths," often used to refer to Psalms 130.

17 The seven phrases spoken by Jesus while hung on the cross.

18 Scherzo means "joke" in German and denotes a lively, playful movement. Allegro-Vivace is a tempo notation meaning to play very fast.

19 Dabbler.

20 Craze.

21 Latin for "the voice of the people is the voice of God."

22 Allegretto is a tempo notation to play at a brisk pace in a music composition.

23 The title appears as "Oratorio of 'The Messiah'" in the table of contents of *A Symphony in Dreamland,* but it appears with the title "Oratorio of 'The Messiah' Sonnet" in the book itself.

24 German phase meaning "spring song."

25 "Sea foam" in German.

26 French for pink-colored. May symbolize gentleness and innocence.

The Singers

Alice Emma Sauerwein Lord

1 "Mrs. Marguerite E. Easter," *Baltimore Sun,* July 5, 1877: 2.

2 "Improved Business," *Baltimore Sun*, Oct. 30, 1894: 4.

3 Yopie Prins, *Victorian Sappho* (Princeton: Princeton University Press, 1999), 226.

4 In Greek mythology, Selene is said to be the goddess of the moon.

5 Nymph, follower of Artemis and pursued by Pan.

6 Latmos refers to a mountain range in what is now modern day Turkey.

7 Philomela was a figure in Greek mythology who represents the arts. She is said to have been the "princess of Athens" and is often associated with the song of the nightingale.

8 In Greek mythology, Hebrus was a river-god of Ciconia in Greece.

9 Faience and delf are types of pottery or ceramics.

10 An ell is a unit of length equal to forty-five inches; lawn is a fine, thin woven cotton fabric.

11 "Ailes de pigeon" (French for "pigeon wings") refers to a type of sleeve that puffs out around the biceps but hugs the forearms. It is also a step in ballet.

12 A song in which a phrase or line is repeated continuously.

13 Here and in the next few lines Easter evokes images and places located in the Spanish colonies of California and central America. Caliente is the highest peak in the Caliente mountain range in Southern California; Contago is a city in Costa Rica; a cordillera (derived from "cordilla," which means rope in Spanish)is long chain of mountains.

14 Adonis was the human lover of the goddess Aphrodite, who was associated with love, beauty, pleasure, passion, and recreation, in Greek mythology.

15 A madrigal is a short medieval lyrical poem that maintains a particular form.

16 Thrace is a region of southeastern Europe in the Balkan peninsula north of the Aegean Sea, home of the ancient Thracian tribes and named after the mythological sorceress Thrace, daughter of Oceanus and Parthenope and sister of Europa.

17 Nighthawk.

18 Arcadia, located on the Pelopnnesian peninsula, takes its name from the mythological figure Arcas and home of the Greek god Pan. As such, the region connotes wilderness and rusticity.

19 Bressay is an Island to the East of Scotland, known for having a large number or migrant birds.

20 In Scotland, skylarks are referred to as laverocks.

Marguerite E. Easter

1 WLCB Meeting minutes, March 6, 1894.

Clara Badger Newman Turner

1 "Heritage" appeared in the *Philadelphia Inquirer* on Sept. 25, 1913 and was published in the *Oshkosh Northwestern* on Oct. 13, 1913.

2 "Knitting" was published in the *New York Times* on Nov. 11, 1917.

3 Reference to the chalk downlands in areas of southern England.

4 A range of chalk hills that extend across the eastern coastal counties of England.

5 French for "bell."

6 French for "morning."

7 A Catholic prayer performed at noon that recalls Mary's yes to God through the angel.

8 Part of the rosary in Catholicism, meaning "hail Mary."

9 "Kike" is a derogatory ethnic slur for a Jewish person. "Wop" is a derogatory ethnic slur for Italians or people of Italian descent.

10 "Noblesse oblige" is in quotation marks in the original.

11 A crown of thorns was placed on Jesus' head prior to his crucifixion.

12 Said by Jesus while on the cross, Aramaic for "My God, my God, why hast thou forsaken me?" (Matthew 27:46).

13 The Rotunda is located on the north side of The Lawn and Old Cabell Hall on the south side of The Lawn on the original grounds of the University of Virginia.

Lucy Randolph Cautley

1 Frances E. Baldwin, "New Honors For Woman Writer," *The Sun* (Baltimore, MD), Oct. 14, 1928.

2 These essays are referenced in biographies of Trail but have yet to be recovered.

3 Paul Lauter, "Race and Gender in the Shaping of the American Literary Canon: A Case Study from the Twenties." *Feminist Studies* 9, no. 3 (1983): 435-63. doi:10.2307/3177608.

4 Susan Glenn. *Female Spectacle: The Theatrical Roots of Modern Feminism.* Cambridge: Harvard UP, 2000.

5 Trail consistently capitalized fields of study such as "History" and "Literature," and "Music." These

terms have been silently emended to follow contemporary usage.

6 A reference to Ephesians 4:13: "Till we all come in the unity of the faith, and of the knowledge of the Son of God, unto a perfect man, unto the measure of the stature of the fullness of Christ."

7 George Eliot, pseudonym of Mary Ann Evans (1819-1880), English poet and novelist. This quote is from her novel *Daniel Deronda* (1876).

8 A quote from French philosopher, Victor Cousin (1792-1867).

9 James Anthony Froude (1818-1894) was an English historian who published *History of England* from 1850 until 1870.

10 Quoted within Henry Thomas Buckle's (1821-1862) book *History of Civilization* (1857).

11 Trail's translation:

> Happy is he who, as his life draws to its close,
> A lover of the fine arts, can cultivate their
fruits!

> He braves injustice, he soothes his weariness,
> He pardons human beings, he laughs at
their delirium,

> And with his dying hand he touches once
more his lyre.

12 William Wordsworth, "Ode to Duty" (1807).

13 "En passant" is a move in chess in which a piece makes a double-step from the starting square and avoids capture from the other side.

14 "Psyche Returning from the Inferno" is a reference to Dante's *Inferno*.

15 "*Zarten*" is the German word for tender and "*weichen Jungfrau*" is translated to gentle maiden.

16 Alfred R. (A. R.) Gaul (1837-1913), English composer of "Great and Marvelous."

17 Italian for whisper.

18 Robert Browning (1812–1889), poet and playwright, "Colombe's Birthday."

19 German for "for a good night."

20 Signor Cetti (1726-1778), Italian Jesuit priest.

21 Elizabeth Barrett Browning (1806-1861), English Victorian poet married to Robert Browning, "A Vision of Poets," lines 25-36.

22 German for storm and struggle.

23 French for know-how.

24 Ancient Indian play by Kalidasa.

25 French for purpose; literally, "reason for being."

26 Major city in northeastern Italy and capital city of the western Roman empire until its collapse in 476 AD.

27 German late-Renaissance composer and one of the most influential musicians of sixteenth century Europe.

28 University professors in medieval Europe; practitioners of scholasticism.

29 Albertus Magnus (1200-1280), German friar and bishop later canonized as a saint; Duns (John) Scotus (1266-1308), Scottish and Catholic philosopher; William of Occam (1285-1347), English friar and philosopher.

30 The first chapter of the Gospel of Matthew begins with a genealogy which leads down to Jesus Christ, which was often set to music.

31 The "L'Homme Armé" was a popular French song of secular origin that was appropriated during the Renaissance for the musical setting of the Ordinary of the Mass. The Agnus Dei (Lamb of God) is part of the liturgy.

32 Giovanni Pierluigi da Palestrina (1525-1594), Italian Renaissance composer of religious music.

33 The Thirty Years' War (1618-1648) was one of the most destructive conflicts in human history. Thuringia was an eastern region of Germany, consisting of medieval villages, including the one where Martin Luther was ordained.

34 Nicola Porpora (1686-1768), Italian composer who taught Joseph Haydn (1732-1809).

35 George Frideric Handel (1685-1759), German composer who lived for a time in London. Giuseppe Domenico Scarlatti (1685-1757) was an Italian composer.

36 Christoph Willibald Gluck (1714-1787), Italian and French opera composer. Pietro Metastasio (1698-1782), Italian poet and librettist.

37 Robert G. Ingersoll (1833-1899), American writer and orator, nicknamed "The Great Agnostic." Anton Seidl (1850-1898), Hungarian conductor.

38 Opera composed in 1859 by French composer Charles Gounod (1818-1893).

39 Wilhelm Richard Wagner (1813-1883), German composer.

40 *Die Meistersinger von Nürnberg* (*The Mastersinger of Nuremberg*), three-act opera composed by Wagner in 1867.

41 *Lohengrin* (1850) and *Tannhauser* (1845) were both three-act operas written by Wagner.

42 Twelfth-century romance.

43 Gabrielle D'Anunzio (1863-1938) was Prince of Montevoso, a general and soldier in World War I, and a prominent Italian poet.

44 *Der Ring des Niebelungen*, also known as the Ring Cycle, written by Wagner in 1874. The cycle has four parts: *Das Rheingold, Die Walkürie, Siegfried*, and *Die Götterdammerung*.

45 *Parsifal* (1882) three-act opera by Wagner.

46 Translation of Horace's passage: "When men in their greed discern their passions as the sole measure of right and wrong."

47 *Belisario* is a three-act opera written by Gaetano Donizetti. *I Lombardi* (1843), *I Due Foscari*

(1844), *La Battaglia di Legnano* (1849), and
Il Trovatore (1853) are all by Giuseppe Verdi.
Masaniello, also known by the title *La Muette de
Portici* (1828) is a five-act opera by Daniel Auber.

48 Quoted from "Diana of the Crossways" by
George Meredith (1885).

49 From *An Account of a Conversation Concerning
a Right Regulation of Governments* by Andrew
Fletcher of Saltoun (1653-1716), a Scottish writer,
politician, and patriot.

Ella Morrow Sollenberger

1　The identity of "Ayesha" is unknown, but she (or
he) was presumably another columnist or correspondent to the *Baltimore American*.

2　Bayard Taylor (1825-1878) was a popular travel
writer and literary figure.

3　The Greek god of marriage.

4　Founded in 1880 in Baltimore to provide women
the opportunity to make money by selling hand-
made items.

5　A Baltimore-based organization dating from at least
the 1870s whose goal was to "elevate the scale of art
appreciation and knowledge among the people" and
"arouse an interest where there is now apathy" ("The
Decorative Art Society," *Baltimore Sun*, May 31, 1879).

6

7　Percy Bysshe Shelley, translation from the Greek
of Homer's "Hymn to Mercury."

8　Mary Martha Sherwood (1775-1851), British
writer of children's literature.

9　Nickname for New York City in the 19th century.

10 This quotation and the several that follow come
from the essay "Manners" by Ralph Waldo Emerson (1803-1882).

11 Alfred, Lord Tennyson (1809-1892), "The Lo-
tos-Eaters" (1832). The Lotos Eaters were a race of
people in Greek mythology who lived on an island
abundant with lotus flowers. Lotus flowers served
as their main food source and acted as narcotics,
causing the inhabitants to be in a constant state of
sleep and peaceful apathy.

12 In Shakespeare's *The Merchant of Venice*, Portia
disguises herself as a lawyer's apprentice to save the
life of Antonio in court.

13 George Alsop, "The Lofty Virtues of the Marylanders" (1666), reprinted in *A Library of American Literature: An Anthology in Eleven Volumes*,
ed. Edmund Clarence Stedman and Ellen Mackay
Hutchinson (New York: Charles L. Webster and
Co., 1891), Vols. I, 404.

Crusaders & Critics

Florence Trail

1　*The Mark of the Beast* was published anonymously, although the editors of *Lippincott's* pointed to
the identity of the author by including a note at
the bottom of the first page of the story reading:
"Author of Metzerott, Shoemaker."

2　Response of Cain, son of Adam, to God's question about the whereabouts of his brother abel in
Genesis 4:9.

3　Revelation 3:17. The "mark of the beast" identi-
fies an individual worshippers of the antichrist.

4　Lord God of the hosts of heaven.

5　"Engel" is "angel" in German. The name may
also be an allusion to Friedrich Engels (1820-
1895), nineteenth-century German philosopher
and co-author, with Karl Marx, of the *Communist
Manifesto* (1848).

6　The Little Pilgrim is a character traveling to the
Celestial City in John Bunyan's religious allegory,
The Pilgrim's Progress, published in the late seven-
teenth century.

7　Psalms 33:6.

8　Acts 5 tells the tale of Ananias and his wife Sap-
phira, who die after lying to the Holy Spirit about
money.

9　Solomon, biblical Israelite king who built the first
Temple of Jerusalem.

10 German for "country squire," member of the
landowning aristocracy of Prussia and eastern
Germany.

11 German grandmother or mother.

12 Where the kings of the earth under demonic
leadership will wage war on the forces of God at
the end of history.

13 Elizabeth Barrett Browning (1806-1861), "A
Lady's Yes."

14 German phrase translating to "My God!"

15 The Decalogue is the Ten Commandments.

16 The legendary prince Cophetua falls in love at
first sight with the beggar Penelophon. The story
was popularized by Edward Burne-Jones's painting
King Cophetua and the Beggar Maid (1884).

17 St. Peter's Basilica in Rome has a height of 448
feet.

18 Abbreviation for Victoria Regina, a colloquial reference to Queen Victoria of England. The Queen
signed her letters "Victoria R."

19 In Matthew 19:24, Jesus says to his disciples:
"It is easier for a camel to go through the eye of
a needle, than for a rich man to enter into the
kingdom of God."

20 Paraphrase of 2 Corinthians 5:17, "if any man

be in Christ, he is a new creature: old things are passed away; behold, all things are become new."

21 French term translating to "hotheaded."

22 In William Shakespeare's play *Hamlet*, Act 1, Scene 2, Hamlet describes his mother's overly hasty second marriage as an occasion where "The funeral baked meats did coldly furnish forth the marriage tables."

23 John 3:15, "Everyone who hates his brother is a murderer, and you know that no murderer has eternal life abiding in him."

24 Russian author and philosopher Leo Tolstoy (1828-1910) was a proponent of non-violence.

25 The word of God, as stated in Ephesians 6:17.

26 After rejecting God's request to preach to the Nivenites, Jonah is thrown off a boat and swallowed by a whale, wherein he sits for three days in prayer and repentance before being expelled on the shores of Niveneh.

27 The mourner's bench is a concept in Methodist and Evangelical churches that involves a special bench, sometimes called a "mercy seat," reserved for either mourners or penitent sinners seeking salvation.

28 Hopkins paraphrases a line from Shakespeare's *A Midsummer Night's Dream*, Act 2, Scene 1, in which Oberon greets Titania, "Ill met by moonlight, proud Titania."

29 A heavy mist, nearly a drizzle.

30 *Macbeth,* Act 2, Scene 1, when a floating dagger, representing his guilt, appears before Macbeth.

31 "Oh! Never, nevermore!"

32 "In full seriousness," in French.

33 French word translating to "regulars" or frequenters.

34 Christian symbol of sacrifice, innocence, and Christ himself.

35 Genesis 4:12. The "brand of Cain," more commonly referred to as the "mark of Cain," indicated that anyone who harmed Cain would receive that damage sevenfold. It was also a warning not to do as Cain did in murdering his brother.

36 To ostracize someone.

37 In Revelation 19:11, Jesus's appearance is described as follows: "And I saw heaven opened, and behold a white horse; and he that sat upon him was called Faithful and True, and in righteousness he doth judge and make war."

38 Song of Solomon 2:4: "He brought me to the banqueting house, and his banner over me was love."

39 John Ruskin (1819-1900), Victorian art critic and artist.

40 Galatians 3: "There is neither Jew nor Greek, there is neither bond nor free, there is neither male nor female: for ye are all one in Christ Jesus."

41 The International Typographical Union was founded in 1852 in New York City; it was one of the first unions to admit women, first doing so as early as 1869.

42 The poem "The Song of the Shirt" (1843) by the English poet Thomas Hood (1799-1845) was a tribute to a widow and seamstress named Mrs. Biddell who lived and died in awful conditions.

43 The House of the Good Shepherd was a nineteenth-century asylum for women in New York City. It was managed by the Congregation of Our Lady of Charity of the Good Shepherd and was composed of a convent, an industrial school, and a reformatory for women and girls, including many accused of prostitution. The Westchester Protectory likely refers to the Catholic Protectory that in Westchester, New York, an asylum for Catholic children.

44 Leonora M. Barry (1849–1923) was an Irish woman who immigrated to the United States who worked for the Knights of Labor and advocated for working women in the nineteenth century.

45 Wanamaker's was one of the first American department stores, opening in 1876. The first location was in Philadelphia, and eventually there were over twenty locations in the United States.

46 The Working Women's Protective Union was founded in 1863 in New York City as an organization that aimed to improve the conditions of women workers in the nineteenth century.

Hester Crawford Dorsey Richardson

1 Ladd-Franklin is writing from New York City. She earned an A.B. at Vassar College in Poughkeepsie, New York, lectured at Columbia University in New York City, and died in New York, New York on March 5, 1930.

2 The Philadelphia Stenographers' Association was an association of stenographers, women and men, established in April, 1889. Members paid initiation and regular dues for the assets provided to them, including furnished workspaces and weekly meetings discussing segregation of duties and events of interest (Francis H. Hemperley, *Philadelphia Stenographer* 1, ser. 1-9 [May 1890], Harvard University Graduate School of Business Administration, Baker Library).

3 The banquet took place at Sydnor's Restaurant on 12th St. in Philadelphia on April 30, 1890, in celebration of the association's first anniversary (Hemperley, *Philadelphia Stenographer*).

4 Stanton Coit (1857-1944) founded the Neighborhood Guild settlement house in the Lower East Side of Manhattan.

5 Presumably a reference to the United Garment Workers of America, a labor union established in

April 1891, in New York.

6 The 1890 New York Convention fostered the establishment of the General Federation of Women's Clubs.

7 Normal Schools, first established in 1839 and aimed primarily at women, provided a general standard of training for aspiring teachers, with a curriculum above the grammar-school education traditionally offered at the time.

8 Thorstein Veblen (1857-1929), a Norwegian-American economist and sociologist who coined the term "conspicuous consumption," paraphrased by Ladd-Franklin as "ostentatious expenditure."

9 Ladd-Franklin's name was printed without the hyphen.

Katharine Pearson Woods

1 Claire Lobdell, "Margaret Sutton Briscoe Hopkins: A Woman of Enterprise and Gusto," The Consecrated Eminence: The Archives & Special Collections at Amherst College, 21 March 2014, https://consecratedeminence.wordpress.com/2014/03/21/margaret-sutton-briscoe-hopkins-a-woman-of-enterprise-and-gusto/

2 Thomas Carlyle (1795-1881), *Past and Present* (1843).

3 Robert Louis Stevenson (1850-1894), "Beggars" (1888).

4 The original uses the term "per cent." throughout the document; all instances have been edited to read "percentage."

Chrsitine Ladd-Franklin

1 "Our School System," *Baltimore Sun*, Dec. 22, 1892: 8.

2 "Five Letters of Reference," Library of Congress, accessed May 7, 2018, https://www.loc.gov/resource/rbpe.17704400/

Margaret Sutton Briscoe

1 Agnes Hooper Gottlieb, "Malloy of the *American*: Baltimore's Pioneer Woman Journalist," *Maryland Historical Magazine* 91.1 (1996): 29.

2 Reed Smoot (1862-1941) was an Apostle of the Mormon Church who served in the United States Senate for thirty years.

3 The Woman's Christian Temperance Movement, founded in 1879, was a highly influential women's group that sought to end alcohol consumption. They also campaigned for labor laws, prison reform, and suffrage.

4 Arthur Gordon Pym is a fictional character from Edgar Allan Poe's *The Narrative of Arthur Gordon Pym of Nantucket*. In the original, the line reads

"Arthur P. G.," which is clearly in error given the reference as well as the rhyme scheme.

5 This phrase comes from typesetting, where lower-case Ps and Qs occupied adjacent receptacles in the typecase and were often confused, as they are mirror-images of one another.

6 The Milesian school of philosophy was founded in Miletus in the sixth century BC.

7 Robert Browning (1812-1889), English poet who achieved great popularity in the United States during the mid- to late-nineteenth century.

8 The peace movement

9 A "fuddist" would be a fuddy-duddy, a person who has old-fashioned ideas or habits.

10 David Garrick (1717-1779), English actor and theatrical manager of the Drury Lane Theatre.

11 Samuel Foote (1720-1777), Cornish actor and poet, a friendly rival to David Garrick and also known for creating satirical sketches of living people through his plays.

12 Peg Woffington (1720-1760), Irish actress who made her debut in *The Beggar's Opera*. She starred alongside many leading actors, including David Garrick. Frank Hopkins, *Rare Old Dublin: Heroes, Hawkers and* Hoors (Harmondsworth Middlesex, UK: CPD Group), 160.

13 I.e., jealousy; Shakespeare, *Othello*, Act 3, Scene 3.

14 Nell is a diminutive of the name Eleanor.

15 Lines from the poem "The Grand Panjandrum." It is said that Foote made these lines up to test the skill of actor Charles Macklin.

16 The Lane was also known as the Theatre Royal in the developing West End in London. David Garrick was the manager of the theater towards the end of his career.

17 William Shakespeare, *Hamlet*, Act 3.

18 The typescript reads "lose."

Mary Noyes Colvin

1 William Wordsworth, "She Was a Phantom of Delight," lines 25-30.

2 The novels *Lady Kitty Bristol* and *The Marriage of William Ashe* are by British novelist Mary Augusta Ward, who wrote under her married name, Mrs. Humphrey Ward. Ward worked to improve education for the poor and became the founding president of the Women's National Anti-Suffrage League.

3 Frances Borkman, "The Visiting Nurse as a Social Force," *Review of Reviews* (1906).

4 *Johns Hopkins Nurses Alumnae Magazine*, 5.1 (1906): 126.

5 Isabel Adams Hampton Robb was an American nursing theorist, author, and nursing school administrator. She wrote several influential

textbooks and helped to found the organizations that became known as the National League for Nursing, the International Council of Nurses, and the American Nurses' Association. Hampton also advanced the social status of nursing through her work in developing a curriculum of more advanced training during her time at the Johns Hopkins School of Nursing.

6   Bellevue Hospital, founded in 1736, is the oldest public hospital in the United States. Early on in its history, it gained notoriety for its psychiatric facilities, where many women were sent if it was believed they were experiencing psychological ailments.

7   Mary Adelaide Nutting was an American nurse, educator, and pioneer in the field of hospital care. She founded a modern nursing program at Johns Hopkins University, from which she graduated in 1891.

8   The University of Maryland Hospital Infirmary was founded in 1823. It is now known as The University of Maryland Medical Center.

9   The Spanish-American War (April 21-August 13 1898) was fought to control colonial territories including Cuba, Guam, and the Philippines.

10 The Hospital for Crippled Children is now known as Shriners' Hospitals for Children, which is a network of twenty-two non-profit medical facilities across North America.

11 Possibly an allusion to William Bradford's description of the Plymouth Colony as a "city upon a hill."

12 Mary J. Putts graduated from the nurses' training school in connection with the Maryland Homeopathic Hospital in 1897. She was the superintendent of nurses at the hospital for three years until she accepted a similar position at Memorial Hospital in VA.

13 The City Hospital was founded in 1874 by the Sisters of Mercy and now operates as Mercy Medical Center.

14 The Institut Pasteur was founded in 1887 by Louis Pasteur, French chemist and microbiologist.

15 The Union Protestant Infirmary School for Nurses trained professionals from 1933-1955. Eventually, the hospital merged with St. Mary's Hospital, and together they became Union Hospital Center.

16 The Baltimore City Health Department was founded in 1793 and is considered the oldest continuously operating health department in the United States. It was established in response to the first recorded yellow fever outbreak in Baltimore at Fell's Point.

17 A physician, educator, and spokesperson for preventive medicine, public health, women's health, childcare. She played a vital role in many women's organizations and clubs, including the Women's Literary Club of Baltimore, and contributed to many medical social movements throughout the state.

18 An American biologist regarded as one of the founders of biogerontology, the sub-field of gerontology concerned with the biological aging process, its evolutionary origins, and potential means to intervene in the process. Pearl was also a prolific writer of academic books, papers and articles, having published over 841 publications throughout his life.

19 The public bath movement began in the 1890s in Baltimore in the area of Canton and continued through the mid-twentieth century, allowing for greater hygiene opportunities for the city's residents.

20 The Mount Wilson State Hospital and Sanitarium was established in 1925 and closed in 1981. Thousands of tuberculosis patients were treated there during the 1950s, '60s, and '70s.

21 The Woman's Medical College of Baltimore opened in 1882. It provided an ambitious curriculum and many well-known physicians as lecturers and teachers but closed in 1909.

22 The Crittenton Home was originally the home of David Carroll, owner of the Mount Vernon Mill Company. In 1925, the Florence Crittenton Mission took over its location and took on a new name. The Mission was started in 1882 by wealthy New Yorker and Protestant evangelist Charles Crittenton, who made his fortune in pharmaceuticals. After losing his four-year-old daughter Florence to scarlet fever, Crittenton dedicated himself to philanthropy, using his wealth to open sanctuaries for unwed mothers. The mission was the first charitable organization to receive a national charter from the United States. At its peak, the Mission had over seventy-five homes internationally.

23 The Maryland Industrial Training School for Girls, alternatively called the Female House of Refuge, was founded in 1866 as a reform school for girls and was later renamed Montrose School for Girls.

24 Long-running American newspaper comic strip created in 1907 by cartoonist Bud Fisher. Cicero was the son of the ne'er-do-well Mutt.

25 According to published proceedings, Anthony's last public address was given on Feb. 7, 1906, during the National American Woman Suffrage Association's 38th annual conference. (Testimony from Dr. Shaw later in the article, however, suggests that Anthony may have spoken on Feb. 8, instead.) The National American Woman Suffrage organization was formed in 1890 by merging two rival organizations, the National Woman Suffrage Association and the American Woman Suffrage Association. NAWSA became the largest voluntary

organization in the nation and played a pivotal role in the passing of the 19th Amendment, which granted women the right to vote.

26 Nellie V. Mark was an American physician and suffragist. In addition to service as vice-president of the Association for the Advancement of Women, Mark was a member of the Just Government League of Baltimore, the Equal Suffrage League of Baltimore, and the National Geographic Society. She was an early member of the Woman's Literary Club of Baltimore and later joined the Arundell Club.

27 The Riggs House hotel was located at 15th and G Streets in Washington, DC. It was torn down in 1911 and replaced with an office building. Streets of Washington, accessed July 24, 2019, http://www.streetsofwashington.com/2009/11/and-one-block-north.html.

28 The Lyric first opened in 1894 as The Lyric Opera House. In 1909, it because known as The Lyric when it was purchased by Otto Kahn. It still exists today as the Modell Performing Arts Center.

29 Julia Ward Howe (1819-1910) was an American poet and author best known for writing "The Battle Hymn of the Republic." She was also an advocate for the abolition of slavery and women's suffrage. Mary Elizabeth Garrett (1854-1915) was an American suffragist and philanthropist. She was the youngest child and only daughter of John W. Garrett, a philanthropist and president of the B & O Railroad.

30 Louisa May Alcott (1832-1888) was an American novelist, poet, and short story writer, best known for her novel *Little Women* (1868). Alcott was also fierce advocate for women's suffrage. She became the first woman to register to vote in Concord, Massachusetts, in a school board election, and addressed women's issues in many of her works. Alcott was also an abolitionist; several of her letters were published in *Commonwealth*, a Boston anti-slavery paper.

31 Bates (1846-1911) was an honorary member of the WLCB who presented on several occasions between 1903-1910, including several translations of French literary works.

32 A reference to an illustration included with the article, a letter from Anthony to Mark, is omitted here.

33 Anna Howard Shaw (1847-1919) was a leader of the women's suffrage movement in the United States. She was also a physician and one of the first ordained female Methodist ministers in the United States. "The Story of a Pioneer," is an autobiography of Shaw that details her life from her birth in Newcastle-on-Tyne, England through her presidency of the National American Woman Suffrage Association.

34 Martha Carey Thomas (1857-1935) was born in Baltimore and attended the Society of Friends School in the city alongside her cousin, Frank Smith. However, after Smith's unexpected death, Thomas's parents moved her to the Howland Institute, a Quaker institute near Ithaca, NY. In her adult life, Smith was an educator, suffragist, and linguist, and served as the second president of Bryn Mawr College. Alongside several other women, Thomas founded the Bryn Mawr School, a preparatory school in Baltimore, in 1885. In 1908, she became the first president of the National College Women's Equal Suffrage League. She was also a leading member of the National American Woman Suffrage Association and advocated the policies of the National Woman's Party.

35 The Arundell Club of Baltimore formed in 1893, possibly in response to the WLCB's decision not to actively engaged in philanthropy and social reform. In 1921, the WLCB began meeting in a room at the Arundell Club.

36 Ira Remsen (1846-1947) was a chemist who, along with Constantin Fahlberg, discovered the artificial sweetener saccharin. He was the second president of Johns Hopkins University.

37 Mary Emma Woolley (1863-1947) was an American educator, peace activist and women's suffrage supporter. She was the first female student to attend Brown University and served as the eleventh president of Mount Holyoke College. Lucy Maynard Salmon (1853-1927) was an American historian and professor of history at Vassar College. She was also the first woman to be a member of the executive committee of the American Historical Association. Mary Augusta Jordan was a professor of English at Smith College from 1884 to 1921.

Louise Molloy

1 Joanne Dobson, "Reclaiming Sentimental Literature." *American Literature* 69, no. 2 (1997): 263-88. doi:10.2307/2928271

Emily Emerson Lantz

1 The major sources of biographical information for Mary Spear Tiernan are Charles B. Tiernan, *The Tiernan Family in Maryland* (Baltimore, 1898), pp. 160-167, and Margie H. Luckett, *Maryland Women* (Baltimore: King Brothers, 1931).

2 "Graves Decorated by Women," *Baltimore Sun*, November 3, 1900.

3 Death of Mrs. Mary Spear Tiernan," *Baltimore Sun*, January 14, 1891.

4 Coleman Hutchison, *Apples and Ashes: Literature,*

Nationalism, and the Confederate States of America (Athens, GA: University of Georgia Press, 2012).

5 Richie D. Watson, Jr., "Mary Spear Tiernan's Unique Contribution to Post-Bellum Virginia Fiction," *Southern Literary Journal* 17.2 (1985): 100-107.

6 In one of Aesop's fables, a wolf upstream from a lamb accuses it of muddying the water he is trying to drink. When the lamb explains, reasonably, that it could not have muddied the wolf's water, the wolf responds by eating the lamb anyway.

7 A variation of the British idiom "set the Thames on fire," meaning to do things that cause a great or remarkable sensation in the world. Frequently used in the negative to indicate the opposite.

8 Reference to 1870 narrative poem "The Heathen Chinee" by Bret Harte. The poem was a satire of anti-Chinese sentiments in northern California. Ultimately, the poem reinforced racism among its readers rather than Harte's intention of challenging it.

9 Confederate currency was hand-signed and hand numbered, and according to Don Kelly, dealer in Confederate currency the back side of currency produced between 1862-1865 was blue (email correspondence, July 25, 2019).

10 A native or resident of the US state of South Carolina.

11 A derogatory word of French origin meaning the common people or the proletariat.

12 Nickname of Thomas Jonathan Jackson (1824-1863), Confederate general.

13 Roland, the legendary nephew of Charlemagne, battled Oliver, another of Charlemagne's knights, to a standstill. Being so evenly matched, a strong friendship subsequently developed between them. The idiom indicates an effective or appropriate retort or response; tit for tat.

14 On the alert or lookout; French.

15 The Richmond Bread Riot took place on April 2, 1863 and was spawned by food deprivation during the Civil War. It was the largest civil disturbance in the Confederacy during the war.

16 The so-called "pétroleuses," derived from the French word for gasoline, *petrol,* were female supporters of the Paris Commune accused of burning down the city in protest in 1871.

17 Joan of Arc.

18 The Battle of Fredericksburg was fought on December 11-15, 1862 in and around Fredericksburg, VA in the Eastern Theater of the American Civil War. It was one of the most one-sided battles of the war, with Union causalities almost twice as heavy as those suffered by the Confederates.

Chroniclers of the Homefront

Mary Spear Nicholas Tiernan

1 Her best works, according to that review, are "The Lamp of Psyche," "Estelle," "The Problem," "A Point of Honor," and "When Least Aware."

2 French phrase meaning "my good fellow" or "my good man."

3 Honoré de Balzac (1799-1850) was a French novelist and playwright known for his sensuality, verging on coarseness. Charles Augustin Sainte-Beuve (1804-1869) was a French literary critic whose work was perceived as cultured and sophisticated.

4 A Latin phrase meaning the force of inactivity, either literally or metaphorically; inertness.

5 Ishmael appears in the Genesis book of the Old Testament as the son of Abraham. At the age of fourteen, Ishmael and his mother are expelled from Abraham's home at the demand of Abraham's wife, Sarah.

6 A French word meaning "narrow-minded."

7 Matthew 6:23.

8 A reference to Matthew 4:3: "If thou be the Son of God, command that these stones be made bread."

9 Johann Paul Friedrich Richter (1763-1825), German romantic writer popular during the nineteenth century.

10 Shakespeare, *Hamlet,* Act 3, Scene 4.

11 In Genesis 25:29-34, Esau sells his birthright for a bowl of lentil stew (a "mess of pottage").

12 Paraphrase of Jaques's monologue in Shakespeare's *As You Like It* , Act 2, Scene 7.

13 Thucydides was an Athenian historian and general.

14 Griselda is a figure in European folklore noted for her patience and obedience.

15 A French phrase meaning complete freedom to act as one wishes or thinks best. Literally, a blank "card" or blank slate.

16 A fuss or disturbance.

17 Shakespeare, *Othello,* Act 1, Scene 2: "But that I love the gentle Desdemona,/ I would not my unhoused free condition."

Ellen Duvall

1 Dorsey is referring to Baltimore, where the Dorsey family (on which the Scarboroughs of this story appear to be based) originally became established. The Baltimore Corn and Flour Exchange, referenced in the subsequent passage, was established in the early 1850s.

2 An eight-day clock was intended to run for eight days per winding, meaning that one would only

need to wind the clock once per week.

3 The "rest cure," popularized by psychologist S. Weir Mitchell and depicted in Charlotte Perkins Gilman's well-known story "The Yellow Wallpaper" (1892), recommended complete abstinence from labor of all kinds—physical, psychological, and intellectual—as a treatment for nervous exhaustion.

4 *Lavandula vera* is commonly known as old English lavender; *Lavandula spica* or *Lavandula latifolia*, commonly known as spike lavender, is grown in Spain and France. The latter produces far more oil and is thus less valued than the English variety.

5 John Milton's *Paradise Lost* (4. 162-3)

Marian V. Dorsey

1 "Mr. H. O. Haughton Dead," *Baltimore Sun*, Feb. 27, 1909: 9.

2 Muller, Amelia. "Carriage-Trade Modiste: Magician with Shears." *Baltimore Sun*, Feb. 29, 1948.

3 Reference to Napoleon Bonaparte's crushing defeat to the British-led Seventh Coalition at the Battle of Waterloo, June 18, 1815.

4 From "Letter V, Confessions," in Eric MacKay's *Love Letters of a Violinist, and Other Poems* (1886).

5 A large public park in Paris.

6 French for "the true tree." It refers to the first tavern created in 1848 by Joseph Guesusquin in Paris. This tavern, inspired by the myth of Robinson Crusoe, was perched in a tree and called "Au Grand Robinson." It featured meals mounted directly in baskets which customers could access via a pulley system.

7 French for "head-to-head." Means to have a private conversation between two persons.

8 "Good-Bye," composed by Francesco Paolo Tosti in 1880.

9 From the one-act play *In a Balcony* (1853), by Robert Browning (1812-1889).

10 Telephone numbers in the United States during the early 1900s named the local exchange (here, Mount Vernon), and the number corresponding to the address in that exchange. Mount Vernon is an area of Baltimore that was once home to the city's most wealthy and fashionable families.

11 Washington, DC.

12 Several concert auditoriums by this name existed at this time. One was in New York City, another in Boston.

Louisa Courtland Osburne Haughton

1 "When Girls of Today Take Up Reading," *Baltimore Sun*, Sept. 19, 1915, p. 1.

2 Fanny K. Reiche, "Baltimore Is the Home of Many Conspicuous Woman Writers," *Baltimore Sun*, Feb. 14, 1909, p. 17.

3 Reiche, "Baltimore Is the Home of Many Conspicuous Woman Writers."

4 Hildegard and Irene are speaking on a party line, a telephone line that was shared by several subscribers. Anyone sharing a line could listen to anyone else speaking on the line by picking up their receiver. Common courtesy dictated that if people were already using the line, one would hang up and wait for the others to finish their conversation.

5 Type of dance party popular in nineteenth-century America, frequently featuring the German quadrille as one of the dances partaken by attendees.

Harriet Lummis Smith

1 "Anne" was read to the WLCB on two occasions. It was read by Reese on June 3, 1890 under the title "Her eyes be like the violets," and a second time on April 13, 1909 in celebration of the publication of *A Branch of May*. "Anne" was also published in her 1891 volume, *A Handful of Lavender*, and was reprinted in a number of periodicals, including the *Savannah Morning News* (1887), the *Indianapolis Journal* (1899), and the *Salt Lake Tribune* (1909).

2 Likely a reference to the meeting house in Sudbury, Massachusetts which was constructed in 1653. New England meeting houses provided a public space for residents to discuss politics, religion, and other town issues. Reese also used Sudbury as a setting in her poem, "Lydia," which was also published in *A Handful of Lavender*.

3 "April in Town" was read for the Club on two occasions: first, on October 7, 1890 by Virginia Woodward Cloud, and second, by Reese on May 20, 1893 in honor of the end of Francese Litchfield Turnbull's term as president of the Club.

4 "Lord, Oft I Come" was recited for the Club on October 7, 1890 by Virginia Woodward Cloud in anticipation of the release of *A Handful of Lavender*.

5 "Lydia" was read for the Club on two occasions: first, it was recited on October 7, 1890 by Virginia Woodward Cloud, and second, by Reese on November 10, 1891.

6 Likely a reference to the historic St. Martin's church in West Baltimore, Maryland. It was built in July 1865 and served Irish and German immigrants.

7 "An Old Song" was recited, with "Lord, Oft I Come," for the Club by Virginia Woodward Cloud on October 7, 1890 in anticipation of the

release of *A Handful of Lavender.*

8 Pierre de Ronsard (1524-1585) was a French poet known for his amatory verse. Reese refers here to his poem titled "Quand vous serez bien vieille," or "When you are old." This poem is published in his 1578 volume, *Sonnets pour Hélène (Sonnets for Hélène)*, which was commissioned by the French Queen Catherine de Medici for her maid of honor, Hélène de Surgeres, who lost her lover in the war. In this volume, de Ronsard compares Hélène de Surgeres' beauty with the beauty of Helen of Troy. Hélène served as de Ronsard's muse and the inspiration for many of his poems.

9 "Thomas á Kempis" was read to the Club on March 17, 1891 by Elizabeth Turner Graham. Thomas á Kempis (1380-1471) was a German-Dutch canon regular and the author of *The Imitation of Christ*, a text advocating for readers to place their full trust in God and his plan for their lives. *The Imitation* has been translated into over fifty languages.

10 "Her Last Word" was read to the Club by Reese on December 8, 1891 prior to its publication in *Scribner's Magazine.* Eliza Ridgely, the recording secretary for the club at the time, described the poem as "sweet, suggestive, half-showing of a woman's feeling for her former lover: as to whether he shall remember—or forget her."

11 This poem was also known by the title "Fra Basil." It was read to the Club on May 15, 1893 and on October 13, 1908.

12 "A Christmas Folk Song" was performed by Reese for the Club on December 17, 1901. One of Reese's best-known poems, it was printed periodicals in states including Wisconsin, Kansas, Oklahoma, and Illinois over a span of just three days, from December 20 to December 23 of 1905. The poem was reprinted in Reese's volume *A Wayside Lute* in 1909, as well as in periodicals and magazines around Christmas time in subsequent years. Many readers celebrated Reese's storytelling and portrayal of the Christmas spirit, but the poem also differs from Reese's customary style in its informality and use of dialect.

13 First published in the *Atlantic Monthly* in June 1904.

14 "The Fold" was possibly read to the Club on April 17, 1900 under the title "In the Fold."

15 The first known publication of "Taps" was in the *Atlantic Monthly* in 1899. It was reprinted in Reese's own volume *A Wayside Lute* in 1909, and again in an anthology titled *Memorial Day Poems* in 1924. "Taps" was read to the Club by Belle Brooks on February 13, 1900. Lydia Crane, the recording secretary, described the poem as telling "of the bugle call of fame, that so often dies away

into the dirge of eternal rest." Taps was read again for the Club by Reese on October 12, 1909.

16 "A Violin at Dusk" was possibly read by Reese at the Club meeting on February 3, 1903 under the title "The Violin."

17 "Lilacs" was read for the Club by Reese on February 3, 1903. Lydia Crane, recording secretary, wrote that the poem's "exquisite tenderness" made it "the favorite" of several poems performed by Reese at that meeting.

18 Huntingdon, now called Waverly, is the neighborhood in which Reese lived as a child and again in adulthood.

19 Old York Way, now known as York Road, dated from colonial times, connecting York, Pennsylvania to the port of Baltimore.

20 *The Old House in the Country* was read by Reese to the Club on February 3, 1914. The sonnet cycle centers around the house where she was born. Club recording secretary Lydia Crane describes the poem as such: "She touched on her ancestors, simple and stern in their creed, but as sure of God as his sunrise. The old churchyard, where they carried armfuls of lilacs, the lane where lovers strolled were described in poignant phrases. The terrors of war-time, when prize portraits were hidden, and the children were afraid to go to bed at night were vividly portrayed. The poem closed in a minor chord, regret for past loveliness."

21 Saint John's Parish is now known as Saint John's Episcopal Church and is located on Old York Road in Reese's neighborhood of Huntingdon (now Waverly). Reese began her teaching career at the St. John's Parish School, and was buried at this church. Her tombstone reads, per her request, "I will sing unto the Lord a new song." She mentions the church by name later in the poem cycle.

22 Old York Lane, now known as York Road, dated from colonial times, connecting York, Pennsylvania to the port of Baltimore.

23 Reese refers to *The Pilgrim's Progress* (1678), a Christian allegory authored by John Bunyan.

24 "Forgiveness" was read for the WLCB by Reese on October 27, 1903 and is included in her book *The York Road* (1931).

25 Govanstown is a neighborhood in northeast Baltimore, Maryland.

Observers of Nature & Humankind

Lizette Woodworth Reese

1 A rag fair is a street market where old or second-hand clothing is sold.

2 Lily of the valley is a poisonous flower that prefers to grow in the shade.

3 This piece, originally titled "Love's House,—A Thought on Materialization," was scheduled to be read by Whitelock at the Woman's Literary Club of Baltimore's sixtieth General Meeting on October 11, 1892, but had to be omitted because they ran out of time. It was not read at the club until their seventy-fifth meeting on Valentine's Day, 1893.

4 1 Kings 18:44.

5 *The House Beautiful: Essays on Beds and Tables, Stools and Candlesticks*, by Clarence Chatham Cook (1878) established the tenets of the Aesthetic Movement in interior design and home decoration. William Randolph Hearst began publication of the magazine titled *House Beautiful* in 1896 a few years after the publication of "Love's House"; the magazine, first of the so-called "shelter magazines," is still in publication today.

Louise Clarkson Whitelock

1 In the book of Genesis in the Old Testament of the Bible, the Israelite Joseph learns that his son Jacob is still alive and well in Egypt, and the ruler sets out to find his son, who had previously thought to be dead.

2 Alternate spelling of Ahmose I, who was the King of Egypt from approximately 1549–1524 BC. He is noted for restoring Theban rule over Egypt and laying the foundations for what is considered to be the "New Kingdom," or a golden age, for Egypt.

3 Thebes was an Egyptian city that now lies in ruins within Luxor, Egypt. It was located along the Nile River, about five hundred miles south of the Mediterranean Sea.

4 Memphis was the ancient capital of Aneb-Hetch, the first division of Lower Egypt. Its ruins are located near the town of Mit Rahina, twelve miles south of Giza. Historically, it was important as it occupied a key position at the mouth of the Nile Delta. It was supposedly founded by the pharaoh Menes.

5 Reference to Jean-François Champollion, a nineteenth-century French scholar and Egyptologist.

6 The Theban Necropolis is a large, elaborate ceremony on the west bank of the Nile. Historically, it was used for burial rituals.

7 In the Eleventh Dynasty of Egypt (21 BC), Amun served as a grand leader of Egypt; he is regarded as the patron god of Thebes, or the tutelary god of Thebes.

8 Amenhotep I was the son of Amhose I and Nefertari. He ruled from about 1525–1504 BC.

9 Deir el-Bahari is a collection of temples and tombs that are a part of the Theban Necropolis.

10 Referring to Amelia Edwards, author of *Pharaohs Fellas and Explorers* (1891), a text from which Early appears to have used as her primary source for this article.

11 Ramases, more commonly spelt Ramesses or Ramses, was the third Pharaoh of the Nineteenth Dynasty of Egypt. He was a celebrated and powerful ruler and is also referred to as "Ramasses the Great" and the "Great Ancestor" (of Egypt).

12 Hatshepsut (1478–1458 BC) was the fifth Pharaoh of the 18th Dynasty of Egypt.

13 Thutmose II (1510 BC-1479 BC) was an Egyptian Pharaoh of the Eighteenth Dynasty.

14 The Bulak (or Bulaq) Museum, what is now the Egyptian Museum, is a museum in Cairo, Egypt, established in 1858 by French scholar Auguste Mariette.

15 Reference to Heinrich Karl Brugsch, a German Egyptologist of the nineteenth century.

16 Thutmose III was an Egyptian Pharaoh of the Eighteenth Dynasty who ruled from 1479–1425 BC.

17 Semenut was an architect and government official of the Egyptian Eighteenth Dynasty. He was a close companion of Hatshepsut and is referred to as the "Steward of the God's Wife."

18 The Land of Punt was a trading partner of Ancient Egypt, known for gold, ebony, ivory, and other valuable resources.

19 Ferdinand de Lesseps was a nineteenth-century French diplomat known for his development of the Suez Canal and his attempt to build a Panama Canal.

20 Édouard Naville (1844-1926) was a Swiss scholar who specialized in the history of Egypt among other areas.

21 Alternate spelling of Akhenaten.

22 Ka, a concept of Ancient Egyptian religion, is the principal aspect of the soul of a human being or of a god.

23 The Peabody Institute Library, known now as the George Peabody Library, was founded in 1866 in the Mount Vernon neighborhood of Baltimore, Maryland.

24 The Karnak Temple Complex is a collection of temples, chapels, and other buildings near Luxor, Egypt.

25 Hathor is an ancient Egyptian goddess considered to be the primeval goddess from whom all others were derived.

26 The Egyptian Museum of Berlin was founded in the early nineteenth century and housed an important collection of Ancient Egyptian artifacts.

27 Amenhotep III was the son of Amenhotep II. He ruled from 1388–1351 BC and was the ninth Pharaoh of the Eighteenth Dynasty of Egypt.

28 Tiye, as her name is now commonly spelt, was the daughter of a wealthy ancient Egyptian who was likely of foreign descent. After marrying Amenhotep III, the couple had at least seven children.

29 Spelled "Keun-a-ten" in the original.

30 Here, Early refers to the Protestant Reformation, a religious movement which swept across Europe following the publication of Martin Luther's Ninety-five Theses in 1517. "Kuen-a-ten," mentioned earlier in the sentence, was spelled "Kuhn-a-ten" in the original.

31 The ankh, also known as the crux ansata, is the ancient Egyptian hieroglyphic symbol used to represent life.

32 According to the Old Testament, Solomon's Temple was the holy temple of ancient Jerusalem until being destroyed in the Siege of Jerusalem of 587 BCE.

33 Heliopolis was a major ancient Egyptian city, known in the past as Iunu.

34 Tell el-Amarna is the site of the ruins and tombs of the city of Akhetaton in Upper Egypt. It was built by the Pharaoh Amenhotep IV around 1348 BCE as the capitol for his new kingdom.

35 Eduard Mahler was a Hungarian-Austrian scholar who dedicated himself to astronomy, mathematics, and history.

36 The Colossi of Memnon are sometimes referred to as the "Vocal Memnon," as there is a legend that these statues occasionally "sung" following their partial destruction due to an earthquake in 27 BC.

37 The British museum of London, England possess the largest collection of Egyptian artifacts outside of Egypt.

38 Cleopatra (69-30 BC) was an Egyptian ruler during the Ptolemaic Dynasty who is remembered for her skills as a general as well as her relationship with the Roman Marc Antony.

39 Helen of Troy is the wife of Greek mythological figure King Menelaus of Sparta; her beauty was, according to legend, the cause of the Trojan War.

Elizabeth Turner Graham

1 Bliss Carman, ed., *The Oxford Book of American Verse* (Oxford: Oxford University Press, 1927).

2 This poem was read during the Woman's Literary Club of Baltimore meeting of October 19, 1909, the entirety of which, according to the minutes was dedicated "to the poems of our honorary member, Miss Grace Denio Litchfield."

3 Read during the Woman's Literary Club of Baltimore meeting of October 19, 1909.

4 Read during the December 3, 1895 meeting of the Woman's Literary Club of Baltimore, along with other poems from *Mimosa Leaves.*

5 The title of Litchfield's novel comes from the Rubáiyát of Persian poet Omar Khayyám (1048-1131), translated into English by Edward FitzGerald in 1859:

The Moving Finger writes; and, having writ,

Moves on: nor all thy Piety nor Wit

Shall lure it back to cancel half a Line,

Nor all thy Tears wash out a Word of it."

Maud Graham Early

1 This story is aligned with this quote said by Jesus in the Bible, "I did not come to bring peace, but a sword" (Matthew 10:34); it was published in Litchfield's collection *As a Man Sows, and Other Stories* (1926).

Grace Denio Litchfield

1 Druid Hill Park, in the northwest quadrant of Baltimore City, was designed by Frederick Law Olmsted in the 1850s and is one of the oldest landscaped public parks in the United States.

1 Woman's Literary Club of Baltimore Meeting Minutes, March 12, 1901.

2 Woman's Literary Club of Baltimore Meeting Minutes, November 19, 1901.

3 Howard Pollack, *John Alden Carpenter: A Chicago Composer* (University of Illinois Press, 2001), 335.

4 Ellen Duvall, "Virginia Woodward Cloud," in *Library of Southern Literature: Biography*, edited by Edwin Anderson Alderman, Joel Chandler Harris, and Charles William Kent (Martin & Hoyt Company, 1909), 979–983.

Elizabeth McCormick Reese

1 Matthew 24:41.

2 Cypress traditionally is a symbol of death and the afterlife.

3 First published in *Century Magazine* in Aug. 1899.

4 Also published in the *Zion Herald* on Dec. 2, 1903, under the title "The Lecturer."

Anne Weston Whitney

1 "Kessler-Atwater," *Baltimore Sun*, February 21, 1895.

2 "How Sammy Went to Coral-Land," *Tennessean* (Nashville), Sept. 26, 1902.

Virginia Woodward Cloud

3 There are in fact five species of rabbits in South America, and twenty million feral rabbits living in Australia.

4 This is called the nictitating membrane and aids in protection of the eyelid as well as lubrication.

5 All rabbits have these, more commonly referred to as "peg teeth."

6 The French word for fox.

7 Also known as white fox, polar fox, or snow fox, and is native to the Arctic regions of the Northern Hemisphere.

1 "Six Bard-Avon Graduates: Each Member of Class to Interpret on Popular Drama," *Baltimore*

Sun, May 30, 1917, p 6.

2 "Society," *Baltimore Sun*, June 23, 1928, p. 4.

3 "The Three Arts: Music, Drama, Painting," *Baltimore Evening Sun*, February 10, 1922, p. 6.

4 "New D. A. R. Chapter Formed: "Washington-Custis Chosen as Name Of Organization," *Baltimore Sun*, February 6, 1910, p. 11.

5 English author Marie Corelli (1855-1924) wrote popular gothic novels, including *The Sorrows of Satan* (1895).

Emily Paret Atwater

1 "Suffragists in Play: Just Government League Also Begins Annual Meetings," *Baltimore Sun*, April 16, 1913, p. 3.

2 "Real Star in Suffrage Play," *Baltimore Sun*, November 2, 1910.

3 The Vagabond Players, founded in 1916 as part of the "Little Theater" movement, remains the oldest continuously operating community theater in the United States.

4 *Baltimore Sun*, March 8, 1915, p 6.

Virginia Berkley Bowie

1 "Miss Evans, 80, Peabody Music Pioneer, Dies," *Baltimore Sun*, Jan. 13, 1947.

2 Ibid.

3 Dale Geiger, "Sisters in Step," *Johns Hopkins Magazine*, April 2000, http://pages.jh.edu/jhumag/0400web/29.html.

4 Bessie Evans and May G. Evans, *Native American Dance Steps* (New York: A.S. Barnes, 1931), 7.

5 Septimus Tustin (1796-1871), Presbyterian clergyman.

6 Neilson Poe (1809-1884) was Poe's cousin and a judge for Baltimore's orphan's court.

7 Either six or seven people are believed to have attended Poe's funeral: those identified by Spence are the Reverend W. T. D. Clemm ("the preacher") and cousin of Virginia Poe; Neilson Poe; and Henry Herring (1792-1868), Poe's uncle by marriage. The unidentified "gentleman" may have been Dr. Joseph E. Snodgrass, an acquaintance of Poe who later popularized the idea that Poe had died of alcoholism.

8 The new monument was designed by George A. Frederick, who was the architect for Baltimore's City Hall, and dedicated on November 16, 1875. The ceremony was attended by Neilson Poe and poet Walt Whitman, among others.

9 Excerpt from Lizette Woodworth Reese's poem "Westminster Churchyard," published in 1910, and is included in the "Tributes" section of this volume.

10 "Red Man" was an offensive name of Native Americans given by Europeans and white people, referring to the color of their skin and implying that they were inferior to the white race.

11 Pueblo is a Native American tribe in Southwestern region of the US.

12 Passage is a reference to Psalm 149.

13 Several paragraphs at the beginning of the section, which explain the forms of notation used throughout the book, are omitted.

14 *Dancing, Ancient and Modern* was published in 1911 by Ethel Lucy Urlin.

15 The eagle was believed to have a connection between heaven and earth, and could control rain and thunder. The dog dance was performed to bring success to battle and was danced by the bravest warriors.

16 J. E. Crawford Flitch (1881-1946) was the author of *Modern Dancing and Dancers* (1912).

17 A glossary of descriptive terms is omitted.

18 The San Ildefonso Pueblo were located within Santa Fe County, New Mexico.

19 The Taos Indians were a Pueblo tribe located in Taos, New Mexico, north of Santa Fe.

20 Dr. Clark Wissler (1870-1947) was an American anthropologist.

21 Pliny Earle Goddard (1869-1928) was an American linguist. The Dog Society is the Native American military.

Corinne Robert Redgrave

1 Desirée Henderson, "The Friendship Elegy," in *A History of Nineteenth-Century American Women's Poetry*, ed. Jennifer Putzi and Alexandra Socarides (New York: Cambridge University Press, 2017), 109, 115.

2 Charles Dickens, *The Haunted Man* (1848).

3 Orphanages.

4 Possibly a reference to William Shakespeare's Sonnet 71, which includes the lines, "if you read this line, remember not / The hand that writ it, for I love you so, / That I in your sweet thoughts would be forgot, / If thinking on me then should make you woe."

5 Longfellow wrote several poems featuring indigenous Americans, the most famous being "The Song of Hiawatha" (1855).

6 Easter's note: "Read before the Woman's Literary Club, of Baltimore, on the Lanier Memorial Day and inscribed to the President of the Club, Mrs. Lawrence Turnbull, a personal friend of the poet, February 3, 1889."

7 Sidney Lanier, "Sunrise," *Poems of Sidney Lanier*, ed. Sidney Lanier and Mary Lanier (New York: Scribner's Sons, 1885).

8 Easter's note: "Read at the Longfellow Memorial meeting of the Woman's Literary Club of Baltimore, February 24, 1890."

9 *Looking Backward: 2000-1887* (1888), bestselling utopian novel, which spurred the creation of the

socialist Nationalist Party.

10 The Anglican priest John Mason Neale (1818-1866) was the author of several histories of the Christian religion, including *A History of the Holy Eastern Church* (1847) and *Medieval Preachers and Medieval Preaching* (1856). John Pearson was another Anglican, whose *Exposition of the Creed* was first published in 1659. Dionysus Lardner's edition of François Arago's *Popular Lectures on Astronomy* was published in 1845.

11 St. Luke's Episcopal Church was established in the mid-nineteenth century and is still located in West Baltimore at 217 N. Carey St.

12 Dorsey Richardson's biography of Woods was published in the same issue of *Lippincott's* in which *The Mark of the Beast*, included in the "Crusaders and Critics" section of this volume, was published.

13 "In Memoriam" was read at a memorial service for Mary Spear Tiernan held on Oct. 20, 1891 organized by the WLCB. Eliza Ridgely's minutes list the following works being read: "Mrs Lord 'In Memoriam of Mary Spear Tiernan'; by Mrs [Marguerite E.] Easter 'So will we think of thee'; by Mrs [Elizabeth Turner] Graham on 'Truth-tellers of Fiction'—a tribute on a conversation with Mrs Tiernan upon *Homoselle*; and by Miss [Jane] Zacharias 'On Expression,' referring to the last address made to the Club by Mrs Tiernan." A printed clipping of Lord's poem was inserted in the scrapbook containing the program for the event in the WLCB collection at the Maryland Historical Society; none of the other poems appear to have been recorded or preserved.

14 Azrael is the Angel of Death and one of four archangels in the Qu'ran, and the Angel of Destruction and Renewal in the Hebrew Bible.

15 Tribute included in the Woman's Literary Club of Baltimore minutes, and read by Lydia Crane before the Club on October 8, 1895.

16 Green Mount Cemetery was established in 1838 and is the resting place of many prominent Baltimoreans. Lydia Crane is also buried in the Crane family plot.

17 Charles County, MD, is located on the Western Shore south of Washington, DC.

18 In March 1839, when she was in her late twenties, Margaret Fuller wrote in her journal, "I . . . made up my mind to be bright and ugly." *The Essential Margaret Fuller*, ed. Michael Croland (Mineola, NY: Dover, 2019), 5.

19 The New Theatre on Holliday Street in downtown Baltimore, at the current site of the War Memorial Building and City Hall, opened in 1795 and was demolished in 1917. Over the course of its lifetime it was also known as the New Holliday, Old Holliday, the Baltimore Theatre, and the Old Drury.

20 Charles Jean Marie Loyson (1827-1912), French priest and theologian.

21 Francese Litchfield Turnbull, longtime president of the WLCB.

22 Maria Clemm (1790-1871) was Poe's aunt and mother-in-law. Sarah Elmira Royster Shelton (1810-1888) was a childhood sweetheart of Poe's who became engaged to him just before his death. She had been married to Alexander B. Shelton, who died in 1844.

23 Woodberry: "Life of Edgar Allan Poe." (Wrenshall's note.)

24 Westminster Church Yard is at the site of the former First Presbyterian Church of Baltimore and was established in January 1787. Important Marylanders are buried here, most notably, poet Edgar Allan Poe. Circumstances surrounding Poe's mysterious death are still ambiguous today, as he was found incoherent near East Lombard Street in Baltimore shortly before his death. He was brought the Church Home and Hospital, also known as Washington Medical College, where he died four days later on October 7, 1849.

25 This line is an allusion to the biblical verse, "Dust thou art, and unto dust shalt thou return" (Genesis 3:19).

26 Professor Killis Campbell (1872-1937) was an American author and professor.

27 Dudley Buck (1839-1909) was an American composer, organist, and writer. *Winter Pictures* (Op. 19), was published in 1866.

28 Sir August Manns (1825-1907) was a German conductor and director of music at London's Crystal Palace.

29 Josef Holbrooke (1878-1958) was an English composer who in fact wrote more than thirty works inspired by Poe—which he called his "Poeana." They included piano pieces, orchestral works, a double concerto for clarinet and bassoon (*Tamerlane*), choral works, and a ballet.

30 The bibliography is not included in this volume.

31 A reference to Poe's poem, "Al Aaraaf."

32 Minnesingers were medieval German lyric poets who sang love songs. Thomas Moore (1779-1852), Irish poet.

33 This region holds Gunpowder Falls State Park, which is one of Maryland's largest state parks, established in 1959.

34 The Church Home and Infirmary was a hospital in Baltimore located South of Johns Hopkins Hospital. It was associated with the Episcopal Diocese of Maryland and is believed to be the site where Edgar Allan Poe died. The hospital closed down in 2000, but was later re-opened as a unit known as the Church Home and Hospital Building of John Hopkins Hospital.

35 The *Republican* newspaper, based in Springfield, Massachusetts, was founded in 1824 by Samuel Bowles, an acquaintance of Emily Dickinson. It played a prominent role in the founding of the United States Republican Party in the nineteenth

century, and still operates today.

36 In Greek mythology, Endymion was variously a handsome Aeolian shepherd, hunter, or king who was said to rule and live at Olympia in Elis.

37 William Henry Rinehart was a renowned American sculptor who worked within the classical style. In 1844 he began an apprenticeship in the stone-yard of Baughman and Bevan on the site of what is now The Peabody Institute in Baltimore, and studied sculpture at what is now called the Maryland Institute College of Art. He then went on to continue his studies in Rome, but later opened a studio in Baltimore and sculpted numerous busts, such as a fountain-figure for the main U.S. Post Office in Washington, DC. As Lantz notes, Reneheardt was buried in Baltimore's Green Mount Cemetary.

38 Green Mount Cemetery is a historic cemetery in Baltimore that was established in 1838. It holds the remains of several prominent Baltimore families and notable figures, such as John Wilkes Booth, Johns Hopkins, and Henry Walters, founder of the Walters Art Museum.

39

40 Eastern High School in Baltimore was established in 1844 to allow female students to advance in education beyond primary schools. Lizette Woodworth Reese, a prominent WLCB member, was an alumna of the school and later taught there.

41 A misspelling of the name of Michelangelo di Lodovico Buonarroti Simoni, an Italian sculptor, painter, architect, and poet of the High Renaissance.

A Provisional Bibliography of Works by Members of the Woman's Literary Club of Baltimore

The bibliography below contains works from authors who were active Club members between 1890-1920, listed chronologically in order of publication. Those holding purely honorary status are excluded. News articles and regular newspaper columns and features by journalists are listed if they are included in *Parole Femine* but may otherwise be incomplete.

The Woman's Literary Club of Baltimore website (http://loyolanotredamelib. org/Aperio/WLCB/) offers a complete, searchable archive of all documented Club member publications.

Atwater, Emily Paret. "Uncle Pete's Christmas." *Short Stories*, 1895.

———. "Colonel Von Winkle's Prowess; The Story of a Family Portrait." *Puritan*, 1897.

———. *How Sammy Went to Coral-Land*. Philadelphia: George W. Jacobs, 1902.

———. *Tommy's Adventures*. Philadelphia: George W. Jacobs, 1905.

———. *Trixsey's Travels*. Philadelphia: George W. Jacobs, 1905.

———. "The Garrett Room." *Cavalier*, 1910.

———. *In Ocean Land*. Chicago: Albert Whitman, 1927.

Atwater, Emily Paret, ed. *The Reminiscences of William Paret, Sixth Episcopal Bishop of Maryland*. Philadelphia: George W. Jacobs, 1911.

Bowie, Virginia Berkley. "How They Met Themselves." *Cosmopolitan*, Sept. 1907.

———. "The Desolating Adventures of Jean Baptiste." *Cosmopolitan*, Oct. 1907.

———. "Dilemma of Patrolman Redmond." *Baltimore Sun*, Oct. 10, 1915.

Briscoe, Margaret Sutton. "A Tea Leaf." *Frank Leslie's Illustrated Newspaper*, Sept. 20, 1890.

———. "Ned." *Overland Monthly*, Feb. 1891.

———. "Through a Glass, Darkly." *Belford's Magazine*, June 1891.

———. "How the Spirit Moved Cynthia." *Christian Union*, July 11, 1891.

———. *Situations*. *Godey's Lady's Book*, serialized in three installments, July-Sept. 1891.

———. "A Chip." *Frank Leslie's Illustrated Newspaper*, Aug. 15, 1891.

———. "An Extravagant Beggar." *Christian Union*, Oct. 1891.

———. "The Gentleman in Plush," *Christian Union*, Dec. 26, 1891 and Jan. 2, 1892.

———. "A Floating Cork." *Frank Leslie's Illustrated Newspaper*, ca. 1892.

———. "At the Door of the Pew." *Frank Leslie's Illustrated Newspaper*, Mar. 3, 1892.

———. "An Open Question." *Harper's Weekly*, Mar. 16, 1892.

———. "Miss Chesilia McCarthy." *Christian Union*, Apr. 1892.

———. "From Bed to Bed: An Afternoon in a Hospital." *Christian Union*, May 14, 1892.

———. "The Tramp Problem in Baltimore." *Christian Union*, Aug. 27, 1892.

———. "Apples of Gold." *Scribner's*, Dec. 1892.

———. "How Many Crimes are Committed in Thy Name!" *Christian Union*, Dec. 17, 1892.

———. "A Victim." *Christian Union*, Dec. 24, 1892.

———. *A Woman's Privilege*. Serialized in the *Christian Union*, 1893.

———. *Links in a Chain*. New York: Dodd, Mead, 1893.

———. *Perchance to Dream, and Other Stories*. New York: Dodd, Mead, 1893.

———. "Becalmed." *Outlook*, Aug. 12, 1893.

———. "An I.O.U." *Scribner's*, Sept. 1893.

———. "A New England Graveyard." *Outlook*, Sept. 16, 1893.

———. "Amateur Dramatics." *Harper's Bazaar*, Mar. 11, 1894.

———. "John Harvey." *Frank Leslie's Illustrated Weekly*, Mar. 22, 1894.

———. "Amateur Tableaux." *Harper's Bazaar*, Apr. 14, 1894.

———. "Amateur Dramatics." *Harper's Bazaar*, Apr. 28, 1894.

———. "Pore Little Pinkey." *Harper's Bazaar*, June 2, 1894.

———. "Amateur Dramatics: Charades." *Harper's Bazaar*, June 30, 1894.

———. "A Chalk-Line." *Outlook*, July 7, 1894.

———. "The Low Sun." *Harper's Bazaar*, July 14, 1894.

———. "Ephphatha." *Harper's Bazaar*, Aug. 18, 1894.

———. "The Garrett." *Outlook*, Sept. 29, 1894.

———. "The Cellar." *Outlook*, Oct. 13, 1894.

———. "Amateur Dramatics." *Harper's Bazaar*, Nov. 3, 1894.

———. "The Kitchen." *Outlook*, Nov. 10, 1894.

———. "A Confidence." *Harper's Bazaar*, Dec. 8, 1894.

———. "The Days We Live In: The Professional Woman." *Harper's Bazaar*, Dec. 22, 1894.

———. "An Unrecorded Miracle." *Frank Leslie's Illustrated Weekly*, Dec. 25, 1894.

———. "Papa's Rod." *Harper's Young People*, Dec. 25, 1894.

———. "The Days We Live In: Ambidexterity." *Harper's Bazaar*, Feb. 2, 1895.

———. "The Days We Live In: Definition." *Harper's Bazaar*, Mar. 9, 1895.

———. "The Days We Live In: A Phase of the Servant Question." *Harper's Bazaar*, Mar. 30, 1895.

———. "A Dinner Engagement: A Closet Play in Two Acts." *Frank Leslie's Illustrated Weekly*, Apr. 18, 1895.

———. "The Days We Live In: The Art of Pleasing." *Harper's Bazaar*, May 11, 1895.

———. "Annie Tousey's Little Game." *Harper's Monthly*, July 1895.

———. "Jimty." *Harper's Monthly*, Aug. 1895.

———. "The Days We Live In: Counting the Cost." *Harper's Bazaar*, Aug. 3, 1895.

———. "Counting the Cost—Suffrage." *Harper's Bazaar*, Aug. 24, 1895.

———. "Aunt Caulfield's Wedding Gown." *Harper's Bazaar*, Nov. 23, 1895.

———. "The Midway." *Harper's Bazaar*, Nov. 25, 1895.

———. "A Goose-Chase." *Harper's Monthly*, Apr. 1896.

———. "The Family Stick." *Harper's Bazaar*, June 6, 1896.

———. "Between Two Years." *Harper's Round Table*, July 4, 1896.

———. "The Violin-Case." *Harper's Bazaar*, Aug. 1, 1896.

———. "Like Mistress, Like Maid." *Harper's Bazaar*, Aug. 22, 1896.

———. "From Line to Kettle." *Harper's Bazaar*, Dec. 5, 1896.

———. "Marriage." *Harper's Bazaar*, Jan. 2, 1897.

———. "Elasticity." *Harper's Bazaar*, Jan. 7, 1897.

———. "Princess I-Would-I-Wot-Not." *Harper's Monthly*, Feb. 1897.

———. "An Entomological Wooing." *Harper's Monthly*, Mar. 1897.

———. "On Choosing Home." *Harper's Bazaar*, Apr. 27, 1897.

———. "Baby Goes to Sleepy Town." *Outlook*, May 1, 1897.

———. "How Sarah Paid for Peace." *Century*, June 1897.

———. "Blue Mondays." *Harper's Bazaar*, June 5, 1897.

———. "Salt of the Earth." *Outlook*, July 8, 1897.

———. "Concealed Weapons." *Century*, Aug. 1897.

———. "Masques: A Play in Three Acts." *Harper's Bazaar*, Aug. 1897.

———. "American Humor." *Harper's Bazaar*, Aug. 28, 1897.

———. "A Southern Market," *Harper's Bazaar*, Sept. 25, 1897.

———. "Amateur Dramatics: Manager." *Harper's Bazaar*, Sept. 25, 1897.

———. "Home Keeping." *Harper's Bazaar*, Oct. 9, 1897.

———. "Amateur Dramatics: A Portable Theater." *Harper's Bazaar*, Oct. 23, 1897.

———. "The Quarter Loaf." *Harper's Monthly*, Nov. 1897.

———. "The Sixth Sense." *Harper's Monthly*, Jan. 1898.

———. "Thedmore." *Frank Leslie's Illustrated Weekly*, Jan. 6, 1898.

———. "A Will and a Way." *Harper's Monthly*, May 1898.

———. "A Petitioner." *Harper's Monthly*, July 1898.

———. "A Question of Methods." *Harper's Bazaar*, July 9, 1898.

———. "On Appealing to a Low Motive." *Harper's Bazaar*, Aug. 27, 1898.

———. "The Code Revised." *Harper's Bazaar*, serialized in eleven installments from Sept. 24, 1898–Jan. 14, 1899.

———. *Jimty, and Others*. New York: Harper & Brothers, 1898.

———. "Club Women." *Century*, Nov. 1898.

———. "The New Race." *Century*, Dec. 1898.

———. "The Code Revised: 'Getting to Work—Peter's Wife.'" *Harper's Bazaar*, Dec. 3, 1898.

———. "Uncle Elijah's Christmas Dinner." *Harper's Bazaar*, Dec. 10, 1898.

———. *The Sixth Sense, and Other Stories*. New York: Harper & Brothers, 1899.

———. "The Code Revised: Manner as a Garb." *Harper's Bazaar*, Jan. 14, 1899.

———. "His Nomination." *Harper's Monthly*, Feb. 1899.

———. "A Temple of Solomon." *Century*, Mar. 1899.

———. "Of Her Own Household." *Harper's Monthly*, Mar. 1899.

———. "Matilda's Address Book." *Harper's Monthly*, July 1899.

———. "The Code Revised: Modesty." *Harper's Bazaar*, July 7, 1899.

———. "Cosmopolitans." *Harper's Bazaar*, serialized in seven installments, July 29–Sept. 2, 1899.

———. "The Animation of Beck Ann." *Harper's Bazaar*, Sept. 12, 1899.

———. "Rounding the Circle; or, How a Hemisphere May Be a Sphere." *Century*, Oct. 1899.

———. "This Mortal Coil." *Harper's Weekly*, Oct. 6, 1899.

———. "A Cosmopolite." *Harper's Bazaar*, Nov. 11, 1899.

———. "The Midway." *Harper's Bazaar*, Nov. 25, 1899.

———. "I Believe." *Century*, Dec. 1899.

———. "The Cuban Cactus." *Harper's Monthly*, Feb. 1900.

———. "His Old Love." *Harper's Monthly*, Aug. 1900.

———. "Mother of the Coming Race." *Harper's Bazaar*, Dec. 8, 1900.

———. "The Chip and the Block." *Delineator*, Mar. 1901.

———. "Oscar and Louise." *Scribner's*, Oct. 1901.

———. "Creating a Vacuum." *Outlook*, Dec. 21, 1901.

———. "Whither Thou Goest." *Harper's Monthly*, Jan. 1902.

———. *The Change of Heart: Six Lovely Stories*. New York: Harper & Brothers, 1903.

———. "His Price." *Harper's Monthly Magazine*, Mar. 1903.

———. "His Opportunity." *Harper's Weekly*, May 9, 1903.

———. "His Prerogative." *Harper's Monthly*, July 1903.

———. "Red Tassels." *Century*, July 1903.

———. "The Matriculation of Courtney." *Harper's Monthly*, Feb. 1904.

———. "In Loco Parentis." *Harper's Monthly*, Mar. 1904.

———. "To Arms." *Good Housekeeping*, Apr. 1904.

———. "The Little Still." *Outlook*, Apr. 2, 1904.

———. "Philanderings." *Ainslee's Magazine*, Sept. 1904.

———. "His Bad Half-Hour." *Harper's Weekly*, Nov. 5, 1904.

———. "To Understand." *Harper's Monthly*, Feb. 1905.

———. "Treasure Cottage." *Good Housekeeping*, Oct. 1905.

———. "Mademoiselle Crapaud." *Ainslee's Magazine*, Jan. 1906.

———. "Visions of an Optimist." *Ainslee's Magazine*, serialized in four installments, Oct. 1906–Jan. 1907.

———. "The Debt of Honor." *Everybody's*, Jan. 1907.

———. "Visions of an Optimist: V. On Remembering." *Ainslee's Magazine*, Feb. 1907.

———. "Made in Heaven." *Harper's Monthly*, Sept. 1907.

———. "Versus the Same." *Harper's Monthly*, Apr. 1908.

———. "Daughter's Heart." *Harper's Monthly*, May 1908.

———. "The Sporting Chance." *Ladies' Home Journal*, Oct. 1908.

———. "His Mother-at-Heart." *Ladies' Home Journal*, Dec. 1908.

———. *The Image of Eve: A Romance with Alleviation*. New York: Harper & Brothers, 1909.

———. "The Girl That Peter Brought." *Ladies' Home Journal*, Mar. 1909.

———. "The Secret." *Harper's Weekly*, Aug. 21, 1909.

———. "Hospitalized Child." *Good Housekeeping*, Nov. 1910.

Briscoe, Margaret Sutton (as Travers Hopkins). "Meditation." *Smart Set*, May 1920.

Briscoe, Margaret Sutton and "M. A. R." "Three Stories of Russian Life: 'How Many Crimes are Committed in Thy Name!'" *Christian Union*, Dec. 17, 1892.

Cautley, Lucy Randolph. "A Unique Charity." *Churchman*, May 30, 1893.

———. *By Giotto's Tower; or, The House of Death: A Drama in Four Acts*, 1901. Listed in *Dramatic Compositions Copyrighted in the United States 1870-1916, Vol. 1,* (Washington, DC: US Government Printing Office, 1918).

———. *Henry Esmond: A Drama in Four Acts*, 1901. Listed in *Dramatic Compositions Copyrighted in the United States 1870-1916, Vol. 1,* (Washington, DC: US Government Printing Office, 1918).

———. "Kipling Notes." *Conservative Review* 5, 1901.

———. "Betrayal." *Harper's Monthly*, June 1901.

———. *The Widow's Might: A Play in Four Acts*. Catalogue of Copyright Entries 11, no. 1 (Washington, DC: US Government Printing Office, 1914).

Coale, Mrs. James Casey. *The Cottage by the Sea*. Baltimore: J. Murphy, 1896.

———. *Leila the Hindoo Girl.* n.p., n.d.

Cloud, Virginia Woodward. "White Marie." *St. Nicholas*, Oct. 1891.

———. "Lizbeth's Song." *St. Nicholas*, Nov. 1891.

———. "Firelight." *St. Nicholas*, Mar. 1892.

———. "Fairy-Land." *St. Nicholas*, May 1892.

———. "What Things Befell the Squire's House." *St. Nicholas*, July 1892.

———. "Rokey's Ginger Jar." *Independent*, Mar. 23, 1893.

———. "A Stradivarius." *Cosmopolitan*, Aug. 1893.

———. "Among the Pines." *Cosmopolitan*, Nov. 1893.

———. "The Belfry Light." *Outlook*, Nov. 11, 1893.

———. "In the Camp of Philistia." *Lippincott's*, Dec. 1893.

———. "Silence and Love." *Cosmopolitan*, Dec. 1893.

———. "The Jester." *Short Stories*, Jan. 1894.

———. "How the Boy Was Prevented." *Short Stories*, July 1894.

———. "The Man Who Died at Amdheran." *Lippincott's*, Nov. 1894.

———. "The Black Duck: Lois, Her Book." *St. Nicholas*, Apr. 1895.

———. *The Witchcraft at Bow Bridge Castle.* *Outlook*, July 6 and July 13, 1895.

———. "An Interlude." *Bookman*, Sept. 1895.

———. "By the Fire." *Bookman*, Oct. 1895.

———. "The Train for Tarrow's." *Lippincott's*, Oct. 1895.

———. "Happiness." *Bookman*, Nov. 1895.

———. "Leonard Bradley and the Wolves." *Outlook*, Jan. 25, 1896; also published in *Christian Observer*, June 10, 1896.

———. "'The Lady or the Tiger?' A New Solution." *Century*, Feb. 1896.

———. "In April." *Bookman*, July 1896.

———. "The Gospel of Love." *Bookman*, Oct. 1896.

———. "The Woman Who Found Things." *Youth's Companion*, Oct. 22, 1896.

———. "The Magnanimity of the Lord Mayor." *Outlook*, Nov. 7, 1896.

———. "An Anonymous Love Letter." *Lippincott's*, Jan. 1897.

———. "Leisurely Lane." *Ladies' Home Journal*, Oct. 1897.

———. *Down Durley Lane and Other Ballads.* New York: Century, 1898.

———. "Penelope's Christmas Dance." *Ladies' Home Journal*, Jan. 1898.

———. "A Witness of War." *Black Cat*, May 1898.

———. "The Story of a Hero." *Independent*, July 7, 1898.

———. "Humour." *Bookman*, Oct. 1898.

———. "Care." *Century*, Oct. 1898; also published in *The American Anthology*, ed. Edmund Clarence Stedman (Boston: Houghton Mifflin, 1900).

———. "Revelation." *Harper's Monthly*, Dec. 1898.

———. "A Red Coat." *Independent*, Dec. 29, 1898.

———. "Exile." *Bookman*, Jan. 1899.

———. "Imitation." *Bookman*, Apr. 1899.

———. "Poor Mrs. Marks." *Century*, July 1899.

———. "An Old Street." *Harper's Monthly*, Aug. 1899; also published in *The American Anthology*, ed. Edmund Clarence Stedman (Boston: Houghton Mifflin, 1900).

———. "Alien." *Bookman*, Oct. 1899.

———. "The Matrimonial Opportunities of Maria Pratt." *Century*, Dec. 1899.

———. "Rebekah Bings' Blighted Life." *Harper's Bazaar*, Dec. 2, 1899.

———. "Prelude." *Bookman*, Jan. 1900.

———. "The Mother's Song," "Youth," "Care," and "An Old Street." *The American Anthology*, ed. Edmund Clarence Stedman. Boston: Houghton Mifflin, 1900.

———. "The Wishing Well." *Successful Recitations*, ed. Alfred H. Miles. London: H. Virtue, 1901.

———. "The Mask of Life." *Cosmopolitan*, July 1900.

———. "Autumn Song." *Atlantic Monthly*, Sept. 1900.

———. "His Godmother." *St. Nicholas*, Oct. 1900.

———. "The Pilgrim." *Cosmopolitan*, Dec. 1900.

———. "The Wishing Well." *Successful Recitations*, ed. Alfred H. Miles. London: H. Virtue, 1901.

———. "Children." *Cosmopolitan*, Jan. 1901.

———. "Cronies." *Smart Set*, Jan. 1901.

———. "The Shirt-Waist Chain." *Century*, Jan. 1901.

———. "At the Gate." *Bookman*, Feb. 1901.

———. "The Song of Joy." *Delineator*, Feb. 1901.

———. "Interlude." *Bookman*, Apr. 1901.

———. "The Blue Ring." *Delineator*, May 1901.

———. "Mistress Nell Williams and Her Soldier." *Ladies' Home Journal*, July 1901.

———. "A Butterfly." *Bookman*, Aug. 1901.

———. "In Tune." *Cosmopolitan*, Aug. 1901.

———. "Liza Wetherford." *Atlantic Monthly*, Sept. 1901.

———. "Dusk." *Bookman*, Sept. 1901.

———. "A Vigil." *Pearson's Magazine*, Sept. 1901.

———. "And Each Man in His Turn." *Delineator*, Oct. 1901.

———. *A Reed by the River.* Gorham Press, 1902.

———. "Misery and Company." *Harper's Monthly*, Feb. 1902.

———. "To Love." *Harper's Monthly*, Apr. 1902.

———. "The Willy-Wispy." *Pearson's*, Apr. 1902.

———. "Songs." *Bookman*, July 1902.

———. "Understudies." *Delineator*, Aug. 1902.

———. "Love's Lenity." *Bookman*, Nov. 1902.

———. "Mrs. Chick." *Century*, Dec. 1902.

———. "From a Little Red Book." *Smart Set*, Feb. 1903.

———. "Paying the Piper." *Bookman*, May 1903.

———. "The Butterfly." *Bookman*, July 1903.

———. "A Sitting." *Short Stories*, July 1903.

———. "Dust." *Smart Set*, Aug. 1903.

———. "The Witch Girl." *Ladies' Home Journal*, Aug. 1903.

———. "The Lecture." *Outlook*, Nov. 14, 1903; reprinted under the title "The Lecturer," *Zion's Herald*, Dec. 2, 1903.

———. "Heart's Inn." *Smart Set*, Dec. 1903.

———. "A Jester's Song." *Smart Set*, Jan. 1904.

———. "The Invisible Prince." *Smart Set*, Feb. 1904.

———. "O'Tara." *Harper's Weekly*, Feb. 6, 1904.

———. "His Good Angel." *Bookman*, Mar. 1904.

———. "Iram's Rose." *Smart Set*, Apr. 1904.

———. "The Dream." *Smart Set*, Apr. 1904.

———. "His Fiancée." *Delineator*, May 1904.

———. "A Special Dispensation." *Smart Set*, June 1904.

———. "After Ravenhoe." *Smart Set*, July 1904.

———. "Mother Earth." *Bookman*, Aug. 1904.

———. "After All." *Smart Set*, Aug. 1904.

———. "The Heart on the Highway." *Bookman*, Sept. 1904.

———. "The Other Thing." *Smart Set*, Nov. 1904.

———. "At the Well." *Smart Set*, Jan. 1905.

———. "A Leaf from Life's Book." *Cosmopolitan*, Feb. 1905.

———. "Birthright." *Booklovers Magazine*, Mar. 1905.

———. "His Honor vs. Cupid." *Delineator*, Mar. 1905.

———. "The King." *Delineator*, Apr. 1905.

———. "Concerning Mr. Penwinkle." *Smart Set*, May 1905.

———. "His Lady to Ronsard." *Smart Set*, July 1905.

———. "Why Patty Hildreth Powdered Her Hair." *Ladies' Home Journal*, Aug. 1905.

———. "The Gate." *Ainslee's Magazine*, Sept. 1905.

———. "A Song at Evening." *Smart Set*, Sept. 1905.

———. "The Things We Say." *Smart Set*, Oct. 1905.

———. "A Ballad of Coronation." *Harper's Bazaar*, Oct. 1, 1905.

———. "If Thou Lovest Me Not." *Bookman*, Nov. 1905.

———. "The Strolling Minstrel." *Smart Set*, Dec. 1905.

———. "A Petition." *Harper's Monthly*, Dec. 1905.

———. "Egypt Land." *Harper's Monthly*, Jan. 1906.

———. "In Bluebeard's Closet." *Smart Set*, Feb. 1906.

———. "In the Way He Should Go." *Delineator*, Mar. 1906.

———. "Paying the Piper." *Scrap Book*, Apr. 1906.

———. "A Life-Saving Service." *Life*, May 3, 1906.

———. "Enter the Blind God." *People's Magazine*, Oct. 1906.

———. "The Blue Kimono." *Delineator*, Dec. 1906.

———. "Pan to His Pipe." *Smart Set*, May 1907.

———. "The Scarecrow." *Smart Set*, Dec. 1907.

———. "The Tenure of Tradition." *Uncle Remus's*, Jan. 1908.

———. "A Witness of War." *People's Home Journal*, June 1908.

———. "Eden's Gate." *Cassell's Magazine of Fiction*, Oct. 1914.

———. "Blue Butterflies." *Smart Set*, May 1915.

———. "A Boy Without a Name." *Bellman*, June 30, 1917.

———. "Her Arabian Night." *Bellman*, Aug. 11, 1917.

———. "Through the Call of Closer Days." *Smart Set*, Oct. 1917.

———. "The Little House." *Bellman*, Dec. 8, 1917.

———. "Isle of Dreams." Bellman, Feb. 2, 1918.

———. "The Laughing Duchess." *Bellman*, Apr. 23, 1918.

———. "The Sword of Solomon." *Bellman*, May 25, 1918.

———. "Robin's Wood." *Bellman*, Jan. 25, 1919.

———. "The Door." *Bellman*, Apr. 12, 1919.

———. "The Rainy Day." *Youth's Companion*, Jan. 13, 1921.

———. *The Collected Poems of Virginia Woodward Cloud.* Baltimore: The Norman, Remington Co., 1922.

———. "Little Things." *Holland's*, Oct. 1923.

———. *Candlelight.* The Norman, Remington Co., 1924.

———. "White Elephant." *Holland's*, Apr. 1924.

Colvin, Mary Noyes, ed. *Godeffroy of Boloyne: Or, The Siege and Conqueste of Jerusalem*, trans. William Caxton. London: Kegan Paul, Trench, Trübner, 1893.

De Valin, Laura. "Parting Ode of 1859." Music by John F. Petri. Baltimore: E. Sachse & Co, 1859.

———. *Elisa, A Drama in Five Acts*, 1892. Listed in *Dramatic Compositions Copyrighted in the United States 1870-1916, Vol. 1*, (Washington, DC: US Government Printing Office, 1918).

———. *The Chaperon; A Comic Opera in Three Acts*, 1892. Listed in *Dramatic Compositions Copyrighted in the United States 1870-1916, Vol. 1*, (Washington, DC: US Government Printing Office, 1918).

Dorsey, Marian V. (Mary Dorsey). "Salutations and Inscriptions." *Decorator and Furnisher*, June 1888.

———. "Poe Monument and Memorial Volume."

Homemaker, Jan. 1893.

———. "A Daughter of the Cavaliers." *Kate Field's Washington*, May 9, 1894.

———. "Mythology in the Public Schools." *Journal of Education*, July 18, 1895.

———. "Birthday Parties for Old People." *Ladies' Home Journal*, Jan. 1899.

———. "Folk Lore." *Dixie*, July 1899.

———. "In Corn Pone Land." *Northwestern Miller*, Apr. 3, 1901.

———. "Decorations of a Boy's Room." *Washington Herald*, Feb. 18, 1902.

———. "'Aunt Tempy's' Maryland Dishes." *Good Housekeeping*, Dec. 1902.

———. "From 'Aunt Tempy,' Again." *Good Housekeeping*, Jan. 1903.

———. "My Lavender Garden." *Good Housekeeping*, Mar. 1904.

———. "From a Southern Kitchen." *Delineator*, Oct. 1904.

———. "Telling the Time at 'Controversie.'" *Northwestern Miller*, July 8, 1908.

———. "Blue China Old and New." *Harper's Bazaar*, Sept. 1908.

———. "Fried Chicken." *Good Housekeeping Everyday Cookbook*, ed. Isabel Gordon Curtis, 1909.

———. "Raising Lavender." *Harper's Bazaar*, May 1910.

———. "Summer Girl Who's Popular." *Minneapolis Star-Tribune*, July 2, 1911.

———. "Maxims for Summer Guests." *Chicago Tribune*, July 30, 1911.

———. "Boyville in Your Back Yard: The Canvas Bungalow and Its Suggestion for Suburbanites." *Suburban Magazine*, Aug. 1911.

———. "Joys for the Stay-at-Homes." *Chicago Tribune*, Aug. 13, 1911.

———. "You Can Easily Be Charming." *Chicago Tribune*, Aug. 27, 1911.

———. "Heirlooms from the Handsomest Drawing Room in America." *Baltimore Sun*, Oct. 8, 1911.

———. "Getting Ready for College." *Washington Herald*, June 9, 1912; also published in the *Atlanta Constitution*, Aug. 9, 1912.

———. "Possibilities of the Veranda." *Atlanta Constitution*, July 21, 1912.

———. "Decorating with House Plants." *Washington Herald*, July 28, 1912.

———. "A Steele Tradition of Lafayette." *Bulletin of the Maryland Original Research Society of Baltimore*, May 1913.

———. "The Washington Bust in the Monument: Is it a Canova or a Ceracchi?" *Patriotic Marylander*, Sept. 1915.

Dorsey, Marian V. (as Constance Chisholm). "Collecting of Old Lustre Ware—Now Is the Time."
Baltimore Sun, Aug. 11, 1912.

———. "Fad for 'Green India,' or Gold Medallion Ware." *Baltimore Sun*, Sept. 29, 1912.

———. "Your Old Silver Spoons—Do You Know Them?" *Baltimore Sun*, Nov. 10, 1912.

———. "Bayberry Candles Burnt at Christmas Bring Good Luck to House." *Baltimore Sun*, Dec. 15, 1912.

———. "The Interest That Attaches to Silhouettes." *Baltimore Sun*, Jan. 26, 1913.

———. "The Bonnet of 1830 Versus the Saucer Hat." *Baltimore Sun*, Mar. 30, 1913.

———. "Why Not the Picture Loan Service from Our Libraries?" *Baltimore Sun*, Apr. 25, 1915.

Dandridge, Danske Carolina. *Joy: And Other Poems*. London: G. P. Putnam's Sons, 1888.

———. *Rose Brake: Poems*. New York: G. P. Putnam's Sons, 1890.

———. *George Michael Bedinger: A Kentucky Pioneer*. Charlottesville, VA: Michie, 1909.

———. *Historic Shepherdstown*. Charlottesville, VA: Michie, 1909.

———. *American Prisoners of the Revolution*. Charlottesville, VA: Michie, 1911.

Duvall, Ellen. "Molière." *Lippincott's*, Sept. 1895.

———. "An Old-Testament Drama." *Lippincott's*, Apr. 1896.

———. "Innocuous Vanity." *Lippincott's*, March 1897.

———. "The Decline of the Hero." *Lippincott's*, July 1897.

———. "Opportunity." *Lippincott's*, Feb. 1898.

———. "The Problem." *Harper's Monthly*, Mar. 1898.

———. "The Open Door." *Atlantic Monthly*, Sept. 1900.

———. "A Point of Honor." *Atlantic Monthly*, Aug. 1901.

———. "The Fourth Gentleman." *Harper's Monthly*, July 1901.

———. "The Lover." *Atlantic Monthly*, Nov. 1901.

———. "Women's Heroes." *Atlantic Monthly*, Dec. 1902.

———. "When Least Aware." *Atlantic Monthly*, Dec. 1904.

———. "Return." *Harper's Weekly*, Dec. 10, 1904.

———. "Estelle." *Smart Set*, Feb. 1907.

———. "The Lamp of Psyche." *Smart Set*, Oct. 1907.

———. "Eye and Hand." *Atlantic Monthly*, Sept. 1909.

———. "The Strategists." *Smart Set*, June 1910.

———. "The Unpainted Portrait." *Atlantic Monthly*, Mar. 1911.

———. "The Persistence and Integrity of Plots." *Atlantic Monthly*, Apr. 1911.

———. "The Tenth Point of the Law." *Woman's Home Companion*, Mar. 1915.

———. "Frewen's Daughter." *Woman's Home Companion*, Apr. 1916.

Early, Maud Graham. "Three Queens of Ancient Egypt." *Southern Literary Messenger* (Washington, DC), June 1895.

———. "The Tale of the Wild Cat: A Child's Game." *Journal of American Folklore*, Mar. 10, 1897.

Easter, Marguerite E. "Yesterday." *New Eclectic Magazine*, Nov. 1870.

———. "Antigone's Farewell to Haemon." *Southern Magazine*, Jan. 4, 1875.

———. *Clytie and Other Poems.* Boston: A.J. Philpott, 1892.

Evans, May Garretson. *A Primer of Facts About Music: Questions and Answers on the Elements of Music for the Use of Teachers and Students.* T. Presser, 1909.

———. "Facts About Mistake in Marking Original Burial Place of Poe." *Baltimore Sun*, Aug. 1, 1920.

———. *American Indian Dance Steps.* New York: A. S. Barnes, 1931.

———. *Music and Edgar Allan Poe: A Bibliographical Study.* Baltimore: Johns Hopkins University Press, 1939.

———. "Poe in Amity Street." *Maryland Historical Magazine,* Dec. 1941.

Goessmann, Helena Theresa. "At All Sacrifices." *Catholic World*, Aug. 1893.

———. *The Christian Woman in Philanthropy: A Study of the Past and Present.* n.p., 1895.

———. *A Score of Songs.* New York: Sadler, 1897.

———. "The Soul of Julius Bittel. " *Catholic World,* Sept. 1911.

Graham, Elizabeth Turner. *Buttercups and Daisies: Songs of a Summer.* Baltimore: D. W. Glass & Co., 1884.

———. *Holly and Mistletoe: Songs Across the Snow.* Baltimore: D. W. Glass & Co., 1885.

Haughton, Louise Courtauld Osburne. "The Ever-Ready Edgar." *Ladies' Home Journal*, Dec. 1906.

———. "The Malachite Collar." *New York Tribune*, July 16, 1911.

———. *The Decision; or The Vacillations of Amelia.* Typescript, US Copyright Office. 1912.

———. *Side-Lights on Maryland History, with Sketches of Early Maryland Families.* Baltimore: Williams and Wilkins, 1913.

Ladd-Franklin, Christine. "On the Algebra of Logic." In Peirce, Charles S., et al., *Studies in Logic.* Boston: Little, Brown, 1883.

———. "The Pascal Hexagram." *Science*, June 29, 1883.

———. "Richet on Mental Suggestion." *Science,* Feb. 13, 1885.

———. "A Method for the Experimental Determination of the Horopter." *American Journal of Psychology*, Nov. 1887.

———. "An Unknown Organ of Sense." *Science,* Sept. 13, 1889.

———. "On Some Characteristics of Symbolic Logic." *American Journal of Psychology*, 1889.

———. "Some Proposed Reforms in Common Logic." *Mind*, Jan. 1890.

———. "The Usefulness of Fellowships." Publications of the Association of Collegiate Alumnae, Oct. 24, 1890.

———. "Eine Neue Theorie der Lichtempfindungen" ("A New Theory of Light Sensations"). *Zeitschrift für Psychologie und Physiologie de Sinesorgane.* Hamburg: 1892.

———. "A New Theory of Light Sensation." *Science,* July 14, 1893.

———. "Color Vision." *Science*, Aug. 9, 1893.

———. "Psychological Literature: The Perception of Light and Color." *Psychological Review*, Mar. 1894.

———. "Psychological Literature: Vision." *Psychological Review*, Mar. 1896.

———. "Color-Blindness and William Pole: A Study in Logic." *Science*, Feb. 19, 1897.

———. "The Reduction to Absurdity of the Ordinary Treatment of the Syllogism." *Science*, Apr. 12, 1901.

———. "Some Points in Minor Logic." *Journal of Philosophy, Psychology and Scientific Methods*, Jan. 7, 1904.

———. "Endowed Professorships for Women." Publications of the Association of Collegiate Alumnae, Feb. 1904.

———. "Minor Logic." *Journal of Philosophy, Psychology and Scientific Methods*, Sept. 1, 1904.

———. "Note on the House of Mirth." *Bookman*, Nov. 1906.

———. "Magazine Science." *Science*, May 1907.

———. *Epistemology for the Logician.* Heidelberg, 1908.

———. "Society Women." *Nation*, Oct. 29, 1908.

———. "On De Morgan's Extension of the Algebraic Processes." *American Journal of Mathematics*, 1910.

———. "Foundations of Philosophy: Explicit Primitives." *Journal of Philosophy, Psychology and Scientific Method*, Dec. 21, 1911.

———. "Explicit Primitives Again: A Reply to Professor Fite." *Journal of Philosophy, Psychology and Scientific Methods*, Oct. 10, 1912.

———. "Implication and Existence in Logic." *Philosophical Review*, Nov. 1912.

———. "The Antilogism—An Emendation." *Journal of Philosophy, Psychology and Scientific Methods,*

1913.

———. "Color Sensation Theory." *American Encyclopedia of Opthalmology* (18 vols). Chicago: Cleveland, 1913-1921.

———. "A Non-Chromatic Region in the Spectrum for Bees." *Science*, Dec. 12, 1913.

———. "On Color Theories and Chromatic Sensations." *Psychological Review*, May 1916.

———. "Color Theories and Chromatic Sensations." *Psychological Review*, May 1916.

———. "An Introduction to the Study of Colour Vision (review)." *Psychological Bulletin*, July 1916.

———. "Freudian Doctrines." *Nation*, Oct. 19, 1916.

———. "Charles S. Peirce at the Johns Hopkins University." *Journal of Philosophy, Psychology and Scientific Methods*, Dec. 21, 1916.

———. "The Logic Test." *Science*, Apr. 23, 1920.

———. "Practical Logic and Color Theories." *Psychological Review*, May 1922.

———. "Tetrachromatic Vision and the Development Theory of Color." *American Journal of Physiological Optics*, Sept. 1923.

———. "L'État Actuel du Probléme de la Nature des Sensations de Couleurs." *L'Année Psychologique*, 1924.

———. "On the Nature of Color Sensations." In Helmholtz, Hermann von, *Treatise on Physiological Optics*, Vol. 2, 455-468. Washington, DC: Optical Society of America, 1924-25.

———. "The Reddish Blue Arcs and the Reddish Blue Glow of the Retina: Seeing Your Own Nerve Currents through Bioluminescence." *Proceedings of the National Academy of Sciences*, June 1926.

———. "A Logic Poem." *Science*, Oct. 8, 1926.

———. "The Physicist and the Facts of Color." *Science*, Dec. 16, 1927.

———. "Visible Radiation from Excited Nerve Fiber Again." *Science*, Feb. 10, 1928.

———. "More Data." *Science*, Apr. 27, 1928.

———. *Colour and Colour Theories*. New York: Harcourt, Brace, 1929.

———. *La Non-Existence de l'existence: l'Idéaliste Pur et le Réaliste Hypothétique*. Paris: A. Cohn, 1931.

Ladd-Franklin, Christine, and Eugene Shen. "The Complete Scheme of Propositions." *Psyche* 9, no. 3, 1929.

Lantz, Emily Emerson. "A Love Song." *Baltimore Sun*, Apr. 1, 1903.

———. "Maryland Heraldry: Tiernan Lineage & Arms." *Baltimore Sun*, Jan. 1, 1905.

———. "Suburban Baltimore: Charles Street." *Baltimore Sun*, Oct. 1, 1905.

———. "A Southern Girl in '61." *Baltimore Sun*, Oct. 9, 1905.

———. "Suburban Baltimore: Ellicott City." *Baltimore Sun*, Oct. 22, 1905.

———. "Suburban Baltimore: Roland Park." *Baltimore Sun*, Nov. 5, 1905.

———. "Suburban Baltimore: West Arlington." *Baltimore Sun*, Nov. 12, 1905.

———. "Suburban Baltimore: Mt. Washington." *Baltimore Sun*, Nov. 19, 1905.

———. "Suburban Baltimore: Catonsville." *Baltimore Sun*, Nov. 26, 1905.

———. "Artist of Talent: Miss Marie Keller." *Baltimore Sun*, Dec. 10, 1905.

———. "Demand the Right to Vote." Jan. 7, 1906.

———. "John Street and Its Celebrities." *Baltimore Sun*, Apr. 8, 1906.

———. "The 'Registered Nurse.'" *Baltimore Sun*, June 24, 1906.

———. "Maryland Heraldry: The Dorseys of Maryland, Descendants of Hon. John Dorsey, Col. Edward Dorset and Joshua Dorsey." *Baltimore Sun*, Jan. 19, 1908.

———. "History of the Steamboat on the Chesapeake Bay: The Story of the Old Lines, Famous Ships, and Celebrated Commanders." *Baltimore Sun*, June 7, 1908.

———. "Eden's Love-Nest, Man's Initial Home, Hence All Mankind Loves a Garden." *Baltimore Sun*, June 12, 1912.

———. "Maryland Holiday in the Olden Time." *Baltimore Sun*, Dec. 6, 1914.

———. "Books of the Day." *Baltimore Sun*, Nov. 22, 1915.

———. "Finding Five-Cent Christmas Opportunities." *Baltimore Sun*, Dec. 5, 1915.

———. "Baltimore's Effort for Healthier Babies through Bureau of Child Hygiene." *Baltimore Sun*, July 12, 1919.

———. "The Prospective Removal of the Academy to a New Home near Roland Park." *Baltimore Sun*, Aug. 3, 1919.

———. "The Long, Long Trail Becomes A Short Cut of Fascinating Byways into the Land of One Adventurous Lady's Dreams." *Baltimore Sun*, Sept. 7, 1919.

———. "Where the Blue of the Visiting Nurse is Seen, Comfort is Being Carried to the Sick and the Helpless." *Baltimore Sun*, Nov. 9, 1919.

———. "Her Centenary Sees Susan B. Anthony's Cause near to Success." *Baltimore Sun*, Feb. 15, 1920.

———. "Mrs. Thomas B. Gresham's Valuable Collection of Confederate War Relics." *Baltimore Sun*, Mar. 7, 1920.

———. "Compared Cost of Home and Restaurant Lunches for Feminine Workers." *Baltimore Sun*, Mar. 14, 1920.

———. "Baltimore High School Girls Solving

Problem of Correct Daily Dress." *Baltimore Sun*, Apr. 4, 1920.

———. "Woman's Literary Club Thirty Years Old This Week, Will Give Lunch." *Baltimore Sun*, Apr. 4, 1920.

———. "The Brief Summer of His Rose." *Baltimore Sun*, Apr. 7, 1920.

———. "Banner Enrollment of Maryland Institute." *Baltimore Sun*, Apr. 11, 1920.

———. "Forgotten Graveyard on North Ave." *Baltimore Sun*, Apr. 18, 1920.

———. "Eight Baltimore Girls New Fraternity Members." *Baltimore Sun*, Apr. 25, 1920.

———. "Baltimore Woman Saves Lives of War Orphans at a Chalet in Swiss Alps." *Baltimore Sun*, May 9, 1920.

———. "This Month Will See the Canonization of Jeanne D'Arc by Pope." *Baltimore Sun*, May 16, 1920.

———. "People's Theatre on Municipal Pier Opens with American Comedy." *Baltimore Sun*, May 30, 1920.

———. "Western High School Girls Make Every Year Thousands of Garments." *Baltimore Sun*, June 13, 1920.

———. "Better Homemakers Is Idea of Bill Extending Work of Public Schools." *Baltimore Sun*, July 5, 1920.

———. "Art Center in Business Section of Baltimore." *Baltimore Sun*, Sept. 5, 1920.

———. "Florence Nightingale,—'Lady with the Lamp'—Honored in Baltimore." *Baltimore Sun*, Sept. 5, 1920.

———. "Jennie Lind's Centenary Recall." *Baltimore Sun*, Sept. 19, 1920.

———. "Good Samaritan Seal and Women Who Embodied Its Ministering Spirit." *Baltimore Sun*, Oct. 3, 1920.

———. "Mother of Women's Clubs in Maryland Finds Rest after an Eventful Life." *Baltimore Sun*, Oct. 24, 1920.

———. "Baltimore's Home of the Friendless Really Is Very Friendly Place." *Baltimore Sun*, Nov. 1, 1920.

———. "Neighborhood House at Curtis Bay Is Factor in American Citizenship." *Baltimore Sun*, Nov. 7, 1920.

———. "Head of Women's Clubs Urges Uniform Divorce Laws as Protective Act." *Baltimore Sun*, May 8, 1921.

———. "Maryland Poet Who Is Little Known in Her Own State Is Lucy Mitchell." *Baltimore Sun*, June 19, 1921.

———. "What We Should Eat in Hot Weather Is Problem." *Baltimore Sun*, July 17, 1921.

———. "Woman Artist Believes That She Is In-spired to Paint Strange Pictures." *Baltimore Sun*, Sept. 25, 1921.

———. "Red-Haired Woman Tells the Story of Her Origin in Her Tresses and Eyes." *Baltimore Sun*, Nov. 5, 1921.

———. "Writers of Baltimore Say Thrills Attended Their Literary Debuts." *Baltimore Sun*, Dec. 18, 1921.

———. "Writers of Baltimore Describe Thrills of Literary Debuts." *Baltimore Sun*, Jan. 15, 1922.

———. "Do You Know the Street On Which You Live?: Calvert Street." *Baltimore Sun*, Nov. 25, 1923.

———. "Heard and Seen in Passing Christmas Crowds." *Baltimore Sun*, Dec. 23, 1923.

———. "Do You Know the Street On Which You Live?: Greenmount-York." *Baltimore Sun*, Apr. 27, 1924.

———. "Her Mother Saw Monument Built." *Baltimore Sun*, Apr. 12, 1925.

———. "Women Ready for Great Council in Capital." *Baltimore Sun*, Apr. 19, 1925.

———. "Murals Adorning Baltimore Court House." *Art and Archeology*, May 1925.

———. "Energy Outstanding Trait of Allegany County." *Baltimore Sun*, Oct. 24, 1926.

———. "Flag House Dedication Tomorrow." *Baltimore Sun*, Nov. 11, 1928.

———. *The Spirit of Maryland: Revealed in Her Twenty-Three Counties from Provincial Days to 1929.* Waverly Press, 1929.

———. "Woman's City Club Active Here." *Baltimore Sun*, June 2, 1929.

Latimer, Elizabeth Wormeley. *Amabel: A Family History.* New York: G.P. Putnam, 1853.

———. *Our Cousin Veronica, or, Scenes and Adventures Over the Blue Ridge.* New York: Bunce, 1855.

———. *Birthday Book.* Baltimore: n.p., 1860.

———. "A Southern Lady of Shalott." *Harper's Monthly*, Sept. 1876.

———. "Punished Enough." *Harper's Monthly*, Feb. 1878.

———. "Old Soup." *St. Nicholas,* May 1878.

———. "An English Bride in Roumania." *Harper's Monthly*, Sept. 1878.

———. *Salvage.* Boston: Roberts Bros., 1880.

———. "St. George and the Dragon." *St. Nicholas,* Apr. 1880.

———. *My Wife and My Wife's Sister.* Boston: Roberts Bros., 1881.

———. *The Princess Amélie: A Fragment of Autobiography.* Boston: Roberts Bros., 1883.

———. *Familiar Talks on Some of Shakespeare's Comedies.* Boston: Roberts Bros, 1886.

———. "The Legend of Saint Nicholas." *Harper's Monthly*, Dec. 1886.

———. "St. Patrick." *Harper's Weekly*, Mar. 17, 1888.

———. "Benvenuto Cellini." *Harper's Monthly*, Feb. 1890.

———. "Saint Anthony." *Harper's Monthly*, Jan. 1891.

———. *France in the Nineteenth Century*. Chicago: A.C. McClurg and Co., 1893.

———. "Archbishop Darboy, the Martyr of La Roquette." *Catholic World*, Mar. 1893.

———. "Polyeuct and Pauline." *Harper's Monthly*, Aug. 1893.

———. "Girl's Recollection of Dickens." *Critic*, Sept. 9, 1893.

———. *England in the Nineteenth Century*. Chicago: A.C. McClurg and Co., 1894.

———. *Russia and Turkey in the Nineteenth Century*. Chicago: A.C. McClurg, 1894.

———. *Europe in Africa in the Nineteenth Century*. Chicago: A.C. McClurg, 1895.

———. "British Power in Africa: Europe in Africa." *Current Literature*, Mar. 1896.

———. *Italy in the Nineteenth Century, and the Making of Austro-Hungary and Germany*. Chicago: A.C. McClurg, 1896.

———. *Spain in the Nineteenth Century*. Chicago: A.C. McClurg & Co., 1897.

———. "In Ohio a Hundred Years Ago." *Lippincott's*, Aug. 1898.

———. *Judea from Cyrus to Titus: 537 B.C.-70 A.D.* Chicago: A.C. McClurg and Co., 1899.

———. *The Last Years of the Nineteenth Century: A Continuation of "France in the Nineteenth Century," "Russia and Turkey in the Nineteenth Century," and "Spain in the Nineteenth Century."* Chicago: A.C. McClurg & Co, 1900.

———. *The Prince Incognito*. Chicago: A.C. McClurg & Co., 1902.

———. "Inner Life of Fra Ugo Bassi." *Chautaquan*, Jan. 1902.

———. *My Wife's Hidden Life*. Chicago: Rand, McNally, 1913.

Latimer, Elizabeth Wormeley, and Baron Gaspard Gourgaud. *Talks of Napoleon at St. Helena with General Baron Gourgaud, Together with the Journal Kept by Gourgaud on Their Journey from Waterloo to St. Helena*. Chicago: A.C. McClurg, 1903.

Latimer, Elizabeth Wormeley, ed. *My Scrap-Book of the French Revolution*. Chicago: A.C. McClurg and Company, 1898.

Latimer Elizabeth Wormeley (translator). *Nanon*, by George Sand. Boston, Roberts Brothers, 1890.

———. *The Love Letters of Victor Hugo 1820-1822*. New York: Harper, 1901.

———. *History of the People of Israel*, by Ernest Renan. Boston: Roberts Brothers, 1895.

Litchfield, Grace Denio. "The Lost Rose." *Post*, Jan. 21, 1881.

———. "The Milky Way." *Lippincott's*, Sept. 1882.

———. "To a Hurt Child." *Atlantic Monthly*, Mar. 1883.

———. "One Chapter." *Century*, Dec. 1883.

———. *Only an Incident*. New York: G.P. Putnam's Sons, 1883.

———. "Good-Bye." *Century*, Jan. 1884.

———. "The Price I Paid for a Set of Ruskin." *Century*, Oct. 1884.

———. "My Lost Baby." *Youth's Companion*, Nov. 6, 1884.

———. "An American Flirtation." *Atlantic*, Dec. 1884.

———. "A Mystery." *Independent*, Apr. 16, 1885.

———. "Hilary's Husband." *Century*, June 1885.

———. "Only One Killed." *Independent*, June 18, 1885.

———. "The Song of the Cricket." *Independent*, July 9, 1885.

———. "Sweet Mother of My Dreams." *Independent*, Aug. 27, 1885.

———. *Criss-Cross*. New York: G.P. Putnam's Sons, 1885.

———. *In the Hospital*. New York: G.P. Putnam's Sons, 1885.

———. *The Knight of the Black Forest*. New York: G.P. Putnam's Sons, 1885.

———. "The Snow-Storm." *St. Nicholas*, Dec. 1885.

———. "Little Delia's Shoes." *Independent*, Dec. 24, 1885.

———. "Love, Now." *Independent*, Jan. 7, 1886.

———. "The Stray Angel." *Independent*, Jan. 28, 1886.

———. "The Storm-King." *Independent*, Mar. 11, 1886.

———. "Almost." *Independent*, Apr. 8, 1886.

———. "The Top of the Ladder." *Wide Awake*, May 1886.

———. "Day Dreams." *Independent*, May 20, 1886.

———. "Daisy-Song." *St. Nicholas*, July 1886.

———. "La Rochefoucauld's Saying." *Independent*, Aug. 12, 1886.

———. "Poor Papa!" *Century*, Oct. 1886.

———. "Tick, Tack." *Independent*, Dec. 12, 1886.

———. "Death of the Old Year." *Independent*, Dec. 30, 1886.

———. "Sympathy." *Independent*, Jan. 27, 1887.

———. "The Beggar." *Independent*, Feb. 2, 1887.

———. "The Earthquake at Menton." n.p., Feb. 27, 1887. Clipping in Grace Denio Litchfield Papers, Box 1, Johns Hopkins University Special Collections.

———. "Only a Match." *Independent*, Apr. 14, 1887.

———. "In the Line of the Earthquake." *Wide Awake*, June 1887.

———. "Song of the Mosquito." *St. Nicholas*, June 1887.

———. "To a Rosebud." *Acorn*, June 1887.

———. "Tweedledee and Tweedledum." *Independent*, July 14, 1887.

———. "An Enigma." *Independent*, July 28, 1887.

———. "How It Really Was." *Independent*, Aug. 18, 1887.

———. "The Grace of Love." *Independent*, Sept. 22, 1887.

———. "My Sun-Lover." *Acorn*, Nov. 1, 1887.

———. "My Other Me." *St. Nicholas*, Nov. 1887; also published in *The American Anthology*, ed. Edmund Clarence Stedman. Boston: Houghton Mifflin, 1900.

———. "Time's Warehouse." *Independent*, Dec. 15, 1887.

———. "Listening." *Independent*, Feb. 2, 1888.

———. "Master Shadow." *Wide Awake*, Apr. 1888.

———. "Wardrobe Talk." *Independent*, Apr. 19, 1888.

———. "Selina's Singular Marriage." *Century*, June 1888.

———. *A Hard-Won Victory*. New York: G.P. Putnam's Sons, 1888.

———. "A Desecrated Memory." *Independent*, June 13, 1889.

———. "Hidden Brook." *Century*, July 1899.

———. "Bin." *Wide Awake*, Aug. 1889.

———. "What the Roses Said." *Independent*, Nov. 7, 1889.

———. "Flowertime Weather." *Independent*, Mar. 20, 1890.

———. "Pain." *Independent*, May 1, 1890.

———. "Swinging." *St. Nicholas*, June 1890.

———. "The Fairy Needle." *Far and Near*, Dec. 1890.

———. *Little He and She*. Boston: D. Lothrop, 1890.

———. *Little Venice, and Other Stories*. New York: G.P. Putnam's Sons, 1890.

———. "Love's Young Dream." *Century*, May 1891.

———. "The Song of the Goldenrod." *St. Nicholas*, Sept. 1891.

———. "An Afternoon's Drama." *Independent*, Nov. 3, 1892.

———. "To the Cicada Septendecim." *Century*, June 1893.

———. "The Poet-Heart." *Century*, June 1893.

———. "The Sunlight." *Century*, June 1893.

———. "In Life's Tunnel." *Century*, Sept. 1893.

———. *Mimosa Leaves*. New York: G.P. Putnam's Sons, 1895.

———. "Courage." *Dial*, Feb. 16, 1896.

———. "Ennui." *Century*, Jan. 1897.

———. *In the Crucible*. New York: G.P. Putnam's Sons, 1897.

———. "In the Forum of Justice." *Century*, May 1900.

———. *The Moving Finger Writes*. New York: G.P. Putnam's Sons, 1900.

———. "My Letter." *The American Anthology*, ed. Edmund Clarence Stedman. Boston: Houghton Mifflin, 1900.

———. "Setting Sun." *Bookman*, Jan. 1901.

———. "Song." *Century*, May 1901.

———. "Bend of the Road." *Century*, Feb. 1902.

———. "One Result." *Outlook*, Jan. 3, 1903.

———. "Women as Advocates." *Independent*, July 9, 1903.

———. "Tangle-Town." *Bookman*, Aug. 1903.

———. *The Letter D*. New York: Dodd, Mead and Co., 1904.

———. *Vita, a Drama*. Boston: R. Badger, 1904.

———. "Song of the Sunrise." *Independent*, Feb. 23, 1905.

———. "The Closed Door." *Independent*, Oct. 24, 1907.

———. "Birthday Song." *Century*, Dec. 1907.

———. *Narcissus, and Other Poems*. New York, London: Putnam, 1908.

———. *The Supreme Gift*. Boston: Little, Brown, and Co., 1908.

———. "Icarus." *Century*, July 1910.

———. *Baldur, the Beautiful*. New York: G. P. Putnam's, 1910.

———. "Frigga's Dirge: From Baldur the Beautiful." *North American Review*, Oct. 1910.

———. *The Nun of Kent; a Drama in Five Acts*. New York, London: G.P. Putnam's Sons, 1911.

———. "Semele." *Century*, Jan. 1913.

———. "Where Am I While I Sleep?" *Century*, Mar. 1913.

———. "Sleep." *North American Review*, Apr. 1913.

———. "A Last Message." *Century*, May 1913.

———. *The Burning Question*. New York, London: G.P. Putnam's Sons, 1913.

———. *Collected Poems*. New York, London: G.P. Putnam's Sons, 1913.

———. "The Hermit Thrush." *North American Review*, Nov. 1915.

———. "To a Thistledown." *Art World*, Mar. 1917.

———. *The Song of the Sirens*. New York, London: G.P. Putnam's Sons, 1917.

———. "The Little Brown Bungalow." *Art World*, Jan. 1918.

———. *As a Man Sows, and Other Stories*. New York: Putnam, 1926.

Lord, Alice Emma Sauerwein. *A Symphony in Dreamland*. New York: G.P. Putnam's Sons, 1882.

————. *The Days of Lamb and Coleridge: A Historical Romance.* New York: Henry Holt, 1893.

————. *A Vision's Quest: A Drama in Five Acts.* Baltimore: Cushing, 1899.

————. *Moods and Tenses.* Richmond: William Byrd Press, 1929.

Malloy, Louise. *The Patapsco: A Comic Opera in Two Acts.* Music composed by Elliott Woods. Baltimore: Baltimore American Job Printing Office, 1894.

————. *The Prince's Wooing.* G. P. Putnam's, 1894.

————. "At 11:59 P.M." and "He was Slow." *Baltimore American,* May 10, 1903: 4.

————. "A Change" and "Lucky Dogs." *Baltimore American,* May 12, 1903: 6.

————. "Good Example" and "Half Truths." *Baltimore American,* May 14, 1903: 6.

————. "Heard at the Horse Show." *Baltimore American,* May 15, 1903: 6.

————. "A Hero," "Unbreakable," and "A New Version." *Baltimore American,* July 9, 1903: 8.

————. *The Player Maid.* 1905. Typescript, Louise Malloy Papers, University of Maryland Special Collections.

————. "A Sea Tale." *Baltimore American,* Sept. 18, 1905: 6.

————. "With Apologies to Poe (E. A.)." *Baltimore American,* Sept. 20, 1905: 8.

————. "A Fruitful Quarrel." *Baltimore American,* Sept. 21, 1905.

————. "At the Wedding." *Baltimore American,* Sept. 23, 1905: 10.

————. "The First One." *Baltimore American,* Oct. 9, 1905: 6.

————. "In the Swim." *Baltimore American,* Oct. 22, 1905: 4.

————. "Traveling in Russia." *Baltimore American,* Oct. 26, 1905: 8.

————. "Her Choice." *Baltimore American,* Nov. 2, 1905): 8.

————. "The Victim." *Baltimore American,* Jan. 5, 1906: 24.

————. "The Modern Writer." *Baltimore American,* Jan. 9, 1906: 8.

————. "The Youthful Diplomat." *Baltimore American,* June 9, 1906: 8.

————. "The Real Expert." *Baltimore American,* March 9, 1907: 8.

————. "The Place for Her." April 19, 1907: 8.

————. "Her Style." *Baltimore American,* Nov. 20, 1907: 6.

————. "The Smile Feminine." *Baltimore American,* June 24, 1908: 6.

————. "Diplomacy." *Baltimore American,* May 10, 1909: 8.

————. "House Cleaning Time." *Baltimore American,* May 20, 1909: 8.

————. "Her Soliloquy." *Baltimore American,* Feb. 10, 1910: 8.

————. "Ideals. Danger." *Baltimore American,* Oct. 4, 1910: 8.

————. "Her Merits." *Baltimore American,* Nov. 18, 1910: 8.

————. "The Woman Question." *Baltimore American,* Feb. 27, 1911: 8.

————. "A Monosyllabic Tragedy." *Baltimore American,* Aug. 8, 1911: 4.

————. "The Picket's Cry." *Baltimore American,* Aug. 20, 1917: 4.

————. *Our Country: Pageant for School Children.* c. 1920s-1930s. Typescript, Louise Malloy Papers, University of Maryland Special Collections.

————. *The Life Story of Mother Seton.* Baltimore: Carroll, 1924.

————. *The Boy Lincoln.* 1940. Typescript, Louise Malloy Papers, University of Maryland Special Collections.

————. "A Forgotten Love Story: An Episode in the Life of Charles, 5th Lord Baltimore." *Maryland Historical Magazine,* Spring 1996.

Mullin, Elizabeth Lester. "Mistress Brent's Bluff." *Baltimore Sun,* Nov. 7, 1915.

Mullin, Elizabeth Lester (translator). "The Codicil: A Comedy in One Act," by Paul Ferrier. *Poet Lore,* 1908.

————. "Missa Solemnis—A Christmas Story (by Adolphe Ribaux)." *Modern Culture,* Feb. 1901.

Redgrave, Corinne Robert. "What Every Amateur Actress Ought to Know." *Ladies' Home Journal,* Oct. 1913.

Reese, Elizabeth Meredith. "A Tulip Story." *Independent,* May 9, 1895.

————. "A Crocus Story." *Johnson's Third Reader.* Richmond: B. F. Johnson, 1899.

Reese, Lizette Woodworth. "The Deserted House." *Southern Magazine,* June 1874.

———— . *A Branch of May.* Baltimore: Cushings & Bailey, 1887.

————. "Tell Me Some Way." *Scribner's,* Dec. 1888.

————. "Daffodils." *Century,* Apr. 1890.

————. "Hallowmas." *Dial,* Feb. 1892; also published in *Gardens, Houses, and People,* Nov. 1934.

————. *A Handful of Lavender.* New York: Houghton Mifflin Company, 1891.

————. "After the Rain." *Poet Lore,* Dec. 1891.

————. "An Old Belle." *Century,* Jan. 1892.

————. "Her Last Word." *Scribner's,* Sept. 1892.

————. "An English Missal." *Atlantic Monthly,* Nov. 1892.

————. "A Song for Candlemas." *Spectator,* Dec. 3, 1892.

————. "Consolation." *Century,* Apr. 1893.

———. "When Polly Takes the Air." *Century*, Sept. 1893.

———. "The Jonquil and the Rose." *Ladies' Home Journal*, May 1896.

———. "Compensation." *Bookman*, Nov. 1896.

———. "Mystery ('Elude Me Still')." *Atlantic Monthly*, Nov. 1896.

———. "Writ in a Book of Celtic Verse." *Bookman*, Nov. 1896.

———. "Trust." *Outlook*, Nov. 28, 1896; also published in *Bookman*, Dec. 1896; *The Critic*, June 12, 1897; *Grit Story Section*, Nov. 15, 1936.

———. "Lavender Woman." *The Nation*, Dec. 10, 1896; also published in the *Living Age*, July 3, 1897.

———. "Love Came Back at Fall of Dew." *Bookman*, Dec. 1896; also published in *Poet Lore*, Jan. 1897.

———. *A Quiet Road*. New York: Houghton Mifflin Company, 1896.

———. "To a Town Poet." *Poet Lore*, Jan. 1897; also published in the *Living Age*, May 29, 1897.

———. "The House of Silent Years." *Atlantic Monthly*, Jan. 1897.

———. "Adam." *Outlook*, Jan. 30, 1897.

———. "Memory." *Dial*, Feb. 1, 1897.

———. "A Valentine." *Scribner's*, Feb. 1897.

———. "On a Colonial Picture." *Living Age*, Apr. 10, 1897.

———. "An English Lad." *Overland Monthly*, Aug. 1897.

———. "A Stay-At-Home Enemy." *Harper's Bazaar*, Nov. 20, 1897.

———. "Darkness in the Nursery." *Independent*, c. 1897; reprinted in the *Saturday Evening Post*, Jan. 29, 1898.

———. "Old Mis' Rich." *Outlook*, Feb. 5, 1898.

———. "Poetry as Factor in Education." *Independent*, Aug. 4, 1898.

———. "The Cry of Rachel." *Lippincott's*, July 1899.

———. "Tears." *Scribner's*, Nov. 1899; also published in *Current Literature*, June 1900; *Canada Magazine*, Nov. 1910; *Literary Digest*, Jan. 10, 1914; and *Onward*, Apr. 11, 1926.

———. "Taps." *Atlantic Monthly*, Dec. 1899.

———. "Timrod." *Atlantic Monthly*, Jan. 1900.

———. "To Art." *Scribner's*, June 1900.

———. "To Song." *Atlantic Monthly*, June 1900.

———. "Wild Geese." *Lippincott's*, Sept. 1900.

———. "The Fold." *Congregationalist*, Apr. 13, 1901.

———. "Cherry Boughs." *Lippincott's*, June 1901.

———. "Herbs." *Atlantic Monthly*, Mar. 1902.

———. "The Lost Teacher." *Dial*, Apr. 16, 1902.

———. "Thistletown." *St. Nicholas*, Aug. 1902.

———. "Lydia." *Harper's Monthly*, May 1903.

———. "Cornelia's Birthday." *Harper's Monthly*, June 1903.

———. "The Young Mother." *Smart Set*, June 1903.

———. "A Christmas Folksong." *Lippincott's*, Dec. 1903; also published in the *Woman Citizen*, Dec. 1926, and reprinted in many newspapers throughout the first few decades of the twentieth century.

———. "The Last Lover." *Smart Set*, Feb. 1904.

———. "Lavender." *Lippincott's*, May 1904.

———. "The Cry of the Old House." *Atlantic Monthly*, June 1904.

———. "The Lark." *Lippincott's*, Sept. 1904.

———. "Dust." *Lippincott's*. Dec. 1904.

———. "Henrietty." *Lippincott's*, Nov. 1905.

———. "A Song ('Scented Apples in the Bin')." *Smart Set*, Feb. 1906.

———. "An April Ghost." *Smart Set*, Apr. 1906.

———. "Daffodils." *Century*, June 1906.

———. "The Mystery ('As up and down the World I Go')." *Smart Set*, Feb. 1907.

———. "Wise." *Harper's Monthly*, Mar. 1910.

———. "Westminster Churchyard." In Wrenshall, Letitia Humphreys Yonge and the Edgar Allan Poe Memorial Association, *Edgar Allan Poe: A Centenary Tribute*. Baltimore: 1910.

———. "Songs of Our Village." *Delineator*, Oct. 1910.

———. "Virgin." *Delineator*, Feb. 1911.

———. "The Old Patch." *Current Literature*, Mar. 1911.

———. "The Dropping Bloom." *Harper's Monthly*, May 1911.

———. "Home from the Fields." *Delineator*, Sept. 1911.

———. "Sunday Afternoon." *Harper's Weekly*, Mar. 30, 1912.

———. "My Mother's Candle." *Harper's Weekly*, Apr. 12, 1912.

———. "Upper Chamber." *Century*, May 1912.

———. "Threnody." *Harper's Weekly*, May 18, 1912.

———. "Old Lavender." *Harper's Weekly*, Aug. 17, 1912.

———. "Week's End." *Harper's Weekly*, Aug. 31, 1912.

———. "Seventy Times Seven." *Lippincott's*, Sept. 1912.

———. "Prophet's Chamber." *Harper's Weekly*, Oct. 26, 1912.

———. "A Wet Spell." *Smart Set*, Nov. 1912.

———. "A Picture." *Smart Set*, Dec. 1912.

———. "Three Kings." *Harper's Monthly*, Dec. 14, 1912.

———. "A Song ('Love along My Garden Went')." *Smart Set*, Mar. 1913.

———. "The Common Lot." *Harper's Monthly*, May 1913.

———. "Sunset." *Designer*, May 1913.

———. "Drought." *Smart Set*, June 1913.

———. "The Gentle Pensioner." *Delineator*, Apr. 1914.

———. "Fog." *Harper's Monthly*, May 1914.

———. "When the Cows Come Home." *Delineator*, Oct. 1914.

———. "All Saints' Day." *Delineator*, Nov. 1914.

———. "The Dropping Leaf." *Smart Set*, Nov. 1914.

———. "Old Houses." *Forum*, Dec. 1914.

———. "Tankle-Tinkle Tank" and "Haworth Parsonage." *Forum*, Jan. 1915.

———. "Monday." *Smart Set*, Feb. 1915.

———. "Burning the Leaves." *Smart Set*, Mar. 1915.

———. "The Secret." *Smart Set*, Feb. 1916.

———. "The Rector." *Smart Set*, June 1916.

———. *A Wayside Lute*. Portland, ME: Thomas B. Mosher, 1916.

———. "All Hallows." *Smart Set*, Nov. 1916.

———. "Arraignment." *Literary Digest,* Mar. 24, 1917; also published in *Current Opinion,* Apr. 1917.

———. "The Ghostly Bugles." *McClure's* Magazine, July 1917; also published in *Current Opinion,* Aug. 1917.

———. "Chloe to Amaryllis." *Bookman,* Dec. 1917.

———. "To Myself." *Bookman*, Feb. 1918.

———. "Little Shoe." *Scribner's*, Apr. 1919.

———. "I Weep for Him." *Ainslee's Magazine*, Mar. 1920.

———. "If." *Ainslee's Magazine*, July 1920.

———. "A Carol." *Maryland Women's News*, Dec. 18, 1920.

———. *Spicewood*. Baltimore: Norman Remington Company, 1920.

———. "The Shot Tower." *Baltimore News-American*, Feb. 15, 1921.

———. "A Girl's Mood." *Smart Set*, May 1921; also published in *Current Opinion*, Aug. 1921.

———. "The Rose." *Lyric*, June 1921.

———. "Young Beauty." *Current Opinion*, July 1922.

———. "White Flags." *Bookman*, Aug. 1922.

———. "Brambles and Dusk." *Bookman*, Aug. 1922.

———. "To Love." *Ainslee's* Magazine, Aug. 1922.

———. "Loneliness." *Bookman*, Aug. 1922.

———. "Red Stars of the Night." *Smart Set*, Sept. 1922.

———. "The Cry." *Smart Set*, Dec. 1922.

———. "Wages." *Smart Set*, Feb. 1923.

———. "Puritan Lady." *Literary Digest*, Mar. 31, 1923; also published in *Bookman*, May 1923.

———. "Foggy Afternoon." *Current Opinion*, May 1923.

———. "Portrait." *Bookman*, May 1923; *Current Opinion*, May 1923; published again in *Bookman*, Dec. 1929.

———. "Sanctuary." *Harper's Monthly*, July 1923.

———. "Lonely." *Harper's Monthly*, Aug. 1923; also published in *Current Opinion*, Oct. 1923.

———. "Kiss." *Nation*, Aug. 9, 1923.

———. *Wild Cherry*. Baltimore: Norman, Remington Company, 1923.

———. "Fortune." *Ainslee's Magazine*, Jan. 1924.

———. "Loveliness." *Harper's Monthly*, Feb. 1924; also published in *Current Opinion*, Apr. 1924.

———. "Last Testament" and "Were I To Love You Less." *Bookman*, June 1924.

———. "To Life." *Harper's Monthly*, July 1924.

———. "Forgiveness." *Outlook*, July 16, 1924.

———. "Sanctuary." *Harper's Monthly*, Sept. 1924.

———. "Chapters from an Unwritten Autobiography." *Bookman*, Sept. 1924.

———. "Two Houses." *Lyric*, Oct. 1924.

———. "Dreams." *Harper's Monthly*, Jan. 1925; also published in *Scholastic*, Nov. 16, 1935.

———. "Old Saul." *Harper's Monthly*, Apr. 1925.

———. "After Disaster." *Saturday Review of Literature*, Apr. 18, 1925.

———. "Tragic Books." *Harper's Monthly*, June 1925.

———. "Wet Grass." *Bookman*, Aug. 1925.

———. "All Hallows' Night." *Lyric*, Nov. 1925.

———. "When Martin Plays Upon the Flute." *Bookman*, Dec. 1925.

———. "Gold." *Saturday Review of Literature*, Mar. 27, 1926.

———. "Gildy." *Southwest Review*, Apr. 1926.

———. "The Second Wife." *Harper's Monthly*, Apr. 1926; also published in *Literary Digest*, May 29, 1926.

———. "Nocturne." n.s., 1926 (FictionMags Index). Reprinted in *Fantasy and Terror* 5 (1985).

———. "Ownership" and "Sheparding." *New Republic*, Dec. 29, 1926; "Ownership" also published in *Saturday Review of Literature*, Nov. 1, 1930.

———. "Your First Love." *New Republic*, Mar. 30, 1927; also published in *Literary Digest*, May 7, 1927.

———. "Thrift." *Harper's Monthly,* Apr. 1927.

———. "Wind at Doorways." *Independent* (Dearborn, MI), Apr. 30, 1927.

———. "Windy Night." *Saturday Review of Literature,* May 14, 1927.

———. "Scent." *New Republic*, June 1, 1927.

———. "Heat." *Independent* (Dearborn, MI), July 9, 1927.

———. "Apples Dropping." *Independent* (Dearborn, MI), Sept. 24, 1927.

———. "Crows." *Saturday Review of Literature*, Oct. 1927.

———. *Little Henrietta*. New York: George H. Doran Company, 1927.

———. *The Selected Poems*. New York: Longmans, Green, 1927.

———. *A Victorian Village: Reminiscences of Other Days*. New York: Farrar & Rinehart, 1927.

———. "Widow." *New Republic*, Apr. 25, 1928.

———. "Surety." *New Republic*, May 9, 1928.

———. "Women." *New Republic*, May 23, 1928.

———. *The Pamphlet Poets*. New York: Simon & Schuster, 1928.

———. "Bound." *New Republic*, July 18, 1928; also published in *Literary Digest*, Aug. 11, 1928.

———. "Bitters." *Harper's Monthly*, Sept. 1928.

———. "Babylon." *Saturday Review of Literature*, Aug. 31, 1929.

———. "For Anice." *Saturday Review of Literature*, May 24, 1930.

———. "Scarcity." *Saturday Review of Literature*, June 28, 1930.

———. "Persimmons." *New Republic*, July 2, 1930.

———. "Brier Goes in Scarlet." *New Republic*, July 23, 1930.

———. *White April and Other Poems*. New York: Farrar & Rinehart, 1930.

———. "Permanence." *Gardens, Houses, and People*, Dec. 1930.

———. "Hill Pasture." *Ladies' Home Journal*, June 1931.

———. "Thorn." *Lyric*, Autumn 1931.

———. "White Birches in Autumn." *Virginia Quarterly Review*, Oct. 1931.

———. "For a Waverly Garden." *Saturday Review of Literature*, Oct. 17, 1931.

———. "The Widower." *Virginia Quarterly Review*, Autumn 1931; also published in *Literary Digest*, July 12, 1933.

———. "Driving Home the Crows." *New Republic*, Oct. 21, 1931; also published in *Literary Digest*, Oct. 31, 1931.

———. *The York Road*. New York: Farrar & Rinehart, 1931.

———. "Impermanence," "A County Doctor," and "Order." *Virginia Quarterly Review*, Apr. 1932.

———. "Quest." *New Republic*, Apr. 20, 1932.

———. "Pastures." *Poetry*, May 1932.

———. "To a Renegade." *New Republic*, Aug. 10, 1932.

———. "Wild Asters." *Virginia Quarterly Review*, Oct. 1932.

———. "Winter Roads." *New Republic*, Jan. 25, 1933.

———. "Prayer." *Ladies' Home Journal*, Feb. 1933.

———. "Yellow Violets." *Carillon*, Spring 1933.

———. "Books." *Library Journal*, June 15, 1933.

———. *Pastures and Other Poems*. New York: Farrar & Rinehart, 1933.

———. "Thrushes in Spring." *Lyric*, Spring 1934.

———. "The Ancient Looking-Glass." *Gardens, Houses, and People*, May 1934.

———. "Soldiers' Epitaph." *Nation*, June 13, 1934; also published in *Literary Digest*, July 7, 1934.

———. "To a Thrush at Twilight." *Nation*, June 13, 1934.

———. "Ghosts." *Nation*, June 27, 1934.

———. "St. John's Night (Midsummer)." *Gardens, Houses, and People*, Aug. 1934.

———. "Indian Summer" and "Two Countries." *Virginia Quarterly Review*, Oct. 1934.

———. "Small Things." *Virginia Quarterly Review*, Apr. 1935; also published in *Literary Digest*, Apr. 20, 1935.

———. "Ancestry." *Virginia Quarterly Review*, Summer 1935; reprinted in *Fiction Parade and Golden Book Magazine*, Sept. 1935.

———. "Crying," "Table Setting," "A Thorn Tree in Spring," and "The Widower." *Fiction Parade and Golden Book Magazine*, June 1935.

———. "Wind" and "Lover to Lover." *Scholastic*, Nov. 16, 1935.

———. "A Christmas Song." *Gardens, Houses, and People*, Dec. 1935.

———. "To an Indecent Novelist." *Gardens, Houses, and People*, Jan. 1936.

———. "Heretics." *Harper's Monthly*, Jan. 1936; also published in *Literary Digest*, Mar. 7, 1936.

———. "Wild Pear Trees." *Fiction Parade and Golden Book Magazine*, May 1936.

———. "Credo." *Fiction Parade and Golden Book Magazine*, Aug. 1936.

———. *The Worleys*. New York: Farrar & Rinehart, 1936.

———. *The Old House in the Country*. New York: Farrar & Rinehart, 1936.

———. "At Their Door." *Lyric* (n.d.; reprinted in *Fiction Parade and Golden Book Magazine*, Feb. 1937).

———. "March Gold." *Argosy*, Mar. 1948.

———. "The Abandoned House," "Bees," "Defeat," "Fagots," "Fixed," and "Sudden Death." *Baltimore Sun*, Jan. 8, 1956.

Richardson, Hester Crawford Dorsey. "The Domestic Service Difficulty." *Good Housekeeping*, Jan. 1888.

———. "Things Woman Can Do." *Baltimore American*, Dec. 15, 1889.

———. "To Keep Men at Home." *Baltimore American*, Dec. 29, 1889.

———. "The Lady in Society." *Baltimore American,* Jan. 5, 1890.

———. "(Fragment)… Early Hours." *Baltimore American,* Jan. 12, 1890.

———. "Author of 'Metzerott, Shoemaker.'" *Lippincott's,* 1890.

———. "The College Settlement." *Lippincott's,* June 1891.

———. *Side-Lights on Maryland History: With Sketches of Early Maryland Families.* Baltimore: Williams and Wilkins, 1903.

———. "Good-By." *Current,* Feb. 28, 1905.

———. "Personal Sketch (on Edwin Warfield)." *Harper's Weekly,* Apr. 15, 1905.

———. "Last Honors to John Paul Jones." *Harper's Weekly,* July 29, 1905.

———. "Scions of Aristocracy in America." *North American Review,* May 1906.

———. *The Origin and Customs of English Manors: With an Account of Feudal Rights and Privileges in the American Colonies.* New York: Order of Colonial Lords of Manors in America, 1913.

Shackleford, Frannie H. *The Great Jew and The Great German or From Paul to Luther: A Historical Study.* New York: William Beverley Harrison, 1896.

Sioussat, Annie Leakin. *Old Manors in the Colony of Maryland.* Baltimore: Lord Baltimore Press, 1913.

———. *John Gardner Murray.* Church Missions Publication Company, 1930.

———. *Old Baltimore.* Maryland Society of the Colonial Dames of America, 1931.

Smith, Emily Anna. *The Life and Letters of Nathan Smith, M.B., M.D.* New Haven, CT: Yale University Press, 1913.

Smith, Harriet Lummis. "Matilda's Good Impression." *Youth's Companion,* Nov. 22, 1906.

———. "A Rush Order." *Zion's Herald,* June 19, 1907.

———. "The Boy's Christmas Tree." *Zion's Herald,* Dec. 18, 1907.

———. "The Picture on the Bare Wall." *Zion's Herald,* Jan. 22, 1908.

———. "Ferguson's Mascot." *Washburn Leader* (ND), Feb. 21, 1908.

———. "Flowering of Vengeance." *Munsey's,* Mar. 1908.

———. "The Promise." *Independent,* Sept. 3, 1908.

———. "The Maze." *Baltimore Sun,* Sept. 10, 1908.

———. "The Lady of the Lantern." *Cavalier,* Feb. 1909.

———. "Humility." *New England Magazine,* Apr. 1909.

———. "A Previous Engagement." *Baltimore Sun,* Apr. 22, 1909.

———. "A Departure in Missionary Work." *Zion's Herald,* Apr. 28, 1909.

———. "How Wallace Got Even." *Christian Observer,* Apr. 28, 1909.

———. "Through the Fire." *Munsey's,* May 1909.

———. "Telephone, The: A Lesson in Neighborliness." *Christian Observer,* May 26, 1909.

———. "The Peculiar Choice of Persis." *New York Observer and Chronicle,* June 17, 1909; also published in *Presbyterian of the South,* July 14, 1909.

———. "Blind Man's Buff." *Baltimore Sun,* June 29, 1909.

———. "Victory." *Youth's Companion,* July 1, 1909.

———. "Jimmy's Opportunity." *Baltimore Sun,* July 21, 1909.

———. "On the Roof." *Baltimore Sun,* Aug. 18, 1909.

———. "Reputation of the 'Bella B.'" *McClure's,* Sept. 1909.

———. "The Blue Pitcher." *Presbyterian of the South,* Sept. 15, 1909.

———. "The Panama Hat." *Baltimore Sun,* Sept. 24, 1909.

———. "A Practical Joke." *Christian Observer,* Oct. 6, 1909.

———. "Old Joe's Apostasy." *Zion's Herald,* Oct. 20, 1909.

———. "The Matchmaker." *Cavalier,* Nov. 1909.

———. "Deaf and Dumb!" *Baltimore Sun,* Jan. 11, 1910.

———. "Boys and Girls." *Zion's Herald,* Jan. 19, 1910.

———. "The Interruption." *Youth's Companion,* Feb. 3, 1910.

———. "At the Matinee." *Baltimore Sun,* Mar. 1, 1910.

———. "How Two Wrongs Made a Right." *Baltimore Sun,* May 10, 1910.

———. "Atwater's Aunt." *Baltimore Sun,* May 21, 1910.

———. "Time's Changes." *New-York Tribune,* May 30, 1910.

———. "Problem of the Destructive Child." *Zion's Herald,* Aug. 10, 1910.

———. "A Debt of Gratitude." *Smart Set,* Sept. 1910.

———. "Guilt Circumstantial." *Cavalier,* Sept. 1910.

———. "Home Circle: Her Own." *Christian Observer,* Sept. 14, 1910.

———. "The Sister of a Genius." *Youth's Companion,* Sept. 29, 1910.

———. "A Random Shot." *Baltimore Sun,* Oct. 13, 1910.

———. "Fifty Dollars Reward." *Baltimore Sun,* Nov. 16, 1910.

———. "Home Circle: Ann and the Temperance Reform." *Christian Observer,* Nov. 23, 1910.

———. "Her Last Half-Year." *Young's*, Dec. 1910.

———. "Home Circle: Two Girls Who Changed Places." *Christian Observer*, Dec. 12, 1910.

———. "Man Wanted." *Baltimore Sun*, Dec. 19, 1910.

———. "An Interrupted Widowhood." *Young's*, Apr. 1911.

———. "The Footprints." *Harper's Bazaar*, Nov. 1911.

———. "Cornelia's Customer." *Baltimore Sun*, Nov. 23, 1911.

———. "The Remedy." *Youth's Companion*, Feb. 22, 1912.

———. *The Girls of Friendly Terrace; or, Peggy Raymond's Success*. Boston: L. C. Page, 1912.

———. "To Gain or Lose It All." *Young's*, Apr. 1912.

———. "Sauce for the Gander." *Cavalier*, Sept. 14, 1912.

———. "When a Woman Will." *Housewife*, Oct. 1912.

———. "Going Up!" *Boys' Magazine*, Jan. 1913.

———. "From the Silence." *Cavalier*, Mar. 15, 1913.

———. "Scientific Methods." *Cavalier*, July 19, 1913.

———. *Peggy Raymond's Vacation; Or, Friendly Terrace Transplanted*. Boston: L.C. Page, 1913.

———. "The First Children's Day." *Herald of Gospel Liberty*, June 11, 1914.

———. "The Gray Tweed Tragedy." *All-Story Weekly*, July 10, 1915.

———. "Food for Thought." Life, Sept. 9, 1915.

———. "Destiny Decides." *Baltimore Sun*, Sept. 19, 1915.

———. "A Study in Hospitality." *Youth's Companion*, Oct. 7, 1915.

———. "Caught on the Roof." *Punta Gorda Herald*, Dec. 9, 1915.

———. "For Margaret's Sake." *Breezy Stories*, Jan. 1916.

———. "The Beat." *Breezy Stories*, Mar. 1916.

———. "The Thoroughbred." *Romance*, June 1916.

———. "By Devious Ways." *All-Story Weekly*, July 22, 1916.

———. *Peggy Raymond's School Days*. New York: Doubleday, Page, 1916.

———. *Other People's Business: The Romantic Career of the Practical Miss Dale*. Indianapolis: Bobbs-Merrill, 1916.

———. "'Take It Back Day' and Ann." *Youth's Companion*, Aug. 24, 1916.

———. "An Outlet for Miss Jane." *Youth's Companion*, Feb. 8, 1917.

———. "Shop Early." *Smith's*, Jan. 1918.

———. "The Singular Case of Sarah." *Detective Story Magazine*, Feb. 5, 1918.

———. "One Lesson Enough." *Youth's Companion*, Sept. 18, 1919.

———. "Fool for Luck." *Detective Story Magazine*, Oct. 28, 1919.

———. "A Golden Silence." *Youth's Companion*, June 24, 1920.

———. *Agatha's Aunt*. Indianapolis: Bobbs-Merrill, 1920.

———. "Taking After Grandmother." *Youth's Companion*, Jan. 27, 1921.

———. "Profit and Loss." *Youth's Companion*, July 24, 1924.

———. "High Water." *Youth's Companion*, Aug. 28, 1924.

———. "Twenty-Five Dollars Reward." *Youth's Companion*, Jan. 29, 1925.

———. "Muddy Creek Overflows." *Youth's Companion*, Apr. 9, 1925.

———. *Pollyanna's Jewels*. New York: Grosset & Dunlap, 1925.

———. "Lizzie to the Rescue." *Youth's Companion*, Mar. 12, 1925.

———. *Pollyanna of the Orange Blossoms*. London: George P. Harrap, 1927.

———. *Pat and Pal*. New England Publishing Company, 1929.

———. *Pollyanna's Western Adventure*. New York: Grosset & Dunlap, 1929.

Sollenberger, Ella Morrow. "Sympathy" and "Heritage." *Lippincott's*, July 12, 1913.

———. "Knitting." *New York Times Current History: The European War*, Vol. 14, Jan. 3, 1918.

———. *Driftwood and Other Verse*. n.p., n.d. (c. 1930s).

Szold, Henrietta. *Legends of the Jews*. Philadelphia: Jewish Publication Society, 1909.

———. *Memoir of Heinrich Leberecht Fleischer*. Washington: Government Printing Office, 1902.

———. "Promised Land." Aug. 13, 1914.

———. *Recent Jewish Progress in Palestine*. Philadelphia: Jewish Publications, 1915.

———. *The Renascence of Hebrew Literature*. Philadelphia: Jewish Publication Society of America, 1909.

Szold, Henrietta (translator). *Jewish History: An Essay in the Philosophy of History*. n.d.

———. *The Ethics of Judaism (1860-1945)*, by M. Lazarus. Philadelphia: Jewish Publication Society, 1901.

Thruston, Lucy Meacham. *Mistress Brent: A Story of Lord Baltimore's Colony in 1638*. Boston: Little, Brown, 1901.

———. *A Girl of Virginia*. Boston: Little, Brown, 1902.

———. *Jack and His Island*. Boston: Little, Brown,

1902.

———. *Where the Tide Comes In*. Boston: Little, Brown, 1904.

———. *Songs of the Chesapeake*. Baltimore: Hoen, Mar. 14, 1905.

———. *Called to the Field*. Boston: Little, Brown, 1906.

———. *Jenifer*. Boston: Little, Brown, 1907.

———. "The Truant Wife." *Illustrated Sunday Magazine*, Apr. 25, 1915.

Tiernan, Mary Spear. "Honi Soit Qui Mal Y Pense." *Scribner's*, May 1881.

———. *Homoselle*. Boston: Ticknor and Company, 1881.

———. *Suzette*. New York: Henry Holt & Co., 1885.

———. "Dirt Pies." *Harper's Monthly*, July 1886.

———. "A Widow, Indeed!" *Godey's Ladies' Book*, Apr. 1887.

———. "Two Negatives." *Century*, Feb. 1889.

———. *Jack Horner*. Boston and New York: Houghton Mifflin, 1890.

Trail, Florence. *My Journal in Foreign Lands*. Baltimore: W.L. Stork & Co., 1884.

———. "Musings in a Crowd." *Lexington Intelligencer*, July 10, 1886.

———. *Studies in Criticism*. New York: Worthington Company, 1888.

———. *Under the Second Renaissance*. Buffalo: Charlie Wells Moulton, 1894.

———. *A History of Italian Literature*. New York: Vincenzo Ciocia Stamperia Italiana, 1903.

———. *History and Democracy; Essays in Interpretation*. Baltimore: Falconer Co., 1916.

———. *Meanings of Music*. Boston: R. G. Badger, 1918.

———. *The Scholar's Italy*. Baltimore: Williams & Wilkins Co., 1923.

———. *An Italian Anthology*. Boston: R. G. Badger, 1926.

———. *A Memorial of Ariana McElfresh Trail*. Boston: R. G. Badger, 1929.

———. *Modern Italian Culture*. Philadelphia: Westbrook, 1931.

———. *Foreign Family Life in France in 1891*. Boston: B. Humphries, 1944.

Turnbull, Francese Litchfield. *Marguerite's Vow*. Baltimore: I. Friedenwald, 1882.

———. *The Catholic Man: A Study*. Boston: D. Lothrop Company, 1890.

———. *Val-Maria: A Romance of the Time of Napoleon I*. New York: Lippincott, 1893.

———. "The Modern Need of the Ideal: An Address Delivered at the Seventh Annual Salon of the Women's Literary Club of Baltimore, June the 2nd, 1896." Baltimore, H. Williams Company, 1896.

———. "A Study of William Watson." *Poet Lore* 9, no. 1, Jan. 1897.

———. *The Bible God, Bible Teachings, and Selections from the Writings of Scientists*. NY: Peter Eckler, 1899.

———. *Golden Book of Venice: A Historical Romance of the 16th Century*. New York: The Century Company, 1900.

———. "For Venice." *Living Age*, June 4, 1901.

———. *A Royal Pawn of Venice*. Philadelphia: Lippincott, 1911.

———. "New Statue of Edgar Allan Poe by Sir Moses Ezekiel." *Art and Archaeology*, May 1917.

Turner, Clara Newman. *Mail from Nowhere: Distributed with the Hope of a Response from the Hearts of My Correspondents*. Privately published, before 1900.

———. Recollection of Emily Dickinson (1896), in *'Reminiscences' of Dickinson in Her Own Time: A Biographical Chronicle of Her Life, Drawn from Recollections, Interviews, and Memoirs by Family, Friends, and Associates*, ed. Jane Donahue Eberwein, Stephanie Farrar, and Cristanne Miller. Iowa City: Univ. of Iowa Press, 2015.

Tyson, Florence MacIntyre (translator). "The Jack-of-All-Trades," by Grazia Deledda. *Short Stories*, Apr. 1903.

———. "The Lost Letter." *Short Stories*, June 1903.

———. "Two Men and a Woman," by Grazia Deledda. *Short Stories*, July 1903.

———. "Waiting," by Jean Madeline. *Short Stories*, Sept. 1903.

———. *Russia*, Vol. 1, by Théophilé Gautier. Philadelphia: J. C. Winston Co., 1905.

———. "Mirline." *Short Stories*, Feb. 1906.

Vanderpoel, Adaline E. *Bermuda Past and Present*. Privately printed in New York, Nov. 28, 1902.

Whitelock, Louise Clarkson (as L. Clarkson). *Violet, with Eyes of Blue*. Philadelphia: J.L. Sibole, 1876.

———. *The Gathering of the Lilies*. Philadelphia: J.L. Sibole, 1877.

———. *The Rag Fair and Other Reveries*. Philadelphia: F.W. Robinson, 1879.

———. *Buttercup's Visit to Little Stay-at-Home*. New York: E.P. Dutton, 1881.

———. *Fly-Away Fairies and Baby Blossoms*. New York: E.P. Dutton, 1882.

———. *Indian Summer: Autumn Poems and Sketches*. New York: E.P. Dutton, 1883.

———. *The Shadow of John Wallace*. New York: White, Stokes, & Allen, 1884.

Whitelock, Louise Clarkson. *A Mad Madonna and Other Stories*. Boston: J. Knight, 1895.

———. *How Hindsight Met Provincialitis*. Boston: Copeland and Day, 1898.

Whitney, Anne Weston. "The Southern Cousin." *American Baptist Publication Society*, 1892.

———. "Captain's 'Harnt.'" *New England Magazine*, Sept. 1888.

———. "De Los' Ell an' Yard." *Journal of American Folklore*, 1897.

———. "Items of Maryland Belief and Custom." *Journal of American Folklore*, Dec. 1899.

———. "Negro American Dialects, Part I." *Independent*, Aug. 22, 1901.

———. "Negro American Dialects, Part II." *Independent*, Aug. 29, 1901.

Whitney, Anne Weston, and Caroline Canfield Bullock. "Folklore from Maryland." 1925.

Woods, Katharine Pearson. *Metzerott, Shoemaker*. New York, T. Y. Crowell & co., 1889.

———. "Dr. Toiseman's Family." *Dawn*, June 1890.

———. "The Mark of the Beast: A Romance." *Lippincott's*, Sept. 1890.

———. *A Web of Gold*. New York: T. Y. Crowell & Co., 1890.

———. "Queens of the Shop, the Workroom, and the Tenement." *Cosmopolitan*, Nov. 1890.

———. "From Leopold's Window." *Harper's Monthly*, June 1892.

———. *From Dusk to Dawn*. New York: D. Appleton, 1892.

———. "Mine and Thine." *Journal of the Knights of Labor*, 1894.

———. "Wild Mag." *Congregationalist*, July 1894.

———. "Hold Me Not False." *Bookman*, June 1896.

———. "Between the Lights at Sea: A Rhapsody." *Bookman*, Oct. 1896.

———. *The Crowning of Candace*. New York: Dodd, Mead and Company, 1896.

———. *John, a Tale of King Messiah*. New York: Dodd, Mead and Company, 1896.

———. *The Son of Ingar*. New York: Dodd, Mead and Company, 1897.

———. "Edward Bellamy: Author and Economist." *Bookman*, July 1898.

———. "Only These." *Bookman*, Sept. 1898.

———. "Twilight Fantasia." *Bookman*, Oct. 1898.

———. "Christmas Silhouette." *Bookman*, Dec. 1898.

———. "A Song of Dawn and Spring-Time." *Bookman*, May 1899.

———. "The Evolution of an Artist." *Bookman*, June 1899.

———. "The Renaissance of Wonder." *Bookman*, Dec. 1899.

———. *The True Story of Captain John*. New York: Doubleday, Page, 1901.

———. "From One Poet to Another." *Harper's Monthly*, Dec. 1901.

———. "Captain John Smith and the American Nation." *Harper's Monthly*, Feb. 1902.

———. "From King Leopold's Window." *Harper's Monthly*, June 1902.

———. "Song of Love and Summer." *Harper's Monthly*, June 1902.

———. "A Song of Sunset." *Harper's Monthly*, Apr. 1904.

Wrenshall, Katharine H. "An American Sculptor in Rome: Sir Moses Ezekiel." *World's Work*, Nov. 1909.

———. "The Bears of Berne." *Travel*, Jan. 1908.

———. "The Parson and the Pick-Pocket." *Smart Set*, Sept. 1910.

Wrenshall, Letitia Humphreys Yonge. "Summer Philanthropy in Baltimore." *New Cycle*, Sept. 1895.

———. "De Clar Pitcher." *Smith's*, Aug. 1906.

———. "A Drive Out from Beautiful Naples to Dead Cities and Lakes of Fire." *Baltimore Sun*, May 3, 1908.

———. "Along the Two Gulfs of Naples and Salerno." Published in two parts, *Baltimore Sun*, June 29 and July 5, 1908.

———. "Traveling in the Radiant Old Mediterranean." *Baltimore Sun*, Apr. 5, 1908.

Wrenshall, Letitia Humphreys Yonge and the Edgar Allan Poe Memorial Association. *Edgar Allan Poe: A Centenary Tribute*. Baltimore: Edgar Allan Poe Memorial Association, 1910.

Zacharias, Jane. *The Newsboys' Christmas Party*. Baltimore: Lord Baltimore Press, 1899.

Apprentice
House Press
Loyola University Maryland

Apprentice House is the country's only campus-based, student-staffed book publishing company. Directed by professors and industry professionals, it is a nonprofit activity of the Communication Department at Loyola University Maryland.

Using state-of-the-art technology and an experiential learning model of education, Apprentice House publishes books in untraditional ways. This dual responsibility as publishers and educators creates an unprecedented collaborative environment among faculty and students, while teaching tomorrow's editors, designers, and marketers.

Outside of class, progress on book projects is carried forth by the AH Book Publishing Club, a co-curricular campus organization supported by Loyola University Maryland's Office of Student Activities.

Eclectic and provocative, Apprentice House titles intend to entertain as well as spark dialogue on a variety of topics. Financial contributions to sustain the press's work are welcomed. Contributions are tax deductible to the fullest extent allowed by the IRS.

To learn more about Apprentice House books or to obtain submission guidelines, please visit www.apprenticehouse.com.

Apprentice House
Communication Department
Loyola University Maryland
4501 N. Charles Street
Baltimore, MD 21210
Ph: 410-617-5265 • Fax: 410-617-2198
info@apprenticehouse.com • www.apprenticehouse.com